D1509445

# Poetry
# Criticism

# Guide to Gale Literary Criticism Series

| For criticism on | Consult these Gale series |
|---|---|
| Authors now living or who died after December 31, 1999 | *CONTEMPORARY LITERARY CRITICISM (CLC)* |
| Authors who died between 1900 and 1999 | *TWENTIETH-CENTURY LITERARY CRITICISM (TCLC)* |
| Authors who died between 1800 and 1899 | *NINETEENTH-CENTURY LITERATURE CRITICISM (NCLC)* |
| Authors who died between 1400 and 1799 | *LITERATURE CRITICISM FROM 1400 TO 1800 (LC)*<br><br>*SHAKESPEAREAN CRITICISM (SC)* |
| Authors who died before 1400 | *CLASSICAL AND MEDIEVAL LITERATURE CRITICISM (CMLC)* |
| Authors of books for children and young adults | *CHILDREN'S LITERATURE REVIEW (CLR)* |
| Dramatists | *DRAMA CRITICISM (DC)* |
| Poets | *POETRY CRITICISM (PC)* |
| Short story writers | *SHORT STORY CRITICISM (SSC)* |
| Literary topics and movements | *HARLEM RENAISSANCE: A GALE CRITICAL COMPANION (HR)*<br><br>*THE BEAT GENERATION: A GALE CRITICAL COMPANION (BG)*<br><br>*FEMINISM IN LITERATURE: A GALE CRITICAL COMPANION (FL)*<br><br>*GOTHIC LITERATURE: A GALE CRITICAL COMPANION (GL)* |
| Asian American writers of the last two hundred years | *ASIAN AMERICAN LITERATURE (AAL)* |
| Black writers of the past two hundred years | *BLACK LITERATURE CRITICISM (BLC)*<br><br>*BLACK LITERATURE CRITICISM SUPPLEMENT (BLCS)* |
| Hispanic writers of the late nineteenth and twentieth centuries | *HISPANIC LITERATURE CRITICISM (HLC)*<br><br>*HISPANIC LITERATURE CRITICISM SUPPLEMENT (HLCS)* |
| Native North American writers and orators of the eighteenth, nineteenth, and twentieth centuries | *NATIVE NORTH AMERICAN LITERATURE (NNAL)* |
| Major authors from the Renaissance to the present | *WORLD LITERATURE CRITICISM, 1500 TO THE PRESENT (WLC)*<br><br>*WORLD LITERATURE CRITICISM SUPPLEMENT (WLCS)* |

ISSN 1052-4851

# Poetry Criticism

*Excerpts from Criticism of the Works of the Most Significant and Widely Studied Poets of World Literature*

## Volume 83

*Michelle Lee*
Project Editor

GALE
CENGAGE Learning

Detroit • New York • San Francisco • New Haven, Conn • Waterville, Maine • London

Hillside Public Library

GALE
CENGAGE Learning™

**Poetry Criticism, Vol. 83**

Project Editor: Michelle Lee

Editorial: Dana Barnes, Thomas Burns, Elizabeth Cranston, Kathy D. Darrow, Kristen Dorsch, Jeffrey W. Hunter, Jelena O. Krstović, Thomas J. Schoenberg, Noah Schusterbauer, Lawrence J. Trudeau, Russel Whitaker

Data Capture: Frances Monroe, Gwen Tucker

Indexing Services: Factiva, Inc.

Rights and Acquisitions: Scott Bragg, Barb McNeil, and Tracie Richardson

Composition and Electronic Capture: Gary Oudersluys

Manufacturing: Rhonda Dover

Associate Product Manager: Marc Cormier

© 2008 Gale, Cengage Learning

ALL RIGHTS RESERVED. No part of this work covered by the copyright herein may be reproduced, transmitted, stored, or used in any form or by any means graphic, electronic, or mechanical, including but not limited to photocopying, recording, scanning, digitizing, taping, Web distribution, information networks, or information storage and retrieval systems, except as permitted under Section 107 or 108 of the 1976 United States Copyright Act, without the prior written permission of the publisher.

This publication is a creative work fully protected by all applicable copyright laws, as well as by misappropriation, trade secret, unfair competition, and other applicable laws. The authors and editors of this work have added value to the underlying factual material herein through one or more of the following: unique and original selection, coordination, expression, arrangement, and classification of the information.

For product information and technology assistance, contact us at
**Gale Customer Support, 1-800-877-4253.**
For permission to use material from this text or product,
submit all requests online at **www.cengage.com/permissions.**
Further permissions questions can be emailed to
**permissionrequest@cengage.com**

While every effort has been made to ensure the reliability of the information presented in this publication, Gale, a part of Cengage Learning, does not guarantee the accuracy of the data contained herein. Gale accepts no payment for listing; and inclusion in the publication of any organization, agency, institution, publication, service, or individual does not imply endorsement of the editors or publisher. Errors brought to the attention of the publisher and verified to the satisfaction of the publisher will be corrected in future editions.

*Gale*
27500 Drake Rd.
Farmington Hills, MI, 48331-3535

LIBRARY OF CONGRESS CATALOG CARD NUMBER 91-118494

ISBN-13: 978-0-7876-9880-5
ISBN-10: 0-7876-9880-6

ISSN 1052-4851

Printed in the United States of America
1 2 3 4 5 6 7 12 11 10 09 08

# Contents

Preface vii

Acknowledgments ix

Literary Criticism Series Advisory Board xi

# Preface

*P*oetry Criticism (*PC*) presents significant criticism of the world's greatest poets and provides supplementary biographical and bibliographical material to guide the interested reader to a greater understanding of the genre and its creators. Although major poets and literary movements are covered in such Gale Literary Criticism series as *Contemporary Literary Criticism* (*CLC*), *Twentieth-Century Literary Criticism* (*TCLC*), *Nineteenth-Century Literature Criticism* (*NCLC*), *Literature Criticism from 1400 to 1800* (*LC*), and *Classical and Medieval Literature Criticism* (*CMLC*), *PC* offers more focused attention on poetry than is possible in the broader, survey-oriented entries on writers in these Gale series. Students, teachers, librarians, and researchers will find that the generous excerpts and supplementary material provided by *PC* supply them with the vital information needed to write a term paper on poetic technique, to examine a poet's most prominent themes, or to lead a poetry discussion group.

## Scope of the Series

*PC* is designed to serve as an introduction to major poets of all eras and nationalities. Since these authors have inspired a great deal of relevant critical material, *PC* is necessarily selective, and the editors have chosen the most important published criticism to aid readers and students in their research. Each author entry presents a historical survey of the critical response to that author's work. The length of an entry is intended to reflect the amount of critical attention the author has received from critics writing in English and from foreign critics in translation. Every attempt has been made to identify and include the most significant essays on each author's work. In order to provide these important critical pieces, the editors sometimes reprint essays that have appeared elsewhere in Gale's Literary Criticism Series. Such duplication, however, never exceeds twenty percent of a *PC* volume.

## Organization of the Book

Each *PC* entry consists of the following elements:

- The **Author Heading** cites the name under which the author most commonly wrote, followed by birth and death dates. Also located here are any name variations under which an author wrote, including transliterated forms for authors whose native languages use nonroman alphabets. If the author wrote consistently under a pseudonym, the pseudonym will be listed in the author heading and the author's actual name given in parenthesis on the first line of the biographical and critical introduction. Uncertain birth or death dates are indicated by question marks. Single-work entries are preceded by the title of the work and its date of publication.

- The **Introduction** contains background information that introduces the reader to the author and the critical debates surrounding his or her work.

- The list of **Principal Works** is ordered chronologically by date of first publication and lists the most important works by the author. The first section comprises poetry collections and book-length poems. The second section gives information on other major works by the author. For foreign authors, the editors have provided original foreign-language publication information and have selected what are considered the best and most complete English-language editions of their works.

- Reprinted **Criticism** is arranged chronologically in each entry to provide a useful perspective on changes in critical evaluation over time. All individual titles of poems and poetry collections by the author featured in the entry are printed in boldface type. The critic's name and the date of composition or publication of the critical work are given at the beginning of each piece of criticism. Unsigned criticism is preceded by the title of the source in which it appeared. Footnotes are reprinted at the end of each essay or excerpt. In the case of excerpted criticism, only those footnotes that pertain to the excerpted texts are included.

- Critical essays are prefaced by brief **Annotations** explicating each piece.

- A complete **Bibliographical Citation** of the original essay or book precedes each piece of criticism.

- An annotated bibliography of **Further Reading** appears at the end of each entry and suggests resources for additional study. In some cases, significant essays for which the editors could not obtain reprint rights are included here. Boxed material following the further reading list provides references to other biographical and critical sources on the author in series published by Gale.

## Cumulative Indexes

A **Cumulative Author Index** lists all of the authors that appear in a wide variety of reference sources published by Gale, including *PC*. A complete list of these sources is found facing the first page of the Author Index. The index also includes birth and death dates and cross references between pseudonyms and actual names.

A **Cumulative Nationality Index** lists all authors featured in *PC* by nationality, followed by the number of the *PC* volume in which their entry appears.

A **Cumulative Title Index** lists in alphabetical order all individual poems, book-length poems, and collection titles contained in the *PC* series. Titles of poetry collections and separately published poems are printed in italics, while titles of individual poems are printed in roman type with quotation marks. Each title is followed by the author's last name and corresponding volume and page numbers where commentary on the work is located. English-language translations of original foreign-language titles are cross-referenced to the foreign titles so that all references to discussion of a work are combined in one listing.

## Citing *Poetry Criticism*

When citing criticism reprinted in the Literary Criticism Series, students should provide complete bibliographic information so that the cited essay can be located in the original print or electronic source. Students who quote directly from reprinted criticism may use any accepted bibliographic format, such as University of Chicago Press style or Modern Language Association (MLA) style. Both the MLA and the University of Chicago formats are acceptable and recognized as being the current standards for citations. It is important, however, to choose one format for all citations; do not mix the two formats within a list of citations.

The examples below follow recommendations for preparing a bibliography set forth in *The Chicago Manual of Style,* 14th ed. (Chicago: The University of Chicago Press, 1993); the first example pertains to material drawn from periodicals, the second to material reprinted from books:

Linkin, Harriet Kramer. "The Language of Speakers in *Songs of Innocence and of Experience*." *Romanticism Past and Present* 10, no. 2 (summer 1986): 5-24. Reprinted in *Poetry Criticism.* Vol. 63, edited by Michelle Lee, 79-88. Detroit: Thomson Gale, 2005.

Glen, Heather. "Blake's Criticism of Moral Thinking in *Songs of Innocence and of Experience."* In *Interpreting Blake,* edited by Michael Phillips, 32-69. Cambridge: Cambridge University Press, 1978. Reprinted in *Poetry Criticism.* Vol. 63, edited by Michelle Lee, 34-51. Detroit: Thomson Gale, 2005.

## Suggestions are Welcome

Readers who wish to suggest new features, topics, or authors to appear in future volumes, or who have other suggestions or comments are cordially invited to call, write, or fax the Associate Product Manager:

Associate Product Manager, Literary Criticism Series
Gale
27500 Drake Road
Farmington Hills, MI 48331-3535
1-800-347-4253 (GALE)
Fax: 248-699-8054

# Acknowledgments

The editors wish to thank the copyright holders of the criticism included in this volume and the permissions managers of many book and magazine publishing companies for assisting us in securing reproduction rights. Following is a list of the copyright holders who have granted us permission to reproduce material in this volume of *PC*. Every effort has been made to trace copyright, but if omissions have been made, please let us know.

**COPYRIGHTED MATERIAL IN *PC*, VOLUME 83, WAS REPRODUCED FROM THE FOLLOWING PERIODICALS:**

*American Literature,* v. 60, May, 1988. Copyright © 1988 by Duke University Press. All rights reserved. Used by permission of the publisher.—*Criticism,* v. 45, fall, 2003. Copyright © 2004 by Wayne State University Press. Reproduced with permission of the Wayne State University Press.—*Exemplaria,* v. XVI, spring, 2004. Copyright © 2004 by Pegasus Press, Asheville, North Carolina. Reproduced by permission.—*Explicator,* v. 53, fall, 1994; v. 54, summer, 1996; v. 64, fall, 2005. Copyright © 1994, 1996, 2005 by Helen Dwight Reid Educational Foundation. All reproduced with permission of the Helen Dwight Reid Educational Foundation, published by Heldref Publications, 1319 18th Street, NW, Washington, DC 20036-1802.—*Modern Language Notes,* v. 113, September, 1998. Copyright © 1998 by the Johns Hopkins University Press. Reproduced by permission.—*Mosaic,* v. 34, March, 2001. Copyright © by Mosaic, 2001. Acknowledgment of previous publication is herewith made.—*Neuphilologische Mitteilungen,* v. 96, 1995 for "Fighting Spirit and Literary Genre: A Comparison of Battle Exhortations in the *Song of Roland* and in the Chronicles of the Central Middle Ages" by John R. E. Bliese. Copyright © 1995 by Modern Language Society, Helsinki. Reproduced by permission of the publisher and the author.—*Papers in Romance,* v. 3, autumn, 1981. Copyright © 1981 by the University of Washington. Reproduced by permission.—*Renascence,* v. 51, spring, 1999. Copyright © 1999 by Marquette University Press. Reproduced by permission.—*Romance Notes,* v. 14, autumn, 1972; v. 14, spring, 1973. Both reproduced by permission.—*Speculum,* v. 76, January, 2001. Copyright © 2001 by the Medieval Academy of America. Reproduced by permission.—*Studies,* v. 87, summer, 1998. Reproduced by permission.—*Tulane Studies in English,* v. XI, 1961. Copyright © 1961 by Tulane University. Reproduced by permission.—*Western Folklore,* v. 64, winter-spring, 2005. Copyright © 2005 by Western States Folklore Society. Reproduced by permission.

**COPYRIGHTED MATERIAL IN *PC*, VOLUME 83, WAS REPRODUCED FROM THE FOLLOWING BOOKS:**

Brownlow, F. W. From *Robert Southwell.* Twayne, 1996. Copyright © 1996 by Twayne Publishers. All rights reserved. Reproduced by permission of Cengage Learning.—Cameron, Elspeth. From "Earle Birney's 'David' and the *Song of Roland*: A Source Study," in *Inside the Poem: Essays and Poems in Honour of Donald Stephens.* Edited by W. H. New. Oxford University Press, 1992. Copyright © 1992 by Oxford University Press Canada. Reprinted by permission of the publisher.—Cook, Robert Francis. From *The Sense of the* Song of Roland. Cornell University Press, 1987. Copyright © 1987 by Cornell University Press. All rights reserved. Used by permission of the publisher, Cornell University Press.—Crosland, Jessie. From *The Song of Roland.* Translated by Jessie Crosland. Cooper Square, 1967. Copyright © 1967 by Rowman & Littlefield Publishers, Inc. All rights reserved. Reproduced by permission.—Garza-Falcón, Leticia Magda. From *Gente Decente.* University of Texas Press, 1998. Copyright © 1998 by the University of Texas Press. All rights reserved. Reproduced by permission of the University of Texas Press.—Goldin, Frederick. From "Time and Performance in *The Song of Roland*," in *Cuny English Forum.* Edited by Saul N. Brody and Harold Schechter. AMS Press, 1985. Copyright © 1985 by AMS Press, Inc. All rights reserved. Reproduced by permission.—Haidu, Peter. From *The Subject Medieval/Modern.* Stanford University Press, 2004. Copyright © 2004 by the Board of Trustees of the Leland Stanford Junior University. All rights reserved. Used with the permission of Stanford University Press, www.sup.org.—Hill, Geoffrey. From *The Lords of Limit: Essays on Literature and Ideas.* Oxford University Press, 1984. Copyright © 1984 by Geoffrey Hill. Reproduced by permission of Oxford University Press.—Janelle, Pierre. From *Robert Southwell: The Writer.* Sheed and Ward, 1935. Reproduced by permission.—Limón, José E. From "The Return of the Mexican Ballad: Américo Paredes and His Anthropological Text as Persuasive Political Performances," in *Creativity/Anthropology.* Edited by Smadar Lavie, Kirin Narayan, and Renato Rosaldo. Cornell University Press, 1993. Copyright © 1993 by Cornell University. All rights reserved. Used by permission of the publisher, Cornell University Press.—Limón, José E. From "Oral

Tradition and Poetic Influence: Two Poets from Greater Mexico," in *Redefining American Literary History.* Edited by A. LaVonne Brown Ruoff and Jerry W. Ward, Jr. The Modern Language Association of America, 1990. Copyright © 1990 by the Modern Language Association of America. Reprinted by permission of the Modern Language Association of America.—McBride, Kari Boyd. From "Gender and Judaism in Meditations on the Passion: Middleton, Southwell, Lanyer, and Fletcher," in *Discovering and (Re)Covering the Seventeenth Century Religious Lyric.* Edited by Eugene R. Cunnar and Jeffrey Johnson. Duquesne University Press, 2001. Copyright © 2001 by Duquesne University Press. All rights reserved. Reproduced by permission.—Mickel, Emanuel J. From *Ganelon, Treason, and the Chanson de Roland.* Pennsylvania State University Press, 1989. Copyright © 1989 by the Pennsylvania State University. All rights reserved. Reproduced by permission of the Pennsylvania State University Press.—Pilarz, Scott R. From "'To Help Souls': Recovering the Purpose of Southwell's Poetry and Prose," in *Discovering and (Re)Covering the Seventeenth Century Religious Lyric.* Edited by Eugene R. Cunnar and Jeffrey Johnson. Duquesne University Press, 2001. Copyright © 2001 by Duquesne University Press. All rights reserved. Reproduced by permission.—Saldívar, Ramón. From *The Borderlands of Culture: Américo Paredes and the Transnational Imaginary.* Duke University Press, 2006. Copyright © 2006 by Duke University Press. All rights reserved. Used by permission of the publisher.—Saldívar, Ramón. From "The Borders of Modernity: Américo Paredes's *Between Two Worlds* and the Chicano National Subject," in *The Ethnic Canon: Histories, Institutions, and Interventions.* Edited by David Palumbo-Liu. University of Minnesota Press, 1995. Copyright © 1995 by the Regents of the University of Minnesota. All rights reserved. Reproduced by permission.—Scallon, Joseph D. From *The Poetry of Robert Southwell, S. J.* Institute Für Englische Sprache und Literatur, Universität Salzburg, 1975. Copyright © 1968 by Joseph D. Scallon. Reproduced by permission.—Sisson, C. H. From *The Song of Roland.* Translated by C. H. Sisson. Carcanet Press Limited, 1983. Copyright © 1983 by C. H. Sisson. Reproduced by permission of Carcanet Press Limited.—Thomas, J. W. From *Priest Konrad's Song of Roland.* Translated by J. W. Thomas. Camden House, 1994. Copyright © 1994 by Camden House, Inc. All rights reserved. Reproduced by permission.

# Gale Literature Product Advisory Board

The members of the Gale Literature Product Advisory Board—reference librarians from public and academic library systems—represent a cross-section of our customer base and offer a variety of informed perspectives on both the presentation and content of our literature products. Advisory board members assess and define such quality issues as the relevance, currency, and usefulness of the author coverage, critical content, and literary topics included in our series; evaluate the layout, presentation, and general quality of our printed volumes; provide feedback on the criteria used for selecting authors and topics covered in our series; provide suggestions for potential enhancements to our series; identify any gaps in our coverage of authors or literary topics, recommending authors or topics for inclusion; analyze the appropriateness of our content and presentation for various user audiences, such as high school students, undergraduates, graduate students, librarians, and educators; and offer feedback on any proposed changes/enhancements to our series. We wish to thank the following advisors for their advice throughout the year.

**Barbara M. Bibel**
Librarian
Oakland Public Library
Oakland, California

**Dr. Toby Burrows**
Principal Librarian
The Scholars' Centre
University of Western Australia Library
Nedlands, Western Australia

**Celia C. Daniel**
Associate Reference Librarian
Howard University Libraries
Washington, D.C.

**David M. Durant**
Reference Librarian
Joyner Library
East Carolina University
Greenville, North Carolina

**Nancy T. Guidry**
Librarian
Bakersfield Community College
Bakersfield, California

**Heather Martin**
Arts & Humanities Librarian
University of Alabama at Birmingham, Sterne Library
Birmingham, Alabama

**Susan Mikula**
Librarian
Indiana Free Library
Indiana, Pennsylvania

**Thomas Nixon**
Humanities Reference Librarian
University of North Carolina at Chapel Hill, Davis
  Library
Chapel Hill, North Carolina

**Mark Schumacher**
Jackson Library
University of North Carolina at Greensboro
Greensboro, North Carolina

**Gwen Scott-Miller**
Assistant Director
Sno-Isle Regional Library System
Marysville, Washington

# Américo Paredes
## 1915-1999

American poet, novelist, short story writer, editor, and translator.

## INTRODUCTION

Paredes was a renowned scholar and folklorist who specialized in the border culture of the American Southwest. In his poetry and in his extensive scholarship on the *corrida*, or Mexican ballad, Paredes sought to correct what he regarded as the misrepresentation of his people and culture.

## BIOGRAPHICAL INFORMATION

One of eight children, Paredes was born on September 3, 1915, in Brownsville, Texas. His father was Justo Paredes, whose family had been ranchers on both sides of the Rio Grande from the middle of the eighteenth century, and his mother was Clotilde Manzano-Vidal, whose family had come to the region from Spain in the middle of the nineteenth century. Paredes learned to read and write in Spanish at home, but received his formal education at the English-language public schools of Brownsville. He began writing poetry while still a student at Brownsville High School and took first prize in a state-wide poetry contest. Paredes graduated from high school in 1934, enrolled at Brownsville Junior College, and began working as a translator and writer for the local newspaper, *The Brownsville Herald*. He also found occasional work as a professional singer and studied piano and guitar during this time. He continued writing poetry and began writing fiction as well, although he did not publish it until much later. In 1939 Paredes married Consuelo Chelo Silva, a local singer; the couple had a son, Américo Paredes, Jr. The marriage lasted only a short time and ended in divorce. During World War II, Paredes again worked as a journalist, serving as reporter and editor with the U.S. military newspaper *Stars and Stripes* in Japan. He remained there after the war and worked for the American Red Cross, where he met Amelia Shidzu Nagamine, whose mother was Uruguayan and whose father was a Japanese diplomat. They married in 1948 and had three children together, two sons and a daughter; the marriage lasted more than fifty years.

In 1951 Paredes returned to Texas and began studying English at the University of Texas at Austin, earning a B.A. in 1951, an M.A. in 1953, and a Ph.D. in 1957 with a specialty in the folklore of the Texas-Mexican border region. For the next several years Paredes held a variety of positions in academia. He taught for a time at Texas Western University, worked as an archivist at the University of Texas at Austin's Folklore Archive from 1957 to 1967, and served as bibliographer for *The Southern Folklore Quarterly* from 1960 to 1965. In the late 1960s Paredes served as editor of the University of Texas Latin American Folklore Series. In 1966 he began teaching at the University of Texas at Austin, where he remained for almost twenty-five years, eventually attaining the rank of full professor.

Paredes's numerous awards include the first prize in poetry from Trinity University (1934); a Guggenheim fellowship (1962); the Charles Frankel Award from the National Endowment for the Humanities (1989); the Order of the Aztec Eagle from the government of Mexico (1990); and the Order of José Escandón (1991), also from the government of Mexico. Paredes died on May 5, 1999, following a long illness.

## MAJOR WORKS

Paredes's poetry was inspired by the ballads and stories passed down to him by his father when he was a boy and was informed by his conviction that his people and his region had been misrepresented in the literature of the dominant American culture. In 1935, the poetry that he had written in high school began appearing in "Los lunes literarios," the literary supplement of San Antonio's Mexican-American newspaper *La Prensa*, as well as in *The Brownsville Herald*. Paredes published his first volume of poetry, *Cantos de adolescencia*, in 1937, at the age of twenty-two. The volume's sixty-two poems recount an adolescent's struggle to fit into a culture that is neither Mexican nor American. Paredes's only other collection of original poetry was the 1991 volume *Between Two Worlds*, consisting of poems written during the 1930s but unpublished at the time of composition. One of the most famous poems in the collection is "The Mexico-Texan" which, according to Paredes, was written while he was in high school and later "became current in manuscript form in south Texas, was used in political campaigns, was reprinted a few times as anonymous, and entered oral tradition locally." Another poem that appeared in *Between Two Worlds* was the politically-charged "Alma pocha," originally written for the 1936 Texas Centennial, but rejected for publication by the editors of *La Prensa*. The poem is a story of defeat and shame for the

Mexican-American who becomes a servant on the land he once owned. In 1958 Paredes produced *"With His Pistol in His Hand": A Border Ballad and Its Hero,* based on his doctoral dissertation and consisting of a scholarly study of the ballad form, passed down as part of the Texas-Mexican border region's oral tradition and performed by anonymous balladeers. Paredes tape-recorded in the field the various versions of one such narrative ballad, "The Ballad of Gregorio Cortez," codified its many variants, and offered his own English translation.

Paredes wrote in a number of other genres besides poetry. In addition to his scholarly studies of folklore, such as *Uncle Remus con Chile* (1993), his most famous contributions to border literature are the novel *George Washington Gomez* (1990) and the short story collection *The Hammon and the Beans and Other Stories* (1994).

## CRITICAL RECEPTION

Critics offer high praise for Paredes as a pioneer in the field of border culture and in what came to be called "border writing." Concerned that the national literature of America misrepresented the experiences of the inhabitants of the Southwest border country, Paredes tried to capture more accurately the culture of his people and his region. Ramón Saldívar points out how far ahead of its time the poetry of *Between Two Worlds* was: "Looking as it does from its liminal present both to the past and to the future, speaking an oddly dual idiom that simultaneously celebrates a lyrical history and forebodes a prosaic future, *Between Two Worlds* might well emblematize the features of . . . postmodern border writing were it not for the fact that it predates the notion by more than half a century." Saldívar believes, however, that Paredes's poetry is even more valuable in illuminating how modernism relates to Chicano literature, as well as to the literatures of other minority groups within American culture. José R. López Morín has studied Paredes's early work and finds an artificial quality to some of his early verse. According to López Morín, the poem "Flute Song" "seems awkward for a young Mexican American activist" and "does not possess any notable qualities that set it apart from other English verse." Saldívar insists, though, that Paredes's poems "function as snippets of cultural critique and social analysis to show how culture, knowledge, and power are interlinked as social constructions that might be challenged and reconfigured. And they do so in a curiously modern and bilingual way."

## PRINCIPAL WORKS

### Poetry

*Cantos de adolescencia* 1937

*"With His Pistol in His Hand": A Border Ballad and Its Hero* (ballad translation and folklore study) 1958
*Between Two Worlds* 1991

### Other Major Works

*Border Country* (short stories) 1952
*Folktales of Mexico* [editor] (folktales) 1979
*George Washington Gomez: A Mexicotexan Novel* (novel) 1990
*Uncle Remus con Chile* (essay) 1993
*The Hammon and the Beans and Other Stories* (short stories) 1994
*The Shadow* (novel) 1998

---

## CRITICISM

### José E. Limón (essay date 1990)

SOURCE: Limón, José E. "Oral Tradition and Poetic Influence: Two Poets from Greater Mexico." In *Redefining American Literary History,* edited by A. LaVonne Brown Ruoff and Jerry W. Ward, Jr., pp. 124-41. New York: The Modern Language Association of America, 1990.

[*In the following essay, Limón analyzes the relationship between folklore and literature, examining the ballads composed and performed by unknown folk artists alongside Paredes's written poetry.*]

> It's a wise child that knows its own father.
>
> *The Odyssey*

> Man is in love and loves what vanishes, What more is there to say?
>
> Yeats

The development of a literary history may involve a combination of strategies, including the rediscovery of forgotten texts, the reevaluation of writers and traditions slighted by mainstream scholarship, and the criticism of criticism in order to open up new conceptual windows onto the literary landscape. This essay proceeds along each of these revisionist lines, and it does so with respect to the literary history of Mexicans in the United States.[1] It may seem premature to speak of *revision* for a literary history still in its infancy, but perhaps emergent histories should be revised from the outset, lest they ossify into undesirable patterns. That some ossification is already occurring will be one point of departure for these remarks. In addition, I will address a more general issue in the construction of any literary history—namely, the relation of folklore, especially oral tradition, to written literature.

I will address these issues by examining one concrete instance in the relation of oral tradition to written literature in Texas-Mexican cultural history. My analysis focuses on the influential relationship between the Mexican ballad, or *corrido,* and one example of the relatively unknown poetic work of an otherwise prominent Texas-Mexican intellectual—the distinguished folklorist, anthropologist, and cultural historian Américo Paredes (see Limón, "Américo Paredes").

I submit that this instance, and perhaps many others that are cross-cultural, cannot be adequately understood through the dominant conceptualizations of the folklore-literature relation. After acknowledging these structures and discussing their limitations, I shall offer Harold Bloom's theory of poetic influence as a more powerful approach for grasping the meaning of this instance.[2] Yet I shall also point to the ultimate inadequacy of Bloom's ideas, inattentive as they are to literature as socially symbolic acts embedded in historical process. By expanding the range of Bloom's interpretive framework, I will make an initial anthropological statement on intergenerational cultural change in Texas-Mexican society.

My reading of the conceptual scholarship on the folklore-literature relation indicates three general tendencies. The first, oldest, and increasingly more marginal of these might be called the *precursory* position. This approach, never quite made explicit but still most evident in literary anthologies, understands folklore primarily as oral tradition that constitutes a kind of ill-formed and ill-informed "literature." The preliterature slowly gives way to well-formed and learned written productions. This position is, as I say, becoming much less prevalent in comparison to the second, which continues to dominate the subject; it is practiced by those whom Roger D. Abrahams has labeled the "lore-in-lit people" ("Folklore" 77). They are fundamentally concerned with folklore as it is found embedded in literary texts. Within this camp, however, we can make a further distinction between those who seemingly rest content with the formal identification of folklore in literature and those, like Alan Dundes, who advocate not only identification but also interpretation, to set out the stylistic and thematic significance of the folklore item for the literary text ("Study").

Before moving to the third position, we might note the influence of the first two on the emergent literary history of Mexicans in the United States, a late product of what has been called the "Chicano literary Renaissance." Since the 1960s, young writers of Mexican descent in the United States have produced a veritable outpouring of literature in all its modern genres, with poetry, perhaps, taking a leading role. The literary flowering occurred in the context of a militant redefinition of the political and cultural relations between the dominant society and a still subordinated Mexican American community. Led principally by a university-based cadre and resting on a generally ethnic nationalist ideology, the Chicano movement sought to better the social conditions of Mexicans in the United States. It also inspired and created the new Chicano literature.[3]

This literature has been accompanied by a scholarship that seeks the critical understanding of the new artistic production as well as its historical enlargement; the latter, which is proceeding largely through efforts to identify undiscovered texts, has an interesting paradoxical character (see, e.g., R. Paredes, "The Evolution"). While such a literary past may be discovered and historically reconstructed, it seems clear that it cannot be an informing tradition, in Eliot's sense, at least not for the Chicano literature produced up to the present. Chicano writers have simply not had the time to digest the recently discovered texts. Indeed, one may wonder whether the quality of the latter is such that they will ever become truly influential.

Chicano literature is indebted, however, to two other traditions—one, Western literary culture, especially North American and Latin American writers; the other, Mexican folk culture, particularly verbal art. Yet while scholarly criticism has paid some attention to the former relation, the literary connection to folk culture has remained almost wholly unexplored. Thus, Juan Rodriguez, an important critic of Chicano letters, can tell us in "El desarollo del cuento Chicano: Del folklore al tenebroso mundo del yo" that the Chicano novelist Tomás Rivera has as his masters "Sherwood Anderson, William Faulkner and Juan Rulfo," but we learn little of folklore in relation to Rivera's fiction (164). The "folklore" in Rodriguez's title refers to what he sees as a local color style in some early, premovement Chicano writers, and it would appear that this critic views folklore as a limiting historical factor in the development of Chicano literature, as the "progressive" movement of his subtitle suggests. Although Rodriguez clearly objects to "folkloristic" writing, it is not clear what his critical views are of folklore in its own right and in relationship to written literature.

To the limited extent that other critics address this relation, they seem to be guided—or misguided—by the two major prejudices inherited from mainstream criticism. One—and there is a hint of this in Rodriguez—is, as noted earlier, to think of folklore as a precursory and secondary form of literature, before the culture develops a "mature" written literature. The powerful, if unconscious, influence of this bias is illustrated in the organization of an important volume devoted to Chicano literature (Sommers and Ybarra-Frausto), which opens with a reprinted article on the "folk base" of the literature, while the rest of the largely original seventeen articles are devoted to written literature. Individual critics as well as editors can demonstrate this prejudice. In a comment that directly applies to the present case, Raymund Paredes tells us that "the *corridos* of border conflict and other types of folk song may be regarded as an *incipient* form of Chicano literature" in which one may find "the components of a *nascent* Chicano sensibility: ethnic pride and strong belief in the group's durability" ("The Evolution of Chicano Literature" 39; emphasis mine). Still another influential critic, Felipe de Ortego y Gasca, acknowledges, in "An Introduction to Chicano Poetry," that at the onset of the Chicano literary Renaissance "the old and traditional forms of Chicano poetry were still vital: *corridos, coplas, redondillas,* all artfully wrought in the tradition of Hispanic poetry" (113). Yet this is the first and last we hear of the "artfully wrought" poetry, because Ortego y Gasca devotes the rest of his essay to the explication of written literature.

Other critics take the lore-in-lit perspective noted earlier. While acknowledging the contemporary presence of folklore, they confine their scholarly task to the textual identification of folklore items in literature, or, at best, they try to demonstrate the stylistic and thematic contributions made by the folklore item to the literary text as a whole. What few appraisals have been made along these lines take the second perspective. Jane Rogers, for example, tells us of the function of *la llorona* in Rudolfo Anaya's fiction, and a few critics have focused on folk speech in Chicano literature.[4]

Nevertheless, the criticism and history of Chicano literature have given minimal attention to its relation to Mexican folklore, even while it is commonly asserted that, somehow, the literature is indebted to such folklore. To the extent that it deals with the relation, however, it does so according to the two dominant models I have outlined, and it necessarily reflects certain limitations in these approaches. In the first position, folklore takes an artistic and thematic backseat role to written literature in a chronological sense, an attitude unacceptable to scholars who still find much folkloric creativity today. And it is precisely this contemporary recognition of folklore's artistic vitality that makes some folklorists uncomfortable with the lore-in-lit perspective, for, in its own way, it too assigns folklore to a secondary role. While the presence of folklore *in* literature may enhance the latter's value, it is clear that the critical focus remains on the written text.

To be sure, Mary Ellen B. Lewis has argued for an expanded view of the folklore-literature relation. Influenced by the folklore-as-performance school, she regards folklore not solely as a text embedded in literature but as a full performance involving text, stylistics, and context, all of which the writer brings to the written literary creation and which the scholar needs to account for in any critical interpretation:

> With reference to literature then, I am suggesting that a creative writer may use folklore on several levels: that is, folklore may enter a work of literature on the *situation, medium,* or *product* level. I think future scholars must not limit their identification and analysis of folklore to *product*; but this will necessitate a well developed understanding of the multifaceted nature of literature.
>
> (345-46)

While certainly an improvement over strictly textualist approaches, this view nonetheless appears to be still fundamentally a lore-in-lit approach, albeit a more sophisticated one. We now have the writer appropriating a full folkloric performance rather than a simple text; the task of the critic is made more interesting and more complex, but the secondary role of folklore still lingers.

I believe that both in general and in Chicano criticism we should reconceptualize the folklore and literature relation to avoid the historically and artistically unwarranted relegation of folklore to a secondary position. The models of folklore as "incipient" literature or as lesser items functioning *in* literature do not do justice to the thematic and artistic complexity of verbal art suggested by the best current work in contemporary folkloristics, particularly performance-oriented folkloristics.

### FOLKLORE AS LITERATURE

We can, however, identify the third general perspective on this issue, one that essentially abandons the folklore as *pre-* or *in* literature in emphatic favor of a folklore *as* literature approach. Adherents of this viewpoint see folklore as sharing the full thematic and artistic weight of written productions. Like Lewis, these theorists depart from a concept of folklore as performance, although it is more accurate to say that they *directly* represent this school of folkloristic thought. Since this approach recognizes the full artistic potential of folklore as performance, it seems only natural that we should find here a symmetrical view of the folklore and literature relation.

We find an early statement of this model in Américo Paredes's 1964 essay "Some Aspects of Folk Poetry," in which he explicitly evokes the concept of performance to point to the range of folk poetry, different from but artistically equal to written forms. In a more recent essay, "Folklore and Literature as Performance," Abrahams invites us to consider both folklore and literature as performances with the parallel artistic power to enlist the attention and sympathy of their audiences. Finally, Susan Stewart, in *Nonsense,* points to the shared, profound ways in which folklore and written literature make sense and nonsense of experience.

Upholding the equality of folklore and literature, however, does not necessarily bring the two domains into a dynamic relationship. While important, this perspective says only that they are equal but essentially separate ways to achieve the artistic experience, sharing the resources of language and human aesthetic consciousness. To the folklore *pre-* and *in* models we can now add folklore *as* equal to but essentially separate from written literature. We need a perspective that brings the two artistically equal domains into a reciprocal relation, for only then can we be cognizant of both the continuity and the diversity of literary endeavor.

In a review of Russian and Prague School semiotics and their connection to folklore, Richard Bauman points to such a necessary relation ("Conceptions"). Along with the other folklore-as-performance theorists, he does not settle for an expanded view of folklore *in* literature but forcefully argues for an understanding of folkloric performance as a full and important artistic elaboration in its own right. Thus he writes that "the folklorist, no less than the scholar of written literature, confronts individual folk poets and unique works of literary creation, worthy of critical attention as such, as artists and works of art" (15). Yet, as noted, one can advocate folklore's equality without asserting a reciprocal bond between the two forms. Those interested in this link cannot settle for separate but equal, and neither does Bauman. Drawing on Mikhail Bakhtin, he notes that both folklore and written literature are dialectically akin to tradition and therefore to each other:

> [Of] course, neither the artists who produce these works of oral literature nor the folklorists who record them are oblivious to their traditionality, to the relationships between these particular texts and others that preceded them, in their own performances and those of others. So too must Milton have been aware of other texts of his tale of *Paradise Lost,* or Goethe of other texts of *Faust,* or Joyce of *Ulysses.* But as Bakhtin has shown us, all texts, oral or written, within a given field of expression or meaning, are part of a chain or network of texts in dialogue with each other. To identify a particular oral text as traditional is to highlight its place in a web of intertextuality that, far from placing it on the opposite side of a boundary that sets it apart from written literature, unites it with written literature still more firmly.
>
> (15)

With the performance theorists, I accord full importance to folklore in relation to written literature. Like Bauman who follows Bakhtin, I am interested in exploring the intertextual connections of these domains, each as a full and significant literary production. However, in developing my particular cultural case, I take perhaps a more radical position that incorporates but also breaks with the others. In a sense I too will speak of folklore as precursory, although not as inferior; I will analyze a performance of folklore as it appears *in* written literature, yet I will posit the independent existence of

an influential folklore outside and prior to the written text. Finally, and most important, I will demonstrate the intertextual relation of folklore and literature but not as fully literary equals. Rather, reversing its traditional role as handmaiden to literature, I shall speak of folklore as a powerful, disturbing, and dominating influence on a written poem. If, as Bauman says, Milton, Goethe, and Joyce were aware of other and presumably prior texts of their tales and if at least some of these were folkloric in character, there is no reason to assume that they were artistically inferior versions—indeed, they may have been superior.

I will argue for such a relationship of influential superiority in the particular cultural case at hand. A folkloric performance—the Mexican ballad—is taken as a dominating mode of artistic expression by a later non-folk poet "within a given field of expression or meaning"—namely, the cultural history of Mexicans in the United States. Before moving to a close examination of this poetic-cultural relation, let us review the character of the Mexican ballad.

### THE MEXICAN CORRIDO

The ballad, or *corrido,* has a prominent place in the folklore and cultural history of the Mexican people on both sides of the border. As formally and thematically defined by its leading students, the *corrido* is a folk narrative composed in octosyllabic quatrains and sung to a tune typically in ternary rhythm and in 3/4 or 6/8 meter. The quatrains are usually structured in an *a b c b* rhyme pattern, and the entire narrative may be framed by formulaic openings and closings. Its most general function is to record those events that have significantly affected the sensibilities of the Mexican masses, including social conflict, natural calamities, political changes, and interpersonal crisis (Mendoza; A. Paredes, "Mexican Corrido").

While distantly related to Spanish medieval *romance* introduced into the New World during the Conquest, the *corrido* as a distinctive form did not fully crystallize until the second half of the nineteenth century; it seems to have done so not in Mexico per se but among the people of Mexican descent who found themselves suddenly living in a subordinated condition in the "United States" after the annexation of 1848. Or so the leading contemporary scholar of the genre suggests, as he goes on to argue that the *corrido* may actually have been a creation of the Mexican community in the United States and later diffused southward as the events of the Mexican Revolution of 1910 provided new narrative themes. While *corridos* of the Mexican Revolution are much better known throughout the greater Mexican folk world, the oldest-known *corrido* tells of competition and conflict between Mexican and Anglo cowboys in south Texas in the 1860s. And some years before the ballad heroes of the revolution seized the Mexican folk imagination, the Mexican-descent community of south Texas was composing songs about local heroes like Gregorio Cortez, who resisted Anglo-Texan persecution "with his pistol in his hand" (see the work, of the same title, by Américo Paredes). Paredes is not dogmatic on this question. "That the Mexican *corrido* went through its first stages on the Lower Rio Grande Border—under the impulse of border conflict—is a thesis that could never be definitely proven" ("Mexican Corrido" 104). But, he maintains, no one as yet has identified any older *corridos* in internal Mexico.

In one sense the issue is of considerable importance, for it identifies this genre as a native Mexican American folk poetry born of social conflict with the dominant society. Thus one has a viable candidate for the beginnings of a Mexican American literary history. In another sense, however, the issue loses some of its significance, if one keeps in mind that most Mexican Americans are actually immigrants or descendants of immigrant/refugees leaving Mexico following the social upheaval of the revolution of 1910 and its aftermath. These people carried their own, similar folk poetry with them, speaking to that social experience. Eventually as natives and immigrants became one people, the two repertoires became as one, at least in the folk mind.

Whatever its origins, the Mexican *corrido* became a major folk poetry; while somewhat diminished today, it is still heard within the greater Mexican community in oral, though more often in popular recorded, form. In its epic character and even in its reduced form, the *corrido* stands as a poetic creation of its community. In addition to Américo Paredes's analysis, John H. McDowell demonstrates the social poetics of the *corrido,* leaving little doubt that this is a complex, socially engaged form.

The appreciation that contemporary Chicano critics and writers felt for the poetic and cultural power of this folk creation first led me to think of it as a dominating influence on subsequent poetry in the same tradition. I have already noted Raymund Paredes's and Ortego y Gasca's somewhat skewed recognition of the *corrido* as the beginning of Chicano literature. We can also note that the prominent Chicano writer Tomás Rivera has acknowledged its powerful influence (Bruce-Novoa, *Chicano Authors* 73, 150), while the noted poet-critic Alurista has demonstrated the clear moral-aesthetic superiority of one ballad hero over a Chicano novel and its hero ("From Tragedy"). Similarly, in the ballad of Gregorio Cortez, Guillermo Hernández finds "the most powerful and symbolic characterization" of the Chicano social experience ("On the Theoretical Bases"). Finally, Erlinda Gonzales Berry accounts for the popularity of poetry among Chicano writers by recognizing that "many of today's poets were undoubtedly nourished on *corridos* and popular verse forms which abound in the oral tradition" (45)—a judgment supported by Sergio

Elizondo when, speaking of the *corrido*'s influence, he tells us that in the Chicano poetry of "Alurista, Abelardo, and Ricardo Sánchez, among the best known, one observes it" (73). It remains to be specified how this influence actually works in contemporary Chicano poetry.[5]

If, as the evidence seems to indicate, a bond exists between the Mexican *corrido* and the work of today's Chicano writers, the link was surely more powerful for a poet who knew the *corrido* intimately and was historically and geographically closer to the epic period of the genre, at the turn of the century, in south Texas and northern Mexico. Later I will describe how a writer of the 1930s responded to the ballad's dominating presence with the poetic attitude that Harold Bloom has called the "anxiety of influence." Before proceeding to this close reading, let us examine Bloom's ideas.

### On Anxiety and Poetic Influence

I shall summarize and, I hope, in the best sense simplify Bloom's position, as expressed in a number of allusive, elusive, terminologically burdened statements and restatements. Great or "strong" poems are produced largely through the influence of stronger precursory poems. (What constitutes strength is unclear, or Bloom may think it self-evident.) Yet the relation between poems and their makers is not a happy one. The genesis of a later poem lies in the poet's act of rebellion against the precursory work, which must be overcome even as the poet senses a deep indebtedness to it. It is the anxiety of influence that underlies the struggle.

Freud informs Bloom's analysis throughout. Indeed, at times Bloom broadly hints that his own critical writing is the result of creative struggle with Freud; the anxiety of influence is not limited to poets and can structure the relation of all manner of discourse (conversely, the concept suggests that all discourse is fundamentally poetic, a point I will exploit later). The earlier poet/poem is *as* parent who dominates the child and stands in the way of the latter's own creativity, dialectically inhibiting and stimulating it. Yet the poetic child, or *ephebe,* to use Bloom's term, knows that originality is impossible, that to a fundamental extent creativity necessarily and paradoxically entails borrowing from that which one is trying to overcome. Poetic life is the continuous rebellion against the poetic parent; poetry, the result of the effort to produce a different and better poem, with the largely unconscious understanding that "different" and "better" are relational terms that imply the superior *other.*

In an effort to escape, the ephebe engages in what Bloom sees as a flexible sequence of defensive strategies. Bloom identifies six such strategies; I shall deal specifically with some of them later. Initially they help the ephebe avoid the precursor's influence but later lead to an acknowledgment of the precursor's influence without wholly negating the ephebe's own poetic existence. These strategies—what Bloom calls "revisionary ratios"—find their analogues in Freudian defense mechanisms, although, as David Gordon has noted, Bloom parts company with Freud at a critical point. For Freud these defenses against the parent usually result in a well-adjusted personality and thus are valuable and necessary. For Bloom, however, the strategies seem ultimately to end in defeat for the ephebe and, paradoxically to result in poems that are strong but always weaker than those of the master of the poetic household.

Nevertheless, the defenses against the precursor are interpretively found in the complex of images that together yield a poem. Any substantial poem and its distinctive images can, in principle, be analyzed as a variety of defensive revisions of a precursory poem within the same linguistic and cultural tradition. For Bloom, the history of Anglo-American poetry represents a series of major revisions, always in rebellion against a past and ultimately leading back to a dominant master poet—Milton. Since *Paradise Lost,* this tradition consists of artistically profitable but nevertheless weakened attempts to deal with stronger precursory poets like Milton. And indeed, Bloom's applications have been largely confined to the Anglo-American heritage and to relations between written poems. In the next section I shall test his notions of the bond between folklore and literature within the greater Mexican tradition.

### THE MEXICAN BALLAD AND "GUITARREROS"

In 1935 Américo Paredes, a twenty-year-old Texas-Mexican poet, wrote the following poem, published thirty years later.

#### "Guitarreros (Guitarists)"

Bajaron el toro prieto
que nunca lo habían bajado

(They brought the black bull down,
Never before brought down.)

Black against twisted black
The old mesquite
Rears up against the stars
Branch bridle hanging,
While the bull comes down from the mountain
Driven along by your fingers,
Twenty nimble stallions prancing up and down the *re-
    dil* of the guitars.
One leaning on the trunk, one facing—
Now the song:
Not cleanly flanked, not pacing,
But in a stubborn yielding that unshapes
And shapes itself again,
Hard-mouthed, zigzagged, thrusting,
Thrown not sung
One to the other.

The old man listens in his cloud
Of white tobacco smoke.
"It was so," he says,
"In the old days it was so."

We could easily analyze this poem using the lore-in-lit approach; even to someone not versed in greater Mexican culture, it is fairly evident that the poem incorporates folkloric elements. As its central image the poem features two guitarists singing in a rural setting, perhaps on a rural theme, although this last point requires the not-too-difficult understanding of bull either as the subject of the song or as a metaphor for song.

Our knowledge of the Mexican *corrido* tradition, however, permits us to identify the folklore in the poem. To begin with, the epigraph the poet provides consists of two lines from the traditional Mexican *corrido* "El Hijo Desobediente" ("The Disobedient Son").[6] I offer a Spanish-language text furnished by Américo Paredes and my own translation:

#### El Hijo Desobediente

Un domingo estando herrando
se encontraron dos mancebos,
echando mano a los fierros
como queriendo pelear;
cuando se estaban peleando
pues llegó su padre du uno:
—Hijo de me corazón,
ya no pelees con ninguno.—

—Quitese de aquí me padre
que estoy mas bravo que un leon,
no vaya a sacar la espada
y la parta el corazón.—
—Hijo de mi corazón,
por lo que acabas de hablar
antes de que raye el sol
la vida te han de quitar.—

—Lo que le pido a mi padre,
que no me entierre en sagrado,
que me entierre en tierra bruta
donde me trille el ganado,
con una mano de fuera
y un papel sobre-dorado,
con un letrero que diga,
"Felipe fue desdichado."

—La vaquilla colorada,
hace un año que nació.
ahi se la dejó a mi padre,
por la crianza que me dió;
los tres caballos que tengo,
ahi se los dejó a los pobres
para que digan en vida,
"Felipe, Diós te perdone."—

Barjaron el toro prieto,
que nunca lo habían bajado,
pero ora sí ya bajó
revuelto con el ganado;
ya con esta me despido

por la estrella del oriente,
y aquí se acaba el corrido
de El Hijo Desobediente.

### The Disobedient Son

On a Sunday during branding
Two young cowboys did meet,
Each going for their steel
Each looking to fight;
As they were fighting
The father of one arrived:
—My beloved son,
Do not fight with anyone.—

—Get away from here my father
I feel more fierce than a lion,
I do not want my knife
To split your heart in two.—
—My beloved son
Because of what you have said
Before the next sunrise
Your life will be taken away.—

—I only ask of my father
Do not bury me in sacred ground,
Bury me in plain earth
Where the stock may keep me company.
With one hand out of the grave
And a gilded paper.
With an epitaph that reads
"Felipe was disgraced."

—The red yearling
Born a year ago,
I leave to my father
My upbringing to him I owe;
My three stallions
I leave to the poor
So that they may say
"May God forgive Felipe."—

They brought the black bull down,
Never before brought down,
But now the bull has come down
With the rest of the stock;
Now with this I say farewell
Guided by the eastern star
This ends the ballad
Of the disobedient son.

We also realize that the guitarists are singing this particular song in the poem; indeed, even without the epigraph we can identify the song based on internal evidence. However, having made this identification, what can we say interpretively from the lore-in-literature perspective?

Clearly the occasion for the song is a folkloric performance and not merely the incorporation of a text. As such, it seems a ready-made example of Lewis's recognition that writers may use folklore events and not just texts. We still have to ask, however, what the thematic and artistic purpose of the event is and how it serves the purposes of the poet. We might call the work an exercise in nostalgia. With consummate detail Pare-

des presents a description of the guitarreros playing a traditional song—a description taking up the bulk of the poem. Indeed, it is one continuous complex sentence ending with the lines "Thrown not sung / One to the other." Another scene, in which an old man says simply, but perhaps nostalgically, "It was so / In the old days it was so," closes the poem. Folklore serves as a symbol of the past in a poem crafted in the present. This is, again, from the lore-in-literature perspective.

However, we can make a more interesting case for this otherwise limited poem if we approach it with Bauman's notion of intertextuality between folklore and literature and Bloom's theory of poetic influence. I suggest that the *corrido* and its anonymous folk poet(s) have a precursor relation to **"Guitarreros"** and conversely that the ephebe maker of this poem is a latecomer struggling against the dominating achievement of the folk poem.

We should note first that this is a poem about singing, about poetic performance. Writing in the 1930s, the ephebe did not have a printed text of the ballad before him as we do; rather, he had seen many *corrido* performances in his native border country of south Texas. The poem is fashioned in response not to what he read but to what he heard and felt. We might assume that Paredes, as he wrote, remembered the performance of the composition. The presence of the *corrido* is manifest in the epigraph, which, like the title, is in the original Spanish. And, of course, the title and opening scene speak explicitly of singing.

For Bloom, no strong latecomer wholly accepts the precursor; in a creative struggle in which defensive strategies are cast as poetic images, the ephebe achieves an artistic work even if it necessarily falls short of complete victory. The six strategies tend to appear in matched pairs. Bloom calls them *clinamen-tessera, kenosis-daemonization,* and *askesis-apophrades* and finds them operating in the poetry of Western culture.

Having established in the epigraph the presence of the poetic forebear, Paredes the ephebe opens his poem with an eight-line section that, in my estimation, constitutes one of Bloom's primary revisionary ratios. The lines execute a *clinamen,* or poetic swerve, with respect to the ballad. In *The Anxiety of Influence,* Bloom tells us that a *clinamen* appears as a corrective move in the ephebe's poem "which implies that the precursor poem went accurately up to a certain point, but then should have swerved, precisely in the direction that the new poem moves" (97). In a later statement Bloom explains that a poem's opening *clinamen*

> . . . is marked by dialectical images of absence and presence, images that rhetorically are conveyed by the trope of simple irony . . . and that as psychic defense assume the shape of what Freud called reaction-formation. . . . Just as rhetorical irony . . . says one

thing and means another, even the opposite thing, so a reaction-formation opposes itself to a repressed desire by manifesting the opposite of the desire.

(97)

Implied error and asserted correction. Absence and presence. Irony and the literal. Desire and repression. These are the dialectical meanings of the first eight lines; it is important to note that the manifest content may be only a secondary key and that we must also be aware of the role of form (a concern that receives Bloom's less-than-adequate attention). Even as the *corrido*'s presence is established through the epigraph, it is quickly removed, at least formally. Having just read (and "heard") two lines from precursory tradition, we immediately find ourselves in a different poem. Spanish gives way to English; the regular meter and rhyme of folk poetry is replaced by a written form that has varying meter and little rhyme. Most important, in contrast to the conventional diction of folk song, Paredes's creation draws on a constellation of modernist imagery—"Black against twisted black"; a mesquite like a stallion; fingers, also like stallions, that drive along a bull as they play a song. These formal choices, the essence of the ephebe's poetic swerve, implicitly and initially say that the poem is different from and better than its precursors.

Yet this new formal presence is necessarily caught in an irony conditioned, paradoxically, by the appearance of tradition. For even as the "correction" of implied error is made, the formal declaration of poetic independence is thematically dominated by the *corrido*. What appears to be an autonomous poem in lines one through five reacknowledges tradition in lines five through eight as two folk singers slowly emerge in the long poetic clause

> While the bull comes down from the mountain
> Driven along by your fingers,
> Twenty nimble stallions prancing up and down the *re-dil* of the guitars.

The ephebe is addressing his precursory poets—"*your* fingers"—as it becomes clear that they are playing their guitars and singing the ballad alluded to in the epigraph. The portrait becomes even clearer with the line "One leaning on the trunk, one facing—."

In explicitly recognizing his precursors, the ephebe is engaging in the revisionary movement Bloom calls the *tessera,* in which the formal swerve of the *clinamen* falters or at least gives way to the emerging presence of tradition in the images of the poem. The *tessera* is an expression of truce between ephebe and precursor. The ephebe talks to and talks only about the earlier poets as they begin to craft their song; the imagery of fingers like "Twenty nimble stallions" reveals the ephebe's admiration for his precursors. In this sense we can say that the precursor exerts control over the ephebe.

However, the folk poets are at the same time within the control of the ephebe, for their singing can be "heard" only through his poetic skill. Only, the ephebe seems to say, through his more modern verse can one make sense of the precursory power. In the movement of *tessera,* Bloom tells us,

> . . . the later poet provides what his imagination tells him would complete the otherwise "truncated" precursor poem or poet. . . . In this sense of a completing link, the *tessera* represents any later poet's attempt to persuade himself (and us) that the precursor's Word would be worn out if not redeemed as a newly fulfilled and enlarged Word of the ephebe.

(*Anxiety* 67)

Having made this temporary adjustment—this compromise—between self and tradition, the ephebe continues the poem by seemingly negating his own poetic presence. In this final negotiation with the precursor—the *kenosis*—the ephebe submits to the authority of tradition while yet exacting a price from the precursor. Although "apparently emptying himself of his own afflatus, his imaginative godhood," the later poet

> . . . seems to humble himself as though he were ceasing to be a poet, but this ebbing is so performed . . . that the precursor is emptied out also, and so the later poem of deflation is not as absolute as it seems.

(14-15)

The *kenosis* begins with the line "Now the song," as the ephebe engages in direct evaluatory encounter with the precursor poem. What does he think of it and, by implication, how does it compare to his own song before us? His description betrays too much, for clearly the young ephebe is overwhelmed and his poem is suffused by the powerful poem from the past, which like a strong bull or cow pony (the metaphor is slightly but perhaps profitably confused here) is

> Not cleanly flanked, not pacing,
> But in a stubborn yielding that unshapes
> And shapes itself again,
> Hard-mouthed, zigzagged, thrusting,
> Thrown not sung
> One to the other.

The reader shares the admiration of the ephebe for his precursor song, but the other effect of the passage is to vitiate the ephebe's own poetic effort. It is still the ephebe, of course, who is in some degree of control as the *tessera* lingers, but it is now quite a shaky truce as the precursor takes over the ephebe and his poem.

Nevertheless, in the revisionary ratio of *kenosis,* the ephebe's voice remains, muted as it may be. In its final poetic analysis, the work empties itself in a way "that the precursor is emptied out also." The ephebe accomplishes the dual movement by the ingenious introduction of an old man in the last four lines:

The old man listens in his cloud
Of white tobacco smoke.
"It was so," he says,
"In the old days it was so."

What are we to make of this conclusion?

First, we must take the old man as what he most probably is—namely, an elder; and, as Paredes the cultural historian has noted, in the greater Mexican culture of early southern Texas, "decisions were made, arguments were settled, and sanctions were decided upon by the old men of the group, with the leader usually being the patriarch" (***"With His Pistol"*** 12). In effect, the elder settles the struggle between the ephebe and tradition but does so in the manner of *kenosis.* That is, although in one sense he represents tradition, he is also speaking for the ephebe, and in the dual role of traditional image and poetic voice, he limits both tradition and the ephebe, "emptying" them out in relation to each other.

The limitation is carried primarily by the old man's "It was so." What "was so"? At one level, the old man is commenting on the powerful singing. As an essentially historical artistic performance, it *was* so, but by clear implication, it is not now. We are left with a different style of singing that is not singing at all—namely, the ephebe's poem. If it is less impressive than the "hard-mouthed, zigzagged, thrusting" song, then we are the poorer for it; yet at the same time, folk tradition has also reached its performative limits. It can no longer speak to us directly; the precursor's voice is muted; and only the ephebe's poem *is so,* for all its inferiority to the powerful song of the past.

At another level of meaning we need to recall the ballad itself—a ballad about sons, fathers, disobedience, and dire consequences, which up to now we have largely neglected. A miscreant son violates the moral hierarchy of his society and meets his fate in a world in which, according to Paredes, "the representative of God on earth was the father" and his "curse was thought to be the most terrible thing on earth" (***"With His Pistol"*** 11). Symbolically, moral order is restored at two levels in the ballad. Even as he calmly accepts his fate, the young *vaquero* affirms the natural order of things by distributing his goods, especially his stock, a prized possession, and by asking to be buried in a secular setting. Second, the *corrido* ends as, presumably, other *vaqueros* establish control over a paradoxical power. Like the *vaquero,* the black bull is strong but potentially dangerous and perhaps, as his color connotes, even evil; therefore society must reestablish the moral order. To this control of potential disorder symbolized by the black bull, the old man, appropriately in a cloud of white smoke, tends his approving but limiting "It was so."

Once again, like the singing, we can understand this moral world only secondhand. For us it is a world no longer possible, and with the ephebe we stand empty before it, knowing that we have to construct our own moral existence. The normative impact of the past has been blunted, and only the ephebe's desire can give us imaginative access to it. It was so.

Both the moral and artistic dimensions of the *corrido* world are captured through the single metaphor of the *guitarreros* driving the song, as the *vaqueros* control the black bull. The *vaqueros* and the singers, of course, must exercise an intermediary control over their "stallions," one group literally, the other through the ability of their fingers to produce a finely crafted artistic whole. This is a world in which moral and artistic disorder is not permitted. Potential disorder must be controlled by human beings lest they suffer the degradation of their kind; but, again, it was so.

We cannot help sensing the ephebe's desire for the world of the *corrido;* after all, he writes of nothing else in this poem. Yet of course he writes about it; it does not come to us in an unmediated form. It is his generosity to tradition in his art that makes it possible to us. Even as he formally violates tradition in the ways noted earlier, he ultimately affirms it. While lending final assent to this dominant influence, he nevertheless implicitly and explicitly demonstrates its historicity, and thus, in Bloom's terms, "the precursor is emptied out also" in relation to the ephebe even as he is being overwhelmed by the precursor.

Perhaps the most poetic evidence of the paradoxical is the existence of the *two* ephebes. Like Felipe, the young hero of the *corrido,* our ephebe has swerved in *clinamen;* he has readjusted in *tessera,* as does the son when he willingly acknowledges his moral error; finally, in *kenosis,* both young men affirm tradition to the point of self-negation. As a poet our ephebe must die under the influence of the powerful moral-artistic order that is his inheritance. For such an order to live in our consciousness, there must be a rebellion, but one that in this instance can end only in the ephebe's willing assent to the superiority of the parent, even while the parent incurs a debt to the child.

In principle the poem need not end here, and we could have a paradise regained. With more time, experience, learning, and self-confidence there should follow the dialectical, antithetical completion of *kenosis* in what Bloom calls *daemonization,* in which the ephebe begins "a movement towards a personalized Counter-Sublime, in reaction to the precursor's Sublime" (*Anxiety* 15) as the "later poet opens himself to what he believes to be a power in the parent poem that does not belong to the parent proper, but to a range of being just beyond that precursor." The ephebe seeks an autonomous voice, and "turning against the precursor's Sublime, the newly strong poet undergoes *daemonization,* a Counter-

Sublime whose function suggests *the precursor's relative weakness*" (120).

Our ephebe's poem ends short of this revision. There is no strong counterassertion, no attempt to articulate a distinctive poem that implicitly denies the adequacy of the precursor. In this poem at least, our later poet cannot find—perhaps chooses not to find—his own distinctive voice. The poem ends with an implicit recognition of the power of tradition made explicit in the dedication of Paredes's other major dialogue with the *corrido* heritage:

> To the memory of my father,
> who rode a raid or two with
> Catarino Garza;
> and to all those old men
> who sat around on summer nights,
> in the days when there was
> a chaparral, smoking their
> cornhusk cigarettes and talking
> in low, gentle voices about
> violent things;
> while I listened.[7]

In the days of Catarino Garza when there *was* a chaparral and when men talked of violent things—here we find our ephebe as a poet with a sense of social history; I turn now to this relationship.

### TEXAS-MEXICAN POETRY AND HISTORY

I have argued for an intertextual relation between a folk poem from oral tradition and a later poem by a Texas-Mexican intellectual. Drawing on Harold Bloom, I have suggested that the written poem is an artistic manifestation of the "anxiety of influence" as the poet engages in a creative struggle with his strong precursor.

While I obviously find Bloom's ideas useful for the explication of at least some intertextual relations, I have a sense of unease concerning the ahistorical and asocial character of Bloom's argument. For while Bloom implicitly appeals to history by way of tradition and chronology when he speaks of "precursor" and "later," there is another, social, sense of history that he almost wholly ignores. In his interpretive world poets deal with each other as pure poets divorced from sociohistorical contexts and constraints. In the *Anxiety of Influence*, he is quite candid on this point: "That even the strongest poets are subject to influences not poetical is obvious even to me, but again my concern is only with *the poet in a poet*, or the aboriginal poetic self" (11). Bloom simply chooses not to consider that his poets and possibly their anxieties are products and producers of the social consensus and contradictions of their historical movement. His wisest critic shares my unease. Frank Lentricchia finds Bloom's idea of "the poet in a poet"

shrewd, disarming, and also question begging and evasive. What about those "influences not poetical"? And what is the poet in a poet? Something isolate and impregnable to all externally originating influences except those literary in character? The unspoken assumption is that poetic identity is somehow a wholly intraliterary process in no contract with the larger extraliterary processes that shape human identity.

(326)

Bloom does not deal with the ways a particular poem may be read simultaneously as a manifestation of the "anxiety of influence" *and* the effects of social change. Permit me to argue this expanded view of influence through the case at hand.

Clearly, the *corrido* of the lower Texas-Mexican border was an expressive product of a culturally homogenous and socially stable folk society that prevailed in this region from its founding in the mid-eighteenth century to the latter half of the nineteenth. As a fundamentally precapitalist society with certain semifeudal characteristics, it was not yet caught up in the transition to agrarian capitalism and the process of cultural change that descended on the area in 1848 and accelerated greatly between 1890 and 1930. This period of intense change was accompanied by physical and psychological violence against those recalcitrant Mexicans who resisted the new social order (see A. Paredes, *"With His Pistol"*; see also Montejano).

The *corrido* as an epic with the symbolic hero "with his pistol in his hand" became one form of folk resistance against the imposition of the new order. The epitome of the ballad of resistance is **"El Corrido de Gregorio Cortez,"** as Américo Paredes has shown us. Such ballads contain the symbolic representations of the new social contradiction and express a manifest ideological content of resistance. There can, however, also be what Fredric Jameson, in *The Political Unconscious,* calls an "ideology of form," in which form itself captures consensus and contradiction (98-102). By this line of analysis we might put forth the speculative notion that at the moment of greatest social contradiction, between 1890 and 1930, the *corrido* as a formal process, and regardless of its particular symbolic content, articulated the principles of social hierarchy, moral order, collectivity, and a rhythmic life process threatened by oppressive and fragmenting social relations. However, as Paredes has also noted, by the 1930s the *corrido* itself entered a period of decline, a process I have elsewhere interpreted as the incorporation of the folk tradition into the hegemonic order and the dissolution of its organic folk base in south Texas (see A. Paredes, "Mexican Corrido," and Limón, "Rise").

As someone who witnessed the end of the *corrido* period in his adolescence, our ephebe experienced two anxieties of influence; one, toward the power of the *corrido* as I have demonstrated it, and, another—not accounted for in Bloom's ahistorical scheme—toward the influence of social change. If there is an ideology of form as well as of symbolic content, we might say that formally and linguistically our ephebe is attempting to swerve away from a tradition no longer serviceable, but is doing so in the direction of a style and language representing the cultural level of the new social order. Whatever its content at a formal level, **"Guitarreros"** is a profoundly modern American poem. Responding to the anxiety of influence fostered by the new order, the ephebe opens himself up almost wholly to it, in the manner of a *kenosis,* and in effect writes a poem for *them* (now really all of us). At the same time, he develops a poetic content that demonstrates an anxiety of influence toward the *corrido* and the traditional past. In 1935, Paredes also wrote **"Flute Song"**:

> Why was I ever born
> Heir to a people's sorrow,
> Wishing this day were done
> And yet fearful for the morrow.

In that year Texas-Mexicans were already experiencing the dilemma and, as a generation, were responding in a variety of ways to the anxiety of influence they felt toward the past and the present. Our ephebe's formal and thematic poetic solution is a particularly fine manifestation of the social contradiction that will continue to haunt the poetry of Mexicans in the United States.

With the increasing production of literature by Mexicans in the United States and the growth of an accompanying scholarship, we can confidently begin to speak of a literary history for this population. Representing the second largest minority group in this country, such a history should inevitably also become part of the literary history of the United States.

My principal concern in this essay has been to contribute to this process in at least three distinctive ways. First, I have presented the work of relatively unknown and largely undiscovered poets—the anonymous folk poet(s) of "El Hijo Desobediente" and the distinguished Texas-Mexican intellectual Américo Paredes. Second, I have offered a critique of the prevalent and limited ways of treating the relations of folklore and written literature, objecting to these approaches both in general and to the degree to which they have dominated the literary history of Mexicans in the United States. Finally, I have argued for an alternative conceptualization of this relation by drawing on the Bakhtin-Bauman notion of intertextuality and, more significantly, on Bloom's theory of poetic influence. Any future intellectually defensible history of literature cannot in principle reject the equal status of folklore and written literature and should be able to accept instances in which the folklore emerges

as a dominant influence on written literature and not merely as something that is *in* the literature. This final point has also involved a revision of Bloom's theory. For as Lentricchia has critically noted, Bloom argues that the "psychic and social life of the poet as a man in the world counts for nothing; history in a big, inclusive sense cannot touch the sacred being of intrapoetic relations," which "constitute an elite and inviolably autonomous body of discourse" (331). Lentricchia correctly observes that, as it stands, Bloom's theory is really the reappearance of the asocial New Criticism in a fresh guise. While I believe that Bloom's ideas offer a useful way to unite literary history, for Mexicans in the United States at least, a history of literary relations cannot ignore their obvious immersion in social process. To this end, I have offered an amplification of his thought. To the degree that I have succeeded I hope to have made a contribution to a new American literary history.

*Notes*

1. I use the word *Mexican* as a simple translation of *mexicano,* the preferred Spanish-language term of self-reference for the Mexican-descent population of the United States, although I am not insensitive to the pejorative misuses of this term by the Anglo-Saxon tongue. This choice also takes into account the genesis of the Mexican ballad, or *corrido,* which is not uniquely the property of those on this side of the border. *Chicano* I shall reserve to designate the political and cultural persons and processes of social activism since the 1960s. For my elaborated views on the always controversial question, see "The Folk Performance of *Chicano* and the Cultural Limits of Political Ideology." Following Américo Paredes, I shall also use the term *greater Mexico* to refer to the movement of people and culture across a political boundary. I read versions of this essay at the 1980 meetings of the Modern Language Association and at the 1983 Symposium on Chicano Popular Art and Literature, University of California, Santa Barbara. I am grateful to Luis Leal and members of the audience for a helpful critical discussion. My particular thanks go to Teresa McKenna and Tomás Ybarra-Frausto.

2. Bloom, *Anxiety, Map, Poetry,* and *Breaking.* My special thanks to Ramon Saldívar for leading me to Bloom's work.

3. Ybarra-Frausto, "Chicano Movement." For a comprehensive treatment of this poetry—or at least the major figures—see Juan Bruce-Novoa, *Chicano Poetry.* This unabashedly "textualist" critic says relatively little about my central

concerns—folklore, influence, history, and social changes. His concern is the "chicano" poetry "text"; the rest he leaves to "social scientists." I accept.

4. Rogers. Studies of folk speech in Chicano literature include Mario Garza and Guadalupe Valdes-Fallis.

5. The present essay is a version of one chapter of a study in press on this influence. Subsequent chapters include analyses of Rodolfo "Corky" Gonzalez, José Montoya, and Juan Gomez-Q.

6. According to Paredes, this is the version he learned as a young man from the *corridistas* of the lower border. It is quite literally his direct influence. For another version, see Mendoza 266-68.

7. Dedication *"With His Pistol."* Catarino Garza was a late nineteenth-century south Texas newspaper editor who led an armed resistance movement against both the dictatorship of Porfirio Díaz in Mexico and the Texas rangers on this side of the border.

## Works Cited

Primary works by African American, Native American, Asian American, and Hispanic writers are listed in the selected bibliographies.

Abrahams, Roger D. "Folklore and Literature as Performance." *Journal of the Folklore Institute* 8 (1972) 75-94.

Alurista. "From Tragedy to Caricature . . . and Beyond." *Aztlan* 11 (1980): 89-98.

Bauman, Richard. "Conceptions of Folklore in the Development of Literary Semiotics." *Semiotica* 19 (1982): 1-20.

Berry, Erlinda Gonzalez. "Perros y Antiperros: The Voice of the Bard." *De colores* 5 (1980): 45-68.

Bloom, Harold. *The Anxiety of Influence: A Theory of Poetry.* New York: Oxford UP, 1973.

———. *The Breaking of the Vessels.* Chicago: U of Chicago P, 1982.

———. *A Map of Misreading.* New York: Oxford UP, 1975.

———. *Poetry and Repression: Revisionism from Blake to Stevens.* New Haven: Yale UP, 1976.

Bloomfield, Leonard. *Plains Cree Texts.* Publications of the American Ethnological Soc. 16. New York: Stechert, 1934.

Bruce-Novoa, Juan D., ed. *Chicano Authors: Inquiry by Interview.* Austin: U of Texas P, 1980.

———. *Chicano Poetry: A Response to Chaos.* Austin: U of Texas P, 1982.

Dundes, Alan. "The Study of Folklore in Literature and Culture: Identification and Interpretation." *Journal of American Folklore* 78 (1965): 136-42.

Elizondo, Sergio. "Sergio Elizondo." Bruce-Novoa, *Chicano Authors* 67-82.

Gordon, David. "Form and Feeling." *Yale Review* 62 (1973): 582-93.

Hernández, Guillermo. "On the Theoretical Bases of Chicano Literature." *De colores* 5 (1980): 5-18.

Jameson, Fredric. *The Political Unconscious: Narrative as a Socially Symbolic Act.* Ithaca: Cornell UP, 1981.

Lentricchia, Frank. *After the New Criticism.* Chicago: U of Chicago P, 1980.

Lewis, Mary Ellen B. "The Study of Folklore in Literature: An Expanded View." *Southern Folklore Quarterly* 40 (1976): 343-51.

Limón, José E. "Américo Paredes: A Man from the Border." *Revista Chicano-Riqueña* 8 (1980): 1-5.

———. "The Folk Performance of *Chicano* and the Cultural Limits of Political Ideology." Bauman and Abrahams, *"And Other Neighborly Names"* 197-225.

———. "The Rise, Fall, and 'Revival' of the Mexican-American Corrido: A Review Essay." *Studies in Latin American Popular Culture* 2 (1983): 202-06.

McDowell, John H. "The Corrido of Greater Mexico as Discourse, Music, and Event." Bauman and Abrahams, *"And Other Neighborly Names"* 44-75.

Mendoza, Vicente T. *El corrido mexicano.* México: Fonda de Cultura Economica, 1954.

Ortego y Gasca, Felipe de. "An Introduction to Chicano Poetry." Sommers and Ybarra-Frausto, *Modern Chicano Writers* 108-16.

Paredes, Américo. "Flute Song." Unpub. poem, 1935.

———. "The Folk Base of Chicano Literature." Sommers and Ybarra-Frausto, *Modern Chicano Writers* 4-17.

———. "Guitarreros (Guitarists)." 1935. *Southwest Review* 19 (1964): 306.

———. "The Mexican Corrido: Its Rise and Fall." Boatright, Hudson, and Maxwell, *Madstones and Twisters* 91-105.

———. "Some Aspects of Folk Poetry." *Texas Studies in Literature and Language* 6 (1964): 213-25.

———. "Tributaries to the Main Stream: The Ethnic Groups." Coffin, *Our Living Traditions* 70-80.

————. *"With His Pistol in His Hand"*: *A Border Ballad and Its Hero*. Austin: U of Texas P, 1958.

Paredes, Raymund. "The Evolution of Chicano Literature." Baker, *Three American Literatures* 33-79.

Rodriguez, Juan. "El desarollo del cuento Chicano: Del folklore al tenebroso mundo del yo." *The Identification and Analysis of Chicano Literature*. Ed. Francisco Jimenez. New York: Bilingual, 1979. 58-67.

Rogers, Jane. "The Function of the *la llorona* Motif in Rudolfo Anaya's *Bless Me, Ultima*." *Latin American Literature Review* 5 (1977): 64-69.

Sommers, Joseph, and Tomás Ybarra-Frausto, eds. *Modern Chicano Writers: A Collection of Critical Essays*. Englewood Cliffs: Prentice, 1979.

Ybarra-Frausto, Tomás. "The Chicano Movement and the Emergence of a Chicano Poetic Consciousness." *New Scholar* 5 (1972). Rpt. in *New Directions in Chicano Scholarship*. Ed. Ricardo Romo and Raymund Paredes. La Jolla: Chicano Studies Center, Univ. of California, 1978. 81-110.

## José E. Limón (essay date 1993)

SOURCE: Limón, José E. "The Return of the Mexican Ballad: Américo Paredes and His Anthropological Text as Persuasive Political Performances." In *Creativity/Anthropology*, edited by Smadar Lavie, Kirin Narayan, and Renato Rosaldo, pp. 184-210. Ithaca, N.Y.: Cornell University Press, 1993.

[*In the following essay, Limón discusses Paredes's influential studies and translations of the folk ballads of the Texas-Mexican border region.*]

This essay's principal argument is that a particular anthropological text and its author, largely ignored in wider anthropological circles, have played a central influential role in the formation and development of a Mexican-American political culture in our time. I refer to Américo Paredes and his ***"With His Pistol in His Hand": A Border Ballad and Its Hero*** (1958, 1971), a study of the Mexican ballad, or *corrido,* and its sociocultural context along the lower Texas-Mexico border. Although an important part of this book's significance stems from its superb scholarship and its anticipation of certain contemporary intellectual practices, in this analysis, I want to call attention to that influence which flows from the author's career and part I of his book as cultural rhetoric, as unified, contextually persuasive, textual performances. Paredes's life and his book, in their narrative organization and poetics, recall the aesthetic politics of their scholarly subject, the Mexican ballad of border conflict; through their artistic transformation of the ballad, they exert a compelling influence on a new generation.

It is not often that an anthropological study and the life of its author become persuasive, artistic, textual performances, if by the latter phrase we at least imply, following Jan Mukarovsky (1977), that a textuality partakes of what he calls "poetic designation," meaning the "every use of words occurring in a text with a predominant aesthetic function" (1977: 65) where this aesthetic function renders "the sign itself the center of attention" (1977: 68). However, Mukarovsky does not wish to be misconstrued on two important issues: one, such a designation and function apply not only to formal poetry or other figurative language; "this function participates, at least potentially, in every human act" (1977: 69), whether poem, ritual, conversation, or anthropology; and, two, that this focus on the sign "itself," while weakening the relationship to any immediate reality, "does not preclude a relation between the work and reality as a whole; on the contrary it is even beneficial to this relation" (1977: 71). He summarizes and concludes in a statement that is a charter for this essay. "The aesthetic function . . . is potentially present in every utterance. The specific character of poetic designation, therefore, rests solely in its more radical exposure of the tendency inherent in every act of designation. The weakening of the immediate relation of poetic designation to reality is counterbalanced by the fact that the poetic work as a global designation enters into relation with the *total* set of the existential experiences of the subject, be he the creative or the perceiving subject" (1977: 72-73).

We are only too aware of the poetic designation inherent in traditional literary practice in its various genres. However, other human acts, and indeed "every human act," are beginning to receive increasing attention in these terms, including those discourses, chiefly intellectual, that often inherently and strongly define themselves with a claim to *non*-poetic designation. The analysis and the self-conscious *practice* of poetic designation in ostensibly non-poetic intellectual discourse, while not yet mainstream, gains increasing prominence, a tendency that Clifford Geertz, one of its exemplary practitioners and theorists, calls "blurred genres" (1980). We also think of Hayden White in history (1973, 1978), Harold Bloom in literary criticism (1982), and in anthropology, with Geertz, others including Boon (1982), Marcus and Cushman (1982), Bruner (1986), and Clifford and Marcus (1986).

I will also argue that, as practice, Paredes's poetically designated anthropology anticipates this contemporary trend toward "blurred genres"; my own essay pretends to be an ethnically keyed, theoretical intervention in this new trend. Thus, in union with Paredes, I want to help allay James Clifford's concern that ethnic marginality may be a necessary constraint on textual experimentation or its theoretical analysis.[1]

Further, this essay proposes to be a modest effort to restore Mukarovsky's full formation, whose social intent is often repressed in contemporary analysis.[2] There is, it seems to me, in such analysis, a too singular concern with the first half of his formulation, with the text as pure sign rendering it the "center of attention," and a relative lack of concern with the poetically designated text "as a global designation" which "enters into relation with the *total* set of the existential experiences of the subject, be he the creative or the perceiving subject." I want to take Paredes's poetically designated text and his career beyond their obvious reference to an immediate reality (the Mexican ballad and a community of ballad specialists) to its more global designation as a persuasive, political cultural text that, marshalling the influence of the ballad, addresses and helps to form a generation of poets, intellectuals and activists all engaged in a political movement. I propose then to focus on the poetics of *"With His Pistol in His Hand"* and its author, firmly taking into account, to paraphrase Mukarovsky only once again, a near totality of the social experiences of those political, creative, and perceiving subjects involved in the textualization of this author and his work.

### THE APPEARANCE OF *WITH HIS PISTOL IN HIS HAND*

Paredes's book is generally a continuation of a scholarly tradition of folk cultural studies on the Mexican-descent population of the U.S. Southwest. When published in 1958, it represented a sharp break with the interpretive politics of this tradition, which consisted either of a conservative formal textualism, as in the case of Aurelio M. Espinosa's work on New Mexico, or a liberal utopian romanticism, as in J. Frank Dobie's work on Mexican Texas (Limón n.d.). As I suggest in this section, Paredes offered a conflictual model of cultural process which took into account, at least implicitly, questions of class, domination, and cultural creation and resistance. In this respect his work was an early alternative in critical anticipation of a body of later, functionalist anthropological work on this population (Rosaldo 1985). However, as I began to suggest earlier, *"With His Pistol in His Hand"* is substantively a study of the Mexican border ballad or corrido as it appears and develops along the lower Texas-Mexico border, South Texas, since the Spanish settlement of the area in the mid-eighteenth century. More specifically, it is a study of the life, legend, and corpus of ballads generated by the activities of one individual, Gregorio Cortez. My interpretation of Paredes's book requires the reader's knowledge and understanding of these events: what follows is the known history of the incident as set out by Paredes.

Until 12 June 1901 Cortez was a rather ordinary Mexican-American in Texas, an agricultural laborer like so many others who, from his own perspective, was witnessing the intensification of a largely Anglo-American and capitalist domination of Texas, including the predominantly Mexican-American region of South Texas. This domination of the native and increasingly immigrant Mexican-descent population took the form of class and racial subordination, the latter evidenced in part in the rough and ready lynching "justice" often administered to Mexican-Americans accused of crimes (Limón 1986). Such was the fate that Cortez undoubtedly expected on 12 June in the moments after he killed Sheriff W. T. Morris in Karnes County in central Texas in an exchange of pistol fire which also left Cortez's brother, Romaldo, seriously wounded. In his last official act, Sheriff Morris, an ex-Texas Ranger, had come out to the farm where the Cortezes, migrants from the border, were sharecropping. The sheriff was looking for reported horse thieves. Because neither he nor his accompanying deputy spoke Spanish well, if at all, they mistakenly accused the Cortezes of the thievery, and the sheriff drew his gun. Probably thinking they were about to be gunned down in cold blood, Romaldo charged the sheriff, not knowing that his brother had a gun hidden behind his back. Morris shot Romaldo but in the next instant was himself cut down by Gregorio, even as the deputy ran for his life and help. With the sheriff lying dead before him, Cortez knew that he faced certain Texas justice. Entrusting his brother to his family, Gregorio began a long horseback ride of escape to South Texas and the Mexican border. Along the way he evaded numerous posses through skillful riding and help from local Mexican-Americans. He also killed a second sheriff. Eventually, Cortez learned that the authorities had incarcerated his wife and children and were carrying out reprisals against those who had helped him. He turned himself in to the authorities near Laredo, Texas, where Mexican-Americans still had some measure of political control. Nonetheless, he was returned to Karnes County where, under constant threat of lynching, he was tried and convicted. In one of those paradoxes characteristic of Texas, he was eventually pardoned by an Anglo governor.

By 1901 the Mexican-Americans of Texas had experienced a half century of domination. Cortez's encounter with this domination and his largely successful, adventurous ride to freedom stirred the folk imagination of this community; its folk singers turned to a traditional musical form—the corrido—to speak to these events. As a song narrative the corrido had as its ancestral form the medieval Spanish *romance* such as those of *El Cid*. Then, as now, this form served communities well in recording important historical events and artistically rendering their perspectives on these events. Soon after, or perhaps even during, Cortez's ride, the folk singers began to compose and sing the ballad of Gregorio Cortez, as Paredes says, "in the *cantinas* and the country stores, in the ranches when men gather at night to talk in the cool dark, sitting in a circle, smoking and listening to the old songs and the tales of other days" (1971: 33). They sang this song in the traditional octosyllabic metre with rhyming quatrains of *a b c b* and in duets of two guitars. One of the better versions of the ballad which Paredes offers as a representative text follows:

### El Corrido de Gregorio Cortez

In the county of El Carmen
A great misfortune befell;
The Major Sheriff is dead;
Who killed him no one can tell.

At two in the afternoon,
In half an hour or less,
They knew that the man who killed him
Had been Gregorio Cortez.

They let loose the bloodhound dogs;
They followed him from afar.
But trying to catch Cortez
Was like following a star.

All the rangers of the county
Were flying, they rode so hard;
What they wanted was to get
The thousand-dollar reward.

And in the county of Kiansis
They cornered him after all;
Though they were more than three hundred
He leaped out of their corral.

Then the Major Sheriff said,
As if he was going to cry,
"Cortez, hand over your weapons;
We want to take you alive."

Then said Gregorio Cortez,
And his voice was like a bell,
"You will never get my weapons
Till you put me in a cell."

Then said Gregorio Cortez,
With his pistol in his hand,
"Ah, so many mounted Rangers
Just to take one Mexican!"

Cortez's epic encounter was neither the first nor the last of such encounters with Anglo-Texan authority, nor was it the first or last to inspire corridos. Ten years before Cortez, Catarino Garza, journalist and guerrilla leader, had taken up organized arms against the Texas Rangers and inspired a balladry. Fourteen years after Cortez, new corridos could be heard along the border about *los sediciosos* (the seditionists), bands of Mexicans who, again, rose up in armed rebellion in 1915-1916 against Anglo-Texan authority. In reprisal the Texas Rangers carried out massive killings of combatants and civilians alike, a practice that even an eminent champion of the Rangers, historian Walter Prescott Webb, felt obliged to criticize as an "orgy of bloodshed" (1935: 263).

In an attenuated form, the tradition of conflict and corridos continues through the present, although by the 1930s the intense conflict and the epic corridos of the past had diminished (Peña 1982: Limón 1983). Nonetheless, the subordination of the Mexican-descent community continued even while new leadership elements emerged to speak on its behalf, albeit in an assimilationist rhetoric. It was in the waning moments of the epic corrido and amid this new assimilationist ideology that Américo Paredes came to maturity. I shall say more of his life later; for now, I note that he is Professor of English and Anthropology at the University of Texas at Austin.

When it appeared in 1958, *"With His Pistol in His Hand"* received its principal attention from the communities of folklorists and scholars of the West and certain elements of the Anglo lay public in Texas. It might have remained another circumscribed, scholarly book for specialists. However, in the 1960s the book found a sociopolitical context and a wider audience of socially-designated perceiving subjects that gave it a far more global meaning. The 1960s provided these when the first significant groups of largely working-class Mexican-American youth attended colleges and universities in the Southwest, and joined with other youth in the political protest and cultural rebellion of the time. For Mexican-American youth, of course, there was a very particular focus on the continuing socioeconomic plight of their native community. This activity among this college youth became the Chicano movement which, in addition to its practical politics, also generated a great deal of intellectual and artistic work on the Mexican-American community (Gomez-Quiñones 1978; Ybarra-Frausto 1977). Published on the eve of this political, intellectual, and artistic florescence, Paredes's book proved to be not only a scholarly, anthropological folklore study but also a text written in such a poetically designated way that, almost as if by design, it became a powerful influence on a new generation of Chicano writers, intellectuals, and activists as they produced a new critical social discourse. The late Tomás Rivera, former chancellor of the University of California at Riverside and still the leading Chicano fiction writer, had this to say concerning his introduction to *"With His Pistol in His Hand."* He writes of a time when he was a graduate student at a small state college in San Marcos, Texas between Austin and Karnes County.

> One day I was wandering through the library and I came across *"With His Pistol in His Hand"* by Américo Paredes and I was fascinated. I didn't even know Paredes existed though we were only thirty miles away . . . but there was no communication at all, because there wasn't a Movement or anything like that. I checked out that book. I was hungry to find something by a Chicano. . . . It fascinated me because, one, it proved it was possible for a Chicano to publish; two, it was about a Chicano, Gregorio Cortez and his deeds

. . . and, the ballads too. I grew up with the *corridos* in Texas. That book indicated to me that it was possible to talk about a Chicano as a complete figure. . . . More importantly, *"With His Pistol in His Hand"* indicated to me a whole imaginative possibility for us to explore. Now that also was in 1958, and it was then I began to think, write, and reflect a hell of a lot more on those people I had known in 1945 to '55.

(Bruce-Novoa 1980: 150)

Taking Rivera's statement as a representative text for the Chicano movement, I now want to examine the persuasive poetics of Paredes's book to suggest interpretively how it could become such influential cultural rhetoric.

Given the account of Gregorio Cortez Paredes has given us in *"With His Pistol in His Hand,"* it is not difficult to see a general and simple basis for the book's appeal to a new audience of young Chicanos. Seeing themselves in a renewed confrontation with the gringos, Chicano community activists would certainly find an inspiring model in the figure of Cortez, his pistol in hand, resisting Anglo authority. For Chicano critical scholars, Paredes's superb, counterhegemonic scholarship would also prove influential, particularly for a group that had precious few examples of such scholarship in its historical background. Finally, as Rivera demonstrates, Chicano creative writers certainly responded affirmatively to Paredes's fine, engaging depiction of Cortez.[3]

However, I submit that, in addition to its political, scholarly, and literary qualities, or better still, subsuming all of these, *"With His Pistol in His Hand"* and its author work as cultural rhetoric, as a total poetic global designation for the Chicano movement. We must understand this influence then beyond the artificial divisions of politics, letters, and scholarship. In their narrative composition, the author/text recall and transform the residual though still powerful social poetics of the Mexican ballad for social subjects who were still keenly aware of this native poetics. As Tomás Rivera attests: "I grew up with the corridos in Texas," and so did many of us. It is as if, through the possession of this traditional aesthetics, *"With His Pistol in His Hand"* and its author were composed as a transformed "ballad," and we, the participants in the Chicano movement, were able to read them as such. Drawing on this shared aesthetic, Paredes and his text may have played an important part in producing the form and character of the Chicano movement as a total cultural enactment. It was a movement that could and did respond to the corrido directly in its "naive" form[4] but one that also needed and found a mediated and transformed corrido that would both evoke the traditional aesthetic yet respond to a new socio-educational reality. As a "model of" the past, this new corrido also offered a "model for" producing a political movement in our time (Geertz 1973).

My analysis will focus on those major elements in the book that, since its publication, have contributed to its rhetorical influence as another ballad of Gregorio Cortez.

### THE RETURN OF THE MEXICAN BALLAD: THE AUTHOR'S TEXT

Paredes's book opens with an unusual dedication, one that is an important part of the public text. His dedication in free verse "to the memory of my father / who rode a raid or two with / Catarino Garza" continues:

and to all those old men
who sat around on summer nights
in the days when there was
a chaparral, smoking their
cornhusk cigarettes and talking
in low, gentle voices about
violent things;
while I listened.

(1971: 6)

This poetic text at the beginning of the book is important because it establishes the author's relationship to his father and to an older generation and their folklore (a point to be pursued later); it also establishes the writer's special authority to recall and transform the past which, on those summer nights, would have included the singing of corridos. In his use of free English language meter and verse and in his evocation of his youth, the author is also establishing his authority to speak to the present generation increasingly educated in a modernist and postmodernist climate.

A brief introduction is next, as if the author is anxious to move us quickly to the main text; its precise economy, however, alerts us to the traditional model that will inform this text. The author uses his introduction to set up his rhetorical strategy in three ways. First, Paredes tells us: "This book began as the study of a ballad; it developed into the story of a ballad hero. Thus it became two books in one. It is an account of the life of a man, of the way that songs and legends grew up about his name, and of the people who produced the songs, the legends, and the man. It is also the story of a ballad, **'El Corrido de Gregorio Cortez,'** of its development out of actual events, and of the folk traditions from which it sprang" (1971: 3). This statement of textual division permits Paredes to present technical, formal scholarship and analysis of the Mexican ballad in a separate, second section, with the strategic rhetorical effect of making available to the reader, should he or she need it, the defining material for understanding this genre. At the same time, by bracketing this more technical, "scholarly" data in a separate and second section, he does not impede the narrative flow of part I for those who may already possess a good deal of the necessary and perhaps native knowledge concerning the corrido form. (For others, the result is an engaging, informative good story.)

Second, as if to alert us explicitly to the style of his text even as he provides useful information, Paredes also provides a brief and general definition of the corrido: "*Corrido,* the Mexicans call their narrative folk songs, especially those of epic themes, taking the name from *correr,* which means 'to run' or 'to flow', for the *corrido* tells a story simply and swiftly, without embellishments" (1971: 3). I suggest that this is precisely what we will recognize when we begin the main text, a story told "simply and swiftly, without embellishments."

Finally, however, it will not be a simple story about just any balladry or for that matter, any Mexican balladry; it will be a story about the balladry of borders and conflict, particularly the border and conflict between those of Anglo and Mexican descent in the United States. With this third rhetorical move, Paredes locates his Chicano readers and appeals to their general experiential sense of this conflict in the same way that a traditional ballad singer along the border might say, as part of his brief introduction, "I'm going to sing a corrido about the americanos," and everyone would understand the social relation he was evoking as the context for his song.

Having just told us that this will be a book about corridos, Paredes next presents us with a partial version of one printed on a single page without commentary (1971: 6). We might say that, on one level, it is there as a useful example of what he will soon be discussing. In my interpretive terms, however, it also has the rhetorical effect of reminding Chicano readers of the style of our traditional folk form and of its sound for those who can read the musical notation that Paredes also provides (not included on p. 6). Moving to the next page, we have the model of the corrido fresh in our consciousness, a visible reminder of the tradition that Paredes is about to transform for our use.

To proceed further in understanding this transformation, we must move momentarily to part II of the book; here, we obtain a fuller definition of the corrido that we can use as context for the corridolike quality of part I and for a comparison of the two corridos, that of tradition and that of scholarly prose. According to Paredes, a "scenic structure . . . is typical of the Border heroic *corrido.* The setting in motion of the action in a few swift lines, the introduction of the hero speaking out his boast in the second scene, after his first exploit, thus giving the whole narrative a middle-of-things feeling, the tendency to tell the story not in a long continuous and detailed narrative but in a series of shifting scenes and by means of action and dialogue—all these are stylistic devices typical of the Border *corrido.*" And, in such ballads, Paredes continues, "a couple of stanzas get the story going and then the hero appears shouting out his boast or his defiance. From that moment on, the story moves swiftly to its conclusion, with point of view shifting rapidly from the hero to his adversaries

and back again, and from one position in space to another if the action covers a great deal of ground" (1971: 187).

To this we might add the following, with which Paredes would not disagree. The corrido of border conflict is embedded in a history of social conflict, and therefore, as a text, it continually signifies and refers to the confrontation of larger social forces defined by ethnicity and class.

Armed with this extended definition of the border corrido, we can now closely examine part I of *"With His Pistol in His Hand"* and its author's biography as they incorporate and transform this traditional poetics into a compelling rhetoric for our time. As a textual transformation of tradition, we should, of course, not expect *"With His Pistol in His Hand"* to *be* a ballad. Rather, as a text, it reveals the stylistic influence of its folk subject, drawing upon its simple power and transforming it for an audience. This audience draws upon its knowledge of this traditional poetics yet needs it transformed to speak to a new social and intellectual political climate.

The first chapter of part I called "The Country," like the first stanzas of a corrido, establishes the setting and scene of the action in a relatively "few swift lines." "Country" here, however, means more than the geographic locale of the story; it encompasses a careful delineation of the opposing social forces—Anglo and Mexican—which a traditional corrido singer could far more easily have assumed to be part of his audience's everyday, intense, social experience. They would have immediately understood the full signification of stanza I of **"The Ballad of Gregorio Cortez,"** where a sheriff has died, and stanza II, where the killer is identified as Cortez, although the particular details of the incident and its aftermath await the rest of the ballad narrative. In our time we require a few more words to delineate a social structure that, while somewhat obscured and mystified, still retains its force today. For as Paredes began to "sing" his corrido to his new audience, he did so within an ongoing social structure that produced segregated barber shops around the University of Texas at Austin in the early 1960s and sanctioned the use of Texas Rangers to break up Mexican farm worker strikes in the Lower Rio Grande Valley. And yet, as I've suggested, like the corrido singer, Paredes is careful not to use too many words lest he lose his audience and distort the clarity of the situation. In only twenty-six simply and elegantly written pages, we who still appreciate corrido-like simplicity are told the essentials of what we need to know to grasp the full social significance of the Cortez incident which is to follow. However, our relative lack of intense social experience—our generation was never lynched—and, paradoxically, our higher education create our need for the longer opening "stanza" of chapter I.

As Paredes has noted, the traditional corrido usually introduces the hero in the next few stanzas in legendary proportions. "But trying to catch Cortez / Was like following a star," which are maintained as the ballad narrative unfolds: Cortez directly addresses and taunts the pursuing Texas Rangers; three hundred surround him at a single moment, yet he escapes. These are the fictive elements permitted to the composer in the exercise of his poetic license. They draw on a larger store of legend with its own independent oral existence, which, present in the community's consciousness, enhances their appreciation of the sparse, sung ballad.

Following the ballad pattern, Paredes introduces us to the legendary Cortez in chapter II called "The Legend," our second "stanza." Amplifying what the ballad suggests, the legend tells us that Cortez was a quiet, polite, good man: a fine horseman, a knowledgeable farmer, and a superb shot with rifle and pistol. He was living a quiet life along the predominantly Mexican border country when his brother, who "was just like the young men of today, loud mouthed and discontented," persuaded him to leave the border country and to "move away from the river and go up above, where there was much money to be made" (1971: 36). This chapter then recapitulates the legendary proportions of the shooting incident in Karnes Country and the dramatic flight southward told in the ballad narrative.

As in chapter I, Paredes takes a few more lines in his "ballad" to accomplish for his audience what a traditional singer in 1901 could assume about his, namely, that the legend of Cortez was in the people's consciousness, and that they would bring it to bear in their appreciation of his sung ballad. Paredes's audience requires a direct, elaborated, albeit economical prose version of the legend; this is his historically necessary way to "sing" his ballad.

Like much folklore, however, the corrido is not simply a narrative of totally mythic fictions. It is an historical account that, within a mythos and an ideological perspective, permits its audience to discover a remarkable range of social reality. Whatever the fictive dimensions of this particular ballad, its audience learns that, in fact, Cortez had killed a sheriff in a place called Karnes County, and afterward claimed his right to do so in defense of his life and that of his brother. They also learn certain true details of the southward flight, of which the most general and important is that Cortez did outride and outshoot the vaunted Texas Rangers who, in fact, "captured" him only when he turned himself in after learning about the reprisals taken against his family and community.

Within his textual narrative constraints, it would have been next to impossible for Paredes to narrate legend alternating with historical fact: he does the next best thing, staying close to the corrido narrative conventions. He separates out the historical facts of the case based on primary research in chapter III, called "The Man." Here we learn, interestingly enough, how remarkably close the legendary aspects of the ballad are to the emergent historical narrative as Paredes discovers and constructs it. In presenting his historical reconstruction, Paredes is also attentive to another corrido convention: telling the story "with point of view shifting rapidly from the hero to his adversaries and back again" (1971: 187). Unlike the Anglo historical reconstructions extant in 1958 and still not much improved, Paredes's ballad narrative actually tells a great deal about the Anglo point of view and, like the corrido brings it to life, a favor rarely returned except in the dubious form of stereotypes. What we discover to some extent in the original corrido and to a larger extent in Paredes's "corrido" is that Anglos are people; they show fear, doubt, anxiety, anger, fairness, meanness, pettiness, and generosity, although frankly, at that historical moment, where Mexicans are concerned, the negatives predominate. Using two chapters then, Paredes reproduces, in his more elaborated version with economical and simple words, the legendary and factual historical narration—the substance of the ballad—and brings it to a conclusion.

But if the ballad and Paredes's transformations of it come to a structural close with chapter III, we would seem to be left with a superfluous final chapter IV in part I called "The Hero's Progress." In this closing chapter Paredes simply reviews the fact and fancy, the variants and versions of the Cortez legend and balladry and demonstrates their intertwined relationship. This chapter, clearly intended as a summary, bears no narrative structural relationship to the preceding three chapters. Yet, from my analytical perspective, it has the interesting rhetorical effect of reading like a conversation, albeit in English prose.

In this final chapter Paredes offers, in his own restrained prose, a summary of the conversations that men might have after a corrido performance as they evaluate the corrido, its hero, its circumstances and try to get at the truth. As a postnarrative review, Paredes's final chapter resembles this kind of polyphonic conversation and as such is as integral a part of his total performance as it would be for a traditional corrido sung to an audience. Hence, I would argue even the seeming "review" character of chapter IV recalls a corrido performance.

I have suggested that *"With His Pistol in His Hand"* constitutes a transforming narrative response to the aesthetic influence of its scholarly subject, the border Mexican ballad. I would now like to amplify this argument by suggesting that to this balladlike anthropological performance, we can add its author's biography. As a social text, it, too, responds and seems shaped by the influence of the border ballad.

THE RETURN OF THE MEXICAN BALLAD: THE
AUTHOR AS TEXT

When Chicano movement people gather and the conversation turns to the subject of Américo Paredes, one can often detect the gradual emergence of what I shall call an unsung proto-ballad-legend of Américo Paredes. Such conversations—a kind of Chicano movement oral tradition—seem to construct the known life and career of this man into a folklore narrative, combining ballad and legend. Like all narratives, this narrative varies from group to group and performance to performance. Certain motifs are sometimes stated, sometimes implied, but an overall narrative structure does emerge, one which recalls the thematic structure of the traditional ballad and legend.

As with the traditional ballad, these conversations first establish a time and place setting, and imply a social context for the appearance of the hero and the central narrative action. This initial narrative sometimes starts with a key incident of confrontation between the hero and the Anglo authorities (Gregorio Cortez and the Sheriff). An Anglo teacher tells the young Paredes that college is not for boys "like him"; has he considered attending vocational school? Or, an assimilationist, middle-class, Mexican-American publisher in San Antonio refuses to publish Paredes's early, stridently ethnic, nationalist poems. Or, perhaps most dramatic of all, the University of Texas Press in the late 1950s refuses to publish *"With His Pistol in His Hand"* unless Paredes deletes all critical references to Walter Prescott Webb, J. Frank Dobie, and the Texas Rangers. Paredes refuses to do so, threatens to publish the book elsewhere, and the University of Texas Press finally relents. When the book does appear, a former Texas Ranger actually tries to get Paredes's address from the press so that he can "shoot the sonafabitch who wrote that book."

This conversational proto-narrative may then fill out the author's background and key aspects of his career in a way that is almost entirely factual and yet has the aura of legend. Our hero was born in the auspicious year of 1915 during the height of the Texas Ranger killings in South Texas. He is said to be a good and simple man, as was said of Cortez, but from the beginning he is a bit extraordinary. As a young man in South Texas, he is something of the bohemian, exceptionally attractive to women and highly respected by men; a well-known popular singer on radio programs, a prize-winning poet and a journalist; a man who could and did defend his family's honor. The narrative continues. The hero is said to be highly gifted intellectually, restless and curious about life beyond South Texas. Like Cortez, Paredes leaves the border country and eventually winds up in central Texas near Karnes County at the University of Texas at Austin, after spending a few years as a cor-

respondent in Japan and China after World War II. "Did you know that Don Américo covered the Chinese Revolution?"

When he does arrive at the University of Texas to study English and creative writing—his central career goal—it is not before another confrontation with those who dominate. This time it is the U.S. government, which initially refuses a visa to his wife, who is a Japanese national. For a moment Paredes thinks of living in Mexico. But the obstacle is overcome, and his advanced college education begins; he has had one year of community college work. Already in his midthirties, he has children; by overloading his course schedule, he completes his B.A. with highest honors in two years, an M.A. in one, and the Ph.D. in two more years in which he teaches several sections of freshman English to support his family. During this period he also publishes a few scholarly articles and writes a prize-winning novel. He also completes a dissertation on the balladry and life of Gregorio Cortez (later *"With His Pistol in His Hand"*), and after teaching one year in El Paso, he is invited to rejoin the Department of English at Texas as a faculty member.

As a faculty member during the period 1958-66, Paredes engages in intellectual politics, continually attacking the dominant society's disparaging view of Mexican-Americans by demonstrating the latter's active historical presence through careful, creative scholarship such as that of *"With His Pistol in His Hand."* He also tries to promote social activism among the university's Mexican-American students, but an assimilationist perspective is still too prevalent among them, and they do not respond to his efforts. Like Cortez, Paredes finds himself engaging the opposition largely alone, although he does find a Romaldo-like brother in Professor George I. Sanchez, a progressive figure in his own right (Garcia 1989: 252-72).

Cortez arouses the consciousness of his community by riding and shooting his way toward them and receiving their help. Paredes's native ideological and cultural community actually begins to come to him in the mid-1960s as the Chicano student movement starts to develop in Texas and in other southwestern universities. The hero and his community struggle in mutual support around issues such as the farm workers, Mexican-American studies, and increased political representation. With this social activism, the dissemination of his book, and visits to other campuses, the hero's legend continues to develop to the present in the conversational form that I have sketched. Though neither a ballad nor a legend in any formal narrative sense, this conversation partakes of both and gives us a sense of a ballad and a legendary hero in formation.

THE RETURN OF THE MEXICAN BALLAD AND
THE CHICANO MOVEMENT

One of the most active participants in and a better observer of the Chicano movement has noted the tendency of this movement to draw on historical models. "The entire Chicano leadership pattern, in fact, closely resembled the pattern of the Mexican Revolution, where revolutionary juntas and local leaders emerged. These leaders took care of their home bases and were supported by their own followers . . . all adhered to this basic pattern, inspiring intense loyalty among their followers" (Acuña 1981: 360).

We can expand this perceptive formulation by considering other historical models and the Chicano movement as a social narrative—to see the movement as an unfolding social enactment that followed the model of the most potent Mexican narrative—the corrido—as it had learned it in mediated form from the widely popular Américo Paredes and his ostensibly anthropological text. Taking this author-text as one of several possible important cultural models, I want to generally trace its influence on the Chicano social narrative.

We may begin by noting that, like our legendary heroes Cortez and Paredes, these Chicano students were also from the border, if not literally from the U.S.-Mexico border, then certainly from the borders and margins of U.S. society. Although by no means from the most deprived sectors of U.S. society, they largely represented a wage-labor, working-class segment, particularly those from the literal border or even close to it—West San Antonio, Albuquerque, Phoenix, East Los Angeles, areas that reflected persistent socioeconomic marginalization. At a critical moment these students also experienced Cortez's journey. According to folk legend and to a considerable degree in historical fact, Cortez and his family had been drawn away from the border by the work made available as a result of the capitalist economic transformation of Texas. Similarly, as a result of new federal civil rights and educational aid policies beginning in the late 1950s, Chicano students found themselves attracted to the new socioeducational "north." For Texas students, as with Cortez and Paredes, such movement for opportunity was perfectly congruent with geography as they left the southern border area to come north to the University of Texas at Austin. (At the University of California at Los Angeles, the movement was east-west.)

This movement "north" brought many of these students into conflict with other aspects of the culture there. For while U.S. society presented new opportunities, it had not done so for the masses of Mexican-American society; the most telling evidence of this clear shortfall was (and is) the continuing plight of border society, and particularly the plight of the farm workers. Further,

from the point of view of the students, who despite their own change in culture were still, in the words of the poet Juan Gomez-Quiñones, "just Mexican enough" (1973: 73), the colleges and universities receiving them were themselves sociointellectual embodiments of the same sociocultural power that dominated their parents and had lynched their grandparents. Not Sheriff Morris of Karnes County, but U.S. society, as these students experienced it, was still a dominating force as it had been for Américo Paredes when he tried to publish his book.

For the students, the most direct confrontation came through the labor struggles of the largely Mexican-American farm workers in the mid-1960s in the Southwest. In Texas, the ballad narratives of the past took on special pertinence when farm workers from the border made a pilgrimage to Austin in 1966, only to be denied a hearing for their grievances by then governor John Connally, certainly as representative a symbol of Anglo-Texan class and cultural power as any symbolic anthropologist could have hoped for. To this denial Connally added injury, and stepped right alongside the models of history by sending the Texas Rangers to break up, with violence, farm worker strikes along the border; parallel confrontations occurred in California.

The student sector of the farm worker movement actively participated, and found its own beginning in these farm labor struggles; in Texas students had confrontations with the Rangers along the border. For, like Cortez, these students returned to the border not to escape but to engage; in so doing, like Cortez, they reestablished their links to their native community. (In Texas this meant literally following the general path that Cortez took as he rode south, except this time the path was taken in car caravans.) This initial participation and linkage with the home community soon widened as students lent their support to other issues in the society, particularly the serious deficiencies of public schooling. Soon Chicano college students throughout the Southwest were organizing strikes in the public schools to protest substandard educational conditions and, in so doing, enlisting public school youth in the movement (Foley et al. 1977). From the wider struggles in the larger community, the students also returned to the universities to bring them to account for their own denial of Mexican-American society, particularly for the failure of higher education to draw more Mexican-Americans into its ranks and to devote more intellectual attention to Mexican-American society and culture.

As in the ballad, legendary heroes to lead the struggle appeared early in the Chicano social narrative. Given the centrality of the farm labor movement, it is not too surprising that Cesar Chavez should be among the foremost of these—a "simple, good man"—but there were others as well, not always simple or good, whose rhetorical powers and personal charisma quickly lent them near legendary status. Rodolfo "Corky" Gonzales of Colorado, Reis Lopez Tijerina in New Mexico, and José Angel Gutierrez in Texas were surely among these (Hammerback, Jensen, and Gutierrez 1985). And, of course, in the political world of intellect and letters there was Américo Paredes, whose personal "ballad" developed dialectically with this movement and whose written "ballad" *"With His Pistol in His Hand"* was, starting in the early 1960s, an influence upon it; countless Mexican-American students read it.

Paredes has suggested that the ballad of border conflict and its hero, such as Gregorio Cortez, epitomize "the ideal type of hero of the Rio Grande people, the man who defends his right with his pistol in his hand, and who either escapes at the end or goes down before superior odds—in a sense a victor even in defeat" (1971: 124). Something like this might be said—and it is only one perspective—of the Chicano movement in 1966-75. While it did "shoot" an institutional "Ranger" or two, its achievements were limited though real; farm labor legislation was passed; more Mexican-American political figures were elected; Mexican-American studies departments were established. Nonetheless, for many Chicanos various versions of a new social order did not come to pass, leading them to judge the movement a failure, though with some compensations of "a victor even in defeat." Even as I write—and my words are perhaps a contribution—discussion and debate are taking place after the performance of our "ballad" (the movement) with its narrative of conflict between a community with its legendary heroes and a dominant social order denying this community. Like others after a performance of a traditional sung ballad, we, too, are asking and debating. "What was the meaning of this ballad?" "How good was it?" "Shall we sing another one?"

I have offered for interpretive consideration the interrelated propositions that Américo Paredes's public career and his major anthropological text, *"With His Pistol in His Hand,"* formally and thematically mediate the influence of the Mexican border ballad and, in turn, become themselves cultural texts that help to shape the character and development of the Chicano movement. By no means were these the only influential cultural models. As Acuña has suggested, the social drama and heroes of the Mexican Revolution were also important, as were the mythic practices of the pre-Conquest peoples of Mexico and the drama of the Conquest itself. I am suggesting that closer to these students' home culture is another cultural model—the corrido available to them as part of their folk tradition and represented to them by Paredes's life and his corrido-like, politically and intellectually elaborated, simple and well-told story, both well known and appropriate to the students' liminal moment. Paredes's textuality had this particular

mission: at this moment, it may be appropriate to assign it another for which it may also be an important text.

### The Return of the Mexican Ballad and the "Experimental Moment in the Human Sciences": "A Last Word"

The purpose of Paredes's last chapter, called simply "A Last Word," is simultaneously to reaffirm the local character of the Mexican border ballad and to demonstrate its clear comparative relationship to world balladry. Of particular importance here is the close parallel that Paredes draws with Scottish balladry and political resistance to English domination. I submit that this chapter also had a rhetorical and instructive effect on its Chicano readership: always to attend finely to the character of the local experience of resistance while locating it as part of a larger pattern in the interest of generalizing and linking struggles. To this end, and in the interest of enhancing its hitherto localized reading, I shall offer my own parallel "last word" on Paredes's textuality by locating it among three broader issues that constitute part of what George E. Marcus and Michael M. J. Fischer, in their subtitle, have called "an experimental moment in the human sciences" (1986).

I alluded above to the first of these, although for my purposes I approach it from a somewhat different perspective than does Marcus in an independent statement (1986). He correctly complains that ethnographers, in describing their various societies and cultures, have not "portrayed the role of these worlds in the sort of events and processes that make history, so to speak. . . . The world of larger systems and events has thus often been seen as externally impinging on and bounding little worlds but not as integral to them" (1986: 166). While Paredes's text is least satisfactory here—for example, we wish to know more about the particular character of the capitalist development that was transforming Gregorio Cortez's world—nonetheless, in his account of a folk world not in a pure state, but responding dialectically to imposed change through the creative process of corrido and legend, Paredes, writing in the mid-1950s anticipates somewhat a new trend toward this desirable sort of ethnography. From another perspective, his consistent effort to locate this local folk resistance in relationship to other world efforts foreshadows a new desire to move beyond the bounds of localized ethnography.

The two remaining issues locate Paredes's text in perhaps sharper anticipation of this experimental moment not only in the human sciences but in literary criticism as well (if the distinction is even warranted). I refer to the personal role of the anthropologist, really the intellectual, in the production of his discourse and, to return to the place where I started, to the poetics of such discourse and its relationship to ethnic marginality.

Here we should recall Clifford's concern that ethnic intellectuals may be more constrained about textual experimentation in the production of their discourse; it is, he suggests, considerations of tenure and promotion and other forms of institutional acceptability that are constraining. Nonetheless, he is, "uneasy with a general notion that privileged discourse indulges in esthetic or epistemological subtleties, whereas marginal discourse 'tells it like it is.' The reverse is too often the case" (1986: 21). He is quite right; the reverse is often the case, and I have tried to suggest as much in the case of Américo Paredes in terms of both his writing and his career. I want to specify this relationship a bit more.

As his own example of the reverse case, Clifford points us to the ethnic works that Fischer discusses in an excellent essay on the ways that ethnic autobiographical writing can enhance experimental writing in anthropology. Fischer argues that such autobiographical writing offers to ethnographers models of desirable writing practices: "intertextuality, inter-reference, and the inter-linguistic modalities of postmodernist knowledge," creative techniques that can "contribute to a reinvigorated ethnographic literature, one that can again fulfill the anthropological promise of cultural criticism" (1986: 202).

By intertextuality Fischer refers in part to the tendency in some ethnic autobiography to shape the present text as an often transforming repetition of "behavior patterns previously established toward some prior significant other," often a father figure (204). This is the psychoanalytical concept of the transference, "the return of the repressed in new forms" (206), which results in the generation of the ethnic text as the "conquest of an anxiety . . . that cannot be articulated in rational language but can only be acted out" (204). In a different version of this essay, I argue that *"With His Pistol in His Hand,"* as a kind of ethnic autobiography, textually reenacts this sort of relationship between Paredes as a younger writer and the ballad world of his father, whom he clearly acknowledges as an influence in the dedication (noted earlier) only to transform him in the figure of Cortez (Limón 1992: 61-80). As Fischer also notes, such relationships are the subject of Harold Bloom's work on the poetics of influence (1973, 1975).

Interreference and the interlinguistic modalities of postmodernist knowledge are, for Fischer, expressed in ethnic autobiography through its creative use of, among other techniques, "multiple voices and perspectives, the highlighting of humorous inversions and dialectical juxtaposition of identities/traditions/cultures, and the critique of hegemonic discourses" (1986: 202). I submit that Paredes's text—both the "ballad" he has written and the "ballad" about him—are exemplary in this regard. I have already noted the multiple voices and perspectives that enter into the construction of a corrido

and the way Paredes's texts are also constructed in this polyphonic way. In *"With His Pistol in His Hand"* this polyphony also involves the clear dialectical juxtaposition of "identities/traditions/cultures," the more obvious one of Anglo vs. Mexicans and the varying identities within the Mexican-descent community itself. A few examples. In chapter II, "The Legend," a fictional traditional figure, recalling the singing of "El Corrido de Gregorio Cortez," says, "That was good singing, and a good song; give the man a drink. Not like these *pachucos* nowadays, mumbling damn-foolishness into a microphone; it is not done that way. Men should sing with their heads thrown back, with their mouths wide open and their eyes shut. Fill your lungs, so they can hear you at the pasture's end" (1971: 34). And we discover that our mythic hero also has varying identities, including some not so mythic, which speak to gender differences and which Paredes handles with a kind of humorous inversion. For when Cortez is finally captured and brought to jail, *several* women show up to claim him as theirs even as his poor wife waits in the jail.

Humor, irony, and inversion, however, best serve Paredes in attacking hegemonic, Anglo, racist discourses about Mexicans in Texas; here too he borrows from the corrido tradition which often makes fun of Anglos. Paredes quotes the dominant Anglo historical authority on the subject of Mexicans. "Without disparagement," says Webb, "there is a cruel streak in the Mexican nature" (1935: 14). Webb attributes this partly to the heritage of the Spanish Inquisition and partly to Mexican Indian "blood," which, however, "when compared with that of the Plains Indian, was as ditch water" (1931: 125-26). Nevertheless, despite his "cruel streak," the Mexican is an inferior warrior; "the whine of the leaden slugs stirred in him as irresistible impulse to travel with rather than against the music" (1935: 14). To all this, Paredes wryly comments: "Professor Webb does not mean to be disparaging. One wonders what his opinion might have been when he was in a less scholarly mood and not looking at the Mexican from the objective point of view of the historian" (1971: 17). Later, in his discussion of the shooting between Cortez and Sheriff Morris, Paredes ironically appropriates and juxtaposes Webb's observations in a new context. After Morris is shot, his deputy runs, according to Paredes, preferring to "travel with rather than against the music" made by "the whine of leaden slugs" (1971: 63).

Multiple voices, inversions, humor and irony, and the dialectical juxtaposition of "identities/traditions/cultures": these are for Fischer substantial elements of the creative imagination found in ethnic autobiography which can be of service to the writing of a new kind of ethnography. I suggest that, at least in some incipient anticipatory way, Paredes's book involves just such practices, as well as a larger juxtaposition, a blurring of genres between ethnic autobiography, historical ethnography and, as I have been particularly concerned to argue, between folk poetic forms and, to borrow a subtitle, "the poetics and politics of ethnography" (Clifford and Marcus 1986).

We need to consider as well another level of the juxtapositions of identities and traditions in the production of discourse. As I come to the end of my own discourse, I am becoming even more convinced, to return to Clifford, that when it comes to ethnicity, and experimental and ultimately subversive writing, the reverse *is* more often the case. From the margins of ethnicity, we may be able to obtain a more reflexive, innovative and critical discourse. We should not, however, be in an insular fortress—ethnicity peering in fear and suspicion at the "out there"—but work rather more as a guerrilla ethnicity, creatively and dialectically at the margins of various discourses. By the same reasoning, this approach need not be confined to the "traditional" ethnic groups, although I suspect that, under present conditions, they will be a more likely source. While certainly not a "trend," there seems to be increasing interest among nontraditional "ethnics" to locate in their respective heritages some resources for the development of new discourses: Harold Bloom returns anxiously to his Jewish Gnostic influences and analyzes the Jewish present (Bloom 1982); Frank Lentricchia recommends that "the intellectual of working class background, or more broadly of a background outside the social, racial, ethnic, economic, gender-biased, and homophobic mainstream . . . retrieve his outsider's experience" and "bring it to bear in critical dialogue with the traditional confirmation he has been given" (1983: 8), referring, by way of example, to his own southern Italian origins. One also thinks of Raymond Williams's engaging discussions of his creative relationship to his working-class Welsh background (1979: 21-38).

If this kind of creative ethnic juxtapositioning in one's career is also an emergent part of the experimental moment in contemporary discourse, then here too we find Américo Paredes anticipating and providing an early model, doing so not as a propagandist for simple ethnicity nor as a community "activist" but as a literary intellectual, a *specific* literary intellectual, as Lentricchia would say after Foucault: "one whose radical work of transformation, whose fight against repression is carried on at the specific institutional site where he finds himself and on the terms of his own expertise, on the terms inherent to his own functioning as an intellectual" (Lentricchia 1983: 6). In the 1950s Américo Paredes was, and he continued to be, this kind of intellectual, drawing creatively on his own cultural background and bringing it to bear in critical dialogue with his traditional intellectual training. His writings and career represent a transformation of his political/poetic past—the cor-

rido—in the service of a radical work of transformation in the present for the Mexican-descent community and as a possible anticipatory model for the emergence of a new critical discourse among intellectuals at large.

For the immediate future, it is for his poetic politics with persuasive reference to the Mexican-descent community in the United States, particularly its activist intellectuals, that Américo Paredes will be best known. This is a considerable achievement in the context of the restricted and transient nature of much contemporary intellectual work. Like his Texas-born and raised contemporary and fellow "outsider" C. Wright Mills, Paredes used and continues to use "the wit of the satirist, the passions of the partisan, the imaginative attention to detail of the novelist" in a fight against repression (Miller 1986: 83). Like Mills, Paredes too, is "a poet of political possibilities" (Miller 1986: 83). With one singular book and career, Paredes also might be described, though in the present tense, in something of the terms that Miller uses for C. Wright Mills: "Dramatizing his political vision in 'sociological poems' that he aimed at the widest possible readership, [he] reached a mass audience and—perhaps more importantly— inspired a handful of young activists. Through these students, who revered his images and took his ideas to heart, he fostered a rebirth of democratic idealism . . . he left a legacy of vivid intellectual style, frequently brilliant social analysis, a beguiling icon of democracy and a seductive new rhetoric of vernacular radicalism" (Miller 1986: 101).

For this and more, we are grateful to Américo Paredes.

*Notes*

1. "It may be generally true," says Clifford, "that groups long excluded from positions of institutional power, like women or people of color, have less concrete freedom to indulge in textual experimentations. To write in an unorthodox way, Paul Rabinow suggests in this volume (Rabinow 1986), one must first have tenure. In specific contexts a preoccupation with self-reflexivity and style may be an index of privileged estheticism. For if one does not have to worry about the exclusion or true representation of one's experience, one is freer to undermine ways of telling, to focus on form over content" (Clifford 1986: 21).

2. This divorce of the sign from society as part of the "postmodern" and the "poststructural" has been the subject of critiques from various perspectives on the left (Anderson 1984; Jameson 1984; Lentricchia 1980; Rabinow 1986; Said 1982).

3. See Saldivar 1990: 26-46.

4. Indeed, this Chicano movement produced corridos of its own (Limón 1983).

## References

Acuña, Rodolfo. 1981. *Occupied America: A History of Chicanos.* New York: Harper and Row.

Anderson, Perry. 1984. *In the Tracks of Historical Materialism.* Chicago: University of Chicago Press.

Bloom, Harold. 1973. *The Anxiety of Influence: A Theory of Poetry.* New York: Oxford University Press.

————. 1975. *A Map of Misreading.* New York: Oxford University Press.

————. 1982. *Agon: Towards a Theory of Revisionism.* New York: Oxford University Press.

Boon, James. 1982. *Other Tribes, Other Scribes.* New York: Cambridge University Press.

Bruce-Novoa, Juan D. 1980. *Chicano Authors: Inquiry by Interview.* Austin: University of Texas Press.

————. 1982. *Chicano Poetry: A Response to Chaos.* Austin: University of Texas Press.

Bruner, Edward M. 1986. "Ethnography as Narrative." In Victor W. Turner and Edward M. Bruner, eds., *The Anthropology of Experience.* Urbana: University of Illinois Press.

Clifford, James. 1986. "Introduction: Partial Truths." In Clifford and Marcus, eds., 1986. Pp. 1-26.

Clifford, James, and George E. Marcus, eds. 1986. *Writing Culture: The Poetics and Politics of Ethnography.* Berkeley and Los Angeles: University of California Press.

Fischer, Michael M. J. 1986. "Ethnicity and the Post-Modern Arts of Memory." In Clifford and Marcus, eds., 1986. Pp. 194-233.

Foley, Douglas, et al. 1977. "From Peons to Politicos: Ethnic Relations in a South Texas Town." Austin: Center for Mexican American Studies Monograph. University of Texas.

Garcia, Mario. 1989. *Mexican Americans: Leadership, Ideology, and Identity.* New Haven: Yale University Press.

Geertz, Clifford. 1980. "Blurred Genres: The Refiguration of Social Thought." *The American Scholar* 29: 165-79.

Gomez-Quiñones, Juan. 1973. "Song." In *5th and Grande Vista (Poems, 1960-1973).* New York: Editorial Mensage. P. 73.

————. 1978. *Mexican Students por la Raza: The Chicano Student Movement in Southern California, 1967-1977.* Santa Barbara, Calif.: Editorial La Causa.

Hammerback, John C., Richard J. Jensen, and José Angel Gutierrez. 1985. *A War of Words: Chicano Protest in the 1960s and 1970s.* Westport, Conn.: Greenwood Press.

Jameson, Fredric. 1984. Foreword. Jean-François Lyotard. *The Postmodern Condition: A Report on Knowledge.* Minneapolis: University of Minnesota Press.

Lentricchia, Frank. 1980. *After the New Criticism.* Chicago: University of Chicago Press.

————. 1983. *Criticism and Social Change.* Chicago: University of Chicago Press.

Limón, José E. 1983. "The Rise, Fall, and 'Revival' of the Mexican-American Ballad: A Review Essay." *Studies in Latin American Popular Culture* 2: 202-07.

————. 1986. "Barbarians, Christians, Jews: Three Narrative Scenes in the Sociolinguistic Legacy of the Mexicans of Texas." Paper presented at the annual meeting of the Texas State Historical Association, Austin, Texas.

————. 1992. *Mexican Ballads, Chicano Poems: History and Influence in Mexican American Social Poetry.* Berkeley: University of California Press.

————. n.d. "Mexicans in the Southwest: The Tropics of Folkloristic Discourse." Unpublished manuscript.

Marcus, George E. 1986. "Contemporary Problems of Ethnography in the Modern World System." In Clifford and Marcus, eds., 1986. Pp. 165-93.

Marcus, George E., and Dick Cushman. 1982. "Ethnographies as Texts." *Annual Review of Anthropology* 11: 25-69.

Marcus, George E., and Michael M. J. Fischer. 1986. *Anthropology as Cultural Critique: An Experimental Moment in the Human Sciences.* Chicago: University of Chicago Press.

Miller, James. 1986. "C. Wright Mills Reconsidered." *Salmagundi,* nos. 70-71: 82-101.

Mukarovsky, Jan. 1977. *The Word and Verbal Art.* New Haven: Yale University Press.

Paredes, Américo. 1971 [1958]. *With His Pistol in His Hand: A Border Ballad and Its Hero.* Austin: University of Texas Press.

Peña, Manuel H. 1982. "Folksong and Social Change: Two Corridos as Interpretive Sources." *Aztlan* 13: 13-42.

Rabinow, Paul. 1986 "Representations Are Social Facts: Modernity and Post-Modernity in Anthropology." In Clifford and Marcus, eds., 1986. Pp. 234-61.

Rosaldo, Renato. 1985. "Chicano Studies." *Annual Review of Anthropology* 14.

Said, Edward W. 1982. "Opponents, Audiences, Constituencies, and Community." *Critical Inquiry* 9: 1-26.

Saldivar, Ramon. 1990. *Chicano Narrative: The Dialectics of Difference.* Madison: University of Wisconsin Press.

Webb, Walter Prescott. 1931. *The Great Plains.* Boston: Ginn.

————. 1935. *The Texas Rangers.* Cambridge: Houghton Mifflin.

White, Hayden. 1973. *Metahistory.* Baltimore: Johns Hopkins University Press.

————. 1978. *Tropics of Discourse.* Baltimore: Johns Hopkins University Press.

Williams, Raymond. 1979. *Politics and Letters: Interviews with New Left Review.* London: New Left Review Books.

Ybarra-Frausto, Tomás. 1977. "The Chicano Movement and the Emergence of a Chicano Poetic Consciousness." *The New Scholar* 6: 81-110.

## Ramón Saldívar (essay date 1995)

SOURCE: Saldívar, Ramón. "The Borders of Modernity: Américo Paredes's *Between Two Worlds* and the Chicano National Subject." In *The Ethnic Canon: Histories, Institutions, and Interventions,* edited by David Palumbo-Liu, pp. 71-87. Minneapolis: University of Minnesota Press, 1995.

[*In the following essay, Saldívar examines Paredes's poetry as an exploration of Chicano culture's relationship to modernism.*]

> Nations, like narratives, lose their origins in the myths of time and only fully realize their horizons in the mind's eye.
>
> —Homi K. Bhabha, *Nation and Narration*

Renowned as an ethnographer, literary critic, and social historian for more than thirty years of magisterial production, Américo Paredes is being hailed at century's end for special accomplishment in the creative arts as well. His artistic endeavors include distinguished work as an arranger, composer, and performer of ballads and popular music, and as a screenwriter, storyteller, and oral historian. Honored in 1989 by the National Endowment for the Humanities as one of the initial recipients of the Charles Frankel Prize, and in 1990 by the Republic of Mexico as one of the first Mexican American inductees to the Orden del Aguila Azteca (Order of the Aztec Eagle), Paredes is one of the most respected of contemporary Chicano intellectuals and the founder and virtually unparalleled practitioner of what has come to be known as Chicano Cultural Studies.[1]

Paredes's fame rests on his foundational work of the 1950s and 1960s on the ballads and everyday folklife of Mexican Americans and on his subsequent elaboration of that work during the seventies and eighties. His initial

scholarly contribution from this early period, *"With His Pistol in His Hand": A Border Ballad and Its Hero* (1958), is a masterful work of intellectual intervention decades ahead of its time. In an epoch when the intellectual modes dictated either an old historicism or a restrictive new critical formalism, *"With His Pistol in His Hand"* went emphatically against the grain of the accepted analytical methods of the day. Combining literary, sociological, ethnographic, and historical analysis of traditional border ballads—*corridos*—it offered, as José David Saldívar has shown, a stinging rebuttal and a devastating "deconstruction of [the] established [white supremacist] authority and hierarchies" that operated as the common wisdom and official histories of the relations between Anglos and Mexicans in Texas and the rest of the West and Southwest (170). "To dramatize his sense of culture as a site of social contestation," Saldívar continues, "[Paredes] located the sources of meaning not in individual subjectivities, but in social relations, communication, and cultural politics" (4).

Richard Bauman notes, in his Introduction to a collection of Paredes's essays, *Folklore and Culture on the Texas Mexican Border* (1993), that Paredes "has carried out extensive field research and published a considerable body of Border folklore and he has produced the most important and influential scholarship of our generation on the folklore of Greater Mexico in general and the Lower Border in particular" (1). Before Paredes, the cultural politics of Texas and the Southwest were the singular product of the Anglo-American imagination, responding exclusively to the hegemony of Anglo-American material interests. But as Michel Foucault reminds us, "Where there is power, there is resistance" (1978, 95). After Paredes, with the publication of his work, the cultural politics of the region began to be cast in the decidedly different mold of biculturalism, reflecting the true, multicultural realities of the American social world. To this immensely influential body of Paredes scholarship, scholars need to add two new works, the collection of essays referred to earlier, *Folklore and Culture on the Texas Mexican Border* (1993), and a comprehensive study of jokes, jests, and oral narrative entitled *Uncle Remus con Chile* (1993).

Paredes's most recently published literary works—a novel and a book of poetry—have added yet another dimension to the imposing array of his contestational work in the historical, ethnographic, and theoretical realms. These literary works also address the predicaments of contemporary Chicano/a cultural politics, identity formation, and social transformation. Given the contemporaneity of their concerns, it is curious to learn, however, that these newly published literary works are not contemporary pieces, nor even products of the fifties and sixties. They are instead works from the thirties and forties, a period decades before that of his mature work.

As products of an era and of literary formations other than those enjoying current vogue, they belie their postmodern, post-Chicano movement thematics and publication dates. The novel *George Washington Gómez* (1990), and the collection of poetry, ***Between Two Worlds*** (1991), both written during the Depression years along the Texas-Mexican borderlands of deep South Texas, anticipate with imaginative force the sophisticated insight of Paredes's later exemplary transdisciplinary work of social criticism and cultural intervention. They prefigure crucial aspects of the growing body of postmodern Chicano writing and cultural studies from a high modernist, *pre*-movement historical moment. Together with the later scholarly work, the novel and the poetry can now be seen as part of a larger imaginative project to study what Héctor Calderón correctly identifies as "the organization of life that was formed out of the New World landscape" (25). It seeks as well, I think, to invent a figural discourse of national epic proportions appropriate to the construction of a new narrative of "American" social and cultural history at the borders of modernity.

*Between Two Worlds* as "Border Writing"

Predating the work of all of the better-known of the present generation of Chicano authors, Paredes's literary productions are richly marked by the flavor of their origins in the era of high literary modernism in both its Anglo-European and Latin American varieties. These works are also self-consciously steeped in an unwavering resistance to the residual effects of nineteenth-century American imperialism and its racist aftermath as well as to the continuing effects of twentieth-century capitalist transformations of production in the Southwest. ***Between Two Worlds,*** especially—border verses composed during the very moment of what could arguably be called the historical divide between the modern and the postmodern—represents the bifurcated, interstitial, indeed one might say differential, quality of the kind of writing that has come to be called "border writing."[2] Looking as it does from its liminal present both to the past and to the future, speaking an oddly dual idiom that simultaneously celebrates a lyrical history and forebodes a prosaic future, ***Between Two Worlds*** might well emblematize the features of that postmodern border writing were it not for the fact that it predates the notion by more than half a century.

Despite what could be shown to be this work's allegiance to a certain aesthetics of modernism, albeit in the modified form modernism acquired in the interstices between the Northern and Southern American hemispheres, I wish to show that the crux of Paredes's work in lyric and narrative poetry lies not in whether or not it is a hybrid product of transcultural or multicultural modernism. Rather, its importance rests on what it shows about the relationship of modernism to Chicano literature, and indeed to other "minority" American literatures in general, to the extent that traditional English and American studies are defined, as they continue to be, in *national* terms.

From this perspective, the ideological victory represented by the canonization of the generation of the post-World War I European and American high modernists as the teleological end point to which their respective national literatures had been aimed represents an absurd terminus to history. It is absurd because that canonization assumed that the end of the era of modernism could be defined with singular temporal certitude and definitive theoretical justification outside of any sociopolitical categories.

The end of modernism, more profitably to be seen coincident with the cataclysmic restructuration of the classical imperialist world system with the onset of World War II than with the arbitrary demarcation of a certain literary period, offers an emblematic break that is less an empirically verifiable matter than a historiographic decision. It is, nonetheless, a decision of great moment in the articulation of the narrative of the Mexican American community's struggle for justice and self-determination in the twentieth century. Paredes's ***Between Two Worlds,*** as product and symptom of the end of modernism at the peripheries of modernization, suggests how the commonly held characterizations of modernist ideologies as ahistorical and apolitical are no longer fully persuasive nor entirely adequate to explaining the cultural productions of writers actively engaged in decolonization struggles on the margins of sanctioned history and at the borderlands of high culture. These productions offer a striking anticipation of Adorno's notion that "modernity is a qualitative, not a chronological, category" (*Minima Moralia,* 218).

Today, near century's end, with many nations once thought fully consolidated now finding themselves challenged and, indeed, sundered by "'sub'-nationalisms within their borders—nationalisms which, naturally, dream of shedding this sub-ness one happy day," as Benedict Anderson puts it, it is quite clear that the end of the era of nationalism is "not remotely in sight" (13). Even as the epoch of multi-, trans-, and even postnational "isms" bears down upon us, the idea of "nationness" remains "the most universally legitimate value in the political life of our time" (13). A work such as Paredes's ***Between Two Worlds*** is crucial to an understanding of modernity precisely because it demonstrates with astonishing clarity the fundamental link between basic political economy and ideas of culture on one hand and the joint constructs of modernism and the nation on the other. Far from apolitical and ahistorical, Paredes's modernity is formed by the very historical and political legacy of the Mexican American communities of the Lower Border.

To gain a sense of the formative effect of the historical and the political on Paredes as a modernist poet, we need first to recognize the peculiar constructions of American nationalism and that its national literature can be seen as "cultural artefacts of a particular kind" (Anderson, 14), constituted as much by alternatively defining pressures from the outside at the peripheral borders as by those from the inner central heartland. The particular constellation of ideologies that demarcate the boundaries of that construct make up, as Homi Bhabha suggests, its imaginative horizon (1).

In his poetry of the 1930s and 1940s, Paredes represents the limits of the Anglo-American cultural and political horizon, limits that are precisely instantiated at its borders by the emergence of a modern "new Mexican," neither Anglo nor Mexican, nor still less the contemporary avatar of Guillermo Gómez-Peña's "Border Brujo" or "Aztec HiTech." Paredes's proto-Chicano consciousness cuts, like Occam's razor, more finely and figures itself more elegantly politically as the product of the newly self-imagined difference between two concrete nationalisms.[3] A lyric poet at the end of the era of high modernism, Paredes sought to create poetic figures to account for what some are today denoting as the post-national Latino subject in the very midst of that subject's formation. This subject in process, the displaced and dispossessed object of official narratives of American history, the Mexican American that Paredes describes, existed in an empty discursive realm: "He no gotta country, he no gotta flag / He no gotta voice, all he got is the han' / To work like the burro; he no gotta lan'" (***Between Two Worlds***, 27).

Paredes's work demonstrates with great imaginative force the filling-in of that empty discursive space. It represents as well the informing presence of the extraliterary, the political, and the economic within the borders of modernist discourse itself to counter the work of one brand of organicist modernism and its concurrent myths of homogeneity. To understand better the dynamics of modernity within the history of the Chicano subject and the manner of its expression in cultural production, however, we must first turn to the narrative of history itself and situate our figures in their social context on the border of modernity.

MODERNITY AND THE CHICANO SUBJECT

On the afternoon of January 6, 1941, with American entry into the war now less than a year away, Franklin Delano Roosevelt entered the Senate chamber to deliver his annual State of the Union address to Congress and the nation. In the days before the event, Roosevelt had fretted over how best to address in one unified line the lingering effects of spiritual and economic crisis, the need for a revaluation of political standards in moral terms, and the real urgency of preparing for the coming war. At the very brink of war, its shadow practically touching the shores of the American continent, Roosevelt urged the Congress to prepare the ground for this "new order" by understanding that national security certainly involved vigilance and action on the international stage and in foreign policy, with the United States continuing to serve as the "arsenal" of democracy (Roosevelt, 668). But Roosevelt was also still profoundly aware of how national security depended on the internal stage of domestic affairs. Therefore, in 1941 Roosevelt argued that "as men do not live by bread alone, they do not fight by armaments alone. Those who man our defenses, and those behind them who build our defenses, must have the stamina and the courage which come from unshakable belief in the manner of life they are defending" (670).

This was no time, Roosevelt pleaded, to stop thinking about "the social and economic problems which are the root cause of the social revolution which is today a supreme factor in the world" (670). Having linked national security and domestic tranquillity in the alleviation of the national Depression, private individual interests thus having assumed public collective significance (Arendt, 33), Roosevelt looked ahead, even beyond the war that the United States had not yet officially entered, to "the ultimate objectives of American policy" (Greer, 12) to sketch a vision of what the nation might one day be. What emerged from that vision was the momentous formulation of the "Four Freedoms." "In the future days, which we seek to make secure," Roosevelt proclaimed, "we look forward to a world founded upon four essential freedoms":

> The first is freedom of speech and expression—everywhere in the world.
>
> The second is freedom of every person to worship God in his own way—everywhere in the world.
>
> The third is freedom from want—which, translated into world terms, means economic understandings which will secure to every nation a healthy peacetime life for its inhabitants—everywhere in the world.
>
> The fourth is freedom from fear—which, translated into world terms, means a world-wide reduction of armaments to such a point and in such a thorough fashion that no nation will be in a position to commit an act of physical aggression against any neighbor—anywhere in the world.
>
> (Roosevelt, 672)

Cynics scoffed that Roosevelt offered here no more than a utopian vision of a distant millennium (Greer, 12). Roosevelt himself, however, insisted in his message to the nation that his grand idea of the Four Freedoms was "a definite basis for a kind of world attainable in our own time and generation" (Roosevelt, 672). Even more grandly, for Roosevelt the Four Freedoms constituted both a renewal of the American commitment to basic human rights and an extension of those personal rights into the transpersonal arena of world politics.

The Four Freedoms—*of speech and expression, of religion, from want,* and *from fear*—represented the culmination of Roosevelt's lifelong commitment to liberal democratic notions of justice and fundamental human rights.[4] The New Deal agenda for American renewal, to be understood as an ethical revaluation for the elimination of spiritual and economic maladies, was now turned outward upon the world in general. Modern social conditions in 1941, on the eve of the American entry into the latest of the great European imperial world wars, precluded that on the international as on the national scale "the social and economic problems which are the root cause of the social revolution" affecting the world could be ignored. "The world order which we seek is the cooperation of free countries, working together in a friendly, civilized society" (Roosevelt, 672). To this end, then, Roosevelt asked "all Americans to respond to that call" (671), concluding that "our strength is our unity of purpose" (672).

What is at stake in Roosevelt's momentous pronouncement of a "world order" to be built on the groundwork of the Four Freedoms is nothing less than a renewed commitment to an ideal vision of a unified American nation working to effect that brave new "world order" under the pressure of "modern [American] social conditions." In a hegemonic move worthy of the most enlightened of liberals, Roosevelt urged the personal liberties guaranteed in the Bill of Rights as the constitutional ground for the construction of both a modern new American nation and a modern new world order formed in the American image. Emerging from an older Republican disorder built on neurotic fears and shaken by real depression, the nation's, and the world's, unity is here called into being as a Democratic system of cultural signification, "as the representation of social *life* rather than the discipline of social *polity*" (Bhabha, 1-2). The narrative of global and national unity that Roosevelt elegantly unravels displays exactly this conceptual divide between lived experience on the one hand and the institutionalized structuration of that experience on the other. It also exemplifies perfectly Benedict Anderson's thesis that "nationalism has to be understood, by aligning it not with self-consciously held political ideologies, but with large cultural systems that preceded it, out of which—as well as against which—it came into being" (12).

That there were profound ambiguities as well as fissures within the ideologies of both the political groundwork and the culturally significant grand unified narrative of American history that underwrites Roosevelt's address to the nation is all too well known. As Tom Nairn has argued, and as the economic conditions of late twentieth-century America have proven, the uneven development of capitalism inscribes within the modern nation social progression in alternate cycle with economic depression, imbricating both "progress and regress in the very genetic code of the nation" (345-46). Consequently, the course of national history and national economies can never run smoothly. Certainly, history offers ample instances of how, in moderate doses, nationalism can provide a positive, collective identity; but it shows concurrently that in immoderate or irrational doses, nationalism creates negative, even lethal, chauvinisms. In either case, what is apparent from a glance at the rhetoric of national discourse—for example, in Roosevelt's use of it in reference to the crisis of the Great Depression—is the psychologistic cast of its tropes and metaphors. There is nothing accidental in this link between the discourses of nationalism and subjectivity, as nationalism explicitly provides one way of joining the subjective conditions with the material modes of production. It is this subjectivity that underwrites as well the legitimacy of Roosevelt's "four essential freedoms."

What is surely less well known than the ambivalences of American nationalist ideology is how the traditional narrative of national destiny that Roosevelt tried to reimagine in liberal bourgeois terminology at the end of one historical era and on the verge of another was received and revised at the margins of the nation, in the borderlands of history, by those other Americans—African Americans, Asian Americans, and Native Americans, for instance—but particularly, by Mexican Americans, the historical subjects of the present discussion. Viewing this response not only allows us to fill in historical gaps in our cultural history but also to understand through dialectical counterreflection the very production of that cultural knowledge itself. ***Between Two Worlds*** offers Américo Paredes's striking response to Roosevelt's millennial vision with his own revision of the Four Freedoms in a Spanish-language poem entitled, in English, **"The Four Freedoms"**:[5]

> Lengua, Cultura, Sangre:
> es vuestro mi cantar,
> sois piedra de los mares
> y muro de hogar;
> este país de "Cuatro Libertades"
> nada nos puede dar.
> Justicia . . . ¿acaso existe?
> La fuerza es la justicia,
> palabras humorísticas: Justicia y Libertad.
> Nos queda sólo la Raza,
> nos queda sólo la Lengua;
> hay que guardarlas siempre
> y mantenerlas vivas
> por una eternidad.

> Language, Culture, Blood:
> my song is of you,
> you are rock of oceans

and commorant wall;
this "Four Freedoms" nation
can offer us nothing.
Justice . . . scarcely exists?
Might is justice, amusing words:
Justice and Liberty.
We have but *la Raza,*
we have but our Tongue;
let's preserve them perpetually
and living maintain them
for eternity.

(58)

In contrast to Roosevelt's universalizing liberal ethico-political discourse of national unity that seeks to extend that local unity globally, Paredes cites the local communal aspects of national culture, language, and "race" as the real mainstays of freedom. In this context, "la Raza" plays an ambivalent role, for, as will become clear with other poems in the collection, what Paredes implies with this deployment of the term is less a *genetic* consanguinity than a culturally *fashioned* collectivity ("la raza" can be translated colloquially as "the people," "the folk," or "the community"). In another, related poem of 1937, **"Mi Pueblo"** (**"My People"**), Paredes had made this localization of culture even more explicit, dedicating the poem **"A mi barrio, El Cuatro Veinti-uno"** (**"To My Barrio, the Four Twenty-One"**):

Eres cierta incertidumbre entre cielo y podredumbre,
del abismo y de la cumbre el destino te formó
citadino y campirano, eres yanqui-mexicano,
eres méxico-tejano,
eres pocho, como yo!

(48-49)

You are a certain incertitude between the heavens and
   putrescence,
destiny shaped you from the abyss and the summit
urbanite and country dweller, you're a Yankee-
   Mexican,
you are a Mexico-Texan,
you are a *pocho* [U.S.-born Mexican], like me!

Like language and culture, and even "race" itself, personal consciousness begins to emerge as a conceptual invention of the community to guarantee "justice" and "liberty" as aspects of lived reality rather than as abstract notions of political economy. It is assuredly not a romantically constructed ideal *Geist* of the *Volk* that provides the subjective repertoire of the Mexican American social mechanism. What real "liberty" might look like is the subject of yet another poem, **"La libertad"** (1942), that also speaks to the Rooseveltian "Four Freedoms":

Raza morena y mestiza
¡oh, semilla de grandeza!
llevas en ti la entereza
que te da la juventud. . . .

Indio descalzo, trigueño,
que llorando vas tu suerte,
indio, ¡qué diera por verte
soberano de verdad!
Con el estómago lleno,
bien vestido y bien calzado
y en tu destino confiado—
ésa es la libertad.

Dark, mestizo race
Oh, seed of grandness!
you bear within you the integrity
that youth gives to you. . . .
Barefoot, dusky Indian,
who weeping bear your destiny,
Indian, what I wouldn't give to see you
Sovereign in truth!
With a full stomach,
well dressed and well shod
and confident in your destiny—
that is liberty.

(62)

"Liberty" here is a material, concrete property of collective interactions, not an abstract reification from an assemblage of personal freedoms. Its features are solid, perceptible, attainable. Its blazon is a well-fed, well-dressed, well-shod *indio,* standing in the sovereignty of truth and the confidence of destiny. Beyond the myths of blood and tongue, the cause of la Raza's (the Folk's) cultural identity lies, as Paredes would have it, in the uneven development of history and world economy, situated on the margins of "cierta incertidumbre," figured in the subjective site of the *pocho,* the hybrid neo-culturo-mestizo, cross-cutting, crisscrossing the seemingly impermeable lines of cultural sovereignty.

The sovereignty of the *pocho's* identity is by no means certified, however. Marked by the "certain incertitude" of local conditions, the *pocho* is undeniably subject to the barbarisms of history. Thus, the poem **"Alma Pocha"** (1936) was written in ironic response to the great and gaudy centennial celebrations of Texas's independence:

En tu propio terruño serás extranjero
por la ley del fusil y la ley del acero;
y verás a tu padre morir balaceado
verás a tu hermano colgado de un leño
por el crimen mortal de haber sido trigueño.
Y si vives, acaso, será sin orgullo,
con recuerdos amargos de todo lo tuyo;
tus campos, tus cielos, tus aves, tus flores
serán el deleite de los invasores;
para ellos su fruto dará la simiente,
donde fueras el amo serás el sirviente.
Y en tu propio terruño serás extranjero
por la ley del fusil y la ley del acero.

(35-36)

In your native homeland a stranger you will be
by the law of the rifle and the law of cold steel;

and you'll see your father shot to death
you'll see your brother strung from a limb
for the mortal crime of having been born dark.
And if perhaps you should happen to live, without
     pride it will be,
with bitter remembrances of what once was yours;
your lands, your skies, your birds, your flowers
will be the delight of the invaders;
for them your fruit will sprout,
where once a master a servant now you will be.
And in your homeland a stranger you will be
by the law of the rifle and the law of cold steel.

The poem counterposes the grim reality of present conditions, "la jornada tejana" ("the arid Texan wastelands"), with the utopian memory of long-lost days. Nature's former beauty, its panoramic vistas, the land's living richness are another's and mock the former master, now a servant, with their fecundity. Calling the "Alma pocha" (the feminine soul of the *pocho*)[6] a stranger in her own homeland, Paredes's speaker, "destiny" ("el destino"), echoes here what, in another poem, another voice describes as "A sad, sad longing / That is almost pain / For something that I one day was / And wish to be again" ("Rose Petals"). Assaulted by "the law of the rifle and the law of cold steel," the "alma pocha" remains, nonetheless, "la que sufre, / la que espera" ("she who suffers / she who hopes").

In another poem from this same period (1935), entitled **"Ahí nomás" ("Just over There")**, Paredes reminds us that the Mexican American's conditions of existence are not by any means unique but constitute a fundamental part of American history:

"Indian, dark brother from whose ancestors
Half of my father's fathers sprang,
You who know all these ragged mountains,
Up to the nests that the eagles hang,
Where do your weary footsteps take you?"
          . . . . .

[W]ith a shrug and a smile he answered,
"Just over there. *Sí ahí nomás.*"
          . . . . .

Should I encounter along my journey
A sister soul that is drawn to me,
Who rhymes with me in a perfect couplet,
Whose voice is pitched on my selfsame key,
Touching my arm, she will stop me, ask me,
"Where are you going? *¿A dónde vas?*"
And with a shrug and a smile I'll answer,
I too shall answer, *"Ahí nomás."*

                                                    (22)

The "alma pocha" here finds kindred souls among native peoples, and among women, all of whom have trod with "weary footsteps" the ages of "bitterness and despair." The "sister soul," in fact, is the very mediator of the alliance among the "dark brother," the poet, and the one "Who rhymes with me." The construction of

the phrase "alma pocha" is a highly unusual one, but the exigencies of the grammatical rule allow for a great deal of figural free play concerning the fecundity, fruitfulness, and erotic destinies of Mexican American life, as this poem makes plain.

### The Borders of Modernity

The "new" Mexican consciousness that Paredes fiercely underwrites in his bilingual poems, a consciousness that resides in the cognitive, social, and political-economic space "between two worlds" and that speaks this bilingual tongue, now arises to contest other discourses for the authority to create new meanings and to assign different meanings and different directions to both the progressivist modernity of Roosevelt's New Deal rhetoric and the assimilative, pluralistic ideology of other Mexican American reformers of the day. In this, as in other matters, Paredes anticipated analytical formations and discursive strategies that lay decades in the future.

Situated on the border, a discursive site of heterogeneity and multiaccentual articulations, Paredes's poetry doubles the signs of "modernity" and the "national" to investigate the nation-space "in the process of the *articulation* of elements" (Bhabha, 3) and to set the scene for a new stage of Mexican American/Chicano cultural and social history. What Paredes will amply accomplish a half century later in his enthnographic and literary studies, he is already working out here in lyrical forms as snippets of cultural critique and social analysis to show how culture, knowledge, and power are interlinked as social constructions that might be challenged and reconfigured. Like Antonio Gramsci, another contemporaneous philosopher of working-class culture, Paredes "grasped the idea that culture serves authority, and ultimately the national State, not because it represses and coerces but because it is affirmative, positive, and persuasive" (Said, 171).

Unlike J. Frank Dobie, Walter Prescott Webb, and other official state intellectuals—Paredes's discursive antagonists, who in their mythological renderings of the American West and Southwest sought to legitimize one particular vision of American culture—and unlike even those oppositional Mexican American writers who sought to pluralize that legitimacy under the sign of assimilation, Paredes sought instead precisely to *de*-legitimize it by showing the production of a modern American "nation-space" in process, in medias res, halfmade, "caught in the act of 'composing' its powerful image" (Bhabha, 3), as it were, and whose modernity was thus subject to a critical reproduction. As Homi Bhabha, in another context, has written:

The marginal or "minority" is not the space of a celebratory, or utopian, self-marginalization. It is a much more substantial intervention into those justifications of

modernity—progress, homogeneity, cultural organi-
cism, the deep nation, the long past—that rationalize
the authoritarian, "normalizing" tendencies within
cultures in the name of the national interest or ethnic
prerogative. In this sense, then, the ambivalent,
antagonistic perspective of nation as narration will
establish the cultural boundaries of the nation so that
they may be acknowledged as "containing" thresholds
of meaning that must be crossed, erased, and translated
in the process of cultural production.

(4)

Perhaps nowhere else than in Paredes's poetry of the
1930s and early 1940s is the future possibility of a Chi-
cano national subject most unambiguously projected.
Like Matthew Arnold in "Stanzas from the Grande
Chartreuse" (1855)—the source of the title and epigraph
to Paredes's collection of lyrics—retracing the poetic
lines of Wordsworth's Alpine journey in *The Prelude,*
Paredes returns to his own undiscovered country, the
borderlands of South Texas. In this poetic return he
repeats the symbolic phrases of his community's master
narrative in the *corrido* but without the historical
amnesia of the original score and in full knowledge of
its possible self-negations.

A word about Arnold's poem is appropriate in conclu-
sion. Arnold's "Grande Chartreuse" is not so much a la-
ment for former times and beliefs as it is an expression
of his hopelessness over the impotence to which
melancholy stoicism reduces us (DeLaura, 20):

> Wandering between two worlds, one dead,
> The other powerless to be born,
> With nowhere yet to rest my head,
> Like these, on earth I wait forlorn.
> Their faith, my tears, the world deride—
> I come to shed them at their side.

In "Grande Chartreuse," Arnold poetically considers
and rejects various historical attitudes: Christian faith,
now simply "gone" (l. 84); his own "out-worn" and
"out-dated" (ll. 100, 106) code learned from his former
"rigorous teachers," whom he calls the "masters of the
mind" (ll. 67, 73); and the attitude of "the kings of
modern thought," who are silent, dumb, passive, and
merely "wait to see the future come" (ll. 116, 119). But
Arnold allows of another historical possibility, one that
he wistfully acknowledges is unavailable to him: the vi-
sion of a future country, now "powerless to be born."

This vision of what we might call, paraphrasing Arnold,
the country of the kings of *postmodern* thought is
unmistakably that which animates Paredes's modernist
revolution. Arnold, "between two worlds," resigns
himself at the beginning of modernism to his former
ethical codes, judging himself totally unfitted for the
life of "action and pleasure" (l. 194) offered by the
burgeoning modern world (DeLaura, 21). Paredes, in
contrast, at the end of modernism, embraces this

undiscovered country, figured in the liminal, differential
status of living "between two worlds." It is a place that
demarcates a spatiotemporal zone of critical deconstruc-
tion, and constitutes the very possibility of "action and
pleasure" for his community. In a poem from 1950,
entitled **"Esquinita de mi pueblo"** (**"My Community's
Corner"**), Paredes reflects exactly on this process of
living an imaginative cartography:

> At the corner of absolute elsewhere
> And absolute future I stood
> Waiting for a green light
> To leave the neighborhood.
> But the light was red.
>
> . . . . .
>
> That is the destiny of people in between
> To stand on the corner
> Waiting for the green.

(114)

With this poem, Paredes brings us to the present
problematic of the post-contemporary. This is the era
after World War II, during which, as Raymond Wil-
liams puts it, the modern shifts its reference from "now"
to "just now" or even "then," and for some time has
been a designation with which "contemporary" may be
contrasted for its presentness (32). "All that is left us,"
adds Williams, "is to become post-moderns." To become
postmodern, however, in this sense at least, is to remain
modern, to keep in step, to be contemporary, to make of
modernity an incomplete project.

What Paredes maps in **"Esquinita de mi pueblo"** as
"the corner of absolute elsewhere / And absolute future"
is precisely the marker and the substitute of the limits
of the modern. Between the emergence of a properly
modernist style and the representational dilemmas of
the new imperial world system, Paredes's verses exploit
their contingency to history—"the destiny of people in
between" and the utopian glimpses of achieved com-
munity, "Waiting for the green," that this contingency
allows. Indeed, in exploring its styles and testing its
ethics, Paredes offers us something very like what Fre-
dric Jameson calls a "cognitive mapping" (1988) of the
social spaces of the imaginary borders of modernity
within the real conditions of existence. The achieve-
ment of his symbolic cartography is confirmed in its
prefigurative tropes, tracing out in aesthetic patterns
relationships that turn out to be all too real social reali-
ties. It is perhaps in this vein, as the anticipatory precur-
sor of the postcontemporary, that we should read the
concluding lines of Paredes's "Prologue": "I am aware
that if this volume finds any favor with the reader it
will be mostly as a historical document. It is thus that I
offer it, as the scribblings of a 'proto-Chicano' of a
half-century ago" (11).

*Notes*

1. For further biographical information on Américo Paredes and excellent indications of his preeminent role in the foundation of Chicano Cultural Studies, see José E. Limón, "Américo Paredes: A Man from the Border" (1980); Héctor Calderón, "Reinventing the Border: From the Southwest Genre to Chicano Cultural Studies" (forthcoming); and José David Saldívar, "Chicano Narratives as Cultural Critique" (1991) and "Américo Paredes and Decolonization" (1993).

2. The problematic of "border writing" deserves an essay unto itself. Nonetheless, as idiosyncratic, not to say self-indulgent, initial explorations of the postmodern quality of contemporary Chicano discourse, see the essay by D. Emily Hicks, "Deterritorialization and Border Writing," and an interview conducted by Coco Fusco with Guillermo Gómez-Peña and Emily Hicks on "The Border Art Workshop/Taller de Arte Fronterizo."

3. On Gómez-Peña, in addition to the interview cited in note 2, see John Phillip Santos, "A Latin Quest for Identity: Performance Artist Guillermo Gómez-Peña Unveils New Work following 'Genius' Award," 19-20.

4. As early as March 1929, Roosevelt had already claimed that "modern social conditions have progressed to a point where such demands [as basic human rights] can no longer be regarded other than as matters of an absolute right" (Greer, 14).

5. Paredes has mentioned to this writer that at one point he considered entitling his collection *The Four Freedoms*. Concerning the claims of Roosevelt's "Four Freedoms," Paredes comments dryly in a footnote to his poem: "Some people were skeptical." Translations of the Spanish are my own.

6. "Alma" ("soul") is a feminine noun, requiring the corresponding feminine ending of the adjectival modifier, "pocha." On the derivation and meaning of the Mexicanism "pocho/a," Santamaría notes (s.v. "pocho/a") that it is "a name designating the northamerican descendents of Mexicans"; it also suggests "someone of limited abilities"; and it can also refer to the "corrupted Castillian tongue, mixture of English and poor Spanish, spoken by northamerican descendents of Mexican origin." Paredes activates all valences of the term and converts their pejorative quality into an honorific.

*References*

Anderson, Benedict. *Imagined Communities: Reflections on the Origin and Spread of Nationalism.* Rev. ed. London: Verso, 1983, 1991.

Arendt, Hannah. *The Human Condition.* Chicago: University of Chicago Press, 1958.

Arnold, Matthew. "Stanzas from the Grande Chartreuse." In *The Norton Anthology of English Literature,* vol. 2. 4th ed. Ed. M. H. Abrams et al. New York: W. W. Norton, 1979.

Baker, Houston, Jr. *Blues, Ideology, and Afro-American Literature: A Vernacular Theory.* Chicago: University of Chicago Press, 1984.

Benjamin, Walter. "Theses on the Philosophy of History." In *Illuminations,* ed. Hannah Arendt. New York: Schocken Books, 1969.

Bhabha, Homi K., ed. *Nation and Narration.* London and New York: Routledge, 1990.

Calderón, Héctor. "Reinventing the Border: From the Southwest Genre to Chicano Cultural Studies." In *Chicano Cultural Studies,* ed. Mario T. García. Los Angeles: University of California Press, forthcoming.

DeLaura, David J. *Hebrew and Hellene in Victorian England: Newman, Arnold, and Pater.* Austin: University of Texas Press, 1969.

Foucault, Michel. *The History of Sexuality.* Vol. 1: *An Introduction.* Trans. Robert Hurley (New York: Pantheon Books, 1978).

Fusco, Coco. "Interview" with Guillermo Gómez-Peña and Emily Hicks in "The Border Art Workshop," *Third Text* 7 (summer 1989): 53-76.

Greer, Thomas H. *What Roosevelt Thought: The Social and Political Ideas of Franklin D. Roosevelt.* East Lansing: Michigan State University Press, 1958.

Habermas, Jürgen. "Modernity—An Incomplete Project." In *The Anti-Aesthetic: Essays on Postmodern Culture,* ed. Hal Foster. Port Townsend, Wash.: Bay Press, 1983.

Hicks, Emily. "Deterritorialization and Border Writing." In *Ethics/Aesthetics: Postmodern Positions,* ed. Robert Merrill. Washington, D.C.: Maisonneuve Press, 1988. 47-58.

Jameson, Fredric. "Cognitive Mapping." In *Marxism and the Interpretation of Culture,* ed. Cary Nelson and Lawrence Grossberg. Urbana: University of Illinois Press, 1988. 347-57.

———. "Modernism and Imperialism." In Terry Eagleton, Fredric Jameson, and Edward W. Said, *Nationalism, Colonialism, and Literature.* Intro. Seamus Deane. Minneapolis: University of Minnesota Press, 1990. 43-66.

Nairn, Tom. "The Modern Janus." In *The Break-up of Britain: Crisis and Neo-Nationalism.* 2d ed. London: Verso, 1981.

Paredes, Américo. *Between Two Worlds.* Houston: Arte Público Press, 1991.

———. *Folklore and Culture on the Texas Mexican Border.* Ed. Richard Bauman. Austin: Center for Mexican American Studies Publications and University of Texas Press, 1993.

———. "Folklore, Lo Mexicano, and Proverbs." *Aztlán* 13:1-2 (1982): 1.

———. *George Washington Gómez: A Mexicotexan Novel.* Houston: Arte Público Press, 1990.

———. "The Mexican *Corrido*: Its Rise and Fall." In *Madstones and Twisters,* ed. Mody C. Boatright. Dallas: Southern Methodist University Press, 1958. 91-105.

———. *A Texas-Mexican Cancionero: Folksongs of the Lower Border.* Urbana: University of Illinois Press, 1976.

———. *Uncle Remus con Chile.* Houston: Arte Público Press, 1993.

———. *"With His Pistol in His Hand": A Border Ballad and Its Hero.* Austin: University of Texas Press, 1958.

Roosevelt, Franklin Delano. "Annual Message to the Congress," January 3, 1940; and "Annual Message to the Congress," January 6, 1941. In *The Public Papers and Addresses of Franklin D. Roosevelt,* vol. 9: *War—and Aid to Democracies, 1940.* New York: Macmillan, 1941.

Said, Edward. "Reflections in American 'Left' Literary Criticism." In *The World, the Text, and the Critic.* Cambridge, Mass.: Harvard University Press, 1983.

Saldívar, José David. "Chicano Narratives as Cultural Critique." In *Criticism in the Borderlands: Studies in Chicano Literature, Culture, and Ideology,* ed. Héctor Calderón and José David Saldívar. Durham, N.C.: Duke University Press, 1991. 167-80.

———. "Américo Paredes and Decolonization." In *Cultures of United States Imperialism,* ed. Amy Kaplan and Donald E. Pease. Durham, N.C.: Duke University Press, 1993. 292-311.

Saldívar, Ramón. *Chicano Narrative: The Dialectics of Difference.* Madison: University of Wisconsin Press, 1990.

Santamaría, Francisco. Diccionario de Mejicanismos. 3d ed. Mexico City: Editorial Porrua, 1978.

Santos, John Phillip. "A Latin Quest for Identity: Performance Artist Guillermo Gómez-Peña Unveils New Work following 'Genius' Award." *San Francisco Chronicle* Datebook (November 3, 1991): 19-20.

Soja, Edward W. *Postmodern Geographies: The Reassertion of Space in Critical Social Theory.* London: Verso, 1990.

Williams, Raymond. *The Politics of Modernism: Against the New Conformists,* ed. Tony Pinkney. London: Verso, 1989.

**Leticia Magda Garza-Falcón (essay date 1998)**

SOURCE: Garza-Falcón, Leticia Magda. "The Poetry of Américo Paredes." In *Gente Decente: A Borderlands Response to the Rhetoric of Dominance,* pp. 165-67. Austin: University of Texas Press, 1998.

[*In the following excerpt, Garza-Falcón provides a brief discussion of Paredes's poem "Alma pocha."*]

Though not well known as a poet until recently, Américo Paredes has been writing poetry since the age of fourteen. In 1989 he referred to his poetry as "the scribblings of a 'proto-Chicano' of a half-century ago," as "no garden of verses . . . but more like an overgrown clearing in the chaparral, with more burrs and thistles than flowers" (1991: 10-11). The theme of dispossession, with the resulting losses of social and political position and of rights as a member of society, emerged early in Paredes's poetry:

> A cit'zen of Texas they say that he ees,
> But then, why they call him the Mexican Grease?
> Soft talk and hard action, he can't understan'.
> The Mexico-Texan he no gotta lan'
>
> (1935: "THE MEXICO-TEXAN")

As Paredes notes in the 1991 publication of this poem in **Between Two Worlds** (note 2), this poem is "perhaps the best known of [his] efforts at versifying" (139). He states that he originally composed this poem in the spring of 1934, "while walking the 21 blocks home from [high] school one afternoon," but eventually as a second, written version, it "became current in manuscript form in south Texas, was used in political campaigns, was reprinted a few times as anonymous, and entered oral tradition locally" (139).

Also printed in **Between Two Worlds** is another "story" of displacement where the destiny speaks to the persona created by this new situation. As Paredes's notes to the text indicate, the poem **"Alma pocha"** was written on occasion of the Texas Centennial celebrations. On this occasion, *La Prensa* of San Antonio, a Mexican American newspaper which had on occasion published Paredes's verses, "declined to print it" (p. 139, footnote 4). This story, told in verse, is about the defeated soul of the Mexicano who has suffered defending the toil of his people, *"el sudor derramado,"* and is now a stranger in his own land. He sees his father shot down, his brother lynched, and everything he once felt an important part of himself—the fields, the skies, the birds, and flowers—are now being enjoyed by the invading stranger. He is haunted always by a history that has made the name of Santa Anna the shame of every Mexican. Destiny's mouth is made despicable when it speaks of the Texas (Texan's) journey:

Alma pocha
ensangrentada,
la sufrida,
la olvidada,
la rebelde sin espada;
alma pocha
salpicada
de tragedia y humorada,
alma pocha.
En tu propio terruño serás extranjero
por la ley del fusil y la ley del acero;
y verás a tu padre morir balaceado
por haber defendido el sudor derramado;
verás a tu hermano colgado de un leño
por el crimen mortal de haber sido trigueño.
Y si vives, acaso, será sin orgullo,
con recuerdos amargos de todo lo tuyo;
tus campos, tus cielos, tus aves, tus flores
serán el deleite de los invasores;
para ellos su fruto dará la simiente
donde fueras el amo serás el sirviente
por la ley del fusil y la ley del acero.
De este modo
habló el destino
en la jornada tejana
¡y la boca se envilece
con el nombre de Santa Anna!
Alma pocha
vas llorando
la verguenza mexicana.
Alma pocha,
alma noble y duradera,
la que sufre,
la que espera.

1936 (35-36)

[Soul of the pocho
the bloodied one,
that which has suffered
and been forgotten,
rebel without a sword;
soul of the pocho
splashed
with tragedy and tempered,
soul of the pocho.
In your own native soil you shall be a stranger
by the law of the gun and the blade;
and you shall see your father die, riddled with bullets
for having defended his poured out sweat;
you shall see your brother hanging from a tree branch
for the mortal crime of having been brown-skinned.
And if by chance you live it shall be without pride,
but with bitter memories of all that was yours;
your fields, your skies, your birds and flowers
shall be the delight of the invaders;
for them the seed will give its fruit;
where you would have been master, you shall be a
 servant
by the law of the gun and the blade.

In this way
did destiny speak
while on its Texas journey
and the mouth becomes despicable
with the name of Santa Anna!
Soul of the pocho
you go crying out
the Mexican shame.
Soul of the pocho
noble and lasting soul,
one that suffers,
one that waits.]

(MY TRANSLATION)

## José R. López Morín (essay date winter 2005)

SOURCE: López Morín, José R. "The Life and Early Works of Américo Paredes." *Western Folklore* 64, nos. 1/2 (winter 2005): 7-28.

[*In the following essay, López Morín examines early influences on Paredes's writing career.*]

> . . . Porque a mí me importa un bledo que me apunten
>  con el dedo,
> que de mí murmure quedo tu correcta sociedad;
> pueblo bajo y barullero, pueblo dulce y romancero,
> yo te juro que te quiero,
> yo te quiero de verdad.
>
> —**"Mi pueblo"** (1935), Américo Paredes

A LONG LIFE AND CAREER AT THE UNIVERSITY
OF TEXAS AT AUSTIN

When the 40-year old Américo Paredes was writing his dissertation that would become the basis of his most famous book, *"With His Pistol in His Hand": A Border Ballad and Its Hero* (1958), he drew on the memories of his youth. He was especially mindful of those quiet "summer nights, in the days when there was a chaparral," when his father and the old men sat around and talked in "low, gentle voices about violent things" (Paredes 1958: Dedication). These stories, especially the performances of *corridos* (narrative folksongs), were never forgotten by Américo Paredes. They nurtured his imagination as a young boy and became the subject of some of his most important research in his adult life. The heroic events of popular song and legend offered him a different picture of historical events from the formal history he learned in school. One of Paredes's main contentions in his long life as a scholar was the fact that North American literature had been offering a distorted view of the history of his region and his people. In order to set things in a way he thought right, he wrote poetry, short stories, and a novel that would better capture and represent the character and psychology of the border folk. The search for a distinct perspective (many years later it would be properly called a

Chicano perspective) is evident throughout much of his early work. His research on the *corrido* was the starting point and the touchstone of his contribution of a people whose children and grandchildren would identify themselves as Mexican Americans and Chicanos. Paredes argued in his thesis that *el corrido de Gregorio Cortez* served as a resistance literature against North American domination. The ballad of Gregorio Cortez challenged both the stereotypical views of Mexicans, and the official versions of recent events in the history of the border. Paredes did not write his book from the perspective of a dispassionate bystander. He felt a moral responsibility to contribute to the cultural survival of his people. As the Mexico-Tejano scholar embarked on a very distinguished career at the University of Texas at Austin, he made it a life-long quest to celebrate the spirit, wisdom, and dignity of his people.

A good portion of this essay is based on two interviews granted by Américo Paredes in Austin, Texas. Juan Gómez-Quiñones, José Limón, Teresa McKenna, and Victor Nelson conducted one interview on August 23, 1984. Twelve years later, despite Américo's failing health, Héctor Calderón and I were privileged with the opportunity to converse with him at his home on July 13, 1996.[1] During two and half hours of a videotaped interview, Américo Paredes spoke candidly about his upbringing in south Texas, his service in the Armed Forces in World War II, his years as a Professor of English and Anthropology at the University of Texas, Austin, and his literary projects in retirement. Throughout the conversation, both Héctor Calderón and I sensed Américo Paredes's outrage at the way in which Mexicans had been treated in south Texas by Anglo-Texans of certain types. But these personal recollections were always offset with his sharp wit and keen sense of humor. In many ways, Américo Paredes personified the spirit and ingenuity of the border folk, who as a people learned to resist in various ways against the hardships and prejudices of the time.

### How Américo Paredes's Life Was Shaped along the U.S./Mexican Border

Américo Paredes Manzano was born on September 3, 1915 in Brownsville, Texas to Justo and Clotilde Manzano-Vidal Paredes. He was born during the peak months of the border troubles between North Americans and Mexico-Tejanos.[2] As a boy, he spent most of his summers with his family relatives across the Rio Grande River in Matamoros, Tamaulipas. There, in a Mexican rural environment, he came to know his people's history as he remembers listening with interest to the legends, ballads, and tales of the border folk. His father don Justo Paredes Cisneros was an anti-clerical *ranchero* with literary inclinations. He imparted to his son with a sense of urgency many of the beliefs and customs of a ranching way of life in evident decline. On many occa-

sions, Don Justo sat and talked for hours with his son about the ways of his own father and grandfather. The oral tradition transmitted from generation to generation, in families like his own, was at the core of a culture Paredes would be instrumental in understanding and disseminating. Among the rich family oral history were tales of the arrival from Spain of his father's clan, a colony of *sefarditas* led by Luis de Carbajal in 1580; the heroic exploits of his great-grandfather in Palo Alto against General Zachary Taylor's troops in the Battle of *La Resaca*; and bitter recollections of the abuses by the Texas Rangers against the Lower Rio Grande border folk (Calderón and López Morín 2000:204). These stories fascinated Américo as a child, and they inspired a large corpus of his writings.

Before enrolling in an English-speaking elementary school in Texas, Américo could already read and write in Spanish. His teachers were his father and his eldest brother. The Paredes family recognized early on Américo's inquisitive nature, and they had high expectations for him. "Este es el que va a hacer algo por nosotros— por nuestra familia. Es el que va a ir a la escuela" [This is the one who will do something for us—for our family. He is the one who will go to school], don Justo was often heard commenting to friends (Paredes 1984). The high expectations weighed on Américo's consciousness and played a role in his growing sense of responsibility toward his family and toward the people along the Lower Rio Grande Border.

In elementary school, Américo took to reading and writing in English with enthusiasm. The quiet life of the *rancho* away from school offered minimal distractions during these years. He enjoyed reading popular literature for young people, including the *Tarzan* novels of Edgar Rice Burroughs, yet he also read serious literary works in both Spanish and English. He was especially fond of his book of Shakespeare's sonnets, a gift from his eldest brother who had taught him to read in Spanish. Thus, at a young age, books became his companions. They allowed him to dream of other worlds, and they were an invitation to explore his own world of fantasy. Américo remembered spending hours recreating the stories he heard from the old men, or making up his own, and imagining he was Gregorio Cortez against the *rinches* (Texas Rangers). Daydreaming allowed him to project himself as a hero for his people and helped him to relieve his anger and frustration over the realities of life for the Mexico-Tejano border folk.

His father's interest in Spanish-language poetry also informed the young Américo's literary formation. Don Justo memorized, read, and even wrote poetry, and he would often recite his own *décima* or *espinela, redondilla,* and the *canto a desafío*. These forms of folk poetry were recited usually during the times when stories were told, and at other times these poems were sung with the accompaniment of a guitar. But for Américo Paredes, "the narrative, which the *décimas* adorned like colorful motifs on a larger design—the narrative was the important thing because it bound the *décimas* together, and all of [the people] as well" (Paredes 1993 [1987]:249).

The ability to read and write effectively in two languages naturally broadened his horizons at a young age. The informal education received at home combined with the more formal one in the Brownsville public school system gave Américo a dual perspective. He appreciated some aspects of his formal schooling, but he did not hesitate to challenge the information he received in the classroom with the knowledge he had gained at home. As his sister and others have recalled, he was generally a quiet and mild mannered individual (García 1991:1B). But he was not afraid to stand up for his culture or his background. Américo said that he protested to the point of becoming unruly when his teachers offered a view of recent history he considered denigrating to his people.

In junior high school, for example, Américo Paredes remembered the time his teacher tried to explain and justify the creation of the Monroe Doctrine. The teacher told a story to the class about a little boy with a lollipop who met a bigger boy: "Suppose . . . [this] big bully comes over and tries to take it away from the little boy. Then the United States is the other boy that comes and beats up the bully." At that moment Américo asked: "Yes, but what if the boy after he beats up the bully starts beating up the boy with the lollipop and takes it away?" (Paredes 1984). According to Américo Paredes, the class celebrated his point with laughter, and he was sent to the principal's office for insubordination.

In junior high school Américo developed another of his many interests—his love for music. One of his favorite musicians was the singer and guitar player Ignacio *Nacho* Montelongo, a border Mexican who would pile his clothes and belongings into an old washtub, swim across the Rio Grande, and visit the Paredes family to sing and play. Years later Nacho would inspire Américo as *Chano* Quintana, a memorable character in the short story Rebeca (Paredes 1994:95).

Nacho Montelongo taught the young Américo to play the guitar, although don Justo was adamantly against the idea. Américo's father had a distaste for popular musicians, whom he considered irresponsible and bohemian. His image of the popular musician was Juventino Rosas, the composer of a celebrated song entitled *Sobre las olas* [Over the Waves]. Don Justo would often remind his son that he had met Mr. Rosas in Monterrey, Nuevo León; and while he saw him once

dressed in a fine suit, conducting an orchestra, he also saw Mr. Rosas lying in the streets *borracho* [drunk]. Américo's father was convinced that all musicians were drunks and that "they were all a lost cause" (Paredes 1984).

Disagreement between father and son over the issue of popular music is the central theme in one of Paredes's first short stories, entitled, quite appropriately, "Over the Waves is Out" (1994 [1952]). He later would learn to play the piano, which was another of his childhood dreams. Many years later Américo was surprised to learn that his father, too, had played the guitar, until *his* father forced him to quit these musical pursuits.

Despite don Justo's wishes, Américo secretly purchased a cheap guitar and began to compose songs at the same time as when he began to write poetry. He frequented musicians and poets along the border to practice, write, and sing. Many of them sometimes crossed the border to Matamoros and met at a lodge called the Texas Bar (Paredes 1984). Food and drink were cheap there, and a group of about eight to ten members reunited outside in the patio area to recite their own poetry. At other times, Américo and his friends driving around in a car frequented different places in Brownsville to sing and write poetry. Paredes became so adept at composing and playing the guitar that he was hired to perform on the radio for fifteen dollars a week.

Américo Paredes pursued his love for reading and writing in high school. Many times his teachers did not receive well his unconventional views. Américo remembered having written an essay in high school on William Shakespeare's *The Merchant of Venice* (1603). Paredes read the play in terms of his own situation, and he sympathized with Shylock's precarious reality as a Jew in a Christian world. In the 1984 interview with Gómez-Quiñones, Limón, McKenna, and Nelson, Américo Paredes recalled a famous passage of the play with which he closely identified. In fact, he believed that Shylock's words had significance to the Mexico-Tejanos of the Río Grande Border: "If you prick us, do we not bleed? if you tickle us, do we not laugh? if you poison us, do we not die? and if you wrong us, shall we not revenge? if we are like you in the rest, we will resemble you in that. If a Jew wrong a Christian, what is his humility? revenge: if a Christian wrong a Jew, what should his sufferance be by Christian example? why, revenge. The villainy you teach me, I will execute; and it shall go hard but I will better the instruction" (Shakespeare 1979:415).

One can see how the young Paredes could read into this passage the frustrations and predicaments of Mexicans living in the United States. His high school essay on the play was never returned, as was the custom of the time, but he knew that it had had an impact. In the same

1984 interview, Américo Paredes commented that other teachers and even members of the community had heard about his essay. He was aware that writing could be an effective tool to challenge conventional views and was determined to be well read in both Spanish and English literature.

Américo Paredes remembered reading an array of Spanish poetry in a newspaper section called the "Lunes Literarios de la Prensa," a literary supplement published by the daily *La Prensa* of San Antonio, Texas. He read well-known poets like Gustavo Adolfo Bécquer, José Santos Chocano, and Rubén Darío, among many others. In English he read the poetry of Henry Wadsworth Longfellow, Walt Whitman, and Edgar Allan Poe. He received a kind of inspiration from this poetry and tried to apply it to his own social reality along the Lower Rio Grande Border. He knew that his poetry would address the border folk's social and economic situation, but he had not found what I would characterize as a distinctive Chicano voice of resistance. There is an artificiality to some of his poetry as the poem **"Flute Song"** suggests:

### "Flute Song"

Why was I ever born
Heir to a people's sorrow
Wishing this day were done
And yet fearful for the morrow.

Why was I ever born
Proud of my southern race,
If I must seek my sun
In an Anglo-Saxon face.

Wail, wail, oh flutes, your dismal tune,
The agony of our birth;
Better perhaps had I never known
That you lived upon the earth.

[Paredes 1991 (1935):24]

Although a sense of humiliation torments the poet who despises North American exploitation, the poem seems awkward for a young Mexican American activist, with verses like *fearful of the morrow* and *Wail, wail, oh flutes, your dismal tune.* The poetry does not possess any notable qualities that set it apart from other English verse, and it is difficult to imagine Américo Paredes with this type of attitude given some of his background and personality. What is apparent here is the young Mexico-Tejano's experimentation with various literary models as he attempts to discover a distinct Chicano perspective that could capture the essence of his divided reality.

A poem that illustrates the dilemma of an in-between existence is The Mexico-Texan. Paredes recalled writing this particular piece "while walking the 21 blocks home from [high] school" in the spring of 1934 (1991

[1935]:139). This detail sheds light on his early life and his ability to identify with his people. A vernacular and sympathetic voice is used to explain the Mexico-Tejano's predicament:

### "The Mexico-Texan"

The Mexico-Texan he's one fonny man
Who leeves in the region that's north of the Gran',
Of Mexican father he born in these part,
And sometimes hes rues it dip down in he's heart.

For the Mexico-Texan he no gotta lan',
He stomped on the neck on both sides of the Gran',
The dam gringo lingo he no cannot spik,
It twisters the tong and it make you fill sick.
A cit'zen of Texas they say that he ees,
But then, why they call him the Mexican Grease?
Soft talk and hard action, he can't understan',
The Mexico-Texan he no gotta lan'.

If he cross the reever, eet ees just as bad,
On high poleeshed Spanish he break up his had,
American customs those people no like,
They hate that Miguel they should call him Mike,
And Mexican-born, why they jeer and they hoot,
"Go back to the gringo! Go lick at hees boot!"
In Texas he's Johnny, in Mexico Juan,
But the Mexico-Texan he no gotta lan'.

Elactions come round and the gringos are loud,
They pat on he's back and they make him so proud,
They give him mezcal and the barbacue meat,
They tell him, "Amigo, we can't be defeat."
But efter election he no gotta fran',
The Mexico-Texan he no gotta lan',

Except for a few with their cunning and craft
He count just as much as a nought to the laft,
And they say everywhere, "He's a burden and drag,
He no gotta country, he no gotta flag."
He no gotta voice, all he got is the han'
To work like the burro; he no gotta lan'.

And only one way can his sorrows all drown,
He'll get drank as hell when next payday come roun',
For he has one advantage of all other man,
Though the Mexico-Texan he no gotta lan',
He can get him so drank that he think he will fly
Both September the Sixteen and Fourth of July.

[Paredes 1991:26]

Here, Américo Paredes the poet begins to explore the concept of what others outside the border culture think of the Mexico-Tejano people. The poem functions as a kind of ethnic slur or slurs, made up of attitudes and phrases about Texas Mexicans.[3] Paredes uses the third person singular and plural, *he* and *they*, to give an opinion of what he believes to be the Mexico-Texan's image of himself based on what others think of him. The poem is insightful because it suggests how an in-between existence muddles and yet shapes the Mexico-Texan's identity.

One of Américo Paredes's better poems which moves closer to the spirit and essence of the old ranching culture along the Lower Rio Grande Border is **"Guitarreros."**[4] The poem begins with an epitaph from one of Américo Paredes's favorite *corridos* entitled "El hijo desobediente" [The Disobedient Son]. The folksong is about a young man who disobeys the advice of his father while in a fight. The boy curses his father by threatening to kill him if he also interferes. Having made these comments, the boy knows he must suffer the consequences of his lack of respect. According to the *corrido* scholar Merle Simmons, a kind of divine punishment awaits him. This *castigo* [punishment] will manifest itself in the form of a violent death (Simmons 1957:61). The boy, therefore, wishes to be buried anywhere but in sacred ground. The epitaph, *bajaron el toro prieto / que nunca habían bajado.* [They brought down the black bull / the one that had never been brought down], alludes to this violent death on the horns of an enraged bull. This didactic work in the style of a folksong highlights the respect one should have towards others, especially one's father. The theme of respect and honor is hinted at in the poem, for the way in which singing was done in the old ranching culture. Apparently, very few *guitarreros* are able to keep this tradition alive as the poem suggests:

### "Guitarreros"

> *bajaron el toro prieto,*
> *que nunca lo habían bajado . . .*
> Black against twisted black
> The old mesquite
> Rears up against the stars
> Branch bridle hanging,
> While the bull comes down from the mountain
> Driven along by your fingers,
> Twenty nimble stallions prancing up and down
> the *redil* of the guitars.
>
> One leaning on the truck, one facing—
> Now the song:
> Not cleanly flanked, not pacing,
> But in a stubborn yielding that unshapes
> And shapes itself again,
> Hard-mouthed, zigzagged, thrusting,
> Thrown not sung
> One to the other.
>
> The old man listens in his cloud
> Of white tobacco smoke.
> "It was so," he says,
> "In the old days it was so."

(Paredes 1991 [1935]:29)

A closer analysis of the poem's title suggests a kind of tribute for the way in which folk poetry was performed in the old days. The images of a ranching way of life combine with those of lyrical music to offer a glimpse of a traditional performance—proud and dignified. The elderly gentlemen do not approve of the way in which folk songs are performed nowadays, and they express their distaste with a traditional performance. Américo Paredes offers a glimpse of the folk poets' attitudes towards some of the changes that have taken place along the Lower Rio Grande region. The ethical world evoked by the *corrido*—one that once made sense—is now pointless in a world were God no longer exists (Pérez-Torres 1995:256).

Américo Paredes's dedication to his poetry helped him win the first place award in a statewide high school poetry contest sponsored by Trinity College (now Trinity University in San Antonio, Texas). The poem, a sonnet entitled Night, came to the attention of Mr. "Red" Irving, Paredes's high school principal who was also the dean of the local junior college at the time. After high school graduation, Mr. Irving noticed Américo standing on a street corner looking for a job. The principal encouraged him to apply for a student assistantship, even though the deadline had passed. Through Mr. Irving's efforts Américo Paredes received a college work-study award that enabled him to pay for his college tuition and enroll at Brownsville Junior College. Paredes started to dream about becoming a university English professor in Texas.

PAREDES'S EXPERIENCES IN JOURNALISM,
MARRIAGE, AND WORLD WAR II

While attending college in the mid 1930's during the Great Depression, Américo Paredes worked long hours. He performed certain tasks at school for the student assistantship award, and he worked at a grocery store for approximately 50 hours a week, for the modest salary of two dollars per week. Notwithstanding, Américo continued to write, and in Mexico he published his first volume of lyric poetry at the age of twenty-two entitled **Cantos de adolescencia** (1937). The poetic voice in this collection is that of a youngster in search of an identity that is neither Mexican nor American, as the prologue suggests:

> *Los versos que en este libro se encierran no son sola-*
> *mente el diario de un adolescente. Son el diario de un*
> *adolescente méxico-texano. ¡Adolescente! Fenónemo*
> *físico causado por la proximidad de dos edades; indi-*
> *viduo que no es niño ni es adulto. ¡México-texano!*
> *Fenómeno sociológico, planta de tiesto, hombre sin*
> *terruño propio y verdadero, que no es ni mexicano ni*
> *yanqui.*

(Paredes Manzano 1937:3)

The verses enclosed in this book are not only *the diary of an adolescent.* They are the diary of a Mexico-Texan adolescent. Adolescent! Physical phenomenon caused by the proximity of two ages; individual that is neither child nor adult. Mexico-Texan! Sociological phenomenon, stubborn plant, man without a true and proper country that is neither Mexican nor Yankee.

*(my translation)*

If earlier the young Américo used the English language to convey his innermost feelings of exile, now he makes a conscious effort to articulate this search in his native tongue:

> *Estas páginas son el resultado de esta lucha de tiempo de decisión. Comencé a escribir verso desde la edad de quince anos pero mis obras fueron todas en ingles. Mis versos en español no comienzan hasta en 1932, dos anos después. Esto se debe a la influencia de una escuela en ingles y de muy pocos libros en la lengua de Cervantes. En verdad, todavía me siento más seguro de mí mismo en la lengua de Shakespeare que en la mía. Por eso encontrará el lector en mis versos errores de gramática . . . La mayor parte fueron corregidos. Los que quedan fueron dejados al propósito, porque en mi concepto, no se pueden remover. Así—en aquellas palabras—sentí lo que quería decir. Decirlo de otra manera fuera no decirlo.*

(Paredes Manzano 1937:4)

These pages are the result of this struggle with time to decide: I began to write poetry at the age of fifteen, but my work was all in English. My verses in Spanish do not begin until 1932, two years later. This is the result of an English-speaking school's influence and of very few books in the language of Cervantes. In truth, I still feel more confident in Shakespeare's language than in my own. That is why the reader will find in my poetry grammatical errors . . . The majority of errors were corrected. The ones left behind were left on purpose because in my view, they cannot be removed. That is how "I felt" what I wanted to say—in those words. To say it another way would have been not to say it at all.

*(my translation)*

The small book consists of sixty-two poems, divided into nine sections: "La lira patriótica" [The Patriotic Lyre], "La música" [The Music], "La naturaleza" [Nature], "La comedia del amor" [The Comedy of Love], "La tragedia del amor" [The tragedy of Love], "In Memoriam," "La voz rebelde" [The Rebellious Voice], "Décimas" [Spanish stanzas in octosyllabic lines], and "L'envoi" [verses placed at the end of a ballad in praise of someone]. And although the poems in *Cantos de adolescencia* are generally weak in poetic style, they do represent Américo Paredes's creative talent and first attempts in Spanish verse.

The poem **"México, La Ilusión del Continente"** [**"Mexico, The Dream of the Continent"**] is a good example of Américo's continued search for a distinct Chicano mode of expression. Here, the poetic voice laments his in-between existence and mourns his southern country's condition; yet, in spite of these circumstances, the poet remains loyal to his native people and homeland, as the final stanzas of the poem suggest.

**"México, La Ilusión Del Continente"**

> *¡Audaz tribuno de las frases bellas!*
> *cuando la Peña o el dolor me hiera,*
> *¡enséñame a ser águila altanera*
> *para volar contigo a las estrellas!*

> *Y si mi espíritu se encuentra yerto,*
> *si un César me consigna en el Calvario,*
> *¡hazme un nopal heróico y solitario*
> *que crece entre las peñas del desierto!*

> *Mi alma que en tinieblas fué indecisa*
> *espera una palabra que la alienta;*
> *quiere ser . . . ¡siquiera una serpiente*
> *que hiere al presuntuoso que la pisa!*

> *Será mi luz, la estrella que me guía,*
> *el águila, el nopal y la serpiente:*
> *¡México! La ilusión del continente!*
> *¡México! La ilusión del alma mía!*

Audacious tribune of beautiful phrases!
when shame and pain may hurt me
teach me to be a proud eagle
to fly with you to the stars!

And if my spirit finds itself dead,
if a Cesar assigns me to Calvary,
make me a lone and heroic cactus
that grows among the destitution of the desert!

My spirit that in darkness was indecisive
awaits a word that will inspire it
it wants to be . . . at least a serpent
that wounds the conceited that steps on it!

It shall be my light, the star that guides me,
the eagle, the cactus, and the serpent:
Mexico! The dream of the continent!
Mexico! The dream of my soul!

*(my translation)*

In the poet's search for guidance and inspiration from the motherland, the eagle, cactus, and serpent (images in the center of the Mexican flag) represent icons of optimism, perseverance, and courage for the poet. Américo Paredes is proud of the fact that he is Mexican, although his country the United States frowns upon his native heritage.

In 1938, Paredes was hired as a translator with the *Brownsville Herald* where he also earned two dollars a week. The new job gave him more time to read and write, and he developed the important skill of typing. In time, Paredes became part of the regular staff at the *Brownsville Herald,* and it was around this time that he met Hart Stilwell. The two became friends and Stilwell used Américo as a resource person for his novel entitled *Border City* (1945). The book, not surprisingly, is about the racial conflict that exists along the Lower Rio Grande Border between Anglos and Mexicans. In the story, Jim Billings—the political boss of Border City— rapes a Mexican girl named Chelo Moreno, and a newspaperman named Dave Atwood takes up her case. Dave uses the newspaper to expose the discrimination against the Mexican people, and, while he makes enemies along the way, he begins to fall in love with Chelo. The climax of the narrative is Dave's ardent campaign to have Billings defeated at the polls. He not only loses the crusade to bring about change in south Texas, but he also loses Chelo Moreno, who decides to move to Mexico because of the racial differences between her and Dave. Undaunted, Dave Atwood is resolved to continue his fight for justice as the novel ends.

In his book, Hart Stilwell states at the beginning that the characters are fictitious and "any resemblance to any person, living or dead, is purely coincidental." But one may wonder if the character of Pepe, a young Mexican American with fair-skin, gray-green eyes, and who "could have passed for pure Spaniard," is none other than Américo Paredes himself. Certain passages in the story suggest this may be the case, and if so, the reader is able to learn about the opinions Paredes had on issues such as Christianity and the Mexican people's socio-economic situation while he was working for the *Brownsville Herald.* For example, an interesting feature of Pepe is his anti-clerical views, and he is oftentimes upset by the lack of political activism demonstrated by the Mexican people due to their religious devotion. When Chelo Moreno gives a crucifix as a gift to Dave Atwood for his assistance, the Anglo newspaperman is moved by her faith and gesture. Dave then shows the cross to his friend and coworker Pepe, who is not impressed. The editor of the Spanish edition of the newspaper bitterly replies:

> Don't let it move you too far . . . It has helped to move my own people into a condition of slavery and keep them there for three hundred years . . . For three hundred years and more—yes, for two thousand years—those who rule have used the Catholic Church to keep the poor people poor, to keep the ignorant people ignorant, to fill them with nameless fears and blind them to reason when they are little children so that they can be herded and driven and worked until they drop dead of exhaustion; still they are afraid to cry out. Show me no crosses, my friend. No crosses.
>
> (Stilwell 1945:52)

These views expressed by Pepe are in line with Américo Paredes's views with regard to the Catholic Church. Earlier in the novel, Pepe says:

> They let him die. They put him there in the hut and then they all went rushing around for a priest. Nobody bothered about a doctor. Nobody thought of taking him to a hospital so they might save his life. They were too busy saving his soul. They all went for a priest. That is the way of my people—but someday they will learn. They will learn, and then—and then officers won't stand and slap them in the face and ask them how they like it.
>
> (Stilwell 1945:56)

Like Américo, Pepe was very anticlerical and usually attended church only for baptisms, weddings, and funer-als. He believed the Catholic Church was too conservative and failed to address the injustices and racism Mexicans endured in south Texas.

At the time, Paredes proofread many articles by J. Frank Dobie, a very distinguished Texas folklorist who published regularly for the newspaper. Paredes was often angered by the content of Dobie's articles regarding the Mexican people and felt that his tone was condescending. Américo Paredes felt a great deal of frustration, since he could not challenge those of Dobie's printed opinions that enraged him. So Paredes's anger and frustration were channeled into his own creative writings. He mocked J. Frank Dobie in a novel (*George Washington Gómez*) he was writing at that time:

> K. Hank Harvey . . . was considered the foremost of authorities on the Mexicans of Texas. . . . Harvey was a self-made man. After he had come to Texas, with only a few years of schooling, he resolved to become an authority on Texas history and folklore. In a few years he had read every book there was on the early history of Texas, it was said, and his fellow Texans accepted him as the Historical Oracle of the State. There was a slight hitch, it is true. Most early Texas history books were written in Spanish, and K. Hank didn't know the language. However, nobody mentioned this, and it didn't detract from Harvey's glory.
>
> (Paredes 1990:270-71)

Although the young Américo at the time did not know Dobie in person, he satirized him in his book. According to Paredes, J. Frank Dobie originated the term *wetback,* a designation for those Mexicans who swam across the Rio Grande River, and this infuriated Paredes (Calderón and López Morín 2000:225).

After gaining an A.A. Degree from Brownsville College, Américo Paredes married Consuelo Chelo Silva, a well known vocalist in the Lower Rio Grande region and a native of Brownsville, Texas. Américo had fallen in love with her, and he composed and sang songs to her. Soon, Américo and Chelo blended their voices artistically as a professional duet, performing traditional music for weddings, parties, and at a local Brownsville radio station, before the onset of World War II. The couple married in the late 1930's and thereafter had their first child, Américo Paredes, Jr. But the marriage was not to last, and the couple soon divorced. Chelo Silva went on to become a well-known singer throughout Greater Mexico and South America.

Américo later obtained a government job with Pan American Airways in 1940, where he inspected fighter jet planes sent to Europe during World War II. This government job kept him from being drafted into the United States Army. He maintained his job with the *Brownsville Herald* on weekends, and he continued playing on the radio in the evenings. This was not a high point in his life, especially after his divorce from Chelo Silva. He wanted to get away from the area and felt guilty because his two brothers, Amador and Eleazar, and many of his close friends were overseas fighting in World War II. As a result, he decided to quit his job with Pan American and volunteered to join the army. In August of 1944, Américo Paredes finally enlisted in the United States Army.

He was stationed in Japan immediately after World War II ended. He chose to remain in Japan where he worked as a journalist for *Pacific Stars and Stripes,* the newspaper of the United States Army. He later was offered the post of political editor for *Pacific Stars and Stripes* and began to cover the war crime trials and other issues of political and legal interest.[5] This exposure to the court system and due process would later inform his famous 1958 work on the Gregorio Cortez *corrido.* As did Américo's training in journalism, his working with newspaper reports, official documents, letters, and interviews having to do with the criminal cases against Japanese officials would help him tremendously with his own scholarly research (Calderón 1994:43).

From the Far East, he also wrote articles in Spanish for Mexico City's *Universal.* These weekly articles consisted of sketches about life in China, Korea, and Japan. Américo Paredes began to study the clash of cultures in other parts of the world. As his article "Desde Tokio" suggests, Paredes was sensitive to issues of American expansionism in other parts of the world:

> *Todo Tokio tiene cierto aire norteamericano. Las calles lucen letreros en inglés y además tienen nombres ahora, o más bien números e iniciales al estilo poco imaginativo de los militares. En las calles se ven autos acabados de recibir de Estados Unidos por los trabajadores que se encuentran en Tokio. En los distritos residenciales hay letreros frente a las residencias, los cuales nos dicen que aquí vive el coronel fulano y acá el general zutano del ejército yanqui. En el centro de la ciudad hay una enorme tienda para el personal de la ocupación, donde se encuentra cualquier cosa, desde pañuelos y jugo de tomate hasta una barbería y un restaurante. Hay más teatros y hay que pagar para entrar, cosa que no era hace seis meses—hay más lugares donde comer. Y hay más distancia entre la población japonesa y la nueva población de Tokio que antiguamente entre los japoneses y los primeros soldados norteamericanos.*

(Paredes 1947:1)

All of Tokyo has a certain North American air. The streets shine billboards in English and have names now, or better yet, numbers and initials with little imaginative style from the military. In the streets one can see automobiles just received from the United States for workers who find themselves in Tokyo. In residential districts there are billboards in front of the residences, the ones that tell us that colonel so-and-so lives here and general so-and-so over here from the Yankee military. In the center of town there is a huge store for the occupation personnel where everything is found from handkerchiefs and tomato juice to a barbershop and restaurant. There are more theaters, and one has to pay to enter, something that was not done six months ago—there are more places to eat. And there is more of a distance between the Japanese population and the new Tokyo population than there was in earlier times between the Japanese and the first North American soldiers.

*(my translation)*

In a socio-cultural setting somewhat like that of the Lower Rio Grande region, Américo was very much interested in the acculturation process taking place in post-war Japanese society, where men, women, and children were soon beginning to learn English and the American way of life. In many ways, Américo Paredes was an expert on the effects of the expansion of US influence, having experienced it first-hand along the Lower Rio Grande Border. There is a feeling of empathy conveyed by the Mexico-Tejano reporter toward the defeated Japanese people.

In 1946 *Pacific Stars and Stripes* reduced its personnel, and Américo Paredes was discharged from active duty. Paredes became a public relations officer for the American Red Cross in China. In his reminiscences about this position, Paredes remembered witnessing much destruction, poverty, and emotional suffering caused by the war, especially in Korea. In 1948, when the communists began to make advances in China, the Red Cross recalled its personnel, and Paredes was again without employment. He returned to Japan and became editor for a small army weekly journal intended for the American troops stationed in Japan.

While in Japan Américo met and married his second wife, Amelia Shidzu Nagamine, in May 28, 1948. She had been educated in Mexico City and returned to Japan to work for the Red Cross. Her contributions to Américo Paredes's success as a journalist, musician, scholar, teacher, and political activist have not been acknowledged sufficiently. She gave selflessly of herself as a wife and mother and, for a time, put aside her own educational pursuits to support her husband's career and dreams.

Américo enrolled in English and American literature through the correspondence program at the University of Texas at Austin. He had access to the library of the United States Armed Forces College, known among the troops as Tokyo College. Paredes borrowed many books from Tokyo College. He discovered several major writers, including William Faulkner. In July of 1950, Américo and Amelia returned to the United States to pursue his literary studies.

Amelia was the daughter of a Japanese father and a Uruguayan mother. Because of her Japanese background, she was not allowed to enter the United States. She obtained a visitor's visa for 6 months, but it was for a maximum stay of one year only. The couple went to live in Matamoros, Tamaulipas, Mexico, with one of Américo's brothers for two months, and later they moved to Austin, Texas in September of 1950.

### A MAVERICK AT THE UNIVERSITY OF TEXAS AT AUSTIN

At the age of 35, Américo planned to complete his Bachelor's Degree in a year at the University of Texas at Austin and then move to northern Mexico, where he had relatives and some connections, and where Paredes did not expect to find prejudice against Asians, such as his wife. He carried a full load of courses which emphasized writing and literary criticism. Amelia helped him tremendously by assuming the majority of the household responsibilities, and thus allowing her husband to devote himself to his studies. Américo earned his B.A. *summa cum laude* in English and Philosophy in 1951. Fortunately, during the year, the immigration law was amended, and Amelia was able to receive permanent residence status. The English faculty encouraged Américo to stay and work on a graduate degree in English and, so, the couple decided to stay in Austin.

Américo Paredes participated in several literary competitions as a way to make extra income for the family, which now included their first child, Alan, born in July in 1951. He received the first place prize in the *Dallas Times Herald* short-story writing contest, with a collection of some his short stories entitled *Border Country* (1952). The prize consisted of five hundred dollars' worth of books. Paredes later (1955) won another first place prize in the D. A. Frank novel writing contest with his short novel *The Shadow* (published in 1998). This time, however, the award was for five hundred dollars in cash, and, according to Américo Paredes "[i]t was a welcome boost to the family bank account and to [his] ego as well" (1998: *Preface).*

In what was to prove to be a crucial shift in his intellectual focus, Américo modified his course of study in graduate school to emphasize folklore. Once, when he was comparing two versions of the traditional Scottish ballad "Sir Patrick Spens" in one of his classes, Paredes remembered his childhood days when the old men gathered in the evenings along the border. He recalled the importance of context in the performance and interpretation of the songs and legends they exchanged. The mood of the group played a fundamental role in the way the ballads and stories were performed. He brought a paper on the *corrido* to his professor of literary criticism, who then referred him to another profes-

sor, Robert Stephenson. A professor in English and Spanish, Stephenson also taught courses in folklore, and Paredes talked to him about the *corrido* of Gregorio Cortez. The two conversed for a time, and Américo decided to switch to the study of folklore for his Master of Arts and Ph. D. Since the subject in which he wished to specialize was balladry, the English Department required him to take courses in medieval balladry and courses on Shakespeare, Chaucer and the history of the English language. Paredes also had to take a number of courses in the Spanish Department, which covered the medieval epic *El Cid,* the history of the Spanish language and *El Siglo de Oro.* In the study of English and Scottish ballads, he studied Francis James Child, Helen Child Sargent, and George Lyman Kittredge and in Spanish, Ramón Menéndez Pidal, Ramón Meléndez Pelayo, and Vicente Mendoza. The education he received was liberal, not concentrated on one particular subject. Many kinds of subjects were reflected in Paredes's library, which included fiction, history, anthropology, and folklore. This learning complemented his oral traditional development with the border folk.

In folklore Américo Paredes received the assistance of Stith Thompson, one of the most highly regarded folklorists in the United States and Europe. Thompson had returned to his alma mater as a visiting professor, and Paredes added him to his committee. Thompson, impressed by Paredes's dissertation, recommended it for publication to the University of Texas Press. At the time, Américo Paredes had left the University of Texas at Austin to teach courses at Texas Western University (now the University of Texas, El Paso). Américo received a call from the director of the Press, informing him that they had received a copy of his manuscript. The director planned to publish it, but for the fear of being sued, the Press asked Paredes to moderate his comments about Dr. Walter Prescott Webb and the Texas Rangers (Calderón and López Morín 2000:220). He refused and asked the director to return the manuscript. Fearing that Paredes might publish it somewhere else, the University of Texas Press conceded and published it in 1958. Today, the book is now in its twelfth printing.

Upon the book's publication, the Press chose to forego its customary reception in honor of the author because the relationship between Paredes and the Press had deteriorated, on account of his refusal to moderate his comments about the Texas Rangers and Walter Prescott Webb. Shortly afterward, according to Paredes, a retired Texas Ranger visited the director of the Press, wanting to learn more about the identity and whereabouts of the author, so that he could pistol-whip him for his comments about the Texas Rangers (Calderón and López Morín 2000:226). Fortunately, this information was kept confidential.

Américo Paredes continued his work in the field of folklore, even though ***"With His Pistol in his Hand"*** received little recognition after its initial publication. He worked as an archivist for the Folklore Archive at the University of Texas at Austin, a post he began in 1957 and held for ten years. From 1960 to 1965, Paredes assumed the position of Bibliographer for a major American folklore journal, *The Southern Folklore Quarterly,* a post previously held for approximately twenty-four years by the renowned folklorist Ralph Steele Boggs. A few years later, he became editor for the University of Texas Latin American Folklore Series, and of another major folklore journal, *Journal of American Folklore,* a post he held from 1968 to 1973. In addition, Américo Paredes was hired in 1966 to teach courses in the Anthropology Department at Austin, and he later organized the Mexican-American Studies program, becoming Director of the Center for Mexican-American Studies (1970-1972). He was also Acting Director of the Center for Intercultural Studies of Folklore and Ethnomusicology from 1974 to 1975. Ironically, the University of Texas at Austin, some said, did not appreciate his many contributions. For approximately 25 years, Américo Paredes oftentimes was at political odds with the administration, taught in basements, and was one of the lowest paid full professors at the University of Texas at Austin for almost his entire career (Bauman and Peña 2000:196).

In his later years, Américo Paredes would edit, co-edit, translate, and publish more than 90 reviews and articles and 10 books on Hispanic and Mexican folklore and culture. Some of his most significant publications in Spanish and English include "Some Aspects of Folk Poetry" (1964), "El folklore de los grupos de origen mexicano en los Estados Unidos" (1966), "Divergencias en el concepto del folklore y el contexto cultural" (1967), "Folk Medicine and the Intercultural Jest" (1968), *Folktales of Mexico* (1970), *Toward New Perspectives in Folklore* (1972), A Texas Mexican *Cancionero: Folksongs of the Lower Border* (1976), "On Ethnographic Work among Minority Groups: A Folklorist's Perspective" (1977), and *Folklore and Culture on the Texas-Mexican Border* (1993). In addition to his scholarly works, his poetry, short stories, and novels have also been recently published. These fictional works include **Between Two Worlds** (1991), *The Hammon and the Beans and other stories* (1994), *George Washington Gomez: A Mexicotexan Novel* (1990), and *The Shadow* (1998).

In addition to his writings, in 1989 Américo Paredes received the Charles Frankel Award from the National Endowment for the Humanities for his contribution to Mexican American studies. In 1990, Mexico honored him with the Order of the Aztec Eagle for preserving Mexican culture—the highest honor given to a foreigner by the Mexican Government. In 1997, the American Folklore Society recognized him as the most significant scholar in Latino, Latin American, and Caribbean folklore and "the most important and influential American folklorist in the field of Mexican American and borderlands folklore" (Peña and Bauman 2000:197).

Américo Paredes died *el cinco de mayo* in 1999, a day of remembrance in Mexico's struggle to maintain its sovereignty against a foreign invasion, and a time of cultural celebration for many Mexican Americans as well. Given the historical importance of the turbulent era in which he was born and the cultural significance of the day of his death, one can see a close link between Paredes's life and career and the history of Mexico and Mexican Americans. Between these years, Américo Paredes strove to understand, preserve, and defend Mexican culture in the United States, and he maintained his "unflinching stand against racial intolerance" (Peña and Bauman 2000:196). But the keeper of the flame was finally called home, leaving behind a legacy of the highest standards for others to follow.

*Notes*

1. See Calderón and López-Morín 2000 for the published version of the July 13, 1996 interview with Américo Paredes.

2. See Sandos 1992 for a discussion of the social and political unrest along the Lower Rio Grande Border during the early twentieth century.

3. Jansen (1965 [1959]) and others have noted that our consciousness of ourselves as a particular group is related to our awareness of other groups besides our own.

4. Limón (1992:45) considers "Guitarreros" to be Américo Paredes's best poem.

5. In the 1984 interview mentioned above, Américo recalled how he obtained the post. The military had discovered that the political editor of the army newspaper at the time was a member of the communist party and had fought for the Republicans in Spain. The army released him and, given Paredes's background in journalism, the administration hired him on the spot.

*Works Cited*

Bauman, Richard and Manuel Peña, 2000. Américo Paredes (1915-1999). *Journal of American Folklore* 113:195-98.

Calderón, Héctor, 1994. Literatura fronteriza tejana: El compromiso con la historia en Américo Paredes, Rolando Hinojosa y Gloria Anzaldúa. *Mester: Literary Journal of the Graduate Students of the Department of Spanish and Portuguese, University of California, Los Angeles* 22-23, 2:1:41-61.

———. 1995. Reinventing the Border. In *American Mosaic: Multicultural Readings in Context,* ed. Barbara Roche Rico and Sandra Mano. 2d ed. Boston: Houghton Mifflin Company. Pp. 512-21.

————and José R. López Morín. 2000. Interview with Américo Paredes. In *Nepantla: Views from South* 1:197-228.

García, Kimberly, Author battles racist views, *Brownsville Herald,* Sunday, 4 August 1991.

Jansen, William Hugh. 1965 [1959]. The Esoteric-Exoteric Factor in Folklore. In *The Study of Folklore,* ed. Alan Dundes. Englewood Cliffs, N.J.: Prentice-Hall. Pp. 43-51.

Limón, José E. 1992. *Mexican Ballads, Chicano Poems: History and Influence in Mexican-American Social Poetry.* Berkeley: University of California Press.

Paredes Manzano, Américo. 1937. *Cantos de adolescencia.* San Antonio: Librería Española.

Paredes, Américo, Desde Tokio, *El universal: el gran diario de México.* Martes 17 de junio 1947.

————. 1958. *With His Pistol in His Hand: A Border Ballad and Its Hero.* Austin: University of Texas Press.

————. 1984. Interview. Juan Gómez-Quiñones, José Limón, Teresa McKenna and Victor Nelson. Austin, Texas.

————. 1987 [1986]. The Undying Love of 'El Indio' (sic) Córdova: *Décimas* and Oral History in a Border Family. Ernesto Galarza Commemorative Lecture. Stanford: Stanford Center for Chicano Research, Stanford University.

————. 1990. *George Washington Gómez: A Mexicotexan novel.* Houston: Arte Público Press.

————. 1991. *Between Two Worlds.* Houston: Arte Público Press.

————. 1994. *The Hammon and the Beans and other stories.* Houston: Arte Público Press.

Pérez-Torres, Rafael. 1995. *Chicano Poetry: Against Myths, Against Margins.* New York: Cambridge University Press.

Porterfield, Billy, Twilight of a great man: Illness makes work harder for Hispanic UT scholar, 74, *Austin American-Statesman,* Friday, 28 July 1989.

Sandos, James A. 1992. *Rebellion in the Borderlands: Anarchism and the Plan of San Diego, 1904-1923.* Norman and London: University of Oklahoma Press.

Shakespeare, William. 1979. The Merchant of Venice. *The Globe Illustrated Shakespeare: The Complete Works Annotated.* Edited by Howard Staunton. New York: Gramercy Books. Pp. 391-442.

Simmons, Merle. 1957. *The Mexican* Corrido *as a Source for Interpretive Study of Mexico (1870-1950).* Bloomington: Indiana University Press.

**Guillermo E. Hernández (essay date winter/spring 2005)**

SOURCE: Hernández, Guillermo E. "On the Paredes-Simmons Exchange and the Origins of the *Corrido.*" *Western Folklore* 64, nos. 1/2 (winter/spring 2005): 65-82.

[*In the following essay, Hernández discusses Paredes's contribution to the collection, codification, and translation of the* corrido, *or Mexican ballad, a verse narrative genre of the border region.*]

Forty years ago, Américo Paredes and Merle E. Simmons engaged in an almost forgotten exchange on the origins and development of the *corrido* (1963). Paredes objected to Simmons' suggestion that the *corrido* had emerged directly from the Spanish ballad or *romance.* Simmons based this claim on the existence of ballads or folksongs displaying stylistic features closely resembling the *corrido,* disseminated throughout Mexico and the United States and antedating the rise of the genre by several hundred years. On the basis of this evidence, Simmons suggested that an unbroken line of transmission connected the Spanish *romance* to the contemporary *corrido.* Paredes dismissed the examples Simmons adduced in support of his thesis as insufficient and isolated evidence. In contrast to a "moribund *romance* tradition," Paredes forcefully argued, the *corrido* represented a living tradition:

> A whole ballad corpus, which by its very weight impresses itself on the consciousness of the people who cultivate it, owing its pervasiveness to the fact that it shapes the way of life or reflects the character of that people.
>
> (1963:231)

This exchange with Simmons provided Paredes with an opportunity to outline his views regarding the origins and development of the *corrido.* Lamenting the lack of evidence to determine whether the survivals of the *romance,* found throughout Latin America, had *crystallized* in a *corrido* tradition, he posited a number of problems, suggesting a solution to this historical quandary. First, he pointed out, the corpus of ballads collected by students in Mexico, from oral and printed sources, failed to include examples recognizable as *corridos* prior to the appearance of the genre in the middle of the nineteenth century in his native Lower Rio Grande Border. Second, his fieldwork in the area—interviewing and collecting *corridos* among family members and community folk—convinced him that some of the early examples he found had served as models in the local development of the genre.[1] Third, the border *corrido,* he argued, served as a cultural expression reflecting the conflicts between Mexicans and Anglo-Americans during the second half of the nineteenth century. To support these views, Paredes drew attention to a number of ballad motifs; he believed were created in the Lower Rio Grande Border, which would have been later incorporated into the tradition of Greater Mexico. Finally, he suggested that the border *corrido* was probably the earliest variety of its kind and, in all likelihood, the precursor of the genre.

The Paredes-Simmons exchange deserves further discussion. The evidence at hand suggests that while both scholars' arguments were convincing, their observations were, as Paredes perceptively pointed out, neither in contradiction nor the final word on the subject. In the pages that follow, I review some new and old evidence that further delves into the complex discussion on the origins and evolution of the *corrido*. Since the Paredes-Simmons exchange took place, a number of regional and thematic collections of *corridos* have been published. Several of these are particularly important to our purposes, given that they were unavailable in 1963, when Paredes and Simmons reflected on the nature and origins of the *corrido*. Particular attention must be paid to the fieldwork conducted by Cuauhtémoc Esparza Sánchez in the early nineteen fifties in the state of Zacatecas, Mexico, published until 1976 as *El corrido zacatecano*. Another significant corpus is the Strachwitz-Frontera collection of commercial phonograph discs, undoubtedly the largest collection of Mexican and Mexican-American popular music in existence, containing a massive number of commercial recordings.[2] Furthermore, in 1960, Olga Fernandez Latour published *Cantares históricos de la tradición argentina* documenting the existence of *corridos* in Argentina prior to the appearance of the genre in Mexico and the United States. This important study by Fernandez Latour was reviewed by Paredes (1962), who found it of great interest to students of the *corrido*.

Esparza Sánchez's meticulous historic field research collection from the state of Zacatecas, Mexico, includes examples from the early nineteenth century, the revolutionary period and the first quarter of the twentieth century.[3] Thus, it is a corpus meeting the *corrido* requirement posed by Paredes concerning a living tradition. Likewise, the Strachwitz Frontera collection includes many early sound performances of *corridos* helpful in the recreation of the path followed by the genre in Mexico and in the United States. One of the titles in the collection is none other than the first known recording of the *corrido* of Gregorio Cortez from 1928, a time when Paredes was a young boy hearing the stories of the Cortez saga told and sung by his elders. Many of the musicians who performed on these phonograph discs were folk performers whose repertoires extended back into the nineteenth century.

The historical ballads in the Argentinean anthology of Fernández Latour include many *décimas* or poetic compositions of ten lines, narrative poems that may not be considered *corridos* due to their contrasting elaborate rhyme schemes. Yet, her collection also contains many pieces that maintain the form and conventions Paredes would demand from a traditional *corrido*. Her work thus supports the notion that a popular epic song tradition existed in the southern cone region, particularly in Argentina and Chile. Many of these songs are stanzaic with octosyllabic lines rhyming *abcb,* as in the *corrido,* and reflect epic and tragic narrative events. Portraying a figure known as *gaucho* or *huacho* (cowboy), theses compositions are known with names such as *corridos, cielitos,* and *videlas*.[4] As in the case of the ballads from the state of Zacatecas, these popular heroic poems adhere to Paredes's requirements of constituting a living tradition. Furthermore, a few of these Argentinean ballads can be documented as early as the eighteenth century.

### Ballad Motifs and Formulaic Language

John McDowell notes the problem involved in studying the formulaic nature of *corridos,* due to the limitations of the corpus at hand, is further compounded by the practice of indiscriminately publishing, next to each other, texts of oral and printed origin without proper attribution. Indeed, in the evolution of the genre oftentimes the researcher finds oral, printed, and discographic versions of texts fused in a complex chain of influences.[5] Nevertheless, McDowell has been able to establish the formulaic character of the *corrido,* suggesting that its corpus allows us to "trace the continuity and innovation of theme and formula along the line of descent from romance to *corrido* and other contemporary forms" (1972:220).

A review of formulaic expressions in *romances* and *corridos* from earlier periods and various regions can be a most enlightening procedure in tracing the formative stages and development of the *corrido* tradition. The evidence, on one hand, supports the soundness of Simmons' proposal that there must be a link between the romance and the *corrido* while, on the other hand, sustains Paredes's assertion of the genre as an expression of local norms and experiences that, in turn, impact the audience as well as the living tradition. For purposes of expediency and to avoid overwhelming the reader, I shall limit my presentation of this formulaic evidence to a few examples, including more instances in appendices.[6]

### The I Am (Yo soy) Formula and the Self-Asserting Protagonist

Epic ballads invariably portray a protagonist representing ideal qualities. In demonstrating strength of character, therefore, self-assertion in the midst of tension portrays a model of behavior most admired by the audience. In claiming: *I am (Yo soy)* characters affirm an undisputed place within their social contexts. The formula *I am* appears in the northern ballad of the legendary hero of the 1880s, Heraclio Bernal, whose exploits precede the 1901 events surrounding the border *corrido* of Gregorio Cortez. Paredes has suggested that this formula in Bernal's ballad might have been influential to the Mexican-Texas border *corrido,* achieving its definite form in the *corrido* of Gregorio Cortez (1958:236). The formula, however, is traditional in the romance and appears in epic, lyric, as well as religious Spanish ballads (Appendix A).

> *Yo soy el conde Dirlos*
>
> (Wolf 1856: II, 129-170)

> I am Count Dirlos
> *Yo soy don Rufo*
>
> (Sarazar 1999: 365-66)

> I am don Rufo
> *Yo soy Gaiferos, señora*
>
> (Wolf 1856:II, 226-28)

> I am Gaiferos, Lady

### "With His Pistol in the Hand" ("Con la pistola en la mano") as a Formula Portraying the Stance of the Heroic Protagonist

Most versions of Cortez's *corrido* portray him defiantly confronting opponents with his pistol in the hand (*con su pistola en la mano*). For Paredes, such defiance is a most distinctive portrait of the border hero, and the figure of Cortez with the pistol in the hand serves as a model to what will be the evolution of border heroic figures. This image, however, is present throughout the *romancero* as a formula that may involve the brandishing of either a sword or a lance.[7] It would only be natural that in modern times the medieval weapons would be replaced by a pistol, as in the romance "La ronda malograda," collected in the province of León, Spain, in 1916. Here a prisoner recounts the events that led him to his present state: *Ech(ar)on mano a sus pistolas* (they took out their pistols [with their hands]). The formula *in the hand* is used in other contexts to hold a variety of objects. In other citations the items included are, respectively; golden arrows, falcons, prey, a staff, knife, arch, candle, dice, cane, letters, or book (Appendix B).

> *Tomó* la espada *en la mano*
>
> (Wolf 1856: II, 96-97)

> [*C*]*on* la espada *en la mano*
>
> (ibid.: 3-7)

> took the sword in hand
> with the sword in hand

While the *in the hand* formulas describe what is being held, there may also be a reference to the holder of the object, in his (her) hand. (*en la su mano*). This pronoun usage may be the direct antecedent to the *pistol in his hand*. The formula may be altered to refer to the first person.

> *gruesa lanza en la su mano*
>
> (Wolf 1856:I, 35-36)

> *y en la su mano derecha*
>
> (Wolf 1856:II, 72-74)

> thick lance in his hand
> in his right hand

> *gruesa lanza con dos hierros en la su mano llevaba*
>
> (Wolf 1856:I, 308-313)

> thick lance . . . in his hand

> *con cartas en la su mano*
>
> (Wolf 1856:I, 241-244)

> *con un libro en la su mano*
>
> (ibid.: 161-174)

> *yo traigo lanza en mi mano*
>
> (ibid.: 51-54)

> with letters in his hand
> with a book in his hand
> I have a lance in my hand

This formula *the sword in hand* portraying the stance of the epic hero passed to the Argentinean tradition, as shown in the following examples:

> *Si Quiroga murió fusilado*
> *no murió por infame y traidor*
>
> *murió* con la espada en la mano
> *defendiendo la federación.*
>
> (Fernández 1960:67)

> If Quiroga died by execution,
> he did not die because of wrong-
>       doing and treason,
> he died with the sword in the hand,
> defending the federal government.

*Vamos allá compañeros,*
*Tomen la espada en la mano,*
*Entren al campo'e batalla*
*Denle muerte al tirano.*

(Fernández 1960:267)

Let's go there, partners,
take the sword in the hand,
go into the battlefield,
kill the tyrant.

### THE HONEY-COLORED OR SORREL HORSE (CABALLO MELADO) AS A FORMULA FOR THE MOUNT OF THE HEROIC PROTAGONIST

Paredes has also pointed out that a horse rider on a honey-colored (*melado*) or sorrel (*alzán*) horse is the distinctive mount of the heroic protagonist from the border. This formula also appears in Spanish *romances* since early times. The protagonist may simply *ride on his horse* or else *on a mare* (*yegua*), There may also be an indication, as in the *corrido,* to a specific color of the horse: sorrel (*alazán or alazano*), *avero* (white paint), *morcillo* (reddish black). The adjective may describe the kind of horse: *rocino* (work horse), *ligero* or *corredor* (fast) or by its name, Babieca, or Boca-negra (Appendix C).[8]

*Ya cabalga Melisenda* en un caballo alazán.

(Wolf 1856:II, 229-48)

Melisenda rides on a sorrel horse

*Ya es salido del palacio* en un caballo alazán

(ibid. 229-48)

He has left the palace on a sorrel horse

*armado de todas armas*, en un caballo alazano

(Wolf 1856:I, 263-65)

fully armed on a sorrel horse

The presence of the hero on his horse may be linked to other formulas, such as the armor of the rider:

*el marqués se fue armar; cabalgara* en su caballo,

(Wolf 1856: II, 171-95)

The Marquis armed himself, and rode on his horse

Ya es armado Montesinos, *ya cabalga* en su caballo.

(ibid. 279-89)

Montesinos has been armed and rides *on his horse*

As shown below, several formulas may be grouped together. In addition to riding on a horse, the protagonist is holding a *lanza, zagaya* (lance), or a *gavilán* (sparrow hawk). A variant shows him with *his face bathed in water* in a metaphoric reference to his tears:

*encima una yegua . . . y en su mano una zagaya*

(Wolf 1856: I, 175-78)

on a mare . . . and on his hand a [small] lance

*caballero en un caballo, y en su mano un gavilan*

(ibid. 100-102)

a knight on a horse, and in his hand a hawk

*Torna a subir en la yegua, su cara en agua bañada*

(Wolf 1856:II, 311-312)

He then climbs atop the mare, his faced bathed with water

### THE ON THE VERGE OF TEARS (COMO QUERIENDO LLORAR) FORMULA IN THE PORTRAYAL OF THE TRAITOR OR THE COWARDLY ENEMY

The figure of someone on the verge of tears (*como queriendo llorar*) is formulaic in the *corrido,* portraying the traitor, the cowardly enemy or the clown. (Paredes 1958:228). According to Paredes, this convention first appears in *Gregorio Cortez* and is later borrowed by other twentieth-century *corridos*. Yet, as with other motifs discussed before, the image of a man or a woman crying or on the verge of crying appears throughout Spanish-language balladry. Such portrayals customarily highlight extreme pain, affliction, suffering, sadness or defeat. Paredes rightly observes that adding the phrase *como queriendo*, literally meaning *on the verge*, or *as if he was about to*, conveys a sense of ridicule. In the *romance* the presence of tears generally demonstrates the reaction of a character who confronts painful events. In the two stanzas below, King Rodrigo portrays this pain as he reportedly laments his loss of Spain as a result of his wrongfully abducting the daughter of Count Julian. The third passage provides a glimpse of the fall of the Moorish kingdom of Granada in the fifteenth century. Other examples illustrate various protagonists whose crying represents intense suffering (Appendix D).

*gran mancilla en sí tenía*
*llorando de los sus ojos*
*de esta manera decía*
*Ayer era rey de España,*
*hoy no lo soy de una villa.*

(Wolf 1856: I, 15-17)

He place great blame on himself:
crying from his eyes,
he would thus say:
Yesterday I was king of Spain,
today I don't even rule a village.

*comenzó a decir llorando:*
*Ya, señora,*
*no sois reina,*
*ya no tenéis ningún mando.*

(ibid.: 19-21)

He began to say, crying:
no longer my lady,
are you a Queen,
you no longer have a reign.

Crying may also be a demonstration of the rage felt by
a character whose feelings of desolation are shared by
the audience. In the stanza below, the Portuguese king
exemplifies the wrath he feels leading him to avenge
the death of his beloved Isabel de Liar.

*Cuando aquesto supo el rey,*
*no hace sino llorar;*
*juraba por su corona*
*que la había de vengar.*

(ibid.: 350-351)

When the king learned of this
he would not stop crying,
he swore by his crown
that he would avenge it.

Because adventuring youths often encounter dangers,
the allusion to young men in perilous conditions is a
topic that causes anguish or great sorrow to the family
at home. The romance of "Mambru," disseminated
throughout the Spanish-speaking world, is widely sung
to this day. The sad news Mambru brings elicits crying:

*Mambrú se fue a la guerra,*
*qué noticias traerá.*
*Las noticias que trae*
*son de hacer llorar.*

(Calvo and Catalán 1993:262)

Mambru (Marlborough) went to war
What news will he bring?
The news he brought
make one cry.

Crying is also a sign of weakness, cowardice or fear. It
is unbecoming of a man to cry whenever such demon-
stration blemishes his reputation or behavior. In the
case of Alfonso XII, his ballad has become well-known
and, like "Mambru," has evolved into a children's song.
Originally it recounted the death of the widely-admired
queen Mercedes. The following stanza is critical of Al-

fonso, warning him that, given the superior qualities of
his deceased wife, he is unlikely to find another spouse
that will equal the departed Mercedes. In a straightfor-
ward and most economic expression, the *vox populi*
praises the dead queen, while reminding the king of his
comparatively inferior traits.

*Llora, llora, Alfonso XII,*
*y no dejes de llorar,*
*que reina como Mercedes*
*no volvieras a casar.*

(ibid. 107)

Cry, cry, Alfonso XII
and don't stop crying
because a Queen like Mercedes
you won't marry again.

The image of a man crying can also be employed to
ridicule his attitude. In the following stanza from "Di-
funta pleiteada," the weeping man declares his failed
aspiration for the love of a woman.

*¡oh!, con los ojos lloraba,*
*¡oh!, con la boca decía:*
*"No se dio para mí*
*rosa tan bien florecida."*

(ibid. 361-62)

Alas!, his eyes cried
Alas!, his mouth said:
"Such a blossoming rose
was not meant for me."

The image of tears may also convey an ironic tone, as
exemplified by a crying young man in "Gaiferos libera
a Melisenda," who, facing a most difficult time, is
subjected to teasing. He cries when his uncle at first
refuses to lend him the arms required to avenge his
father. But when the uncle accedes to his request, there
is a nuanced tone with lighthearted humor.

*Llorando como un niño*
*volvió los ojos hacia atrás.*
*"Ven acá, sobrino mío,*
*yo te los voy a emprestar."*

(Catalán et al. 1991:I, 81-82)

Crying like a child
he turned his eyes to the rear
"Come here, nephew of mine,
I will lend the [weapons] to you."

The crying formula has been borrowed by the Argen-
tinean ballad tradition. In the following stanzas from
"Difunta pleiteada" this motif is employed to mock
enemies who lack dignity and resolve.

*Lloró don Valentín Castro*
*viendo en peligro su vida*
*ayudaba al sentimiento*
*ese don Doroteo Díaz.*

(Fernández 1960:105)

Valentín Castro cried
seeing his life in danger,
his feelings were assisted
by that man Doroteo Díaz.

The formula appears as early as the second half of the nineteenth century in a number of Mexican ballads from the state of Zacatecas. Here the example is closer to "Gregorio Cortez":

*Entonces corrió el minero*
*como queriendo llorar,*
*a decirle a don Jesús*
*lo que acabó de escuchar.*

(Esparza 1976:44-45)

Then the miner ran,
on the verge of crying,
to mention to Don Jesús
What he had just heard.

*Andaban los pobres gringos*
*como queriendo llorar:*
*a veinte pesos el muerto,*
*el que se anime a bajar.*

(ibid. 48)

The poor gringos found themselves
on the verge of crying
Twenty pesos for each dead body
To anyone who risks going down.

### CONCLUSIONS

As its is evident in the present discussion, the exchange between Merle E. Simmons and Américo Paredes is of fundamental importance in the definition of the *corrido,* its evolution, and any future research on the genre. In order to trace the history of the *corrido,* however, a working definition of the genre is necessary. Such objective will allow: (a) to identify its antecedents, (b) to locate early and significant examples, and (c) to distinguish major traits throughout its distinct periods.

Any discussion on the evolution of the *corrido,* however, must take into account the oral, printed and electronic, visual, and digital dissemination of the genre. Although these methods of transmission often overlap, it is necessary to recognize their distinct venues, contexts, and conventions. The oral *corrido* emerges within an artistic verbal network of close interaction between composer, performer, and audience. Oral

performances are contextually rich and provide variable versions, as the song is transmitted along diverse listeners. Inevitably, therefore, oral compositions produce multiple interpretations of a *corrido* and are subjected to frequent fusion or blending among similar types of lyrics and melodies. Such is not the case with printed versions, in broadsheets or in songbooks, which preserve a single version of the lyrics and sometimes the musical notation, and are lacking the benefit of the aural and visual live interpretations of a performer. These limitations are circumvented in electronic, visual and digital renditions of a *corrido,* which maintain the lyrical and musical interpretation but lack the spontaneity and informality of the oral creation. A closer experience is the concert, impromptu or scheduled performance offered by professional musicians, whose livelihood depends on pleasing a discriminating audience. These diverse contextual conditions have had a profound impact on the creation, transmission, preservation, appreciation, and evolution of the *corrido.*

As Paredes recognized in his article, he and Simmons shared more areas of agreement than dissent. Yet, as the above examples suggest, there is strong evidence supporting Simmons' argument for a continuous tradition linking the Spanish ballad with the *corrido.* Indeed, the presence of similar formulaic expressions throughout a geographic and chronological ballad continuum—motifs Paredes had identified as distinctive of the border *corrido*—leaves no doubt that the Spanish-language ballad has close bonds with the romance tradition. Yet, this assertion does not deny the inherent truth in Paredes's claim that the study of the *corrido* involves issues of a living tradition, while the romance has been largely preserved as an artistic expression of earlier times. That is, the role of local folk has been a major factor in the creation, dissemination and survival of the genre.

In addition to formulating a central problem in the study of the *corrido,* Paredes and Simmons helped outline its prominent textual and contextual boundaries. It is significant to recall that the first substantive effort in this regard was Vicente T. Mendoza's *Romance y Corrido,* a musical-based comparative approach intended to define the *corrido* in terms of a new world version of the Spanish romance. The Paredes and Simmons exchange was a next step in the tradition of conducting serious research and analysis of the genre. Beginning in the late 1980s, several conferences brought together an international group of scholars, creators and performers of the *corrido* who have shared their interpretations, knowledge and research.[9] This new generation continues the important contributions of Américo Paredes, Merle E. Simmons and Vicente T. Mendoza, among others.

In his 1963 article, Merle E. Simmons suggested that further research on the *corrido* was necessary to attain a clear outline of the chronology of the genre:

[I]f we can find from other areas texts of early ballads which show substantial affinities to late nineteen-century *corridos* in truly basic fundamentals such as subject matter, literary form and style, we are justified in considering these to be links in a *continuing and unbroken* ballad tradition that was common to much if not all of the New World

(Simmons 1963:2).

Paredes agreed with Simmons that such a search was necessary and his words fittingly conclude this essay written in Paredes's honor:

Folkloric theories—even more than other theories—are always based on incomplete data; so that the folklorist must always keep on searching. I am, consequently, in complete agreement with Simmons as to the necessity of further investigation to discover *corrido*-like texts in Mexico and elsewhere

(Paredes 1962:356).

### APPENDIX A

The *I am* (*Yo soy*) formula and the self-asserting protagonist

*Yo soy aquel Roldán*

(Wolf 1856: II, 401-408)

I am that Roldán

*Yo soy el moro Bramante*

(Wolf 1856: II, 401-408)

I am the Moor Bramante

*que yo soy el moro Muza*

(ibid.: 306-308)

I am the Moor Muza

*Yo soy el moro Mazote*

(Wolf 1856: II, 42-43)

I am the Moor Mazote

*Yo soy el buen Jesús, mira*

(Salazar and Salazar 1999:267)

I am Jesús, the good one, look

*Yo soy la Virgen del Carmen*

(ibid.: 347-349)

I am the Virgin of Carmen

*Yo soy la Virgen*

(Catalán et al. 1991: I, 347-49)

I am the Virgin

*Yo soy Rosalina*

(ibid.: 225-26)

I am Rosalina

*Yo soy tu esposa Ana*

(ibid.: 29-30)

I am your wife Ana

*Yo soy aquel don Francisco*

(ibid.: I, 58)

I am that don Francisco

### APPENDIX B

*With his pistol in his hand (con la pistola en la mano)* as a formula portraying the stance of the heroic protagonist

*Rodrigo lanza en la mano*

(Wolf 1856: I, 96-99)

Rodrigo sword in hand

*saetas de oro en la mano*

(Wolf 1856:II, 43-45)

gold arrows in the hand

*y su halcín en la mano*

(ibid.: 273-78)

and his falcon in the hand

*con un falcón en la mano*

(Wolf 1856:I, 99-100)

with a falcon in the hand

*caza que tengo en la mano*

(Wolf 1856:II, 358-71)

game I have in the hand

*toma la vara en la mano*

(Wolf 1856:I, 161-74)

takes staff in the hand

*la vara tiene en la mano*

     (Wolf 1856:II, 72-74)

he has the stick in the hand

*púsole daga en la mano*

     (Wolf 1856:I, 348-49)

[he] placed a knife in his hand

*no toma el arco en la mano*

     (Wolf 1856:II, 13-14)

[he] does not take the bow in the hand

*y la candela en la mano*

     (Wolf 1856:I, 113-114)

and the candle in the hand

*Los dados tiene en la mano*

     (Wolf 1856: II, 229-48)

[he] has the dice in the hand

*con su bordón en la mano*

     (ibid.: 346-57)

with his cane in the hand

*Echó la mano a la espada*

     (ibid.: 353-55)

He placed the hand on the sword

*Echó mano a su espada*

     (Wolf 1856: I, 316-318)

He placed his hand on his sword

*y echa mano a la su espada*

     (Catarella 1993:20-21)

He places his hand on his sword

*echara mano a su espada*

     (Salazar and Salazar 1999:85-87)

placing his hand on the sword

*Echan mano a las espadas*

     (Wolf 1856:II, 326-34)

placing a hand on their swords

*Echaron mano a las lanzas*

     (ibid.: 401-408)

placing a hand on their lances

*Echaron mano a las lanza*

     (ibid.: 401-408)

placing a hand to their swords

*y echó mano al tablero*

     (ibid.: 269-73)

he placed a hand on the board

*tomara cuchillo en mano*

     (ibid.: 23-24)

he would take a knife in hand

*que no tome arma en mano*

     (Wolf 1856:I, 3-5)

let him not take weapon in hand

*en la espada puso mano*

     (Wolf 1856:II, 279-89)

placing a hand in the sword

*en a māno à espada mettia:*

     (ibid.: 76-77)

and placing a hand to the sword

*ponen mano a las espadas*

     (Wolf 1856:I, 42-47)

they place a hand in the swords

*sacan ambos las espadas*

     (Wolf 1856:II, 408-413)

both take out their sword

*Sacó la espada de cinta*

     (ibid.: 45-48)

he took out the sword from the belt

*De presto tomó la espada*

　　　　　　　　　(Wolf 1856: I, 72-75)

he suddenly took the sword

*blandiendo una gruesa lanza*

　　　　　　　　　(ibid.: 42-47)

brandishing a thick lance

*blandeando la su lanza*

　　　　　　　　　(ibid.: 237-239)

brandishing his lance

*el cual blandiendo su lanza*

　　　　　　　　　(ibid.: 308-313)

he was brandishing his lance

*la lanza iba blandiendo.*

　　　　　　　　　(ibid.: 293-95)

the lance he was brandishing

*las lanzas van blandeando*

　　　　　　　　　(ibid.: 124-27)

the lances he was brandishing

## From the Argentinean tradition:

*El año cuarenta y dos*
*empuñó la espada Urquiza*
*y el año cuarenta y seis*
*hizo brillar su divisa.*

　　　　　　　　　(Fernández 1960:122)

The year of forty two
Urquiza brandished the sword
and the year of forty six
his banner stood out

*Caballero mi don Juan,*
*una espada en cada mano,*
*en una ¡Viva la patria!*
*en la otra ¡Muera el tirano!*

　　　　　　　　　(Fernández 1960:189)

Gentleman, Don Juan,
a sword in each hand:
On one of them Long live the fatherland!

On the other: Death to the tyrant!

*Una espada en cada mano*
*en una ¡Qué viva Rosas!*
*en otra ¡Muera el tirano!*

　　　　　　　　　(Fernández 1960: 244)

A sword in each hand:
On one of them Long live Rosas!
On the other: Death to the tyrant!

## APPENDIX C

The honey-colored or sorrel horse (*caballo melado*) as a formula for the mount of the heroic protagonist

　　*cabalgara en su caballo:*

　　　　　　　　　(Wolf 1856:I, 248-50)

he would ride on his horse

*Caballero en su caballo*

　　　　　　　　　(Wolf 1856: II, 27-29)

a knight on his horse

*caballero en una yegua, que caballo no quería*

　　　　　　　　　(Wolf 1856: I, 241-44)

A knight on a mare, for he did not want a horse

*caballero en una yegua que ese día la ganara*

　　　　　　　　　(ibid.: 276-78)

a knight on a mare that he won that day

*descabalga de una mula y cabalga en una yegua*

　　　　　　　　　(ibid.: 276-78)

descends from a mule and rides on a mare

*Muy gallardo sale el moro, caballero en una yegua*

　　　　　　　　　(ibid.: 279-82)

The handsome Moor leaves, a knight on a mare

*él encima de una yegua muy herido se escapaba*

　　　　　　　　　(ibid.: 283-88)

he was wounded as he escaped riding on a mare

*armado de piezas dobles en un caballo morcillo*

　　　　　　　　　(ibid.: 143-45)

armed with double weaponry on a reddish black horse

*bien armado, que salía en un caballo morcillo*

(Wolf 1856:II, 102-110)

well-armed he went out on a reddish black horse

*Garcilaso se había armado, y en un caballo morcillo*

(Wolf 1856: I, 302-306)

Garcilaso had armed himself, and on a reddish black horse

*encima un caballo overo.*

(Wolf 1856:II, 35-36)

on top of a white paint horse

*tel buen rey en su caballo, y Vellido en su rocino*

(Wolf 1856:I, 134-37)

the good king on his horse, and Vellido on his work horse

*armado de piezas dobles en un caballo ligero*

(Wolf 1856: II, 35-36)

armed with double weaponry on a swift horse

*caballero a la gineta en un caballo corredor,*

(ibid.: 72-74)

a knight riding a la jineta [with short stirrups and bent legs] on a running horse

*en su caballo Babieca ¡oh qué bien que parecía!*

(Wolf 1856: I, 105-106)

on his horse Babieca, oh, he looked so fine!

*cabalgara en su caballo, que le decían Boca-negra:*

(ibid., 248-50)

rode on his horse named Boca-negra

### APPENDIX D

The *on the verge of tears (como queriendo llorar)* formula in the portrayal of the traitor or the cowardly enemy

*cayó el Cegrí desmayado:*
*mucho lo sintió el rey moro;*

*del gran dolor ha llorado.*

(ibid. 300-302)

the Cegrí fell and fainted:
the Morís king suffered it greatly;
from such great pain he has cried.

*En gran pesar y tristeza*
*era el valiente Bernaldo,*
*por ver a su padre preso,*
*y no poder libertallo.*
*Vestidos paños de duelo,*
*y de sus ojos llorando.*

(ibid.:I, 32-35)

Great weight and sorrow
had the brave Bernaldo
seeing his father in prison
unable to free him
dressed in clothing of mourning
and crying from his eyes.

*Lloraba de los sus ojos,*
*de la su boca decía:*
*"Oh ciudad, cuanto me cuestas*
*por la gran desdicha mía!*

(ibid.: 332-333)

His eyes were crying
His mouth was saying:
Alas, City, how dear you've been to me
due to my immense grief!

*cuando los quintos soldados*
*se marchan para la guerra,*
*unos cantan y otros lloran*
*y otros llevan mucha Peña.*

(Catalán et al. 1991:II, 15-16)

when the draftees
go to war
some sing and others cry
and others carry great hurt.

### The crying formula in the Argentinean ballad tradition.

*El peludo para Salta*
*se ha soltado chicoteando*
*sin pisar en los estribos*
*tristemente lagrimeando.*

(Fernández 1960:166)

The "hairy one" has gone to Salta
whipping (the horse) without restraint,
without touching the stirrups,
tear-eyed and sad.

### The crying formula in the Mexican ballad tradition from the state of Zacatecas.

*Iba José María*
*como queriendo llorar,*
*diciendole al Santo Niño:*
*"¡No me vayan a mater!"*

(Esparza 1976:29)

José María was going
on the verge of crying
saying to the Holy Child:
"Don't let them kill me!"

*Siguió diciendo este Antonio*
*como queriendo llorar:*
*Muchachos, ¡tráiganme al padre,*
*que me quiero confesar!*

(ibid.:44-45)

Antonio continued saying
on the verge of crying
"Boys, bring the father
Because I want confession."

*Andaba don Jesús Casas*
*como queriendo llorar,*
*diciendole a su señora:*
*"¡Dónde me voy a quedar!"*

(ibid.:64)

Don Jesus Casas found himself
on the verge of crying
telling his wife:
"Where am I going to stay?"

## Notes

1. I am employing two of Paredes's terms as well as the definitions he ascribed to them: "Lower Rio Grande Border" and "Greater Mexico." Accordingly, the first, sometimes referred as "Lower Border" or simply "border," includes the area along both banks of the Rio Grande from the two Laredos to the Gulf; while the second term refers to all the areas of Mexican culture, not only within the present limits of the Republic of Mexico but in the United States as well, in a cultural rather than a political sense.

2. The Strachwitz Frontera Collection—presently being digitized at UCLA—consists of commercial phonograph recordings made between 1904 though 1950. The collection includes approximately 15,000 78-rpm, 20,000 4-rpm and 3,000 $33^{1/3}$-rpm disc recordings illustrating contemporary styles and regional traditions.

3. Esparza Sánchez did not intend to provide a comprehensive corpus of the *corridos* of this region. The state of Zacatecas, however, has an abundant corpus of *corridos,* forming a continuing and unbroken tradition from the beginning of the nineteen century to the present. It should also be noted that both Paredes and Esparza Sánchez conducted their respective fieldwork interviews during the early nineteen fifties.

4. In his *Romance and corrido* (1939), Vicente T. Mendoza discussed the existence of South American romance survivals. Many of these had affinities with the *corrido* tradition, and some examples evidently composed by local authors reveal oral composition and transmission.

5. I discuss the printed, oral and discographic versions of the *corrido* "La punitiva" in Hernandez 1985. The discographic version of this *corrido* is the oldest and longest collected and helps understand the oral and printed versions.

6. The following citations are from the valuable Internet database organized and maintained by Suzanne Petersen: March 2003. http://depts.washington.edu/hisprom/index.html.

7. I have highlighted the recurring formula *en la mano* to indicate its pervasiveness as a recurring expression. I follow this convention in my discussion, designating those expressions to which I wish to draw attention, due to their repetition or formulaic nature.

8. For a discussion of the various terms for horse colors in Spanish, see: http://www.oni.escuelas.edu.ar/2001/bs-as/desfile-criollo-artesanal/caballos.htm.

9. To date, the following local institutions have organized international conferences on the *corrido*: Consejo Cultural de Nuevo León, Monterrey (Mexico) in 1992; The University of Texas at Austin, 1996; University of California, Los Angeles, 1998; Museo de Culturas Populares, México D. F, 2000; Universidad Autónoma de Sinaloa, Culiacán, 2003.

## Works Cited

Calvo, Raquel and Diego Catalán. 1993. Romancero general de Segovia. Series: Tradición romancística castellana. Madrid: Seminario Menéndez Pidal, Universidad Complutense de Madrid—Diputación Provincial de Segovia. In *Pan-Hispanic Ballad Project,* ed. Suzanne Petersen (March 2005): <http://www.bctex.com/suzy/>.

Catalán, Diego and M. de la Campa Deb. Catalán, P. Esteban, A. Ferrer y M. Manzanera, eds. 1991. Tradiciones orales leonesas. In *Romancero general de León I. Antología 1899-1989.* 2 volumes. Madrid: Seminario Menéndez Pidal, UCM y Diputación Provincialde León. In *Pan-Hispanic Ballad Project* edited by Suzanne Petersen (March 2005): <http://www.bctex.com/suzy/>.

Catarella, Teresa, ed. 1993. El romancero gitano-andaluz de Juan José Niño. Sevilla: Fundación Machado. In *Pan-Hispanic Ballad Project,* edited by Suzanne Petersen (March 2005): <http://www.bctex.com/suzy/>.

Esparza Sánchez, Cuauhtémoc. 1976. *El corrido zacatecano.* Mexico: Instituto Nacional de Antropologia e Historia.

Fernández Latour de Botas, Olga. 1960. *Cantares históricos de la tradición argentina.* Buenos Aires: Instituto Nacional de Investigaciones Históricas.

Hernández, Guillermo E. 1986. La punitiva: el corrido norteño y la tradición oral, impresa y fonográfica. Mexico City: *Estereofonía, Conservatorio Nacional de Música,* 29 (3):46-64.

McDowell, John Holmes. 1972. The Mexican Corrido. Formula and Theme in a Ballad Tradition. *Journal of American Folklore* 85:205-220.

Mendoza, Vicente T. 1939. *El romance español y el corrido mexicano.* México: Universidad Nacional Autómoma dc Mexico, Instituto de Investigaciones Estéticas.

Paredes, Américo. 1962. Review of Cantares históricos de la tradición argentina, by Olga Fernández Latour. *Journal of American Folklore* 75:356.

————. 1963. The Ancestry of Mexico's Corridos: A Matter of Definitions. *Journal of American Folklore* 76:231-35.

————. 1958. *'With His Pistol in His Hand': A Border Ballad and its Hero.* Austin: University of Texas Press.

Petersen, Suzanne H. Ed. 1982. Voces nuevas del romancero castellano-leonés. Series: Archivo Internacional Electrónico del Romancero. 2 vols. Madrid: Seminario Menéndez Pidal-Gredos. In *Pan-Hispanic Ballad Project,* edited by Suzanne Petersen (March 2005): <http://www.bctex.com/suzy/>.

Salazar, Flor and Diego Salazar. Eds. 1999. El romancero vulgar y nuevo. Madrid: Fundación R. Menéndez Pidal-Seminario Menéndez Pidal. In *Pan-Hispanic Ballad Project,* edited by Suzanne Petersen (March 2005): <http://www.bctex.com/suzy/>.

Simmons, Merle E. 1963. The Ancestry of Mexico's Corridos. *Journal of American Folklore* 76:1-15.

Wolf, Fernando José, and Conrado Hofmann. Eds. 1856. Primavera y flor de romances o colección de los más viejos y más populares romances castellanos. 2 vols. Berlin: A. Asher & Co. In *Pan-Hispanic Ballad Project,* ed. Suzanne Petersen (March 2005): <http://www.bctex.com/suzy/>.

### Ramón Saldívar (essay date 2006)

SOURCE: Saldívar, Ramón. "Bilingual Aesthetics and the Law of the Heart." In *The Borderlands of Culture: Américo Paredes and the Transnational Imaginary,* pp. 264-88. Durham, N.C.: Duke University Press, 2006.

[*In the following excerpt, Saldívar discusses the poetry of* Between Two Worlds.]

There are no shadows. Poetry
Exceeding music must take the place
Of empty heaven and its hymns,
Ourselves in poetry must take their place,
Even in the chattering of your guitar.

—Wallace Stevens, "The Man With the Blue Guitar"

Empieza el llanto
de la guitarra. . . .
Es inútil callarla.
Es imposible
callarla.
Llora monótona
como llora el agua,
como llora el viento . . .
Llora por cosas
lejanas.

—Federico García Lorca, "La guitarra"

In folk poetry, not only does the performer have the task of bringing the "part" assigned him to temporary life, but he can re-create the text at will. In the end, it is the performer who is the poet—for the brief moment that he performs.

—Américo Paredes, "Some Aspects of Folk Poetry"

Américo Paredes's reputation as a scholar rests in no small part on his lifelong project of overturning the historical strategies of containment that have limited the modes through which everyday Mexican American life has been described historically. His critical project was decades ahead of its time in its resolve to overturn the narrative clichés and historical commonplaces through which Anglo writers and historians had formerly represented Mexican American life. What was true of the scholarship of the late 1950s, 1960s, and 1970s is also true of his last published works, including the novel *George Washington Gómez,* the volumes of poetry *Cantos de adolescencia,* and *Between Two Worlds,* the collection of short stories *The Hammon and the Beans and Other Stories,* and a final novel, *The Shadow*—all of which were written in the 1930s, 1940s, and early 1950s. These works offer a striking confirmation of Adorno's notion that "modernity is a qualitative, not a chronological, category" (*Minima Moralia* 218).

In a variety of fascinating ways, these imaginative works address the predicaments of contemporary ethnic cultural politics, identity formation, and social transformation in the context of what I am here calling a bilingual modernity and transnational modernization. Paredes's lyrical forms already function as snippets of cultural critique and social analysis to show how culture, knowledge, and power are interlinked as social constructions that might be challenged and reconfigured. And they do so in a curiously modern and bilingual way. To exemplify this bilingual modernity, I turn now to the beautifully evocative lyrics of a poem written in 1935 and collected in *Between Two Worlds* entitled **"Guitarreros"** (Guitarists).

> *Bajaron el toro prieto,*
> *que nunca lo habían bajado . . .*
> [They brought the black bull down never before brought down]
> 　Black against twisted black
> 　The old mesquite
> 　Rears up against the stars
> 　Branch bridle hanging,
> 　While the bull comes down from the mountain
> 　Driven along by your fingers,
> 　Twenty nimble stallions prancing up and down
> 　　the *redil* of the guitars.
>
> One leaning on the trunk, one facing—
> Now the song:
> Not cleanly flanked, not pacing,
> But in a stubborn yielding that unshapes
> And shapes itself again,
> Hard-mouthed, zigzagged, thrusting,
> Thrown not sung,
> One to the other.
>
> The old man listens in his cloud
> Of white tobacco smoke.
> "It was so," he says,
> "In the old days it was so."
>
> 　　　　　　　　　　　　　　(29)[1]

Paralleling the allegorical course of his river songs and the human geographies and social spaces that they represent, Paredes's many poems about music, singing, and poetry also involve ideas concerning social space, temporality, and Mexican American modernity in a multilingual mode. As we have seen in the preceding discussion, some of the poems from *Between Two Worlds* are entirely in Spanish, some entirely in English. Others, such as **"Guitarreros,"** are subtly bilingual. In the instance of this poem, the title and the epigraph are in one language, while the rest of the poem—except for one crucial word—is in another. The point of Paredes's bilingual aesthetic is precisely to direct our attention to this play between languages and cultures as sites where modes of consciousness are made and unmade in the dialogical space between cultures and traditions. Its goal is to incite critical inquiry by reflecting on the ways that one may use poetry—and its central sensorium, the heart—as a tool of cognition.

Quite apart from the starkly modernist imagery of the first few lines, reminiscent of Pound's or Stevens's most sublime moments, **"Guitarreros"** is of great interest for its elegantly self-conscious representation of the complex interplay among history, geography, poetry,

language, and what I want to call the transnational modern in two cultural and linguistic registers. It speaks of male relationships and the sensuous experience of shared song and poetry. It is also about the havoc wrought by changing modes and relations of production with the advent of twentieth-century capitalist economies (modernization, corporate agribusiness, and capital markets) within the ranching communities of the Southwest at the end of the nineteenth century. Cormac McCarthy's trilogy consisting of *All the Pretty Horses, The Crossing,* and *Cities of the Plain* has chronicled these themes and values as features of the postmodern borderlands.[2] Paredes's fiction and poetry address them as a project of social aesthetics five decades earlier.

In **"Guitarreros,"** the human geography and the social structure related in Paredes's river poems—figuring a divided social space that both encompasses and includes—is reduced to the ritualized performance site of the song itself. The poem locates us beneath the "branch bridle hanging" canopy of an "old mesquite." Two *corridistas*—traditional ballad singers—perform in this rich sociopoetic pastoral space a traditional ballad, "El corrido del hijo desobediente" (The Ballad of the Disobedient Son), some verses from which are cited as the epigraph to the poem: "Bajaron el toro prieto, / que nunca lo habían bajado." Simple as the poem may seem, closer examination quickly reveals that the symbolic implications of the song and its unitary scene far exceed its locally circumscribed sociotextual space, even while the bilingual aesthetics of the moment remain the paramount concern of the poet.[3] In Spanish, the word *guitarrero* implies much more than its literal English equivalent, *guitarist.* For the term *guitarist,* Spanish offers us two alternatives. In the first option, a guitarist could be a *guitarista,* someone who aspires to the artistry of the instrument. In the second option, a guitarist might also be a *guitarrero,* that is, someone who has attained the full mastery of artistic performance with the guitar. To get a sense of the subtleties of the bilingual aesthetics exploited by the poem, however, we must first turn briefly to the traditional nineteenth century *corrido* to which Paredes's poem refers. The most instructive form of this exercise would be to listen to a musical performance of the classical ballad, since performance is what is at issue in both the song and the poem. Failing that, I cite the lyrics of the *corrido* in full here.[4]

El hijo desobediente

> Un domingo, estando herrando,
> se encontraron dos mancebos,
> echando mano a sus fierros
> como queriendo pelear.
>
> Cuando se estaban peleando,
> pues llegó su padre de uno:
> —Hijo de mi corazón,
> ya no pelees con ninguno.—

—Quítese de aquí, mi padre,
que estoy más bravo que un león
no vaya a sacar la espada
y le parte el corazón.—

—Hijo de mi corazón,
por lo que acabas de hablar
antes de que raye el sol
la vida te han de quitar.—

—Lo que le pido a mi padre,
que no me entierre en sagrado,
que me entierre en tierra bruta,
donde me trille el ganado.

Con una mano de fuera
y un papel sobre-dorado,
con un letrero que diga,
"Felipe fue desdichado."

—La vaquilla colorada,
que hace un año que nació,
ahí se la dejo a mi padre
por la crianza que me dió.

De tres caballos que tengo,
ahí se los dejo a los pobres,
para que siquiera digan en vida,
"¡Felipe, Diós te perdone!"—

Bajaron el toro prieto,
que nunca lo habían bajado,
pero 'ora si ya bajó
revuelto con el ganado.

Y a ese mentado Felipe
la maldición le alcanzó
y en las trances del corral
el toro se lo llevó.

Ya con ésta me despido,
con la estrella del oriente,
esto le puede pasar
a un hijo desobediente.

[The Disobedient Son

On a Sunday afternoon branding
Two young cowboys did meet,
Each going for their blades
Each looking to fight.

As they were fighting,
The father of one arrived:
—My dearly beloved son
Do not fight with anyone.—

—Get away from here my father
I feel more fierce than a lion,
I do not want to draw my sword
And split your heart in two.—

—My dearly beloved son,
Because of what you have said
Before the next sunrise
Your life will be taken from you.—

—I only ask of my father
That you not bury me in sacred ground,
That you bury me in common earth,
Where the stock may break and tame me.

With one hand out of the grave
And in my hand a gilded sheet of paper,
With an epitaph that reads
"Felipe was accursed."

The red yearling,
Born but a year ago,
I leave there to my father
For the upbringing that to him I owe.

My three stallions
I leave there to the poor
So that at least they may pray,
"May God forgive you, Felipe."

They brought the black bull down
Never before brought down,
But now indeed the bull is down
Thrown in among the herd.

And as for this cursed Felipe
The sacrilege caught up with him
And within the confines of the corral
The bull took him away.

With this I say farewell,
By the light of the eastern star;
This can happen to
A disobedient son.]

## In the Chattering of Your Guitar

In the "corrido del hijo desobediente," a prodigal son disobeys his father's plea that he not fight another young cowboy. The son then compounds his misfortune when, in the heat of the moment, he not only disregards his father but even threatens him with the same phallic violence that the disobedient son wishes to inflict on his antagonist: "Quítese de aquí mi padre / que estoy más bravo que un león / no vaya a sacar la espada / y le parte el corazón." The son's words threatening his father represent a supreme violation of patriarchal authority, of the phallocentric system, and of communal protocols. They manifest a complete failure of respect for the uncompromisable quality of paternal authority and the ritual law of the elders. Moreover, they express an unguarded flaunting of the symbolic oedipal order. Given the primal nature of the son's insolence, the words, not surprisingly, bring down on the young man's head the father's heavy curse and doom the fractious son to death before the next sunrise. So fierce is the certainty of this doom, and the power of the symbolic word of the father that calls it forth, that the song's diachronic narrative of male-on-male violence abruptly halts with the father's curse in the fourth quatrain. Nothing remains for the disobedient son but to lie down and be buried. So the narrative jumps ahead elliptically in the fifth quatrain to the disobedient son's synchronic acceptance of his foretold death, and to his despairing attempts to salvage what honor he can from his disgrace. As he lies dying, he makes his final requests—to be buried among his livestock in unsanctified ground ("Lo que le pido a mi padre . . . que me entierre en tierra bruta / donde me trille el ganado") with one hand out of the grave ("con una mano de fuera"), holding as his epitaph a gilded sheet on which is to be written, "Felipe fue desdichado."[5]

With his dying breaths, the disobedient son then wills away his most prized possessions, a red yearling to his father and three stallions to the poor of the community, so that they might pray for his forgiveness ("¡Felipe, Diós te perdone!"). In most versions, the *corrido* ends with the two lines that Paredes cites as the epigraph to his poem: "Bajaron el toro prieto, / que nunca lo habían bajado." These last verses tell of the breaking of a black bull, one never before brought down, to graze with the rest of the livestock ("revuelto con el ganado"), presumably in fulfillment of the disobedient son's last testament, donating his cattle to the poor, but also suggestive of the breaking of symbolic masculine sexual force.

José E. Limón points out in an excellent reading of the structure of the "anxiety of influence" in Paredes's poem that in identifying the epigraph as a verse from "El corrido del hijo desobediente," we realize that the *guitarreros* of Paredes's poem are singing this specific song. The poem is "about the imagined singing of this particular corrido" (*Mexican Ballads, Chicano Poems* 49). However, the focus of Paredes's English-language poem is not, as we might expect, the Spanish-language *corrido* itself, but rather the ritualized performance of the *corrido,* the artistry of its composition, the enacted communal ties that the performance ritual instantiates, and the nostalgic remembrance of a time when, as the poem in its concluding verse says, "It was so . . . / In the old days it was so." The bilingual modernity of **"Guitarreros"** emerges less from its overt linguistic features such as code switching, interlingual references or puns, or the use of vernacular Chicano argot, than from the deeply embedded bicultural elements of the discursive moment it represents. How and why this is so forms the crux of Paredes's bilingual aesthetic and a key to the modernity of its keynote themes.

In one of his later works, a scholarly monograph titled *A Texas-Mexican Cancionero,* Paredes would argue that the nineteenth-century ballad form popularly termed *corrido* is based on the medieval *romance corrido*. With its sources in medieval ballads, the *corrido* is chiefly a male performance genre whose pragmatic vernacular aesthetics sought to instruct and delight its audience with stories that celebrated, interpreted, and dignified the symbolic values of the community. Its special quality in the United States-Mexico borderlands is as the chronicle of that community's attempt to resist the encroachment of dominant Anglo culture in the last half of the nineteenth and the early part of the twentieth century.[6]

Of major significance in both *corrido* performance in general and in Paredes's poem in particular is the gendered nature of this bilingual scene. While women might occasionally perform *corridos,* especially in the "organized audience" situation of the intimate family setting, more often than not, and especially in extended family gatherings or in formal ceremonial settings, "men were the performers, while the women and children participated only as audience" (Paredes, *Texas-Mexican Cancionero* xxi). In these special ceremonial occasions, only the "oldest and wisest men had the privilege" (xxii) of narrating the histories that situated the song and of singing the *corrido* tales drawn from the heroic worldview of masculine virtue and value. In **"Guitarreros,"** Paredes takes this point of the performance aesthetic as the central feature of his poem. The specific ritual of performance—male elders only in a rural, pastoral setting sharing the pleasure of song and recollection—more so than the song itself draws our attention and mediates the achievement of a collective, masculine-gendered, subtly homoerotic *mexicano* identity.

Citing "El corrido del hijo desobediente" as the epigraph to his poem, Paredes thus activates as an element of the present the entire expressive tradition of the Spanish-language *corrido* genre, as well as of its gendered oral performance ritual. These traditions then become the latent narrative of a manifest narrative of celebration in English-language poetic verse. Why this is significant becomes apparent when we recall the social function of the *corrido* genre in the Mexican American community. As the oral folk history memorializing the late nineteenth-century conflict between Mexican American tradition and Anglo-American hegemony, a socially symbolic intervention into subjective and collective identity construction, the *corrido* constitutes a crucial illustration of the residual cultural order continuing as an effective element of the present.[7]

Through the citation of "El corrido del hijo desobediente," Paredes wishes to show how certain experiences, meanings, and values of a lapsed agrarian, precapitalist, patriarchal order now no longer entirely verifiable in terms of the dominant culture are nonetheless still imaginatively lived and practiced through the residue of the cultural institution of the *corrido*. They are also active in the social formations still marginally figured by the *guitarreros* of the song and by the old man in the poem who affirms that "It was so . . . / In the old days it was so." The apparent simplicity of **"Guitarreros"** masks the complexity of its multiply layered scores that resonate deeply with the fullness of stories, songs, and local histories. Like the allegorical course of the bordering river in others of Paredes's poems, here the flow of the song's poetic speech is polytemporal, multiply accentuated, and surges along—bound not by the unidirectional, single axis of grammatical forms, but by the polychromatic, multidimensional axes of musical form and notation.

In a high modernist mode, it evokes cultural institutions and social formations abstractly, with the forceful clarity of one of Picasso's paintings of guitars and guitarists, with the most economical of lines, the starkest of images: "the bull comes down from the mountain / Driven along by your fingers, / Twenty nimble stallions prancing up and down the *redil* of the guitars." Uniting history and lyrical song in one complex figure—"Hardmouthed, zigzagged, thrusting, / Thrown not sung"—the river poems and this and others of Paredes's ritual performance songs serve as figural markers of the power of poetic language to evoke residual elements within the contemporary human geography. All in all, the depicted scene certainly seems to represent a comfortingly nostalgic image of organic male consciousness celebrating its rich historical patrimony, *macho a macho,* in premodern time and space. At once a song, a manifesto, and a memory, the poem offers a strong opening for a unitary celebration of that macho ethos.

## MACHO CHIASMUS

But before we get too comfortable with this manly reading, we would do well to note that at first glance, because the citational structure and memorializing tone of the poem predominate so powerfully, it is easy to underestimate the profound discomfort with which Paredes's poem regards this nostalgic scene of male bonding and tradition sharing. Two features of the cited *corrido* and Paredes's poem should give us pause: first, we should not overlook the strangely enigmatic equality of the epigraphic citation itself, *"Bajaron el toro prieto, / que nunca lo habían bajado."* Nor should we ignore, second, the bizarre image in the cited *corrido* of the disobedient son's hand protruding from the grave and gripping in stony rigor mortis the script of his own epitaph, "Felipe fue desdichado." The strikingly graphic qualities of epigraph and epitaph work here hand in hand to effect a powerful deconstruction of certain aspects of the traditional, male, Spanish-language residual culture that both song and poem seem to celebrate without qualification. Let us see how this is so.

We will recall that in "El corrido del hijo desobediente" the disobedient son dies making an oddly catachrestic final request. He wishes to be buried among his livestock in unsanctified ground so that, in a complete reversal of his former relation to them, in death he might now be broken and tamed by his wild stallions and cattle, as he once broke and tamed them. This is the figure of chiasmus, "a grammatical figure by which the order of words in one of two parallel clauses is inverted in the other," as the OED states, and a special instance of the trope of catachresis, "the application of a term to a thing or concept to which it does not properly denote." In this instance we have a special case of a borderlands crossing, a chiasmus, in which the disobedient son exchanges places with his wild animals and as the former tamer of the herd, now becomes the tamed. Ultimately, these new pairings challenge the validity of defining relations of mastery in any binaries: father/son, old/young, obedience/disobedience, inheritance/disinheritance, and more obliquely perhaps, but still operative in this instance, the binaries of masculine/feminine, heterosocial/homosocial.

As if that catachresis were not weird enough, the disobedient son also gruesomely requests to be buried with one hand protruding from the grave, holding his own epitaph. The epitaph gilds the grim reality of the fact that the disobedient son's supplication is surely, at best, only an ambiguous acknowledgment, if not in fact a partial denial, of his own responsibility for his unpardonable sin. In Spanish, to be *desdichado* means, as I have noted, "to be ill-fated, or wretchedly sorrowing." As it happens, *desdichar,* the root verb form of the participle, also means, "to contradict oneself, to gainsay by word or deed." The Spanish-language *corrido* indirectly acknowledges, then, that Felipe is certainly ill-fated, but he is so not through the power of some transpersonal destiny, but because in the agency of his own historical being the disobedient son contradicts and denies the very values of manhood, patriarchy, patrimony, and respect defending which, presumably, he died in the first place.

Traditionally, why do machos fight one another to the death if not to defend their challenged or insulted masculinity? In doing so, they reveal a repressed anxiety and desire for recognition in the fullness of (sexual) being. To paraphrase Saint Luke, then, Felipe in death is, as he was in life, a sign which shall be spoken against, a sign of contra-diction (*desdicho*), in fact, the very sign of his own contradiction (*desdichado*).[8] In the undoing of his life and the body of his contradictions, represented by the synecdoche of his hand equivocally signing from the grave, the disobedient son literally loses his integrity.

The final, enigmatic verse of the *corrido,* the first two lines of which Paredes cites as the epigraph to his poem, is likewise charged with suggestive ambiguity. In the *corrido* proper, these concluding verses telling of the breaking of an unbroken black bull seem almost irrelevant to the story of the disobedient son. Indeed, this quatrain seems so distantly connected to the archetypal narrative of filial disobedience within the pastoral patriarchal order that some variants of the song simply excise it, cutting out the bull, so to speak. One early anthology of Chicano literature reprints the ballad precisely in this manner (Castañeda Shular, Frausto, and Sommers 179). That is to say, in the uncut versions of the song, the lines about the black bull supersede the primary narrative of the son's disobedience. They introduce by metonymy a larger theme, that of the closing of a mythical epoch.

Because of these variations, excisions, and perplexing ambiguities, it is very tempting to read the relationship between the disobedient son and the black bull as simply a contrivance of emplotment. In fact, however, the relationship between the symbolic "toro prieto" and the paradigmatic "hijo desobediente," as Paredes would have us see, is anything but contrived. A quick reference to the *Diccionario de mejicanismos* reveals what Paredes, who grew up in the transnational borderlands of south Texas and *norteño* Mexican ranches, obviously knew, namely, that the verb *bajar* used in the song in reference to the bull, has the vernacular, northern Mexican, south Texas usage of "breaking and taming livestock." In short, it is exactly synonymous with *trillar,* the verb naming Felipe's reversed relation to his animals (111; 1087). Moreover, the verbs *trillar* and *bajar* that the song uses to indicate the taming of wild stallions, bulls, and disobedient sons also share another meaning, expressly, "to subdue," as in the exercise of power implied in the subjection of a beaten warrior to the victor, or a people to a ruler, or a bride to a man. All of these meanings share a place in the now sharply compromised phallocentric system of the song; its vanity and pride subdued.

In both the *corrido* and the poem, then, what at first sight seems like an unremarkable and uncritical celebration of a utopian masculine absolute past of unitary sociocultural value is instead something else. Both the *corrido* and the poem exhibit the taming and breaking of a social formation under the weight of its own "contradictory" (*desdichado*) value structure. In displaying that economic and social collapse, rather than celebrating masculine power, the poem contrives to unravel an entire system of values. In complete dialogic reversal, the young buried macho, former breaker of stallions and bulls, now lies broken and subdued by them. The rising intensity of the song leads directly to this virtuoso turnabout of those meanings, especially as the chiasmus reverses the direction of the subjection. What is more, the gilded script naming the self-contradiction of his values by his own actions, which in death he embodies, openly marks his grave. This unraveling critique is performed in the mode of bilingual metonymy, through the science of the beautiful (aesthetics), in the provenance of the modern. With dialogic intensity, *corridos* such as that of the disobedi-

ent son contradict and negate the very truths and authenticities that they desire to uphold. Surely, this is the point of the mediated image of macho chiasmus here.

In point of fact, many years after having written this poem, as a scholar of the *corrido* form, Paredes would argue precisely that by the 1930s "when Mexico's Tin Pan Alley took over the *corrido* . . . its decay was inevitable" and the genre no longer clearly served its former critical function. The demands of the modern, newly consolidated global American culture industry and its dependent Mexican counterpart, claimed Paredes, "wore the folk material thin" to produce what he came to call "a pseudo-*corrido*" ("Mexican Corrido" 138-39). Laboring to meet the needs of the modern consumer, mass entertainment, the culture industry under the growing demands of the developing commercial radio, film, and audio recording industries for more and more products, the anonymous folk balladeers of the *corrido* were overwhelmed by commercial songwriters. Mexican Tin Pan Alley commercial songwriters creating products for consumption in the newly commercialized form of the *corrido* in the 1920s and 1930s produced music that mimicked a tradition, simulated the gestures of a tradition, or simply invented one if it did not exist.

### DOWN A DARK TIN PAN ALLEY

This "invention of tradition" was especially true, Paredes would argue decades later as an ethnographer of Greater Mexican culture, for the fabrication of a Mexican national identity and its link to Mexican masculinity.[9] In an essay originally published in Spanish as "Estados Unidos, México y el machismo" (1967), Paredes offers a devastatingly critical genealogy for the absurdly exaggerated version of Mexican masculinity notoriously identified as machismo. Far from representing a traditional type of masculinity in opposition to a debased modern version, Paredes argues, machismo as an expression of the gun-toting, braggart and bully, facing death with false bravado was an invented tradition, a product of cultural romanticism, reflecting the ideological needs of a newly emergent state groping for a distinctive national subject identity. As the anthropologist Kate Crehan concludes, "the context for this particular 'invention of tradition' was the very specific one of Mexican nationalism and its struggle to define, always in the shadow of its powerful northern neighbor, an autonomous Mexican identity" (198). It reflected, moreover, the class structures of that emerging society, especially in the *corridos* promulgated by commercialized Mexican popular song and film:

> Then appear the *corridos* for which Mexico is known abroad, the same ones cited repeatedly by those who deplore *machismo*. . . . Such *corridos* were disseminated in Mexico and abroad by the voice of popular singers like Pedro Infante and Jorge Negrete.

That is to say, these were moving-picture *corridos*. And when one says moving-pictures, one says middle-class. These have been the songs of the man from the emergent middle class, a man who goes to the movies, has enough money to buy a car, and enough political influence to go around carrying a gun. During World War II, it was the middle class that became emotional hearing Pedro Infante sing:

*¡Viva México! ¡Viva América!*
*¡Oh pueblos benditos de Dios!*

("The United States, Mexico" 221)


Long live Mexico! Long live America!
Oh, nations blessed by God!


Paredes points out the class basis of this notion of masculinity and the influence of the United States in its construction. Not the least of the contentious arguments that Paredes makes in this essay is for the close genealogical relationship between Mexican machismo and the figures of the North American frontiersman and cowboy whose supposed manliness was venerated by myth, legend, history, and Hollywood, as well as celebrated by American presidents from Theodore Roosevelt at the beginning of the twentieth century to George W. Bush at the beginning of the twenty-first century. In both instances, the Mexican and the American one, Paredes claims, "machismo betrays a certain element of nostalgia; it is cultivated by those who feel they have been born too late" ("The United States, Mexico" 234).

In "El corrido del hijo desobediente," this nostalgia disguises a mystified desire for an archetype that the economic and social history of the Southwest will simply not entertain. This is the point of Paredes's bilingual aesthetics. Having become so powerfully identified with the failed ideologies of a defeated ranchero, patriarchal, and precapitalist world, unable to resist the encroaching hegemony of modern cultural commoditization, the *corrido* in both its newly commodified and traditionally residual forms from this time forward would either have to evolve or give way to new symbolic constructions that could layer different, richer, and more viable alternatives to the lyrics of former songs.

Likewise, the failed virtues celebrated in countless *corridos,* graphically monumentalized in this instance by the disobedient son's epitaphic hand holding not the archetypal pistol in hand but the gilded pronouncement of his contradiction, are replaced now by a modernist poetic aesthetic and script that memorialize even as they supersede. Unbending patriarchal authority and uncompromising male violence such as that celebrated, or at least memorialized, in a *corrido* like the one discussed could not prevent the destruction of that

former way of life that had now receded into the legendary past ("In the old days it was so"). Nor could it contest the modern historical erasures that Paredes in the 1930s was witnessing and documenting in his poetry. This may well explain in part why neither the patriarchal social formations nor the heroic border *corrido* survive to oppose the processes of twentieth-century modernization. Other versions and newer forms authored by different persons would have to arise to fulfill that function in another age.[10]

Moreover, his recognition of this historical process explains why Paredes sings a song about the ritual of singing rather than simply singing the song of patriarchal authority itself. He is, finally, less concerned with representing the decline of a particular community and the nostalgia for a premodern world than with rendering the very processes of change and creative adaptation. The cultural critic Robert E. Livingston thus correctly points out that "whatever might be said about its ultimate political allegiances, the movement of literary modernism derives much of its energy from its resistance to an institutionalized cultural order and its ever-keener awareness of the transnational dimension of aesthetic production" (152). The case of Américo Paredes's modernism illustrates Livingston's point precisely about the links between modernism and the critique of an officially sanctioned institutional order and an emerging insight to the transnational character of aesthetic production.

### Llora por Cosas Lejanas

The transnational character of aesthetic production in Paredes's poetry emerges constantly, but not always in the use of a bilingual idiom. When the poems are bilingual, however, we are on special notice that something distinctive is about to occur. This is particularly the case in **"Guitarreros."** *Redil,* as the only Spanish-language word in Paredes's poem apart from the epigraph, requires our special attention because of the web of transnational allusions it justifies. First, the "*redil* of the guitars" as a figure in the poem for the livestock pens and enclosures of ranches that once existed (in the "old days it was so") makes the guitars synecdoches of an economic and social formation that also no longer exists. Second, since *redil* comes from *red,* meaning "net," it may also be a metaphor for the ten strings and fretted necks of the two guitars. This metaphor in turn creates a visual corral for the guitarists' eerily disembodied fingers, represented as "twenty nimble stallions prancing up and down the *redil* of the guitars." Third, in addition to being a synecdoche for the guitars themselves, the "*redil* of the guitars" is also the small circle of men whose song brings the bull down from the mountain, "driven along by your fingers." A fourth strand of allusions created by *redil* refers to the character constellation of the poem. If there are three characters in the poem, two guitarists singing, "One to the other," and an old man who listens to their song and comments about the "old days," then the poem reproduces exactly the reduced character constellation as well as the confining topoi of "El corrido del hijo desobediente," with only its two fighting cowboys and an intransigent patriarch making up its entire cast. As in the ballad, the poem hints at another perspective beyond the nostalgic old man and the *guitarreros* with their guitars yearning for faraway things, namely, that of a poet who stands aside to witness and record the alignments of their mutually defining circumstances. Together, these multiple strands of allusions emanating from the *rediles* of the guitars form the fold of its intertextual *red,* or poetic net of the poem and the song.[11]

### BAD GUITARS AND LYING WOMEN

A poem written almost a decade later and half a world away adds yet a fifth component to the figures of the guitar and the guitarist that Paredes explores here in **"Guitarreros."** In **"Guitarras y mujeres"** (**"Guitars and Women"**), the poet mocks his own macho blindness by recalling some painfully sententious lines that in full naïveté he had once composed about women and guitars: "Las mujeres mentían / como las guitarras malas" (women lied / like bad guitars). Another male voice immediately challenges the disingenuous poet by asking with archirony whether it is perhaps not the other way around, that "mienten las guitarras / como las malas mujeres" (guitars lie / like evil women) (**Between Two Worlds** 69).[12] With this coy reversal, we find ourselves back in the problematic trope of "El corrido del hijo desobediente" and its macho chiasmus. In this instance, with the chiasmus of a crisscrossed exchange between lying guitars and evil women, how are we to know which way the irony cuts? In that of the lying women or of the bad guitars? Lying guitars or evil women? Or, is this instead a conundrum to be resolved only uniquely, concerning the particular individual, woman, or guitar? The poem concludes with precisely that question: "¿Es cuestión del individuo? / ¿la mujer? /¿o la guitarra?" (is it a question about the individual? the woman? or the guitar?). As in the earlier instances of macho chiasmus, the figure reproduces the stereotype while simultaneously undercutting its implications. We are once again in a situation that explicitly challenges the validity of defining relations of mastery in terms of the hierarchical binaries of masculine/feminine, truth/falsehood, or good/evil. In retrospect, from the vantage point of this later image of the *guitarras malas,* the good guitars of **"Guitarreros"** can hardly be regarded as unambiguous instruments of truth telling. Instead, Paredes's personified guitars should be understood as near avatars, embodied representations of the principle that expressions of what is good or bad, or truth or lie, are corralled in the *rediles* of the very cultural gestures that they presume to signify.

While the *guitarreros* of the poem and the singers of ballads celebrate nineteenth-century economies and mourn the passing of their enmeshed social-gender relations and negotiations, the modernist poet cannot commemorate the world within which they lived without being aware of the constraining nature of its cultural idioms and forms of sociability. Perhaps nowhere else in his poetry of the 1930s and early 1940s than here with his guitars is Paredes most consummately a modern.

### THE KINGS OF MODERN THOUGHT

We should recall at this point that the source of the title and epigraph to Paredes's **Between Two Worlds** is Matthew Arnold's great poem of 1852, "Stanzas from the Grande Chartreuse."[13] In this poem, Arnold retraces the near elegiac contours of Wordsworth's alpine journey limned in the "Prelude," "the convent of Chartreuse / Received us two days afterwards, and there / We rested in an awful solitude—" (Prelude [1805], Bk vi, lines 422-24). Like Arnold following Wordsworth poetically, Paredes returns to his own undiscovered country between two worlds, the borderlands of south Texas and northern Mexico. In this poetic reprise, he reiterates the symbolic phrases of his community's master narrative of the *corrido,* but without the historical amnesia of the sexual politics of the original score and in full acknowledgment of its rhetorical and tropological self-negations. *Anamnesis,* not amnesia, drives Paredes's revisionary song.

The literary critic David DeLaura has pointed out that Arnold's "Stanzas from the Grande Chartreuse" is not so much a lament for former times and beliefs as it is an expression of Arnold's hopelessness over the impotence to which melancholy stoicism reduces us (20). Here are Arnold's lines:

> Wandering between two worlds, one dead,
> The other powerless to be born,
> With nowhere yet to rest my head,
> Like these, on earth I wait forlorn.
> Their faith, my tears, the world deride—
> I come to shed them at their side.
>
>                                                    (lines 85-90)

In the "Stanzas from the Grande Chartreuse," Arnold imaginatively considers and rejects various historical attitudes that in former times he feels have served effectively to stave off the dread of the unknown future. He enumerates them in order to refuse them in sequence. First, he rejects Christian faith, now simply "gone" (line 84). Then, he sees the flaws in his own codes of conduct and ethics, which he had absorbed from his former "rigorous teachers . . . masters of the mind" (lines 66, 73) and sees them as now "outworn" and "out-dated" (lines 100, 106). Finally, Arnold turns away even from the mentalities of "the kings of modern thought" because they are merely silent, dumb, and passive as they "wait to see the future come" (lines 115, 118). Bound as he is between two worlds, Arnold still does allow of another historical possibility. It is one, however, that he wistfully acknowledges is ineluctably unavailable to him: the poetic vision of a future realm, "powerless to be born" (285).

This vision of what we might call, paraphrasing Arnold, the realm of the kings of *post*modern thought is unmistakably what animates Paredes's antinostalgic, counterdiscursive modernist work. Arnold, "between two worlds," dispiritedly resigns himself to his former ethical codes, judging himself totally unfit for the life of "action and pleasure" (line 194) offered by the fearsomely burgeoning modern world of the mid-nineteenth century (DeLaura 21).

As cultural historian Regenia Gagnier notes, by the time that Arnold published *Culture and Anarchy* (1869), he had resolved his fears by turning to aesthetics, or "Culture," as a solution to faithlessness, anomie, and the machinery of modernity. In *Culture and Anarchy,* "Culture" for Arnold means "trying to perfect oneself and one's mind as part of oneself." But human perfection as culture conceives it, writes Arnold, "is not possible while the individual remains isolated" (qtd. in Gagnier, *Insatiability* 107-8). Paredes, too, turns to culture as a solution. But unlike Arnold, Paredes embraces the idea of the undiscovered country, figured in the differential condition of life between two worlds. That liminal space marks a zone of critical deconstruction and constitutes the site where Arnoldian "action and pleasure," unattained even by the cultured individual, might be finally realized. As a master performance artist at the peripheries of modernism, Paredes sees the shared activity of culture, figured here in the performance of the *corrido* and the poem about the performance, as a profoundly social activity.

With the breaking and taming of the disobedient son in the Spanish-language *corrido,* and the singing of his story in an English-language poem, Paredes tells a heteroglossic lyrical narrative: of the collapse of a feudal, patriarchal, and sexual social order under the weight of its own contradictory values, hastened by the corrosive power of the modern. History is one name for the dialectical play between these mutually complicit values and ideologies, dystopias constructed from within utopias. And the site of this utopia is the human geography of critical social space, played out here in poem and song as the fatally resolved oedipal conflict between father and son and the fracturing of the pastoral patriarchal order under the mark of modernity.

Where does the critique of this social order leave us, however? If the eroticized warrior hero of a former era lies dead and buried with his contradictions exposed,

who then is to take his place? With the ironic debunking of patriarchal macho values, are we left only with the irony of modern poetic vision? The English-speaking poet who serves up the contradictions and their unresolved tensions does not quite seem up to the role of cultural hero, warrior or otherwise. In contrast to the two patrimonies, one based on male violence and power, the other on male performance genres in rigidly stratified gender and sexual patterns, the bilingual discursive space of the poem offers an alternative figurative domain.[14] As in the archeological work of folklore itself, we are left here to deal with the exposed historical signs of the past and the curriculum of its contradictory flows.

A new vision of self and society, a dialogic world not based on static notions of male privilege and desire, nor of unitary concepts of self or community, emerges from the bilingual space of the poem. It is not present *in* either Spanish or English, but situated in the critical mediation *between* the two languages, interlingually as it were, an early version of what Arjun Appadurai has termed "transnational public culture" emerging in the new global "diasporic public spheres" (21). It is what Heidegger in the book on Nietzsche, talking about Descartes, means when he claims that modernity is not in the subject or the object but in the relational *situatedness* and *positionality* of the two.[15] In **"Guitarreros"** that situational modernity rises from the realm of the transnational public culture and the social aesthetic between two languages and cultural discourses.

### THE LAW OF THE HEART

A word about this social aesthetic seems necessary, then. Heidegger argues that as logic comports itself toward the true, and ethics toward the good, so aesthetics comports itself toward the beautiful (78). Aesthetics is consideration of the beautiful in relation to peoples' state of feelings and is thus at home in the realm of the human visceral sensorium. In an essay on ethics, *Theory of Moral Sentiments* (1759), the eighteenth-century philosopher Adam Smith held that virtuous actions were also by definition beautiful. Virtue is beauty, and beauty virtue. Now, recalling etymologies with the help of the OED one more time, we should recollect that *virtue* is derived from the Latin *virtus,* meaning "manliness, valour, worth, etc." "Human society," writes Smith,

> when we contemplate it in a certain abstract and philosophical light, appears like a great, an immense machine, whose regular and harmonious movements produce a thousand agreeable effects. As in any other beautiful and noble machine that was the production of human art, whatever tended to render its movements more smooth and easy, would derive a beauty from this effect, and on the contrary, whatever tended to obstruct them would displease on that account: so virtue, which is, as it were, the fine polish to the wheels of society,

necessarily pleases; while vice, like the vile rust, which makes them jar and grate upon one another, is as necessarily offensive.

(qtd. in Eagleton, Ideology of the Aesthetic 37)

In this way of thinking about the beautiful, the whole of social life, including ethics and politics, is aestheticized into a harmoniously encompassing social aesthetic. Terry Eagleton thus points out that virtue is the easy habit of goodness. A good society is one in which people conduct themselves gracefully, where the law is not external to individuals but lived out in the heart, as the very principle of one's free identity. "Such an internal appropriation of the law is at once central to the work of art and to the process of political hegemony. The aesthetic is in this sense no more than a name for the political unconscious; it is simply the way that social harmony registers itself on our senses, imprints itself on our sensibilities" (Eagleton, *Ideology of the Aesthetic* 37). Critique and sensibility thus unite in judgment and help create the law of the heart.

While one way to read this aestheticization of the social totality in the unity of critique and sensibility is to see it as justification for the way things are, it may also, alternatively, "be read as a discourse of utopian critique," contends Eagleton (38). If this is so, then, we would expect that from the margins of the social whole a very different reading would emerge, respecting the function of aesthetics as something other than a tool of hegemony. Regenia Gagnier points out that "from Kant on, modern aesthetics was seldom about the beautiful object alone (formalism) but rather about the relation between the receptive subject and the object" (Gagnier, "A Critique of Practical Aesthetics" 264). Elsewhere, Gagnier notes that for this reason, the "Kantian judgment of taste is neither simply subjective, relating to the consumer, nor objective, relating to the object" ("Critique" 264).[16] Aesthetic judgment resides precisely in the conceptual space of the relation between subject and object. But what exactly is at stake in this alternative reading of the relation between the receptive subject and the perceivable object?

In aesthetic judgment, says Kant, we put our own prejudices aside, and we put ourselves in everyone else's place.[17] A portrait of *enchiladas de mole* is not beautiful because I happen to enjoy eating *enchiladas de mole*. If we judge it beautiful, it is because it meets other, community, standards for judging it beautiful. My saying it is beautiful, does not make it so. As opposed to mere egoism and selfish judgment, the aesthetic is communal. It points to a utopian alignment of subjects united in the deep structure of their shared field of being. In the political realm, individuals are bound together for external, instrumental ends. Social life would collapse if it were not held together by force. The cultural aesthetic domain, by contrast, is one of

noncoercive consensus. Culture and the aesthetic thus promote unity based on their effectuating human responses of mutuality in their most intimate subjectivity in relation to the object world. They allow us to internalize the social consensus in an uncoercive way.

With this way of reading the Kantian aesthetic and its role in the construction of meaning and critique, the beautiful turns out to be just the political order lived out on the body—in the way it strikes the eye, pleases the ear, soothes our skin, and stirs the heart. However, Paredes is not trying to aestheticize morality and society in quite this way. Instead, he wishes to elicit that state of feeling—as a practice, and as a way of life.

Kant's notion of the aesthetic as the *relation* between a receptive subject and a perceived object warrants in Paredes's poetry a relation always to be understood in the context of a specific historical moment and profoundly situated societal locale, what I am calling a social aesthetic.[18] As a lived experience, its political motivation unfolds from its attempts to present historically and dialectically contextualized views of these states of feeling as phenomena of consciousness. As a practice, its formal and rhetorical impetus appears, not surprisingly, as understatement, contradiction, parody, satire, burlesque, and most frequently, irony. Paredes accesses and enacts the social aesthetic through all of these modes.

Writing about contemporary Mexican folk art, the anthropologist Néstor García Canclini notes that if we could free the concept of the aesthetic from its elitist and Eurocentric connotation to include the more "rustic" arts and crafts, then we would be able to "include under the name of art expressions that handle in a different manner the tangible and imaginary relations of individuals with other individuals and their environment" (*Transforming Modernity* 107). In providing social experience in this differently mediated way, Paredes offers a strikingly distinctive form of aesthetics, a bilingual vernacular aesthetics that asks us to be able to reside comfortably between two worlds. His bilingual aesthetics is in the fields of sensuousness and feeling what dialectics is in the area of thinking, which is why we may regard it as a kind of dialectics of sensuousness. The articulation of this dialectics of sensuousness in idioms of refractory male violence and power allows us to envision an alternative, if surely utopian, model of identity to ones based on the monological word of the father. Guiding us through complex structures of feeling, this dialectic of sensuousness offers an alternate mode of analysis, one linked not to the logic of the intellect but to the logic of the heart. Art, community, and critical moral culture are at least in part the substantial products of that modernist bilingual aesthetic.

In a poem entitled **"Esquinita de mi pueblo"** (**"The Corner of My Community"**), composed in 1950 in the weeks after his return from Japan, Paredes reflects exactly on this process of living the cartographic imaginary between two worlds:

> At the corner of absolute elsewhere
> And absolute future I stood
> Waiting for a green light
> To leave the neighborhood.
> But the light was red. . . .
> That is the destiny of people in between
> To stand on the corner
> Waiting for the green.

(*Between Two Worlds* 114)

Unable to sanction fully (nor live uncritically) the ideological structures that the "old man" of **"Guitarreros"** and the other inhabitants of the poet's "neighborhood" occupy, Paredes sings instead of twentieth-century constructions of narratives about narratives and the revisions of history that such metanarratives might allow: "Not cleanly flanked, not pacing, / But in a stubborn yielding that unshapes / And shapes itself again."

This process of shaping and unshaping is precisely the marker and the substitute of the limits of a monolingual aesthetics. It charts what in **"Esquinita de mi pueblo"** Paredes alternately maps as "the corner of absolute elsewhere / And absolute future." That is, between the emergence of a properly modernist style and the representational dilemmas of the new capitalist world system, Paredes's verses exploit their contingency to history, "the destiny of people in between," and the utopian glimpses of achieved community, "Waiting for the green" that this contingency allows. Indeed, as I have tried to show, in exploring its styles and testing its ethics, Paredes offers us something very like what Jameson calls a "cognitive mapping" of the imaginary borders of modernity within the real conditions of existence.[19] At moments such as this, tracing out in aesthetic figures relationships that turn out to be all too real social affinities, Paredes's poetry accomplishes Wallace Stevens's requirement that poetry must "exceed music" and "take the place of empty heaven and its hymns" ("The Man With the Blue Guitar" 167).

The concluding lines of Paredes's prologue to the collection **Between Two Worlds** say: "I am aware that if this volume finds any favor with the reader it will be mostly as a historical document. It is thus that I offer it, as the scribblings of a 'proto-Chicano' of a half-century ago" (11). These "scribblings" annotate one way that the desire for social harmony registers itself on our senses, imprints itself on our sensibilities, and becomes the law of the heart at the borders of language in the transnational spaces between two worlds.

## Notes

1. Composed in 1935, this poem was first published in the *Southwest Review* (Autumn 1964): 306.

2. See also the discussion of McCarthy in Moya and Saldívar 14-16.

3. I first presented a version of this chapter at the conference "Bilingual Aesthetics" organized by Doris Sommer at Harvard University. For an elaboration of some of the themes of that seminal conference, see Sommer, *Bilingual Aesthetics*.

4. "El corrido del hijo desobediente" is one of the most widely known of Mexican ballads. This version of the *corrido* combines the versions of the song performed by Américo Paredes as transcribed in Limón, *Mexican Ballads*; the version paraphrased in Paredes's novel, *The Shadow*; other variants of the song, including my transcript of the verses from a 1921 recording; and the version collected in Kuri-Aldana and Martínez 446-47. Limón notes that Paredes informed him in personal correspondence that "El corrido del hijo desobediente" was his favorite *corrido*. The Archive of Recorded Sound at Braun Music Library, Stanford University, has one of the earliest recorded versions of the song. Aurora Perez, operations manager and archivist there, helped me locate a pristine copy of a seventy-eight RPM recording of the *corrido* by Martin y Malena con Mariachi, recorded April 7, 1921. The classic Mexican movie, *Flor silvestre* (1943), directed by Emilio "El Indio" Fernández (1904-86), the greatest filmmaker of the Golden Age of Mexican cinema, and starring the luminous Dolores del Río and macho par excellence Pedro Armendáriz, includes a scene in which *guitarreros* perform the *corrido* with exquisite emotive flair. Julia Tuñón comments that *Flor silvestre* tells "the unhappy love story of a couple from different social classes who face the opposition of [the hero's] wealthy *hacienda*-owning parents at a time of Revolutionary violence and confusion. This romance alludes to the conflictual encounter between tradition and the modern values implied by the desire for equality that [the hero] discovers in Revolutionary ideas" (182). In Paredes's poem and in his rendition of the ballad, the focus is on violence, confusion, and contradiction in a time of revolutionary change rather than on irresolvable romantic woes.

5. Variants of the *corrido* use the words *desgraciado* (wretched) and *desdichado* (ill-fated) interchangeably. Even if we choose as the preferred reading of the song *desgraciado* instead of *desdichado,* a similar case can be made concerning the ambiguity, indeed contradictory nature, of the word. The crucial issue here is the use of the verb *fue* (he was), rather than the alternate form, *era* as the operative modal. The first possibility implies passive force—Felipe was disgraced/ill-fated (by something/someone); the second denotes continu-

ity of condition—Felipe was disgraced/ill-fated (as a state of being).

6. See my discussion of this theme in *Chicano Narrative* 36-38.

7. For a more complete discussion of the *corrido* as a "socially symbolic act," see my discussions under the headings "The Folk Base of Chicano Narrative" and "Paredes, Villarreal, and the Dialectics of History" in *Chicano Narrative* 26-73.

8. See Luke 2:34, where Christ is described as "a sign that is rejected" (Jerusalem Bible); "a sign which shall be spoken against" (King James Version); or "signum cui contradicetur" (Biblia Vulgata). In the later poem "Tres faces del pocho," Paredes's narrator sings to Mexico "un himno extraño / . . . para que sepas bien lo desdichado / que pueden ser los hijos de tus hijos" (an odd hymn / so that you may know the wretched (contradiction) / that the children of your children can be), *Between Two Worlds* 40.

9. The phrase is Hobsbawm's from his classic study of the relationship between modernity and tradition, *The Invention of Tradition.* See Hobsbawm and Ranger 54. On Mexican masculinity, see Irwin, who describes the shifting constructions of masculinity in the early twentieth century.

10. This is not to say that other kinds of *corridos* might arise to serve the function of symbolic action and vernacular critique that the *corrido* of border conflict had formerly performed. For discussions of the function of the *corrido* in the contemporary period, see Herrera-Sobek; and J. Saldívar, *Border Matters.* See also my discussion of the transnational theme and the contemporary function of the *corrido* in "Transnational Migrations." On critical vernacular culture, see also Kymlicka, *Politics in the Vernacular.*

11. As one of the anonymous readers of this book for Duke University Press points out, García Lorca's beautiful poem, "La guitarra" from *Poema del cante jondo* (1931), about the yearning for "cosas lejanas" (faraway things) may be part of the intertextual *red* or *redil* of "Guitarreros." García Lorca's poem links the image of the guitar with yet another "transfixed heart," that of the Virgin of Sorrows, pierced by swords. See the lovely illustration of the Virgin of Sorrows and her pierced heart adorning the title page of García Lorca's "Poema del canto jondo" 92.

12. The contrapuntal subtext to Paredes's line about "malas mujeres" is certainly Lydia Mendoza's protofeminist recording of the classic tango, "Mal hombre" ("Evil Man"), first recorded in 1934:

"Mal hombre / tan ruin es tu alma que no tiene nombre, / eres un canalla, eres un malvado, / eres un mal hombre" (Evil man, / your soul is so vile it has no name, / you are despicable, you are evil, / you are an evil man). See Mendoza 19-21.

13. Arnold wrote the "Stanzas from the Grande Chartreuse" (285) sometime between 1851 and 1855, probably mainly in 1852. Another of Arnold's poems, "The River," roughly from this same period, is also noteworthy in relation to Paredes. It is probably more than coincidence that Paredes's river poems echo Arnold's when he speaks of his soul seeking "immunity from my control" as it "wander[s] round the world" (Arnold, "The River" 232).

14. For a discussion of the changing role of the Chicano warrior hero under the impact of feminism, see Rosaldo, *Culture and Truth* 150-66.

15. Fredric Jameson made this point in a lecture titled "Aesthetic Autonomy in the Age of Capitalism," delivered at Stanford University on January 26, 1998. The lecture has been published in *A Singular Modernity* 42-55.

16. See also Gagnier's exceptionally insightful account of Kant's ethical aesthetics in *The Insatiability of Human Wants* 124-25.

17. See *Critique of Judgment,* First Book, Analytic of the Beautiful, Part VI. "The beautiful is that which, apart from concepts, is represented as the Object of a Universal delight" 292.

18. I follow and am deeply indebted here to the illuminating discussion of Smith, Shaftesbury, Hume, Burke and the Kantian imaginary in Eagleton, *Ideology* 31-66. Also on Kant's aesthetic, see Jameson, *A Singular Modernity* 175-76. And see Robert Kaufman's wonderfully suggestive idea that Kant "began and executed much of his critical project—the *Third Critique* most obviously" from the impasses into which intellectual rigor had led him and was fully aware that these impasses "corresponded to the structure of the real." In "Red Kant" 688-89.

19. Jameson discusses "cognitive mapping" in several places, most notably in "Cognitive Mapping." See also the concluding chapter of his *Postmodernism* 409-13. Jameson's proposition there is that the stages of capitalism, from its classical market form to that of monopoly capitalism in the stage of imperialism to the moment of late capitalism and the multinational network "generate a type of space unique to it." The conceptual spaces that Jameson refers to are not literal terrains but "are all the result of discontinuous expansion of quantum leaps in the enlargement of capital,"

especially in its "penetration and colonization of hitherto uncommodified areas" (410).

## Works Cited

Adorno, Theodor. *Minima Moralia: Reflections from Damaged Life.* Trans. E. F. N. Jephcott. London: New Left Books, 1974.

Appadurai, Arjun. *Modernity at Large: Cultural Dimensions of Globalization.* Minneapolis: University of Minnesota Press, 1996.

Arnold, Matthew. *The Poems of Matthew Arnold.* Ed. Kenneth Allott. London: Longmans, 1965.

Castañeda Shular, Antonia, Tomás Ybarra Frausto, and Joseph Sommers, comps. *Literatura chicana: Texto y contexto/ Chicano Literature: Text and Context.* Englewood Cliffs, NJ: Prentice-Hall, 1972.

Crehan, Kate. *Gramsci, Culture, and Anthropology.* Berkeley: University of California Press, 2002.

DeLaura, David J. *Hebrew and Hellene in Victorian England: Newman, Arnold, and Pater.* Austin: University of Texas Press, 1969.

Eagleton, Terry. *The Ideology of the Aesthetic.* Oxford: Blackwell, 1990.

Gagnier, Regenia. "A Critique of Practical Aesthetics." *Aesthetics and Ideology.* Ed. George Levine. New Brunswick, NJ: Rutgers University Press, 1994. 264-82.

———. *The Insatiability of Human Wants: Economics and Aesthetics in Market Society.* Chicago: University of Chicago Press, 2000.

García Canclini, Néstor. *Consumers and Citizens: Globalization and Multicultural Conflicts.* Trans. George Yúdice. Minneapolis: University of Minnesota Press, 2001.

———. *Transforming Modernity: Popular Culture in Mexico.* Trans. Lidia Lozano. Austin: University of Texas Press, 1993.

García Lorca, Federico. *Collected Poems: Bilingual Edition.* Trans. Catherine Brown et al. Ed. Christopher Maurer. New York: Farrar, Straus and Giroux, 2002.

Herrera-Sobek, María. *The Mexican Corrido: A Feminist Analysis.* Bloomington: Indiana University Press, 1990.

Hobsbawm, Eric, and Terence Ranger, eds. *The Invention of Tradition.* Cambridge: Cambridge University Press, 1983.

Jameson, Fredric. "Cognitive Mapping." *Marxism and the Interpretation of Culture.* Ed. Cary Nelson and Lawrence Grossberg. Urbana: University of Illinois Press, 1988. 347-57.

———. *Postmodernism; Or, the Cultural Logic of Late Capitalism.* Durham, NC: Duke University Press, 1991.

———. *A Singular Modernity: Essay on the Ontology of the Present.* London: Verso, 2002.

Kant, Immanuel, and Carl J. Friedrich. *Critique of Judgment.* 1790. *The Philosophy of Kant's Moral and Political Writings.* New York: Modern Library, 1993.

Kaufman, Robert. "Red Kant; Or, the Persistence of the Third Critique in Adorno and Jameson." *Critical Inquiry* 26 (2000): 682-724.

Kuri-Aldana, Mario, and Vicente Mendoza Martínez. *Cancionero popular mexicano.* 2 vols. Mexico City: Consejo Nacional para la Cultura y las Artes, 2001.

Kymlicka, Will. *Politics in the Vernacular: Nationalism, Multiculturalism, and Citizenship.* Oxford: Oxford University Press, 2001.

Limón, José E. *Mexican Ballads, Chicano Poems: History and Influence in Mexican-American Social Poetry.* Berkeley: University of California Press, 1992.

Livingston, Robert Eric. "Global Knowledges: Agency and Place in Literary Studies." PMLA 116.1 (2001): 145-72.

McCarthy, Cormac. *All the Pretty Horses.* New York: Knopf, 1992.

———. *Cities of the Plain.* New York: Knopf, 1998.

———. *The Crossing.* New York: Knopf, 1994.

Mendoza, Lydia. *Lydia Mendoza: A Family Autobiography.* Eds. Chris Strachwitz and James Nicolopulos. Houston: Arte Público Press, 1993.

Moya, Paula, and Ramón Saldívar, eds. "Fictions of the Trans-American Imaginary." Spec. issue of *Modern Fiction Studies* 49.1 (2003).

Paredes, Américo. *Between Two Worlds.* Houston: Arte Público Press, 1991.

———. "Estados Unidos, México y el machismo," *Journal of Inter-American Studies* 9 (1967): 65-84.

———. *George Washington Gómez: A Mexicotexan Novel.* Houston: Arte Público Press, 1990.

———. "The Hammon and the Beans." *Texas Observer,* April 18, 1963.

———. "The Mexican Corrido: Its Rise and Fall." 1958. *Folklore and Culture on the Texas-Mexican Border.* Ed. Richard Bauman. Austin: Center for Mexican American Studies, University of Texas at Austin, 1993. 129-41.

———. *The Shadow.* Houston: Arte Público Press, 1998.

———. "Some Aspects of Folk Poetry." 1964. *Folklore and Culture on the Texas-Mexican Border.* Ed. Richard Bauman. Austin: Center for Mexican American Studies, University of Texas at Austin, 1993. 113-28.

———. *A Texas-Mexican Cancionero: Folksongs of the Lower Border.* Urbana: University of Illinois Press, 1976.

———. "The United States, Mexico, and *Machismo.*" 1971. Trans. Marcy Steen. *Folklore and Culture on the Texas-Mexican Border.* Ed. Richard Bauman. Austin: Center for Mexican American Studies, University of Texas at Austin, 1993. 215-34.

Paredes Manzano, Américo. *Cantos de adolescencia.* San Antonio: Librería Española, 1937.

Rosaldo, Renato. *Culture and Truth: The Remaking of Social Analysis.* Boston: Beacon, 1989.

Saldívar, José David. *Border Matters: Remapping American Cultural Studies.* Berkeley: University of California Press, 1997.

Saldívar, Ramón. *Chicano Narrative: The Dialectics of Difference.* Madison: University of Wisconsin Press, 1990.

Sommer, Doris. *Bilingual Aesthetics: A New Sentimental Education.* Durham, NC: Duke University Press, 2004.

Stevens, Wallace. *Collected Poems.* New York: Knopf, 1954.

Tuñón, Julia. "Emilio Fernández: A Look behind the Bars." Trans. Ana Lopez. *Mexican Cinema.* Ed. Paulo Antonio Paranagua. London: British Film Institute, 1995. 179-92.

Wordsworth, William, et al. *The Prelude 1799, 1805, 1950: Authoritative Texts, Contexts, and Reception, Recent Critical Essays.* New York: Norton, 1979.

# FURTHER READING

## Biography

Peña, Manuel Richard Bauman. "Américo Paredes." *Journal of American Folklore* 113, no. 448 (spring 2000): 195-98.

Overview of Paredes's life and career as writer, performer, political activist, folklorist, and teacher.

## Criticism

McDowell, John H. "Chante Luna and the Commemoration of Actual Events." *Western Folklore* 64, nos. 1/2 (winter/spring 2005): 39-64.

Explores the relationship between folklore and historical events, particularly Paredes's treatment of the legend of José Mosqueda, an important figure in Texas-Mexican border culture.

Saldívar, Ramón. "The Borderlands of Culture: Américo Paredes's *George Washington Gómez* and Chicano Literature at the End of the Twentieth Century." *American Literary History* 5, no. 2 (summer 1993): 272-93.

Discusses Paredes's work on Chicano cultural studies, praising him for having "established the very ground for 'border writing'" in America.

———. "Américo Paredes." In *Updating the Literary West*, pp. 633-37. Fort Worth: Texas Christian University Press, 1997.

Brief analysis of Paredes's literary publications of the 1990s, including the 1991 poetry collection *Between Two Worlds*.

**Additional coverage of Paredes's life and career is contained in the following sources published by Gale:** *Contemporary Authors,* **Vols. 37-40R;** *Contemporary Authors—Obituary,* **Vol. 179;** *Dictionary of Literary Biography,* **Vol. 209;** *Exploring Poetry*; *Hispanic Writers,* **Ed. 1; and** *Literature Resource Center.*

# The Song of Roland

(*La Chanson de Roland*) French poem, c. 1170.

## INTRODUCTION

A popular medieval narrative and possibly the earliest extant *chanson de geste,* the *Chanson de Roland,* or *Song of Roland,* is a representation of the battle of Roncevaux in 778, in which a large part of Charlemagne's forces were ambushed and slaughtered. According to some accounts, the poem was written by an anonymous author (or authors) in the early part of the 12th century, with c. 1170 the date most often used by critics.

*The Song of Roland* consists of almost 4,000 lines divided into approximately 300 strophes, or *laisses,* of different lengths—from as few as five lines to more than thirty. The unifying factor of the individual laisses is assonance, which varies from one laisse to another. Many of the laisses are followed by the letters AOI, which according to some scholars may have been a battle cry or exhortation, although this is not certain. The text is also characterized by shifts in tense—a feature that has sometimes fueled the debate over whether the epic was composed by a single author or by a number of authors over a long period of time.

## TEXTUAL HISTORY

The story of Roland's exploits in a battle fought in 778 became a popular narrative passed down orally through several generations and preserved in written form by an anonymous author or authors as the *Chanson de Roland.* Although the original has not survived, the text has been preserved in several different languages in later versions that were not exact translations of the French—for example, the German *Rolandslied* (Konrad, late 12th c.), taken from a Latin text, or the Middle English *Song of Rouland* (anon., late 14th-early 15th c.). Other manuscript versions include the Chateauroux, Venice VII, Paris, and the oldest, the Oxford. The Oxford *Song of Roland* has long been considered the definitive text, taken from the "Digby 23" manuscript, donated by Sir Kenelm Digby sometime in the seventeenth century, and first published by Francisque Michel in 1837.

## PLOT AND MAJOR CHARACTERS

Charlemagne, King of the Franks and Holy Roman Emperor, embarked on his first campaign into Spain at the age of thirty-six, accompanied by approximately 5,000 of his men, in the spring of 778. On the army's return to France, traveling through the Pyrenees, the rear guard, led by Charlemagne's nephew Roland, was ambushed by the Saracens of Saragossa at Roncevaux. As many as 1,000 of Charlemagne's men were killed in the attack, including Roland.

The principal characters of *The Song of Roland,* in addition to Charlemagne and Roland, are Roland's friend Oliver, Roland's stepfather, Ganelon, and the Saracen King Marsile, who offers a treaty to Charlemagne and promises to convert to Christianity if the Franks will end the siege of Saragossa and leave Spain. Roland nominates Ganelon to serve as emissary to Saragossa. Ganelon, fully aware of how dangerous such a mission will be, becomes enraged and vows revenge against his stepson. Betraying his countrymen because of a personal dispute with Roland, Ganelon delivers the rear guard into an ambush. Oliver begs Roland to summon help from Charlemagne when it becomes clear that they are outnumbered five to one, but Roland refuses. When the situation is completely hopeless, he at last sounds the alarm and Charlemagne and his army turn back to help them, but it is too late to save the brave knights of the rear guard. Roland, wounded by the final blast of the *oliphant,* or horn, advances to the front of the battlefield so that Charlemagne can see that he died bravely. Charlemagne's main force defeats Marsile's army and then defeats the pagan Baligant. The last part of *The Song of Roland* concerns the trial of Ganelon, who defends himself by claiming that his actions amounted to personal revenge rather than treason. Although his defense garners some support among the Frankish nobility, he is ultimately found guilty and drawn and quartered. As the poem ends, Charlemagne, still in mourning for the loss of his knights, is summoned to another crusade.

## MAJOR THEMES

On the most basic level, the principal themes of *The Song of Roland* are good versus evil, honor, courage in battle, and loyalty to one's ruler. The idea of keeping one's promises under any circumstances, or what Robert Francis Cook calls "responsible commitment," also plays a major role in the epic. When Roland assures Charlemagne that he may "cross the pass in total safety" and that he "need fear no man while I am alive," Roland is committing to that promise regardless of the overwhelming number of Saracens he encounters or the complications caused by Ganelon's betrayal. Gerard J. Brault (see Further Reading) lists good versus evil, betrayal, conversion, and victory as the most prominent themes in the epic, and he adds that these themes "provide important links between [the work's] various parts."

Robert A. Eisner, in his discussion of theme, shifts the focus from Roland to Charlemagne, contending that the Frankish king is inconsistently represented—at times he is authoritarian and at other times completely impotent. As Eisner sees it, the poem's "tragic theme is reflected in the way in which Charles, the representative of the old order, constantly weeps and sighs. As his lamentations become the keynote of the poem, his visions illustrate his inability to check the evolution of the new society."

Thematic elements vary among the different versions of the *Song*. The German *Rolandslied,* for example, transforms a narrative of nationalism and patriotism into a religious epic "dominated by Crusade ideology," according to J. W. Thomas. Brewster E. Fitz, however, sees strong religious elements even within the Oxford *Chanson de Roland.* He contends that the text "projects a new order of Christianity, which stands in relation to the pre-crusading order as the New Testament era to the Old Testament era." For Fitz, the narrative's "*telos* is to judge, convict, slay or convert all forms of the Other, whether within or without."

## CRITICAL RECEPTION

Scholarly debate on *The Song of Roland* commonly involves the actual date of the poem, its origins, the historical accuracy of the events it supposedly represents, and the authenticity of the various versions. One of the most persistent critical controversies involves the question of unity. There is disagreement as to whether the narrative was the work of a single poet or a composite of several versions of the story evolving over many years, even centuries. Jessie Crosland explains that the latter theory had long been accepted—based on the notion that songs about the battle were composed shortly after the event and were "repeated and amplified from generation to generation" over the course of three centuries. According to Crosland, this theory was discredited early in the twentieth century in favor of one put forth by Joseph Bédier, who argued that such "an agglomeration of episodes composed at diverse times by diverse people and merely welded together" was an impossibility. But scholars have long wondered why the epic does not end with the death of its eponymous hero, but instead continues for another 115 laisses. Guy R. Mermier (see Further Reading) addresses that issue, insisting that there is no gap between

the two parts of the poem, but rather that the action forms a continuum which "justifies the sublime aesthetic unity of *The Song of Roland.*" Brault acknowledges the complexity of the epic, but reports that if there is one point of agreement among critics, it is that it "is a well-structured poem."

Critics have also debated the nature of the characterization of Roland, as well as of Charlemagne, and some have concluded that one or both of them bears responsibility, in varying degrees, for the massacre of so many brave knights. Cook reports that some critics feel that Roland's "pathological concern for his reputation" and his "pathetic sense of his own superiority" led him "to scorn obviously reasonable advice, and to bring on a disaster that he could have prevented by the proper exercise of his leadership." Cook, however, disagrees, contending that for contemporary audiences the idea of promises and the accomplishment of those promises would be of paramount importance. "Personal pride," claims Cook, "—even if Roland did exhibit such pride—would be irrelevant to the theme of responsibility and sacrifice in a context of promises and ensuing, related acts." Cook, therefore, finds Roland's actions "exemplary." Susan E. Farrier (see Further Reading), however, notes that different versions of the text arrive at different conclusions regarding the character of Roland and/or Charlemagne, and that the Oxford version "has often been perceived as morally ambiguous" in that regard. According to Farrier, both Konrad's *Rolandslied* and the anonymous *Song of Rouland* take firmer stances regarding the culpability of both Charlemagne and Roland in the massacre of the troops; the former finds them both innocent and the latter finds them both guilty.

The historical accuracy of *The Song of Roland* also continues to be debated among scholars. Some contend that the invasion of Spain up until the battle at Roncevaux was successful, with the Franks capturing every pagan city except Saragossa. W. S. Merwin (see Further Reading) disagrees, asserting that "even the royal chroniclers would have difficulty in trying to describe [Charlemagne's] ambitious summer campaign in Spain as though it had been a success." C. H. Sisson concurs, insisting that "contrary to what the *Chanson* tells us— the expedition was not a success." Moreover, reports Sisson, the rear guard was ambushed by Basques, not by Saracens, as the epic claims.

Several critics believe that *The Song of Roland* represents a transition between two cultures, two versions of Christianity, and/or two notions of literacy. In addition to Eisner's study of Charlemagne as a representative of the old, authoritative order unable to embrace, or even understand, the changes taking place in his society, there is also Fitz's suggestion that the text ushers in a new religious order based on crusade ideology and committed to eliminating all non-Christians. Additionally, Eugene Vance (see Further Reading) contends that the work is "an epic which is quite obviously both a preeminent vestige of an oral tradition . . . and a precious written monument inaugurating nothing less than a new order of vernacular literacy in France. The *Chanson de Roland* may be considered, therefore, as a threshold to a culture of the text which in some deep way is very much our own today." Andrew Taylor makes a case for *The Song of Roland*'s importance much later in history, tracing what he calls the epic's "editorial construction" in nineteenth-century France as part of a "quest for national origins." According to Taylor, "*Roland* soon became a symbol of the very spirit of France." He concludes: "Given the pressing need of postrevolutionary France for a national epic, had the *Chanson de Roland* not existed, it would have been necessary to invent it."

# PRINCIPAL WORKS

*La Chanson de Roland* [*The Song of Roland*] c. 1170

## Principal English Translations

*The Song of Roland* (translated by Dorothy L. Sayers) 1957
*The Song of Roland* (translated by Robert Harrison) 1970
*The Song of Roland* (translated by Gerard J. Brault) 1978
*The Song of Roland* (translated by Frederick Goldin) 1978
*The Song of Roland* (translated by D. D. R. Owen) 1981
*The Song of Roland* (translated by Glyn Burgess) 1990
*The Song of Roland* (translated by Patricia Terry) 1998
*The Song of Roland* (translated by W. S. Merwin) 2001

# CRITICISM

## Jessie Crosland (essay date 1967)

SOURCE: Crosland, Jessie. Introduction to *The Song of Roland,* translated by Jessie Crosland, pp. ix-xxiii. New York: Cooper Square, 1967.

[*In the following introduction, Crosland discusses some of the critical controversies surrounding* The Song of Roland—*for example, its date of composition and the question of whether it was originally a unified poem or a composite of a number of songs modified over the course of several generations.*]

The *Chanson de Roland* has received much attention from scholars of late years, and the difficult question of its origin and date has been discussed from every possible point of view. Recent investigators have succeeded in throwing a flood of light on the genesis of the famous Old French epic and in drawing closer the limits between which the date of its birth may be supposed to fall.

### RELATIONS OF *THE SONG OF ROLAND* TO HISTORY.

The bare framework of the *Chanson de Roland* rests upon a historical event which took place 300 years before the poem itself was composed. In 778 Charlemagne was returning from Spain after a successful campaign. His rear-guard, which was separated from the main army, was attacked in the passes of the Pyrenees and every man in it was killed. Amongst the number was a personage of high rank named Roland. Einhard, in his *Vita Caroli,* ch. IX, relates the fact as follows:—"In quo prœlio Eggihardus, regiæ mensæ præpositus, Anshelmus, comes palatii, et *Hruodlandus, Brittannici Limitis Præfectus,* cum aliis conpluribus interficiuntar."[1] It was this Roland who became the symbol of French knighthood in after years and whose exploits, according to the chronicler Wace, were celebrated by Taillefer in 1066 at the battle of Senlac:

> Taillefer, qui moult bien chantout
> Sor un cheval qui tost alout
> Devant le duc alout chantant
> De Karlemaigne e de Rolant
> E d'Oliver e des vassals
> Qui morurent en Rencesvals.[2]

### COMPOSITION AND DATE OF *THE SONG OF ROLAND.*

Until quite recent years the view generally accepted concerning the origin of the *Chanson de Roland,* was that the defeat and death of those who formed the rear-guard of Charles's army in 778 moved their contemporaries so profoundly that songs, either lyric or lyrico-epic in character, were composed immediately after the event and sung about them, and most of all about Roland, who soon became a popular hero. These songs, repeated and amplified from generation to generation, grew by degrees to epic dimensions, until, after 300 years, they appear in the form which we now know as the *Chanson de Roland.* This theory of the composite nature of the poem has been discredited of late years, largely owing to the investigations and critical insight of M. Joseph Bédier, whose book on the "Epic Legends" was epoch-making in the history of this subject.[3] M.

Bédier shows the fallacies contained in the theory of the growth of the epic by slow degrees from an original short poem, or poems, composed by contemporaries or eye-witnesses of the event. He insists on the obvious unity of the poem, and the impossibility of such a work consisting of an agglomeration of episodes composed at diverse times by diverse people and merely welded together rather skilfully by a *jongleur* of the 11th century. M. Bédier connects the **Chanson de Roland** very closely with the French expeditions against the Saracens in Spain which took place at the end of the 11th and the beginning of the 12th centuries. The French knights would follow the very route which Charlemagne had followed 300 years before and would in all probability halt at the same stages—at Bordeaux, at Dax, at Blaye and at Roncevaux—where the monks and the *jongleurs* joined forces in seeking to entertain the travellers by means of their relics and their songs. Some poet of genius among the *jongleurs* chanced perhaps upon that very page of Einhard's chronicle containing the short account of the battle and the death of Roland, and round this theme, with the local colouring to guide him and the warlike spirit of the Crusades to inspire him, he wove the whole soul-stirring legend that we speak of now as the **Song of Roland.**

As regards the actual date of the poem, M. Bédier, in his recent edition of the manuscript of Oxford (the earliest complete manuscript that we possess), supports those critics who place the composition of the poem "vers l'an 1110," rather than thirty or forty years earlier as former scholars had done. A more recent writer still, M. Boissonade, would retard the date another decade and place the **Chanson** in the neighbourhood of the year 1120, the year in which the crusades in northern Spain reached their culminating point. M. Boissonade attaches even more importance than his predecessor to the expeditions into Spain, and points out the extraordinary accuracy of the author with regard to the geography of Northern Spain at that period. If, as both M. Bédier and M. Boissonade conjecture, the Turoldus who signs his name at the end of the Oxford manuscript ("Ci falt la geste que Turoldus declinet") was the author of the poem, we may assume that this Norman "clerc-jongleur" (for such his language and style would indicate him to be) had either taken part in one of the expeditions himself, or had received detailed information from someone well acquainted with that region.

THE POEM OUTSIDE FRANCE.

The sentiments which animate the **Song of Roland,** namely the struggle for the propagation of Christianity and the love of France, which is hardly distinguishable from the veneration due to Charlemagne, give the poem both a European and a national character. Its religious character was certain to make it acceptable to the other nations; in Germany, for instance, Roland, under Pfaffe

Chuonrat's pen, was converted into the Christian hero who burns with one love, namely, the love of God, and whose one desire is to die a martyr's death:

> The noble Roland spoke: he raised his hand. Did I not know that it would distress thee, dear companion, I would swear by an oath that I will not sound my horn; to-day is the last day of the heathen, however great be their number; I tell thee in truth, they are judged before God; thus the martyrs of the Lord will be purified by blood; willingly would I submit to become a martyr, if God grant that I be worthy to obtain this name. Happy is he whom God has chosen to die in His service, for He gives him the kingdom of heaven. I will not sound my horn for these vile heathen; they would think that we were afraid, or that we had need of succour to resist them; they are the worst nation in the world, and I will give their flesh for a prey to the ravens, and their joy shall not be of long duration. God will show His marvels here, and good Durandal will give proof of great valour.[4]

Similarly, it was in order to impress upon his subjects' minds the grandeur and the heroism of Christianity that the king of Norway, Haakon Haakonson (1217-1263), incorporated the song of Roncevaux into the *Karlamagnus Saga.*[5]

In Italy there was another cause which tended to ensure the popularity of this poem, viz., the prestige attaching to the French language and the facility with which it was understood in that country. Two manuscripts written in Italy, now at Venice, contain versions of the greatest value for the reconstruction of the critical text. Moreover, the Song is one of the sources of the *Spagna* and of the *Rotta di Roncisvalle,* a *remaniement* of the *Spagna in rima,* which was composed between 1350 and 1380. It is also one of the sources of Pulci's *Morgante,* and we find Roland again in the works of the great epic poets: in the *Orlando innamorato* of Bojardo (1486); in the *Orlando furioso* of Ariosto (1516); and in the *Orlando innamorato* of Berni.

In Spain Roland's heroism in the cause of fair France was naturally felt to be rather galling. It was thought necessary to provide him with an auxiliary, and the Spaniards created Bernard del Carpio,[6] Charlemagne's nephew, an illegitimate son of his sister and a Spanish count whom she had met on a pilgrimage to Saint-Jacques. Then the legend of Bernard del Carpio underwent a transformation. His mother became the sister of Alphonso the Chaste. Alphonso, threatened by the Saracens, called Charlemagne to his aid, but his Spanish subjects revolted at the mere idea of being helped by the French, and Alphonso was forced to tell Charles that he could do without him. The King of France, indignant, declared war against the Spaniards, and they, rather than yield to the hated Frenchmen, solicited the alliance of Marsile and the heathens. The alliance was concluded by Bernard del Carpio. Then the

French, overwhelmed by two armies, or rather two races, were defeated, and Roland was killed. Bernard del Carpio was afterwards reconciled with Charlemagne, who made him King of Italy.

The **Chanson de Roland** penetrated into England through the medium of Anglo-Norman. The Oxford MS., 1624 (Digby 23) dates from the 12th century, and the Cambridge MS. (Library of Trinity College, R. 3. 32) was written in the fifteenth. It was translated into English, but unfortunately only a fragment of the English adaptation has been preserved. This fragment, which was written in a South-west Midland dialect, probably at the end of the fourteenth century, is to be found in the Lansdowne MS. 388. This version differed considerably from that contained in the Oxford MS., as may be seen from the following analysis. The beginning of the fragment[7] corresponds to *laisse* LV. of the French poem, where Ganelon brings Charles the message of the Sultan, "declaring that Marsile will himself repair to France within sixteen days, there to do homage to Charles and to embrace Christianity:

> Within xvj days thedur he will hym hye,
> and all the hethyn statis in his company,
> a thoussond of his lond of the best;
> all will be cristenyd & leve on Jhesu Crist.
> ther law will they lef sone anon,
> And at thy comandment þey will done.
> of Saragos the cete he sent þe key
> And all thes faire ladys with the to pley:
> echon of them is a lordis doughtur.
> And her ys good wyn; drink þer-of after.
> and thou wisly wirche, thou failid nought,
> there is no prow to pryk þer men pece sought!
> If that mercy and myght mellithe togedur
> he shall have the mor grace ever aftur.

> (21-34)

Charles is delighted, and gives orders for an immediate return home. The army starts, and after marching ten miles encamps for the night. In the night Charles has two dreams, warning him of treachery, which disturb him greatly. The next morning he holds a council, and reminding his knights of the dangers of Roncevaux, desires them to arrange who shall take command of the rear-guard, the post of danger. Ganelon proposes that that duty shall be assigned to Roland, and much against the king's wish, Roland declares his willingness to accept the post. The other *douzeperes* declare they too will go with Roland. Leaving them behind with 20,000 men, Charles and the rest of the army start for France, Ganelon commanding the van-guard. The Saracens prepare to attack Roland. He sees them and warns his fellows. Sir Gauter is sent forward with 10,000 men to reconnoitre, but is surprised and every one of his men slain. He warns Roland of treachery. Meanwhile Charles is alarmed at the delay of his rear-guard, but is reassured by Ganelon, and goes on to Cardoile. The Sa-

racens appear, and Oliver presses Roland to blow his horn for help, but he refuses:

> Ye knyghtis, for shame shon ye never.
> have ye broken eny bone or any harm tid?
> may ye schew in your sheld any strokis wid?
> is not your compony hole as they come?
> Flee fast þat is afferd, þat he wer at home:
> I will fight with them that us hathe sought.
> And or I se my brest blod throughe my harnes ryn
> blow never horn for no help then.

> (560-567)

At daybreak Turpin celebrates Mass, after which the fight begins. Roland, Oliver, and the others perform prodigies of valour."[8] By sunset there is not a single Saracen left. On the following day they come more numerous than ever. A new fight begins.

> Sithe God spek with mouthe on the mountaigne,
> And taught Moyses his men to preche,
> In so litill whille was never mo marrid, I you teche,
> As wer drof to dethe at the dais end,
> not in the battaille of Troy, who so will trouthe find.
> But while our folk fought togedur,
> ther fell in Fraunce a straunge wedur,
> A great derk mist in the myd-day-tym,
> Thik, and clowdy, and evyll wedur thene,
> And thikness of sterris and thonder light.

> (840-849)

The Saracens again attack the French; Ingler, Bradmond, Sampson, Dalabern of Valern, the King of Africa, Cadwen, and many others are slain.

> Then was the Soudan woo in his hert,
> That so many of his men were slayn hym about.

The Saracens attack Roland, who "drof hem into a daile." Others come:

> When Roulond se hem, he grevyd sor.
> He had but few men, allas þerfor!
> The lest part of men þer had he,
> And þey wer woundid, it is mor pete.
> He praid hem rest, and hove þer stille:
> 'Herkenyt now, rist here unto they cum us till,
> Yonder is a gret host and a compony
> As ever cristyne man se with his eye;
> And we ar but few, and hathe fought long,
> Our horse wery, and we not strong.
> I red we send a man to feche our lord;
> Say we be sore hurt, and socour we wold.
> But if he cum and help us anon
> our lyves be lost, and the lond gone.'
> then answerd Olyver with a rufful stevyn,
> Angry in hert thus gan he nevyn:
> 'Broder, let be all siche sawes!'

> (1033-1049)

Here the fragment ends, and it is impossible to trace with any certainty the relation which it bears to the different versions of the **Song of Roland** which have been handed down to us.

Works dealing with *The Song of Roland*.

It would be vain to attempt to enumerate the works which have appeared in France on the **Chanson de Roland** during the last century, so numerous are they, whether in book-form, or in the nature of articles in the learned periodicals. A bibliography of the earlier ones will be found in Léon Gautier, *Les Epopêes Françaises, Bibliographie des Chansons de Geste* (1897), pp. 170-198, and for more recent ones it must suffice to call attention again to the masterly analysis and appreciation to be found in Vol. III of Bédier, *Les Lêgendes Epiques,* and to the short *Introduction* to the same author's edition of the Oxford manuscript. In England the Oxford manuscript was first brought to notice by I. Tyrrwhitt in his edition of the *Canterbury* Tales, London, 1775. In a note to l. 13, 741 (Vol. IV, p. 318) we read: "This romance (**Chanson de Roland**), which in the manuscript has no title, may possibly be an older copy of one which is frequently mentioned by Du Cange under the title of *Le Roman de Roncevaux.*" In the *Gentleman's Magazine* of August, 1817, J. Conybeare announced his intention of publishing a work entitled *Illustrations of the Early History of English and French Poetry,* and he went on to say: "Among the notices on early French poetry will be found an account of a poem on the well-known subject of the Rout of Roncesvalles, which, from various circumstances of internal evidence, I am led to regard as the earliest specimen in this line at present known to exist among the manuscript treasures of our libraries" (p. 103, col. 2). T. Wright gave a few extracts of the English fragment in Michel's edition, *La Chanson de Roland ou de Roncevaux, publiêe pour la première fois d'après le manuscrit de la Bibliothèque à Oxford,* Paris, 1837. It was published for the first time in its entirety, and carefully studied by Sidney J. Herrtage in Part II of the English Charlemagne Romances, quoted above. It has been translated several times both in England and America, the most notable translation of recent years being that of C. K. Scott Moncrieff (1919), in which the author attempts to reproduce the metre of the original. Finally, critical appreciations of the Song by the late Professor W. P. Ker will be found in his books, *Epic and Romance* (Macmillan, 1897), and *The Dark Ages* (Blackwood, 1904), in a few pages which will be read with pleasure by every student.

## Notes

1. *cf.* Eginhard, Vie de Charlemagne. Ed. by Halphen, Paris, Champion, 1923.

2. As regards Taillefer see *Carmen de Hastingæ prælio,* II.931-44, by Gui de Ponthieu, Bishop of Amiens (d. 1074), edited by Francisque Michel, *Chroniques anglo-normandes,* I., 38; Henry of Huntingdon, *Historia Anglorum,* lib. viii.; Geoffroi Gaimar, *L'Estorie des Angles*; Benoit, *Chron. des ducs de Normandie,* II., 37497-37507. Wil-

liam of Malmesbury does not mention Taillefer's name, but says: "Tunc cantilena Rollandi inchoata ut martium viri exemplum pugnaturos accenderet . . . prœlium consertum est."

3. *Les Légendes Epiques,* Recherches sur la formation des Chansons de geste, par Joseph Bédier, Paris, Champion, 1912.

4. For this and also for the *Stricker* and *Karl Meinet, cf.* Gaston Paris, *Histoire poétique de Charlemagne,* pp. 120-3. For Karl Meinet, *cf.* also Bartsch, *Ueber Karl Meinet. Ein Beitrag zur Karlsage.* Nürnberg, 1861.

5. This has been translated into Swedish and Danish.

6. The story of Bernard del Carpio will be found in the *Chronicon,* by Lucas de Tuy (d. 1250); in *De rebus Hispaniæ,* by Roderic of Toledo (d. 1247); and in the *Crônica general* of Alphonse X. (second half of the thirteenth century.)

7. See Early English Text Society, Extra Series, XXXV., Part II., and Schleich, *Prolegomena ad Carmen de Rolando anglico.* Berolini, 1879 (*cf. Romania,* 1879, p. 479).

8. E.E.T.S. [Early English Text Society], p. xxxvi.

## Robert A. Eisner (essay date autumn 1972)

SOURCE: Eisner, Robert A. "In Search of the Real Theme of *The Song of Roland." Romance Notes* 14, no. 1 (autumn 1972): 179-83.

[*In the following essay, Eisner suggests that the main theme of* The Song of Roland *is hinted at in its inconsistent representation of Charlemagne, which serves as an indication that the old order is giving way to a new, less authoritarian society.*]

The central contention of this essay is that traditional preoccupation with the origin and unity of the **Song of Roland** has obscured the main theme of the poem.[1] The key problem to be considered is the apparent inconsistency in the portrait of Charlemagne: why is he represented as both strong and weak, authoritarian and impotent?

In the first council, which Charles calls to decide what answer should be given to Marsilion's offer of peace, he is decidedly peremptory. Shortly thereafter Roland and Oliver argue about which one of them should go as ambassador to Marsilion; the king tells them in no uncertain terms that neither they nor any others of the twelve peers will go on the mission. Nevertheless, despite his evident power, Charles demands that the council assume the responsibility of choosing an ambassador. When Roland nominates his father-in-law, Ganelon, Charles does not demur. Either he is content with the choice or he is unwilling or unable to alter it.

In the second council, called to decide who will lead the rear-guard as the Franks march out of Spain, Charles again asks, or rather demands, advice. When Ganelon returns the favor by nominating Roland, Charles' sudden outburst of fury seems incomprehensible, especially in the light of his refusal (or inability) to do anything about the choice. Charles' role is admittedly a delicate one: he cannot be blind or impotent, but neither can he be too imperious. A word from him would put an end to Ganelon's machinations. Nevertheless, this powerlessness clashes with features attributed to Charles at other points in the poem. For example, during his struggle with Baligant all the forces of Christianity seem to be epitomized in him.

Erich Auerbach is troubled by the ambivalent portrait of the emperor. He characterizes Charles as "sonambulistically paralyzed"[2] and goes on to develop this disparity: "The important and symbolistic position—almost that of a Prince of God—in which he appears as the head of all Christendom and as the paragon of knightly perfection, is in strange contrast to his impotence."[3]

The ambivalence in the portrait of Charles is, then, a real problem. The historical Charles was, according to historians, an exceptionally strong ruler. He had complete command; he held assemblies and consulted his barons, but the initiative and the decisions were his alone. It should be evident that the historical Charles is equal to only one dimension of the poetic Charles: the omnipotent, hieratic emperor of the latter part of the poem.

We know that every male over the age of twelve had to swear fealty to Charles.[4] Because of the religious nature of the society, the oath was considered indissoluble. Subsequent to his coronation as emperor, Charles commanded that every man in his kingdom pledge to him the fidelity which he had previously promised to him as king; and all those who had not yet taken any oath should do likewise, down to those who were twelve years old.[5] This second oath, though more specific than the first, nevertheless does not imply a strict bond of obedience to Charles, as a vassal would swear to his lord, but rather only loyalty, and that in mostly negative terms; that is, the subject swears not to interfere with Charles' government.[6] It is thus not to be considered adequate for someone directly in the king's service, who must promise to serve with aid and counsel. This will be an interesting point to consider when we approach the problem of Ganelon's alleged treason, within the context of his relationship to Charles.

Now let us see what aspects of the eleventh century may be detected in the political and social climate of the poem. This will allow us to determine what elements found in the poem are contemporary with the world of the poet. To bridge the gap between the eighth and the eleventh centuries, we should point out that Charles established a strong central government, but himself contributed to its inevitable downfall after him by allowing the aristocracy to distribute benefices to the people, as he did to the aristocracy. Thus, each lord became the protector of a small group of people, all ostensibly faithful to the king. In reality, the nobles' growing authority was confirmed by Charles' order that the men enlist in the army under the command of their lords. Charles hence ensured the future rise of feudalism.[7]

Feudalism was fine in principle, but in practice it usually meant anarchy. Of the reign of Philip I (1060-1108), almost certainly the time during which the *Song of Roland* took its final poetic form, it has been said that "the greater, of the king's alleged vassals never came near his court, whether to perform homage or to render any other service. France, obviously, had ceased to be a state in any proper sense of the word. Rather, it had been split into a number of states whose rulers, no matter how they styled themselves, enjoyed the substance of the regal power."[8] Here it is evident that we have a description of the world of the later feudal epics, such as *Raoul de Cambrai, Girart de Roussillon,* and *Renaut de Montauban.* However, the forces that later produce the revolted barons are already at work in the *Song of Roland.* The rise of individuality can be seen here, especially in the person of Ganelon, and the latter's trial illustrates the revolt of a powerful family of barons who do not feel themselves subject to the emperor's will. As Marc Bloch defines the sort of absolutism with strings that prevailed in the eleventh century, it sounds very much like the situation that obtains during the two councils and later in Ganelon's trial: "Selon le code de bon gouvernement alors universellement admis, aucun chef, quel qu'il fût, ne pouvait rien décider de grave sans avoir pris conseil."[9]

Our study of the ambivalence in the portrait of Charles has thus led us to the conclusion that there are elements in the poem that unmistakably reflect the eighth century, as well as others that can only be a reflection of the time when the poet lived—the late eleventh century. This attitude toward the *Song of Roland* leads naturally to a multiple interpretation of the main themes. There is not only a struggle between Christianity and Islam; within the empire there are new forces to contend with: the rise of individuality and the rise of France as an entity. It may be that Charles' mythical age in the poem, his "dous cens anz," is intended to encompass the period of the Carolingian dynasty, from 768 to 987. In this sense, Charles symbolizes the entire dynasty, both its absolutism of the eighth century and its decline in the tenth. He represents the old, authoritarian order, but the action has its setting in the new order. The figure of Charles is equivocal, as if to embody the transition. The central theme of the poem is the decay of the historical Charles' world. Duty in the new order is no longer clear. Roland is an anachronism, an exemplar of the earliest feudal ideal, no longer valid in the realities of the eleventh century. The poet admires him, bestows a beautiful death on him, but makes clear nevertheless the incongruity of his actions. Whereas Roland represents a past age, Ganelon reflects the new, which the poet deplores. The clash of old and new values provides the conflict.

The poet has conceived Roland as the perfect knight, the flower of chivalry. In the portrait of the hero there is a naïveté that gives one the impression that Roland exists within the framework of an early age of innocence, at least in the eyes of the poet. That would be the eighth century, a time that has left its imprint on the poem as being one of simplicity and clearly drawn societal behavior. In the context of the eighth century a perfect knight is, above all, a faithful vassal. The poem abounds with evidence that the poet sees his hero in just that light. There is no question about his sense of loyalty toward his emperor. The personality trait that causes a conflict between his individual objectives and that sense of loyalty is, as every reader must recognize, his desire for fame.

As for Ganelon, though he is assigned the role of villain, he is by no means unattractive. The poet stresses his splendid appearance and the impression he makes. He betrays, but he is in no sense a vile traitor. The treason he commits is unwitting. In his mind, he is doing nothing more than following the dictates of feudal life, marked by war among barons and sworn vengeance against anyone who offends or insults.

We have already seen that the oaths required of a subject in Charles' time were of a negative character, requiring the swearer not to meddle in government affairs. These oaths do not appear to have been adequate for someone directly in the king's service. One is tempted to apply the lessons of history to the fictitious Ganelon and infer from them that he did not feel bound to any extraordinary degree of loyalty to his sovereign. In any case, Ganelon's treason does no harm to the person of Charles; it is avenged because it hurts Charles' *maisnee,* i.e., his lineage. But Ganelon never admits that he has been disloyal to Charles. Thus, what is ultimately tragic in this refusal to see any conflict of interests in his loyalty to his sovereign and his private vendetta against Roland is that it creates a situation that exceeds the confines of Ganelon's person to envelop his entire society. That Ganelon is almost acquitted attests to the disorder of the feudal world. A baron could with impunity destroy another one and with him his men as well, as long as he observed the code of proper challenge. In every respect, Ganelon reflects the mentality of the tenth or eleventh century rather than the time of Charlemagne. He is the incarnation of that later individualism. In the *Song of Roland* this individualism clashes with the old, superannuated world of the autocratic emperor.

The tragedy of Roncevaux is the result of the breakdown of societal values, and the tragic theme is reflected in the way in which Charles, the representative of the old order, constantly weeps and sighs. As his lamentations become the keynote of the poem, his visions illustrate his inability to check the evolution of the new society; he cannot grasp their details. Charles is still Charles, but the world in which he must function is no longer the authoritarian empire of the eighth century.

*Notes*

1. This paper was read, in a somewhat longer form, at the Fifth Biennial Conference on Medieval Studies held in May 1970 at Western Michigan University, Kalamazoo, Michigan.

2. *Mimesis,* trans. Willard Trask (Garden City, 1957), p. 87.

3. *Ibid.*

4. Louis Halphen, *Charlemagne et l'Empire Carolingien* (Paris, 1947), p. 165.

5. From a royal capitulary on the *Missi,* quoted by Norman F. Cantor, *The Medieval World: 300-1300* (New York, 1963), p. 154.

6. C. E. Odegaard, "Carolingian Oaths of Fidelity," *Speculum,* 16 (1941), 291.

7. Victor Duruy, *Histoire de France* (Paris, 1905), I, 191.

8. Carl Stephenson, *Medieval Feudalism* (Ithaca, 1942), p. 78.

9. *La Société Féodale* (Paris, 1949), II, 197.

**Kathleen M. Capels (essay date spring 1973)**

SOURCE: Capels, Kathleen M. "The Apple Incident in Laisse XXIX of *The Song of Roland.*" *Romance Notes* 14, no. 3 (spring 1973): 599-605.

[*In the following essay, Capels explains the significance of Roland's presentation of an apple, symbolizing the crowns of all the pagan kings, to Charlemagne.*]

Interspersed in the *Song of Roland* (Oxford version) are several small stories, each only a few lines long, describing seemingly minor events from the past. For example, there is the story of the origins of Turpin's horse (vv. 1488-89),[1] and the one concerning the battle of Noples where Roland washed away the blood from the fields (vv. 1775-79). A third example, the one which will be the basis for this study, is the tale Ganelon tells Blancandrin about Roland giving a red apple, representing the crowns of all the pagan kings, to Charlemagne (vv. 383-88):

> 383 Er matin sedeit li emperere suz l'umbre,
>     Vint i ses niés, out vestue sa brunie,
> 385 E out predet dejeste Carcasonie;
>     En sa main tint une vermeille pume:
> 387 "Tenez, bel sire, dist Rollant a sun uncle,
>     De trestuz reis vos present les curunes."

This third story, and probably the others also, is not just an ornamental element adding a bit of color to the poem. It has other meanings as well, and the purpose of this study is to explore these other meanings.

T. Atkinson Jenkins feels that this incident is a jest on Roland's part. Roland's "idea of amusement is to present Charlemagne with all the crowns in the world, typified by a bright red apple."[2] In a footnote, Jenkins states that the apple represents the golden orb that is one of the signs of an emperor's power, along with his crown and sceptre.[3] Martín de Riquer[4] and Jessie Crosland both see this incident as an allusion to Roland's pride. As Miss Crosland says, in speaking of Noples and of the apple incident:

> We may not, perhaps, attach too much credence to Ganelon's account of his [Roland's] daring and rather childish exploits. . . . These may be merely the accusations of an aggrieved man anxious to prove that Roland's actions were dictated by pride and folly.[5]

Gerard J. Brault is the first scholar to devote a lengthy article, and not just a passing reference, to the apple incident as well as to the story of Noples. He sees the apple as a temptation symbol. Roland is tempting the Franks to disaster by urging them to conquer all the pagan world. He presents Charles with a symbol of the crowns of the conquered pagan kings, hinting that the Franks could and should actually conquer these kingdoms so Charles can be given the kings' real crowns. In Ganelon's eyes,

> Roland, le brillant jeune homme, qui va de succès en succès, mène en réalité Charles et tous ses hommes au désastre aussi sûrement que le Tentateur qui offre sa pomme et tous les royaumes du monde. Mais, nous dira Charlemagne plus tard dans un moment de lucidité extraordinaire [v. 746], le démon c'est Ganelon et non pas Roland.[6]

Blancandrin speaks of the bad advice given to Charles by his counselors:

> 379 Mult grant mal funt e cil duc e cil cunte
>     A lur seignur, ki tel cunseill li dunent.

Ganelon replies that this bad advice was only given by Roland:

> 381 Guenes respunt: "Jo ne sai veirs nul hume,
>     Ne més Rollant, ki uncore en avrat hunte."

Ganelon could then tell the story of the apple to show that Roland was tempting the Franks to do the wrong thing. Brault sees a parallel between Roland giving bad advice to and tempting the Franks, and the devil tempting Christ in the desert (Matthew 4.1-11). The devil was telling Christ to do the wrong thing when he offered Christ all the kingdoms of the world, just as Roland was—according to Ganelon—misleading Charles and the Franks by offering them all the kingdoms of the pagan world.

The apple incident can hardly be viewed as a jest, for then there is apparently no reason why Ganelon should recount this story. He himself would certainly not be in a mood for jesting when he tells this tale to Blancandrin, for he is on his way to what he fears will be certain death at the hands of the Saracens in their camp. The anecdote could plausibly illustrate Roland's role as tempter, especially when linked with the idea of bad advice. It could also be an example of Roland's pride, for immediately following the apple story Ganelon speaks of this pride:

> 389 Li soens orgoilz le devreit ben cunfundre,
>     Kar chascun jur de mort s'abandunet.

Brault, however, disagrees with this opinion. He feels that these two verses refer to verse 391, where Ganelon says there will be peace if Roland is killed, rather than to the preceding verses about the apple incident. In other words, Ganelon switches directly from the anecdote of the apple to another train of thought. In this second group of thoughts Ganelon claims that if Roland—who, because of his pride, often puts himself into situations where he could easily be killed—is actually killed by someone, the war would stop.

I believe, however, that there is another aspect to this little story, for the apple may be interpreted as an insult to Blancandrin and to the Saracens. To understand this new aspect, we must go further back in the poem, to the council Charles holds with his knights to decide how to reply to Marsile's proposal of peace. Roland offers his advice, and then Ganelon gives an opinion opposite to that of Roland. Ganelon says:

> 228 Cunseill d'orguill n'est dreiz que a plus munt;
>     Laissun le fols, as sages nus tenuns! AOI.

Thus Ganelon has insulted Roland by calling his advice foolish. Roland has his chance to return the insult later on during the council. He states:

> 294   Mais saives hom, il deit faire message:
>        Si li reis voelet, prez sui por vus le face!

Roland is saying that it takes a wise man to deliver the message, and that he is wise and capable of delivering it to Marsile. Thus he has countered Ganelon's accusation that Roland is foolish, and added another insult by implying that while Ganelon might be afraid to go to Marsile, he, Roland, is not afraid.[7] Ganelon angrily lashes out and threatens Roland, but Roland merely laughs:

> 300   "Einz i frai un poi de legerie
>        Que jo n'esclair ceste meie grant ire."
>        Quant l'ot Rollant, si cumençat a rire. AOI.

Ganelon is still smarting from Roland's insults when he rides towards Marsile's camp with Blancandrin. Blancandrin comments that the Franks did a great wrong towards their king by counseling him not to accept Marsile's offer (vv. 378-79). Since it was only Roland who gave this "bad" advice to Charles, this statement is an additional reminder of what started the round of insults between Roland and Ganelon. Blancandrin adds:

> 380   Lui e altrui travaillent e cunfundent

implying that it was a bad idea to suggest continuing the war, since the pagans will naturally win. Therefore he is insulting Ganelon the warrior, as well as Charles and the rest of the Frankish army. In the council scene with Roland, Ganelon responded to Roland's insults by returning them. Especially because he was just reminded of this previous series of insults by Blancandrin (vv. 378-79), it would seem logical for Ganelon to follow this pattern and counter the pagan's insult by another one, which in fact he does.

In a study of depreciatory comparisons, A. Robert Harden writes:

> The general policy in the selection of a suitable object is to choose something which underlines the inadequacy of a person or thing because it is too soft, too small, too old or so altered as to be incapable of self-preservation.[8]

A little later on in the essay (p. 68) he states: "Larger but equally soft fruit also inspire unflattering comparisons, as for instance, the apple." Tobler and Lommatzsch's *Altfranzösisches Wörterbuch* also lists several examples of an apple being used as a derogatory comparison in various epic poems. Thus the apple is an insult to the pagans, for by comparing the crowns of their king to a worthless apple, the implication is drawn that the pagan kings—and also their subjects—are worth next to nothing. There are also other derogatory remarks

in the *Song of Roland,* such as Abisme's shield not being worth a red cent after Turpin strikes it (vv. 1504-05) or Charles saying that the pagans' religion is not worth a penny (v. 3338), so this apple insult is not a unique example of an unflattering reference.

However, why does Ganelon attribute the comparison, and thus the insult, to Roland? Roland is Charles' most powerful warrior, and a derogatory comparison from a valiant knight would be more insulting than one from a lesser knight. Also, if Ganelon were afraid for his life, which would be reasonable, as two other messengers Charles sent to Marsile—Basan and Basile—were murdered by the pagans (vv. 207-09), he would not want it to seem like the insult came from him. It is very likely that Blancandrin will be angered by the insult. If his ire is directed towards Roland, he might not do anything to Ganelon, who is merely telling the story. Thus Ganelon can insult the pagans, but save himself from harm by having the insult supposedly come from Roland.

Some critics feel that Ganelon has already planned to betray Roland. The Saracens are war-weary, so Ganelon would have to reawaken their desire to fight if he wants them to kill Roland.[9] One of the best ways to do this is to anger them by an insult. Ganelon still considers himself a loyal vassal to Charles, as demonstrated by his defense at his trial (vv. 3769-78). In Ganelon's eyes, he has publicly challenged Roland during the first council scene with Charlemagne, and thus has a legal right to personal vengeance.[10] He only wants to avenge himself upon Roland, and does not want to betray Charles. Therefore, since the insult supposedly came from Roland, it is against Roland, and not Charles, that the pagans' anger and lust for war will be directed.

Even if Ganelon has not, at this point, definitely planned to *betray* Roland, he could be looking for *some* way to get revenge for Roland's insults. Blancandrin has hurt Ganelon's pride as a warrior by implying that the Franks are no good and would lose to the pagans. Hinting that the Saracens are worth little by comparing their kings' crowns to an apple is a balm for Ganelon's wounded *soldierly* pride. Roland's insults have wounded Ganelon's *personal honor.* Ganelon, by having the apple insult come from Roland, paints him in an unfavorable way for the Saracens. By making Roland seem insulting and prideful—because he certainly appears that way to Ganelon—Ganelon is soothing his own insulted pride. Roland degraded Ganelon in front of the other Franks, and now Ganelon degrades Roland in front of Blancandrin.

It has been shown, then, that the apple incident in laisse XXIX of the *Song of Roland* is not a mere ornamental device attached to the poem. It could be a way of demonstrating Roland's pride, and also a means of portraying Roland in the role of a tempter, or devil. It could also be an insult given in response to the one Blancandrin says. The reason why Ganelon attributes the insult to Roland depends upon the way one views Ganelon's character. If Ganelon is afraid for his own life, he is protecting himself from the wrath of the pagans—and also saving himself from possible murder—by saying that it was Roland, and not he, who insulted the pagans. If Ganelon wants to deliberately provoke the Saracens to war, he could insult them. Since the insult apparently comes from Roland, and not from Ganelon or Charles, they would only wage war on and hopefully kill Roland. Thus Ganelon could have his personal vengeance satisfied, but he would not have betrayed Charles because the Saracens would not have attacked Charles and the main army. If Ganelon only feels the need for revenge, without having definitely formulated the idea of betraying Roland, he could still use the insult to show Roland in a bad light to the pagans. The insult is a balm for Ganelon's wounded soldierly pride, and the attribution of the insult to Roland is a balm for his wounded personal pride.

*Notes*

1. This verse reference, as well as the others noted in this essay, is taken from Joseph Bédier's edition of *La Chanson de Roland* (Paris, 1964).

2. *La Chanson de Roland: Oxford version,* revised ed. (Boston, 1965), p. xxv.

3. *Ibid.,* p. 39.

4. *Les Chansons de geste françaises,* trans. Irénée Cluzel (Paris, 1957), p. 95.

5. *The Old French Epic* (Oxford, 1951), pp. 78-79.

6. "Ganelon et Roland: deux anecdotes du traître concernant le héros," *Romania,* 92 (1971), 398.

7. Critics such as Jules Horrent, *La Chanson de Roland dans les littératures française et espagnole au moyen âge* (Paris, 1951), p. 270; Eugene Vance, *Reading the Song of Roland* (Englewood Cliffs, New Jersey, 1970), p. 13; and Eugene Dorfman, *The Narreme in the Medieval Romance Epic* (Toronto, 1969), pp. 89-90, agree with this idea of a double insult between Roland and Ganelon during the council scene.

8. "The depreciatory comparison: a literary device of the medieval French epic" in *Mediaeval Studies in Honor of Urban Tigner Holmes, Jr.* (Chapel Hill, 1965), p. 65.

9. Jenkins (pp. xxix-xxx), Dorfman (p. 98), and Edmond Faral, *La Chanson de Roland* (Paris, 1948), p. 210.

10. Horrent (p. 271), Jenkins (p. 38), and Winifred Mary Hackett, "La féodalité dans la *Chanson de*

*Roland* et dans *Girart de Roussillon,*" in *Société Rencesvals: IVᵉ Congrès International* (Heidelberg, 1969), pp. 22-23.

## Jeffrey T. Chamberlain (essay date autumn 1981)

SOURCE: Chamberlain, Jeffrey T. "Diachronic Syntax in the *Song of Roland*: The *Faire*-Causative and the *Baligant* Episode." *Papers in Romance* 3, no. 3 (autumn 1981): 145-51.

[*In the following essay, Chamberlain offers evidence supporting a later date for the* Baligant *episode of* The Song of Roland.]

A question which has repeatedly been raised in **Roland** criticism deals with the authenticity of the so-called 'Baligant episode' (generally understood to comprise laisses 189 to 202 and 214 to 267).[1] The arrival of the Emir Baligant, who is not mentioned in the poem before laisse 189, has been viewed as a late interpolation in the composition and the redaction of **Roland,**[2] and has been no less successfully defended as an integral part of the poem's structure.[3] Most research has addressed textual, stylistic, and socio-historical considerations, but some analysts have dealt with matters of language, such as the assonances and the use and frequency of certain syntactic features of the language of the poem. Allen (1974), for example, offers statistical evidence that the definite article in the **Roland,** while it occurs fairly consistently in the non-*Baligant* sections, is considerably more frequent in the *Baligant* episode. This finding suggests a later time of composition for *Baligant* than for the remainder of the epic, since the generalization of the use of the definite article characterizes a more recent period in the development of the French language.

This paper offers additional syntactic evidence in support of a later composition of the *Baligant* portion with respect to the remainder of the **Roland,** by means of an analysis of the causative construction with *faire* plus infinitive; for example:

(1) Li emperere *fait* ses graisles *suner*

(**Rol.** 2443)

(2) Li emperere i *fait suner* ses graisles

(**Rol.** 3301)

'The emperor has his trumpets sounded'

Sentences (1) and (2), with identical meaning, exhibit a syntactic alternation which is no longer possible in modern standard French. Only sentences like (2), in which the causative verb *faire* immediately precedes the dependent infinitive, are grammatical in the modern language. Transformational analyses (Kayne 1975, Saltarelli 1976) have postulated a monoclausal structure for this construction in modern French, based on the generally impermeable nature of the double-verb complex. A transformation called VERB-RAISING or CLAUSE-UNION (referred to hereafter as CU) derives a monoclausal structure in which *faire* and the infinitive function together as the single verb in the sentence. This situation contrasts with that observed in sentence (1), in which each of the two verbs *fait* and *suner* functions individually, the main verb *fait* governing the subordinate constituent *ses graisles suner.* Sentence (1) reflects the situation characteristic of double-verb constructions in Latin, which for certain verbs (*iubeo, veto, sino;* cf. Harris 1978:226) exhibited an infinitive complementizer (sentence 3) in favor of the more frequent sentential complement (sentence 4):

(3) iubeo te ire 'I order you to go'
(4) impero ut eas 'I order that you go'

The accusative-infinitive construction occurred somewhat infrequently with *facere* in the classical language, but it became common in late Latin and prefigures the Romance construction (cf. Väänänen 1963:149):

(5) qui nati coram me *cernere* letum *fecisti*

(Virg., *Aen.,* 2, 538-39)

'(you,) who forced me to witness the murder of my son'

(6) *facite* homines *discumbere*

(Vulg., *Ioh.,* 6, 10)

'have the men sit down'

Analyses for Latin (Lakoff 1968, Pepicello 1977) have suggested a biclausal structure for the Latin causative with *facere* plus infinitive, described by a transformation called SUBJECT-TO-OBJECT RAISING (SOR), which promotes the subject of the lower clause into the position of object of the main verb while leaving the biclausal sentence structure intact. These analyses suggest a gradual diachronic development from the biclausal, or SOR, structure in Latin to the corresponding monoclausal, or CU, structure in modern French (Chamberlain 1980, Saltarelli 1980). The *Song of Roland,* set down in the period of transition, exhibits both SOR (sentence 1) and CU (sentence 2) structures in its causatives with *faire* plus infinitive.

An analysis of all the occurrences of the causative *faire* in the *Roland* reveals an *état de langue* in which the Romance monoclausal construction had become productive, but it had not completely eliminated the Latin-type biclausal structure. The 54 occurrences of *faire* plus infinitive in the *Roland* may be accordingly classified as follows:

(7) A. SOR construction: 16 examples; e.g.:[4]

679 E. XX. hostages, *faites* les ben *guarder*
701 Franc desherbergent, *funt* lur sumers *trosser*
1060 Si l'orrat Charles, *ferat* l'ost *returner*
2593 *Fait* sei *porter* en sa cambre voltice
3849 *Fait* cels *guarder* tresque li dreiz en serat

B. CU construction: 38 examples; e.g.:[5]

57 De nos ostages *ferat trencher* les testes
678 Mult grant aveir vos en *faz amener*
1610 Sun bun ceval i *ad fait esdemettre*
1856 En saintes fleurs il les *facet gesir*
3749 Li emperere devent sei l'*ad fait traire*

The CU sentences, which constitute approximately two thirds of the *faire* causatives in the *Roland,* appear relatively normal to the modern reader. The SOR sentences are no longer possible in modern French, with the exception of 679, which exhibits the idiosyncratic clitic pronoun placement which still occurs in the modern affirmative imperative. The exception, which requires the placement of object pronouns (but not nouns) between the two verbal elements, may derive from tonic considerations involving the stressed pronoun, or it may represent a construction fossilized in the modern language by grammatical prescription. It is evident, however, that both the SOR and the CU constructions were valid in a variety of syntactic environments in the French of the time of the *Roland,* with the monoclausal structure well on its way to replacing the Latin-type biclausal structure.

Just as the more modern syntax of the definite article in the *Baligant* episode (cf. Allen 1974) suggests that this portion was composed later than the remainder of the poem, so also will the syntax of the *faire*-causative reflect a similar diachronic differentiation. An immediate problem arises in the definition of what constitutes the *Baligant* portion of the *Roland.* The logical beginning of the episode is at laisse 189, which offers a reprise of laisse 1 and mentions, in a somewhat 'deux ex machina' fashion, Marsile's now seven-year-old request for Baligant's aid; the episode ends at laisse 267, where Charlemagne leaves Saragossa and returns to France to begin Ganelon's trial. Charlemagne's two dreams (laisses 185 and 186) should also be included in *Baligant,* especially laisse 185, which prefigures the entire episode. For this study at least, the question is immaterial, since there are no occurrences of the causative *faire* in the laisses in question.

The *Baligant* portion, which in any event constitutes approximately one fourth of the *Roland*'s 4,002 lines, also contains approximately one fourth of the poem's occurrences of the causative *faire*; i.e. 12 of the 54 occurrences. Two of these 12 occurrences exhibit the biclausal structure characteristic of the earlier stages of the language:

> (8) 2613 Al premer an *fist* ses brefs *seieler*
> 3137 Par tute l'ost *funt* lur taburs *suner*

The remaining 10 causatives in *Baligant* show the monoclausal structure found in modern French; e.g.

> (9) 2624 Ses granz drodmunz en *ad fait aprester*
> 2678 El destre poign si li *faites chalcer*
> 3661 A mil Franceis *funt ben cercer* la vile[6]

Table 1 summarizes the occurrences of biclausal and monoclausal causatives in the entire *Roland,* and in the *Baligant* and non-*Baligant* portions of the text.

TABLE 1

*FAIRE-CAUSATIVES IN THE SONG OF ROLAND*

|  | BICLAUSAL (SOR) | MONOCLAUSAL (CU) | TOTAL |
|---|---|---|---|
| *BALIGANT* | 2 (17%) | 10 (83%) | 12 |
| NON-*BALIGANT* | 14 (33%) | 28 (67%) | 42 |
| ENTIRE *ROLAND* | 16 (30%) | 38 (70%) | 54 |

The percentage of occurrences of the SOR structure in *Baligant* is approximately half that of the occurrences in the remainder of the poem. These figures suggest a later composition of *Baligant,* since the direction of the evolution of French was in favor of CU at the expense of SOR. The figures must be viewed with caution, however, inasmuch as the *Roland* is a poetic text subject to limitations of meter and assonance, among others. In many instances, the word order could not be freely determined, but was conditioned by constraints of poetic composition. The two examples of SOR in *Baligant,* for example, are revealing when cited in the context of the laisses in which they occur:

> (10) *2613* Al premer an fist ses brefs seieler,
> 14 En Babilonie Baligant ad mandet,
> 15 Ço est l'amiraill, le viel d'antiquitet

> (11) *3137* Par tute l'ost funt lur taburs suner
> 38 E cez buisines e cez greisles mult cler:
> 39 Paien descendent pur lur cors aduber

In line 2613, the poet could have preposed the object *ses brefs: Al premer an ses brefs fit seieler* (cf. 2627 *Tut sun navilie i ad fait aprester*), thereby incorporating the supposedly preferred CU structure while observing the assonance; or the line could have read *fist seieler ses brefs* without contradicting the assonance (a line in the same laisse ends in *nefs*). Line 3137 could in like manner have read *lur taburs funt suner,* thereby avoiding an additional SOR structure. In spite of the preference for the CU causative, these two examples demonstrate that the choice of word order undoubtedly involved factors

such as emphasis, euphony, and formulaic composition, and the SOR construction may have been used as a deliberate archaism long after it had been abandoned by the spoken language as a productive structure.

The figures in Table 1 may be falsified by an 'unnatural' word order characteristic of the poetic form. It is impossible to establish precisely the nature and the extent of the constraints involved, but examples such as lines 2613 and 3137 can be identified, for which alternative structures could have been employed without contradicting the assonance or, in some cases, interfering with the caesura, which in medieval verse constitutes a genuine pause separating syntactic units (Verluyten 1981). In fact, more than half of the causatives in the *Roland* do occur under unavoidable prosodic constraints; for example:

> (12) 1610 Sun bun ceval ‖ i ad fait esdemettre
> =?I ad fait ‖ sun bun ceval esdemettre (misplaced caesura)
>
> 1796 Li empereres ‖ ad fait suner ses corns
> =?Li empereres ‖ ad fait ses corns suner (incorrect assonance)

With the caveat that other unverifiable factors must have operated in the choice of word order, it is nonetheless possible to identify 25 of the 54 causatives in the *Roland* as being free of the constraints observed in lines 1610 and 1796. These examples offer alternatives, such as those discussed for lines 2613 and 3137, and it is appropriate to assume that they will demonstrate the predilection of the language for one construction over the other without the limitations imposed by assonance and meter. Table 2 illustrates the figures for the 25 such 'free-word-order' causatives in the two portions of the *Roland*:

TABLE 2

*'WORD-ORDER-FREE' CAUSATIVES IN THE SONG OF ROLAND*

|  | BICLAUSAL (SOR) | MONOCLAUSAL (CU) | TOTAL |
|---|---|---|---|
| *BALIGANT* | 2 (25%) | 6 (75%) | 8 |
| NON-*BALIGANT* | 9 (53%) | 8 (47%) | 17 |
| ENTIRE *ROLAND* | 11 (44%) | 14 (56%) | 25 |

The table shows, as expected, a much smaller percentage of SOR causatives in the *Baligant* portion than in the remainder of the text. The figures are too small to be statistically valid, although a preference for CU in *Baligant* is clearly apparent. This tendency occurs in marked contrast to that which appears here in the non-*Baligant* portion, which in fact appears to favor slightly SOR over CU in the free-word-order causatives. The difference between the two parts of the poem is more pronounced when the word order is not subject to certain identifiable prosodic constraints, but as Table 1 shows, the preference in *Baligant* for the monoclausal causative remains all the more pronounced even in spite of the limiting prosodic conditions under which most of the examples occur.

Allen (1974:70) suggested that future investigation following his study of the definite article would discover other differences between the *Baligant* and the rest of the **Roland.** The grammar of the causative with *faire* plus infinitive adduces new evidence for a later addition of *Baligant,* although the numbers involved may prevent anything but a general conclusion regarding tendencies. In his study of the assonances in the **Roland,** Hall (1959:159) suggests that if *Baligant* was a late interpolation, it must have been added to the poem at some time before the final redaction, since the episode shows no difference in the types of assonances employed from those found in the remainder of the poem. Syntactic features such as the causative *faire,* however, are particularly significant indicators of the circumstances of composition, because, unlike features of vocabulary, prosodics, or even style, they represent low-level surface phenomena over which the user of the language exercises little conscious control. The strong predilection in the *Baligant* for the monoclausal structure reflects, the conservatism of the written language notwithstanding, the situation which was to prevail in the modern language. Within the framework of the diachronic syntactic development suggested above, the evidence offered by the syntax of the *faire*-causative in the **Song of Roland** supports the hypothesis that the *Baligant* episode was composed later than the remainder of the text.

### Notes

Paper delivered at the Fifth International Conference of Historical Linguistics, Galway, Ireland, April, 1981. The author gratefully acknowledges travel grants from the Department of French and the Graduate College of the University of Illinois which made possible his attendance at the Conference.

1. Laisse and verse numbers refer to the Bédier 1937 edition of the Oxford manuscript of the *Roland.*

2. For late interpolation, see, e.g.: Jenkins 1924, Fawtier 1933, Horrent 1951, Rychner 1955, Menéndez Pidal 1959, Hall 1959, Allen 1974.

3. For integral structure, see, e.g.: Bédier 1912, Faral 1934, Siciliano 1940, Aebischer 1949, Delbouille 1954, Burger 1964, Uitti 1973.

4. SOR structure: lines 610, 679, 700, 701, 1060, 1203, 2451 (2 infinitives), 2443, 2593, *2613,* 2962, 2965, *3137,* 3692, 3849. Examples in *Baligant* are underlined.

5. CU structures: lines 57, 89, 158, 159, 160, 213, 678, 852, 1249, 1468, 1610, 1796, 1816, 1856, 2450, 2506, *2624, 2627, 2678, 2774,* 2920, 2947, 2958, 2964, *2992, 3148, 3266, 3301, 3661, 3670,* 3749, 3853, 3895, 3903, 3917, 3919, 3943, 3964. Examples in *Baligant* are underlined.

6. As in modern French, inverted subjects, adverbs, and certain other modifiers do not constitute an interruption of the single-verb structure. The significant feature of the analysis is the position of the logical subject (or object) of the infinitive used with *faire.*

### References

Aebischer, Paul. 1949. *Pour la défense et illustration de l'épisode de Baligant.* Paris: Société d'édition 'Les Belles Lettres'.

Allen, J. R. 1974. "On the authenticity of the Baligant episode in the *Chanson de Roland." Computers in the humanities,* ed. by J. L. Mitchell, 65-72. Minneapolis: University of Minnesota Press.

Bédier, Joseph. 1912. *Les Légendes épiques,* vol. III. Paris: Champion.

———, ed. 1937. *La Chanson de Roland,* publiée d'après le manuscrit d'Oxford. Paris: L'édition d'art H. Piazza.

Burger, André. 1964. *Remarques sur la composition de l'épisode de Baligant.* Mélanges de linguistique romane et de philologie médiévale offerts à M. Maurice Delbouille, vol. II.56-69. Gembloux: Duculot.

Chamberlain, Jeffrey T. 1980. "Syntactic evolution of the French causative with *faire*: evidence in the *Song of Roland."* Read at the 1980 Conference of the Committee for the Advancement of Early Studies, Ball State University. MS.

Delbouille, Maurice. 1954. *Sur la genèse de la Chanson de Roland.* Brussels: Palais des Académies.

Faral, Edmond. 1934. *La Chanson de Roland: étude et analyse.* Paris: Mellottée.

Fawtier, Robert. 1933. *La Chanson de Roland: étude historique.* Paris: Boccard.

Hall, Robert A., Jr. 1959. "Linguistic strata in *The Song of Roland." Romance Philology* 13.156-161.

Harris, Martin. 1978. *The evolution of French syntax: a comparative approach.* London: Longman.

Horrent, Jules. 1951. *La Chanson de Roland dans les littératures française et espagnole au moyen âge.* (Bibl. de la Fac. de Philosophie et Lettres de l'Univ. de Liège, 120.) Paris: Société d'édition 'Les Belles Lettres'.

Jenkins, T. Atkinson. 1924. *La Chanson de Roland.* Boston: D. C. Heath. Rpt. 1977 American Life Foundation.

Kayne, Richard S. 1975. *French syntax: the transformational cycle.* Cambridge: MIT Press.

Lakoff, Robin T. 1968. *Abstract syntax and Latin complementation.* Cambridge: MIT Press.

Menéndez Pidal, Ramón. 1959. *La Chanson de Roland y el neotradicionalismo: orígenes de la épica románica.* Madrid: Espasa-Calpe.

Pepicello, W. J. 1977. "Raising in Latin." *Lingua* 42.209-218.

Rychner, Jean. 1955. *La Chanson de geste: essai sur l'art épique des jongleurs.* (Publications romanes et françaises, 53.) Geneva: Droz.

Saltarelli, Mario. 1976. "Theoretical implications in the development of accusativus com infinitivo constructions." *Current studies in Romance linguistics,* ed. by Marta Luján and Fritz Hensey, 88-99. Washington: Georgetown University Press.

———. 1980. "Syntactic diffusion." *Papers from the 4th International Conference on Historical Linguistics,* ed. by Elizabeth C. Traugott et al., 183-191. (Amsterdam studies in the theory and history of linguistic science, 4; Current issues in linguistic theory, 14). Amsterdam: John Benjamins B.V.

Siciliano, Italo. 1940. *Le origini delle canzoni di gesta: teorie e discussioni.* Padua: Dottore Antonio Milani.

Uitti, Karl D. 1973. *Story, myth, and celebration in Old French narrative poetry, 1050-1200.* Princeton: Princeton University Press.

Väänänen, Veikko. 1963. *Introduction au latin vulgaire.* Paris: Klincksieck.

Verluyten, S. Paul. 1981. "Historical metrics: the caesura in French." Read at the Fifth International Conference of Historical Linguistics, Galway, Ireland.

## C. H. Sisson (essay date 1983)

SOURCE: Sisson, C. H. Introduction to *The Song of Roland,* translated by C. H. Sisson, pp. 7-11. Manchester, England: Carcanet Press Limited, 1983.

[*In the following essay, Sisson provides a concise introduction to* The Song of Roland's *textual history and the scholarly controversies surrounding the text.*]

The story of the **Chanson de Roland** has its origin in the obscure history of the eighth century. In 778 Charlemagne, then the most powerful figure in the western world, undertook an expedition into Spain, which was already largely over-run by Muslims from North Africa. Although in the **Chanson** this enterprise is represented as a crusade, this was hardly the nature of it. The year

before, Charlemagne had been approached by some of these intruders, who had sought his help against their co-religionists further south in the country, and it was in response to this appeal that he ventured over the Pyrenees. Moreover—and contrary to what the **Chanson** tells us—the expedition was not a success. Charlemagne took Pamplona, a Christian city, and afterwards razed it to the ground. Before Saragossa, which was held by the Saracens, he failed, and had to turn back to meet trouble nearer home. It was during this withdrawal that, in the narrow pass of the Roncesvalles, the rear-guard was ambushed and Roland, the Warden of the Breton Marches, was killed—not by Saracens, as the story is told, but by Basques who no doubt saw an opportunity for plunder. Out of this slender material the epic of **Roland** was made, but not before the passage of time had made it possible to improve on history without fear of contradiction.

It seems that the chroniclers, both Christian and Muslim, are laconic on the subject, neither party finding in the events much that they wished to advertise. The antecedents of the poem itself have been the subject of much enquiry and much argument by scholars since the work first re-emerged into the light of day in the first half of the nineteenth century, but the findings, truth to tell, are largely negative. The authorship has been the subject of debate. All in all, there seems to be no sufficient reason for the ordinary reader not to take it that the poem is the work of one Turoldus, who in effect signs it in the last lines. He was a poet of great genius and originality. The **Chanson de Roland** is not only the first, but incomparably the best, of the *chansons de geste*. It stands as it were on the threshold of French literature, the first great work we encounter. We have the *Cantilène d'Eulalie* of the ninth century:

> Buona pulcella fut Eulalia,
> Bel auret corps, bellezour anima.

In the tenth and eleventh centuries we have—less impressively—the lives of St Leger and St Alexis. The date of the **Chanson de Roland**—another subject of controversy—is certainly somewhere in the neighbourhood of 1100.

What we have, therefore, in the **Chanson,** is a re-handling, about the time of the First Crusade, of events from the age of Charlemagne. This meant that the author of the poem was much more preoccupied with the notion of a Christendom set against the pagan world than could have been the case in the eighth century. If the events are those of the earlier time, the sentiments, one might say the politics, are those of the later. The matter is more complicated than that, however. Whatever the precise pre-history of the story of the **Chanson,** there is no doubt that during the three or more centuries that had passed since Charlemagne's expedition the heroes of it had become larger than life. It is not a falsification of history that Turoldus gives us but a world of legend, yet it is a legend around which enough reality still clings to engage not only a sense of wonder but a sense of actuality. That this double effect still operates on us at the present time is due to the poet's profound grasp of his themes. He understands these characters who think nothing is more creditable than to split someone's brains in two or to raze a city to the ground, and exhibits great sophistication in his delineation of their loyalties and jealousies. One is reminded again and again of that singular combination of vigour and clarity of line which marks Romanesque architecture and sculpture. Anyone who has mooched around churches in England or France knows how the work of the period stands out among the still beautiful but fussier work of the later Middle Ages. All this grace, strength and sureness of touch are to be found in the work of Turoldus.

The story moves with great rapidity, for Turoldus does not give us more than the essentials. A sight of the high mountains and the deep valleys of the passes, of Ganelon throwing back his marten-skins in a moment of anger, are given us in a flash. Charlemagne's councils, the councils of the pagan king Marsilie, are presented so that we see the actors and feel the ominous weight of the business transacted. The battle scenes are told as by someone who 'remembers with advantages' what feats were done there, but the exaggerations are never allowed to destroy the solidity of the actors. When Roland and Oliver die after the desperate battle in the Roncevalles, it is not as over-sized heroes, but as any pair of young comrades-in-arms dying in a far country after having done their uttermost. The *Chanson* is a sombre and relentless poem, as well as an extraordinarily lively one. Fantastic in some respects, it is in a profound sense true not only to the spirit of the times from which it emerged, with their absolute and menacing demands and feudal loyalties, but to that of any time in which violence is not far away.

There are invincible oddities. The Saracens are represented as idolaters, who smash up their gods when they fail them. Charlemagne is not merely the emperor, but a sort of priest-king who can give absolution to his men at the start of a great enterprise. There is a world of darkness and ignorance under the glittering surface of the poem, but it is because rather than in spite of this that we are left with so strong an impression of the depth and grasp of the poet's mind.

The strangeness and remoteness of the world from which the legend, and the poem itself, well up, present some difficulties to the translator. For in a translation the *tone* is, if not everything, at least something he must be sure of, if he is to produce a version which carries any conviction. This is a matter not of conscious working out—whatever work the translator may have to put in on details of the text—but of direct perception. The translator has to feel at home with the mind of the author; he has also—and this is the translator's difficulty *par excellence*—to see how he can say the things the author says in the language of an utterly different time, moving among utterly different superficial assumptions, whatever profound affinities may lurk below. The world of Lucretius and Catullus, or of Horace and Virgil, was very different from our own, but these poets were at the centre of a great urban civilization, full of sophistication of the kind we understand. The world of Dante was different again, but however strange his cosmology may be to us, the people he presents to us so vividly have all the concerns which still lie at the heart of our civilization. With the world of Roland things are otherwise. Turoldus's sharp delineation of character is such that, despite the unfamiliar circumstances we can recognize the types we know, but their assumptions and the general content of their minds are so unlike our own that it is hard to pick the language in which we could talk to them. What does one say to a man whose greatest glory is to hit someone else over the head, or to be the leading hand in a massacre, and who thinks it natural that a traitor should be pulled limb from limb by cavorting stallions? These things are not as far from us as we should like to think, but they are pleasures from which we avert at least our conversation. The solution of using a garbled and sham antique language, which no one ever spoke, to suggest that people were different in those old times, is not open to us—at least if we believe in the continuing life of old literatures and the radical unchangeability of the human race. One has to learn to live with the assumptions of heroic legend without finding them all that strange; and in fact, they are not that strange.

The qualities of the language and verse of the poem present us with difficulties of a lesser but by no means negligible order. The Old French or Norman-French in which it is written had emerged over the preceding centuries from the vulgar Latin spoken by Caesar's soldiers and the colonists, with some admixtures. What Turoldus gives us is a speech of comparatively limited vocabulary, by modern standards, as it were presided over by radical Latin meanings which had changed colour more or less with the passage of time and the development of the feudal and ecclesiastical systems. So narrow a range is not easily accommodated in the English of our own day, but at least it points in the direction of a language as simple and direct as may be. As to the verse, there can be no question of adopting exactly the form of the original, though something like that has been attempted in more than one twentieth-century version. The *Chanson* is written in what are called *laisses*—bundles or stanzas—of ten-syllabled assonanced verse. This may call for as many as twenty or thirty rhymes or half-rhymes in a stanza—an absurdity in modern English and one which is bound to distort the language so that anything like a natural directness is lost. As to the number of syllables, the classic line in French is of twelve syllables, and it is this which corresponds to the classic English line of ten syllables. The ten-syllable line in French is a *short* line, and the nearest equivalent in English is the line of eight syllables. A great deal more of the speed of the original—an essential characteristic one may reasonably hope to preserve in translation—is lost by ignoring this point. Given all these considerations, my solution has been to use a basic octosyllabic couplet, not however counting on my fingers for every line.

I first became interested in the ***Chanson de Roland*** through Joseph Bédier's edition of the Oxford manuscript and this edition, with its sensitive prose version *en face,* is probably still the best starting point for anyone who has access to modern French and wishes to explore the text further. The essential supplement is the volume of commentaries Bédier published some years later (in 1927). Bédier is at once immensely scholarly and immensely literate, and his work has an enduring attraction for the general student of literature. Of course debate did not cease with his volumes. Among more recent books I have consulted are Paul Aebischer's *Préhistoire et protohistoire du Roland d'Oxford* (Berne, 1972) and André Burger's *Turold, poète de la fidelité* (Geneva, 1977).

My version was commissioned by the BBC in 1981 and originally broadcast on Radio 3 in October and November 1982 with brilliant incidental music by Nigel Osborne. I should like to thank Fraser Steel, to whose grasp of its literary, dramatic and musical possibilities the project owed so much from its inception, as well as the actors, Garard Green, Christopher Neame, Andy Rashleigh, Geoffrey Banks, Ann Rye, Bert Parnaby and above all John Franklyn-Robbins, the narrator, for the manner in which they made it come to life.

### Frederick Goldin (essay date 1985)

SOURCE: Goldin, Frederick. "Time and Performance in *The Song of Roland.*" In *CUNY English Forum,* Vol. 1, edited by Saul N. Brody and Harold Schechter, pp. 129-53. New York: AMS Press, 1985.

[*In the following essay, Goldin examines the numerous tense shifts in* The Song of Roland *and their effect on audiences' understanding of the poem.*]

One of the most striking characteristics of ***The Song of Roland*** is that it keeps on switching from one tense to another without any apparent system. The brief seventh *laisse* provides a good example. There are ten verbs in these seven lines, and each one seems to lack any relation to the others as far as its tense is concerned:

Dis blanches mules fist amener Marsilies,
Que li tramist li reis de Suatilie.
Li frein sunt d'or, les seles d'argent mises.
Cil sunt muntez ki le message firent;
Enz en lur mains portent branches d'olive.
Vindrent a Charles, ki France ad en baillie;
Nes poet guarder que alques ne l'enignent. AOI.[1]

Anyone who likes to have a story told in proper sequence—or in *any* sequence—must find this passage hard to explain: "Marsilion *had* (preterite) ten white mules led out, which the King of Suatilie *sent* (preterite) him. The reins *are* (present) of gold, the saddles encrusted with silver. Now the men *are* (present) mounted, who *delivered* (preterite) the message. In their hands they *carry* (present) olive branches. They *came* (preterite) to Charles, who *has* (present) France in his keeping. He *cannot* (present) prevent their *tricking* him (present subjunctive) somewhat."

The attempt to account for this disorienting non-sequentiality of time and tense began almost a century ago, and we now have several valuable studies dealing with this problem in ***The Song of Roland*** and in Old French narrative generally.[2] In this paper I shall concentrate on what I consider the chief effect of this continual change in the designation of time—an effect that has not, so far as I know, been adequately noted and that still needs to be defined. For once we have renounced our lineal, eye-minded, reader's expectations—once we have freed our notion of sequence from our notion of time—we are able to see that the distribution of tenses in the Oxford ***Roland*** is not haphazard at all, that it reflects a coherent pattern of history and necessity in which every event—every act, every gesture—finds its inevitable place.

To begin with, it is important to note how concerned the Oxford poet is to tell things correctly. ***The Song of Roland*** is based on a disastrous event, the destruction of the baggage train of Charlemagne's army and the killing of every man in the rear guard on August 15, 778. The event was reported in Christian and Saracen chronicles both during and after Charlemagne's lifetime, though it was only after his death that the full scope of the disaster was revealed in the West—an indication of how bitter this defeat was to the King of the Franks. Though the epic has changed every detail of this chronicled event except for the location and the circumstances of the massacre—the rear guard falls in the Pyrenees as Charlemagne's grand army is withdrawing from Spain and returning to France—it, too, refers several times to a chronicle, the *Gesta Francorum,* which it calls the *Geste Francor,* the Great Deeds of the Franks, or simply the *geste* (vv. 1443, 1685, 2095, 1684, 3181, 3262, 3742), and which it regards as ancient (*l'anciëne geste*) and a precious repository of documents and charters. *Il est escrit es cartres e es brefs, / Ço dist la Geste* (1684f), it declares, to support its affirmation that Roland, Oliver, and Turpin had killed more than four thousand Saracens. Furthermore, this chronicle is one of several (*en plusurs gestes*, 3181).

In *laisse* 155 (2095-2098) the poem tells about the last great deed of Archbishop Turpin, mortally wounded, who struck a thousand blows before he died and killed four hundred of the enemy, whose corpses Charles later found lying at the feet of this great warrior and holy man. "*Ço dit la Geste*," says the poet, "and one who was on that field, the baron Saint Gilles, for whom God makes miracles, and who made the charter in the minster at Laon—whoever does not know this has understood very little." Thus the story of the great battle of Rencesvals has been preserved by a miracle—the presence of St. Gilles as a witness on the field; by a double miracle, in fact, since St. Gilles lived and died two hundred years before the battle. For every man on that field was killed, and were it not for the Charter deposited by that holy witness (or perhaps by God himself), no one would have known the true history of their loyalty and their tremendous sacrifice, and posterity would have been deprived of their glorious example. The Saint deposited this document in the monastery at Laon, and this same document was one of the *cartres e brefs* upon which the *Geste Francor* is based and which authenticate the story that the **Song** relates.[3] Thus the **Song of Roland** insists upon its own reliability as history, its truthfulness, its authenticity.

Now the *Geste Francor* was a written document (*il est escrit*), presumably meant to be read. **The Song of Roland,** on the other hand, was always meant to be sung—before the text we now have, it existed as an oral poem dating, perhaps, from the historical event itself, or soon after; and when the Oxford text was composed and fixed, removing at least this version of the **Song** from the continual mutations of oral poetry, it was still composed as a song to be *performed*, before an audience in attendance—witness the word *nostre* in the very first line: *Charles the King, our Emperor, the Great*! And it may be just this circumstance—the condition in which the poem was presented to the public—just this essential element of *performance*, that accounts for one of the most perplexing features of the poem: the apparent absence of any sequence or any concordance in the tenses of the verbs, so that a verb in the present and a verb in the preterite are often found in the same line, even though they refer to two contemporaneous or rigorously sequential actions. Furthermore, this (to us) disturbing absence of tense coordination is characteristic of old French narrative poetry in general, including the courtly romances.[4] And that is why I say that the circumstance of the performance is a necessary condition of this freedom in the use of tenses. When one is telling a story to an attending audience—to people whose eyes meet the eyes of the reciting narrator—one often instinctively switches from preterite to present to

make the narrative more vivid, to make the time in which the narrative is set coincide dramatically with the time in which the audience listens to it and so, in a way, to "involve" them, to transform them from listeners into witnesses.

The performance situation explains what makes this constant shifting of tenses possible, but it does not reveal any pattern in the appearance of these tenses or explain the dizzying frequency with which they change. And yet there is good circumstantial evidence of such a pattern. There are many places, for example, where one or another tense could have been used without changing the number of syllables or the position of the tonic accents—as in v. 2217, where *a (d)* present, or *out* preterite, would fit equally well. Since one or another tense could have been used, one had to have been chosen; and if there was a choice, there must have been a principle governing that choice.

Such instances are enough to refute the idea that the use of tenses was determined by the metrical demands—that the present perfect might be used when three syllables are needed, for example, and the simple past when the verse needs only one. As soon as one reaches for that comforting theory, he is stopped cold by another extraordinary feature of the Oxford **Roland**. Well over half of the poem consists of dialogue—terse, brilliant, powerful dialogue that lends the poem its great dramatic force. Now in all of these conversations (except one), in the face of the same metrical demands, there is a perfect concordance in the tenses of the verbs, even when the speaker is telling a story to others in his presence. The flawless coordination of tenses in the dialogues contrasts sharply with the non-sequential use of tense in the narrative; the dialogues prove that the constant refraction of time in the narrative was the result of a deliberate choice, for the poem could have told its tale just as its characters tell theirs, with all the verbs in perfect order.

By way of orientation, I would like to list some of the principles that govern the choice of tense in the narrative.[5]

1) The tense changes within the *laisse* when the point of view changes, or when a new aspect of the action, or a new motif is introduced. We find a clear example in the sixty-fourth *laisse*:

> 792. Li quens Rollant est muntet el destrer. AOI.
>       Cuntre lui vient sis cumpainz Oliver.
>       Vint i Gerins e li proz quens Gerers,
> 795. E vint i Otes, si i vint Berengers
>       E vint i Astors e Anseïs li veillz,
>       Vint i Gerart de Rossillon li fiers;
>       Venuz i est li riches dux Gaifiers.
>       Dist l'arcevesque: "Jo irai, par mun chef!
> 800. E jo od vos, ço dist li quens Gualters;
>       Hom sui Rollant, jo ne li dei faillir."
>       Entr'els eslisent.XX. milie chevalers. AOI.

(792. Count Roland is mounted on his war horse,
        Oliver, his companion, comes to him.
        Gerin came, and the brave Count Gerer,
795. Oton came, and there came Berenger,
        And Astor came, and Anseïs the old,
        and Gerart came, of Roussillon, fierce and
        proud;
        Gaifier, that mightly duke, has come.
        Said the Archbishop: "I shall go, by my head!"
800. "And I with you," said Walther the Count;
        "I am Roland's man, I must not fail him."
        Together they choose 20,000 men.)

This *laisse* consists of three parts, each part marked by a change in tense. Roland and Oliver are introduced in the present. Then there follows, in the preterite and bound by anaphora, a catalogue of the great nobles who joined these two leaders (794-797); and in order to signal the end of this catalogue, v. 798 is in the present perfect. The third part of the laisse contains the speeches of Turpin and Gautier del Hum, introduced by the preterite. Finally, in the last line, a new aspect of the action is narrated in the present (802). Not only is the design of the *laisse* clearly marked out by the arrangement of the tenses, but the four most important men are distinguished. Roland and Oliver are placed on a different temporal plane from the others; Turpin and Gautier are separated from the others by the intervening present perfect in v. 798 and by the fact that they are quoted. In this way, the four greatest warriors—those who will stand together and all alone at the end, and be the last to die—are united at the very beginning.

It is thus the arrangement of the tenses that reveals the structure of the *laisse*. That is one of the most important functions of the distribution of the tenses, one that, as far as I know, has never been noticed, and one that produces deeply moving effects. At least fifty entire *laisses* and the greater part of the narrative can be analyzed in this way. Not only entire *laisses* but many series of lines within a *laisse* follow the same principle. Even in a single line containing verbs in different tenses—perhaps the most striking cases of all—the confusion is cleared up when one remembers that the tenses define aspects of an action. So, for example, in v. 1005, the beginning of an action is narrated in one tense, the conclusion in another, and the change in tense marks a change in point of view: *Granz est la noise, si l'oïrent Franceis*—"Great is the noise (made by the pagans), and the French heard it." Or v. 162: *La noit demurent tresque vint al jur cler*—"They remain there that night till the bright day came."

2) When a certain action produces both immediate and far-reaching consequences, the immediate and temporary succession is related in one tense (usually the present or present perfect), the enduring and persistent succession in another (usually the preterite or imperfect). We shall see an example of this in connection with the next principle.

3) The preterite is sometimes used to tell of an event that is inevitably going to happen. It has not happened yet, but it will ineluctably take place. For, from the point of view of the audience, it is already a part of the history of that distant time, it has already taken place. This use of the past tense has been called the "epic anticipatory preterite,"[6] and as a sign of anticipation it is distinguished in two ways from the future tense. *In most cases* the future indicates an event that may happen or not, an eventuality: the essential uncertainty of the future tense is part of the meaning of the statement. *Jo vos durrai un pan de mun païs* (3207), says Baligant to his son, "I shall give you a portion of my land"—a promise that takes on an ironic nuance by the time it reaches the ears of the audience, for the audience knows that he never had the chance to make his promise good. On the other hand, the future *is* occasionally used to designate a necessary future; in such cases it is distinguished from the epic anticipatory preterite in that it represents the future not from the point of view of the audience (as does the preterite) but from the perspective of the agent. In the fifty-third *laisse*, the arrangement of the tenses begins in the present:

661. Li empereres aproismet sun repaire.
        Venuz en est a la citet de Galne.
        Li quens Rollant, il l'ad e prise e fraite;
        Puis icel jur en fut cent anz deserte.

(661. The Emperor approaches his domain.
662. He has come to the city of Galne. [Immediate
        succession.]
663. Count Roland stormed it, destroyed it.
664. From that day forth it stood a hundred years laid
        waste.)

In the last line the preterite reveals the inevitable and enduring consequence stretching into the remote future—an accomplished future from the point of view of the audience, and a condition that will continue beyond the time defined by the narrative.

In *laisse* 109 we can see how the poem exploits the difference between the two signs of the future.

1401. Tant bon Franceis i perdent lor juvente!
        Ne reverrunt lor meres ne lor femmes,
        Ne cels de France ki as porz les atendent. AOI.
        Karles li magnes en pluret, si se demente.
1405. De ço qui calt? N'en avrunt sucurance,
        Malvais servis le jur li rendit Guenes
        Qu'en Sarraguce sa maisnee alat vendre;
        Puis en perdit e sa vie e ses membres;
        El plait ad Ais en fut juget a pendre,
1410. De ses parenz ensembl'od lui tels trente
        Ki de murir nen ourent esperance. AOI.

(1401. So many good men of France lose their young
        lives there!
        They will not see their mothers or wives again,
        Or the men of France who await them at the

passes.
Charlemagne weeps, wails for them.
1405. What does that matter? They'll get no help from
him.
Ganelon served him ill that day
He went to Saragossa to sell the barons of his
house.
He lost his life and limbs for what he did;
He was doomed to hang in the trial at Aix,
1410. And thirty of his kin with him
Who never expected to die.)

Verses 1402-1405 tell of what lies ahead from the point of view of those who are about to die; here the future is used for *representation,* dramatizing the situation of the young men of France and defining their prospects in terms of their losses, the things they long to see again and never shall. The two following lines concern Ganelon's treason, the cause of their hopeless future, and this change in perspective is indicated by the change in tense to the preterite. This is the simple preterite, designating the past, for the plot forged by Ganelon and Marsilion is completely included in the temporal perspective of the agents: it is part of their past, even though they know nothing about it. But from line 1408 until the end of the *laisse* facts are reported that cannot be located by the temporal and spatial coordinates that originate in the agents, facts that are beyond their ken, beyond their time and space. Here is the preterite that designates the remote, invisible, and enduring consequence, the preterite that "has not yet become the future";[7] from the point of view of the audience, it is the preterite of the accomplished future, the preterite of the chronicler.

Coming back now to the seventh *laisse,* we can see these principles at work. Each new aspect of the narrative is signaled by a change of tense: (I) Marsilion *had* the mules led out; (II) the messengers *are* mounted; (III) they *came* to Charles; (IV) he *can*not prevent their tricking him. In v. 94 there is a dramatic change in the point of view: the messengers who have been shown leaving Marsilion are now seen approaching Charlemagne, and this change is signaled not only by the choice of the verb (*venir*) but by the striking change in tense: *Vindrent a Charles, ki France ad en baillie,* "They came to Charles, who has France in his keeping."

In v. 92 two tenses are used to distinguish two kinds of succession. Once the treason is sworn, Marsilion begins the action by ordering the mules led out. Immediate succession: *Cil sunt muntez.* Ultimate, historic, momentous succession: *ki le message firent.* Since the message will be delivered beyond all doubt—since it was *in fact* delivered—this action is narrated in the preterite rather than in the future.

Now it is clear from these examples that tense is not used exclusively for the designation of time. Different tenses are used to distinguish different aspects of an ac-

tion, or different points of view; to differentiate inevitability from eventuality, or to establish moral categories. The one principle that seems to be based on the linear succession of time is the one that distinguishes between immediate and distant succession, and therefore between two temporal levels. But here, too, it is not time as such that is the ultimate object of this distinction. For these two kinds of succession distinguish two kinds of statement: the fact that the messengers are on their horses and that their accouterments are of gold and silver is of a different order from the other fact narrated in the preterite, namely, that the message was delivered, a fact that arises from historic necessity and reveals the eternal significance of these men: they are forevermore, until the end of time, the men who brought the traitorous message to the Emperor of Christendom. Thus—to judge for the moment from these examples—the present, the present perfect, and the future are employed in order to communicate details whose primary purpose is to create and maintain the mimetic illusion; while the preterite and the imperfect are reserved for facts of a different order, facts that are not, like the others, minutely dramatized or mimetically represented. And so even in this apparently temporal distinction one can see a principle at work, an essential and defining principle of the narrative technique of the *chanson de geste*: the use of tense to indicate modality. At the most decisive moments, it is by representing actions on different temporal planes that the narrative indicates their function, their necessity or their contingency, or the point of view and the moral commitment of their agents.

But it will not do to call these planes simply the present and the past since, as we have seen, time as such has only an intermediary function in the passages we have considered; furthermore, these terms—present, past—suggest a coherent and continual flow of time instead of different modal planes, non-contiguous and non-sequential, upon which the several moments of the story are variously situated. It is better to distinguish them according to their function:

1) the mimetic or representational plane, which governs the mimetic tenses—the present, the future, the present perfect—where the story is vividly dramatized in order to evoke or to sustain the mimetic illusion. On this plane, the messengers are mounted, the golden reins and olive branches in their hands; and Charlemagne, who cannot prevent them from fooling him, is still our Emperor;

2) the chronicle plane, which governs the chronicle tense—the preterite, the imperfect—and which abstracts certain moments from the narrative present and situates them in the historic past. On this plane are all those facts which, for quite different reasons, are distinguished from those that are being dramatized—either because

the details in the past tenses are preliminary or supplementary or recapitulative with regard to the dramatized action, or else because they define the monumental facts of the past in order to reveal the pattern of the future: on this plane, Marsilion ordered out the mules, thus putting the treasonous plot into action, and the ten messengers brought the message to Charlemagne.

The illuminating and dramatic interplay of these two planes can be seen in one famous line, v. 179, the concluding line of the twelfth *laisse*: *Des ore cumencet le cunseil que mal prist,* "Now here begins the council that went wrong." The chronicle tense records only completed actions, never actions in the course of taking place, because the process—the succession of moments that constitute an action—is the object *par excellence* of mimetic representation. That is why *cumencet* is here, as virtually everywhere throughout the poem, in the present tense, for the explicit mention of a beginning implies a continuing action. But the completion of this action and its immeasurable consequence are reported in the documentary tense, the preterite.

It must be emphasized that in speaking of the preterite and the imperfect we speak of a relatively infrequent element in the temporal pattern of **The Song of Roland**—it is precisely from its relative infrequence that it derives its effect. The chronicle tenses—the preterite, the imperfect—comprise only about twenty-five percent of the verbs in the poem, a fact that indicates that the present tense is the normal tense of narration. It is therefore the preterite, not the present, that demands an explanation: it is exceptional, an element that glistens in the web of the narrative because it is unexpected. It is, therefore—just because of its rarity—an essential phenomenon of the narrative function, a means of signaling at various times both that which is subordinate to the action being represented and that which is too important to be limited to a momentary condition. I would like to talk now of the global effect of this phenomenon; and here we shall see that the preterite, even as it retains its non-temporal functions, preserves its capacity to indicate the past.

What makes it possible to use the preterite to indicate the future—the epic anticipatory preterite? In *laisse* 231 (vv. 3201-3213), Baligant calls his son Malpramis: "If you can kill that proud spirit of the Franks, I shall give you a part of my land." And Malpramis—

> . . . Cil respunt: "Sire, vostre mercit!"
> Passet avant, le don en requeillit,
> Ço est de la tere ki fut al rei Flurit;
> A itel ore unches puis ne la vit,
> Ne il n'en fut ne vestut ne saisit.

> (He replies: "Lord, thank you!"
> He comes forward; he received the gift—

> It is the land that belonged to King Flurit—
> In a bad hour, for he never saw it,
> Was never vested, he never got the land.)

For, as we are going to learn—or rather, as we already know—he never left the battlefield, he was killed by Roland. Thus the death of Malpramis, a future event from the point of view of the agents, is in the past for us—that is, with regard to the time in which we listen to the **Song,** with regard to *our* present. For the epic anticipatory preterite absolutely demands the presence of an audience; it could not exist without listeners in attendance for whom the entire course of events—from the false embassy of the Saracens to the trial and execution of Ganelon—has already taken place and is therefore present all at once; an audience to whom all the furious and manifold action of a distant age appears static, accomplished, necessary, locked immutably in the frame of history.

This use of the preterite establishes and confirms a certain temporal and moral relation between the narrator and the audience. They become, in a certain way, contemporaries, no matter how much time intervenes between them, because they are drawn together by their distance from that which they both contemplate. The action is in the past for both of them. For both the audience and the narrator, the action is already complete, already inserted into an historic pattern that transcends the vision of the agents. This means that even we, today, share the poet's moral perspective, at least to this extent: we both contemplate the action under the aspect of necessity, we both see the story as *history.*

In her provocative book *Die Logik der Dichtung,*[8] Käte Hamburger has argued that in a fictional narrative the tenses of the verb are no more than a substratum: the preterite loses its grammatical function as tense, it no longer designates the past but rather a "fictive present" which is to be distinguished from the temporal present. The fictive present has nothing to do with time: it is rather a spatial present, it designates the state of *being* present, the *Da-sein,* the static and non-temporal *Gegenwart* of a painting—all that is conveyed by the romance concept *representare.* And this non-temporality of the preterite is the unmistakable sign of a narrative that is fictional, one that represents the field of experience—the "I-origo"—of fictional characters.

It is in a work of history, according to Käte Hamburger, that the preterite retains its function of indicating the past, and so the historian can exploit the judicious use of the "historic present," the present in the sense of the past. In a fictional narrative, she insists, the historic present has no function and can—and should—always be replaced by the preterite, since the preterite is the proper sign of a fictional narrative and has no temporal sense. But in a work of history, where the tenses really do indicate time, the preterite and the present can make an effective contrast. In that kind of factual narrative, the historic present can be used to produce a *Vergegenwärtigung,* a dramatic representation. It presents the characters as though they were acting of their own free will, it creates the illusion of history in the making, while the preterite reports accomplished actions, the established facts.

Now here one will recognize a precise description of the use of these two tenses throughout the *Song of Roland.* In this poem the preterite has retained its function as a grammatical tense, as a sign of historical narrative. It is the preterite that reveals beyond question that the action belongs to the past, that the action is already complete even as it is being narrated. These preterites are not determined by the temporal and spatial coordinates that issue from the position of a created character: they are spoken from the perspective of a real I, that of the narrator, the teller of history. For it is clear that the narrator of this poem is not, like the narrator in certain novels of our own time, a character like the others; he is rather the performer, the trouvère-jongleur as recorder and chronicler. It is therefore the preterite and the imperfect which convey the monumental facts of the past and define the historic frame of the poem, and which constitute a sign that *The Song of Roland* does not come forth as a fictional narrative. This narrative claims authenticity; it is what it insists it is, a work based on written documents, divinely ordained. It is no parable, uninvolved in history. It is chronicle and epic at once.

But it is not only through the narrative technique that one can establish the real anteriority of the preterit; one can detect it as well on the existential level of the *Song.* The people in the audience attend the performance of a story that they already know, an account of the most fateful event in their past: this is the necessary condition of performed epic. And it is just *this* part of their long past that is now narrated because the characters and events that appear in it are exemplary and prefigurative: this vision of the past is at the same time a vision of the future enjoined upon the audience: whoever hears this *Song* is enlisted in the struggle to reestablish the divinely ordained empire that Charlemagne once governed, in order to restore all that has been lost. The audience is witness to a moral precedent, a model by which one can judge the condition of his present, a model to emulate, a model to restore. Now there cannot be an injunctive moral precedent of this sort—a condition demanding restoration—without historical anteriority, and it is just this exemplary aspect of the past that the preterit of the chronicle conveys.

The characters in the *Song of Roland* transcend every fictive grid: we recognize them, we experience them as those who lived before us, and we react to them as we would to the personalities of a chronicle. That is because history is not simply the matter—the *matière*—of this poem, the substratum of the fictive system, as for example, the War of 1812 is the matière of Tolstoy's novel. The history of Charlemagne and of the Empire is itself a part of the redemptive drama that the divine Author has revealed to us: it could never be transformed into fiction, its nature as an event of the historic past could never be replaced by the temporal and spatial coordinates that issue from a created character.

One may ask whether, in the last analysis, there is *anything* fictional in *The Song of Roland,* even when we are told what people said to each other in certain unchronicled moments or the things they felt and remembered. The term "mimetic" that I have been using may very well be a begging of the question; for the dramatizing, representation aspect of the poem is not necessarily fictional. Everything in the poem is history—either documented history such as that which the *Geste Francor* has preserved for us; or inferred history, history as it must have happened, the authorized assumptions that enable us to perceive history's redemptive pattern. No matter who composed the Oxford version, the history that the *Song of Roland* relates is a precious and ordained heritage, the history of the mission of the Franks, preserved from generation to generation. As such it is immune to every process that would transform it into fiction, although the narrator, like every historian, may use the techniques of *Vergegenwärtigung,* of representation. He draws his authority for the narration of the undocumented parts of his story from the necessary coherence of God's plan.

It is in the frame of necessity erected by time that the audience can contemplate the providential design of the past and the future. It is by studying the great events sworn to and inscribed that each one will learn the history of a great nation, dear to God, which was betrayed by one of its own; and which, after the great losses and the great griefs that followed this betrayal, became even dearer to that God who had foreseen everything. These are the great upheavals and the great restorations that mark the path of human progress, and that we study in order to trace the design of Providence; and they are all inscribed in the book, the chronicle.

For there is a chronicle embedded in the temporal texture of *The Song of Roland,* the ultimate reference of all its vivifying details. If we set apart the introductory first *laisse,* where Charles appears in his eternal present, here is the story related in the chronicle:

> King Marsilion was in Saragossa (*laisse* II). Blancan-
> drins, who was among the wisest of the pagans and a
> good warrior, said to the King: Send false promises of
> faithful service and great love to Charles (III, IV).
> King Marsilion ended his council; he summoned ten

men to go as ambassadors and present their proposals to Charlemagne (V, VI). Marsilion ordered ten white mules brought forth for the men who delivered the message. The ambassadors came to Charles (VII). In the Christian camp there were Roland and Oliver and the Twelve Peers around the King. The pagan messengers got down on foot and greeted the King in all love and good will (VIII). And Blancandrins said to the King: Here is the message of King Marsilion (IX). And after that, the Emperor bowed his head; he never spoke hastily, without reflecting; and the look on his face was proud and fierce; and he said to the messengers: How can I put my trust in my great enemy? And the Saracen said: He will give you hostages (X). The next morning, the great barons assembled—there were Duke Oger, Turpin the Archbishop, Richard the Old and his nephew Henri, Acelin of Gascony, Thibaud of Reims, and Milon, his cousin; and there too were Gérier and Gérin, and with them there came Count Roland, and Oliver, the brave and noble. And Ganelon came, who committed the treason. This was the council that went wrong.

(XII)

This is the story that the chronicle tells in the first 179 verses of **The Song of Roland,** in the chronicle tenses, the preterite and the imperfect. Here, too, one notes certain apparently mimetic details, but it is clear that these details have been chosen because they have a significance beyond what they denote: the Emperor's slow and pensive gesture expresses his office as the King of Christendom. Practically all of the poem can be reduced in this manner to the tale told by its preterites, without the omission of any important moment in the historic event. It is only in the trial of Ganelon, at the end of the poem, where the preterite narrative loses its continuity. I think that the unusual infrequence of the preterite in the last 300 lines of this 4000-line poem is explained by the ceremonial and ritual nature of the trial itself, which is the subject of these lines. Each phase of the trial is prescribed by ancient customs that are painstakingly represented in the poem—customs which, if Ruggero M. Ruggieri is correct, take us back to the end of the ninth century.[9] The traditional nature of the trial, therefore, suffices to evoke the sense of the past and to sustain the belief in the historic reality of the event, in that sworn-to and documented history of which the **Song,** by its own word, gives the true representation.

Otherwise there are, to be sure, one or two lacunae of little importance in the preterite aspect of the narrative. But can one tell a story equally coherent and equally concise on the other plane? Here is an extract of the present-tense narrative in the same part of the poem:

The Emperor is full of joy and exultation, he has taken Córdoba and shattered its walls; his knights get great plunder from that. Not a single pagan has remained who is not killed or turned into a Christian. Around the King, the men of France: The knights are seated on fabrics of white brocaded silk; the wisest ones and the old men are playing at tables and at chess; the young men are fencing. Beneath a pine, near a hawthorne, a throne has been set up: there sits the King who governs sweet France. His beard is white, his body fair, his bearing is proud and fierce. If anyone should ask for the King, there is no need to point him out. Blancandrins has spoken, the first to speak: Here is what King Marsilion says to you (IX). It is the King's custom to speak in his own good time. He gets up. He answers: Marsilion can still save his soul (X). The King orders a tent to be set up; there he has the ten messengers lodged. Twelve serving men have provided for their needs. They remain there till the dawn. The Emperor has arisen early in the morning, has heard mass and matins. The King has gone beneath a pine, he calls his barons to hold his council; he wants, in all things, to proceed with the aid of the men of France.

(XI)

In this extract, the present and present-perfect are the mimetic tenses *par excellence*. In these tenses all of those details are conveyed that dramatize the action so tersely reported on the chronicle plane, details of which the greater part—the marble steps, the reins of gold, the white brocaded silk, the lodgings of the messengers—reveal their significance only when seen in the light of the preterite chronicle, which defines the significant event. This is not to say that everything related in the preterite derives directly from the chronicles to which the story alludes. It is rather that the function of the preterite is to remind the audience that these events are a part of history, that they have already taken place and, in their essential outlines, been recorded. The preterite in **The Song of Roland** thus represents a claim to authenticity, like the narrator's allusions to the *Geste Francor,* which is itself based on irrefutable documents—*written* documents—including the depositon of the baron Saint Gilles. That which is said in the preterite is endowed with the qualities of a written text: immutability, duration, authority—the qualities of truth itself.

Now it is clear by the very miracle that preserved this history for future generations—a miracle of writing—that this chronicle records more than the actions of men: it is the chronicle of the nation's future as well as of its past, for the cycle of suffering and amelioration that it reveals will continue till the last age, when the state ruled by Charlemagne shall be restored exactly as it was in the past, and Charles will once again be *nostre emperere*—an age prefigured in the great apocalyptic battle with Baligant. In other words, the past revealed in the chronicle is not simply the historic past but also the providential past, the past foreseen by providence, the past that defines the pattern of the future.

Now this point of view, which enables us to regard events of the past in the context of the future, is inconceivable without the attendance of an audience, for the audience's present lies in the future envisaged by the narrative. It is the audience that knows that what a character thinks about doing he has in fact already done or refused to do. It is the audience, by its presence, that establishes the pastness of the event. From the perspective of those in attendance upon the *Song,* every event, every moment, every gesture takes place by necessity, because they know that it has *already* taken place. Their point of view participates to this extent in Providence: by virtue of their position in time, those who hear the song consider all the moments of an action, and all the actions of an event, simultaneously, knowing everything at once from beginning to end, seeing every moment framed in a necessary and immutable design. It is therefore the performance situation which is the ultimate context of the tenses of the verb in *The Song of Roland,* and generally in the *chansons de geste.*

Once seen in the transfiguring perspective of Providence, action loses its essential quality and is transformed into its opposite. For when it is perceived as part of a vast and invariable pattern, it too becomes static: every action is transformed by necessity, it cannot change or develop, it can never be different from what it was; all chance, every alternative possibility, every potential but unrealized consequence is excluded forever. For the action is accomplished and chronicled, it is now perceived whole and so appears as a fixed element, no longer as a succession that unrolls in time. In this stasis the two genres of lyric and epic are joined.

For the sake of this demonstration, the preterite has been abstracted from the whole temporal design; now it must be put back into the fabric of the narrative. And as soon as it resumes its relation to the other tenses, one will perceive that *all* of the tenses of the verb in *The Song of Roland* would be appropriate in a chronicle, that the chronicler, too, uses a mixture of tenses to enliven his history. All of the tenses are at once chronicle tenses and mimetic tenses, and it is the function of the preterite to make us continually aware of this fundamental truth.

There are two seminal works on time and tense—one quite recent, the other from a distant age—whose distinct perspectives enable us to test our perception of the temporal design in *The Song of Roland.*

In his book *Tempus,*[10] Harald Weinrich distinguishes between the *besprechende* and the *erzählende Tempora,* the tenses of commentary and the narrative tenses, each group defined by the kind of reaction it is supposed to evoke. In using the tenses of commentary, the speaker signals to the receiver that his message should be heard with a certain tension, for he is speaking of things that concern them both directly, even as he speaks. They are both *engagé,* for the frame of reference of the message is the situation in which they find themselves together, and what the speaker has to say may affect their very

survival. On the other hand, in using the narrative tenses the speaker indicates to the receiver that the subject of the speech lies outside their common situation; his words have to do with something more or less remote and may be heard with a certain *détente,* for no effective reaction is expected from the receiver: the situation in which they communicate with each other is not the arena in which the action takes place. The tenses of commentary are the present, the present perfect, and the future; the narrative tenses are the simple past, the past perfect, the imperfect, and the conditional. This view of the function of the tenses accords with our own distinction between the mimetic and the chronicle tenses in the performed epic; for the mimetic tenses locate the action in the spatial and temporal realm of the performance situation—the audience "sees" an historical moment taking place—whereas the chronicle tenses enclose the action in the frame of the distant and accomplished past.

Both Harald Weinrich and Käte Hamburger, for all their considerable differences, are alike in insisting that in a fictional narrative the preterite is not used primarily to designate the past. But they both fail to point out that the use of the preterite in fictional narrative derives directly from its normal grammatical function as "the past tense." In ordinary, everyday discourse, when an action is related in the past, that means that it has run its course. It is perceived as immutable, incapable of further development through accident or intention. But once an event is over and done with, it inevitably takes on a form: it is abstracted from the endless, metamorphosing welter of experience and framed in our perception. Now that is how the preterite came to be used as a fictional narrative tense: it is a sign to the audience that the action being narrated has a determined and perfected from, a beginning and an end, even though at any given moment we may be attentive only to one part of that form. A person speaking in the past tense may ramble on and on, having lost sight of the end—but the end is there, and the action that he is describing is defined forever, redeemed from the formlessness of actual experience by the aestheticizing effect of distance. The preterite thus comes to be the sign of a certain aesthetic discourse, narrative, essentially distinguished from the potentially infinite desultoriness of ordinary conversation.

But the most profound and the most fundamental study of time and tense is contained in Book XI of St. Augustine's *Confessions.* I believe that in this work we can find the truest perspective on the relation of time and performance.

It begins with the question that taunts us all: *Quid est ergo tempus?*

> If no one asks me what it is, I know; if someone asks me and I wish to explain it to him, I know not. I only know for sure that if nothing passed away, there would

be no past time; and if nothing were yet to come, there would be no future time; and if nothing were, there would be no present. But these two times, past and future, how can they *be,* since the past is no longer, and the future is not yet? As for the present, if it were always present and did not move continually into the past, it would no longer be time, but eternity. If then, the present, in order to be time, only comes into existence because it goes into the past, how can we still say that it exists, since the reason why it exists is that it shall exist no longer; and so, to speak truly, we can only say that time *is* because it tends continually *not to be.*

(XI, xiv, 17)

And yet, we perceive intervals of time, and we compare them and say that some are shorter and some longer (xvi, 21). But how can that be, how can we measure time, since the only time that exists is the present, and the present, passing instantaneously into the past, is a point without extension? "And yet, who would tell me that there are not three times, as we learned as boys, and as we have taught boys—past, present, future. . . ." (xvii, 22)

> For where do they who foretold future things see those things, if those things do not yet exist? For that which is not, cannot be seen. And those who relate (*narrant*) things past surely could not relate the truth if they did not discern those things in the mind; now if none of those things existed, they could not be discerned. Things past and things future, therefore, exist.
>
> (*Ibid*)

But wherever they exist, they cannot be there as future or as past, but only as present, for only present time can be measured (xviii, 23). Where, then, is that present extended so that it can be measured? When one narrates past things truly, one draws from the memory not the things themselves, which are past, but words conceived through the images that those things imprinted as traces (*vestigia*) on the mind, imprinted them through the senses as they passed. My childhood is past, but its image, when I evoke it, is present, because it is still in my memory (*ibid.*). Similarly, when we think of future things, our fore-thinking (*praemeditatio*) is present (*ibid.*).

> What now is clear and plain is that neither future things nor past things exist, not is it properly said that there are three times, past, present, and future. But perhaps it might be properly said: there are three times, a present of things past, a present of things present, a present of things future. For these three times are somehow in the soul, and I do not see them elsewhere: the present of things past is the memory; the present of things present is the sight (*contuitus*); the present of things future is expectation.
>
> (xx, 26)

These three times, being present, can be measured. But it is not only presence that is necessary before a thing can be measured, there must also be dimension, or

extension, as well. Therefore, time is a certain extension, *quandam distentionem* (xxiii, 30)—but of what? It must be an extension of the mind itself (xxvi, 33).

*In te, anime meus, tempora metior* (xxvii, 36), "It is in you, my mind, that I measure times." The impression (*affectionem*) that things produce in the mind as they pass remains in the mind even after they have passed; and it is this *affectionem* that I measure, for it is present, not the things that have passed by to make this impression: this is what I measure, when I measure time.

Let us suppose that someone intends to utter a sound of some fixed length. Before he speaks he has already composed a space of time, in silence; and then, committing it to memory, he begins to utter that sound, which goes on till it reaches the end already fixed. In the course of this performance it *has* sounded and it *will* sound, for so much of it as is completed has already sounded, and the remainder will sound. Thus it goes on, as the present intention (*praesens intentio*) causes the future to move on into the past until, through this diminution of the future and enlargement of the past, the future is consumed and all is past (*ibid.*).

In doing this the mind performs three acts: *expectat, adtendit, meminit*—it expects, it considers or is attentive, it remembers; that which it expects passes through that to which it is attentive into that which it remembers. It is in this way—it is in the mind, that past, present, and future are all both present and extended and therefore measurable.

> I am about to recite a psalm—a psalm that I know. Before I begin, my expectation is extended over the entire text; but when I have begun, whatever part of that psalm I have plucked away from my expectation and gathered into the past is now extended along my memory; and so the life of this activity of mine is now stretched out between memory and expectation—memory, because of what I have recited; expectation, because of what I am going to recite. But my attention is present all the while, and through it passes that which was future so as to become past . . . till all expectation is consumed, when the act is accomplished and has passed into memory. Now that which takes place regarding the whole psalm takes place as well for each of its parts and for each syllable. And the same holds true in every act of greater length, of which this psalm is perhaps a small part; and it holds true for the whole life of man, of which all the acts of man are parts; and it holds true for the whole age of the sons of men, of which all the lives of men are parts.
>
> (xxviii, 38)

Now this last splendid sentence must give us pause, for we must ask: Whose is the mind whose faculty of attention considers the *saeculum totum,* the whole age of the sons of men? Whose faculty of expectation is stretched toward it, who sings it, who conveys its moments progressively into the memory till expectation is consumed and memory enlarged? St. Augustine clearly cannot be looking beyond this *saeculum,* for he would never attribute this discursiveness to the mind of God. "Far be it," says he (xxx, 41), "far be it that you, Author of the Universe, Creator of souls and bodies, should come to know all things past and future in this way, like one who sings or hears a song that he knows, in whom the expectation of the words to come and the memory of the words already sung cause his feelings to vary and his senses to be distended." For there is no change in God's knowledge and no change in His action, He is beyond time, eternally present. It was to demonstrate God's transcendence of time that Augustine undertook this meditation upon past, present, and future. Past, present, and future exist only in the realm that God created: "Let them see," he prays God, "that time cannot exist without the creature." (xxx, 40)

From this we may see that the divisions of time, the alternation of tenses, the very existence of tense in our language and of anticipation, attention, and memory in our minds is a sign of our discursive and contingent existence. This, I believe, is the final truth revealed in every celebration of man's great deeds and monuments. Epics and chronicles proclaim us creatures, they foretell the death of the warrior, or detail the degradation of his ideal, or find a cause for admiration in the weariness of God's faithful servant.

When St. Augustine speaks of the mind's anticipation, consideration, and memory of the whole age of the sons of men, he can only be thinking of the human mind focused upon history. Here he shows us the way to understand the activity of the epic poet and the epic audience, and the relation between time and performance.

For in the performance, once the epic song is begun, and even before it is begun, the common memory of poet and audience evokes the entire story, from beginning to end, and at once their common expectation is charged. Their memory performs the two functions defined by St. Augustine: it apprehends at once all the things that are about to be told verse by verse in the song—the song that they know—and it retains all of the things that have been told, the parts that have passed before their *contuitus,* their "sight." It is by this phenomenon of performance that we can account for the mixture of tenses in the *chanson de geste.* The representational tenses, the mimetic tenses—the present, the future, the present perfect—direct the action toward the *contuitus,* the vision focused on each moment at the instant of its passage from the future into the past, so that this action unfolds in the present of things present. The chronicle tenses—the preterite, the imperfect—refer to the whole action, its beginning and end already contained in the memory, where it is understood as history and continues to exist in the present of things past.

And just as there is a double function of the memory in the performance in the epic song—one that records the performance and one that extends beyond it to the historical past—so there is a double function of anticipation or expectation, that faculty which apprehends the present of things future. Expectation anticipates the future of the performance, but it extends beyond the performance to the historical future as well, the future of history.

For memory contains the whole age of the sons of men, from the Creation to the Fall to the Redemption, to the establishment of the Christian Empire, to the dissolution of that Empire after Charlemagne's death. All these things are present in the memory as images—as vestiges left in the memory, not by the things themselves which passed away long before the epic audience was born, but by the recounting of these things from generation to generation in chronicles and songs. Now those in attendance on the performance remember the providential history of mankind, which is the true subject of **The Song of Roland.** And remembering it, their expectation is aroused, for they know that the whole age of the sons of men lies only partly in the past, that its total form will be completed in the future—the future revealed by the past. And so they anticipate, at once, the completion of the song in performance, and the completion of the age prefigured in the song, the last days, when the Christian Empire shall be restored, and all time shall cease—and tense shall have no meaning.

One of the most striking features of St. Augustine's Book XI is that it explains the human experience of time in terms of performance—"I am about to recite a psalm—a psalm that I know." The terms that he uses can help us see that the performance of epic song is a moving model of time built upon the expectation, attention, and memory of the audience. It is through these acts that the human mind becomes capable of measuring—that is to say, of *experiencing*—the past, the present, and the future of its own life and of the whole age of the sons of men. These dimensions of time are at first circumscribed by the little circle of the performance, coinciding with the beginning and end of the *Song,* and then extended to the very limits of time, the resumption of eternity.

Here, finally, we can see the redeeming effect of memory and anticipation in the temporal world, whose defining trait is that it tends continually not to be, a world saved from disintegration only by God's gracious admonition—*admonitio*—calling the plummeting soul to draw upon the truth and the power in the treasure of its memory. It is only through memory and anticipation that the disintegrating effect of time can be halted, and time itself extended. And memory is the basis of all, even of anticipation—there could be no anticipation, if there were not first memory. Roland himself anticipates *our* memory and the performance in which we are witnesses to his great deeds, as he calls upon his companions and vows that the songs that men will make of him will never portray him as a coward. To be commemorated is the hero's last and greatest victory; to commemorate, the epic poet's supreme calling. Only through memory and performance can the epic world create a shelter for its monuments and a space for its community—through memory, which, as St. Augustine says, is the mediator between time and eternity;[11] and through performance, the actualization of communal memory.

### Notes

1. *La Chanson de Roland,* ed. Gérard Moignet (Paris, Brussels, Montreal, 1969), vv. 89-95.

2. See the bibliography in Friederike Stefenelli-Fürst, *Die Tempora der Vergangenheit in der Chanson de geste* (Vienna, 1966). The following studies should be added: Michel Blanc, "Le présent épique dans la Chanson de Roland," *Actes du Xe congrès de linguistique et philologie romanes,* II (Strasbourg, 1962), 565-578; "Time and Tense in Old French Narrative," *Archivum Linguisticum,* 16 (1964), 96-124; L. Peeters, "Le présent épique dans la Chanson de Roland," *Revue des langues romanes,* 81 (1974), 395-423; "Syntaxe et style dans la Chanson de Roland," *ibid.,* 80 (1972), 45-59; Minette Grunmann, "Temporal Patterns in the Chanson de Guillaume," *Olifant,* 4, 1 (1976), 49-62.

3. See Martin de Riquer, *Les Chansons de geste françaises,* tr. I. Cluzel (Paris, 1957).

4. See Karl von Ettmayer, *Analytische Syntax der französischen Sprache,* 2 vols (Halle, 1930), pp. 688, 886; and Tatiana Fotitch, *The Narrative Tenses in Chrétien de Troyes: A Study in Syntax and Stylistics* (Washington, D. C., 1950), especially pp. 20-24, 43-44. As Fotitch notes, the alternation of tenses was a recognized procedure of Latin rhetoric. See, for example, Meusel's analysis of Caesar's *De Bello Gallico,* cited by Heinrich Blase in *Tempora und Modi (Historische Grammatik der lateinischen Sprache,* ed. Gustav Landgraf, III, 1 (Leipzig, 1903), p. 104; the technique of describing battles, for example, closely resembles that of the *chansons de geste*: "Die einzelnen Momente des Kampfes werden durch das Präsens gegeben, das Ergebnis durch das Perfekt." Also: "Die Verba des Glaubens und Meinens stehen selten im Präsens, ebenso die des Meldens während das, was infolge der Meldung geschieht, präsentisch ausgedrückt wird."

5. I present a fuller treatment of these principles in my communication, "Le Temps de chronique dans la Chanson de Roland," in: *VIII Congreso de la Société Rencesvals, 1978* (Pamplona, 1981), pp. 173-183.

6. See Grunmann, cited in note 2 above.

7. Anna Granville Hatcher, "Tense-Usage in the Roland," *Studies in Philology,* 39 (1942), 597-624.

8. 2d. ed., Stuttgart, 1968.

9. *Il processo di Gano nella Chanson de Roland* (Florence, 1936).

10. *Tempus: besprochene und erzählte Welt,* 2d. ed. (Stuttgart and Berlin, 1971).

11. See the comments of R. C. Taliafero in his translation of the *De Musica* (Fathers of the Church, Vol. 4), pp. 163-164; cf. pp. 375-376, n. 21. *Cf.* Robert Jordan, "Time and Contingency in St. Augustine," *Review of Metaphysics,* 8 (1954-55), 394-417.

## Robert Francis Cook (essay date 1987)

SOURCE: Cook, Robert Francis. "Rereading the *Song of Roland*" and "The Characters: Words and Deeds." In *The Sense of the* Song of Roland, pp. 127-46; 160-77. Ithaca, N.Y.: Cornell University Press, 1987.

[*In the following excerpts, Cook studies the contemporary implied audience of* The Song of Roland, *and examines the epic's main characters.*]

[It] can be a difficult task to discover what sort of hero Roland is in the Oxford *Song of Roland,* or how his story embodies (as it is said to do) the spirit of its age. He is surely an energetic man and a paladin, a great fighter. The reader scarcely needs a literary critic's help to notice that. But when one does read what critics have had to say about him, far more often than one reads of some perversity—a tragedy, a failure, built into his very character, making all his prowess hollow. Pierre Le Gentil, the most influential recent interpreter of the *Song,* implies that he puts his own civilization in jeopardy: "At the last moment, abandoning all caution, surer than ever of his prowess—perhaps unmindful of the fate of his men and of the greater interests of Christianity [*la Chrétienté,* Christendom]—he blindly rushes into a battle that from the start is doomed by his own fault. . . . Roland, in his eagerness to answer his stepfather's challenge, exposes Christendom to a catastrophe."[1] He does these things, we are told, because of a pathological concern for his reputation, a pathetic sense of his own superiority, a *démesure* that leads him to boast when he cannot perform, to scorn obviously reasonable advice, and to bring on a disaster that he could have prevented by the proper exercise of his leadership.[2]

Any reader curious about medieval life and thought may very well ask how such a tale of narrow, selfish pride fits the framework of a time like the late eleventh and early twelfth centuries—a time of endemic local struggles, of uncertain central government, of baronial privilege, all of which temporarily threatened Europe with political instability, economic stagnation, and a patchy cultural future. What sort of response is the self-centered heedlessness we find in Roland supposed to have awakened in the hearers for whom he was created? He is said to look upon man's deadliest occupation as a sport or game. What does this have to do with the ethos of the elite around the year 1100? A story of o'erweening pride may have held the interest of its hearers then, but did it do more than entertain them? Can "a tale of personal grudge and feud leading to treachery and national disaster" (Owen) have spoken to the age of Europe's emergence with any moral force?

The usual answer to such questions is to posit the poem of culpable rashness and then read it as an example of behavior to avoid. As Le Gentil puts it, "The Oxford poem criticizes Roland, or causes him to be criticized, in unequivocal fashion."[3] There have been apologists for Roland the character, including Le Gentil, who have argued that, though unthinking and prideful, the hero is not beyond redemption (eschatologically or aesthetically). But it is still traditional to claim that the text teaches us that the disaster of Roncevaux is the wages of Roland's pride: "It cannot be too often stressed that the drama of Roncevaux is at heart [*par ses origines*] a human drama, initiated by Roland's pride [*C'est la démesure de Roland qui l'explique*]."[4]

When we, at least, contemplate the announcement of Roland's failure and the statement that his humanity lies in his flaw, we are satisfied. It seems proper to us to express an ideal such as that of "measure" by showing the sad effect of its opposite; and, though earlier medieval literature, and epic in particular, tend to a straightforward portrayal of heroism (or saintliness), that is indeed no reason to insist that a Turold could not have essayed, instead, a more familiar, apparently more sophisticated, negative form of exemplum.

Still, important questions remain, for some readers at least—questions that the tradition of scholarly interpretation of the *Song of Roland* has never answered and in some measure has failed to address. Are Roland's preternatural soldierly skills, his sublime prowess, his firm statements of feudal principle, his translation to heaven, really caveats? Is that how they link functionally with the other elements in the *Song of Roland* to lend weight and closure to the narrative? And more immediately important: is Roland really such a fool? Does he talk and act like one within the text and within what we know of the duties of his caste? If these and other questions of the sort no longer inspire perfect consensus among *Roland* scholars, it is not just because Roland's fate is what Le Gentil calls an "apparent paradox"; it is in large degree because so much of what happens in the

*Song of Roland* seems to have little relevance to the theme of overbearing pride and its consequences, or no congruity with it at all. The disparity is quite large, as I have tried to suggest in the Commentary. Among its effects in criticism has been an exaggerated disdain for the way the work is constructed. Even so great a partisan of its unity as Joseph Bédier did not hesitate to call the Oxford *Roland* "enigmatic," to declare parts of the poem "obscure, nearly unintelligible," to claim that the poet, "too human to choose," never makes clear his own attitudes toward the *"preux"* Roland and the *"sage"* Oliver.[5] In the *Song of Roland,* then, the hero's misguided bravura is thought to be evident, but once that is posited, the narrative means used to express *démesure* are often described as vague.

The purpose of the foregoing Commentary and these supplemental essays is to explore how the *Song of Roland* makes sense as a different story. The intensity of scholarly commentary on this most famous of French epics has not always been matched by any great breadth of curiosity about why its contents and sequence are precisely what they are. The traditional reading of the poem was established and elaborated under the strong influence of late nineteenth- and early twentieth-century concepts of realistic narrative. Methodological innovations have since proceeded apace, both in criticism and in the writing of narrative itself. Yet the entrenched conception of the *Song* as a psychological drama, and the insistence on psychology—Roland's character and his interaction with the others—as the main validating feature for interpretation, have survived even in the work of those who mistrust the philological methods of our predecessors.

Not that I mean to apply any innovative calculus to the narrative values of the *Song of Roland.* There are two reasons to stick to a more prosaic algebra instead. First, if a new reading is to gain acceptance, it must be put into terms accessible to the broadest possible interested audience. Second, my analysis is meant to form a contrast with the reading generally given from Léon Gautier's time (if not Fauriel's or Grimm's) to Le Gentil's, and to permit comparison with that reading it should be cast in a form compatible with it. For those reasons I chose to begin with an old exercise whose advantages should not be underestimated: that of the explanatory paraphrase. The foregoing Commentary is similar in form (though not in scope) to the summaries every reader learns when first encountering a lengthy and ancient work of narrative art. It resembles, as well, the sort of mental paraphrase on which readers tend to rely, for some purposes, as much as they do on the whole text. This is not, then, a "new reading" in the sense become traditional in some critical circles—applying some category of modern thought (Marxism, Freudianism, deconstructionism) to a poem created without overt attention to such things.[6] Behind the paraphrase lies instead a deep curiosity about the author's and the audience's habits of literary thought, and their attitudes toward heroic subjects.

If the *Song of Roland* is not primarily a study in psychology, then what should we take it to be, and how should we take on the task of interpreting it, which (for an epic narrative at least) is the preliminary to other forms of understanding? My answer—temporary as all such answers are—is that it should be read as certain other works of art of its time are "read," as an ethical statement, embodying values in a framework that is no less aesthetically satisfying for all that it conveys ideas. Recognizing its power means admitting that our ancestors may have been moved, even excited, by ideals whose aesthetic status is greatly diminished today. Coming to grips with such historical particulars is a prerequisite for any reading that aims to discern where the poem's universal appeal may actually lie.

The appeal to history as a guide to interpretation is an important feature of philological method, and as such it has often been decried by proponents of various forms of New Criticism and by some structuralists. Some "Poststructural" theorists, on the other hand, have been less inclined to insist that something intrinsic to literary texts allows us to interpret them without ever referring to how their makers and audience thought and lived. The available space does not allow me to discuss at any length the ways concepts associated with reader-response criticism and reception theory echo the historical philologist's concern with the text's effects in the past. I can only note briefly that in the case of a work like the *Roland,* the practical, mediating interpretations medievalists give may be strengthened by considering such notions as the variability of communities or the implied audience.

Thus, for example, Stanley Fish has invoked the authority of "interpretive communities" to help explain how conflicting readings arise and come to supplant each other (an implicitly historical notion). In Fish's strategy, the concept of interpretive community permits us to avoid the impasse created by the insistence that meaning is specified either by isolated readers or by the text itself taken in isolation.

The solution will not seem particularly strange to literary historians who know, say, Gaston Paris's work on the relationships between Arthurian literature and the court of Champagne, Curtius's on vernacular literature and the medieval intellectual community, Robertson's on the milieu for which Chaucer wrote, or Stock's on textual communities.[7] Decisions about what counts in a text are made according to prevailing assumptions that stem not from individuals but from the "interpretive communities" to which they belong. As Fish puts it:

> What was normative for the members of one community would be seen as strange (if it could be seen at all) by the members of another. In other words, there is no single way of reading that is correct or natural, only "ways of reading" that are extensions of community perspectives. . . . This meant that the business of criticism was not (as I had previously thought) to determine a correct way of reading but to determine from which of a number of possible perspectives reading will proceed. . . . The business of criticism, in other words, was not to decide between interpretations by subjecting them to the test of disinterested evidence but to establish by political and persuasive means (they are the same thing) the set of interpretive assumptions from the vantage of which the evidence (and the facts and the intentions and everything else) will hereafter be specifiable.[8]

For the purposes espoused by the present community of readers of the *Song of Roland*—primarily a community of persons curious about other, medieval persons—the preferable reading is the one probably attributable to another community, a medieval one. The "perspective" or point of view from which the hermeneutical ball is set rolling is a perspective created by our knowledge of the past. It is often claimed that we cannot know the attitudes of the past, but such claims apparently stem from overarching philosophical assumptions about knowledge itself, rather than from any actual demonstration that history is a total failure. A different assumption unites such divergent theorists as Hans-Georg Gadamer and E. D. Hirsch, who allow us the capacity to recognize and grasp meanings that are not the meanings we originally had in mind—even if they come from the past.[9]

Fish, like most of his colleagues in reader-response criticism, does not put the question historically, but it is more important to note that, in his formulation, two communities' criteria for right reading differ and can be identified:

> Given the notion of interpretive communities, agreement more or less explained itself: members of the same community will necessarily agree because they will see (and by seeing, make) everything in relation to that community's assumed purposes and goals; and conversely, members of different communities will disagree because from each of their respective positions the other "simply" cannot see what is obviously and inescapably there. This, then, is the explanation for the stability of interpretation among different readers (they belong to the same community). It also explains why there are disagreements and why they can be debated in a principled way: not because of a stability in texts, but because of a stability in the makeup of interpretive communities and therefore in the opposing positions they make possible.[10]

Fish, therefore, does not merely postulate the interpretive community. He explicitly gives it a form of authority for textual meaning, and this decision has clear application in medieval studies. Indeed, it is easier to understand historically why two communities differ in their assumptions than it is to understand why contemporaries constitute more than one community (Fish seems to define communities pragmatically, more by the interpretations they give than by any other features they may have).

A formulation such as Fish's allows us to pursue our curiosity about authors and early audiences, not as ultimate arbiters of meaning, but as the putative authorities on what the text meant to them. Deciding how they would have exercised their authority, without confusing our own with theirs, remains a difficult task, but the difficulty itself is historical and subject to historical rules. Where there is little or no evidence of how medievals actually first reacted to a work—as is the case for the *Roland* among many others—there is at least evidence for the preoccupations and attitudes of a medieval community, and that evidence can be applied according to the usual canons of probability.[11] (In the Commentary, I have followed the rough working consensus according to which the overt content of the *Roland* implies a knightly, or soldierly audience, an idea to which I will return.) Error is possible in the exercise, and anachronism is specifically an error, since it means assuming an authority over medieval readings as historical events that belongs properly to medieval people. Before attributing a reading of the *Song of Roland* to Turold or Henry Plantagenet, the medievalist must do whatever can be done to specify anachronism—study language as the interpretive community under consideration used it; discern the place of the text's elements of reference in the community's mentality; and even judge the implicit claims of critics that the text corresponds to essentially postmedieval frames of reference.

A historical reading of the *Song of Roland,* then, seeks to reconcile the text with a time and place, with people not ourselves, as we know them. It is a type of reconstruction, not an immanent reading; what it tries to reconstruct is one or more versions of the text's meaning that have already existed—especially those likely to have been natural to the intended audience and the author, whose reactions and achievements interest us profoundly. Intuition does not offer any form of guarantee that we are sharing anything; analogical criticism asks us above all to acquiesce in the analogy; but a historical reading can draw on what has become a considerable mass of studies on medieval habits and society. I have only scratched the surface of that mass, and yet in the preceding pages the constraints of terrain, time, and physical strength, the practicality of vows and hardihood have easily taken the place of assumptions and intuitions about personality and honor in the *Song of Roland.* The substitution allows parts of the work to be analyzed as functional where traditionally they were hardly analyzed at all. On the other hand, to posit a historical context and characterize a likely medieval audience does not solve all our problems.

It is essential for us to use the medieval predicate of meaning—to speak of "What the *Song* meant to a medieval audience"—but that is not entirely adequate. There is every reason to think that there were multiple meanings for real medieval people just as for us. One thinks of the heresies described by Stock, of the fourteenth-century disagreements about the *Roman de la Rose,* of clerical condemnations of apparently rather orthodox romances, or, more immediately, of the medieval remakers of the Roland legend, who gave parts of it length and complexity of a sort it does not have in the Oxford version and probably did not have in the *remanieurs*' models. One may even imagine, and not idly, that there were medieval hearers who sympathized with Ganelon and felt he was entitled to wipe the rear guard out.

In this sense we may still teach and describe more than one *Song of Roland,* within certain limits: a monastic one condemning the sin of pride in one or more characters; an individualistic one defending Ganelon's right to put personal interest above the group's; a monarchical one wherein Charlemagne's court in the *Song* is identified with the kingship of Louis VI or Louis VII of France. All we need to do, it would seem, is posit an audience that would most likely have heard the work as we wish to describe it, and then speak from that audience's vantage point.

The risk is that the interpreter will attempt (in Robert Crosman's words) "to impose on modern readers responses [the critic] is not certain of being able to persuade them to adopt on the evidence of their own reading of the text."[12] It is not enough to posit a likely past community or "homogeneous past" and then derive statements about the text's meaning from the characteristics of that community rather than from the text's content and procedures directly. Here another theoretical concept comes to our aid: that of the "implied reader" (here, "implied audience"), which allows us to pay close attention to the text's allusions and to how the narration unfolds, without requiring us to abandon our curiosity about how the work was perceived in the Middle Ages.

The implied reader or audience is neither a hypothetical extratextual construct nor a real audience, but a feature of the text. In W. Daniel Wilson's handy definition, it is "the behavior, attitudes and background—presupposed or defined, usually indirectly, in the text itself—necessary for a proper understanding of the text."[13] A literary work will not always exhibit an imaginary reader (Wilson's "characterized fictive reader") to whom the narrator actually speaks. It is well known that narratorial asides are rare in the *Song of Roland,* although they do occur. But a text will always have an audience whose anticipated reaction guides the author.[14] That implied audience's characteristics will be discernible from the way the text goes about informing it—or not informing it—of things it needs to know in order to understand: in the Oxford text, the pagans' intentions at the outset, the dangers of the Pass of Cize, or the wording and results of Roland's promises, of Turpin's, or of Chernuble's.

The concept of implied audience is rooted in the study of literature as communication, not just in literary phenomenology. By definition, the implied audience of the *Song of Roland* is that with which it communicates fully and effectively; by inference, it is those hearers for whom it was designed. In my example above, a real reader sympathetic to Ganelon must consider what the text asks of the implied audience when it shows an angel guiding his accuser's hand. The angel's presence implies a religion, and his act implies a judgment. "An interpretation of the implied or intended reader's role in a work must aim at what the author intended (in a wider sense) to communicate, and historical circumstances will condition this intention," says Wilson.[15] On the other hand, the implied audience is, again, a formal feature of the text in that its state of knowledge about events is what the narrative communicates. (This is one of the ways in which it may differ from any real audiences that had heard a *Song of Roland* more than once.) To concentrate on it is to give ourselves the advantage of not having to postulate, as sole guides to a historical reading, either an author about whom we know nothing specific or an audience about whose actual composition we are ill-informed. We may rely instead, as we would in any reading, on observations and inductions.

A glance at my Commentary will show that what I have referred to as "the hearers" or even as "we" is often the implied audience, not a hypothetical one reading the *Song of Roland* through Freudian, structuralist, or even Augustinian categories. I consider the limitation an important one in the first stages of choosing a reading. It would be possible, though burdensome, to show that *Roland* criticism has at times shifted from the implied or intended audiences to hypothetical real ones and back for reasons of convenience. But when we have deliberately described what we think was the implied audience of the *Song,* it has not always been incongruous with the probable real one. The implied audience of which the text informs us is only a clue, "no more authoritative and restrictive on our own right to establish a new interpretation than other aspects of a work are."[16] But it is an important, even irreplaceable, clue to the existence of a definable group with which the author worked to communicate—a "most likely medieval audience," or a historical interpretive community, as we might put it with Stanley Fish's terms in mind.

Observation of the Oxford text then leads us to a picture of the audience, implied and probably real, that is not unfamiliar, since we have at least partly been guided by the text's implications all along. To judge by what the *Song* talks about overtly, its audience was knowledgeable about feudal practices; anyone who can follow the text's feudal allusions will also have certain historically real knowledge of the system that is its setting. I will also reason, in Chapter 5, from the presupposition that the audience was not only conversant with the rules of society but also interested in them, that is, that the poem did not bore its intended audience. (This assumption, a safe one in the case of the *Roland,* is coming to be acceptable for a growing number of other medieval texts, as indeed it should be.) Furthermore, on similar grounds, the implied audience grasps Christian eschatology, is comfortable with formulaic style, and is familiar with campaigning and fighting on horseback and on foot. Its interests do not seem, on the face of things, to be primarily ecclesiological—another old observation—but it is neither pagan nor German nor even Carolingian. In short, the implied audience has interests a great deal like those that many of the Oxford redactor's contemporaries had: the needs of feudal society suffice to explain them. And—if we accept the account of its knowledge and likely reactions that I have given in the Commentary—the implied audience is not hostile to didactic concerns, any more than many real contemporaries of the Digby redactor were.

Gerard Brault has already argued at length that the numerous restatements of the traditional interpretation "fail to do justice to the poem's religious dimension or misconstrue its techniques of character portrayal,"[17] and I do not intend to attempt gleaning after him in the fields of iconographical or exegetical analysis. But I believe that one need not acquiesce entirely in Brault's postulate of a conflict between "Christian" and "feudal" values in this masterwork from an age notorious for its disinclination to separate religion from daily life. Thus, without any desire to minimize the importance of the religious atmosphere that is so clearly a major aspect of the poem, I have preferred to apply my curiosity principally to the nominally secular questions of responsibility, to the matters of government and social principle that furnish the immediate setting of the action. For convenience, I have called the set of relationships involved "feudal," though there is no great uniformity among scholars—especially literary scholars—in the use of that term. I understand by it the system of vassal and lord, of homage and mutual service, discussed more fully in Chapters 5 and 6.

The structural key to the Roncevaux episode is the relationship, through time, between promises and their accomplishment. (This is the general burden of Chapters 2 and 3 in this part.) Roland's promises are qualified ones, and their context is broader than the battle of Roncevaux. These facts, though not always appreciated, are essential. Roland carries out his promises as qualified, while his enemies neither limit theirs nor succeed in fulfilling them. There is little to be gained by contorting these elements of the text, or ignoring them, for the sake of a scholarly doctrine of heroic pride. Personal pride—even if Roland did exhibit such pride—would be irrelevant to the theme of responsibility and sacrifice in a context of promises and ensuing, related acts.

"The problem of vassaldom is at the very heart of the **Chanson de Roland**."[18] The construction of the work—Roland's context as a character—has the highest possible likelihood of resonance with a larger context, that of a relatively early medieval society in which the oral vow, homage and its analogues, represented the knight's primary way of shaping the future. This resonance (treated primarily in Chapters 4 and 5) requires even more thorough consideration than **Roland** criticism has already given it. This is not to say that Roland, Oliver, and Aude "do not have" a psychology. Any human action can probably be described in the terms psychologists use. But the **Song**'s structure cannot be deduced from psychological categories, for the **Song of Roland** is not a drama of personalities. It is a drama of the sworn word. It exalts neither a nation nor a religion so much as the power and efficaciousness of faith: faith in the bonds of promises kept, between persons and God, of course, but also among persons.

Feudal ideas have been associated with the **Song of Roland** for a long time,[19] but to apply them in a systematic inquiry into its meaning is another matter. Breadth of definition is a strength rather than a weakness here, as I will argue in Chapter 5, since we cannot discern precisely when or where the **Song of Roland** took shape. Various forces coexisted uneasily within feudal society, throughout the period of the **Roland** and far beyond it, and we tend to emphasize the tension where we might with equal accuracy emphasize the coexistence.

Feudalism, as it pertains to literary interpretation, is a strong tendency for people who lived together under a common general arrangement to take the argument as natural. It is very much like what most historians now recognize as a "mentality" (or set of shared attitudes)[20] Any such set of attitudes will probably contain some profound contradictions, but experience, and numerous studies, show that the contradictions do not prevent the mentality from functioning—it, rather than some radically different system, will most likely occur even to highly intelligent and thoughtful people as a point of reference. Such a tendency of thought may manifest itself in literature in quite general terms.

That a mentality of reference, despite the great strength of its original appeal, may have lost the favor it once enjoyed is axiomatic in the history of ideas, but we have been slow in applying that insight to the study of *belles lettres*. Medieval ways of conceiving and idealizing a set of relations among people are surely as vital an element of "alterity" as are medieval genres or styles of composition. And (to borrow R. S. Crane's terms) they affect the "pre-constructional" and "constructional" phases of poetics as well as the "post-constructional" ones.[21]

At this point, the problem of reading for meaning overlaps with questions of history. The fact that the **Song of Roland** does not say explicitly how its parts are related to its themes does not mean that its construction is loose or confused. Many of the questions that arise as we read it can be answered by information about its historical setting. That is an obvious alternative to the postulate that the **Song** is an unclear or ambiguous work. Yet numerous critics have chosen to follow another tradition of explanation, that exemplified by Erich Auerbach's well-known claim that the paratactic line or sentence structure of the **Song** is mirrored in a mystifying absence of logic in the story itself. Paul Zumthor offers a convenient summary:

> Opposition between the stripped-down precision of the utterance, and what appears to be a lack of clarity on the plane of narrative causality, an ambiguity deriving from the uncertainty into which the hearer is plunged: which of the previous propositions gives rise to the one now being heard? Perhaps the order of causality and implication is reversed: because Roland must be avenged, he dies; because he is to die, he must be betrayed. The text can be understood only imperfectly, or not at all.[22]

This expresses both a hermeneutic stance and an aesthetic position. In the atmosphere created by such presuppositions, the characters' hidden motives and unspoken thoughts may come to seem as important as anything they actually say or do. The protagonists are seen as vehicles of a kind of complexity, even ambiguity, whose evocation lends the work a misleading air of aesthetic familiarity. Guesses about what Roland, Charlemagne, or Ganelon is thinking (when the **Song** does not say) may then replace scrutiny of sequence and juxtaposition, cause and effect as instruments for understanding it.[23] To analyze the **Song of Roland** has long meant assuming (as Auerbach in fact did; see Chapter 4) that uncertainty about circumstances is a real feature of the narrative, and one that any implied audience may presumably be expected to accept. On the other hand, arguments against incoherence and for the work's unity of structure have been made primarily in terms of psychological categories—Roland the proud (or, in Roger Pensom's terms, the neurotic), Oliver the wise, Charles the weak—rather than by reference to the situations the characters are in and to the potential for constraint those situations involve.

Furthermore, the reluctance to explore allusions to the situation, and the appeal to assumptions about the psychology of the characters, are intertwined with each other and with the *démesure* theory in the history of *Roland* interpretations, since any of the three can serve as a postulate apparently authorizing the other two. Whatever in the text does not match the requirements of the received interpretation can be laid to the incoherence of the narration. Concern for cause and effect can be transferred to the realm of character study. The three ideas of incoherence, psychological deduction, and foolish pride work together to make empirical, inductive, close reading seem either unnecessary, or unlikely to give significant results. For these and other reasons, there has never been a full-dress exposition of the *Song* from the vantage point of its likely historical setting—even in the simplified form I have adopted here. On the contrary, its place in history has usually been assigned on the basis of the often-repeated *démesure* hypothesis.

In other words, the interpretations found in the secondary literature of medieval studies are borrowed for use in other contexts *as though* their referents were historical. The use of imaginative literature as a tool for exploration of the past is a well-known tenet of the "*Annales* school," as Calin has recently recalled;[24] thus it is no surprise that, let us say, Philippe Ariès gives a particular interpretation of the *Song of Roland* status as an element of medieval culture. "The death of Roland," he says, "became the death of the saint" and was so regarded "by the clergy as well as the laity."[25] Neither is it especially surprising that Philippe Contamine can state that "the notions of sacrifice, and absolute devotion, seem alien to medieval mentality,"[26] although when he does so he is taking an implicit stance (perhaps unintentionally) against sacrifice as the rear guard's reason for dying at Roncevaux.

In an older but equally famous study, J. H. Randall adopted the *démesure* convention as an important element in his summary of premodern civilization. At the same time, he repeated the incompatible but equally traditional description of Roland as *bon vassal*:

> The knight was first and last a warrior. Hence valor, personal and physical, was his prime quality. The reckless courage of Roland, who from pride and confidence refused to blow his mighty war-horn for Charlemagne when the Moors ambushed the rear guard of the Frankish army, and thus doomed his fellows to destruction, had its counterpart in many of the great fighters, like Godfrey of Bouillon and Richard the Lion-Hearted; it was forever making impossible anything like sound military tactics. . . . Of equal importance was loyalty; for the performance of the numerous vows of medieval society, the very structure of feudal obligations, depended upon it. . . . Roland expresses this feudal loyalty admirably as he goes into battle.[27]

Here Randall has in effect attributed literary *démesure* to a pair of Crusaders (one of whom may have shown it, one of whom, Godfrey, almost certainly did not). And so it is that the early Romanists' descriptions of literary texts find strong echoes in such diverse publications as the *Annales,* the *Dictionnaire de théologie catholique,* and Ezra Pound's *Spirit of Romance.*[28] In similar fashion but in a more literary context, Georges Duby and Erich Köhler have integrated accepted notions of courtly love into their discussions of twelfth-century French society.[29] "All critical schools adopt in practice, without question, the findings of literary history," says Goulemot.[30] He does not explicitly include interpretation in his definition of literary history (borrowed from Raymond Picard), but observation shows that literary historians rarely eschew interpretation, indeed probably cannot. In the context of their statements about authors' ideas, biographies, and achievements, their interpretations tend strongly to be passed on, as part and parcel of the history.

To reread the *Song of Roland* means to apply systematically the hypothesis that Roland may be strikingly right in what he does and says, even where that is not immediately clear. This heroic hypothesis of interpretation assumes the text is largely coherent and that it presents information about events that orients our reading, though inconsistencies may seem to occur or have habitually been posited in it. In other words, like its predecessor, the reading of the *Song* as exemplary is a tendentious reading. We may thank hermeneutic criticism for reminding us that tendentiousness is not some avoidable defect, but a feature common to all readings, at least all those that seek coherence in sequential narratives.[31] The question is which tendency of reading is most consistent with the contents of the text. In the case of a tale devised for an audience from a lost culture, we must ask which tendency matches what can be known of the context in which the tale was designed to be heard. The answers to those questions are supplied by public testing of coherent readings that can claim a basis in the text and also in what we know of its times.[32]

My analysis does not, I have said, seek to apply any special method, but it does make some claims about the poem's content and its implications that have not been made frequently. A few words about the assumptions behind them are in order. I began with the suspicion, aroused by the work of Alberto Del Monte, Alfred Foulet, Gerard Brault, L. S. Crist, Norman Cartier, Emanuel Mickel, and William Kibler, that what is at stake in the *Song of Roland* is not persons and their short-term survival but a social system or set of ideas about society, thought to transcend immediate personal concerns. Rather than seek to explain *why* Roland would boast, or would pursue a course leading to an incomprehensible death, I have tried to show the important senses in which those things do not occur at all in the text. Arguments to that effect may seem forced or conjectural unless we distance ourselves from the secondary literature and take the measure of *démesure* in the poem.

That, in turn, requires us to remember that the *démesure* interpretation is itself a hypothesis, not an argument, and has a traceable history. It was affirmed very early without extensive confrontation with the text. Early specialist reports—those of Paulin Paris, Léon Gautier, Gaston Paris, and Louis Petit de Julleville—make roughly identical claims about the work's import and Roland's place in it, but they cite only isolated lines and psychological surmises as evidence. The ubiquity of the interpretive hypothesis of Roland's pride hides the fact that throughout the better part of the nineteenth century it was purveyed by authors who never thought to test it against any alternatives. By the twentieth century, the hypothesis seems to have been considered as having been established at some earlier time. It is assumed, as a basis for deductions and arguments, in the fuller analytical work of Bédier and Menéndez Pidal. Both the hypothesis and the confidence with which it is repeated lead us to expect elements in the poem—exaggerated claims, missed opportunities—whose presence is not revealed by close reading.

Upon examination, the poem appears neither to exalt heedlessness nor to express a grudging acceptance of it. The heroes often criticized for presumed errors are in fact, and in context, aware and foresighted, as leadership in any age requires. Neither Roland nor Charles is marked by any fatal flaw. But they are marked by their places in the story and in a fairly well known, historically localized structure of leadership. If Roland and Charles do not act to prevent Roncevaux, it is because their freedom to act is limited by military and political reality. There cannot be an immediate, iron-clad demonstration of this, less because society in a large sense has nothing to do with narrative literature than because there is no eleventh-century handbook of procedure—civil or military—with which the *Song of Roland* might be compared in detail. What I can do is examine the text for congruency with the feudal system as I understand it as a nonspecialist—through the general works of Frédéric Ganshof, Marc Bloch, Georges Duby, Jean-François Lemarignier, David Herlihy, Joseph Strayer, and others. In so doing, I use such terms as *rules* or *principles* in the looser senses applicable to historical feudalism as those authors describe it. These tendencies of thought stand as points of reference for reading the poem. They occupy the place usually occupied by broad claims about human psychology as a universe, or about the protagonists' own characters, which in my view are not givens but points at issue. I have tried to limit my assumptions to the nearly obvious, and my deductions to those that allow for a consensus of informed readers. Though I cannot speak with the authority of an institutional historian, I am convinced that a reading more closely related to feudal ideals is one that offers better textual and historical credentials than the *démesure* hypothesis can show. That is, in sum, a recognition that the latter reading had

its own assumptions (Roland's autonomy in the field, the mutability of his promises, and the finality of his death, for example) and that these may be found anachronistic not merely in the abstract but in comparison with the text we know, the situations it contains, and the ideas it names.

The many forms and manifestations of the *démesure* hypothesis make testing it a particularly complex task. The idea that Roland causes a disaster at Roncevaux through self-destructive error is one of the oldest ideas in medieval literary studies. The tragic error is implicit in the summary Francisque Michel gave of the poem when he first published it in 1837: "The most prominent hero is Roland, who, through the advice he gives Charlemagne, brings about Ganelon's betrayal, his own death, and that of the twelve peers at Roncevaux."[33] The idea is made explicit at least as early as Gaston Paris's *Histoire poétique de Charlemagne* (1865): "[Oliver] asks Roland to sound his ivory horn. . . . Roland refuses out of an exaggerated sense of honor."[34] In Louis Petit de Julleville's edition (1878), it has taken on something like its modern form: "Roland destroys the entire rear guard, and himself, at Roncevaux, through his foolish obstinacy. . . . [Such flaws] lend his character [the effect of] life and truth."[35] Having attained the status of a given in *Roland* scholarship early on, the tragic principle of interpretation has served for generations as an element of argumentation or proof in studies on the poem's origins, poetics, politics, and genre. Now that *démesure* itself has come under occasional attack, it is not surprising that the aesthetic and historical arguments that *démesure* helped establish long ago are sometimes invoked themselves as givens that make it inevitable. This network of interdependent arguments in various areas makes the *Song of Roland* both a strikingly illustrative work to interpret correctly and a burdensome work to treat with anything approaching thoroughness.

Under most circumstances a summary or paraphrase of the *Song of Roland* would stand or fall virtually alone, depending on whether it is accurate, complete, and respectful of historical context. But to establish a reading where another, very different one has long been accepted and is so thoroughly enmeshed in a vast secondary literature is a more problematic business. To say practically anything about the *Song of Roland* is to repeat someone and to contradict someone else. To say anything about its content, organization, and meaning, in the context of such a complex set of critical reactions, is to imply some stance on its origins, its intended audience, their literary and social mores and outs, and so on. Heroism, obviously, and the feudal system, less obviously, have aesthetic standing, and their very importance in the *Song* can thus be denied on grounds that appear to override history. Merely to consider them is to raise the general question of how reactions are related to the text. It is incumbent upon the reinterpreter not only to state what lies behind the new reading but to explore the implications of his conclusions. Hence some closing arguments (Chapters 7 and 8) to the effect that the *Song of Roland,* as it is described here, deserves all our efforts of understanding and explanation.

I cannot pursue all the threads of this tangled skein to final conclusions, but it will be clear to anyone interested in any of the broader questions I have referred to that I would be remiss in my duty as an interpreter if I gave them short shrift. The reading is its own best argument, even if it cannot quite stand alone. Nonetheless, in the vast body of criticism specifically devoted to the *Roland,* there are elements that clearly must be treated in greater detail. . . .

* * *

The narrator's voice in the *Song of Roland* is every bit as laconic about characters as it is about events and their causes or effects. With rare exceptions ("Ganelon . . . who committed the treason" [178]), we must derive our notions of them from a narrative that prefers showing to telling. But the characters are not mute themselves. "The knights are valourous, their words are noble" (1097): promises, boasts, battlefield taunts and scornful replies are part of the technique of representation in the work, and not a matter of ornament.

This brings me back at once to a point that any revisionist reader of the *Song* must face over and over. Just as we associate the structure of the work with pathos and tragedy, all experienced readers also recall the impression Roland's speeches made on first reading. That impression—as the secondary literature abundantly confirms—is negative. The hero's words seem brash, impetuous, and offensive. They appear to express a limitless self-confidence and an arrogant sense of superiority that refers every event and every character to itself.[36]

It has then been natural to assume that Roland makes rash promises and fails disastrously to carry them out. This aspect of the standard interpretation requires a presupposition that has almost never been discussed explicitly before. Roland must be the victim of a well-known form of narrative irony. His martyrdom is at best the unintended consequence of an attempt at earthly conquest. The glorious victory of which he boasts is impossible, and the finality of death awaits him instead. If he is accepted into the company of the angels, it is because he has stumbled into sublimity by mistake. D. C. Muecke has called this "self-betraying irony," "where the false image a character has formed of himself clashes with the image that the work enables the reader to form."[37] I have suggested in the Commentary that

this irony, like the pathos just discussed, has been supplied not by the work's events but by a prior hypothesis of reading, and that when Roland's speeches appear to reinforce the notion of an irony working against his expectations, our impression needs to be corrected.

It is true, once again, that sophisticated commentators, sensitive to the tension between the foolish Roland and the heroic legend, have combined the character and the legend in complex ways, a reaction that flows more or less naturally from our first impressions of Roland. We may then read that Roland is prideful or foolish, but not culpably so; or that he is guilty, but partly lucid; or that he is initially foolish but later humble and clearsighted.[38] As I have said, the presumption of complexity is then reflected in considerations of structure, and we are obliged to posit anagnorisis or ambiguity where they are not otherwise necessary. In fact, as I hope to show, we need not assume either structural ambiguity or confusion in the heroic protagonist in order to recognize the text's inclusion of human diversity. But the diversity is in the characters that surround Roland, not in him. The speeches of Oliver, Ganelon, and Naimon express precisely that diversity, not authorial disapproval of Roland's vision.

It is axiomatic that, in the absence of explicit comments, the text will convey Roland's character to us by his words and deeds.[39] That makes it all the more imperative to examine these in detail without trusting to general impressions. I have said that some consequences of Roland's actions are comprehensible only with respect to certain ideas. The eschatological framework into which we are to fit the many deaths, though stated, is never systematically expounded. But the promises Roland makes are set in a complete narration, and, once we have examined their style closely enough to have gained a clear idea of their import, we may compare them with the textual events they refer to, and to other characters' claims about those events.[40] The results may well make us uneasy with the assumption that the hero's statements are designed to reveal an inadequate understanding of his fate.

In particular, if we do not take up Roland's speeches in the First Horn Scene with the presupposition that they will lead him into unexpected catastrophe, then we will realize that what he says contains no exaggeration. Roland is in fact more nearly given to understatement, even in the most flamboyant of his remarks: "I will strike great blows; my sword will be bloody along the whole length of its blade" (1055-56, 1065-67, 1077-79), when in the event he does not merely strike, but slays, and cripples even Marsile without having boasted of it as the pagan peers had done just before. The *gabs,* then, are on the enemy side.[41] Roland's promises are characterized rhetorically by a consistent meiosis, a reverse Delphism in which he raises minimal expectations and then exceeds them. *Démesure* characterizes the claims of his foes, and not his, as the comparison of laisses 69-78 with laisses 83-88 has shown. Here I would like to explore one of two ramifications of this presentation of the First Horn Argument.

Roland's replies to Oliver's suggestions are sometimes said to show not only his overconfidence, but also his overbearing nature. It is true that this is not the way we would like our neighbors to talk to us. Furthermore, our humanist sentiment is that it is not a good thing to be impatient with what we take for weakness in others. But the primary observation we must make on the text, one that goes far toward answering the claims of Roland's detractors, is that even in this emergency Roland speaks not to Oliver's character but to his suggestions: *Ne dites tel ultrage* ("Don't say such a dishonorable thing"; 1106; cf. 1113). His sharpest line, *Mal seit del cuer ki el piz se cuardet* ("Cursed be the cowardly heart"; 1107), is a generalization, though it may be read as a reference to a suspicion on Roland's part (in fact an accurate one) that Oliver may not be quite himself at the moment (cf. 1036 and the commentary to laisse 81). But Roland never indulges in the accusations that Oliver will employ against him in the Second Horn Scene. Roland's first-person pronouns, his references to his own honor and his own family (which appear only here), may be the better part of discretion in this sense, and not signs of egotism. After all, he has the choice between tempering his remarks by putting the problem in terms of himself ("If I were to do what you suggest, I would be wrong") or replying directly to his temporarily shaken friend ("*You* are wrong; you are making a shameful suggestion").

As for humanism and tolerance, if Roland is right in any degree, then there is every reason for us to accept his sense of urgency. The poem up to this point has led to this: when the expected attack has actually come to pass, will Roland carry out his promises? Will he, unlike Ganelon, meet the challenge of exemplary behavior? Oliver has just seen how very many pagans there are. We are not told what his reaction was to the nomination of Roland and the choosing of the rear guard, whether he understood the danger as Charles, Roland, probably Turpin and perhaps Gautier del Hum did, or whether he is only just now grasping it. But to judge by his way of describing what he has seen from the hilltop, Oliver is unsettled specifically by the large number of Saracens (1035-36, 1049-52). The issue in the First Horn Scene, as Oliver puts it (and as Bédier's interpretation, for instance, puts it by implication) is this: is Roland to carry out his promise to defend Charles and his goods even though the pagans are more numerous than Oliver expected? And the answer must be: yes, of course. Oliver is himself an important character, but his opinion on the number of pagans involved is an irritating side issue. Nothing else has

changed. The statement of the meaning of Roncevaux was made when Roland accepted his task, with no qualifying reference to numbers. If he meant what he said when he made that statement, then it is no wonder Roland is adamant about holding to it now.

Let us recall the words of Roland's original, controlling promise, as they appear in lines 755-59. "Charles the king will, in my view of things, lose not a palfrey nor charger in the rear, not a mule, not a packhorse, without a decision of arms—unless things have been decided by the sword." These future tenses constitute an authentic prediction. Roland has not said that Charles will not lose a single warhorse or beast of burden at Roncevaux or in the mountains—though this prediction, had he made it, would have come true as the others do. He says, instead, that Charles will suffer no loss without a fight, without resistance. That is not a boast, but rather a minimal statement of assent, a definition of the rear guard's duty to which Roland will hold consistently. Given our knowledge of feudal proceedings and of the importance of form in fixing a vassal's responsibility, we may not assume such precision to be insignificant; indeed, we must give serious consideration to it, as we always have to the precisely worded oaths of Guenevere or Iseut.[42]

Only afterward, as if to suggest his awareness that he has been betrayed, does the hero speak three angry lines to Ganelon, echoing Charles's. "Evil man (renegade?), did you think the glove would fall from my hand in public, as the wand did from yours?" (763-65). The comparison with the earlier scene underscores what the text is about to show; that Roland's mission will begin with a good augury, not with an ill omen. He does not drop the token he receives (a bow, in fact, not a glove—hardly a telling inconsistency). Showing how strongly he suspects a risk whose existence he cannot prove, Charles offers his nephew half the army instead of a detachment. Roland refuses this expedient as unworthy and makes a final, precisely qualified promise: "Cross the passes in total safety. You need fear no man while I am alive" (790-91). Again, he has bound himself by a promise he can keep, if his will is strong enough, though he may not live, a possibility to which his last words allude. Roland is angry, perhaps deeply saddened (again *irascut*, Naimon's word, can mean both),[43] but there is no sign of heedlessness. To produce any such signs, we would have to modify what he says.

The issue is vitally important, for if Charles or Roland were to try to change the course of events (implicit from the Council Scene on), it would mean in effect accusing Ganelon of the highest of crimes without proof. Circumstantial evidence indicates, early on, that any promise Roland makes here will be tested to the extreme limits he evokes, even to death. But that is the logic of a situation and not the dictate of personalities. Roland's character is no different from the ideal character of his whole class. He must, in the end, do as he says, with no regard for the immediate circumstances—betrayal, the overwhelming size of the army sent against him—or bend his vows to his own point of view, as Ganelon does.[44] Roland chooses the ideal, and when he might have modified his choice, in the Horn Scene, he reaffirms it explicitly again and again.

It is helpful to recall briefly what sort of limitations his commitment places on Roland. It is not, perhaps, until we review the histories of the art of warfare (at least the more recent histories, which allow the feudal age some tactical sense) that we realize how the limits on maneuverability and the difficulties of communication—the mountains and the breath that blows the horn—affected the medieval soldier's task. As noted in the Commentary, it could be of the utmost importance that one stick firmly to one's plan or assigned place. Chaos threatened the feudal army's line of march and its plan of battle as inevitably as fire threatened wooden cities. In the Commentary, I have taken the Crusades not as a direct explanation of the Saragossa campaign but as a well-documented, nearly contemporary example of the need for and the respect given to strict discipline among both footsoldiers and knights. The movements of the latter could, at need, be firmly subordinated to the needs of the army as a whole, as R. C. Smail makes clear in his discussion of what he calls "fighting on the march."[45] We may understand the habitual Turkish tactics of harassment as attempts to destroy a necessary order in the Western armies, and we may admire the discipline that allowed the retreat from Bosra in 1147 or the march from Acre to Jaffa in 1191, through hostile territory and under intermittent attack. Apparently (though it will not do to insist too strongly on the coincidence) the Muslims considered the rear of the moving army to be its weak point and directed their attacks especially against the rear guard.[46] Individual initiative could save the day, but to an extent that the *chanson de geste* rarely shows, it could lose it as well. Hence the period's slow movement away from autarchy in social organization may be thought to have parallels in warfare.

Therefore, once we remember that Roland is not a general but a lieutenant, and commands not an army but a detachment with its own function, we see that the question before him is eminently understandable in tactical terms. Is he to carry out his promise to stand fast, or is he to modify his position in difficult (but not entirely unforeseen) circumstances? The poem shows the former choice and its consequences, but it cannot simultaneously show what the consequences of the latter decision would have been. Criticism has often assumed that the consequence of the horn-call would have been a victory, and survival for the rear guard.[47] I have suggested that if we think of how the army as a whole (not the mounted force that accompanies Charles on his

mission of vengeance) travels in the Pyrenees, we may find that conclusion overly hasty. But even if it is correct, it leads us back to a platitude that the *démesure* theory could never entirely hide: when attacked by a superior force, one should call for help, and live to fight another day. We must consider that the feudal system, as a set of social and political ideas, may have generated more sophisticated arguments than that.[48]

This raises an essential point for our understanding of what is expected of Roland at Roncevaux and of what he is referring to in his speech of acceptance. What is the function of a rear guard in general, and how does it govern this rear guard in particular? It is a question to which the poem gives only very limited space. That is not in itself proof that the question is negligible. There is an excellent chance that the brevity of Charles's allusion to the crossing of the Pyrenees is, rather, an indication of the intended audience's familiarity with the nature of Roland's task. Unfortunately for the application of that well-known principle of historical criticism, any such familiarity is long lost, along with a number of other things that our forebears neglected to write down. The personal and oral nature of the knightly apprenticeship may have made its codification in written form superfluous. But it is not quite true to say that the poem itself gives no indication of what the rear guard is needed for. If we are to understand the text's brief invocation of this crucial matter, however, we will have to rely to a certain extent on historically conditioned common sense.

The mountains, the Pyrenees, may be in the work for any of a number of reasons, all well chronicled elsewhere, but it may also be that the poem makes a particular use of the Pyrenees as a locus of action, a use that we have not yet considered thoroughly. Edging toward the pathetic fallacy, we speak of the high peaks and the dark vales of Roncevaux as a poetically evocative setting for great and hopeless deeds. But the mountains may also have suggested something else to the minds of hearers with more immediate knowledge of campaigning in the age of muscle power.

The Pyrenees are rough mountains indeed, in many places bare and unforgiving. The medieval track that crossed such terrain was uncertain, steep, and narrow. Einhard's famous passage reminds us precisely of the dangers such a crossing may involve. It must have been a struggle to bring an army across a mountain pass in the eleventh and twelfth centuries, what with laden pack animals, problems of supply and organization, and no doubt dust, thirst, and heat in the best of seasons. Like many other tasks we no longer appreciate, that of moving an army efficiently or safely at the time the poem was written must have required skill and energy even when the terrain and weather were favorable. Any difficulty may have called forth in concentrated fashion the initiative and stamina which, in theory, had created personal leadership in the distant past.

But none of those considerations, now beyond absolute proof, is necessary for the understanding of what is involved in the return from Spain in the *Song of Roland.* We need only consider two obvious points. First, an army did not travel in armor ready to fight—even the pagans must arm and equip themselves before attacking Roland—and, second, it did not and could not travel through mountains in defensive formation: its order of march was dictated by the terrain. Much more likely than not, a medieval army went over a high pass in something like single file. One never knows how to judge medieval tactics; they depended too much on the particular combatants involved. But it cannot have been good to ignore the possibility of danger implied by the relatively defenseless posture of an army entering the high mountains, with undefeated enemies behind.

It is this context of potential danger that gives their full meaning to Charles's two sentences concerning the crossing of the pass:

You see the defiles and the narrow passages.
Choose now who shall be in my rear guard.

(741-42)

It also makes clear why Roland speaks unstintingly of resistance and never of victory. Victory is not his assignment. It is not part of the context of Roncevaux. Neither does he require any orders. The nature of his job is clear on its face, and he sums it up himself. If an attack comes, when it comes, he must stand his ground between the attackers, with their advantage of surprise, and his comrades, and in the crudest of terms buy time for the army to cross the passes safely (as it does) even at the cost of his life.[49]

Roland promises nothing more, but the text underscores the urgency of his situation in various ways. Naimon knows that in this extremity things will be hard and that they cannot be changed: the rear guard is Roland's—no baron can or will change that—but send good men to make a stand with him! (778-81). And Gautier del Hum echoes, as compactly as possible, Roland's own words of commitment in the face of danger: "I am Roland's man, I must not fail him" (801). In an embedded replica of Charles's choice, Roland then does an obvious thing. He sends his vassal onto the high ground, with a detachment, "lest the emperor lose any man of his there." The narrator here adds the same qualification Roland used in his acceptance. Gautier will not come down, however rough the going, until many swords have been used (810-11). When his men are dead, and he has done all he can, Gautier still does not flee. Critics have wrongly accused him of cowardice, as they have been wrong to accuse his captain of heedlessness.[50] Instead, Gautier rides down into the thick of a hopeless battle, fights on, and is killed, one of the very last, at Roland's side.

I will not discuss Roland's speeches in the Second Horn Scene or the Council of Charlemagne in detail here; both are treated at length in the Commentary. Where the council in particular is concerned, it has now become commonplace to recognize that Roland, not Ganelon, has grasped the situation rightly and that his arguments from long experience of Marsile's perfidy are justified. Surely the analysis already given suffices to show that, despite our impressions, the exhibition of heedless pride is not Roland's function in the Oxford text. We must admit that Roland not only does not *do* the sort of thing we have ascribed to him without full study of the context; upon close examination it is clear that he does not *say* the sort of thing our criticism has implied. I do not doubt that it is beyond the power (and outside the proper domain) of scholarship to prove that Roland never makes any statement that cannot conceivably be interpreted as prideful. But the textbook description of his character requires him to be consistently and blatantly prideful, and that I think the text does not allow. Primarily, he does not boast, at least if boasting means to proffer exaggerated statements of one's own prowess and importance. We may not like all the overtones of what Roland says, and the results may unsettle us, but what he says is true nonetheless, in the only context in which we can know him. From the very first he calls for vengeance and war, which is unpleasant of him, but he does so, and he is the only character to do so, on the basis of experience.

Roland is neither Hotspur nor Custer.[51] Despite the overtones of the adjectives applied to him in criticism, the intensity of his speeches is a response to the challenge of his situation and not to the excitement of bloodlust. His words are strong because he is using them (and his exemplary swordstrokes) to urge his men to their duty, in circumstances where hesitation means more than momentary embarrassment. The only irony in his speeches is the controlled irony of his grim jests—the reference to Oliver's broken lance (1360-62), perhaps his exclamation when the rash Saracen seizes him: "I don't think you are on our side!" (2286). It is a point of view he shares with those around him, with Oliver at first (1006-7) and with Turpin. This is no more and no less than the battlefield humor of any and all fighting men, who laugh as they set to work, and laugh ironically because they know only too well what is ahead.

In arguing that Roland's role in the *Song* is exemplary, I am of course also suggesting reevaluation of the roles of the characters who disagree with him or comment otherwise, by word or deed, on his acts. I have had occasion, [elsewhere] to speak of Charlemagne in connection with the work's most significant and decisive scene, that of the hero's nomination to the rear guard, since Charles's situation and Roland's are closely bound in that scene. I will speak briefly of Aude and Gautier del

Hum at the end of this chapter. But first a few words about two other major characters—Ganelon and Oliver—are in order.

I have described Ganelon's double betrayal in the Commentary. Ganelon's machinations have two sets of victims: the rear guard, and the pagans who believed his claim that Charles was fighting only because Roland spurred him to it. ("Whoever betrays a man brings death to himself and to others" [3959], though the reference there is to Ganelon's compurgators; see the commentary to laisses 287-89). That turn of events naturally helps give us a sense of his character. But the most important thing from the point of view of the theme of duty and responsibility is surely the lie he tells Charlemagne upon his return from Saragossa (laisse 54). Not only does Ganelon avoid his mission in this particular as in others, but worse than that, his falsehood covers up the infidelity of the enemy. In the long run, he betrays even Naimon's good sense, by making it impossible for the Franks to know what the hostages really mean. It is therein that the larger significance of his character lies. As the *Song* shows him, he is not only a traitor in the mechanical or functional sense; above all, he serves as a constant reminder of the vulnerability of the feudal community of trust.

Yet the issue in describing Ganelon is not precisely that of individualism versus something else. Rather, through the figure of the traitor, the text shows how an individual's shortsightedness can do great harm, while simultaneously showing, through the example set by Roland, how the individual can further the general good by accepting necessary constraints. But Roland, with Charles, Turpin, Gautier, and his detachment solidly behind him, is no more isolated than any epic hero, and perhaps less so than many. Critics working deductively from the *démesure* theory have sought to assign something very like Ganelon's role to the hero instead and have parsed an unbridled individualism as the cause of the Roncevaux tragedy.[52] But that role—the heedless pursuit of private ends and personal status—is the traitor's. Of the two, he is the one who uses his free choice from the beginning. In a major departure from the traditional procedure, Roger Pensom has provided a remarkably similar restatement of Ganelon's position relative to Roland in the poem: "Ganelon is dedicated to his own freedom, and Roland to the acknowledgement of the constraints that bind him and which order his life."[53] But despite his numerous remarks on the "common-sense" aspects of the narration, Pensom appears to share at least some of the mistrust of the story to which I have referred. . . . He relies on analogies with the categories of psychoanalysis as warrants for his interpretation of this passage and others. Thus, further along, he classifies Roland's sense of responsibility as "neurotic."[54] I will continue to stick as closely as I can to the poem's events and words, which do not

suggest to me the sort of internal conflict Pensom describes in the hero.

Roland is the first to speak in the Council Scene, but he names no names except Marsile's, and insults no one in particular (unless we make the large assumption that the unexpressed plural subject of the verb *loerent* in line 206 is Ganelon and not the plural *Franceis* from 205). The hero's argument is historical, and the necessities to which he refers have no personal dimension. Only a very strong extratextual hypothesis like *démesure* can invest his words with insulting qualities. Ganelon chooses to fling the first insult of the poem in response, and his counsel flies in the face of reality as established by the Franks' prior experience of Marsile. He chooses to make a cutting reply to a reasonable if energetic evocation of the situation as it stands. Following a principle discussed in Chapter 2, Ganelon's first choice then governs at least his own later choices, including the choice to betray, since his embassy is the logical but impractical result of the counsel he gave in his first speech. What happens to him is clear without our having to extrapolate, from his allusions when cornered, some idea of a long-standing quarrel between him and Roland. The quarrel that is in the text is enough.[55]

In general, then, our understanding of the text has little to gain by our injecting either great subtlety or lonely nobility into Ganelon's reactions in the Council Scene and the later actions that follow from them.[56] There is no longer much risk (as perhaps there once was) that, if we decide Ganelon is wrong, critics unsympathetic to ancient narrative forms will mistake him for the mustache-twisting villain of some simplistic melodrama. Like the setting in which he appears, the character may be thought univocal without being considered simplistic. His initial insistence on treating with an untrustworthy enemy leads him into prolonged opposition to his society's best interests. He makes a mistake, and hews to it; there is, unfortunately, nothing unrealistic in that. We should not forget that Ganelon was created in an age when error had overtones of commitment to evil and that (much like the pagans) he cannot desist from perversity. But we do not have to take that fact as a starting point for discovering what he does in the text. There have been numerous apologias for him, but none has reconciled him with all the facets of his manifestation in the *Song*. Thus Moignet, for example, follows Ruggieri's lead in saying that Ganelon's challenge to Roland before leaving on his mission is legitimate because it is couched in technically valid terms; yet this fails to address a larger issue. No *desfi* is valid except as a response to sufficient provocation, as Ganshof implies.[57] Even without reference to the fact that both Roland and Ganelon are on campaign in Charles's service, even without recalling (as Ganelon does not) that he swore to aid an enemy, the pretext Ganelon uses is far from adequate. Roland's suggestion, followed by a procedurally correct ratification from the group, is nothing but the consequence of Ganelon's own arguments, and no provocation at all.

A certain body of secondary literature nonetheless argues that Ganelon never committed treason and that an attack on Roland was (as Ganelon claims when on trial) a matter of private vengeance, not implying betrayal of Charles or the army. We have no way of knowing what Ganelon was thinking when he explained to Blancandrin and Marsile how to deprive Charles of his right arm (laisses 29-30, 41-45). But we can at least compare Ganelon's claims about the act with what the poem shows. His claim, made after we have seen the bloody consequences of what he did, is not at all compelling, even if we were to decide that conflict between king and "overmighty subject" is a generic attribute of heroic epic.[58] Let us grant that in reference to the much more tenuous relations of twelfth-century political life, with its multiple homages, treason is a difficult term to apply. Local laws in the eleventh or twelfth century may have been quite as complicated as the situations they had to resolve. But feudalism is the setting and not the theme of the *Song*. The theme is responsibility: the knight's duty to serve God and one suzerain as a knight. Like any trial, Ganelon's may bring to mind any number of potentially relevant analogies and arguments. But the Oxford poet's art is, once again, an art of reduction. As he settled the Spanish question on the battlefield, he proves by unanswerable violent device that the right can prevail even when men's prevarications hinder it. The issue in the Trial Scene is the power of Ganelon's family and friends to prevent or delay judgment—summed up in the threatening presence of Pinabel, who has sworn to champion Ganelon without any reference whatever to law. The barons do not acquit Ganelon; they fail to judge at all. They are *felun*, as Charles puts it, deficient in feudal morality, offering no *consilium*. It is their abdication and not any uncertainty about Ganelon's guilt that gives rise to the duel, making Thierry's confrontation with Pinabel every bit as necessary as the fight at Roncevaux, and (for much the same reasons) every bit as significant.

Oliver is not like Ganelon. He is clearly different from Roland, but not his opposite. However, a reaffirmation of the primacy of sacrifice as an ideal in the poem means a reevaluation of Oliver's stance, one that will be at least as thorough as the one to which Ganelon's must be subjected. The classic view of Oliver is that he embodies *sapientia*, thought, while Roland knows only action.[59] The deduction behind that opposition seems to be based on Oliver's pleas for release from what he says is an unnecessary combat. Critical tradition assumes, minimally, that because Oliver expresses concern with saving lives, Roland must be throwing them away. The hero does not answer Oliver because he is unable to.

But the famous, ink-drowned scenes of argument become clearer if we recognize that Roland and Oliver are not talking about the same things. They are not taking the opposing sides of a single argument; their premises are different.[60] Oliver is expressing the urgency of the immediate situation, while Roland looks beyond the circumstances to their consequences. Oliver may be concerned with saving lives, but Roland is concerned with why men may not care whether they die. If anyone were to blow the horn, it would have to be Roland, but that is not the same as saying that Oliver furnishes him good reasons to. As ever, the hero argues from principle, while his companion can, for the moment, see only the approaching Saracens and their unexpectedly vast numbers. As Ganelon's and Naimon's wills to peace strike a chord in us, so does Oliver's anxiety. It seems cruelly insufficient for Roland to say or imply that if only we do our duty everything will work out in the end. Yet what appears to be prudence, like what appears to be peace, may turn out to be something else in the long term. I repeat that the paradoxical nature of this idea may explain why the **Song of Roland** is ordered the way it is: not because the point it has to make is simplistic, but because it is a challenging idea and needs to be presented as strongly as possible. For within the **Song,** everything does work out. At the end, Spain is rid of the foes of Christendom, and Thierry at last sees to it that justice can be done.

Thus the consideration of how the principal characters are related brings us back to matters of structure. The traditional reading of the **Song,** in assigning to Oliver (if not to Ganelon) virtues as a soldier and counselor that Roland does not possess, furnishes a paradox that competes with the paradox of duty. It yields a complex arrangement of two heroic or exemplary protagonists. Their precise values have proven difficult to fix, but generally speaking, Oliver is said to be superior in wisdom and both are thought about equal in prowess.[61] The present reading clarifies things in this area, as it does elsewhere, by placing Oliver on another level, giving him the role that Ganelon's defenders, by and large, have sought to assign the latter: that of a noble man who makes a mistake only under great pressure. The complexity is not entirely lost; only the emphasis changes. For this and other reasons, I have felt free to describe the poem as didactic and its hero as exemplary without any fear of diminishing its interest thereby. The attractive notion of a worthy but flawed knight who falters in his duty to a comrade is still in the work, but the poem's range has been extended. It still includes three types of protagonists, but at a greater remove from one another. Ganelon does ill, Roland does good, fairly consistently, but there is still room for the recognition that these are extremes. Roland is what has sometimes been called an *actor,* Ganelon is an *opposer,* but Oliver is a foil (*repoussoir*).[62]

Blind to the implications of what is happening, the hero's comrade lashes out verbally at him more than once. Later, when physically blinded, he will symbolically strike Roland an unjustified sword-blow and receive his forgiveness. A bit like Ganelon, he knows only one kind of danger. Yet he does not commit treason. He does not hear Roland's statement of principle well, but he knows his duty in spite of that.[63] That is why he is *esguaret,* disturbed, at the thought that he must stand his ground. But when Roland dies for duty's sake in a large sense, Oliver dies too, for the sake of that smaller duty of comradeship.

That is enough. As long as Roland knows his responsibility as lieutenant and leader and holds to his promises in the face of adversity, then Oliver will in fact follow him and meet his fate also. This could be pathetic, but only in another setting. Roland dies the death of knowledge. He has spoken of the danger and sworn to discount it, from the first. That is a form of *sapientia*—possibly the implication of the line that calls him *proz.*[64] Oliver's strength is in the fortitude of adherence in the face of doubt, and that could, just possibly, be a meaning of *sage.*

Roland can see what Oliver cannot. He speaks not of the moment, but of the potential effects of his actions in the future. If he fears *malvaises cançuns,* it is because his deeds will live after him in exemplary form (he is already inside an epic) and readers and hearers will learn from them. This is, by implication, one of the civilizing principles behind feudalism: that a promise can be held binding beyond the present; that a knight can describe a future for himself and then hold to it. Roland's death, then, implies the survival of his principles. That means we must consider the Baligant and Trial episodes, whatever their ultimate origins, as being at home in the poem we have. They do not merely prolong the battle of Roncevaux, but make its meaning explicit. They are, at least, clearly foreshadowed in Oliver's accusation: *Ja mais Karlun de nos n'avrat servise* ("Never again will Charles receive our service"; line 1727). That has been taken as a self-evident condemnation of Roland, but the text shows it to be as irrelevant in the mouth of the doubting Oliver as in the mouth of the boasting pagan Escremiz: *De bons vassals avrat Carles suffraite* ("Charles will be short of good men"; 939). The sequence may originally have been the result of historical accident. The Baligant episode may not be as old as the rest. But once we recognize the theme of sacrifice in the work, we will see that the army's victory over Baligant's men (see 3511-16, 3543-59), like that of Thierry over Pinabel, is meant to show the consequences of the sacrifice the poem advocates.

Finally, the death of Gautier del Hum and Aude's refusal to live after Roland's death are elegantly embedded echoes of the principal theme of responsible commit-

ment, expressed through the same sense of hierarchy. Gautier's decision depends in the first instance on Roland's, and his story is set within the story of the rear guard. Aude dies because Roland has died, and beyond all sentimentality the thing she says is perfectly adequate to the situation. Roland was pledged to her, and whatever the pledge she made in her turn, she considers that situation purely and simply binding. "May it not please God, his saints, or his angels, / That I remain alive after Roland" (3718-19). Aude echoes Roland's refusal of the easier alternatives Charles offers, and her assent to duty is as straightforward as his. She does not die of a broken heart, but as Roland and Gautier died: in witness to a principle.

Thus even if the question had any bearing on interpretation, we would not need to agree that an exemplary **Song of Roland** lacks interest or even complexity of texture, where either structure or the relationships among characters are concerned. To bend a cliché, it is Romanesque in its way: a powerfully stark architectonics that sometimes stands alone and is sometimes highly decorated.[65] To be more direct, it is a straightforward story set in complicated circumstances, which is, perhaps, one of the ways we can distinguish moral art from naive propagandizing. It may even be to our advantage as humane critics to exchange the old Roland for the new. It may make Ganelon or Oliver seem more at the mercy of their fears and hesitations.[66] But in return, we get a poem in which numerous interlocking gestures are structurally decisive and are not obscure bits of byplay. Above all, we receive a hero of towering stature, exaggerated at times as Romanesque figures are, yet whose exaggerated traits are appropriate to the size of the challenge he faces. Time has tried, in its unsettling way, to diminish his stature, but the path he chooses leads to an authentically heroic destiny. Maybe the name of the narrow place where Roland's road ends can come to stand for something besides a grandiose debacle.

*Notes*

1. Le Gentil, *Song,* 89, 94.

2. "Roland's braggadocio is the epitome of his haughtiness (2316-34)," says Jones (*Ethos,* 67; as Brault points out, the example is ill-chosen [Brault, *Song,* 1:97]). For the claim that Roland boasts, see, among many others, Cartier, 62 (who justifies it); Kibler, "Roland's Pride," 152-54; Siciliano, 348, 351; Boatner, 577; Jones, "Lament," 13-14; Owen, "Secular Inspiration," 391; Donohoe, 255; Renoir, "Roland's Lament," 576. For the claim that Roncevaux is a disaster, and the rear guard is wasted, see Van Emden, "Guarant," 31; Owen, "Secular Inspiration," 390.

3. Le Gentil, "A propos de la démesure," 204. Cf. Boatner, 575, 576: "In the name of feudal loyalty [Roland] betrays every aspect of the feudal code

. . . his total misunderstanding of his feudal obligations is due to the blindness of pride." Roland "fails to live up to his contract; indeed, he perverts it." Scattered affirmations of the contrary have appeared in the works of critics not immediately concerned with refuting the *démesure* hypothesis in any detail. See Guiette, "Deux Scènes," 96; Battaglia, 126-40; Yves Bonnefoy, "Sur la *Chanson de Roland,*" *L'Ephémère,* 4 (1967), 62-65; Farnham, 164 ("a great warrior whose martyrdom is a supreme act of feudal loyalty"); Williamson, 557; Picherit, 265; Owen, "Secular Inspiration," 398; Payen, *Le Motif du repentir,* 127 ("in an epic perspective, [Roland's] conduct appears nearly beyond reproach"). Mickel points out parallels between Roland's role and those of the Virtues in Prudentius (Mickel, "Parallels in Prudentius's *Psychomachia,*" 440-42). See also the works cited in note 4 to the Preface, above.

4. Le Gentil, *Song,* 87.

5. See Bédier, *Légendes,* 3:388-90, 439, 444, and below, Chapter 4.

6. See Martin Steinmann, Jr., "What's the Point of Professional Interpretation of Literature?" *Philosophy and Literature,* 8 (1984), 267-68.

7. See Stock, 88-240, esp. 88-92, and D. W. Robertson, *A Preface to Chaucer* (Princeton, 1962), e.g., vii-ix, 3-6; and cf. Daniel Poirion's measured remarks on literary communication in the Middle Ages in his introduction to *Précis de littérature française,* esp. 13-15.

8. Stanley Fish, *Is There a Text in This Class?* (Cambridge, Mass., 1980), 15-16. It is not my present business to delineate the complex and interesting relationships between this statement of Fish's, the "literary anthropology," associated with Roland Barthes, the "traditions" associated with Hans-Georg Gadamer, or Jauss's various applications of the idea of "horizons of expectation."

9. H.-G. Gadamer speaks of "mediation between past and present" and of the possibility of avoiding historical error (in connection with legal history), in *Truth and Method* (New York, 1984), xxi; E. D. Hirsch discusses "bracketing" of "alien meaning" in *The Aims of Interpretation* (Chicago, 1976), 3-6.

10. Fish, 15.

11. The crucial role of probability in historical reasoning is described by, among others, G. R. Elton, *The Practice of History* (New York, 1967), 83-87. For the equally vital distinction between the probable and the plausible, see Jacques Barzun and Henry Graff, *The Modern Researcher,* 3d ed. (New York, 1977), 125-46, esp. 133.

12. Robert Crosman, "Some Doubts about 'the Reader of *Paradise Lost,*'" cited by W. Daniel Wilson, "Readers in Texts," *PMLA,* 96 (1981), 857. The "fallacy of the homogeneous past" is discussed by Hirsch, 40-41. It is perhaps the error of which Joseph Duggan would accuse Brault; see Duggan's review of Brault's *Song* in *Speculum,* 56 (1981), 355-58.

13. Wilson, 848; I will follow here Wilson's useful summary and definitions. Reference to the medieval audience (a collectivity, not an individual) is inevitably clumsy in this context, but I have retained the term where it seems appropriate, even though "member of the audience" or "hearer" might be more accurate at times. One way of framing the question of interpretation, then, is to ask which points a medieval audience would have recognized and recalled as salient as the Oxford story unfolded.

14. Ibid., 851-52.

15. Ibid., 851.

16. Ibid., 858.

17. Brault, *Song of Roland,* 1:xiii.

18. Dufournet, 142.

19. The most cogent discussion of this is by John Benton, "Nostre franceis n'unt talent de fuïr: The *Song of Roland* and the Enculturation of a Warrior Class," *Olifant,* 6 (1979), 237-58.

20. For discussion and summary definitions, see Georges Duby, "L'Histoire des mentalités," in Charles Samaran, ed., *L'Histoire et ses méthodes* (Paris, 1961), esp. "L'Outillage mental," 952-57; Philippe Ariès, "L'Histoire des mentalités," in Jacques Le Goff, ed., *La Nouvelle Histoire* (Paris, 1978), 402-3; Jacques Le Goff, "Les Mentalités: Une Histoire ambiguë," in J. Le Goff and Pierre Nora, eds., *Faire de l'Histoire* (Paris, 1974), 3:76-94.

21. See R. S. Crane, *Critical and Historical Principles of Literary History* (Chicago, 1971), 11, and W. D. Wilson's remarks on the relationship between author and "implied audience" (p. 851).

22. Paul Zumthor, *Essai de poétique médiévale* (Paris, 1972), 337. "*La Chanson de Roland* . . . is, on the political and psychological levels, a far more sophisticated, ambiguous work than, say, Auerbach would want us to believe," says Calin, 437. For further statements on the text's ambiguity, see, e.g., Frederick Whitehead, "L'Ambiguïté de Roland," *Studi in onore di Italo Siciliano* (Florence, 1966), 1203-12; R. A. Hall, Jr., "The Individual in Relation to His Society: *The Chanson*

*de Roland,"* in *Cultural Symbolism in Literature* (Ithaca, N.Y., 1963), 17-32. For Evelyn Birge Vitz, however, the poem is coherent on the level of narrative syntax or "plot in comprehensible human terms," despite features that undermine the "ontological solidity" of causality; see her "Desire and Causality in Medieval Narrative," *Romanic Review,* 71 (1980), esp. 222-23.

23. Paulin Paris insisted early that the characters were consistent, and he stated their importance for interpretation ("Roncevaux," *Histoire littéraire de la France,* 22 [1852], 740). Cf. Le Gentil, *Song,* 82; "[the] lives of the principal characters . . . are psychologically intense lives" (Horrent, *Chanson de Roland et geste de Charlemagne,* 7); "emotions hidden beneath the [political] surface . . . never come directly into view" (Calin, 20). For surmises about the hidden thoughts or intentions of the characters, see, among many others, Bédier, *Légendes,* 3:418ff.; Siciliano, 334, 347, 352; Boatner, 577, 579; Crosland, 75-76, 78-79, 81, and passim; Faral, *Chanson,* 94-95; Burger, "Deux Scènes," 114-15, 122; Donohoe, 252-53; Foulet, in Bédier, *Chanson de Roland commentée,* 148; Pensom, 78, 80, 85, 98 (but cf. 99), 104, 131, and esp. 132ff.; Stranges, 338-39, 344, 365; Brault, *Song,* 1:110, 129, 133, 322 (the Franks), 141 (Blancandrin), 152 (Marsile), 160 (Roland), 168 (Charles). D. W. Robertson protested energetically against the assignment of psychological motivations to the characters (*Preface to Chaucer,* 162-71). Cf. Battaglia, 356; Goldin, "Die Rolle Ganelons," 134-35; Crist, 17, "[Roland] has no autonomous mental processes." Hunt also states the position I prefer: "The 'exposition' of the *Roland* consists of a chain of reactions to what is openly *said:* it is not a revelation of character" ("Character and Causality," 32). Hunt does not eschew surmise entirely (cf. pp. 8, 14, 19, and 22 of the same article), but his remarks on pp. 11-12 are questions rather than guesses.

24. Calin, 13.

25. Ariès adds various statements on the meaning of details: "[Roland] does not have a single thought for Aude, his betrothed, who falls dead when she learns of his cruel end, nor for his fleshly parents" (*The Hour of Our Death,* trans. Helen Weaver [New York, 1981], 5, 14; cf. 143-46, 213).

26. Contamine, 255.

27. J. R. Randall, *The Making of the Modern Mind,* 2d ed. (1940; reprint ed., New York, 1976), 85-86.

28. For the *Annales,* see the following note; for the *Dictionnaire,* see L. Salembier's bitter denunciation of the *Roman de la Rose* in his article "Jean

Gerson" (6:1324). Like Randall, Pound repeats the *démesure* hypothesis: the "bombastic" Roland, "splendid and absurd," is "Galliffet at Strasbourg," and he falls victim "not to the treachery of Ganelon, but to that pride which forbade him to sound the horn for aid" (Ezra Pound, *The Spirit of Romance* [New York, 1910], 74-75, 77).

29. See Duby, "Dans la France du Nord-ouest au XIIᵉ siècle"; Erich Köhler, "Observations historiques et sociologiques sur la poésie des troubadours," *Cahiers de civilisation médiévale,* 7 (1962), 27-51; and cf. Evelyne Patlagean on Köhler in Jacques Le Goff, ed., *La Nouvelle Histoire,* 257.

30. Jean-Marie Goulemot, "Histoire littéraire," in Le Goff, *La Nouvelle Histoire,* 309.

31. See the discussion of historical interpretation and criticism in Gadamer, *Truth and Method,* 258-74; David Linge's introduction to Gadamer *Philosophical Hermeneutics* (Berkeley and Los Angeles, 1976), xvi; and David C. Hoy, *The Critical Circle* (Berkeley and Los Angeles, 1978), esp. 141-46.

32. I like to think that a reading capable of passing such tests could also be a "valid" reading according to the tests recently proposed by Armstrong (inclusiveness, "intersubjectivity," and efficacy or fruitfulness); see Paul Armstrong, "The Conflict of Interpretations and the Limits of Pluralism," *PMLA,* 98 (1983), 341-52.

33. Francisque Michel, *La Chanson de Roland ou de Roncevaux* (Paris, 1837), xi. On Roland's presumed responsibility (or guilt) for his own death and that of others, see, e.g., Vance, *Reading,* 3 ("his decision causes the destruction of all Charles's most beloved vassals"); Donohoe, 259 ("[Roland's] insufferable pride is the real underlying cause of the tragic occurrence"); Le Gentil, "A propos de la *démesure,*" 203; Van Emden, "Guarant," 31; Scully, 229; Siciliano, 348 ("the single responsible party"); Brault, *"Sapientia,"* 108; Hall, "Ganelon and Roland," 266n.; Stranges, 333; Kirsch, 390; Whitehead, 1206-11. But cf. Uitti, 112 ("Ganelon, not Roland, is guilty of the massacre").

34. 2d ed., Paris, 1905; Reprinted ed. 1974. Quotation from p. 273.

35. Petit de Julleville, *Chanson de Roland,* 59.

36. Cf. Pensom, 126; Kibler, "Roland's Pride," 148, 152; Hunt, "Roland's 'vermeille pume,'" 207; Horrent, *Chanson de Roland dans les littératures* . . . ; Brook, "Le Forfait de Roland," 123. Renoir calls his "uncouth" speeches "embarrassing" ("Roland's Lament," 576). For Siciliano (p. 354; cf. p. 351), he is "trenchant, quarrelsome . . .

rancorous . . . even . . . perfidious." Calin, 21-22, finds him impulsive and simple as well as tactless. Mermier, 101, speaks of his "rude impatience." For further expressions of irritation, see Burger, "Rire," 8-9; Boatner, passim; Donohoe, passim; Halverson, 662. Does this irritation explain the energy with which numerous commentators have defended Ganelon? ("It is not difficult for us to be in sympathy with Ganelon": Owen, "Secular Inspiration," 391).

37. D. C. Muecke, *Irony and the Ironic,* 2d ed. (New York, 1982), 87. Hunt recognizes that the traditional Roland must be a victim of irony ("Tragedy," 798; cf. Nichols, 166-68, 172).

38. Roland changes his mind, or atones: Le Gentil, "A propos de la *démesure,*" 206; Le Gentil, *Song,* 90-93; Van Emden, "Guarant," 35; Burger, "Deux Scènes"; Renoir, "Roland's Lament," 579; Boatner, 580; Atkinson, 271-84; Calin, 19, 24; Mermier, 99; Jenkins, xlii; Nichols, 172-73, 177; Renoir, "Heroic Oath," 254, 258; Bernard Huppé, "The Concept of the Hero in the Early Middle Ages," in Norman T. Burns and Christopher J. Reagan, eds., *Concepts of the Hero in the Middle Ages and the Renaissance* (Albany, 1975), 1-26. Roland and Oliver exchange characters during the battle: Vance, *Reading,* 51 ("Roland is at last wise and Oliver is at last bold"); cf. Boatner, 581, and Donohoe, 261. For Pensom, 137, Roland is changed (but Oliver is not), but not transformed into a saint (pp. 154-59). Roland does *not* change: Owen, "Secular Inspiration," 393, 396; Alfred Foulet, "Is Roland Guilty?" 146-48. For Vance, Roland is "right for the wrong reasons" (*Reading,* 11-12). See also the works cited in notes 11 and 12 to Chapter 2, above.

39. Faral, *Chanson,* 229-30, clearly states the opinion I will refute: "Roland knows, and is not afraid to say, what he is worth. . . . He does not doubt the worth of his sword for an instant, and in the death threats he makes to the enemy, we find almost the same boastful mockery with which the insane challenges of the twelve pagan peers were filled." Again, Léopold Peeters argues that words and deeds cannot be separated for purposes of interpretation ("Le 'Faire' et le 'dire,'" 383-92; see also Pensom, 83; Hunt, "Character and Causality").

40. On the audience's power of recall, see the Preliminary Note. Cf. Paul Zumthor's useful remarks (based, however, on a broader concept of public memory or commemoration) in *La Poésie et la voix dans la civilisation médiévale* (Paris, 1984), esp. 105-12. Peeters, 391-92, has also argued that the text shows Roland to have told the truth and that Ganelon has lied.

41. For discussions of the concept of the *gab,* see the works referred to in note 77 to the Commentary.

42. Most recently in Barbara Nelson Sargent-Baur, "Truth, Half-Truth, Untruth: Béroul's Telling of the Tristan Story," in Leigh Arrathoon, ed., *The Craft of Fiction: Essays in Medieval Poetics* (Rochester, Mich., 1984), 393-421. On the importance of form in medieval law, see M. Bloch, 360.

43. See Kleiber, *Le Mot "ire,"* 145-54, 329-31.

44. In another narrative sequence, Oliver might well be thought right, but his recommendation to Roland is wrong in this context. That is why it is not really a question of a hierarchy of values.

45. Smail, *Crusading Warfare,* 156-65.

46. Ibid., 164.

47. Exceptions are Cartier and Del Monte.

48. I see I am approaching from its negative side a point made by Benton: "Even though disciplined retreat can sometimes be the best strategy, every commander wants troops who will risk, indeed sacrifice, their lives if necessary" (John Benton, "Nostre franceis n'unt talent de fuïr," 245-46).

49. The risks Charles and his men run in returning to Spain to answer the horn-call are not Roland's fault but Ganelon's.

50. See the works cited in notes 72, 73, and 119 to the Commentary.

51. It is not without relevance to the present study that Rosenberg once chose Roland as metonym for the unfortunate cavalryman, see Bruce Rosenberg, *Custer and the Epic of Defeat* (University Park, Pa., 1974), xi (cf. 175-81), and Goldin, "Die Rolle Ganelons," 140-41. This may remind us that Custer actually *was* in command and on the offensive. For comparisons between Roland and Hotspur or Young Hal, see note 4 to Chapter 2.

52. Among many others, Gérard, 445, 464-65; Hunt, "Structure," 306 (Roland's individuality versus Charles's); Pensom, 91 (Ganelon's versus Roland's), 92-93 (poet favors society); Waltz, e.g., 51-56, 61-65. Pensom, 131, also defines Roland's neurosis—a basic concept for him—as "the repressed conflict between his identity as a 'clan-member' and his identity as a servant of the state." Kirsch, 396, speaks of a tension in Roland between incompatible concepts of vassaldom and sovereignty. The ideas that Roland and Ganelon have the same individualistic ethos, are similarly heedless, and share the responsibility for Roncevaux appear in various forms; see, e.g., Hall, "Ganelon and Roland," 266; Sarah Kay, "Ethics

and Heroics in the *Song of Roland*," *Neophilologus,* 62 (1978), 480; Mermier, 93-94 ("both Roland and Ganelon display a certain lack of responsibility"); Gérard, 452ff.; Halverson. But Calin, 18, no doubt following Waltz here, attributes two different, competing ethics to them. See also Battaglia, Stranges, and Robert Eisner, "In Search of the Real Theme of the *Song of Roland,*" *Romance Notes,* 14 (1972-73), 179. To explain the author's apparent preference for Roland, Kay, 487-88, postulates a "transformation of ethics" that makes legitimate in Roland's case acts that would be unethical in real life. Roland fights for personal and family honor (Kibler, "Roland's Pride," 151, 154). Cf. Gaston Paris, *La Poésie du Moyen Age,* vol. 1, 2d ed. (Paris, 1887), 109 ("from personal pride, first of all, and from family pride, but also from a sense of national honor"); Mermier, 95; Burger, "Deux Scènes," 113.

53. Pensom, esp. 84-95.

54. Ibid., 133ff.

55. The idea that something we never learn about must precede the Council Scene in order for it to possess coherence goes back at least to Petit de Julleville (in his 1878 ed., 67) and is still repeated with some regularity despite such arguments as Hall's.

56. The "good Ganelon" motif in criticism is another very old one. Paulin Paris, 740: "Even as a criminal, Ganelon possesses a sort of heroic grandeur: he has his reasons for wishing to include the entire council in his vengeance" (this passage also furnishes a typical example of affirmation without argument). On the Ganelon problem, see the works cited by Brault, *Song,* 1:378, nn. 539-40, and J. Thomas's summary, 91; Thomas suspects Ganelon's defenders among critics are more numerous than those who condemn him. For examples, see Le Gentil, *Song,* 82-87, 114-16; Eisner, 182-83 (his treason "unwitting"); Stranges, 334, 340-41, 343 (forced to betray by circumstances); Burger, "Rire," 9; Moignet, 45, 49; Waltz, 31-32; Halverson, 666; Ruggieri's study on the trial, cited in note 132 to the Commentary. Others find him partly good or ambiguous: Petit de Julleville, 66-69; Léon Gautier, "L'Epopée nationale," in Louis Petit de Julleville, ed., *Histoire de la langue et de la littérature française,* vol. 1, part 1 (Paris, 1896), 96 ("he is struggling with himself"); Owen, *Song of Roland,* 20-21; Marianne Cramer Vos, "Ganelon's *mortel rage,*" *Olifant,* 2 (1974-75), 16; Horrent, *Chanson de Roland dans les littératures . . . ,* 270-71. For another group of scholars, Ganelon is clearly evil (Robertson, *Preface to Chaucer,* 163-65; Golden, "Die Rolle Ganelons"; Pensom, 94ff.; Brault, *Song,* 1:100; Kellogg.

57. Ganshof, 98-99, discusses only relationships between lord and vassal, not among equals, but the gravity of situations leading to *diffidatio* is unmistakable (cf. Lemarignier, 138-39).

58. For such a claim, see Jackson, esp. 129.

59. The idea that "Roland's behaviour may be dictated by an ethos which invests action with positive moral value" is expressed most recently in Kay, 483.

60. J. M. Enders, "La Logique des débats dans la *Chanson de* Roland" (M.A. thesis, University of Virginia, 1979), shows that their forms of argumentation are significantly different also. As we might expect by now, Roland's is deductive, beginning with principles, and Oliver's is inductive, beginning with an immediate situation. Of course, inductive arguments are local, while deductive arguments are general in their applications.

61. On the *proz-sage* dichotomy, see the commentary to laisse 87, and also Brault, *Song,* 1:11-15; Misrahi and Hendrickson, 359-61, 364-67; Uitti, 109-12; Wendt, 290-96; Jean Subrenat, ". . . e Oliver est proz," *Etudes de philologie romane et d'histoire littéraire offertes à Jules Horrent* (Liège, 1980), 461-67. The idea of Oliver's superiority is again both ancient and very well entrenched. Léon Gautier, "L'Epopée nationale," 89, spoke of his "tranquil valor, alongside [Roland's] frantic bravery"; Paulin Paris, 741, claimed that "Oliver seems to prevail, because he adds caution and calmness to [Roland's] warlike fearlessness." The idea can be traced down to Fox, 68-69: "The poet clearly expected his audience to admire Roland . . . but to approve rather of Oliver and his saner, more practical approach." Further examples may be found in Le Gentil, *Song,* 110-11 (our "secret preference" for Oliver); Mermier, 98-99; Pauphilet, *Legs,* 76; Faral, *Chanson,* 218; Siciliano, 346-47; Gérard, 448-49; Halverson, 664 (Roland "is not quick"; Oliver "thinks . . . in terms of the common good" and is "something of a new man"); Williamson, 557 (Roland is "selectively deaf" to Oliver's advice); Calin, 23 (Oliver is Roland's "better conscience").

62. For a summary of this "modèle actantiel," energetically applied to the study of narrative about a decade ago, see Oswald Ducrot and Tzvetan Todorov, *Dictionnaire encyclopédique des sciences du langage* (Paris, 1972), 290-91. Ducrot and Todorov do not mention the term *foil*; its use here is a matter of induction.

63. See Brault, *"Sapientia,"* 101; Crosland, 82; Uitti, 109, Del Monte, 234.

64. On *proz,* see also Brault's different arguments in his *"Sapientia,"* 105-8. Thomas Aquinas's later definition of *fortitudo* may include traditional elements. "For Saint Thomas Aquinas courage [la force, *fortitudo*] is . . . both firmness of mind in the accomplishment of a duty and, in consequence, the condition for all virtue. . . . Fortitude is *a kind of golden mean* [*conduite du juste milieu*; my trans., emphasis added; see original, p. 407], 'a virtue which moderates fear and boldness for the common good.'" (Contamine, 251.) Niles cites a definition of *fortitudo* that includes forbearance and patience, from the Anglo-Saxon Wulfstan; see John Niles, *Beowulf* (Cambridge, Mass., 1983), 224-25. On *sapientia,* see Brault, *"Sapientia,"* 108ff., and McCash, 143-44.

65. On Romanesque aesthetics in the visual and literary arts, see Robertson, *Preface,* 138-71; Brault, *Song,* 1:44-47; Farnham; Nichols; Charles F. Altman, "Interpreting Romanesque Narrative: Conques and the *Roland,*" *Olifant,* 5 (1977-78), 4-28.

66. I would not go so far as to endorse Van Emden's claim that Cartier's analysis "runs the risk . . . of turning Oliver, Charles and Naimon into imbeciles and cowards" ("Guarant," 26). Cf. note 9 to this chapter. Among the Christians there are not two systems at odds, but two ways of reacting to stress and challenge—*pace* Halverson.

### Works Cited

Altman, Charles F. "Interpreting Romanesque Narrative: Conques and the *Roland.*" *Olifant,* 5 (1977-78), 4-28.

Ariès, Philippe. "L'Histoire des mentalités." In Jacques Le Goff, ed., *La Nouvelle Histoire.* Paris: CEPL, 1978. Pp. 402-23.

———. *The Hour of Our Death.* Trans. Helen Weaver. New York: Knopf, 1981.

Armstrong, Paul B. "The Conflict of Interpretations and the Limits of Pluralism." *PMLA,* 98 (1983), 341-52.

Atkinson, James C. "Laisses 169-70 of the *Chanson de Roland.*" *Modern Language Notes,* 82 (1967), 271-84.

Barzun, Jacques, and Henry F. Graff. *The Modern Researcher.* 3d ed. New York: Harcourt, 1977.

Battaglia, Salvatore. "La Glorificazione di Orlando." In *La Formazione della lingua francese.* Rome: Perella, 1945. Pp. 126-40. Reprinted in *Filologia e letteratura,* 17 (1971), 355-67.

Bédier, Joseph. *La Chanson de Roland commentée.* Paris: Piazza, 1927.

———. *Les Légendes épiques.* 2d ed. 4 vols. Paris: Champion, 1914-21.

Benton, John. "Nostre franceis n'unt talent de fuïr: The *Song of Roland* and the Enculturation of a Warrior Class." *Olifant,* 6 (1979), 237-58.

Bloch, Marc. *Apologie pour l'histoire ou le métier d'historien.* Paris: Colin, 1952.

———. *Feudal Society.* Trans. L. A. Manyon. Chicago: University of Chicago Press, 1964.

Boatner, Janet W. "The Misunderstood Ordeal: A Re-Examination of the *Chanson de Roland.*" *Studies in Philology,* 66 (1969), 571-83.

Bonnefoy, Yves. "Sur la *Chanson de Roland.*" *L'Ephémère,* 4 (1967), 55-65.

Brault, Gerard J. *La Chanson de Roland: Student Edition.* University Park, Pa.: Pennsylvania State University Press, 1984.

———. *"Sapientia* dans la *Chanson de Roland.*" *French Forum,* 1 (1976), 99-118. Also in *Société Rencesvals: Proceedings of the Fifth International Conference.* Salford, Eng.: University of Salford, 1977. Pp. 85-104.

Brook, Leslie C. "Le Forfait de Roland dans le procès de Ganelon: Encore sur un vers obscur de la *Chanson de Roland.*" In *Société Rencesvals: IVe Congrès International.* Heidelberg: Carl Winter, 1969. Pp. 120-28.

Burger, André. "Les Deux Scènes du cor dans la *Chanson de Roland.*" In *La Technique littéraire des chansons de geste.* Paris: Belles Lettres, 1959. Pp. 105-25.

———. "Le Rire de Roland." *Cahiers de civilisation médiévale,* 3 (1960), 2-11.

Calin, William C. *A Muse for Heroes: Nine Centuries of the Epic in France.* Toronto: University of Toronto Press, 1983.

Cartier, Norman R. "La Sagesse de Roland." *Aquileia: Chestnut Hill Studies in Modern Languages and Literatures,* 1 (1969), 33-63.

Contamine, Philippe. *War in the Middle Ages.* Trans. Michael Jones. Oxford: Blackwell, 1984.

Crane, R. S. *Critical and Historical Principles of Literary History.* Chicago: University of Chicago Press, 1971.

Crist, Larry S. "A propos de la *desmesure* dans la *Chanson de Roland*: Quelques propos (démesurés?)." *Olifant,* 1 (1974), 10-20. Also in *Société Rencesvals: Proceedings of the Fifth International Conference.* Salford, Eng.: University of Salford, 1977. Pp. 143-55.

Crosland, Jessie. *The Old French Epic.* Oxford: Black-well, 1951.

Del Monte, Alberto. "Apologia di Orlando." *Filologia romanza,* 4 (1957), 225-34.

Donohoe, Joseph. "Ambivalence and Anger: The Human Center of the *Chanson de Roland.*" *Romanic Review,* 67 (1971), 251-61.

Duby, Georges. "Dans la France du Nord-ouest au XIIe siècle: Les 'jeunes' dans la société aristocratique." *Annales,* 19 (1964), 835-46.

————. "L'Histoire des mentalités." In Charles Samaran, ed., *L'Histoire et ses méthodes.* Paris: Gallimard, 1961. Pp. 937-66.

Ducrot, Oswald, and Tzvetan Todorov. *Dictionnaire encyclopédique des sciences du langage.* Paris: Seuil, 1972.

Dufournet, Jean. *Cours sur la Chanson de Roland.* Paris: Centre de Documentation Universitaire, 1972.

Eisner, Robert A. "In Search of the Real Theme of the *Song of Roland.*" *Romance Notes,* 14 (1972-73), 179-83.

Elton, G. R. *The Practice of History.* New York: Crowell, 1967.

Enders, Jody May. "La Logique des débats dans la *Chanson de Roland.*" M.A. thesis, University of Virginia, 1979.

Faral, Edmond. *La Chanson de Roland: Etude et analyse.* Paris: Mellottée, [1934].

Farnham, Fern. "Romanesque Design in the *Chanson de Roland.*" *Romance Philology,* 18 (1964), 143-64.

Fish, Stanley. *Is There a Text in This Class?* Cambridge, Mass.: Harvard University Press, 1980.

Foulet, Alfred. "Is Roland Guilty of *desmesure?*" *Romance Philology,* 10 (1956-57), 145-48.

Gadamer, Hans-Georg. *Philosophical Hermeneutics.* Trans. David Linge. Berkeley and Los Angeles: University of California Press, 1976.

————. *Truth and Method.* New York: Crossroad Press, 1984.

Ganshof, Frédéric L. *Feudalism.* Trans. Philip Grierson. 3d ed. New York: Harper and Row, 1964.

Gautier, Léon. "L'Epopée nationale: La *Chanson de Roland.*" In Louis Petit de Julleville, ed., *Histoire de la langue et de la littérature françaises des origines à 1900.* Vol. 1: *Moyen Age,* part 1. Paris: Colin, 1896. Pp. 80-98.

Gérard, Albert. "L'Axe Roland-Ganelon: Valeurs en conflit dans la *Chanson de Roland.*" *Le Moyen Age,* 75 (1969), 445-66.

Goldin, Frederick R. "Die Rolle Ganelons und das Motiv der Worte." In Kurt Baldinger, ed., *Beiträge zum romanischen Mittelalter.* Tübingen: Niemeyer, 1977. Pp. 128-55.

Goulemot, Jean-Marie. "Histoire littéraire." In Jacques Le Goff, ed., *La Nouvelle Histoire.* Paris: CEPL, 1978. Pp. 308-13.

Guiette, Robert. "Les Deux Scènes du cor dans la *Chanson de Roland* et dans les *Conquestes de Charlemagne.*" *Le Moyen Age,* 69 (1963), 845-55. Reprinted in *Forme et senefiance.* Geneva: Droz, 1978. Pp. 172-80.

Hall, Robert A., Jr. "Ganelon and Roland." *Modern Language Quarterly,* 6 (1945), 263-70.

————. "The Individual in Relation to His Society: The *Chanson de Roland.*" *Cultural Symbolism in Literature.* Ithaca, N.Y.: Linguistica, 1963. Pp. 17-32.

Halverson, John. "Ganelon's Trial." *Speculum,* 42 (1967), 661-69.

Hirsch, E. D. *The Aims of Interpretation.* Chicago: University of Chicago Press, 1976.

Horrent, Jules. *Chanson de Roland et geste de Charlemagne.* In Hans Robert Jauss et al., eds., *Grundriss der Literaturen des romanischen Mittelalters,* Vol. 3, tome 1, fascicle 2.A.I.1. Heidelberg: Carl Winter, 1981. Pp. 5-12.

————. *La Chanson de Roland dans les littératures française et espagnole au Moyen Age.* Paris: Belles Lettres, 1951.

Hoy, David C. *The Critical Circle.* Berkeley and Los Angeles: University of California Press, 1978.

Hunt, Tony. "Character and Causality in the Oxford *Roland.*" *Medioevo romanzo,* 5 (1978), 3-33.

————. "Roland's 'vermeille pume.'" *Olifant,* 7 (1980), 203-11.

————. "The Structure of Medieval Narrative." *Journal of European Studies,* 3 (1973), 295-328.

————. "The Tragedy of Roland: An Aristotelian View." *Modern Language Review,* 74 (1979), 791-805.

Huppé, Bernard F. "The Concept of the Hero in the Early Middle Ages." In Norman T. Burns and Christopher Reagan, eds., *Concepts of the Hero in the Middle Ages and the Renaissance.* Albany: State University of New York Press, 1975. Pp. 1-26.

Jackson, William T. H. *The Hero and the King.* New York: Columbia University Press, 1982.

Jenkins, T. Atkinson, ed. *La Chanson de Roland: Oxford Version.* 2d ed. Boston: Heath, 1924.

Jones, George Fenwick. *The Ethos of the Song of Roland.* Baltimore: Johns Hopkins University Press, 1963.

———. "Roland's Lament: A Divergent Interpretation." *Romanic Review,* 53 (1962), 3-15. Cf. "La Complainte de Roland: Une Interprétation divergente." *Cultura neolatina,* 21 (1961), 34-47.

Kay, Sarah. "Ethics and Heroics in the *Song of Roland.*" *Neophilologus,* 62 (1978), 480-91.

Kellogg, Judith L. "Ganelon: The Poetics of Guile and Greed." *Olifant,* 8 (1980), 161-79.

Kibler, William W. "Roland's Pride." *Symposium,* 26 (1972), 147-60.

Kirsch, P. "La Condition du héros dans la *Chanson de Roland.*" In *Mélanges de philologie romane offerts à Charles Camproux.* Montpellier, France: Centre d'Estudis occitans, 1978. Pp. 385-99.

Kleiber, Georges. *Le Mot "Ire" en ancien français.* Paris: Klincksieck, 1978.

Köhler, Erich. "Observations historiques et sociologiques sur la poésie des troubadours." *Cahiers de civilisation médiévale,* 7 (1962), 27-51.

Le Gentil, Pierre. "A propos de la démesure de Roland." *Cahiers de civilisation médiévale,* 11 (1968), 203-9.

———. *La Chanson de Roland.* Paris: Hatier, 1955; 2d ed. 1967. Translated by Frances Beer under the title *The Song of Roland.* Cambridge, Mass.: Harvard University Press, 1969.

Le Goff, Jacques. "Les Mentalités: Une histoire ambigüe." In Jacques Le Goff and Pierre Nora, eds., *Faire de l'histoire.* 3 vols. Paris: Gallimard, 1974. 3:76-94.

Le Goff, Jacques, ed. *La Nouvelle Histoire.* Paris: CEPL, 1978.

McCash, June Hall Martin, "*Scientia* and *Sapientia* in the *Chanson de Roland.*" *Medievalia et Humanistica,* n.s. 11 (1982), 131-47.

Mermier, Guy: "More about Unity in the *Song of Roland.*" *Olifant,* 2 (1974-75), 91-108.

Michel, Francisque. *La Chanson de Roland ou de Roncevaux.* Paris: Silvestre, 1837.

Mickel, Emanuel J. "Parallels in Prudentius' *Psychomachia* and *La Chanson de Roland.*" *Studies in Philology,* 67 (1970), 439-52.

Misrahi, Jean, and William L. Hendrickson. "Roland and Oliver: Prowess and Wisdom, the Ideal of the Epic Hero." *Romance Philology,* 33 (1979-80), 357-72. See also Hendrickson.

Moignet, Gérard, ed. *La Chanson de Roland: Texte original et traduction.* Paris: Bordas, 1969. Cf. *La Chanson de Roland: Extraits.* Paris: Bordas, 1970.

Muecke, D. C. *Irony and the Ironic.* 2d ed. New York: Methuen, 1982.

Nichols, Stephen G. *Romanesque Signs: Early Medieval Narrative and Iconography.* New Haven: Yale University Press, 1983.

Niles, John D. *Beowulf.* Cambridge, Mass.: Harvard University Press, 1983.

Owen, D. D. R. "The Secular Inspiration of the *Chanson de Roland.*" *Speculum,* 37 (1962), 390-400.

Owen, D. D. R., trans. *The Song of Roland: The Oxford Text.* London: Allen and Unwin, 1972.

Paris, Gaston. *La Poésie du Moyen Age: Leçons et lectures.* 2 vols. 2d ed. Paris: Hachette, 1887.

Paris, Paulin. "Roncevaux." *Histoire littéraire de la France,* 22 (1852), 727-55.

Pauphilet, Albert. *Le Legs du Moyen Age: Etudes de littérature médiévale.* Melun, France: D'Argences, 1950.

Payen, Jean-Charles. *Le Motif du repentir dans la littérature française médiévale.* Geneva: Droz, 1968.

Peeters, Léopold. "Le 'Faire' et le 'dire' dans la *Chanson de Roland.*" *Revue des langues romanes,* 81 (1975), 376-93.

Pensom, Roger. *Literary Technique in the Chanson de Roland.* Geneva: Droz, 1982.

Petit de Julleville, Louis. *Histoire de la littérature française des origines à nos jours.* 10th ed. (1st in one vol.). Paris: Masson, 1895.

Petit de Julleville, Louis, ed. *La Chanson de Roland.* Paris: Lemerre, 1878.

Picherit, Jean-Louis. "Le Silence de Ganelon." *Cahiers de civilisation médiévale,* 21 (1978), 265-74.

Poirion, Daniel, et al. *Précis de littérature française du Moyen Age.* Paris: Presses Universitaires de France, 1983.

Pound, Ezra. *The Spirit of Romance.* London: Dent; New York: Dutton, 1910.

Randall, J. R. *The Making of the Modern Mind.* 2d ed. Boston and New York: Houghton Mifflin, 1940. Reprint. New York: Columbia University Press, 1976.

Renoir, Alain. "The Heroic Oath in *Beowulf,* the *Chanson de Roland,* and the *Nibelungenlied.*" In Stanley B. Greenfield, ed., *Studies in Old English Literature in Honor of Arthur G. Brodeur.* Eugene, Ore.: University of Oregon Press, 1963. Reprint. New York: Russell and Russell, 1973.

———. "Roland's Lament: Its Meaning and Function in the *Chanson de Roland.*" *Speculum,* 35 (1960), 572-83.

Robertson, D. W. *A Preface to Chaucer.* Princeton: Princeton University Press, 1962.

Rosenberg, Bruce A. *Custer and the Epic of Defeat.* University Park, Pa.: Pennsylvania State University Press, 1974.

Ruggieri, Ruggero M. *Il Processo di Gano nella Chanson de Roland.* Florence: Sansoni, 1936.

Sargent-Baur, Barbara N. "Truth, Half-Truth, Untruth: Béroul's Telling of the Tristan Story." In Leigh Arrathoon, ed., *The Craft of Fiction: Essays in Medieval Poetics.* Rochester, Mich.: Solaris Press, 1984. Pp. 393-421.

Scully, Terence. "The Ordeal at Roncesvalles: 'Francs e paiens, as les vus ajustez.'" *Olifant,* 7 (1980), 213-34.

Siciliano, Italo. *Les Chansons de geste et l'épopée: Mythes, histoire, poèmes.* Turin: Società Editrice Internazionale; Paris: Picard, 1970.

Smail, R. C. *Crusading Warfare, 1097-1193.* Cambridge, Eng.: Cambridge University Press, 1956.

Steinmann, Martin, Jr. "What's the Point of Professional Interpretation of Literature?" *Philosophy and Literature,* 8 (1984), 266-70.

Stock, Brian. *The Implications of Literacy.* Princeton: Princeton University Press, 1983.

Stranges, John A. "The Character and the Trial of Ganelon: A New Appraisal." *Romania,* 96 (1975), 333-67.

Subrenat, Jean. ". . . e Oliver est proz." *Etudes de philologie romane et d'histoire littéraire offertes à Jules Horrent.* Liège: n.p., 1980.

Thomas, Jacques. "La Traitrise de Ganelon." *Romanica Gandensia,* 16 (1976), 91-117.

Uitti, Karl D. *Story, Myth, and Celebration in Old French Narrative Poetry.* Princeton: Princeton University Press, 1973.

Vance, Eugene. *Reading the Song of Roland.* Englewood Cliffs, N.J.: Prentice-Hall, 1970.

Van Emden, Wolfgang C. "E cil de France le cleiment a guarant: Roland, Vivien, et le thème du *guarant.*" *Olifant,* 1 (1974), 21-47. Also in *Société Rencesvals, VIe Congrès International: Actes.* Aix-en-Provence: Université de Provence, 1974. Pp. 31-61.

Vitz, Evelyn Birge. "Desire and Causality in Medieval Narrative." *Romanic Review,* 71 (1980), 213-43.

Vos, Marianne Cramer. "Ganelon's *mortel rage.*" *Olifant,* 2 (1974-75), 15-26.

Waltz, Matthias. *Rolandslied, Wilhelmslied, Alexiuslied: Zur Struktur und geschichtlichen Bedeutung.* Heidelberg: Carl Winter, 1965.

Wendt, Michael. *Der Oxforder Roland: Heilsgeschehen und Teilidentität im 12. Jahrhundert.* Munich: Fink, 1970.

Whitehead, Frederick. "L'Ambiguïté de Roland." In *Studi in onore di Italo Siciliano.* Florence: Olschki, 1966. Pp. 1203-12.

———. "*La Chanson de Roland* et l'esprit héroïque." *Cahiers de civilisation médiévale,* 3 (1960), 115-17.

———. "Charlemagne's Second Dream." *Olifant,* 3 (1975-76), 189-95.

Williamson, Joan B. "Trust and Kinship in the *Chanson de Roland.*" In *VIII Congreso de la Société Rencesvals.* Pamplona: Institución Principe de Viana, 1981. Pp. 553-60.

Wilson, W. Daniel. "Readers in Texts." *PMLA,* 96 (1981), 848-63.

Zumthor, Paul. *Essai de poétique médiévale.* Paris: Seuil, 1972.

———. *La Poésie et la voix dans la civilisation médiévale.* Paris: Presses Universitaires de France, 1984.

## Mary Ann C. Curtis (essay date May 1988)

SOURCE: Curtis, Mary Ann C. "*The Sun Also Rises*: Its Relation to *The Song of Roland.*" *American Literature* 60, no. 2 (May 1988): 274-80.

[*In the following essay, Curtis contends that Ernest Hemingway's apparent familiarity with* The Song of Roland *influenced the plot, characterization, and general structure of* The Sun Also Rises.]

In the abundant critical attention which Ernest Hemingway's *The Sun Also Rises* has received, very little of it has been directed to the structural basis of the novel. Most of the critical discussion has centered on theme and character, an emphasis which is very often divided on the two sides of an issue suggested by the novel's epigraphs, that of "lost generation" versus "the abiding earth." But, as Peter Brooks points out in his recent book-length study of plot and narrative, "plot is somehow prior to those elements most discussed by most critics."[1] Why an author arranges his material in one way and not another is of some literary interest.

Angel Capellán refers to the Spanish portion of *The Sun Also Rises* in his study of Hemingway and the Hispanic world. After discussing the Burguete trip as a prelude to the Pamplona festival, he says: "Besides the preparatory nature of the entire Burguete episode, there is an added element. The continuous presence of the Monastery of

Roncesvalles—the locale for the *Chanson de Roland*—provides the episode with a mythical-heroic dimension that can hardly be missed."[2] But here he lets the matter drop. Actually, a close comparison reveals that *La Chanson de Roland* and the Spanish portion of Hemingway's novel bear a remarkable resemblance in plot.

Hemingway has given his reader a key leading into this perspective on the book, in Jake's use of the word "Roncevaux." As he and Bill approach Burguete, Jake narrates:

> As we came to the edge of the rise we saw the red roofs and white houses of Burguete ahead strung out on the plain, and away off on the shoulder of the first dark mountain was the gray metal-sheathed roof of the monastery of Roncesvalles.
>
> "There's Roncevaux," I said.
>
> "Where?"
>
> "Way off there where the mountain starts."
>
> (P. 108)[3]

This is not the first time Jake has been to Burguete, and it appears that he has been watching for the monastery to come into view. Since this is the only time in the book that Roncesvalles is referred to as Roncevaux, the name by which the monastery is called in *The Song of Roland,* we can assume that Jake has that medieval French epic in mind when he uses the name. And since Bill shows no surprise or question about "Roncevaux," it is likely that he catches the allusion.

But before launching upon an analysis of *The Song of Roland* vis-à-vis *The Sun Also Rises,* it would be well to establish that a connection between them would not have been foreign to the author at the time of his writing. And, in fact, there are several things which point to just such a supposition. When Hemingway's letters were published, Carlos Baker, the editor, appended a footnote to a letter written in 1956 to Harvey Breit, in which Hemingway exclaims, *"Ah que cet cor a long haleine."* Baker says: "How this handsome line came into [Hemingway's] possession is not clear, although he had long been interested in the exploits of Roland and alluded to the monastery of Roncesvalles in *The Sun Also Rises,* chapter 11." Baker then goes on to thank Victor H. Brombert and John Logan for identifying the original of Hemingway's line as line 1789 of *La Chanson de Roland.*[4] What Mr. Baker does not remark is that the line immediately preceding in Hemingway's letter is, "But Pauline and I once drove from Madrid to San Sebastian arriving in plenty of time for the bull fight." The jump from driving plans, to a memory of Spain, to *The Song of Roland* is more than interesting; it is one of the clues to Hemingway's creative mind.

According to Michael S. Reynolds' research into Hemingway's reading, Eric Dorman-Smith wrote to Carlos Baker stating that he discussed *The Song of Roland*

with Hemingway after the Pamplona festival in July of 1924.[5] This may have been the basis for Baker's comment that Hemingway "had long been interested in the exploits of Roland." But more than that, it places the discussion of *The Song of Roland* within the time-frame of the raw material for *The Sun Also Rises.*

Reynolds also points to Hemingway's sustained interest in medieval literature, which he says "reveals one other warrior, little connected with Hemingway, whom we should have suspected long ago: the medieval knight." No one, he says, followed up Baker's mention of Colonel Cantwell's "chivalric code," and critics did not take seriously Fitzgerald's 1934 letter to Maxwell Perkins expressing curiosity about Hemingway's novel, and about which Fitzgerald says, "I hope to God it isn't the crusading story he once had in mind."[6]

Peter Brooks recaps a study done on the component parts of fairy tales as part of his overall study of plot. The relevant point is that sequence of action is the unifying thread among various stories, and that functional action may be carried by any number of different characters from story to story. This "'functionalist' view of narrative structure"[7] may be applied to a comparison of *The Song of Roland* and *The Sun Also Rises.* Although there are obvious equivalents between the characters in the novel and those in the epic poem, they do not necessarily remain constant. There is no question here of *The Sun Also Rises* being a retelling of *The Song of Roland*; it is not. But it does appear that Hemingway had the French epic in mind in choosing some of his details, and in ordering the sequence of events in his novel. For example, in the poem the Twelve Peers of France engage in battle at Roncevaux with the Twelve Peers of the Saracens. Hemingway has continued the pattern by giving Jake the "biblical name" of Jacob—the father of the Twelve Tribes of Israel. Another example, closer to the tone of Hemingway's novel, is the famous incident of Roland lifting up his oliphant and blowing three tremendous blasts upon it to recall Charlemagne to the battle (*laisses* 133-35).[8] This is ironically mirrored in Jake's tipping up of the Spanish wine skin (shaped like an oliphant) to drink from it, and being startled by the Basque's imitation of "a klaxon motor-horn" (p. 103), a feat the Basque repeats several times before the bus gets started for Burguete.

In the basic plot of the poem, Ganelon goes to Saragossa and parleys treacherously with the pagan forces. He then arranges for Roland and his troops to go to Roncevaux without him, as Charlemagne's rear-guard. In the novel, Robert Cohn goes to San Sebastian where he has a brief affair with Brett. He later arranges for Jake and Bill to go on the fishing trip to Burguete without him. Dewey Ganzel has done a thorough job of describing Brett as the "complete pagan,"[9] and it is not difficult to see Cohn as the traitorous Ganelon.

At the battle of Roncevaux, the principal heroes are Roland, his good friend Oliver, and the warrior-prelate, Archbishop Turpin. In the same setting of Roncevaux and environs, Jake and Bill go fishing; like Roland and Oliver, they are good friends. They meet Harris, who rounds out the trio, and seems to be added to the story for no other purpose than to represent Archbishop Turpin. Several details of this section of the novel are equivalent to the poem. There are five engagements in the battle, and the fishing trip lasts for five days. In the first fishing scene, there is a certain wry humor, with fish-hooks replacing lances, and with the description of fish entrails replacing the human entrails so graphically described in the poem. Roland and Oliver's quarrel is turned into the nonsensical argument between Jake and Bill (pp. 122-23), and they catch ten fish on the first day, the exact number of Saracen Peers killed in the first engagement. Roland "climbs a hill and halts beneath two beautiful trees," where he falls down on the green grass in a swoon (lines 2267-70); Jake stretches out on the ground beneath two trees and goes to sleep (pp. 120, 123-24).

In the fifth engagement Oliver is killed, and Roland and Archbishop Turpin are mortally wounded. Turpin tries to climb the hill to Roncevaux, where there is a "running stream," in an attempt to get water for the dying Roland (*laisse* 165). In the novel, on the fifth day, Jake, Bill and Harris climb the hill to the monastery of Roncevaux, and finding a pub there, they quench their thirst together. Harris insists on paying because they've had "such a jolly good time" together (pp. 128-29). This displacement of tragic, legendary epic into the lives of drunken but friendly comrades-at-fishing instead of comrades-at-arms gives a piquant and wryly comical reading to the whole scene. When Harris says, "I've not had much fun since the war," it's hard not to imagine the shades of Roland, Oliver and Turpin sitting around the table drinking at Roncevaux.

After Charlemagne arrives at Roncevaux, the remnants of the Saracen forces are routed, and the scene changes to the judgment of Ganelon. The young Thierry takes up the cause of Roland's family in a contest that has all the accoutrements and ceremony of a bullfight with "pics rising like lances" (p. 212). Before the contest, Thierry and the other knights go to confession and mass, just as Jake Barnes goes to mass and confession during the festival and prior to Cohn's attack on him. Although Thierry is smaller and weaker than the knight who fights for Ganelon, he overcomes his opponent through sheer nerve and determination. This is Cohn's fight with Jake and Mike Campbell, and especially with the young Romero, during the festival in Pamplona; his moral defeat by Romero, and his banishment from the story by Romero's threat to kill him, is equivalent to the execution of Ganelon.

In his comments on Hemingway's reading of medieval literature, Reynolds is mistaken when he says that pre-1929 Hemingway characters have no relationship to medieval heroes because they "do not love well and do little heroic but survive."[10] In the *chansons de geste,* the chivalric code has nothing to do with courtly love, and the heroics of a medieval knight of the crusades are measured only by adherence to a code which demands loyalty to feudal lord and the Christian faith. Ganelon is a traitor, not merely because he arranges for Roland's death but because he strikes against the code of feudal order. The code of behavior for Jake and his friends is just as rigid as the chivalric code; it is unsentimental and unromantic. Cohn breaks this code not merely because he "slept" with Brett—Mike tells him, "she's slept with lots of better people than you" (p. 142)—but because he uses "bad form" in his open and persistent romantic attachment to Brett. Both Brett and Jake say that Cohn has "behaved very badly" (pp. 143, 181). The awful death of Ganelon is displaced into Cohn's banishment from the group, but the judgment pronounced in the poem could be the same for both cases: "Any man who betrays another must not be allowed to brag about it!" (line 3974).

At the end of **The Song of Roland,** Charlemagne has established peace in his empire, and is resting quietly. Then an angel appears and recalls him to arms; his help is needed again in distant lands. After the close of the festival in Pamplona, Jake Barnes is also resting quietly, alone in San Sebastian. Then a telegram comes from Madrid. It is Brett asking for his help once again. Unlike Charlemagne, who bemoans his call to resume his labors, saying, "God! . . . my life is so full of suffering" (line 4000), Jake merely sends a return wire saying he is on the way, signs it "with love," and goes in to lunch (p. 239). In the final scene of the novel the "pagan" Brett's unselfish act of giving up Romero makes her feel good about herself, which she says is "sort of what we have instead of God." This is as close as Hemingway lets her come to the conversion of the pagan queen, Bramimonde, Charlemagne's "noble prisoner" who "wishes to believe in God" (lines 3978-80), and the novel ends with Jake and Brett on their way somewhere else. Both the poem and the novel leave a final impression of the restless round of life going on.

Although we have the conversation with Dorman-Smith as evidence that Hemingway was familiar with **The Song of Roland** as early as 1924, it is, of course, impossible to know exactly what text or texts he had read. Joseph Bédier's modern French translation of 1921 was well known, and there was a new French edition published in Paris in 1924, translated from the Old Norman French by Edmond Aubé. These would have been available to Hemingway in addition to other, older texts in both French and English. However, an English translation of **The Song of Roland** which came out in

1919 holds some interesting implications. It was published by Dutton, and is a translation by Charles Scott Moncrieff, who says he carried the little book of Roland with him through the trenches of France and Belgium during the war. That idea would have appealed to Hemingway. G. K. Chesterton's introduction to Scott Moncrieff's book would also appeal to an author's imagination with its story of Taillefer the Jongleur, who at the Battle of Hastings in 1066 "went in front of the Norman Army throwing his sword in the air and singing the **Song of Roland.**" He declares that the "bard in front of their battle line was shouting the glorification of failure." Whether Hemingway read Chesterton's introduction or not, the idea of Roland as the epitome of the defeated hero bears some relation to Jake Barnes.

There is one last item to be mentioned about the 1919 edition of **The Song of Roland.** Scott Moncrieff dedicates his book to three friends who died during the war: "To Three Men / Scholars, poets, soldiers / Who came to their Rencesvals / In September, October, and November / Nineteen Hundred and Eighteen." The names of these men are Philip Bainbrigge, Wilfred Owen, and Ian Mackenzie. With a little imagination, one can read the names of Jake Barnes, Bill Gorton, and Mike Campbell, the Scotsman.

## Notes

1. *Reading for the Plot: Design and Intention in Narrative* (New York: Knopf, 1984), p. 4.

2. *Hemingway and the Hispanic World* (Ann Arbor: UMI Research, 1985), p. 54.

3. Page numbers in parentheses refer to *The Sun Also Rises* (New York: Scribners, 1970).

4. *Ernest Hemingway: Selected Letters 1917-1961* (New York: Scribners, 1981), p. 870. The original line which Baker quotes in his footnote, *"cil corz at longe aleine,"* is from Jenkins' text of the Oxford manuscript, and is in Old (Norman) French. It is doubtful that Hemingway could read Old French, and a modern French translation comes much closer to the line as he used it: *"Ce cor a longue haleine."* (This is numbered as line 2009 in Aubé's 1924 translation.)

5. *Hemingway's Reading 1910-1940: An Inventory* (Princeton: Princeton Univ. Press, 1981), p. 93. A letter from Hemingway to Ezra Pound from Burguete on 19 July 1924 describes the Pamplona festival which he has just left, and mentions Dorman-Smith ("Chink") as being one of the party.

6. *Hemingway's Reading 1910-1940,* p. 26.

7. *Reading for the Plot,* pp. 14-16.

8. Lines and *laisses* in parentheses refer to Gerald J. Brault, trans., *The Song of Roland: An Analytical Edition: Oxford Text and English Translation* (University Park: Pennsylvania State Univ. Press, 1978).

9. *"Cabestro* and *Vaquilla*: The Symbolic Structure of *The Sun Also Rises," Sewanee Review,* 76 (1968), 26-48.

10. *Hemingway's Reading 1910-1940,* pp. 26-27.

## Emanuel J. Mickel (essay date 1989)

SOURCE: Mickel, Emanuel J. Introduction to *Ganelon, Treason, and the* Chanson de Roland, pp. 1-24. University Park: Pennsylvania State University Press, 1989.

[*In the following essay, Mickel explains the importance of the trial of Ganelon in the critical controversies regarding the origin and date of* The Song of Roland.]

From the earliest efforts of scholarly research devoted to medieval French literature and history, the **Chanson de Roland** has played a prominent role in intellectual controversies concerning both historical and literary subjects. One might also state that the trial of Ganelon, more than any other portion of the **Roland,** has been used by scholars in support of historical and literary positions they hold. In 1872, at the height of Franco-Prussian enmity, Léon Gautier[1] reaffirmed the argument he had made in 1869,[2] and which many supported, that the French epic was Germanic in origin. As a major proof Gautier noted that a close analysis of the episodes of Ganelon's trial revealed that there was not a single element of Roman law in it. The purely Germanic origin of the epic could be demonstrated by the fact that no element of Roman legislation or canon law could be found in any segment of the trial. To prove his point Gautier then divided the trial and arrest of Ganelon into seven "actes" or "tableaux," whose relevant legal elements he found in various Germanic law codes dating from the sixth to the thirteenth centuries. Not only was there no late addition or influence from canon law, but the trial seemed to fit particularly well with archaic Germanic traditions, thus bolstering the idea that the epic was the product of the Germanic people and had been brought into Gaul by the invading tribes. That the epic appeared as French literature was merely the result of the Frankish conquest of Gaul, their subsequent adoption of the *lingua romana,* and the composition of these stories centuries later in the adopted language.

In a slightly later version of the question of the origins of the epic, the trial continued to play a significant role. Joseph Bédier countered traditional arguments that the epic,[3] created in the aftermath of the historical event it recounted, was recited orally from generation to generation until it was written down in the eleventh and twelfth centuries. Bédier argued that eleventh- and twelfth-century poets created the epic poems from accounts in Latin chronicles and histories in which the nearly forgotten events had been recorded.[4] Motivated by relics which were found in shrines along the pilgrimage routes, enterprising hostels encouraged the creation and narration of stories which provided a historical framework for the treasures of church and monastery. This thesis caused many opposing scholars to analyze the poems carefully to see how well the pilgrim-route theory held up as a primary motivation for creation of the genre, and many studied the earlier chronicles and histories to find evidence of an oral vernacular poetry in the long period between event and text which Bédier characterized by the phrase "silence des siècles." Others analyzed the Latin histories and chronicles to determine whether or not they could account for the material in the many quasihistorical poems of the genre.[5] Menéndez Pidal, Paul Aebischer, and others laid emphasis on the fact that more accurate historical detail could be found in the Oxford version of the *Chanson de Roland* than in the official Latin accounts of the period.[6] Here the events surrounding Ganelon's treason played a major role in several ways. Scholars pointed to later Arab chroniclers who stated that Ganelon's treason was prompted mainly by greed and Arab bribery, a point included in the epic but not given primary emphasis as the motive for his treason.[7] In this and other details traditionalists perceived a remnant layer of historical truth in the epic text which was to be found nowhere in the Latin documents of the period. Thus, they reasoned, the epic must have had an oral life stemming from a period close to the epic events themselves.

But the trial itself and the treason of Ganelon seemed to some to offer even more persuasive proof of the text's early provenance and led to a full-length book on the subject. In 1936 Ruggero Ruggieri argued that the trial of Ganelon not only demonstrated the Germanic origin of the Oxford *Roland,* but revealed a law which was antiquated even in Charlemagne's time.[8] This argument, if correct, would have profound influence on many important issues addressed by *Roland* scholarship. Ruggieri asserted that Ganelon's defense reflected a Germanic legal concept which had been replaced in the Carolingian period by a new law which sought to eliminate the traditional right of vengeance. Thus the original author of the *Roland* must certainly have composed the principal elements of the text in the eighth or ninth century, and even then some of the ideas he employed were archaic for the time. Ruggieri's analysis of the trial contributed both to the question of the Germanic origins of the epic and to its probable oral existence prior to the eleventh- or twelfth-century version found at Oxford.

Scrutiny of the Oxford *Roland,* generally conceded to be the oldest extant version and one of the oldest, if not the oldest, extant epic poem, has placed its earliest date of composition in the late eleventh or early twelfth century, with a minority of scholars arguing for a later, twelfth-century date.[9] The problem becomes more difficult when one departs from the idea that the Oxford *Roland* was written by one author at a given time. If one conceives of the extant Oxford version of the text as the last in a series of versions either composed orally or rewritten by various authors in different periods, then the *Roland* becomes a kind of layered palimpsest. Not only can one conceive of episodes being added or deleted at different periods, but *remanieurs* probably altered details concerning warfare, weapons, costume, and social relationships to make the text more familiar or understandable to their own audience, or they may have added what they thought were archaic customs appropriate to that "ancient" period. This fact, of course, does not complicate so much the question of dating the Oxford version itself as it does the assessment of the age of any given episode or even the language or visual and intellectual detail used in its composition. Thus the elements of the trial, which Ruggieri used to argue for the antiquity of the Oxford *Roland,* could indeed, if he is right, be evidence of the early composition of this aspect of the epic, or it could be the archaizing influence of a later poet. Close analysis of the trial should help one distinguish the period of law involved, especially if there is consistency.

The question of dating the poem extends far beyond the issue of establishing the period in which the version found in the extant manuscript was first composed in its current form. In attempting to analyze the meaning of the poem, many scholars have sought to place it within a historical context. Aebischer and Menéndez Pidal have developed arguments based on details from the expedition of 778 which the *Roland* shares only with later Arabic chronicles; Fawtier, Ganshof, and Aebischer have attempted to demonstrate that the condition of Charlemagne's kingdom immediately after the expedition was truly precarious, thus reflecting a serious defeat of the Frankish forces; others see the politics of a later period reflected in the text.[10] In 1943 Emile Mireaux set forth the idea that the *Chanson de Roland* reflected events and characters associated with the Angevin house, especially in the years just after 1150.[11] Mireaux's thesis did not find much support from scholars of that period because of the way in which he used and conceived of the influence of twelfth-century history on the poem.[12] But the later study of Karl-Heinz Bender, who proposed that the *Roland* reflects the politics of the late eleventh century more than it does that of Charlemagne's own period,[13] has been received more favorably. Bender's thesis takes into account that the *Roland* might reflect political realities at the time of the poet's composition. Was not the priest-king portrayal of Charlemagne an image more suitable to the thought of the late eleventh and twelfth centuries, a likely grafting onto the text by the final *remanieur* of the Oxford version, Turoldus? In fact this idea of the king contrasts sharply with the ideal feudal king, the *primus inter pares* Germanic ruler who recognizes and observes the rights of the barons. Bender sees all the real, not the idealization of eleventh-century politics, in the *Roland.* Not only does one have the major theme of the war against the Infidel, a fact every king and prince had to confront, but there is the tension present between the barons and the crown.

However, this argument recalls Ruggieri's own thesis that the tension between barons and crown in the Ganelon trial reflected the principal transformation of Germanic society from its earlier tribal condition to that of a kingdom where family and regional loyalties come into conflict with loyalty to the realm or the increasingly powerful monarchy. The idea was not original with Ruggieri, of course, but derived from the nineteenth-century development of prehistoric and feudal Germanic society. In his *Origines de l'ancienne France* Jacques Flach saw the same conflict between family loyalty and the crown in the combat between Pinabel and Thierry:

> L'appel de faux jugement s'y montre comme une con-séquence de ce fait capital que la justice féodale, au XI$^e$ siècle, oscille entre la protection mutuelle que se doivent les pairs et la fidélité qu'ils doivent à leur seig-neur. C'est un troisième élément, le concours des proches, qui fait pencher la balance d'un côté ou de l'autre.[14]

Flach saw a dilemma for barons who wish to give help to one of their own and yet remain loyal to the king.

Ruggieri believed that Germanic tribal society was identified with baronial authority and the regional orientation of power prior to the rise of the Carolingian monarchy under Charlemagne's centralizing and unifying influence. This imperial idea of kingship, which he saw as a reflection of Roman and Church influence on the kingdom, was, he argued, detrimental to the Germanic idea of traditional governance. In both Bender's and Ruggieri's thesis the trial of Ganelon becomes a focal point where the conflict is played out. The rights of the crown, transgressed by Ganelon's alleged act of treason, come into conflict with what Ganelon sees as his private right of vengeance. For Ruggieri, in fact, the earliest version of the *Roland* had probably focused on this conflict more than on Roland's death and martyrdom, a later orientation under the influence of the crusade movement. Ruggieri suggested that the original conception of the text placed Ganelon at the center as a kind of tragic hero, an admirable Germanic warrior, who was provoked by his boastful stepson and brought to his tragic conclusion when he allowed his anger and

desire for vengeance to lead him to commit a crime against the king. On these interpretations the legal questions involved in the trial and the concepts of Germanic and Roman law play a major role. At times a close analysis of the legal traditions which pertain can be most helpful in determining if such issues are really at work in the text or if the modern reader perceives relationships which, when analyzed more closely, no longer seem so apparent or yield a different interpretation.

Recently the *Roland* and the epic genre in general have been perceived as important documents reflecting the changes taking place in eleventh-century France. Recent studies of Léopold Genicot, K. F. Werner, Georges Duby, and others have focused attention on the nobility in France after the collapse of the Carolingian Empire and the formation of the territorial principalities.[15] It is noted that, although there was no discontinuity in the noble families as once believed,[16] regional families, no longer deriving power from links to the crown, became more concerned with vertical ancestry. With a strong central authority, as in the time of Charlemagne and Charles the Bald, genealogies are characterized by a kind of horizontal lineage emphasizing marriage ties to the royal family. As the authority of the crown weakened, families perceived that the land once held from the crown had, in reality, become their own.[17] In the early eleventh century one can see the consciousness of this fact in the regional histories sponsored by important baronial families living in the areas of Anjou, Normandy, and Flanders. As Duby points out in his discussion of the *Historia comitatum Ghisnensium,* Lambert traces the family's lineage back to 928. At that point he introduces a Scandinavian, one Sifridus, who seduces the daughter of the Count of Flanders and becomes the founder of the line.

This same pattern can be seen in the *Chronica de Gestis Consulum Andegavorum,* written in various stages at the behest of the house of Anjou.[18] The chronicler traces the lineage back to Foulque le Roux II (886-941) and then turns to the youthful Ingelger, the legendary founder of the house (not verifiable historically) who successfully defends Countess Adela in single combat against her accuser, Guntram. Abandoned by her own kin, Adela is saved by the young man, related to her only through a baptismal ceremony. Before retiring to the convent, Adela has Ingelger named her heir.[19]

Duby sees in these early chronicle narratives a strong influence from *chanson de geste* literature, with its emphasis on ancestry and a proclivity for foreign heroes who save a family and marry the heiress.[20] The conscious patronage of literature and history which begins in Anjou and Normandy at this time is witness to a growing class of literate laymen aware of their own increasing independence and the importance of recording that history. There are those who attribute the wide interest in Arthurian romance in the late twelfth century to Angevin/English patronage. The rivals of the king of France took strong interest in a literate, courtly kingdom which gave the British a distinguished ancestor whose renown would rival even the legendary fame of Charlemagne. Seen in this light, texts of the period must be viewed closely in terms of the audience or patrons who wished to inspire them. Even if one can argue that traditional narratives were used and much of the substance could be transmitted intact, such political use of the text would make it subject to alteration in many small and subtle ways. It is precisely in such matters that the presentation of a treason trial would become so important, for how it is presented and the nature of the conflict within the legal perspective of the text determine the meaning to be derived from the outcome of the trial. In this regard it is fascinating that only the Oxford and Lyon versions of the *Roland* give such prominence to the trial in the epic.[21] Some have no trial at all and scarcely consider the issue. In the Oxford version it is central to the poem's meaning. If the Oxford *Roland* were written with the political problems of another age in mind, it is through study of the trial that the intended use of the poem is seen.

The medieval bent for reading typologically compels one to be aware of another force at work in the composition of the *Roland.* As Robert Folz demonstrated over thirty years ago and Stephen Nichols only recently, the medieval legend surrounding Charlemagne and the religious context in which he was perceived were extensive.[22] Though many would not agree with the numerous direct biblical correspondences which Michael Wendt presented in his exegetical study, there is no doubt that the large number of biblical and religious overtones make one aware that the *Roland* was shaped by an audience steeped in biblical iconography and accustomed to seeing history in typological terms.[23] It is well known that histories and annals of the period were shaped by concepts of time and space generated by Eusebius, Jerome, Orosius and Bede. The Christian chronicler saw historical time within a context of eternity.[24] As Boethius discussed in his *De Consolatione Philosophiae,* time represents man's perspective, his way of measuring existence according to his own finite perspective. Even Creation and Last Judgment have meaning as temporal moments only to a creature for whom these events mark a beginning and an end. Thus the medieval historian attempted to understand history in a larger sense. He tried to see history temporally and spatially through God's eyes, on the one hand enclosed by God's perspective and, on the other, within a continuum which reduces the events of temporal existence to insignificance and places great importance on the moral decisions (made in a timeless present) which lie behind the temporally framed human actions. In this perspective man himself becomes a mor-

ally timeless figure who can be seen in numerous figural repetitions throughout history. Literary and historical figures foreshadow or recall other types of which they are examples. Every man essentially plays out the drama of life within the ephemeral, temporal moment called life. Even though historical circumstances may differ, he faces the same eternal moral questions. And, since historical events as such pass away and are of little consequence, it is the eternal moral question which matters.

As much as one may see actual political realities of the tenth or eleventh century reflected in the *Roland,* one must also recognize that the typological vision of the Middle Ages had much to do with the shaping of the characters, events and moral issues. Just as Clovis was seen as a new Constantine who had led his people to conversion, so was Charlemagne another David, Roland a type of Christ or David depending upon the part of the poem, and Ganelon a type of Judas.

Thus historical questions become further complicated by these multiple perspectives of history. When Ganelon receives gifts from a long line of Saracens, some see evidence of the true issue at Roncevaux in 778: the Franks did not leave the field of battle because the Saracens had agreed to surrender and be converted but because the Franks had been bribed. Others see the many *laisses* which describe a Saracen giving a gift to Ganelon as the author's way of emphasizing the resemblance between Judas and Ganelon, further highlighted by the reminiscences of the Passion in Roland's death scene. In this context an analysis of the trial becomes especially important. Is the trial conducted in a way which recalls ordinary treason trials of a given period? Or can one see a myth-maker at work? Are there elements of the trial and its procedure which give special meaning to the events or cast the characters in figural roles? The answers to questions concerning the authenticity of the trial as a credible event in a specific period contribute to our understanding of the trial's meaning in the text.

If the trial plays an important role in historical questions pertaining to the origins of the *Roland* or the historical framework which encompasses it, it has also been important to many historians as a vital document in scholarly discussions about feudalism and legal procedure. Even in earlier years, when historians were loath to cite literary texts as evidence concerning historical issues, the *Roland* always seemed to be regarded as a worthy historical document of the times, often revered as a text which seemed to preserve the very essence of medieval feudal reality. Marc Bloch referred to it in his discussion of feudalism, Duby in his *Trois Ordres,* K. J. Hollyman in his study of feudal vocabulary, and Boutrouche in his study of feudalism.[25] Most historians of the period have cited the *Roland* for one reason or another. Legal historians often turn to the *Roland* trial to prove a point of procedure or to underscore some understanding of the nature of treason.[26] The trial in the *Roland* seems to be a classic case of treason against the state as defined by the later medieval understanding of *laesa maiestatis,* a concept derived primarily from Roman law. Yet the defense offered by Ganelon was purely Germanic in character, given its understanding of treason as the transgression of one's oath or formal feudal tie to another. Then how does one reconcile the somewhat elaborate trial procedure of a later period with a defense which, scholars argue, represents an early Germanic understanding of justifiable vengeance, i.e., after lawful disengagement from any feudal ties and fair warning through open defiance?

Ultimately this question affects the interpretation of the Oxford *Roland.* Critics have long disputed how the *Roland* was intended to have been received, how it was performed or read, or how the audience of the twelfth century actually perceived it. Is Roland presented as a kind of tragic hero, courageous and loyal yet flawed by his own pride and stubbornness? Is he guilty of *démesure* in his failure to blow the horn and in his conduct toward Ganelon? And is Olivier, who is considered by some to be as brave and loyal as Roland, the wise and prudent knight held up for emulation, an exemplary companion whose contrary virtues accentuate Roland's weakness? When the author describes the glorious Ganelon preparing to embark on the mission he fears will be fatal, are we supposed to share his anger at Roland? Did the author or singer expect his audience to agree that Roland had insulted Ganelon and that his wrongful treatment of his step-father gave Ganelon just cause to seek vengeance? And if we believe that Ganelon had just cause for vengeance, are we supposed to have sympathy for this trial defense as a legitimate argument in the eyes of an early Germanic audience? Or do we accept the Ruggieri analysis which makes Ganelon into a kind of tragic hero himself, perhaps the central figure in an earlier Germanic version.[27] In such a version Roland's own *desmesure* becomes less an issue, for it is Ganelon, worthy and trusted knight of Charlemagne, who allows his all-consuming desire for vengeance to lead him into treason against his beloved king and nation, thus tragically ruining his reputation and destroying his clan. For some Ganelon's treason was invented by poets seeking to explain the French defeat against the Infidel at Roncevaux. Given the fact that, in the view of a medieval poet, God would certainly favor the Christian cause against the pagans, how could one account for the loss except to imagine a betrayal from within? In Ruggieri's view this provided the *jongleur* with a perfect opportunity to center the action at Roncevaux on a figure like Ganelon.

In all these questions the trial of Ganelon plays an essential role. In this concluding episode, the final redactor or singer of the epic renders his judgment on the events which led to Ganelon's defense and conviction. A close study of the stages of the trial in the light of normal medieval trial conditions and practices often reveals how the trial may have been perceived by contemporaries or how the trial fits within the context of the narrative.

Previous studies of law and French literature in the Middle Ages have been too broad, have dealt with later literature, or have mentioned the *Roland* only in passing.[28] Historical discussions of treason often mention the *Roland,* but they have tended to focus on materials considerably later than the Oxford text.[29] Studies which have pursued the questions of the ordeal, trial procedure or scenes of single combat in Old French literature refer only to a certain element of the *Roland* trial or cite some aspect of the trial out of context.[30] Both Gautier and Ruggieri analyzed the trial very carefully, Ruggieri with great care to establish the trial within the traditions of the Germanic law codes allegedly of the pre-Carolingian era. There is no doubt that Ruggieri knew both the primary and secondary scholarly materials pertaining to the early period, including a broad knowledge of general issues, such as the history of the ordeal. However, Ruggieri was convinced that the Oxford *Roland*'s version of the trial essentially preserved an ancient legal position which, he confidently surmised (based on the accepted assessment of the nature of an oral legal tradition), virtually reached back to prehistoric Germanic society.[31] Not only did he tend to see old traditions undergirding all important aspects of the trial, but he assumed, as did most scholars, that the more ancient the custom the cruder and crueler it would be. Thus harsh treatment, even if not found in the older documents, was accepted as an early practice and leniency was naturally assumed to represent a more enlightened period.[32] And Ruggieri tended to find evidence which supported his theory, just as Gautier had argued previously that the Germanic origin of the epic could be seen in the fact that the trial contained only Germanic law.

Every period tends to see literature through its own eyes; there is a tendency to shape the questions of the past in terms of the vital issues of the present. Nineteenth-century anti-clericalism and Darwinian thought shaped the history of medieval French drama and continues to be a factor in the historical interpretation of that literature even today.[33] Republican fervor of the nineteenth century made Vercingetorix one of the early heroes of French freedom, a symbol of Germanic independence from Roman, imperial domination. Troubadour love poetry represented a spirit of secular freedom from the stifling homogeneity of Christian morality and the Church.[34] The undercurrent of a pre-

Christian pagan society associated with the Germanic spirit fit well into the developing psychology of the nineteenth and twentieth centuries, which equated the subconscious, source of originality and the true self, with the folkloric pre-history of the European peoples. The rational mind, only capable of imitation and craftsmanship, was equated with the dominant order of society (the Church, the monarchy, the values of the bourgeoisie, *et cetera*), an outside force which sought to repress the natural impulses of society or, in human terms, of the inner self. The nineteenth-century revolutionary myth, which pits the individual against society and yearns for a pre-lapsarian utopia in which men lived in natural harmony without government or private ownership, has shaped much of our own history-making. Thus in George F. Jones's thesis, Roland becomes an other-oriented individual living in an old order where the individual's personality and being take definition from the group.[35] In a psychological sense shame and honor thus become such dominant forces because they represent the code values of the group from which the individual is defined. In this view Ganelon and Roland curiously become close partners, both sharing the same values. It is Olivier who becomes the champion of a new order, one which accords more with our own ideal. Olivier is the inner-directed man, one not obsessed with the values of the group, able to see the realities of the situation and to take appropriate action despite fears of what society may think. Gérard's article, a variation on the Jones theme, puts Roland with the old clannish values of the traditional ethic, whereas Olivier represents the new centralizing order of the monarchy:

> Face à cette morale à la fois individualiste et clanique, se dresse en la personne d'Olivier, une morale d'Etat, où le triomphe de la nation et la puissance de son chef passent avant toute autre considération.[36]

There is no doubt that Roland is concerned about his family and how his actions will be perceived. However, the context should not be limited to our view of the situation. Roland and Olivier both live in an absolute world where the standard of conduct is set by God. The purpose of the *judicium dei,* in fact, was to have that absolute perspective revealed in order to avoid human consequences that only appeared to be true. All men lived under the absolute scrutiny of God and no man could hide from his omniscience. Thus, for Roland it was vital that his conduct reflect the absolute standards of that reality. But the oral society in which Roland lived judged more by appearance and oral report than by documents and internal evidence. It was not a society which expected the true motives of one's actions always to lie beneath the surface. Lacking the psychological perspective which developed in the nineteenth century, eleventh- and twelfth-century man, while acknowledging that men are often devious and hide their designs, as did Ganelon, did not perceive all men as being dominated by inner, selfish drives. He did not expect a priori to find a difference between man's inner motives and his outer presentation. A case of presumption or notoriety was easily accepted as the best evidence of guilt. The man holding the dagger dripping with blood was acknowledged with confidence as the murderer of the victim lying prone beneath him. Moreover, in a society which depended on visual witness and the oral recounting of events to establish proof, it was vital that appearances reflect reality. In modern society, heavily dependent on documents and records, one relies less on oral report than documentary evidence to establish truth. But in the eleventh and twelfth centuries, the event became historically what man thought it was.

Roland is very conscious of this fact. He and his men are faithful in an absolute sense. They are all willing to fight to the death, which they all affirm on more than one occasion in proclaiming that none will desert for fear of death. Yet Roland also wishes the truth of his conduct and theirs to be known. This is why he emphasizes to Olivier that he will never conduct himself in such a way that "bad songs" might be sung. The "malveise chanson" of the eleventh or twelfth century was not just fiction, it was history. It was the only knowledge of events that man would have. In a world-view where man saw this reality as an enigma which must be deciphered in order to see that greater order of God's plan (of which temporal reality was only a momentary part), the real truth of an event in absolute terms was important to mankind in a way modern man can hardly appreciate. Roland is far from having a self-ish attitude or of being concerned only with his own reputation and the reputation of his family. Roland is the *garant* of his men and the Franks. That is, he is the champion who goes into combat on behalf of his people confident that the cause he upholds is right and that he will, therefore, be granted victory. For Roland, his family, and the Franks as a nation, it is important that his faith and courage be what they are thought to be. Thus Roland's last acts are not selfish but designed to establish the absolute truth of the event as it happened. He is careful to find the bodies of the peers and to face them in the direction of Spain. He does not wish anyone who witnessed the carnage to imply in his account of the battle that some had died in flight with their backs toward the enemy. It is important that no "bad songs" report the events falsely. Finally, after Roland has arranged the dead, he himself walks toward Spain, a symbolic gesture to show his leadership and to show that he was the *garant* that he was supposed to be. When Roland's horse is killed in the final assault, the author notes that he does not pursue the fleeing Saracens only because he has lost his horse. At the end Roland does move toward the fleeing Saracens to indicate the true nature of the situation.[37] In a world-view where the thoughts and deeds of characters deliberately reflect such a reality, one loses much of the density of character and place if one employs a modern psychological construct which looks for motives and meanings belonging to another perception of character delineation or reality. Such an analysis often seems to oversimplify the reading of the material and reduces the dimensions of the text. Since the logic of the character's personality is based on a different set of premises and another way of thinking about man, it is no wonder that a richness of context is lost and that the text, the period, and the characters no longer seem to mesh.

In recent years historians have become more and more fascinated by the relative nature of history.[38] With increasing sophistication they have tried to take into account various contexts in which the historian wrote and the controlling cultural and intellectual conditions which shaped his perspective. When Chrétien de Troyes says in the Prologue to his romance, *Cligés,* that *clergie* and *chevalerie* have passed from the Greeks and Romans to the French, one must try to understand these words and ideas within a specific intellectual and historical context. One must try to fathom the transformation of materials and ideas which are part of a twelfth-century understanding of this idea. In a sense the medieval lack of historical awareness naturally caused an, at times, unconscious transformation of past materials into a modern context. Without a sense of the differences between Greece and Rome or between pre-Christian Rome and twelfth-century France, many important distinctions were lost. Furthermore, twelfth-century immersion in its own philosophical and theological perspective caused writers to alter the shapes of materials and ideas. A different and absolute view of history made them read multiple patterns into texts and events. Moreover, the predominantly oral character of society produced a constantly but subtly changing texture of law, philosophy, and social attitudes within a framework which perceived itself as unchanging. Custom law by nature considers itself the good old law, the law of one's ancestors. Yet modern anthropological and ethnographical studies have shown that contemporary oral societies are in a constant state of flux, though the inhabitants perceive their customs to be unchanging. Oral societies tend to alter their laws, customs and memory of history imperceptibly and without being aware of it to fit the needs of contemporary reality.

To the medieval writer of the **Chanson de Roland,** it would have been natural to recast the legal conditions into those he knew in his own time. He would not have done so consciously to disturb the conditions of the text, nor would he have been aware that the law in Charlemagne's day might have been different. In his mind, he was providing a legal context which dated back to time immemorial, as far back as anyone could remember.[39] He also would have been unconcerned about retaining the exact authenticity of a previous version. The written word had not yet imprinted the notion of historical authenticity to the exact printed word, nor had the idea of authorship yet commingled with originality to make the specific version of the original author artistically sacred. The idea that translation from one language to another automatically alters a text's authenticity was unknown. Ideas and texts were public domain for the next author to amplify and abbreviate as he saw fit.

An oral society lives in a kind of eternal present. Current values and laws are perceived as those of one's ancestors in a kind of timeless, seamless connection with a nebulous past, not as vestiges of a specific past moment. A charter does not represent a moment in the past when some scribe penned the document, but is a vehicle which contains an everpresent, timeless agreement whose importance lives for contemporaries. The moment when it was conceived matters little; what counts is that it was spoken and has living force in the present. In an oral society lineages and history become foreshortened. As time goes by the memory retains only the truly significant features and individuals from the past. This telescoping of events has the effect of bringing one's ancestors and past into a more immediate proximity and of giving greater relevance to current events. Moreover, in theological terms God sees man and the world within a timeless present. "Crusades" to Spain in the eighth and ninth centuries have a closer relationship to similar events in the eleventh century than seventeenth-century events would to us moderns. To us the periods are historically distinct, and our cause-and-effect mentality makes any connection between events then and now only indirectly and remotely connected. Within the eternal perspective of a society which tries to see reality as God sees it, the moral questions which face man remain the same. Charlemagne and Godefroi de Bouillon faced the same decisions, and these decisions concerned questions pertaining to material things far less than issues involving courage and moral commitment. It would matter little to the twelfth-century reader or writer that Charlemagne's expedition could not really be called a crusade in the eleventh-century sense. In their eyes his confrontation with Marsile and then Baligant replayed vivid moments of a history whose immediacy and relevance made it seem as though it were happening before one's eyes. As Rupert Pickens has observed, the **Chanson de Roland**'s author betrays no sense of historical distance in his narrative style.[40] To some this would mean that the **Roland** belongs to an oral tradition. Its lack of historical perspective would then reflect the fact that it had been created at the time of the event and therefore had no historical distance to show. In my view the immediacy of the **Roland** reflects an oral society's perspective more than oral composition itself. In this sense the **Roland** does represent an old order, whereas the romance, and the Arthurian material in general, represent the new literate society of an age which has become historically self-conscious. The historical awareness in Marie and Chrétien reflects the distance which they perceived between contemporary reality and the Arthurian world. Even here the literature is used for contemporary purposes and comments on eternal questions, but there is no mistaking the fact that the author is looking back on a past time. In the **Roland** there is the immediacy of the cinema or a drama. Roland stands in the pass in an eternal present searching his own soul and facing odds which the veterans who had survived the siege of Antioche would have recognized and relived with him during the recitation. And so would the unfortunate father of Stephen of Blois, who saw the vast Saracen host besieging the enclosed crusaders in Antioche, deemed the situation hopeless, and assumed that the better part of valor lay in withdrawal.

The modern writer can hardly escape his keen sense of history, and yet he has a deep-seated understanding that this awareness may be truly illusory. He knows only too well that he is a prisoner of his own intellect, education, and self-absorption into his own period of modernity. Yet it is the fascination of what we perceive as history that it offers us a chance, or, one might say, the hope of moving beyond ourselves. We aspire to know something beyond the self, and what we read and see in the literature, art, and history of previous periods makes us acutely aware of different and captivating modes of understanding and patterns of existence based on entirely different philosophical premises. And even if one knows intellectually that he can never really know or become the other, one also senses that the attempt to know changes the self: that the effort to understand a previous period's art and thought in its own terms expands one's perspective. And this is not changed by our realization that what we are studying is not "history" but only extant documents which are the product of men attempting to manipulate reality and being manipulated by their cultural and social context. For the more historical reality becomes the protean image of relative perspective, the more fascinating it is to trace the complex threads which form the fabric of that vision.

In this study of the **Roland** I shall attempt to see the trial of Ganelon within a complex context of historical and legal traditions. I shall try to see the trial against the background of medieval law codes and trials from the fifth to the fourteenth centuries and in the light of the procedure and disposition of treason cases found in the chronicles of both France and Anglo-Norman England. In such an assessment one must avoid, as much as possible, broad assumptions about the primitive Germanic social unit and the legal conditions of prehistoric Germany if one is to escape conclusions which merely confirm one's pre-existing ideas. Ruggieri's work on the trial of Ganelon has been considered standard for decades.[41] Although his knowledge of

medieval Germanic law is impressive, Ruggieri's conclusions about the **Roland** depend on his assumptions about primitive Germanic society and kingship. Indications that later legal tradition might be involved remained unperceived because Ruggieri was certain that the essentials of the trial reached back to a period too early for documentation. In this study I shall challenge some of the hypotheses and conclusions drawn by earlier scholars. In general I am now of the opinion that the elements of Ganelon's trial tend to reflect later rather than earlier legal practices. Some of the conclusions or interpretations which would seem to follow such findings bear on many important questions in **Roland** scholarship.

*Notes*

1. *La Chanson de Roland* (Tours, 1872).

2. "Idée politique dans les Chansons de geste," *Revue des questions historiques* (1869), 101ff.

3. Gaston Paris, *Histoire poétique de Charlemagne* (Paris, 1865).

4. Joseph Bédier, *Les Légendes épiques,* 4 vols. (Paris, 1908-13).

5. Ferdinand Lot, "Etudes sur les légendes épiques françaises," *Romania* 54 (1928), 357-80.

6. Ramon Menéndez Pidal, *La Chanson de Roland y el neotradicionalismo: Origenes de la épica románica* (Madrid: Espasa-Calpe, 1959); Paul Aebischer, *Préhistoire et protohistoire du Roland d'Oxford* (Berne: Francke, 1972).

7. Gerard Brault stresses Ganelon's greed in his commentary on the *Roland* (*The Song of Roland,* vol. 1, *Introduction and Commentary*. University Park, PA, 1978). See also T. A. Jenkins, "Why Did Ganelon Hate Roland?" *PMLA* 36 (1921), 119-33. Jenkins argues that Ganelon was really motivated by envy of Roland's greater wealth.

8. *Il processo di Gano nella Chanson de Roland* (Florence: Sansini, 1936).

9. For arguments asserting a later date of composition, see Hans Erich Keller, "La Place du *Ruolantes Liet* dans la tradition rolandienne," *Moyen Age* 71 (1965), 215-46; "*La Chanson de Roland,* poème de propagande pour le royaume capétien du milieu du XII$^e$ siècle," *Travaux de Linguistique et Littérature* (Strasbourg) 14 (1976), 229-41; and "La version dionysienne de la *Chanson de Roland,*" in *Philologica romanica. Erhard Lommatzsch gewidmet* (Munich: Fink, 1975), 257-87. Based on his numismatic study, A. Blanchet suggested a date between 1075 and 1090. Others have cited the reference to the use of camel and drums and thus point to the battle of Zalaca in 1086 as a

determining date. In his article in the *Coloquios de Roncesvalles* (1956), "Il silenzio del *Roland* su Sant'Iacopo: Le vie dei pellegrinaggi e le vie della storia," A. Roncaglia argues for a date between 1049 and 1095, the period of conflict between the Papacy and the Bishop of Santiago.

10. Robert Fawtier, *La Chanson de Roland: Etude historique* (Paris: Boccard, 1933), first argued that the loss of the rearguard had been a serious defeat covered up by the official annals. F. Ganshof's many studies on the Frankish period support Fawtier's thesis. Bédier considered the defeat a minor setback for the Carolingian leader.

11. *La Chanson de Roland et l'histoire* (Paris: Michel, 1943).

12. See, for example, the rejection of Jesse Crosland, *The Old French Epic* (Oxford: Blackwell, 1951).

13. *König und Vasall* (Heidelberg: Winter, 1967).

14. Jacques Flach, *Origines de l'ancienne France* (Paris: Larose, 1886-1917), vol. 1, 242.

15. Léopold Genicot, *L'Economie namuroise au bas moyen age* (Louvain: Bibliothèque de l'Université, 1960); especially F. W. Werner, "Untersuchungen zur Frühzeit des französischen Fürstentums (9-10 Jahrhundert)," *Die Welt als Geschichte* 18 (1958), 256-89; 19 (1959), 146-93; 20 (1960), 87-119. Georges Duby, *Hommes et structures du moyen âge* (La Haye: Mouton, 1973) and *Les trois ordres ou l'imaginaire du féodalisme* (Paris: Gallimard, 1978). One should also mention the early seminal work of Guilhiermoz, *Essai sur l'origine de la noblesse en France au moyen âge* (Paris: Picard, 1906). For pertinent scholarship concerning the Germanic artistocracy, see K. Leyser, "The German Aristocracy from the Ninth to the early Twentieth Century: A Historical and Cultural Sketch," *Past and Present* 41 (1968), 25-53. For Capetian France, see Andrew W. Lewis, *Royal Succession in Capetian France: Studies on Familial Order and the State* (Cambridge, MA: Harvard University Press, 1981); Louis Halphen, *Le comté d'Anjou au XI^e siècle* (Paris: Picard, 1906); J. Dhondt, "Henri I^er et l'Anjou, 1043-1056," *Revue belge* 25 (1947), 87-109; J. Chartrou, *L'Anjou de 1109 à 1151* (Paris, 1928).

16. Marc Bloch, *La Société féodale. La Formation des liens de dépendance* (Paris: Michel, 1940).

17. For a recent study of Germanic kinship which rejects the traditional belief in patrimonial and unilineal descent as the norm in prehistoric Germanic society, see A. C. Murray, *Germanic Kinship Structure* (Toronto: Pontifical Institute of Medieval Studies, 1983). Murray believes that the bilateral descent found in the ninth and tenth centuries was not a change of tradition but a continuation of what had always been.

18. Louis Halphen and René Poupardin, eds. *Chroniques des comtes d'Anjou et des seigneurs d'Amboise* (Paris; Picard, 1913). This edition replaced the 1856 edition of Marchegay and Salmon.

19. Paul Marchegay and André Salmon, eds. *Chroniques d'Anjou* (Paris, 1856), 41-46; Halphen and Poupardin, 135-39. Text drawn from ms. 6005.

20. For an excellent example, see *Le Chevalier au Cygne,* ed. Jan Nelson, *The Old French Crusade Cycle* (Tuscaloosa: University of Alabama Press, 1985), vol. 2. The Swan Knight arrives in time to save Ida, beleaguered by Renier. Subsequently they marry and their heirs include the famous Godefroi of Bouillon.

21. The other versions of the *Roland* will be discussed in the final chapter.

22. Robert Folz, *Le Souvenir et la légende de Charlemagne dans l'empire germanique médiéval* (Paris: Les Belles Lettres, 1950); Stephen Nichols, *Romanesque Signs. Early Medieval Narrative and Iconography* (New Haven: Yale University Press, 1983).

23. Michael Wendt, *Der Oxforder Roland. Heilsgeschehen und Teilidentität im 12. Jahrhundert* (Munich: Fink, 1970).

24. See Robert W. Hanning, *The Vision of History in Early Britain* (New York: Columbia University Press, 1966) and Antonia Gransden, *Historical Writing in England c. 550 to c. 1307* (Ithaca: Cornell University Press, 1974). For an interesting discussion of medieval historiography, see Roger Ray "Medieval Historiography Through the Twelfth Century: Problems and Progress of Research," *Viator* 5 (1974), 33-59.

25. Marc Bloch, *La Société féodale*; Georges Duby, *Les Trois Ordres*; K. J. Hollyman, *Le Développement du vocabulaire féodale en France pendant le haut moyen âge* (Geneva: Droz, 1957); Robert Boutrouche, *Seigneurie et féodalité,* 2 vols. (Paris: Aubier, 1968 and 1970).

26. M. Pfeffer, "Die Formalitäten des gottesgerichtlichen Zweikampfs in der altfranzösischen Epik," *Zeitschrift für romanische Philologie* 9 (1885), 1-74. Pfeffer studies the procedures of numerous treason trials involving trial by combat. The later the text the more elaborate the ritual seems to have been. Ruggieri sees the lack of religious ceremony in the Ganelon trial as proof that early medieval trials had no such ceremonies (Ruggero Ruggieri, *Il Processo*).

27. See the final sections of Ruggieri, *Il Processo.* André Burger considers Roland clearly guilty of humiliating Ganelon when he laughed at him. In his view Ganelon also becomes a kind of tragic figure because he has the right to take vengeance on Roland but cannot do so and remain faithful to the emperor ("Le Rire de Roland." *Cahiers de Civilisation médiévale* 3 [1960], 2-11).

28. F. Carl Riedel, *Crime and Punishment in the Old French Romances* (New York: Columbia University Press, 1938) focuses on French romances of the thirteenth century and refers to the *Roland* in only a couple of places. R. Howard Bloch, *Medieval French Literature and Law* (Berkeley: University of California Press, 1977) also focuses on the period of literature after the *Roland.* Bloch is primarily concerned with the change in trial procedure away from so-called irrational to rational proofs. He was interested in demonstrating a correlation between the growing late medieval preoccupation with intent and inquiry into rational proofs and the fictional representation of trials in thirteenth-century romances.

29. J. G. Bellamy, *The Law of Treason in England in the Later Middle Ages* (Cambridge: Cambridge University Press, 1970) has an excellent first chapter on "The Medieval Concept of Treason," but the volume is oriented toward the thirteenth century and later. S. H. Cuttler, *The Law of Treason and Treason Trials in Later Medieval France* (Cambridge: Cambridge University Press, 1981) is a fine study of treason in thirteenth-century France and later, but treatment of the crime in earlier periods is not included.

30. G. Baist, "Der gerichtliche Zweikampf, nach seinem Ursprung und im Rolandslied," *Romanische Forschungen* 5 (1890), 436-48; Stefan Hofer, "Das Verratsmotiv in den chansons de geste," *Zeitschrift für romanische Philologie* 44 (1924), 594-609; Hermann Nottarp, *Gottesurteilstudien* (Munich, 1956).

31. For a stimulating discussion about the reliability of transmission in illiterate oral societies and about the alleged antiquity of what is remembered, see M. T. Clanchy, *From Memory to Written Record* (Cambridge, MA: Harvard University Press, 1979). In his article, "Remembering the Past and the Good Old Law," *History* 55 (1970), 165-76, Clanchy makes a number of important comparisons between the medieval oral tradition of law and contemporary illiterate societies. See especially Brian Stock's *The Implications of Literacy* (Princeton: Princeton University Press, 1983), particularly chapters 1, 4, and 5.

32. The progressive ideas of post eighteenth-century European intellectual history are so ingrained in modern man that it is difficult for us not to accept them without question. The same assumption is made about the question of intent versus deed and the use of rational versus irrational proofs. Even the terms we use to distinguish between the various modes of proof show our natural bias. For a classic example of the assumption that modern ideas are superior to what preceded and can be used even to identify higher cognitive attainment in man, see Charles M. Radding, *A World Made by Men. Cognition and Society, 400-1200* (Chapel Hill: University of North Carolina Press, 1985). Another perspective on proofs can be found in Rebecca B. Colman, "Reason and Unreason in Early Medieval Law," *Journal of Interdisciplinary History* 4 (1974), 571-91; Colin Morris, "Judicium Dei: The Social and Political Significance of the Ordeal in the Eleventh Century," *Studies in Church History* 12 (1975), 95-111. For speculation on the manipulative use medieval society made of supernatural proofs, see Peter Brown, "Society and the Supernatural: A Medieval Change." *Daedalus* 104 (1975), 133-51. O. B. Hardison's exposition of the influence of Darwin and biological thought on nineteenth- and twentieth-century scholarship is classic (*Christian Rite and Christian Drama in the Middle Ages* [Baltimore, 1965]).

33. See especially the excellent introductory chapters of O. B. Hardison, *Christian Rite and Christian Drama in the Middle Ages.*

34. Much interest in the ribald humor of the fabliau and the presence of devils in medieval drama stem from this same sense that these are vestiges of an earlier, pre-Christian secular society struggling to remain alive.

35. *The Ethos of the Song of Roland* (Baltimore: Johns Hopkins University Press, 1963).

36. Albert Gérard, "L'axe Roland-Ganelon: valeurs en conflit dans la *Chanson de Roland,*" *Le Moyen Age* 76 [1969], 451. The reading of John Halverson ("Ganelon's Trial," *Speculum* 42 [1967], 661-69) also presents the text through Jones's lens. Olivier is the new man of a new order which has a broader vision than the narrow, parochial view of feudal, Germanic society.

37. Stephen Nichols paraphrases Augustine when he writes that "God's grace consists . . . in allowing man to apprehend, in the multiplicity of his human acts, a coherent pattern relating human deeds to divine purpose" (*Romanesque Signs,* 193). Nichols notes that, as the text develops the theme of Roland as martyr saint, where human events

are interpreted in eternal terms, the final scene becomes important as "a textual monument valorizing the word-as-deed of the hero" (Ibid., 195).

38. Paul Zumthor's *Essai de Poétique médiévale* (Paris: Editions du Seuil, 1972) comes to the bleak conclusion in the chapter titled, "La Nuit du temps," that there is so little remaining from the past that one cannot hope to reconstruct events within their own construct. In the past twenty years, many scholars have taken the position that the idea of an objective history is an illusion. In a relative sense every document can only reflect events as the beholder perceived them. Every word and observation thus becomes prisoner to the ideological perspective, the general culture, and relative position, etc. of the historian. Others see "history" as the written record left by power structures using the literate word to promote and maintain their own perspective and base of power. These critics do not see the historical record that is left merely as the product of man's relative perspective, but as the deliberate creation of a fiction which can be used to perpetuate power and wealth.

39. Note that Marie de France did the same thing in her trial in *Lanval*.

40. Rupert T. Pickens, "Historical Consciousness in Old French Narrative," *French Forum* 4 (1979), 168-84.

41. For a recent assessment, see Joseph J. Duggan, *A Guide to Studies on the Chanson de Roland* (London: Grant and Cutler, 1976), 67, item 285.

*Bibliography*

Aebischer, Paul. *Textes norrois et littérature française du Moyen Age.* Geneva: Droz, 1954.

Baist, G. "Der gerichtliche Zweikampf, nach seinem Ursprung und im Rolandslied." *Romanische Forschungen* 5 (1890), 436-48.

Bédier, Joseph. *Les Légendes épiques.* 4 vols. Paris, 1908-13.

Bellamy, J. G. *The Law of Treason in England in the Later Middle Ages.* Cambridge: Cambridge University Press, 1970.

Bender, K. H. *König und Vasall.* Heidelberg: Winter, 1967.

Bloch, Marc. *La Société féodale. La Formation des liens de dépendance.* Paris: Michel, 1940.

Bloch, R. Howard. *Medieval French Literature and Law.* Berkeley: University of California Press, 1977.

Boutrouche, Robert. *Seigneurie et féodalité.* 2 vols. Paris: Aubier, 1968 and 1970.

Brault, Gerard. *The Song of Roland.* 2 vols. University Park: Penn State Press, 1978.

Brown, Peter. "Society and the Supernatural: A Medieval Change." *Daedalus* 104 (1975), 133-51.

Burger, André. "Le Rire de Roland." *Cahiers de civilisation médiévale* 3 (1960), 2-11.

*La Chanson de Roland.* Ed. Léon Gautier. Tours: Mame et fils, 1872.

Chartrou, J. *L'Anjou de 1109 à 1151.* Paris, 1928.

*Le Chevalier au Cygne.* Ed. Jan A. Nelson. Vol. 2, *The Old French Crusade Cycle.* Ed. Jan Nelson and Emanuel Mickel. 9 vols. Tuscaloosa: University of Alabama Press, 1985.

*Chroniques d'Anjou.* Ed. Paul Marchegay and André Salmon. Paris: Renouard, 1856.

*Chroniques des comtes d'Anjou et des seigneurs d'Amboise.* Ed. Louis Halphen and René Poupardin. Paris: Picard, 1913.

Clanchy, M. T. *From Memory to Written Record, 1066-1307.* Cambridge: Harvard University Press, 1979.

Clanchy, M. T. "Remembering the Past and the Good Old Law." *History* 55 (1970), 165-76.

Colman, Rebecca B. "Reason and Unreason in Early Medieval Law." *Journal of Interdisciplinary History* 4 (1974), 571-91.

Crosland, Jesse. *The Old French Epic.* Oxford: Blackwell, 1951.

Cuttler, S. H. *The Law of Treason and Treason Trials in Later Medieval France.* Cambridge: Cambridge University Press, 1981.

Dhondt, J. "Henri I$^{er}$, l'Empire et l'Anjou, 1043-1056." *Revue belge* 25 (1947), 87-109.

Duby, Georges. *Hommes et structures du moyen age.* La Haye: Mouton, 1973.

Duby, Georges. *Les trois ordres ou l'imaginaire du féodalisme.* Paris: Gallimard, 1978.

Duggan, Joseph J. *A Guide to Studies on the Chanson de Roland.* London, Grant and Culter, 1976.

Fawtier, Robert. *La Chanson de Roland: Etude historique.* Paris: Boccard, 1933.

Flach, Jacques. *Origines de l'ancienne France.* 4 vols. Paris: Larose et Forcel, 1886-1917.

Folz, Robert. *Le Souvenir et la légende de Charlemagne dans l'empire germanique médiéval.* Paris: Les Belles Lettres, 1950.

Ganshof, François Louis. *The Carolingian and the Frankish Monarchy.* London: Longman, 1971.

Gautier, Léon. "L'Idée politique dans les Chansons de Geste." *Revue des questions historiques* 8 (1868), 79-114.

Genicot, Léopold. *L'Economie namuroise au bas moyen âge.* Louvain: Bibliothèque de l'Université, 1960.

Gérard, Albert. "L'axe Roland-Ganelon: valeurs en conflit dans la *Chanson de Roland.*" *Le Moyen Age* 76 (1969), 445-65.

Gransden, Antonia. *Historical Writing in England c. 550 to c. 1307.* Ithaca: Cornell University Press, 1974.

Guilhiermoz, Paul. *Essai sur l'origine de la noblesse en France au moyen âge.* Paris: Picard, 1902.

Halphen, Louis. *Le comté d'Anjou au XI<sup>e</sup> siècle.* Paris: Picard, 1906.

Halverson, John. "Ganelon's Trial." *Speculum* 42 (1967), 661-69.

Hanning, Robert W. *The Vision of History in Early Britain.* New York: Columbia University Press, 1966.

Hardison, O. B. *Christian Rite and Christian Drama in the Middle Ages.* Baltimore: Johns Hopkins Press, 1965.

Hofer, Stefan. "Das Verratsmotiv in den chansons de geste." *Zeitschrift für romanische Philologie* 44 (1924), 594-609.

Hollyman, K. J. *Le développement du vocabulaire féodal en France pendant le haut Moyen Age.* Geneva: Droz, 1957.

Jenkins, T. A. "Why Did Ganelon Hate Roland?" *PMLA* 36 (1921), 119-33.

Jones, George F. *The Ethos of the Song of Roland.* Baltimore: Johns Hopkins University Press, 1963.

Keller, Hans-Erich. "La *Chanson de Roland,* poème de propagande pour le royaume capétien du milieu du XII<sup>e</sup> siècle." *Travaux de Linguistique et de Littérature* (Strasbourg) 14 (1976), 229-41.

Keller, Hans-Erich. "La Place du *Ruolantes Liet* dans la tradition rolandienne." *Moyen Age* 71 (1965), 215-46.

Keller, Hans-Erich. "La Version dionysienne de la *Chanson de Roland*" in *Philologica romanica, Erhard Lommatzsch gewidmet* (Munich: Fink, 1975), 257-87.

Lewis, Andrew W. *Royal Succession in Capetian France: Studies on Familial Order and the State.* Cambridge: Harvard University Press, 1983.

Leyser, K. "The German Aristocracy from the Ninth to the Early Twentieth Century: A Historical and Cultural Sketch." *Past and Present* 41 (1968), 25-53.

Lot, Ferdinand. *Études sur le règne de Hugues Capet et la fin du Xe siècle.* Paris: Champion, 1903.

Menéndez Pidal, Ramon. *La Chanson de Roland y el neotradicionalismo: Origenes de la épica románica.* Madrid: Espasa-Calpe, 1959.

Mireaux, Emile. *La Chanson de Roland et l'histoire.* Paris: Michel, 1943.

Morris, Colin. "*Judicium Dei*: The Social and Political Significance of the Ordeal in the Eleventh Century." *Studies in Church History* 12 (1975), 95-111.

Murray, Alexander. *Germanic Kinship Structure: Studies in Law and Society in Antiquity and the Early Middle Ages.* Toronto: Pontifical Institute of Mediaeval Studies, 1983.

Nichols, Stephen. *Romanesque Signs, Early Medieval Narrative and Iconography.* New Haven: Yale University Press, 1983.

Nottarp, Hermann. *Gottesurteilstudien.* Munich: Kösel, 1956.

Paris, Gaston. *De Pseudo-Turpino.* Paris: A. Franck, 1865.

Pfeffer, M. "Die Formalitäten des gottesgerichtlichen Zweikampfs in der altfranzösischen Epik." *Zeitschrift für romanische Philologie* 9 (1885), 1-74.

Pickens, Rupert T. "Historical Consciousness in Old French Narrative." *French Forum* 4 (1979), 168-84.

Radding, Charles M. "A World Made by Men." *Cognition and Society,* 400-1200. Chapel Hill: University of North Carolina Press, 1985.

Ray, Roger D. "Medieval Historiography through the Twelfth Century: Problems and Progress of Research." *Viator* 5 (1974), 33-59.

Riedel, F. Carl. *Crime and Punishment in the Old French Romances.* New York: Columbia University Press, 1938.

Ruggieri, Ruggero. *Il processo di Gano nella Chanson de Roland.* Florence: Sansini, 1936.

Stock, Brian. *The Implications of Literacy.* Princeton: Princeton University Press, 1983.

Wendt, Michael. *Der Oxforder Roland. Heilsgeschehen und Teilidentität im 12. Jahrhundert.* Munich: Fink, 1970.

Zumthor, Paul. *Essai de poétique médiévale.* Paris: Editions du Seuil, 1972.

**Elspeth Cameron (essay date 1992)**

SOURCE: Cameron, Elspeth. "Earle Birney's 'David' and the *Song of Roland*: A Source Study." In *Inside the*

*Poem: Essays and Poems in Honour of Donald Stephens,* edited by W. H. New, pp. 60-9. Toronto: Oxford University Press, 1992.

[*In the following essay, Cameron considers* The Song of Roland *as a major source for Birney's 1941 poem "David," a fact directly acknowledged by Birney.*]

Ironically, Earle Birney was not sanguine about the success of "David,"[1] the poem which, more than any other, was to ensure his reputation as a major poet. "I've just finished a narrative of about 275 ll., about mountain climbing in the Canadian Rockies," he wrote on 24 April 1941 to James McLaughlin, the editor of the American journal *New Directions,* who was compiling an anthology of contemporary verse. "E. J. Pratt, the only 'known' Canadian poet," Birney continued:

> thinks it's swell, but he can't suggest a place that would take it. The material is strange for an easterner, and the west has no magazines. The form is an assonantal five-beat stanza, abba—and nobody has, apparently, written in that form, so it's out! And the damned thing tries to be understandable and tragic and pictorial, and nobody but a duffer would want to read that kind of thing nowadays.[2]

Birney's peevishness stemmed from his disappointment that E. J. Pratt, though exuberantly enthusiastic about the poem, thought it too long for his *Canadian Poetry Magazine.* It seemed to Birney, however, that a more sophisticated editor like McLaughlin might be more likely to publish it. In a letter a month later, by which time he had compressed his poem from 275 to 184 lines, he wrote: "I am honestly trying 'new directions' of my own in "David," and I hope that you will find it good enough for your anthology."[3]

"David" was indeed a "new direction" for Birney. It was the result of an idiosyncratic fusion of an astonishing number of exotic elements—some personal, some literary—the twelfth-century *Song of Roland* among them. "David" owed much, of course, to Birney's mountaineering experiences as an adolescent in Banff, Alberta, and to climbing accidents he had heard of or read about there and in the coastal mountains near Vancouver, where he climbed during his undergraduate years at the University of British Columbia.

Among his literary sources, Birney directly acknowledged three narratives: Archibald MacLeish's Pulitzer prize-winning saga of the conquest of Mexico by Cortés, *Conquistador* (1932), and Stephen Vincent Benét's Civil War epic, *John Brown's Body* (1928), as well as the *Song of Roland,* a *chanson de geste* based on Charlemagne's crusade against the Saracens in northern Spain.[4]

Aside from these acknowledged literary influences, there is sufficient evidence to conclude that Birney's poem also owed much to Scottish long poems, such as

Burns' classic romp "Tam o' Shanter" and Hugh Mac-Diarmid's philosophical and political musings in *A Drunk Man Looks at the Thistle* (1926) and "The Glass of Pure Water" (1937)[5]; and, closer to home, the narratives of Pratt himself, particularly "Brébeuf and his Brethren," which Birney had fulsomely praised as the poem of the year in September 1940 (*Canadian Forum,* 80), only a month or so before he began writing "David."

Of "David"'s specifically named literary antecedents, however, the most surprising is probably the *Song of Roland.* MacLeish and Benét were Birney's contemporaries, North Americans whose narratives had proven popular and successful. But *Roland* was a work remote in time, language, and sensibility; it was eight centuries since the Old French heroic epic had eulogized events that took place three centuries before that. For this reason, the case of *Roland* and the unique influence it may have on a modern poem is intriguing.

Birney encountered the *Song of Roland* in the course of his highly specialized training as a Chaucerian scholar. Though it is not clear exactly when he first read the poem, his capacity to read it in the original Old French versions was acquired in 1936 at the University of Toronto where he studied Old French, Old Norse, Gothic, and Anglo-Saxon, languages which comprised the minor in Germanic Philology and Linguistics for the Ph.D. he completed that year. That he knew the poem intimately, along with the main body of critical literature which interpreted it, is clear from his undated lecture notes[6] on "Romance," "The Epical Tradition in Old English and Middle English," and *"Romans de France."*

The most extensive notes on *Roland* consist of a one-page outline which mentions the historical basis of the poem (the Battle at Roncevaux in 778, in which Charlemagne's rearguard, returning from a successful expedition against the Moors in Spain, is ambushed and destroyed by Basque mountaineers); a list of eight characters of which Roland is the "only one individualized," a "tragic epic hero" whose "glorious fault [is] an excess of soldierly zeal"; and comments about the treatment of content ("national religious epic—la douce France & a holy war, monotonous repetition of incident, elementary epic characterization, and passion for [the] marvellous"). Elsewhere among notes that repeat some of these points, Birney observes that *Roland* is the "Carolingian counterpart of the Grail theme."

The only aspect of the *Song of Roland* that Birney clearly admits drawing on is the form of the poem. In a letter responding to literary critic Desmond Pacey's request for information to be used in his forthcoming book about Canadian poets,[7] Birney wrote, "In 'David' itself I am conscious of minor formal influences of the

*Song of Roland* and *Conquistador*."[8] Precisely what Birney meant by this statement (which Pacey did not refer to in his book) is not entirely clear, and he does not elaborate by example. He may, for instance, have meant that the formal influences from both sources was "minor"; or he could have meant that the influence was not necessarily minor, but that it stemmed from minor, as opposed to major, formal elements in these two antecedents.

Certainly, a comparison of "David" with *Roland* reveals many formal similarities—both major and minor—and suggests, beyond these, that Birney's poem may owe more to this literary source than these purely formal characteristics.

Although *Roland* is roughly twenty times longer than "David," and is, consequently, much greater in scope and complexity, formal similarities are numerous. Both poems describe a simple Rise-Climax-Fall pattern. Though *Roland* develops a binary plot-line (Brault, 49-51) and "David" a single story, the Ascent/Death of the Hero/Expiation story provides an overall structure within which minor episodes are presented with—to borrow Gerard Brault's description of *Roland*—a "geometric" effect (Brault, 76-7). The *Song of Roland* is made up of *laisses,* or stanzas, which present self-contained scenes where stylized attitudes and gestures "convey abstract ideas in visual terms" (Owen, 31). Though Birney's poem differs formally in that he regulated his stanzas to four lines each, whereas in *Roland* the *laisses* vary in length from fewer than five lines to over twenty; and Birney grouped his stanzas into five numbered sections (presumably to echo the five acts of classic dramatic tragedy), whereas *Roland*'s *laisses* simply follow one another, both poems have the same effect of presenting a variety of scenes through one or more stanzas without transitional links. In both poems, too, each stanza, or *laisse,* is unified by assonance: in *Roland* by the use of the same vowel (usually) in the last word of each line, in "David" through an a-b-b-a pattern.[9] Birney lengthens the five-beat decasyllabic line standard of *Roland* to a five-beat line of usually twelve or thirteen syllables.

This technical comparison of formal elements cannot, however, do justice to the suppleness of either *Roland* or "David." Though Birney, like the author of *Roland*,[10] presents a succession of self-contained, memorably simple, unlinked scenes, the effect in both poems is "an impression less of individual 'frames'" punctuated by laconic dialogue "than of a running film strip synchronised with a resonant, pulsating and evocative sound track" (Owen, 31). This is due partly to the fact that the *Song of Roland* was in all likelihood, as its title suggests, a poem to be sung or chanted by *jongleurs,* and that many of its formal elements (such as assonance, strong rhythms, epithets, and formulaic phrasings) were intended as mnemonic devices or musical cues. As D. D. R. Owen observes:

> in modern terms, the structure of the poem might be called symphonic. It has distinct movements, and between and within them are the tonal variations: lyrical passages alternate with rousing periods of full orchestra; there are the crescendos and diminuendos, changes of pace and key within the general flow; and of great importance are the continual statements and restatements of themes and phrases, which bind the whole composition together and strengthen its formal unity.
>
> (29-30)

It is for reasons such as these that the *Song of Roland* is considered the greatest *chanson de geste.*

Birney, possibly because of his advanced linguistic training, was able to imitate this peculiarly "oral" vividness of *Roland.* Like its twelfth-century antecedent (and unlike either *Conquistador* or *John Brown's Body,* both of which seem more literary and less emphatic to the ear), "David" has striking auditory effects (its pounding rhythms, modulating pace, and proliferation of onomatopoetic and alliterating words, for example) and seems meant to be read aloud. In fact, its first impact on a wide audience was in a radio airing on 4 January 1942, a month after the poem's original publication in *The Canadian Forum.*[11]

Aside from these formal common denominators between *Roland* and "David," there are a number of ways—some rather important—in which Birney's poem may have been influenced by this *chanson de geste.* But before turning to these, some clear dissimilarities must be noted. Because these are manifold and significant, Birney's "David" can in no way be understood to be modelled on the *Song of Roland,* nor to copy or parody it. Aside from the striking differences in length and complexity already mentioned, the *Song of Roland,* unlike "David," aggressively vindicates Christianity, not only in theme but also in texture (events in *Roland* are commonly understood to be deliberate parallels of Biblical happenings, for example); it is—to use today's terminology—explicitly nationalistic and racist, glorifying France at the expense of the Muslim Saracens; it develops a story involving several minor characters, different settings, and the movements of large groups; and it takes for granted a connection between "heroism" and military prowess.

Only one section of *Roland*—the middle section concerning the ambush in the mountain pass of the rearguard led by Charlemagne's nephew Roland, his death, and the death of his comrade-in-arms Oliver—can be seen as a source for elements other than formal ones in "David." This climactic section presents a debate between Roland and Oliver about whether or not Roland should sound his horn to call Charlemagne and the troops proceeding through the pass ahead of them to return and help. Oliver urges Roland to do so; Roland refuses, on grounds that his honour would be sullied. In the ensuing battle, the French, who are vastly outnumbered by the Saracens, go down to bitter and bloody defeat. When defeat becomes inevitable, Roland and Oliver debate again about whether or not Roland should sound his horn. Oliver now argues against blowing it; Roland, wounded and desperate, sounds the horn with such force that his temples burst and bleed. Oliver is mortally wounded and dies, to Roland's great distress. Then Roland himself dies in battle.

Even from this thumbnail sketch a number of echoes in "David" can be detected. Among these, one of the most striking is the quality of friendship between two young men. The relationship between Roland and Oliver in the *Song of Roland* is frequently hailed as the finest example of *compagnonnage,* a relationship defined by D. D. R. Owen as follows:

> Two young men, not related by birth . . . might freely pledge to each other loyal comradeship and brotherhood in arms. Their pact was not necessarily formal; but its effect was to link the knights' destinies as firmly as any feudal tie or even blood connection . . . neither history nor legend offers any more illustrious pair of [such] companions than Roland and Oliver.
>
> (11)

According to C. M. Bowra, such a friendship is "a partnership of a special kind," possibly the highest order of love possible between humans: "The participants share both dangers and glory, and the honour of one is the honour of the other . . . A hero's love for his friend is different from his love for his wife or his family, since it is between equals and founded on an identity of ideals and interests" (65). There is more than a hint of such *compagnonnage* between David and Bob as they move up and away from "the ruck of the camp" into a shared idealism. Peter Aichinger notes a parallel between David and King Arthur, and between Bob and Sir Bors, but the parallel between the two mountaineers and Roland and Oliver is more convincing.[12] David, like Roland, leads and teaches his companion in ways that have overtones of a chivalric code of behaviour; and the affection and loyalty demonstrated under duress is of an exceptionally rarified sort.

Like the *Song of Roland,* too, "David" focuses on a single hero. By Bowra's definition, the hero of epic and romance "differs from other men by his peculiar force and energy":

> [H]e has an abundant, overflowing, assertive force, which expresses itself in action, especially in violent action. . . . [T]he great man must pass through an ordeal to prove his worth and this is almost necessarily some kind of violent action, which not only demands

courage, endurance, and enterprise, but, since it involves the risk of life, makes him show to what lengths he is prepared to go in pursuit of honour. . . . [T]he story passes from the record of bold achievements to something graver and grander and suggests dark considerations about the place of man in the world and the hopeless fight which he puts up against his doom. . . . The splendour which irradiates a hero in the hour of defeat or death is a special feature of heroic poetry.

> (97, 48, 118, 128)

Despite some obvious differences in content—mountainclimbing, though risky, is by no means the same thing as a battle—there is much in "David" that could have been suggested by such characteristics of heroic poetry in the *Song of Roland.* That we are to focus on a central hero, the meaning of his attitude to life, and the significance of his death, is implied by the title.[13] The aura surrounding David, which gives the impression that he is exceptional, particularly in terms of his "courage, endurance and enterprise," resembles our impressions of Roland. "[M]ountains for David were made to see over." Certainly the violence and horror of David's accident and death equals that of Roland and Oliver's deaths in battle. The sense of a terrible waste of splendid young manhood, and, beyond that, a sense of "dark considerations about the place of man in the world," is common to both poems. As in many heroic poems—*Roland* among them—the story in Birney's poem centres on an ethical test in which the hero must make an "agonizing choice" (Brault, 104) for which he must accept responsibility. That Birney locates this aspect of his source not in David, the character who most resembles Roland, but in Bob, who resembles Oliver, is an interesting twist that does not in any way diminish the connection between the two poems.

More than one commentator on the *Song of Roland* has noted its author's "art of adapting the background to the tone and temper of events." One of the main ways in which this correspondence is struck is by relating Roland and Oliver's climbing of the Pyrenees to their ascent into the abstract code of chivalric honour, national pride, valour, and loyalty. *Roland* dramatizes, through its scenery, the heights to which Roland aspires, and, through the use of panoramic vistas, suggests the aristocracy of the fellow-knights, the spiritual dimension of their crusade, and the magnitude of their farreaching ambitions. As Brault observes, *Roland*'s narrative moves "literally from elevation to elevation, the story reverberating from peak to peak, as it were, like the sound of the hero's oliphant [horn]" (81). Birney may have derived some aspects of this technique from *Roland* (Pacey found Birney's irregular lines and anapestic rhythms "well chosen to give the effect of climbing" [306]), though his personal mountaineering experience and his other formal source, *Conquistador,* are so thoroughly intertwined that specific influence is impossible to discern. Certainly, if he drew on **Roland,** he outdid that source both in his majestic description of the Rockies and in the way in which his mountains, valleys, lakes, and swamps *are* his theme and characters. This amplification can be seen by comparing parallel passages from the two poems:

> Halt sunt li pui e li val tenebrus
> Les roches bises, les destreiz merveillus.
>
> [The mountains are high and the valleys are shadowy,
> The rocks dark, the defiles frightening.]
>
> (***Song of Roland,*** *laisse* 66, ll. 814-15)

> The peak was upthrust
> Like a fist in a frozen ocean of rock that swirled
> Into valleys the moon could be rolled in.
>
> ("David," II, ll. 17-19)

In several small details, too, there are echoes of **Roland** in "David." The episodes of the "skull and the splayed white ribs of a mountain goat" and the suffering "wing-broken" robin which David kills, though clearly used by Birney as foreshadowing, correspond roughly to the several scenes of carnage on the battlefield at Roncevaux. The most salient feature of the description of Oliver's death is the lance that pierces his chest right through from back to front, a blow that may have suggested the "cruel fang / Of the ledge thrust in his back" that David endures. And Oliver's inadvertent sword-blow to Roland's head, struck when Oliver cannot see because he is bleeding so much, and the poignant dialogue in which Roland forgives his friend for mistakenly attacking him, may have suggested the central incident of David, when Bob slips because he is "heedless / Of handhold" and unwittingly causes David's fall when David loses his balance as a result of reaching out to steady his friend. Certainly Roland's remorse and distress at Oliver's death (caused ultimately by Roland's refusal to sound his horn for aid) anticipates Bob's guilt and grief at David's death.

Why Birney used the **Song of Roland** as a source for "David" poses an interesting literary challenge. His engagement with early Germanic literatures in preparation for the Ph.D. and his ongoing use of these works in his university teaching kept the **Song of Roland** fresh in his mind. But in his own life, too, there was a curious parallel to the twelfth-century poem; Birney had been serving on a crusade as intense and far-reaching as Charlemagne's. For close to a decade, he had devoted himself to Trotsky's cause as a member of the Independent Labour Party in anticipation of a new world order to be ushered in by the Fourth International. Birney had joined the "Church" (as the Trotskyist movement referred to itself) in 1933, after sampling a number of left-wing political organizations in the early 1930s, and had dedicated his energies to speeches, reading groups,

arrangements for speakers, and the dissemination of party publications, with nothing less than missionary zeal. His abandonment of Trotskyist politics in January 1940 as a result of Trotsky's endorsement of Russia's invasion of Finland the previous November constituted a wrenching disillusionment. "I have broken with POLITICS," he wrote to a friend at the time.

> For a while I carried on a fight against the Old Man's [Trotsky's] Finnish policy—he wanted the Reds to win, at the same time piously "condemning" the invasion. But I finally had to face a lot of ugly facts I had been forced to admit for along [sic] time: that the Old Man's organization is growing as bureaucratic as the next one, that up here the whole organizational approach is quixotic and suicidal . . . I still think the ultimate choice is socialism or barbarism. But as for me, I've spent more than eight year's [sic] leisure time, and sacrificed more than I care to think of, for [a cause] that seems pretty futile now. . . . My spare time, if I can find any, is going to be writing, and not political writing . . . you know me well enough to know that a break like this doesn't come easy, not without a lot of thought.[14]

Though Birney had dabbled in poetry and short story writing since he was an undergraduate at UBC in the mid-1920s, it was only in the winter of 1940-41 that he turned his best energies to creative writing, as if to fill the vacuum left by abandoning "POLITICS."

It was out of this clear turning point in his life that "David" and most of the other poems that would eventually be collected in *David and Other Poems* (1942) were forged. This context suggests that "David" was an expression of the end of youthful idealism: "That day," as Bob puts it, "the last of my youth, on the last of our mountains." The **Song of Roland** may have suggested itself as a model partly because the high point of Birney's Trotskyist experience was the visit he and his fellow-traveller Ken Johnstone (using their party pseudonyms, Comrade Robertson and Comrade Alexander) paid to Trotsky in Hønefoss, Norway, in November 1935: like two fellow-knights sworn to a chivalric code, they were received at court and sent onwards in the great crusade. There was a more subtle parallel, too, between the two Trotskyites and Roland and Oliver. Just as Oliver's sister is Roland's fiancée, Johnstone's sister was Birney's wife.[15] And the **Song of Roland** may have seemed appropriate, specifically, because Birney intended to treat it both seriously and ironically: seriously, in that **Roland** captured the uplifting spiritual euphoria of naive youthful commitment and the special bonding that tied compatriots to their crusade; ironically, in that surviving the loss of idealism (as Bob does, whereas Roland and Oliver do not)[16] means carrying on in a real world no longer glorious, but diminished and ugly. Even in defeat and death, Roland and Oliver vindicate idealism; their honour is not only unsullied, but augmented. But Bob, whose "agonizing choice" evokes an act of mercy-killing, which may represent a higher moral order shared by David, but is, none the less, a "crime" and may represent reversion to a lower moral order, must carry forward the burden of a shameful self-knowledge which is profoundly repellent.

Birney recognized that "David" would probably strike contemporary readers as old-fashioned. Hence his remark to McLaughlin that "nobody but a duffer would want to read that kind of thing nowadays." As he explained further to E. K. Brown, on submitting it to the *University of Toronto Quarterly,* the poem was "written in conscious antipathy to the fashionable obscurancy, the Audenian didactics and the pedantic allusiveness of the sons of Eliot."[17] He was disappointed, but not surprised, that Brown didn't accept it, that McLaughlin found its form "too traditional,"[18] and that poet Kenneth Rexroth in San Francisco suggested sending it to England since "the market for such literature is almost entirely English."[19] It was the *Song of Roland,* more than any of Birney's other literary sources, that caused his poem to "lapse," as he put it regretfully, "into the cliché of melodrama."[20]

Yet the experiment was bold, and ultimately successful. By going back to the *chanson de geste,* Birney brought to Canadian poetry a refreshing vigour achieved through oral effects and the restoration of English words to their roots in early Germanic languages. Partly intent on making a mark for western Canadian poetry—which he thought of as non-existent in any modern sense—he turned naturally to a classic poem of national self-glorification as a model for what he called gently "western nostalgia."[21] And, in adapting an aristocratic, chivalric brotherhood to a contemporary ethical situation, he signalled, as he intended, a new voice in Canadian poetry:[22] a voice paradoxically romantic and realistic, at once intelligent, secular, philosophical, democratic, and passionate.

Despite the many self-deprecating comments Birney made to friends ("I'm a rather lightminded beginner";[23] "I've somewhat shamefacedly published a little"[24]) as "David" found its way to its audience, it was not long before the poem was acclaimed as a classic on its own terms. Birney, at his lowest ebb after "twelve tantalizing personal letters of rejection"[25] for "David"'s publication, wrote to Frank Wilcox, a former University of British Columbia professor:

> most of my verse, as you might guess, stinks. . . . Some of it is so bad that I put it out anonymously. One effusion ["David"] that I acknowledge will appear in the Canadian Forum next week, but I doubt if I will send it to you. It is a piece of ornate melodrama, and I would have you think better of me than that I published it.[26]

But once the poem was published and broadcast by radio, it was quickly appreciated in terms such as these by poet James Wreford Watson, who wrote to Birney without having any idea who he was:

> I was very attracted to ["David"], arrested and elevated. It has something of the grand manner about it, with all the classical virtues of austerity, architecture and abstraction, and yet with an organic structure and a vital freedom that fuses content and form in a very organic way. . . . As for the verse itself, it strikes me both for its discipline and its freedom. . . . The trick of carrying one verse over into the other, the clever use of assonance, the organic variation of rhythm, the nice choice of words impress me with a mastery of the best from the classical and romantic traditions, and their fusion into something original, necessary and in advance of them.[27]

*Notes*

1. "David" was first published in *The Canadian Forum,* which did not please Birney, because he had been literary editor of the journal until December 1940 and suspected that it was accepted there for that reason. The version I use in this article is the first version to appear in book form in *David and Other Poems.*

2. Earle Birney to James McLaughlin, letter 24 April 1941, Birney Collection, Thomas Fisher Rare Book Collection, University of Toronto.

3. Birney to McLaughlin, 23 May 1941, Birney Collection, Toronto.

4. The text used here is the "Oxford" text generally accepted by scholars as the most authentic version. The edition used is Brault.

5. For a full exploration of these influences, see my "The Influence of the Scottish Long Poem on Earle Birney's 'David'," *British Journal of Canadian Studies* 7.1 (1992): 59-73.

6. See Box 79, Birney Collection, Toronto.

7. See Desmond Pacey, *Ten Canadian Poets. A Group of Biographical and Critical Essays* (Toronto: Ryerson, 1958).

8. Birney to Pacey, 4 Feb. 1957, Birney Collection, Toronto.

9. It is worth noting here that MacLeish uses a 3-line assonantal stanza with an a-b-a pattern in *Conquistador,* and links his stanzas assonantally by using the "b" vowel from each stanza as the "a" vowel in the following one. In other words, Birney's form in "David" is a hybrid, merging the self-contained assonantal *laisses* of *Roland* with some aspects of the more structured stanzas of MacLeish's *Conquistador.*

10. Despite much scholarly speculation, the author of the *Song of Roland* is unknown, though, because of the poem's last line "Ci falt la geste que Turoldus declinet" ("Here ends the story that Turoldus tells"), he is usually referred to as Turoldus.

11. Lacey Fisher read "David" for the Western Canada Network of CBC radio at 10:15 p.m. (Pacific Coast Time), Monday, 4 Jan. 1942.

12. Aichinger writes: "in Part VII all these boyish things are left behind and a new note of high seriousness creeps in. David becomes the 'chevalier sans peur et sans reproche' who has undertaken many adventures with his squire (Bob) but who must now go forth to dreadful and final battle with the Finger. As he passes, 'the quiet heather flushed' like a maiden blushing for her warrior knight. David yodels at the mountain sheep and sends them fleeing as a brave knight would drive in the enemy's pickets and sound a defiant trumpet challenge to the enemy himself" (89).

13. In fact, among Birney's acknowledged and probable literary influences, all but *Conquistador* use proper names in their titles: *John Brown's Body,* "Tam o' Shanter," "Brébeuf and his Brethren," and the *Song of Roland.*

14. Birney to Hilton Moore, 29 Jan. 1940, Birney Collection, Toronto.

15. Though the marriage had been annulled almost at once, Birney and Sylvia Johnstone were still technically married at the time Birney and Johnstone visited Trotsky.

16. That Birney intended this clear difference between *Roland* and "David" is suggested by Bob's words when he trips on his way down the mountain and back to the camp: "but I did not faint," for much is made of the fact that Roland faints on seeing his dead friend, Oliver.

17. Birney to E. K. Brown, 30 May 1941, Birney Collection, Toronto.

18. McLaughlin to Birney, 5 July 1941, Birney Collection, Toronto.

19. Kenneth Rexroth to Birney, 5 Sept. 1941, Birney Collection, Toronto.

20. Birney to G. G. Sedgewick, 5 April 1942, Birney Collection, Toronto.

21. Birney to Frank Wilcox, letter n.d. [probably mid-May] 1941, Birney Collection, Toronto. Even the notion of "western nostalgia" may have been suggested by the *Song of Roland,* which nostalgically glorifies events that occurred three centuries earlier.

22. Birney had explained in his letter of 30 May 1941 to Brown: "what I want most to see in Canadian letters is poetry which is not following English or American fashions, however timely, but is striking out for itself."

23. Birney to Brown, 30 May 1941, Birney Collection, Toronto.

24. Birney to Wilcox, letter n.d. [probably mid-May] 1941, Birney Collection, Toronto.

25. Birney to Sedgewick, 5 April 1942, Birney Collection, Toronto. The rejections, as listed by Birney in his copy of *David and Other Poems,* Birney Collection, Toronto, were from: *Sewanee Review, Atlantic Monthly, Penguin New Writing, Poetry* (Chicago), *Queen's Quarterly, Twice A Year, New Directions, New World, National Magazine, University of Toronto Quarterly,* and *Horizon.* The twelfth was *Canadian Poetry Magazine.*

26. Birney to Wilcox, 20 Nov. 1941, Birney Collection, Toronto.

27. James Wreford Watson to Birney, 3 March 1942, Birney Collection, Toronto.

### Works Cited

Aichinger, Peter, *Earle Birney.* Twayne's World Authors Series. Boston: Twayne, 1979.

Benét, Stephen Vincent. *John Brown's Body.* New York: Rinehart, 1928.

Birney, Earle. "Canadian Poem of the Year." *The Canadian Forum* (Sept. 1940): 180. Rpt. in Birney, *Spreading Time: Remarks on Canadian Writing and Writers, Book I: 1904-1940.* Montreal: Véhicule, 1980: 51-2.

———. "David." *The Canadian Forum* (Dec. 1941): 274-6.

———. *David and Other Poems.* Toronto: Ryerson, 1942.

Bowra, C. M. *Heroic Poetry.* London: Macmillan, 1952.

Brault, Gerard J., trans. and ed. *The Song of Roland: An Analytical Edition* (2 vols). University Park and London: Pennsylvania State Univ. Press, 1978.

MacDiarmid, Hugh. *A Drunk Man Looks at the Thistle.* Edinburgh: Blackwood, 1926.

MacLeish, Archibald. *Conquistador.* Boston: Houghton Mifflin, 1932.

Owen, D. D. R., trans. *The Song of Roland.* Bury St. Edmunds: Boydell, 1990.

Pacey, Desmond. *Ten Canadian Poets: A Group of Biographical and Critical Essays.* Toronto: Ryerson, 1958.

### J. W. Thomas (essay date 1994)

SOURCE: Thomas, J. W. Introduction to *Priest Konrad's* Song of Roland, translated by J. W. Thomas, pp. 1-15. Columbia, S.C.: Camden House, 1994.

[*In the following essay, Thomas compares the* Rolandslied, *the German version of the* The Song of Roland, *with the original, finding that while the French version emphasizes the nationalist aspect of the French forces securing their border with Spain, the German version treats the incident as a religious victory of Christianity over Islam.*]

Perhaps the most important contribution of the twelfth century to Western culture was the development of belletristic literature in the vernacular languages of Western and Northern Europe. In the German-speaking lands the process took place during the reigns of Emperors Konrad III and Friedrich Barbarossa in what is called the pre-courtly period (ca. 1150-ca. 1175). Prior to this time, written German was, with few exceptions, solely an instrument of the Church: in lyric and narrative verse clerics composed hymns, sermons, and versions of Old and New Testament stories for the spiritual edification of the general public. Latin, of course, was the standard written language and, for many purposes, remained so until well past the Middle Ages.

About the middle of the century a few noblemen, inspired perhaps by Middle Latin lyrics, began to compose in German simple love songs, that were recorded by their scribes. These poets were followed a decade or so later by others, whose more sophisticated verse forms—influenced by Provençal troubadours—were used by a still younger generation to create the immortal minnesongs of the courtly period. A second literary genre that began to flourish in German during the pre-courtly decades was the *Legende,* the story of a saint. Several German *Legenden* had appeared earlier, but these short narratives did not become a significant part of the vernacular literature until the second half of the twelfth century. They exerted an appreciable influence on the development of the secular verse tales of the following century.

No true drama is extant from the transition period; it first appears in the late Middle Ages—which is perhaps surprising when one considers the popularity of the Latin liturgical plays. But everything written in German was dramatic in that it was composed for performance: to be read and acted out before an audience.

The most important genre of the pre-courtly period was the longer verse narrative, and its principal representatives were a lost version of the Hilde-Kudrun story, *König Rother,* the *Alexanderlied,* and the *Rolandslied.* The first two—based on native Germanic legends dealing with the abduction of a bride—were the forerunners of the so-called "heroic" and "gleeman" tales, respectively, of the late twelfth and the thirteenth century. The latter two—German versions of French stories—exerted a pronounced influence on the courtly romances that followed. A significant innovation common to all four works, and others of the period, is that they have secular heroes, appeal largely to secular interests, and thereby

have become more than simply religious documents, although the ecclesiastical stamp is still apparent.

In borrowing its material from France, the *Rolandslied* turned the attention of the younger poets toward the ultimate source of all of medieval Germany's numerous chivalric romances, including the many Arthurian tales. For France was already making use of Classical stories and the rich store of British folklore, as well as its own historical past; it led its eastern neighbor by a generation in the development of belles-lettres. As the first literary work of Germany to treat Charlemagne, the *Rolandslied* also exerted a significant, though in many cases indirect, influence on the scores of medieval and modern literary treatments of the emperor by German authors.

The *Rolandslied* is memorable as a social document, for no other medieval work portrays so vividly the religious zeal, indeed one might call it the religious fanaticism, that prevailed in many quarters after the Second Crusade. Its depiction of the Christian warrior as a *miles dei* may well have contributed to the literary concept of knighthood in the chivalric romances of Germany. The intent of the work was to reveal the true spirit of a Crusade, but it was probably because of the lurid battle scenes that the work became popular throughout the German-speaking lands. In a thirteenth century revision, it is extant in many manuscripts.

The battles that are central to the *Rolandslied* and its French source are based on a conflict described by Einhard, a German historian and adviser to Charlemagne. In his *Vita Caroli* he reports that, when the emperor's army was returning from a Spanish campagne in 778, the rearguard was attacked in the Pyrenees by Basques and completely destroyed. Among the dead was a Count Roland of Brittany. Nearly four centuries later the Norman poet Wace in his *Geste des Normanz* (ca. 1160) wrote that a minstrel named Taillefer sang of Roland and his companions to William the Conqueror and his troops at Hastings. This suggests that the battle in which Roland fell may have become a well-known piece of French folklore by the time it found literary treatment, although one cannot know to what extent the song influenced the epic poem.

This latter work, the **Chanson de Roland,** was composed about the year 1120—perhaps by an otherwise unknown Turoldus whose name appears at the end of the chief manuscript—and may have been inspired in part by the French Crusades against the Saracens in Spain that were taking place at that time. The situation described in the **Chanson** differs greatly from that recorded by Einhard. The enemy is not the Christian and relatively obscure Basques but the combined forces of heathendom, and the loss of the rearguard does not go unavenged, for Charlemagne turns back, defeats the Saracen armies, and forces the survivors to accept Christianity.

The author of the *Rolandslied* identifies himself as "Priest Konrad," without making clear—at least to a modern audience—where he lived or the specific period of the twelfth century in which he composed. As a result, much research has been devoted to determining the proper place of the work in the history of medieval literature. At first the language of the extant manuscripts and fragments was of little help in revealing Heinrich's homeland, for each was written in a different dialect, but later a careful examination of their rhymes indicated that the original had been in Bavarian.[1] This conclusion is supported by recent studies of the manuscripts' illustrations—apparently influenced by this original—which show them to belong to a school of art associated with Regensburg, the medieval capital of Bavaria and the only city of the duchy that is mentioned in the *Rolandslied.*[2] It is therefore generally assumed that Konrad was a Bavarian and dwelt mainly in Regensburg.

There is less unanimity of opinion with regard to his dates. The epilogue speaks of the work's sponsor: a Duke Heinrich who brought its French source from France at the request of his wife, "the daughter of a mighty king," but the twelfth century produced three dukes of Bavaria named Heinrich whose consorts were the children of kings. They were Heinrich the Proud (1126-1138); Heinrich Babenberg (1143-1156)—usually called Jasomirgott, English: "Yes-by-God," after his favorite expression—and Heinrich the Lion (1155-1180). Further comments in the epilogue seem to fit best Heinrich the Lion, whose wife was Mathilde—daughter of Henry II of England and Eleanor of Aquitaine, a well-known patron of French literature.

Still some scholars object to identifying Konrad's duke with this Heinrich because to do so would place the date of composition of the *Rolandslied* after 1168, the year of his marriage, whereas the prosody and language of the work are more characteristic of an earlier generation of German poets.[3] Like them, Konrad often employed assonance instead of pure rhyme, used irregular meter, and was apparently not familiar with the language and customs of chivalry that had begun to appear in certain other German works of the seventies. The refinements of verse and style that are found in another romance of the decade, the *Strassburg Alexander,* were quite foreign to the *Rolandslied.*

But the new literary trends came largely from France, and Regensburg was far from the Rhine. In fact Konard's knowledge of French was apparently quite

limited, for he says that he first translated the *Chanson* into Latin and from there into German. The priest's reading seems to have been mainly in Latin and restricted almost entirely to sermons and other Biblical treatises. Indeed, the only work in the vernacular that exerted a significant influence on him was the *Kaiserchronik,* which was completed in Regensburg about the year 1147, well before the innovations that marked the early courtly narratives of Germany. Everything considered, it is more than likely that Konrad's duke was Heinrich the Lion, which means that his *Rolandslied* was composed about 1170. A date much later is precluded by the fact that, in praising his sponsor's Christian piety, the author does not mention Heinrich's having taken a pilgrimage to Jerusalem in 1172.[4]

Although Konrad was not in the literary mainstream, he was by no means isolated from the important political and religious movements of his day. It is assumed that he was not a parish priest but was employed in some capacity in the Bavarian chancellery, where he would have been aware of most of the important events in the German lands. Since Heinrich the Lion was also duke of Saxony, the nobleman's personal interests stretched from the Alps to the Baltic, and his close relations to his cousin, Emperor Friedrich Barbarossa—that lasted until about 1174—kept him involved with many of the activities of the Empire. A reference in the *Rolandslied* to a patron saint of a Brunswick church suggests that Konrad may have spent some time at Heinrich's court in Saxony.[5]

The duke's participation in the Wendish Crusade of 1147 and his twenty years of intermittent warfare against the heathen Slavs in the Northeast, which resulted in the Christianization of much of the Baltic area, would doubtless have made a significant impression on the priest who was to compose the first Crusade verse novel of German literature.[6] And Friedrich's conception of his imperial title as a grant from God to lead Christendom—a view which he supported in 1165 by bringing about the canonization of his illustrious predecessor, Charlemagne—might also have been influential.[7] If Konrad was middle-aged or older when the *Rolandslied* was written, as his somewhat archaic language suggests, he would have recalled and perhaps been affected by the impassioned sermons with which Bernard of Clairvaux supported the Second Crusade.

The studies that have linked characters in Konrad's work with certain historical individuals of the twelfth century have not been convincing, nor have those that have attempted to discern the author's sympathies with respect to the quarrels of Friedrich with Pope Adrian and Pope Alexander III.[8] Nevertheless it seems clear that he was strongly affected by contemporary events and that he reflected with some accuracy a wide-spread religious fervor of the period between the Second and the Third Crusade.

The *Chanson de Roland* is a national epic in which the French Emperor Charles, with the aid of certain vassal states, secures his southern border by defeating the Moslems of Spain. Although its author occasionally reminds us that the French are Christians and their foes are heathens, he is primarily concerned with the glory of France rather than with the spread of religion. But Konrad's work is dominated by Crusade ideology, not by patriotism.[9] His Karl is the divinely appointed head of the Holy Roman Empire and as such is the leader of the entire Christian world in its struggle against the powers of darkness. Always guided by prayer, he is portrayed like an Old Testament patriarch. Through an angel messenger God has given him the mission to convert the heathen, if need be with the sword.[10]

The plot is more clearly defined in the German work. The course of the campaign is determined by a family conflict. A rivalry between Roland and his stepfather, Genelun, in their attempts to influence the emperor—who is the uncle of one and the brother-in-law of the other—leads to ill-feelings that are exacerbated when Genelun becomes convinced that Roland is planning his death and intends to seize the inheritance of Genelun's son. Each of the three main characters is defined mainly in terms of his relationship to the Crusade.

Karl is the ideal ruler and crusader. Seeking neither wealth nor fame, he wants only to be an agent in carrying out the divine will; his strength comes from God.[11] Although the others are not directly compared to him, he sets the standard according to which they are judged. Roland is his able and zealous lieutenant, but one with a serious fault: he is proud of his prowess as a warrior and eager to defend and enhance his personal honor. The first indication of Roland's overweening pride comes from the emperor, who refuses to employ him as an emissary to the enemy because he is too quick to wrath. At the same time Genelun accuses his stepson of becoming so angry at his Bavarian allies when they pressed through the city gates ahead of him during the battle for Cordova that he had to be restrained from attacking them. Neither Roland nor the leader of the Bavarians denies the charge. Roland's desire for fame is later expressed in his words before the attack on his forces. "The great arrogance of the heathens won't help them," he declares. "So many will die today that the story may well be told until the Last Judgment." And when his friend Olivir, having seen that their troops are hopelessly outnumbered, asks him to save them by summoning aid from the main army, Roland replies: "I'll not sound the horn because of this foul carrion; they would think we were afraid and needed help to withstand them, the worst of cowards. . . . I'll feed their carcasses to the ravens." This concern for his personal honor results in the death of all of his comrades, the complete annihilation of his army of twenty thousand men, and the imperiling of the entire Crusade.

Mortally wounded, Roland tries in vain to break his sword to keep it from falling into enemy hands—which would blemish his renown. Then he recalls his many victories with the sword and also remembers that an angel had brought it to Karl to give to his nephew so that he might protect widows and orphans.[12] Realizing at last that the God who sent the sword is responsible both for it and for his success, he addresses the weapon. "How could I be so blind!" he exclaims. "May the Lord of heaven forgive me for wantonly trying to break you! Dying, I return all I have from Him and yield myself to His mercy!" He then lifts up his glove, the symbol of his mission, and an angel carries it away.[13]

Genelun is handsome, powerful, and well regarded by the nobles assembled at Karl's court. At first he may have gladly supported the Crusade, but after seven years of warfare and the loss of many of his troops, he sympathizes with the desire of the remainder to return home to their families and is no longer concerned with converting the heathens. When Roland proposes him as an emissary to their king, who had beheaded two previous messengers, he becomes enraged and publicly declares himself an enemy of his stepson. He remains loyal to Karl, and his secret alliance with the heathen Marsilie is not directed against the emperor, only against Roland and his followers. At a hearing before a tribunal of his peers he maintains that, having publicly declared a feud, he could not be guilty of treachery, and most of the French agree with him. But in the trial by combat that follows he is defeated by a much weaker man, and it becomes clear that his crime was not against Roland but against God, for he had betrayed the Crusade.

The Crusade concept that pervades the *Rolandslied* has to do not only with the conversion of heathens but also with Christian martyrdom, as the surest means of winning salvation and eternal bliss.[14] Karl, Roland, and Bishop Turpin inspire their troops with promises of eternal life amid the joys of heaven as a reward for fighting as God's warriors in the age-old struggle against the minions of the devil. This readiness, even eagerness to die for their cause implies a certain rejection of worldly pleasures and institutions. Genelun is the only Christian who is drawn by his home and family.[15]

The scope of the Crusade grows throughout the hostilities. At first the Christians are opposed only by the Spanish King Marsilie and his vassals; later he is joined by allies from neighboring lands and from islands in the sea; and at last Paligan, king of Persia and leader of all the heathen lands, gathers a great armada at Alexandria and sails to his aid. Then Karl's army faces the combined might of the heathen world in a battle that could be viewed as a symbol of Armageddon.

Due in part to the introduction and sustaining of the Crusade theme, the German work is more than twice as long as the **Chanson de Roland.** Konrad begins his version by adding a scene that explains why Karl decided to invade Spain, and throughout the work he reminds his audience of the true nature of the campaign by interpolating commentaries on the action and references to parallel situations in the Old Testament. He also expands the story by developing and embellishing elements of his source and by bringing in explanatory and transitional material to correct its episodic nature. Several new incidents are included simply for their intrinsic interest. A significant stylistic change is the use of longer sentences with subordinate clauses; the French work could be punctuated with a period at the end of each verse.[16] The German version has more description, most of which has a symbolic function. The ornate armor of the heathens with its gold and jewels is an expression of their arrogant pride and obsession with material wealth. On the other hand, the splendor of Karl's military camp illustrates his greatness and likeness to Solomon. The black skin of some of the heathens is, of course, a sign of evil.[17] And the large and powerful stature, handsome face, and rich attire of Genelun at once evoke the medieval picture of Lucifer, the fallen angel.

The most distinctive and controversial feature of Konrad's style is his Biblical language, which—together with situations modeled after those in the Scriptures and some 170 references to Biblical persons and events—raises questions as to the presence or extent of symbolism, allegory, or deliberate postfiguration in the work.[18] Perhaps it is best to assume that Konrad was a simple priest whose reading was restricted almost entirely to the Scriptures and Bible commentaries and that he wrote in the only literary language that he knew.

Certainly the fact that his German version was translated from an intermediate Latin step, rather than directly from French, would have increased the tendency to use Biblical phrases and examples. Moreover, much of the material borrowed from the Old and New Testaments seems primarily intended to embellish or add significance to a situation without interpreting it; the earthquake, thunder, and signs in the skies that accompanied the death of Roland, for example, do not necessarily make him a Christ figure. In any case, it is clear that the *Rolandslied* has no extended allegory and that its author was less interested in using the characters and occurrences of his story to illustrate a host of Biblical passages than in presenting effectively its central spirit.

Like many narrative poets of medieval Germany, Konrad took care to give his story a symmetrical structure.[19] There is a prologue—in which he praises Karl and declares that the emperor has won the kingdom of heaven for having forcefully converted the heathens—and an epilogue that speaks highly of Duke Heinrich, commends him for spreading Christianity by his campaigns against the heathens, and predicts that he will be assigned to endless happiness on Judgment day. Following the prologue comes a scene at Karl's court in which the emperor takes counsel with his advisers concerning the invasion of Spain, and directly preceding the epilogue there is a second meeting of the lords at the imperial court, this time to determine the fate of the traitor Genelun.

The main body of the work consists largely of four battles. At the end of the first two, The Christians under Roland's command are completely annihilated and their leader dies. In the later conflicts Karl's troops destroy the heathen armies and Karl kills Caliph Paligan. Within this overall framework of combat there are dozens of parallel episodes in which the actions of one side are mirrored by those of the other.[20] The reader or listener is thereby constantly reminded of the duality of the human situation in the struggle between good and evil. But in shifting back and forth between the two hosts, Konrad reveals a weakness that he shares with other poets of his day: the tendency to record simultaneous events as if they had occurred consecutively.[21] Also in other respects he is as careless with time as he is meticulous with structure. For example, his audience does not learn until well into the story that seven years passed between the initial invasion and the treachery of Genelun.

The author is for the most part not concerned about details. Sometimes the renowned twelve heroes of Roland's army include Olivir, Turpin, and him; occasionally there are twelve in addition to one or more of the three. Opposed to these twelve is a like number of heathen warriors, but when they are named one by one, three are missing. Another group of twelve heathens appears to have only seven members. Such discrepancies are excusable since obviously it is the symbolic number twelve that is important. But Konrad's casual attitude toward minor matters is not limited to mathematics. In one battle the heathen King Grandon slays the Christian warrior Beringer and is himself slain by Roland, yet both Grandon and Beringer take part in a subsequent conflict. It is of course possible that these errors may have appeared in the author's source; still the more precise poets of the following generation would have noticed and corrected them.[22] In any event the author is consistent where it really matters, for he never loses sight of his theme: the divinely ordained Crusade.

Konrad's chief source, of course, was the French epic, but it was not one of the extant versions and was perhaps older than they.[23] His work therefore is of interest to scholars who attempt to reconstruct the original **Chanson de Roland.** Second in importance for the priest's work was the Bible, from which he drew heavily for comparisons and commentaries. His quotations from the Scriptures are almost never quite exact, and it seems likely that Konrad is repeating the verses as they appeared in hymns, homilies, or patristic writings.[24] The one secular work in German to exert a strong influence on Konrad, the *Kaiserchronik,* apparently served the priest as a literary model. There are hundreds of verbal borrowings—names, words, phrases, even sentences—and the general styles of the two works are so similar that some earlier scholars assumed them to have been composed by the same person.[25] Whether or not Konrad was indebted to the Latin *Pseudo-Turpin* (ca. 1150), especially for his introductory scene, is debatable.[26]

A verse that Konrad lifted almost unchanged from *Das himmlische Jerusalem* and another that came from *Salomos Lob* tell something about his general literary background. The former poem, an allegory, is based on Revelation 21; the latter is a fanciful account of the building of Solomon's temple. Both are from the first half of the twelfth century. A reference to the warrior Wate of the early, lost version of the Hilde-Kudrun story suggests that the spirit of Konrad's crusaders may have been borrowed in part from Germanic heroes and that his conflicts might even owe something to the famous struggle on the Wülpensand. The battle exhortations of Karl, Turpin, Roland, and Olivir—that promise their men a heavenly reward, a martyr's crown, earthly and heavenly fame, eternal joy, and victory over the devil—may reflect the fiery Crusade sermons of Bernhard of Clairvaux.[27]

The *Rolandslied* is extant in two manuscripts and four fragments, all from the late twelfth century. These numbers, large for the period, and the fact that each is from a different dialect-region indicate that the work was very popular for a time. But literary tastes with regard to both subject matter and style changed rapidly during the last quarter of the century as laymen began to replace clerics as poets and noblemen with secular interests became their chief sponsors. So it was that only a single product of the courtly Classical Period of Medieval German literature (ca. 1175-1225) drew significantly from Konrad's work. This was Wolfram von Eschenbach's *Willehalm* (ca. 1218), that also had a French source and treated battles between the French and the Spanish Saracens.

The influence of the earlier narrative on Wolfram's verse romance is seen particularly in the introduction and in the presentation of the war as a momentous struggle to preserve the Christian West from the assembled forces of the Moslem East. *Willehalm* also contains numerous references to the *Rolandslied* as well as passages and situations that parallel those in Konrad's work. But the spirit of *Willehalm* is that of a more secular and tolerant age: its Moslems are not evil minions of the devil but are men driven by the same inexorable sense of duty as that which impels the Christians.[28]

Not long after the appearance of Wolfram's poem, the *Rolandslied* was revised by a very prolific writer who used the pseudonym Stricker. In his *Karl* (ca. 1225) he adapted Konrad's verse to the contemporary taste by using pure rhyme and courtly language and by adding unaccented syllables to create a regular rhythm. The style of the older work also was altered, chiefly by eliminating the paratactic sentence structure that had been taken over from the **Chanson** and supplying brief introductions to persons and events. With regard to content, a fictional account of Karl's youth was added, the omissions of the *Rolandslied* were filled in, and its errors were meticulously corrected. Yet in spite of the many apparent improvements, Konrad's poem did not gain by this revision, for it now was somewhat lacking in intensity and vitality. Nevertheless the new version was very popular—as witnessed by over forty extant manuscripts and fragments—and almost completely supplanted the earlier one.[29]

The story of Karl and Roland, as it appears in such fifteenth-century works as the *Weihenstephaner Chronik*, Heinrich von München's *Weltchronik*, the *Zürcher Buch vom heiligen Karl*, and *Karl der Grosse*, was taken from Stricker's *Karl*. But the anonymous *Karlmeinet* (ca. 1300) borrowed directly from Konrad's work for its compilation, that used four earlier works to form a fictional life of Charlemagne.[30] As one might expect, the religious zeal of Konrad's account is less apparent in these later works—composed by laymen long after the Crusades—and the invasion of Spain is viewed for the most part as one of many legendary adventures of a great emperor. Konrad's other hero is remembered especially in the many (ca. 40) medieval statues of him in North Germany. These so-called Roland columns apparently signified certain special privileges that were granted by an emperor or ruling prince to the town or city in which they stand.[31]

The *Rolandslied* is well-known among art historians for the illustrations of its chief manuscript (Heidelberg University cod. pal. germ. 112). The calligraphy places it in the last quarter of the twelfth century; the language is South German; the iconography is typical of the Regensburg-Prüfening school. Especially during the century from 1150 to 1250 the Prüfening Monastery of

Regensburg produced manuscripts in which pen sketches without frames were inserted into the texts to accompany the epic narration and emphasize its dramatic moments. The effect is that of a twice-told tale. The illustrations are strictly two-dimensional without any sort of background and, like much medieval art, tend to be symbolic. For example, a small group of closely packed warriors may represent an entire army. More often than not, scribe and artist did not work together; one left blank spaces on the pages, the other filled them in at a later date. Presumably it was the former who decided what was to be depicted.

Unlike some of his colleagues, the illustrator of the Heidelberg manuscript was fully acquainted with the text and drew on it for considerable detail. Some scenes were chosen especially for their symbolic or emblematic importance. The very first sketch, showing Bishop Turpin baptizing the heathen, presents the Crusade theme; the scene depicting Turpin pierced by enemy spears emphasizes the martyr motif; the illustration in which the dying Roland slays the heathen with his horn reminds us that he and all his men could have been saved if his pride had not kept him from sounding the horn in time; the final sketch, where Karl sentences his brother-in-law to death, not only brings the plot of family conflict to an end but also reinforces the oft repeated motif of the Last Judgment.

Wanting to have his figures as large as possible, the illustrator often left out feet and lower legs and in one sketch sacrificed part of two heads. Although the characters are identified primarily by their attire, he gave distinctive features to the most important ones, so that there is seldom any question as to the scenes portrayed. Unfortunately many of the thirty-nine drawings have become faded and discolored. The ten included in the translated text are representative of the illustrations produced by the monastery.

Konrad composed in the traditional narrative verse form of his time—rhymed couplets in which iambic tetrameter predominates—and, like most of his contemporaries, used line and rhyme fillers. Moreover, since he was not skillful at versifying, he often introduced elements in other than normal thought sequence and occasionally even shuffled sentences about in order to gain a rhyme. His language is simple and has none of the Romance borrowings used by the courtly poets that followed him. In rendering his verse into idiomatic prose, the translator has felt free to leave out such words and phrases as served only the interests of prosody and, in several instances, has put clauses in a more logical order. He has avoided sophisticated vocabulary and words that are obviously of Romance origin, has sometimes added an adverb to distinguish between simultaneous and sequential actions, and has provided chapter divisions and headings. Place names appear in their modern

equivalents only when there could be little doubt as to the locality intended.

The translation was made from the edition of Carl Wesle, that gives the texts of the extant manuscripts and fragments of the *Rolandslied*. For the most part the translator followed the Heidelberg Manuscript, but on occasion the wording of another text was used. He wishes to express his appreciation to the University of Kentucky for a research grant.

*Notes*

1. Carl Wesle, "*Kaiserchronik* und *Rolandslied,*" *BGDSL* [*Beiträge zur Geschichte der Deutschen Sprache und Literatur*] 48 (1924): 223-58.

2. Rita Lejeune and Jacques Stiennon, *La légende de Roland dans l'art du moyen âge* (Brussels: Arcade, 1967), I, 117. The assumption that the original manuscript was illustrated and in a specific style is based on the fact that the two manuscripts that survived (one only until 1870) had similar pen sketches although neither had been copied from the other.

3. Peter Wapnewski, "Der Epilog und die Datierung des deutschen Rolandsliedes," *Euphorion* 49 (1955): 261-82, agrees with the majority of earlier scholars, who assumed that Konrad wrote during the reign of Heinrich the Proud; Friedrich Neumann, "Wann entstanden *Kaiserchronik* und *Rolandslied,*" *ZDA* [*Zeitschrift für Deutsches Altertum und Deutsche Literatur*] 91 (1962): 263-329, maintains that the *Rolandslied* was composed while Jasomirgott and Gertrud were duke and duchess of Bavaria; Christian Gellinek, "The Epilogue of Konrad's *Rolandslied*: Commission and Dating," *MLN* [*Modern Language Notes*] 83 (1968): 390-405, argues for a somewhat later period, when Jasomirgott was married to Theodora, the niece of the emperor of Byzantium. Other scholars of the last few decades believe that Konrad's sponsor was Heinrich the Lion.

4. Ferdinand Urbanek, "The *Rolandslied* by Pfaffe Conrad: Some Chronological Aspects as to its Historical and Literary Background," *Euphorion* 65 (1971): 234, concludes that certain lines in the epilogue refer to the impending pilgrimage.

5. Hans-Dietrich Keller, "Der Pfaffe Konrad am Hofe von Braunschweig," in *Wege der Worte: Festschrift für Wolfgang Fleischhauer* (Cologne: Böhlau, 1978), pp. 143-66, conjectures that Konrad composed his epic poem at Brunswick over a long period of time and completed it about 1195.

6. The relation between the *Rolandslied* and the Slavic wars is treated by Jeffrey Ashcroft, "Konrad's *Rolandslied,* Henry the Lion, and the Northern Crusade," *FMLS* [*Forum for Modern Language Studies*] 22 (1986): 184-208.

7. Horst Richter, "Das Hoflager Kaiser Karls: Zur Karls Darstellung in deutschen *Rolandslied*," ZDA 102 (1973): 81-101, discusses Charlemagne's role in Friedrich's "Empire metaphysics."

8. Helmut Röhr, "Die politische Umwelt des deutschen *Rolandsliedes*," BGDSL 64 (1940): 1-39, describes the political background of the *Rolandslied*, discusses its pro-Empire orientation, and attempts to identify various characters in the work with Konrad's contemporaries. Dieter Kartschoke, *Die Datierung des deutschen Rolandsliedes* (Stuttgart: Metzler, 1965), pp. 135-40, and Gustav A. Beckmann, "Der Bischof Johannes im deutschen *Rolandslied*: Eine Schöpfung des Pfaffen Konrad?" BGDSL (Tüb.) 95 (1973): 289-300, link Konrad's Bishop Johannes with two different historical figures, and several scholars connect his Karl and Roland with Emperor Friedrich and Duke Heinrich.

9. "Wir müssen von Kreuzzugsfrömmigkeit sprechen," says Helmut de Boor, *Von Karl dem Grossen zum Beginn der höfischen Dichtung 770-1170* (Munich: Beck, 1966), p. 242, "einer neuen Form kämpferischer Glaubensglut, die in Deutschland erst durch die Predigt Bernhards von Clairvaux geweckt worden ist." "Der nationale Heidenkrieg der Chanson," writes Friedrich-Wilhelm Wentzlaff-Eggebert, *Kreuzzugsdichtung des Mittelalters: Studien zu ihrer geschichtlichen und dichterischen Wirklichkeit* (Berlin: De Gruyter, 1960), p. 79, "ist zum gottgewollten Vollzug christlichen Glaubenseifers umgewandelt."

10. "Konrad regards the past and relates it to the present on the level of *Heilsgeschichte*," writes Jeffrey Ashcroft, "Questions of Method—Recent Research in the *Rolandslied*," FMLS 5 (1969): 275. "The story of Charlemagne and his warriors demonstrates the working out of a divine purpose in history; they represent the typological fulfillment of biblical prefigurations and promises. For the present they provide ethical and redemptive paradigms of Christian kingship and chivalry." Waltraut-Ingeborg Geppert, "Christus und Kaiser Karl im deutschen *Rolandslied*," BGDSL (Tüb.) 78 (1956): 349, defines the theme of the work thus: "In den Schlachten Karls und seiner Helden erweisen sich der ewige Sieg und die zeitliche Niederlage des Gottesstaates gegenüber dem Herrschaftsbereich des Widersachers. Es vollzieht sich in der endgültigen Vernichtung der heidnischen Kriegsmacht der Sieg Christi über die Gewalt des Teufels."

11. It should be noted that Konrad gave no title to his work. This was supplied by Wilhelm Grimm, who called his 1838 edition *Ruolandes Liet*. Eberhard Nellmann, "Pfaffe Konrad," *Verfasserlexikon* V (1985), col. 121, speaks for many scholars when he maintains that the title is misleading with respect to Konrad's concept of the relative importance to his story of Roland and Karl.

12. Jeffrey Ashcroft, "*Miles dei—gotes ritter.* Konrad's *Rolandslied* and the Evolution of the Concept of Christian Chivalry," FMLS 17 (1981): 146-66, views this conferment of Durendart as "a historical prototype for the *Schwertleite*" and considers Konrad to be "the first vernacular author to make Christian chivalry the main theme of an epic work."

13. The death scene is treated at some length by Karl Bertau, "Das deutsche *Rolandslied* und die Repräsentationskunst Heinrichs des Löwen," DU [*Der Deutschunterricht*] 20 (1968), ii: 4-30.

14. Herbert Backes, "Dulce France—Suoze Karlinge," BGDSL (Tüb.) 90 (1968): 23-42, considers the winning of the heavenly kingdom by Charlemagne and his vassals to be the main theme of the work and states that Konrad presented them to his contemporaries as examples to be followed. Ferdinand Urbanek, "Lob- und Heilsrede im *Rolandslied* des Pfaffen Konrad: Zum Einfluß einer Predigt-Spezies auf einen literarischen Text," *Euphorion* 71 (1977): 209-29, disagrees with the latter conclusion. "Aber auch die Belehrung als solche, obwohl gelegentlich hervortretend, steht nicht im Vordergrund des Werkes, entspricht nicht der Textintention seines Verfassers," he writes. "Dies wird deutlich, wenn man die Reden des *Rolandsliedes* mit inhaltlich entsprechenden Textphrasen der . . . geistlichen Dichtungen des 12. Jhs. vergleicht."

15. Elizabeth Mager, "Der Standescharakter der Tapferkeit: Ein Vergleich zwischen *Chanson de Roland* und *Rolandslied*," WZUG [*Wissenschaftliche Zeitschrift der Ernst Moritz Arndt-Universität Greifswald. Gesellschaftswissenschaftliche Reihe*] 15 (1966): 545-50, points out the difference in the spirit of the *Chanson* heroes, who would rather die than live without honor, and that of Konrad's warriors, who look forward to death as a martyrdom that will give them a heavenly reward.

16. Danielle Buschinger, "Le Curé Konrad, adaptateur de la *Chanson de Roland*," CCM [*Cahiers de Civilisation*] 26 (1983): 95-115, compares the styles of the two works in detail.

17. Alfred Noyer-Weidner, "Farbrealität und Farbsymbolik in der 'Heidengeographie' des *Rolandsliedes*," RF [*Romanische Forschungen*] 81 (1969): 22-59, discusses the discrepancy between Konrad's symbolic colors and factual colors.

18. Brian Murdoch, "The Treachery of Genelon in Konrad's *Rolandslied*," *Euphorion* 67 (1973): 372-

77, suggests that Konrad comes near to allegory in his account of the betrayal of Roland by Genelun, who is compared to Judas. Kathleen Harris, "Das Problem der Spiegelbildlichkeit im *Rolandslied*," *Neophilologus* 48 (1964): 11, writes: ". . . die laufend auftauchenden Bezüge auf biblische Persönlichkeiten und Geschehnisse . . . sollen dem Leser bzw. Hörer die Bedeutung der ewigen Wahrheiten, die in dieser Geschichte eines Kreuzzuges immanent sind, lebending vor Augen halten."

19. According to Hans Eggers, "Zahlenkomposition im deutschen *Rolandslied*?" *Interpretation und Edition deutscher Texte des Mittelalters* (Berlin: Schmidt, 1981), pp. 1-12, Konrad's work is carefully structured in units or multiples of 120 that suggest possible religious symbolism. His chart is interesting but not entirely convincing.

20. Kathleen Harris, "Das Problem der Spiegelbildlichkeit im *Rolandslied*," treats these parallel episodes.

21. Konrad's treatment of simultaneous action is discussed by Hans-Hugo Steinhoff, *Die Darstellung gleichzeitiger Geschehnisse im mittelhochdeutschen Epos: Studien zur Entfaltung der poetischen Technik vom 'Rolandslied' bis zum 'Willehalm'* (Munich: Edos, 1964), pp. 96-119, 124-6.

22. Diether Haacke, "Konrads *Rolandslied* und Strickers *Karl der Grosse*," *BGDSL* (Tüb.) 81 (1959): 274-94, points out various discrepancies in Konrad's account. Karl-Ernst Geith, "'das buch . . . gescriben ze den Karlingen'—zur Vorlage des deutschen 'Rolandsliedes'," *Kontroversen, alte und neue,* 9 (Tübingen: Niemeyer, 1986), pp. 137-42, believes that the German poet conscientiously followed a faulty French manuscript.

23. Karl-Ernst Geith, "Rolands Tod: Zum Verhältnis von *Chanson de Roland* und deutschem *Rolandslied*," *ABäG* [*Amsterdamer Beiträge zur Älteren Germanistik*] 10 (1976): 1-14, compares several scenes of Konrad's work with the extant manuscripts of the *chanson* and concludes that his version, when one disregards obvious additions and changes, is closer to the original than they. A. G. Krüger, "Die Bestattung der bei Ronceval gefallenen kaiserlichen Paladine nach dem Rolandsepos und seiner Übertragung durch den Pfaffen Konrad," *ZDP* [*Zeitschrift für Deutsche Philologie*] 58 (1933): 105-16, judges Konrad's source to have been some twenty years older than the Oxford *Chanson de Roland* manuscript. He uses the burial description in the *Rolandslied* to support French versions that differ from the Oxford manuscript with respect to this passage.

24. The influence of the Bible on the *Rolandslied* is treated especially by Herbert Backes, *Bibel und ars praedicandi im Rolandslied des Pfaffen Konrad* (Berlin: Schmidt, 1966); Horst Richter, *Kommentar zum Rolandslied des Pfaffen Konrad* (Bern and Frankfurt: Herbert Lang, 1972); and David Sudermann, "Meditative Contemplation in the MHG *Rolandslied*," *MP* [*Modern Philology*] 85,3 (1988): 225-44. Unfortunately Richter's work is incomplete, covering only a third of the epic.

25. The most informative studies of the relationship between the *Rolandslied* and the *Kaiserchronik* are those by Carl Wesle, "*Kaiserchronik* und *Rolandslied*," and Georg Karl Bauer, "*Kaiserchronik* und *Rolandslied*," *ZDP* 56 (1931): 1-14, who agree that Konrad was the borrower. Georges Zink, "*Rolandslied* et *Kaiserchronik*," *EG* [*Etudes Germaniques*] 19 (1964): 1-18, is almost alone among the scholars of the past forty years in believing the *Rolandslied* to be the older work.

26. Cola Minis, "Der *Pseudo-Turpin* und das *Rolandslied* des Pfaffen Chunrat," *MitJ* [*Mittellateinisches Jahrbuch*] 2 (1965): 85-95, presents arguments to show that Konrad occasionally made use of the Latin work; Wolfgang Decker, "Über *Rolandslied* und *Pseudo-Turpin*," *Euphorion* 72 (1978): 133-42, surveys the literature dealing with the possible relationship between the two works and suggests a means by which the *Pseudo-Turpin* might have become available to Konrad. In any event, the evidence that Konrad drew from the *Pseudo-Turpin* is not very convincing.

27. Friedrich-Wilhelm Wentzlaff-Eggebert, *Kreuzzugsdichtung,* p. 90, cites passages that appear to have been influenced by Bernard of Clairvaux, the Bible, certain hymns, and liturgy.

28. Rudolf Palgen, "*Willehalm, Rolandslied,* und *Eneide*," *BGDSL* 44 (1920): 191-241, points out the passages and situations in Wolfram's work that appear to have been influenced by Konrad. He believes that Rennewart and his fate owe much to the character and the end of Roland.

29. Clifton D. Hall, "The *Saelde*-Group in Konrad's *Rolandslied* and Stricker's *Karl der Grosse*," *Monatshefte* 61 (1969): 347-60, notes that Stricker uses *sælde* almost half of the time with the secular meaning of "good fortune," while Konrad uses it only to mean a God-given blessing or happiness. Hall believes this indicates a somewhat greater orientation on the part of Stricker toward affairs of this life. Diether Haacke, "Konrads *Rolandslied* und Strickers *Karl der Grosse*," compares the styles of the two poets in considerable detail.

30. Udo von der Burg, "Konrads *Rolandslied* und das Rolandslied des *Karlmeinet*," *RhV* [*Rheinische Vierteljahrblätter*] 39 (1975): 321-41, compares the

two works and concludes that the *Karlmeinet* author had an older version of Konrad's epic poem than the one Stricker used.

31. The various theories concerning the origins of the Roland columns are discussed by Theodor Goerlitz, *Der Ursprung und die Bedeutung der Rolandsbilder* (Weimar: Böhlau, 1934).

### Select Bibliography

#### MAJOR EDITIONS

*Das Rolandslied.* Ed. Karl Bartsch. Deutsche Dichtungen des Mittelalters, 3. Leipzig: Brockhaus, 1874. Normalized according to MS. A.

*Das Rolandslied des Pfaffen Konrad.* Ed. Carl Wesle. 1928; 2nd rev. ed. by Peter Wapnewski. Tübingen: Niemeyer, 1967. Presents the single complete manuscript together with the fragments of four other manuscripts. Bibliography includes many works of the nineteenth and early twentieth century.

*Das Alexanderlied des Pfaffen Lamprecht. Das Rolandslied des Pfaffen Konrad.* Ed. Friedrich Maurer. Deutsche Literatur in Entwicklungsreihen. Geistliche Dichtung des Mittelalters, 5. 1940; rpt. Darmstadt: Wissenschaftliche Buchgesellschaft, 1964.

*Das Rolandslied.* I: 121 leaves. II: Wilfried Werner and Heinz Zirnbauer. *Einführung zum Faksimile des Codex Palatinus Germanicus 112 der Universitätsbibliothek Heidelberg.* Wiesbaden: Reichert, 1970. Facsimile of Manuscript P.

*Das Rolandslied des Pfaffen Konrad: Mittelhochdeutscher Text und Übertragung.* Ed. Dieter Kartschoke. Munich: Fink, 1971.

*Das Rolandslied des Pfaffen Konrad.* Ed. Horst Richter. Darmstadt: Wissenschaftliche Buchgesellschaft, 1981. Revises Maurer's text and adds a detailed summary in Modern German.

### John R. E. Bliese (essay date 1995)

SOURCE: Bliese, John R. E. "Fighting Spirit and Literary Genre: A Comparison of Battle Exhortations in the *Song of Roland* and in the Chronicles of the Central Middle Ages." *Neuphilologische Mitteilungen* 96, no. 4 (1995): 417-36.

[*In the following essay, Bliese examines the exhortations to battle that appear in* Roland *and compares them to speeches intended to motivate knights in medieval chronicles.*]

#### A COMPARISON OF BATTLE EXHORTATIONS IN THE *SONG OF ROLAND* AND IN CHRONICLES OF THE CENTRAL MIDDLE AGES

The chansons de geste have often been used as sources of information about the knights and nobles of the central middle ages. Léon Gautier's description of the life of the medieval knight is based chiefly on the chansons in which, he believes, are found "la peinture la plus exacte de la Chevalerie et des temps chevaleresques." The poets were sincere and "n'ont peint en réalité que *ce qu'ils avaient sous les yeux*" (1884: xiii; emphasis in the original). George Fenwick Jones approves of a claim by Alfred North Whitehead: "'It is in literature that the concrete outlook of humanity receives its expression. Accordingly, it is to literature that we must look . . . if we hope to discover the inward thoughts of a generation'" (1963: 1). Jones then applies this principle to the epic poetry of the middle ages. The chansons de geste and especially the *Song of Roland,* he contends, are the best sources "to ascertain the 'inward thoughts' of twelfth-century humanity . . . [Such epics] enjoyed far wider reception than did any monastic writing; and consequently they give us a better picture of the ideals and aspirations of the people in general, or at least of the fighting and ruling classes" (1963: 1).

On the other hand, in his study of chivalry Maurice Keen draws a distinction between the knights of "fiction" and the knights of the "real world" (1984: 2-3). Bernard S. Bachrach goes even farther and contends that there is a "gulf between . . . reality and chivalric literature" (1988: 193). J. F. Verbruggen, in one of the best works on medieval warfare, emphatically rejects certain aspects of the typical portrayal by the poets which, he contends, are not good evidence for the psychology of knights on the battlefield. The common notion that the knights had "a gigantic and insatiable lust for fighting" is based merely on the "lyrical effusions" of some poets, which "have made some scholars think that the knight felt contempt for human life and suffering" (1977: 39-40; 1954: 97-8). He cites Gautier and Huizinga as examples. According to Gautier, "Nos chevaliers aiment trop souvent la bataille pour elle-même, et non pour la cause qu'ils y défendent" (1884: 67; quoted in Verbruggen 1977: 40; 1954: 99). Huizinga refers to the knights' "'pure courage in combat: shuddering withdrawal from narrow egotism to the emotion of life-danger, the deep tenderness about the courage of the comrade, the voluptuousness of fidelity and self-sacrifice'" (quoted in Verbruggen 1977: 41; 1954: 99; in Huizinga's English edition, the wording is slightly different; 1924: 65). Verbruggen rejects such conclusions which are based on literary sources:

Without wishing to detract from the courage, daring and self-sacrifice which the knights so freely displayed both in battles and on many other occasions, especially in the East, it is nevertheless necessary to contradict this often-repeated, usually biassed, praise of their warlike spirit and their contempt for death. Despite their great and sometimes wholly admirable gallantry, the knights were still human beings who feared for their lives in the presence of danger, and who behaved as men have always done in battle—in fear of death, mutilation, wounds and captivity.

(1977: 41; 1954: 99-100)

He then turns to eye witness accounts of battles in the chronicles for better evidence of the psychology of the knights of the real world.

Implied in Verbruggen's argument is a larger question: just exactly what are the differences between the chronicles and the epic poems in their portrayal of the knightly mentality in combat? It is to this question that I want to direct my investigation here.

One might compare and contrast all relevant statements by poets and chroniclers, but it would be very difficult to draw conclusions from such random comments. It would be much better if we could use a directly comparable type of evidence, and we have just such a type in battle orations—exhortations to armies before battles begin or during combat. Battle orations constitute a recurrent rhetorical form that is found in both types of writing, and will allow us to do a more detailed comparative analysis of the two genres.

The chronicles of the central middle ages contain literally hundreds of battle speeches. I have found some 360 in ninety-two histories written in western Europe between approximately 1000 and 1250 (Bliese 1989). These speeches, of course, are not "reports." They are the literary products of the chroniclers themselves, who were expected to embellish their narratives with all sorts of rhetorical devices. But these speeches are not mere flights of fancy. One of the most important prescriptions for rhetorical historiography is that it must be plausible (as measured, of course, by the standards of the time).[1] The chroniclers used those persuasive strategies and emotional appeals which they thought would be most appropriate and effective in stimulating fighting spirits. Battle orations, thus, are a rhetorical form that concentrates and focuses the authors' concepts of the psychology of courage and morale in combat.[2]

Some of the poets also wrote battle speeches, allowing us to make direct comparisons. For a complete analysis, one would have to collect battle speeches from many epics as well. Here, I can only start such a study by looking at just one poem, and the obvious one to examine is the Oxford version of the *Song of Roland*. It is the most famous piece of literature from the central middle ages, and there is much exhortation in its battle scenes.[3] Moreover, songs about Roland, in some form or other, seem to have had some influence on the medieval concept of courage. For example, before the Battle of Hastings, we are told, the story of Roland was sung to bolster the Normans' fighting spirit (William of Malmesbury 1889, 2: 302; Wace 1971: 183).

I will not attempt to offer any new interpretation of the poem, nor will I presume to criticize the literary analyses by the many great *Roland* scholars. All I intend to do here is to compare motive appeals used in the poem to those in the chronicles of the central middle ages, noting similarities and differences in their portrayal of the psychology of combat. All the battle speeches from the chronicles are addressed to western knights, so from the poem I will consider only the speeches to the French, not those to the Moslems.

First, some differences in form need to be noted briefly. In the chronicles, almost all of the harangues to armies are set-piece speeches, usually presented before a battle begins, but occasionally given during combat to rally fleeing troops. There is seldom any dialogue, and where there is, it merely sets up a following speech. Speeches vary in length, from just a few lines to several pages in the printed editions. They can be in either direct or indirect discourse.

In the *Song of Roland,* by contrast, the exhortations in the battle scenes are numerous and all are very short. They occur throughout the battle scenes and often involve dialogue. The speaker frequently begins by taunting an enemy, and then turns to exhorting his friends. Sometimes the speaker begins with remarks that are apparently to himself alone, and then encourages his comrades. It is not always clear exactly where the discourse becomes exhortative. Some of the speeches in the poem are directed to specific individuals, which is rare in the chronicles. All are in direct discourse. Thus, the forms of the battle orations are considerably different.

To compare and contrast the content of the exhortations, I will focus on the motive appeals or rhetorical topoi used. What sorts of things do the speakers say to build morale? The chroniclers' speeches are generally constructed from a relatively short inventory of motive appeals. There are 16 topoi that recur with some frequency in these orations (Bliese 1989). In decreasing order of frequency, they are as follows (with a brief typical example of each):

1. Most common are appeals to the martial, manly virtues: bravery, valor, prowess. Intimately connected with these motives is the public recognition that goes with them: honor, glory, renown. Fulcher of Chartres has King Baldwin address his crusaders, showing the close connection between the martial virtues and the fame they produce. "Fear nothing. Conduct yourselves manfully and you will be mighty in this battle . . . If you survive as victors you will shine in glory among all Christians" (1866: 392; 1969: 157-8). These appeals can have a negative side as well, asking the knights to avoid disgrace, not to be cowardly. As Richard Lion Heart was leading his crusaders on a march, the Turks

kept harassing the rear. When the knights there could take it no longer, some of their leaders called out:

> . . . "Seignors, poignomes!
> L'en nos tendra por malvès homes.
> Tel honte ne fu mes venue,
> N'onques mes par gent mescreue
> Nen ot nostre ost tel reprover."
>
> (Ambroise 6395-9)

Nearly half of the speeches—156—contain appeals from this category and I have counted only speeches where the motive is developed as a separate appeal. Adjectives and adverbs from this category are liberally scattered throughout other appeals as well.

2. In 109 speeches there is a claim that the cause for which they are fighting is a just one.[4] Typically, the speaker says that the enemy are bad people and have committed all sorts of evil deeds. In one version of William the Conqueror's speech at Hastings, the duke tells his men that Harold has committed the terrible crime of perjury and so has to be punished (Henry of Huntingdon 1853: 211; 1879: 202).

3. In 108 orations, the army is assured that God is on their side and will help them win this battle. Typical is William the Breton's account of King Philip speaking before the Battle of Bouvines: "We ought faithfully to trust that God will be merciful to us sinners and give us the victory over his enemies and ours" (1882: 273).

4. Sixty-nine speakers attempt to boost their armies' confidence by telling them that they have some decisive military advantage over the foe. According to Wace, Harold encouraged his men at Hastings by comparing the weapons of the two sides.

> Longues lances ont e espees
> que de lor terre ont aportees,
> e vos avez haches agues
> e granz gisarmes esmolues;
> contre vos armes, qui bien taillent,
> ne qui que les lor gaires vaillent.
>
> (1971: 174; lines 7769-74)

5. It is rather surprising to find, in fifty speeches, that the commander has to plead with his men not to run away. There are two possible approaches. The speaker can be purely pragmatic, telling his men that flight is impossible or more risky than standing their ground. A typical instance of this type appears in the chronicle attributed to Benedict of Peterborough: "Moreover, there is one thing, bravest nobles, that I want to stress firmly: it is not possible to turn back as fugitives. We are surrounded from all sides by our enemies. Therefore, since there is no hope of flight, this alone remains, that we conquer or we fall" (1867, 1:53). Alternatively, the speaker can ask his men to transcend their fears, ap-

pealing to their courage or sense of honor. Helmold records a speech in which a count concludes, "the shame of flight . . . demands recourse to battle" (1935: 185; 1937: 127). The pragmatic approach is clearly dominant (Bliese 1991b).

6. Naturally, one of the important motives for fighting was for plunder and it appears in forty-eight speeches. At Hastings, William the Conqueror promises his men:

> e quant nos vencu les avron,
> que nos feron legierement,
> lor or avron e lor argent
> e lor aveirs donc plenté ont
> e les maneirs, qui riches sont.
>
> (Wace 1971: 161; lines 7742-6)

7. In forty-six speeches there is a claim that the men are fighting to defend themselves and all that is dear to them. In the war against Cnut, Edmund Ironside exhorts his men "to bear in mind that they are about to contend for their country, their children, their wives and their homes" (Florence of Worcester 1848, 1: 174; 1854: 128).

8. In forty-five speeches, the speaker tries to stimulate fighting spirit by reminding the knights of their past victories. Before the Battle of the Standard, Aelred of Rievaulx claims that a long exhortation was given to the Anglo-Norman army in which the past victories of the Normans all over the world, from England to Italy and the Holy Land, were given in detail (1886: 185-6).

9. Forty-two speeches contain the simple promise of victory, the assurance that they will emerge from the coming battle as conquerors. Richer has a commander assure his men that they have nothing to fear, for victory is not in doubt (1967, 1: 88).

10. Thirty-nine speakers call on their men to take revenge on the enemy for injuries of some sort. Before the walls of Jerusalem, the first crusaders are exhorted to take vengeance: "If some foreigner kills any of your relatives, will you not avenge your blood? By much more ought you to avenge your God, your father, your brother, whom you see blamed, outlawed, crucified; whom you hear crying and forsaken and begging for aid" (Baldric of Bourgueil 1879: 101).

11. The speaker can ask his men to bear in mind the glorious reputation of their country or ancestors. This is a general appeal, found in thirty-seven speeches, in which no specific achievements are given. Before the Battle of Hastings Duke William reminds the Normans "of their fatherland, of its noble history, and of its great renown" (William of Poitiers 1952: 182; 1953: 225).

12. When an army confronts a considerably larger enemy force, the commander must reassure his men that it is possible for a few to emerge victorious over a

multitude. Ralph of Caen has a speaker exhort his men: "Do not let your small numbers terrify you; victory is not in numbers but in the strength of God" (1886: 716). This appeal appears in thirty-six speeches.

13. Also in thirty-six speeches, the leaders promise their men that they will gain eternal rewards from the coming battle. Guibert of Nogent writes of the princes encouraging the crusaders: "If you should perish in this place, the heavenly kingdom awaits you, you would die a fortunate death" (1879: 161). These appeals are most common, of course, in accounts of the crusades, but they are by no means limited to crusading.

14. Crusaders, in twenty-three speeches, are asked to fight for Christ or the Holy Sepulcher. On the crusade against the Albigensians, Count Simon exhorts his men and reminds them that "the cause of Christ depends entirely on this battle" (Pierre de Vaulx-Cernay 1926: 268).

15. In twenty-three cases the commander exhorts his men to follow his example in combat. The *Gesta Consulum Andegavorum* describes a duke haranguing his men: "Behold I am your brother, lord and master; and what you see your lord doing, you also do likewise" (1856: 149).

16. Finally, in twelve orations, the commander reminds his men that this battle is precisely what they have long wanted. This appeal is not used to show lust for combat, but rather to overcome reluctance when finally face to face with the enemy. Orderic Vitalis writes of some French knights trying to decide whether to confront their foes. One advises them not to fight, but the others persuade him: "Have we not hoped for long enough to meet the English forces in open country? And here they are" (1980, 6: 350-1).

The exhortations in the **Song of Roland** include 14 of the chroniclers' motive appeals. The claim that the men have long wanted this battle (number 16) would probably be irrelevant in any of the battle scenes. But since the job of a rear guard is to protect the main army, it is a bit surprising not to find any use of defense (number 7) as a motive in the first battle. Roland had earlier said that he would fight to protect the last mule and pack horse (755-9). We can now examine the topoi that the **Song of Roland** uses in common with the chronicles, and then consider some appeals in the poem that do not appear in the histories.

The dominant appeal in the **Song of Roland** as in the histories is to the manly, martial virtues (appeal number 1), and it is used both positively and negatively. Roland exhorts Oliver and claims that Charlemagne selected for the rear guard

Itels.XX. milie en mist a une part,
Sun escïentre, n'en i out un cuard.

(1115-6)[5]

He concludes this speech with praise of Durendal and himself:

Se jo i moerc, dire poet ki l'avrat
. . . que ele fut a noble vassal.

(1122-3)

During the battle, Roland admires a blow by Turpin, and says to Oliver: "itels colps me sunt bel" (1395). Turpin says to Roland:

Asez le faites ben!
Itel valor deit aveir chevale.

(1877-8)

Before the second battle, Charles tells his men: "Barons franceis, vos estes bons vassals" (3335). And his men reply: "Icist reis est vassals" (3343).

All these appeals are rather weak. But when we turn to the negative side of this motive, the poet is much more forceful. Roland exclaims: "Mal seit del coer ki el piz se cuardet" (1107). At a crucial point in the battle, Turpin has to plead with the knights: "Seignors barons, n'en alez mespensant" (1472). Charlemagne says of his army: "Asez est fols ki entr'els se demente" (3010). And in one of the strangest speeches of all, Ogier speaks to Charlemagne:

Veez paien cum ocient voz humes!
Ja Deu ne placet qu'el chef portez corone,
S'or n'i ferez pur venger vostre hunte!

(3537-9)[6]

The poet depicts the French knights as very concerned that they do not get a negative reputation—that bad songs not be sung about them. Roland says:

Or guart chascuns que granz colps i empleit
Que malvaise cançun de nus chantet ne seit!

(1013-4)

Roland asks Oliver to strike, and says about Durendal and Halteclere: "Male chançun n'en deit estre cantee" (1466). And Turpin begs the knights not to flee, "Que nuls prozdom malvaisement n'en chant" (1474). There is no mention of honor or glory to be won, no mention of good songs that might be sung about their noble exploits.

Perhaps the strangest feature of the poem is the way in which it uses this motive. As George Fenwick Jones notes, the strongest appeals in the poem are decidedly negative: "most of its actions are motivated by fear of shame" (1963: 97). The stress in **Roland** is not on winning glory but on avoiding disgrace. Rather unheroic motives, one would think, for the greatest heroes in Christendom, but there they are.

Although the poem's portrayal of warrior society features shame as the dominant sanction on behavior, the chroniclers of the time show the knights' motivation rather differently. The chroniclers' approach to this category of motives is overwhelmingly positive. They use appeals to win glory and honor, to show valor and courage, to exercise manliness and daring far more often than they use negative pleas to avoid disgrace. Consider two typical examples, in addition to the quotation from Fulcher of Chartres given above. Before the Battle at Assandun, Edmund Ironside exhorts the English army to remember their former valor (Florence of Worcester 1848, 1: 177; 1854: 130). On the first crusade, during a battle near Antioch, Bohemond sends in his reserves with an exhortation to its leader: "Charge at top speed like a brave man and fight valiantly . . . be very brave, as becomes a champion of Christ" (*Gesta Francorum* 1962: 36-7).

The chroniclers do, of course, use the sanctions of shame and disgrace in their battle speeches. We have seen one example from Ambroise quoted above. In King Philip's speech at Bouvines, he asks each of his knights "to take care not to lose his own honor" (William the Breton 1885: 314). As a battle is about to begin, William the Marshal calls out to his men: "Errez! . . . Honiz seit qui plus [i] demore!" (*Histoire de Guillaume le Maréchal* 16577, 16580).

However, of the chroniclers' 156 speeches that include this motive appeal, only thirty-five (22%) take the negative approach, and many of those balance it with affirmations. Fighting against the French, William the Marshal tells his men that anyone who does not challenge the foe will be shamed, but

> E se nos le[s] vencons, sanz fable,
> Nos avrons enor pardurable
> Conquise a trestoz nos eages,
> A nos & a toz nos lignages.
>
> (*Histoire de Guillaume le Maréchal* 16284-5, 16295-8)

Before the Battle of Hastings, William of Poitiers has Duke William exhort his Normans: "If you bear yourselves valiantly you will obtain . . . honor . . . If not, . . . you will incur abiding disgrace" (1952: 182-4; 1953: 225). The *Song of Roland* does not balance the two sides of this appeal and as a result its use of this motive is much more negative than is the chroniclers'.

Jones concludes that the poem "expresses a way of life known as a 'shame culture'" (1963: 97). The chroniclers, however, believed that the knights were much more concerned with obtaining honor and glory than with merely avoiding disgrace—and that alone would make for a very different profile of motives.

The justice of the cause the knights are fighting for (appeal number 2) plays as important a role in the poem as in the chronicles. In the *Song of Roland* it appears eight times. The first case is Roland's famous and often quoted claim that "Paien unt tort e chrestïens unt dreit" (1015). This is repeated a few lines later: "Nos avum dreit, mais cist glutun unt tort" (1212). In the middle of the battle, Turpin kills Siglorel and says: "Icist nos ert forsfait" (1393).

When Charles and his men hear Roland's horn, they hurry back. Since daylight will soon be gone, Charles prays to God to stop the sun, and an angel exhorts the emperor, calling the enemy "la gent criminel" (2456). Before the second battle starts, Charles exhorts his men, telling them that the pagans are "felun" (3337). Early in the battle the French exclaim: "Carles ad dreit "(3359). After the next pagan is killed, they say again:

> Carles ad dreit vers la gent . . .
> Deus nus ad mis al plus verai juïs.
>
> (3367-8)

Later in the battle, Charlemagne calls out to the French: "Ja savez vos cuntre paiens ai dreit" (3413).

In the poem, the claim that they are fighting for a just cause often takes the form of a general ideological assertion that Christians are right and Moslems are wrong. In the chronicles, by contrast, the speakers normally claim that the enemy are evil or have committed some evil deeds for which they should be punished.[7]

While divine aid in battle (appeal number 3) plays a major role in the chroniclers' harangues, it plays only a very minor role in speeches in the *Song of Roland.* In the first battle, only Oliver uses it: "Seignurs Franceis, de Deu aiez vertut" (1045). In Charlemagne's battles, the French call on God to protect Charles (3277) and later they call on God for help for themselves (3358). Of course, God does intervene, sending dreams to Charles, prolonging the day, preserving Christian heroes from specific blows; but assurance of his aid plays little role in motivating the French in the poem.

It is rather surprising to find the commanders in their battle harangues frequently pleading with their men not to run away (appeal number 5). It is perhaps even more disconcerting to find it in the *Song of Roland,* but there it is, twice. The French first respond to Oliver's scouting report with a brash threat—"Dehet ait ki s'en fuit" (1047)—which would seem to be a tacit admission that some of them just might. Later, when they see the second wave of the enemy approaching, the men implore Oliver and Roland and the Peers to protect them, in an expression of fear that is entirely realistic (see Verbruggen 1977: 41-7; 1954: 100-7). Turpin has to plead with them:

Seignors barons, n'en alez mespensant!
Pur Deu vos pri que ne seiez fuiant,
Que nuls prozdom malvaisement n'en chant.
Asez est mielz que moerjum cumbatant.

(1472-5)

John Benton believes that this plea plays a role of "en-culturation," its function is to teach "the virtues desired for an ideal warrior." It attempts to instill "a code of honor and glory that condemns flight as shameful," since "every commander wants troops who will risk, indeed sacrifice, their lives if necessary" (1979: 245-6).

But the plea not to flee is also, of course, a simple reflection of military reality: when the going got really tough for an army, the knights of the real world often did turn and flee. Duke William had to rally his fleeing knights at Hastings (e.g., William of Poitiers 1952: 190; 1953: 226; [Guy of Amiens] 1972: 28-31), as did Duke Robert at Dorylaeum on the first crusade (e.g., Henry of Huntingdon 1853: 229; 1879: 221). And the examples could easily be multiplied. Verbruggen uses such instances to show that the knights were not fearless unfeeling fighting machines but human beings, just as warriors have always been (1977: 47-50; 1954: 107-10).[8]

The chroniclers stress the pragmatic reasons for standing one's ground: it is in most instances less dangerous than turning one's back in flight, and in some cases it is impossible to flee (Bliese 1991b). In support of Benton's interpretation of these lines in the *Song of Roland,* we may note that Turpin appeals only to the knights' sense of honor and reputation, and the earlier collective condemnation of anyone who flees implies the same.

Neither the poet nor the chroniclers seem to think that there was anything shameful about warning an army not to run away. And the poem's juxtaposition of statements that no one in the rear guard was a coward (1116) with the plea not to flee, jarring as it may seem, may also be found in the chronicles. In the passage quoted above from the chronicle attributed to Benedict of Peterborough the speaker calls his men "bravest nobles" ("fortissimi proceres") and then tells them that it is impossible to escape by fleeing (1867, 1: 53). In Wace's version of William's speech at Hastings, the duke tells his men that they are the bravest army ever assembled, and then proceeds to explain to them in great detail just exactly why they cannot save themselves by running away (1971; 161-2).

The medieval man at arms fought in great part for the opportunities for plunder, and promises of booty are important motivators in the chroniclers' battle speeches (motive appeal number 6). But the role of plunder as a motive in the *Song of Roland* has been disputed. At two points, unambiguously, the Christian army acquires huge amounts of plunder: after taking Cordres (99-100) and after Marsile's army has been cut down or drowned in the Ebro (2478). Later, Charlemagne plays on materialistic motives when he says that he owes his men rewards ("gueredun") for their past service (3409-10). In the passage that is disputed, Roland says to his men:

Encoi avrum un eschec bel e gent,
Nuls reis de France n'out unkes si vaillant.

(1167-8)

Most scholars take "eschec" to mean booty:

Today our booty will be rich and rare,
More precious than French king has ever won.

(Owens trans., 1990: 75)

T. Atkinson Jenkins offers the note: "'eschec' is plunder; it plays an important role in the poem; cf. vv 99, 2478" (1929: 94). George Fenwick Jones (1963: 76) and Dorothy Sayers (1957: 97), among others, likewise take the word to mean booty. Of the modern French versions, Gérard Moignet translates "eschec" as "butin" (1969: 103) as does Joseph Bédier (1924: 91; see also 1929a: 435).

Robert Francis Cook, however, believes that the term is not meant literally here. It "is a figurative reference to the martyr's privilege of heavenly acceptance. It is not some unprecedented vast treasure somehow to be won on this desert field, but a metaphoric treasure such as no king of France ever had, for it is not of this world" (1987: 75). Patricia Terry accepts Cook's argument because she believes there would be no booty for a rear guard (1989: 160).

If the rear guard is going to cover the main army as it crosses the mountains and then retreat behind it (as in Richard Lion Heart's march from Acre to Jaffa; see Verbruggen 1977: 210-20; 1954: 376-90), they would have no opportunity for plunder. But if the Franks expect to fight a battle and defeat the Moslem army, and Terry indicates that they expect to do exactly that (1989: 160), there would be plenty of booty. They would have the horses, weapons, armor and camp of a 400,000 man army to plunder, just as the camp of Kerbogha offered immense booty to the crusaders at Antioch.[9]

Gerard Brault, however, goes even farther in rejecting the normal interpretation of this passage. Although he indicates that under certain circumstances booty has Biblical approval (1978, 1: 416), he believes that this reading attributes "an unworthy thought" to Roland. "Filled with thoughts of striking a mighty blow for Christianity and twirling the pure white banner symbolizing the rightness of his cause, Roland appears to sound a jarring note here" (1978, 1: 187). Although Brault takes "eschec" to mean booty in lines 99 and 2478, he argues that it can also mean "battle" (1978, 1: 188), so he translates the passage:

> Today we shall have a fine and noble battle,
> No king of France ever had such a worthy challenge.

Brault's argument is analyzed and rejected by Ian Short, who notes that Brault "cites no parallel examples and omits any specific reference to the [*Altfranzösisches Wörterbuch*] which, as it turns out (III, 890f., s.v. eschiec), registers nothing remotely similar" (1981: 55).

Perhaps the chroniclers' speeches can shed some light here. The Norman knight who relates his experiences on the first crusade includes a marvelously luminous passage in his description of the Battle of Dorylaeum. The knights encouraged each other by passing a message along their line: "Stand fast all together, trusting in Christ and in the victory of the Holy Cross. Today, please God, you will all gain much booty" (*Gesta Francorum* 1962: 19-20). Guibert of Nogent sees nothing disgraceful or jarring in having Raymond of Saint Gilles urge his men on as Jerusalem falls to the crusaders: "Why do you delay here? Don't you see the Franks, having obtained the city, are now rejoicing about all the plunder they have taken?" (1879: 227). Medieval warriors and chroniclers apparently did not have Brault's scruples about fighting for God and booty at the same time.

An army's glorious achievements are frequently used to stimulate fighting spirits (appeal number 8). In *Roland,* there are several extensive references to past victories, but they are usually egocentric, with Roland bragging about his own great exploits.[10] Only three times are they used in exhortation. Roland calls on Oliver to strike with his sword Halteclere, as he himself will strike with Durendal.

> En tanz lius les avum nos portees!
> Tantes batailles en avum afinees!

(1464-5)

Charlemagne reminds his men:

> Tantes batailles avez faites pur mei,
> Regnes cunquis e desordenet reis!

(3407-8)

Earlier, Charles seems to imply this when he says to his men: "Tantes batailles avez faites en camps" (3336).

Vengeance is a very important motive (number 10 in the chronicles) in the *Song of Roland.* When Roland informs Oliver that Engelier is dead, Oliver replies (in one of those exclamations that may or may not have an

exhortative function): "Deus le me doinst venger" (1505). After Roland summons Charles to return, Turpin calls on the few remaining men to strike hard, and says that the Emperor "ben nus vengerat" (2145). When Charlemagne comes back, revenge is a dominant motive in his battles, and it is mentioned in six speeches. When they see the dust raised by the battle at Roncevaux, Duke Naimes exhorts the Emperor: "Vengez ceste dulor" (2428). After prolonging the daylight, God sends an angel to exhort Charles:

> La flur de France as perdut ço set Deus.
> Venger te poez de la gent criminel.

(2455-6)

During the battle Charles tells his companions: "La mort Rollant lur quid cherement rendre" (3012). Later he calls on all his men:

> Vengez voz filz, voz freres e voz heirs
> Qu'en Rencesvals furent morz l'altre seir!

(3411-2)

Near the end of the battle, in the strangest of speeches, Count Ogier tells Charles he is unworthy of his crown, "S'or n'i ferez pur venger vostre hunte" (3539). At last, as they pursue the fleeing pagans, Charles calls on all his men to "vengez voz doels" (3627).

The role of revenge in the motives of the French army has been variously interpreted. For George Fenwick Jones, it is one of several decisive proofs that the poem portrays a secular, pagan, Germanic culture, not a Christian one. Christianity "proclaims a God of peace and forgiveness" (1963: 82). "[B]asic to Christianity . . . are the tenets that . . . love is better than hate, and that forgiveness is better than vengeance. Such tenets are not expressed in the [*Song of Roland*]" (1963: 100-1). In the poem, revenge is usually presented "as a matter of personal satisfaction" (1963: 82), a most unChristian motive.

Robert Francis Cook, on the other hand, believes that vengeance was a purely political motive, not a matter of personal spite. A feudal leader was responsible for protecting his men, and ideally that meant bringing all necessary force to bear to ward off any threat. But "a leader cannot, in all circumstances, protect the men who are his allies . . . Yet he will eventually make it clear that anyone who harms his men will not escape in the long run. Thus vengeance . . . is a political act with abstract implications, not an emotional response" (1987: 12).

Comparison with the chroniclers' battle speeches may be of interest here. The chroniclers see no inconsistency between Christianity and vengeance, even when it is treated as a personal, vindictive motive. Thus Helmold puts into the mouth of "a most steadfast priest" a speech in which he harangues an army: "Plunge your swords into their vitals . . . and be avengers of your blood . . . Let them not go back with a bloodless victory" (1935: 179; 1937: 121). Fully half of the instances in their speeches draw a direct connection between religion and revenge. Crusading armies are often asked to avenge injuries to God or Christ, as in the passage from Baldric of Bourgueil quoted above. But avenging God is not limited to the crusades. The saintly Aelred of Rievaulx relates that the Anglo-Norman army at the Battle of the Standard was told that Christ had chosen their hands to avenge his injuries (1886: 188).

Many of the chroniclers' calls for vengeance thus do not seem to be abstractly political. Moreover, many of them link religious motives with revenge. In contrast to the clear differentiation Jones seeks to draw, these instances seem to illustrate John Benton's conclusion: "The idea that there could be a sharp distinction between secular and religious culture in the crusading period seems to me to be a false dichotomy" (1979: 253).

The promise of eternal rewards (appeal number 13) is developed twice and mentioned a third time, and clearly plays an important role in encouraging the French at Roncevaux. Turpin says:

> Asoldrai vos pur voz anmes guarir.
> Se vos murez, esterez seinz martirs,
> Sieges avrez el greignor pareïs.

(1133-5)

Later, he proclaims:

> Ultre cest jurn ne serum plus vivant.
> Mais d'une chose vos soi jo ben guarant:
> Seint pareïs vos est abandunant,
> As Innocenz vos en serez seant.

(1477-80)

And Roland says: "Ci recevrums matyrie" (1922). The use of this appeal is especially prominent in chronicles of the crusades, but in the mentality of the central middle ages, eternal rewards are by no means limited to battles against Moslems.

The other appeals from the chroniclers' inventory play only minor roles in the *Song of Roland*. There is only one reference to their nation's reputation (number 11). The chroniclers normally use this motive in a positive manner, asking the army to remember the glorious reputation of their nation and ancestors. In the poem, however, just like the approach to personal honor, it is negative.

> Ferez, seignurs, des espees furbies,
> Si calengez e vos cors e voz vies,
> Que dulce France par nus ne seit hunie!

(1925-7)

Roland and his rear guard obviously enjoy no military advantage over the pagans (appeal number 4), so no comparative claim is made. Charlemagne, however, uses this topos when he tells his men that the enemy are cowardly ("cuart") (3337).

When facing a numerically superior enemy, the chroniclers' commanders often claim that a few can be victorious over a multitude (number 12). Oliver implies as much in his remarks when he returns from scouting. He reports that he has seen an enormous number of pagans, with a force of one hundred thousand in the forefront (1039-41). He then exhorts the army: "El camp estez, que ne seium vencuz" (1046). However, he immediately turns to Roland and expresses grave reservations about the chances of so few against so many in the famous first horn scene (1049-50; 1083-7). Later, Charlemagne uses this topos, but rather weakly, when he says: "S'il unt grant gent, d'iço, seignurs, qui calt?" (3339)

The French are twice asked to fight for Christ (appeal number 14). Turpin calls on them: "Chrestïentet aidez a sustenir" (1129). When facing Baligant's forces, the French threaten the enemy and encourage themselves. After calling on God to protect Charles, they say: "Cest bataille seit . . . en sun num" (3278).

Sometimes commanders try to set themselves up as examples for their men to emulate, and call on them to "follow me" (appeal number 15). There is some of this motive in the poem. Roland first approaches the idea from the negative side: "Malvaise essample n'en serat ja de mei" (1016). During the battle, he says: "Ferez, Franceis, car jol vos recumenz" (1937). Later, Charlemagne uses this motive in a negative way: "Ki or ne voelt a mei venir, s'en alt" (3340).

If the commander can assure his men that they will win the battle, they will take heart (motive appeal number 9). Hopeless as Roncevaux might seem, this topos appears a couple of times. As the battle is about to begin, Roland asks his men to advance and says: "Cist paien vont grant martirie querant" (1166). Cook contends that this is not a true promise of victory (1987: 74-5), but Oliver does assure the men that they will win. Early in the battle, he strikes Falsaron and calls out: "Ferez i, Francs, kar tres ben les veintrum" (1233).

In the later, fully developed concept of chivalry, knights fight valiantly to impress the ladies. But it has often been remarked that women play little role in the *Song of Roland.* Never are the knights urged to fight to please or impress their women. Likewise, in the chroniclers' speeches, even those written as late as the middle of the thirteenth century, the commanders do not appeal to their knights to consider their reputation with the fair ladies.[11]

As we have now seen, there is a considerable overlap in the use of motive appeals in exhortations in the *Song of Roland* and in the chronicles of the central middle ages, although there are some major differences in the ways in which these appeals are developed. But there are also a number of interesting topoi in the poem that are not found in the chronicles.

Most notable are the assertions of what a vassal owes his lord. In a passage that Janet Boatner calls "one of the greatest of all speeches on vassalage" (1969: 576), Roland says:

> Pur sun seignor deit hom susfrir destreiz
> E endurer e granz chalz e granz freiz,
> Sin deit hom perdre e del quir e del peil.
>
> (1010-2)

This is repeated almost verbatim few lines later:

> Pur sun seignur deit hom susfrir granz mals
> E endurer e forz freiz e granz chalz,
> Sin deit hom perdre del sanc e de la char.
>
> (1117-9)

Turpin adds:

> Seignurs baruns, Carles nus laissat ci,
> Pur nostre rei devum nus ben murir . . .
>
> (1127-8)

There is also a very general instance in the second battle, where the French say of their emperor: "ne li devom faillir" (3359). These are often interpreted as summaries of the ideal feudal relationship of vassal to lord (e.g., Cartier 1968: 44; Cook 1987: 62; Boatner 1969: 576), and they are clearly used as motivators in the poem.

This sort of claim is almost entirely absent from the historians' battle harangues, and they are very weak appeals compared with the *Song of Roland*'s. For example, Florence of Worcester has Bishop Wulfstan exhort some knights to "be firm in your loyalty to the king" (1848, 2: 25; 1854: 190). While the poet treats a knight's duty to his lord as a key to motivation in combat, the chroniclers apparently believe it is hardly relevant at all.

In the first battle, two speakers exclaim that the French have the first blow. As the two forces clash, Roland kills Aelroth and says to his army: "Ferez i, Francs, nostre est li premers colps" (1211). Shortly after, Turpin kills Corsablix and calls to his men to strike: "Cist premer colp est nostre, Deu mercit" (1259). The chroniclers do not use this topos, but the forms of discourse they usually write (orations before the battles begin or rallying an army in flight) would almost automatically exclude it.

Also striking about the exhortations in *Roland* is the number of times the speakers condemn anyone who misbehaves in any way. The French say: "Dehet ait ki s'en fuit" (1047). Roland exclaims: "Mal seit del coer ki el piz se cuardet" (1107). Condemnation is called down on anyone who "slacks off" in the battle:

> . . . n'avons guaires a vivre,
> Mais tut seit fel cher ne se vende primes.
>
> (1923-4)

Late in the battle, Roland calls on the French to strike and Oliver adds: "Dehet ait li plus lenz" (1938). Turpin says: "Fel seit ki ben n'i ferrat" (2144). In the final battle, Charles asks whether the men will help him now and they reply: "Trestut seit fel ki n'i fierget a espleit" (3559).

Again, such a negative approach seems rather strange in this poem about heroic French knights. It does not appear in the chronicles, except for a very few instances where commanders threaten their men to keep them from fleeing. For example, in Ralph of Coggeshall's account of the third crusade, King Richard speaks to his men as the Turks are about to attack. He swears by almighty God that if he sees anyone flee, he will cut off his head (1875: 47). But a general condemnation, like the poet's "dehet ait" or "fel seit," is not used by the chroniclers.[12]

Much weaker, but still within the negative approach to motivation, is Turpin's encouragement of Roland that begins by praising his valor and ends by saying that if a knight does not have such valor

> . . . ne valt IIII deners,
> Einz deit monie estre en un de cez mustiers,
> Si prierat tuz jurz por noz peccez.
>
> (1880-3)

There is nothing similar in the chroniclers' speeches.

Finally, one cannot overlook a very strange case, with no parallel in any of the historians' speeches. At the critical moment of the final battle, Charlemagne has been hit and is about to lose his fight with Baligant. Gabriel speaks to him and uses no motive appeal at all: "Reis magnes, que fais tu?" (3611)[13]

When Thomas McGuire compared the knight as portrayed in several chansons de geste with the knight as portrayed by a few contemporary histories, he concluded that they were basically similar (1939: 112-3). A more detailed analysis of motives in battle orations in both genres, however, allows us to see not only similarities but also some significant differences in the portrayal of the mentality of the knights. The knight of the *Song of Roland* and the knight of the chronicles both fight for booty in this life and eternal rewards hereafter. They both seek revenge for wrongs done to them. And they are stimulated to fight by the memory of their past victories.

The differences, on the other hand, are far more interesting. The knight of the *Song of Roland* fights to avoid shame and disgrace, a bad reputation, having bad songs sung about him. Neither does he want his "nation" to get a bad name. And he wants to avoid being condemned for being a "slacker" or "shirker." His motivation is, thus, predominantly negative. The chroniclers of the central middle ages do not corroborate this pattern of motives at all. The knight of the chronicles, by striking contrast, is motivated to be brave and courageous as a positive goal. He fights largely for a favorable reputation—to win honor and glory and to carry on his "nation's" reputation. Both knights are motivated to fight if their cause is just. But the knight of the chronicles, even of the crusade chronicles, stresses the evil deeds of the foe. The knight of the *Song of Roland* is more "ideological," stressing that his side is "right." The knight of the chronicles is often promised help from Heaven in the battle, but this plays little role in bolstering the fighting spirit of the knight of the *Roland* poet. Both the knight of the chronicles and the knight of the *Song of Roland* have to be warned not to run away. But the chroniclers stress purely pragmatic reasons: it is safer to fight than to flee. The poet stresses, again, the bad reputation they will get if they flee. The knight of the epic is motivated to fight by thinking of his feudal duties which he owes to his lord. For the knight of the chronicles, this is virtually irrelevant when facing combat. Likewise, it is important for the poet's knight to know that his side strikes the first blow in battle. The chroniclers do not apparently think this is important.

This comparison of battle speeches in the *Song of Roland* and in the chronicles of the central middle ages suggests that the two genres, with their different purposes and constraints, produce rather different pictures of the mentality of the knights and the psychology of combat. For a definitive conclusion, of course, one would have to compare the chroniclers' speeches with battle rhetoric from a number of epic poems. But the *Song of Roland* is in many ways the most important one, so the ways in which it differs from the chronicles is significant.

The chroniclers were writing within the long tradition of rhetorical historiography.[14] As noted earlier, one primary constraint on the authors was the criterion of plausibility. Their battle rhetoric, consequently, shows us what the authors thought was a believable portrayal of the psychology of combat for contemporary knights.

The primary purpose of the chansons de geste, on the other hand, was to entertain (Jackson 1960: 37; Muir

1985: 4). Presumably, therefore, the use of motives in their battle speeches shows us the picture of the knights which the poets thought would have been most entertaining to an audience composed largely of warriors. The epic portrayal of medieval warfare is often exaggerated, sometimes even a "burlesque" of real war (Daniel 1984: 18), to make it more entertaining. Can we not expect that the epic portrayal of motives in combat has been likewise altered? It is often said that the chansons de geste embody the values and ideals of their audiences (e.g., Jackson 1960: 37-8; Cook 1987: 130). This may indeed be the case, but those ideals are presumably presented in the way the poets thought would be most entertaining. For comparison, one may note that American ideals, such as individualism and self-reliance, are often embodied in western movies that are anything but realistic pictures of the lifestyle or mentality of real cowboys.

There seem to be, in sum, major differences between the purposes, expectations and constraints operating on the authors of the chronicles and on the *Roland* poet. These have produced some major differences, as well as some similarities, in their respective portrayals of the knights in combat. Is the Oxford *Roland* a representative medieval epic in this respect? This question could be answered only after a comparison using speeches from many of the poems. Such an analysis might also help to determine whether Jones or Verbruggen is closer to the mark in their respective contentions about the utility of the two genres as evidence for the mentality of the knights of the real world. But this investigation of one poem gives good indication that the knight of the chronicler and the knight of the epic poet are rather different men.

## Notes

1. Plausibility was a primary criterion by which rhetorical devices and embellishments were judged. Nancy Partner even refers to it as a "rhetorical imperative" (1985: 12; see also Ray 1985: 66, 83-4). For relevant precepts from the two most popular texts for the study of rhetoric at the time, see Cicero, *De Inventione* 1.7.9; 1.19.27—1.20.28; 1.21.30 and *Rhetorica ad Herennium* 1.2.3.; 1.8.11—1.9.16.

2. There is, moreover, reason to believe that the chroniclers had a good basis for composing "realistic" battle orations. Some of the authors were knights themselves and had fought in wars; others had accompanied armies, especially on the crusades. Some chroniclers were attached to courts where they would have had frequent contact with knights. Even those who were monks knew something of the psychology of war. Monks normally came from the same social background as the knights. Monasteries were social centers

where knights and nobles often gathered, and there were frequently converted knights in the monasteries. As a result, John Gillingham concludes, "it was natural for observant monks to be well informed about war" (1989: 143). Maurice Keen reaches a similar conclusion: "knights and clerks sprang from the same stock and understood each others' world better than is often allowed for" (1984: 32).

3. The battle speeches in the *Song of Roland* have received little scholarly attention as examples of medieval rhetoric. Some lines within the speeches are among the most famous of all and they, of course, have been extensively analyzed by many *Roland* scholars. But only a few have discussed the orations as rhetoric. Eugene Vance, for example, considers the speeches but dismisses them, claiming that none of the heroes is eloquent. Moreover, he says, the author may not have thought that the vernacular tongue would favor grand orations (1967: 612). Albert Pauphilet briefly discusses a couple of the orations. He, too, says that the characters are not particularly eloquent but they choose their arguments well and put them in good order. However, he singles out Charlemagne's harangue before the battle with Baligant, which he thinks is a remarkable model of military eloquence, worthy of Caesar or Napoleon (1950: 86).

4. This motive appeal does not correspond at all closely to the theological and legal concepts of the just war (Bliese 1991a).

5. All quotations from the *Song of Roland* are from the edition by Gerard J. Brault.

6. Brault comments on this passage: Ogier's "tense nerves are much in evidence as he bluntly informs the Emperor he must strike now or risk incurring the wrath of God . . . 'For a moment, Charlemagne seems paralyzed . . . and his chief barons must wake him to a sense of his peril.' . . . Ogier makes it clear that . . . God will be angry if Charles does not intervene. Ogier's role, then, is not to shake the Emperor from a perilous torpor but to remind him, prophetlike, of his duty. Old Testament prophets were usually counselors of royalty, proclaiming not what pleased their clients but what God told them to do" (1978, 1: 307; his quotation is from Jenkins).

7. William A. Henning claims that the motivation in the first battle is predominantly feudal, in the later battles predominantly religious (1976: 233-5; see also Paden 1989: 355). Yet clear and strong ideological statements also appear in speeches from the first battle scene.

8. The standard military manual of the time takes careful account of this normal human reaction in face of danger. Vegetius specifically advises a commander never to corner an enemy. If the foe has a route for escape, he will think of running for safety and can be cut to pieces while in flight (3.21). For the use of Vegetius' 4th or 5th century military manual in the middle ages, see Bachrach 1985; Wisman 1979; Shrader 1979 and 1981.

9. "The Turks fled in terror and we pursued them right up to their camp . . . The enemy left his pavilions, with gold and silver and many furnishings, as well as sheep, oxen, horses, mules, camels and asses, corn, wine, flour and many other things" (*Gesta Francorum* 1962: 70).

10. This is the traditional interpretation of Roland's bragging. Robert Francis Cook, however, contends that "his claim is not exaggerated." Roland was field commander in these attacks, so "by synecdoche, as Charles's designated agent, he won those cities by leading the Franco-Christian army that attacked them" (1987: 12-3).

11. For the one and only exception of which I am aware, see Duby 1973: 22 and the passage in William the Breton's *Philippidos* to which he refers (1885: 323).

12. Jenkins indicates that this condemnation was a severe one. "*Dehet ait* must have been a crushing malediction, for it translated the ecclesiastical *odium Dei habeat*" (1929: 86). This phrase is also discussed by Paris 1889 and Sheldon 1903; see also the Godefroy and Tobler-Lommatzsch dictionaries. For "fel" see Jones 1963: 28-30 as well as the dictionaries.

13. Jenkins comments: "The appearance of Saint Gabriel at this critical moment might have been suggested by Luke xxii.43 . . . As it was difficult for the poet to imagine words suitable to the mouth of an archangel, he may have derived some aid from the legend of the miraculous bird which, leading Charles through a wilderness, called out to him, 'France, quid dicis?'—a phrase which is suitably vague in meaning" (1929: 249). Jenkins refers to Bédier (1929b: 123) for this story. Pierre Le Gentil comments: "Dieu s'est borné à les exhorter d'un mot ou d'un signe. . . . Il n'en a pas fallu davantage pour que le vieux monarque retrouvât, avec l'espoir de vaincre, la vigueur nécessaire pour abattre son ennemi" (1955: 145).

14. For the rhetorical tradition of historiography, see Partner 1985; Southern 1970; Ward 1977 and 1985; Wiseman 1979; Ray 1974 and 1985.

*Works Cited*

Aelred of Rievaulx. 1886. *Relatio de Standardo*. In Richard Howlett, ed. *Chronicles of the Reigns of Stephen, Henry II and Richard I*. 4 vols. London. Rolls Series. 3: 179-99.

Ambroise. 1897. *L'Estoire de la Guerre Sainte*. Ed. Gaston Paris. Paris.

Bachrach, Bernard S. 1985. "The Practical Use of Vegetius' *De Re Militari* during the Early Middle Ages." *The Historian* 47: 239-55.

————. 1988. "*Caballus et Caballarius* in Medieval Warfare." In Howell Chickering and Thomas H. Seiler, ed. *The Study of Chivalry*. Kalamazoo. 173-211.

Baldric of Bourgueil. 1879. *Historia Hierosolymitana. Recueil des Historiens des Croisades: Historiens Occidentaux*. Paris. 4: 1-111.

Bédier, Joseph, ed. and trans. 1924. *La Chanson de Roland*. Paris.

————. 1926a and b, 1929a and b. *Les Légendes Epiques*, 3rd ed. 4 vols. Paris.

[Benedict of Peterborough.] 1867. *The Chronicle of the Reigns of Henry II and Richard I*. 2 vols. Ed. William Stubbs. London. Rolls Series.

Benton, John F. 1979. "'Nostre Franceis n'unt talent de fuïr': The *Song of Roland* and the Enculturation of a Warrior Class." *Olifant* 6: 237-58.

Bliese, John R. E. 1989. "Rhetoric and Morale: A Study of Battle Orations from the Central Middle Ages." *Journal of Medieval History* 15: 201-26.

————. 1991a. "The Just War as Concept and Motive in the Central Middle Ages." *Medievalia et Humanistica* N.S. 17: 1-26.

————. 1991b. "When Knightly Courage May Fail: Battle Orations in Medieval Europe." *The Historian* 53: 489-504.

Boatner, Janet W. 1969. "The Misunderstood Ordeal: A Re-examination of the *Chanson de Roland*." *Studies in Philology* 66: 571-83.

Brault, Gerard J. 1978. *The Song of Roland, An Analytical Edition*. Vol. 1, *Introduction and Commentary;* Vol. 2, *Old French Text and English Translation*. University Park, Pennsylvania.

————, ed. and trans. 1984. *La Chanson de Roland*. University Park, Pennsylvania.

Cartier, Normand R. 1968. "La Sagesse de Roland." *Aquila: Chestnut Hill Studies in Modern Languages and Literatures* 1: 33-63.

Cicero. 1968. *De Inventione*. Trans. H. M. Hubbell. Cambridge, Mass. Loeb Classical Library.

Cook, Robert Francis. 1987. *The Sense of the Song of Roland*. Ithaca, New York.

Daniel, Norman. 1984. *Heroes and Saracens: An Interpretation of the Chansons de Geste*. Edinburgh.

Duby, Georges. 1973. *Le Dimanche de Bouvines*. Paris.

Florence of Worcester. 1848. *Chronicon ex Chronicis*. 2 vols. Ed. Benjamin Thorpe. London.

————. 1854. *The Chronicle of Florence of Worcester*. Trans. Thomas Forester. London.

Fulcher of Chartres. 1866. *Historia Hierosolymitana. Recueil des Historiens des Croisades: Historiens Occidentaux*. Paris. 3: 311-485.

————. 1969. *A History of the Expedition to Jerusalem*. Ed. Harold S. Fink; trans. Francis Rita Ryan. Knoxville, Tennessee.

Gautier, Léon. 1884. *La Chevalerie*. Paris.

*Gesta Consulum Andegavorum et Dominorum Ambaziensium*. 1856. In Paul Marchegay and André Salmon, ed. *Chroniques d'Anjou*. Paris. 34-157.

*Gesta Francorum et Aliorum Hierosolymitanorum*. 1962. Ed. and trans. Rosalind Hill. London.

Gillingham, John. 1989. "William the Bastard at War." In Christopher Harper-Bill, Christopher J. Holdsworth and Janet L. Nelson, ed. *Studies in Medieval History Presented to R. Allen Brown*. Woodbridge, Suffolk. 141-58.

Godefroy, Frédéric. 1880-1902. *Dictionnaire de l'Ancienne Langue Française*. 10 vols. Paris.

Guibert of Nogent. 1879. *Gesta Dei per Francos. Recueil des Historiens des Croisades: Historiens Occidentaux*. Paris. 4: 113-263.

[Guy, Bishop of Amiens.] 1972. *The Carmen de Hastingae Proelio of Guy Bishop of Amiens*. Ed. and trans. Catherine Morton and Hope Muntz. Oxford.

Helmold of Bosau. 1935. *The Chronicle of the Slavs*. Trans. Francis Joseph Tschan. New York.

————. 1937. *Cronica Slavorum*. Ed. B. Schmeidler. *Monumenta Germaniae Historica Scriptores in Usum Scholarum*, 32. Hannover.

Henning, William A. 1976. "Concepts of Warfare in the *Chanson de Roland*." In Charles L. Nelson, ed. *Studies in Language and Literature: The Proceedings of the 23rd Mountain Interstate Foreign Language Conference*. Richmond, Kentucky. 233-7.

Henry of Huntingdon. 1853. *The Chronicle of Henry of Huntingdon*. Trans. Thomas Forester. London.

————. 1879. *History of the English*. Ed. Thomas Arnold. London. Rolls Series.

*L'Histoire de Guillaume le Maréchal, Comte de Striguil et de Pembroke, Régent d'Angleterre de 1216 à 1219*. 1891-1901. 3 vols. Ed. Paul Meyer. Paris.

Huizinga, J. 1924. *The Waning of the Middle Ages*. London.

Jackson, W. T. H. 1960. *The Literature of the Middle Ages.* New York.

Jenkins, T. Atkinson, ed. 1929; reprint 1977. *La Chanson de Roland.* Boston; reprint Watkins Glen, New York.

Jones, George Fenwick. 1963. *The Ethos of the Song of Roland.* Baltimore.

Keen, Maurice. 1984. *Chivalry.* New Haven.

Le Gentil, Pierre. 1955. *La Chanson de Roland.* Paris.

McGuire, Thomas A. 1939. *The Conception of the Knight in the Old French Epics of the Southern Cycle with Parallels from Contemporary Historical Sources.* East Lansing, Michigan.

Moignet, Gérard, ed. and trans. 1969. *La Chanson de Roland.* Paris.

Muir, Lynette R. 1985. *Literature and Society in Medieval France.* New York.

Orderic Vitalis. 1969-80. *The Ecclesiastical History.* 6 vols. Ed. and trans. Marjorie Chibnall. Oxford.

Owen, D. D. R., trans. 1990. *The Song of Roland.* Woodbridge, Suffolk.

Paden, William D. 1989. "Tenebrism in the *Song of Roland.*" *Modern Philology* 86: 339-56.

Paris, Gaston. 1889. "Dehé." *Romania* 18: 469-72.

Partner, Nancy. 1985. "The New Cornificius: Medieval History and the Artifice of Words." In Ernst Breisach, ed. *Classical Rhetoric and Medieval Historiography.* Kalamazoo. 5-59.

Pauphilet, Albert. 1950. *Le Legs du Moyen Age.* Melun.

Pierre de Vaulx-Cernay. 1926-39. *Hystoria Albigensis.* 3 vols. Ed. Pascal Guébin and Ernest Lyon. Paris.

Ralph of Caen. 1866. *Gesta Tancredi in Expeditione Jerosolymitana. Recueil des Historiens des Croisades: Historiens Occidentaux.* Paris. 3: 587-716.

Ralph of Coggeshall. 1875. *Chronicon Anglicanum.* Ed. Joseph Stevenson. London. Rolls Series.

Ray, Roger. 1974. "Medieval Historiography Through the Twelfth Century: Problems and Progress of Research." *Viator* 5: 33-59.

———. 1985. "Rhetorical Scepticism and Verisimilar Narrative in John of Salisbury's *Historia Pontificalis.*" In Ernst Breisach, ed. *Classical Rhetoric and Medieval Historiography.* Kalamazoo. 61-102.

*Rhetorica ad Herennium.* 1968. Trans. Harry Caplan. Cambridge, Mass. Loeb Classical Library.

Richer. 1967. *Histoire de France, 888-995.* 2 vols. Ed. Robert Latouche. Paris.

Sayers, Dorothy L., trans. 1957. *The Song of Roland.* Baltimore.

Sheldon, E.-S. 1903. "Dehé, Dehait." *Romania* 32: 444-5.

Short, Ian. 1981. "Re-interpreting the 'Roland': *Per Litteram, Sensum, et Sentiam.*" *Romance Philology* 34 (Special Issue): 46-63.

Shrader, Charles R. 1979. "A Handlist of Extant Manuscripts Containing the *De Re Militari* of Flavius Vegetius Renatus." *Scriptorium* 33: 280-305.

———. 1981. "The Influence of Vegetius' *De Re Militari.*" *Military Affairs* 45: 167-72.

Southern, R. W. 1970. "Aspects of the European Tradition of Historical Writing: I. The Classical Tradition from Einhard to Geoffrey of Monmouth." *Transactions of the Royal Historical Society* 5th series 20: 173-96.

Terry, Patricia. 1989. "Roland at Roncevaux: A Vote for the Angels." *Olifant* 14: 155-64.

Tobler, Adolf and Erhard Lommatzsch, ed. 1925-. *Altfranzösisches Wörterbuch.* 10+ vols. Wiesbaden.

Vance, Eugene. 1967. "Spatial Structure in the *Chanson de Roland.*" *MLN (Modern Language Notes)* 82: 604-23.

Vegetius, Flavius Renatus. 1967. *Epitoma Rei Militaris.* Ed. C. Lang. Stuttgart.

Verbruggen, J. F. 1954. *De Krijgskunst in West-Europa in de Middeleeuwen.* Brussels.

———. 1977. *The Art of Warfare in Western Europe During the Middle Ages.* Trans. Sumner Willard and S. C. M. Southern. Amsterdam.

Wace. 1970-3. *Le Roman de Rou de Wace.* 3 vols. Ed. A. J. Holden. Paris.

Ward, John O. 1977. "Classical Rhetoric and the Writing of History in Medieval and Renaissance Culture." In Frank McGregor and Nicholas Wright, ed. *European History and Its Historians.* Adelaide. 1-10.

———. 1985. "Some Principles of Rhetorical Historiography in the Twelfth Century." In Ernst Breisach, ed. *Classical Rhetoric and Medieval Historiography.* Kalamazoo. 103-65.

William of Malmesbury. 1887-9. *De Gestis Regum Anglorum.* 2 vols. Ed. William Stubbs. London. Rolls Series.

William of Poitiers. 1952. *Histoire de Guillaume le Conquérant.* Ed. and trans. Raymonde Foreville. Paris.

———. 1953. "The Deeds of William, duke of the Normans and king of the English." In David Douglas and George W. Greenaway, ed. and trans. *English Historical Documents.* London. 2: 217-31.

William the Breton. 1882. *Gesta Philippi Augusti.* In H.-François Delaborde, ed. *Œuvres de Rigord et de Guillaume le Breton, Historiens de Philippe-Auguste.* 2 vols. Paris. 1: 168-320.

———. 1885. *Philippidos Libri XII.* In H.-François Delaborde, ed. *Œuvres de Rigord et de Guillaume le Breton, Historiens de Philippe-Auguste.* 2 vols. Paris. 2: 1-385.

Wiseman, T. P. 1979. *Clio's Cosmetics.* Leicester.

Wisman, Josette A. 1979. "L'*Epitoma Rei Militaris* de Végèce et sa Fortune au Moyen Age." *Le Moyen Age* 85: 13-31.

## Brewster E. Fitz (essay date September 1998)

SOURCE: Fitz, Brewster E. "Cain as Convict and Convert? Cross-Cultural Logic in the *Song of Roland.*" *Modern Language Notes* 113, no. 4 (September 1998): 812-22.

[*In the following essay, Fitz notes that Muslims, Jews, and pagans are not differentiated within* The Song of Roland *and suggests that this signifies a new order of Christianity committed to abolishing or converting the Other regardless of religious affiliation.*]

In the Oxford *Chanson de Roland* Muslims and Jews are designated as "pagans" and differentiated only from Christians but not from one another. Indeed, after having defeated Baligant and taken Saragossa, Charlemagne has the "idols" smashed in synagogue and mosque alike, and converts the "pagans" who remain alive—except Bramimunde—to Christianity at sword's point (O [Oxford], 3660-70). This apparently "naive" indifferentiation among Muslim, Jew and pagan may stem from an intentional erasure of difference between the exterior Muslim enemy and the interior Jewish enemy, who owing to a God-given sign, had lived in relative peace among Muslims and Christians up until the time of the First Crusade.

It is my hypothesis that the narrative of the *Song of Roland* projects a new order of Christianity, which stands in relation to the pre-crusading order as the New Testament era to the Old Testament era. Such a narrative is guilt-driven. Its *telos* is to judge, convict, slay or convert all forms of the Other, whether within or without, while sacrificially absolving radical guilt.

Gerard Brault has speculated that the *olive haute* under which Ganelon begins his conversation with Blancandrin on their way to Saragossa may serve to link Ganelon to the Jewish nation, to the treason of Judas in the Garden of Olives, and to the despair of Judas, who according to tradition, hanged himself in an olive grove

(69). It can hardly be denied that Ganelon is a Judas figure. Indeed, Conrad's *Ruolandesliet* not only explicitly compares Ganelon to Judas (Conrad, 1925, 1936-1939, 6102-04), but hyperbolically suggests that Ganelon's treason is even greater. The Heidelberg manuscript of Conrad's text also contains three illustrations in which a person, whom Rita Lejeune has identified as Ganelon (124), is wearing a curious bonnet. Professor Lejeune has called this headgear "une sorte de bonnet catalan" (124). She suggests that the illustrator may have coiffed Ganelon with this "Spanish" headgear in order to distinguish him from the Franks. That the bonnet does distinguish Ganelon from the Franks is undeniable. It also distinguishes him from the Saracens. The distinction made, however, may be somewhat different from the one Professor Lejeune had in mind, for this bonnet resembles one of the kinds of headwear frequently used in the Middle Ages to designate the wearer as a Jew. Cain, Abraham, Aaron, Noah, the doctors disputing with Christ in the temple, the mockers of Christ, Caiphas, and occasionally even Judas are often depicted wearing this or other forms of *Judenhut* in medieval illustrations.[1]

Given the increase in violent anti-semitic incidents linked to recruitment for the First Crusade—some historians like Riley-Smith even refer to this period as the "first Holocaust" (34, 50-51)—it would not be entirely unreasonable to speculate that the illustrator of the Heidelberg manuscript may have depicted Ganelon wearing a *Judenhut* not just to distinguish him from the Franks, but also to underline his felonious relation to Judas, Cain and Jewry, and vice versa, to underline the Jews' relation to Ganelon.

Whatever might have been the intention of the illustrator of Conrad's text, Ganelon starts as a Christian in all versions of the *Song of Roland*. I will argue, though, in a reading of three episodes from the Oxford text, that Ganelon's attitude toward Roland, toward *caritas,* and toward the Muslims, is figuratively, i.e. typologically, Jewish.

### 1. THE BRICUN AND THE BRANCHES D'OLIVE

After seven years of war the Saracens know they are defeated. Blancandrin proposes to pretend to request mercy, *caritas,* while sending to Charlemagne treasures that use *cupiditas* to turn the Christian army around. In other words, Blancandrin proposes a gift whereby the Christian army will be unwittingly "converted" by the pagans' alleged "faith." Crucial to blinding the Christians to the falsity of the "faith" to which this double conversion is directed are the *branches d'olive,* which the Saracen emissaries will carry to signify *pais e humilitet,* and the Saracens' offering of their sons, whom they know will be killed:

> "Enveiu[n]s i les filz de noz muillers:
> Par num d'ocire i enveierai le men.

Assez est melz qu'il i perdent le chefs
Que nus perduns l'onur ne la deintet,
Ne nus seiuns conduiz a mendeier." AOI

(O, 42-46)

The Saracens' preference for this-worldly honor and possessions over the lives of their own sons is only to be expected from a people who, as the Châteauroux manuscript makes clear, belong to the *ligneage de Cain* (C [Châteauroux], 6066-84). But just as Charlemagne has difficulty distinguishing Christian dead from Saracen dead at Roncevaux (in C), and must therefore ask for a divine sign to mark the *ligneage de Cain*—God causes briars and thorns to grow up around the Saracens' corpses—so Charlemagne needs some sign that links Marsilie's and Blancandrin's words to their "faith":

Dist as messages: "Vus avez mult ben dit,
Li reis Marsilies est mult mis enemis.
De cez paroles que vos avez ci dit,
En que mesure en purrai estre *fiz*?"

(O, 143-46, my italics)

The Saracens' sons are that sign:

—"Voet par hostages," ço dist li Sarrazins,
"Dunt vos avrez ú dis, ú quinze, ú vint.
Pa[r] num de ocire i metrai un mien filz,
E sin avrez, ço quid, de plus gentilz."

(O, 147-50)

The pagans' offer to give their sons is not, however, an unambiguous sign, as it is unclear whether it is grounded in *caritas* or *cupiditas*. Typologically speaking, it is unclear whether Blancandrin's decision to offer his son is figured by Abel's heartfelt intention in sacrificing his lamb or by Cain's murderous intention in dispatching his brother into the realm of typology, thereby transforming their sacrifice into the most common medieval illustration of felony.[2] Hence, Charles can only declare his inability to know Marsilie's heartfelt intention, "Mais jo ne sai quels en est sis curages" (O, 192), and assemble his barons and ask for *exegetical* assistance.

Roland offers an exegesis of Marsilie's signs and words—his *plait*—that rejects these in terms of a counsel not to *believe* an "evil sign:" "Ja mar crerez Marsilie!" (O, 196). The name *Marsilie* itself, since it repeats *mar* (from *mala* and *hora*) functions etymologically as an evil sign of a past false request for conversion which was grounded in felony rather than in *caritas*, as Roland's citing the murder of Basan and Basilie demonstrates. His exegesis signals the evil sign of false belief. His counsel embodies the logic of the Crusade as vengeance for the death of Christians stemming from felony:

"Faites la guer[re] cum vos l'avez enprise:
En Sarraguce menez vostre ost banie,
Metez le sege a tute vostre vie.
Si vengez cels que li *fels* fist ocire!"

(O, 210-13, my italics)

Ganelon also offers an exegesis, which rather than clearly identifying a sign, parodies Roland's words while replacing the obviously evil sign, the name *Marsilie* itself, with the unclear, pluri-referential, disparaging term, *bricun*:

Franceis se taisent, ne mais que Guenelun:
En piez se drecet, si vint devant Carlun,
Mut fierement cumencet sa raisun,
E dist al rei: *"Ja mar crerez bricun,
Ne mei ne altre, se de vostre prod nun."*

(O, 217-21, my italics)

In this brilliant piece of exegetical rhetoric, *bricun* can refer to Roland, to Marsilie, to Ganelon, or to anyone. Ganelon has erased the difference between Marsilie and Roland, between Marsilie and himself, between Roland and himself. Or, in terms of faith, between pagan, Christian, Muslim and Jew. This indifferentiation sets the scene for a sacrifice that will restore differences.[3]

Some scholars have contended that Ganelon is "unaware of the treacherous nature of the pagans' peace proposals" (Hunt, 203). Yet, given his becoming *mult anguisables* when Roland judges him to be emissary to Marsilie, Ganelon must know the significance of Blancandrin's proposal; he is one of a kind with the pagan in that he prefers this-worldly honor and possessions over the life of one of his own "brothers" who, like Basan and Basilie, is sure to be murdered by the felonious Saracens. Ganelon's argument is that the Christians should embrace the same "faith" that he, Blancandrin and, typologically, Cain hold, and demonstrate their "belief" in it, if it is to their this-worldly benefit, for their *prod*. Part of demonstrating this "belief" constitutes their willingness to send a "brother" to be killed. *Guenes,* as he is called in subject case, is viewing fratricidal sacrifice from Cain's point of view, not Abel's.

Furthermore, in proposing this exegesis that erases difference, Ganelon is rejecting belief in Roland, whose death is an *Imitatio Christi*. Hence, he is rejecting the logic of the Crusade, the quest for a martyr's death while taking vengeance on the enemies of Christ, and the quest for penance and absolution provided by the Crusade. Typologically speaking, he is imitating the Jew's rejection of Christ, Who often in the iconography of the Crusade was depicted riding in the vanguard with sword in mouth.[4]

Ganelon is looking back, not just on *France la dulce*, but more importantly on an old order of pre-crusading faith, an order which is to the new crusading order what the Old Testament is to the New Testament. In that old order Jews lived in relative peace among Muslims or Christians. In the new order Muslim, Jew and pagan all stand to be judged, slain or converted (Riley-Smith, 54). Ganelon judaicizes himself in regard to his *filastre,* the number one exponent of this new crusading order. I agree with Professor Lejeune that Charlemagne's unspeakable secret sin, for which the campaign in Spain can be penance, is woven "in filigrane" into the relation between Ganelon and Roland.

Despite Ganelon's mastery of exegetical rhetoric, Roland's judging him to be emissary to Marsilie marks a victory of the logic of crusading in the debate. Roland cleverly converts his figuratively Jewish *parastre* into a potential good Jew—a Joseph or a Jesus instead of a Judas—a pious victim of God's will to whom martyrdom offers a chance to re-convert, to re-establish the differences between pagan and Christian his rhetoric has erased. Naimes' acceptance of the wisdom of Ganelon's words, once they have been glossed according to *caritas,* prepares the way for Roland's crusading victory in providing his *parastre* with his own *Imitatio Christi* at the hands of Cain's lineage. Having conceded effectively that Roland has won the debate by "turning a false judgment" on him, having refused the company of his own knights, Guenes rides away under the ambiguous *olive halte.*

## 2. Olive Halte and Vermeille Pume

On the way to Saragossa Ganelon recounts the famous apple *exemplum,* which has occasioned much scholarly debate. This *exemplum* provides further testimony to Ganelon's interpreting passages from the Old and New Testament to reject Roland as a Christ figure and concomitantly to reject the theologic of the Crusades. Blancandrin has initiated the conversation by praising Charles and the Franks, while stating that those who counsel crusading are doing evil. Ganelon praises Charlemagne and takes this occasion to designate Roland as the sole stumbling block:

> Guenes respunt: "Jo ne sai veirs nul hume,
> Ne mès Rollant, ki uncore en avrat hunte.
> Er matin sedeit li empereere suz l'umbre;
> Vint i ses nies, out vestue sa brunie,
> E out predet dejuste Carcasonie;
> En sa main tint une vermeille pume:
> 'Tenez, bel sire,' dist Rollant a sun uncle,
> 'De trestuz reis vos present les curunes.'
> Li soens orgoilz le devreit ben cunfundre,
> Kar chascun jur de mort [il] s'abandunet.
> Seit ki l'ociet, tute pais puis avriúmes." AOI

(O, 381-91)

Scholars have speculated that this *vermeille pume* that Roland allegedly held out before his uncle is Constantinople, the world, a *Weltherrschaftssymbol* (Hunt, 207).

Roland himself says that it is "the crowns of all the kings" that he is presenting to his uncle. Like *bricun, vermeille pume* is pluri-referential in Ganelon's mouth. As an apple it obviously calls to mind the forbidden fruit which Satan encouraged Eve and Adam to eat. As "the crowns of all the kings" it recalls Satan tempting Christ with "all the kingdoms in the world" (Matthew 4:8). Thus, Ganelon is implying that Roland is to Charles as Satan was to Adam and Eve and as Satan was to the second Adam. Ganelon typologically links Satan and Roland. At the same time he is suggesting that Charles, unlike Christ, cannot resist temptation. Charles' secret sin, of which Roland is the *fruit,* is woven in filigrane into this passage that is grounded in Ganelon's hate for his *filastre* as well as for the Crusade that would absolve this sin.

Ganelon's rhetoric implies that Roland is a literal incarnation of Christ's enigmatic words describing Himself:

> Think not that I am come to send peace on earth: I came not to send peace, but a sword.

> For I am come to set a man at variance against his father, and the daughter against her mother, and the daughter in law against her mother in law.

> And a man's foes shall be they of his own household.

(Matthew 10: 34-36)

Within this system of in-laws and households Roland is a foe of Ganelon.

Thus, while riding under the *olive halte,* Ganelon weaves an ambiguously "Christian" interpretation through one passage in the Old Testament and at least two passages in the New Testament. The result of this exegetical rhetoric is Blancandrin's and Ganelon's pledging adherence to the same felonious "faith:" "Tant chevalcherent Guenes e Blancandrins, / Que l'un a l'altre la sue feit plevit" (O, 402-03). It now remains for Ganelon to "convert" Marsilie to this projected Judasity. He must erase the differences between Marsilie and himself.

## 3. Charles' Destre Braz del Cors

Ganelon uses his *grant saver,* his rhetorical talent, to manipulate comically—though dangerously—the arrogant and irascible Marsilie. Nevertheless, without the help of Blancandrin, Ganelon would have gone the way of Basan and Basile, backed up against a pine tree and brandishing his sword in response to Marsilie's son's threatening request to "administer justice" (O, 495-500). It is in terms of the *profitable* "faith" pledged to him by Ganelon that Blancandrin seeks the reconciliation of Marsilie and Ganelon: "De nostre prod m'ad plevie sa feid" (O, 507). During the subsequent council in the Garden, Ganelon turns Christ's words figuratively against the Crusade in a passage where the peace between the traitor and the pagans is sealed with a kiss that recalls and gives an additional twist to the sign of Judas' betrayal:

> —"Chi purreit faire que Rollant i fust mort,
> Dunc perdreit Carles le destre braz del cors,
> Si remeindreient les merveiluses óz;
> N'asemblereit jamais Carles si grant esforz;
> Tere Major remeindreit en repos."
> Quan l'ot Marsilie, si l'ad baiset el col,
> Puis si cumencet a venir ses tresors. AOI

(O, 596-602)

In this vertiginous world opened between new order and old order by judaicizing rhetoric, it is Ganelon, the potential imitator of Christ, whose act of Judasity is ironically reflected in his being kissed. The designation of Roland as Charlemagne's right hand continues Ganelon's ambiguous Christian exegesis as it calls to mind the words of Christ: "And if thy right hand offend thee, cut it off, and cast it from thee: for it is profitable for thee that one of thy members should perish, and not that thy whole body should be cast into hell" (Matthew 5:30).

The rest is literature. Roland is placed in charge of the rearguard; *Roland est proz e Oliver est sage*; Roland blows his olifant, consummating his *Imitatio Christi*, converting Charles' army, turning the rearguard into the vanguard; Ganelon is chained up *altresi cum un urs*; Marsilie loses his right hand and his son to Roland's sword in the sacrificial irony that underpins the narrative; and Charlemagne takes Saragossa, smashing idols in synagogue and mosque alike, re-founding differences and slaying or converting by the sword all "pagans" except Bramimunde.

## 4. Whose Trial?

At the end of the trial, after Basbrun and one hundred *serjanz*s have hanged the thirty hostages, the narrative places the blame on Ganelon not only for Roland's death, but also for his own death, as well as for the deaths of Pinabel and of his own family: "Ki hume traïst sei ocit e altroi. AOI" (O, 3959).

Thus far I have suggested that Guenes is both a Cain and a Judas figure, and that his treason amounts to his having Judaicized himself rhetorically. Unlike Cain, Guenes does not literally murder his *per*, Pinabel. The latter's death is effected vicarially by Thierry's sword as God renders his judgment of Ganelon. Indeed, like Cain, Thierry receives from slaying Pinabel a mark which coincides with the revelation of God's will that he not be killed:

> Mult par est proz Pinabel de Sorence;
> Si fiert Tierri sur l'elme de Provence:

> Salt en li fous, que l'erbe en fait esprendre;
> Del brant d'acer la mure li presentet,
> Desur *le frunt* li ad faite descendre,
> Parmi le vis (li ad faite descendre):
> La destre joe en ad tute sanglente:
> L'osberc del dos josque par sum le ventre.
> *Deus le guarit, que mort ne l'acraventet.* AOI

(O, 3915-23, my italics)

Seen in a post-Roncesvallian mode, Thierry is a divinely sanctioned, vicarial murderer—a sacred executioner—a perfect Crusader in whom the Word is the sword. Abel's death, Christ's death, Roland's death, Pin*abel*'s death are all necessary to convict Cain and his lineage literally, to avenge the deaths of Abel, Christ and Roland, to restore difference between pagan and Christian, and to convert and mark the new Cain with the sign of the *Croi*sade.

### Notes

1. Ruth Mellinkoff has studied the *Judenhut* in medieval iconography; according to her, "that this cap had intensely negative meaning both in general and for Jews is demonstrated by its portrayal on Judas at the Last Supper . . . Judas, linked typologically with Cain, was considered in some Christian circles the most despicable of all New Testament Jews" (32).

2. Mellinkoff shows two depictions of Cain and Abel as an example of felony (figures 26 and 27, 34-35).

3. The *Chanson de Roland* lends itself to being read as a sacrificial crisis, either from the point of view of Ganelon, who is seeking peace, or from the point of view of Roland who is seeking war (see Girard, 63-101).

4. For such an illustration see Roland Bainton, I, figure 53.

### Works Cited

Bainton, Roland H. *Christendom*. 2 vols. New York: Harper and Row, 1964.

Brault, Gerard J. *The Song of Roland: An Analytical Edition*. 2 vols. University Park: Pennsylvania State University Press, 1978.

Girard, René. *La Violence et le sacré*. Paris: Grasset, 1972.

Hunt, Tony. "Roland's 'Vermeille Pume'." *Olifant* 7 (1980): 203-11.

Lejeune, Rita, and Jacques Stiennon. *La Légende de Roland dans l'Art du Moyen Age*. 2 vols. Bruxelles: Arcade, 1967.

Mellinkoff, Ruth. "Cain and the Jews." *Journal of Jewish Art* 6 (1978): 16-38.

Mortier, Raoul, ed. *Les Textes de la Chanson de Ro-
land: La Version d'Oxford.* 1. Paris: La geste francor,
1940.

———. Vol. 4, *Le Manuscrit de Châteauroux.*

———. Vol. 10, *Le Texte de Conrad.*

Riley-Smith, Jonathan. *The First Crusade and the Idea
of Crusading.* Philadelphia: University of Pennsylvania
Press, 1986.

## Andrew Taylor (essay date January 2001)

SOURCE: Taylor, Andrew. "Was There a *Song of Ro-
land*?" *Speculum* 76, no. 1 (January 2001): 28-65.

[*In the following essay, Taylor provides an extensive
textual history of* The Song of Roland, *and concludes
that France's desire for a national epic in the period
following the French Revolution led to its "construc-
tion."*]

In 1835 a young philologist named Francisque Michel,
who had been commissioned by the minister of public
instruction, François Guizot, to visit England and
transcribe a number of medieval works, turned his at-
tention to a poem on the Battle of Roncevaux in the
Bodleian Library. Two years later Michel published *La
chanson de Roland ou de Roncevaux du XIIe siècle
publiée pour la première fois d'après le manuscrit de la
Bibliothèque Bodléienne à Oxford,* and the poem entered
French literary history.[1] Henceforth the standard version
of the poem would be the text of the Oxford manuscript,
and it would bear the title Michel had given it. The
*Song of Roland* had been born.

Of course, the history of Roland's death had never been
entirely forgotten, especially in France. It was known
through Dante, Ariosto, and Cervantes and through a
popular tradition still potent enough for Rouget de Lisle,
author of the "Marseillaise," to draw on it for another
revolutionary song, "Roland à Roncevaux," which had
the defiant refrain "Mourons pour la patrie."[2] Scholars
knew the account of the Pseudo-Turpin and of numer-
ous other medieval references to the exploits of Roland,
Oliver, and Charlemagne, and they knew that these
exploits had been the subject of chansons de geste,
including one version allegedly sung at Hastings by a
member of Duke William's household, sometimes
identified by the name Taillefer.[3] The best-known ac-
count was that offered by the twelfth-century Anglo-
Norman chronicler Wace, in his *Roman de Rou.* Wace
describes Taillefer singing the Normans into battle:

> Taillefer, qui mult bien chantout,
> sor un cheval qui tost alout,
> devant le duc alout chantant

> de Karlemaigne e de Rollant,
> e d'Oliver e des vassals
> qui morurent en Rencevals.[4]

(Taillefer, who sang very well, was mounted on a horse
that raced along, and he went in front of the duke sing-
ing of Charlemagne, Roland, and Oliver and the knights
who died at Roncevaux.)

The story of Taillefer's performance was noted by
Claude Fauchet in his influential *Recueil de l'origine de
la langue et poésie françoise* of 1581, by Voltaire, and
by the British antiquarians Thomas Percy and Joseph
Ritson, for whom it evoked the power and fascination
of a lost oral tradition.[5] This lost work was what so
many early scholars hoped to find, not just another
poem about Charlemagne and his twelve peers, but the
very song of Taillefer.

By Michel's day, the search for this work had already
been going on for some time. In 1777, the marquis de
Paulmy, chief editor of the *Bibliothèque universelle des
romans,* a popular series devoted to summaries of
"romances," published an account of the stories of Char-
lemagne and Roland based on the Pseudo-Turpin. In
this account Paulmy speculated that French troops go-
ing into battle might have sung the lost *Chanson de
Roland,* and he actually went so far as to offer a pos-
sible reconstruction, with the following refrain:

> Soldats François, chantons Roland;
> De son pays il fut la gloire,
> Le nom d'un guerrier si vaillant;
> Est le signal de la victoire.[6]

According to Paulmy, the *Chanson de Roland* could
scarcely deal with all of Roland's great deeds, and it
therefore chose to present him as a model to imitate.
His reconstruction praises Roland as a paragon: brave,
modest, obedient, a good Christian, a moderate drinker,
reluctant to seek a quarrel but a terror to his enemies—
all in all, a perfect officer and gentleman ("Roland fut
d'abord Officier, / Car il étoit bon Gentilhomme").[7]

Although Charles Burney was sufficiently impressed
that he reprinted "Soldats François" in its entirety and
provided music, for the most part the poem won little
praise.[8] It may have provided inspiration for Rouget de
Lisle when he composed his anthem "Roland à Ron-
cevaux," however, and it certainly drew renewed atten-
tion to the story. In 1814 Charles Nodier speculated in
the *Journal des débats* about the possible survival of
the epic in some library, and in 1831 Chateaubriand
suggested more specifically that fragments might
survive in one of the former royal libraries.[9] The search
to recover the work had begun in earnest. Although the
story of this search has been told by Léon Gautier and
Joseph Bédier among others, and will be familiar to
most Old French scholars, it is worth reviewing it once
more to see just how extensively a certain preconcep-

tion of what the poem should look like guided its discovery. For Gautier and Bédier this editorial history is the story of the discovery of a medieval poem. I will suggest that it is also the story of this poem's modern invention.

The earliest account of the story of Roland to draw on a specific medieval manuscript is that offered by Louis de Musset, marquis de Cogners, grand-uncle of the poet Alfred Musset, in his "Légende du bienheureux Roland, prince français" of 1817. Musset had access to what is now known as the Châteauroux manuscript and drew on it to retell the story of Charlemagne, Roland, and the Battle of Roncevaux.[10] Guyot des Herbiers, a family relation, began to prepare an edition of this manuscript, but died in 1828 without having finished.[11] It was not until 1832, when Louis-Henri Monin, a student at the Ecole normale, published his *Dissertation sur le roman de Roncevaux* that a full version of the poem at last appeared in print.[12] Monin based his edition on the Paris text (now Bibliothèque nationale de France, MS Français 860), which he compared with the Châteauroux manuscript, using the transcription of Herbiers.

For some time scholars had also been aware of the existence of an earlier version of a poem about Charlemagne and Roland in a manuscript in the Bodleian, although they were not quite sure what this poem was.[13] The poem appears to have been known to John Josias Conybeare, formerly professor of Anglo-Saxon at Oxford, who in 1817 announced his intention of publishing "some account of a poem on the well-known subject of the Rout of Roncesvalles" from an early manuscript but never actually did so.[14] Abbé Gervais de la Rue, who had worked in the Bodleian while in exile in England, also knew the Oxford poem, which he classified as "un *Roman de la bataille de Roncevaux* qu'on appelle encore le *Roman des douze pairs de France*."[15] He found it not without its interest, primarily for its age, and thought it a pity that Monin had not known of it, since it would have provided a fine example of the early state of Old French.[16] De la Rue actually published a few samples from the Oxford text in his *Essais historiques sur les bardes, les jongleurs et les trouvères*, and it is here that the famous opening lines first appear in print, although publication was delayed until 1834, years after he had examined the manuscript.[17] But de la Rue never connected the Oxford poem to Taillefer; indeed, he lamented that he had never been able to find even a fragment of Taillefer's song and poured scorn on those like Paulmy who claimed to have found traces of the song in later romances.[18] When Michel came to Britain in 1835, then, both French and British scholars had been dreaming of discovering Taillefer's lost performance for at least half a century, but nobody yet believed he had found it.

Guizot sent Michel to Britain as part of an extensive cultural mission to find fragments of early French literature and history.[19] As one of the many treatments of Charlemagne, the Oxford poem justified a trip up from London, where Michel was copying Gaimar's *Estoire des Engleis* and Benoît de Sainte-Maure's *Chronique des ducs de Normandie*. On 13 July Michel announced the discovery that would eclipse the rest of his voyage in a triumphant letter to his patron, Louis-Jean-Nicolas Monmerqué, a member of the Académie des Inscriptions et Belles-Lettres, and Monmerqué quotes from this "cri d'exultation jeté au moment d'une découverte" in his own letter to Guizot a week later. Michel believed he had found not just a poem about Roland that was older than any of the others that survived but something far more precious, a copy of the great lost chanson de geste of Taillefer itself:

> Je vous écris de la ville d'Alfred, à deux pas de la Bodléienne, où je viens de trouver . . . quoi? . . . Devinez! . . . La Chanson de Roland!! C'était presque la quadrature du cercle!

> Ce n'est autre chose que le *Roman de Roncevaux* rimant par assonances comme *marches, corages, vaille, homme* . . . etc., mais c'est le Roman de Roncevaux dans un manuscrit du commencement du XIIe siècle, et chaque couplet se termine par *aoi*, que vous m'expliquerez; ne serait-ce pas le cri *away*, cri d'élan sur l'ennemi?[20]

This letter was soon followed by a more cautious report to Guizot.[21] Here, too, Michel suggested the "AOI" might be a kind of battle cry, and in the title he adopted for his edition—a title that appears nowhere in the manuscript—he made the connection to Taillefer's lost battle song explicit:

> On peut croire aussi que, par ces mots **Chanson de Roland,** nous avons voulu donner à penser que nous regardions le poème de Turold comme étant celui dont Taillefer chanta des morceaux à la bataille d'Hastings. Nous ne cacherons point que nous avons l'intime persuasion que le chant du jongleur normand étoit pris d'une chanson de geste; nous dirons même que cette chanson pourroit bien être celle de Turold.[22]

Over the years the fascination with Taillefer and his performance has faded or lost much of its scholarly credibility; but in its broad outlines, Michel's understanding of the poem in the Oxford manuscript remains in force to this day. This particular version of the poem, in its entirety, is imagined as a chanson, something that a minstrel might sing, chant, or recite. As Michel noted when queried on his imposition of the title, the work is clearly a chanson de geste and Roland its chief hero; although the title does not appear anywhere in the manuscript, it fits.[23]

Michel realized that he had made an important discovery, but his scholarly edition was not intended for a general readership and gives little sense of the widespread excitement the **Roland** would generate or of the role it would soon play in the canon of French literature.

Others made the larger claims for it. The **Roland** was hailed both by scholars and by the popular press as a national epic—"peut-être notre plus ancienne, notre véritable épopée nationale."[24] As such, the **Roland** filled an important lacuna: without its own epic, French literature could never match the classical tradition; with the publication of the **Roland,** it could. The need to reach a broader public was soon recognized, and in 1850 François Génin published a popular edition with a translation, the first major step toward enshrining the poem as a literary classic.[25] As Génin declared, "Désormais on ne reprochera plus à la littérature française de manquer d'une épopée: voilà le **Roland** de Theroulde."[26]

The search for Taillefer's song was not just about establishing a literary canon; it was part of a broader quest for a national literature to renew a languishing France. The social conflict of the Revolution and the demise of the First Empire brought a strong demand, often explicitly articulated, for poetry that would revitalize the country, restoring political harmony by evoking the lost glories and the nobler conduct of earlier times. This desire appears perhaps most forcefully in the eight-volume series *La Gaule poétique* of Louis Antoine François de Marchangy, a collection of historical sketches designed for the use of painters, sculptors, and poets, of which the first two volumes appeared in 1813.[27] Marchangy's romantic medievalism was part of a widespread resurgence of interest in things medieval (the following year, for example, saw the first French translation of Walter Scott's novels), but it also had strong nationalistic overtones.[28] Marchangy argued that medieval French history, and the courage and love of its knights, provided a noble exemplar for a poet of any nation.[29] Admittedly, for Marchangy, the Battle of Roncevaux was but one medieval topic among many; there were other battles, like Charlemagne's siege of Narbonne, and other heroes, notably Joan of Arc, who would serve an artist just as well. Roland's death at Roncevaux did, however, have a particular emotional force. France, as Marchangy had proclaimed, is greatest in her misfortunes, and courage is the one constant element in her history.[30] The story of Roland's reckless chivalry and noble defeat was ideally suited for the moral revival Marchangy envisaged.

For Marchangy the Middle Ages was a period of vibrant contrasts that could stir the poetic imagination, but it was also the age of chivalry and provided a moral code that might still be revived through new orders, decorations, and public ceremonies.[31] Later editors like Léon Gautier might find him risible—"On ne peut guère nommer sans rire M. de Marchangy et la *Gaule poétique*"[32]—but their visions of the Middle Ages were not that far removed from his, and their editorial projects shared much of his moral and nationalistic fervor. In the end it was to be the editors, not the poets, who would fulfill Marchangy's call for a literature of chivalric revival, not by writing poems but by shaping them.

Nineteenth-century philologists, conservative Catholics and staunch Republicans alike, shared a view of the Middle Ages as a period of simpler, nobler virtues, and that view played a crucial role in their editorial construction of medieval literature. They believed that the vigor of the simple, youthful age was matched by the vigor of a simple, youthful language, French before it became sophisticated, and they extolled Old French poetry as a kind of folk art, a direct expression of the national spirit, in a pure and original state, free of the corrupting influences of later civilization.[33] Sainte-Beuve, for one, praised Paulin Paris's early edition of *Berte aus Grans Piés* for its "naïveté charmante."[34] The *Chanson de Roland* would offer the preeminent example of such simplicity. In his edition of 1850 Génin expressed openly the qualities both critics and philologists were seeking: "Le caractère essentiel de l'épopée, c'est la grandeur jointe à la naïveté; la virilité, l'énergie de l'homme fait unies à la simplicité, à la grâce ingénue de l'enfant: c'est Homère."[35]

The *Chanson de Roland,* then, was more than just a literary monument. Its editorial construction was part of the quest for national origins that dominated French romantic philology. Gaston Paris insisted that while Old French literature could appeal to readers of the most diverse political temperaments, its recovery was nonetheless a unifying project inspired by piety toward the tradition of one's ancestors.[36] For Gautier, true epics always presuppose "l'unité de patrie, et surtout l'unité de religion."[37] The **Roland** soon became a symbol of the very spirit of France. For Ludovic Vitet, writing in 1852, "Roland, c'est la France, c'est son aveugle et impéteux courage."[38] As the century progressed, this totemic value increased. The threat of German scientific industrialism in both the military and scholarly fields, culminating in the humiliation of the Franco-Prussian War, strengthened the tendency to see the **Roland** as an expression of the French genius for doomed gallantry.[39] During the siege of Paris of 1870, Paris lectured on "La *Chanson de Roland* et la nationalité française" and called to his audience, "Faisons-nous reconnaître pour les fils de ceux qui sont mort à Roncevaux et de ceux qui les ont vengés."[40] Gautier in his edition of 1872 called the poem "La France fait homme." Writing "au milieu des malheurs de la Patrie," he drew attention to the poem's early patriotism as a direct rebuke to the Germans:

> Jamais, jamais on n'a tant aimé son pays. Et écoutez bien, pesez bien les mots que je vais dire, O Allemands qui m'entendez: IL EST ICI QUESTION DU XIe SIÈCLE. A ceux qui étouffent aujourd'hui ma pauvre France, j'ai bien le droit de montrer combien déjà elle était grande il y a environ huit cents ans.[41]

The *Roland* was given the highest form of official sanction when in 1880 it was assigned to students in *seconde*.[42] In 1900 a teacher from the prestigious Lycée Henri IV echoed the praise of three generations of French philologists when he told his audience at the academy for staff officers at Saint-Cyr, "*La Chanson de Roland* est notre *Iliade*."[43]

### SUNG EPIC AND THE SÉANCE ÉPIQUE

From the moment of its rediscovery this poem has been associated with minstrel performance; that is what it means to call it a song. Both its epic dignity as a French *Iliad* and its patriotic value as a repository of martial valor depend upon this classification. It has become an article of faith that the poem was recited by minstrels to largely illiterate knights in a series of linked sessions, so that over several days the audience might hear the poem in its entirety. Jean Rychner first suggested that these sessions might typically have extended for a thousand to two thousand lines, from dinner to dusk, and a figure in this range has been widely accepted.[44] Ian Short, in a popular edition, sums up the consensus:

> Véhiculés par des chanteurs spécialistes de la récitation (il s'agit des jongleurs), les poèmes épiques se déclamaient en fait, avec accompagnement musical et devant un auditoire, à raison de quelques 1000 à 1300 vers par séances. Epopées jongleresques, donc, à écouter, plutôt que textes épiques à lire.[45]

This epic dignity was closely associated with a vision of what the poem was, how it was received, and by whom. In his edition of 1872 Gautier described a wandering minstrel reciting a heroic epic at length while the isolated baron, a man of simple faith, and his knights listen enthralled:

> Ils se retrouvaient tout entiers dans ces vers. Cette poésie était faite à leur image. C'était le même feu pour la Croisade, le même idéal ou le même souvenir de la Royauté française et chrétienne, le même amour pour le sang versé et les beaux coups de lance. *Roland* n'est, pour ainsi parler, qu'un coup de lance sublime . . . en quatre mille vers.[46]

Edmond Faral echoes this association of epic simplicity with oral delivery, describing the jongleur as a wandering light that illuminates the monotonous life of the knights.[47] Faral recognizes that the jongleurs performed before all classes but insists that for that very reason they were obliged to stick to healthy old traditions and could not embellish, as later court-based minstrels could, so that their art retained its elemental simplicity.[48] Later scholars, such as Rychner, drawing on the work of Milman Parry, insist on the complexity of oral poetry rather than its simplicity but still maintain the connection between orality and epic.[49]

A major shift in the attitude to the poem comes with the work of Joseph Bédier and his insistence that the poem is primarily the work of a single artistic genius rather than the amalgamation of earlier materials. For Bédier, the beauty of the *Chanson de Roland,* like the beauty of Racine's *Iphigénie,* lies in its unity, and this unity came from the poet, Turold, who, in a flash of genius, discovered the central theme of the conflict between Roland and Oliver.[50] Bédier envisaged Turold as a man of letters, one who works "à sa table de travail," but his reassessment of the poem's composition did not cause him to reassess how it might have been delivered, a subject on which he is distressingly vague.[51] No one seems to have directly challenged the notion that the *Chanson de Roland* was performed by jongleurs, although some may have harbored suspicions. Eugene Vance, for example, has shown how the figure of Charlemagne embodies textual attitudes and argued that the final poem documents "a historical transition from an oral *épistémè* to one of writing."[52] Hans-Erich Keller and Gabrielle Spiegel have argued persuasively that the latter part of the poem, especially the trail of Ganelon, reflects the ideology of the Capetian monarchs as formulated by Abbot Suger of Saint-Denis, thus providing a possible milieu for a clerical writer.[53] All this might raise questions about how the final work would have been delivered, but the prevailing assumption that, as a chanson de geste, it actually was sung has not been seriously questioned. The oral performance of the text is central in Paul Zumthor's account of *mouvance,* in which the regular alteration between oral performances and free copyings and reworkings produces the flowing tradition; "le texte n'est que l'occasion du geste vocal."[54] For Peter Haidu, the Oxford manuscript of the poem, Digby 23, "freezes one instant of a fluid, ongoing oral tradition."[55]

For many modern readers the vision of the chanting minstrel is a crucial part of the experience of reading the poem. Zumthor's account of his own response brings this out clearly:

> I take down from my library an edition of the *Song of Roland.* I know (or assume) that in the twelfth century this poem was sung to a tune that, for all intents and purposes, I have no means of reproducing. I read it. What I have before my eyes, printed or (in other situations) handwritten, is only a scrap of the past, immobilized in a space that is reduced to the page or the book.[56]

To read and enjoy the poem, therefore, involves us in historical speculation. We are "forced to come up with an event—a text event—and to *perform* the text-in-action, and integrate this representation with the pleasure that we experience in reading—and take this into account, if the need arises, in our study of the text."[57] We hold a book in our hand, but we listen for a lost song.

The reconstruction of this surmised oral tradition formed a crucial part in the early construction of the poem. In *Les épopées françaises,* for example, Gautier describes in some detail the performance of a jongleur who sings a chanson de geste at a castle, and it is here that he introduces into Old French philology the notion of the "séance épique."[58] But it is in his study *La chevalerie* of 1895 that Gautier offers his fullest account of minstrel recitation. He describes a wedding feast:

> Au repas de noces . . . on avait invité trois jongleurs "chantants"; mais aujourd'hui on n'en entendra qu'un seul. Il est vrai que c'est le meilleur du pays et que, dans sa vie comme dans ses chants, il ne ressemble point aux autres. C'est un chrétien (ce seul mot suffit à son éloge), et qui regarde son métier comme une sorte de prêtrise de second ordre, encore auguste et presque sacrée. . . . "Que voulez-vous que je vous chante ce soir?" ditil en donnant son premier coup d'archet, vigoureux et sonore. L'hôte, réfléchit un instant, et répond: "Je viens d'avoir une idée, que je vous soumets. Au lieu de nous réciter ce soir une seule chanson (ce qui semble parfois un peu long), je vous prierai de nous chanter les plus beaux passages de nos plus beaux poèmes."[59]

Responding to this request, the jongleur works through a series of great moments in French epic. Finally, for the day is passing, he offers one last song, this time of Ogier the Dane recapturing Rome; but as the minstrel reaches the end and recounts the pope's triumphal entry, the barons are reminded of the religious politics of their own day. A voice cries out that Philip does not love Pope Innocent so well, the host speaks of their reconciliation, and this response brings the performance to a close:

> Ce mot termine l'après-midi, qui devenait longue. Le jongleur, très applaudi et très fêté, reçoit du seigneur un mulet d'Arragon et un bliaut en *paile* rouge.
>
> La séance épique est achevée; la nuit tombe.[60]

Gautier's imagination conjures up a lengthy recitation, one that continues throughout the afternoon until dusk. Admittedly, Gautier sees this recitation as exceptional, but his account presupposes two situations as norms: the performance of the less exalted "others," whom Gautier's minstrel in no way resembles, and who presumably offer more vulgar entertainment, command less strict attention, and play to humbler audiences, and that of the normal "séance épique," where a single minstrel would recite or sing a single epic in the great hall to an audience that might grow a little restless but would nonetheless provide him a reasonable chance to complete his song.

Gautier draws support from references to performance in the chansons de geste themselves, but his "séance épique" is actually modeled upon an eighteenth-century work, André Chénier's *L'aveugle,* and its account of an extended performance by Homer, in which the blind bard sings in succession the great moments of Hellenic epic. And, before returning to his account of the Middle

Ages, Gautier quotes from the beginning of Homer's song. The simple shepherds welcome the stranger, and he repays their charity by singing, while they listen rapt:

> Commençons par les dieux: Souverain Jupiter,
> Soleil, qui vois, entends, connais tout, et toi, mer,
> Fleuves, terre, et noirs dieux des vengeances trop
>   lentes,
> Salut! Venez à moi, de l'Olympe habitantes,
> Muses. Vous savez tout, vous déesses, et nous,
> Mortels, ne savons rien qui ne vienne de vous.[61]

Gautier objects only to Chénier's underlying paganism: "Ah! Si nous avions un Chénier qui, au lieu d'être païen dans ses moelles, fut vraiment chrétien et Français! un Chénier s'inspirant de **Roland**!"[62] So Gautier casts himself as Chénier's Christian surrogate and offers an elaborate fantasy of an honored minstrel's sustained performance. Echoing Homer's opening prayer to Jupiter and his stilling of nature, Gautier's minstrel begins, after a short exposition, with Charlemagne praying to God to stop the sun. In the 1895 edition the lines from Chénier appear directly beneath an engraving of this very scene, further emphasizing the parallel Gautier draws between the medieval and Homeric invocations. . . .

Like Chénier, Gautier offers a vision of social and spiritual integration in which audience, song, and singer become one. In the chivalric tradition this unity is achieved when the poet's words are re-embodied in the knights' valiant deeds. This continual cycle of chivalric narrative is figured in the Oxford poem itself when Roland says to his men:

> Or guart chascuns que granz colps [i] empleit,
> Mal[e] cançun de nus chantét ne seit!
>
> (Now let each man take care to deal great blows,
> Lest a bad song be sung of us!)[63]

But even before these lines were recovered from the Bodleian manuscript and brought into wider circulation, the image of the unified band of warriors linked in song was powerful. As I have shown, Paulmy, in one of the earliest modern evocations of the lost *Song of Roland,* imagined it as the marching song of the Norman soldiers. The image remains strong through the nineteenth century and beyond. It is not just Gautier who sees the Roland as "un coup de lance sublime." Génin refers to Homer and Turold as "[g]uerriers comme poëtes," whose grandeur lay in their simplicity.[64] Charles Lenient notes that *geste* can refer not just to a deed but to a noble group, linked "non pas seulement par les liens du sang, mais par la communauté d'exploits et de caractères," the **Chanson du Roland** forming the noblest of such heroic genealogies.[65] In these accounts the epic material merges with the warrior class it celebrates in the full embodiment of oral tradition.

In this vision of medieval culture the orality of the epic is crucial. Gautier's baron, with his "simple, vigorous, almost brutal" faith and his simple pleasures, untainted by gallantry, cannot read. The epic, as Gautier understands it, matches its audience in the purity of its primitivism:

> L'époque qui leur convient, ce sont uniquement les temps primitifs, alors que la Science et la Critique n'existent pas encore, et qu'un peuple tout entier confond ingénument l'Histoire et la Légende. Une je ne sais quelle crédulité flotte alors dans l'air et favorise le développement de cette poésie que la science n'a point pénétrée, que le sophisme n'a point envahie. Les siècles d'écriture ne sont pas faits pour ces récits poétiques qui circulent invisiblement sur les lèvres de quelques chanteurs populaires . . . on ne lit pas ces épopées: on les chante.[66]

The grandeur of oral epic is thus part of the long history in which writing marks a fall from some lost state of primal unity. In the jongleur's song the political body of early France is reconstituted, spiritually, racially, and politically.[67] The epic is not read, it is sung.

### THE MANUSCRIPT

The simplest means of connecting the 4,002 verses preserved in Bodleian Library, Digby 23, to this putative performance history is to claim that Digby 23 itself once belonged to a minstrel or jongleur.[68] This is exactly what Léon Gautier did when he distinguished between the great illuminated manuscripts of the late Middle Ages and the earlier and simpler ones of the twelfth century, which he called "manuscrits de jongleur," a category in which he included Digby 23.

What is striking about this classification is how widely it has been accepted when even a cursory examination of the codex raises the gravest doubts. The classification of Digby 23 as a "manuscrit de jongleur" went unchallenged until 1932, when Charles Samaran, in his introduction to the facsimile edition, offered the first full codicological description of the manuscript, in the process raising doubts about Gautier's identification. Samaran agreed with Gautier that Digby 23 is a cheap and somewhat worn manuscript, composed of poorly prepared parchment that was carelessly ruled, but he also pointed out that careless compilation, small size, and the wear and tear that suggests widespread circulation are not alone sufficient grounds for associating a manuscript with a jongleur. There are numerous Latin manuscripts that are equally carelessly executed and equally battered. Samaran noted as well that the Digby copyist shows little familiarity with French epic material, frequently confusing the names of the great heroes, and that the unknown reviser shows even less, which tends to suggest that neither the copyist nor the reviser was a jongleur.[69]

This leaves the possibility that the Oxford manuscript was written by a cleric for the use of a jongleur. The difficulty here is that Digby 23 is in fact a composite volume; the second half is the *Roland,* but the first half is a glossed copy of Chalcidius's translation of the *Timaeus,* complete with diagrams. . . .[70] Since the *Timaeus* scarcely seems likely reading material for a jongleur, the possibility that the *Roland* belonged to a jongleur rests to a large extent on how early the two sections were bound as one. Both date from roughly the same period, sometime in the twelfth century, but earlier commentators believed that the two had only been brought together at a late date.[71] Samaran, however, noted that a thirteenth-century hand had added several verses from Juvenal's eighth Satire on one of the flyleaves, folio [74]r, suggesting that by this point the *Roland* section of the manuscript belonged to someone who knew Latin, and that the same hand added what Samaran believed to be the word "Chalcidius" on the last page of the *Roland,* folio [72]r, suggesting that by this point the two sections had been united.[72] As Samaran points out, Juvenal and Chalcidius are hardly the kinds of material one would associate with a jongleur. The possibility that at some earlier point the manuscript might have belonged to a jongleur cannot be entirely ruled out, but there is nothing about the manuscript to encourage such a speculation. Digby 23 is a cheap, portable volume; jongleurs were itinerant and were not wealthy—that, and the prevailing assumption that the poem must be associated with a jongleur, is all the basis there has ever been for Gautier's classification of Digby 23 as a minstrel's manuscript. Since the first century of the manuscript's circulation remains largely unaccounted for, the classification cannot be disproved; but it is based not on a consideration of the codicological evidence but on an almost willful indifference to it.

A closer investigation of the manuscript can provide glimpses of the world in which the poem probably circulated and even suggest some of the ways in which it might have been enjoyed. This evidence does not bear directly on the question of whether the *Roland* was sung before knights in the manner of the "séance épique," but it does suggest something of the range of ways in which the poem might have been delivered as well as illustrating the sophistication of at least one baron and the interpretation of clerical and chivalric culture—all points the traditional understanding of the poem tends to deny or at least to minimize. The first approach is through the copyist, who writes a hand that has often been criticized for its awkwardness (Fig. 3). M. B. Parkes attributes this awkwardness to the scribe's attempts to modify a large bookhand, of the kind used for Bibles and Psalters, to the demands of the smaller reading text, and he provides other examples of comparable hands in small single-column manuscripts, many of which seem to have emanated from the Norman or Anglo-Norman schools. The scribe, Parkes suggests, may well have been "someone trained in the schools, who found service as chaplain or clerk in a bishop's *familia* or a baronial household."[73] The conjunction of "worldly-oriented clerics and a sophisticated, urbane baronry" that was particularly marked in England, and which has been offered as one reason for the strength of the Anglo-Norman hagiographic tradition, ensured that there were households where the *Roland* might have found an audience.[74]

Orderic Vitalis has left us a picture of one such household, that of Hugh of Avranches, earl of Chester and one of William the Conqueror's chief supporters, who surrounded himself with "swarms of boys of both high and humble birth."[75] At many of these courts it was the custom when the knights and squires were gathered to have selected members read aloud from some improving book. At Hugh's court this was the responsibility of the chaplain, Gerold:

> To great lords, simple knights, and noble boys alike he gave salutary counsel; and he made a great collection of tales of the combats of holy knights, drawn from the Old Testament and more recent records of Christian achievements, for them to imitate. He told them vivid stories of the conflicts of Demetrius and George, of Theodore and Sebastian, of the Theban legion and Maurice its leader, and of Eustace, supreme commander of the army and his companions, who won the crown of martyrdom in heaven. He also told them of the holy champion, William, who after long service in war renounced the world and fought gloriously for the Lord under the monastic rule. And many profited from his exhortations, for he brought them from the wide ocean of the world to the safe harbour of life under the Rule.[76]

As Marjorie Chibnall notes, these legends represent "a point in eleventh-century culture where hagiography shaded into epic and even romance."[77] Numerous legends circulated about the deeds of the warrior saints Demetrius, George, and Theodore, and there was a chanson de geste of the life of St. Eustace.[78] The "holy champion William" can only be Guillaume d'Orange, also known as Guillaume Courtnez, second only to Charlemagne and Roland among the heroes of Old French epic. The story of Roland would have suited a similar collection admirably. Roland, too, was a "holy champion," often regarded as a saint.[79] If the twelfth-century Digby copyist was indeed "someone trained in the schools, who found service as chaplain or clerk in a bishop's *familia* or a baronial household," his career would have been very similar to that of Gerold, and he might well have used the Digby *Roland* to entertain and improve his own patron's household, just as Gerold used his "great collection of tales" to entertain and improve Hugh's.

Certainly there are numerous passages in the poem that deliver an emphatic moral, such as Archbishop Turpin's address to the knights before their last battle, which the poet appropriately enough calls a sermon:

> Franceis apelet, un sermun lur ad dit:
> —Seignurs baruns, Carles nus laissat ci;
> Pur nostre rei devum nus ben murir.
> Chrestïentét aidez a sustenir!
> Bataille avrez, vos en estes tuz fiz,
> Kar a voz oilz veez les Sarrazins.
> Clamez voz culpes, si preiez Deu mercit!
> Asoldrai vos pur voz anmes guarir.
> Se vos murez, esterez seinz martirs:
> Sieges avrez el greignor pareïs.

(Lines 1126-35)

(Turpin addressed the Franks and gave them a sermon. "Charles has placed us here. It is our duty to die well for our king. Help Christianity to survive! There will be a battle, you may be sure, for you can see the Saracens with your own eyes. Confess your sins and call on God for mercy! I will absolve you to save your souls. If you die, you will be holy martyrs and will have a seat in paradise.")

Here the poem presents an exalted vision of those who fight, but it ensures that religious counsel is incorporated into this vision through the figure of Turpin, a prince of the church who is also a mighty warrior and who combines the two roles with absolute moral certainty.

There are numerous other passages where one can easily hear a chaplain's voice ringing out with moral conviction, reciting lines that tell of the triumph of militant Christianity and attribute the final defeat of the Saracens to divine intervention: "Pur Karlemagne fist Deus vertuz mult granz, / Car li soleilz est remés en estant" ("For Charlemagne God performed a great deed, for he stopped the sun" [lines 2458-59]). Like the saints' lives, the *Roland* tells of miracles, faith tested through violence, and the triumph of bellicose Christianity over its opponents. What is harder to imagine is a chaplain delivering one of the innumerable blow-by-blow descriptions of slaughter, such as *laisse* 104, in which Roland finally draws Durendal:

> La bataille est merveilluse e cumune.
> Li quens Rollant mie ne s'asoüret;
> Fiert de l'espiét tant cum hanste li duret:
> A .xv. cols l'ad <e> fraite e perdue;
> Trait Durendal, sa bone espee, nue,
> Sun cheval brochet, si vait ferir Cher[n]uble.
> L'elme li freint u li carbuncle luisent,
> Trenchet le [chef] e la cheveleüre,
> Si li trenchat les oilz e la faiture,
> Le blanc osberc, dunt la maile est menue,
> E tut le cors tresqu'en la furcheüre.
> Enz en la sele, ki est a or batue,
> El cheval est l'espee aresteüe:
> Trenchet l'eschine, hunc n'i out quis jointure,
> Tut abat mort el pred sur l'erbe drue.
> Aprés li dist:—Culvert, mar i moüstes!
> De Mahumet ja n'i avrez aiude.
> Par tel glutun n'ert bataille oi vencue.

(Lines 1320-37)

(The battle was fierce, and all were engaged. Count Roland did not hold back. He struck with his spear as long as its shaft remained, but he broke it completely by the fifteenth blow. He drew out the naked blade of Durendal, his good sword, spurred on his horse, and struck Chernuble. He cut through his helmet, where the carbuncles shone, and through his head and his hair. He cut through his eyes and his face, his shining mail hauberk, and all his body, to the trunk, and then into his saddle, which was decorated with gold, and into his horse and through its spine, without looking for the joints. He left both dead in the thick grass. Then he said, "Wretch, you did wrong to come. You will never have aid from Mohammed. Battle will never be won by such a coward.")

It is much easier to imagine these lines being delivered by a minstrel or jongleur, who could supply appropriately histrionic gestures and perhaps even go so far as to twirl a sword (as Taillefer is said to have done in one account).[80] As we shall see, however, there are grounds for serious doubt about whether minstrels or jongleurs ever had much opportunity to deliver more than short fragments. If we wish to imagine the conditions under which the poem might have been delivered more or less in its entirety, we must think in terms of someone like the chaplain Gerold, however much this may clash with the clichés of medieval culture we have inherited.

At least a century must pass until we get evidence that ties the manuscript to a specific owner. On an opening leaf of the *Timaeus,* folio [2]r, there is an inscription in a thirteenth-century hand informing us that one Master Henry of Langley bequeathed it to the Augustinian canons of St. Mary of Oseney.[81] Master Henry is in all probability the Henry Langley who was a canon and prebendary of the king's free chapel in Bridgnorth Castle, Shropshire, and who disappears from the surviving records by 1263.[82] If this is the same Henry Langley, he was a lucky man. The prebends of Bridgnorth were worth in the neighborhood of twelve pounds a year and were often used for rewarding valued royal servants such as the king's physician or the clerks of the wardrobe, who held at least five of them during the mid-thirteenth century. This attractive sinecure was one that Henry would have acquired through the influence of his father, Geoffrey.

While Henry remains largely a cipher, his father was notorious. Geoffrey Langley was chief justice of the king's forest, one of the king's most trusted counselors, an infamous purchaser of land, and at one point possibly the most hated man in England. According to Matthew Paris, he was stingy and "lessened as far as possible the bounty and accustomed generosity of the royal table."[83] Geoffrey fought in the Gascon campaign of 1242-43 and was promoted on his return, rising to chief justice of the forest in the year 1250. In this position he enforced the harsh forest laws with unusual vigor.[84] In 1254, as a senior member of the king's council, he was put in charge of the English and Welsh

lands of Prince Edward. His high-handed treatment of the Welsh has often been cited as one of the causes of the rebellion of 1256.[85] It would have been Geoffrey's influence that would have won his son the lucrative prebendary. There is no evidence to link Geoffrey Langley directly with the Digby manuscript (and even his son probably owned only the *Timaeus*), but Geoffrey is an interesting figure in his own right, in part because he stands in such stark contrast to the recurring image of the medieval baron as a semiliterate noble savage. Geoffrey was skilled not just in political and legal machinations but also in the business of land speculation in an inflationary economy. He was one of those larger landholders who made a fortune by lending money to lesser knights who were living off fixed rents and then acquiring their lands through foreclosure, a practice that led to increased social tensions, culminating in the Barons' Revolt of 1263, when Langley's lands were among the first to be pillaged.[86] The money generated by this aggressive speculation was presumably part of what supported his son in his comfortable prebendary at Bridgnorth, where he could read of the celestial harmonies described in the *Timaeus.*

It is not clear quite when the two parts of the manuscript were joined. Henry's name appears only in the opening ex libris, but this appears, on paleographical grounds, to be much later than the word "Chalcidius" or the verses of Juvenal; that is, it comes after the two parts are thought to have been brought together. For what it is worth, Samaran dates the word "Chalcidius" and the verses from Juvenal to the thirteenth century, but with such short examples it is hard to be sure.[87] The joint manuscript might just possibly have belonged to Henry Langley, but it could equally well have belonged to one of the Austin canons, possibly a friend of Henry's, in which case the canons kept Henry's name in remembrance for at least a few generations and then entered his name.

At first it might appear that the two halves of the manuscript have little in common and that their juxtaposition is of interest only as a reflection of the possibly idiosyncratic taste of an early owner. Indeed, some scholars have been at pains to disassociate the two even further, suggesting that the conjunction is largely accidental and that the canons kept the **Roland** out of respect for a donor or simply to add weight to the collection, rather than out of any desire to actually read the poem.[88] Yet the two parts are closer in spirit and form than they might seem. Both are scholars' books, plain, cheap, unadorned texts written in a single column, and they belong to the same cultural milieu. The first, the *Timaeus,* was copied by a Norman, or northern French, scribe, probably in the schools, and was intended for the use of a scholar; in the hands of this scholar, or one of his colleagues, the book made its way to England, where, roughly a century later, we find it in the hands of a royal prebendary. He donates it to the Austin canons living on the outskirts of Oxford, who had regular dealings with students, renting them housing and possibly hearing their confessions.[89] The second, the **Roland,** was copied by an Anglo-Norman scribe, who might well have received his training in the French schools; its format is a little simpler than that of the Digby *Timaeus,* but it, too, may have been intended for a scholar—in its rough script and simple format it resembles cheap copies of Boethius, Cicero, Seneca, and Juvenal, as well as other copies of the *Timaeus.* It is hardly that surprising then to find this book in the hands of the Austin canons of Oxford a century later. The *Timaeus* and the **Roland** might seem to belong to different worlds, but the Norman and Anglo-Norman scribes who copied them lived in the same one.

The northern French and Anglo-Norman clergy were closely connected. There was regular contact between the Norman schools and England; Parkes notes, for example, that the canons of Laon raised money by appealing to their English alumni in 1113.[90] Norman scribes provided England with a steady flow of books during the century after the conquest.[91] As for the clergy's military interests, one need go back only seven years, to the scandals surrounding the election of the bishop of Laon in 1106, to see how strong they could be. The successful candidate was Gaudry, chancellor of Henry I, who, if we are to believe Orderic Vitalis, acquired the bishopric, although he was only in minor orders, because he took Duke Robert of Normandy prisoner at the Battle of Tinchebrai.[92] Guibert de Nogent condemns Gaudry as "more of a soldier than a clerk. . . . In word and manner he was remarkably unstable, remarkably lightweight. He took delight in talk about military affairs, dogs, and hawks, as he had learned to do among the English."[93] The disputes between Bishop Gaudry and his rivals ultimately led to a revolt of the commune, in which "the bishop and the people who were aiding him fought [the attackers] off as best they could by hurling stones and shooting arrows."[94] If soldiers could become clerics and clerics could fight like soldiers, it is scarcely surprising that clerics enjoyed reading or hearing of deeds of arms. Indeed, the interpenetration of chivalric and clerical culture is a commonplace of medieval scholarship—and I would not labor the point were it not that the modern construction of medieval literature has so often tacitly assumed that the two were quite distinct.

The Digby scribe appears to have had at best a limited knowledge of epic material, judging by his misspellings of famous names, but not all clerics were so ill informed. Saints' lives were often recited by minstrels, while clerics told stories of the lives of knights.[95] According to his biographer, Abbot Suger kept his monks awake in this way: "As he was a most cheerful man, he would tell them of the deeds of strong men, sometimes in his own compositions, sometimes in those of others, recounting deeds which he had either seen or learned about, and sometimes he would continue until the middle of the night."[96] Medieval preachers often referred to the epic heroes and their *gesta* to stir up their audience or drive home a point—thus providing one of the major sources of evidence for the circulation of these stories. Orderic may have been shocked by the frivolities of jongleurs, but his work is filled with allusions to Charlemagne, Roland, and the legends of Troy and Thebes; and he often echoes the themes and conventions of the chansons de geste,[97] just as a preacher in thirteenth-century Paris "made a habit of referring to the deeds of Charlemagne, and Roland, and Oliver to stir up his listeners."[98] Although the references may have been scornful, the preacher could scarcely have made them without some knowledge of the epic stories. Similarly, Hugh of Avranches's chaplain Gerold was not the only cleric to sing the praises of Guillaume d'Orange. Orderic tells how Anthony, a monk from Winchester, "complying with our eager desire," brought the story of Guillaume to Orderic's monastery of St. Evroul one winter, and how Orderic managed to copy only part of it because of the cold.[99] The monks of Saint-Guilhem-le-Désert identified their founder, a Count William, with Guillaume d'Orange; and when, in about 1122, they composed a life of their founder as a means of supporting their claim to independence, they drew on the chansons de geste to flesh out his story.[100] The library of St. Augustine's, Canterbury, contained four copies of the *Gesta Guydonis de Warewik in Gallico* as well as a *Gesta Guydonis de Burgundia in patria lingua,* a story of Charlemagne's knight Guy of Burgundy that survives in French but not in English.[101] The Benedictines of Peterborough owned a book "de bello Vallis Runcie cum aliis Gallice."[102] The combination of clerical and chivalric interests in Digby 23 was in no way anomalous.

Of course, any effort to reconstruct medieval reading practice must be highly tentative, but the manuscript does suggest a coherent and not implausible story of how the poem might have been delivered. It suggests that the Oxford **Roland** was never far from clerical hands, and that it may have had something of the status of a saint's life, serving as an inspirational moral poem to read aloud, or possibly even to chant, to the canons and their guests at the refectory. John Stevens notes that "a very likely occasion for the recitation or chanting of a saint's life would be when the monks were gathered in the refectory—in silence, be it remembered—for meals."[103] Perhaps, on occasion, it was read by a canon himself, for this cheap volume could easily have been one canon's private property.[104] This is the reading history that has been almost systematically rejected, so that the song can be preserved in all its martial and national purity as a French epic.

The attitude of Old French scholars to the Digby manuscript has been curiously conflicted. On the one hand, there has been a determined effort to preserve the classification of Digby 23 as a *manuscrit de jongleur,* since this preserves the text's status as a close reflection of an oral performance for a chivalric audience. At the same time, the French poem must be extracted from the English manuscript and saved from its taint, which means that although the actual words on its pages are reproduced with scrupulous care, the manuscript as a social document is dismissed as soon as possible. As a result there are a large number of Old French scholars, from Léon Gautier to Paul Zumthor, who have pronounced on the status of the manuscript without ever examining it closely.

With the **Roland** the taint of writing is compounded by the taint of the foreign and the provincial. It is a singular embarrassment that the earliest written version of France's national epic survives in an manuscript copied by an Englishman in an Anglo-Norman dialect, and it was imperative that the early editors distance the true, original, and national poem from this corrupt witness.[105] Gautier confronts the problem in his first edition, claiming that "le dialecte d'un manuscrit est le fait du copiste, et non point de l'auteur. C'est dans le fond, et non dans la forme de la Chanson, qu'il convient donc de chercher ici quelque lumière."[106] In his school edition of 1887 he takes a curiously convoluted path, insisting on his fidelity to the manuscript ("jamais UN SEUL MOT n'a reçu une forme orthographique QUI NE SOIT PAS OFFERTE PAR LE MANUSCRIT D'OXFORD,") while at the same time undertaking to restore more than five hundred lines to produce "un texte conforme aux lois de notre dialect."[107] L. Clédat "francisized" the vowels in his edition of 1886 on the grounds that the **Chanson de Roland** was "d'origine *française.*"[108] Joseph Bédier, the poem's most prolific editor and popularizer after Gautier, was highly critical of such normalization, but he, too, distinguished between the original poem and the actual written text that survives, "une tardive transposition en français insulaire d'une œuvre écrite d'abord dans un autre idiome."[109] Thus the manuscript was effectively dismissed in favor of the pristine original. As one admirer put it, "After the work of Bédier no one again will surely ever dispute that the **Chanson de Roland,** French in language and French in spirit, was a product of the essential genius of France."[110]

Samaran's doubts about the function of the Digby manuscript have not prevailed. We call the poem it contains the **Chanson de Roland,** accepting the title Michel first provided, one that occurs nowhere in the manuscript. We refer to the words preserved in this specific manuscript, and we mean that these words, with some variation, were once sung, as Gautier's minstrel sang them, in a great hall one long afternoon or through a series of repeated performances.

## Was There Ever a *Song of Roland*?

Given the pressing need of postrevolutionary France for a national epic, had the **Chanson de Roland** not existed, it would have been necessary to invent it, much as Marchangy demanded French poets and artists invent new works by drawing on medieval subjects. And the **Chanson de Roland** was, if not invented, at the very least, constructed. By supplying it with an appropriate epic title, isolating it from its original codicological context, and providing a general history of minstrel performance in which its pure origin could be located, the early editors presented the 4,002-line poem as sung French epic, fashioning the poem they desired.

There is, then, an important sense in which if there ever was such a work as the **Chanson de Roland,** it does not survive. If the 4,002 lines now preserved in the Digby manuscript ever were a minstrel's song, that is not what they were in the manuscript during the twelfth century when they were copied, nor during the thirteenth, when they came to rest alongside the *Timaeus.* If there ever was a **Song of Roland,** it was not the late Anglo-Norman "transposition" but an earlier poem in a slightly different dialect. But this raises a further question. Was there ever such a song, a song of 4,002 lines that was recited or sung by a minstrel and that more or less corresponded to the version preserved in the Digby manuscript? This in turn depends on whether there ever was a tradition of extended or serial recitation in which a work of this kind could have been performed.

Now there is no doubt that minstrels performed poems about the deeds of epic heroes, including Roland, and that these were often called chansons de geste. In a much-cited passage in his early-thirteenth-century penitential, Thomas of Chobham, subdean of Salisbury, writes of three classes of *histriones*: those who distort their bodies through shameful gestures, those who follow the courts of great lords and speak shameful and opprobrious things of those who are not there, and those who play on musical instruments. This third category he then subdivides into those who sing songs that provoke lasciviousness and those "who sing of the deeds (*gesta*) of great men and the acts of saints," whom he calls *joculatores.*[111] Of course, Chobham was a scholastically trained theologian, not an ethnological reporter, but there are enough surviving references to confirm his picture of the range of what minstrels might do, even if few real minstrels could be fitted so neatly into this rationalized grid. The work of Gautier and Faral, who gathered many of the passing references to minstrel performance in sermons and chronicles as well as romances and epics, has now been supplemented by scholars such as Christopher Page, who has brought to light much evidence from sermons and sermon literature from Paris, and all of this material provides abundant references to minstrels singing of Roland.[112] When the

Dominican Daniel of Paris preached in the city in 1272, for example, he mentioned that "A great deal is sung about Roland and Oliver," but that their blows were as nothing to that of St. Martin when he divided his cloak in two.[113] One anonymous sermon goes so far as to specify location and audience response: "When the voice of the jongleur on the Petit Pont [variant: 'in the streets'] tells how those mighty ancient warriors, namely Roland and Oliver and the others, were slain in battle, the people who are standing nearby are moved to pity and sometimes to tears."[114] The examples could be multiplied.

Nor is there any shortage of references that specify that the minstrels *sang* of these heroes.[115] *La vie de seint Josaphaz,* for example, refers scornfully to those who would much rather hear someone sing of Roland, Oliver, or the *douz pers*:

> Ke plus tost orrium chanter
> De Rolant u d'Oliver,
> E les batailles des duze pers
> Orrium mut plus volenters.[116]

When minstrels, or characters who assume the guise of minstrels, boast of their repertoire, one of their most common claims is that they can sing of Roland. Renart, disguised as an English minstrel, assures a patron:

> Moi saver bon chançon d'Ogier,
> Et d'Olivant et de Rollier
> Et de Charlon le char chanu.[117]

Gilles de Paris, in his twelfth-century *Carolinus,* writes:

> De Karolo, clari praeclara prole Pipini,
> Cujus apud populos venerabile nomen in omni
> Ore satis claret et decantata per orbem
> Gesta solent melicis aures sopire viellis.[118]

(The deeds of Charlemagne, the most famous offspring of famous Pepin, whose name is venerated by the people, sounds in every ear, and is sung throughout the world, are accustomed to lull the ears to the accompaniment of melodious viols.)

There are numerous other references to *gesta* being delivered to the accompaniment of instruments, most commonly the viol, and the chansons de geste and saints' lives often refer to themselves as being sung.[119] Of course, these expressions are often largely formulaic and "sing" might mean no more than "tell" or "recite," but some references furnish additional details.[120] The *Roman de la Violette* (1225), for example, tells how the hero sings twenty-four lines about Guillaume Courtnez from the chanson de geste *Aliscans* "a clere vois et a douch son."[121] The late-twelfth-century troubadour Guiraut del Luc claims that one of his sirventes was written "el son Beves d'Antona," suggesting not only that some version of the story of Bevis of Hampton was sung, but that this tune was distinct enough to be bor-

rowed.[122] It is even possible to re-create some of the lost music.[123] Then there is the evidence for the singing of saints' lives, which may have resembled that of the chansons de geste.[124]

There can be little doubt, then, that there existed a tradition of singing about the great epic heroes, including Roland. What is troubling is that the numerous references to minstrel performance at secular festivities such as chivalric feasts never suggest that this singing lasted very long.[125] A case in point is the famous description of the wedding feast of the count of Archimbaud and a Flemish princess, Flamenca, in the Provençal romance that bears her name. After the second feast of the day is over and the tables cleared, the guests are brought fans and cushions. Now is the time for the fifteen hundred jongleurs who are in attendance to perform:

> Apres si levon li juglar;
> Cascus se volc faire auzir.
> Adonc auziras retentir
> cordas de manta tempradura.
> Qui saup novella violadura,
> ni canzo ni descort ni lais,
> al plus que poc avan si trais.
> L'uns viola[.l] lais del Cabrefoil,
> e l'autre cel de Tintagoil;
> l'us cantet cel dels Fins Amanz,
> e l'autre cel que fes Ivans.
> L'us menet arpa, l'autre viula;
> l'us flaütella, l'autre siula;
> l'us mena giga, l'autre rota;
> l'us diz los motz et l'autre.ls nota;
> l'us estiva, l'autre flestella;
> l'us musa, l'autre caramella;
> l'us mandura e l'autr'acorda
> lo sauteri ab manicorda;
> l'us fai lo juec dels bavastelz,
> l'autre jugava de coutelz;
> l'us vai per sol e l'autre tomba;
> l'autre balet ab sa retomba,
> l'us passet sercle, l'autre sail;
> neguns a son mestier non fail.

(Lines 592-616)

(Afterwards the jongleurs rose up, each one wanting to make himself heard. Then you could hear many tunes. Anyone who knew a new tune for the viol, whether a *canzo* or a *descort* or a *lai,* tried more than ever. One played on the viol the *lai* of Chevrefeuil; another that of Tintagel; one sang that of the Noble Lovers, and the other of the deeds of Yvain; one played the harp and the other the lute; one played jigs and one played the rote; some sang the words and some the notes; one played the flute and one the fife; one the mandolin, the other the accompaniment; one played the psaltery and one the monocord; one makes games with marionettes; the other juggles knives; one leaps on the ground and the other tumbles; one jumps; one dives through hoops; nobody fails at his craft.)[126]

We have here the full range of minstrelsy: the music of all conceivable instruments, storytelling to musical accompaniment of various kinds, and tumbling and jug-gling. The noise of the fifteen hundred jongleurs fills the hall:

> Cascus dis lo mieil[z] que sabia.
> Per la rumor dels viuladors
> e pel brug d'aitans comtadors,
> hac gran murmuri per la sala.

(Lines 706-9)

(Each sings as best as he knows. With the sound of the viol players and of each of the storytellers, there was a great noise in the hall.)

Some lines earlier, the poet stresses equally the wealth of choice of stories that the guests were offered.

> Qui volc ausir diverses comtes
> de reis, de marques e de comtes,
> auzir ne poc tan can si volc.

(Lines 617-19)

(He who would hear diverse accounts of marquesses and kings and counts may hear as many as he wants.)

It is possible that the jongleurs are conceived as reciting well-known passages from famous works, but equally possible that the songs they are singing would have borne only the most tangential connection to the famous poems about the same heroes that have survived. In either case, their performances do not appear to have been of any duration. Soon the king calls for the guests to join him in jousting and then dancing. The situation is utterly different from that imagined by Gautier in his account of the *séance épique*.

This passage from *Flamenca* is filled with names famous in French literature: the heroes of all five of Chrétien's romances are mentioned, and Yvain is referred to by the title Chrétien gives him, the Knight of the Lion. The "lais del Cabrefoil" might be Marie de France's *Chevrefeuil*. Yet under these conditions, the jongleurs could not have expected to deliver even one of the Old French *lais,* let alone an Arthurian romance, or a large section from a chanson de geste. The time was too short and the status of any single performer too lowly. As Joseph Duggan notes, it does not seem "that the author of *Flamenca* meant his readers to imagine the jongleurs presenting the works in question in their entirety or in an orderly fashion."[127] At such a feast, no single jongleur could expect to command the attention of any but a small group of guests and even that not for long.

Nor are the circumstances depicted in *Flamenca* such as to permit the jongleur to work through a longer piece over a series of performances. The jongleurs and their audience have been assembled to add dignity to a single ritual occasion; once the feast is complete, they will disperse. To the extent to which *Flamenca* offers a cred-ible depiction of the performance conditions at a royal feast, the implication is that the minstrel versions of *lais,* chansons de geste, or romances differed radically from those that have been preserved in manuscript. As Page notes, "short melodic *fragments* of the *chanson de geste* . . . seem to have loomed large in the repertory of French professional *viellatores* during the thirteenth century."[128] The controversial question would be whether their repertory also included full-length versions or was always limited to fragments.

The example of *Flamenca* is telling because it does seem to reflect established chivalric ceremonial, albeit filtered through literary conventions of plenitude that exaggerate the numbers of minstrels. Accounts of historical feasts, when they survive, show that the number of minstrels was considered a reflection of the dignity of the occasion. A hundred and nineteen minstrels appear on the pay record for the feast held for the knighting of the English Prince Edward in 1302, for example, and of these over 80 are explicitly classified as musicians.[129] Few other feasts are as well documented, but large numbers of minstrels are recorded: 426 minstrels were paid for performing at the marriage of Princess Margaret to John of Brabant in 1290.[130] Nor did the more exalted minstrels who attended the great feasts necessarily stay in the area much longer than those in *Flamenca.*[131]

In fact, the feast was perhaps the least suited of all these occasions for extended recitation. The audience was often disruptive, and there was too much competi-tion; the more prestigious the occasion, the more competition there would be.[132] Humbler situations might have been easier for the performer. At an isolated castle, priory, or country house, or at a village gathering, a jongleur would have stood a better chance of holding the sustained attention of the entire audience, as he does in Gautier's vision. Even here he would have been obliged to modify and curtail his performance to retain interest and suit the occasion.

This, indeed, is a recurring accusation against jongleurs, that they distort the truth by singing whatever they think will please their listeners. Chrétien de Troyes, for example, in the introduction to *Eric et Enide,* accuses "those who live by telling stories" of corrupting the story:

> d'Erec, li fil Lac, est li contes,
> que devant rois et devant contes
> depecier et corronpre suelent
> cil qui de conter vivre vuelent.[133]

(The tale is about Eric, the son of Lac [and it is one] that those who live by telling stories are accustomed to break apart and corrupt in front of kings and nobles.)

The term "depecier" could be taken to mean no more than that the *conteurs* are accustomed to mangle a good story; but taken more literally, it accuses them of break-ing the story into pieces, which is exactly what perform-ers must often have been obliged to do as they anticipated and played upon their audience's response.[134] The story of Taillefer, however legendary it may be, provides a more plausible instance of what an actual performance at a wedding feast might have been like than Gautier's vision of the dignified *séance épique.* Under normal conditions, a jongleur might hope to sing fifty, or a hundred, or at best a few hundred lines, with little prospect of picking up where he left off.

This is not to claim that the notion of sustained recita-tion is merely the product of the romantic imagination. The main source of evidence is the chansons de geste themselves. Zumthor notes that "Plusieurs textes font allusion à l'heure de la déclamation: on commence après déjeuner, on finit avant la nuit tombée."[135] In fact, explicit allusion to the time of performance in Old French epic is not that common, and much discussion has focused on a single example, that of *Huon de Bor-deaux,* where the narrator tells his audience that it is growing dark and that he is getting thirsty and will stop for the night, but that if they pay him well enough he will return on the morrow:

> Segnor preudomme, certes, bien le veés,
> Pres est de vespre, et je sui moult lassé.
> Or vous proi tous, si cier com vous m'avés
> Ni Auberon ne Huon le membré,
> Vous revenés demain aprés disner;
> Et s'alons boire, car je l'ai desiré.[136]

> (Lords, certainly, you see well that it is almost evening and I am very tired. I pray you all, as you love me, or Auberon, or the renowned Hugh, to come back tomor-row after dinner. Let's go and drink, for that is what I wanted.)

Apparently they do return, but not with quite enough money, for the narrator resumes the tale but after only five hundred lines stops to make his pitch again, this time threatening to use the power of Oberon, the fairy king, to excommunicate those who did not fill his purse when his wife brings it around:

> Or faites pais, s'il vous plaist, escoutés;
> Se vous dirai cançon, se vous volés.
> Je vous dirai, par les sains que fist Dés,
> Me cançon ai et dite et devisé,
> Se ne m'avés gaires d'argent donné.
> Mais saciés bien, se Dix me doinst santé,
> Ma cançon tost vous ferai definer.
> Tous chiaus escumenie de par m'atorité,
> Du pooir d'Auberon et de sa disnité,
> Qui n'iront à lour bourses pour ma feme donner.[137]

> (Be silent please and listen. If you like I will tell you a chanson. By the saints God made, I will tell you the chanson that I have told and devised if you give me lots of money. Know well, if God gives me health, I will soon finish my song for you. All those who will

not dip into their purses to give to my wife I excom-municate by the authority given to me by the power of Auberon and his dignity.)

Here would seem to be a persuasive example of sequential performance.[138] But the example is not without difficulties. It is clearly impossible for a poet to predict in advance just when a jongleur might find it appropriate to appeal to his audience, so a jongleur would be singularly ill advised to attempt to deliver *Huon de Bordeaux* verbatim. If we are to read the ap-peals as strictly functional, therefore, the only plausible explanation seems to be that the lines were copied directly from a specific live performance in which a particular jongleur improvised them. As Duggan argues, this scene "requires us to imagine a scenario in which an orally composed text was taken down from live performance."[139] However, there is little evidence to suggest that this kind of ethnographic reporting was at all common in the Middle Ages.[140] It was not that the technology was lacking: although full systems of shorthand were not developed until the sixteenth century, the combination of systems of heavy abbrevia-tion, such as those first developed in Tironian notes, with a trained memory certainly allowed for detailed *re-portationes* of sermons.[141] But the desire to reproduce an authentic transcription of a specific oral performance, down to its appeals for drink and money, reflects concerns for ethnographic exactitude that would be surprising in a medieval cleric.[142]

The alternative explanation is that a text like *Huon de Bordeaux* is not a transcription but an evocation of an oral performance and that the jongleur narrator and his listeners are a fiction, just as implied audiences so often are.[143] This possibility has frequently been suggested for later periods.[144] Michel Zink, for example, in his recent history of French literature, notes that written texts can preserve the oral style: "The indications of oral enuncia-tion—an appeal to the audience, a request for silence, an announcement that the performer is going to break off in order to pass the hat, to rest, or to get a drink— were carefully recopied in the silence of the *scripto-rium.* The artifice is patent."[145] It is the word "artifice" that may help explain why Zink, like so many others, accepts these references as literary conventions when they occur in romances but takes them more literally when they occur in the chansons de geste, which he classifies earlier in his history as "sung narrative po-ems."[146] Artifice is exactly what the chanson de geste, as the direct expression of a simpler age, cannot have. This is the scandal of the canons of Oseney, the scandal of English clergymen reading the **Roland**—not just that they are the wrong audience, but that they reveal all too clearly that even at this early period the writer's audi-ence is indeed a fiction.

I have argued that minstrel recitation was usually short and subject to interruption and, more controversially, that the very notion of sustained recitation is a nostalgic myth and that such recitation rarely occurred, unless it entailed a cleric reading, or possibly even chanting, from a book. How disruptive is such a suggestion? It tends to support those, from Bédier on, who see the *Roland* as essentially a writerly composition. It presents a direct challenge to those, such as Zumthor, who assume a relatively stable textual core that, at some stage, is being sung more or less in its entirety. This is not to reject the idea of *mouvance* but to suggest that its classic formulation underestimates how brutally the lines would be altered as they moved between page and song.[147] My position with regards to oral-formulaic theory is similar. I would accept that the *Roland*'s paratactic and formulaic style ultimately derives from the practice of oral composition.[148] The external evidence of performance practice certainly suggests that the jongleurs must have been capable of considerable improvisation (and thus would have drawn on formulaic systems). I would insist, however, that the written chansons de geste differed radically from these short performances and cannot be regarded as transcriptions of them. Oral-formulaic scholars might resist an argument that places the surviving *Roland* so far from a minstrel's song, but most would now admit, however reluctantly, that a literate poet may compose in an oral style and that the presence of a high level of formulaic density cannot tell us how a given poem was composed or transmitted.[149] At the same time, the notion of tradition has become more complicated and powerful, and the audience has been credited with an ever more important role in maintaining and shaping that tradition. John Miles Foley, for example, argues that the "heightened exchange and intelligibility" of a poetic tradition depends on "a working fluency on the part of not only the performer, but also and crucially the audience and then reader."[150] The evidence of fragmented minstrel performance encourages us to place a similar emphasis on the role of the audience, thinking in terms of *viellatores* who delivered snatches of song about Roland while the audience's knowledge of the overall story provided the governing context. What I wish to stress is that the extended versions of the chansons de geste, the ones that come down to us, were essentially clerical creations, that they were not just copied, but compiled and delivered by clerics, since only if it took the form of a written text would a poem have the prestige or authority to command a listener's attention for four thousand lines.

It is the social status of the text that is the crux of this problem. There is no doubt that oral performers in certain societies, by relying on improvisational systems, trained memories, or some combination of the two, can compose and deliver poems of great length and complexity. What is not clear is whether minstrels of the high Middle Ages could command an audience's attention for the same length of time. The evidence of medieval performance practice is frustratingly tenuous,

and it would seem dangerous to rule out on the basis of an argument *ex silentio* the possibility that on occasion some minstrels recited at length. But, unlike the presence of minstrels and their music, without which no chivalric feast was complete, extended recitation does not appear to have been regarded as a central part of chivalric ceremonial. Passages like the one in *Flamenca* that describe a plethora of apparently short performances are numerous, but for an account of anything approaching the full *séance épique* we must turn to the nineteenth century.

As we have seen, the image of the *séance épique* comes in large part from Gautier's response to André Chénier's evocation of Homer's Orphic performance. But the nostalgia for an age when oral recitation could unite society and restore true chivalry did not originate with Gautier or the anxieties of nineteenth-century France. It is layered upon texts that are themselves already nostalgic for lost origins and a simpler and nobler time. As Gabrielle Spiegel argues, the thirteenth-century Pseudo-Turpin offered the beleaguered Flemish aristocracy an image of "a lost, idealized world of chivalric potency and aristocratic valor," displacing "to a fictive past aristocratic anxiety over a world in social confusion."[151] This may explain why these written texts preserve such strong traces of systems of oral delivery. The Anglo-Norman clerics who copied, read, and heard the Digby *Roland* may have found in both its themes and its style an image of a simpler, nobler time, when they might have been closer to the knightly audience the text evokes.

The notion of *The Song of Roland,* inherited from the nineteenth-century editors and still remarkably tenacious, appeals to a vision of social union in which a band of warriors reconstitutes itself by its attendance at a dignified ritual. This account stresses the power of oral culture but limits its extreme fluidity, giving the song some of the stability of a book; subtending this vision is an implicit social history in which esteemed jongleurs recite monumental national epics for hours upon end, with only slight breaks, so that the epic is transformed gradually over the years rather than brutally from day to day or moment to moment. Without the stability of the *séance épique,* the breach between written transmission and oral delivery widens even further, the forms of performance become more varied, and the relation between oral and written streams can even become hostile, as it is in Chrétien de Troyes's account of the *conteurs* who break and corrupt the true story.

Just as the very possibility of extended oral poems of quality is difficult to comprehend within a literate culture, whose images of aesthetic achievement are deeply grounded in the fixity of writing, so is the fragmentation of minstrel performance. If it was only rarely that listeners could hear a complete version of a poem, and then only when it was supported by the authority of a book, how could the story become a common point of reference for predominantly illiterate societies? It requires an imaginative leap to conceive of a "text" that does not have a relatively stable core but exists as a social property, a series of retellings with no single point of origin performed for communities in which the well-known lines have immense evocative power. We can, however, gain some sense of this broader circle of tellings through its traces—in sculptural programs, in stained glass windows, in the names given to children and to churches, and in local traditions that survived into the eighteenth century.[152] Given such wide circulation, a medieval audience could have supplied the context for even a short fragment from the greater story.

Was there a **Song of Roland**? There were *songs* of Roland, certainly: cantilenas, chansons de gestes, gestes: short songs whose broader context existed in the minds of the people. There was a *tradition* of Roland, transmitted in a stream of tellings and retellings that was as broad as chivalric culture, and the short fragments were given meaning by this broader tradition. There is a *poem* of Roland, a major epic that incorporates the formulae of the oral performer into the fixity of the literary form and whose formal unity and cultural authority are both dependent on the authority of the book. This poem, the one that survives in the Oxford manuscript, might better be termed the *legend* of Roland, a bellicose Christian poem, suitable for reading aloud in the refectory or the hall. But was there an epic *song* of 4,000 lines in oral circulation? The evidence of performance conditions that we have is, admittedly, allusive and fragmentary, but it does form a reasonably coherent picture. It suggests that minstrel recitation was common, both at chivalric feasts and in the marketplace, but that, at least on most occasions, it was short and subject to extreme duress. Under these conditions, the sustained recitation necessary to give a 4,000-line poem voice as song would scarcely have been possible.

### Notes

1. Michel's edition (Paris, 1837) is now available in reprint (Geneva, 1974). Michel mentions his debt to Guizot on p. xvii; the history of the project is laid out more fully by Léon Gautier in *La chanson de Roland, texte critique accompagné d'une traduction nouvelle et précédé d'une introduction historique* (Tours, 1872), pp. clxix-clxxiii, and by Joseph Bédier in "De l'édition princeps de la *Chanson de Roland* aux éditions les plus récentes: Nouvelles remarques sur l'art d'établir les anciens textes," *Romania* 63 (1937), 433-69, and 64 (1938), 155-244 and 489-521.

2. On the history of "Roland à Roncevaux," see Gautier, *Chanson de Roland,* p. clxi, and Harry Redman, Jr., *The Roland Legend in Nineteenth-*

*Century French Literature* (Lexington, Ky., 1991), pp. 29-31. Redman provides an invaluable guide to the interest in Roland among French poets, men of letters, and cultural administrators from the late eighteenth century to the First World War. On popular traditions of Roland in France after the Middle Ages see Gaston Paris, *Légendes du moyen âge* (Paris, 1903), chap. 1, and J. P. Picquet, *Voyage dans les Pyrénées françoises* (Paris, 1789), pp. 285-86, who claims that those living in the region around Tarbes went on regular pilgrimages to Roncevaux and Blayes and still told stories about Roland.

3. William of Malmesbury in his *De gestis regum Anglorum* (ca. 1125), Geffrei Gaimar in his *Estoire des Engleis* (ca. 1139), Henry of Huntington in his *Historia Anglorum* (ca. 1150), and Benoît de Sainte Maure in his *Chroniques des ducs de Normandie* (ca. 1175) all refer to such a performance (*Willelmi Malmesberiensis monachi de gestis regum Anglorum libri quinque,* ed. William Stubbs, Rolls Series 90 [London, 1887-89], vol. 2, book 2, par. 242; *L'estoire des Engleis by Geffrey Gaimar,* ed. Alexander Bell, Anglo-Norman Texts 14-16 [Oxford, 1960], lines 5265-5302; Henry of Huntington, *Historia Anglorum,* ed. Thomas Arnold, Rolls Series 74 [London, 1879], p. 202; Benoît de Sainte Maure, *Chroniques des ducs de Normandie,* ed. Carin Fahlin [Uppsala, 1951-54]], lines 39725 ff.). What may be the earliest reference to this performer comes in the *Carmen de Hastingae Proelio,* which refers to a "histrio" or "mimus" called "Incisor ferri," who rides out to taunt the Saxon troops juggling a sword, but makes no reference to his singing. Catherine Morton and Hope Muntz, editors of the *Carmen de Hastingae Proelio of Guy, Bishop of Amiens* (Oxford, 1972), pp. xv-xxx, argue that the work is indeed that of Bishop Gui (d. 1068), a position accepted by William Sayers, but disputed by R. H. C. Davis, "The *Carmen de Hastingae Proelio,*" *English Historical Review* 93 (1978), 242-61. See also D. D. R. Owen, "Epic and History: *Chanson de Roland* and *Carmen de Hastingae Proelio,*" *Medium Ævum* 51 (1982), 18-34. The different versions of the legend of Taillefer are discussed by William Sayers, "The Jongleur Taillefer at Hastings: Antecedents and Literary Fate," *Viator* 14 (1983), 77-88; David Douglas, "The *Song of Roland* and the Norman Conquest of England," *French Studies* 14 (1960), 99-116; and Hans-Erich Keller, "La chanson de geste et son publique," in *Mélanges de philologie et de littératures romanes offerts à Jeanne Wathelet-Willem,* ed. Jacques de Caluwé, special issue of *Marche Romane: Cahiers de l'A.R.U.Lg.* (Liège, 1978), pp. 257-85, an expanded version of his "Changes in Old French

Epic Poetry and Changes in the Taste of Its Audience," in *The Epic in Medieval Society: Aesthetic and Moral Values,* ed. Harald Scholler (Tübingen, 1977), pp. 150-77. On the practice of minstrels playing to inspire knights or advancing before them into battle, see Bernard Gitton, "De l'emploi des chansons de geste pour entraîner les guerriers au combat," in *La chanson de geste et le mythe carolingien: Mélanges René Louis,* 2 vols. (Saint-Père-sous-Vézelay, 1982), 1:3-19.

4. *Le roman de Rou de Wace,* ed. A. J. Holden, Société des Anciens Textes Français (Paris, 1971), 2:183, lines 8013-18.

5. Claude Fauchet, *Recueil de l'origine de la langue et poésie françoise: Rymes et romans. Livre 1er (Paris, 1581),* ed. Janet G. Espiner-Scott (Paris, 1938), p. 113; Voltaire, *Essai sur les moeurs et l'esprit des nations et sur les principaux faits de l'histoire depuis Charlemagne jusqu'à Louis XIII,* ed. René Pomeau, 2 vols. (Paris, 1963), 1:468; Thomas Percy, *Reliques of Ancient English Poetry,* ed. Henry B. Wheatley, 3 vols. (London, 1885), 3:354; and Joseph Ritson, "An Essay on Minstrels," first published in *Ancient Songs and Ballads* (London, 1790), and reprinted in *A Dissertation on Romance and Minstrelsy to Which Is Appended the Ancient Metrical Romance of Ywaine and Gawain* (Edinburgh, 1891), p. xxxvi. Arthur Johnston provides a fine introduction to the eighteenth-century British antiquarians in *Enchanted Ground: The Study of Medieval Romance in the Eighteenth Century* (London, 1964).

6. Antoine René de Voyer d'Argenson de Paulmy, "Fin de l'histoire de Roland," in *Bibliothèque universelle des romans . . .* (Paris, December 1777, sometimes numbered as volume 40), pp. 203-16 at p. 212). For a discussion see Redman, *Roland Legend,* pp. 24-28, and on the project in general see Roger Poirier, *La Bibliothèque universelle des romans: Rédacteurs, textes, public* (Geneva, 1977). Both Redman and Charles Burney (cited below, n. 8) reproduce the complete text.

7. Paulmy, "Fin de l'histoire de Roland," p. 215.

8. Charles Burney, *A General History of Music from the Earliest Ages to the Present Period (1789),* ed. Frank Mercer, 3 vols. (New York, 1957), 1:597-600. Another chivalric fighting song that also contains the refrain "Soldats français, chantons Roland," and may well be plagiarized from Paulmy, appeared in a small pamphlet of the kind known as "bibliothèque bleu" in about 1837 and may indicate a widespread popular circulation ("Roland: Chant Guerrier," number 2 in a collection identified by the first item, "Le ménestrel: Chansonnier pour 1837, chanté par Rousseau" [Paris, 1837]).

9. Charles Nodier, *Journal des débats* (8 January 1814), and François René de Chateaubriand, *Œuvres complètes* (Paris, 1859), 9:440, discussed in Redman, *Roland Legend,* pp. 3 and 76-77.

10. Louis de Musset, "Légende du bienheureux Roland, prince français," in *Mémoires et dissertations sur les antiquités nationales et étrangères,* 1 (Paris, 1817), pp. 145-71, esp. pp. 151-60; cf. 10:412-14. Musset's version is discussed by Redman, *Roland Legend,* pp. 4-7. The manuscript, formerly known as the Versailles manuscript, is now in the Bibliothèque municipale de Châteauroux. See Raoul Mortier, ed., *Les textes de la Chanson de Roland,* 1: *La version d'Oxford* (Paris, 1940), p. xi.

11. The manuscript's owner, the Swiss collector Antoine Jean-Louis Bourdillon, eventually produced a translation and an extremely free edition, *Le poème de Roncevaux, traduit du roman en français* (Dijon, 1840).

12. H. [Louis-Henri] Monin, *Dissertation sur le roman de Roncevaux* (Paris, 1832).

13. According to Michel, the first to reveal the existence of the manuscript was Thomas Tyrwhitt in one of the notes to his *Canterbury Tales* of 1778 (*Chanson de Roland,* p. vi). See Thomas Tyrwhitt, *The Canterbury Tales of Chaucer,* 3 vols. (Edinburgh, 1860), 3:302, n. to line 137421. As Bédier observed, "il convient d'abord de rendre homage à ce savant d'Angleterre qui, dès le temps de Georges III et de Louis XV, lut de bout en bout le poème" ("De l'édition princeps," p. 450).

14. *The Gentleman's Magazine* (August 1817), p. 103, col. 2. Josias's brother, William Daniel Conybeare, discusses the circumstances of this proposed publication in his introduction to the more limited version, *Illustrations of Anglo-Saxon Poetry* (London, 1826), which eventually appeared under both their names after Josias's death.

15. Gervais de la Rue, *Essais historiques sur les bardes, les jongleurs et les trouvères normands et anglo-normands,* 3 vols. (Paris, 1834), 2:58.

16. Ibid., 1:133 and 2:65.

17. Ibid., 2:60-62.

18. Ibid., 1:132-33.

19. See Guizot's account in his *Mémoires pour servir à l'histoire de mon temps,* 8 vols. (Paris, 1858-67), 3:177-84, 406, and 410. On Guizot's efforts to preserve both medieval documents and buildings, see Gabriel de Broglie, *Guizot* (Paris, 1990), pp. 171-74; Dominique Poulot, "L'archéologie de la civilisation," in *François Guizot et la culture*

*politique de son temps,* ed. Marina Valensise, Colloque de la Fondation Guizot-Val Richer (Paris, 1991), pp. 265-89; and C. O. Carbonelli, "Guizot, homme d'Etat, et le mouvement historiographique français du XIXe siècle," in *Actes du colloque François Guizot (Paris, 22-25 octobre, 1974)* (Paris, 1976), pp. 219-37 (at p. 221). Guizot's anglophile sympathies are discussed by Pierre Reboul, *Le mythe anglais dans la littérature française sous la Restauration* (Lille, 1962), pp. 286-98. Guizot himself had been an indefatigable editor of medieval chronicles, published in *Collection des mémoires relatifs à l'histoire de France,* 29 vols. (Paris, 1823-26).

20. Monmerqué's letter is reproduced by Bédier in "De l'édition princeps," pp. 464-65. The original in the Archives Nationales in the collection F 17 3296 and is stamped 8 August 1835.

21. Michel's two reports on his work in Britain were published in the *Journal des débats* 19 (September 1835) and the *Journal général de l'instruction publique* (26 October 1837), also published as *Rapports M. le Ministre de l'Instruction Publique sur les anciens monuments de l'histoire et de la littérature de la France qui se trouvent dans les bibliothèques de l'Angleterre et de l'Ecosse* (Paris, 1838). Whether Guizot recognized the broader importance of the Oxford manuscript is not clear. According to Gautier, Guizot "comprit toute l'importance de notre Chanson et désira la voir publiée en son texte original" *Chanson de Roland,* p. clxxiii), but Guizot makes only the most passing reference to Michel in his memoirs and does not even mention the Oxford *Roland.* See further W. Roach, "Francisque Michel: A Pioneer in Medieval Studies," *American Philosophical Society Proceedings* 114 (1970), 168-78, and Bédier, "De l'édition princeps," pp. 457-66.

22. Michel, *Chanson de Roland,* p. xi-xii.

23. Ibid., p. xi.

24. Xavier Marmier, review of Francisque Michel's edition in *Le monde* (originally published as *Le monde: Journal quotidien consacré à la politique, à la littérature, aux sciences, aux intérêts du commerce et de l'industrie*), 17 February 1837, p. [3], quoted by Joseph Duggan, "Franco-German Conflict and the History of French Scholarship on the *Song of Roland,*" in *Hermeneutics and Medieval Culture,* ed. Patrick J. Gallacher and Helen Damico (Albany, N.Y., 1989), pp. 97-106 (at p. 98). My discussion of the nationalist inspiration in the early editorial history of the *Roland* owes much to Duggan's study; see also Hans Ulrich Gumbrecht, "'Un souffle d'Allemagne ayant passé': Friedrich Dietz, Gaston Paris and the Genesis of National Philologies," *Romance Philology* 40 (1986), 1-37; Howard Bloch, "'Mieux vaut jamais que tard': Romance, Philology, and Old French Letters," *Representations* 36 (1991), 64-86; idem, "Naturalism, Nationalism, Medievalism," *Romanic Review* 76 (1986), 341-60; and Antoine Compagnon, *La Troisième République des lettres, de Flaubert à Proust* (Paris, 1983).

25. F[rançois] Génin, *La chanson de Roland: Poëme de Theroulde* (Paris, 1850). One of the most forceful calls for a more popular edition came from Ludovic Vitet, the former *inspecteur général des monuments historiques* in his review of Monin's and Génin's editions, "Chanson de Roland," *Revue des deux mondes* (June 1852; vol. 14, bound as vol. 2 for 1852), 817-64, esp. pp. 821-22.

26. Génin, *Chanson de Roland,* p. vi.

27. Louis Antoine François de Marchangy, *La Gaule poétique ou l'histoire de France considérée dans ses rapports avec la poésie, l'éloquence et les beaux-arts,* 8 vols. (Paris, 1813-17).

28. Useful background is provided by Janine R. Dakyns, *The Middle Ages in French Literature, 1851-1900* (Oxford, 1973), esp. pp. 10-15; Paul T. Comeau, *Diehards and Innovators: The French Romantic Struggle, 1800-1830* (New York, 1988), pp. 36 and 78; Michael Glencross, *Reconstructing Camelot: French Romantic Medievalism and the Arthurian Tradition* (Woodbridge, Suff., 1995); and, on the revival of "troubadour taste" in the second half of the eighteenth century, N. H. Clement, *Romanticism in France* (New York, 1939), pp. 95-99.

29. Marchangy, *Gaule poétique,* 3:214.

30. Ibid., 1:15 and 4:9.

31. Ibid., 6:463-64.

32. Gautier, *Chanson de Roland,* p. clxiii.

33. As Howard Bloch argues, much of the appeal of medieval literature was that it provided "a language of beginnings, a poetic vehicle that remains to its object invisible and, therefore, innocent, pristine, unencumbered by artifice, unmannered, and unrepressed" ("Naturalism, Nationalism, Medievalism," p. 347). Bloch discusses the fabliau as the "limit case" of this view of medieval writing as an unliterary literature in which signifier and signified, body and meaning, are united in *The Scandal of the Fabliaux* (Chicago, 1986), esp. pp. 6-10.

34. *Revue des deux mondes* 2 (1832), 598-600 (at p. 598).

35. Génin, *Chanson de Roland,* p. i. Cf. the lament of Edgar Quinet, "notre épique homérique . . . nous est encore inconnue comme si elle n'eût jamais

été" (*Rapport à M. le Ministre des travaux publics sur les épopées françaises du XIIe siècle restées jusqu'à ce jour en manuscrits dans les bibliothèques du roi et de l'Arsenal* [Paris, 1831], p. 21).

36. Gaston Paris, presidential address to the Société des Anciens Textes Français in the *Bulletin de la Société des Anciens Textes Français* 3 (1877), 53-58, esp. pp. 55-56.

37. Léon Gautier, *Les épopées*, 2nd ed. (Paris, 1878), pp. 10-11.

38. Vitet, "Chanson de Roland," p. 864.

39. See, for example, Charles Félix Lenient's critique of "le pangermanisme" and its "invasion" of learned societies, reviews, and universities in *La poésie patriotique en France au moyen âge* (Paris, 1891), pp. 10-11.

40. Gaston Paris, *La poésie du moyen âge: Leçons et lectures,* 7th ed. (Paris, 1913), p. 118.

41. Gautier, *Chanson de Roland,* p. lxxvi.

42. John F. Benton, "'Nostre Franceis n'unt talent de fuïr': The *Song of Roland* and the Enculturation of a Warrior Class," *Olifant* 6 (1979), 237-58 (at p. 237). See also Stephen G. Nichols, Jr., "Poetic Reality and Historical Illusion in the Old French Epic," *French Review* 43 (1969), 23-33 (at p. 23).

43. Lecture on the *Chanson de Roland* by Paul Lehugeur in *L'armée à travers les âges: Conférences faites en 1900* (Paris, 1902), p. 65, cited in Benton, "Enculturation of a Warrior Class," p. 237.

44. Jean Rychner, *La chanson de geste: Essai sur l'art épique des jongleurs* (Geneva, 1955), pp. 48-49 and 54.

45. Ian Short, ed. and trans., *La chanson de Roland* (Paris, 1990), p. 12. The figure of 1,000-1,300 lines was first suggested by Paul Zumthor (*Essai de poétique médiévale* [Paris, 1972], p. 457), who attributed it somewhat inaccurately to Jean Rychner.

46. Gautier, *Chanson de Roland,* p. lxxii.

47. Edmond Faral, *Les jongleurs en France au moyen âge* (Paris, 1910), p. 96.

48. Ibid., p. 221: "Ce qui caractérise la littérature, tant qu'elle est entre les mains des jongleurs, c'est sa vigueur et la richesse de son fonds, vertus fondamentales qui s'évanouiront lorsque, devenant l'affaire d'un public spécial et d'auteurs trop raffinés, elle voudra se faire plus ingénieuse qu'émouvante. . . ." See also p. 225.

49. Rychner, *La chanson de geste,* p. 17.

50. Joseph Bédier, *Les légendes épiques: Recherches sur la formation des chansons de geste,* 3rd ed., 4 vols. (Paris, 1926-29), 3:447-48.

51. As Alain Corbellari argues, Bédier "ne prend la peine de réellement préciser l'idée qu'il se fait du métier de jongleur" (*Joseph Bédier: Ecrivain et philologue* [Geneva, 1997], p. 362).

52. Eugene Vance, "Roland and the Poetics of Memory," in *Textual Strategies: Perspectives in Post-Structuralist Criticism,* ed. Josué V. Harari (Ithaca, N.Y., 1979), pp. 374-403 (at p. 400), and "Roland, Charlemagne, and the Poetics of Illumination," *Olifant* 6 (1979), 213-25, esp. p. 223.

53. Keller, "*La chanson de Roland* d'Oxford" (below, n. 71), and Gabrielle M. Spiegel, *The Past as Text: The Theory and Practice of Medieval Historiography* (Baltimore, 1997), pp. 120-25 and 138-62. Keller goes so far as to date the composition of the original northern French poem to the period of the Second Crusade (1147-49), when Suger was regent of France, or to its immediate aftermath. This argument requires a somewhat later dating of the manuscript than many would allow, but the dating remains far from precise (see further below, n. 71). Among other efforts to locate the proto-*Roland,* see Maurice Delbouille, *Sur la genèse de la Chanson de Roland (travaux récents-propositions nouvelles)* (Brussels, 1954), who dates it to ca. 1100 (p. 73) and locates the poet in the area near Chartres (p. 96).

54. Paul Zumthor, "Jongleurs et diseurs: Interprétation et création poétique au moyen âge," *Medioevo romanzo* 11 (1986), 3-26 (at p. 3). For his account of *mouvance* see esp. *Essai,* pp. 70-75; the book has now been translated by Philip Bennett as *Toward a Medieval Poetics* (Minneapolis, 1992).

55. Peter Haidu, *The Subject of Violence: The "Song of Roland" and the Birth of the State* (Bloomington, Ind., 1993), p. 136.

56. Paul Zumthor, "The Text and the Voice," *New Literary History* 16 (1984), 67-92 (at p. 71).

57. Ibid.

58. Gautier, *Les épopées,* 2:102-42 and, on the "séance épique," pp. 226-71.

59. Léon Gautier, *La chevalerie,* 3rd ed. (Paris, 1895), pp. 656-57.

60. Ibid., pp. 668-69.

61. Ibid., p. 658. Gautier quotes Chénier no further, but the lines that follow immediately afterwards illustrate the full Orphic power that Chénier attributed to Homer, as he stills nature and unites

man with his song. See André Chénier, *Œuvres complètes,* ed. Gérard Walter (Paris, 1950), p. 46. On this tradition, see Brian Juden, *Traditions orphiques et tendances mystiques dans le romantisme français (1800-1855)* (Paris, 1971; repr. 1984).

62. Gautier, *La chevalerie,* p. 658.

63. Cesare Segre, ed., *La chanson de Roland* (Milan and Naples, 1971), lines 1013-14. All further quotations from the poem are taken from this edition.

64. Génin, *Chanson de Roland,* p. ii.

65. Lenient, *Poésie patriotique* (above, n. 39), p. 24.

66. Gautier, *Les épopées,* 1:10-11.

67. Katie Trumpener, *Bardic Nationalism: The Romantic Novel and the British Empire* (Princeton, N.J., 1997), p. 3, describes an analogous vision in the works of Irish and Scottish antiquaries, who "reconceive national history and literary history under the sign of the bard." The bard's performance "binds the nation together across time and across social divides; it reanimates a national landscape made desolate first by conquest and then by modernization, infusing it with historical memory."

68. I offer here a summary of an argument I have laid out more fully in "The Myth of the Minstrel Manuscript," *Speculum* 66 (1991), 43-73.

69. The facsimile edition, *La chanson de Roland: Reproduction phototypique du manuscrit Digby 23 de la Bodleian Library d'Oxford,* with Samaran's introduction, was first published in a limited edition for the Roxburghe Club (Paris, 1932) and then by the Société des Anciens Textes Français (Paris, 1933).

70. For a discussion of this second section of Digby 23, see Paul Edward Dutton, "*Illustre ciuitatis et populi exemplum*: Plato's *Timaeus* and the Transmission from Calcidius to the End of the Twelfth Century of a Tripartite Scheme of Society," *Mediaeval Studies* 45 (1983), 79-119 (at pp. 99-101).

71. The most common paleographical dating of the *Roland* is the second quarter of the twelfth century, the date proposed by Samaran and accepted, with caution, by M. B. Parkes. Ian Short has argued for a date in the late twelfth century in "The Oxford Manuscript of the *Chanson de Roland*: A Palaeographical Note," *Romania* 94 (1973), 221-31, but his argument rests on a single feature, the so-called "*de* monogram," for which M. B. Parkes provides much earlier examples in "The Date of the Oxford Manuscript of *La chanson de Roland* (Oxford,

Bodleian Library, MS. Digby 23)," *Medioevo romanzo* 10 (1985), 161-75 (at pp. 162-63). Hans-Erich Keller has also long supported a date in the last quarter of the century, on the grounds of both paleography (the use of the form *í,* with an *accent aigu* and its similarity to the fragments of the *Roman de Brut* in Bodleian Library, MS Rawlinson D 913) and orthography (the form of the masculine past participle in *ee* seen in the word *truvee* in line 3986, which Mildred Pope finds occurring sporadically "from the later twelfth century on"). See Keller, "*La chanson de Roland* d'Oxford et son public," in his *Autour de Roland: Recherches sur la chanson de geste* (Paris, 1989), pp. 93-94 (a revised version of "The *Song of Roland* and Its Audience," *Olifant* 6 [1979], 259-74), and Mildred K. Pope, *From Latin to Modern French, with Especial Consideration of Anglo-Norman,* 2nd ed. (Manchester, Eng., 1952), p. 460.

72. Samaran, *La chanson de Roland,* pp. 26-27 and 24. Samaran's reading of "Chalcidius" is partly conjectural, since the bottom halves of the letters are lost in a fold and the writing is faded.

73. Parkes, "Date of the Oxford Manuscript," p. 174.

74. The phrase is that of William Calin in *The French Tradition and the Literature of Medieval England* (Toronto, 1994), p. 88, summarizing the argument of M. Dominica Legge, *Anglo-Norman in the Cloisters: The Influence of the Orders upon Anglo-Norman Literature* (Edinburgh, 1950) and *Anglo-Norman Literature and Its Background* (Oxford, 1963).

75. *The Ecclesiastical History of Orderic Vitalis,* ed. and trans. Marjorie Chibnall, 6 vols. (Oxford, 1969-78), 3:216: "Huic maxima semper adherebat familia, in quibus nobilium ignobiliumque puerorum numerosa perstrepebat copia." For a discussion of this account see Keller, "La chanson de geste et son publique" (above, n. 3), pp. 263-64.

76. *Ecclesiastical History,* 3:216: "Praecipuis baronibus et modestis militibus puerisque nobilibus salutares monitus promebat; et de ueteri testamento nouisque Christianorum gestis imitanda sanctorum militum tirocinia ubertim coaceruabat. Luculenter enim enarrabat conflictus Demetrii et Georgii, Teodori et Sebastiani; Mauricii ducis et Thebeae legionis, et Eustachii precelsi magistri militum cum sociis suis, qui per martirium coronari meruerent in coelis. Addebat etiam de sancto athleta Guillelmo, qui post longam militiam abrenunciauit seculo; et sub monachali regula gloriose militauit Domino. Multis igitur profuit eius exhortatio, quos ad tutam regularis uitae stationem e mundiali protraxit pelago."

77. *Ecclesiastical History,* 3:216-17, n. 3.

78. H. Delehaye, *Les légendes grecques des saintes militaires* (Paris, 1909), and Paul Meyer, "Fragment d'une vie de Saint Eustache," *Romania* 36 (1907), 12-28.

79. A thirteenth-century passional refers to "Sanctus Rolandus, comes et martyr in Roncevala." See Maria Chiara Celletti, "Rolando, Oliviero," in *Bibliotheca sanctorum,* 12 vols. (Rome, 1961-70), 11:303. On the twelfth-century canonization of Charlemagne and his appearance in English lectionaries, see Jeanne E. Krochalis, "History and Legend at Kirkstall in the Fifteenth Century," in *Of the Making of Books: Medieval Manuscripts, Their Scribes and Readers. Essays Presented to M. B. Parkes,* ed. P. R. Robinson and Rivkah Zim (Aldershot, Eng., 1997), pp. 230-56 (at p. 239).

80. Gerard Brault offers a fine discussion of this lost repertoire of gestures in "Oral Interpretation: The Gestural Script," in *The Song of Roland: An Analytical Edition,* 2 vols. (University Park, Pa., 1978), 1:111-15.

81. "Liber ecclesiae Sancte Marie de Oseneya, ex legato magistri Henrici de Langeleya." The few references we have to Henry Langley are collected by A. B. Emden, "A Biographical Register: Additions and Corrections," *Bodleian Library Record* 6 (1957-61), 677. Some other donations of books to Oseney are listed by David Postles, "The Learning of the Austin Canons: The Case of Oseney Abbey," *Nottingham Medieval Studies* 29 (1985), 32-43 (at p. 40), and the contents of the library are described by Neil Ker, *Medieval Libraries of Great Britain,* 2nd ed. (London, 1964), pp. 140-41. On the general character of the order, see J. C. Dickinson, *The Origins of the Austin Canons and Their Introduction into England* (London, 1950).

82. *The Victoria History of the Counties of England: A History of Shropshire,* ed. A. T. Gaydon, 2 (Oxford, 1973), p. 125.

83. *Matthaei Parisiensis monachi Sancti Albani chronica majora,* ed. Henry Richards Luard, Rolls Series 57, 7 vols. (London, 1872-83), 5:136-37: "regalis mensae minoravit pro posse dapsilitatem et consuetam curialitatem." See P. R. Coss, "Sir Geoffrey de Langley and the Crisis of the Knightly Class in Thirteenth-Century England," *Past and Present* 68 (1975), 3-37, and his edition *The Langley Cartulary,* Publications of the Dugdale Society 32 (Stratford-upon-Avon, 1980).

84. *Chronica majora,* 5:136-37. Coss describes Geoffrey as "a particularly odious forest justice" ("Sir Geoffrey de Langley," p. 30) but cites this passage in the chronicle as the only evidence.

85. According to Maurice Powicke, Geoffrey was one of several insensitive royal officials whose "indif-ference to Welsh customs and Welsh feeling" played into the hands of Llywelyn (*The Thirteenth Century: 1216-1307* [Oxford, 1953], p. 401).

86. Coss, "Sir Geoffrey de Langley," pp. 28-29.

87. Samaran, *La chanson de Roland,* p. 27; cf. Parkes, "Date of the Oxford Manuscript," p. 162.

88. See M. Dominca Legge's discussion of the manuscript in "Archaism and the Conquest," *Modern Language Review* 51 (1956), 227-29.

89. According to Legge, the chapters of the Austin canons suggest that the "Abbot of Oseney apparently had some jurisdiction over the students" (*Anglo-Norman in the Cloisters,* p. 67). See further H. E. Salter, *Chapters of the Augustinian Canons* (Oxford, 1922). Postles notes that Oseney abbey leased both halls and rooms to the scholars and allowed students who were not members of the order to use the refectory and cloister ("The Learning of the Austin Canons," pp. 32-33 and 37).

90. Parkes, "Date of the Oxford Manuscript," p. 172.

91. Anne Lawrence, "Anglo-Norman Book Production," in *England and Normandy in the Middle Ages,* ed. David Bates and Anne Curry (London, 1994), pp. 79-93, esp. p. 91.

92. *Ecclesiastical History* (above, n. 75), 6:90, discussed in *Self and Society in Medieval France: The Memoirs of Abbot Guibert of Nogent,* ed. John F. Benton (1970; repr. Toronto, 1984), p. 151, n. 3.

93. *Venerabilis Guiberti de vita sua sive Monodiarum libri tres,* ed. Georges Bourgin, *Guibert de Nogent: Histoire de sa vie (1053-1124)* (Paris, 1907), 3.4: "Galterius enim non clericum, sed militarem se semper exhibuerat. . . . In verbo namque et habitu, mire instabilis, mire levis extiterat. De rebus nempe militaribus, canibus et accipitribus loqui gratum habuerat, quod apud Anglos didicerat" (*Memoirs,* pp. 151 and 156).

94. *De vita sua* 3.8, "Porro episcopum insolens vulgus aggrediens, cum pro moenibus aulae prostreperet, episcopus cum quibusdam qui sibi opitulabantur, jactibus lapidum sagittarumque ictibus, quoad potuit, repugnavit" (*Memoirs,* p. 175).

95. Faral, *Jongleurs* (above, n. 47), pp. 168-77.

96. *Guillaume, Sugerii vita,* in *Œuvres complètes de Suger,* ed. A. Lecoy de la Marche (Paris, 1867), p. 389: "Narrabat vero, ut erat jocundissimus, nunc sua, nunc aliorum, quae vel vidisset vel didicisset gesta virorum fortium, aliquotiens usque ad noctis medium."

97. *Ecclesiastical History,* 1:37-38; 4:xxiv-xxvii; 5:xvi-xix; and 6:xxii-xxiv.

98. "Solent gesta Caroli, Rolandi et Oliveri referri ad animandum audientes." Cited by Edmond Faral, "A propos de la *Chanson de Roland*: Genèse et signification du personnage de Turpin," in *La technique littéraire des chansons de geste* (Paris, 1959), pp. 271-79, at pp. 277-78.

99. *Ecclesiastical History,* 3:218-19.

100. *Vita sancti Wilhelmi,* in *Acta sanctorum Ordinis Sancti Benedicti,* saec. IV, 1:72, and in *Acta sanctorum,* May, 6:798. In *Les légendes épiques* (above, n. 50) Joseph Bédier describes the struggle between Saint-Guilhem-le-Désert and its mother-house, the creative hagiography that was used to support their conflicting claims (1:100-147), and the monks' use of contemporary chansons de geste (1:124-47). See also Wilhelm Cloëtta, ed., *Les deux rédactions en vers de Moniage Guillaume,* 2 vols. (Paris, 1906-11), 2:21-53.

101. M. R. James, *The Ancient Libraries of Canterbury and Dover* (Cambridge, Eng., 1903), pp. lxxiii and 372, discussed in R. M. Wilson, *The Lost Literature of Medieval England,* 2nd ed. (London, 1970), pp. 110-11. The largest collection of French romances belonged to Thomas Arnold, a fourteenth-century monk of St. Augustine's, who also made an elegant copy of Ranulph Higden's *Polychronicon* (Cambridge University Library MS Ii.2.24).

102. Madeleine Blaess, "Les manuscrits français dans les monastères anglais au moyen âge," *Romania* 94 (1973), 344. The catalogue dates from the late fourteenth century.

103. John Stevens, *Words and Music in the Middle Ages: Song, Narrative, Dance and Drama, 1050-1350* (Cambridge, Eng., 1986), p. 247.

104. For examples of such portable personal volumes, which became more common in the thirteenth century, see Adelaide Bennett, "A Book Designed for a Noblewoman: An Illustrated *Manuel des péchés* of the Thirteenth Century," in *Medieval Book Production: Assessing the Evidence,* ed. Linda L. Brownrigg (Los Altos Hills, Calif., 1990), pp. 163-81; P. R. Robinson, "The 'Booklet': A Self-Contained Unit in Composite Manuscripts," *Codicologica* 3 (1980), 46-69; and Judith Tschann and M. B. Parkes, introduction to *Facsimile of Oxford, Bodleian Library, MS Digby 86,* EETS [Early English Text Society] SS 16 (Oxford, 1996).

105. See Bédier's critique of the "chasse aux anglo-normannismes" of earlier editors in "De l'édition princeps," pp. 490-91. Michael Camille notes a similar pattern in Gaston Paris's editing of the *Vie de Saint Alexis*: "Philological Iconoclasm: Edition and Image in the *Vie de Saint Alexis,*" in *Medievalism and the Modernist Temper,* ed. R. Howard Bloch and Stephen G. Nichols (Baltimore, 1996), pp. 371-401, esp. p. 383.

106. Gautier, *Chanson de Roland,* p. lxviii.

107. Léon Gautier, *La chanson de Roland,* Edition classique à l'usage des élèves de seconde (Tours, 1887), p. 1 (emphasis in the original).

108. L. Clédat, ed., *La chanson de Roland* (Paris, 1886), pp. i-ii (emphasis in the original).

109. Joseph Bédier, ed., *La chanson de Roland* (Paris, 1922), p. ii.

110. Douglas, "The *Song of Roland* and the Norman Conquest of England" (above, n. 3), p. 108.

111. *Thomae de Cobham: Summa confessorum,* ed. F. Broomfield, Analecta Mediaevalia Namurcensia 25 (Louvain and Paris, 1968), pp. 291-93. For commentary, see John W. Baldwin, *Masters, Princes, and Merchants: The Social Views of Peter the Chanter and His Circle,* 2 vols. (Princeton, N.J., 1970), 1:199-204, and "The Image of the Jongleur in Northern France around 1200," *Speculum* 72 (1997), 635-63 (at pp. 642-44); Christopher Page, *The Owl and the Nightingale: Musical Life and Ideas in France, 1100-1300* (London, 1989), pp. 19-33; Helen F. Rubel, "Chabham's *Penitential* and Its Influence in the Thirteenth Century," *PMLA* 40 (1925), 225-39; and Faral, *Jongleurs,* p. 67. Page dates the *Summa* as c. 1216 (p. 20); see also Baldwin, *Masters, Princes, and Merchants,* p. 139, n. 193.

112. See also Michael Chesnutt, "Minstrel Reciters and the Enigma of the Middle English Romance," *Culture and History* 2 (1987), 48-67, and Andrew Taylor, "Fragmentation, Corruption, and Minstrel Narration: The Question of the Middle English Romances," *Yearbook of English Studies* 22 (1992), 38-62.

113. Bibliothèque nationale de France, MS lat. 16481, fol. 17v, cited in Page, *Owl and Nightingale,* pp. 11 and 71-72.

114. Bibliothèque nationale de France, MS lat. 14925, fol. 132r, and MS lat. 3495, fol. 192r, cited in Page, *Owl and Nightingale,* p. 177: "Cum voce joculatoris, in parvo ponte [var. in plateis] sedentis, quomodo ille strenui milles antiqui, scilicet Rolandus et Oliverius, et cetera, in bello occubuere recitatur, populus circumstans pietate movetur et interdum lacrymatur."

115. Jacques Chailley, "Etudes musicales sur la chanson de geste et ses origines," *Revue de musicologie* 27 (1948), 1-27; Stevens, *Words and Music,* pp. 222-

34; J. Győry, "Réflexions sur le jongleur guerier," *Annales Universitatis Scientiarum Budapestinensis de Rolando Eötvös nominatae: Sectio philologica* 3 (1961), 47-60.

116. Chardri, *Josaphaz, Set dormanz und Petit plet: Dichtungen in der anglo-normannischen Mundart des 13. Jahrhunderts,* ed. John Koch (Heilbronn, 1879), lines 2933-36.

117. Lines 2853-55, cited in Faral, *Jongleurs,* p. 301.

118. Gaston Paris, *Histoire poétique de Charlemagne* (Paris, 1865), p. 106.

119. For an extensive listing of such references, see Christopher Page, *Voices and Instruments of the Middle Ages: Instrumental Practice and Songs in France, 1100-1300* (Berkeley, Calif., 1986), esp. appendices 2 and 3.

120. See the cautions of Sylvia Huot in "Voices and Instruments in Medieval French Secular Music: On the Use of Literary Texts as Evidence for Performance Practice," *Musica disciplina* 43 (1989), 63-113.

121. Stevens, *Words and Music,* p. 223.

122. Ibid. The story survives in the Anglo-Norman *Bueve de Hantone,* copied around 1200 and composed in *laisses*; the Middle English *Beues of Hamtoun*; and a fifteenth-century Irish tradition (see Wilson, *Lost Literature* [above, n. 101], p. 119).

123. J. van der Veen, "Les aspects musicaux des chanson de geste," *Neophilologus* 41 (1957), 82-100.

124. One of the richest sources is a troped epistle for the Mass of St. Stephen's Day, December 26, in Chartres MS 520 (destroyed during the bombing of 1944). This epistle includes a French life of St. Stephen in *laisses* beginning "Seignors, oiez communement car entendre poez brefment / la passion et le torment de saint Esteinvre apartement," which Jacques Chailley offered not only as an example of a musical performance of a vernacular life, but as a more general indication of how the saints' lives might have drawn on the office for their melodies. See Chailley, "Etudes musicales sur la chanson de geste," pp. 1-27, and Stevens, *Words and Music,* pp. 239-49.

125. One of the best-attested examples of extended performance is that of the minstrel Jehan of Beauvais, who, according to an episcopal cartulary, was "tenus de faire chanter de geste ou cloistre de l'eglise saint Pierre de Beauvez le jour de Noel, le jour de grans Pasques, et le jour de Penthecoustes depuis prime lasquie jusques atant qu'on com-

menche l'Evangile de la grante messe ou cas que il puet recouvrer de chanteur en le ville de Beauvez" (cited in Faral, *Jongleurs,* p. 45). Gautier discusses these arrangements at Beauvais at much greater length, citing several of the original documents, but curiously omits this vital passage (*Les épopées,* 2:180-83). At Pentecost the minstrel might have had two and a half hours or more in which to play. According to Andrew Hughes, "The time of day at which the services were held differs: the *horarium* for winter and summer was designed to accommodate the length of the days and nights. . . . However, we should know that on Sundays and feasts the principal Mass of the day was said after Terce" (*Medieval Manuscripts for Mass and Office: A Guide to Their Organization and Terminology* [Toronto, 1982], par. 115). On Christmas, Easter, and Pentecost, the difference between the end of prime (*prime lasquie*) and the main mass after terce would therefore have been two canonical hours, roughly 180 minutes at Pentecost, but only half that at Christmas (since daylight time was evenly divided into twelve hours regardless of the season). Since prime was not a lengthy office, and the minstrel might have begun as soon as the office was completed, rather than at the end of the hour itself, the time available might have been somewhat longer. I would like to thank Richard Gyug and Peter Ainsworth for guiding me through these matters.

126. *Le roman de Flamenca: Nouvelle occitane du 13e siècle,* ed. Ulrich Gschwind, 2 vols. (Bern, 1976). My translation draws on the translation of Merton J. Hubert in *The Romance of Flamenca,* ed. Marion E. Porter (Princeton, N.J., 1962), and on the notes in Gschwind's edition for the definitions of the musical instruments.

127. Joseph J. Duggan, "Oral Performance of Romance in Medieval France," in *Continuations: Essays on Medieval French Literature and Language in Honor of John L. Grigsby,* ed. Norris J. Lacy and Gloria Torrini-Roblin (Birmingham, Ala., 1989), pp. 51-61 (at p. 57).

128. Page, *Voices and Instruments,* p. 129, my emphasis.

129. Constance Bullock-Davies, *Menstrellorum multitudo: Minstrels at a Royal Feast* (Cardiff, 1978), p. 10.

130. Ibid., p. 12.

131. The minstrels who helped celebrate Edward's knighting on Whitsunday 1302 may have stayed in London until Thursday, when the king's granddaughter was to be married, but then the knights,

and presumably the minstrels as well, would have dispersed to ready themselves for the campaign against the Scots. Ibid., p. 175.

132. The account of two rival performers vying for attention in the thirteenth-century farce *Les deux bourdéors ribauz* provides a good example of how disruptive such behavior could be. See Gaston Raynaud, ed., *Recueil général et complet des fabliaux des 13e et 14e siècles imprimés ou inédits, publiés d'après les manuscrits par Anatole de Montaiglon*, 6 vols. (Paris, 1872-90), 1:1-12.

133. *Les romans de Chrétien de Troyes: Erec et Enide*, ed. Mario Roques (Paris, 1963), lines 19-22.

134. We may actually have one example of this, an account preserved at the end of a fifteenth-century Spanish chronicle of a performance of pieces from *El libro de buen amor.* If the short fragments are indeed the traces of a *joglar*'s performance, which is a plausible explanation but no certainty, than the *joglar* began by calling out to Jesus, then recited several short moral truisms, then offered short sections from *El libro de buen amor,* and finally ended with more truisms and a call for money. The text is reproduced by R. Menéndez Pidal, *Poesía juglaresca y juglares* (Madrid, 1924), pp. 462-67, who entitles it "Fragmentos del programa de un juglar cazurro." This attribution is questioned by A. D. Deyermond, *The Middle Ages, A Literary History of Spain* (London, 1971), p. 115.

135. Zumthor, *Essai,* p. 457.

136. Pierre Ruelle, ed., *Huon de Bordeaux* (Brussels, 1960), lines 4976-81. Passages in which jongleurs stop to ask for payment before continuing are more common. A good example occurs in some manuscripts of *Aliscans.* See Claude Régnier, ed., *Aliscans* (Paris, 1990), lines 4579-80.

137. *Huon de Bordeaux,* lines 5510-19.

138. One of the first to make this point is Martín de Riquer, "Epopée jongleuresque à écouter et épopée romanesque à lire," in *La technique littéraire des chansons de geste* (above, n. 98), pp. 75-84. Marguerite Rossi summarizes critical responses to the passage in *Huon de Bordeaux et l'évolution du genre épique au XIIIe siècle* (Paris, 1975), pp. 128-29.

139. Joseph Duggan, "Performance and Transmission: Aural and Ocular Reception in the Twelfth-and Thirteenth-Century Vernacular Literature of France," *Romance Philology* 43 (1989-90), 49-58 (at p. 51). An alternative possibility is that the jongleur dictated to a scribe but retained some oral conventions when he did so. Peter Haidu

envisages the "halting and continually interrupted dictation of an illiterate jongleur to a more or less distracted cleric inscribing what he heard (possibly not exactly what was being said, chanted, or intoned) on the parchment before him" (*Subject of Violence* [above, n. 55], p. 137).

140. Perhaps the closest example is Charlemagne's project to have the "ancient barbaric songs, which sing of the deeds and battles of ancient kings," copied down and committed to memory ("barbara et antiquissima carmina, quibus veterum regum actus et bella canebantur, scripsit memoriaeque mandavit," Einhard, *Vita Karoli Magni Imperatoris* 29, ed. and trans. Louis Halphen [Paris, 1923], p. 82). The passage is discussed by Michael Richter, *The Oral Tradition in the Early Middle Ages* (Turnhout, 1994), pp. 37-40.

141. A tenth-century copy of the notes attributed to Seneca, now in the British Library, provides a good example of their range. For discussion, see Jacques Stiennon, *Paléographie du moyen âge* (Paris, 1973), pp. 129-33. The standard survey is that of Arthur Mentz, "Die Tironischen Noten: Eine Geschichte der römischen Kurzschrift," *Archiv für Urkundenforschung* 16 (1939), 287-384, and 17 (1942), 150-303. For later examples and other methods of rapid transcription, see René Havette, *Les procédés abréviatifs et sténographiques employés pour recueillir les sermons à l'audition du XIIe au XVIIe siècles* (Paris, 1903); Giorgio Cencetti, *Lineamenti di storia della scrittura latina* (Bologna, 1954), pp. 353-475; and Paul Lehmann, *Sammlungen und Erörterungen lateinischer Abkürzungen in Altertum und Mittelalter* (Munich, 1929), who provides examples from as late as the fifteenth century.

142. Examples of meticulous recording of oral narrative occur, often in hagiographic or legal contexts, such as Bernard of Angers's reports of local accounts of the miracles of St. Foix in the early twelfth century or Bishop Fournier's inquisition into Montaillou between 1318 and 1325. These accounts capture much of the dynamic of oral narrative but, despite Bernard's claim to reproduce what he heard "non solum sensum e sensu, sed etiam verbum e verbo," do not reproduce the full range of verbal mannerisms. For a discussion of Bernard's attitude to orality, see Brian Stock, *The Implications of Literacy: Written Language and Models of Interpretation in the Eleventh and Twelfth Centuries* (Princeton, N.J., 1983), pp. 65-66.

143. Dominique Boutet suggests as much in *La chanson de geste: Forme et signification d'une écriture épique du moyen âge* (Paris, 1993), p. 74. The classic account of the general phenomenon is

Walter Ong, "The Writer's Audience Is Always a Fiction," *PMLA* 90 (1975), 9-21.

144. See, for example, Carol Fewster's claim that "the placing of minstrel references in [Middle English] romance is conventional, so too is their own phraseology. . . . [Such lines] recall an older means of transmission" (*Traditionality and Genre in Middle English Romance* [Cambridge, Eng., 1987], p. 28).

145. Michel Zink, *Medieval French Literature: An Introduction,* trans. Jeff Rider (Binghamton, N.Y., 1995), p. 31.

146. Ibid., p. 18.

147. In Zumthor's account of *mouvance,* oral performance and scribal reproduction alternate regularly, producing a series of versions not one of which can claim preeminence, and only this history of oral and written versions constitutes the work in the fullest sense (*Essai* [above, n. 54], p. 73). However, the variation this model posits is gradual not abrupt. While Zumthor stresses the importance of performance, his schema is marked out along a line of manuscripts, each containing a complete or near complete version of the poem. To produce the regular alteration that Zumthor envisages as the normal form of *mouvance,* therefore, one must postulate a series of regular performances covering the different sections of the poem in sequence.

148. See Joseph J. Duggan, *The Song of Roland: Formulaic Style and Poetic Craft* (Berkeley, Calif., 1973), and Edward A. Heinemann, *L'art métrique de la chanson de geste: Essai sur la musicalité du récit* (Geneva, 1993).

149. In "Perspectives on Recent Work on the Oral Traditional Formula," *Oral Tradition* 1 (1986), 467-503, Albert B. Lord concedes that formulaic density indicates only "the degree of involvement of any poem in the oral traditional style" (p. 480), while in *Traditional Oral Epic: The Odyssey, Beowulf, and the Serbo-Croatian Return Song* (Berkeley, Calif., 1990), John Miles Foley concedes that "the formulaic test *as it has been generally carried out* cannot prove oral provenance" (p. 4, emphasis in original). Foley's qualification seems to me misguided. It should be clear by now that no test will ever be able to establish that a particular written text is the direct and uncontaminated transcription of a single oral performance.

150. John Miles Foley, *The Singer of Tales in Performance* (Bloomington, Ind., 1995), esp. pp. 2-11 and 208-10.

151. Gabrielle M. Spiegel, *Romancing the Past: The Rise of Vernacular Prose Historiography in Thirteenth-Century France* (Berkeley, Calif., 1993), pp. 81 and 86.

152. Emile Mâle, *Art et artistes du moyen âge* (Paris, 1927), p. 88; Linda Seidel, *Songs of Glory: The Romanesque Façades of Aquitaine* (Chicago, 1981), pp. 68-69.

## Mark Burde (essay date spring 2004)

SOURCE: Burde, Mark. "Francisque Michel, Joseph Bédier, and the Epic History of the First Edition of the *Song of Roland* (1837)." *Exemplaria* 16, no. 1 (spring 2004): 1-42.

[*In the following essay, Burde discusses the major issues surrounding Joseph Bédier's 1922 edition of the* Oxford Song of Roland.]

The editorial history of the **Song of Roland** is well known and, because of the iconic nature of the work, probably the best documented of any medieval French text. Although the work circulated in at least two forms between the twelfth and the fifteenth centuries, and six complete manuscripts have survived, only one manuscript copy has a twelfth-century pedigree and can make a plausible claim to approximating the lost original.[1] The editorial triumph of what is known as the Oxford **Roland** manuscript by every possible criterion—anteriority of linguistic and poetic forms, literary value, nationalistic iconicity—is measured by the fact that its competitors for a brief time in the 1830s and 1840s, the later continental romance versions then referred to as the "Roman de Roncevaux," have largely vanished from critical discussion as offering anything other than various degrees of corruption of the original text.[2] Not surprisingly, the moment of recovery of the Oxford manuscript, in the form of Francisque Michel's 1835 transcription and subsequent publication of it, has been told and retold—often in sacralizing tones—as a heroic moment of origin for French medieval studies.[3]

The fundamental issue in editing the **Roland** has boiled down to how much weight to give the Oxford manuscript against the other surviving copies and, within the Oxford manuscript itself, how much reliability to grant the sometimes careless scribe against an original authorial position, necessarily conjectural.[4] After a series of late-nineteenth-century German editions attempted to produce a composite text in the name of philological reconstruction, the extreme degree of fidelity to the Oxford manuscript was famously established by Joseph Bédier, who over the course of his illustrious career not only produced a landmark edition of the Oxford **Roland** in 1922 but ceaselessly strove to refine the same text through five subsequent revised editions (one accompanied by a five-hundred-page companion volume of detailed textual commentary).[5] It is not an exaggeration to see in the Oxford **Roland** the alpha and the omega of Bédier's career, and even to postulate that the nature of his relationship to the text went far beyond the professional.[6] Awarded a copy of Léon Gautier's classic 1872 edition as a school prize in his teens, Bédier would devote three long articles at the end of his life to an overview of the hundred years' worth of editorial attention lavished on the *Roland.* If Bédier's famous non-interventionist theory of textual editing was first enunciated in the name of the *Lai de l'ombre,* it was the Oxford *Roland* manuscript that again and again became the showcase for Bédier's ideas in practice.[7]

When Bédier died suddenly in August of 1938, his 167-page trilogy of Roland articles in *Romania* became his de facto critical testament. Entitled "De l'édition princeps de la *Chanson de Roland* aux éditions les plus récentes: nouvelles remarques sur l'art d'établir les anciens textes" ("From the First Edition of the *Song of Roland* to the Most Recent Editions: New Remarks on the Art of Editing Old Texts"), the series began with a detailed account of the entry of the Oxford manuscript into modern criticism.[8] This prosaically entitled first installment (the "Premier article") is unique in Roland criticism: Bédier's seemingly exhaustive archivally-based account of the events surrounding Francisque Michel's recovery and publication of the Oxford *Roland* manuscript affords a wealth of insights unequaled before or since into this pivotal episode in the growth and advancement of French medieval literary studies. Indeed, virtually all current understanding of Francisque Michel's mission to England of 1833-36 derives from Bédier's presentation of the archival documents.[9] Suffused with the tender affection characteristic of the commemorative tribute, Bédier's salute to Michel's first edition on the centennial of its publication contrasts sharply in tone and content with the second and third articles, which appeared the following year and reiterated matter-of-factly and in line-by-line philological detail the case for the pre-eminence of the Oxford manuscript.

The obstinacy of Bédier's refusal to accept any but a handful of suggested editorial changes to his beloved Oxford manuscript (rejecting almost all of the "environ 5000 opérations chirurgicales qu'a subies jusqu'ici ce texte martyr," "approximately 5000 surgical operations that this martyred text has undergone to date," as he put it) would in time draw exasperated rebuttals from dissenting critics, but the saga of Francisque Michel presented in the first article has settled into uncontroversial existence as an important piece of straightforward—if at times anecdotal—medievalism scholarship.[10] In actuality, Bédier's thirty-six-page reconstruction of the Michel mission to England is a far less straightforward piece of criticism than the charming collection of anecdotes embellishing a solid core of archival fact that it purports to be. Despite Bédier's pledge to have avoided excessive fictionalizing and to have respected basic facts, a careful examination of several key source documents he used in reconstructing the mission and its aftermath reveals a subtle but recurrent pattern of selective and out-of-context quotation, imaginatively inaccurate attribution of roles, and even chronological modification that collectively belie any claim to purely historical reliability. Illustrating this assertion, and assessing its implications for a thorough understanding of Michel's contribution to Roland scholarship, is the primary goal of this article.

Nothing suggests that Bédier set out willfully to mislead his readers, nor could one legitimately posit a post-retirement, premortem ebb of his mental acuity. His article does contain an oddly high number of purely typographical and citational errors, but of exclusive interest here are what could be called Bédier's *interventions,* the choices of emplotment that any narrator, historical or literary, is called upon to make when synthesizing copious original documents, and to which Bédier in this instance devoted himself with particular relish and liberality.[11] As a brilliant prose stylist whose modern reconstruction of the Tristan legend won him admission to the French Academy, Bédier never respected any distinct demarcation between criticism and imaginative narration, as a recent biography devoted to him has demonstrated.[12] All evidence suggests that, under cover of the centennial tribute genre, Bédier could not resist taking a number of liberties and "Rolandizing" Michel's feat, thereby making one of the bolder ventures into artful, plot-driven critical reconstruction of his career. Assessing what he gained from fashioning a "Song of Francisque Michel" and what larger, otherwise inaccessible truths he was able to express in so doing are the secondary goals of this article.

ROMANCING THE ROLAND RECOVERY

Bédier was far from the first critic to recount the events of Michel's spectacular first mission to England, Michel having long been a considered a pioneer of medieval literary studies. Precociously prolific, Michel was the most energetic of the first generation of French medieval scholars to be trained not as classicists but through courses offered at the newly-founded *École des Chartes* in Paris in the paleographical skills necessary for dating and deciphering the texts of their field. He was also adroit to the point of opportunism, having realized that 1833, his twenty-fourth year, was a particularly propitious moment for an ambitious young man to nominate himself for a governmental grant. The details are sketchy, but Michel apparently took advantage of a modest budgetary provision to encourage research in the sciences and letters ("encouragements aux sciences et aux lettres") at a moment when François Guizot, the new Minister of Public Instruction and a prominent medievalist historian, was about to implement a number of major additional initiatives to recuperate historical monuments deemed crucial to the national heritage.[13]

As the grantor of Michel's request, Guizot became the recipient of the first of a long series of accounts of Michel's solo expedition to England, in this case the dryly prosaic, end-of-mission *Rapports à M. le ministre de l'Instruction Publique sur les anciens monuments de l'histoire et de la littérature de la France qui se trouvent dans les bibliothèques de l'Angleterre et de l'Écosse* of 1838.[14] In this brochure, Michel outlined in essence how he had profited from a vaguely-worded clause in his official mission statement—to report back on the catalogued medieval holdings of various English archives—in order to go far beyond his formal mandate of transcribing two vernacular verse chronicles deemed important to French history, namely Geoffrey Gaimar's *Estoire des engleis* and Benoît de Sainte-Maure's *Histoire des ducs de Normandie*.[15] The fact that Michel's mention of the **Roland** manuscript occupied no more than a prosaic paragraph in this report no doubt signals his awareness of Guizot's relative indifference towards the work and, indeed, to medieval literary study as a whole.[16]

Concurrently a parallel heroic mode was also developing, however—much simpler in its focus and more effusive in its tone. Michel himself had inaugurated this mode in a private letter to Louis-Jean-Nicolas Monmerqué, one of his Parisian mentors and collaborators, a letter in which Michel had placed the sole recovery of the **Roland** at the center of the mission's goals and the pinnacle of its accomplishments.[17] The vaguely Archimedian echoes to Michel's triumphal cry ("Je vous écris de la ville d'Alfred, à deux pas de la Bodléienne où je viens de trouver . . . quoi? Devinez . . . **La Chanson de Roland**!" C'est presque la quadrature du cercle!" ["I am writing from Alfred the Great's city, right next to the Bodleian, where I have just come across . . . what? Guess . . . the **Chanson de Roland**! It's almost the squaring of the circle!"]) signaled his enthusiastic conviction that he had solved a burning historico-literary conundrum of his day—namely recovery of an epic supposedly sung by invading Norman troops at the battle of Hastings.[18]

It was, however, in the name of broader national heritage and esthetic value, not as solution to a specialists' conundrum, that his feat would soon come to be sacralized. Immediately several reviewers of Michel's edition had recognized, in the poem's "rudesse sauvage" and "noble simplicité homérique" ("untamed ruggedness" and "noble, Homeric simplicity"), the value of the **Roland** as a foundational work for national poetry.[19] Fifteen years later a second edition of the Oxford manuscript was published, providing Paulin Paris with the opportunity to refer to the work as "ce précieux monument littéraire," "this precious literary monument," in an 1851 review article.[20] The same review contained the first detailed reconstruction of the recovery of the **Roland**, tracing the process by which the sequential ef-

forts of five researchers—the Abbé de La Rue, Jean-Louis Bourdillon, Paris himself, Henri Monin, and Francisque Michel—had culminated in Michel's bringing home "une si précieuse relique," "such a precious relic." "Les difficultés de lecture, pour grandes qu'elles fussent, ne pouvaient arrêter un aussi bon linguiste," Paris wrote ("The interpretive problems, however great, were unable to stop such a competent linguist"). Two decades yet again later the preface to the first general-readership luxury edition of the **Roland,** issued in the aftermath of the calamitous French defeat of 1870, embellished considerably on this heroic emplotment. Léon Gautier's fancifully nationalistic account imagined a crisply efficient Michel charged by his government and guided by God in an inexorable mission to bring a national treasure back to its rightful home:

> Il s'installa à la Bodléienne d'Oxford, plaça devant lui le fameux manuscrit 23 du fonds Digby, copia notre vieux poëme, et, moins de deux ans plus tard, fit paraître la première édition de notre grande Épopée nationale. Grâces en soient rendues à Dieu, dont la Providence s'étend aux études littéraires: c'est un Français qui eut cette gloire et non pas un Allemand![21]

> He sat down in Oxford's Bodleian library, placed before him the famous Digby 23 manuscript, copied out our old poem, and, less than two years later, published the first edition of our great National Epic. Thanks be to God, whose Providence extends to literary studies, that it was a Frenchman who earned this glory and not a German!

In a more sober context, Gautier also promoted the more general assessment of Michel's work that would be seconded by many successor critics, finding in Michel's Roland edition a representative milestone of the first major movement in modern textual editing—"la méthode paléographique," an approach, in Gautier's words, that was "naïve mais sûre."[22]

If not quite yet a genre, then, the recounted Michel mission had become something of an academic set piece amenable to a surprisingly varied range of critical fashionings by the time Bédier set out to write his centennial salute in 1937. Although Gautier's account, by far the most detailed before Bédier's, had also posited a sequence of heroic acts, it had focused on the recovery of the manuscript itself as the pivotal event in a teleology of long-term critical evolution ("Époque de préparation ou d'intuition," followed by a "Période d'invention," followed by the "Période de vulgarisation," and so on—"Era of Preparation or Intuition," "Period of Invention," "Period of Popularization"). Bédier, by contrast, puts people, not the manuscript, at the center of his investigation. The main character, not surprisingly, is Michel, a veritable transcription machine on two legs, who bedazzles Bédier with his scholarly *prouesse* ("Tant de livres lui sont dus. . . . Quelle prodigalité de bienfaits!" ["He produced so many books. . . . A prodigious contribution to the field!" 469]); the year Michel turned twenty-five, his publications—mainly editions of medieval manuscripts—surpassed his age in number.[23] Even Michel, however, could not have seized on the **Roland** project by dint of sheer personal initiative. Investigating the relatively simple question Bédier sets out for himself ("qui a donné l'éveil à Francisque Michel? qui l'a aidé?" ["who alerted Francisque Michel? who assisted him?" 433]) thus becomes an exercise in reconstructing a vast network of academic relationships in the early days of medieval studies.

On general points, such as evidence of the *Zeitgeist* for things medieval in early 1830s French academic and literary circles, Bédier cleaves to information available in previous accounts: he notes how a renewed interest in medieval literature had permeated the academy, with dueling pamphlets by the young scholars Jules Michelet and Edgar Quinet demonstrating that a generalized Romantic interest in recovery of foundational works of national literature was transforming into specialists' interest. Key secondary figures, ur-medievalist sexagenarians such as Claude Fauriel and François-Just-Marie Raynouard, hover about as they had in Gautier's account, ready to intervene at propitious moments.[24] Where Bédier's singularity emerges is in the degree to which he draws the heroism topos out to its logical conclusion, peopling his narrative with warrior-scholars whose portraits are resurrected from material lying in state archives.[25] Henri Monin, duly credited in earlier accounts with having published the first study ever of any of the **Roland** manuscripts in 1832, is not simply the young *normalien* whose *Dissertation sur le Roman de Roncevaux* provided Michel with a book to review and the occasion for his first documented engagement in the **Roland** recovery effort.[26] Bédier's Monin becomes three-dimensional, having garnered a cluster of heroic-sounding epithets from his École Normale professors, from whose archived evaluations Bédier coaxes epic effusiveness:

> Excellent esprit. De la pénétration, mais surtout de la force, de la suite, de la persévérance. Travail indéfatiguable, connaissances déjà variées. Il sait plusieurs langues modernes et prodigieusement de faits.
>
> 452 n1

> Fine mind. Perceptive, but, in particular, strong and persevering. Indefatigable work habits, broad general knowledge already. He knows several modern languages and a huge quantity of facts.

Such an epic profile befits a figure who already in Gautier's account had marked a rupture with a generation of amateurish pseudo-scholarship on the **Roland** legend by actually consulting some of the **Roland** manuscripts (the current rhymed C and P versions) he was presuming to evaluate.[27]

Embellishing liberally on this topos, Bédier places Monin's originality under the sign of the triumphal advance—in a literal sense—of empiricism. His imaginative reconstruction reads as follows:

> Soit que tel ou tel de ses maîtres l'y ait engagé, soit qu'il ait agi de son propre mouvement, on voit [Monin] franchir la porte de son École, alors sise rue de La Harpe, et s'acheminer au loin vers une région mystérieuse. Là-bas, sur l'autre rive de la Seine, le Cabinet des manuscrits du roi n'attend que sa venue. Il y demande et reçoit des mains de quelque attaché, Paulin Paris peut-être, deux manuscrits: l'insigne manuscrit du XIIIe siècle, jadis manié par Du Cange . . . et une copie récente . . . du manuscrit de Versailles: elle avait été donnée depuis peu à la Bibliothèque par Guyot Desherbiers, qui avait renoncé à son projet d'édition.
>
> 443

> Whether this or that teacher had requested his assistance or whether he was acting on his own initiative, we can envision [Monin] walking out the door of his School (then located on rue de La Harpe) and venturing forth towards a mysterious region. Over there, on the other bank of the Seine, the Office of Royal Manuscripts awaits his coming. He requests and is given two manuscripts by some archival assistant (perhaps Paulin Paris): the notable thirteenth-century manuscript, which Du Cange had held . . . and a recent copy . . . of the Versailles manuscript. It had recently been deposited at the Library by Guyot Desherbiers, who had abandoned his intention to edit it.

Surely the justification for this interpolated fancy is the parallel it establishes between Monin's symbolic crossing of the French capital's geographical dividing line and Michel's expedition across the English Channel the following year. Innocuously illustrative, Bédier's imagined anecdote, through its factitiousness, celebrates the casting off of outdated paradigms and the march of scholarly progress into realms of terra incognita.

In his role as foil to Michel, Bédier's Monin may inhabit the same rarefied heroic universe as his exact contemporary, but in his circumspection he plays Olivier to Michel's Roland; Monin owed practically all of his early success, Bédier maintains, to Fauriel's generous patronage. In particular, Bédier details at length his theory of how Monin's aforementioned *Dissertation,* a second-year student's humble independent study project, was guided by Fauriel all the way to unheard-of publication with doctoral honors. Everything about Bédier's Michel, by contrast, connotes a bursting of bounds and heroic *démesure* attributable largely to internal drive: he is medievalist passion personified and the first specimen of a new breed of professional scholar who intuitively understands the concept of fundable research. Under cover of a precise and timely project, this researcher, in Bédier's account, will turn himself loose on the rich bounty of scores of medieval manuscripts far outside the range of his official mandate, as well, of course, as tracking down the precious Oxford *Roland* manuscript. Michel's literal eccentricity, furthermore, extends to his institutional marginality, since he received his training in Old French paleography and diplomatics as an auditor at the *École des Chartes* after failing to obtain an entrance exam score ranking him among the first eight students, to whom admission would be offered.

The echoes of epic—and of the plot of the *Roland* in particular—are not limited to the pairing of Michel with Monin. In Bédier's telling, Michel's efforts were met with generalized scorn and mockery; as an epic of defeat, the sad story of the fate of the first edition of the *Song of Roland* reads like Bédier's contribution to this age-old genre.[28] Bédier quotes the opinionated pronouncement of Jean-Louis Bourdillon, an antiquarian and gentleman scholar who had long been at work on an as-yet unfinished edition of one of the continental manuscripts when Michel's edition appeared, as representative of what could be printed with impunity concerning the Oxford *Roland*:

> Absurdités, bévues, mots jetés au hasard, expressions impropres, vers estropiés, raison sans rimes et rimes sans raison, je ne crois pas que, dans aucune langue, on ait jamais présenté au public un fatras pareil.
>
> 468
>
> Absurdities, gross errors, words thrown about, incorrect expressions, mutilated verses, reason without rhyme and rhyme without reason, I do not believe that, in any language, the public has ever been presented with such a jumbled mess.

Fifteen years of scholarly evolution did little to soften the barbs, according to Bédier, who goes so far as to imply that Michel's overall contribution to medieval studies was not appreciated for its full value until his own centennial tribute.[29]

Answering the question of who tipped off Francisque Michel to the Oxford *Roland*'s existence and how things went from there leads Bédier to evoke to some degree or another many other motifs reminiscent of the plot of the *Roland* as well. The benighted forces of paganism receive symbolic representation in Bédier's account of Guizot's dismissive evaluation of medieval literature as a whole; caught in a moment of intellectual Saracenism, Bédier's Guizot confides to one of his female correspondents, "A mon avis, la vraie littérature française ne remonte pas au delà du xvɪᴇ siècle, Montaigne et Rabelais" ("In my opinion, real French literature does not extend back earlier than the sixteenth century with Montaigne and Rabelais," 462).[30] Even the arcane workings of the machinery of state bureaucracy reveal their poetic potential in Bédier's hands: the gross irregularities in the process by which Monin's independent study project gets published by the royal press constitute a "privilège insolite," "unusual privilege" (438) and a suspension of procedure as miraculous, in its own way, as the sun standing still.

Such a heroicization of the characters and actions involved in the recovery of the Oxford *Roland* manuscript seems, on the face of it, completely appropriate to the celebratory overtones of the commemorative genre, and at any rate hardly surreptitious, since Bédier foregrounds the whimsical alacrity with which he puts himself to the task of plunging into this rich past, "cette période héroïque de nos études," "this heroic period of our discipline" (467). An eclectic mix of ancient, medieval and modern narrative touches is evident from the opening paragraph's vague invocation of the muse ("[Cette histoire] est complexe, et, par endroits, obscure. Puissé-je la retracer correctement!" 433) to the carefree recourse to self-consciously dramatic reconstruction of events (in addition to the example cited above, Bédier writes "on imagine quelle dut être la fierté des normaliens quand ils purent se passer glorieusement de main en main les épreuves encore humides d'un livre, dont la page de titre portait: *Dissertation sur le Roman de Roncevaux,* par H. Monin, élève de l'École normale," 436), to Bédier's jocular comparison of himself to a medieval narrator of heroic deeds ("En vérité, dans le recul du temps, Francisque Michel fait grande figure parmi ses contemporains. Mais je n'ai voulu conter que ses «enfances», 469).[31]

The implicit function of these narrative touches is to enliven the tribute without ever compromising its factual validity. On initial inspection, Bédier's account seems to respect all conventional rules of evidentiary engagement; his categorical declaration of allegiance to the rules of factual inquiry ("L'histoire romancée est chose haïssable, et notre récit, nécessairement conjectural par endroits, veut rester véridique," ["Inventive history is a despicable thing, and our account, although necessarily conjectural in places, aspires to truthfulness," 436]) is often scrupulously respected. At several points, for example, he makes no attempt to paper over the gaps in the written record, such as upon uncovering inconclusive evidence suggesting that in the early 1830s Fauriel drew lecture points from a since-vanished complete transcription of one of the continental manuscripts: "Elle ne nous a pas été conservée: l'avait-il prise lui-même? ou quelqu'un l'avait-il prise pour lui? Monin peut-être? On ne sait" ("It has not survived; had he copied it himself, or had someone copied it for him? We do not know," 446).[32] At other times, Bédier brings the scientific apparatus of manuscript editing techniques to bear in elucidating some particularly nebulous questions about what Michel knew about the Oxford manuscript and when he knew it. Thus, to pinpoint the six-week window during which the existence of the Oxford manuscript surfaced in Michel's writing, Bédier locates minute yet telltale differences in two sequential reviews Michel devoted to Monin's *Dissertation* in the autumn of 1832. In the later version of the review, Michel added a paragraph chiding Monin for not having mentioned the Oxford manuscript in his study—a manuscript, Michel somewhat pedantically pointed out, referred to quite plainly in an eighteenth-century edition of the *Canterbury Tales* by Thomas Tyrwhitt. Here, Bédier concludes, Michel reveals his one and only possible source of awareness of the Oxford manuscript to have been Tyrwhitt's mention of it: using the method of common error, Bédier notes that a line quoted by Michel in his review contains a transcription error common to the half-dozen Oxford *Roland* lines imperfectly reproduced by the Englishman.[33]

Why, one might wonder, does Bédier delve into such minutiae? Given that the number of men of letters who had laid eyes on the Oxford *Roland* manuscript in the early 1830s was limited to a single-digit group generally of English nationality, the question of how awareness of the work crossed the channel is a valid one. Previous to his *Romania* article, Bédier had followed the commonsensical assumption that one of these precursors had simply told Michel of the manuscript, the most logical candidate being the Abbot Gervais de La Rue.[34] Here, however, Bédier takes advantage of the opportunity to showcase the principles of scientific rigor that undeniably structure much of the article. Declaring himself bothered by the lack of evidence for the Abbé de La Rue connection, Bédier sets out a revised explanation in his commemorative tribute: Michel, following his omnivorous interests, had been researching a certain figure from Germano-Scandinavian mythology important to another project. Tyrwhitt having published on this matter, Michel must have serendipitously come across the Oxford *Roland* footnote while checking what Tyrwhitt had to say on the initial question. Bédier's revised explanation thus has the double merit not only of correcting the original hypothesis through considerable attention to detail, but also of making Michel the originary agent of his own passion for the *Roland* recovery.[35]

### Behind Bédier's Song of Michel: The Archival Evidence

To sum up my argument so far: a critical narrative premised on the assumption that the archives are the locus of acts of heroism certainly befits a centennial tribute, and Bédier clearly enjoys playing the epic bard, even to the point of drawing inspiration from the plot of the *Roland* itself, while simultaneously assuring his readership of the veracity of the essential facts presented and offering implicit proof of his commitment to standards of scholarly investigation. The first two-thirds of Bédier's exposition gives every indication of having respected the balance of this basic formula.[36] In the final third, however, Bédier's narrational liberties surpass the standard one would expect from a heavily-footnoted piece of scholarship. This final portion, which constitutes the climax of the narration, spans the point from which Michel's eagerness to recover the Oxford *Ro-*

*land* manuscript led him to propose his England mission to Guizot up to the appearance of the work in print. Over this two-year period (1833-35), more than a hundred documents, mainly letters Michel wrote Guizot from the field and drafts of Guizot's responses, accumulated in a single file now preserved at the Archives Nationales.[37] Checking Bédier's reconstruction against the originals reveals the degree to which he indulged in his temptation to diverge from the prosaic details of the record.

Bédier's portrayal of the planning and execution of Michel's mission relies heavily in particular on the validity of four propositions: first, as I have implied above, that the project for recovery of the Oxford *Roland* manuscript had an air of secrecy about it and needed, at least initially, the camouflage of more immediately fundable research; second, that Michel's youthful vigor was accompanied by a heroic youthful impetuousness accentuated by occasional naïveté; third, that an avuncular Fauriel unwaveringly played a crucial mentoring and nurturing role (as attested by what Bédier calls "sa charitable maïeutique," "his selfless nurturing role," 460); and finally, as I have noted, that the reception of the Oxford manuscript was chilly if not outright hostile for years after it first appeared in print. In reality, however, each of these propositions is questionable if not demonstrably false, a fact attributable in the aggregate to Bédier's decision to mold the facts to fit his heroic narrative framework. Examination of each in turn will reveal a great deal about the structure of the article as a whole.

Concerning the first point, Bédier is vague about exactly how Michel presented his project to Guizot, noting that it was done by letter but failing to reproduce any of what one would expect would be a crucial missive.[38] Instead, he sketches Michel's goals by quoting the next best thing in the dossier, namely a long and informal evaluation of the project furnished by Fauriel at Guizot's request (458-59). According to what in essence is Fauriel's letter of recommendation in support of the project, Michel had one vague and general goal—the completion of bibliographical references—and one specific one—the copying of two vernacular verse chronicles by Benoît de Sainte Maure and Geoffrey Gaimar. Conspicuously absent from Fauriel's evaluation is any mention of the *Roland* project.

Fauriel's semi-confidential correspondence with his old friend Guizot cannot legitimately substitute for Michel's own presentation of his ideas, however. Bédier's failure to quote from the source is probably attributable to the fact that Michel's initial letter of solicitation was misfiled in the Archives Nationales dossiers for an indeterminate period of time.[39] In this crucial originary document, Michel clearly states his intention at the outset to take copies of both the work now known as the *Pèlerinage de Charlemagne* and the Oxford ***Roland*** manuscript, which he refers to as "le roman de Roncevaux rédigé dans les premières années de la première moitié du XIIe siècle" ("the *Romance of Roncevaux* written in the early years of the first half of the twelfth century").[40] Michel does mark his concession to the reality of the times by emphasizing the works' linguistic and historical rather than literary value, but the proposition that Michel concealed his true ambitions in presenting his project can now be shown to be incorrect.[41] In fostering what has become a modern critical fallacy, namely that Michel's intention to copy the ***Roland*** manuscript constituted a secret agenda about which he had informed no one, Bédier imbues the whole mission with an air of mystery generative of dramatic suspense and suggestive that from the outset the true value of the ***Roland*** relic could be appreciated only by enlightened initiates.

Granted, given the gap in the documents with which Bédier was likely confronted, it would be unfair to make too much of such factual liberties—were it not for the treatment Bédier accords the other three aforementioned points. Here the narrative does indeed contravene readily-available evidence that supported a contrary interpretation, a fact that will be evident from an examination of Bédier's reconstruction of what happened in the crucial first ten months of the mission. On the issue of Michel's naïveté and even immaturity, Bédier speculates that although this brash and cocky 24-year-old may have amused the Minister during his interview (after all, writes Bédier, he coined the charmingly self-deprecating designation of "ancien élève refusé de l'École des Chartes"), once in the field Michel later exasperated Guizot with his gauche appeals for more generous funding, which Bédier illustrates by reproducing Michel's supposedly guileless exclamations about the price of postage in England.[42] When not bemoaning the cost of living abroad, Bédier's Michel is brazenly trying to collect a double salary on the grounds that his work in England complements an archivist's position he had already held in Paris, and, as though recognizing the unseemliness of these solicitations, he tries to right the listing ship of his indecorous manners with the conciliatory ballast of frenetic updates on his search for an early print edition of a work in which Guizot had expressed momentary interest.[43] Even his signature efficiency and tirelessness work against him: "on le surveille en effet" ("he is being closely monitored"), writes Bédier after quoting a remark Guizot pencilled to an aide in the margin of one of the letters: "Je ne veux rien faire de nouveau pour lui qu'en étant sûr du travail déjà fait" ("I want to offer no new support to him until we are assured of the quality of the work already done," 462).

If Bédier's Michel at times resembles a bumbling Perceval, his youthful energy and Rolandian resolve

eventually convince a skeptical Guizot to loosen much of his initial bureaucratic restraint. Bédier locates this shift mid-way through the mission; writing of Guizot, he remarks:

> Peu à peu, il comprend. Jadis, au XVe siècle, les humanistes s'étaient lancés «comme des limiers», selon l'expression de l'un d'eux, à la chasse des manuscrits grecs: ce jeune homme leur ressemble.
>
> 463

> Little by little, he comes to understand. The fifteenth-century humanists had thrown themselves "like bloodhounds," as one of them put it, into the search for Greek manuscripts; this young man resembles them.

Furthermore, the intervention of first Fauriel and later Monmerqué will be instrumental in effecting this balance. Recounting the point just before the tension is resolved, one of Bédier's paragraphs more than any others illustrates the key compositional strategies of the article's method as it reaches its climax. In full, this paragraph reads as follows:

> La vérité est que Guizot s'inquiète de la multiplicité toujours croissante des travaux que Francisque Michel lui annonce. Il veut bien encourager les lettres et les sciences, mais un ministre de Louis-Philippe doit se montrer bon ménager des deniers publics: ce missionnaire se croit-il donc missionnaire pour la vie? «J'ai l'orgueil de penser, ose lui écrire Fr. Michel (29 mai 1834), que je passe dans votre opinion pour quelque chose de plus qu'un copiste ordinaire», et par la même occasion il l'entretient de nouveaux projets. Guizot consulte une fois de plus Fauriel, qui en approuve plusieurs (lettre du 12 juin), mais convient aussi qu'il y a lieu de modérer tant d'ardeur. Guizot s'y emploie (le 28 juin): «Au lieu de vous mettre à copier un peu au hasard les divers manuscrits qui vous tombent sous la main, je vous engage, toutes les fois qu'un manuscrit vous paraîtra intéressant, à le parcourir et à me transmettre une notice sur sa nature, son contenu, son âge, etc., afin qui je puisse consulter ici le conservatoire de la Bibliothèque du roi et vous donner des instructions en conséquence.»
>
> 462-63

> In truth, Guizot is worried by the ever-increasing number of projects Francisque Michel is announcing. Of course he wants to encourage the study of literature and the sciences, but as one of Louis-Philippe's ministers he must prove himself a good steward of public funds; does this envoy think he has been granted a lifetime appointment? "I am presumptuous enough to think," Michel dares to write him (May 29 1834), "that I rate as something other than an ordinary copier of manuscripts in your estimation," and goes on in the same letter to speak of new projects. Again Guizot consults Fauriel, who approves several of them (letter of June 12), but concedes also that there is good reason to moderate such zeal. Guizot conveys the news (June 28): "Instead of your copying willy nilly the various manuscripts you happen to encounter, I would like for you to skim each manuscript that interests you and

inform me what kind of manuscript it is, as well as its contents and age, etc., so that I can check here with the conservatory of the Royal Library and give you further instructions."

Although Guizot did indeed at certain moments express alarm at Michel's omnivorous interests and impulsive tendencies, the fact is that the quotation Bédier attributes to Guizot's letter of June 28 actually appears as a postscript to a much earlier missive—that of November 7, 1833, a mere two months after Michel's arrival in England.[44] Aside from freely rearranging chronology, Bédier has here also quoted Michel out of context and simplified the engagement of Fauriel, whose actual report to Guizot not only approved none of Michel's projects outright but explicitly recommended the cancellation of two of them.[45]

A full reconstruction of the complex negotiations on worthwhile archival projects conducted among Michel, Guizot, and the Parisian scholars Guizot consulted is beyond the scope of the present article, as it would have been for Bédier's as well. But even a cursory and celebratory account such as Bédier's could have alluded to role reversals evident in the epistolary exchanges, such as Michel's occasional impulse to question or correct Guizot in the name of efficient use of time. After indeed having put Michel on a probationary period, as Bédier notes, by June of 1834 Guizot was actually sending him occasional requests to pursue specific projects outside his original mandate, some of which Michel reported to be redundant or based on erroneous information.[46] Moreover, while it is true that Guizot's June 28, 1834, letter, as cited by Bédier, denied Michel's request for permission to copy a number of manuscripts, in this he was merely relaying, often verbatim, the written recommendations Fauriel had provided him in the letter delivered to Guizot's office five days earlier, on June 23 (presumably the model for what Bédier calls the letter of June 12). That Bédier preferred to establish, in place of this complexity, a polar opposition between a zealous Michel and a reticent Guizot, with Fauriel mediating, conforms to narrative exigencies more than it does to the nuances of the surviving record. A self-assured Michel who proudly flaunts his "orgueil" cannot but evoke, however dimly, a heroic Roland to Bédier's readership, and Guizot, by extension, becomes a vaguely suzerain figure holding the purse strings of the July Monarchy bourgeois state, the lord in the service of whom one must "endure great cold and tremendous heat alike," as the ***Roland***'s famous formula has it:

> Pur sun seignur deit hom susfrir granz mals
> E endurer e forz freiz e granz chalz.[47]

The problem is that Michel did not in this instance flaunt his "orgueil" any more than his youthful exuberance led him to complain about the cost of everyday life in England in a naïve and exclamatory way. Michel spent a good deal of his career bemoaning, sometimes bitterly, what he deemed his unmerited fate, and his considerable pride is occasionally as evident in the 1833-35 correspondence as it is in that of his mature years, but Bédier's account completely elides a great deal of information favorable to the construction of another Michel.[48] This other Michel was bearing the unpoetic brunt of severe limits on research funding even as Guizot launched radically ambitious new projects, with the result that he, Michel, was expected to absorb costs that went far beyond the amount of his occasional stipend. The catch-all budgetary provision under which Michel was awarded funding never surpassed twelve thousand francs per year until 1842, and during the period Michel spent in England Guizot had faced stiff parliamentary resistance to his request that ten times this amount be allocated to his new domestic historical research program.[49] Behind Michel's claim of "orgueil" lay the bitter reality of the life of a new breed of professional medievalist, dependent on state largesse to make up for the personal fortunes on which many of the gentlemen scholars of previous generations had relied, but not yet lucky enough to live at a time of full state commitment to funding this research.[50] In the postage stamp incident mentioned above, what Bédier portrays as Michel's "plaintes naïves" ("guileless complaints," 462) could more prosaically be called an understandable reaction to the requirement that he dispense nearly a full day's wages for the right to receive a message via the sole means of international communication available to him. In glossing over Michel's dire financial straits, Bédier fails to give full consideration in his narration to Michel's modest social class, which he notes only in passing (457).

This fact becomes abundantly clear when one examines the actual context of the "orgueil" remark. On May 29, 1834, Michel wrote Guizot the fourth or perhaps fifth letter in a crescendoing series of attempts to convey the depths of his financial need. Gingerly and in impeccably elegant prose he complained that his episodic stipends of 500 francs were of insufficient amount and regularity. What he wanted—a salary both decent and regular—touched on material and moral considerations, both of which he expressed succinctly in the letter written just before he finally exploded and requested to be reposted to Paris in July of 1834 after ten months in the field.[51] In each of his reports from the field, after several paragraphs devoted to the state of his work, Michel turned to devote the second half of the missive to material concerns. This portion of the May 29, 1834, letter reads as follows:

> Souffrez maintenant, Monsieur le ministre, que je vous parle de moi et que je réclame de vous une nouvelle indemnité proportionnée à mes dépenses et à mes besoins. La dernière que vous avez daigné m'accorder est du 15 mars, c'est-à-dire date de deux mois et demi, temps durant lequel, outre mes frais nécessaires, j'ai

été obligé d'en faire d'extraordinaires pour aller à Cambridge, y séjourner huit jours et en revenir. Dans une précédente j'ai eu l'honneur de vous parler du taux élevé des logements et des objets de première nécessité à Londres; un exemple que je vous en donnerai dans celle-ci est que l'un des archivistes du gouvernement anglois chez qui je viens de placer M. Berbrugger, *ancien élève, refusé comme moi, de la seconde école des chartes,* s'est cru obligé de le prévenir que la livre Sterling qu'il lui donnoit chaque jour de travail pourroit s'augmenter par la suite, et que maintenant il ne devoit songer qu'à rentrer dans ses frais de séjour en Angleterre. Quant à la place elle-même, si je l'ai donnée au lieu de la garder pour moi, c'est que j'ai regardé celle que j'occupe maintenant comme l'effet d'une convention que je ne puis violer sans crime, et *qu'outre que j'ai l'orgueil de penser que je passe dans votre opinion pour quelque chose de plus qu'un copiste ordinaire,* j'ai l'espoir de vous engager par mon travail à vous intéresser dans la suite à ma position. Pour le présent, elle m'a forcé à vous adresser ma dernière demande: car je suis absolument sans argent.

Please now permit me, sir, to speak of myself and to request from you a new allocation commensurate with my expenses and my needs. The last one you were so good as to grant me dates from March 15—in other words, from two and a half months ago, during which time, in addition to my necessary expenses I, was forced to make unexpected ones in travelling to Cambridge, spending a week there, and returning. In an earlier letter I had the honor of speaking of the high cost of lodging and of the most basic necessities in London; this time, allow me to note that one of the archivists of the English government, in whose employ I have just found a position for Mr. Berbrugger, who is, *like me, a rejected graduate of the second École des chartes,* felt obliged to inform him that the one pound Sterling he paid him for each day worked might later be increased, and that he now must not expect any better than to break even financially for his stay in England. As for the position itself, if I gave it away instead of keeping it for myself, it is because I considered the one I hold now the result of an agreement that I am duty-bound to honor. *In addition to being so presumptuous as to think that I rate as something other than an ordinary copier of manuscripts in your estimation,* I hope to be able, through my work, to convince you of the importance of continuing my position. For the time being, this position has forced me to make my last request: for I am utterly out of money.

Restored to their original context, the two italicized phrases convey very different meanings from the ones Bédier assigns to them. In Bédier's assessment, Michel's self-designation as an "ancien élève refusé de l'École des Chartes" signaled the colorful self-assuredness of a quirky outsider capable of talking his way into a boldly innovative mission, whereas the "orgueil" remark, reproduced as an anecdotal snippet, illustrated Michel's unbounded youthful zeal. In fact, as is plainly evident from the original, both lines were embedded in subordinate clauses carefully calibrated to stress the larger rhetorical point about Michel's sense of honor, duty, commitment and generosity in the face of

daunting material hardship. "Once already," Michel seems to say, "my capabilities were not recognized by state institutions; will the same injustice be repeated?" That such an insinuation smacks of self-pity, grudge-nursing and even a persecution complex does not invalidate Michel's fundamental point: assuming the accuracy of the basic facts he recounts, the archivist's salary of a pound set for Michel's friend Berbrugger by the British government represented, at the exchange rate of the time, a sum of 25 francs a day, or, presuming a six-day work week, between 600 and 700 francs a month.[52] Although deemed a subsistence wage at best by the employer, this amount nonetheless far exceeded the two or three allotments of 500 francs Michel had received from Guizot's ministry over the course of that spring.

Michel, of course, did not follow through on his July 1834 declaration of intent to return to Paris in disgust. Later that month, at Monmerqué's urging, Guizot approved a regular monthly salary of 500 francs for Michel—renewable after four months—thus allowing for a significantly less turbulent second year of the mission (although Michel took advantage of subsequent occasions to shame the French bureaucracy for its niggardly support).[53] To the extent that the full details of Michel's messy financial negotiations constitute a seamy underside to the glorious aura the mission has acquired, one can understand Bédier's decision to elide them. What is remarkable, as I have been claiming, is his determination to recuperate a selected few of them, shorn of their contextual nuance, in the service of a heroic emplotment patterned loosely on the characters and events of the most paradigmatic of French medieval epics.

On the final point of the reception of Michel's edition, it would indeed be hardly correct to call the book a best seller; prior to 1850, the indifference of the non-specialist reading public to actual medieval literary works—as opposed to medievally-inflected modern fantasies—is well enough documented for France.[54] Fifty years before Bédier, Léon Gautier had already pointed out the split between the actual scientific value of Michel's Roland work and its unenthusiastic reception outside of a small circle of specialists.[55] Bédier's emplotment considerably embellishes upon and reworks this established episode in the stock of Micheliana motifs, however; four witnesses are called to testify that indifference to Michel's edition extended even to specialists of the day, who, as Bédier would have it, shared the reaction previous accounts had attributed only to the general public. Of these four, one—Michel himself—is again quoted out of context, two are highly unrepresentative, and one is not who Bédier says he is. "L'édition princeps de la *Chanson de Roland* . . . n'avait valu à l'éditeur que peu de renom et encore moins de profit" ("The first edition of the *Song of Ro-*

*land* earned its editor but little renown and even less profit"): this sentence does indeed appear in the preface to Michel's second edition (1869) of the Oxford *Roland* manuscript, as Bédier notes, but it serves tartly to set up a contrast between the minimal financial support Michel received with the immense state largesse bestowed upon François Génin for his highly idiosyncratic and controversial 1850 edition.[56] It does not, as Bédier implies, signal that Michel regarded his first edition as a failure with his specialist readership; in fact, he held just the opposite.[57] Nor was Jean-Louis Bourdillon's vitriolic denunciation of the text of the Oxford manuscript representative of anything other than the last gasp of a moribund tradition of gentleman scholarship whose aim was a full restoration of the poetic gem long lost under the muck of scribal alteration.[58] Bédier quotes his third witness, Raynouard, also in very specific circumstances not representative of general scholarly opinion.[59] As for the acerbic assessment of the Oxford *Roland* text contained in the quotation Bédier incorrectly attributes to his fourth witness—Francis Guessard—the citation is faulty and I have not been able to determine its source.[60]

Bédier further notes mournfully that the print run for this first edition was minuscule and had to be financed by Michel himself:

> Il l'avait fait imprimer à ses frais et tirer à 200 exemplaires seulement . . . et il faut remarquer que ces 200 exemplaires suffirent pendant treize ans et plus à «la curiosité de l'Europe savante.»
>
> 468

> He had it printed at his own expense, a print run of a mere 200 copies . . . and we must note that these 200 copies satisfied "scholarly curiosity in Europe" for over thirteen years.

The fact that only two hundred copies of Michel's first edition were printed is, alas, all too unremarkable, as print runs for editions of medieval works in the 1830s and 1840s were minuscule and catered to the rare "hommes de goût," "men of good taste," whom Michel mentioned in his 1869 re-edition. William Roach, commenting on exactly the same glass as Bédier, finds it to have been half full: "Michel's edition of the Roland, although it was printed in only two hundred copies, remained in print for more than a dozen years after it was issued."[61] That a print run of 200 copies can elicit two competing interpretations—one optimistic, the other pessimistic—certainly falls within the bounds of conventionally-accepted interpretive latitude. Bédier's more radical interventions concerning both the reception of the work and the content of Michel's correspondence become only more striking by contrast. What does it benefit a scholarly exposition to venture so deliberately into the realm of imaginative emplotment? Why would Bédier construct a proud, impetuous,

Roland-like Michel who is a champion of archival endurance, bound for the gloriously heroic failure of an epic battle lost?

### THE MORAL OF THE STORY

First of all, Bédier's Michel becomes a double of Bédier himself: the discoverer of the Oxford *Roland* manuscript becomes, intellectually speaking, an ancestor of its most ardent promoter, and the latter pays due homage to the former. The implicit familial model is only strengthened by the fact that Michel's first mission also brought back important early transcriptions of the other defining corpus of Bédier's career, the Tristan romances. More broadly, Bédier's tendentious ideas of manuscript editing can be seen to rest on assumptions very similar to those underlying Michel's, insofar as both valorized the material coherence of individual manuscripts.[62] In light of these implied familial and methodological bonds, the more Bédier can trumpet Michel's failure to garner the immediate recognition his edition deserved, the stronger the implication that Bédier's own daring obstinacy will, in time, be proven to have been just as prescient and heroic a devotion to the same true artifact. Viewed from this perspective, the "Premier article" turns out to share the ideological architecture of the second and third articles in the *Romania* trilogy, so different at first glance in scope and tone.

Furthermore, insofar as Michel's paradigmatic heroism presupposes not just great deeds of prowess, but also tragic flaws, cruel turns of fate, and a rupture between individual and society, it epitomizes a bittersweet reflection Bédier permits himself on the workings of the academy and several of its early visionaries. Bédier's Monin may be Michel's opposite in productivity, but like Michel he reveals himself to have been an institutional misfit and an outsider by the terms of Bédier's epic of marginality. Not only was his 1832 *Dissertation,* the seminal study of two continental Roncevaux manuscripts, the only publication that ever appeared on the drearily static annual productivity reports he was required to file over the course of his university career, but Bédier homes in on such seeming trivia as the imagined pathos caused by a promised but never published review of the work. Although Monin boasted in print the year following the publication of his *Dissertation* of having garnered no fewer than four reviews from a man of letters named Saint-Marc Girardin, Bédier reports that archived issues of the journal in question contain but three successive articles that never got around to the intention, stated clearly enough in the introductory piece, of reviewing Monin's *Dissertation sur le Roman de Roncevaux*. "Mais il peut légitimement attendre un quatrième article qui, celui-ci, lui sera consacré," Bédier comments. "Il attend et les jours passent. Hélas! Tout un siècle a passé depuis: Monin attend toujours" ("But he is justified in expecting a fourth article that will finally be devoted to him. He waits and time passes. Alas! An entire century has now passed and Monin is still awaiting his review," 454).[63] The cover of the jocular remark here does not completely obscure Bédier's more sober fascination with the troubled juncture where hope and desire and youthful excitement abut the material realities of scholarly production. Bédier reconstructs an epic world not just of heroism in the archives but of school essays being rushed into print, of naïve young scholars condemned to never-ending patience, of research projects pursued on the side of official funding by *Chartiste* rejects, and of meteoric rises and cruel returns to earth. If Bédier's Michel and Monin are resolutely ahead of their time, they also end more often than not behind the eight ball; such is the bitter truth about scholarship's irregular and unpredictable spurts and advances, carried forward by fate-trampled heroes.[64]

Readers and admirers of Bédier's criticism, who have grown more numerous in the past two decades, will recognize here the signature skepticism that this fiercely individualistic and even contrarian scholar brought to so many of his better known endeavors.[65] Interdisciplinary in his method, witty and ironic in his delivery, often delighting in the chance to expose as invention what his predecessors had trumpeted as their discoveries, Bédier brought radical skepticism to bear on the dogma and ossified consensus that had grown up around the topics of his major interests.[66] Bédier's *Légendes épiques* in particular had famously rejected the premise of the oral origins of the medieval epic by attributing the persistence of the historical memory of Roland and Charlemagne in the eleventh-century Pyrenees to the mythopoetic use value these figures afforded churches along the major pilgrimage routes. In a similar fashion, the Michel commemorative tribute likewise makes a foray into institutional history—or Bédier's idiosyncratic formulation of it—as a way of emphasizing the importance of materialist and institutional considerations in the understanding of history.

Curiously absent from this treatment, however, is any of the acerbic edge with which Bédier set out to demolish his opponents' theories in most of his previous work.[67] Whereas Bédier had twice before in his career aimed withering jibes at Claude Fauriel, for instance, the Fauriel who graces Bédier's 1937 tribute to Michel has been transformed into an altruistic midwife of great medieval scholarship, as nurturing of Monin as he is of Michel.[68] The third and final benefit Bédier realizes from adopting his creative turn, considerably more subtle than the previous points, lies in the transformation of Fauriel from irritating apologist for the oral origins of epic into an admirable and grandfatherly embodiment of orality itself, the emblematic figure of a lecture-based oral scholarship in the sunset of its currency proudly passing the torch to a younger generation

of print-oriented researchers. Fauriel was after all, as Bédier recounts with unexpected affection, "l'homme de son temps qui devait mettre en circulation le plus d'idées" ("the man destined to launch the most ideas of his era," 460). Proffered throughout the nineteenth century as evidence of both Fauriel's fertile mind and his selfless generosity, as Bédier explains in a detailed footnote, this cliché also contains a sinister implication Bédier declines here to investigate: namely, that he who lectured much published little, that the pioneering professor of medieval literary studies in the French academy functioned best as a font of anonymous ideas whose fixity and substance would be developed by others. A contemporary of Fauriel's even went so far as to declare that his own study on the troubadours was inevitably inferior to the potential one that Fauriel might write, but the event would never come to pass, Fauriel being "incapable d'amener rien à terme," "incapable of ever finishing anything."[69] If Bédier steers away from any such pejorative scholarly observations, it is not because he has succeeded at absolving Fauriel of the taint of an amateurish orality but, rather, because he has chosen to accentuate the positive and laud Fauriel's farsighted encouragement of a paradigm shift from oral propagation of academic ideas to publications-based scholarship. What better way for Bédier to celebrate the birth of the *Song of Roland* in print than to wed it to a definitive coming of age in scholarly publication itself?

Admittedly, this idea is far from explicit in Bédier's article, since as I noted above Bédier queries the archives at length to try to establish, in the frequent absence of formal publications, a paper trail for Fauriel. The traces he finds in Fauriel's lecture notes of a vanished teaching copy of a Roncevaux manuscript do, however, by their very inconclusiveness, tend to associate Fauriel with the evanescence of the oral. What is more, Bédier makes no secret of the fact that he has pinned his hopes on Fauriel in his search for preciously rare evidence of actual first-hand knowledge of the Roman de Roncevaux manuscripts among scholars of the early 1830s.[70] For him to have to admit that he has turned up empty handed is thus all the more significant. Likewise, Bédier's most blatant reconstructive intervention of the whole article also cuts two ways, at once praising Fauriel's human qualities but also hinting at his growing professional deficiencies as the academy around him evolved. In answer to the question Bédier pursues at length of why Monin's teachers would have so avidly sponsored this neophyte's work, namely his 1832 *Dissertation*, Bédier merrily postulates that sheer magnanimity led Fauriel to want to make the public believe that his disciple had beaten him to the continental Roland manuscripts, and that to promote this illusion Fauriel even delayed publication of his own recently-delivered lectures on the topic until after Monin's "petit livre," "little book," had been in print for two months.[71] Underneath the celebratory tones, however, lurks the more damning implication that Fauriel felt uncomfortable working with manuscripts—especially Northern French ones—and that he may well have willingly left it to his disciple to make the heroic crossing of the Seine to the Bibliothèque Royale that Bédier recounts in imagined detail.[72]

What Bédier seems not to be able to bring himself to say, Michel had written in a stinging letter to La Rue in January of 1833.[73] Absent this dramatic conclusion, Bédier's reader, kept in suspense for several pages as to what answer Bédier will propose to his stated conundrum ("pourquoi un tel souci de mettre en lumière si hâtivement ce modeste travail?" ["why such haste to publish this modest piece of work?" 447]), can feel only anticlimax. Deducing this conclusion through an implied readerly privilege bestowed and encouraged by Bédier's own free invention leads to a rich complexification of the narrative, which subsequently assumes the characteristics of an allegory about the eclipse of an almost pure scholarly orality by an archivally-based academic writing produced by trained specialists.

The readerly privilege underpinning the analysis presented in this article will, I hope, seem entirely justified and appropriate in light of the evidence I have brought in support of my argument. The privilege I am claiming in having queried the archives for a story other than Bédier's is not to have "set the record straight" so much as to have revealed its fundamentally crooked and circuitous nature when the totality of Bédier's concerns are taken into account. The most important truths Bédier expresses—sometimes tendentious and partial, always probing—do not lie in the accumulation of a sequence of more or less objective factual observations about archival discoveries. To the degree that Bédier and Michel are each a figure of towering importance to French medieval studies, each deserves to be understood in the full complexity of his contributions to the profession—a complexity indissociable in the two instances from a headstrong personality unwilling to be bounded by conventions (intellectual or methodological) and confident of the rewards accruing to warrior scholars who are naturally inclined to buck and transgress them.

### Notes

A portion of this argument was presented at the International Congress on Medieval Studies, Kalamazoo, Michigan, in May 2001, and I thank the session participants for their comments. I would also like to thank Jeffry Larson for bibliographical assistance, John Lytle for research assistance, Howard Bloch, Keith Busby, Edwin Duval, Elizabeth Emery, and Michelle Warren for collegial colloquy, and the Griswold Foundation at Yale for its non-Guizotesque munificence in research funding. I also extend my gratitude to the staff members of the Archives Nationales in Paris, the University of Michigan at Ann Arbor, and Wayne State University in Detroit.

1. On the manuscript tradition of the *Roland*, see T. Atkinson Jenkins, *La chanson de Roland* (Watkins Glen, N.Y.: American Life Foundation, 1977), xcv-xcviii, and P. Le Gentil, *La chanson de Roland* (Paris: Hatier-Boivin, 1955), 9-16; the numbers I cite do not include the numerous medieval-era translations made into other European languages. Throughout this paper, I will use the title *Song of Roland* (sometimes abbreviated *Roland*) in a general sense to designate a family of manuscripts of which the text of Oxford's Bodleian Library MS Digby 23 has become the canonical exemplar. When it is necessary to distinguish between the Oxford manuscript and the later rhymed (rather than assonanced) continental redactions, I will adopt the nineteenth-century convention of calling them the *Roman de Roncevaux*. The somewhat problematic status of the title "Song of Roland"—which appears in none of the manuscripts and was adopted gradually over several decades beginning in the 1830s—is beyond the scope of this article; on this point, see Andrew Taylor, "Was There a Song of Roland?" *Speculum* 76 (2001): 28-65, and Paul Aebischer, *Préhistoire et protohistoire du Roland d'Oxford* (Berne: Francke, 1972), 187-203.

2. Exceptions are William W. Kibler, "The *Roland* After Oxford: The French Tradition," *Olifant* 6 (1979): 275-92; and Joseph J. Duggan, "L'épisode d'Aude dans la tradition en rime de la *Chanson de Roland*," in *Charlemagne in the North*, ed. Philip E. Bennett et al. (Edinburgh: Société Rencesvals, 1993), 273-79.

3. Michel's edition, entitled *La chanson de Roland ou de Roncevaux du XIIe siècle*, was published in 1837 by Silvestre, a small Parisian bookseller. Aside from Bédier's account of the project—the subject of this article—see the following studies: William Roach, "Francisque Michel: A Pioneer in Medieval Studies," *Proceedings of the American Philosophical Society* 114.3 (1970): 168-78; and Claudine I. Wilson, "A Frenchman in England: Francisque Michel," *Revue de littérature comparée* 17 (1937): 734-49. Countless single-page synopses of Michel's mission also appear in the prefaces of numerous editions and studies of the *Roland* (cf. P. Le Gentil, *Chanson de Roland*, 8-9).

4. For precise philological detail on this point, see Frederick Whitehead, "The Textual Criticism of the *Chanson de Roland*: An Historical Review," in *Studies in Medieval French* (Oxford: Clarendon, 1961), 76-89; and T. B. W. Reid, "The Right to Emend," *Medieval French Studies in Memory of*

*T. B. W. Reid*, ed. Ian Short (London: Anglo-Norman Text Society, 1984), 1-32. Interestingly, of the great national European epics—*Beowulf, El cantar de mío Cid, Das Nibelungenlied, La chanson de Roland*—the *Roland* alone presents these problems. *Beowulf* and the *Cid* survive in a single manuscript, whereas the extreme variance of the *Nibelungenlied* manuscripts has resulted in the publication of three separate versions and a consequent lack of a single definitive textual version.

5. Bédier's edition was reprinted with corrections in 1924, 1927, 1928, 1931, 1938 and, posthumously, in 1944. Consultation of the commentary volume, informally referred to as the "Commentaires," is complicated by the fact that this text is officially entitled *La chanson de Roland, commentée par Joseph Bédier,* and hence easily confused with the title of the edition itself (*La chanson de Roland, publiée d'après le manuscrit d'Oxford et traduite par Joseph Bédier*).

6. There is evidence Bédier's earliest engagement with the text as a youth while growing up on the Ile de la Réunion marked him deeply. See Michelle R. Warren, "*Au commencement était l'île*: The Colonial Formation of Joseph Bédier's *Chanson de Roland,*" in *Postcolonial Approaches to the European Middle Ages: Translating Cultures,* ed. Ananya J. Kabir and Deanne M. Williams (Cambridge, forthcoming).

7. For a useful overview of theories of textual edition and Bédier's role in it, see Alfred Foulet and Mary Blakely Speer, *On Editing Old French Texts* (Lawrence: Regents Press of Kansas, 1979).

8. See *Romania* 63 (1937): 433-69 for the "Premier article"; *Romania* 64 (1938): 145-244 for the "Deuxième article"; and ibid., 489-521 for the "Troisième article." All future references to the contents of the "Premier article" will be provided parenthetically in the text by page number. All translations are my own.

9. To my knowledge, the only archival research on this mission carried out independently of Bédier's dates from the 1930s and was presented with much less detail by Claudine I. Wilson in "A Frenchman in England." See also her "Francisque Michel and his Scottish Friends," *Modern Language Review* 30 (1935): 26-35. The numerous other accounts prior to Bédier's that I mention below did not attempt archival reconstruction of the events, relying instead on the authors' personal knowledge of people and events.

10. Bédier, "Troisième article," 520. For the anecdotal charge, see Alain Corbellari, *Joseph Bédier: Écriv-*

*ain et philologue* (Geneva: Droz, 1997), 364. For a rebuttal, see Whitehead, "Textual Criticism," especially 83.

11. It would be tedious and petty to draw up a list of Bédier's errata. On the other hand, the reliability of his Michel narrative is at the center of the present analysis. Balancing the first against the second criterion and omitting a goodly number of typographical errors, I offer this abbreviated list of two particularly noteworthy slips: a quotation clearly misdated and almost certainly incorrectly attributed to Francis Guessard ("Premier article," 469 n1), and the initial omission—corrected later, but only in passing, via a footnote—of the third clause in the official 1833 ministerial decree authorizing Michel's trip to England (461; corrected on 466 n1). Since the third clause stipulated that Michel's transcriptions were to be deemed property of the state, requiring permission for publication, Bédier's initial omission of this fact tends to underplay the constraints within which Michel was operating. I will investigate both of these points at greater length below.

12. For an examination of the detail of this point concerning his monumental four-volume work *Les légendes épiques,* see Corbellari, *Joseph Bédier,* 380ff.

13. Desperate to attain a political stability that had eluded France for decades, the July Monarchy was seeking an affirmative historical narrative of national origins in the largely unwritten history of the bourgeoisie. To this end, a national cultural census of sorts was soon to be launched in the provinces; see Pim Den Boer, *History as a Profession: The Study of History in France, 1818-1914,* trans. Arnold J. Pomerans (Princeton: Princeton University Press, 1987), chapter 2, and Gabriel de Broglie, *Guizot* (Paris: Perrin, 1990), 171. For the original documentation on Guizot's initiatives, see Xavier Charmes, *Le comité des travaux historiques et scientifiques: Histoire et documents,* 3 vols. (Paris: Imprimerie Nationale, 1886), vol. 2. On budgetary provisions, see Marie-Elizabeth Antoine, *Bulletin de la section d'histoire moderne et contemporaine,* fascicule 10 (Paris: Bibliothèque Nationale, 1977), 37-38.

14. Francisque Michel, *Rapports à M. le ministre de l'Instruction Publique sur les anciens monuments de l'histoire et de la littérature de la France qui se trouvent dans les bibliothèques de l'Angleterre et de l'Écosse* (Paris: Imprimerie Royale, 1838). The portion of this report dealing with the 1833-35 mission had earlier been published in the *Journal des débats* 19 (September 1835).

15. Michel reproduces the terms of the official *arrêté* in his brochure, *Rapports,* 1. By the end of his

mission, Michel was to transcribe hundreds of thousands of lines from over two dozen works.

16. Guizot took a functional approach to the value of literary manuscripts, which he tended to view as useful documents for studying language change or forgotten beliefs and customs; tellingly, his progress report to the king of December 1835 did not see fit to mention the *Roland* manuscript among Michel's more notable achievements (which in the aggregate he found to be "considérables"). See Charmes, *Le comité des travaux historiques,* 2:45. See also Charles Augustin de Sainte-Beuve, *Premiers lundis,* 3 vol., vol. 3 (Paris: Calmann Lévy, 1891), 378-83.

17. The contents of this letter were, however, not destined for publication and were first rendered public only when Bédier published Monmerqué's summary of it in his 1937 *Romania* article. For the original missive (Michel to Monmerqué, rather than Monmerqué to Guizot), see Gerald Brault, "'C'est presque la quadrature du cercle': Francisque Michel's Letter Announcing his Discovery of the Oxford Manuscript of the *Chanson de Roland* (1835)," *Olifant* 5.4 (May 1978): 271-75.

18. Ibid. Numerous medieval historical sources had made vague reference to such a song, and finding a plausible surviving work that fit the bill had become something of a Grail quest by Michel's day. For the sources, as well as the nineteenth-century imaginative works to which they gave rise, see Harry Redman, Jr., *The Roland Legend in Nineteenth-Century French Literature* (Lexington: University Press of Kentucky, 1991), and Taylor, "Was There a Song of Roland?" Although critics generally accord Michel the distinction of having "discovered" the Oxford *Roland* manuscript, it is more correct to say that he was the first of the four or five or men of letters who had up to then examined the manuscript to recognize its great importance and to publish a complete transcription of it (for details on Michel's predecessors, see Taylor). For this reason, I prefer to speak of Michel's "recovery" of the Oxford *Roland* manuscript, rather than his "discovery" of it.

19. Quotations are from L. Amiel's review in *Le Journal de Paris,* 25 April 1837. Likewise, Xavier Marmier wrote, "C'est là, peut-être, notre plus ancienne, notre véritable épopée nationale" ("This is perhaps our oldest and most authentic national epic," *Le Monde* 17 February 1837), quoted in Joseph Duggan, "Franco-German Conflict and the History of French Scholarship on the *Song of Roland,*" in *Hermeneutics and Medieval Culture,* ed. Patrick J. Gallacher and Helen Damico (Albany: SUNY Press, 1989), 97-106, at 98. Although it is generally true that "Francisque Michel avoided

any semblance of nationalistic fervor," as Duggan writes (97), near the end of his 1838 *Rapports à Monsieur le ministre,* Michel permitted himself this comment about a late-twelfth-century Anglo-Norman historical poem: "Un autre sera plus heureux que nous, et publiera bientôt, nous le souhaitons vivement, l'ouvrage de Jordan Fantosme. Dieu veuille que cet éditeur soit un Français!" ("Someone else more fortunate than we will soon publish, or so we urgently hope, the Jordan Fantosme work. May God grant that this editor be French!" 21).

20. Paulin Paris, "La Chanson de Roland (Edition de M. F. Génin)," *Bibliothèque de l'École des Chartes* 2, 3rd ser. (March-April 1851): 297-338, at 297. Paris was reviewing the notoriously controversial third edition of the Oxford *Roland* published in 1850 by François Génin. His antipathy to Génin's project seems to have crystallized his respect for the Oxford manuscript, which he had ranked as inferior to one of the continental rhymed manuscripts (MS P) as recently as three years earlier (although he had simultaneously stated his preference for Michel's edition of the lesser manuscript to Bourdillon's pseudo-edition of the better one). See Paris's *Les manuscrits françois de la bibliothèque du roi* (Paris, 1848), 7:26.

21. Léon Gautier, *La chanson de Roland, texte critique accompagné d'une traduction nouvelle et précédé d'une introduction historique* (Tours: Mame, 1872), clxxiii. The agency and engagement Gautier ascribes to Guizot—"M. Guizot . . . comprit toute l'importance de notre Chanson et désira la voir publiée en son texte original"—is pure wishful thinking. Not only was the *Roland* manuscript absent from the list of works deemed of primary importance to Michel's mission, but Guizot did not see fit to mention Michel's work in his memoirs years later. See François Guizot, *Mémoires pour servir à l'histoire de mon temps* (Paris: Michel Lévy, 1858-67), 3:177-84, 406, 410.

22. Léon Gautier, *Les épopées françaises: Étude sur les origines et l'histoire de la littérature nationale,* 2nd ed. (1878-97; reprint Osnabrück: [Otto] Zeller, 1966), 1:254. Michel as philological pioneer has become a standard motif in recent criticism. See Roach, "Francisque Michel," and Bernard Cerquiglini, *Éloge de la variante: Histoire critique de la philologie* (Paris: Seuil, 1989), 73-74. For an expansion of this idea into a laudatory assessment of the whole of Michel's career, see Michel Espagne, *De l'archive au texte: Recherches d'histoire génétique* (Paris: PUF, 1998), chapter 7. Espagne's treatment is, to my knowledge, the closest thing that currently exists to an intellectual biography of Francisque Michel.

23. For a full list, see the bibliography in Roach, "Francisque Michel."

24. Fauriel (1772-1844) renounced politics for a life of study and went on to make his name as a comparative philologist with specializations in Provençal literature and the popular oral poetry of modern Greece. Raynouard (1761-1836), a lawyer by training and also active in revolutionary politics in his youth, pioneered the philological study of troubadour poetry. For a short biographical sketch, see Charles Ridoux, *Evolution des études médiévales en France de 1860 à 1914* (Paris: Champion, 2001), 21-28.

25. He had used the warrior-scholar topos before; see Per Nykrog, "A Warrior Scholar at the Collège de France: Joseph Bédier," in *Medievalism and the Modernist Temper,* ed. R. Howard Bloch and Stephen G. Nichols (Baltimore: Johns Hopkins University Press, 1996), 286-307.

26. Francisque Michel, *Examen critique de la dissertation de M. Henri Monin sur le Roman de Roncevaux* (Paris: Silvestre, 1832).

27. Deriding in particular Louis Antoine François de Marchangy's *La Gaule poétique ou l'histoire de France considérée dans ses rapports avec la poésie, l'éloquence et les beaux-arts* of 1813-17, Gautier had written, "tant de travaux n'avancent point la grande question. Ce ne sont là que des préludes ou, pour mieux dire, des balbutiements. Personne encore n'a eu l'audace de regarder notre Épopée en face. C'est un Français qui eut cette hardiesse en 1832" ("so many studies make no progress on the fundamental question. All these are nothing but preludes or, more precisely, the first faltering attempts at speech. No one has yet been bold enough to look directly upon our Epic. It was a Frenchman who was daring enough to do so in 1832," *La chanson de Roland,* clxiix).

28. For a perceptive treatment of the narrative topoi shared by accounts of losing epic battles fought at Roncevaux, Kosovo, the Alamo and Little Big Horn, see Bruce A. Rosenberg, *Custer and the Epic of Defeat* (University Park: Pennsylvania State University Press, 1974).

29. "Quelle prodigalité de bienfaits! Personne pourtant, que je sache, ne l'a jamais dit, que, s'il n'était pas venu, l'admirable Dictionnaire de Godefroy serait beaucoup moins riche et que l'oeuvre de Gaston Paris elle-même ne serait pas tout ce qu'elle est." ("What a prodigious contribution to the field! Yet no one, to my knowledge, has ever remarked that, if he had not come along, Godefroy's admirable dictionary of Old French would be much the poorer and that even the work of Gaston Paris would not be what it is," "Premier article," 469).

30. Bédier could have pursued his point even further in noting that, written as it was in May of 1836, the remark summarized the opinion of the most recently inducted member of the Académie Française on some very recent discoveries of medieval treasures. (Guizot was elected to the Académie on April 28, 1836.)

31. Translations, in order: "This story is complex, and occasionally obscure. May I recount it correctly!"; "one can imagine the pride felt by the students of the École Normale when they were able gloriously to pass around the still-damp proof sheets of a book whose title page read: *Dissertation on the Romance of Roncevaux,* by H. Monin, student of the École Normale"; "Truly, with the passing of time, Francisque Michel stands as a giant among his contemporaries. Here, however, I have recounted only his early exploits."

32. Fauriel's lectures were given at the Sorbonne. He had earned France's first university appointment in medieval literature in being named professor of "littérature étrangère" by the July Monarchy in October of 1830.

33. Tyrwhitt had made a gender mistake, mistakenly recording "le geste" for "la geste" in the final line of the Oxford manuscript ("Ci falt la geste que Turold' declinet"). See Thomas Tyrwhitt, *The Canterbury Tales of Chaucer, with an essay upon his language and versification, an introductory discourse, notes, and a glossary* (1775-78; London, 1822), 448-49. (Incidentally, Bédier himself mistakenly records "copie" for Tyrwhitt's "copy" and "no" for his "not.") The reason Tyrwhitt was citing the Old French text in the first place was to elucidate the jocular oath "by Termagaunt" appearing in Chaucer's "Tale of Sir Thopas"; the form "Tervagan," Tyrwhitt noted, appears frequently in "an old Romance, Ms. Bod. 1624."

34. La Rue was a cleric from Caen who, during several decades of self-imposed exile after the Revolution, combed the English archives for Old French manuscripts and finally published a monumental synopsis of his research in 1834, *Essais historiques sur les bardes, les jongleurs et les trouvères normands et anglo-normands.* See Keith Busby, "Three Frenchmen Abroad: La Rue, Michel, and Meyer in England," *Nineteenth-Century French Studies* 22.3-4 (1994): 348-63.

35. Michel's surviving correspondence with La Rue (which covers the crucial period in question) lends credence to Bédier's hunch. In a July 1832 letter to La Rue, Michel mentions having been unable to consult La Rue's study on Anglo-Norman poets (presumably then circulating in draft form), which included a section on "Turold," and at no point

does he thank La Rue for communicating what one would assume Michel would have valued as precious information on the *Roland* manuscript. See Caen, Bibliothèque du Musée des Beaux Arts, Collection Mancel MS 113, fols. 252-83.

36. The first twenty pages of Bédier's "Premier article" draw on a sufficiently varied number of archival sources as to have put their verification beyond the scope of the current analysis; in the absence of evidence to the contrary, I am not calling into question the factual propositions made in this portion of Bédier's reconstruction.

37. The dossier in question, labeled "Francisque Michel" and entitled "Recherches philologiques en Angleterre," is filed in box F17 3296 in the Archives Nationales; all subsequent references to the Michel correspondence will concern the contents of this file. In all, the records of approximately 150 research projects ("projets de publication") proposed by individual scholars between 1833 and 1906 have been preserved in a half-dozen boxes.

38. At the point at which one would logically expect a quotation from this letter, Bédier has recourse to free indirect discourse in the interrogative. The paragraph revealing the genesis of the mission reads as follows; I have italicized the crucial phrases:

> Francisque Michel dresse un programme des tâches qui lui semblent le [sic] plus urgentes. Il se fait recommander au ministre de l'Instruction publique, Guizot; *ne pourrait-on pas le charger d'une mission, rétribuée par le Gouvernement? Il en fait la demande par lettre.* Guizot le fait venir. Il semble que ce bachelier, «ancien élève refusé de l'École des chartes» (comme il se qualifie lui-même), ait intéressé le ministre ou plutôt l'ait amusé quelques instants. L'entretien est tombé par hasard sur Jean Scot Érigène: Guizot a dit (ou du moins son interlocuteur a cru comprendre) qu'il tiendrait beaucoup à être mieux renseigné sur un certain traité du Docteur subtil. Le ministre prend bonne note de la demande et congédie le solliciteur.
>
> 458
>
> Francisque Michel draws up a list of the projects that he deems most urgent. He has himself recommended to the Minister of Public Instruction, Guizot; *could he not be entrusted with a research mission, funded by the government? He makes this request in writing.* Guizot agrees to meet with him. Apparently, this holder of the Baccalaureate degree, a 'rejected graduate of the École des Chartes' (as he dubs himself), intrigued the minister or perhaps amused him briefly. The interview turned by chance to John Scotus Eriugena: Guizot said (or at least his interlocutor understood him to say) that he wanted very much to be better informed on a certain treatise by the learned Doctor. The minister duly noted Michel's request and then dismissed his guest.

Michel's witticism played on the conventional honorific phrase "ancien élève *pensionnaire* de

l'École des Chartes" (roughly, "graduate who benefited from boarding privileges").

39. In researching this article, I came across this letter in the papers of a certain "Magnoncourt," Archives Nationales, F17 3295; it has since been returned to Michel's file. Given that the current files were constituted between 1906 and 1935, it seems probable that the misfiling antedates Bédier's research by at least several years.

40. Francisque Michel to François Guizot, received 10 June 1833 (no date of composition specified):

> De même, Monsieur le Ministre, l'histoire fabuleuse de Charlemagne et l'état de la langue romane d'oil au 11e et 12e siècles n'ont pu encore être suffisamment déterminés, attendu que le poëme anglo-normand composé vers le milieu de l'XIe se [sic] sur le voyage de Charlemagne à Constantinople et que le roman de Roncevaux rédigé dans les prémieres [sic] années de la prémière [sic] moitié du XIIe siècle n'existent pareillement qu'en Angleterre.
>
> Furthermore, sir, the mythical history of Charlemagne and the state of the *langue d'oïl* in the eleventh and twelfth centuries have not yet been sufficiently established, given that the Anglo-Norman poem composed around the middle of the eleventh century on the voyage of Charlemagne to Constantinople and that the *Romance of Roncevaux* written in the first years of the first half of the twelfth century also exist only in England.

41. Implicit in Bédier, this suggestion becomes increasingly explicit in accounts given by Roach and Busby. Bédier speculates that Michel was concerned with concealing his enthusiasm first and foremost from himself, so as to avoid crushing disappointment.

42. Bédier, quoting Michel, offers this example of what he terms one of Michel's "plaintes naïves": "Deux ou trois de vos lettres, Monsieur le Ministre, me sont arrivées, affranchies par l'Etat de Paris à Calais, mais de Dover à Londres grevées d'une surtaxe énorme . . . de 28 francs!" ("Two or three of your letters, sir, were delivered to me, postage paid by the government from Paris to Calais, but from Dover to London surtaxed at an enormous rate . . . of 28 francs!" "Premier article," 462). The line as it actually appears in Michel's letter of 12 June 1834, with the important part of Bédier's omission italicized, reads

> *Je ne vous parlerai point ici, Monsieur le Ministre, des frais de bureau qui en Angleterre sont fort élevés, ni de ceux que m'ont coutés* deux ou trois de vos lettres qui mises à la poste avec une enveloppe recouvrant en outre une lettre de mon père déposée à votre hôtel, me sont arrivées affranchies par l'état, de Paris à Calais, mais de Dover à Londres grevées d'une surtaxe énorme (22 francs).
>
> *I shall not speak here, sir, of the administrative surcharges that are very high in England, nor of those that I was obliged to pay* for two or three of your let-

ters which, posted with an envelope also containing a letter my father delivered to you, were delivered to me, postage paid by the government from Paris to Calais, but from Dover to London surtaxed at an enormous rate (22 francs).

Aside from the fact that Bédier has caricatured Michel by adding a pregnant pause and exclamation point and by revising the sum upward by more than a quarter of the actual figure (28 instead of 22), he has shorn the original quotation of its introductory preterition and deprived Michel of his actual rhetorical agility and maturity.

43. This particular claim, it must be acknowledged, is a well-founded if easily overemphasized point from the epistolary record. Bédier quotes Michel's initial offer ("Je suis prêt à rechercher l'ouvrage de Scot Érigène, auquel, Monsieur le Ministre, vous paraissez tant tenir," "I am ready to search for the Scotus Eriugena work which, sir, seems to interest you so much") and Guizot's pencilled marginal response to an aide ("Je n'ai nul besoin qu'il achète, ni qu'il copie l'ouvrage de Jean Érigène," "I have no need for him either to buy or to copy the work by John Eriugena," "Premier article," 461).

44. I stress that concerning letters sent by Guizot, I continue to refer to the drafts contained in the file, all the final copies having of course been sent to Michel.

45. Fauriel changed his mind on the desirability of the Geoffrey Gaimar manuscript he had earlier recommended and categorically rejected the idea that a fourteenth-century romance Michel had requested permission to copy—the *Histoire des seigneurs de Gavre*—could deliver the desirable historical information promised by its title. The reason for Fauriel's about-face is unclear from the archival evidence I have so far consulted. An ancillary point: Bédier's reported date of June 12, 1834, for this supposed Fauriel missive corresponds to no letter in Michel's file. The only surviving letter written by Fauriel during the month of June of that year bears no date of composition but is stamped as having been received by Guizot on 23 June. Since it begins "Je réponds à la fois aux deux dernières lettres que vous m'avez fait l'honneur de m'écrire" ("I am responding to both of the recent letters you kindly wrote to me") and since the rate of exchange of correspondence in the whole file almost never exceeded one letter per week, the existence of a letter dated 12 June seems highly dubious, whether or not it would have disappeared from the file since Bédier examined it some sixty-five years ago.

46. For instance, on April 10, 1834, Michel announced his decision to refrain from copying a manuscript

Guizot had designated as noteworthy (under the fluctuating title of "Les usages/usances de Romanie") on the grounds that it had already been published. Exactly a month later, Michel noted that what Guizot had assumed from other sources to be a rare and desirable law code contained in a Bodleian manuscript, the "Assises de Jérusalem," was actually a common work then known as the *Roman de Vespasien,* now referred to as the *Vengeance de Nostre Seigneur.*

47. Laisse 88; Joseph Bédier, *La chanson de Roland publiée d'après le manuscrit d'Oxford et traduite par Joseph Bédier* (Paris: L'Édition d'Art, 1944), 96. The effect is heightened by Bédier's noting that Michel addressed his first letters to Guizot from his sickbed, having fallen deathly ill upon arrival in London.

48. Michel never resigned himself to the indignity of having been relegated to what he deemed a distant provincial university post in Bordeaux and feuded bitterly at the end of his career with the minister of public education over having been denied a promotion, a fact attributable largely to his habitual absenteeism. In essence, Michel published and perished. For details, see Espagne, *De l'archive au texte,* and Archives Nationales, F17 21325.

49. Guizot notes in his memoirs that when he proposed creating a Comité des Travaux Historiques in 1834, liberal deputies suspected a subversive conservative plot to siphon the best and the brightest out of political careers and spirit them off to dank and dark archives (Guizot, *Mémoires,* 3:179-81). Opponents may have voiced outrage, but would-be recipients found cause for hilarity. Prosper Mérimée, recruited to help conduct Guizot's national cultural census, recounts the following illustrative anecdote in a letter to a mentor in January 1835:

> M. Guizot, à la première séance, nous dit que nous devions faire un catalogue de *tous* les monuments de la France actuellement existants. Je me récriais, il me dit: «Figurez-vous que ni le temps ni l'argent ne vous manqueront.» Je fus réduit au silence, et mon voisin, homme au pis, m'écrivit sur un morceau de papier: «Le temps? il ne sera pas ministre dans trois mois. L'argent? il n'a plus un sou des cent vingt mille francs votés pour 1835.» En attendant, nous nous réunissons fréquemment pour blaguer.

> M. Guizot informed us at the first meeting that we were to draw up a catalogue of *all* the monuments currently in France. When I cried out in surprise, he said, "Of course you will lack neither time nor money in this endeavor." After I had been reduced to silence, the man seated next to me, of a cynical nature, passed me a note reading, "Time? He will no longer be minister in three months. Money? He has not one *sou* left of the 120,000 francs appropriated for 1835." While we wait, we've been getting together often to tell jokes.

See *La revue de Paris* 27 (May-June 1898): 233.

50. It is true that the French state had funded scientific missions episodically since the seventeenth century. Medieval research under the Ancien Régime, however, was often conducted in a patrician atmosphere by aristocrats who sometimes provided their services free of charge and by Benedictine monks who always did; see Lionel Gossman, *Medievalism and the Ideologies of the Enlightenment* (Baltimore: Johns Hopkins University Press, 1968), 186-87 and 220. Michel alludes to his situation, albeit not without a fillip characteristic of the manipulative supplicant, in a February 23, 1834, letter to Guizot from London:

> Comme je n'ai aucune fortune personnelle, je me vois forcé, monsieur le ministre, d'en apeller [sic] à votre sagesse et à votre justice. La première sait qu'en Angleterre, à Londres surtout, les choses de première nécessité sont d'un prix qui ne peut être comparé à celui qu'elles ont en France; et votre justice ne souffrira point qu'un voyage que j'ai entrepris dans le but d'ajouter un rayon de plus à notre gloire historique et littéraire, et d'obtenir une part de l'intérêt que vous avez toujours accordé à la jeunesse studieuse et paisible, devienne pour moi une cause de découragement et de ruine.

> As I have no personal fortune, I find myself, sir, forced to call upon your wisdom and your sense of fairness. Your wisdom knows that in England, and London especially, the high cost of the most basic necessities cannot be compared to prices in France. Your sense of fairness will not allow that travel I have undertaken with the goal of adding one more ray to our country's historical and literary glory and of receiving a portion of the attention you have always granted to studious and well-behaved young people should become for me a cause of discouragement and financial ruin.

51. On June 12, 1834, he had written to Guizot: "Je termine en vous suppliant de m'accorder la nouvelle indemnité que je vous demande et de la convertir en un traitement régulier et conforme à la valeur de l'argent ici, à ma position sociale et à mon travail" ("I shall end in begging you to grant me the new lump sum payment that I am requesting and to convert it into a regular salary commensurate with the value of money here, with my social status and with my work"). His July 3, 1834, expression of his desire to give up the England project resulted in his achieving his goal: a 500-franc-per-month stipend, beginning that same month.

52. The exchange rate of 25 francs to one pound sterling is supplied by a July 1834 memo in the hand of one of Guizot's aides, commenting on Michel's demand for a regular stipend. Achille Jubinal, a contemporary of Michel's, noted wryly in 1850 that early codicological work he had done for the French state was remunerated at a rate

one-third to two-thirds less than the standard wages of a mason. See Charles-Olivier Carbonell, "Guizot, homme d'État, et le mouvement historiographique français du XIXe siècle" in *Actes du colloque François Guizot, Paris, 22-25 octobre 1974* (Paris: Société de l'histoire du Protestantisme français, 1976), 219-37, at 225. By contrast, Jean-François Champollion had received a royal navy escort and 180,000 francs, half from the French Crown, to undertake his mission to Egypt in 1828; see Jean Lacouture, *Champollion: Une vie de lumières* (Paris: Grasset, 1988), 397-98.

53. In his one-year self-evaluation letter of October 1, 1834, Michel wrote the following to Guizot:

> Vous savez sans doute, Monsieur le Ministre, que le gouvernement anglois a ouvert les yeux sur les encouragements que vous donnez à la science historique. A l'imitation de vos actes, il a fait envoyer par la <u>records commission</u>, à Heidelberg, à Paris et à Lisbonne des jeunes-gens chargés de travaux analogues aux miens. En revenant, leurs recherches seront publiées aux frais de la commission, qui a plusieurs millions par an pour mettre en lumière les documents historiques relatifs à l'Angleterre, enfouis dans les archives et les bibliothèques. Quant à ceux relatifs à la France que je publierai par vos ordres, je vous promets, Monsieur le Ministre, de ne jamais recourir aux presses du gouvernement tant que, pour en supporter les frais, je trouverai des libraires, desquels cependant je ne puis attendre aucun salaire et qui eux-mêmes comptent sur votre appui lors de la mise en vente.

> As you must know, sir, your encouragement of historical research has opened the eyes of the English government, and in imitation of your actions, the *Records Commission* has dispatched young people to Heidelberg, Paris and Lisbon with missions analogous to mine. Upon their return, their research will be published at the expense of the commission, which receives several million a year to publish historical documents related to the history of England that are recovered from archives and libraries. As for those works concerning France that I will publish upon your orders, I promise, sir, never to call upon the government's press as long as I can find booksellers to provide subventions. I cannot, however, hope for any salary from them, and they depend upon your support at the time the book appears.

54. See Dorothy Doolittle, "The Relations Between Literature and Mediaeval Studies in France from 1820 to 1860" (Ph.D. dissertation, Bryn Mawr College, 1933), 68 and 89.

55. Gautier rapidly summarized the editorial history of the *Roland* in the introduction to his 1887 student edition. After noting approvingly Michel's contribution to study of the *Roland*, Gautier writes: "Mais l'opinion publique ne s'émut point de cette découverte, et l'on peut dire que la seconde popularité de notre Chanson ne date vraiment chez nous que de l'édition et de la traduction de Génin" ("Public opinion, however, was

indifferent to this discovery, and one can thus date the second period of popularity of our *Song* to Génin's edition and translation"). See Gautier, *Chanson de Roland,* xliv-xlv.

56. Francisque Michel, *La chanson de Roland et le Roman de Roncevaux des* xɪɪᵉ *et* xɪɪɪᵉ *siècles* (Paris: Firmin Didot, 1869), xvi. Among other things, Génin, who held a high post in the Ministry of Public Instruction, not only had his book (in which Michel was nowhere mentioned) printed at state expense but also had free review copies distributed to a large number of journalists. On the Génin edition, see Jean-Claude Faucon, "La bataille (du poème) de Roncevaux ou l'exquise aménité des médiévistes du xɪxe siècle," in *Chemins ouverts: Mélanges offerts à Claude Sicard,* ed. Sylvie Vignes (Toulouse: Presses Universitaires du Mirail, 1998), 13-23.

57. In the same 1869 preface Bédier draws upon (ibid., xiv-xv), Michel emphatically professes his pride at his accomplishment:

> Le premier des poëmes que nous donnons ici a été imprimé à la suite de l'une de nos missions en Angleterre. Le bruit que fit cette publication, tout de suite appréciée par les hommes de goût, engagea un amateur d'anciens manuscrits [i.e. Jean-Louis Bourdillon] à produire par la même voie celui qu'il possédait; mais en dépit de tous ses efforts, assaisonnés d'une aigreur que rien ne justifiait, le public s'obstina dans son admiration pour le texte de Turold, et en même temps que M. Bourdillon publiait le *rifacimento* qu'il prétendait mettre au-dessus, MM. Delécluze, Vitet, Génin, Saint-Albin, Jônain, et d'Avril, s'en tenant à la vieille chanson de geste, la faisaient passer plus ou moins heureusement dans notre langue actuelle.

> The first poem in this edition was published as a result of one of our missions to England. Immediately appreciated by men of good taste, this publication caused a stir that prompted a lover of old manuscripts also to publish the one he owned. But in spite of all of his efforts, which were leavened with a completely unjustified virulence, the public remained steadfast in its admiration for the Turold text, and at the same time that M. Bourdillon published the revised version which he claimed superior, Messers Delécluze [et al.], remaining faithful to the old *chanson de geste,* were largely successful in transposing it into our current tongue.

58. Gautier rightly accorded Bourdillon considerably less authority than did Bédier (*Chanson de Roland,* clxxvi).

59. Raynouard, who found himself reviewing competing editions done by two of his students—Michel and Monin—quite predictably found something positive to say about each: "S'il s'agissait de comparer le poème dont M. Monin a publié l'analyse avec celui-ci [i.e. Michel's], je ne craindrais pas de dire que les faits contenus dans les manuscrits français sont en général plus intéressants et les

récits plus poétiques que ceux qu'on trouve dans le manuscrit anglo-normand; mais celui-ci offre quelques détails heureux et surtout un dénoûment plus satisfaisant" ("If one were to compare the poem of which Mr. Monin has published an analysis with this one, I would not hesitate to say that the deeds contained in the French manuscripts are generally more interesting and the narration more poetic than those found in the Anglo-Norman one; but the latter offers some nice touches of its own and in particular a more satisfying conclusion"; quoted in Bédier, "Premier article," 468-69). By contrast, the eight or so reviews Michel's edition received in the general and specialized presses made laudatory comments almost without exception. Some examples: "Puisse ce livre obtenir tout le succès qu'il mérite!" ("May this book receive all the success it deserves!" Xavier Marmier, *Le Monde,* 17 February 1837). "It is, in every respect, a most extraordinary poem; it abounds with the most splendid imagery: its fable is interesting; it contains many of the most venerable traditions of the middle ages; and it faithfully reflects the manners and opinions of the age" (*The Dublin Review,* 4 [January 1838]: 130). "Ein älterer und . . . besserer Codex wurde in der Bodleianischen Bibliothek zu Oxford aufbewahrt. Durch die dankbar anzuerkennende Unterstüzung des französischen Ministeriums . . . ward es Herrn Michel möglich gemacht, nach England zu reisen und eine auch äusserlich würdig ausgestattete Ausgabe zu liefern" ("An older and better codex was to be found in Oxford's Bodleian Library. Through the fortunate support of the French ministry, it was possible for Mr. Michel to travel to England and to deliver an extremely richly endowed edition"; Wilhelm Grimm, *Göttingische gelehrte Anzeigen,* 29 March 1838, 493). The closest thing to a negative review came in Raimond Thomassy's reproach that Michel's edition did not make sufficient accommodations for non-specialist readers. For references to all reviews, see Emil Seelmann, *Bibliographie des Altfranzösischen Rolandsliedes* (Heilbronn: Gebr. Henninger, 1888), 7.

60. According to Bédier, Guessard opined acerbically as follows: "La *Chanson de Roland* paraît à M. Génin tout ce qu'il y a de plus suave et de plus harmonieux; c'est un chef-d'oeuvre, ou peu s'en faut. Il ne tarit pas sur les mérites de cette vieille rhapsodie, et il y voit tout ce qui n'y est point" ("Mr. Génin sees in the *Song of Roland* the most exquisite and most harmonious work—a masterpiece, almost. He is effusive about the qualities of this ancient epic and sees in it everything that it lacks"), 469. Bédier's footnoted source—a Guessard article of 1840—obviously cannot support his claim that resistance to the Oxford *Roland* was

still continuing strong *fifteen* years after Michel's 1837 edition. Nor does Guessard's 1851 contribution to the Génin controversy contain the words Bédier attributes to him. It is Bourdillon's characteristically terse contribution to the same dispute ("Le manuscrit d'Oxford ne vaut absolument rien," "The Oxford manuscript is completely worthless") that comes closest to the spirit of Bédier's quotation, but if the Guessard source ever existed, it remains a mystery to me. (The Bourdillon quotation is found on page 62 of his *Remarques sur quelques passages de l'édition du poème de Roncevaux sortie récemment de l'imprimerie nationale à Paris,* an 1851 pamphlet housed in the collection of the Bibliothèque Méjanes, Aix-en-Provence, call no. P 12836.)

61. Roach, "Francisque Michel," 171.

62. On this point, see Corbellari, *Joseph Bédier,* 522.

63. It should be noted that numerous critics, one as recently as 2001, take Monin at his word, crediting his *Dissertation* with having elicited multiple reviews. Again, Bédier can indeed claim exhaustivity and archival exactitude on certain points.

64. Nothing proves that Bédier personally identified with these portraits of marginality, but Ferdinand Lot's startlingly frank memorial homage written the year after Bédier's death implies a few possible points of resemblance. Lot depicts a scholar surprisingly uneasy with the institutions in which he rose to such prominence (driven to agony by his stylistic perfectionism, for example), whose idiosyncratic notion of scholarly productivity led him more than once to return to familiar material when his peers expected new work from him. See Lot's sometimes exculpatory *Joseph Bédier* (Paris: Droz, 1939), especially 12, 27-28, 30-32, and 34.

65. For important recent studies on Bédier as a critic, see the brilliant article by Hans Aarsleff, "Scholarship and Ideology: Joseph Bédier's Critique of Romantic Medievalism," in *Historical Studies and Literary Criticism,* ed. Jerome J. McGann (Madison: University of Wisconsin Press, 1985), 93-113; and Alain Corbellari, "Joseph Bédier, Philologist and Writer," in *Medievalism and the Modernist Temper,* 269-85.

66. Bédier had a Voltairean knack for cutting straight to the risible. To cite just one example, he culled this line on the problematic origins of epic poetry from Gaston Paris's *Histoire poétique de Charlemagne* (1865) as a subtle way of calling attention to the unflatteringly dated terms in which the effusions of a positivist forebear found expression: "De même que toute combinaison chimique est accompagnée d'un dégagement de chaleur, toute combinaison de nationalités est accompagnée d'un dégagement de poésie" ("Just as every chemical mixture releases heat, every mixture of national peoples releases poetry"); Joseph Bédier, *Les légendes épiques: Recherches sur la formation des chansons de geste,* 4 vols., 3rd ed. (Paris: Champion, 1926), 3:240.

67. On Bédier's negativity, see in particular Nykrog, "A Warrior Scholar."

68. A young Bédier under the temporary spell of the positivistic claims of philology had lumped Fauriel in with a group of ineffectual, pre-scientific bumblers: "Après les généralisations hâtives, brillantes et inutiles de l'école de Raynouard, de Fauriel, d'Ampère et de Villemain, alors que l'intelligence du moyen âge était compromise par l'à-peu-près et le clinquant romantiques, il fallait que cette réaction érudite se produisît" ("After the hasty, brilliant and useless generalizations of the school of Raynouard, Fauriel, Ampère and Villemain, and at the time that appreciation of the Middle Ages was compromised by Romantic flashiness and approximation, this erudite reaction was natural"); "Les lais de Marie de France," *Revue des deux mondes* 107 (1891): 835-63, at 842. More damningly, the mature Bédier of the *Légendes épiques* had derided Fauriel as an unoriginal thinker slavishly devoted to promulgating wrongheaded German Romantic theories of the popular origins of epic (3:204-11).

69. J. C. L. Simonde de Sismondi, quoted in Michael Glencross, *Reconstructing Camelot: French Romantic Medievalism and the Arthurian Tradition* (Cambridge: Brewer, 1995), 121.

70. Referring to the romance contained in these manuscripts, Bédier writes, "à la façon dont Raynouard présente ce roman dans le *Journal des Savants,* il est visible que les «savants» euxmêmes ne le connaissaient, pour la plupart, que par ouï-dire. . . . Il en va autrement, peut-être, de Fauriel" ("given the manner Raynouard presents this romance in the *Journal des Savants,* it is obvious that the 'experts' themselves generally know it only by second-hand reports. . . . Fauriel is, perhaps, in a different category"; "Premier article," 443).

71. "Fauriel aura voulu laisser à la *Dissertation* le temps de se propager; il aura eu à coeur de persuader le public que son jeune disciple l'avait devancé." The following paragraph begins, "Cette conjecture est peu assurée, certes, mais inoffensive, et j'ai pris plaisir à la façonner" ("Fauriel may have wanted to give the *Dissertation* time to become known, wanting to persuade the public that his disciple was one step head of him." / "This

is a speculative conjecture, certainly, but harmless, and I have enjoyed creating it"; "Premier article," 447).

72. In Sorbonne lectures published in 1832, Fauriel, evoking the large number of unpublished epic and romance manuscripts, had made the following admission: "Ces romans sont en grand nombre, et pour la plupart encore enfouis dans de vieux manuscrits, difficiles à déchiffrer, où ils semblent braver la patience et la curiosité des littérateurs" ("These romances are numerous and for the most part still buried in old, difficult-to decipher manuscripts, where they seem to defy the patience and the curiosity of literary scholars"); Fauriel, "Origine de l'épopée chevaleresque du moyen âge," *Revue des deux mondes* 7 (1832), 513-75, at 516.

73. Michel's letter of January 1, 1833, reads in part:

> "[J]e vous dirai ce qu'est ce monsieur Fauriel. Il est professeur de littérature étrangère à la faculté de lettres de Paris, où pour remplir ses fonctions, il fait un cours de littérature provençale; il a publié un recueil de chansons grecques modernes, de plus, il est conservateur adjoint aux manuscrits de la Bibliothèque Royale où il n'a jamais mis le pied qu'une seule fois. Vous voyez qu'il a tout ce qu'il faut pour disserter savamment sur les épopées du moyen-âge. proh! pudor!"
>
> I'll tell you who this Fauriel is. He is a professor of foreign literature at the University in Paris, where he carries out his duties by teaching a course on Provençal literature. He has published a collection of modern Greek songs; he is, moreover, assistant manuscript librarian at the Royal Library, where he has set foot only once. As you can see, he has everything necessary to write knowledgeably about *medieval epic*. For shame!"

Caen, Bibliothèque du Musée des Beaux Arts, Mancel MS 113, fol. 270. Paulin Paris had been equally dismissive of Fauriel on this point; see his *Li romans de Garin de Loherain,* 2 vols. (Paris: Techener, 1833-35), 1:iii.

## Peter Haidu (essay date 2004)

SOURCE: Haidu, Peter. "Epic and the King's Peace: *The Song of Roland* and *Louis's Coronation.*" In *The Subject Medieval/Modern,* pp. 57-78. Stanford, Calif.: Stanford University Press, 2004.

*[In the following essay, Haidu examines the presentation of violence in medieval epics, specifically in* The Song of Roland, *claiming that such texts "addressed violence as a social and textual problem, from the perspective of a state in the process of creation and the recasting of subjectivity."]*

War itself requires no special motive but appears to be engrafted on human nature; it passes even for something noble.

*Immanuel Kant*

Violence is inscribed at the deepest, most constitutive structural levels of the epic chansons de geste's warrior heroism. An oversimple identification of matter, meaning, and structure has led to a generalized impression that the epic universally glorifies the violence it portrays. That is confusing meaning with problematics. Epic explores violence: Is this automatically a glorification? Does Sophocles' *Oedipus Rex* endorse incest? Epic explores violence and its structures; in some cases, it projects symbolic solutions to the political problem of violence. Violence is epic's central concern, not the object of its praise. It is a matter toward which epic takes a stance, not an identitarian embrace. That stance is often complex, a mix of admiration and critique.

How paradoxical this can be appears in one of the earliest Old French poems extant. Itself not an epic, the *Voyage of Saint Brendan* was written early the twelfth century. Its hagiographic background winds through an exotic fantasy quest, en route to paradise—far from the motifs of contemporary epics. Nevertheless, their topic is inscribed in the poem's dedication to Lady Alice the queen. Through her will divine law prevail, growing an earthly law to make

> multitudinous wars disappear,
> Thanks to the weapons of Henry the King
> And the counsels you will deliver.[1]

The law of God and human counsel will pass through the queen to the king, human and divine laws will be respected, peace will arrive, war will disappear—thanks to the king's intervention with the weapons of war. The king brings an end to war by making war: war ushers in peace. The paradoxes of twelfth-century governance, and of governance ever since, are inscribed in this brief dedication. Hagiography rejected a warring world for the sake of salvation. The *Voyage of Saint Brendan* offers a glimpse of paradise within the framework of this life, one terminus of an escapist fantasy. The other terminus is that nexus of peace, power, and war as the means to achieve the peace.

After the Oaths of Strasbourg, the thin series of Old French texts are all of religious inspiration for nearly three hundred years, translated from Latin: the *Vie de saint Alexis* is merely the most imposing. Then, in the north, secular narrative predominated, in epics focused on transactions of violence and power. As is normal in oral culture, the content and even structures of individual poems evolved and changed continuously. Their actual manuscript inscription did not begin until the late twelfth and thirteenth centuries. Different manuscripts of the same text can bear substantive variations. *Manuscripts* can sometimes be dated; *works* are best "dated" by a temporal bracket.

The epic, in Greece, Rome and medieval Europe, thematizes war and its effects. Issuing from societies modernity deems "primitive," it can be extraordinarily sophisticated, complex, and highly articulated. The poems prize the heroic, lauding physical prepossession, technical fighting skills, courage, and loyalty above all, in recognizable conventions that can give rise to ideas of "genre." But conventions are often used in profoundly discordant ways. Seemingly conventional "war poems" may harbor structures pointing to peace and its disciplines, such concerns for peace being hidden by textual circumspection toward traditional conventions. Some of the most archaic stories are embedded in texts revised much later. The same *story* could be told in purely constative or admirative veins; its act of *narration* could reveal a sense of tragic loss deriving from a mingling of identification with distance—as in the case of *Raoul de Cambrai,* which aspectualizes its narrative through perspectivalism.[2] Different, even contradictory subjects of enunciation are implied by different tellings.

The Old French epic was class-specific, but the noble class was a complex one, and the jongleurs who were its entertainers were marginals. The oral epic, as it appears through later written recensions, was the cultural field within which segmental differences of the dominant political class were deployed and negotiated in ideological semiosis. Women, peasants, merchants, clerics, even the pope, make only occasional appearances, especially in the early poems. The essential, paradigmatic axis of the texts is that which defines feudalism: that between vassal and lord, often promoted to king or prince. Although feudalism has come under skeptical scrutiny as a principle of historical explanation, there is no doubt of its ideological reality in vernacular narrative. Not only does it structure most narratives: a subcategorization organizes the epic in three cycles according to a structural analysis of the fundamental feudal relationship. The texts are distributed according to legendary genealogical ancestors of heroes: Charlemagne, Garin de Montglane, Doon de Mayence.[3] The specific roles of heroes and kings, subjects and destinators, reveal an axiological surface distribution of positive and negative value to the two paradigmatic actors of feudalism: lord and vassal.

In "the matter of France," the king's cycle (for example, *Song of Roland*), both vassal and lord are given positive markers on the surface: both Roland and Charlemagne appear as "good guys." In the Garin de Montglane or William of Orange cycle, the king is weak, young, incompetent: he is negativized; his vassal, Count

William or another, is the hero. In the last cycle, that of the rebellious barons, both lord and vassal are negatively valorized: both are "bad guys." The distribution is as follows:

|                          | lord | vassal |
|--------------------------|------|--------|
| King's cycle:            | (+)  | (+)    |
| William of Orange cycle: | (-)  | (+)    |
| Rebellious baron's cycle:| (-)  | (-)    |

The texts envisage three narrative possibilities: both king and vassal are admirable, and only a traitor explains tragic defeat; the king lacks the requisite qualities, but is supported by a great vassal; or the king's weakness or ill will leads to the dreadful cycle of revenge, both antagonists assuming negative markings. One further subtype is logically possible: the king would be given positive value, and the vassal negativized. That possibility does not actually materialize, marking the class enunciatory position.

The validity of this distribution is limited. As texts bespeaking a complex class, they are not only accounted for by a simple, binary ethic. Surface values "cover" the text's more serious exploration of fundamental political issues. The surface binary is an enabling condition for the textualization of the culture's "political unconscious." That unconscious operates, not at the level of surface verbalizations, but in developing complex political content for deeper narrative structures. Epic discourse is one of competing values and loyalties, where plural and contradictory value schemes take advantage of the enlarged framework of fiction to explore the constitutive aporias of feudalism—conflicts that can extend over generations without finding a resolution. Sometimes only the participants' exhaustion allows a cessation of devastating warfare.

### THE SONG OF ROLAND

Narrative logic undergoes specific modulations in the Middle Ages, sometimes ignored in favor of the new twelfth-century interest in dialectics.[4] It is characterized by episodic construction, in ill repute since Aristotle. Purely episodic narrative, which consists merely of "one thing after another" without differentiation of initial and terminal states, can only leave things as they are: it is inherently conservative. Only as a culture grasps the principle of narrative transformation does it obtain ideological purchase on its own historicity: its dependence on prior states of social forms, its potential for change that may flicker as glimpses of desire or, indeed, as tremulous threats or warning signs of degradation. "Narrative," as it grasps its own potential to move from a *state (a)* at the beginning, through a process of change at *state (b),* so as to arrive in conclusion at a *new state (c),* bears a potential of imagining historicity. Insofar as it embraces its own force, it attains a threshold of narrative performativity, the possibility of impinging on social praxis, so as to change the socius. The transformational narrative potential of the text also defines its potential of performative historical intervention.

Such narrative offers a "principle of hope" that can nourish people, texts, and political developments. A secular, vernacular culture inscribed its potential for historical transformation in complicated ways that coordinated contradictory imperatives. Epic deployed the ideological force of a distant Carolingian mythology to address more recent issues with a view to a cruelly "utopian" future. No text fuses the antinomies of warrior heroism with the transformative hope for peace more intently than the Oxford manuscript of the *Song of Roland.* The fundamental structural integrity of the text is precisely the reason it appears to moderns to transcend its own historicity, *and* the reason its transformations apparently had the historically performative power they did.

The *Song of Roland* is readily mined for ideology in the classic sense. Thus,

> A vassal must suffer great hardship for his lord,
> Endure sharp cold and great heat,
> Lose his blood and his flesh.[5]

Not only hortatory discourse, but the poem's narrative content furnish *exempla* of feudal ideology. All the Franks of the rearguard die for their lord, courageously performing vassalic duty at the mountain pass of Roncevaux. Oliver and Roland, for all their momentary differences, as well as the Archbishop Turpin, are merely the most individualized of the poem's vassalic heroes. What better examples to illustrate feudal ideology? And yet, the poem is equally cited as monarchical propaganda and testimony of religious hegemony—both inimical to feudalism.[6] None of these perspectives is entirely misplaced, but none takes account of the problem posed if all are somehow relevant to the interpretation of the text: the key terms—feudalism, monarchy, religion—imply different social systems and contradictory value schemes.

The poem's crucial ideological negotiation occurs at the structural level, when the entire narrative trajectory is examined as the relationships of constitutive parts.[7] That is where the poem organizes the multiple value-systems it incorporates and makes a deeper critique of its own surface representations of feudal, monarchical and religious values. Its beginning offers an idealized version of feudal nobility, heroically submitted to a wise and powerful leader marked off from ordinary men by communications with the divine. A surface reading lays the responsibility for the disaster awaiting in a mountain pass, where the returning army's rearguard is entrapped and decimated, on the shoulders of the traitor Ganelon. In fact, the violence of the feudal order is amply demonstrated as a self-generating mechanism, destroying individual lives as well as the service owed a higher authority. Hero and traitor both are courageous and loyal to feudal ideals. That is the paradox: feudalism self-destructs. When he returns to the battlefield to find his nephew Roland stretched out in death among the flowers of the field, Charlemagne bemoans the military and political disaster that has befallen him: it will weaken him in future politics. Neither the sincerity of his grief nor the severity of the disaster is open to doubt, in the affective rhetoric of his sorrow.

Nevertheless, Charlemagne mounts a new army, replacing Roland and Oliver, great heroes trailing the refulgence of past exploits, as if by verbal magic, with unknowns, Rabel and Guineman, reorganizing the army in effective divisions that will follow his orders precisely. Short the great heroes of the past, it begins to resemble the regimented, anonymous armies of the future, its soldiers not only serving a royal chieftain, but subjected to him. With this new army and God's help, Charles wins against a reinforced enemy: the emir Baligant's arrival from the east with huge, fresh contingents turns the conflict from a local skirmish to cosmological totalization. After Charles' victory, the text returns to unfinished business: the formal trial of the traitor Ganelon, which redefines the relations of feudalism and monarchy. Found guilty by a jury of his peers under pressure from the emperor, he is drawn and quartered at the latter's order. Ganelon's torture is both the unmaking of the feudal world, in Elaine Scarry's phrase, and the assertion of the approaching dominance of royalty spearheading the disciplinary society.[8] Extreme judicial punishment is governmental terror as policy, from the *Roland* to Damiens in 1757.

The argument that convicts Ganelon defines an important principle in politics and law. It is voiced by an unknown, an everyman. Heroes are blond and prepossessing; Thierry is slight, dark, and swarthy. He proclaims the hierarchical superiority of the king's service over any noble right or prerogative:

> Whatever wrong Roland did Ganelon,
> being in your service, that was his protection.
> Ganelon is criminal in that he betrayed him.
> Toward you, he's perjured in bad faith.[9]

Thierry, asserting the priority of royal claims over and against feudal values, defines the legal meaning of the trial. The *Roland* establishes a principle that does not obtain in the reality of the day. While the king's special aura was generally acknowledged, in cold hard fact, local vassals rebelled: the princes of adjoining principalities readily warred against their king as a merely equal antagonist. The poem argues a position of hierarchical superiority that is not evident in contemporary historical reality. It transforms the initial feudal context, in which the emperor-king performs as little more than parliamentary chair of the meeting, into a position of political preeminence. That will become a historically crucial transitional type, the "feudal monarchy," a stepping-stone toward the absolute monarchy and, ultimately, the modern nation-state.

The logic of the poem's narrative structure thus follows a sequence of four stages:

1. feudalism's self-destruction;

2. universalize the conflict [the Baligant episode];

3. resolve issues of culpability [Aude's death, Ganelon's trial];

4. suggest the new order.

A monstrous political economy structures the first stage. Although the traitor is nominally responsible for the disaster at the mountain pass, his performance as the king's messenger to the enemy reveal him to be a courageous, headstrong knight similar to the hero, his stepson Roland. Alone in the enemy camp, he is entirely prepared to fight and die for his king's honor. He and Roland share warrior traits and values; only in loyalty is there a difference, and even that remains problematic. Ganelon follows established feudal rules: a noble, he has the right to personal vengeance and issues the proper public challenge, before Charlemagne as witness, no less! He achieves vengeance in what seems to him a correct observance of judicial norms. The hecatomb of feudalism at Roncesvals is produced by the logical, systemic self-destruction of feudal ideology.

An issue remains as a narrative excess. The king, as feudal lord of his troops, owes them protection, a duty spelled out in frontline arguments with the enemy. The narrative repeatedly signals the emperor's burden of culpability and the legal principle that condemns him. Charlemagne remains the feudal lord who did not succor his vassals, hence an unresolved culpability. The enemy's entrapment, the traitor's obvious guilt, the self-destruction assigned Roland, do not relieve the emperor. Culpability pursues him to the last laisse of the poem, where he undertakes yet further missions, in a punishment he himself ascribes to God: *"si penuse est ma vie!"* (l. 4,000).

The text thus tracks a transformation from its initial feudal stage, to a historically later stage of monarchical predominance—a stage that would not be achieved for about one hundred years after the traditional dating of the poem (ca. 1100). The poem, along with other epics, (re)marks the problematic character of feudalism, producing feudal violence as an effect of the warrior

class' character and ideology. It also designates the structure by which the present will be transformed into its futurity: monarchy will surpass the feudal order by taking every possible advantage of existing feudal norms. It will respond to feudal calls for help in solving feudal problems, thus overcoming the aporias of "the feudal system" over a period of centuries.

That the *Roland*'s narrative transformation had a performative effect on the historical social text is not demonstrable in evidentiary terms: as a hypothesis, it is not falsifiable. That is true for most fundamental notions of social life. It must retain the status in which it is proposed, a hypothesis that can be supported with various kinds of argument and subscribed to with greater or lesser certainty and conviction, but that cannot be established as positivistic fact: only vectors of likelihood are available. What is more certain is that this shift represents an ideological transformation. This was not unprepared in Latin discourses on the responsibilities of kingship. The effectivity of such discourse on peasants or knights was indirect and limited: the *Roland*'s language and narrative force was available to the entire population. It is in the vernacular that ideological transformations affecting the general populace, or a largely illiterate segment like the knights, had to be worked.[10] Most knights, even when agents of a prince's administration, remained ignorant of Latin.[11] And it was the knights who were the target of the ideological effort to instill the value of peace in nascent subjectivity.

The *Song of Roland* posed the effective subjection of the nobility to the monarchy as a desideratum: in historical context, it expressed a utopian hope. Elements of ideological fantasy are present: the transformation of violence against clerics, women, and peasants into military heroism against foreign invaders; creating a new army out of nothing; the assertion of continuing feudal loyalty as a military norm as against the historical introduction of mercenaries, accompanied by the princes' and kings' obsession with garnering money to pay these troops-for-hire; stopping the course of the sun, at the convenience of the Christian king and deity. Such narremes are ideologically oriented. Behind the fiction lay far less heroic social performances, structures of force, authority, and taxation—incipiences of the state disregarded by the narrative. The poem's response to the sociopolitical problem of violence mingled admiration for an aesthetic ethics of heroism, recognition of the feudal nobility's self-destructive mechanism (a sociological reformulation of the principle of tragedy), and an optative narration in which the hierarchical priority of the sovereign figures as a supersession of feudal fragmentation: it proposed a re-totalization of the political field that subsumed feudalism rather than discarding it, under the domination of an ideologized mythology of kingship.

The **Roland**'s narrative structure states a starting point and an end point. It demonstrates the ideological starting point; it limns the new man required *after* the revolution (Rabel, Guineman) and the fundamental ideology that will generate him (Thierry). What it omits is the practical question: *How?* Just *how* is the switch in ideology and the resultant change in subjectivity and behavior to be achieved? What the poem does not envisage, what was perhaps unimaginable in its own historical context, was the process by which this subjection of violent warriors to a rule of state could come about. What would lead these creatures of violence, trained to violence, to find profit and gratifications in horsebacked violence, constructing violent identities in the close-knit fortress troop—what would lead these rough-hewn warriors to subject their taste for violence, the social status and financial advantages it won them, to the rule of a distant king? Psychic investments had been made in the practices and value-systems that made the warriors what they were. What was required was a fundamental shift of psychic adhesions—the kind of subjective shift at a level fundamental to society, where its ideological cement provides communal adhesion.

### LOUIS' CORONATION

The question would not be addressed until the arrival of "romance" on the cultural scene. In the meanwhile, a cultural problem of a different order blocked the conceptualization of a solution to the antinomy of power and legitimacy—its imagination, taking that word as a gerund. It is a lack in the world of cultural forms that impeded an imagined political solution. Characteristic of early epics (outside the **Roland**) is their entrapment in the irresolution of purely episodic form. In later narratives such as the novel, episodic differentiations do exist and yield a coherent structural paradigm.[12] Episodic structures may be overlaid with shifts of perspective, under the influence of the new romance discourse, with appeals to feelings over physical actions, attention to romantic emotions tangled in feudal conflict, and the priority of individual moral value over social status defined by legal criteria, as well as the insertion of pilgrimage and adventure into the traditional epic framework.

But these syncretisms prove insufficient to respond to the problematics of violence. So too, the installation of new aspectualities does not in itself allow for the operation of a crucial narrative potential. That is the fusion of anthropomorphic representation and sequential logic that offers a transformative potential. The early-twelfth-century poem, *Louis' Coronation,* belongs to the second epic subtype, the William of Orange cycle, traced genealogically to Garin de Montglane. Louis, a weak, frightened boy, is crowned king during his father's lifetime according to custom, in spite of evident inadequacies, by William, Duke of Aquitaine, who performs as guarantor of the throne and Louis's personal safety. In repeated episodes, William fights off attacks from external and internal enemies:[13] only thanks to his courage and loyalty does Louis survive multiple besetting dangers. A weak, inept superior survives to triumph over his enemies thanks to the personal heroism and military support of a vassal, a great prince of his realm.

Principalities such as Anjou, Champagne, Flanders, and Normandy were better organized, more powerful, less plagued by the insubordination of theoretical vassals, than the putative "kingdom." The king's domain, the Ile-de-France, was itself one of half a dozen major principalities in northern France. It was marked by relative weakness, and the survival of a vague, inchoate sense of the king's preeminent legitimacy. No cohesive theory of kingship had general currency in the eleventh and twelfth centuries to sustain royal preeminence: only hints of such a theory glimmer in Suger's writings. *Louis' Coronation* resolves the split between the two levels of rulership by the willing, loyal subordination of a principality's prince, the locus of real political power at the time of the text's composition, to legitimate kingship.[14] It is in the structures of the text, which organize its oppositions and narrative sequences, that its political (un)conscious, and that of the period, are inscribed. No distinction, in any polity, is more fundamental than that between violence and legitimacy. Their conjunction is all that distinguishes the king of France from his equals or superiors in power before 1180. Insofar as *Louis' Coronation* textualizes the political unconscious of the period, it is structured as a subject split between power and legitimacy.

The division of the textual subject is doubled by the indeterminacy of the narrative subject. The narrative subject is known as "William of Orange" in scholarship, but in this poem he is variously named. He is Shortnosed Bill (Guillelme al Cort Nés); William son of Amory of Narbonne the Proud and brother of Bernard of Brabant the Warrior; Strongarm Bill (Guillelmes Fierebrace); or just plain Strongarm. Each name is imbricated in narrative. Shortnosed William is explained in the narrative, as his first major antagonist, the pagan Corsolt, cuts off the tip of his nose along with his nosepiece, his shining hauberk and the hair on his forehead (ll. 1037-41). This may be an etiological narrative for the odd name of "Short-nosed," which looks like a misreading, striking in a supposedly oral text: "Guillelmes al Cort Nés" would be a misreading of an original "Guillelmes al Corb Nés," marking the Roman nose frequent in the South. The nose is turned to fun as it is subjected to Saracen sarcasm and William's own irony, who "avenges" his nose by killing a Saracen who insults him.

"Strongarm William" is also etiologized by narrative. In the poem's initial episode, William comes to court and finds already seated at the king's side one Arneïs of

Orleans, the internal enemy who offers himself as regent during the weak prince's youth. Arneïs, in fact, is on the point of successfully tricking his lord and becoming the regent. Wild William stalked through the crowd to stand in front of the traitor. Rather than decapitate him with his sword—he suddenly remembered that killing is a mortal sin—William rolled up his sleeves:

> He grabbed him by the hair with his left,
> Raised the right, and slammed it back on his neck:
> He broke his jaw in half,
> And knocked him to the ground, dead at his feet.[15]

Names, like subjects, are produced by stories. Unlike the modern, medieval man is not onomastically trapped: identity and names are social constructs, sometimes individual choices or socially attributed "nicknames." William's onomastic dispersal parallels the split of power and legitimacy in the poem, and royalty's aporetic reliance on a rival for political support. Such an aporia marks a site of weakness and potential conflict in the political domain.

### THE PROBLEMATICS OF PEACE

The desire to overcome violence made itself felt, not only among men of the church, among peasants distraught at having their labors come to naught as fields were burned, cattle stolen, themselves and their families beaten, harassed, even killed. Peace was integrated into the slow recapture of centralized power by princes and kings. The church had launched the Peace of God in the absence of a king capable of controlling excessive violence. Its failure left hanging the task of peace it had begun. The king's inability to rule (*rex inutilis, imbecilitas regis*), the church helpless in spite of alliances with secular power, peace turned into an instrument, a sign of achieved rule: an ideologeme.

Peace was not the absence of war. Peace had a structure, a political structure that incorporated political calculations and economic class. It was an ongoing project, engaged in negotiation and conflict, including *werra*. No polls exist, of course, but it is a reasonable supposition that at least a rough peace was heartily desired by the silent majority of the population. Its peasantry, fearful or angry at being ravaged by unpredictable irruptions of violence, whether in war, local terror, or the pure pleasure or aggression expressed by Bertran de Born, probably preferred the labor of the fields and the pleasures of its homes.

Differences of ethos dug a wide gulf between the warriors and the others of their society. Along with violence, overspending—largesse—was the knightly ethic. Going into debt was chic, in conspicuous consumption mimetic of the great aristocrats. Peasants resembled the monastic clergy in one respect: both accumulated value and valued peace. Abbeys and monasteries laid up treasure: foodstuffs in granges and larders, gold and silver in treasuries. Such accumulations of value made excellent targets of opportunity, inviting the devastatory proclivities that knights could also gratify in burning peasant fields and destroying their huts. These too turned a profit. Stolen metal implements could be resold, to be melted down and recast as knightly armor: ploughshares could be beaten into swords. How does one repress violence when its pleasure is doubled by profit? What the rest of society hated was both appetizing and lucrative to the knights.

The limited, punctual alliance between clerics and peasantry was based both on common economic interest and the religious ideology that cast the church as shepherd of the poor and the weak, the commonality disarmed in the knights' attempt to monopolize the means of violence. That alliance consolidated in the Peace Movement to face a dominant class that was fundamentally divided, economically, socially, and politically. The economic interests and culture of mounted warriors differed from those of great aristocrats, proud of ancient genealogies that legitimated status and fortresses.[16] By contrast, castellans and their bands of warriors were rank *parvenus,* pretentious, arrogant but dangerous Johnny-come-latelies. Local powers, they had to be negotiated with, both necessary instruments of the princes' power and their competition.[17] Legitimacy and power were split. The aristocracy saw its power base sapped as castellans acceded to local power. The lesser nobility had only weak and recent claims to legitimacy: all the more reason to assert these claims violently.

That split was a constitutive fissure in the political dominance of the nobility. The effort to impose unity on inherently contradictory class segments by ideological consolidation took several forms. The dubbing of knights became a sociosemiotic act so generalized among both segments that it can be studied as historical anthropology.[18] The upper nobility adopted the designation of its lower servants: all members of the new, compound class were now "knights," a mounted *chevalerie.* The horse gave mobility, increased height that leveraged the weapons of violence, and became the living symbol of sociopolitical superiority, both instrument and sign of the new order and ideology of "chivalry."[19] Most important, the knights, functionally armed retainers and enforcers, were inducted into the nobility as new members of an ancient class, endowing them with a new legitimacy and making them "free" men: free of onerous taxes levied on plebeians. The upper nobility exchanged the lower-level knights' customs for sociolegal promotion, conjoining what had formerly been two separate class segments competing for surplus value into a new class, "universal" insofar as it excluded peasants as quasi animals, monks as quasi women, and women as women. These semiotic and ideological exchanges, around the turn of the eleventh century, asserting the unity of the newly complex nobility, guaranteed the continuity of surplus value extraction for all of the newly constituted class. The abyss between the "two levels of feudalism"[20] was papered over by class unity, however factitious. The constitution of a new class also inched toward another phenomenon, only dimly perceived initially: the creation of a "disciplined" society, even as the social formation was producing new social types.[21] Society was becoming increasingly complex. Its constituent classes were forming a new kind of civilization, of governance, discipline, and ideology.

This ideological rapprochement resolved the problem of class unity at one level. The tension in the texts, however, was not only between the two levels of feudalism: it was also between the feudal class, especially the great feudatories, and the king. The status and effective power of the king decreased considerably during the devolutionary period. Earlier, attendance at the royal court had been a privilege, a sign of high status and authority, an occasion to participate in the interplays of influence and decision making, in the acquisition, creation, and strengthening of power. Great princes and bishops attended, and signed the king's charters and diplomas. But the rank of those in attendance dropped, first to chatelains and knights, and by the end of the eleventh century, to burghers, clerics, or monks, even farmers and village mayors: "very obscure characters."[22] Dialectically, the degradation of the court had advantages: the king's multiple links with people of little importance gave him deeper roots in the country—a royal populism. For administrative purposes, absent bishops and counts are replaced by the king's officers: seneschal, *connetable, chambrier,* and *bouteiller* take leading roles under Philip I (r. 1060-1108). Permanent members of the royal entourage, they came from the midlevel aristocracy of the Ile-de-France. They formed the kernel of governance in a turbulent political world as governance passed from bishops to laymen, from independent powers to more manageable subordinates.

A renewed conception of royal authority was affirmed under Suger and Louis VI (r. 1108-37): sacrality played a diminished role, political superiority in the kingdom a greater one. Nevertheless, in spite of these quiet developments in royal administration, the king's effective powers remained limited. Suger's *Life of Louis VI* shows the king spending an inordinate amount of time and energy on horseback, battling the rebellious barons of his own principality, establishing feudal control over his own territory only by dint of unceasing effort. Conflicts with great neighboring princes who were technically the king's vassals were normal and structured the initial phase of verbal ideology.

## REQUIRED: SUBJECTS AND KINGS

Max Weber's sociological theory of the state named as its essential elements territory, monopolistic control of violence, and the bureaucratic apparatus that incorporates not only policy but the very identity principle of statehood.[23] It elides an essential component. "A state exists chiefly in the hearts and minds of its people."[24] It requires the willing submission of its population. Such submission is taken for granted in the First World, constituted by populations who experience their "voluntary servitude"—produced by centuries of discipline and ideology—as freedom.[25] Such a population does not occur by nature or by accident: it is created. The *Song of Roland* did not benefit from centuries' worth of hindsight. That text addressed its futurity, stretching toward an imagined polity with tragic recognition of its ineluctable cost, but without specifying the process by which the requisite subjection would be achieved. It was not deluded into a purely idealized, optimistic utopianism. A new world was to be elaborated, requiring new kinds of subjects, to be constituted as integral to political (re)construction. Out of the fragmented seigneurial regime would be erected structures of state: the state's first form was *as* a seigneury![26] The process was neither linear nor uninterrupted. Violently cruel, often sudden and erratic, subject to losses, erasures, reversals, and rediscoveries, not at all an elegantly incremental progressive self-fashioning, what can seem merely accidental beginnings of state formation are discernible ex post facto; particular innovations lead to the political formation we inhabit. The inventors themselves were too busy dealing with concrete, ad hoc empirical issues on the ground to theorize.

These (re)beginnings take the form of a (re)centralization of power, but with a difference. The past was appealed to as ideology in the political mythology of Charlemagne, as well as in cultural commonplaces: *translatio studii, translatio imperii.* At the Carolingian court, clerics had been agents of royal publicity and ideology. Theocracy had served both kingship and church. But starting in the twelfth century, and reaching its apogee under Philip the Fair (r. 1285-1314), another ideology developed, that of a royalty that refused submission to ecclesiastical power. Medieval clerics in royal service created the first discursive ideologies of state.[27] In spite of Daniel Bell, history "consists of a long series of ideological conflicts": we are nowhere close to "the end of ideology."[28] Recurrent appeals to the past must not blind us to medieval pragmatism, oriented to the legitimation of the present.[29] Reference to the past in the Middle Ages is neither merely conventional or commemorative: it is addressed to the present inflected by an imagined future, desired or feared. Invocation of the past is a present force.

"Peace" was an ideologeme associated with rulership, from Charlemagne to Robert the Pious, who was told in 1023 that justice and peace were the roots of his office.[30] As with the Peace Movement, ideological discourse has to be apprehensible to the population addressed. That population, in the twelfth century, was a lay population, mostly "Christian" in the sense of overt adhesion and minimal beliefs, but which necessarily negotiated ideological issues in its own vernacular. Latin ideology was inadequate to the task of constituting subjects of the state—a task requiring endless repetition, variation, and adaptation. Some in the clergy realized this. During the century between 1150 and 1250, the ideology of the three orders was adapted in a variety of vernacular texts, including history, fiction, didacticism, and Etienne de Fougères' *Livre des manières.*[31] No discursive counterideology developed during the twelfth century: no authentic, self-generated discursive representations of the knights' or the peasants' political beliefs against the claims of clerics surfaced—hence the impression that the latter represented all of society. No vernacular prose discourse appeared in the twelfth century until its very end: just lyric poems, poetic epics, verse narratives, verse histories.

Ideological modes for the *illiterati* developed. While reserving ideational discourse in exclusionary Latin, the church developed nonverbal practices, rituals that marked public life with sacred sanction. The royal coronation became a major ritual, establishing the king's legitimacy.[32] Although ritual does not create the king, it is the symbolic instrument of his legitimacy. Before his death in 1226, Louis VIII urged rapid coronation of his oldest son. Joan of Arc's mission in the fifteenth century was to have the king crowned at Reims to assure his legitimacy. The coronation's judicial principle was retained even though the dynastic principle replaced royal election as of the birth of Philip Augustus in 1165. A descendant of Charlemagne through his mother Adèle of Champagne, he was saluted as "Karolid" by contemporaries, his reign hailed as a return to Carolingian roots (*redditio ad stirpem Karoli*). Ritual and genealogy responded to ideology.

Prepared and staged by the clergy, this royal propaganda stressed neither principles of monarchy nor the abstract idea of the state, but the concrete effect of the real person of the king in majesty presented as audio-visual ceremonial. The royal insignia, differentiated from feudal symbols by their religious aspect, represented the functions of power: military attributes, symbols of command, judicial power. Like the crown, they were concrete objects. The holy character of the sacred unction evoked the king's ecclesiastical nature, in analogy to a bishop's consecration. The coronation was presented as nearly miraculous. The legend of Saint Remy, the holy unction of Clovis, played decisive roles in making the king of France the successor, not only of Clovis and Charlemagne but also of David. Even absent directly political or social vernacular discourse, the king's clerics produced a panoplied symbolism of power. Ceremonial ritual and the production of insignia endowed secular power with the requisite touch of the sacred. King and state were identified: the concrete specificity of the former, enhanced by ecclesiastical symbolism, predominated. Suger records the coronation of Louis VI in an ABA form: words, ritual, words.[33] From the very first sentence, Suger uses the vocabulary of the Peace Movement, and has Louis enact its key ideologemes: protect the church; succor "the poor," peasantry and clericality melded together; repress violences of upstart tyrants, knights, and castlemasters who wield power illegitimately.[34] The ritual followed, in three major phases: the royal dubbing; application of the unction; grant of the royal insignia (tunic, ring, scepter, the hand of justice); at the end, the coronation itself and installation on the raised throne, symbol of the primordial mountain as the cosmic seat of power.[35]

The same topics recur at the beginning of the chapter that follows the coronation, with one difference. For the suppression of tyrants, Suger substitutes the young king's devotion to peace and the defense of the kingdom (*paci et regni defensioni insistere*). The substitution identifies two sides of the same coin: to subdue "tyrants," the nobles who pillage, rob, and murder, *is* to establish and defend the peace of the kingdom. Thus, restatements of the ideology of the Peace Movement frame the coronation. The Movement's triumph was to have produced a program that, though it failed in its own terms, became the ideology of the monarchy's return to a recentralized exercise of power. While this recentralization was only part of the momentous civilizational change under way, it was an integral and a necessary part: perhaps its kernel and backbone. Ideological packaging linked the exercise of the king's business of war with pastoral protection of the poor and the defenseless in the name of peace.

The drama of ritual, with music and imagery, with royal insignia, holidays, royal entrances, and the king's coronation, had a powerful effect. Ritual symbolism suggested a royalty of awesome nature, seemingly dependent on ecclesiastical structures for political and economic strength as well as legitimation. Strict limitations blocked the theocratic potential. The Capetian was not, and did not seek to become, a *rex sacerdos*. He remained a layman, to whom were granted "a few crumbs of ecclesiastical dignity."[36] The coronation ritual created a fiction, the image of an all-powerful sovereign.[37] In fact, none of the twelfth-century kings—Louis VI, his son Louis VII, or Philip II "Augustus"—was all-powerful, in spite of the implicit claim of unlimited powers lodged in the person who symbolized the *res publica.*

This is the limitation of ritual. Awesome and imposing, its effects are gross, not subject to subtlety or qualification. From the perspective of ideology, ritual falls short in formulating and articulating specificities. Verbal discourse is the only means of defining a program or imposing a policy.[38] Suger's own account frames the description of the ritual with two statements of the specific values Louis VII incarnated: he explicates the ritual's meaning verbally. Language allows for more specificity than other means of semiosis and remains the best medium for the development of ideology that provides performative models of behavior and the constitution of subjects.

There was also a practical problem with rituals, even when successfully staged. Their effectivity was limited by the requirement of physical presence. Ideological subjectivation is fragile and requires repeated reinforcement. Coronations were rare, particularly among the long-lived Capetians, who did not die and succeed each other frequently enough: only three during the twelfth century. Coronations fell into ineffectual forgetfulness. This limitation was parried. "Crowned courts" (*curiae coronata*) developed, held on great festival days where the king's coronation was renewed by the public wearing of the royal diadem.[39] Such ritual repetitions were not necessarily devoid of substance. At the *curiae coronata* of Bourges in 1145, the second crusade was initiated.[40] A decade later, in 1155, at Soissons, the historical process came full circle: the pale, semiclerkly figure of Louis VII who had lost glamorous Eleanor and Aquitaine to Henry II, reclaimed the historic function of centralized power by proclaiming, for ten years, "the King's Peace."

This was neither a completely unforeseen development, nor an anomalous one. Already in Louis VI's reign, great nobles had recognized the king's right to judge infractions of the kingdom's peace.[41] The specific contribution of Louis VII's reign was the "decisive strengthening of the king's prerogative as protector of churches and pacifier of his kingdom."[42] Although educated as a cleric who became heir apparent on the death of his older brother, Louis was capable of horrendous violence. In 1142, he invaded Champagne and set siege to Vitry, the main town of the Perthois, dependent on Thibaud de Champagne. His army despatched the burghers' militia, spread through the streets, pillaging and setting houses on fire. Soon, both city and castle were an inferno. Fifteen hundred villagers who sought refuge in the church died in the flames: the resemblance to Raoul de Cambrai's massacre at Origny is striking. The king wept over the event, which did not prevent him from carrying devastation into the very heart of Champagne with extreme violence: "Almost all that belonged to count Thibaud was pil-

laged, burnt and depopulated," wrote one cleric. Violence perdured as part of the king's effort to establish "peace."

Nevertheless, Louis VII's reign is remarkable for the dual development of ideology and efforts for internal peace. As in the coronation, he himself was sign of his own kingship and its main ideological vehicle. In spite of the debacle of the Second Crusade and the loss of Aquitaine, he came to figure in the popular imagination as a lay saint. This iconization masks the finesse that allowed him to conciliate three policies: a continuing alliance with the church; the independence of secular royalty as the church's equal; and increasing emphasis on peace.

In 1141, Innocent II affirmed the papacy's superiority over temporal power, at least in spiritual matters, subordinating the secular prince to the church and lowering kingship to a limited, purely lay power. Louis refused this conception and asserted the equality of sacerdotal and royal powers. The principle of dual powers was supported by Suger, regent during the Second Crusade. Addressing the pillage and ransoming of the Brabançons—unemployed mercenaries turned bandits, in a transformation to become familiar during the Hundred Years' War—Suger invoked the ideological symbol of two swords, "material and royal," on the one hand, "spiritual and ecclesiastical," on the other. The abbot of Saint Denis wrote the archbishop of Reims in 1149:

> The glory of the Church consists in the indissoluble unity of the regnum and the *sacerdoce*; what is of benefit to one benefits the other, and it is obvious that the temporal kingdom lives by the Church of God, just as the Church of God prospers and grows by the temporal kingdom.[43]

After Suger's death in 1151, from 1154-55, Louis lay down the bases of a complex policy, incorporating the interdependence of war and peace. He attempted to unite his own vassals in new alliances to contain Plantagenet ambitions. Blois-Champagne was turned into an ally: Count Thibaud became the seneschal of France. Securing justice and peace in the kingdom is the duty and prerogative of the king:

> The honor of the king, attentive to dispensing justice, should procure peace and tranquility to all, extending his long hands for the protection and care of all.[44]

The king's mission of justice, peace, and tranquility extends to the protection and care of his population: it (re)establishes the pastoral function of the state.

The *rex pacificus* was associated with new political alliances, eliciting the sympathy and adhesion of the churches and enlarging the royal purview. In the King's

Peace, secular power took over a policy that had failed in the hands of the clergy: it became the lynchpin in a complex ideological image of a kingdom (re)united in sociopolitical peaceability. On June 10, 1155, an assembly of prelates and barons met at Soissons. Its final act resembles the legislations of the Peace Movement. At the request of the clergy, with agreement of the barons, Louis establishes "peace for the entire kingdom":

> We order that, as of next Easter [March 1156], and for a period of ten years, all the churches of the kingdom, with all their possessions, all the peasants with their livestock and herds, and all merchants, in all places, and the men dependent upon whomsoever, insofar as they are ready to seek justice from their ordinary judges, shall always have peace and full security. In full council and before all, by the royal word, we have said that we would hold inviolable this peace, and that, if there were infractions of this peace thus decreed, would make justice in their respect, according to our ability.

Those present swore support, "so that justice be done to the violences."[45] Two years later, a council of bishops (Reims) gave judicial definition to the policy of 1155. A lord refusing to enact justice will be considered "infractor" of the peace. Recourse to the king would be available to victims: "the king has the power to constrain evil people to amend themselves, from his office by virtue of which he must defend churches."[46]

A new order is being sketched out. The responsibility for a peace that had been God's through ecclesiastical intermediaries is turned into "a mission of public order" shared by bishops and princes, the king of France as its supreme arbiter. The mission was difficult. Its enforcement had to respect the kingdom's feudal structure.[47] Patient negotiations and compromise were required, between the ideology of the King's Peace and the realities of mid-twelfth-century power. But the essential step had been taken. Soissons substituted the King's Peace for the Peace of God.[48] A function that had been imperial before feudalism now returned to the monarch. Royalty assumes effective responsibility for peace and the welfare of its population. Foucault's "pastoralism of power" begins to take form with the nascent state.

The weakness of the marginal can be a strength. Latin continued as the language of official policy: vernacular texts did not encroach on its protected precincts. Lay, vernacular culture developed practices of fictional representation that possessed a great tactical benefit: the virtue of deniability. Vernacular writing was the cultural medium in which the essential ideological work of the nascent state was done, taking forms seen as mere amusements and distractions: poetry, epic, romance, vernacular history, and chronicle. Although men of the church disliked these texts, the danger they posed to the church's monopoly on ideological discourse did not appear until the beginning of the thirteenth century. Lay, vernacular culture developed for nearly a century, eluding dominant opponents before being subjected to concerted pressures that warranted changes in the way it transacted its ideological business.

What modernity misreads as the incomprehensible monstrosities of medieval epic violence, or the light-heartedly fantastic amusements of narrative romance, were a major ideological workspace of medieval society. These texts addressed violence as a social and a textual problem, from the perspective of a state in the process of creation and the recasting of subjectivity. Postmodernity lives the unwinding of the nexus whose complex construction began in the Middle Ages. That it will discover the solution to the question human violence poses to reflexive consciousness is not evident.

### Notes

1. "Donna Aaliz la reïne, / Par qui valdrat lei divine, / Par qui cresitrat lei de terre / E remandrat tante guerre / Por les armes Henri lu rei, / E par le cunseil qui ert en tei" (Benedeit, *Le voyage de Saint Brandan,* ed. Ian Short [Paris: UGE (10/18), 1984], ll. 1-6). The queen named in l. 1 varies according to the king's marriages.

2. See below, Chapter 7.

3. This is the epic world according to Bertrand de Bar-sur-Aube's *Girart de Vienne* and *Doon de Mayence,* in Ulrich Mölk, *Französisches Literarästhetik des 12. und 13. Jahrhunderts* (Tübingen: Niemeyer, 1969), pp. 9f., 13f.

4. Foremost among these: Tony Hunt, "The Dialectic of *Yvain*," *Modern Language Review* 72 (1977): 285-99; Tony Hunt, "Aristotle, Dialectic and Courtly Literature," *Viator* 10 (1979): 95-129; and Eugene Vance, *From Topic to Tale, Logic and Narrativity in the Middle Ages* (Minneapolis: University of Minnesota Press, 1987).

5. "Pur sun seignur deit hom susfrir granz mals / E endurer e forz freiz e granz chalz, / Sin deit hom perdre del sanc e de la char" (*La Chanson de Roland,* ed. Joseph Bédier [Paris: UGE: 10/18], ll. 1117-19). Bédier's edition remains authoritative.

6. Hans-Erich Keller, "*The Song of Roland*: A Mid-Twelfth Century Song of Propaganda for the Capetian Kingdom," *Olifant* 3 (1976): 242-58; Stephen G. Nichols, "Fission and Fusion: Meditations of Power in Medieval History and Literature," *Yale French Studies* 70 (1986): 21-42; and Stephen G. Nichols, *Romanesque Signs: Early Medieval Narrative and Iconography* (New Haven, Conn.: Yale University Press, 1983).

7. Haidu, *The Subject of Violence . . . : The Song of Roland and the Birth of the State* (Bloomington: Indiana University Press, 1993).

8. Elaine Scarry, *The Body in Pain: The Making and Unmaking of the World* (Oxford: Oxford University Press, 1985); Michel Foucault, *Surveiller et punir: Naissance de la prison* (Paris: Gallimard, 1975).

9. "Que que Rollant a Guenelun forsfesist, / Vostre servise l'en doüst bien garir. / Guenes est fels d'iço qu'il le traït; / Vers vos s'est parjurez e malmis" (ll. 3827-30).

10. The progress of education in the twelfth century affected secular knowledge of Latin only marginally. The beneficiaries of the cathedral schools and the later university were clergy, many headed toward secular careers.

11. The exchequer inscribed their presumption of "illiteracy": see below, Chapter 8.

12. Haidu, "The Episode as Semiotic Module in Twelfth Century Romance," *Poetics Today* 4, no. 4 (1983): 655-81.

13. Haidu, "Toward a Socio-Historical Semiotics: Power and Legitimacy in the *Couronnement de Louis,*" *Kodikas/Code* 2 (1980): 155-69.

14. See Jean Dunbabin, *France in the Making 843-1180* (Oxford: Oxford University Press, 1985-91).

15. "En talent ot qi'il li colpast le chief, / Quant li remembre del glorios del ciel, / Que d'ome ocire est trop mortel pechiez. / Il prent s'espee, el fuere l'embatié, / Et passe avant; quant se fu rebraciez, / Le poing senestre li a meslé el chief, / Halce le destre, enz el col li assiet: / L'or de la gole li a par mi brisié; / Mort le trebuche a la terre a ses piez" (*Le couronnement de Louis,* ed. Ernest Langlois, 2d ed. [Paris: Champion, 1966] ["Classiques Français du Moyen Age," no. 22], ll. 125-33).

16. This split grounded Erich Köhler's analyses of feudal literature: *L'aventure chevaleresque: Idéal et réalité dans le roman courtois* (Paris: Gallimard, 1956); "Observations historiques et sociologiques sur la poésie lyrique des troubadours," *Cahiers de civilisation médiévale* 7 (1964): 27-51.

17. Other classes were internally differentiated as well, including the clergy (not a class in the Marxist sense) and the peasantry. Imposing impossible standards of theoretical purity on an analytic concept such as "class" is a polemical weapon in the effort to discard it as an instrument of reflexion.

18. Jacques le Goff, "Le rituel symbolique de la vassalité," *Pour un autre Moyen Age: Temps, travail et culture en Occident* (Paris: Gallimard, 1977), pp. 349-420.

19. Robert Bresson's *Lancelot du Lac* explores the centrality of the horse's point of view to the culture of this class. The self-destruction of a polity by its highest ideal (passionate "chivalric" love) is shot in moral and cinematic darkness from the perspective of the horse's eye: the symbol of the class becomes the means of its perspectival deconstruction.

20. Joseph Strayer's classic essay, originally in *Life and Thought in the Early Middle Ages,* ed. R. S. Hoyt (Minneapolis: University of Minnesota Press, 1967).

21. See the remarks on Etienne de Fougères and Hugh of St Victor, below.

22. Jean-François Lemarignier, *Le gouvernement royal aux premiers temps capétiens (987-1108)* (Paris: 1965); Jean-François Lemarignier, "Aux origines de l'état français. Royauté et entourage royal aux premiers temps capétiens," in *L'Europe aux IXe-XIe siècles: Aux origines des Etats nationaux* (Warsaw: Panstwowe Wydawnictwo Naukowe, "Institut d'Histoire de l'Académie Polonaise des Sciences," 1968), pp. 43-55; and Eric Bournazel, *Le gouvernement capétien au XIIe siècle, 1108-1180: Structures sociales et mutations institutionnelles* (Paris: PUF, 1975).

23. Max Weber, *The Theory of Social and Economic Organization,* ed. Talcott Parsons (Oxford: Oxford University Press, 1947-64), p. 156f.

24. Joseph R. Strayer, *On the Medieval Origins of the Modern State* (Princeton, N.J.: Princeton University Press, 1970), p. 5.

25. Etienne de la Boétie, *Le discours de la servitude volontaire* (Paris: Payot, 1976-93).

26. Jacques Krynen, *L'empire du roi. Idées et croyances politiques en France. XIIIe-XVe siècle* (Paris: Gallimard, 1993), p. 68.

27. Pierre Riché, "Les Clercs carolingiens au service du pouvoir," in *Idéologie et propagande en France,* ed. Myriam Yardeni (Paris: Picard, 1987), pp. 11-18.

28. Ibid., p. 17f.; Daniel Bell, *The End of Ideology—On the Exhaustion of Political Ideas in the Fifties* (Glencoe, N.Y.: Free Press, 1960).

29. Georges Duby, "Remarques sur la littérature généalogique en France aux XIe et XIIe siècles," *Hommes et structures du moyen âge* (The Hague: Mouton, 1973), pp. 287-98.

30. Krynen, p. 36.

31. Jean Batany, "Du *bellator* au chevalier dans le schéma des 'trois ordres' (étude sémantique)," in *La guerre et la paix au moyen âge* (Lille: Actes du 101e congrés National des Sociétés Savantes, 1976), pp. 232-34.

32. Aryeh Graboïs, "La royauté sacrée au XIIe siècle: manifestation de la propagande royale," in *Idéologie et propagande en France,* ed. Myriam Yardeni (Paris: Picard, 1987), pp. 31-41; Jacques le Goff, "Aspect[s] religieux et sacré[s] de la monarchie française du Xe au XIIIe siècle," *Pouvoirs et libertés au temps des premiers capétiens,* ed. Elisabeth Magnou-Nortier (Editions Hérault, 1992), pp. 309-22.

33. Suger, *Vie de Louis VI le Gros,* ed. Henri Waquet (Paris: Les Belles Lettres, 1964), ch. xiv, pp. 84-89.

34. Krynen, p. 38.

35. Le Goff, p. 311f.

36. Ibid., p. 313.

37. Graboïs.

38. Riché, p. 13. On the limitations imposed on ritual's ability to form consensus by political, rhetorical, and strategic manipulations, see Philippe Buc, *Dangereux rituel. De l'histoire médiévale auxx sciences sociales,* Paris: PUF, 2003.

39. A. Luchaire, *Histoire des institutions monarchiques sous les premiers Capétiens (987-1180),* 2 vols. (Paris: Picard, 1883), 1:69.

40. Graboïs, p. 39.

41. Krynen, p. 39.

42. Details on Louis's reign from Yves Sassier, *Louis VII* (Paris: Fayard, 1991).

43. Ibid., pp. 205-7.

44. Ibid., p. 258.

45. Ibid., p. 263f.

46. Ibid., p. 265.

47. Krynen, p. 42.

48. Jacques le Goff, "Genèse de la France (milieu IXe-fin XIIIe siècle): Vers un état monarchique français," in *Histoire de la France,* ed. André Burguière and Jacques Revel (Paris: Seuil, 1989), p. 34.

---

# FURTHER READING

## Criticism

Brault, Gerard J. Introduction to The Song of Roland: *An Analytical Edition,* pp. 1-116. University Park: Pennsylvania State University Press, 1978.

Discusses the complex structure of *The Song of Roland* as well as its metaphorical consistency and thematic unity.

———. *"The Song of Roland* 778-1978." *Olifant* 6, nos. 3 & 4 (spring & summer 1979): 201-11.

Examines what is known of the battle represented in *The Song of Roland* and summarizes the views of various historians and scholars regarding what actually took place.

Cook, Robert Francis. "Translators and Traducers: Some English Versions of the *Song of Roland* Stanzas 83-85." *Olifant* 7, no. 4 (summer 1980): 327-42.

Discusses the complexity of translating and interpreting "a lost language and a lost civilization" in the study of *The Song of Roland.*

Duggan, Joseph J. "Formulaic Language and Mode of Creation." In The Song of Roland: *Formulaic Style and Poetic Craft,* pp. 16-62. Berkeley: University of California Press, 1973.

Examines poetic language in *The Song of Roland,* contending that the formulas used in its creation were both necessary and effective, and refuting the common critical assumption that oral poetry is inferior to written texts.

———. "Franco-German Conflict and the History of French Scholarship on the *Song of Roland.*" In *Hermeneutics and Medieval Culture,* edited by Patrick J. Gallacher and Helen Damico, pp. 97-106. Albany, N.Y.: State University of New York Press, 1989.

Examines the history of scholarship on *The Song of Roland* during the period 1837 to 1945—years marked by hostility between France and Germany—and the effect of that hostility on the interpretation of the poem.

Farrier, Susan E. *"Das Rolandslied* and the *Song of Roulond* as Moralizing Adaptations of the *Chanson de Roland.*" *Olifant* 16, nos. 1 & 2 (spring & summer 1991): 61-76.

Contends that two versions of *The Song of Roland*—one late 12th c. German and one late 14th or early 15th c. Middle English—should be termed adaptations rather than faithful translations.

Jones, George Fenwick. "Ethical Origins and Ideological Environment." In *The Ethos of the* Song of Roland, pp. 96-158. Baltimore, Md.: Johns Hopkins Press, 1963.

Explores the prevailing ideology regarding public opinion, honor, and shame motivating the heroes of *The Song of Roland.*

Keller, Hans-Erich. *"The Song of Roland* and its Audience." *Olifant* 6, nos. 3 & 4 (spring & summer 1979): 259-74.

Examines the dating controversy surrounding the Oxford version of *The Song of Roland.*

Kunkle, Roberta A. "Time in *The Song of Roland.*" *Romance Notes* 13, no. 3 (spring 1972): 550-55.

Examines the temporal structure of *The Song of Roland,* suggesting that dividing the work into seven one-day segments provides the most plausible framework for the historical events it depicts.

Mermier, Guy R. "More about Unity in the *Song of Roland.*" *Olifant* 2, no. 2 (December 1974): 91-108.

Studies the critical controversy surrounding the unity of *The Song of Roland,* suggesting that the problem should be approached from an aesthetic viewpoint.

Merwin, W. S. Introduction to *The Song of Roland,* translated by W. S. Merwin, pp. vii-xv. New York: The Modern Library, 2001.

Provides the historical context for *The Song of Roland* as well as a brief review of the various versions of the poem that exist today.

Paden, William D. "Tenebrism in the *Song of Roland.*" *Modern Philology* 86, no. 4 (May 1989): 339-56.

Contends that Roland, like Charlemagne, emerges as a hero at the end of *The Song of Roland* because "he strove mightily to reach the light in a shadowy world."

Thomas, P. Aloysius. "The Structural and Aesthetic Heroes in the *Song of Roland.*" *Neuphilologische Mitteilungen* 81 (1980): 1-6.

Responds to Guy R. Mermier's 1974 essay on unity in *The Song of Roland,* contending that Mermier's essay, while valuable, does not really settle the controversy that has long been the subject of so much scholarly debate.

Vance, Eugene. "Roland, Charlemagne, and the Poetics of Illumination." *Olifant* 6, nos. 3 & 4 (spring/summer 1979): 213-25.

Explores *The Song of Roland*'s cultural status as both an important part of an older oral tradition and a written text introducing a new era of vernacular literacy.

———. "Style and Value: From Soldier to Pilgrim in the *Song of Roland.*" *Yale French Studies* 80 (1991): 75-96.

Contends that an ethical and semantic disjunction occurs at the halfway point in *The Song of Roland,* with the replacement of Roland as the hero with Charlemagne.

---

**Additional coverage of *The Song of Roland* is contained in the following sources published by Gale: *Classical and Medieval Literature Criticism,* Vols. 1, 50; *Epics for Students,* Vol. 1; *European Writers,* Vol. 1; *Literature Resource Center*; and *Reference Guide to World Literature,* Ed. 2.**

# Robert Southwell
## 1561-1595

English poet and religious writer.

## INTRODUCTION

A Jesuit priest executed for treason during the reign of Elizabeth I, Southwell was canonized as a saint in 1970. He is known for devotional poetry that is unusually passionate and charged with emotion. His most famous poems are *Saint Peters Complaint* (1595) and "The Burning Babe" (1595).

## BIOGRAPHICAL INFORMATION

Southwell was born into a wealthy country family in 1561 at Horsham St. Faith's in Norfolk, England. He was the fifth of eight children—the third and youngest son—of Richard Southwell and Bridget Copley. Details of his early education are unknown, but by 1576 he was sent to Douai in France where he began attending a Jesuit school. Two years later, he became a novice in the Jesuit order in Rome. In 1584 Southwell was ordained and in 1586 he was sent to England, returning to his native land after an absence of ten years. A year earlier, a statute had been passed in England making it a treasonable offense to be a Catholic priest or to administer the sacraments. Thus Southwell was forced to operate in secret, and for the next six years he served as a pastor, usually in the vicinity of London. During this time he was writing both poetry and prose, much of it designed to reach his religious congregation via the printed word, since the proclamations of the English government precluded public preaching. Southwell was captured in June, 1592, by Richard Topcliffe, a favorite of Queen Elizabeth, notorious for tracking down and torturing Catholic priests. After a month in Topcliffe's hands, Southwell was imprisoned in the Tower of London, where he stayed for the next two years before being moved to a cell in Newgate Prison prior to his trial. On February 20, 1595, he was found guilty of treason and was hanged, drawn, and quartered the following day; he was 33 years old. In 1970, Southwell was canonized by Pope Paul VI.

## MAJOR WORKS

Southwell's earliest works, written when he was very young, were his Latin poems, some of which were unsuccessful attempts at the epic form in imitation of Virgil. Although historians have had great difficulty dating any of the individual poems, most scholars believe that most of his poetic work was written during the six years he served as a pastor in England before his arrest. In 1595, shortly after the poet's execution, *Saint Peters Complaint, with Other Poems* appeared, as well as *Moeoniae,* published with just the initials "R. S." on the title page, although it was well known that the volume was the work of Southwell. His shorter pieces, fifty-two in all, appear in three different manuscripts: Stonyhurst, Virtue and Cahill, and the British Library. A fourth manuscript, known as the Harmsworth Manuscript, contains twelve additional poems, but some scholars question whether Southwell actually wrote them. *The Poems of Robert Southwell* (1967), edited by James H. McDonald and Nancy Pollard Brown, includes various other poems, some of them undoubtedly earlier versions of published works, for a total of seventy short verses. Of these, many deal with the lives of Christ and Christ's mother, Mary. Among the poems devoted to the early life of Mary are "The Virgins Salutation," "The Virgine Maries Conception," "Her Nativity," and "The Visitation." These poems were apparently in keeping with the Catholic Counter-Reformation's emphasis on devotion to Mary and to the rosary. In addition, events from the early life of Christ are represented in "His Circumcision," "The Presentation," "A Childe My Choyce," and his most famous individual poem, "The Burning Babe." The last two, along with "New Heaven, New Warre" and "New Prince, New Pompe," are often treated as a unit known as the nativity poems.

Southwell's other poetry appeared in the volume *Saint Peters Complaint.* It contains a number of poems devoted to the subject of repentance, many of them featuring images of imprisonment and torture, and may have been written during his own captivity, although many scholars contend that Southwell could not possibly have been composing verse after his arrest. Still, the content of some of the poems suggests otherwise. Harry Morris has studied a group of five poems from the volume—"Life Is but Losse," "I Die Alive," "What Joy to Live," "Life's Death, Love's Life," and "At Home in Heaven"—and points out that "they refer to imprisonment, anguish, pain, and torment; they employ images of stripes, wounds, and blood." Additionally, Morris notes that "The stanza forms, the meter, the diction are all extremely simple, direct, and well-suited to the frailty of the man and to his situation." He finds it difficult to believe that if Southwell were composing such lyrics in the comfort of his study, he would have been able to achieve such a sense of urgency about his impending death.

## CRITICAL RECEPTION

Southwell's poetry was heavily influenced by the theories of the Jesuits, which called for literature that was based on the neo-classicism of the Renaissance, was "morally harmless," and was completely devoid of innovation or "passion." Art could never serve as an end in itself, but must always serve the cause of religion. Pierre Janelle has studied Southwell's work and traces the influence of the Society of Jesus, claiming that although "its ardent piety no doubt fanned his poetical flame into a blaze," Southwell's lyricism was "damped into frigidity" by its restrictions. These restrictions, however, were primarily apparent in Southwell's Latin verse and in his early English verse; in his later work, according to Janelle, he was able "to shake off the leading-strings of literary orthodoxy." Morris, in fact, finds Southwell's "deathbed" poems, particularly "I Die Alive," filled with the passion denigrated by the Jesuits. The poem is based on the antithesis between life and death with "the paradox of the title . . . carried out so well in the imagery of the poem," in addition to being "furthered through the rhymes." But F. W. Brownlow, who has studied Southwell's poetry extensively, concludes that fewer than half of the short pieces represent the quality work the poet was capable of producing. "Southwell had embarked on a campaign to convert contemporary secular love poetry to religious ends," writes Brownlow, and "it had unfortunate effects upon his poetic writing." Many of the poems were riddled with clichés and borrow so heavily from the work of other poets that some critics have charged Southwell with plagiarism.

"The Burning Babe," much admired by Ben Jonson, and possibly inspiring a line in William Shakespeare's *Macbeth*, is Southwell's most frequently anthologized poem. Joseph D. Scallon explains that the work "employs the conventions of vision poetry to elicit a response to the pathos surrounding the child Jesus." According to Scallon, "Southwell evidently believed that English Catholics needed to be reminded of the poverty and humility of Jesus to strengthen their wills to accept the sacrifices laid upon them for fidelity to their religion." Scott R. Pilarz, who has studied the motivation behind Southwell's poetry, maintains that "he writes as a pastor, not as a polemicist, and he is confident that his literary efforts will help souls by promoting reconciliation." Geoffrey Hill claims that Southwell's poetry, particularly "The Burning Babe," possesses a quality of "mystical pragmatism."

The poem "New Heaven, New Warre" has long been the subject of scholarly debate since it is unclear whether Southwell intended it to be a single poem or two separate poems that were printed as one in error. Karen Batley believes that it is a single poem because it is one of a group of four known as the nativity poems, which are "characterized by a single factor—the poet's wonder at the incarnation and the paradoxical power of the apparently helpless infant to save humankind." According to Batley, "the structure and meaning of 'New Heaven, New Warre' obviously depend on this very paradox," which she considers evidence that the poem should not be treated as two separate works.

Southwell's poetry is rarely read today, although it is still studied by literary historians and critics. Kari Boyd McBride believes that it "has a continuous, if marginal, history, perhaps guaranteed by Ben Jonson's comment that he would have destroyed many of his own poems to have written 'The Burning Babe.'" Aside from that, however, McBride reports that "scholarly interest in Southwell's poetry peaked" in the mid-twentieth century and "more recent studies tend to concentrate on Southwell's recusancy and his prose works and letters." Gary M. Bouchard contends that "although Robert Southwell's literary 'canonisation' occurred more-or-less simultaneously with his religious canonisation . . . , he remains a relatively obscure footnote in the Tudor period of literature."

---

# PRINCIPAL WORKS

## Poetry

"The Burning Babe" 1595

*Moeoniae; or, Certaine Excellent Poems and Spirituall Hymns: Omitted in the Last Impression of* "Peters Complaint" 1595

*Saint Peters Complaint, with Other Poems* 1595

*The Complete Poems of Robert Southwell* 1872

*The Poems of Robert Southwell* 1967

## Other Major Works

*An Epistle of Comfort, to the Reuerend Priestes, & to the Laye Sort Restrayned in Durance* (prose) 1587

*Mary Magdalens Funeral Teares* (prose meditation) 1591

*An Humble Supplication to Her Maiestie* (prose) c. 1591-92

*The Triumphs over Death; or, A Consolatorie Epistle* (prose) 1595

# CRITICISM

## Pierre Janelle (essay date 1935)

SOURCE: Janelle, Pierre. "A Jesuit Neo-Classic." In *Robert Southwell: The Writer,* pp. 116-41. London: Sheed and Ward, 1935.

[*In the following excerpt, Janelle discusses the Jesuits' theory that artistic beauty should never be an end in itself, and the influence of that theory on Southwell's poetry.*]

The influence of the Society of Jesus upon Southwell the writer was two-fold: its ardent piety no doubt fanned his poetical flame into a blaze; but at the same time, his lyricism was to some extent, during the former part of his career, damped into frigidity by the literary theory which the Jesuits had evolved. The latter was part of the plan of action through which they sought to extend their influence to every branch of human activity, art being of course included. It was practical and utilitarian. It made no attempt to innovate, but following the directions of the Council of Trent, struck the easier path, and confirmed the classicism of the Renaissance, while attempting to make it morally harmless; but the very fact that it banished "passion" from literature and tried to substitute methodical reflection for inspiration, explains why it took the heart out of those very forms of poetry to which it sought to give new life.

The *Ratio studiorum,* which was being prepared while Southwell was a student at Rome, and embodies the experience of the first forty years of the Society, makes it clear that neo-classicism was the main prop of the educational edifice which was being raised: "It was thanks to the help of those [classical] studies, rather than that of the higher faculties, that the Society was rapidly propagated in the main parts of Christendom; nor can it be better or more firmly maintained in those parts, than by that same branch of knowledge, on account of which it was first admitted."[1] The *Ratio* then proceeds to exhort the members of the Society not to fall into "Barbarity" and to preserve that "noble ornament [of classical culture] with which God has deigned to honour the Society." Practical rules are laid down accordingly. Among candidates to membership or teaching offices, those must be preferred who, other qualifications being equal, "excel more in humanities"; while even the teachers of theology are scarcely to rank above the professors of "inferior sciences," i. e., of classical letters.[2]

Such professors were to be found in all Jesuit colleges from their foundation; Southwell came under their influence at the Collège de Clermont. Whether he attended their classes at the Roman college or not, the whole atmosphere of the place would work upon him. Jesuit neo-classicism was ever present in the daily life of the scholastics at Rome; it was especially manifested on solemn or joyful occasions, such as liturgical feasts, anniversaries, distributions of prizes, visits of the pope or cardinals; and then the professors and students would vie with one another, in composing "orationes" or "carmina" which gave proof of the purity and elegance of their Latin. Very few facts have come down to us concerning the presence at the Roman College of the great theorists of Jesuit poetry. Whether Southwell knew any of them personally is uncertain, but he may quite likely have come into touch with one of the most notable among them, father Benci, better known as Franciscus Bencius.[3] This father was an Italian, born at Acquapendente in 1542. He had studied at Rome for seven years under the famous Antonius Muretus, who after belonging to the old school of Renaissance humanists, had become in his latter years a "convert" to the Jesuit view of literature as a handmaiden of religion. Bencius himself was instrumental in Muretus' conversion, and induced him to break off with the freedom of a worldly life and to seek ordination as a priest. The pupil later became a master himself, and after joining the Society as a novice in 1570, taught eloquence at Siena, Perugia and Rome. He had become a professor at the Roman college by 1573, first teaching classics for six years, then rhetoric, in which work he apparently continued until his death in 1594. He was at the Roman College all through Southwell's stay there, and apparently in a position of high esteem. He took part in many public ceremonies, and on November 8th, 1584, recited before his colleagues and students a Latin poem *On the best means of enjoying a quiet life.*[4] By that date Southwell, who in his "wisdom" lyrics was to handle kindred themes in the same spirit, had left for the English college; but it seems likely that their paths had met in the preceding years. Anyhow, the influence of such men as Bencius upon the English Jesuit cannot be doubted; what it mostly consisted in, we shall now attempt to show.

The documents available for such a purpose are not to be sought before or during Southwell's student years, but after. It would indeed have been more gratifying to be able to state definitely that he had known before himself setting to work, such or such a treatise on poetry or eloquence. But this is impossible, and the reason is a simple one. Literary theories only take a formal shape in set tractates years after their first appearance, when they have already been alive and at work for a long period. Southwell's Roman years were still for the Society of Jesus, in respect of its literary activities, years of adjustment and stress. The time for stocktaking, for analysis, for conclusions, was still somewhat ahead. It was only in the last decade of the XVIth century that critics supplied sets of rules, extracted from the literary practice of the last fifty years. Bencius, Possevinus, Pontanus, all began to legislate on poetry at the same time. Pontanus[5] is the most typical and noteworthy of the whole group of lawgivers, because he wrote, not detached fragments or jumbled remarks on various authors or "genera," but a real, deliberate "Ars Poetica," his *Poeticae Institutiones*.[6] All of them however will help us towards a fuller understanding of the Jesuit ideal, theory and plan in regard to the use of poetry.

* * *

Of course, even between Jesuit critics there are individual differences of temperament; but on one point all are strikingly agreed. Poetry, they say, like painting or music, like artistic beauty in general, is not an end in itself. Its position is subordinate. Indeed it may give pleasure; but that pleasure is not to be cultivated or enjoyed for its own sake; it is only legitimate in so far as it is made to serve the cause of virtue or religion, to concur in the greater glory of God. Horace had left the door open for future controversies, when ambiguously writing in his *Ars Poetica*:

> Aut prodesse volunt, aut delectare poetae.[7]

The Renaissance, the quattrocento, had laid the stress on the second verb; and now the art critics of the Counter-Reformation threw it back on the former. For Pontanus, who quotes the line, "delectare" is subsidiary to "prodesse." "What we must consider, he says, is not whom the poets represent, what story they tell, what play they act; but to what end, in what mind, for what reasons . . . Let us define poetry, he adds, an art which represents the actions of men, and sets them forth in verse, for the better ordering of man's life."[8] And Possevinus states no less clearly: "The first purpose of the poet must be, to make his reader better; his second only, to delight him."[9] The true nature of poetry therefore is not really artistic; its main element is not beauty or charm, but wisdom. It is a branch of moral philosophy. Let the poet, Pontanus says, borrow as much as he may need from the masters of morals, so that "of writing well the source and fount be wisdom."[10]

Why then, it may be asked, should poetry exist at all? why should writers trouble to indite in verse instead of adopting the purely didactic method of philosophers? Because some concession must be made to the fallen condition of human nature, which is not strong enough to abide the nakedness and severity of eternal truth. Moral principles are like a bitter draught that the patient will not swallow unless it be sweetened. "Let the poet, Pontanus writes, teach duty in the following way: he should thoroughly reject all divisions, definitions, reasonings; and by means of a most adorned diction, and most beautiful examples, either first imagined by

himself, or amplified, illustrated and somehow fashioned anew through ingenious fictions, he should rouse in turn various motions of the soul, and either entice, or carry away the readers or spectators whither he pleases. Hence it is, that wise men have asserted that poetry is some kind of philosophy, cloaked over with the covering of fables."[11] Should those words not appear clear enough, the Jesuit critic expresses his thought even more explicitly a few lines further on. If the poet, he says, is intent on "delectare" instead of merely "prodesse," it is "to gratify the vulgar, who are always fonder of pleasant than of useful things, and easily spurn wholesome doctrine unless it is besprinkled with charms and delights of many kinds."[12]

It appears clearly from the above why the Jesuits welcomed the literary discipline of classicism, and even improved upon it. For one thing, it tallied with that ideal of well-ordered life which the Society had made its own. Besides, if the chief purpose of art be to edify, if outward beauty be only a concession to vulgar minds unacquainted with the higher, unsullied splendour of naked spiritual truth; if the poet be like an apothecary, who prepares wholesome drugs for humble, ignorant patients, and cheats them with the sugared coating of his bitter pills; why then! there must be formulae for those drugs and pills,—that is, for the automatic production of artistic emotion. The poor innocent folk will be carried away, though unaware of the means used; but the enlightened, superior few know how such effects are produced; they know the tricks, they know the "rules." For the word is out at last: a literature which is merely meant to achieve a coldly-calculated result cannot be other than a literature of "rules." An Italian writer, Giuseppe Toffanin,[13] has clearly shown the process through which Aristotle, after dominating the theology of the Middle-Ages, was unceremoniously requested in the sixteenth century to lend the weight of his authority to the new, moralizing conception of literature. His *Poetica* supplied all requirements: from it were extracted both a statement of the ethical purpose of poetry, and the laws which were henceforth to regulate the work of the poet, now a craftsman in the true sense of the word.[14]

What room could be left in such a scheme for the ardent breath of inspiration? Of course it would have been too preposterous to deny it altogether, and it was coldly and guardedly mentioned in the opening pages of literary treatises. But no sooner had the concession been made, than it was withdrawn. The Sybils, the prophets, all those who seemed to be possessed with some divine fury, might well, as in Benci's *Orationes,* be praised—in the past.[15] But according to the same writer, the ideal, for the young scholar of the Roman college, was to imitate illustrious classical models

> mid leisure fair,
> Which brings no storm to trouble placid life.[16]

Pontanus is even more positive; for him the enthusiasm, the sublime madness which carries the poet away should be avoided at all costs. It is advisable on the contrary to set about the work of composition with "a mind appeased, a mind emptied of any other cares whatever, released and free from any anguish or emotion. For a distracted spirit can in no wise perform its task fitly and properly."[17] And just as religious emotions can be fostered by the "compositio loci," a suitable environment should produce the necessary detachment of the soul and freedom of the mind: "Such places, as those where we find a pleasantness alluring for the senses, forests, gardens, groves, country farms, where trees break into leaf, where wines ripen, where fields yield bountiful crops, where

> down the rill
> The trembling water swiftly flees."[18]

In other words the poet must carefully refrain from indulging in those emotions which he tries to awaken in others. Though some shrewd truth may lie hidden in such advice, nevertheless the real source of lyricism is ignored. And Pontanus betrays his total lack of understanding of what poetry really means, when stating that Ovid's *Tristia* rank below his other works, because, he says, they were composed, not in pleasant surroundings, but in the unpropitious dreariness of his sad exile.[19] The discreet versifier whom Jesuit critics substitute for the "vates" is of course nothing but a good Jesuit applying his efforts to a certain type of work, while remaining inwardly true to the ideal of his order. "Passion" is out of the question, and so therefore, is inspiration; "self" is to be suppressed, and so, therefore, lyricism, which is so largely the expression of self.

As a matter of fact, Pontanus makes a distinction between two faculties, "ingenium" and "judicium,"—inspiration, creative genius on the one hand, and judgment on the other. The latter, he says, is immeasurably superior;[20] for the poet, in his peaceful retirement, is not to be compared to a painter, whose work takes shape in a flash of creative light, but to a patient craftsman who fills in a mosaic, choosing one precious stone here and one precious stone there. Neither the material nor the pattern are his own; both are supplied by classical antiquity. For imitation, Pontanus says, is his chief task; not the imitation of nature indeed, but of suitable Latin or Greek models.[21] After providing himself with a sufficient supply of words and expressions—"conquirendum prius rerum ac verborum supellectilem"[22]—the poet will drill himself to the use of the material thus acquired through a series of exercises, from which inspiration is wholly banished. The sense remaining the same, now the phrasing will be different, and now the language used; now again the "genus" selected;[23] the whole culminating in the least original form of poetry, in which "judicium" has completely ousted "ingenium," the cento, made up wholly of elements borrowed from one or several authors, as in those prayers to God or the Virgin Mary, in which every single line is taken from Virgil.[24] However, no acknowledgement is to be made, and this plundering of ancient writers is to pass for original work; for Pontanus concludes with this delightfully naïve remark: "We must strive with all our labour, so that those things we spoke of, appear not theirs, but ours; though where we took them from, learned men cannot be unaware."[25] In other words, if the Jesuit critic is to be understood literally, the only task open to the poet is the manufacture of patchwork pieces, for the refined delight of connoisseurs, and for the wonderment of the vulgar. He is forbidden to strike a personal line. The *Ars poetica* is but a cookery-book, with recipes for the manufacture of beauty, "the straight and easy path to Helicon;"[26] the poem a disguised sermon, with "ornaments" awkwardly tacked on in places: "Let us lay on purple, sprinkle flovers."[27] Patience, discrimination, taste even, are allowed to the poet; but imagination, invention, originality, are denied.

\* \* \*

Such is the literary theory, which certainly inspired the teaching of Southwell's Jesuit professors, both at the Collège de Clermont and at the Roman college. A repellent and absurd theory indeed, which is the very negation of poetry, thus stripped of its life, robbed of its very soul; yet one which was to meet with such success in Jesuit educational circles, that it came to be generally considered as the official and current doctrine of Jesuit art. According to this doctrine, poetry was not the expression of anything really deep in the spiritual life of man; the part assigned to it might be brilliant, but it remained that of a menial. Yet it was not in the power of any cut and dried principles to stifle the love of beauty and the natural emotions that are inborn in the human heart. Even Jesuit professors of "rhetoric" (which included both prose and verse) were unable to take such a coldly utilitarian view of art as Pontanus. In all fairness be it said, and with no mean praise, though still widely removed from the theory of "art for art's sake" some of them had a notion of the value of beauty as such. Take Bencius, who was at the Roman college all through Southwell's years there, and whose influence was paramount upon many generations of students. He does believe that poetry has a favourable effect upon man's conduct; not merely, however, because it conveys artfully veiled advice, but because its charm has a soothing effect upon the passions. He is transported with this thought, and breaks out into verse:

> Do greed, and coveting, set thy heart afire?
> We know some words, and sounds, will soothe thy
>   pain
> And drive away most part of thy disease.

Art swoll'n with love of praise? But chastely read
Some booklet thrice, and peace restores and heals.
The envious, angry, sluggish,—tipplers, lechers,
Are none so fierce, but may not soften, if
To verse refined they lend a patient ear.[28]

But poetry does not only share, and more than share, music's soothing influence upon the heart of man; it does more, it inspires, it elevates: "It seems to be some divine force, which lifts up the spirit of man, so as to mingle it with the heavenly choirs."[29] Its excellence, its dignity, its beauty, "may never enough be praised, will never be praised according to their worth."[30] It must be defended against its detractors, who attack it on the ground of its appeal to the senses, "those headlong men, who inveigh against her with insolent abuse, and fear not to defile themselves with such a monstrous parricide."[31]

For Bencius, the moral efficacy of poetry is less a justification of its existence, than a confirmation of its proper value. The delight derived from literary composition is not merely to be tolerated on account of its improving purpose, but to be enjoyed for its own sake. That "liquida voluptas," it is true, is not inebriation; it is more like the conscientious satisfaction of the skilful workman; yet it is some sort of an artistic pleasure all the same. And one is glad to reflect that if Southwell's early poetical development was cramped by neo-classical "rules" and prescriptions, on the other hand Bencius may have imparted to him some of his genuine, though oratorical, enthusiasm for those "elegantes et ingenuae artes,"[32] some of his love of pure, perfect form, of smooth, easy verse, "flowing like a tranquil and crystalline river, without any ruggedness, without tortuous bends."[33]

Note that Bencius, in his *Orationes de laudibus poeticae,* does not merely praise poetry; he defends it—and this is not a sham fight for the sake of rhetoric, but a real one—against those who would now condemn it altogether, because the Renaissance writers had turned it to wicked uses. He scouts the notion that it is only the unworthy servant of religion. Not a servant indeed, but a sister. Does not its sublimity join hands with that of eternal truth? Is not the "vates" divinely inspired? That lifting upward of poetry and indeed of the whole of man, in so far as every man is to some extent a poet, is far truer, wiser and nobler, far more akin to Southwell's real spirit, than Pontanus' distrust of human nature, of its love of beauty, of its ardent emotions. Poetry, then, being truly divine, can be no other than Christian; it was Christian in classical antiquity, despite all appearances to the contrary; and the continuance of classical forms in the future will be no hindrance to its being more definitely Christian than ever. To the proving of this double and, in part at least, paradoxical thesis, Bencius devotes a large part of his *Orationes.*

His demonstration is worth reproducing, for it explains the curious, and sometimes preposterous way, in which the Jesuit professors and writers, and Southwell himself among others, attempted to adapt the poetical lore of pagan ages to the needs of a newly-reformed Catholicism.

First, the invention of metrical speech is to be ascribed, not to Orpheus or other classical characters, but to the writers of the Old Testament.[34] Bencius goes the length of stating that Moses composed a song in hexameters, and that whatever chronology may have to say to it, David wrote his psalms long before the appearance of any Greek hymnographer.[35] In the Bible and out of the Bible, the Jesuits insist on the considerable mass of non-pagan poetry which is actually extant. Yet the great heathen classics are the soul of humanism, and they cannot be ruled out. But why should one be afraid of them? Do not their writings evidence their sense of the supernatural and divine? Are they not to be compared to the worshippers of the unknown God at Athens? What is more, are there not many among them who school us to virtue and piety? In that respect, all Jesuit critics are agreed to give the first place to the serious, God-fearing and virtuous Virgil, "the chief of Latin poets,"[36] "the choir and dance leader, as it seems, of all others."[37] His moral qualities earn him admiration and praise; he has more "judicium" than Homer,[38] he "nods" less frequently[39]: "what fulness and richness in his speech, what weightiness in his thoughts, what dignity and beauty in his words!"[40] Besides, in his fourth eclogue, he clearly sings the glories of the Virgin mother and the infant Christ.[41] What is true of him is also true of others in a lesser degree. Bencius lavishes praise on Catullus' *Epithalamium of Thetis and Peleus,* the brilliant "ornaments" of which, he says, "bring to the readers marvellous delight, joined with equal profit,"[42] and "implant in their souls the love of virtue, and the desire of glory."[43] Glory beside virtue! here the old and the new humanism are curiously blended, and the mere fact that the two words appear here together casts a flood of light on the process of assimilation which the Jesuits were engaged in.

In one respect, however, there is a line of cleavage between the Jesuit critics and the theorists of seventeenth century classicism. The fervour of the latter has clearly cooled down; for them, religion has ceased to be all-absorbing and all-important; they feel, or pretend to feel, such awe-stricken respect for it, that they keep it confined to the temple, and refuse to consider it as supplying suitable matter for literary composition; they allow its place to be taken by the frigid inventions of a dead and unmeaning antiquity.[44] The former on the contrary have no intention of lending a new and unnatural life to the beliefs and manners of pagan ages; they do, indeed, take over the whole of the classical vocabulary, and even make a free use of non-Christian names for Christian characters and objects; they turn to their own convenience all the stage machinery of ancient poetry; but the subject must be Christian: "Who would not be moved, Bencius writes, by those things which happen after death, even though they be known to be feigned, the boat's journey across Acheron, the dull roar of Cocytus, the barking of Cerberus, the sight of men's shades, that dark and precipitous place, the monstrous, bottomless pit of Hell, and lastly that trial, that each man must stand before most stern judges, alone in the midst of a huge multitude. If those things have great power, as they certainly have, to teach and move our spirit, how much greater weight, how much greater authority, are to be found, where we know that the most absolute truth resides? in what holy singers, with conceits clearly inspired from Heaven, have indited to the praise of the only God, and of things divine?"[45]

The whole passage had to be quoted here: it will soon help us to realize how closely Bencius' advice, or advice similar to his, was followed by Southwell. The same author's choice of Christian subjects for his *Carmina* is especially striking: *De Christi domini precatione in horto*; *De imagine Deiparae* (the latter word betrays the humanist); *De beatissima virgine*; *De eadem in coelum ascendente*; *De Sancta Maria Magdalena*; *Ad effigiem Christi redimiti spinis*; *Ad Christum, dum cruci suffigitur.*[46] That Southwell took the lead from such masters is clear enough in a general way, from the fact that he chose kindred subjects for his English lyrics. But there is an even more surprising coincidence which seems indeed to be something else than a mere coincidence: among a list of themes which he recommends for Christian hymnology, Pontanus includes a series of poems on the various liturgical feasts of the Virgin Mary, which is exactly similar to the Virgin "cycle" in Southwell's English poems.[47] Here again the Jesuit appears as true to the spirit of his order.

\* \* \*

Both the genuine love of beauty of some of the early Jesuits, and the utilitarian view of poetry held by others, were to have a real influence all through Southwell's poetical career, the former gradually gaining the upper hand. They are however best illustrated in his Latin poems. These were written while their author was still a very young man, and are largely to be considered as college exercises. Yet they should not therefore be summarily dismissed; for, as well as the Latin devotions, they are a fitting introduction to the English works, the qualities of which they already foreshadow. Nor are they lacking in merits of their own. Southwell's classical studies had not been wasted; for while he had obediently subjected himself to the literary drill prescribed by his masters, he had come to realize the proper value of ancient poetry, and to understand its harmonies. In his Latin pieces therefore, he appears as

endowed with a capacious and retentive memory, a knack of imitation, a musical ear; his "supellex verborum" is a rich store of idiomatic phrases, and like Bencius, he has a nice sense of the balance and proportion of the line. On the other hand, his range of metrical forms is a limited one, and he already betrays less desire to vary the music of the verse, than to use its narrow limits to the best advantage, for the ingenious expression of his thought.

His Latin compositions belong to three distinct "genera," the epic, the elegy, the epigram. The first of these suited his temper but ill, and his juvenile attempt to emulate Virgil's grander vein ends in utter failure. It was indeed preposterous to handle the themes of the Assumption and Pentecost in the style of the Æneid. The former subject lent itself to the expression of tenderly or rapturously devout feelings, of enthusiasm, of loving bliss. Yet Southwell merely makes it the occasion for servile imitation of some of the Latin poet's coldest and most conventional descriptions and allegories. The poem *De Assumptione* opens with a few lines on the Creation (ll.1-6), but our first parents are soon forgotten, while Southwell describes the garden of Eden (ll.7-27) in a pastoral vein strongly reminiscent of classical pictures of the golden age. Then we are briefly informed that Lucifer (this pagan name being naturally preferred to that of Satan) has made Adam and Eve the slaves of the Stygian court. Pluto raises his victorious ensign, and inexorably rules over the whole of mankind. Yet a Virgin is born, who cannot be made to share the common lot; for Mary is here granted, not merely the privilege of immaculate conception, which the Jesuits already held as real, and which rescued her from spiritual perdition, but also that of perpetual health:

> Her well-attempered
> Body, her vigorous limbs, her lively strength,
> Still whole, to deadly sickness bar access.[48]

Death, here personified, then makes her appearance upon the stage, in surroundings which at once recall the Sybil's cave in the sixth book of the Æneid, "spelunca alta fuit vastoque immanis hiatu . . ."

> A cave there is, oft-winding, vast, and rough,
> Untouched of sunrays, gaping out below,
> And branching, awe-bewrapt, to jagged recesses.
> There Lethe's stream from open cleft outpours,
> And roaring loud beneath the sounding vaults
> 'Mid eddies miry rolls a headlong flood,
> And shivers on the rocks that block its course.
> Now, here, now there, the sooty roof outspreads,
> And rugged halls, with sickness-breathing air,
> Lie deep in gloom of death perpetually.
> Amidst them stands a throne, all unadorned,
> Bedaubed with shapeless mud, besmeared with slime,
> On props which ancient rust hath eaten out.
> There, hoary-bristling all, sits aged Death,
> Her visage lean, her cheeks with putrid gore

Decayed, her eyes deep-sunk, and round her teeth,
Lips livid, gaping out in shameful leer.

(ll.58-74)[49]

The passage of course appears at first sight as a Virgilian cento of the approved type. What follows borrows some interest from the fact that Milton was to choose a curiously parallel theme for epic treatment. Death, like Satan in *Paradise lost,* calls up a council of her retainers, whose help and advice are requested, in the present case, against the blessed Virgin. But where the greater poet brings individual characters upon the stage, Southwell merely parades a host of allegories—the comical array of diseases introduced with their medical names. Death then, with

eyes darting flames,
With gnawed-out nostrils blowing stinking fumes,

(ll.89-90)[50]

addresses the infernal army:

Black cohort, aye most faithful to our rule,
What glory Lethe's reign did once obtain
Above, where Phoebus, where the golden Moon
Their chariots drive; what crowds in war we slaugh-
     tered,
How many kings we slew, and eke how oft,
We swept the world of men all clear of life,
Since' neath your darts most fell, is known to you.
For well I wot, to Tartarus you drove
Thick clouds of souls in headlong rush, and glutted
With plenteous crops of men devouring Orcus.

(ll.91-99)[51]

Death's speech thus proceeds for some time, in a vein that recalls Cicero as well as Virgil. She exhorts her followers, whom she calls "cives," to remember their past glory, and warns them of the danger with which the Virgin threatens them. She then stops, with a foaming mouth, her words stifled by rage; the "citizens" raise the tumult of war and swear to take up arms against Heaven. But the epic vistas thus opened out soon close up again. Another allegorical character appears upon the stage. Old Age steps forward, and in one more rhetorical speech, endeavours to dissuade the infernal legions from the hopeless undertaking suggested by Death. Their noble enterprise, he says, is doomed to failure. Let them remember the sad fate of the Giants and of Lucifer, who in succession tried their strength against the "divi" or "superi." It is wiser far to bring the cause before him whose justice cannot fail, the thundering God (Tonans) himself. From now on Southwell's poetical imagination seems to flag. The narrative flows on swiftly. Death appears before God to plead her cause, and Gabriel to speak on behalf of the Virgin. She is born of Adam, Death says, and like all men, must submit to the power of the Parcae. But she is without sin,[52] says Gabriel, and besides she is the mother

of Christ and "sponsa Tonantis," the spouse of the thundering God,—one is almost betrayed into translating "the spouse of Jupiter" (ll. 170-205). After both speeches God renders judgment: the soul of the Virgin will leave her body painlessly, and "rise to the stars." Death shudders in wrath, yet requests permission at least to dissolve the Virgin's corpse; but

Against her claim the highest take their stand
And limbs unspotted aye, fair ornaments
Of blissful soul, to Heaven straight up fly.
     Th'all pow'rfull God agrees. Resounds with glee
The court of godly ones; of Heaven queen
The Virgin sits, and Death in rout is fled.[53]

Thus is the Assumption casually brought in at the last moment, and disposed of in a couple of prosaic lines. The Christian warmth of feeling which one had every reason to expect is equally absent from Southwell's other epic fragment in Latin hexameters, *For the feast of Pentecost, May 21st, 1580 (In festem Pentecostes, Anno Domini 1580, 21 Maii)* which he in fact wrote before he was twenty. We need not dwell at length on this unripe attempt, in which the wretched men left on earth after the Ascension complain that they alone remain without a solace, which Heaven and Hell have enjoyed. The whole is classical in character, and it will be enough to quote one line, in which God is besought to devise some means of comforting his children, so that

Te triplici laudet coelum, Styx, terra, camena,

(l. 29)[54]

Praise thee, Heav'n, Styx and earth, a threefold muse
. . .

Obviously, Southwell's genius did not lie that way. Though he might at times be soberly grave, he was not winged for the sublime flights of epic poetry; its largeness, its ampleness, were beyond his powers. His imitations of Virgil are indeed curious, entertaining even, as samples of the kind of work which might be turned out by a conscientious pupil in a Jesuit college; but they have little value of their own. Southwell himself soon realized his own limitations, and was well-advised enough to remain henceforth on safer ground.

\* \* \*

If Southwell failed in the epic *genre,* this was due to his inability to rise to the highest summits of poetry, and not to any awkwardness in the use of classical forms of speech; for as soon as he touches elegy, the sweetness and harmony of his Latin are scarcely less than those of his English lyrics. Christian subjects are now handled, if not in a purely Christian key, at any rate in a mood of pious lovingness. Such is the case for the first one among the elegiac pieces printed by Grosart, *A Letter to His Father, Written by the Prodigal Son while Tending His Swine* (*Filii prodigi procos pascentis ad patrem epistola*). In the former half of the piece, the prodigal son describes his wretched fate:

> Like gusty winds all things have passed away,
>    All things have changed the face they bore.
> Woe! Fortune turned her wheel, and freed the storm,
>    And bent on hurting, broke my raft.
> The golden age gives place to iron days,
>    And merry hours are turned to sorrows;
> The sails which once were pushed of favouring winds,
>    Which tamed the seas like placid lakes,
> Twixt Scyllas now and' twixt Charybdes rush,
>    Are rent and torn of hostile waves . . .
>
>                      (ll. 17-26)

> The days of rest have gone, and sad days follow;
>    The last of joy was first of pain;
> This fate is hard, but due to my misdeeds;
>    A fiercer wrath my faults deserved.
>
>                     (ll. 29-32)[55]

The prodigal son, having enlarged upon the profligate life he used to indulge in, proceeds thus:

> All o'er this main my wandering sail did roam,
>    While high the water bore my hull.
> But soon, upon a shore of rugged reefs,
>    A crumbling wreck, my craft was stranded.
>
>                     (ll. 51-54)[56]

In the second part of the poem, the prodigal son addresses his father and throws himself upon his mercy:

> O sole, o highest hope, o father mine,
>    A father, guard thy son from hurt.
> With tears he now declares his woeful crimes;
>    Forgiving is the part of love.
> I sinned, t'is true, my soul repentant mourns,
>    For each misdeed each limb atones,
> But pardon now my soul repentant craves,
>    Nor ought but sin can love forgive. . . .
>
>                   (ll. 91-98)

> Thy offspring now thou seest turned to rebel:
>    Wilt then, from father, turn to judge?
> But hadst thou been my judge, ne'er would my days
>    Have been condemned to bear such woe.
> Why did I leave thy threshold once beloved,
>    Withdraw my mournful eyes from thine? . . .
>
>                  (ll. 101-106)

> Ah God, see what I bore; restrain the waves,
>    My hull becalm in long'd for bays;
> Through reefs and seas and dread Charybdes toss't,
>    Guide her at last to gentler courses. . . .
>
>                  (ll. 109-112)[57]

More real pathos now appears. While he is yet unforgiven, the prodigal son might die; he imagines his father's sorrow on hearing the tidings:

> Should then a letter soon bring news to thee
>    Of my sad fate, what wilt thou think,
> What feel, if limbs that once were sprung of thee
>    Have been of raging beasts devoured.
> Perhaps thou wilt, with sighs, seek but his grave,
>    Whom now thy home might keep alive.
> If thou hast spurned, thy spurning thou shalt rue,
>    A double rain will wet thy cheeks;
> Thy dead son's face will oft appear to thee,
>    And thou shalt weep, and utter plaints;
> But shadows sad alone will watch thy tears,
>    Thy moans will vanish on the wind;
> Thy heart, yet whole, will grieve, and from thy sore
>    Thy buried love will rise again;
> 'T will rise, 't will rise, too late, alas, for me,
>    When hopes of long'd for help have gone. . . .
>
>                  (ll. 129-144)[58]

Here again, the poet's faults are too obvious to be concealed. Where we look for the direct and natural expression of sincere, genuine feeling, we still meet with far too much that is merely conventional. The style especially is artificial, this being due, as previously, to that "imitation" which was soon to be, in Pontanus' eyes, the very essence of poetry. Southwell knows his Ovid by heart, and exudes the *Tristia* and *Epistolae ex Ponto* at every pore. Once again, he deserves praise less for his own poetical imagination than for the careful keeping of a written or mental notebook of Latin phrases, and for the skilful way in which he extracts from it words of the needed quantity. Lastly, no translation, however painstaking, will veil the fact that part of the poem is utterly pedestrian.

At the same time, it cannot be denied that the *Letter of the Prodigal Son,* despite the preposterous unlikelihood of its subject, stands on a definitely higher level than the two epic fragments. Nor is this merely due to the soft plaintiveness of the model which Southwell was so faithfully following. At any rate, he would not have provided such a happy reproduction of Ovid's harmonious sadness, if his own mood had not been in a way akin to that of the Latin writer. Both the despondent grief of the elderly courtier, and the devotional sentimentalism of the adolescent Jesuit, find expression in the same vague wistfulness. Yet the colour is not exactly the same in both cases. Ovid is cringingly earnest in his complaints, whereas Southwell's pleading is of a gentler kind; it wins love through its own amiableness; it disarms anger and compels leniency through its half-smiling gracefulness. The **"Ah Deus, ecce tuli,"** with its weary trustfulness, reminds one of the Latin meditations, and foreshadows the concluding part of *Saint Peters Complaint.* Here already, we find a moving charm which is Southwell's own.

\* \* \*

In the *Letter of the Prodigal Son,* while the poet's emotion is touching indeed, its expression is neither direct nor plain; and we already find in it an element which will come to the forefront in the other elegies and in the epigrams, the peculiar Southwellian blend of gentle feeling and mannered expression. His Jesuit education naturally fostered his natural neatness and skilfulness in the arrangement of ideas and words. Preciosity is the supreme form of Pontanus' "ingenium," and was of value, for the teachers of the Society, as supplying a motive of literary interest to take the place of passion and sensuousness. Besides, its appearance in religious writings was scarcely a novelty; it was the direct outcome of patristic rhetoric; it had flourished in the Middle-Ages, in the course of which pious conceits were more than once introduced into the hymns of the Church.

The preference of the Jesuits for non-lyrical forms of poetry explains their partiality for the epigram, that favourite pastime of the humanists. "We are wont to admire the epigram, Pontanus writes, not only on account of its perfection of style, of its gracefulness, of its numbers falling in sweet succession, of its brevity . . . but also on account of its subtlety and cleverness." He then makes a distinction between simple and "adorned" epigram; in the latter, he says, there are two terms, one of which is related to the other, being greater, or smaller or equal, or different, or contrary. As an illustration of this he quotes Cicero on parallelism and opposition of terms, whether they be of like nature or antithetical; such parallelism and opposition being extended not only to single ideas, but also to series of corresponding ideas. We find here some of the most essential elements of preciosity, those which are most conspicuous in Southwell's works.

As a matter of fact, the scholars of the Society were profuse in the composition of such concise and witty pieces. One of Southwell's fellow-prisoners in the tower, John Ingram, not a Jesuit himself it is true, but a grateful pupil of the Jesuits at Pont-à-Mousson and Rome, covered the walls of his dungeon with epigrams. These do not testify to very high powers, even of the kind here referred to, but they prove with what gusto the neo-humanists cast into the mould of "elegant" conceits their most intimate, deepest and even most tragic emotions.[59] Thus also did Southwell when he came to the writing of epigrams. His preciosity already appears in its full-blown form in what Grosart calls the *Fragment of a Series of Elegies.* This fragment consists of three pieces, headed Elegies VII, VIII and IX respectively, the middle one alone being complete. Grosart erroneously referred N° VII to the defeat of the Armada, and also mistakenly supposed N° VIII to be an imaginary speech of Mary Queen of Scots. In fact, the whole set seems to have been written to commemorate the life and death of Saint Margaret, queen of Scotland,

a holy woman who for various reasons appears to have held a prominent place in the affections of English Catholics in the late XVIth century. She was the wife of King Malcolm, of Shakespearian memory, a wild barbarian whom she won over to Christianity, by her lovingness and charm, and whom she constantly guided in the pious exercise of his rule over his subjects. When the fragment opens, the saint has just died; Elegy VII describes the whole universe mourning for such an irreparable loss. It is placed in the mouth of Malcolm himself, who laments the death of "Margaris" or "Margareta" in such words as the following:

I mourn, let Heaven be witness! My Margaret, alack!

(l.34)

Should I not mourn? My life with Margaret flees!

(l. 36)

I faint, I fall! O grief, o grief, I die!
No more! Kind eearth, o hide my pain!

(ll. 40-41)[60]

The idea expressed in these lines is further developed in Elegy VIII, also placed in the mouth of the husband of the saint. This piece is a rather graceful but over-skilful display of verbal agility, centring round a conceit, namely that the beloved woman being one with her lover, either she cannot be said to have died since he remains alive, or he cannot be said to remain alive since she is dead. The theme of the elegy is earthly love, but earthly love so free from any sensuousness, so thoroughly blended with Christian piety, so ethereal, as to be indistinguishable from divine love. Lastly, Elegy IX, which is short and of small interest is entitled: **"The Shade of the Queen Teaches Her Noblemen, What Is to be Thought of These Fleeting Things below"** (**"Umbra reginae nobiles viros docet, quid sit de rebus hisce fluxis sentiendum."**) It is an oration, full of sensible moral advice, and a forerunner of Southwell's lyrics of wisdom.

Elegies VII and VIII are sweetly touching in places, but they are marred by conceits which are no better than puns, and poor ones at that; they supply proofs, both of Southwell's childish immaturity at the time and of the absurd lengths to which preciosity was pushed by his literary compeers. He stoops to such playing upon words as: "Heu, dicunt periisse Peru!" (Elegy VII, 1.22: Alas, they say that Peru perished!) or the following distich, in which the husband speaks to himself:

Sic quod amas animas? quod amas sinis ecce perire;
Si sinis hoc cinis est, nam calor inde fugit

(El. VIII, ll.7-8)

The conceit on "sinis" and "cinis" is untranslatable, the meaning being as follows:

Thy love thou quicknest? No, thou lettest her die;
    Let'st her turn to ashes: from her flees heat.

But the climax is reached with the following comical
joke:

Quid quod et Æthiopes membris nigrantibus horrent.
    A luctu credo provenit ille color

(El. VII, ll. 20-21)

Th'Ethiopians shudder in their swarthy limbs.
Methinks their mourning bred their colour.

But once again, the lad Southwell may be forgiven for
his passing concession to the debased tastes of the age.
At the same time that he was thus unwittingly provid-
ing amusement for future readers, he was already sup-
plying instances of another kind of wit, which was far
more natural to him. The following lines contain an
intellectual conceit, one in which the central motive is
not verbal likeness or contrast, but the opposition of
two ideas—here represented by the words "one" and
"two":

Now countest well? I, thou: think'st two names.
    But in those two one soul is seated;
One soul: thus hearts embrace, and minds are wed:
    Thou, I, not two, though two our hearts.
I thine, thou mine: twin bonds will join us both;
    Here both of us, and yet not twain.
Why mourn? shalt live, one body holds us both,
    A living body hast in mine;
Or else I'm dead; one body holds us both,
    My limbs are buried in thy grave.

(El. VIII, ll. 15-24)[61]

The next passage is musically touching; yet, though
free from actual conceits, it remains delicately subtle:

Of all things fairest thou, thus spokest dying:
    "Thy heart for e'er my name shall keep.
Though hence I go, let spouse and spouse be near.
    I die; in death live still with me. . . ."

(ll. 27-30)

Thou shalt for e'er be mine, though deemed afar,
    Aye shall my breast thy last words hold;
And like thy words, for e'er thou'lt cleave to me,
    Thy words, my days, one death will meet.
Of mourning e'er no light shall make me weary:
    Who would forget such light as thine?. . . .

(ll.33-38)[62]

Such, then—uniting tender lovingness with clever
trifling—is Southwell's one contribution to the poetry
of human love. Even where the feeling is most genuine,
the main conceit on "life" and "death" is not forgotten;
an age-old conceit, which appears everywhere in the
literature of the time, Continental as well as English,
but which must have possessed rare charms in the eyes
of the Jesuit; for he reverted to it again and again. Its
pious interpretation lay in the contrast between earthly
life, which is so often tantamount to spiritual death, and
the death of the body, which opens out the portals of
everlasting life. To this religious use Southwell turned
in two Latin epigrams. In the former of these, *For the
renewing of his vows at Christmas-time* (*In renova-
tionem votorum, festis natalis Domini*),[63] he even
improves upon it, by adding to it an untranslatable
double pun on "vota" and "vita," (the poet's religious
vows, and life, taken now in its proper sense, and now
as an equivalent for God)[64]—the two words and the
three ideas interlacing with each other throughout the
piece. The same thought again, though worked out in a
simpler way, supplies the central motive for the tracery
work of the second epigram, **"To God in Affliction: An
Elegy"** (**"Ad Deum in afflictione: Elegia"**)—this
description being an obvious misnomer. This short poem
runs as follows:

Thou seest my silent tears, my wounded heart,
    The secret fire with which I burn;
How oft my breast in sadness heaves up sighs,
    How oft I'd welcome death for thee.
And yet I live, if life be life, to whom
    'T is death to live, and life to die.
The life, which I would live, takes flight afar,
    A life unsought for, cruel, comes:
My chase one flees, one follow when I flee.
    I chase and flee: here grief, there grief;
Nor fleeing am I caught, nor catch who flees.
Alack for me, who'll change my fate?[65]

This is not, indeed, the only Latin poem in which South-
well expresses his distress upon earth, and his pining
for his heavenly home. In the short piece headed **"To
Saint Catherine, Virgin and Martyr"** (**"Ad sanctam
Catherinam, virginem et martyrem"**).[66] he addresses,
instead of God, one of the dwellers in Paradise, but the
feeling is the same as previously. He prays that he may
be freed from his "biting grief," his "weeping," the
"silent fires that inwardly burn him." Conventional im-
ages are now borrowed from the common store of Pe-
trarchan love poetry. And yet, who would doubt his
sincerity? It is vouched for by his Latin devotions, by
his English poems, by the way in which he raised his
own life so near to the purely spiritual and supernatural,
by the radiant bliss that lit up his death at Tyburn.
Therefore, while casting his most intimate and ardent
feelings into the artificial mould of preciosity, he was
giving the lie to Pontanus' theory, according to which
the neo-classical poet should be wholly detached from
himself, and his hand know nothing of his heart.

Whether this holds good of other precious authors as
well, must be decided in each individual case. Suffice it
for the present to have shown that genuine feelings may
quite easily clothe themselves in an artificial garb, when
fashion prescribes as much. This will have to be

remembered when we come to the study of Southwell's Italian models, or of his own English compositions. Nor is the reaching of such a conclusion the only justification for a detailed study of his Latin prose and verse. The latter is indeed of small literary value; its interest is chiefly that of a document on Jesuit education. Yet it throws light upon influences that Southwell was slow in rejecting, and which are still strongly felt in **Saint Peters Complaint** and in *Mary Magdalens teares.* They illustrate what we have called the weaker side of his personality, in which a taste for neatness, for prettiness, for poetical fretwork and arabesque, combines with a tenderness which is sweet and touching indeed, yet too clever in its expression to sound really deep. They bear witness to the poet's gift of adaptability, to the fineness of his taste and ear and to his musical sense; they offer, as yet, little that may be called original.

On the whole, Southwell's years of literary preparation present a curiously mixed picture, and largely account for the various phases of his progress. The literary spirit of the Society of Jesus, its insistence on the minor sides of poetical craftsmanship, were not alone responsible for his preciosity; yet their influence was felt in the early English works as well as in the Latin verse. At the same time it was not possible for any theory to stifle the emotions aroused in juvenile hearts when they came into direct touch with the beauties of ancient poetry. Southwell had felt them, and tried to emulate them. His natural lyricism was strengthened at Rome, as well as his belief in the divine mission of the poet. The inspiration thus awakened in him was soon to shake off the leading-strings of literary orthodoxy.

## Notes

1. *Ratio studiorum et Institutiones Scholasticae Societatis Jesu..* collectae.. a G. M. Pachtler S. J. (*Monumenta Germaniae Paedagogica . . .* herausg von Karl Kehrbach, vol. 5, and 11) Tomus II, p. 144 (from the *Ratio* of 1586) "Tandem horum studiorum adminiculo potius, quam superiorum facultatum Societas breui propagata est in praecipuas orbis Christiani partes: neque in ijs melius ac firmius conseruari potest, quam ijsdem artibus, ob quas initio admissa fuit . . ." The *Ratio Studiorum* was begun in 1581, while Southwell was a Scholastic at the Roman College; but the *Constitutions* first published in 1558 stressed the necessity for the Scholastics to cultivate their style. (*Constitutiones Societatis Iesv,* Antverpiae apud Ioannem Mevrsivm, 1625, p. 165, § 13).

2. *Ratio Studiorum,* ed. cit., p. 145: "Quare in vestibus, in cubiculis, in libris, alijsque rebus necessarijs nihil fere intelligatur esse discriminis inter istos et illos Professores . . . In ijs, qui vel in Societatem cupiunt admitti, vel admissi iam ad Superiores facultates profitendum promouendi sunt, alijs

(si caetera valde imparia non sint) praeferantur, sedulo etiam quaerantur ij, qui literis humanioribus magis excellunt."

3. The fullest biographical source for Bencius is Alegambe, *Bibliotheca Scriptorum Societatis Jesy, Antverpiae,* M.DCXLIII, which unfortunately dwells more upon the religious than upon the literary side of the life of the Jesuit professor. Cf. also De Backer-Sommervogel, vol. I, col. 1285 sqq. Those two works have supplied us with several of the particulars mentioned here. As to Bencius' professorship at the Roman College, cf. in the Archives of the Society of Jesus two catalogues of the Roman province, dated 1579 and 1584. The former has the following mention of Bencius: "Docuit litt. hum per sex annos legit Rhet."; the latter confirms the initial date with these words: "legit Rhetor. 9 annos." I was able to obtain these extracts from the archives owing to the kindness of Fr. Newdigate, S.J. and Father Kleyser, S.J. It is to be presumed that in the catalogue of 1584, the nine years of rhetoric include the six years of humanities mentioned in the catalogue of 1579.

4. *Carmen quo quaeritur quae sit optima ratio tranquillioris vitae instituendae,* in Franciscus Bencius, *Carmina, libri quatuor,* Ingolstadii, 1592, liber primus, p. 1.

5. Jacobus Pontanus (Spanmuller), born at Bruck in Bohemia in 1542, became a Jesuit in 1562. He was a professor of humanities and rhetoric for 27 years and died at Augsburg in 1626. He does not appear ever to have been connected with the Roman college and I have been unable to find out whether he came to Rome, but he had begun the series of his published works, all on the art of writing, as early as 1573, and anyhow he is but the most typical mouthpiece of a doctrine which was to prevail in the Society for nearly two hundred years. Cf. De Backer-Sommervogel, vol. VI, col. 1007 sqq.

6. The first edition of this work dates back to 1594 (Cf. de Backer-Sommervogel, vol. VI, col. 1011) and is entitled: *Jacobi Pontani Societatis Iesv Poeticarvm Institutionvm libri III . . .* Ingolstadii; ex typographia Davidis Sartorii, 1594 (8vo). The edition we shall refer to here is that of 1595, which bears the same title, with the following addition "editio Secunda emendatior." (8vo) The printer was Adam Sartorius.

7. *Ars Poetica,* l.333.

8. PONTANUS, *op. cit.,* p. 6: "Non quem imitentur, quid narrent, quid agant poetae; sed quamobrem, qua mente, quibusque rationibus, hoc intuendum est . . ." p. 5: "Sit ergo poetica, *Ars, hominum actiones effingens, easque ad vitam instituendam carminibus explicans.*"

9. *Antonii Possevini Societatis Iesv Tractatio De poesi & Pictura ethnica, humana, & fabulosa collata cum vera, honesta, & sacra.* Lugduni, M.D.XCIIII. p. 474: "Poetis autem hoc maximè propositum esse debeat, ut Lectorem reddant meliorem: secundo loco, ut delectent."

10. PONTANUS, *op. cit.,* p. 14: "Assumet igitur poeta quamtumcunque opus fuerit à magistris illis moralibus. . . . vt scribendi rectè, sapere sit & principium & fons." (This last line from Horace, *Ars poetica,* 1.309)

11. *Ibid.* pp. 14-15: "Eoque modo officium docebit, vt divisiones, definitiones, ratiocinationes, interrogationes, funditus repudians, compositissima oratione, exemplisque pulcherrimis à se vel primum excogitatis, vel ingeniosis fictionibus amplificatis & illustratis, & quodammodo conditis, etiam diversos animi motus misceat, & lectores siue spectatores vel alliciat, vel rapiat, quo placerit. Hinc est, quod viri sapientes poesin quandam esse philosophiam, fabularum involucris tectam asseruerunt."

12. *Ibid.,* pp. 17-18: "vulgo gratificantes, cui semper iucunda magis quam vtilia sunt in amoribus: & quod salutarem doctrinam nisi leporibus & oblectamentis multimodis respersam facilè aspernatur."

13. Cf. Giuseppe TOFFANIN, *La fine dell' umanesimo,* Torino 1920.

14. ARISTOTLE'S *Poetica* of course applied to the drama, and so did the rules more or less justifiably extracted from it; but the same legislating spirit which enforced the rules was to prevail in other branches of literature as well.

15. BENCIUS, *op. cit.,* p. 114-115.

16. *Ibid., Carmen quo quaeritur* etc., concluding lines:

> . . . otia pulchra
> Quae placidam nullo perturbent turbine vitam . . .

17. PONTANUS, *op. cit.,* p. 40 "Vnum est, mens pacata, mens alia quavis sollicitudine vacans, angore & perturbatione omni soluta prorsus atque libera. Animus distractus, nulla in re munus suum fungi probe, ac decenter potest . . ."

18. *Ibid,* p. 41: "Illi loci, in quibus est sensibus blandiens amoenitas, syluae, horti, memora, ruscula, vbi frondescunt arbores, pubescunt vites, segestes largiuntur fruges, vbi obliquo laborat lympha fugax trepidare riuo . . ." The last words from Horace, Carmen III, ad P. Dellium, l. 11-12.

19. *Ibid.* p. 41.

20. *Ibid.,* see the whole of Chapt. XIII, pp. 42-45.

21. *Ibid.,* p. III, and Chapt. X, pp. 28 sqq.

22. *Ibid.,* Chapt. XII, p. 38.

23. *Ibid.,* Chapt. IX, pp. 24-28.

24. *Antonii Possevini Societatis Iesv Tractatio De Poesi & Pictura ethnica, humana, & fabulosa collata cum vera, honesta, & sacra . . .* Lvgdvni, Apvd Ioannem Pillehotte, 1594, pp. 480 (cento quid sit), 503 and 504.

25. PONTANUS, *op. cit.,* p. 32: "Omnis labor eo impendendus, ne, quae dicimus, illorum, sed nostra videantur: quamuis doctos viros, vnde illa hauserimus, non fallat."

26. *Ibid.,* sig (2ᵃ): "Verum et commodum ad Heliconem iter."

27. *Ibid.,* p. 26: "Fucum addamus, flores inspergamus."

28. BENCIUS, *op. cit.,* p. 113:

> Feruet auaritia, miseroque cupidine pectus?
> Sunt verba, & voces, quibus hunc lenire dolorem
> Possis, & magnam morbi depellere partem.
> Laudis amore tumes? Sunt certa piacula, quae te
> Ter pure lecto poterunt recreare libello.
> Inuidus, iracundus, iners, vinosus, amator,
> Nemo adeo ferus est, vt non mitescere possit,
> Si modo culturae patientem accommodat aurem.

This is of course a commonplace of antiquity, ever since Orpheus charmed the wild beasts; the difference from Pontanus is none the less notable.

29. *Ibid.,* p. 114: "Poëtica videlicet ipsa divina quaedam vis est, quae extellit hominis animum, vt superum plerumque choris immisceat . . ."

30. *Ibid.,* p. 117: "Nunquam laudatae satis, nec pro dignitate laudandae . . ."

31. *Ibid.,* p. 92: ". . . praecipiti homines . . . qui in illam . . . contumeliose inuehuntur, nec verentur se tam immani parricidio inquinare."

32. BENCIUS, *op. cit.,* p. 54.

33. *Ibid.,* p. 42: "Vt sedatum & dilucidum amnem, sine salebris & vllo anfractu fluere . . ."

34. Cf. *Ibid.,* pp. 93 sqq.

35. Cf. *Ibid.,* Liber Secundus, Caput XXXI, de Hymno, pp. 142 sqq.

36. *Ibid,* p. 31: "Poetarum latinorum imperator."

37. BENCIUS, *op. cit.,* p. 115: "Qui coryphaeus quidam & praesultor videtur esse ceterorum." Cf. also p. 117: "Fulgor ille poëtarum, & Romani magister eloquij."

38. PONTANUS, *op. cit.,* p. 45.

39. *Ibid.* "Virgilius rarius dormitat."

40. BENCIUS, *op. cit.,* p. 105: "Quanta sit orationis vbertas, quae pondera sententiarum, quanta dignitas speciesque verborum . . ."

41. *Ibid.,* pp. 115-116, and POSSEVIN, *op. cit.,* p. 488.

42. BENCIUS, *op. cit.,* p. 117: "Tam multa habet ornamenta artis intimae, quae miram afferunt voluptatem legentibus, cum pari vtilitate coniunctam."

43. *Ibid.,* p. 118: "Earumque rerum . . . quae . . . ingenerant amorem virtutis, & gloriae cupiditatem in animis . . ."

44. Cf. in BOILEAU's *Art poétique* the passage beginning: "De la foi d'un Chrétien les mystères terribles . . ."

45. BENCIUS, *op. cit.,* p. 98: "Quem non permoueant illa post mortem, etiamsi ficta esse credantur, transuectio Acherontis, Cocyti fremitus, Cerberi latratus, vmbrarum aspectus, locus ille obscurus & praeceps, immanis & nunquam explebilis vorago inferorum, illa denique quae erit vnicuique pro se apud senerissimos iudices maxima in corona hominum, caussa dicenda? Quod si haec magnam habent vim, vt certe habent, ad erudiendos animos & commouendos, quanto maius in iis inesse debet pondus, grauiorque auctoritas, quae scimus esse verissima? in iis etiam quae ad vnius Dei laudem, ac rerum divinarum, sacrosancti pepererunt vates conceptu plane divino . . ."

46. *Ibid,* pp. 165, 177, 177, 177, 180, 184, 184, respectively.

47. Cf. PONTANUS, *op. cit.,* pp. 151, 152, and *infra,* chapt. x.

48. *Complete poems,* GROSART's ed., pp. 192-193.

> quod corporis aequa
> Temperies, vegetique artus, et vivida virtus
> Lethiferis aditum praecluderet integra morbis

49. This is a translation, as accurate as possible, of the lines in the *Complete poems,* GROSART's ed., p. 193, which run as follows:

> Est vastum scabris sinuosum anfractibus antrum,
> Solis inaccessum radiis, fundoque dehiscens,
> Et ruptas reserans immani horrore cavernas.
> Propatulo hic fluvius surgit Lethaeus hiatu,
> Ingentique ruens per concava saxa fragore,
> Proecipitante rotat limosa volumina cursu,
> Et dirum aggeribus spumans fremit unda repertis.
> Hinc atque hinc atrata patent fuligine tecta,
> Et loca senta situ, varios spirantia morbos,
> Aeternum spissae squalent caligine mortis.
> In medio solium, nulla spectabile pompa,
> Informi obductum limo, sanieque perunctum,

> Eminet, exesis diuturna aerugine fulcris.
>   Hic annosa sedet canis mors horrida saetis,
> Os macie taboque genas confecta, cavisque
> Immersos fossis oculos et livida circum
> Dentes labra gerens turpique patentia rictu.

"Solis inacessum radiis" is from the description of Cacus' cave, *Æneid* VIII, 195: "Loca senta situ" refers to Tartarus, *Æneid,* VI, 462; Southwell has made a patchwork collection of all the caverns in Virgil's epic. Cf. also, for the description of Death, *Æneid* III, 590 and VIII, 197.

50. *Ibid,* p. 194:

> . . . oculis jaculantibus ignes,
> Atque olidum truncis fumum de naribus efflans . . .

51. *Ibid:*

> Atra cohors, nostris semper fidissima sceptris,
> Olim quanta fuit Lethei gloria regni
> Qua Phoebus, qua luna suos agit aurea currus,
> Quas bello edidimus strages, quot funere reges
> Mersimus, et totum quoties consumpsimus orbem
> Non latet, et vestris cecidit pars maxima telis.
> Vos etenim spissos animarum ad Tartara nimbos
> Proecipites egisse subit, plenisque voracem
> Exsatiasse hominum functorum messibus Orcum.
>
>                                    *(Ibid.)*

52. It is of course well-known that the Society of Jesus was strongly in favour of the dogma of the Immaculate Conception. St John Berchmans, S.J., who belonged to a slightly later generation, but who was like Southwell in many ways, wrote in his private devotions a promise, signed with his own blood, "everywhere and always to affirm and defend it." (Hippolyte DELEHAYE, *Saint Jean Berchmans,* Paris, 1921.)

53. *Complete poems,* GROSART's ed., p. 109.

> Ast superi contra insurgunt, et nescia labis
> Coelo (sic) membra petunt, animae decora alta beatae.
>   Annuit Omnipotens. Divum sonat aula triumphis.
> Virgo poli regina sedet, mors victa fugatur.

54. *Ibid.,* p. 213.

55. *Ibid.,* p. 200:

> Omnia nimboso fluxere simillima vento,
>   Nec facies rebus, quae fuit ante, manet.
> Hei volvit fortuna rotam, ventisque solutis
>   Disrupit nostram perniciosa ratem.
> Aurea deperiit, nunc ferrea prodiit aetas;
>   Sunt laeta in tristes tempora versa dies.
> Quaeque prius ventis pergebant vela secundis,
>   Et pontum ut faciles edomuere lacus,
> Acta ruunt inter Scyllas interque Charybdes
>   Et fracta adversis dilacerantur aquis . . .
> Jam placidae periere dies, tristesque secutae;
>   Ultima laetitiae prima doloris erat.

Sors ea dura quidem, sed nostris debita factis,
    Immo est errato lenior ira meo . . .

On the whole, the poem is a close imitation of OVID's *Tristia* and even more so of the *Epistolae ex Ponto,* of their vocabulary, style, harmony and feeling. Compare with the above passage the following lines:

En ego, non paucis quondam munitus amicis
    Dum flavit velis aura secunda meis;
Ut fera nimboso tumuerunt aequora vento
    In mediis lacera puppe relinquor aquis . . .

      (*Epist. ex Ponto,* lib. II, Ep. III; ll. 25-29.)

56. *Ibid.,* p. 201:

Hoc mea lustravit nimium vaga carbasus aequor,
    Alta quoad plenam sustulit unda ratem:
Sed modo saxosi portus anfractibus haerens,
    Corruit ablatis naufraga puppis aquis.

57. *Ibid,* p. 203:

O pater, O nati spes summa et sola salutis,
    Sis pater et nati sit tibi cura tui.
En scelus agnoscit, lacrimis commissa fatetur,
    Parcere peccanti munus amoris erit:
Peccavi, fateor, sceleris mens conscia luget,
    Erroresque luunt singula membra suos;
Scilicet et veniam sceleris mens conscia poscit
    Nec nisi peccanti parcere posset amor . . .
Nec quia me cernis factum de prole rebellem,
    Tu fieri judex ex genitore velis.
Quamvis si fieres, nunquam te judice tantis
    Esset, credo equidem, subdita vita malis.
Cur tua deserui redamati limina tecti!
    Cur mea subtraxi lumina maesta tuis! . . .
Ah, Deus, ecce tuli, saevos jam comprime fluctus,
    Et petat optatos lassa carina sinus.
Per mare, per scopulos, per mille agitata Charybdes,
    Mitius ah tandem, te duce, pergat iter . . .

The parallel use of *limina* and *lumina* in lines 105-106 is a typical play upon words, which cannot be rendered in English.

The passage is again strongly reminiscent of the *Epistolae ex Ponto,* as the following quotation will show:

Poenitet o! Si quid miserorum creditur ulli,
    Poenitet, et facto torqueor ipse meo!
Quumque sit exsilium, magis est mihi culpa dolori;
    Estque pati poenas, quam meruisse, minus.

      (*Epist. ex Ponto,* I, i, 59-62.)

The prodigal son's graceful way of imploring leniency recalls the manner in which Ovid begs for the Emperor's forgiveness:

Difficile est, fateor; sed tendit in ardua virtus,
    Et talis meriti gratia major erit

      (*Ibid.,* II, ii, 113-114)

Cf. also *ibid.,* 117-122, and I, i, 75.

58. *Complete poems,* GROSART's ed., pp. 204-5:

O si forte brevi tales tibi littera casus
    Adferat, et nati talia fata tui,
Quae tibi mens, quis sensus erit, cum, te orta parente,
    Audieris rabidas membra vorasse feras?
Tunc fortasse gemens sobolis vel busta requires,
    Quam poteras vivam nuno habuisse domi.
Tunc, si me renuas, memorans renuisse dolebis,
    Atque tuo duplex imber ab ore fluet.
Obvia saepe animo defuncti occurret imago,
    Junctaque cum lacrimis plurima verba dabis,
Ast aderit nullus nisi tristes fletibus umbrae
    Et rapiet gemitus ventus et aura tuos.
Tunc dolor invadet quem non invaserat olim,
    Quique sepultus erat, vulnere surget amor.
Ille quidem surget, sed nostros serus in usus,
    Cum nulla optatae spes opis esse potest.

The peculiar use of "litera" is from Ovid (Ibid., II, vii, I) The description of the father's weeping may recall *Tristia,* I, iii, 17-18..

59. John INGRAM's Epigrams (scribbled by him on the walls of his dungeon in the Tower) in *C. R. S.,* vol. V, pp. 270-281.

60. *Complete poems,* GROSART's ed., p. 207:

Ah doleo! testes superi! Mea Margaris, eheu! . . .
Non doleam? mea vita fugit, mea Margareta! . . .
Deficio, subsido: dolor! dolor! expirabo!
    Jam satis est, luctus tu tege, terra, meos.

61.    An bene dinumeras? Ego, tu; duo nomina fingis:
    Ast unum duplici nomine numen inest.
Numen inest: cor corde premit, mentemque maritat;
    Non duo tu vel ego, sint duo corda licet,
Sim tuus et mea sis, sint vincula bina duorum:
    Simus et hic ambo; non tamen ambo sumus.
Quid queror? haud moreris; duo sunt nam corpore in uno,
    Sic vivum nostro corpore corpus habes:
Aut ego jam perii, duo sunt nam corpore in uno;
    Sic mea sunt tumulo membra sepulta tuo.

62.    Hoc est, quod moriens, rerum pulcherrima, dixti:
    Nomen tu memori pectore semper habe!
Et licet hinc absim, sit praesens conjuge conjux:
    Defungor: functa tu quoque vive mihi.
Jam mea semper eris, licet hic mea diceri absens;
    Pectoribus statuam dicta suprema meis.
Quamque mihi dictum, tam tu mihi semper adhaeres,
    Et dicti et vitae mors erit una meae.
Non mihi votorum reddet lux ulla tuorum
    Taedia; quis tantae non meminisse potest?

      (*Ibid.,* p. 209)

63. GROSART, p. 214.

64. The opposition between *vota* and *vita* runs throughout this short poem, the last two lines reading as follows:

Des igitur tua vota Deo, dabit ipse seipsum,
    Et reddet votis praemia vita tuis.
(Give thou thy vows to God, he'll give himself,
    And *Life* will bless thee for thy vows.)

In a footnote GROSART says (p. 214): "The MS. reads 'vita', but wrongly; and we substitute 'viva'. "There seems no reason for this, the meaning being perfectly clear with vita=Deus, while Grosart's correction destroys the conceit in the last line.

65.     Tu tacitas nosti lacrimas, tu saucia cernis
            Pectora, secreto quod cremer igne vides;
        Tu, quoties tristi ducam suspiria corde,
            Tu, quoties pro te mors mihi grata foret.
        Vivo tamen, si vita potest quam duco vocari,
            Quippe cui mors est vivere, vita mori.
        Namque procul mea vita fugit, qua vivere vellem,
            Et fera qua nollem vivere vita venit:
        Haec me dum fugio sequitur, fugit illa sequentem.
            Persequor et fugio, luctus utrinque mihi;
        Nec fugiens capior, nec euntem carpere possum.
            Hei mihi, qui versa vivere sorte dabit! (52)

                                                    (GROSART, p. 212)

66. *Complete poems,* GROSART'S ed., p. 213.


## Harry Morris (essay date 1961)

SOURCE: Morris, Harry. "*In Articulo Mortis.*" *Tulane Studies in English* 11 (1961): 21-37.

[*In the following essay, Morris examines the deathbed repentance poems of Southwell, Raleigh, and Donne, giving special consideration to Southwell's "I Die Alive."*]

In religious verse only occasionally does a poem reproduce passions similar to those of deathbed repentance—repentance *in articulo mortis*. Yet in a period of forty years, three poems appeared in England that capture the emotions of mortality *in extremis*. Deathbed repentance is in part a reaffirmation of faith that has been with the sinner always. On Mount Purgatory, all Dante's late-repentant—the excommunicate, the indolent, the violently cut-off, the pre-occupied—were in life firm believers who, for one reason or another, had put aside repentance until moribund. The sinner who waits until the final moments of life before seeking absolution and salvation, led mostly by fear of damnation, sometimes by love of God, gives testimony to a long-held credo. Whether it comes from extremity of terror or depth of love or simply because it is accompanied by the pangs of death, repentance *in articulo mortis* is an intensely moving act. The concentration of the dying person is unbroken; soul and body are in fervent union. The mind's focus upon salvation dims the torment in the flesh. The emotions evoked in an observer are similar to the emotions of the dying man in that the living sees in the other's death his own inescapable doom.

In 1595, John Wolfe published **St. Peter's Complaint,** a volume of poetry by Robert Southwell who earlier that year was hanged, drawn, and quartered at Tyburn for treason, more exactly for practicing his faith as a Roman Catholic priest of the Society of Jesus. In 1604, a book, called *Daiphantus* by an An. Sc. included a poem now attributed almost universally to Sir Walter Ralegh. Although Ralegh had not died by the time of its publication, it was only the whim of James I that kept the poem from a posthumous first issuance. In 1635, a second edition of the poems of John Donne appeared, four years after the death of their author. The first edition of 1633 did not include the poem that concerns us here. The three poems which came to light almost from the tomb, we might say, were Southwell's **"I Die Alive,"** Ralegh's "The passionate mans Pilgrimage," and Donne's "Hymne to God my God, in my sicknesse." Although these poems are not made up of the expressions of sin, remorse, and contrition that usually dominate the final prayers of the sinner on earth, they are concerned with The Four Last Things, with death, judgment, heaven and hell; they are confessions of faith delivered under circumstances that liken the poet to the late-repentant.

According to tradition, two of these poems were composed by writers near death.[1] The third, **"I Die Alive,"** may be of more doubtful authenticity as a poem *in articulo mortis*. Scholars argue that Southwell, suffering continual grievous torture, would have little inclination to write verses.[2] But there is a group of five poems in **St. Peter's Complaint** that have as their plea that death come quickly. They refer to imprisonment, anguish, pain, and torment; they employ images of stripes, wounds, and blood. The stanza forms, the meter, the diction are all extremely simple, direct, and well-suited to the frailty of the man and to his situation, from which the hours and labor needed for poetic composition could be wrung only with great effort. This is not to say that the poems lack art, for to my mind their simplicity is their virtue and their strength. More importantly, all five are charged with an emotional tension that may be the only evidence we can bring to bear in establishing them as verses of a "dying" man.[3] I have chosen **"I Die Alive"** from among them because it seems aesthetically the most successful. That the other four poems do not come off as thoroughly satisfying poems would argue that the agonies of death by themselves are not sufficient to create the kind of poem about which I am writing, even though a poet of proved skill attempts to capture them. We may be moved by pity, but we are not struck by the art. There must be that fusion required in any great poem: language appropriate to the experience, imagery proper to the purpose, and form harmonius with the meaning.

I am convinced that these poems by Southwell, Ralegh, and Donne were composed under special conditions which approach the state I have called *in articulo mortis,* but whether I prove correct or not—if conclusive evidence is ever forthcoming—matters little. If these men wrote in the comfort of their studies, enjoying perfect health, and little thinking that, in fact, they must die on the morrow, they have so well fabricated the fiction of their desperate state that we believe nonetheless in Southwell's torturer, Ralegh's headsman, and Donne's physicians. We cannot agree always with Johnson that "Where there is leisure for fiction there is little for grief." I do not think that Johnson would have cared to hold that his dictum was inescapably true, made aware, say, of a work like Mozart's *Requiem* or Michelangelo's *Last Judgment*. If an artist—a musician, a sculptor, a poet—is given a form within which he must work (I think we must concede here that organic form is a modern concept and one which never would have occurred to Southwell or to any Elizabethan), why may not whatever emotion his faculties are charged with find expression within the restrictions established? Or to approach from another direction, why may not a poem poured out in anguish of spirit be reformed under some measure of tranquility without greatly diminishing the emotional infusion? Would anyone like to disclaim at this date that some similar explanation accounts for the very moving section of *In Memoriam*?

**"I Die Alive"** is constructed upon elaborate antithesis, and that the most fundamental of all: life and death. Balanced syntax and structural parallels are met commonly in Elizabethan verse, and for this reason the charge that Southwell's art is more than his matter must be anticipated. Many poems that rely heavily upon the devices of rhetoric appeal more by their wit than by their feeling. Such is the case with the poem following, a poem ideal for comparison with **"I Die Alive"** since it too opposes life to death:

> The lenger lyfe, the more offence:
> The more offence, the greater payn:
> The greater payn, the lesse defence:
> The lesse defence, the lesser gayn.
> The losse of gayn long yll doth trye:
> Wherefore come death, and let me dye.

The poem appears in *Tottel's Miscellany,* and its author is unknown; but it is only one of hundreds of its kind. As another, Googe's "The oftener seen, the more I lust" springs immediately to mind. Furthermore many students of Southwell point out that by design he was attempting to use the devices of poetry ordinarily devoted to love of the flesh for saintlier verses glorifying *caritas,* and so he announces his purpose in the preface to *St. Peter's Complaint*:

> Poets by abusing their talent, and making the follies and faynings of loue the customarie subject of their base endeuours, haue so discredited this facultie, that a poet, a louer, and a lyer, are by many reckoned but three words of one signification. . . . And because the best course to let them see the errour of their works is to weaue a new webbe in their owne loome, I have heere laide a few course threds together.[4]

But whether or not Southwell succeeds in writing good religious poetry in the secular modes is not entirely the point. To match the achievement of the anonymous writer who penned the poem above or the achievement of Googe is, as I have said, to allow ornament the triumph over emotion. The real question here is whether at the hand of Southwell these forms permit his passion and his agony to come through, and perhaps part of the proof can be found in the successes of others. Without great difficulty several poems can be gathered in which the rhetoric is formidable yet the emotion tangible. Greene's song from *Menaphon* (1589), wherein the grief is of a lesser order than that which usually accompanies the death poem, unites happily the formal and the affective:

> The wanton smilde, father wept:
> Mother cride, babie lept:
> More he crowde, more we cride:
> Nature could not sorowe hide.
> He must goe, he must kisse
> Childe and mother, babie blisse:
> For he left his pretie boy,
> Fathers sorowe, fathers ioy,
> Weepe not my wanton smile vpon my knee:
> When thou art olde ther's griefe inough for thee.[5]

But going to a poem believed to have been written under the very conditions I claim here for Southwell, we find in Chidiock Tichbourne's "elegy written with his own hand in the Tower before his execution" a lyric as rigidly formalized as it is possible to imagine. Yet few have read the piece without experiencing something of the sense of utter waste, the poignancy of the execution of a man so young, so vigorous, and so talented:

> My prime of youth is but a frost of cares,
> My feast of joy is but a dish of pain,
> My crop of corn is but a field of tares,
> And all my good is but vain hope of gain;
> The day is past, and yet I saw no sun,
> And now I live, and now my life is done.[6]

Tichbourne, executed in connection with the Babington plot in 1586, an ill-fated attempt to murder Elizabeth and to release and put upon the throne the Catholic Mary Stuart, was possibly known to Southwell.[7] But whether or not Southwell knew him, he must have known the poem, since he uses the metaphor from Tichbourne's second line: "life as Feast." Southwell has added to the feast image the word *done,* the word that Tichbourne employs as a refrain, the word that rings in our ears as a funeral bell that tolls the poet to his grave. Since Southwell's entire poem is not long and since it is possibly not so well known as Ralegh's and Donne's I reproduce it here in full:

> O life! what letts thee from a quicke decease?
> O death! what drawes thee from a present praye?
> My feast is done, my soule would be at ease,
> My grace is saide, O death! come take awaye.

I live, but such a life as ever dyes;
I dye, but such a death as never endes;
My death to end my dying life denyes,
And life my living death no whitt amends.

Thus still I dye, yet still I do revive;
My living death by dying life is fedd;
Grace more than nature kepes my hart alive,
Whose idle hopes and vayne desires are deade.

Not where I breath, but where I love, I live;
Not where I love, but where I am, I die;
The life I wish, must future glory give,
The deaths I feele in present daungers lye.

(p. 84)

Perhaps the first thing that strikes our attention about the total poem is the play upon antithesis already mentioned; perhaps it is the metrical regularity. I am not sure that these do not go hand in hand. But after we have read the poem, which progresses through three and a half stanzas of almost perfect iambics, we have the feeling that somewhere the measure had not run so smoothly. If we search again, we find that the first two lines are the place. But whether we read the poem again or not, the irregularity has served its purpose. As I make out the scansion, "O life! what letts" and "O death! what drawes" are each double spondees. These four opening syllables of each of the first two lines carry a great deal of the poem's emotion. First we are moderately moved by the conjunction of the lamenting "O" with the word "life," ordinarily a word to be associated with joy. Then the paradox, which asks that life be taken quickly away, develops our pity. The long, soul-fed plea for death which follows puts us in the same state of suffering as the poet. Continued life is tedious, and the tedium is echoed in the near-perfect iambic measure of the rest of the poem.

Another spot at which the meter varies is the opening of line eleven: "Grace more than nature." But the trochaic opening is associated with grace, the only benediction the poet craves. He will not commit suicide, thereby removing himself from a state of grace and losing the paradise he seeks. Grace is the one spark, the one beatitude that starts him out of his lethargy, out of near-despair, and appropriately it is mirrored in the meter.

Grace serves still a greater function in the structure of the poem. It is the concluding element of the first stanza, where it is used to good advantage. The feast image allows for grace to function almost in the four-fold manner of scriptural interpretation. Feast, allegorically, is life, and Southwell's life is really over. It remains only for death to "take away," to come and to put the actual seal upon his living death. In some practices, grace is said after the meal instead of or as well as before. Tropologically, Southwell has made his final act of

contrition and he stands in a state of grace. He is prepared for death to "take away." At a mystical or anagogical reading, we may take feast to be associated with the communion. In such a sacrament, the very act of feasting places the communicant in a state of grace, and thus the grace follows the feast.

Southwell achieves his greatest tension in this poem through the paradox implied in the feast image. He wishes the banquet to end. All the joy, the festivity, the *life* which we associate with feasting is denied; instead, through the mystical sacrament of communion, especially in its sense of *last* supper, Southwell looks forward to dining with Christ in Heaven. But this tension, inherent in the single symbol, is extended through use of the feast image in two other places as well. In the second line, Southwell seems to be inviting Death to join the poet in an immediate, if grisly, dinner, through the carrion image of "present praye" where, we might say with Hamlet, he is "not where he eats, but where he is eaten." That Death will be the only one left at the close of the meal is suggested through the fourth line: "O death! come take awaye." By splitting the two appeals to death with the life-feast image, Southwell draws the two contrasting feasts brilliantly into tension. But neither of the feasts is over though Southwell has cried "My feast is done." In stanza three, we are reminded that his "living death by dying life is fedd." And as he has to deny that his "feast is done," so also he must modify the claim that his "grace is said." Since living death continues, the attempt to remain in a state of grace must be the never-ceasing labor of the poet, for there are great "daungers" that through lapsing into despair he will go from a state of grace to one of reprobation and thus lose his salvation-feast.

Finally, it may be pointed out that the paradox of the title **"I Die Alive,"** carried out so well in the imagery of the poem, is also furthered through the rhymes. Almost every line-end keeps up the tension by loosely alternating words that can be associated with life and death. Separating them into these two categories, in the first we might list *ease, amends, revive, fedd, alive, live, give*; in the second *decease, praye, take awaye, dyes, endes, denyes, deade, die, lye.* This totals to all sixteen endings, but admittedly *give* in the first group and *lye* in the second are weak.

As I have said, any of the five poems in the group to which **"I Die Alive"** belongs could be used to illustrate Southwell's desire to embrace death. In all five there is much of this quality of deathbed emotion that I am trying to illustrate. I believe all were composed very close to each other in time, perhaps even as a single act of composition. The first, **"Life Is But Losse,"** has certain similarities to Hamlet's "who would fardels bear," except that Southwell's answer does not include a "dread of something after death":

Who would not die to kill all murdringe grieves?
Or who would live in never-dyinge feares?
Who would not wish his treasure safe from theeves,
And quite his hart from pangues, his eyes from teares?
Death parteth but two ever-fightinge foes,
Whose civill strife doth worke our endles woes.

(p. 82)

Southwell would not "rather bear those ills we have / Than fly to others that we know not of":

Come, cruell death, why lingrest thou so longe?
What doth withould thy dynte from fatall stroke?
Nowe prest I am, alas! thou dost me wronge,
To lett me live, more anger to provoke.

(p. 82)

The image of pressing may well have occurred to South-well from his experience with Topcliffe, his torturer. While it seems quite clear that the poet was never pressed nor racked his complaints at his trial over his torture indicate that he uses *prest* as a synecdoche for all torments. The anger that Southwell fears to provoke carries a three-fold meaning; primarily it refers to the *Dies Irae* or God's wrath at the moment of the sinner's death; but in the context of this poem, it refers also to the cruelty of Death, who out of anger with the priest withholds the fatal dart. Biographically it may refer to the hatred Topcliffe apparently bore for the Catholic, leading to his outrageous tortures (symbolically, the pressing).[8]

**"I Die Alive"** is the second of the five poems. The third is **"What Joy to Live."** Most conventional of the group, it is least moving. The second line is an overworked Petrarchism: "I hope, I feare, I fry in freesing colde"; but the opening line as well as that beginning the final paragraph carry the ring of passion that we have associated with the other poems:

I wage no warr, yet peace I none enjoy;
. . . . .
O who would live so many deaths to trye?

(pp. 85, 86)

The fourth poem, **"Life's Death, Love's Life,"** is lower in key than **"What Joy to Live,"** but it is a more nearly perfect poem. Although the emotion is subdued, it is pervasive, and all eight stanzas show a deep desire to leave this world for the next. The poem is based on the antithesis not between life and death, but between life and love. Still, the burden of the poem is that love is death. Only through the death of the body may the man of faith achieve his happiness in the love of Christ:

Mourne, therfore, no true lover's death,
Life onely him annoyes;
And when he taketh leave of life,
Then love beginns his joyes.

(p. 87)

The final poem, **"At Home in Heaven,"** which some perhaps would not include in the group, is somewhat removed from the physical, from the flesh which, because of his torture, Southwell weaves so importantly into the other four. The focus is instead upon the disembodied soul, and for the last six of this seven-stanza poem, the body is not mentioned and hardly even implied. But in the opening stanza, we catch again Southwell's poignant desire to dissociate whatever in him is immortal from this mortal coil:

Fayre soule! how long shall veyles thy graces shroud?
How long shall this exile withold thy right?
When will thy sunn disperse this mortall cloude,
And give thy glories scope to blaze their light?
Oh that a starr, more fitt for angells' eyes,
Should pyne in earth, not shyne above the skyes!

(p. 88)

Southwell cries out for death not only because of the torment he undergoes in life but also because of an inner conviction in the potency and mercy of his God. Most men professing faith have their moments of doubt, both about the validity of their beliefs and about the disposition of their own souls. Southwell appears never to have wavered, though he dare not assume his salvation for fear of lapsing into pride. He too has his poems of terror, but terror only over death and Christ's anger, not over the state of his soul or its final haven:

O Lord! my sinne doth overchardge Thy breste.

(**"Sin's Heavy Load,"** p. 105)

If none can 'scape Death's dreadfull dart,
    If rich and poore his becke obey;
If strong, if wise, if all do smart,
    Then I to 'scape shall haue no way.
Oh! grant me grace, O God! that I
    My life may mend, sith I must die.

(**"Vpon the Image of Death,"** p. 157)

Southwell's calm is mystical, originating from a belief in the redemptive virtue of the blood of Christ. The modern evangelist, crying "Are you washed in the blood of the Lamb?" might find new imagery, new metaphors in **"Man to the Wound in Christ's Side"**:

O pleasant port! O place of rest!
O royal rift! O worthy wound!
Come harbour me, a weary guest,
That in the world no ease haue found!
. . . . .

Here would I view that bloudy sore,
Which dint of spiteful speare did breed:
The bloudy woundes laid there in store,
Would force a stony heart to bleede.
. . . . .

Oh, happie soul, that flies so hie
As to attaine this sacred caue!

Lord, send me wings, that I may flie,
And in this harbour quiet haue!

(pp. 153, 154)

Southwell, with blood as his "argument," remained "charitably" disposed since he was a man of peace; though he died violently and suffered bloodily before the end ("My garmentes gives, a bloody feilde my bedd" ["**David's Peccavi**," p. 103]), he kept no rancor. But Ralegh had been a man of war, a man of intrigue, a man of blood. He saw his own violent end in a horrifying image based on a crimson fountain issuing from his decapitated trunk: "Iust at the stroke when my vaines start and spred / Set on my soule an euerlasting head." Agnes Latham points out that "the poem itself so perfectly fits Ralegh's circumstances after his trial in 1603 that it is not easy to put it aside as the freak of a fantastic imagination."[9] It is these circumstances, I believe, that give the poem its peculiar intensity. Not only is the poet going to his death, but he goes with a bitterness that is missing from Southwell's pieces. Certainly no saint, Ralegh is not charitably disposed towards the men who tried him; the poem, which movingly develops a "hope for heaven" in terms of Christ's sacrifice, in terms strikingly similar to Southwell's ("Blood must be my bodies balmer"), does not achieve real passion until he complains of his enemies. The charge is phrased through triumphant scorn, through the indirect method of praising Christ's mildness, mercy, and grace, thereby castigating the un-Christian fierceness, vengeance and guilt of his persecutors.

From thence to heauens Bribles hall
Where no corrupted voyces brall,
No Conscience molten into gold,
No cause deferd, nor vaine spent Iorney,
For there Christ is the Kings Atturney.

(p. 50)

The blood balm of line 7 is implicit in the argument that Christ, as Ralegh's attorney, pleads in the defendant's cause:

When the grand twelue million Iury,
Of our sinnes and sinful fury,
Gainst our soules blacke verdicts giue,
Christ pleades his death, and then we liue.

(p. 51)

The poem concludes then with the image of Ralegh's own blood, already mentioned, thus utilizing blood imagery as a unifying device.[10]

Initial tension in Ralegh's poem comes from a union of the barely suppressed rage of these sections with the calm opening and the joyous, rich, and visionary descriptions of heaven. The blood of Christ which will make possible a peaceful pilgrimage along those holy paths "Strewde with Rubies thicke as grauell" mingles with the poet's own blood as it starts from his veins. He cannot leave his mortal pilgrimage until his own blood is spilt, and he cannot travel "to the land of heauen" until "healed" in Christ's. Further tension comes from a wealth of images associated with the vigor of life, a life the poet must leave shortly. Compared to the mystical love of God, which is all that Southwell looks forward to in heaven, Ralegh's expectations must seem somewhat misguided:

And there Ile kisse
The Bowle of blisse,
And drink my eternall fill
On euery milken hill.
My soule will be a drie before,
But after, it will nere thirst more.

(p. 50)

Thirst and its quenching are followed by the pilgrim's impatient divestment of the clogging earth:

More peaceful Pilgrims I shall see,
That haue shook off their gownes of clay,
And go appareld fresh like mee.

(p. 50)

The brilliant Ralegh of the Queen's court, whom all the portraits show heavily bejewelled, can think of heaven in no other terms but "siluer mountaines," ruby paths, "Seelings of Diamonds, Saphire floores, / High walles of Corall and Pearle Bowres." There is great motion in the poem. In addition to the acts of kissing the bowl of bliss and drinking often at "euery milken hill" and from the "Christall buckets," the pilgrim is traveling continually. In every stanza but one there is a verb of motion: *walke*, *take* (my pilgrimage), *trauels*, *goe*, *bring*, *trauell*, *from thence* (verb of motion implied), *tread*. Even in that one stanza where there is no actual movement of the pilgrim, Ralegh uses the verb *mouest* in substitution for *plead*. The great restless spirit cannot think of the grave or its aftermath as a place of rest. There must be room to bustle in still.

In contrast to Ralegh's poem, one of the central images of Donne's "Hymne" involves the poet's lying flat on his back. Near death under circumstances considerably more peaceful than either Southwell's or Ralegh's, Donne is not beset by either the priest's wrenched flesh nor the courtier's perturbed spirit. We do not therefore find tension in Donne's poem based on a tug of war between rest and anguish; but tension is there, and the achievement thus seems the greater.

In the first stanza the poet acknowledges his awareness of coming death. He has no fear concerning the outcome:

with thy Quire of Saints for evermore,
I shall be made thy Musique.

(p. 50)

Donne was not always so serene in the conviction that his eternal home was to be heaven. He struggled long apparently to achieve some measure of hope in salvation; during that same sickness of 1623 he reverently jested about some gnawing doubts in the "Hymne to God the Father," punning on his name in the manner of Shakespeare's Gaunt:

> Wilt thou forgive that sinne where I begunne,
> Which is my sin, though it were done before?
> Wilt thou forgive those sinnes through which I
> runne,
> And doe them still: though still I doe deplore,
> When thou hast done, thou hast not done,
> For, I have more.
>
> (p. 51)

And yet the "Hymne to God my God, in my sicknesse" exhibits as much composure in the face of death as any poem in the language. There is time still for the finer preparation of the soul, time for thought, time for joy in the anticipated reward:

> As I come
> I tune the Instrument here at the dore,
> And what I must doe then, thinke now before.
> . . . . .
> I joy, that in these straits, I see my West.
>
> (p. 50)

It is this verb *joy,* almost at the spatial center of the poem, about which the "Hymne" revolves. It is the joy, the expectation of blessedness, the experiencing in this life of the felicities, the happiness, the delight of the next that gives the poem its emotional impact. Donne becomes one with the visionary saint, who, in the act of martyrdom, smiles upon his executioner and turns a beatific gaze toward heaven.

At this point we must notice, however, that though Donne means to answer in the affirmative when he asks himself rhetorically "What shall my West hurt me," the dependent clause preceding sounds an ancient note of dread:

> For, though theire currants yeeld returne to none,
> What shall my West hurt me?
>
> (p. 50)

The straits that lead to a "South-west discoverie" are narrow, and the current is strong, so strong that no boat can push back against it once through. Even passage forward is accomplished only with difficulty and with some discomfort: *"Per fretum febris."* This note is subdued, but it is to be picked up later and amplified. Meanwhile, Donne's joy, in the face of death, is produced by the certain knowledge of an eternal life to follow. Death is not the final act; and, as it is not the end, so also in the poetry the image of death is never allowed to exist without an accompanying image of life, eternal life:

> As West and East
> In all flatt Maps (and I am one) are one,
> So death doth touch the Resurrection.
>
> (p. 50)

The proper order is observed: West (death) before East (rebirth), death before resurrection. Furthermore, there is no lapse of time or space between. East is right up against West in the map conceit, and resurrection *touches* death. The straits of the fourth stanza, through which the voyager must go in order to reach his haven, do not stretch over space or time after death and before the new life. They are the final sickness which leads to death. At the opening on the far side of "*Anyan,* and *Magellan,* and *Gibraltare*" the pilgrim comes immediately to the particular paradise for which he is destined: the Pacific sea, the Eastern riches, or Jerusalem. Of course, to say that Jerusalem lies adjacent to Gibraltar is to deny known geographical facts. But Donne is not dealing with the earth's topography; he has not compared himself to the great globe itself; he specifically identifies himself with a map, a flat map; and on paper it is a good deal easier to get from Anyan to the Pacific sea[11] than it is in a sailing vessel. The diminution of space between distant places which Donne achieves consciously by using the map image is only part of traditional Christian mysteries. Death touches the resurrection, and Jerusalem "touches" Gibraltar in the same way that wood from the Tree of Knowledge of Good and Evil found its way into the True Cross:

> We thinke that *Paradise* and *Calvarie,*
> *Christs* Crosse, and *Adams* tree, stood in one place.
>
> (p. 50)

Donne has Christ's crucifixion to take place on that very spot where Adam had transgressed four thousand years before. The place of redemption, Calvary, "touches" the place of the fall. The mortal sweat of Donne-Adam mingles with the divine blood of Christ:

> Looke Lord, and finde both *Adams* met in me;
> As the first *Adams* sweat surrounds my face,
> May the last *Adams* blood my soule embrace.
>
> (p. 50)

Donne employs blood imagery in the same way that Southwell had in a dozen poems and Ralegh had in blood as balm. The number of Donne's sermons without some reference to blood is small, and in one we find what is very close to a prose paraphrase of Southwell's **"Man to The Wound in Christ's Side"**:

> I shall finde my self, and all my sins enterred, and
> entombed in his wounds, and like a Lily in Paradise,

out of red earth, I shall see my soule rise out of his blade, in a candor, and in an innocence, contracted there, acceptable in the sight of his Father.[12]

In the "Hymne" redemption is signalized by complete immersion in the blood of the Savior: "So, in his purple wrapp'd receive mee Lord." The traditional purple of Christ's robe is unmistakably identified with Christ's blood. The act of dying, even for the man awaiting the end placidly in the clean, white sheets of his own bed, surrounded by love ("my Physitians by their love are growne / Cosmographers"), in perfect hope of salvation, involves the human condition of ordeal. Implicit still is the sweat of mortality, which, however composedly he die, attends man in the difficulty he has in letting go his clutch on life. Implicit still is the spilling of blood, if only symbolically in that "The trilling wire in the blood /. . . . The dance along the artery" is stilled. Even some blood from Donne is mixed with that of Christ and both, in turn, with the sweat that surrounds the poet's face. But it is at this point that a magnificently rendered paradox becomes apparent. The raging fever, that earlier introduced the subtle note of discomfort, has given way to sweat. Beads stand out on the poet's face. The fever is broken. The sickness is at an end. But simultaneously with the appearance of sweat is the blood that stands upon Donne's forehead also:

> By these his thornes give me his other Crowne.

> (p. 50)

The blood that streams down Christ's brow from the wounds made by the thorns may be said to stand anagogically upon the forehead of any man caught in the passion of his death. There can be no closer fusion of the metaphors for death and resurrection which appear throughout the poem than in the mingled sweat and blood. That the idea of ordeal is implicit can be seen in the last line of the poem:

> Therfore that he may raise the Lord throws down.

> (p. 50)

The act of dying is in part the price of redemption. It is every man's contribution to the wages of original sin. He cannot pay the entire debt alone; Christ's sacrifice was necessary; but justice must still be served. Justice demands that man become mortal; and death, the punishment, was never meant to be easy. The pain, the fear, the awe that accompany the *ars moriendi,* no matter how beautifully, how serenely it is accomplished, are what give to poetry *in articulo mortis* its unique quality.

### Notes

1. Izaak Walton records in his life of Donne that the "Hymne to God my God, in my sicknesse" was written eight days before the poet's death in 1631 and that it was his last poem. A subheading to "The passionate mans Pilgrimage" reads "Supposed to be Written by One at the Point of Death." Modern scholarship has denied to Walton his dramatic claim, urging that the "Hymne" was written probably in 1623. But this was the year of the poet's serious illness, the year of the meditations that brought forth the *Devotions upon Emergent Occasions.* Insofar as thought and feeling in the "Hymne" are concerned, it matters little that Donne recovered, since he believed fully that he was under interdict of death when writing it. A complete summary of the arguments over the date of the "Hymne" can be found in *The Divine Poems,* ed. Helen Gardner (Oxford, 1952), pp. 132-135. All references to Donne's poems will be to this edition.

   Ralegh's case is similar. Although his sentence was commuted and his execution not carried out until 1618, his certain belief that his head was to come off "next noone" gives to "The passionate mans Pilgrimage" the intensity expected of a condemned man.

2. Mario Praz has given also strong evidence to show that the title piece "St. Peter's Complaint" was written before Southwell went to prison in 1592. But he does not extend his argument to include other poems in the volume. See "Southwell's 'Saint Peter's Complaint' and Its Italian Source," *MLR* [*Modern Language Review*], XIX (1924), 273-290.

3. It might be urged also about these poems of Southwell, in attempting to establish their provenance in death, that they carry perhaps the mystical burden that goes with anticipated martyrdom. The Jesuit priest could not have kept out of his mind for long at any time after his return to England that capture meant death, and that the death he suffered would be an ordeal, during which he would many times hope for the end merely as a stop to bodily pain. In administering the sacraments of his church surreptitiously to a small gathering of the faithful in hiding, he might have said as T. S. Eliot's Becket, "I do not think I shall ever preach to you again."

4. *The Complete Poems of Robert Southwell,* ed. A. B. Grosart (London, 1872), pp. 4-5. All references to the works of Southwell will be to this edition.

5. *The Plays & Poems of Robert Greene,* ed. J. C. Collins (Oxford, 1905), II, 251.

6. *Tudor Poetry and Prose,* ed. J. William Hebel, H. H. Hudson, F. R. Johnson, A. W. Greene, and R. Hoopes (New York, 1953), p. 196.

7. See Christopher Devlin, *The Life of Robert South-well: Poet and Martyr* (New York, 1956), pp. 110, 121, 248.

8. See Devlin, pp. 309-310.

9. *The Poems of Sir Walter Ralegh* (London, 1951), p. 141. All references to Ralegh will be to this edition.

10. For a similar concept see M. W. Askew, *Explicator,* XIII (1954), No. 9.

11. I associate Anyan with the Pacific sea, though Grierson, supporting himself with vast learning and considerable research, maintains that these straits lead to the Eastern riches and those of Magellan to the Pacific sea. *The Poems of John Donne* (Oxford, 1912), II, 249-250. He is seconded by Clay Hunt, *Donne's Poetry* (New Haven, 1954), pp. 105, 244. It is inconceivable to me that Donne would break up the parallelism. The order in which he presents the straits is Anyan, Magellan, Gibraltar; the order of the places to which they lead is Pacific sea, Eastern riches, Jerusalem. To this must be added the order of the sons of Noah. Donne reverses this list, but order is kept: Japhet, Cham, Sem. It was a commonplace of this device of rhetoric to maintain balance through an exact reversal of order. Hundreds of poems might be cited in proof, but Donne himself employs the figure in Paradise and Calvary which is balanced by Christ's cross and Adam's tree. Schematically Donne's intended associations might be represented as follows:

> Anyan—Pacific sea—Sem
> Magellan—Eastern riches—Cham
> Gibraltar—Jerusalem—Japhet

The association of Cham with either the Eastern riches or the Pacific sea is a difficult one since he is always represented as the founder of the black races of Africa. Yet even here I believe I have the slight edge on the grounds that the darker skins of India (whether of India proper or the East Indies) fit the relationship better than the skins of any of the inhabitants of the Pacific sea. Donne wrote often of the riches of India, as in "The Sunne Rising": "both the 'India's of spice and Myne." He may have meant one of these Indias to be the nation and not the islands. Although Grierson identifies both these Indias as the East and West Indies, I cannot see that his is the only possibility. It was not very much later that Milton wrote

> High on a Throne of Royal State, which far
> Outshon the wealth of *Ormus* and of *Ind,*
> Or where the gorgeous East with richest hand
> Showrs on her Kings *Barbaric* Pearl & Gold,
> Satan exalted sat.

12. *The Sermons of John Donne,* ed. G. R. Potter and E. M. Simpson (Berkeley, 1955), II, 211.

## Joseph D. Scallon (essay date 1968)

SOURCE: Scallon, Joseph D. "'Himnes and Spirituall Sonnets': The Reform of Poetry." In *The Poetry of Robert Southwell, S.J.,* pp. 62-150. Salzburg, Austria: Institute für Englische Sprache und Literatur, Universität Salzburg, 1968.

[*In the following excerpt, Scallon evaluates Southwell's importance as a man of letters.*]

[Southwell's] poetry played an important part in his missionary work, especially in his apostolate to the cultured aristocrats he came in contact with in London, which was the center of his priestly work.

Southwell wrote most, if not all, of the poems which have come down to us during the years between his arrival in England and his capture, 1586-1592. These six years were filled with exhausting missionary activity and daily danger from informers and priest hunters. Why, then, did the busy apostle add to his burden and intensify the danger of his position by challenging his adversaries by writing for an illegal printing press? We have already shown that Southwell resorted to the printed word because the government of Elizabeth had deprived him of a public pulpit from which he could proclaim his message. But the question still remains: why did he choose to spend himself writing poetry rather than limit himself to prose exposition of his position?

The answer to this question is not quite as obvious as it might seem to those of us who have inherited some of the Romantic notions of the Pentecostal character of poetic inspiration which were popular in the nineteenth century. In the sixteenth century, the question of whether poetry or indeed any of the arts are licit for a Christian was hotly debated.[1]

In the intoxicating atmosphere of the revival of classical learning men turned their talents to the production of verse to demonstrate their mastery of the arts of language. The excesses of some would-be restorers of the pagan culture of the ancient world forced Christians to re-examine the whole question of the relationship between religion and art. Some of the more radical reformers of religion saw in all art a presumptuous mockery of the divine work of creation and a sign of Rome's desire to retain the delights of paganism at the expense of the undiluted word of God. Stained glass windows, statues, illuminated texts, solemn chants, epics of cruel men tempted by filthy devils, paintings and plays which re-created the very temptations that overcame the ancient pagans—what place have all these in the life of a Christian whose God forbids the making of any graven image and commands the use of simple "yea yea" and "nay nay" (Matt. v. 37) to the exclusion of all ornaments of speech? Inspired by St. Paul's exhortation to his converts not to let uncleanness be mentioned among them (Eph. v. 3), fervent reformers were proclaiming that the time had come for the true children of Israel to give over their shameful hankerings after the fleshpots of Egypt. The Church, in this view, long sunk in the hopeless slavery of trying to serve both God and Mammon, had now to be set free and purified of every taint of paganism. How those Christian bodies on the continent which broke away from Rome in the sixteenth century resolved the conflict between art and religion is outside the scope of this study even though the effects of their efforts are still perceptible in some twentieth-century poetic theories.[2]

The writings of Robert Southwell provide a good sample of how the Roman Church, in the throes of a Counter-Reform, sought to work out a solution. The Jesuit poet was totally committed to the work of making it possible for Englishmen to recognize Christ in the Roman Church and to bringing them the consolations he believed that Church had to offer. His spiritual journal, as we have seen, shows that he was aware of the evils plaguing the church; and that same document proves that he seized upon the best elements in the efforts for reform to achieve a high degree of sanctity: the discipline of mental prayer and a sound asceticism, intensive use of the Sacraments of Penance and the Eucharist, personal commitment to the Savior, and that peculiarly Counter-Reformational habit of mind of viewing material reality in spiritual terms and spiritual realities in very concrete and individual terms.[3]

That reform was desperately needed in the Roman Church cannot be doubted. Her administrative processes required reorganization, her doctrinal positions had to be clarified, and her changed position in society as a whole demanded that she undergo a radical cultural reorientation. The successes of the Counter Reformation in achieving a new and viable cultural stance for the Roman Church are reflected in Father Southwell's success in turning his fellow English poets away from the vanities of courtly love themes to the verities of divine love and the need of repentance. His failures, his occasional lapses into sentimentality and bathetic excess, reflect the failure of certain post-Tridentine popular devotions in which the line between genuine religious feeling and grotesque enthusiasm is not carefully observed.

The guidelines for the artistic program of the Counter Reformation emerged from the directives of the Council of Trent.[4] That the changes in the doctrinal and moral atmosphere of the Roman Church which resulted from the deliberations of the Fathers at Trent were strikingly paralleled in the world of art might be a source of surprise, but there were several contributing factors. First of all, it should be remembered that for centuries the Church had been the most important patron of the arts. Until the sixteenth century a large portion of the paintings and sculptures produced in Europe were created as decorations for places of worship. Music and drama emerged very slowly from the liturgy of the Church. During the first heady days of the pagan Renaissance, churchmen were among the chief patrons and practitioners of the arts. The reform of the clergy, which was probably the single most important achievement of the Council of Trent, was bound to have a tremendous impact on the development of art.

Secondly, it is sometimes forgotten that the paganism of the ancient world was really dead before Christianity became the dominant religion of Europe and Asia Minor. The revival of paganism at the time of the Renaissance was not as serious a threat to Christianity as it may have seemed to be. Corruption and superstition had weakened the hold of true Christianity on the minds of men, but there was not much chance that the cult of Jupiter and Juno was going to take its place. What good men of the age were looking for was a purified form of what they believed to be "true religion," religion based on the revealed word of God. Only a few pedantic dilettantes and grossly sensual aristocrats ever imagined that the salvation of the world and the reform of society could be accomplished by bringing back the dead gods of Greece and Rome. The whole point of More's *Utopia* is that the Utopians were capable of achieving their high degree of culture, not because of, but in spite of the fact that they did not have the advantages of possessing the truths of revelation. The more profound of the so-called humanists were Christian and were in the front ranks of those calling for a renewal of society by a return to basic Christian principles. In their educational programs they stressed the necessity of building upon the foundations of the truths contained in the Scriptures.

The Counter Reformation was a success to the extent that its leaders balanced the instinctive horror of the Christian for vain worldliness, a horror which would have banished all art from Catholic culture, with a recognition that poetry and the fine arts can be a powerful aid in teaching men revealed truths and in preparing them to respond to these truths with appropriate emotions. Thus the Counter Reform within the Church of Rome shielded artists from the charges of frivolity hurled at them by the iconoclasts of the more rigid forms of Protestantism by reminding them (sometimes rather ominously) of their responsibility to the truth. That the truth which artists were called upon to serve was at times conceived of in terms of somewhat narrow categories by the clerics who assumed charge of the reform is an undeniable historical fact—not a particularly surprising one, however, considering the limitations of ordinary men in carrying out grandly conceived programs and the tendency of the important and radically new insights of one generation to become the tired old dogmas of succeeding ones.

Artistically the Counter Reformation was a period of considerable achievement. Although its influence was concentrated in the so-called Catholic countries of southern Europe and Latin America, it was by no means limited to these areas. The poetry of seventeenth-century England especially reflects many of the tenets of Counter Reform. Milton himself, in spite of the sincerity of his renunciation of Rome and all her works and all her pomps, subscribed to the basic principle of the reform that an artist has a duty to use his talents to help men raise their minds to the contemplation of eternal truth and, by presenting this truth in striking ways, to enable men to embrace it with all their powers. The judgment passed by the Son of Man in Milton's *Paradise Regained* on the relative significance of the literature of Greece and Israel has scandalized many neo-humanists, but it cannot be doubted that it represents the deep conviction of the last great poet of the English Renaissance:

> Our Hebrew Songs and Harps in *Babylon*
> That pleas'd so well our Victors' ear, declare
> That rather *Greece* from us these Arts deriv'd;
> Ill imitated, while they loudest sing
> The vices of thir Deities, and thir own
> In Fable, Hymn, or Song, so personating
> Thir Gods ridiculous, and themselves past shame.
> Remove their swelling Epithets thick laid
> As varnish on a Harlot's cheek, the rest
> Thin sown with aught of profit or delight,
> Will far be found unworthy to compare
> With *Sion's* songs, to all true tastes excelling,
> Where God is Prais'd aright, and Godlike men,
> The Holiest of Holies, and his Saints;
> Such are from God inspir'd, not such from thee;
> Unless where moral virtue is express'd
> By light of Nature, not in all quite lost.[5]

The reform of Catholicism called for by the Council of Trent involved many liturgical and pastoral changes as well as doctrinal clarifications, but it could only be brought about by a vast educational program.[6] Perhaps the most significant innovation by the Council was its legislation which eventually created a system of seminaries devoted exclusively to the formation of an educated clergy, a clergy trained to impart to the faithful the new forms of spirituality which emerged in response to the revitalization of Catholic thought and practice. These new forms of spirituality, Carmelite, Jesuit, and a little later on, Salesian, were not developed in a vacuum. They represent the Catholic response to Protestantism. Private devotions in the form of medita-

tion and spiritual reading, regular reception of the Sacraments of Penance and the Eucharist, special devotions in honor of the Blessed Sacrament, a new more personalized cult of the saints, and the countless other phenomena which characterize sixteenth- and seventeenth-century Catholic life were, in large part, the result of the natural reaction of Catholics to the Protestant insistence on man's fundamentally private relation to his Maker.

Of equal importance, however, in the development of these new forms of Catholic thought and practice, was the fact that the Reformation brought about a state of affairs which was completely new in Christian Europe. In the sixteenth century, for the first time in centuries, it was possible not to be a Catholic. Previously, one could choose to be a good or a bad Catholic; but now, as a result of the religious upheavals in the various parts of Europe, one could choose to withdraw from the ancient organization of Christendom and join a new form of Christianity with claims to be more Christian than Rome or choose to belong to no church and devote oneself to the principles of the new scientific and political philosophies which were being offered by daring innovators like Niccolo Machiavelli or Giordano Bruno. Indeed, in large sections of Europe, especially in the northern parts, because of harsh laws aimed at the eradication of Roman Catholicism, to remain faithful to the Old Church had become not only legally not necessary but extremely hazardous and expensive. In these new circumstances, Roman Catholics naturally felt a need to concentrate on the private motives for the practice of religion and to express their faith in personal forms of devotion.

Thus, although they later developed in quite diverse ways and their theoretical bases were quite different, the several branches of Christianity manifested some, superficially at least, similar qualities. Perhaps the most striking instance of this similarity is the heavy emphasis on repentance which appears in the religious writings emanating from both Catholic and Protestant camps in the last decades of the sixteenth century and the first half of the seventeenth. Much of Father Southwell's poetry deals with the subject of repentance, but he was by no means a solitary weeper. Many of the minor poets of England and the continent contributed to the flood of tears to be encountered by even a casual reader in the popular literature of the period.[7] *Saint Peters Complaint* and Southwell's other poems on repentance will be discussed in Chapter Three.

Another important common element of the various reform movements was a vigorous attempt on the part of the reformers to provide religious instruction. Towards the end of the Middle Ages popular preaching had fallen upon bad days. Theology, tainted with nominalism and scepticism, had become an abstruse science to be guarded and argued about within the walls of universities by clerics. In pre-Tridentine days, ordination of parish priests was commonly not preceded by a systematic course of theological and philosophical studies. All too frequently pastors did not have enough education to be able to read and understand the Missal, and quite often they were as ignorant of religious matters as were the members of their flocks.[8]

It is not surprising then that the reformers of the sixteenth century found eager audiences for their new doctrines. Their rejection of a sacramental system which had become encrusted with crude superstitions and their appeal to the sole authority of the Scriptures forced them to rely upon preaching of the word of God. Having eliminated the Mass, the reformed churches devoted a great part of their services to sermons and hymn singing.

In reaction to these new developments as well as in response to her own awareness of a need for renewal, the Roman Church began again to encourage preaching in parishes and the production of books and pamphlets to bring her message to the masses. She undertook a great educational project with astonishing vigor. The new seminaries prescribed by Trent provided priests capable of giving sound instruction, but the vanguard of the movement was from the start the new orders which arose in remarkable profusion in the sixteenth century. The Theatines, St. Phillip Neri's Oratory, the Capuchins (a reformed branch of the Franciscans), and many others eagerly took up the work of teaching and ministering to the neglected laity; but, in terms of numbers and influence, the newly founded Society of Jesus, which received special confirmation at the Council of Trent, where two of its most distinguished theologians, Diego Lainez and Alonzo Salmeron, wielded tremendous influence, was surely the most important.[9]

Mention was made in Chapter One of Pierre Janelle's claim that there existed a Jesuit poetic, as if the Order had evolved a set of clearly delineated artistic principles parallel to its famous *Ratio Studiorum*. An examination of the writings the early Jesuit poetical theorists cited by Professor Janelle—Possevinus, Bencius, and Pontanus—does not seem to verify his claim.[10] The vague norms expressed by these Jesuits merely echo the commonplaces of Renaissance thinking on the subject of the relationship between art and religion. Practically every point concerning the duty of the artist to edify which Janelle attributes to the Jesuits of the Roman College can be found in Sidney and other Renaissance writers. In Southwell's day, everyone who wrote on the subject of literature agreed that the purpose of poetry was to teach delightfully. There were disagreements concerning what poetry ought to teach, but no one denied that a poet owed it to his audience to show them the truth. Professor Janelle, when he attempts to isolate

a "Jesuit neoclassic" pattern for literature, appears to be using categories which do not apply to the literary scene of the Renaissance.

Walter J. Ong has shown that the science of literary criticism as we know it was not possible until the time when the vernaculars became the ordinary vehicles of instruction—a time considerably after the Renaissance.[11] An indication of the difference between contemporary literary criticism and the kind of writing about literature practiced by our forebears is the fact that the word *rhetoric* has gradually ceased to be used to describe the activity of men of letters. The Greek *rhetorike* designated the art which governs the skills of an orator or *rhetor*; and, as long as discussion of literature was conceived of in terms of effective public statement rather than "evaluation of literary performance on its own terms, gathered from the interior economy of the work itself,"[12] what we call literary criticism did not really exist. This is not to say that "rhetoricians" had nothing valuable to say about literature or failed to provide training for literary artists. It merely asserts that what they did was different from what modern critics and teachers of literature do.

There is, of course, a sense in which one can speak of a Jesuit poetic, inasmuch as the schools of the new Order did attempt to teach the humanities in accordance with the norms laid down by the Council of Trent and specifically to present artistic principles which would conform with the general rule for the use of creatures proposed by St. Ignatius in "The First Principle and Foundation." To the founder of the Society of Jesus it seemed axiomatic that

> Man was created to praise, reverence and serve God Our Lord and by this means to save his soul; and the other things on the face of the earth were created for man's sake, and in order to aid him in the prosecution of the end for which he was created.[13]

From this general principle, Ignatius argued that a man has a duty to use things in so far as they help him to achieve his goal and to withdraw from them whenever they prove to be a hindrance. The "indifference to creatures," which Ignatius urges the exercitant to cultivate, does not imply that material things and human activity are not important in themselves. It is based upon a profound awareness that the choices of means one makes affect his success in attaining ends.

Learning and the arts, in this context, belong to the category of the useful and are to be cultivated in so far and only in so far as they help one to serve God. As a matter of fact, Ignatius and the members of the Society which he founded were convinced from the start that learning, sacred as well as secular, and the arts could be powerful instruments in the prosecution of the end which they had set for themselves, the defense of the Church by preaching and teaching.

Of course any means which can help can also be used in a way that will hinder the attainment of a given end. Art that can lead a man to the contemplation of spiritual truths can be employed to focus his attention on the purely carnal. This is especially true in the case of the young; and so, in the schools of the Society, which were for the most part secondary schools, the learning of the Ancient World was presented in carefully selected and, when it was thought necessary, expurgated texts of classical writers.[14] Christian doctrine and morality were taught not only directly from Christian texts and from the history of the Church and the saints but also by means of the pagan poets and philosophers who were treated as unconscious and partial witnesses to the full truth of Christian revelation. While there is no evidence that there was any fear of what we now vaguely call "the beautiful," the Jesuits of the sixteenth century unquestionably did look upon art as a means of teaching rather than an end in itself. They sometimes manifest a shocking lack of concern for "art for art's sake." The practical needs of the Church, in the concrete circumstances of her mission to preserve and spread the truth, tended to be the norm by which the Society governed her involvement with the arts.

The attitude of the Society towards art is discernible in the paintings and sculptures produced by artists who were influenced by Jesuit educational activities.[15] As the Counter Reform began to take hold, the self-contained perfection to be found in the works of the masters of the High Renaissance was replaced by the deliberately elongated and distorted compositions of Mannerist and Baroque artists who force the viewer to look for the truth behind the picture and to form a judgment on it. The new styles draw the viewer into the scene depicted and demand that he share the emotions of the original situation.

This shift in the relationship between artifact and audience from passive admiration of classic perfection to active participation in the emotion of the event, which Baroque and Mannerist artists sought to evoke, must have seemed to the early Jesuits a providential development. Here was a working out in art of an important aspect of Ignatian ascetical practice, the so-called "composition of place." Ignatius, in presenting scenes from the life of the Savior for contemplation, directs the exercitant to place himself in the scene. In the contemplation on the Nativity, for example, he offers the following advice:

> The first point is to see the persons; that is to say, to see our Lady, and St. Joseph, and the serving-maid, and also the Infant Jesus, after His birth, accounting myself a poor and unworthy servant, looking at and contemplating them and tending them in their necessities as though I were present there, with all possible homage and reverence; and after that to reflect on myself in order to derive some profit.
>
>                                                      (p. 39)

The preachers and teachers of the Society of Jesus were, of course, eager to encourage new developments in the arts. The churches erected by the Jesuits were designed so as to place as much emphasis as possible on the altar where the Mass, which Trent reaffirmed as the central act of the Church's worship, was celebrated and on the pulpit from which Catholic doctrine was preached to the faithful. By eliminating the obligation to choir and therefore the need for choir stalls, Ignatius made it possible for his Society to erect churches in which the laity could be present at Mass without being shut out by a choir screen. The walls and ceilings of these new open and well-lighted churches required some sort of decoration to avoid being forbiddingly austere and were obvious spaces for paintings. These paintings were intended to be pleasing to the eye and, at the same time, capable of eliciting appropriate emotional responses from the worshippers.

In their schools, which rapidly spread all over the continent, the Jesuits aimed at imparting not only learning and culture but also moral training and motivation to prepare their students to become leaders in the revival of Christian and Catholic society. They formed Sodalities, organizations in which the basic spiritual formation of a Jesuit was adapted to fit the needs of a devout layman, and vigorously encouraged retreats in which laymen went through *The Spiritual Exercises* which contain the theological and ascetical principles upon which the Jesuit way of life and most of the reform of Catholicism were based: repentance for sin; devotion to Christ the King, the model of all Christian virtue; compassion with the sufferings of the Savior; and a desire to share in His work of salvation and to attain to the ability to view all of creation as a manifestation of God's love and to make as perfect as possible a return of love.

To understand Southwell's poetry it is, necessary to view it in context of the first decades of the Counter Reformation and of the early years of the Society of Jesus. The years Southwell spent in Rome coincided with the period when that city was the center of the most vigorous achievements in painting, architecture, and sculpture. The Roman College was the center of the Church's intellectual life, and it is inconceivable that Southwell should not have been impressed by the ferment going on around him and that he should not have hoped to bring England into it. This rather lengthy *excursus* into Renaissance history, therefore, has been intended to cast some light on the motives of the Jesuit missionary for writing poetry.

It seems safe to assert that his primary purpose was apostolic.[16] He believed that poetry, like the decorative arts and music, could play a part in bringing men into contact with God; and he was convinced that bad poetry caused men to ignore God. The fact is that Southwell's efforts to produce religious literature seemed important enough to his co-religionists to make them risk a great deal, even their lives, to preserve the fruits of his literary labors.

History has not recorded the names of the hundreds of devout persons who exposed themselves to terrible danger by handing about manuscript copies of Southwell's works at a time when mere possession of such literature was grounds for charges against them which could have ruined them. We do, however, know the names of some heroic men and women who paid heavily for their cooperation with the Jesuit writer in his apostolate of letters. Mention was made in Chapter One of Anne Dacres, the faithful wife of Philip Howard. Her conversion to Roman Catholicism had won for her the unrelenting disfavor of the Queen; but she dared to give Southwell, who was her chaplain, shelter in an unused part of Arundel House on the Strand where he could write and financial aid in setting up his printing press. The Venerable James Duckett, a publisher and bookseller, and a printer by the name of Collins were executed in 1602 for producing copies of *An Humble Supplication.*[17] Clearly Southwell's Catholic contemporaries valued his work very highly and found in his writings consolation and encouragement.

But Southwell was concerned for the spiritual welfare of all Englishmen not just Roman Catholics. As we have seen, he, like most of his fellow missioners, was convinced that England was in danger of falling from heresy into atheism. He felt that the poets of England had to bear a part of the responsibility for this state of affairs. That Southwell's fears were shared by the government is shown by the persecution inflicted upon suspected atheists. The genesis of this new atheism has been suggested by J. M. Stone.[18] According to her, many Englishmen seem to have been unwilling or unable to pay the price of remaining faithful to Roman Catholicism and were also unwilling or unable to accept the Calvinistic elements in the doctrines of the newly established Church of England and the various splinter groups of Protestants. Quite naturally, a profound scepticism set in. If Rome was wrong, how was one to know who was right? Several years after Southwell's death, John Donne was still looking for light on the perplexing problem:

> Show me, dear Christ, Thy spouse so bright and clear.
> What! is it she which on the other shore
> Goes richly painted? or which, robbed and tore,
> Laments and mourns in Germany and here?
> Sleeps she a thousand, then peeps up one year?
> Is she self-truth, and errs? now new, now outwore?
> Doth she, and did she, and shall she evermore
> On one, on seven, or on no hill appear?
> Dwells she with us, or like adventuring knights
> First travel we to seek, and then make love?[19]

Donne found an answer to his question in an assiduous cultivation of asceticism and devoted service to his flock; but many others, it would seem, less sensitive than he to the demands of the spirit, gave up the search and settled for a torpid conformity. The theology of great and sincere reform-minded men like Spenser and Sir Philip Sidney was infected with the radical philosophy of Giordano Bruno, to the distress of some of Elizabeth's more orthodox counsellors; but it was the arrogant Sir Walter Raleigh, whose association with the "school of night" had rendered him suspect, who was chosen as the scapegoat.

Just how much the new intellectual ferment influenced the thinking of the ordinary Englishman of the last two decades of the sixteenth century is, of course, impossible to assess at this late date; but Southwell, who was on the scene, thought that a very real danger existed. It is notable, I think, that his defense of Catholicism is almost completely free from the painful polemics which mar the religious writings of most of his contemporaries. He does not attempt to prove the theological soundness of the Roman position or attack the doctrines of the Protestants. His approach is primarily pastoral. In *An Epistle of Comfort to the Reverend Priests, and to the Honourable, Worshipful, and Other of the Lay Sort, Restrained in Durance for the Catholic Faith,* his longest prose work, he proposes eleven causes "of comfort in tribulation," including such arguments as:

> that it [tribulation] sheweth us to be God's children, tenderly beloved by him . . . that death is comfortable to the good . . . [and] that Martyrdom is glorious in itself, most profitable to the Church, and honorable to the Martyrs.[20]

Southwell's pastoral concern causes him to note the unhappiness of the lapsed Catholics, the so-called schismatics; and he warns his readers to beware their example:

> Let them triumph in their imaginary happiness and true misery. Let them rejoice in their wickedness and glory in their destruction. Let us comfort ourselves in our passions and afflictions for Christ, which we know will advance us to an eternal reward, and to those glorious titles before mentioned which undoubtedly are due unto the martyrs in our cause and to no other.

(p. 211)

In this age of ecumenism and the new morality, Southwell's concern to revive what seems to us to have been a rather narrow form of Roman Catholicism may cause us to see him as an alarmist with an overly sensitive conscience. Many of his contemporaries probably viewed him in the same way. Such an Englishman as John Donne would certainly have judged that he was a classic example of the pseudo-martyr. It is beyond the scope of this study to attempt to render a decision in that controversy.[21] The aim of this discussion has been to show that Southwell looked upon his poetry as a means of carrying out his mission to reunite English Catholics and, if possible, all Englishmen with their spiritual and cultural center, the Church of Rome. This conception of his mission gives form and matter to all his literary efforts.

All of Southwell's poems which have come down to us were inspired by his apostolic zeal. Although it is now impossible to establish the chronological order in which his shorter poems were written, his most recent editor, Nancy Pollard Brown, has shown that the arrangement of the shorter lyrics which is found in the Stonyhurst and several other manuscripts derives from a conscious effort by the compiler (possibly Southwell himself) to present "an intelligible series, so that the impact of the spiritual teaching they contained might be intensified."[22]

Southwell himself explicitly affirmed his belief, fostered by his education in the centers of the Counter Reform, that poetry can be of service in evoking those passions which render a man's soul more receptive to the influence of divine grace. In the Preface to his first printed work, *Marie Magdalene's Funerall Teares* (1591), he wrote:

> Passions I allow, & loues I approoue, onely I would wish that men would alter their object and better their intent. For Passions beeing sequels of our nature, and allotted vnto vs as the handmaides of reason: there can be no doubt, but that theyr authour is good, and their end godly: so their vse tempered in the meane, implyeth no offence. . . . And therefore sith the finest wits are now giuen to write passionate discourses, I would wish them to make choise of such passions, as it neyther should be shame to vtter nor sinne to feele.[23]

If pious sentiments are good, bad ones are harmful; and, as we have seen, Southwell felt that poets who glorify these are no better than panderers. He tried to show how the evil of such verse might be counteracted by spiritualizing the themes of poems devoted to what he called "lewd love." In **"What Joy to Live?"** (40) for example, Southwell took over a theme from Petrarch's *Rime*, No. 134, which had been used several times by earlier and contemporary English poets[24] and substituted for the anguish of being separated from a cruel mistress the longing of a devout Christian to be united with God:

> I wage no warre yet peace I none enjoy,
>    I hope, I feaer, I frye, in freesing cold:
> I mount in mirth still prostrate in annoy
>    I all the world embrace yet nothing holde.
> All wealth is want where cheefest wishes faile,
> Yea life is loath'd where love may not prevaile.
>
> For that I love I long, but that I lacke,
>    That others love I loath, and that I have:
> All worldly fraights to me are deadly wracke,
>    Men present hap, I future hopes doe crave.

They loving where they live, long life require,
To live where best I love, death I desire.

*(ll. 1-12)*

The Jesuit missioner does not hesitate to labor his point by extending the fourteen lines of Petrarch's Italian and/or Wyatt's English version to thirty in which he elaborates upon the harmful effects of purely human affection:

> Heere beautie is a baite that swallowed choakes,
>    A treasure sought still to the owners harmes:
> A light that eies to murdring sights provokes,
>    A grace that soules enchants with mortall charmes,
> A luring aime to Cupids fiery flights,
> A balefull blisse that damnes where it delights.
>
> O who would live so many deathes to trye?
>    Where will doth wish, that wisdom doth reprove:
> Where nature craves, that grace must needes denie,
>    Where sence doth like, that reason cannot love,
> Where best in shew, in finall proofe is worst,
> Where pleasures upshot is to die accurst.

*(ll. 13-30)*

The weaknesses of this rather forced baptism of a secular love lyric are obvious. Southwell fails to give concrete substance either to the real object of his desires, heavenly bliss, or to the object which he rejects, purely temporal things. The reader must provide the "objective correlatives" which would render the emotion of the poem valid; Southwell merely refers vaguely to "that I love" and "that others love." Love, friendship, wealth, joy, honor, and even physical beauty are treated only on the level of abstractions, so that the argument Southwell attempts to make never seems to be very real. In short, in **"What Joy to Live?"** Southwell appears to have fallen into the error which William Lynch has described as the fallacy of "the univocal mind."[25] He attempts to bypass the complexity of material reality to arrive immediately at the spiritual, but the result is that the spiritual lacks reality and is merely a negative abstraction.

Fortunately, Southwell rarely committed this same error in his other verses. His experience in prayer and on the English Mission provided him with insights which he gradually learned to incorporate into his poetry. His most striking success in this process is his only long poem, *Saint Peters Complaint,* in which he gives expression to his peculiarly poetic awareness of both the human and the divine aspects of the experience of what it is to repent of a sin. Discussion of that poem, however, belongs to another chapter.

**"A Phansie turned to a sinner's complaint"** (30), as it is called in the manuscripts, represents an attempt by Southwell at even closer imitation of a contemporary poem, Sir Edward Dyer's "A Fancy." Southwell used the same verse form that he found in his model and many of the same images, but these images are more appropriate to the emotion of a Christian penitent than of a disappointed lover. Dyer's lover seems to be indulging in merely conventional hyperbole, partly because he rambles on at such length to tell us how unhappy he is and partly because of the faintly blasphemous terms in which he describes himself:

> As one that lives in shewe,
> But inwardlye doth dye,
> Whose knowledge is a bloody field,
> Where all help slaine doth lie;
>
> Whose harte the Aulter is,
> Whose spirit the sacrifize
> Unto the Powers, whome to appease
> Noe sorrowes can suffize.[26]

The cause of all the misery of Dyer's fancied lover is, it turns out, quite unworthy of such suffering. She is, after all, but a woman who has chosen someone else:

> Forsaken first was I,
> Then utterly foregotten,
> And he that came not to my faith,
> Lo, my reward hath gotten.
>
> . . . . .
>
> O fraile unconstant kynd,
> And safe in trust to noe man!
> Noe woomen angels be,
> And loe, my mystris is a woeman.

(*ll.* 77-80, 93-96)

Southwell's sinner, on the other hand, has a rational basis for his grief. He is one "Whom grace and vertue once advaunc'd / Now sinne hath cast away" (*ll.* 43-44). Similarly, the resolve taken by Dyer's lover to remain faithful to a woman he knows is not worthy of him is hardly reasonable; but the penitential vows of Southwell's sinner are at least adequately motivated:

> I cannot set at naught
> Whom I have held so deere:
> I cannot make him seeme afarre,
> That is in deede so neere.
>
> . . . . .
>
> Yet that shall never faile,
> Which my faith bare in hand:
> I gave my vow, my vow gave me,
> Both vow and gift shall stand.
>
> But since that I have sinn'd,
> And scourge none is too ill;
> I yeeld me captive to my curse,
> My hard fate to fulfill.

(*ll.* 109-12, 117-24)

Here again Southwell is somewhat vague in describing particulars, but the fault probably lies in the fact that in these verses he was attempting a very close imitation.

In the last two stanzas of his parody, Southwell appears to acknowledge the problem, for he warns the reader not to judge the reality of his feelings by the artificiality of his style:

> And though I seeme to use
> The faining Poets stile,
> To figure forth my careful plight,
> My fall, and my exile:
>
> Yet is my greefe not fain'd,
> Wherein I starve and pine,
> Who feeleth most, shall think it least
> If his compare with mine.

(*ll.* 145-52)

Part of the pleasure Elizabethan readers derived from exercises in imitation like this deliberate parody of a popular court poet was probably the recognition of the wit involved. Comparison of Dyer's "Fansie" and Southwell's religious parody of it shows, however, not only that Robert had learned how to ape the conventions in vogue among the poets of his day, but also that his assertion that poets were abusing their talents by devoting them to unworthy subjects was an accurate diagnosis of the state of poetry in the 1580's.

The suggestion has been made that those poems of Southwell which have direct literary inspiration are probably the fruits of his earliest efforts at writing English verse on his return to England in 1586.[27] At the English College at Douai, it is true, exercise in English was a part of the training of the future missioners; and very likely Southwell's years in houses of studies of the Society, in which Latin and Italian would have been the languages most commonly used, left his readiness in English somewhat rusty and caused him to feel a need to practice a bit. His pastoral purpose, however, also provides an adequate explanation for his imitations of contemporary popular poets. He wished to show his fellow poets that changing over to sacred subjects need not involve a switch in poetic conventions because, Southwell believed, the language hitherto used to celebrate human mistresses was really much more appropriate to the praise of God and His saints.

When Southwell gathered his lyrics into a manuscript collection, he set down his thoughts on the relationship between poetry and his mission in an introductory essay, "The Author to his loving Cosen." Aware of his own limitations as a poet, limitations which were probably a result of the fact that he only rarely had peace and leisure in which to develop his talent rather than the absence of a poetic gift, he wrote:

> . . . because the best course to let hem see the errour of their workes, is to weave a new webbe in their owne loome; I have heere layd a few course threds together, to invite some skillfuller wits to goe forward in the

same, or to begin some finer peece, wherein it may be seene, how well verse and vertue sute together. Blame me not (good Cosen) though I send you a blamewoorthy present, in which the most that can commend it, is the good will of the writer, neither Arte nor invention, giving it any credite.

(p. 1)

The identity of Southwell's "loving Cosen" has been the subject of much ingenious speculation. Whether it really was William Shakespeare, as Devlin and several others are inclined to believe, is probably irrelevant and certainly unverifiable.[28] What is significant in this letter is Southwell's succinct statement of the post-Tridentine Church's vindication of poetry:

. . . the authority of God, who delivering many partes of Scripture in verse, and by his Apostle willing us to exercise our devotion in Himnes and Spirituall Sonnets, warranteth the Arts to bee good, and the use allowable. And therefore not onely among the Heathens, whose Gods were chiefly canonized by their Poets, and their Painim Divinitie Oracled in verse: But even in the Old and New Testament it hath bene used by men of greatest Pietie, in matters of most devotion. Christ himselfe by making a Himne, the conclusion of his last Supper, and the Prologue to the first Pageant of his Passion, gave his Spouse a methode to immitate, as in the office of the Church it appeareth, and all men a paterne to know the true use of this measured and footed stile.

(p. 1)

The insistence here on the pastoral motives of Southwell's verse ought not be taken as a denial of more subjective elements. Robert Southwell, like most poets, seems to have found in poetry an outlet for his personal emotions and feelings. We have already seen how he reacted to the rejection of his first application for admission into the Society of Jesus by writing his **Quaerimoniae**. While Grosart's belief that many of Southwell's poems were written in the Tower can no longer be accepted, it is not hard to surmise that at times the harried missioner to the imprisoned and impoverished Catholics of London found solace by submitting himself to the discipline of setting down his thoughts in verse. In his introductory verses **"To the Reader,"** the Jesuit acknowledged that he found versifying relaxing:

DEARE eye that doest peruse my muses style,
With easier censure deeme of my delight:
Give sobrest countenance leave sometime to smyle,
And gravest wits to take a breathing flight:
Of mirth to make a trade may be a crime,
But tyred spirites for mirth must have a time.

The lofty Eagle soares not still above,
High flightes will force her from the wing to stoupe,
And studious thoughtes at times men must remove,
Least by excesse before their time they droupe.
In courser studies tis a sweete repose,
With poets pleasing vaine to temper prose.

(*ll.* 1-13)

The subject of all Southwell's verses, however, is religious; he takes the Psalmist rather than the courtly poets as his model:

Prophane conceites and fayning fits I flie,
Such lawlesse stuffe doth lawlesse speeches fit:
With *David* verse to vertue I apply,
Whose measure best with measured wordes doth sit
It is the sweetest note that man can sing,
When grace in vertues key tunes natures string.

(*ll.* 13-18)

Professor Martz has shown that there is a close relationship between the structure of several of Southwell's poems and that of an Ignatian meditation.[29] It is certain that Southwell practiced meditation carefully, and it seems natural to suppose that the habits of thought formed by this practice carried over into his poetic composition to give rise to "meditative poetry." This is not to say that Southwell, or any other conscientious cultivator of the art of prayer, ever knelt down to make his meditation in order to discover the theme or structure of a poem on some sacred subject. Prayer, for holy men, is always primarily an act of worship which transforms the worshiper's mental faculties by focusing them more intensively on God. Southwell, whose whole life was devoted to the service of God in the Roman Church and the Society of Jesus, quite naturally found relaxation by writing out in his spiritual notebook and in his verses the thoughts and feelings which he stirred up methodically during his hours of mental prayer.

Just which poems of Southwell are the direct result of particularly fruitful meditations is, of course, impossible to discern. If we are to believe the mystics, the illuminations which arise out of the higher forms of mental prayer are largely nonconceptual and are therefore incapable of being communicated by means of language. There is no evidence that Southwell ever experienced any of the extraordinary forms of prayer described by Teresa of Avila or John of the Cross. His only vision poem, his much anthologized **"The Burning Babe"** (17), is clearly not a record of a personal experience but a concretization of an abstract idea—that the intense love of God for men which was the motive for the Incarnation is repaid for the most part by cold indifference:

Alas (quoth he) but newly borne,
    In fierie heates I frie,
Yet none approach to warme their harts,
    Or feele my fire, but I.

(*ll.* 13-16)

The conclusion which seems most plausible is that most of the shorter lyrics of Southwell which do not have direct inspiration in the verses of other Renaissance poets or in public events probably represent the Jesuit's poetic elaboration of ideas upon which he had made formal meditations. It is also probable that, having found that others to whom he showed these poems were helped by them, he began to compose verses on subjects which were dictated more by his zeal than by the concerns of his own spiritual life.

Before considering the body of Southwell's shorter poems, a few remarks ought to be made on those few poems of his which were called forth by events of public interest in the late 1580's, the execution of Mary Queen of Scots in 1587 and the sentencing to death of the Earl of Arundel in 1589. As a spokesman for the Catholics in England, it was natural for Southwell to express a viewpoint on these important public events in order to counteract the propaganda of the official interpretation placed upon them. In the body of Southwell's verse these two poems belong immediately after the poems on repentance (Nos. 25-33 in Brown's edition) and are obviously intended to present examples of heroic constancy in keeping the faith.

The death of Mary Stuart and the condemnation of Howard were not directly connected, although the Earl's father, the fourth Duke of Norfolk, had been hanged as a result of his intrigues on behalf of the Scottish Queen whom he had hoped to marry. There was, however, an indirect link between the two events. Arundel was judged guilty of treason because it was alleged that he had caused a Mass to be offered for the success of the Spanish Armada which was sent to avenge the judicial murder at Fotheringhay.

**"Decease Release: *Dum morior orior*"** (34) presents an Elizabethan Catholic's point of view on the beheading of Mary Stuart. Historians have been arguing about the virtue and intelligence of that tragic and beautiful princess for centuries now; but to Southwell, who believed that all of her sufferings derived from her fidelity to her religion, she was a martyr. The executioner's axe placed the robe of martyrdom upon her and thereby covered all of her sins. Her death freed her from the griefs which attended her earthly queenship and brought her to the joy of reigning in Heaven. In Southwell's poem, the dead queen describes herself and her sad history in terms of one of the fundamental paradoxes of Christianity: "unless the grain of wheat falling into the ground die, it remaineth alone. But if it die, it bringeth forth much fruit" (John xii.24-25):

> THE pounded spice both tast and sent doth please,
> In fading smoke the force doth incense shewe,
> The perisht kernell springeth with encrease,
> The lopped tree doth best and soonest growe.
>
> Gods spice I was and pounding was my due,
> In fadinge breath my incense savored best,
> Death was the meane my kyrnell to renewe,
> By loppinge shott I upp to heavenly rest.
> Some thinges more perfect are in their decaye,

> Like sparke that going out gives clerest light,
> Such was my happ whose dolefull dying daye
> Beganne my joy and termed fortunes spite.
>
> Alive a Queene, now dead I am a Sainte,
> Once N: calld, my name nowe Martyr is,
> From earthly raigne debarred by restraint,
> In liew whereof I raigne in heavenly blisse.

> (*ll.* 1-16)

The omission of the name of the subject of this poem from the manuscripts and from the early editions suggests that it began to circulate fairly shortly after the execution of Mary when the government was very suspicious of any who might have sympathized with the dead queen. If these verses actually were written in 1587, it is difficult to accept Professor Janelle's norm for dating Southwell's lyrics on the basis of style. According to Janelle, as Southwell developed as a poet, he gradually eliminated from his verses the strained conceits and rhetorical tricks he had been taught to admire by his Jesuit teachers and began to write in a chaste, straightforward manner.[30] As a matter of fact, these verses on Mary Stuart are as dignified, and manifest as great a competence in handling the decasyllabic line as any which Southwell wrote. As will be seen in another chapter, *Saint Peters Complaint,* which was probably the last poem Southwell ever wrote, contains some of his most extravagant images.

**"I Dye without desert"** (35) was thought by Grosart and earlier nineteenth-century editors to be a companion piece to **"Decease Release"** and, like the latter, concerned with the death of the Queen of Scots. There are some reasons for this judgment, but more recent students of Southwell agree that these lines were inspired by the condemnation of Philip Howard to death for treason in 1589. The reference in line 27 to "A noble peere for prowess" would seem to eliminate the possibility that the poem concerns Mary Stuart. Moreover, it was perfectly natural for Southwell to have commented on what he thought was the injustice done to the Earl of Arundel because he was chaplain to Anne Dacres, the faithful wife of that unfortunate man. Southwell had already addressed *An Epistle of Comfort* to Philip Howard, and there can be no doubt but that he felt that Arundel was one "restrained in durance for the Catholic Faith."

Southwell takes Howard's condemnation as an occasion for his sharpest criticism of Elizabethan justice:

> Rayne downe, yee heavens, your teares this case
>    requires,
> Mans eyes unhable are enough to shedd,
> If sorow could have place in heavenly quires
> A juster ground the world hath seldome bredd.
> For right is wrong'd, and vertue wag'd with blood,
> The badd are blissd, god murdred in the good.

> (*ll.* 19-24)

In view of this monstrous miscarriage of justice, Southwell indulges in moralizations suggested by the ruin of one of the wealthiest peers of England. Fortune's maddening arbitrariness in permitting the fall of the great is ratified by the viciousness of men, and therefore one must look to God, the sower and the harvester of good seed (Matt. xiii.24-30), to settle accounts:

> Thus fortunes favors still are bent to flight,
> Thus worldly blisse in finall bale doth end,
> Thus vertue still pursued is with spight,
> But let my fall though ruefull none offend.
> God doth sometymes first cropp the sweetest floure,
> And leaves the weede till tyme do it devoure.

*(ll. 31-36)*

A third occasional poem by Southwell ought to be mentioned here because of its connection with Philip Howard. In August of 1591, Margaret Howard Sackville, Philip's beloved half-sister, died at the age of 29. Lady Margaret, a devout Catholic, is a good illustration of the strange religious and marital patterns of the late sixteenth century. She was the daughter-in-law of Sir Thomas Sackville, a poet, a statesman, and a rather militant Protestant, who had sat in judgment on both her father, the Duke of Norfolk, and her half-brother. He also had the terrible task of announcing to Mary Stuart her death sentence. According to Father Thurston, Southwell intended his translation of Diego de Estella's *The Hundred Meditations of the Love of God* for the use of Lady Margaret.[31] At her death, Southwell addressed a letter of consolation to her half-brother, Philip Howard, which was printed by Valentine Sims for John Busby in 1595 under the impressively long title:

THE

Triumphs ouer Death:

OR,

*A Consolatorie Epistle, for afflicted*
mindes, in the affects of
dying friends.

First written for the consolation of one: but now
published for the generall good of all, by *R. S.*
the Author of ***S. Peters Complaint,*** and ***Maeoniae***
his other Hymnes.[32]

The letter ends with a twenty-four line epitaph, a graceful tribute to a great lady, which subtly contrasts worldly fortune, which is largely a result of fortuitous accidents, with the glories of Heaven, which are the reward of free cooperation with grace:

> Death aymed too high, he hit too choise a wight,
>   Renowned for birth for life, for lovely partes,
> He kill'd her cares, he brought her woorths to light,
>   He robd our eyes, but hath enricht our hearts:
>     He let out of the Arke a *Noyes* dove,
>     But many hearts are arkes unto her love.
> Grace, Nature, Fortune did in her conspire

> To shew a proofe of their united skill:
> Slie Fortune ever false did soone retire.
>   But doubled Grace supplied false Fortunes ill:
> And though she raught not to her fortunes pitch,
>   In grace and nature few were found so rich.[33]

These three occasional poems, which can be assigned with some certainty to the second, fourth, and sixth years of Southwell's brief career as a poet and missioner, manifest very little variety in style. All three employ subdued but dignified diction, and the statement is made with a minimum of rhetorical embellishment. It is impossible to find in them any evidence in support of Professor Janelle's assertion that Southwell progressed steadily from a naive dependence on a neoclassical poetic of artificial figures to a self-confident chastity of style in which he expresses himself with dignified simplicity. These three poems show rather that Southwell used a simple style at all stages of his career when he felt that his subject matter demanded it.

The rest of the short poems contained in the Stonyhurst Manuscript fall into two general divisions. The first twenty-two concern events in the lives of the Savior and His mother; the remaining twenty-five, which deal with themes of repentance, the soul's yearning for union with God, and the vanity of worldliness, are separated from the preceding by two dogmatic poems on the Blessed Sacrament.

The first fourteen poems of the collection, all in the so-called Venus and Adonis stanza pattern, form a series on the life of the Blessed Virgin and the infancy of Christ from the Conception of Mary to her Assumption. Professor Martz has shown that these verses ought to be associated with the emphasis of the Counter Reformation on devotion to Mary, particularly with the popular devotion of the Rosary.[34] No one can argue with the reasoning which makes a connection between these poems and the Catholic effort to keep alive in the hearts of Englishmen the centuries old devotion to Mary. What is questionable is the effort to link these poems with the Rosary. No one as yet has shown that there ever existed a form of the Rosary which included exactly those mysteries which Southwell has written about. The rather loose kind of unity which seems to characterize the poems in this series, the fact that they appear to be sets of three or four more or less independent stanzas on different aspects of the mysteries they deal with rather than successive points in developed meditations, would seem to suggest that they were intended, not to provide pious Catholics with considerations for the mental prayer which is supposed to accompany the recitation of the beads, but rather to show how the poetic conventions associated with the epigram could be transformed and used in the service of religion.

The epigram, taken over by the Latins from the Greeks, had been used for centuries as a vehicle for satire and scatological comment. Southwell must have welcomed the opportunity to turn the verbal wit associated with the art of the epigram to the service of God and his devotion to Mary.

> SPELL *Eva* backe and *Ave* shall you finde,
> The first began, the last reverst our harmes,
> An angels witching wordes did *Eva* blinde,
> An angels *Ave* disinchants the charmes,
> Death first by womans weakenes entred in,
> In womans vertue life doth now begin.[35]

Here, in the six-line stanza Southwell used in most of his verse, are contained three neat epigramatic statements on the first and second Eve. This play on *Eva* and *Ave* has an ancient ancestry, going all the way back to the times of the Latin Fathers. For centuries it has been enshrined in the liturgical life of the Church by its use in one of the ancient Latin Marian hymns, the *Ave Maris Stella,* written sometime between the sixth and ninth centuries, which is still the hymn assigned for Vespers on most feasts of Our Lady:

> *Sumens illud Ave*
> *Gabrielis ore,*
> *Funda nos in pace,*
> *Mutans Heave nomen.*[36]

According to Walter J. Ong, there is a natural affinity between wit poetry, which he defines as "that poetry which characteristically employs conceit, that is, paradoxical or curious and striking comparison and analogy, and which favors the development of word-play," and revealed mystery.[37] The poetry which attempts to celebrate the ineffable workings of God accepted by Christian faith quite naturally resorts to various rhetorical figures (which can easily be mistaken by one who is unfamiliar with Christian faith for mere verbal trickery) to suggest truths which are beyond the power of the unaided human intellect to grasp and can only be apprehended by the intellect illuminated by faith by means of analogies with visible reality.

The second stanza of Southwell's **"The Virgins Salutation"** (6) is further illustration of the kind of wit poetry Father Ong seems to have had in mind. In an apostrophe to the womb of the Virgin, which Faith teaches is the receptacle of the Lord of Heaven, the poet makes a sudden switch and calls that same womb Heaven itself. Then, in the closing line, he draws an analogy between the relationship of the sun to the stars (which Southwell thought derived their light from the sun) and that of the Incarnate Word to the virtues:

> O virgin breast the heavens to thee incline,
> In thee their joy and soveraigne they agnize,
> Too meane their glory is to match with thine,
> Whose chaste receit God more then heaven did prize,
> Haile fairest heaven, that heaven and earth dost blisse,
> Where vertues starres God sunne of justice is.
>
> (*ll.* 7-12)

In the third stanza Southwell returns to the contrast of the first; but here the contrast is between the pride of man which robbed him of happiness and the surpassing love of God which was the motive for the Incarnation and our redemption:

> With hauty minde to godhead man aspirde,
> And was by pride from place of pleasure chac'de,
> With loving minde our manhod God desired,
> And us by love in greater pleasure plac'de,
> Man labouring to ascend procurde our fall,
> God yeelding to discend cut off our thrall.
>
> (*ll.* 13-18)

Here the natural divisions of the stanza are followed. The first four lines, rhyming *abab,* set forth the contrast between human pride and divine love in a rather complete form; and a final couplet restates it in a tight epigram. The wit of this artful contrast helps one to apprehend the mysterious workings of God, Who in the Incarnation definitively intervened to change the doleful course of human history set for mankind by the sin of Adam. The seeming frivolity of Southwell's epigrammatic style is intended to alert the reader to the fact that something supernatural is being treated which cannot be apprehended by unaided reason.

The last stanza of **"The Virgine Maries Conception,"** the first poem in the sequence, is an example of a self-contained, six-line epigram on the Immaculate Conception:

> Four only wights bred without fault are namde
> And al the rest conceived were in sinne,
> Without both man and wife was *Adam* framde,
> Of man, but not of wife did *Eve* beginne,
> Wife without touch of man Christs was,
> Of man and wife this babe was bred in grace.
>
> (*ll.* 13-18)[38]

The doctrine is completely orthodox, yet the expression is deliberately "witty" to suggest the secret working of God's Providence which can only be known by faith.

The suggestion here is not that Southwell, in this sequence of poems on the mysteries of the life of the Virgin and the infancy of Jesus, has taken a new approach to religious verse. What I have been attempting to indicate is that, in these poems, he has been following that tradition in medieval Latin hymnody which employed wit to emphasize the mystery. This tradition grew out of the great theological revival emanating from the Monastery of St. Victor which found expression in the verse of Adam of St. Victor (fl. 1140). The hymns of St. Thomas Aquinas are in this same tradition, which was taken up again, possibly as a result of Southwell's example, by the great metaphysical poets of the seventeenth century.

Alongside this tradition there existed another, the so-called Franciscan tradition, which concentrated on the more emotional aspects of events narrated in the gospels and on the psychological factors in the dealings of man with his Redeemer. Jacopone da Todi's *Stabat Mater* and Thomas of Celano's *Dies Irae* were the most famous products of this tradition in Latin; and it would seem, from a cursory survey of the religious verse of fifteenth- and sixteenth-century England, that it was this tradition which inspired most of the religious poetry in English before Southwell.[39] As will be pointed out, much of Southwell's verse belongs to this tradition; yet there is scarcely a trace of it in these epigrammatic stanzas on the mysteries of the Mother of the Savior.

These fourteen poems also illustrate some of the characteristics of emblematic verse, although there is no evidence at all that they were ever accompanied by a set of emblems or indeed that they were intended to be.[40] Emblematic verse had been vigorously employed by the Jesuits and Benedictines on the continent since the middle of the sixteenth century as a means of religious instruction. The emblem books drew upon visual symbols to present spiritual truths concerning not only the secret operations of a man's spiritual faculties but also the hidden significance of events in the lives of Jesus and Mary and of the saints. To be effective the emblems had to be recognizable by reason of traditional and established typological associations and symbols. Invocations from various litanies and phrases from the scriptures were often used by the makers of emblem books, but traditional symbols drawn from medieval bestiaries and other sources of Renaissance knowledge were also popular. Phoenixes, flaming hearts, storm-tossed ships, pelicans, and hundreds of other conventional symbols abound in the books of emblems which are extant; but it must be confessed that these collections scarcely ever rise to the level of great art either poetically or pictorially. In their day they served the efforts of the Counter Reformation to give instruction and stir up devotion; to later generations, their chief interest arises from the light they throw upon the contribution the emblematic tradition made to the poetic technique of men like Southwell and George Herbert.

Southwell's stanzas on the birth of Mary, **"Her Nativity"** (2), contain several examples of the kind of symbolic and typological allusion the emblematists were accustomed to use to set forth the glories of the Mother of God:

> JOY in the rising of our Orient starre,
> That shal bring forth the Sunne that lent her light,
> Joy in the peace that shall conclude our warre,
> And soone rebate the edge of Sathans spight,
> Load-starre of all engolfd in worldly waves,
> The card and compasse that from ship-wracke saves.
>
> The Patriarchs and Prophets were the flowers,
> Which time by course of ages did distill,
> And cul'd into this little cloud the showers,
> Whose gratious drops the world with joy shall fil,

> Whose moisture suppleth every soule with grace,
> And bringeth life to *Adams* dying race
>
> For God on earth she is the royall throne,
> The chosen cloth to make his mortall weede,
> The quarry to cut out our corner stone,
> Soile ful of fruit, yet free from mortall seede,
> For heavenly flowre shee is the *Jesse* rod,
> The child of man, the parent of a god.

Mary is called a star in accordance with an ancient and traditional etymology which derived her name from the Hebrew phrase meaning "star of the sea."[41] In lines one and two she is called the "Orient starre," the *Stella Matutina* of the Litany of Loretto, because her birth heralds the rising of the sun who is, of course, Christ; and Mary's Son gives His light to His herald (Mary) just as the natural sun lends light to the planet Venus. The possible associations between the cult of Venus and devotion to Mary are intriguing,[42] but I find it hard to imagine that they would have been of much interest to Southwell.

In lines five and six the notion of the star of the sea, the *Stella Maris,* is taken up. Mary is called "load-starre" or North Star, the star which mariners use to set their courses. Thus she is the *Consolatrix Afflictorum* and *Refugium Peccatorum* because she reminds "all engolf'd in worldly waves" of their true destiny and by her example gives them "The card and compasse that from shipwracke saves."

The traditional exegesis of Genesis iii.14, which identifies Mary as the woman whose foot will crush the head of the Serpent, is alluded to in lines three and four. The reference to "the peace that shall conclude our warre" may also be an echo of Mary's title *Regina Pacis.*

In the second stanza Southwell places Mary in the context of the whole history of salvation. The prophets and patriarchs are seen as flowers whose perfume is distilled into the little cloud which appeared in answer to the prayers of Elias (I [III] Kings xviii.41-46). This cloud is a type of Mary, and the rain which falls from it is a type of her Son who restores life to the children of Adam as that rain saved the children of Israel from famine. Perhaps a brief quotation from St. Ambrose will shed more light on the kind of thinking that lies behind Southwell's compact statement than any elaborate explication could hope to do:

> As a cloud Mary rained upon the earth the grace of Christ. . . . The shower of this sacred cloud our fathers announced to us would be the world's salvation. . . . This rain quenched the appetite of Eve: this unguent wiped away the stench of hereditary error.[43]

The final stanza continues the description of Mary's peculiar relationship with the Savior. The phrase "royal throne" (*l.* 13) for the Incarnate Word, "God on earth," recalls another of title from Litany of Loretto, *Sedes Sapientiae*. The Second Person of the Trinity has been associated with Wisdom since the beginnings of Christianity.

"The Word became flesh" (Jn. i.14) when He was conceived in Mary's womb, and therefore she is "The chosen cloth to make his mortall weed" (*l.* 14). This image, for which I am unaware of any scriptural or patristic source, suggests to Southwell another drawn from Matthew xxi.42 and Psalm cxvii.22. Mary is the quarry from which Christ, "The stone which the builders rejected . . . [and which] is become the head of the corner," is cut. It is possible that Southwell, who had an easy familiarity with the Scriptures, intended an allusion to another Messianic text, the prophet Daniel's "stone . . . cut out of a mountain without hands," which destroys the monstrous giant with feet of clay (Dn. ii.31-45).

Whether or not Southwell intended an allusion to Daniel, he makes a clear reference to a third Messianic text in line 17 where he calls Mary "the *Jesse* rod" which blossoms forth a "heavenly flowre." The Vulgate version of Isaiah xi.1 employs the same image Southwell used: "Et egredietur virga de radice Jesse, et flos de radice ejus ascendet." The whole of Isaiah xi is devoted to a description of wonders of the Golden Age of the Messiah.

Because Jesus is, in the words of the Ave Maria, "the fruit of [Mary's] womb," she is "Soile ful of fruit" (*l.* 16). Yet, inasmuch as the Son of God has no earthly father, this soil is "free from Mortall seede." All of the mystery and the glory that Mary represented to Southwell and to devout Roman Catholics is summed up in the paradox of the concluding line of the poem. She is "The child of man, the parent of a God" (*l.* 18).

The point of this type of poetry, it would seem, is the pleasure it gives by heaping praises upon Mary, the object of special Catholic devotion and love. Southwell makes scarcely any attempt to justify by logical argument the assertions he makes about Mary; to him, she is the "PROCLAIMED Queene and Mother of a God, / The light of earth, the soveraigne of Saints" (**"The Visitation,"** *ll.* 1-2).

Although these verses in honor of Mary would certainly have had their strongest appeal to Roman Catholics, they probably also struck a responsive chord in the hearts of the great majority of Englishmen who, with characteristic conservatism, deplored the disappearance of the cult of the Virgin in the newly established religion and the destruction of her shrines in the isle which in earlier centuries was proud to style itself "the dowry of Mary."[44] John Donne's sonnets on the Annunciation, the Nativity, and the finding of the Child Jesus in the

Temple in his *La Corona* sequence and especially the stanza on the Virgin Mary in "The Litanie" are evidence that the Mother of Jesus retained a special place in the hearts of religious Englishmen of the early decades of the seventeenth century. Southwell himself would surely have approved of the sentiments which Donne expressed with a poetic gift more perfectly developed than the Jesuit ever achieved:

> For that faire blessed Mother-maid,
> Whose flesh redeem'd us; That she-Cherubim,
>   Which unlock's Paradise, and made
> One claime for innocence, and disseiz'd sinne,
>   Whose wombe was a strange heav'n, for there
>     God cloath'd himselfe, and grew,
> Our zealous thankes wee poure. As her deeds were
> Our helpes, so are her prayers; nor can she sue
> In vaine, who hath such titles unto you.[45]

In "To all Angels and Saints," George Herbert, Donne's disciple and friend and one of Anglicanism's most convinced and devout sons, expressed a sense of nostalgic loss because of the failure of the new religion to find scriptural sanction for the cult of the Virgin:

>               I would addresse
> My vows to thee most gladly, Blessed Maid,
> And Mother of my God, in my distresse.
> Thou art the holy mine, whence came the gold,
> The great restorative for all decay
>               In young and old;
> Thou art the cabinet where the jewell lay:
> Chiefly to thee would I my soul unfold:
> But now, alas, I dare not; for our King
> Whom we do all Joyntly adore and praise,
>               Bids no such thing:
> And where his pleasure no injunction layes
> ('Tis your own case) ye never move a wing.
> All worship is prerogative, and a flower
> Of his rich crown, from whom lyes no appeal
>               At the last houre:
> Therefore we dare not from his garland steal,
> To make a posie for inferiour power.
> Although then others court you, if ye know
> What's done on earth, we shall not fare the worse,
>               Who do not so;
> Since we are ever ready to disburse,
> If any one our Masters hand can show.[46]

Southwell never felt anything akin to Herbert's reticence. He obviously addressed his vows to Mary with considerable joy. "To Jesus through Mary" was the natural progression for him, and therefore seven of the poems in the opening sequence, numbers six through twelve, are devoted to the infancy of Jesus. As in the verses on the Virgin, these poems abound in verbal wit, intended not so much to inform as to recall to the pious the wonderful paradoxes implicit in the mystery of the Incarnation. In **"The Nativitie of Christ"** (6), for example, Southwell dwells lovingly on the *exinanitio* of the Second Person of the Trinity become a helpless infant:

BEHOLDE the father, is his daughters sonne:
The bird that built the nest, is hatched therein:
The olde of yeares, an houre hath not out runne:
Eternall life, to live doth now beginne.
The word is dumme: the mirth of heaven doth weepe:
Might feeble is: and force doth faintly creepe.

(*ll*. 1-6)

This is purely devotional poetry, the art of rhetoric placed in the service of God to call men to recognize their Savior. Southwell twists his grammatical structures into almost incomprehensible forms to emphasize the great benefit conferred upon fallen man when his God undertook his redemption:

O dying soules, beholde your loving spring:
O dasled eyes, behold your sonne of grace:
Dull eares, attend what word this word doth bring:
Up heavie hartes: with joye your joye embrace.
From death, from darke, from deafenesse, from dis-
     paires:
This life, this light, this word, this joy repaires.

(*ll*. 7-12)

Southwell loves to repeat in poem after poem the theological basis of his devotion to Mary, her unique relationship to the Incarnate Word and her sharing in His redemptive work. In **"His Circumcision"** (7), the closeness of Mother and Son in suffering is delicately described:

With weeping eies his mother rewd his smart,
If blood from him, teares ran from her as fast,
The knife that cut his flesh did pierce her heart,
The paine that Jesus felt did *Mary* taste,
His life and hers hung by one fatall twist,
No blow that hit the sonne the mother mist.

(*ll*. 13-18)

Yet Southwell is always orthodox. Mary is not the redeemer, nor is she a goddess. She remains a creature, but the noblest and most precious. Southwell makes this important distinction very gracefully in **"The Presentation"** (9):

O virgin pure thou dost these doves present
As due to law, not as an equall price,
To buy such ware thou wouldst thy life have spent,
The world to reach his worth could not suffice,
If God were to be bought, not worldly pelfe,
But thou wert fittest price next God himself.

(*ll*. 13-18)

The Infant Savior is also the subject of the four (really five) hymns which immediately follow the opening sequence in the Stonyhurst Manuscript. Three of these, **"A Childe My Choyce"** (15), **"The Burning Babe"** (17), and **"New Prince, New Pompe"** (18), are written in fourteeners; **"New Heaven, New Warre"** (16), which is actually two separate poems, consists of two sets of four six-line stanzas of rhymed octosyllabics. All of these poems, which have been the most frequently reprinted of Southwell's verses, were obviously intended to be sung as Christmas songs.

**"A Childe My Choyce"** seems to have derived its title at least from a poem which Southwell may have seen in manuscript, "Love Thy Choice," by Edward de Vere, Lord Oxford.[47] Like Arundel and Southampton, the young de Vere had been a ward of Lord Burghley. If Southwell did see a manuscript of Oxford's poem, we have another hint of a link between him and the Southampton Circle, and **"A Childe My Choyce"** emerges as another of the Jesuit's attempts to persuade by his example his fellow poets to cease "expressing such passions as onely serue for testimonies to what unworthy affections they have wedded their wils" and devote their talents to writing good poetry on such themes as would show "how well verse and vertue sute together."[48] In place of a fictitious lady of incredible beauty and wit, Southwell offers the holy Child of Bethlehem as the perfect subject for praise and song:

LET folly praise that fancie loves, I praise
          and love that child,
Whose hart, no thought: whose tong, no word:
          whose hand no deed defiled.
I praise him most, I love him best, all praise
          and love is his:
While him I love, in him I live, and cannot
          live amisse.
Loves sweetest mark, Lawdes highest theme,
          mans most desired light:
To love him, life: to leave him, death: to
          live in him, delight.
He mine, by gift: I his, by debt: thus each,
          to other due:
First friend he was: best friend he is: all times
          will try him true.

(*ll*. 1-8)

The simple directness of Southwell's statement places this poem in sharp contrast with the artificiality of so much of the love poetry of the 1580's. He feels no need to rationalize his devotion by constructing fanciful comparisons between his beloved and the sun or the moon. The Child he loves really is the light of the world and, in the strictest theological sense, the proper object of adoration. This solid theological basis accounts, I think, for the tone of quiet assurance that pervades the poem. In taking the Incarnate Word as the subject for his praise, Southwell felt no need to apologize for any hyperbole:

Though young, yet wise: though smal, yet strong:
          though man, yet God he is:
As wise, he knowes: as strong, he can: as God,
          he loves to blisse.
His knowledge rules: his strength, defends: his
          love, doth cherish all:

His birth, our Joye: his life, our light: his death,
      our end of thrall.

                           *(ll. 9-12)*

The calm assurance Southwell felt in singing the praises of the Christ Child gives life to the "clumsy" fourteener measure he employed in his song. Southwell's characteristic habits of language—his use of *that* for *that which,* his dropping of copulatives and suspension of predicates to make one verb serve for several—which sometimes render his verses rather monotonous—are quite appropriate in this hymn about the Infant Jesus because part of Southwell's point is that devotion to this Child frees one from bondage to tired old literary conventions. He seems to be saying to his fellow poets, "If you would only choose to honor this Child, whose perfection surpasses your powers of expression, you would not have to waste your time on contrived techniques." What saves this very dubious theory that sublimity of subject matter will redeem unskilled writing, in Southwell's case, is the fact that his genuine fervor lends freshness to the rather trite conventions he uses.

In the final quatrain, Southwell leaves the somewhat abstract and theological considerations he has been presenting to turn our gaze upon the Savior Himself:

Alas, he weepes, he sighes, he pants, yeat doo
      his Angels sing:
Out of his teares, his sighes and throbs, doth
      bud a joyfull spring.
Almightie babe, whose tender armes can force all
      foes to flie:
Correct my faultes, protect my life, direct me
      when I die.

                          *(ll. 13-16)*

The transition is abrupt, and the pathos the poet is striving for threatens to emerge as mawkish sentimentality.[49] But the juxtaposition of the fretful Child and the angelic choir suggests a paradox. We do not ordinarily conceive of angels as singing for joy at the sight of an unhappy baby. In this case, however, the fact that the Son of God took upon Himself the frustrations of the human condition is reason for great rejoicing because in this way the foes of man were forced to flee. The sufferings taken upon Himself by the God-man were the means by which our salvation was accomplished. Using a figure suggested perhaps by the root of Jesse (Isaiah xi) perhaps by Moses striking the rock in the desert (Exodus xvii.6), Southwell describes the joyous effect of Christ's childish tears. The slight ambiguity arising from the two possible meanings of "spring" (*l.* 14) provides just enough tension in this section of the poem to keep the tenderness of the emotion from getting out of hand. The simple and direct prayer of petition which brings the poem to a close restates the motives which should move one to choose this Child.

"**New Heaven, New Warre**" is, as was stated above, really two poems. The first four stanzas set forth the theme that Bethlehem's manger, by reason of the presence of Jesus, has become a new Heaven. Since men fail to render homage to their newborn God, the poet calls upon the angels to make up the deficit because, endowed with superhuman intellects, "His borrowed weed lets not your sight" (*l.* 23). These stanzas contain allusions to passages in both the Old and New Testament which deal with the angels: "Seraphins" (*l.* 8) whose images were carved in gold over the Ark of the Covenant (I [III] Kings vi.19-28); "Raphaell" (*l.* 11) who guided the younger and healed the elder Tobias, as is narrated in the Book of Tobias; and "Gabriell" (*l.* 13) who announced the births of Jesus and his cousin John the Baptist (Luke, 1).

In the four stanzas which make up the second poem, **"New Warre,"** Southwell applies to the Infant Savior some ideas from two of the most important meditations of the Second Week of *The Spiritual Exercises,* "The Meditation on Two Standards" and the consideration of "The Three Degrees of Humility." In the third point of "Two Standards," Ignatius asks the exercitant

> to consider the address which Christ our Lord makes to all His servants and friends, . . . recommending to them that they desire to help all, by guiding them first to the highest degree of poverty of spirit, and even to actual poverty, if it please His Divine Majesty, and He should choose to elect them to it: leading them, secondly, to a desire of reproaches and contempt, because from these two humility results; so that there are three steps: the first, poverty, opposed to riches; the second, reproaches and contempt, opposed to worldly honour; the third, humility, opposed to pride: and from these three steps let them conduct them to all other virtues.

                          *(pp. 46-47)*

Ignatius' description of the third degree of humility likewise stresses imitation of the mysterious abjection of the Savior:

> The third degree is the most perfect humility: when, . . . supposing equal praise and glory to the Divine Majesty, the better to imitate Christ our Lord, and to become actually more like to Him, I desire and choose rather poverty with Christ poor than riches; contempt with Christ contemned, than honours; and I desire to be esteemed as useless and foolish for Christ's sake, Who was first held to be such, [rather] than to be accounted wise and prudent in this world.

                          *(p. 53)*

Southwell, like the founder of the Jesuits, saw in the Incarnation a reversal of the values of secularism. Poverty and humility were the weapons the Savior wielded in the battle He waged for our souls, "For in this weake unarmed wise, / The gates of hell he will surprise" (*ll.* 29-30).

In *The Spiritual Exercises,* Ignatius proposes the "Two Standards" and the "Degrees of Humility" as preparatory considerations for the election, the moral commitment he wishes to elicit from the exercitant. They are intended to be interspersed with contemplations on the infancy and public life of Christ. In **"New Warre,"** Southwell likewise calls upon his reader to make a response to the Child in the manger:

> My soule with Christ joyne thou in fight,
> Sticke to the tents that he hath pight;
> Within his Crib is surest ward,
> This little Babe will be thy guard:
> If thou wilt foyle thy foes with joy,
> Then flit not from this heavenly boy.

> *(ll. 43-48)*

Southwell's insistence on the characteristically Ignatian idea that a Christian must be willing to imitate Christ in humility and suffering if he wishes to share in His joy and triumph had very real pertinence in Elizabethan England. The heavy fines and civil disabilities imposed upon those who refused to conform to the government's settlement of the religious question forced Roman Catholics to accept political anonymity and, in many cases, actual poverty. Southwell hoped to convince these staunch confessors of the faith that the sacrifices they were making were worthwhile and capable of rendering them more like the Savior and more worthy to have a share in His final triumph.

To the worldly minded man, poverty, meekness, and contempt are the great obstacles to achieving happiness; but, to one who has understood the significance of Christ's birth in the squalor of a hillside cave, they are occasions for joining battle on the side of Him to Whom the Father has given "that name which is above all other names," because He emptied Himself on our behalf. The imagery of **"New Warre"** emphasizes the paradox of genuine Christian warfare in which the leader is a weeping baby:

> This little Babe so few dayes olde,
> Is come to ryfle sathans folde;
> All hell doth at his presence quake,
> Though he himselfe for cold doe shake:
> For in this weake unarmed wise,
> The gates of hell he will surprise.

> With teares he fights and winnes the field,
> His naked breast stands for a shield;
> His battring shot are babish cryes,
> His Arrowes lookes of weeping eyes,
> His Martiall ensignes cold and neede,
> And feeble flesh his warriers steede.

> His Campe is pitched in a stall,
> His bulwarke but a broken wall:
> The Crib his trench, hay stalks his stakes,
> Of Sheepheards he his Muster makes;

> And thus as sure his foe to wound,
> The Angells trumps alarum sound.

> *(ll. 25-42)*

**"New Prince, New Pompe"** repeats Southwell's conviction that the scene at Bethlehem is a refutation of false notions of what constitutes real splendour. After describing the misery of the manger upon which the Savior was laid, Southwell warns the reader not to judge the persons by those standards according to which the world is accustomed to pass judgment. The clothes a man wears, the house in which he lives, and the people with whom he associates do not always reflect his real quality:

> Despise not him for lying there,
>     First what he is enquire:
> An orient pearle is often found,
>     In depth of dirty mire.

> Waigh not his Crib, his wooden dish,
>     Nor beasts that by him feede:
> Waigh not his Mothers poore attire
>     Nor Josephs simple weede.

> This stable is a Princes Court,
>     The Crib his chaire of state:
> The beasts are parcell of his pompe,
>     The wooden dish his plate:

> The persons in that poore attire,
>     His royall livories weare,
> The Prince himselfe is come from heaven,
>     This pompe is prized there.

> With joy approach o Christian wight,
>     Doe homage to thy King;
> And highly prise this humble pompe,
>     Which he from heaven dooth bring.

> *(ll. 9-28)*

**"The Burning Babe,"** which Ben Jonson admired so much and from which Shakespeare possibly derived his image of ". . . pity, like a naked new-born babe / Striding the blast,"[50] employs the conventions of vision poetry to elicit a response to the pathos surrounding the child Jesus:

> AS I in hoarie Winters night
>     Stoode shivering in the snow,
> Surpris'd I was with sodaine heate,
>     Which made my hart to glow;

> And lifting up a fearefull eye,
>     To view what fire was neare,
> A pretty Babe all burning bright
>     Did in the ayre appeare;

> Who scorched with excessive heate,
>     Such floods of teares did shed,
> As though his floods should quench his flames,
>     Which with his teares were fed:
> Alas (quoth he) but newly borne,
>     In fierie heates I frie,

Yet none approach to warme their harts,
　Or feele my fire, but I.

. . . . .

With this he vanisht out of sight,
　And swiftly shrunk away,
And straight I called unto minde,
　That it was Christmasse day.

(*ll.* 1-16, 29-32)

These Christmas hymns are more than just contemplations of the Crib; they are calls to the Christian reader to accept the values implicit in the mystery of the birth of Christ. Southwell evidently believed that English Catholics needed to be reminded of the poverty and humility of Jesus to strengthen their wills to accept the sacrifices laid upon them for fidelity to their religion. . . .

### Notes

1. For a brief but very illuminating discussion of the controversies concerning the art of poetry in England in the sixteenth century, see the "Introduction" to *Elizabethan Critical Essays,* ed. G. Gregory Smith (London, 1904), I, xi-xcii.

2. Amos N. Wilder, *Modern Poetry and Christian Tradition: A Study in the Relation of Christianity to Culture* (New York, 1952), pp. 190-204.

3. Wylie Sypher, *Four Stages of Renaissance Style* (New York, 1955), pp. 180-251.

4. "On the Invocation, Veneration, and Relics of Saints, and on Sacred Images," Twenty-fifth Session, Dec. 3-4, 1963, *Canons and Decrees of the Council of Trent: Original Text with English Translation* by H. J. Schroeder (St. Louis, 1957), p. 523.

5. *Paradise Regained,* IV, 336-52, *John Milton: Complete Poems and Major Prose,* ed. Merritt Y. Hughes (New York, 1957), p. 523.

6. Pierre Janelle, *The Catholic Reformation* (Milwaukee, 1949), pp. 139-66.

7. Richard Gappa, "Tears and a Jesuit: A Study of Robert Southwell's *Marie Magdalens Funeral Tears,*" an unpublished monograph (St. Louis, 1964), p. 10.

8. Janelle, *The Catholic Reformation,* pp. 1-19.

9. Janelle, *The Catholic Reformation,* pp. 111-38.

10. *Robert Southwell the Writer,* pp. 116-41. The works of the Jesuit poetic theorists cited by Janelle which I have been able to examine are: Franciscus Bencius, *Orationes et Carmina cum Disputatione de Stylo et Scriptione,* 2nd ed. (Ingolstadt, 1595); Jacobus Pontanus (Spanmuller), Poeticarum Insti-

tutionum Libra III, 2nd ed. (Ingolstadt, 1597); and Antonius Possevinus, *Bibliotheca Selecta de Ratione Studiorum ad Disciplinas et ad Salutem Omnium Gentium Procurandam* (Venice, 1603).

11. "The Vernacular Matrix of the New Criticism," *The Critical Matrix,* ed. Paul R. Sullivan (Washington, D.C., 1961), pp. 3-35.

12. Ong, "The Vernacular Matrix," p. 9.

13. "First Principle and Foundation," *The Text of the Spiritual Exercises of St. Ignatius,* trans. John Morris, 4th ed. rev. (Westminster, Md., 1943), p. 9. Page numbers in my text after quotations from *The Spiritual Exercises* will refer to this edition.

14. In Chapter xiv of the Fourth Part of *The Constitutions of the Society of Jesus* the following rule is set down:

    In regard to the books in the classical languages of Latin and Greek let the universities as well as the colleges, as far as possible, abstain from reading to youths books in which there is anything that can hurt good morals unless the objectionable words and subjects are expurgated.

    Trans. Mary Helen Mayer, *St. Ignatius and the Ratio Studiorum,* ed. Edward A. Fitzpatrick (New York, 1933), p. 107.

15. Harold J. Grimm, *The Reformation Era 1500-1650* (New York, 1954), pp. 603-15, gives a brief survey of the effects of the Reformation (Catholic and Protestant) on the arts.

16. Robert John McAuley, "The Aesthetic and Spiritual Functions of Robert Southwell's Writing" (an unpublished M.A. thesis for Loyola University, Chicago, 1953), discusses the motives of Southwell's literary activity.

17. John Hungerford Pollen, "A Rare Catholic Tract," *The Month,* XCIX (1902), 93-96.

18. "Atheism under Elizabeth and James I," *The Month,* LXXXI (June, 1894), 174-87.

19. "Sonnet XVIII," *The Poems of John Donne,* ed. H. J. C. Grierson (London, 1933), p. 301.

20. Margaret Waugh, ed. (Chicago, 1966). The phrases quoted are from the table of contents, pp. xxi-xxii, and describe respectively Chapters Two, Five, Nine and Eleven. My next quote is also from this edition.

21. Wylie Sypher, in *Four Stages of Renaissance Style,* pp. 100-179, discusses Donne in connection with Mannerist art. His discussion highlights those aspects of Donne which differentiate him most dramatically from Southwell. It may make sense to speak of Donne's "incapacity to commit himself wholly" (p. 122), but not of Southwell's.

22. *The Poems of Robert Southwell, S.J.,* p. xciii.

23. The passage quoted is taken from the 1602 edition (*STC* 22952), sig. A2$^v$-A3$^r$ and A5$^r$.

24. Southwell, of course, could have translated directly from the Italian, but this sonnet of Petrarch's was already at home in English in at least three versions. *Tottel's Miscellany* (1557) contained two translations of it: one by Wyatt (No. 49. "Description of the contrarious passions in a lover") and one by an unknown poet (No. 301. "The duiers and contrarie passions of the louer.") There is another version by Thomas Watson, Sonnet 40 in his *Hecatompathia* (1582). See Hyder Edward Rollins, ed., *Tottel's Miscellany (1557-1587)* (Cambridge, Mass., 1929), II, 168.

25. William F. Lynch, *Christ and Apollo: The Dimensions of the Literary Imagination* (New York, 1960), pp. 113-32. Father Lynch's only reference to Southwell is worth quoting:

> Blessed Robert Southwell went to England with a passion for martyrdom, but when he got there he found that he was too busy with the manifold shapes of the literal to die too quickly. Even in death, therefore, we must not go too quickly from the many to the one . . .
>
> (p. 195)

26. Lines 25-32 quoted from *The Poems of Robert Southwell, S.J.,* pp. 135-36. Brown gives the text of Dyer's "A Fancy" in short lines rather than in the long lines ordinarily used for poems in the poulter's measure. See Ralph M. Sargent's printed version of the poem from MS Ashmole 781 in *At the Court of Queen Elizabeth: the Life and Lyrics of Sir Edward Dyer* (London, 1935), pp. 184-87.

27. Brown, ed., *The Poems of Robert Southwell, S.J.,* "Textual Introduction," p. lxxix.

28. Christopher Devlin, *Life of Southwell,* pp. 257-73. See also K. C. McDonald, "Blessed Robert Southwell, S.J., and William Shakespeare," *The Month,* CLVII (1931), 349-52; and a most extraordinary argument identifying Robert Southwell as the young man of Shakespeare's Sonnets in John William Trotman's edition of Southwell's *The Triumphs over Death,* pp. 110-36.

29. *The Poetry of Meditation,* pp. 179-210. William T. Noon, in *Poetry and Prayer* (New Brunswick, N. J.: Rutgers University Press, 1967), pp. 36-41, offers an interesting and, I think, a sound evaluation of Professor Martz's approach. At any rate, Father Noon's book should provide material for the continuing discussion of the fascinating question of the relationship between poetry and prayer.

30. *Robert Southwell The Writer,* pp. 156-70.

31. "A Memorial for Two Lady Margarets," *The Month,* XCV (1900), 596-607. Father John Morris, S.J., unaware of the fact that Southwell was

32. *STC* 22971. See James McDonald, *Poems and Prose Writings of Robert Southwell, S.J.,* p. 111.

33. "Epitaph on Lady Margaret Sackville," lines 7-18, *The Poems of Robert Southwell, S.J.,* ed. McDonald and Brown, p. 101.

34. *The Poetry of Meditation,* pp. 101-7.

35. "The Virgins Salutation" (4), lines 1-6.

36. Quoted from *The Hymns of the Breviary and Missal,* ed. Mathew Britt, O.S.B. (New York, 1924), p. 317.

37. "Wit and Mystery: A Revaluation in Medieval Latin Hymnody," *Speculum,* XXII (1947), 310-41.

38. Brown, *The Poems of Robert Southwell, S.J.,* p. 108, reprints another version of this poem from the Harmsworth Manuscript, "Conceptio B. Virginis sub porta aurea," which she believes is an earlier form of "The Virgine Maries conception."

39. Ong, "Wit and Mystery," pp. 321-23.

40. The standard work on emblematic literature is Rosemary Freeman's *English Emblem Books* (London, 1948).

41. The name Mary certainly does not mean "star of the sea." This explanation of the name is based upon a misreading of Jerome's attempt to explain it as *stilla maris.* "Mariam plerique aestimant interpretari inluminant me isti uel iluminatrix uel zmyrna maris. Sed mihi nequaquam uidetur. Melius est autem ut dicamus sonare eam stillam maris siue amarum mare." *Liber Interpretationis Hebraicorvm Nominvm, Corpus Christianorvm: Series Latina* LXXII (Turnholt, 1959), 137. For a modern study on the significance of the name Mary, see E. Vogt, "De Nominis Mariae Etymologia," *Verbum Domini,* XXVI (1948), 163-68.

42. Brown, ed., *The Poems of Robert Southwell, S.J.,* p. 119.

43. *In Librum de Institutione Virginis et Sanctae Mariae Virginitate Perpetua ad Eusebium Liber Unus* (c. 392 a.d.), xiii, 81-84, *Sancti Ambrosii Mediolanensis Episcopi Opera Omnia.* Tomi Secundi Pars Prior, p. 339. This is volume XVI of *Patrologia Latina,* ed. J. P. Migne (Paris, 1880). My quotation is from Thomas Livius, *The Blessed Virgin in the Fathers of the First Six Centuries* (London, 1893), pp. 51-52. Father Livius' first

chapter, "The Primitive Patristic Idea of Mary as the Second Eve," pp. 35-59, is full of quotations which shed light on Southwell's mode of thinking about Mary.

44. John R. Roberts, "The Rosary in Elizabethan England," *The Month,* XXXII (1964), 192.

45. "The Litanie," lines 37-42, *The Poems of John Donne,* ed. H. J. C. Grierson, pp. 309-10.

46. Lines 8-30, *The Works of George Herbert,* ed. F. E. Hutchinson (Oxford, 1941), p. 78.

47. C. R. Mangam, "Southwell and the Council of Trent," *Revue anglo-américaine,* XII (1935), 485.

48. "The Author to His Loving Cosen," ed. Brown, p. 1.

49. In *The Poetry of Meditation,* p. 104, Professor Martz cites lines 13 and 14 in his slighting remarks on "A childe my Choyce."

50. *Macbeth,* I.vii.21-22, ed. Keneth Muir, *The Arden Edition of the Works of William Shakespeare,* 8th ed. (Cambridge, Mass., 1957), p. 40.

## Geoffrey Hill (essay date 1979)

SOURCE: Hill, Geoffrey. "The Absolute Reasonableness of Robert Southwell." In *The Lords of Limit: Essays on Literature and Ideas,* pp. 19-37. New York: Oxford University Press, 1984.

[*In the following essay, originally delivered as a lecture in 1979, Hill contends that Southwell's work contains elements of "mystical pragmatism."*]

When Robert Southwell wrote of the 'inhuman ferocity'[1] with which Catholic recusants were treated in Elizabethan England he was not toying with hyperbole. 'Grinding in the Mill, being beaten like slaves, and other outragious vsages' were, again in his own words, but 'ordinary punishments'[2]; and from the extraordinary, the 'more fierce and cruell'[3] penal torments inflicted upon certain priests and laymen, our powers of contemplation recoil. Ours, but not his. Southwell's prose writings, with the exception of the brief but crucial *Spiritual Exercises and Devotions,* were not intended primarily for his own ascetic meditational practice; they were, as the title of his major prose work makes explicit, epistles of comfort 'to the Reverend Priestes, & to the Honorable, Worshipful, & other of the Laye sort restrayned in Durance for the Catholicke Fayth'[4]; but they are not without indications that by such means he was able to apply Ignatian practice to a double purpose, 'seeing in imagination the material place where the object is that we wish to contemplate'.[5] The 'object contemplated'

was most frequently and formally the Passion of Christ; but there can be little doubt that for Southwell it was also his own 'almost inevitable martyrdom'.[6] The pioneering modern historian of recusancy, A. O. Meyer, remarked that a 'yearning for martyrdom' was 'the only fault that can be found with the priests of the Elizabethan age'; but in adding that 'the death of the martyrs ever remained the catholic mission's most effective means for achieving its purpose'[7] he may be thought to have annulled the force of the criticism and to have provided, albeit obliquely, a means for understanding the quality of mystical pragmatism which illuminates much of Southwell's work. I would justify my use of the dangerous term 'mystical' by referring to J. R. Roberts's statement that, in Southwell's poem, **'The Burning Babe'**, 'there is a note . . . of his having lost himself in ecstatic delight, the goal of Ignatian methodology',[8] although I have certain reservations about Roberts's emphasis and although I would not wish to claim this as the keynote for Southwell's work, or even as the prime characteristic of the Ignatian method practised by the Jesuit missionaries in Elizabethan England. Southwell, as his letters to Aquaviva, Agazario and Robert Persons reveal, was minutely and meticulously practical in his conduct of missionary matters, seeking permission, for instance, to 'bless 2,000 rosaries and 6,000 grains, for here all are asking for such objects'.[9] Southwell's predecessor in the field, Edmund Campion, had 'particularly recommended . . . that such of the Society as should be sent upon the *English* Mission, should be able Preachers' and Southwell's own suggestions were fully in accord with this precedent. He wrote to Fr Agazario in Rome: 'Every priest here is useful, especially those who are well skilled in moral theology and controversy . . . Preachers are here in great request: hence it is most important that the students should practise themselves, so as to acquire readiness of speech and a plentiful supply of matter'.[10] As the editors of the Clarendon Press text of his poems remind us, 'English was for him the language of his apostolate'. After years of exile he needed to apply himself 'with much diligence to the study of his native tongue'.[11]

Southwell does not shirk the word 'controversy'; and neither should we. Louis L. Martz has written of 'an England shaken by a threefold controversy, Catholic against Anglican against Puritan'[12]; but Meyer refers to 'the internal divisions within the catholic camp';[13] and more recent studies confirm this view. Dr John Bossy has drawn attention to the 'mutual recrimination'[14] and 'stress between [recusant] clergy and laity'; and his assessment is endorsed by J. C. H. Aveling's suggestion that 'amongst English Catholics' in general there existed an 'anti-Jesuit opposition of a powerful and virulent kind'.[15] 'Threefold' must therefore become 'fourfold' and the statement rephrased to read 'Catholic against Catholic against Anglican against Puritan'.

Such statements must, at the least, be allowed as caveats against the 'special pleading' of the 'English Catholic legend',[16] as Aveling calls it. Even Pierre Janelle, in his justly esteemed study *Robert Southwell the Writer* (1935), associates certain admirable qualities—'a cheerful and loving patience, a gentle and restrained manliness'[17]—too exclusively with pre-Reformation Englishness and with Elizabethan recusant Englishness in particular. That such tones are manifestly present, in the key-works of Edmund Campion and Robert Southwell, one would not for a moment dispute. What is disputable is the contention that these qualities are simply attributable to heredity or national characteristics. Martz is on surer ground in associating that 'mild, moderate, and cheerful temper',[18] which characterizes some of Southwell's finest work, with Franciscan tradition and practice. Janelle himself is aware that Franciscan ascetical writings were 'in great favour among the early Jesuits. Southwell was at one with his order in this respect'.[19] If we adopt Janelle's terms, we migh call 'a cheerful and loving patience' Franciscan, a 'gentle and restrained manliness' Ignatian; and say that both strands are united in the prose and verse of Southwell and in Campion's brief masterpiece, his 'Challenge' or 'Letter to the Council', vulgarly known as 'Campion's Brag'.[20]

Southwell composed his *Humble Supplication* 'rapidly and vehemently'; Campion's 'Challenge' was 'written without preparation, and in the hurry of a journey',[21] but one would hesitate to call such works 'spontaneous effusions'.[22] They have nothing in common with that facile 'self-expression' which so debases the current acceptance of 'spontaneity'. Such ease and rapidity as they manifest are the issue of years of arduous rhetorical and meditational discipline, both classical and Ignatian. They are, moreover, the fruit of a 'well-ordered will';[23] impulse and effect are at one. Fr Christopher Devlin has written that 'the deliberate refusal to allow desire and choice to be separated was the main inspiration of seventeenth-century religious art and poetry'[24] and his words might be justly applied to the work of these two sixteenth-century Jesuits. 'Cheerful . . . patience' and 'restrained manliness' have to be seen as, at one and the same time, the expression of 'desire' and the choice of a 'suitable controversial means of expression'.[25]

The Proclamation of 1591, 'A declaration of great troubles pretended against the Realme by a number of Seminarie Priests and Iesuists . . .', demonstrated the prescience of Campion's 'Challenge', written some ten years earlier, before the full spate of persecutions, in anticipation of just such accusations and slanders.[26] 'Brag' was itself a term of abuse foisted by the opposition on Campion's apologia. The 1591 Proclamation, to which Southwell made an immediate reply, attacked the missionary priests as 'dissolute young men' disguised in a variety of 'apparell', 'many as gallants, yea in all colours, and with feathers . . . and many of them in their behauior as Ruffians . . .'[27] Edmund Campion, after his capture, had been addressed by his Anglican adversaries in public disputation as *'miles gloriosus'*,[28] that is, as the strutting and braggart mercenary of Plautine and Renaissance comedy. It is in such a context that one must interpret the truism that 'the most important weapons for mission work were casuistry and controversy'.[29] Southwell's controversialist skill, like Campion's, took effect in appearing non-controversial. They abstained from what Helen C. White has pithily termed 'the creative art of denigration'[30] and practised instead a polemic of rapprochement. It was possible, of course, to be master of both styles. In the preface to the 1585 edition of his *Christian Directorie guiding Men to their Salvation,* Fr Robert Persons pleaded that 'a spirite of contradiction and contention . . . for the most parte hindereth devotion'[31] but between 1592 and 1594 he was directing what have been called 'uncompromising and inflammatory writings',[32] some of them against his co-religionists. It was possible, also, for a particular rhetorical gesture to be the mask of a quite contrary intent. The title-page of the 'Rhemes' New Testament (1582), reads like an epitome of this method. 'Translated faithfvlly into English', the work claims to have been undertaken 'for cleering the Controversies in religion, of these daies'; but in the light of the quotation from St Augustine, which serves as one of its two epigraphs, 'cleering . . . Controversies' means confounding 'Heretikes: vvhose deceites cease not to circumuent and beguile . . . the more negligent persons'. The 'Rhemes' 'annotations' are also thoroughly contentious.[33]

'Controversy', says Meyer, 'had its poets too'.[34] One of these, the 'witty and courageous martyr' Richard Gwynne, wrote a number of so-called 'carols' in Welsh. Of Gwynne's song of triumph at the assassination of the Protestant Prince William of Orange, Fr J. H. Pollen remarks that 'it is plainly wanting both in forbearance and in good feeling'.[35] Meyer calls it 'a terrible example of the lengths to which religious excitement can drive a man' but presents it as 'a solitary case, an ugly discord breaking in upon the pure harmony of the poetry of English catholics'.[36] The 'carol' is in fact far less 'terrible' in tone and content than Meyer suggests and, as an example of controversialist rhetoric, seems scarcely remarkable. Even so, those apologetical arguments which attribute fanatical enthusiasm to none but Puritan extremists and 'caddish'[37] behaviour only to erastian deans and time-serving judges and magistrates are notably unfair; and that vision of the pre-dissolution Church, movingly evoked by a modern Catholic historian ('the intimate religion of the little shrines . . . God's Presence in tranquillity in the fields'),[38] is a beautiful but nostalgic image for which some Englishmen already possibly 'hankered'[39] as early as the mid-sixteenth century, and which perhaps bore, and bears, little resemblance to late medieval and early Tudor reality. As Dr Christopher Haigh has cogently argued, in a closely-documented survey, in pre-Reformation Lancashire 'local communities met together only in the churches' and, 'violence was even more likely [there] than elsewhere'. There is a violence of morbid religious excitement, and Dr Haigh gives instances of this.[40] There is also something that Wordsworth called 'savage torpor', concomitant with 'sluggishness of spirit', 'spissa ignorantia'.[41] Elizabethan and Jacobean Catholicism not only endured both kinds, it also perpetuated them, or sank into them,[42] and it is a fair inference that Southwell recognized that the contest to which he had been summoned was to be fought upon a number of fronts.

Richard Topcliffe, the government's chief pursuivant and inquisitor, was an atrocious psychopath, 'homo sordidissimus',[43] as one missionary priest called him, 'a man most infamous and hateful . . . for his bloody and butcherly mind',[44] according to another. When such a creature calls Southwell's cousin Anthony Copley 'the most desperate youth that liveth', one cannot accept the statement without reserve, as Fr Thurston has equably remarked.[45] There is independent evidence, however, to substantiate Janelle's description of Copley as 'a wayward, hot-headed, uncontrollable scapegrace'.[46] Whatever emotional stability he came to possess seems to have been due to Southwell's influence.

Southwell's great predecessor, too, had known similar young Catholics of 'ardent temperament and keen literary appreciations'.[47] Richard Simpson, in his *Edmund Campion: a Biography* (1867), names the members of an 'association' of 'young gentlemen of great zeal and forwardness in religion' who acted as guides and 'lay assistants' to the first generation of Jesuit missionaries on their journeys around England.[48] Numbered among this ardent and appealing company were Anthony Babington and the young poet Chidiock Tichborne. It is surely not without significance that one of Babington's harshest critics was to be Robert Southwell. In a letter to Aquaviva he wrote of 'that wicked and ill-fated conspiracy, which did to the Catholic cause so great mischief';[49] and in the *Humble Supplication* he referred, with a more aloof contempt, to 'greene witts . . . easily . . . ouerwrought by Master Secretaries subtill and sifting witt'.[50]

It must be acknowledged that the 1591 Proclamation, in its mocking use of the word 'feathers', though false in tone is probably correct on a point of fact. Southwell was by no means the only missionary priest to concede, uneasily, that it was frequently necessary to appear in 'apparell' quite at odds with 'the graue attire that best suteth our Calling'.[51] To the reasonable question how a turn of phrase can be at once false and true, there is the answer that it is a matter of context; that equity requires

a respect for context. It was one thing for Fr Gerard, in hourly peril of arrest, torture and a protracted death, to go about 'garnished with gold or silver lace, satin doublets, and velvet hose of all colours';[52] it was quite another for the not unlikeable young Anthony Copley, when a student at the English College in Rome, to appear in the pulpit with a rose between his teeth.[53] But slander, no respecter of persons or contexts, would have little difficulty in seeming to equate the one with the other; and in making both appear as gestures of braggart panache, the preening of a *miles gloriosus,* a self-vaunting *os impudens.*

Southwell's necessary choice, therefore, was the achievement of a style ardent yet equable, eloquent and assured yet without 'panache', that is, not tricked out with 'feathers'. It is worth saying again that he was nonetheless a controversialist for sounding non-controversial. Dr William Allen, founder and president of the English College at Douay, had written that, since 'heretics', Protestant controversialists, were wont to 'plume themselves' on their mastery of the vulgar tongue, the future missionaries should practise to 'acquire greater power and grace' in the vernacular.[54] Janelle suggests, a little tendentiously, that in the penultimate chapter of *An Epistle of Comfort* 'Southwell carefully avoids the threatening tone that was so common a feature in the polemical writings of contemporary Puritans'.[55] Ernst Cassirer, it is true, once called puritanism 'a thoroughly quarrelsome and quarrel-seeking religion';[56] but Christopher Morris fairly reminds us that Archbishop Whitgift's chaplain 'the "saintly" Lancelot Andrewes could make a cruel joke in execrable taste' at the expense of the imprisoned Puritan separatist Henry Barrowe, whose response was 'you speak philosophically but not Christianly'. Catholic and Puritan alike fell victim to Elizabeth's penal laws and Anglicanism was 'as Erastian as Elizabeth herself'.[57] Meyer has remarked that 'no puritan could have surpassed in bitterness and hatred'[58] the vituperation of the 1591 Proclamation whose 'contumelious termes'[59] occasioned from Fr Robert Persons 'a reply full of bitterness, hatred and scorn'[60] and from Fr Robert Southwell *An Humble Supplication.*

In confronting the strategy of the Proclamation Southwell undertook a double defence. Edmund Campion, in his great 'Challenge' of 1580, had appealed for 'fair light', 'good method' and 'plain dealing' to be 'cast upon these controversies, that possibly her zeal of truth and love of her people shall incline her noble Grace to disfavour some proceedings hurtful to the Realm, and procure towards us oppressed more equitie'.[61] The Proclamation lards its threats and vilifications with well-timed cynical gestures of mock reasonableness and tolerance, appealing in the name of all that is 'naturall' and 'honorable' against that which is 'wilfull' and 'monstrous', 'the slanderous speeches and Libelles of the Fugitiues abroade'. In the England of Elizabeth, say the authors of the Proclamation, those 'professing contrary religio[n]' who 'refuse to come to Church' 'are knowen not to be impeached for the same . . . but onely by payment of a pecuniary summe . . .'[62] Answered even in its own terms, without reference to executions and incarcerations, this is the most wilful and monstrous cant. Such travesties of 'fair light', 'good method' and 'plain dealing' are of course far more numbing than the most savage vituperation. Southwell's double defence, I suggest, required him to ensure not only that Campion's pedal-note 'equitie' continued to resonate freely but also that the Proclamation's speciously equable tone was refuted by a 'power and grace' able to judge such a travesty, not so much by attack as by being simply yet manifestly on the level. Southwell appeals, in the manner of Campion, directly to Elizabeth herself, to 'measure [her] Censure with reason and Equity'[63] and to weigh a 'sound beliefe' against a 'shadow of likelihoode':

> For to say we doe [the alleged treasons] vpon hope to be enritched with those possessions that others now enjoy hath but very small semblance of probability, considering how much likelyer we are to Inherit your Racks and possesse your places of Execution, then to surviue the present Incumbents of spirituall livings, or live to see any dignities at the King of Spaines disposition.[64]

In its poise and resolution, phrase taking the measure of phrase, this passage both seeks and obtains satisfaction for the injury received; but it is a sign of Southwell's unflaunted mastery that the satisfaction does not seem to be the effect of a rhetorical 'turn' or the consummation of a mere *reductio ad absurdum*. We are persuaded that Southwell, in every sense, delivers a just sentence. 'Let it be scanned with Equity, how little seeming of truth [the Proclamation's charge of sedition] carrieth'.[65]

It is noteworthy to what extent Southwell, across the range of the prose and verse composed during his six years' active apostolate, sounds and resounds the simple clear note of Campion's 'Challenge' calling for 'more equitie' towards the oppressed recusant minority. Time and again the word is spoken with direct, unaffected eloquence; and yet, ironically, involved in the term there remains a virtually insoluble ambiguity both of primary definition and of circumstantial application. 'For a long time', F. W. Maitland observes, 'English equity seem[ed] to live from hand to mouth'. He also says that 'no one was prepared to define by legislation what its place should be'.[66] The *OED* article on 'equity' defines it as 'the recourse to general principles of justice (the *naturalis aequitas* of Roman jurists) to correct or supplement the provisions of the law'; but it remains a moot point whether such 'recourse' signifies an attainable legal process or a hypothetical 'notion of an appeal to "higher law"'.[67] There is a particular passage in

Southwell's work where the citing of 'equitie' strikes one with the full force of a parable, an exemplary figure bearing witness to a sustainable reality. In the beautiful prose meditation, printed in 1591, *Marie Magdalens Funeral Teares,* the weeping penitent standing before the empty tomb is supposed, for the argument's sake, to consider it an 'impeachment' of her 'right' for Christ thus to 'conuey himselfe away without thy consent'. Since it is a 'rule in the lawe of nature' that a donor cannot 'dispose of his gift without the possessors priuitie', 'thou maiest imagine it a breach of equitie', 'if he hath take[n] a way himself'.[68] In the induction to his long poem **Saint Peter's Complaint** there are, again, lines which have an emblematic containment:

> If equities even-hand the ballance held,
> Where *Peters* sinnes and ours were made the weightes:[69]

Elsewhere, however, in other sections of *Marie Magdalens Funeral Teares,* in the *Humble Supplication,* also of 1591, in the 'Letter to Sir Robert Cecil', of 6 April 1593, and in the *Short Rules of a Good Life* (1595) Southwell employs the term 'equity' in what we may refer to as an 'appealing' pattern: 'Thogh I were to sue to the greatest tyrant, yet the equitie of my sute is more then halfe a grant'; 'And as the equity of the cause, doth breath courage into the defendors'; '. . . might in equity Challenge all mens penns to warne you of soe perilous Courses'; '. . . and incline you to measure your Censure with reason and Equity'; '. . . so far as with justice and equity they can demand'; 'For though an indifferent arbiter . . . could not in equity disprove my courses'.[70]

According to Hugh Trevor-Roper, the 'great age of the recusants was . . . the age of their greatest dilemma'.[71] The Papal Bull of 1570, *Regnans in Excelsis,* pronouncing sentence of excommunication upon Elizabeth, was sufficiently hasty in conception and 'uncanonical'[72] in its terminology to permit some seeming latitude in the matter of negotiation and compromise. The 'declaration of allegiance' of 1585, submitted by the wealthy and influential Catholic layman Sir Thomas Tresham, was 'an attempt to work out some kind of acceptable division between the spheres of influence which might be covered by a Catholic gentleman's relation to his queen and his relation to his priest'.[73] And for the next twenty years, during which some one hundred and eighty Catholic priests and laymen went to the scaffold[74] and while his own feelings grew increasingly hostile towards the Jesuit mission, Tresham, with exemplary patience or remarkable obtuseness, persisted in his attempts to effect a compromise between conscience and 'acceptability'. Such a compromise was, in fact, unattainable because, as Christopher Morris has argued[75] with cogent irony, the government, in Machiavellian fashion, proceeded 'in accordance with "reason of state", which was somehow different from normal reason'.

When Robert Southwell, having already been tortured several times, was brought for interrogation before the Privy Council, he was complimented on the courtesy of his demeanour and was asked why he had not behaved with equal reasonableness to his tormentor Topcliffe. 'Because,' he answered, 'I have found *by experience* that the man is not open to reason.'[76] This strikes one as being the most crucial of confrontations, the most searching of contexts. The mission-priests faced a situation in which the 'normal reason' of men like Tresham was compromised at every turn by 'reason of state'. Southwell's retort, in an instant, both judges the travesty and redeems the word. Equity was, indeed, forced to live 'from hand to mouth'. Where it chiefly endured, sustained and sustaining, was in printed 'supplication' and 'challenge', in the extempore but nonetheless deeply meditated speeches in court, in enforced 'conferences' and on the scaffold; and, of course, in Southwell's poems. Maitland[77] has said that 'after the brilliant thirteenth century . . . Law was . . . divorced from literature'. Through the nature of a paradox, a glimpse of reunification was made possible, in the age of Elizabeth, by the work of those whose lives were forfeit to a more savage kind of divorce. It has been argued that 'during Shakespeare's lifetime equity[78] was both an important ethical principle and, through the Court of Chancery, an increasingly strong legal force'. *Measure for Measure* has been called a 'masterpiece of comedy on the theme of administering the law with justice and equity'. But for the arraigned priests and laymen there was no Court of Chancery and the only theatre in which they could enact their 'theme' of the weighing of justice with equity was the public arena of controversy, trial and execution. The strength of the creative paradox turns, then, upon the legal helplessness of the petitioners. As Paul Vinogradoff has shown,[79] there was a forensic precedent in Roman Law, going back at least as far as the Bologna law school of the late eleventh century, in which Irnerius defined 'equity' as 'the mere enunciation of a principle of justice'. 'Mere enunciation' in the work of Campion and Southwell had not only to proclaim the inviolability of an ethical principle but also to appear invested in the authority of 'strong legal force', even though its only court of appeal was the appeal of its own eloquence. It is our recognition of this fact which justifies Pierre Janelle's allusion to Southwell's conduct at his trial and execution as being 'a work of art of supreme beauty'.[80]

Our concern is with the style of Robert Southwell, a poet in both verse and prose. Style is not simply the manner in which a writer 'says what he has to say'; it is also the manner of his choosing not to say. There is a distinction to be drawn here between the manner of not-saying and the demeanour of silence. At his trial in 1535 Sir Thomas More had made what R. W. Chambers calls his 'great plea for the liberty of silence'.[81] The Elizabethan missionaries were, in all humility, proud of their silence under torture. The seminary-priest John Ingram, soon to be executed at Newcastle upon Tyne, reported that Topcliffe had called him a 'monster' of 'strange taciturnity'.[82] Robert Cecil told how he had seen Southwell, subjected to 'a new kind of torture', 'remain as dumb as a tree-stump; and it had not been possible to make him utter one word'.[83] This very 'taciturnity' and 'dumbness' are in themselves powerful coadjutors to the eloquence of the polemical and meditative writings. But 'choosing not-to-say', just as much as choice of words, presupposes a 'hinterland'[84] of style, a 'back-country' of what might, for better or worse, have been said. In our necessary exploration of the 'back-country' of Southwell's eloquence we encounter violence and coarse preciosity and disgust, and what he himself significantly referred to as 'wittye crueltye'.[85]

There is a passage in Thomas Nashe's *The Unfortunate Traveller* (1594) describing a public execution:

> The executioner needed no exhortation herevnto, for of his owne nature was he hackster good inough . . . At the first chop with his wood-knife would he fish for a mans heart, and fetch it out as easily as a plum from the bottome of a porredge pot.[86]

A modern scholar has written that 'the pleasure in a job well done palliates some of the unpleasantness of the description';[87] which seems a cruelly inept comment on Nashe's 'witty cruelty'. At the execution of Fr Edmund Gennings in 1591, 'the martyr crying upon St Gregory his patron to assist him, the hangman astonished said with a loud voice, "God's wounds! His heart is in my hand and yet Gregory is in his mouth"'.[88] There is a world of difference between talk of pleasure palliating unpleasantness and Janelle's suggestion that Southwell made of his own execution 'a work of art of supreme beauty'; it is the difference between collusion and transfiguration. It has already been remarked that the Ignatian exercise of 'seeing in imagination the material place where the object is that we wish to contemplate' must, for Southwell, have involved the 'seeing' of his own almost inevitable martyrdom. In the *Epistle of Comfort* he writes:

> And as a cunninge imbroderer hauinge a peece of torne or fretted veluet for his ground, so contryueth and draweth his worke, that the fretted places being wroughte ouer with curious knottes or flowers, they farr excel in shew the other whole partes of the veluet: So God being to worke vpon the grou[n]de of our bodyes, by you so rente & dismembred, will couer the ruptures, breaches, & wounds, which you haue made, with so vnspeakable glory, that the whole partes which you lefte shalbe highlye beautifyed by them.[89]

An immediate objection would be that Southwell is too much the 'cunning embroiderer', that he 'contriveth and draweth' too 'curiously'; but a more patient consideration would have to concede that the 'ground' upon which he weaves his variations could not be more plainly stated: 'our bodyes . . . rente & dismembred'. Southwell is foresuffering his own agony even as he rises serenely above the fear and the violence: 'Our teares shalbe turned into triumphe, our disgrace into glorye, all our miseryes into perfect felicitye'.[90]

Violence of one kind Southwell not only allows but approves. In his Latin *Spiritual Exercises and Devotions,* which belong to the years of his novitiate, he writes:

> It is a great hindrance to refrain from using violence to oneself, to offer but a feeble resistance to the passions and other obstacles, or to adopt remedies which are almost useless. 'For the kingdom of heaven suffers violence and the violent bear it away.' Moreover experience shows that even the most powerful means are scarcely sufficient for our cure.[91]

This reflection turns upon a scriptural text, Matthew 11:12, which 'had particular significance for Southwell':[92] *Regnum coelorum vim patitur, et violenti rapiunt illud.* This is a text which is recognized by modern commentators to be notoriously 'difficult', 'enigmatic'. Who are 'the men of violence'? The modern 'consensus' agrees that the term must be glossed in a pejorative sense: they are the men of 'hostile intent': Herod, the Pharisees, 'official Israel', the persecutors of both John the Baptist and Christ.[93] This reading would have been so apposite at a time when 'official England' seemed bent on out-Heroding Herod, that one must with some astonishment concede that Southwell, who quotes the text several times, everywhere glosses it in a favourable allegorizing sense. In the *Epistle of Comfort,* where the text is also used as the epigraph on the title-page,[94] he writes 'and though our champions, be of more courage, and our foes more enfeebled, since our redemption, yet doth *the Kingdome of heauen still suffer violence, and the violent beare it awaye*'. There might seem to be a transient ambiguity here; but my feeling is that Southwell resolves it by adding a phrase from 2 Timothy 2: 5, *'and none shall be crowned, but they that haue lawfullye foughte for it'*.[95] The second stanza of the lyric **'At Home in Heaven'** also turns upon the Matthean text. Addressing the aspiring soul Southwell writes:

> Thy ghostly beautie offred force to God,
> It cheyn'd him in the lynckes of tender love.[96]

He is in no way at odds here with the reading established by the early Church Fathers or with the scriptural exegesis of his time, whether Catholic or Protestant. Luther had written, quoting this text, 'in my judgment,

prayer is indeed a continuous violent action of the spirit as it is lifted up to God'.[97] The so-called 'Evangelical Catholic' Juan de Valdés commented on the text thus: 'if you wish to take the Kingdom of Heaven, do violence to yourself, and so you will fear nothing'.[98] The 'Rhemes' New Testament of 1582 does not annotate the text; but the Jesuit commentator, Cornelius à Lapide, provides a detailed allegorizing gloss. Though only six years younger than Southwell, he cannot truly be considered as being of the same 'generation'. He became Professor of Exegesis at Louvain in 1596, the year after the martyr-poet's death, and his New Testament *Commentaries,* begun in 1616, were not published until 1639. It is not unreasonable to suppose, however, that Lapide's seventeenth-century *Commentaries* drew upon the kind of Biblical exegesis prevalent in Jesuit circles in the closing years of the previous century. Lapide's interpretation states that 'for the Kingdom of Heaven's sake worldly men do violence to themselves by the cultivation of repentance, poverty, continence, mortification'. He further interprets 'violence' as the heroism necessary to endure the sufferings of martyrdom: 'Thus let each believer consider that with his utmost energy he must struggle up to Heaven by means of a ladder hedged about with knives'.[99]

Although Southwell's unquestioning gloss on 'violence' in Matthew 11:12 seems too bland and too partial when read in the light of modern New Testament criticism, in other contexts he clearly associates the word with Herodian savagery and with the disorders of the private will. He writes, in one passage, of 'tiranical persecution . . . most violentlye bent' against Catholics, in another of 'violent tortures', and, in a third, of those who 'haue with violence martyred and oppressed vs'. He depicts the 'violence' of Mary Magdalen's grief as well as her 'violent' love. There is indeed a suggestion that he associates 'violence' with the temptation to do wrong in a good cause: 'if thy Lord might be recouered by violence . . . wouldest thou aduenture a theft to obtaine thy desire'.[100] When, in the brief but most beautiful 'A prayer in temptation', he writes, 'I am urged against my will and violently drawn to think that which from my heart I detest'[101] it is as though we have found the focus upon which these different lines of emphasis converge. One might risk the suggestion that in these radical changes of connotation, Southwell is instinctively probing, more keenly than he would consciously recognize, his own conformity with doctrine and the limits of his own rhetoric; as though in matters theological his poetic vision had a prescient advantage over his theology. But the contrary suggestion is equally tenable: that the range of possibility in 'violence' in no way eludes him; that his method is simply and profoundly eloquent, 'speaking out', 'making clear', the complex hazards of equity:

[A]s not to feel sorrow in sorrowful chances is to want sense, so not to bear it with moderation is to want understanding; the one brutish, the other effeminate.

Janelle is quite right, however, to suggest that here 'mere reasonableness [is] raised to a divinely spiritual plane'.[102] Southwell's style is equity made palpable; it is also, as I have already implied, an art of 'transfiguration'. The term connotes both 'metamorphosis' and 'elevation'. What, one may ask, is to be transfigured? And one may answer: the violence, the preciosity and disgust, the 'witty cruelty', the 'hinterland' of Elizabethan mannerism and atrocity. In a significant sense, for the devout recusant the medium of 'transfiguration' already existed in the form of the reliquary: 'Of the venerable martyr [Thomas] Bolliquer . . . a little piece of his heart . . . some of his praecordia . . . some papers greased with his fat . . .' Richard Simpson commented in 1857—and Dom Bede Camm quotes him with approval—'these relics were not the less venerable on account of the disgusting processes they had gone through; the horror does not attach to them, but to the brutes who presided over the butchery'.[103] This is well said, but the very strength of Simpson's emphasis registers the intensity of the 'horror' and the 'disgust' which are there to be overcome. A manuscript 'Catalogue of Martyrs', written *c.* 1594, probably in the hand of Southwell's friend and co-worker John Gerard, records the martyrdom of Fr Thomas Pilchard, 'quartered' in 1587. The 'officers retorninge home, many of them died presently crying out they were poisoned with the smell of his bowells . . . A laye man was executed there some 4 years after . . . whoe beinge asked at his deathe, [what] had moved him to that resolution, etc., he saide, "Nothinge but the smell of a pilcharde"'. This is the kind of thing that Southwell 'lived with' in every sense. In 1584, while still at the English College in Rome, he received, from a friend who had been standing 'under the gibbet', a detailed account of the martyrdom of George Haydock.[104] For Southwell the 'ladder hedged about with knives' could never have been a mere emblem;[105] and, in this, I believe, is one of the sources of his rhetorical strength. To speak of his 'fastidiousness' in the face of such atrocious business might seem to imply a wincing kind of sensitivity. What he attains is rather an eloquent moderation, neither 'brutish' nor 'effeminate'. He too could contrive a 'conceit' out of disembowelling but his witty exercise has none of the cruel flippancy of Nashe and differs markedly from the coarse and acrid punning in the 'Catalogue of Martyrs'. In a letter of December 1586 to Fr Agazario, he writes: 'You have "fishes" there [i.e. in Rome] greatly wanted here, which, "when disembowelled, are good for anointing to the eyes and drive the devils away," while, if they live, "they are necessary for useful medicines"'.[106] Southwell's letters from England were sometimes written in a 'veiled style' for reasons of security; but these words are not so much

like a 'code' as like a serenely witty form of tact. They resemble what an Elizabethan musician would have called a 'division upon a ground', a variation upon some verses from chapter 6 of the Apocryphal Book of Tobias:

> Then sayd the Angel to him: Take out the entralles of this fishe, and his hart, and gal, and liuer, keepe to thee: for these are necessarie and profitable for medecines . . . If thou put a little peece of his hart vpon coales, the smoke therof driueth out al kinde of diuels, either from man or from woman, so that it cometh no more vnto them.[107]

A recusant martyr's 'entralles' were, of course, 'taken out', his heart was burned, fragments of his body were kept by the faithful as 'necessarie . . . medecines'. Southwell, significantly, adapts his source to suggest the virtues of the living priest as well as those of the 'embowelled' martyr. It is noteworthy too that both the minatory 'exemplum' of Pilchard's bowels and Southwell's 'conceit' of ministration and martyrdom must surely refer to the same scriptural source. The first, however, is pitched at the level of Tudor chapbook or even jest-book; it is, literally, a 'vulgar spectacle'. I have said that Southwell 'lived with' this kind of thing in every sense; and he was also capable of exploiting vulgar spectacle. His *Epistle of Comfort* contains 'a warning to the persecutors' as blatantly *ad hominem* as anything in the 'Catalogue of Martyrs' or Bunyan's *Grace Abounding*:

> Remember the sodayne and horrible deathe of one Yonge an Apostata and Pourswivaunt who pursuing a Catholike at Lambeth fell doune on the sodayne, ere he could laye handes on him that he persecuted and foming at the mouthe presentlye dyed.[108]

Even though, as is well known, Southwell worked mainly among the nobility and gentry, and though Arundel House must have provided an exceptionally cultured spiritual environment, he was nonetheless 'hedged round' with sordid violence; he knew that his own execution would be a 'vulgar spectacle' too. I do not imply that he was 'sceptical' of these popular marvels (indeed, he challenges anyone who might doubt that the Thames stood still on the day of Campion's martyrdom).[109] I do suggest, however, that one of the achievements of his own polemical style is its ability to turn both injustice and 'revenge' in the direction of equity; towards 'the reparation of wrongs rather than the punishment of offences'.[110]

More than one authority has described Southwell's characteristic method as that of 'transformation',[111] and it is a word which matches the terminology of Biblical scholars discussing another of Southwell's texts: Philippians 3:21. 'Transformation' can be read both as an acknowledgement that a significant amount of Southwell's work comprises 'translations, adaptations . . . imitations' and 'parodies' and as a recognition of a process that he himself called 'wonderful alteratio[n]'.[112] Strictly interpreted, this means the radical change in 'mens maners' engendered by the blood of martyrs. Figuratively applied, it could be said to describe a crucial 'turn' which is a feature of his style:

> And this is that which Saint *Paule* sayd: *Reformabit corpus humilitatis nostrae, configuratum corpori claritatis suae*: He shall reforme the body of our humility confygured vnto the bodye of his brightnesse. Whiche phrase of speache argueth, that the more the body for him is humbled in torments, the more shall yt be partaker of hys brightnesse in glorye.[113]

'Reform' is the 1582 'Rhemes' reading of the text which a modern scholar paraphrases as '[He] will refashion our body of lowliness to share the form of his body of glory'.[114] The doctrinal point which is currently stressed—'that Paul does not think of his eternal blessedness in terms of the separation of the soul from the body'—is not the matter upon which Southwell concentrates. His concern is to affirm both that the 'scattered parts' of the martyrs will be 'reformed', restored, put together again; and that in due proportion as the body is disfigured for His sake on earth so it shall partake of 'transformation' at Christ's Parousia.[115] Southwell's 'phrase of speech' is one that 'argues' for ultimate equity. But again, it is a sense of equity which turns upon a meticulous attention to sequence and context. As he is at pains to make clear, the transfiguration upon Mount Tabor preceded the Passion. It was more a sign of an initiation to extremity of suffering than a reward for suffering endured and transcended. The word 'reason' itself becomes part of the sinew of Southwell's argument here:

> There is no reason, that Christe shoulde shew him selfe more fauorable to vs, that haue bene his enemyes, then to his owne bodye, neyther can we iustlye complayne, if ere we find him, he giue vs a sipp of that bitter chalice, of which for our sakes he was contente to drincke so full a draught. Yea we may be hartelye glad, if after long teares and deepe syghes, we maye in the ende fynde him at all, whether it be in the pouertye of the cribb and maunger, or in the agonyes of his bloodye sweate in the gardeyne, or in the middest of blasphemyes, reproches, and false accusations at the tribunals, or in the tormentes of a shamefull death vpon the Crosse.[116]

Christ 'transfigured in *Mounte Thabor* . . . was also at the same time, heard talkinge *de excessu* of his bitter passion'.[117] Christ 'transfigured', therefore, is not the Christ-in-glory of the Parousia. What Yeats was to call 'Calvary's turbulence'[118] was perhaps better understood by Southwell. His 'turns' are models of, and ways of mastering, the turbulence in 'the air around him' and in his own spirit: 'For Thy sake allow me to be tortured, mutilated, scourged, slain and butchered' he had written in his early *Spiritual Exercises and Devotions,* adding 'I refuse nothing'.[119] These three words are of radical significance: they are the 'wonderful alteration' of a hovering morbidity into a positive oblation.

I have referred earlier to the 'hinterland' of Southwell's style and to the violence and preciosity and disgust which we encounter there. There was also, in Elizabethan as in modern literature, a disgustingly violent preciosity. We are assured that Southwell knew a fair amount of Ovid by heart;[120] and in the *Metamorphoses* the Elizabethan student could find, drawn with 'lingering-out sweet skill',[121] the flaying alive of Marsyas by Apollo. In Seneca's *Thyestes,* 'faythfully Englished' in 1560 by Jasper Heywood, the future Jesuit Provincial: 'From bosomes yet aliue out drawne the trembling bowels shake . . .' In John Studley's translation of the same dramatist's *Hippolytus,* the protagonist is trampled and torn to pieces amid the wreckage of his chariot:

> From bursten Paunch on heapes his blouddy bowells tumble thick . . .[122]

In the Elizabethan 'hinterland', where spectacular 'closet' horror can at any time become the routine hideousness of public spectacle, how can one say where metaphor ends and reality begins?

This weak rhetorical question is out of keeping, however, with Southwell's power to distinguish and affirm. At the heart of his own eloquent style stands a patristic text which, in the *Epistle of Comfort,* he attributes to St Cyprian confronting his persecutors:

> Whye doest thou turne thee to the fraylty of our bodyes? Why stryuest thou with the weaknesse of our fleshe? Encounter with the force of our minde; impugne the stoutnesse of our reasonable portion; disproue our faythe; ouercome vs by disputation if thou canst, ouercome vs by reason.[123]

It is here that we encounter the paradigm for that 'absolute reasonableness' to which my argument alludes. The 'force of our minde' is a key-term for Southwell's form of argument as Donne's 'masculine perswasive force'[124] is a key-term for his; but the differences of implication between the two phrases are greater than any apparent similarities. For Southwell, 'force of . . . minde' is manifested in the power to remain unseduced and unterrified, whereas Donne's words relish their own seductive strength. Dame Helen Gardner has fairly remarked that Donne forbids us to 'make any simple equation between the truth of the imagination and the truth of experience'.[125] If that is so we may regard Southwell as Donne's antithesis, for his constant practice is to show 'how well verse and vertue sute together'[126] and the 'simple equation' which Donne precludes is the 'equity' to which Southwell appeals in phrases which are like emblems of his faithful reason: 'Whose measure best with measured wordes doth sit'; 'Where vertues starres God sunne of justice is'; 'And though ech one as much as all receive, / Not one too much, nor all too little have'.[127]

The correlative of equity is sacrifice and Southwell sacrifices a great deal, even the poet's delight in self-sustaining, self-supporting wit. Helen C. White has written of his predilection for 'Baroque . . . transformation'[128] but, as I see it, the matter turns more upon his sensitivity to a secular domain of 'baroque' inequity, of 'uneven accompt', which he seeks, in his poetry as in his prose, to 'reform' to a 'just measure':[129] 'the affections ordinate, and measurable, all the passions gouerned by reason, and settled in a perfecte calme' and 'in the syghte of God'.[130] It is entirely characteristic of Southwell's art, however, that, 'ordinate and measurable' though it is, it brings us face to face with violent contradictions. We are bound to assent both to its mediocrity and its monotony, for 'mediocrity' is essentially nothing more nor less than 'measured conduct or behaviour' and 'monotony' is 'sameness of tone or pitch'. If, however, we take this latter term to mean 'wearisome sameness of effect, tedious recurrence of the same objects, actions, etc.', we give our assent to Southwell's indictment of our carnal world. In his eyes it is a world vacuously full of 'loathed pleasures', 'disordred order', 'pleasing horror', 'balefull blisse', 'Cruell Comforts'.[131] The existence of the carnal sinners is an oxymoronic treadmill; and their only means of redemption is by way of the divine paradox. As J. R. Roberts reminds us, Saint Ignatius was particularly 'awestruck' 'by the fact that the Creator had become man'[132] and Southwell is in this, as in all things else, Ignatian. God disadvantaged himself for man's advantage and the priest-poet is concerned to stress both sides of the redemptive equation:

> This little Babe so few dayes olde,
> Is come to ryfle sathans folde;
> All hell doth at his presence quake,
> Though he himselfe for cold doe shake:
> For in this weake unarmed wise,
> The gates of hell he will surprise.[133]

Jeffrey Wainwright draws attention to the 'naïve though winning concession' which he finds in one of Southwell's turns of phrase ('Passions I allow, and loues I approue . . .')[134]. 'Winning' is exquisitely apt. 'Naïve' calls for more care; but is justifiable, I believe. Wainwright directs us to the crux of Southwell's circumstance and achievement. Southwell is 'naïve', if 'witty cruelty' is the world's alternative; but if he is so, it is by choice; and the choice is doubly purposeful. His 'naïvety' is to some extent penitential, submitting the upstart creative 'will' to 'bonds' of humility; and it is, to a further extent, evangelistic. His Nativity Poems, wholly in keeping with Ignatian precept, as Roberts has shown, weigh the harshness and the tenderness of the scene at Bethlehem in order to win men to repentance and love.

One cannot choose 'naïvety', however, if one has no sophistication from which to turn. Southwell, as Janelle and Thurston have amply demonstrated, was a highly sophisticated master both of classical rhetoric and of the modern Euphuistic style. In 'New heaven, new warre' such words as 'ryfle' and 'surprise' are placed with a beautiful tact; and though the rhyme 'quake/ shake' may sound naïve we should not assume that naïvety is the cause. That 'complexity of association'[135] which Helen C. White detects elsewhere in Southwell's writings is here the 'ground' upon which he 'works', instead of 'curious knots and flowers', the lilt of a child's catechism. The paradox of the naked new-born babe, the shivering child who shivers the gates of hell, is at the heart of his vision. It is ultimately a vision of great serenity, but, as I have tried to show, that serenity is achieved in the full awareness of the realities of spiritual and legal violence.

There is a sad irony in the fact that Antonin Artaud, godfather of the 'theatre of cruelty', translated Southwell's **'The Burning Babe'** ['Le Bébé de Feu'] during his incarceration in the asylum at Rodez.[136] Southwell would not grudge him that grace; but it would be a matter for regret if the violent preciosities of extremism were to set their seal of approval on Southwell's profoundly different understanding of the condition of both the tormented and the ecstatic soul. 'Christe was . . . heard talkinge *de excessu* of his bitter passion'. 'Excessus' signifies 'ecstasy'.[137] The word was so used by Saint Bernard, the author closest perhaps to Southwell's heart, whose works he cited in *An Epistle of Comfort*; which were also his 'solace' during his imprisonment in the Tower.[138] We may seem here to have returned to J. R. Roberts's suggestion with which we began, that Southwell, in **'The Burning Babe'**, appears to have 'lost himself in ecstatic delight'. The circle is not quite closed, however. The 'pretty Babe all burning bright', the Christ Child, is 'scorched with excessive heate' which emanates from his own 'faultlesse breast'.[139] There is certainly more 'complexity of association' here than either Janelle or the Clarendon text editors allow. He dismisses it as 'the most hackneyed of all conceits'; they properly point out that it 'parodies . . . Petrarchan tradition';[140] but something further needs to be said. One would read 'excessive' heat simply in the *OED*'s 'neutral' sense, i.e. 'exceeding what is usual' not 'exceeding what is right', if one were not so aware of the striking parallels, detected by Martz, between this poem and such contemporary Jesuit devotional exercises as Puente's *Meditations* . . . The

Christ Child may indeed be talking 'de excessu' from amid a fiery ecstasy of sacrificial love; but I am unable to share Roberts's view that Southwell himself is 'lost . . . in ecstatic delight'. There is a note of deliberate naïvety in the poem which substantiates Martz's suggestion that it should be read as a 'variation . . . on the medieval nativity-ballad, done after the Jesuit manner'.[141] This fact would in no way preclude a sensitive apprehension of the nature of ecstatic experience. St Ignatius himself was much influenced by mystical tradition.[142] But deeply versed though Southwell may have been in the methodology of 'excessus', he was alert to the dangerous implications of excessive behaviour. 'Excesse of minde' is the 'Rhemes' translation of the term in Acts 10: 10, which the Authorized Version renders as 'trance'. Even so, Southwell, in his *Short Rules of a Good Life,* wrote that 'excess in the voice and immoderate loudness are always certain signs of passion and therefore ought to be used but upon some extraordinary necessity'.[143] For Southwell to have 'lost himself' merely in a poem would have required more self-centredness than he was capable of. This keenly witty man who was so properly sceptical of 'fancie' and 'selfe delight'[144] employed all the resources of his wit to moderate between grace and perll in this most dangerous area of the religious life. 'Let vs but consider, the last tragicall pageant of [Christ's] Passion, wherein he wone vs, and lost him selfe. And marke the excessiue loue shewed therin . . .'[145] he wrote in *An Epistle of Comfort.* 'Excess', 'excessive', 'de excessu', 'Passion', 'passion', 'violence', 'equitie': these are all cruces, the little crosses upon which the passion of his reasonableness is enacted for us. We have it on the authority of Fr Christopher Devlin that 'the Jesuit discipline, in the design of St Ignatius, sets up an interior tension which can only be resolved by crucifixion. At the heart of it there is an element of supernatural wildness . . .'[146] In the words 'discipline' and 'wildness' we confront that paradox which Southwell perfectly understood, as I believe he also understood the fulcrum of Ignatian 'design'. I would further suggest that the radical pun perceivable in 'ecstasy', in being 'beside oneself', either with a frenzy of egoistic inclinations or with a disciplined indifference to them, would not be lost on him.[147] When he was brought out to endure 'the torments of a shameful death' Southwell could speak, with perfect calm and tact, in the idiom of his own *Epistle of Comfort*: 'I am come hither to play out the last act of this poor life'.[148] Even at that moment he could retain his grasp on 'complexity' and yet speak with absolute simplicity. And it was such complex simplicity, I would finally claim, that enables this man of discipline to concede, in *Marie Magdalens Funeral Teares,* the 'wonderful alteration' of 'wildness' itself: 'Loue is not ruled with reason, but with loue'.[149]

## Notes

1. 'inhuman ferocity' / *Publications of the C[atholic] R[ecord] S[ociety]* (London, 1905-), vol. v: J. H. Pollen, SJ (ed.), *Unpublished Documents Relating to the English Martyrs,* 1 (1908), 325. Pollen's translation of Southwell's Latin.

2. 'Grinding . . . punishments' / Robert Southwell, *An Humble Supplication to Her Maiestie,* ed. R. C. Bald (Cambridge, 1953), 34

3. 'more fierce and cruell' / *CRS* v, 208: Richard Verstegan's Dispatches.

4. 'to the reverend . . . Fayth.' / *An Epistle of Comfort, To The Reverend Priestes, & to the Honorable, Worshipful, & other of the Laye sort restrayned in Durance for the Catholicke Fayth . . . Imprinted at Paris.* See Pierre Janelle, *Robert Southwell the Writer,'* reprint of the 1935 UK edition (Mamaroneck, NY, 1971), 310: 'really printed, perhaps, at a secret press in England' (London? 1587-8).

5. 'seeing . . . contemplate' / J. R. Roberts, 'The Influence of *The Spiritual Exercises* of St Ignatius on the Nativity Poems of Robert Southwell', *Journal of English and Germanic Philology,* LIX (1960), p. 452; cf. Janelle, op. cit., 109.

6. 'almost inevitable martyrdom' / *Humble Supplication,* xvii. Editorial introduction.

7. 'yearning . . . purpose' / A. O. Meyer, *England and the Catholic Church under Queen Elizabeth,* authorized translation by J. R. McKee (London, 1916), 190, 212.

8. 'there is a note . . . methodology' / Roberts, op. cit., p. 455; cf. Janelle, op. cit., 110, 'mystical outpourings'; Louis L. Martz, *The Poetry of Meditation,* revised edition (New Haven and London, 1962), 36, 69, 78, 83.

9. 'bless . . . objects' / *CRS* v, 319: Pollen's translation of Southwell's Latin. 'particularly . . . Preachers' / [Richard Challoner], *Memoirs of Missionary Priests* ([London] 1741), 42. Brotherton Library, University of Leeds: Special Collections.

10. 'Every priest . . . matter' / *CRS* v, 318, 316: Pollen's translation of Southwell's Latin.

11. 'English . . . tongue' / *The Poems of Robert Southwell, SJ,* ed. James H. McDonald and Nancy Pollard Brown (Oxford, 1967), xix-xx.

12. 'an England . . . Puritan' / Martz, op. cit., 9.

13. 'the internal . . . camp' / Meyer, op. cit., 171.

14. 'mutual recrimination' . . . laity'; / John Bossy, *The English Catholic Community 1570-1850* (London, 1975), 32.

15. 'amongst . . . kind' / J. C. H. Aveling, *The Handle and the Axe: the Catholic Recusants in England from Reformation to Emancipation* (London, 1976), 68.

16. 'special . . . legend' / ibid., 72, 67.

17. 'a cheerful . . . manliness' / Janelle, op. cit., 3.

18. 'mild . . . temper' / Martz, op. cit., 205.

19. 'in great favour . . . respect' / Janelle, op. cit., 109-10.

20. 'Campion's Brag' / cf. A. C. Southern, *Elizabethan Recusant Prose 1559-1582* (London, 1950), 151, 153-6.

21. 'rapidly . . . journey' / *Humble Supplication,* xvii; Richard Simpson, *Edmund Campion: A Biography,* new edition 'reprinted from a copy corrected by the learned Author before his death' (London, 1896), 225.

22. 'spontaneous effusions' / Janelle, op. cit., 109.

23. 'well-ordered will' / ibid., 111. The phrase is apt; though more recent scholarship seriously doubts Southwell's authorship of the translation from Estella.

24. 'the deliberate . . . poetry' / *The Sermons and Devotional Writings of Gerard Manley Hopkins* ed. Christopher Devlin, SJ (London, 1959), 118.

25. 'suitable . . . expression' / Janelle, op. cit., 153.

26. accusations and slanders / See Simpson, op. cit., 224-5.

27. The 1591 . . . Ruffians . . .' / *Humble Supplication,* xi, 60, 64.

28. *'miles gloriosus'* / Simpson, op. cit., 365, 367.

29. 'the most . . . controversy' / Meyer, op. cit., 210.

30. 'the creative art of denigration' / Helen C. White, 'Some Continuing Traditions in English Devotional Literature', in *Publications of the Modern Language Association,* 57, ii (1942), p. 966.

31. 'a spirite . . . devotion' / Quoted in Martz, op. cit., 8; cf. White, op. cit., p. 967.

32. 'uncompromising . . . writings' / R. C. Bald, 'Donne and Southwell', in *Humble Supplication,* 79.

33. The title-page . . . thoroughly contentious. / *The Nevv Testament of Iesus Christ, translated faithfvlly into English . . .* Printed at Rhemes . . . 1582. Brotherton Library, University of Leeds: Special Collections. For example, p. 182: '[Heretikes] may by penal lawes be co[m]pelled to the Catholike faith.'

34. 'Controversy . . . poets too' / Meyer, op. cit., 221.

35. 'Witty . . . feeling' / *CRS* v, 90-1.

36. 'a terrible . . . catholics' / Meyer, op. cit., 222.

37. 'caddish' / C. C. Martindale, SJ, 'Edmund Campion', in Maisie Ward (ed.), *The English Way* (London, 1933), 240: 'In Elizabeth's time the State became the cad as such'.

38. 'the intimate . . . fields' / David Mathew, 'John Fisher', ibid., 208.

39. 'hankered' / Bossy, op. cit., 11.

40. 'local . . . instances of this. / Christopher Haigh, *Reformation and Resistance in Tudor Lancashire* (Cambridge, 1975), 54, 64, 85, 145.

41. 'sluggishness . . . ignorantia' / Bossy, op. cit., 102, 223; cf. *CRS* xxxix (1942), *Letters and Memorials of Fr. Robert Persons,* I, 108.

42. Elizabethan . . . sank into them, / See Aveling, op. cit., 74, 151-3.

43. 'homo sordidissimus' / Henry Garnet, SJ, quoted in C. Devlin, *The Life of Robert Southwell Poet and Martyr* (London, 1956), 210.

44. 'a man . . . mind' / *John Gerard: The Autobiography of an Elizabethan,* translated from the Latin by Philip Caraman (London, 1951), 230.

45. 'the most desperate . . . equably remarked. / H. Thurston, 'Father Southwell the Euphuist', in *The Month,* 83 (1895), p. 243.

46. 'a wayward . . . scapegrace' / Janelle, op. cit., 55; cf. Devlin, *Life of Southwell,* 11, 74, 257n.

47. 'ardent . . . appreciations' / Thurston, op. cit., p. 243.

48. 'association . . . England. / Simpson, op. cit., 223.

49. 'that wicked . . . mischief' / *CRS* v, 314. Pollen's translation of Southwell's Latin.

50. 'greene witts . . . witt' / *Humble Supplication,* 18.

51. 'apparell . . . Calling' / ibid., 8.

52. 'garnished . . . colours' / Caraman, op. cit., 18n.

53. Anthony Copley . . . between his teeth / Devlin, *Life of Southwell,* 257n. *os impudens* / Simpson, op. cit., 368.

54. Dr William Allen . . . vernacular. / Janelle, op. cit., 7-9 and 9 n. 20. T. F. Knox's translation of Latin MS, English College, Rome.

55. 'Southwell . . . Puritans' / ibid., 198.

56. 'a thoroughly . . . religion' / Ernst Cassirer, *The Platonic Renaissance in England,* translated by J. P. Pettegrove (London, 1953), 74.

57. Christopher Morris . . . Elizabeth herself' / Christopher Morris, *Political Thought in England: Tyndale to Hooker* (London, 1953), 174-5, 126, 195.

58. 'no puritan . . . hatred' / Meyer, op. cit., 350.

59. 'contumelious termes' / *Humble Supplication,* 2.

60. 'a reply . . . scorn' / Meyer, op. cit., 351.

61. Edmund Campion . . . equitie'. / Southern, op. cit., 154-5.

62. The Proclamation . . . pecuniary summe . . .' / *Humble Supplication,* 60-1, 63.

63. 'measure . . . Equity' / ibid., 3.

64. 'Sound beliefe . . . disposition. / ibid., 14.

65. 'Let it be scanned . . . carrieth' / ibid.

66. 'For a long time . . . should be' / *Selected Historical Essays of F. W. Maitland,* chosen and introduced by Helen M. Cam (Cambridge, 1957), 133, 131. 'Its' refers to the Court of Chancery which dispensed equity.

67. 'notion . . . law'' / L. L. Fuller, *Legal Fictions* (Stanford, California, 1967), 87.

68. In the beautiful . . . himself'. / *Marie Magdalens Funeral Teares* [1591] by Robert Southwell, a Facsimile Reproduction with an Introduction by Vincent B. Leitch (Delmar, NY, 1975), 32 and 32 verso (henceforward *MMFT*).

69. If equities . . . weightes: / *Poems,* ed. cit., 75.

70. 'Thogh I were . . . disprove my courses'. / *MMFT,* 39 verso; 40 verso; *Humble Supplication,* 2-3; Robert Southwell, SJ, *Two Letters and Short Rules of a Good Life,* ed. Nancy Pollard Brown (Charlottesville, Va., 1973), 33, 79.

71. the 'great age . . . dilemma' / H. R. Trevor-Roper, *Historical Essays* (London, 1957), 92.

72. 'uncanonical' / Meyer, op. cit., 79.

73. 'declaration . . . priest' / Bossy, op. cit., 37.

74. And for the next . . . scaffold / *CRS* v, 8-17.

75. as Christopher Morris has argued / op. cit., 106.

76. 'Because . . . reason' / Devlin, *Life of Southwell,* 287.

77. Maitland has said / Maitland, op. cit., 125.

78. 'during Shakespeare's . . . equity' / J. W. Dickinson, 'Renaissance Equity and *Measure for Measure*', in *Shakespeare Quarterly,* XIII (1962), p. 287; W. Dunkel, 'Law and Equity in *Measure for Measure*', ibid., p. 285.

79. As Paul Vinogradoff has shown . . . / *Roman Law in Medieval Europe,* second edition (Oxford, 1929), 55-6, 66; see also 106: 'justitia est constans et perpetua voluntas jus suum cuique tribuendi. [the definition of justice as given in the Digest]'.

80. 'a work . . . beauty' / Janelle, op. cit., 286-7.

81. 'great plea . . . silence' / R. W. Chambers, *Thomas More,* second edition (London, 1938), 336.

82. 'monster . . . taciturnity'. / *CRS* v, 283.

83. 'a new kind . . . one word' / Janelle, op.cit., 66-7.

84. 'hinterland' / This term was suggested to me by D. W. Harding's brilliant essay, 'The Hinterland of Thought', in *Experience into Words,* paperback edition (London, 1974), 176ff. In fairness to Harding and myself it must be added that I employ it in a different sense.

85. 'wittye crueltye' / *Epistle of Comfort,* 125 verso, translating St Cyprian.

86. The executioner . . . porredge pot. / *The Works of Thomas Nashe,* Edited from the original texts by Ronald B. McKerrow, reprinted from the original edition with corrections and supplementary notes edited by F. P. Wilson, 4 vols (Oxford, 1958), II, 327.

87. 'the pleasure . . . description' / G. R. Hibbard, *Thomas Nashe: A Critical Introduction* (London, 1962), 174.

88. 'the martyr . . . his mouth'' / *CRS* v, 207.

89. And as a cunninge . . . by them. / ed. cit., 203 recto, verso.

90. 'Our teares . . . felicitye' / ibid., 113 recto.

91. It is a great . . . our cure. / Bd. Robert Southwell, SJ, *Spiritual Exercises and Devotions,* edited by J.-M. de Buck, SJ, and translated by P. E. Hallett, abridged edition, English text only (London, 1974), 29. Hallett's translation of Southwell's Latin.

92. 'had particular significance for Southwell' / *Poems,* ed. cit., 146.

93. The modern 'consensus' . . . Christ. / F. V. Filson, *A Commentary on the Gospel According to St. Matthew* (London, 1960), 138; D. Hill (ed.), *The Gospel of Matthew* (London, 1972), 200; J. C. Fenton, *The Gospel of St. Matthew* (Harmondsworth, 1963), 179-80. Hopkins reads the text in Southwell's spirit. See *The Sermons and Devotional Writings of Gerard Manley Hopkins,* ed. Christopher Devlin, SJ (London 1959), 96.

94. epigraph on the title-page / ed. cit. cf: 'And from the dayes of Iohn the Baptist vntil novv, the kingdom of heauen suffereth violence, and the violent beare it avvay.' *Rhemes NT, 1582,* ed. cit., 29.

95. 'And though . . . foughte for it' / ed. cit., 31 verso, 32 recto.

96. Thy ghostly . . . tender love. / *Poems,* ed. cit., 55.

97. 'in my judgment . . . to God' / Luther, *Lectures on Romans,* newly translated and edited by W. Pauck, The Library of Christian Classics xv (London, 1961), 349.

98. 'if you wish . . . fear nothing' / *Spiritual and Anabaptist Writers,* ed. G. H. Williams and A. M. Mergal, The Library of Christian Classics xxv (London, 1957), 369.

99. 'Thus . . . knives' / *The Great Commentary of Cornelius à Lapide,* translated by T. W. Mossman (London, 1876-97): *St Matthew's Gospel, chaps X to XXI,* 58, 60. I am grateful to Fr Martin Jarrett-Kerr CR for discussing this and other questions with me though I am, of course, solely responsible for any errors of fact or interpretation.

100. 'tiranical persecution . . . thy desire' / *Epistle of Comfort,* ed. cit., 79 verso; *MMFT,* ed. cit., 25 recto; *Humble Supplication,* ed. cit., 4; *MMFT,* 58 recto; ibid., 7 recto; ibid., 38 recto, verso.

101. 'I am urged . . . detest' / *Two Letters . . . ,* ed. cit., 56.

102. [A]s not . . . spiritual plane'. / Southwell, *Triumphs over Death,* quoted Janelle, op. cit., 233. Janelle's comment, 232.

103. 'Of the venerable martyr . . . butchery'. / *The Rambler,* NS VIII (1857), 114, quoted in Dom Bede Camm, *Forgotten Shrines,* second edition (London, 1936), 359 and 361n.

104. The 'officers . . . George Haydock. / *CRS* v, 288-9, 57-62.

105. For Southwell . . . emblem / cf. J. Morris, SJ, *The Troubles of our Catholic Forefathers related by themselves,* First Series (London, 1872), 98: (the execution of Fr Cuthbert Maine, 1587) 'a very high gibbet . . . and all things else, both fire and knives, set to the show and ready prepared'.

106. In a letter . . . medicines"'. / *CRS* v, 318. Pollen's translation of Southwell's Latin; p. 301, Pollen's note on 'veiled style'.

107. Then sayd the Angel . . . them. / *The Holie Bible Faithfvlly Translated into English . . .* (Douai, 1609-10), 998.

108. Remember . . . dyed. / *Epistle of Comfort,* ed. cit., 201 recto.

109. indeed . . . martyrdom. / ibid., 202 verso. For a caveat on 'Catholic major gentry portraits' see Aveling, op. cit., 150-4.

110. 'the reparation . . . offences' / Maitland, op. cit., 131.

111. 'transformation' / cf. Janelle, op. cit., 190; Helen C. White, 'Southwell: Metaphysical and Baroque', in *Modern Philology,* 61(1963-4), p. 161; cf. F. W. Beare, *A Commentary on the Epistle to the Philippians,* third edition (London, 1973), 140: 'Even now [Paul] tells us, the transformation is proceeding within us'.

112. 'translations . . . alteratio[n]' / Janelle, op. cit., 184; *Poems,* ed. cit., xcvi, 135; *Epistle of Comfort,* 154 recto.

113. And this . . . glorye. / *Epistle of Comfort,* 203 verso, 204 recto.

114. [He] . . . glory' / Beare, *Commentary,* 138.

115. Christ's Parousia / Cf. Beare, 138, 140.

116. There is no reason . . . the Crosse. / *Epistle of Comfort,* 32 recto, verso.

117. 'transfigured . . . passion'. / ibid., 32 recto.

118. 'Calvary's turbulence' / 'The Magi': *The Collected Poems of W. B. Yeats,* second edition, with later poems added (London, 1950), 141.

119. 'For Thy sake . . . nothing'. / *Spiritual Exercises and Devotions,* 74: Hallett's translation of Southwell's Latin.

120. a fair amount of Ovid by heart / Janelle, op. cit., 135.

121. 'lingering . . . skill' / I apply a phrase of Hopkins, 'Deutschland', st. 10./*Poems,* ed. Gardner and MacKenzie (London, 1970), 54.

122. 'From bosomes . . . tumble thick . . . / *Seneca His Tenne Tragedies translated into Englysh* (London, 1581), 33 recto (*Thyestes*), 72 recto (*Hippolytus*).

123. Whye doest . . . reason. / *Epistle of Comfort,* 205 recto.

124. 'masculine perswasive force' / 'On his Mistris', John Donne, *The Elegies and the Songs and Sonnets,* ed. Helen Gardner (Oxford, 1965), 23.

125. 'make . . . experience' / ibid., xviii

126. 'how well . . . together' / 'The Author to his loving Cosen', *Poems,* ed. cit., 1.

127. 'Whose measure . . . too little have' / *Poems*, ed. cit., 2, 5, 28.

128. 'Baroque . . . transformation' / White, loc. cit.

129. 'uneven accompt' . . . 'just measure': / *Poems*, ed. cit., 79, 77.

130. 'the affections . . . God'. / *Epistle of Comfort*, 191 recto, 190 verso.

131. 'loathed pleasures . . . Cruell Comforts' / *Poems*, ed. cit., 50, 41, 54; *Humble Supplication*, 34.

132. 'awestruck . . . man' / Roberts, op. cit., 454.

133. This little Babe . . . surprise. / 'New heaven, new warre', *Poems*, ed. cit., 14.

134. 'naïve . . . concession' / *Agenda*, 13, no. 3 (Autumn 1975), 32. For Southwell's phrase see *MMFT*, ed. cit., p. A3 verso.

135. 'complexity of association' / White, op. cit., p. 166.

136. Antonin Artaud . . . Rodez / Charles Marowitz, *Artaud at Rodez* (London, 1977), 73.

137. 'Excessus' signifies 'ecstasy'. / Etienne Gilson, *The Mystical Theology of Saint Bernard*, translated by A. H. C. Downs (London, 1940), 26. See also Gordon Rupp, *The Righteousness of God* (London, 1953), 143: '"Excessus mentis," [Luther] says, means "either the alienation of mind . . ." or "the rapture of the mind into . . . faith," and this is really what is meant by "ecstasis".' *A Study of Wisdom: Three Tracts by the Author of 'The Cloud of Unknowing'*, translated into Modern English . . . by C. Wolters (Oxford, 1980), 21: '"Ibi Benjamin adolescentus in mentis excessu' [Psalm 68:28. Vulgate] which means in English, "There is Benjamin, the young child, transported out of mind".'

138. 'solace' . . . Tower / Janelle, op. cit., 68.

139. 'pretty Babe . . . breast' / *Poems*, ed. cit., 15.

140. 'the most hackneyed . . . tradition' / Janelle, op. cit., 168; *Poems*, ed. cit., 124.

141. 'variation . . . manner' / Martz, op. cit., 81-3, 364. Puente's work was first published in 1605. John Heigham's English translation was not issued from St Omer until 1619.

142. St Ignatius . . . tradition. / Janelle, op. cit., 109.

143. 'excess . . . necessity' / *Two Letters* . . . ed. cit., 36.

144. 'fancie' . . . 'selfe delight' / *Poems*, ed. cit., 50.

145. 'Let vs . . . therin . . .' / ed. cit., 37 verso.

146. 'the Jesuit discipline . . . wildness . . .' Devlin, *Life of Southwell*, 85.

147. I would further suggest . . . not lost on him. / cf. Etienne Gilson, *The Spirit of Medieval Philosophy*, translated by A. H. C. Downs (London, 1936), 290-2; Rupp, op. cit., 143; C. Wolters, *Three Tracts* . . . , 21.

148. 'I am come hither . . . poor life'. / Devlin, *Life of Southwell*, 321.

149. 'Loue . . . loue'. / *MMFT*, 52 recto, verso.


## Karen Batley (essay date fall 1994)

SOURCE: Batley, Karen. "Southwell's 'New Heaven, New Warre.'" *Explicator* 53, no. 1 (fall 1994): 7-10.

[*In the following essay, Batley explores the poem "New Heaven, New Warre," refuting the common critical notion that the work is actually two separate poems erroneously printed as a single work.*]

Is **"New Heaven, New Warre"** a single poem or two poems printed in error as one? The answer makes a significant difference to our interpretation of the poem. It contains two distinctly different tones, one devotional (lines 1-24) in admiration of the newly incarnated Christ, the other (24-28) military and obviously in the Jesuit tradition of portraying Christ as the leader of an army. Louis Martz (524-5) attempts to prove rather inconclusively that the poem accords with the structures of devotional meditation. He maintains a two-part structure by leaving a space at lines 24-25 (the close of the manger scene and the beginning of the military section), thereby avoiding a decision on what Southwell's intentions might have been. Helen Gardner, on the other hand, is far more definite, stating (39) that "although printed as a single poem, this is two parallel poems on the Nativity, or possibly on the Nativity and the Circumcision." However, a close examination of the text reveals no reference to the circumcision. Further, despite her conviction that there are two poems, Gardner makes no separation between them in her printed version (40), opting for a "single" poem, at least in appearance. Similarly, Pollard Brown maintains that "the single title was apparently given in error to two separate poems linked only by metrical form and subject. There is distinct change in theme, tone and imagery in the last four stanzas of the poem, ll.25-48" (124). However, Jean Robertson shows that the poem is more likely to be a single one (82-3). Basing her argument on Southwell's use of appropriate and witty titles, she points out that Southwell, like Donne and Herbert, followed the practice of providing titles that deliberately created an integrated effect for the poem as a whole. In the light of this, and considering the thematic structure of the poem, the title **"New Heaven, New Warre"** would suggest that Southwell intended a single poem.

**"New Heaven, New Warre"** belongs to a group of four nativity poems. The other three are entitled **"A Childe My Choyce,"** **"New Prince, New Pompe"** (a title echoing the rhythm and structure of that of **"New Heaven, New Warre"**) and **"The Burning Babe."** The group as a unit is characterized by a single factor—the poet's wonder at the incarnation and the paradoxical power of the apparently helpless infant to save humankind.[1] The structure and meaning of **"New Heaven, New Warre"** obviously depend on this very paradox. My own view, reinforced by these observations, is that **"New Heaven, New Warre"** is almost certainly a single poem based on a scriptural account and that the "new heaven" and "new warre" of the title actually refer compositely to the incarnation and its purpose for salvation. There cannot be a "new heaven" or "new warre" without there having been a previous one. This is illustrated in Scripture. The first war in Heaven took place when Lucifer challenged God's authority and was consequently expelled from Heaven. That Christ was present during this war is shown by his own words in Luke 10:18[2]:

And he said to them, I saw Satan as a lightening fal from heaven.

In Rev. 12:7-9 we are told:

And there was made a great battel in heaven, Michael and his Angels fought with the dragon, and the dragon fought and his Angels: and they prevailed not, neither was their place found any more in heaven. And that great dragon was cast forth, the old serpent, which is called the Devil and Satan, which seduceth the whole world: and he was cast into the earth, and his Angels were throwen down with him.

This is the first, or old war, caused presumably by Satan's attempt to rifle God's fold and challenge his authority. Now, with the incarnation, Heaven has come to earth to challenge Satan in a return bout (the baby has come "to ryfle sathans folde"). Thus the new heaven, to which the Angels, Seraphs, and Cherubs, as well as the Archangels Raphael, Gabriel, and Michael, accompanied by the Graces, are summoned, is earth. The call in lines 8-18 for all these heavenly beings to take up their places is the start of the "new warre," the military campaign for salvation which takes place in the second part of the poem. This is the integrating factor for the two different "tones" in the poem. In the first, heavenly war, Michael was Lucifer's chief opponent; in the "new warre" he will "stand in his [Christ's] defence" (15) because the latter must now himself defeat "sathan" in order to achieve humanity's salvation.

The text itself also offers some internal evidence in favor of a single poem. The first section, lines 1-24, could possibly stand as a complete unit, but the second,

military section would, standing alone, start very abruptly. Its "first" line, "This little Babe so few dayes olde," seems logically to refer to the infant described in lines 1-24. The war described in the second half explains why Michael should need to "stand in his defence" in the first section. Further, if lines 25-48 were to be considered as a complete unit, the reference in line 29 would beg explanation. "For in this weake unarmed wise" implies that the condition has been explained, which of course it has, in the first section. Finally, the concluding stanza of the poem draws the two different sections together—the incarnation and the battle for souls, thereby suggesting further that this is a single poem and should be interpreted as such.

> My soule with Christ joyne thou in fight,
> Sticke to the tents that he hath pight;
> Within his Crib is surest ward,
> This little babe will be thy guard:
> If thou wilt foil thy foes with joy,
> Then flit not from this heavenly boy.

## Notes

1. Southwell states the paradox in a single line in "A Childe my Choyce": "Almightie babe whose tender armes do force all foes to flie." He is obviously concerned with the concept as the motivating principle of the group of poems.

2. All scriptural references are taken from the Douay-Rheims (1582) version of the New Testament, edited by L. A. Weigle.

## Works Cited

Brown, Nancy P. and McDonald, J. H., eds. *The Poems of Robert Southwell, S. J.* Oxford: Clarendon, 1967.

Gardner, H. ed. *The Metaphysical Poets.* Harmondsworth: Penguin, 1964.

Martz, L. *The Meditative Poem.* New Haven: Yale UP, 1963.

Weigle, L. A., ed. *New Testament, Rheims 1582 in (The) New Testament Octopla: Eight English Versions of the New Testament in the Tyndale-King James Tradition.* New York: Thomas Nelson and Sons.

## Mary Lowe-Evans (essay date summer 1996)

SOURCE: Lowe-Evans, Mary. "Southwell's 'Christ's Bloody Sweat.'" *Explicator* 54, no. 4 (summer 1996): 199-202.

[*In the following essay, Lowe-Evans discusses the fluid and fire imagery of Southwell's poem "Christ's Bloody Sweat."*]

Armed with the doctrines of Counter Reformation Catholicism, Robert Southwell, SJ, had been given permission by his Order to use poetry as a means of spreading the rejuvenated dogma among English Catholics. A. D. Cousins contends that Southwell consistently articulated "a world-view centered on the divine agape [rather than devout eros] and on Christ whose principles he expounds . . . and (or) within which he explores the manifestations of God's selfless love" (38). I hope to demonstrate how Southwell's exegesis on the nature of divine love in **"Christ's Bloody Sweat"** is conveyed in fluid and fire imagery, which in turn suggests the two apparently opposing characteristics of Counter Reformation style: extravagance and conservatism. The traditions of Counter Reformation devotional style include the "plain," or conservative, rhetorical mode deriving from Tudor times, and the more extravagant theories of emblematic verse inspired by Renaissance emblem art. These speciously contrary poetic urges are reconciled in Southwell's poem as he demonstrates God's determination both to create love and to keep it in existence, even as energy is kept in existence when it changes form.

The opening stanza introduces the various fluids that represent the creative effusions of Christ's love. The extravagant reiteration of images emphasizes the extravagant love:

> Fat soile, full spring, sweete olive, grape of blisse,
> That yeelds, that streams, that pours, that dost distill,
> Untild, undrawne, unstampt, untoucht of presse,
> Deare fruit, clear brookes, faire oile, sweete wine at will:

Like the fecund earth of the Garden of Olives, Christ is the "fat soile," full partaker in our earthly nature; the "full spring," eternal source of living water, the "sweet olive" promising peace on earth and the holy chrism used to anoint the newly baptized and the newly ordained; the "grape of bliss," whose sweet wine intoxicates all who imbibe it with a divine drunkenness wherein the "self" is lost.

The restatement of effusion images foregrounds the spontaneity of Christ's love. Christ both "streams" and "dost distil" or exude love, involuntarily it would seem. The implied involuntariness is contradicted, however, by the phrase "at will" in the fourth line. Christ's choice was an important issue in Counter Reformation discussions regarding the theological implications of the Agony in the Garden. Christ's submitting to his Father's will in the Garden was deemed sufficient to redeem mankind. In the stanza's closing couplet this doctrinal issue is repeated:

> Thus Christ unforst prevents in shedding blood
> The whips, the thornes, the nailes, the speare, and roode.

In the Garden, Christ chooses to drink the cup ("not my will, but thine be done"); his choice, motivated by love, manifests itself in the bloody sweat. As it falls to the earth the blood renews God's covenant with humankind and "prevents" (anticipates and precludes the need for) the Passion and Crucifixion. As Karen Batley notes, "during the sixteenth century 'prevent' often meant 'to appear before time'" (1).

In the second stanza, Southwell borrows classic types, like the Church fathers before him, to express an "incomprehensible certainty" (Batley 4), as he combines fluid with fire imagery:

> He Pelicans, he Phenix fate doth prove,
> Whom flames consume, whom streames enforce to die,
> How burneth bloud, how bleedeth burning love?
> Can one in flame and streame both bathe and frie?
> How could he joine a Phenix fiery paines
> In fainting Pelicans still bleeding vaines?

Here Southwell reiterates the sufficiency and efficacy of Christ's love as exemplified in his act of the will. The choice Christ made in the Garden combines the "Pelican's" and the "Phenix fate." On one hand, Christ merits for humans all the grace that the bloody sacrifice of the cross would merit as the pelican had merited by her blood the lives of her children. On the other hand, he anticipates the phoenix's fate—the resurrection of the body—a manifestation of the principle of divine conservation.

Next Southwell reverses the experience of the love poet who typically asks his lady to change. Southwell is the poet of a Lover who cannot change. Thus, in asking "can one in flame and streame both bathe and frie?" Southwell attempts to help the reader understand the extravagant and conservative love Christ offers.

The third stanza continues the quest to understand divine love by tracing Southwell's personal attempt to know God, which is also always an attempt to teach the faithful. Here he provides an answer (suggested by the experiences of Elias) to the question posed in the second stanza's closing couplet:

> Elias once to prove gods soveraigne powre
> By praire procur'd a fier of wondrous force
> That blood and wood and water did devoure,
> Yea stones and dust, beyonde all natures course:
> Such fire is love that fedd with gory bloode
> Doth burne no less then in the dryest woode.

In calling upon Elias, Southwell moves from classical to Old Testament types, thereby teaching the reader how the fates of the phoenix and the pelican are joined. Through prayer, Elias was able to call down fire from heaven which consumed the captains and men of the king who had come to apprehend him. The fire demonstrates the efficacy and sufficiency of God's love as the fluid images in the first stanza have done. In the biblical account. Elias, taken into heaven in a fiery chariot, is thus preserved from death, and the principle of divine conservation again becomes operative. The emphasis on the prayer of Elias is implicit in the meditation on the Agony in the Garden in general. Christ's intensely human prayer that the "cup" pass away ends in submission to his Father's will. By his prayer, Christ "prevents" and yet merits all the grace of the Passion and death on the cross. Similarly, by the power of his prayer, Elias overcomes death and enters heaven in a whirlwind of fire. Thus, prayer becomes man's answer to the question of the phoenix and the pelican. Through prayer humans partake of the consequences of the Crucifixion and the Resurrection.

Southwell successfully transmutes the fluids of the first stanza into the fire of the third by moving from Christ at prayer in the Garden of Gethsemane, through the questioning of the pelican's and phoenix's fates in the second stanza, to the prayer of Elias in the third. Prayer, shored up by faith and submission to God's will, allows participation in both the effusiveness and the conserving quality of divine love.

Since the fourth stanza is itself a prayer, Southwell puts into practice the principle he has established:

> O sacred Fire come shewe they force on me
> That sacrifice to Christe I maye retorne,
> If withered wood for fuell fittest bee,
> If stones and dust, yf fleshe and blood will burne,
> I withered am and stonye to all good,
> A sack of dust, a masse of fleshe and bloode.

Like Elias, Southwell calls down the sacred fire of divine love the force of which will equip him to offer a sacrifice like Christ's. In the final line, Southwell reconciles all the poem's images by equating himself with "a sack of dust, a masse of fleshe and bloode." We know that Christ too fits this description, for we have been told that "He Pelicans, he Phenix fate doth prove." Finally, Southwell seeks identity with Christ through the prayer he offers in this meditation.

### Works Cited

Batley, Karen. "Southwell's 'Christ's Bloody Sweat': A Jesuit Meditation on Gethsemane," *UES* [*Unisa English Studies*] 30.2 (1992): 1-7.

Cousins, A. D. *The Catholic Religious Poets from Southwell to Crashaw: A Critical History,* Westminster, MD: Christian Classics, 1991.

### Bibliography

"Conservation, Divine." *New Catholic Encyclopedia.* 1967 ed.

Eliade, Mircea. *Images and Symbols: Studies in Religious Symbolism.* New York: Sheed and Ward, 1969.

Fairbridge, Maurice H. *Studies in Biblical and Semitic Symbolism.* New York: KTAV Publishing, 1970.

Janelle, Pierre. *Robert Southwell, the Writer.* Marmaroneck, NY: Paul P. Appel, 1971.

McDonald, James H., ed. *The Poems of Robert Southwell S. J.* Oxford: Clarendon, 1967. 18-19.

### F. W. Brownlow (essay date 1996)

SOURCE: Brownlow, F. W. "Southwell's Poetry: The Shorter Lyrics." In *Robert Southwell,* pp. 97-124. New York: Twayne Publishers, 1996.

[*In the following excerpt, Brownlow contends that Southwell's reputation as a poet rests on fewer than half of the shorter poems he composed, the remainder being characterized by cliched lyrics and, in some cases, plagiarism.*]

#### THE CANON

Except for the initials "R. S." on the title page of **Moeoniae** (1595), Southwell's publishers did not attribute his poems to him until the Jesuits of St. Omer produced their second edition in 1620. Nor is there any ascription of the poems to Southwell in the manuscript copies. In that context of silence, John Trussell's eagerness to blazon Southwell's name over his edition of *The Triumphs over Death* is all the more surprising. Nonetheless, despite the silence, Southwell's authorship of his various works was well known. A note among the Bacon papers identifies **"Decease Release"** as "des vers de Mr. Southwell" (*Poems,* lxxvii), and Ben Jonson certainly knew who wrote **"The Burning Babe"** when he told Drummond of Hawthornden "that Southwell was hanged, yet so he had written that piece of his **The Burning Babe** he would have been content to destroy many of his."[1]

The three principal manuscripts (Stonyhurst A.v.27, Virtue and Cahill, British Library MS Additional 10422), each providing the same 52 poems in the same order, plus the poem **"To the Reader,"** fix the basic canon of Southwell's shorter pieces. In Nancy Pollard Brown's opinion, one of these poems, a clumsy translation of St. Thomas Aquinas's Corpus Christi hymn, "Lauda Sion salvatorem," may not be Southwell's. Brown included it in her edition "mainly out of respect for the compiler's judgment" (*Poems,* lxxviii). The Harmsworth Manuscript includes an additional 12 poems, of whose authenticity Brown is equally skeptical. The first two, **"Conceptio B. Virginis sub porta aurea"** and **"Praesentatio B. Virginis,"** appear at the beginning of the manuscript and are meant to be part of a sequence on Mary and Jesus. The first of them is an earlier version of **"The Virgin Mary's Conception,"** the first poem of the sequence. The two versions have the same riddling, witty third stanza, but one can see that the abstract grandeur of the Harmsworth version's first two stanzas, based on figures from the litanies of the Virgin, is not a suitable preparation for it:

> A golden gate was her conceiving place,
> That was the gate unto the golden age;
> The mine, the mint, the treasury of grace;
> Our gold to coin, and for to keep in gage,
> Wherewith the ransome of our sins was paid,
> Our pardon got, and all our debts defrayed.

*(Poems, 108)*

**"The Presentation of the Virgin,"** on the other hand, may well belong to the sequence, as Brown suggests, since the feast of the Presentation of the Virgin was reintroduced into the Roman calendar, 1 September 1585 (*Poems,* lxxxiii), and because the poem looks finished. The last of the additional poems is yet another version of a sequence poem, **"The Annunciation Altered from That before."** Brown believes it is spurious, but without objective evidence, and there seems to be no strong reason not to believe that this is an early version too. Indeed, all these additions to the set of 52, except the sequence poem on the presentation of the Virgin, have the look of either early work or drafts. Three of them appear in *Moeoniae*: **"The Virgin Mary to Christ on the Cross," "Man to the Wound in Christ's Side,"** and **"Upon the Image of Death."** Their appearance in Busby's volume, printed from a different source (*Poems,* lxxxi) seems to guarantee their genuineness. There is also a four-stanza elegy for Lady Margaret Howard printed in *The Triumphs over Death,* and a stanza translated from Prudentius in *An Epistle of Comfort.* Including **"The Author to the Reader"** prefacing *Saint Peter's Complaint,* this makes a total of 70 short poems as printed in Brown's edition, not a large body of work.

### THE NATURE OF THE COLLECTION

As copied in the manuscripts, the poems' order reflects predominantly a grouping by theme and subject matter. First comes a sequence of 14 poems on the mysteries encoded in the mother-son relationship of Mary and Jesus. Then come four poems on the nativity and the Christ-child, followed by three on Christ's agony in the garden of Gethsemani. The next three poems belong to no grouping, and seem placed arbitrarily: **"Joseph's Amazement,"** a very peculiar and "incredibly bad" poem (Martz, 186) on Joseph's reaction to Mary's pregnancy; **"An Holy Hymn"** (a translation of Aquinas's "Lauda Sion salvatorem"), and **"Of the Blessed Sacrament of the Altar."** A group of nine

poems on sin occupies the central place in the collection. Although the central positioning of the group is not quite exact, it may be evidence of the design of Southwell's original collection. Then come eight poems on death or the wish to die, two on heaven in relation to the soul, and a final miscellaneous group of nine consisting of six gnomic poems and three persuasions against love, **"Love's Servile Lot," "Lewd Love Is Loss,"** and **"Love's Garden Grief."**

Although the compiler made an attempt to group the poems according to kind or theme, no arrangement, however careful, can obscure the essentially miscellaneous character of the collection. Experience of reading it does not support Brown's belief that "the fifty-two lyrics have been arranged with sensitive awareness of the place of each in a framework of training in the spiritual life" (*Poems,* xcix). There is no particular reason why the last poems in the collection should conclude a training in the spiritual life, or why **"Joseph's Amazement"** at Mary's pregnancy should come after the nativity poems, or be followed by two poems on the sacrament. Then there is the sheer disparity in the quality of the poems to be recognized; as materials for spiritual training, some are decidedly second-rate. It seems that not only the compiler, but Southwell himself, intent upon his program of literary conversion, failed to make some critical distinctions.

This failure of self-criticism, which in a writer as gifted as Southwell is really a failure of self-protection, even of self-esteem, may have been a consequence of his submission of himself and his faculties to his order and his mission. Warren Maurer, comparing Southwell to the German Jesuit poet Friedrich von Spee (1591-1635), produced a very interesting case parallel to Southwell's. Like Southwell, von Spee was of good family, was schooled in Continental humanism, was a missionary to his homeland, wrote a tract appealing for toleration, and left behind unpublished vernacular poetry whose similarity to Southwell's is due to "a very similar religious and literary environment": "The calculated intention to sermonize, combined with the burdensome need to sugar-coat the sermon to make it more palatable for the weak and fickle reader, all but stifles originality. The course often followed by our poets is to imitate popular profane models and render them morally harmless by turning them to the service of God. All too frequently, we see in their work the fabrications of literary craftsmen who, in their anxiety to hold the reader, stray from the path of inspiration."[2] Maurer agrees with Martz that the practice of meditation influenced sixteenth- and seventeenth-century poetry, but he suspects that in the case of the two Jesuits "their lifelong and rather regimented preoccupation with the art of meditation seems to have conditioned their creative powers along certain almost predictable lines" (16). And he adds that "it is hardly surprising that poetry written as an apostolic sideline should deal almost exclusively with God and things divine" (20).

This criticism has the accuracy of hostility. Joseph Scallon, who admires Southwell's poetry, also concludes that Southwell "began to compose verses on subjects which were dictated more by his zeal than by the concerns of his own spiritual life" (90). There is no doubt either, that Southwell had embarked on a campaign to convert contemporary secular love poetry to religious ends, and that it had unfortunate effects upon his poetic writing. This campaign was quite different from his other one for a new and original kind of religious literature, because its whole point was not to be original, but to appropriate others' writing for his own purposes. In many cases, he simply adopted a well-tried manner and preserved all its clichés, as in **"S. Peter's Remorse"**:

> Remorse upbraids my faults,
> Self blaming conscience cries,
> Sin claims the host of humbled thoughts,
> And streams of weeping eyes.

> (*Poems,* 33)

The worst that can be said about this conversion of a weeping Petrarchan lover to a weeping sinner is that as poetry it is boring, and, because bad literature never did anyone much good, as material for religious reading it would surely encourage smugness. Four of Southwell's poems express a wish to escape this sinful life by death (**"Life Is but Loss," "I Die Alive," "What Joy to Live," "Life's Death, Love's Life"**); in them Southwell has similarly converted the anthologies' Petrarchan lover who wishes to die into the sinful but repentant Christian who, while waiting for death and heaven, fills in the time by telling everyone how glad he will be to leave worldly love and transient beauty behind him (Janelle, 261-67).[3]

In a few cases, Southwell appropriated an actual poem for his sermonizing purposes. The most striking example is Sir Edward Dyer's "A Fancy." By deft substitutions, Southwell turns this graceful lament of a jilted lover (which is probably about Dyer's own loss of favor at Elizabeth I's court) into "a sinner's complaint." Martz, who admires the result, calls the process "parody" and relates it to Herbert's conversion of a love poem by the Earl of Pembroke (Martz, 189-91, 316) under the title **"A Parody." "Content and Rich"** (*Poems,* 67-69), another moralizing poem, is based on Dyer's "My mind to me a kingdom is"; **"Love's Garden Grief,"** one of three persuasions against love, is probably based on Nicholas Breton's "A Strange Description of a Rare Garden Plot," published in *The Phoenix Nest* in 1593, but written much earlier (Thurston 1895, 239). Although neither of these poems is a line-by-line substitution of new text for old, South-

well's dependence on the originals is clear enough. **"Love's Garden Grief,"** as Brown observes, is metrically experimental (lxxix), but apart from that it is an unpleasant poem, betraying an almost hysterical distrust of the natural body:

> Your coolest summer gales are scalding sighings,
> 　Your showers are tears,
> Your sweetest smell the stench of sinful living,
> 　Your favors fears,
> Your gardener Satan, all you reap is misery:
> Your gain remorse and loss of all felicity.

> (*Poems,* 64)

Martz's description of Southwell's appropriation of other poets themes, style, and poems as "sacred parody" drew a sharp response from Rosamund Tuve. Martz (186n) claimed to be using "parody" in a neutral sense authorized by Herbert's use of the word as the title of his religious adaptation of a love poem by the Earl of Pembroke. Tuve responded by pointing out that all seventeenth-century definitions of the word "parody" "stress the element of mockery, burlesque, or at least some sidelong denigrating comment on the original author's sense," a meaning that does not fit Herbert's title at all, since Herbert is in no way mocking or caricaturing Pembroke's poem.[4] According to Tuve, there is no neutral meaning of "parody" in the period, and Martz was mistaken in trying to find one. If Herbert was following Southwell's "campaign to convert the poetry of profane love into the poetry of divine love" (Tuve, 252), then his use of "parody" is no more innocent or neutral than if he had written downright travesty. "No attitude toward another man's work is much less neutral than an intention to displace it entirely" (253)—a remark as acute as it is profoundly true.

The only meaning of parody that might help, Tuve argues, is the musical one: "replacement of text for a known tune," as well as the term *missa parodia* to describe masses using well-known tunes as thematic material. She then points out that serious "parodies" of this kind were not news in Southwell's or Herbert's time, and that they had been part of the great campaign of the Protestants—Luther, Marot, Bourgeois, Coverdale, and the authors of *The Gude and Godlie Ballatis*. The reformers used "a musical practice to fulfill intentions they had as religious leaders: the intention does not inhere in the practice . . ." (259). To be fair to Southwell, providing words for music is probably exactly what he was doing: as he writes to his "loving cousin," "I send you these few ditties, add you the tunes" (*Poems,* 2). A ditty or song lyric provides the one notable success among his religious travesties of love poetry: **"Marie Magdalen's Complaint at Christ's Death"** can match any of the songs or "ditties" of the period for metrical skill and graceful statement:

O my soul, what did unloose thee
From thy sweet captivity?
God, not I, did still possess thee:
His, not mine, thy liberty.
O, too happy thrall thou wert,
When thy prison was his heart.

(*Poems,* 46)

Thomas Morley recognized the quality of this poem by setting three of its stanzas to music in his *First Book of Ayres* (Martz, 192n). Another modest success owed to the writing of words for music seems to be **"Man to the Wound in Christ's Side,"** a poem found in *Moeniae* and the Harmsworth manuscript, but not in the other manuscripts. The poem is an expansion of a petition in the prayer "Anima Christi," which precedes Ignatius's *Exercises*: "Within thy wounds hide me." It sounds more like an eighteenth-century evangelical hymn than an Elizabethan poem, and it illustrates C. S. Lewis's point that Southwell often seems to belong to no period:

O pleasant port, O place of rest,
  O royal rift, O worthy wound,
Come harbor me a weary guest,
  That in the world no ease have found.

(*Poems,* 72)

Even so, and with all allowances made, Southwell's versified moral and religious commonplaces erected upon other poets' work add nothing to his poetic reputation. The same is true of the gnomic poems, a group that includes **"Times Go by Turns," "Loss in Delays," "Fortune's Falsehood," "From Fortune's Reach,"** and **"Scorn Not the Least."** It may be, as Brown suggests (lxxix), that these exercises in the style of the popular anthologies had a "hidden relevance" for the persecuted Catholics. Christopher Devlin (180) makes a similar point about some lines from **"Times Go by Turns,"** applying them to Southwell's own relief at a respite from persecution:

Not always fall of leaf, nor ever spring,
No endless night, yet not eternal day:
The saddest birds a season find to sing,
The roughest storm a calm may soon allay.

(*Poems,* 58)

Nonetheless, the poetic temperature is low in all these poems, with the exception of the last of them, **"Scorn Not the Least."** The concluding couplets of these four six-line stanzas redeem them from the general dullness of the genre; they convey a sweet, rueful charm in which, at last, one may hear Southwell's own voice: "Yet higher powers must think, though they repine, / When sun is set: the little stars will shine."

The phrase "higher powers" is from Saint Paul's Epistle to the Romans, 13.1: "Let every soul be subject to higher powers," an injunction echoed by Southwell himself in his *Short Rule*: "Next my duty to God, it behooveth me to consider my duty to my superiors, whom I must account as his vicegerents and substitutes in the things wherein I am subject unto them" (*Letters,* 33). If for once there is a touch of wry humor in the use of the phrase in the poem, it is very acceptable.

These "second-hand" poems account for half of the collection. It is tempting to excuse the worst of them (**"Joseph's Amazement"** or **"The Prodigal Child's Soul-Wrack"**) as early work, even as exercises in English versification. We know that Southwell began writing about St. Peter and St. Mary Magdalen while he was in Rome, and so **"Mary Magdalen's Blush"** might date from that time of his life. Most of these poems, though, probably date from his English years; Scallon (90) may well be right to suspect that Southwell simply allowed himself to be tempted into pious versifying for the good of the faithful. One thing is certain. Contemporary poets, such as Shakespeare, who admired *Saint Peter's Complaint,* would find nothing to interest them in these poems. Martz (184) thought that Southwell's attempt to convert love poetry to religious uses had influenced George Herbert, but there is nothing very specific about the parallels he adduces, and, as Tuve pointed out, there was nothing original about Southwell's activities. Even if there were, it would not improve the quality of the results, nor would it remove the taint of arrogant high-handedness attaching to the method. Plagiarism is not improved by being high-minded.

Southwell's poetic reputation rests upon the other half of the collection, which includes the 14 poems of the sequence on Mary and Jesus in six-line epigrammatic stanzas, the four nativity poems, the three Gethsemani poems, **"A Vale of Tears,"** and two poems on heaven, **"At Home in Heaven"** and **"Look Home."** All these poems except the last three are from the first part of the collection. Whether that means they were written first or last, or whether their position is merely coincidence, is something we shall never know.

### THE SEQUENCE ON MARY AND JESUS

No external evidence survives to explain why this sequence exists, and no one has ever read it as a whole to find out how or why it is a sequence at all. Martz (101-7) speculated that it might be related to the devotion of the rosary, in particular to a version of it called "the *corona*" of Our Lady. Scallon responded to this suggestion by saying that "no-one has yet shown that there ever existed a form of the Rosary which included exactly those mysteries which Southwell has written about" (97). In Scallon's opinion, the poems are better considered as sacred epigrams, in the tradition of metaphysical and witty hymnody associated with Adam of St. Victor and Aquinas (100). Even so, one would like to know why Southwell wrote a sequence of them, and how many poems should be in it.

Because the publishers of the first collections broke the sequence up, Southwell's earliest readers did not know that the poems formed a sequence at all. Wolfe printed two of the poems, and Busby printed 10 more. The last two, **"The Death of Our Lady,"** and **"The Assumption of Our Lady,"** omitted from the first English editions because they were too obviously Catholic, were not printed until 1856. If we include **"The Presentation of the Blessed Virgin,"** preserved in the Harmsworth manuscript, the complete set would number 15 poems. Even with that poem added, there is a question whether the sequence forms a whole. If it is supposed to be on events in the joined lives of Mary and Jesus, why is there no poem on the deposition from the cross or on the miracle at Cana?

The first thing to be noticed about the sequence is that it is framed by poems on Mary's conception and birth, death and assumption; moreover, eight of the poems are about her as opposed to seven about Jesus. Since those are about his infancy and childhood, it seems clear enough that this is a Marian sequence, stressing the mystery as well as the motherhood of Mary—no reader of the printed text, however, could have known that until 1856. Indeed, Brown is the first editor to print the poems in the right order as a unit; and even she, because of her low opinion of the Harmsworth manuscript, omits **"The Presentation of the Blessed Virgin,"** which has all the appearance of a complete, finished poem. Added to the set, that fifteenth poem determines the Marian bias of the whole, and equally important, provides the sequence with a center in the eighth poem on the circumcision.

The first poem, **"The Virgin Mary's Conception,"** is in many ways characteristic of the set. There are three stanzas, each a completed statement in itself. The first imparts the mystery of the Immaculate Conception and its meaning:

> Our second *Eve* puts on her mortal shroud,
> Earth breeds a heaven, for God's new dwelling place,
> Now riseth up *Elias*' little cloud
> That growing shall distil the shower of grace:
> Her being now begins, who ere she end,
> Shall bring the good that shall our ill amend.

> (**"The Virgin Mary's Conception,"** ll. 1-6)

The language is plain, the word order natural, and the form neat, yet the tone is mysterious and exalted. That Mary is a second Eve is a commonplace, but Southwell's mind is focused on the thought that if Eve has come again, the event means a new birth for the world, but a new death for her; she "puts on her mortal shroud." Even the common expression "puts on" acquires mystery in this context (as it does in Shakespeare's use of it, *Macbeth* (4.3.238-39): "The powers above / Put on their instruments"), first because it implies a decision to be conceived, and second because what is put on can be put off: this first line and its verb prefigure the end of the sequence with Mary's death and assumption. Meanwhile the earth that fell with our first Eve prepares to rise with the second, and in Mary it prepares a heaven for God to dwell in on earth. Mary, therefore, is already being spoken of as a microcosmic earth that contains a microcosmic heaven. The smaller contains the larger. Then, as the poem itself prefigures the whole sequence's end, so Southwell announces to us the mystery by which sacred history prefigured the Immaculate Conception as rain after drought in "Elias Little Cloud." The scriptural reference is to 3 Kings 18.42-45, where Elias (Elijah, *A. V.*) prays for rain, and instructs his servant to look towards the sea seven times: "And at the seventh time, behold a cloud arose out of the sea like a man's foot." The implication is that history, past, present, and future, is contained in this moment, which is therefore its microcosm. All that history, moreover, will be redeemed by the good that Mary will bring. The second and central stanza of the poem then spells out the central mystery of all: the making of this baby and this moment is the supreme work of grace and nature. "Both grace and nature did their force unite, / To make this babe the sum of all their best" (**"Conception,"** ll. 7-8). As Brian Oxley first noticed, "A recurrent idea in Southwell's poetry is that of a place or person being a 'sum of beauty and delight'" (Oxley 1985b, 331). Here the phrase not only expresses Mary's microcosmic nature, but also looks forward to the end of the sequence when, in **"The Death of Our Lady,"** "the world doth lose the sum of all her bliss" (l. 2).

In this sequence, Southwell presents his reader with the idea that the world in which the Incarnation is the central event is a world of figures, correspondences, symmetries, antitheses, and paradoxes, all wrought by God as artificer in the medium of life through the agency of time, grace, and nature. Therefore, as if to amaze us with the curiosity, neatness, and sheer cleverness of the world's art, Southwell ends his poem with an ingenious last stanza:

> Four only wights bred without fault are named
> And all the rest conceived were in sin,
> Without both man and wife was *Adam* framed,
> Of man, but not of wife did *Eve* begin,
> Wife without touch of man Christ's mother was,
> Of man and wife this babe was bred in grace.

> (**"The Virgin Mary's Conception,"** ll. 13-18)

If there is to be a quarterity of sinless beings in this world, then no two must come into it the same way: Southwell's God is not only an artist, but, like his poet, he is a mannerist artist, who enjoys being ingenious in detail.

Southwell's sources for these poems are the Bible, the patristic commentaries, and the liturgical texts (missal, breviary, hours and litanies of the Virgin). Enjoyment of the poems requires a taste for intricacy, wit, splendor, and exaltation—in a word, for the baroque. The elaborate art of the poems imitates the art of the cosmos they celebrate. The Bible may be the artist's book of plans and patterns, but the art itself engages just about every kind of art and craft. Here in three lines are tailor, quarryman, and architect:

> For God on earth she is the royal throne,
> The chosen cloth to make his mortal weed,
> The quarry to cut out our corner stone.

> ("**Her Nativity,**" ll. 13-15)

The cornerstone is Christ, as in Ephesians 2. 20: "Jesus Christ himself being the chief corner stone." God as architect has also made Mary, "A glorious temple wrought with secret art" ("**Presentation of the Blessed Virgin,**" l. 1). Time, one of God's adjutants in the art of human history, is the learned chemist and physician who has extracted the significance from the words of the patriarchs and prophets, and applied it to our hurt souls:

> The Patriarchs and Prophets were the flowers,
> Which Time by course of ages did distil,
> And culled into this little cloud the showers,
> Whose gracious drops the world with joy shall fill,
> Whose moisture suppleth every soul with grace,
> And bringeth life to *Adam*'s dying race.

> ("**Her Nativity,**" ll. 7-12)

The God who cures us is a surgeon: "The head is lanced to work the body's cure" ("**His Circumcision,**" l. 1), and a chemist: "The vein of life distilleth drops of grace" (l. 7). His angels prove to be connoisseurs: "Such dainty drops best fit their nectared cup" (l. 12). God is a gardener, too, who plants his tree of life in the paradise-garden he trusts to Joseph's care ("**Her Spousals**"), and who transplants his flower from Egypt to Nazareth because Nazareth means "flower" ("**Christ's Return out of Egypt**"). Even rhetorical, grammatical, and logical art has its place, expressing the mystery and surprise of life in puns, paradoxes, and antitheses: "Spell *Eva* back and *Ave* you shall find, / The first began, the last reversed our harms" ("**The Virgin's Salutation,**" ll. 1-2).

The artist of Southwell's cosmos has no objection to incongruity, either, and happily dresses himself in farm laborer's clothes in order to place a syllogism in a stable:

> Man altered was by sin from man to beast:
> Beast's food is hay, hay is all mortal flesh:
> Now God is flesh, and lies in manger prest
> As hay, the brutest sinner to refresh.
> O happy field wherein this fodder grew,
> Whose taste, doth us from beasts to men renew.

> ("**The Nativity of Christ,**" ll. 19-24)

Above all, the art of Southwell's cosmos is an art of surprise, and of dramatic reversals: "Behold the father, is his daughter's son: / The bird that built the nest, is hatched therein" ("**The Nativity of Christ,**" ll. 1-2). His art delights in disappointing normal expectation: "Man laboring to ascend procured our fall, / God yielding to descend cut off our thrall" ("**The Virgin's Salutation,**" ll. 17-18). Nor does it hesitate to work its transformations upon the most recalcitrant materials. There is even a place in its workshop for Herod's murdered babies to sing a silent song of blood to the accompaniment of tears and swords:

> O blessed babes, first flowers of Christian spring,
> Who though untimely cropped fair garlands frame,
> With open throats and silent mouths you sing
> His praise whom age permits you not to name,
> Your tunes are tears, your instruments are swords,
> Your ditty death, and blood in lieu of words.

> ("**The Flight into Egypt,**" ll. 13-18)

The cosmic artist's masterpiece of reversal and paradox is the crucifixion, the "good that shall our ill amend" prefigured in the first poem of the sequence. Centered in time and place, its centricity expressed in the form of the cross and in the figure of the body sacrificed upon it, Southwell has situated the crucifixion at the center of his sequence in the form of "**His Circumcision,**" a poem whose treatment of the circumcision as a type of the crucifixion is focused in the poem's central, third stanza:

> The vein of life distilleth drops of grace,
> Our rock gives issue to an heavenly spring,
> Tears from his eyes, blood runs from wounded place,
> Which showers to heaven of joy a harvest bring,
> This sacred dew let angels gather up,
> Such dainty drops best fit their nectared cup.

The blood and the water running into the cup prefigure the crucifixion and the mass. The water of the crucifixion that flowed from Christ's wound is the "shower of grace" foretold in "*Elias*' Little Cloud" and Moses' striking of the rock (Exodus 17.6). In the third stanza, the line "The knife that cut his flesh did pierce her heart" emphasizes the typology of the scene of the circumcision by its reference to the words of Simeon to Mary, always taken as a prophecy of the crucifixion: "And thy own soul a sword shall pierce" (Luke 2.35).

Although Mary's role at the crucifixion is that of the watching, suffering mother, her role in this sequence devoted to her is to be the vessel in whom all this history is contained. She is the mother of human history, and when to human eyes she puts off her mortal shroud in death, she resumes her place with the immortal company of heaven. **"The Death of Our Lady"** therefore begins, "Weep living things, of life the mother dies, / The world doth lose the sum of all her bliss"; **"The Assumption of Our Lady"** ends:

> Gem to her worth, spouse to her love ascends,
> Prince to her throne, queen to her heavenly king,
> Whose court with solemn pomp on her attends,
> And choirs of saints with greeting notes do sing.

The sequence therefore has a form and a subject. It is a celebration of Mary embodying in its own art ideas that profoundly moved and stimulated Southwell's imagination—above all his sense, as Oxley expresses it, "of the artifice of holy things, and indeed, of the holiness of artifice." "Rich and gorgeous" (Praz, 289) in its harmony of types, allegories, and paradoxes, but plain and elevated in language, the sequence is unique in English poetry. The irony of it, seen against the background of Southwell's dogged campaign to kidnap Tudor love poetry for the Church, is that in form and structure, the sequence is really Southwell's own love poem and its beloved is Mary as the "sum" of all human beauty and meaning. A conviction of the centrality of love was fundamental to Southwell's life, and first appears in his writing, before he was a professed Jesuit, in one of his Latin elegies, Elegia VIII. At the center (ll. 31-32) of this poem of 62 lines, in which a husband mourns his wife, are two of the most moving lines Southwell ever wrote:

> Dixi ego, ne dubita, memori vivemus amore,
> Quam tuus ipse tuus, tam mea semper eris.
> [I said, Doubt not, we shall live in the memory of
>    love,
> As I am yours, truly yours, so you will always be
>    mine.][5]

The reciprocity of love itself finds verbal form in these lines, in the paired words, in the effortlessly graceful movement of their language, in the interlinking of sounds (so that there is something like a pun on memori/ amore), and in the antithesis that expresses the unity of "mine" and "thine." The same kind of writing appears in the sequence: "Her being now begins, who ere she end, / Shall bring the good that shall our ill amend," and "Our most, her least, our million, but her mite" (**"The Virgin Mary's Conception,"** ll. 5-6, 9). Why, then, has so little attention been paid to the form and content of this sequence? Undoubtedly because until Brown published it almost intact for the first time in 1967, no one had seen it for nearly 400 years.

### Sacred Epigrams: The Gethsemani Group and Others

Southwell's epigrammatic style appears again in three poems in six-line stanzas on Christ's agony in the garden of Gethsemani. They appear together in the manuscripts; Busby printed two of them, **"Christ's Bloody Sweat"** (omitting the second two stanzas) and **"Christ's Sleeping Friends."** The other, **"Sin's Heavy Load,"** was first printed in Cawood's expanded edition of *Saint Peter's Complaint* (1602).

Martz thought that **"Sin's Heavy Load"** was one of the poems that revealed the influence of the Ignatian *Spiritual Exercises* on Southwell's poetics; the first two stanzas "suggest the acts of composition and memory, with a few touches of paradoxical analysis that prepare the way for the operations of the understanding" (Martz, 40-41). Yet the whole poem is a colloquy with Christ, and there is no sign of a "mental representation of the place" at all. In the second part of the poem, Southwell's control of his argument obviously slackens, a fault that has more to do with poetic form than with techniques of meditation. Brown, however, accepted Martz's suggestion, adding that the poem is "a meditation of the kind enjoined in the First Week of the Spiritual Exercises when the retreatant contemplates his own sin" (*Poems,* xcv). Most readers would probably agree with Martz that with its concentration on a single subject, and its argumentative, paradoxical approach, the entire poem foreshadows the methods of Donne.

The poem is based on verses found in the gospels according to St. Mark and St. Luke: "And when he was gone forward a little, he fell flat on the ground" (Mark 14.35); "And his sweat became as drops of blood, trickling down upon the ground" (Luke 22.44). Southwell incorporates the Douay-Rheims English texts into his first stanza with his usual accuracy, but what is really striking in this poem is that he puts himself into the stanza as the cause of Christ's fall:

> O Lord my sin doth over-charge thy brest,
> The poise thereof doth force thy knees to bow;
> Yea flat thou fallest with my faults oppressed,
> And bloody sweat runs trickling from thy brow:
> But had they not to earth thus pressed thee,
> Much more they would in hell have pestered me.

The essential paradox of the poem is that Christ, who holds the world in His hand, and supports the globe with a finger, is brought to the ground by the weight of one man's sin:

> O sin, how huge and heavy is thy weight,
> Thou weighest more than all the world beside,
> Of which when Christ had taken in his freight
> The poise thereof his flesh could not abide;
> Alas, if God himself sink under sin,
> What will become of man that dies therein?

In its best stanzas, then, the poem is really a strong, effective epigram based upon a conceit. It weakens in the fourth through sixth stanzas because Southwell departs from his original idea to develop the more elaborate conceit that, having fallen flat to earth at his arrival into Mary's womb, Christ now falls flat again in order to kiss the earth goodbye. This idea is too ingeniously pretty for the context, and might suggest to some readers that the first conceit is equally insubstantial, despite appearances. It is interesting, nonetheless, to see Southwell applying the charged, epigrammatic style of the sequence poems to other subjects.

The third poem, **"Christ's Sleeping Friends,"** is a companion piece, similarly composed of seven six-line stanzas and based on the story of the apostles' falling asleep during Christ's agony. This time Southwell has avoided the excessive development of the first poem's conceit by devoting the first two stanzas to a plain narrative account of the disciples' sleep, and reserving the rest of the poem for the development of a single typological image based on the story of Jonas. He treats Jonas's sleep through the storm as a type of the disciples' carelessness, and the withering of Jonas's ivy tree as a type of the disciples' loss of Christ.[6]

The strength of both poems is in the powerfully emotive use of conceit and figure, which take on a life of their own, virtually independent of the thing figured. "Alas, if God himself sink under sin, / What will become of man that dies therein?" asks the speaker of **"Sin's Heavy Load,"** having himself invented the conceit that it was his sins that made Christ fall in the first place. The speaker of **"Christ's Sleeping Friends"** addresses the disciples in the poem's last stanza as if they were learned in typological commentary, and were themselves become typological:

> Awake ye slumbering wights lift up your eyes,
> Mark *Judas* how to tear your root he strives,
> Alas the glory of your arbor dies,
> Arise and guard the comfort of your lives.
> No *Jonas'* ivy, no *Zacheus'* tree,
> Were to the world so great a loss as he.

The plain, energetic English suggests the presence of an author whose mind is on his subject, but his figure has so displaced the subject it was ostensibly introduced to explain that inevitably a reader will wonder exactly what the real subject of the stanza is. Is it a warning to people in a state of careless inattention, perhaps the less keen recusants? Is Christ himself figurative in this poem, standing for a threatened way of life? There is no way of knowing. What is clear is that the plain, narrative opening stanzas are in Southwell's plodding, Tottelian style ("From frighted flesh a bloody sweat did rain," l. 2), and that the language comes alive as it turns figurative. Southwell's most intricate figurative structures often seem to come untethered from the reality they should stand for, with the result that the poems can acquire an air of fantastic, ingenious abstraction.

The central poem of this set, **"Christ's Bloody Sweat,"** a truly remarkable performance, is simultaneously a demonstration of the power and the danger of figurative language in Southwell's writing. Here there is no narrative exposition at all.[7] The translation of the event into figures begins immediately in the first stanza, an example of *carmen correlativum*:[8]

> Fat soil, full spring, sweet olive, grape of bliss,
> That yields, that streams, that pours, that dost distil,
> Untilled, undrawn, unstamped, untouched of press,
> Dear fruit, clear brooks, fair oil, sweet wine at will:
> Thus Christ unforced prevents in shedding blood
> The whips, the thorns, the nails, the spear, the blood.

The compiler of the Harmsworth manuscript wrote the first four lines in four columns, so that the reader immediately sees that the sentences read down as well as across. In this poem, the intense compression of the technique corresponds to the intensity and concentration of Christ's experience as a "prevention" or anticipatory experience of the Passion. The figures of soil, spring, olive, and grape contain compressed references to Old Testament texts interpreted as messianic prophecy, such as Isaias 12.3, "You shall draw waters with joy out of the saviour's fountains," and 63.2, "Why then is thy apparel red, and thy garments like theirs that tread in the winepress?" The bloody sweat is a compression of the entire Passion, summed in its instruments: whips, thorns, nails, spear, and cross. The root conception of the stanza seems to be the idea that Christ's agony was voluntary, and that by its very nature, it was also the kind of experience we call contemplative or mystical. Hence it will have come about, as the gospel narrative would suggest to a mind like Southwell's, by means of contemplative prayer. This first stanza therefore establishes a close parallel between the speaker and Christ. As Christ contemplated His own Passion in prayer, and proleptically entered into it through the realized figure of His own blood, so the poet contemplates Christ's Passion and prepares for his own figural embodiment of it. In that sense, the poem is the poet's equivalent of Christ's blood because it prays for and prefigures his martyrdom. There is, though, an important distinction to be made; although Christ's experience is a mystical one, similar to the Transfiguration, the poet's is not. He is the observer and imitator, not—as yet—the protagonist.

The second stanza is emblematic:

> He Pelican's, he Phoenix' fate doth prove,
> Whom flames consume, whom streams enforce to die,
> How burneth blood, how bleedeth burning love?
> Can one in flame and stream both bathe and fry?
> How could he join a Phoenix' fiery pains
> In fainting Pelican's still bleeding veins?

Southwell's fellow Jesuit, John Gerard, describes a crucifix decorated with the symbolism of phoenix and pelican (Gerard, 195). The phoenix, immolated in its own flames, is a symbol of resurrection, and the pelican, according to the bestiaries, revived its young by opening its own breast and feeding them its blood. Southwell treats both birds as examples of loving sacrifice, and the question he asks through the emblematic symbolism seems to be, how can one act combine two different sacrifices, the one motivated by a burning love and desire of a new life, the other by the wish to give oneself for others?

The answer comes in the third stanza with another shift in the mode of the poem, this time to Old Testament typology. In his contest with the priests of Baal (3 Kings 18.38), Elias produced a fire "that blood and wood and water did devour, / Yea stones and dust, beyond all nature's course" (ll. 15-16); the poet declares that "such fire is love." The last stanza is a prayer to that fiery divine love, and though the elaborate style has gone, the figures remain:

> O sacred Fire come show thy force on me
> That sacrifice to Christ I may return,
> If withered wood for fuel fittest be,
> If stones and dust, if flesh and blood will burn,
> I withered am and stony to all good,
> A sack of dust, a mass of flesh and blood.

This is no less than a prayer to be subsumed into figures, to have one's body transformed into a text of typological correspondences, and, of course, it is a preparatory contemplation of the nature of Southwell's own martyrdom. **"Christ's Bloody Sweat"** may be Southwell's finest poem, its tightly wrought web of figures finally enclosing the speaker inescapably in the determinist logic of typology. For that reason, it is also a terrible and tragic poem.[9]

Three other poems should be mentioned here. **"Decease Release:** *dum morior orior,*" almost certainly about the beheading of Mary, Queen of Scots, on 8 February 1587, is the only accurately datable poem in the collection, and it shows Southwell as a master of his figurative, even riddling style quite soon after arriving in England—another hint that his career as an English poet had begun in Italy. The poem, spoken by the spirit of the dead queen, is another of his statements on martyrdom as a transforming sacrament: "God's spice I was and pounding was my due, / In fading breath my incense savored best" (ll. 5-6):

> Rue not my death, rejoice at my repose,
> It was no death to me but to my woe,
> The bud was opened to let out the rose,
> The chains unloosed to let the captive go.
>
> (ll. 25-28)

This poem in particular is notable for the strength and limpidity of its language, showing what the so-called plain, or "drab," style is capable of in the hands of a poet with as musical an ear as Southwell.

**"At Home in Heaven"** and **"Look Home"** are a pair in the manuscripts. The first is about the love of God for the human soul, the second about the soul as a creature made for the love of God. They provide a glimpse of the kind of poet Southwell might have become had he lived a normal English life in his times. As Janelle remarked, the poems reveal a Platonic strain in their author. The soul of **"At Home"** is in exile in this life, its beauty shrouded by veils of mortality; yet its beauty drew God down from heaven to become incarnate in human form: "Thy ghostly beauty offered force to God, / It chained him in the links of tender love." The link suggested between beauty and force, chains and tender love, has the ring of the metaphysical style in the mingling of extremely sensuous feeling and excited, even slightly kinky thought. Unfortunately, like most of Southwell's poems, this one has a didactic purpose—to dissuade its reader from earthly love—and after four superbly disciplined stanzas, it loses itself in prosy sermonizing. In the complementary poem, **"Look Home,"** Southwell writes that "Man's mind a mirror is of heavenly sights, / A brief wherein all marvels summed lie"; although the mind is a creature, it can also create, "To nature's patterns adding higher skill." This is possible because the mind is made in the image of God, Himself a craftsman "of endless skill and might."

Like **"At Home,"** **"Look Home"** is not as benign as it looks at first. Its implication, spelled out Herbert-like in the title, is that since God made the soul to reflect himself, the sooner it turns its back to the world, the better.

### The Nativity Group

The four poems on the nativity include Southwell's best-known lyrics, much anthologized. Benjamin Britten set words from two of them in his *Ceremony of Carols*. Part of the reason for their popularity is their simplicity. **"New Heaven, New War"** is in six-line stanzas made up of octosyllabic couplets; **"New Prince, New Pomp"** and **"The Burning Babe"** are in ballad meter. **"A Child My Choice"** is in fourteeners, and though written in an elaborated syntax nonetheless gives an effect of simplicity:

> Alas, he weeps, he sighs, he pants, yet do his angels sing:
> Out of his tears, his sighs and throbs, doth bud a joyful spring.
> Almighty babe, whose tender arms can force all foes to fly:
> Correct my faults, protect my life, direct me when I die.
>
> (ll. 13-16)

Janelle, who argued that Southwell's writing developed from an overelaborate, conceitist, and artificial style towards plainness and simplicity and who thought that the simpler poems were the later and better ones, praised **"New Prince, New Pomp"** for being "tender and plain," but criticized **"The Burning Babe"** for its hackneyed conceits (168). His predecessor, H. J. Thurston, also thought that Southwell's "affected style" was at odds with "the perfect earnestness and simplicity of Father Southwell's character" (Thurston 1895, 238), and naturally preferred the plainer poems. The taste of both these earlier critics, predating the modernist movement and its interest in the metaphysical style, was formed on different models from any that Robert Southwell knew. There is no reason at all to believe that in Southwell's mind a simple style was ever intrinsically better than a complex one. His nativity poems are probably more simply written for reasons of decorum; a plain ballad or carol-like style suits the subject of the nativity. Whether the poems were written earlier or later in his short poetic career is something we do not know.

In any case, simplicity of style does not necessitate simplicity of content. The first four stanzas of **"New Heaven, New War"** summon the angels to leave home and follow their God's move to the stable on earth where He now is, and each angel is instructed to perform his traditional service there. The fiery seraphim who guard the ark of the covenant are invited to warm the Christ-child because the ark was one of His prefiguring types, and "This little ark no cover hath." Raphael, whose symbol is a fish, and who looked after Tobias, is asked to "provide our little Toby meat." Gabriel, who as angelic groom, "took up" the baby's first "earthly room" in Mary's womb, is to continue in the same employment. Michael the soldier is to guard him. The graces can rock him and all the other angels can sing his lullaby. The combination of angelology and typology with extremely simple, homely language is as clever as it is charming. The poem's fourth stanza announces to the angels the fundamental paradox of the nativity, that the baby in the manger is the God who made and sustains the cosmos or, as G. K. Chesterton expressed it, "The hands that made the sun and stars were too small to reach the huge heads of the cattle":[10]

> The same you saw in heavenly seat,
> Is he that now sucks Mary's teat;
> Agnize your King a mortal wight,
> His borrow weed lets not your sight.

With the second part of the poem, "new war," Southwell mobilizes another paradox, based on Matthew 10.34: "Do not think that I came to send peace upon earth: I came not to send peace, but the sword." The birth in the stable has opened a new front in the war against evil, mobilizing weakness against strength: "This little babe so few days old, / Has come to rifle Satan's fold"; that is, to plunder Satan's sheep-fold of its sheep. There follows a series of bold, even startling conceits:

> With tears he fights and wins the field,
> His naked breast stands for a shield;
> His battering shot are bab'ish cries,
> His arrows looks of weeping eyes,
> His martial ensigns cold and need,
> And feeble flesh his warrior's steed.

These conceits, a variant of St. Paul's instructions to the Ephesians to "put on the armour of God" (6.11), bring one very close to the basis and center of Southwell's own life and beliefs. The Christ child, as the God "Whom love hath linked to feeble sense" (l. 16), is the embodiment of life under the rule of love; and love, in the metaphysical warfare of the Christian soul with "principalities and powers, against the rulers of the world of this darkness,[11] against the spirits of wickedness in the high places" (Ephesians 6.12), is undefeatable because, according to a verse of one of Southwell's favorite biblical books, "Love is as strong as death" (Canticles 8.6). In the final stanza, Southwell addresses his own soul:

> My soul with Christ join thou in fight,
> Stick to the tents that he hath pight;
> Within his Crib is surest ward,
> This little Babe will be thy guard:
> If thou wilt foil thy foes with joy,
> Then flit not from this heavenly boy.

This apparently simple little poem, like *Saint Peter's Complaint* and **"Christ's Bloody Sweat,"** is another version of Southwell's *imitatio Christi*, another stage in his contemplation of martyrdom. In form and content it belongs with his richest and most complex epigrammatic poems.

In its form at least, **"New Prince, New Pomp"** is a genuinely simple poem, carol-like in form and style. This is the poem that Martz used to demonstrate the presence of Ignatian meditative structures in sixteenth- and seventeenth-century poetry, the first two stanzas devoted to "composition, seeing the spot," the next four to "analytical acts of the understanding," and the last to arousing the affections to action in an exhortation (Martz, 39-40). An exhortation, however, is not the same as the colloquy with which a meditation is supposed to end and, furthermore, a meditation is a long and difficult form of prayer. This poem is very short and simple, and it is not a prayer. Its form could, nevertheless, reflect meditative technique; but if it does, then Ignatian meditation only formalized and schematized deeply ingrained mental habits in the service of Christian indoctrination. **"New Prince, New Pomp"** is typical of nativity carols and pageants in setting the scene, explaining it, and inviting the reader—or audience or congregation—to come and worship. As set by the English composer John Ireland, with a traditional "Nowell" for prelude,[12] it fits easily among other nativity carols such as the traditional Staffordshire carol,

"The babe in Bethlehem's manger laid" (*Oxford Carols*, no. 69), or more modern examples such as Edward Caswall's "See amid the winter's snow"[13] and Christina Rossetti's "In the bleak mid-winter" (*Oxford Carols*, no. 187).

No true nativity carol, however, can ever be intellectually simple; simplicity of form is always at odds with miraculous content, as in each of these three examples. The unsophisticated little Staffordshire carol almost takes the mystery for granted, but allows the angels their amazement at seeing God as a baby:

> The babe in Bethlehem's manger laid
>     In humble form so low;
> By wondering angels is surveyed
>     Through all his scenes of woe.

Christina Rossetti hints at the mystery ("A stable-place sufficed / The Lord God Almighty / Jesus Christ"), and Caswall spells it out: "Lo, within a manger lies / He who built the starry skies." In Southwell's case, the setting of the scene in its traditional detail is the prelude to the announcement of the mystery; in the baby shivering in a manger on a freezing winter night, the world is refigured according to His mother's own prophecy: "He hath put down the mighty from their seat, and hath exalted the humble" (Luke 1.52).

> This stable is a Prince's Court,
>     The Crib his chair of state:
> The beasts are parcel of his pomp,
>     The wooden dish his plate.
>
> The persons in that poor attire,
>     His royal liveries wear,
> The Prince himself is come from heaven,
>     This pomp is prized there.

The simple, humble style suits the occasion; the poem, one suspects, is Southwell's own gift to the child. Yet despite its simplicity, the miracle is fully acknowledged, and at the poem's turn from poor appearance to rich reality, the style rises to a tone of exalted conviction: "Weigh not his mother's poor attire, / Nor Joseph's simple weed. / This stable is a Prince's court. . . ."

The most famous of these poems, **"The Burning Babe,"** combines the epigrammatic force of **"New Heaven, New War"** with the carol-like simplicity of **"New Prince, New Pomp"** to produce a figure that has so far eluded all attempts to explain it. Standing shivering in the snow on a frosty winter's night, the poet feels a sudden warmth that makes his heart glow. Looking up to see where the fire might be, he sees in the air a burning, weeping baby, who speaks to him, explaining what he is. The explanation complete, the baby vanishes, "And straight I called unto mind, / That it was Christmas day."

Janelle (168) said of the poem that "despite its prettiness and sweetness, [it] contains the most hackneyed of all conceits" in the lines on the baby's tears and flames—a view that, besides leaving the poem unexplained, disposed of its central mystery entirely. More recently, it has been suggested that the image of the burning baby derives mostly from the emblem book tradition, where such images as flaming hearts, fiery hearts in furnaces, and fountains pouring blood are to be found.[14] Unfortunately, although the baby certainly explains himself as if he were familiar with emblem book practice, no emblem of a burning baby has been found. In any case, Southwell's baby does not behave like an emblem. Another scholar has suggested that the image of the burning babe derives from a typological reading of the burning bush as prefiguring the Virgin and the Incarnation, with an implication that Queen Elizabeth is a new pharaoh, Southwell a new Moses.[15] A burning bush, however, is not a burning baby; it may be an analogue, but it is not a precedent. Martz produced passages from the *Meditations* of Luis Puente on the fire of love in Jesus' heart as context for his argument that this poem, too, was the product of Ignatian meditation, "an application of the senses" following upon a meditation, and beginning with "a particularly vivid 'composition'" (Martz, 81-82). Martz is almost certainly right in thinking that the poem is the result of meditation, even if the technical language is out of place. For instance, the poem does not begin with a "composition" or "mental representation of the place"; it begins with a vision, and ends with its disappearance. John R. Roberts, who accepts Martz's view of the influence of the *Spiritual Exercises,* believes that the poem records a mystical experience: "There is a note here of his having lost himself in ecstatic delight, the goal of Ignatian methodology,"[16] a view with which Geoffrey Hill disagrees: "For Southwell to have 'lost himself' merely in a poem would have required more self-centredness than he was capable of" (Hill, 36).

Practice of the Ignatian exercises could lead to mystical experience, but that was not their purpose, which was instead to discipline and indoctrinate the retreatant. If the experience in **"The Burning Babe"** were the poet's, he would have undergone a physical phenomenon well-known to adepts in mysticism as the incendium amoris, or fire of love, which was by no means uncommon in the fervent atmosphere of Counter-Reformation Catholicism. Saints Philip Neri, Catherine of Genoa, Stanislaus Kostka, and Veronica Giuliani all claimed to experience it. It was a sensation of intense heat in and about the heart, which St. Veronica Giuliani is said to have experienced to the extent of being "stigmatized" with a curved right shoulder. A surgeon's affidavit of 1673 from Naples claims that an autopsy upon a nun, Sister Maria Villani, revealed "smoke and heat which exhaled from the heart, that veritable furnace of love." The surgeon even burned himself on the heart, in which he found a wound "made with a spear of fire."[17]

Southwell would have known of this phenomenon, just as he was familiar with the devotional language of blood, wounds, hearts, and flames. The baby of the poem certainly seems to be experiencing "the fire of love." Southwell uses English precisely, and as Geoffrey Hill observes, the baby's "excessive heat" (l. 9) means heat accompanying, or associated with, "excess," used in the Latin sense of "being outside oneself," in "ecstasy."[18] The poet, standing in the heat radiating from the baby, feels his heart glow—but that is all. Indeed, in the structure of its thought, this poem is similar to "Christ's bloody sweat." In both poems Christ, here the burning Christ-child, undergoes the experience: the poet observes it. The implication is that the poet must imitate it, first in his poem, then in his life.

At the poem's center is a vision of the mystery of divine love as it is expressed in the gospel of St. John, 3.16: "For God so loved the world, as to give his only begotten Son; that whosoever believeth in him, may not perish, but may have life everlasting"; and once again Southwell presents God as an artist or craftsman, this time working his transformations in metal:

> My faultless breast the furnace is,
>    The fuel wounding thorns:[19]
> Love is the fire, and sighs the smoke,
>    The ashes, shame and scorns;
>
> The fuel Justice layeth on,
>    And Mercy blows the coals,
> The metal in this furnace wrought,
>    Are mens' defiled souls.

The lines resist close paraphrase, but one gathers that justice or law fuels the fire of divine love with man's cruelty and inhumanity, and that mercy or compassion intensifies the fire as it smelts and refines the impurities out of souls: the Christian who imitates this Christ will have to go into some very dark corners of the human scene indeed.

How is a reader to understand the factual, expository opening and close of the poem? We know from the prefatory material to *Mary Magdalen's Funeral Tears* that Southwell did not care for fictions, and so we should probably allow that in some sense, if only in his mind's eye, Southwell saw this baby on Christmas night. For him, the stable of the nativity, usually imagined as a scene of peace and joy, prefigured the Passion of Christ and the martyrdom of His disciples. Helen White, who distinguished between the "discursive development of the meditative" and "the total-working immediacy of the contemplative" thought that **"The Burning Babe"** was a truly contemplative poem.[20]

### "A Vale of Tears"

For twentieth-century readers, the most impressive of Southwell's short poems is probably **"A Vale of Tears,"**

a 19-stanza *paysage moralisé* of the troubled mind quite unlike anything else to be found in Elizabethan poetry. It is based (like a famous passage of Byron's *Journal to Augusta*[21]) on Southwell's own experience of crossing the Alps twice, on his way to and from Italy. "The poem most likely reveals the deep impression produced upon him by the wild, majestic and weird scenery in the neighbourhood of the St. Gothard pass" (Janelle, 278). Janelle is surely right; indeed, the first thing to strike one about the poem's form is its composed objectivity, as if the scene had been "photographed" by the poet's memory. The first two stanzas fix its outlines visually, and the attention paid to the movement of the eye in comprehending the scene is especially interesting:

> A vale there is enwrapped with dreadful shades,
> Which thick of mourning pines shrouds from the sun,
> Where hanging clifts yield short and dumpish glades,
> And snowy flood with broken streams doth run,
>
> Where eye-room is from rocks to cloudy sky,
> From thence to dales with stony ruins strowed,
> Then to the crushed water's frothy fry,
> Which tumbleth from the tops where snow is thowed.

The next three stanzas supply the sounds of this enormous, but enclosed place, "Where ears of other sound can have no choice" but wind, water, and thunder: "And in the horror of this fearful choir, / Consists the music of this doleful place."

Having provided a general picture of the valley, Southwell then spends four stanzas on the response of travelers to it. No-one goes there, he says, but pilgrims—people like himself, that is, going to and from Rome. The valley terrifies them, and "They judge the place to terror framed by art"; but they are wrong: "Yet nature's work it is of art untouched, . . . / A place for mated minds," that is, for the terrified and helpless. Four stanzas of detail follow:

> Huge massie stones that hang by tickle stay,
> Still threaten fall, and seem to hang in fear,
> Some withered trees ashamed of their decay,
> Beset with green, are forced gray coats to wear.

This part of the poem closes with a pair of stanzas announcing that this valley, "Where sorrow springs from water, stone and tree," is a place for "pangs and heavy passions," and for "plaining thoughts."

Only in the last four stanzas, in an address to his own soul, does the poet relate the landscape to himself. For him it is a place for tears and repentance, and it becomes clear when he says "Set here my soul main streams of tears afloat" that "here" can only be a mental place, and that this is a mental landscape. Is Martz right, then, to argue that "This is no romantic landscape" but an allegorical setting for a meditation; specifically, that it represents the two "preludes" for the meditation upon one's sins (Martz, 207-8)? In this as in other poems, Southwell may have been influenced by his Jesuit training, but no objective evidence exists anywhere that Southwell made poems out of meditations. To use the word "romantic" to dispose of the contrary view sets up a straw man; no one would mistake this poem for a work of the romantic period. On the other hand, most readers have seen some preromantic tendencies in it, not only in the detailed evocation of a wild alpine landscape and the projection of unhappy states of mind onto it, but in Southwell's aesthetic description of the place, with its "disordered order" and "pleasing horror." Few readers will wish to confine so original a poem within the form and purpose of Jesuit meditation.

In this connection, the most interesting feature of the poem is its musical imagery, which appears in the first stanza in the phrase "dumpish glades," a "dump" being a sad piece of music as well as a generally sad state of mind. The sounds of wind, water, and thunder make the "music of the place"; the pleasant songbirds have left it, and only heavy notes have any "grace"—a musical term meaning ornament. The phrase "disordered order" is an invitation to think of a certain kind of chromatic music, greatly favored in Southwell's time to express melancholy and distress. Music is mentioned in all the last four stanzas addressed to the poet's soul. In the first, the ditties, or words, are to be set to solemn tunes in the saddest kind of music, and in the second, *"Echo,"* a common imitative effect in music, will repeat "thy plainful cries." "Dumps" return in the third of these stanzas, and in the last, tears are to be set to tunes and pains to plaints, and the whole acquires a burden or refrain: "Come deep remorse, possess my sinful brest: / Delights adieu, I harbored you too long."

In a context of so much intensely musical imagery, the line "Set here my soul main streams of tears afloat" also becomes musical, the phrase "streams of tears" evoking a musical composition that, if ever realized, would have been akin to the best-known song of the period—also popular in instrumental form—the *lacrimae,* or "tears," of the great recusant lutenist, John Dowland.[22] Dowland, born in 1563, was almost exactly contemporary with Robert Southwell. **"A Vale of Tears"** is a text for an expressive musical setting; the poem is full of invitations to musical word-painting on the part of a composer:

> A place for mated minds, an only bower,
> Where every thing doth sooth a dumpish mood.
> Earth lies forlorn, the cloudy sky doth lower,
> The wind here weeps, here sighs, here cries aloud.

This being so, the text transcends any origin some elements of its form might have had in meditative habits, or in Southwell's campaign to convert secular verse. The burden, "Delights adieu, I harbored you too long,"

places the poem firmly in a social context, however pious. Its speaking voice is not necessarily Robert Southwell's, but the voice of its singer, and for that reason the poem almost certainly exceeds in significance any intention Southwell himself might have had for it. As a distinguished musicological critic has written of this kind of introspective composition for words and music, "The Elizabethan's delight in the wonders of the physical universe is explicitly related to his preoccupation with his own mind and senses. Exploring nature and exploring the self are the same activity, *both opposed to antique theological dogma*" (my italics).[23] Southwell probably intended his poem to be another encouragement to repentance for sin, but the nature of the landscape and the range of responses possible to it engulf the intention. There is no better evidence of the strength and originality of Southwell's poetic gift than this strikingly forward-looking, even prophetic poem.

*Notes*

1. Ben Jonson, *Works,* ed. C. H. Herford and Percy Simpson, 11 vols. (Oxford: Clarendon Press, 1925-52), 1:137.

2. Warren R. Maurer, "Spee, Southwell, and the Poetry of Meditation," *Comparative Literature* 15 (1963): 16; hereafter cited in text.

3. See, however, Harry Morris, "In Articulo Moris," *Tulane Studies in English* 11 (1961): 21-37, who acknowledges that the poems are imitations of love poetry but treats them (mistakenly) as autobiographical and written at the point of death, and singles out "I die alive" for close analysis.

4. Rosamund Tuve, "Sacred 'Parody' of Love Poetry, and Herbert," *Studies in the Renaissance* 8 (1961): 250; hereafter cited in text.

5. Brown did not print the Latin poems in her edition. They survive in manuscript at Stonyhurst and are available only in *The Complete Poems of Robert Southwell, S.J.,* ed. A. B. Grosart (Blackburn, 1872), 189-215. I owe my knowledge of these poems to two articles by Brian Oxley, "'Simples Are by Compounds Farre Exceld,'" cited previously, and "The Relation between Robert Southwell's Neo-Latin and English Poetry," *Recusant History* 17, no. 3 (May 1985): 201-7.

6. "Jonas" and the "ivy" are the Douay-Rheims, and Southwell's, equivalents of the more familiar King James version's "Jonah" and "gourd."

7. The near-complete subsumption of event into figure in this poem misled Carolyn A. Schten, "Southwell's 'Christ's Bloody Sweat': A Meditation on the Mass," *English Miscellany* 20 (1960): 75-80, into arguing that Nancy Brown was mistaken to link the poem with the other two

Gethsemani poems. Schten mistook Southwell's treatment of Christ's sweat as a prefiguration of Calvary as a treatment of Calvary itself.

8. See Joseph G. Fucilla, "A Rhetorical Pattern in Renaissance and Baroque Poetry," *Studies in the Renaissance* 3 (1956): 23-48; cited by Brian Oxley, "The Relation between Robert Southwell's Neo-Latin and English Poetry," *Recusant History* 17, no. 3 (May 1985): 206. According to Fucilla, after being boycotted under Bembist influence in the midsixteenth century, this extremely mannered technique became popular again after about 1575.

9. The Harmsworth manuscript includes two extra stanzas that are probably discarded drafts. They do not belong in the finished poem as it appears in the other manuscripts.

10. G. K. Chesterton, *The Everlasting Man* (ca. 1925; reprint, New York: Dodd, Mead, 1946), 201-2.

11. τους κοσμοκρατορας του σκοτους τουτου, "cosmocrats of the dark aeon," in Christopher Dawson's translation, cited by John Lukacs, *Confessions of an Original Sinner* (New York: Ticknor and Fields, 1990), 306.

12. *The Oxford Book of Carols,* comp. Percy Dearmer, R. Vaughan Williams, and Martin Shaw (London: Oxford University Press, 1928), no. 170; hereafter cited in text as *Oxford Carols.*

13. Set by John Goss (1800-1880) and first published with the music in *Christmas Carols New and Old,* ed. Henry Ramsden Bramley and Sir John Stainer (London: Novello and Co., n.d.), 64-65. The text in *The New Oxford Book of Carols,* ed. Hugh Keyte and Andrew Parrot (Oxford: Oxford University Press, 1992), 340-41, is severely abridged.

14. Peter M. Daly, "Southwell's 'Burning Babe' and the Emblematic Practice," *Wascana Review* 3 (1968): 29-44.

15. Andrew Harnack, "Robert Southwell's 'The Burning Babe' and the Typology of Christmastide," *Kentucky Philological Association Bulletin* 4 (1977): 25-30.

16. J. R. Roberts, "The Influence of *The Spiritual Exercises* of St. Ignatius Loyola on the Nativity Poems of Robert Southwell," *Journal of English and Germanic Philology* 59 (1960): 455.

17. Herbert J. Thurston, "Some Physical Phenomena of Mysticism: Incendium Amoris," *The Month* 141 (1923): 535-47.

18. Hill (33) cites *Epistle of Comfort* as an example of Southwell's familiarity with the word: "If *Christ* was seen transfigured in *Mount Thabor* in glorious manner, he was also at the same time heard talking *de excessu* of his bitter passion" (32a).

19. As a friend pointed out to me, in an otherwise symbolic fire, the thorns have a very concrete look about them. One is tempted to associate them with the crown of thorns, but if the thorns too are symbolic, then they are probably the parabolic thorns of Matthew 13.22 and signify "the care of this world and the deceitfulness of riches." The same friend says that there may be a suggestion in "Justice" and "Mercy" of the Old and New Testament dispensations.

20. Helen C. White, "The Contemplative Element in Robert Southwell," *Catholic Historical Review* 48 (1962): 10.

21. *Byron's Letters and Journals,* ed. Leslie Marchand, 12 vols. (London: John Murray, 1973-82), 5:102: "Passed *Whole woods of withered pines—all withered*—trunks stripped & barkless—branches lifeless—done by a single winter—their appearance reminded me of me & my family.—"

22. Three keyboard settings of Dowland's "lacrimae"—by Byrd, Farnaby, and Morley—appear in the recusant collection of virginal music, *The Fitzwilliam Virginal Book,* ed. J. A. Fuller Maitland and W. Barclay Squire, 2 vols. (New York: Dover Publications, 1963), 2:42, 172, 472.

23. Wilfird Mellers, *Harmonius Meeting* (London: Dennis Dobson, 1965), 43.

## *Selected Bibliography*

The standard bibliography of Southwell's writings is James H. McDonald, *The Poems and Prose Writings of Robert Southwell, S.J.* (Oxford: Printed for the Roxburghe Club, 1937). It has been superseded, for the poetry, by Nancy Pollard Brown's work on the Clarendon Press edition of the poems.

Southwell's letters, written mostly in Latin, and surviving in a variety of sources and repositories, await a scholarly editor and translator. McDonald's list is now out of date, and published letters are scattered in various volumes in variously reliable texts and translations. About 40 years ago, Philip Caraman, S.J., found 12 letters in the Jesuit archives, Rome (*Fondo Gesuitico,* 651), to be published in *Archivum Historicum Societatis Iesu* (1995) in an edition by Thomas M. McCoog, S.J. Henry Foley, S.J., *Records of the English Province of the Society of Jesus.* 7 vols. (London: Burns and Oates, 1877), 1: 301-87 printed several of Southwell's letters and an eyewitness narrative of his trial and execution. Another group of letters is available in "The Letters of Father Robert Southwell" in John Hungerford Pollen, S.J. (editor), *Unpublished Documents Relating to the English Martyrs,* Publications of the Catholic Record Society 5 (1908): 293-333.

For a bibliographical guide to works on Southwell, see Vittorio F. Cavalli, "St. Robert Southwell, S.J.: A Selective Bibliographic Supplement to the Studies of Pierre

Janelle and James H. McDonald," *Recusant History* 21 (1993): 297-304; see also John N. King, "Recent Studies in Southwell," *English Literary Renaissance* 13 (1983): 221-27.

PRIMARY SOURCES

*An Epistle of Comfort.* London: secretly printed, 1587. Facsimile reprint. In *English Recusant Literature, 1538-1640.* Selected and edited by D. M. Rogers. London: Scolar Press, 1974, vol. 211.

*An Humble Supplication to Her Majestie.* Edited by R. C. Bald. Cambridge: University Press, 1953.

*Spiritual Exercises and Devotions.* Edited by J.-M. De Buck and translated by P. E. Hallett. London: Sheed & Ward, 1931.

*Mary Magdalen's Funeral Tears.* London: Gabriel Cawood, 1591. Facsimile reprint. Edited by Vincent B. Leitch. New York: Delmar, 1975.

*The Complete Poems of Robert Southwell.* Edited by Alexander B. Grosart. London: Printed for Private Circulation [by Robson and Sons], 1872. Includes the Latin poems.

*The Poems of Robert Southwell.* Edited by James H. McDonald and Nancy Pollard Brown. Oxford: Clarendon Press, 1967. The standard edition. Excludes the Latin Poems. Inadequate commentary.

*The Triumphs over Death.* Edited by J. W. Trotman. London: Manresa Press, 1914. The only available text, fussily paragraphed, with an eccentric introduction.

*Two Letters and Short Rules of a Good Life.* Edited by Nancy Pollard Brown. Charlottesville: University Press of Virginia, for the Folger Shakespeare Library, 1973.

SECONDARY SOURCES

Beales, A. C. F. *Education under Penalty.* London: Athlone Press, 1963. A good account of English Catholic schools and colleges, including the English College, Rome.

Bossy, John. *The English Catholic Community, 1570-1850.* New York: Oxford University Press, 1976. An exceptionally good introduction to the world of the Catholic recusants and the missionary priests.

Brown, Nancy Pollard. "Paperchase: The Dissemination of Catholic Texts in Elizabethan England." *English Manuscript Studies* 1 (1989): 120-43. Excellent bibliographical detection, tracking the clandestine production of some Catholic texts in circles familiar to Southwell.

———. "The Structure of Southwell's 'Saint Peter's Complaint.'" *Modern Language Review* 61 (1966): 3-11. A useful but excessively didactic interpretation of the poem.

Cousins, A. D. *The Catholic Religious Poets from Southwell to Crashaw: A Critical History.* London: Sheed & Ward, 1991.

Devlin, Christopher. *The Life of Robert Southwell, Poet and Martyr.* London: Longmans, Green and Co., 1956. The only modern life of Southwell, well researched though sketchily documented, and well written, but from a strongly Catholic point of view.

———. "Southwell and Contemporary Writers. I." *The Month.* New Series 4, no. 3 (1950): 169-180.

———. "Southwell and Contemporary Writers. II." *The Month.* New Series 4, no. 5 (1950): 309-19. These articles give more detailed versions of material used in chapter 18 of Devlin's *Life.*

Hill, Geoffrey. "The Absolute Reasonableness of Robert Southwell." In *The Lords of Limit.* New York: Oxford University Press, 1984. A subtly argued analysis of the integrity of Southwell's prose by an important and sympathetic modern English poet.

Hughes, Philip. *The Reformation in England.* 3 vols. New York: Macmillan, 1954. The best modern Catholic history of the subject, indispensable to students of recusant writing.

Janelle, Pierre. *Robert Southwell the Writer: A Study in Religious Inspiration.* New York: Sheed & Ward, 1935. The first scholarly study, dated, but thoroughly researched and still useful.

Lewis, C. S. *English Literature in the Sixteenth Century Excluding the Drama.* Oxford: Clarendon Press, 1954. Contains a brief but generous notice of Southwell.

Martz, Louis. *The Poetry of Meditation.* Rev. ed. New Haven: Yale University. Press, 1962. Although not specifically about Southwell, this book argues that he is at the source of a tradition of Jesuit influence on English seventeenth-century lyric poetry.

Maurer, Warren R. "Spee, Southwell, and the Poetry of Meditation." *Comparative Literature* 15 (1963): 15-22. A refreshingly critical comparison of Southwell to a similar German Jesuit poet of the period.

Oxley, Brian. "The Relation between Robert Southwell's Neo-Latin and English Poetry." *Recusant History* 17, no. 3 (May 1985): 201-7.

———. "'Simples Are by Compounds Farre Exceld': Southwell's Longer Latin Poems and 'St Peters Complaint.'" *Recusant History* 17, no. 4 (October 1985): 330-40. These two short articles contain the most illuminating commentary and criticism on Southwell so far published.

Partridge, A. C., ed. *The Tribe of Ben: Pre-Augustan Classical Verse in English.* 1966. Reprint, Columbia: University of South Carolina Press, 1970. A brief but acute comment on Southwell's English.

Pollen, John Hungerford, S.J., and William MacMahon, S.J., eds. *The Ven. Philip Howard, Earl of Arundel 1567-95: English Martyrs II.* Catholic Record Society Publications 21 (1919). Gives a documented account of Southwell's relationship with Arundel.

Praz, Mario. "Robert Southwell's 'Saint Peter's Complaint' and Its Italian Source." *Modern Language Review* 19 (1924): 273-90. Places Southwell's long poem in its Counter-Reformation, Roman context.

Puhl, Louis J., S.J. *The Spiritual Exercises of St. Ignatius.* Chicago: Loyola University Press, 1951. An excellent scholarly translation for the student curious to know what the Exercises entail.

Raspa, Anthony. *The Emotive Image: Jesuit Poetics in the English Renaissance.* Fort Worth: Texas Christian University Press, 1983. The introductory chapter on the baroque worldview is particularly useful, though clumsily written.

Roberts, J. R. "The Influence of *The Spiritual Exercises* of St. Ignatius Loyola on the Nativity Poems of Robert Southwell." *Journal of English and Germanic Philology* 59 (1960): 450-56. Praises Southwell for the authenticity and simplicity of his religious feeling; an old-fashioned piece much influenced by Martz.

Robertson, Jean. "Robert Southwell's 'New heaven, new warre.'" *Huntington Library Quarterly* 45 (1982): 82-83. An important demurral about the Clarendon editors' handling of one of the most famous poems.

Scallon, Joseph D. *The Poetry of Robert Southwell, S.J.* Salzburg: Institut für Englische Sprache und Literatur, 1975. An excellent, well-informed, balanced book.

Sundaram, L. J. "Robert Southwell's 'St. Peter's Complaint'—An Interpretation." In *Studies in Elizabethan Literature: Festschrift to Professor G. C. Bannerjee.* Edited by P. S. Sastri. New Delhi: S. Chand, 1972, 4-9. Argues successfully that apostasy is an important theme of the poem.

Thurston, Herbert J. "Catholic Writers and Elizabethan Readers. II. Father Southwell the Euphuist." *The Month* 83 (1895): 231-45.

———. "Father Southwell, the Popular Poet." *The Month* 83 (1895): 383-99.

———. "Father Southwell and His Peter's Plaint." *The Month* 106 (1905): 318-21. These pioneering articles by an exceptionally learned Jesuit scholar are still worth reading for their historical interest and for the information they contain.

White, Helen C. *Tudor Books of Saints and Martyrs.* Madison: University of Wisconsin Press, 1963. Includes a general essay on Southwell relating his prose to the traditions of martyrological writing.

———. "Southwell: Metaphysical and Baroque." *Modern Philology* 61 (1964): 159-68.

———. "The Contemplative Element in Robert Southwell." *Catholic Historical Review* 48 (1962): 1-11. Helen White's interest in Southwell seems to have been chiefly religious, though her work is always learned and informative and has the great virtue of always taking him seriously.

## Gary M. Bouchard (essay date summer 1998)

SOURCE: Bouchard, Gary M. "Robert Southwell and Hopkins." *Studies* 87, no. 346 (summer 1998): 156-63.

[*In the following essay, Bouchard finds numerous parallels between the poetry of Southwell and that of Gerard Manley Hopkins, both of whom were "full-time priests and part-time poets."*]

Robert Southwell, S.J. (1561-1595) and Gerard Manley Hopkins, S.J. (1844-1889), are two of the least likely individuals to have had an influence upon any literary tradition. Both men lived short lives of essential exile. Southwell was educated in seminaries on the European continent before residing undercover for nearly a decade as a recusant priest in London until his capture, torture and execution. Hopkins, an Oxfordian-Newman convert, lived his latter years as a Jesuit Englishman teaching Greek in an Irish University. Both died having achieved no literary reputations. However, these two full-time priests and part-time poets influenced subsequent generations of poets, and both may be regarded as harbingers of modern English verse.

Twentieth century literary criticism has long recognised this in Hopkins. Although Robert Southwell's literary "canonisation" occurred more-or-less simultaneously with his religious canonisation at the beginning of this century, he remains a relatively obscure footnote in the Tudor period of literature. He is a one-man, literary counter-reformation pleading with English poets to embrace sacred themes and lift poetry from the pagan mire. His efforts had unpredictable, unlikely and uncanny success. Not only did Ben Jonson and Shakespeare's patron, the Earl of Southampton, pay attention to him, but when no fewer than six editions of his poetic works were printed following his execution in 1595, Southwell became the unintentional and unconsecrated father of English metaphysical poetry. His intimacy with and reliance upon Ignatius's *Spiritual Exercises,* which prescribe an application of the five senses to the art of meditation, gave birth in English to the meditative verse which would characterise much of the poetry of the early seventeenth century. We find in his poetry the characteristics of metaphysical poetry—the dramatic opening, the argued metaphor, the eccentric conceit, self introspection and spiritual ascent.

> Elsewhere I have attempted to help rescue Southwell from the literary shadows of his martyrdom[1]. My focus here is Hopkins' recognition and specific reliance upon Southwell, his only English Jesuit literary ancestor. There is a profound and substantive similarities in the lives of the two poets, as well as echoes of Southwell's poetry in Hopkins. However, Hopkins' only specific mention of Robert Southwell comes in a letter to Dixon . . . In England we had Fr. Southwell a poet, a minor poet but still a poet; but he wrote amidst terrible persecution and died a martyr, with circumstances of horrible barbarity: this is the counterpoise of his career.
>
> (Correspondence, 94)

That Hopkins has no more to say elsewhere, either in his journals or correspondence, about Southwell has apparently discouraged any consideration of their similarity[2]. What Hopkins does say of Southwell indicates a familiarity with the details of the young Jesuit's persecuted life, and his assertion that Southwell was "a minor poet but still a poet" could only have come from a first-hand knowledge of the poet's works.

The Hopkins family library contained only a volume of Southwell's sermons (*Twelve Sermons,* Robert Southwell, 1692), so it is likely that Hopkins' first sampling of Southwell's poetry may have come during his time at Oxford. In any case, he had ample opportunity to read Southwell's poetry both at Stonyhurst and at St. Beunos (1870-1874). There were as many as five editions of Southwell's Poems in the Library at Stonyhurst when Hopkins was there. At least two volumes of Southwell's works, both prose and poetry, were available to Hopkins when he was a student of Theology at St. Beuno's.

The renewed interest at Oxford and elsewhere in the metaphysical poets would have fuelled Hopkins' interest in Southwell. How reassuring it must have been to Hopkins to find at the origins of this newly popular devotional verse of the seventeenth century a Jesuit priest urging poets to take the church back into their fold instead of busying "themselves in expressing such passions, as only serve for testimonies to how unworthy affections they have wedded their wills" (*Poems,* 1). Southwell's resolution in this familiar letter "to his loving Cosen," which appears at the front of all of the above editions of Southwell, is to "weave a new webbe in their own loome" to which end he says he has "layd a few course threds together, to invite some skillfuller wits to goe forward in the same, or to begin some finer peece, where in it may be seene, how well verse and vertue sute together" (*Poems,* 1). Though Southwell had likely known the young Jack Donne, he cannot

have anticipated the "skillfuller wits" who would take up his invitation to write religious verse; he could have predicted neither the resulting "metaphysical" school which his letter and poems inadvertently inaugurated, nor the next young Jesuit to lay his coarse threads together some two hundred and seventy-five years later.

The likes of Topcliffe the Priest-hunter did not pursue Hopkins, but one can accurately describe both men as exiles from their native England. Southwell's barbarous torture and execution came after arrest had suddenly but predictably ended his career as poet. While living incognito in and around London prior to that and writing poetry, his relationship with his native England was much like Hopkins' own, one of banished affection.

Southwell's mother had been a childhood playmate of Queen Elizabeth and at his execution he declared his loyalty to the Roman Catholic Church, the Jesuit Order and the Queen of England. It was a paradox which Hopkins shared with Southwell. He would ask, as Southwell most did in his determination to return to England as a missionary: "What shall I do for the land that bred me, / her homes and fields that folded and fed me?" (*Unfinished Poems* 156, 1-2) and declare as Southwell had "Call me England's fame's fond lover, / her fame to keep, her fame to recover./ Spend me or end me what God shall send me, / But under her banner I live for her honour" (*Unfinished poems* 156, 11-14). Hopkins' conflicting loyalties cost him the affection of his family—". . . Father and mother dear, / Brothers and sisters are in Christ not near" (66, 2-3), as well as a career in his native "England, whose honour O all my heart woos, wife / To my creating thought . . ." (66, 5-6).

A second aspect of the two poet's shared "counterpoise" is their priesthood. W. H. Gardner noted the similarity between Southwell's line "The God of hoastes in slender hoste doth dwell" (**"Of the Blessed Sacrament of the Aulter"**, 61), and Hopkins' "Low-latched in leaf light housel his too huge godhead" ("The Bulger's First Communion" 12). The parallel between the two passages, Gardner observes, is either reminiscent of Hopkins' early reading or a remarkable coincidence (*GMH: A Study of Poetic Idiosyncrasy,* 169). The line may be a direct borrowing by Hopkins as he would certainly have an interest in reading and remembering a poem treating this subject; in any case, if it is "a remarkable coincidence" it belongs to the broader coincidence of the two men's' priesthood. In fact sacramental imagery abounds in the poetry of both.

Hopkins was not preoccupied with the nativity—his sonnet, "The Starlight Night" being his only possible nativity poem—but even more so than Southwell the essential movement and meaning of Hopkins' poetry is with the Word made flesh. Hopkins' accomplishes this in a post-Romantic fashion; nature, in the form of a kestrel, a well and virtually everything else, being the living presence of the Christ. The "theme" of both poets' is the theme of the sacraments themselves: the inevitability of death and the eternal fullness of eternal life. The most important ingredient belonging to these two poets' common circumstance is their practice of Ignatian meditation and its predictable poetic results. In Jerome Bump's essay "Hopkins, Metalepsis, and the Metaphysicals," he notes that Hopkins, "Heaven Haven" recalls Herbert and Vaughn, as well as these lines from Southwell's **"Seeke flowers of heaven"**

> Graze not on worldly withered weede
> It fitteth not thy taste,
> The flowers of everlasting spring
> Doe grow for thy repast
>
> Whose soveraigne sent surpassing sense
> So ravisheth the minde,
> That worldly weedes needs must be loath,
> That can these flowers find.
>
> (stanzas 2 and 6)

Bump concludes that the echoes between these poets can be traced to "the common source . . . the psalms, especially Psalm 107" (311). While this may be the case in this instance and elsewhere in their work, a daily reading of the Psalms by Southwell, Herbert and Hopkins is an important aspect of their spiritual disciplines. The practice of Ignatian meditation was a central part of the lives of Southwell and Hopkins and consequently their art. Martz summarises "the elaborately detailed explanation of the Jesuit 'application of the sense' to the art of meditation":

> Everyday life must come to play its part, for the meditative man must feel that the presence of God is here, now, on his own hearth, in his own stable,
>
> and in the deep centre of the mind: thus (in St. Ignatius's words) "we may help ourselves much to the framing of spiritual conceits, if we apply unto our matter familiar similitude's, drawne from our ordinary actions, and this as well in historicall, as spirituall meditations."
>
> (introduction, English Seventeenth Century Verse, V 1.

"Framing of spiritual conceits" by sensing and depicting the immediacy of God in ordinary things may be an excellent prescription for spiritual meditation or a formula for writing poetry. Making the word flesh was not only the daily sacramental work of their priesthood, but the prescribed purpose of their life and the essential source and aim of their poetry.

General similarities in subject and theme in their poetry is inevitable. That both were exiles from their own country and its literary canon yields an even more likely correspondence in their tone and theme. An argument from thematic similarities, therefore, is interesting; it would, however, not persuade one of any direct influence of Southwell's work upon Hopkins. There are several specific instances of portions of poetry where one can recognise a common voice in these poets' works.

Robert Southwell, as the innovator of sacred parody in English verse, wrote most of his poems in a conventional manner; many being Petrarchan in tone and deliberately "Elizabethan" in music, imagery and form. I shall draw attention in Southwell's poetry to moments of particular poetic eccentricity where the poet creates monosyllabic lists, invents unusual images, odd juxtapositions and compound nouns or turns simple verbs into nouns and otherwise subverts the grammar of his own syntax.

Consider first the opening stanza of **"Christ's Bloody Sweat"**:

> Fat soile, full spring, sweete olive, grape of blisse,
> That yeelds, that streams, that pours, that dost distil,
> Untild, undrawne, unstampt, untoucht of presse,
> Dear fruit, cleare brookes, faire oile, sweete wine at will:
> Thus Christ unforst prevents in shedding blood
> The whips, the thornes, the nailes, the speare, the roode.

The meditation which yields the images is decidedly Ignatian. The conventional iambic arrangement, as in the final line, is not striking, but in a couple of tensive phrases—"full spring", "faire oile"—and in the impossible image—"Fat soile"—we may hear a voice which we before have recognised as Hopkins' own. So too in the negative string of adjectives: "Untild, undrawne, unstampt, untoucht of presse."

The poem, presents Christ as an agricultural composite of untilled soil, undrawn Spring, unpressed olives and unstamped grapes which nonetheless yield dear fruit, clear brooks, faire oile and sweet wine. Hopkins' in his poem "New Readings" creates a similar composite, his being two rather than four-fold; "I read the story rather / How soldiers platting thorns around CHRIST'S Head / Grapes grew and drops of wine were shed" (3-5) and "From wastes of rock He brings / Food for five thousand: on the thorns He shed / Grains from His drooping Head" (11-13). In "Barnfloor and Winepress" Hopkins' describes Christ as grain "scourged upon the threshing-floor" (6) and "The wine . . . racked from the press" (18). Jerome Bump notes that "the editors of the fourth edition of Hopkins' poems cite Herbert's influence on "New Readings" and "Barnfloor and Winepress":

The lines from Herbert's "The Sacrifice" to which Bump refers are spoken by Christ in the first person:

"Then on my head a crown of thorns I wear: / For these are all the grapes Sion doth bear, / Though I my vine planted and watred there." The two Hopkins' poems, I contend, bear much greater similarity in tone, imagery and voice to Southwell's **"Christ's Bloody Sweat"** than to Herbert's "The Sacrifice." Nor is this surprising since the poem originates in the Ignatian meditation that the two practised. "The basic form" of a series of New Testament" interpretations to which Bump refers was a prescriptive part of Ignatius' *Spiritual Exercise* practised routinely by Southwell and Hopkins. Southwell's **"Christ's Bloody Sweat,"** in fact, is followed by **"Christ's Sleeping Friends."** I do not wish to disregard Herbert's influence upon Hopkins, but to attend in these particular poetic passages to the literary predecessor of both men who, in the case of Hopkins, was, as Jesuit and Catholic, a more intimate religious predecessor as well.

Southwell's poem **"Mary Magdalens Blush"** is a specimen of sacred parody, turning a scriptural narrative into a conventional Petrarchan complaint. In stanza three, for example, Magdalene declares: "All ghostly dynts that grace at me did dart, / Like stubborn rocke I forced to recoyle" (13-14). The next line, however, contains a small but unusual ingredient found elsewhere in Southwell and frequently in Hopkins, the grammatical conversion of a verb to a noun: "To other flights *an ayme* I made my hart" (15, italics mine). In stanza five of this poem this technique, combined with the creation of a peculiar compound noun, the use of all alliteration and the choice and arrangement of other words results in poetry which—if not for its bouncing conventional metre—might be mistaken as Hopkins' own:

> O sence, O soule, O had, O hoped blisse,
> You wooe, you weane, you draw, you drive me back.
> Your cross-encountering, like their combate is,
> That never end but with some deadly wrack.
> When sense doth winne, the soule doth loose the field,
> And present happes, make future hopes to yeeld
>
> (25-30)

The peculiar declaration "O had" in the opening line of this stanza can carry over as a past-perfect verb whose object is blisse, as in "Oh had blisse and Oh hoped for blisse", or, stated simply" Oh past happiness and future happiness." The curiosity of the syntax is that grammatically and metrically "O had" can argue its place as a noun in a list of four others, each preceded by the declarative oh!: "O sense, O soule, <u>O had,</u> O hoped for blisse." The arrangement of a simple verb or article to function ambiguously with noun-like properties is a recognisable grammatical eccentricity, among the many in Hopkins' poetry. I offer four examples from his poems: the use of "have" and "get" in "Spring", "Have, get, before it cloy, / Before it cloud, Christ, lord, and

sour with sinning" (11-12); the use of "any" and "some" in the riddled opening lines of "The Leaden Echo", "How to keep—is there any way, is there none such, nowhere known some, bow or brooch or braid or brace, lace" (1-2); the stirring "let me be fell" (1.8) from sonnet "65". And finally the memorable, haunting final words of Sonnet 66: "This to hoard unheard, / Heard unheeded, leaves me a lonely began" (13-14).

The almost excessive alliteration of the first three lines of the stanza from **"Mary Magdalens Blush"**—sense, soule, had, hoped, wooe, weane, draw, drive, crosse, combate—punctuates the grammatical force of the first three lines which then give way to prosaic and less disruptive declaration in the final three lines. Besides the use of the word "had" in the stanza's opening line, the stanza's alliteration also highlights another innovation which gives a reader of Hopkins' pause. Line three "Your crosse-encountering, like their combate is" relies upon the eccentric creation of the powerful compound noun, "cross-encountering". The sense of this noun carries in the context is conventional, something like, "my sense, soul, memory and hopes all fight unsuccessfully against your cross when they encounter it." Such paraphrase diminishes the effect which Southwell has achieved with the conversion of "encountering" from a present-participle into the second half of a compound noun. The resultant "cross-encountering" would likely have stayed in the mind of Hopkins, the relentless purveyor of compound words, who gives us such nouns as "martyr-master", and "starlight-wender", and who uses the same grammatical conversion by which Southwell created "cross-encountering" to construct compound adjectives like "world-mothering", "widow making", "Cuckoo-echoing", "Blue-beating", and "day-labouring-out".

The word "wrack", while it contributes to the Hopkins-like sound of this stanza, does not, in fact, appear in Hopkins' poetry except in "shipwrack" from "The Wreck of the Deutschland". The final lines of the stanza, in contrast to the first four, sound, like the majority of Southwell's poetry, quite conventionally Petrarchan. There are, however, several other instances in Southwell in which the nearest kindred verse to the sound and sense of a particular Southwell passage is found in the poetry of Hopkins.

There are instances in Southwell's **"A Vale of Tears"** which, for a sixteenth century poem, contains unusually detailed descriptions of nature. The opening stanza reads:

> A vale there is enwrapt with dreadfull shades,
> Which thicke of mourning pines shrouds from the
>    sunne,

Where hanging clifts yeld short and dumpish glades,
And snowie floud with broken strames doth runne.

(1-4)

Southwell's sorrowful valley of repentance brings comfort to the world-weary soul because "sorrow springs from water, stone and tree" (59) and "everie thing with mourners doth conspire". By contrast, Hopkins' "Penmaen Pool" is the quaint guestbook poem which it is intended to be, and his "In the Valley of the Elwy" a forgiving landscape: "Lovely the woods, waters, meadows, cobes, vales", a place where "God, lover of souls" complete his creatures where they fail. "Binsey Poplars" and "Inversnaid" are inviting Romantic landscape meditations, not the terrifying locus of Southwell's **"Vale"**. Nonetheless, there are, in lines like "Where waters wrastle with encountering stones" (16), some vague suggestions of Hopkins' nature. So too in the compound noun "eie-roume", ("Where eie-roume is from rockes to cloudie skie," 5), or "the crushed waters frothie frie" (7) of stanza two, and in the phrases "an onely bower" (33), "a dumpish mood" (34), or "pibble stones," (39), as well as in the declaration of the poem's final stanza: "Let tears to tunes, and paines to plaints be prest" (73).

Those who have insisted upon the spiritual despair of Hopkins' later sonnets, seem to have read neither the Book of Psalms nor the poetry of Herbert, and certainly not the poetry of Robert Southwell. Southwell's **"A Phansie Turned to a Sinners Complaint,"** contains the spiritual and emotional distress of Herbert's and Hopkins' laments; three or four of its stanzas in particular may have served as a source for Hopkins. Stanza twelve of that poem reads:

O thoughts, no thoughts, but wounds,
Sometime the seate of joy,
Sometime the store of quiet rest,
But now of all annoy.

(45-48)

The disrupted syntax of the stanza's opening line and the emphatic resolution of thoughts as wounds, punctuated by the verb "annoy" used as a noun in the stanza's final line suggest a number of moments in Hopkins' poetry. In the opening line of Southwell's next stanza he inaugurates an agricultural metaphor of a bad harvest to describe his spiritual despair:

I sow'd the soyle of peace,
My blisse was in the spring;
And day by day the fruite I eate,
That Vertues tree did bring.

To Nettles now my corne,
My field is turn'd to flint;
Where I a heavie harvest reape,
Of cares that never stint.

(49-56)

How much more concisely and powerfully does Hopkins' utilise this very metaphor for the same purpose in "Carrion Comfort": "Why? That my chaff might fly; my grain lie, sheer and clear" (9).

Stanza seventeen of **"A Phansie"** contains the use of simple verbs as nouns, the peculiar syntax and the stark statement of spiritual despair and paradox which, combined, suggest particular influence upon Hopkins:

In was, stands my delight,
In is, and shall my woe,
My horrour fastened in the yea,
My hope hangd in the no.

(65-71)

Here is a reasonable summary of Hopkins' Dark Sonnets whose "lonely began" and searching for "God knows when to God knows what" (69, 1. 12) belong very much to both a poetic and spiritual convention which here his Jesuit predecessor in both quite clearly shared.

I offer as a final sampling stanza eleven of **"St. Peters Remorse"**:

I was, I had, I could,
Are wordes importing want:
They are but dust of dead supplies,
Where needful helpes are scant.

(41-44)

The lines, from which I have taken this essay's title, contain again the conversion of three verbs, into nouns as the syntax unfolds. The reference to these words, and perhaps words in general, "dust of dead supplies" hints at the ultimate futility of language in the face of stark, overwhelming spiritual or worldly realities. Southwell's legendary eloquence would, in the end, not be enough at his so-called trial to preserve him from the inevitable end of his "counterpoise". That his poems would serve as "Dead supplies" to Herbert, Donne and other seventeenth century poets is frequently overlooked; that this influence came compounded in the haunting weight of martyrdom is rarely considered. Where both literary influence and specific "counterbalance" are concerned Southwell's most important descendent was Gerard Manley Hopkins. They are together England's two Jesuit poets, and it is my small hope that the echoes I have sounded here might cause lovers of Hopkins' poetry to extend their affections and studies to "the dust of the dead supplies" furnished him by his fellow exile, poet and brother, Father Robert Southwell, S.J.

### Notes

1. My own argument for the impact of Southwell's life and death upon the seventeenth century poets

is made in *Robert Southwell, the Original Self-consuming Artefact* in a collection of essays on recusant poets, edited by John Roberts, University of Missouri.

2. An exception is Mother Eleanor, SHCJ, *Hopkins, 'Windhover' and Southwell's 'Hawk'* in Renaissance (v. 15) in 1962.

## Gary M. Bouchard (essay date spring 1999)

SOURCE: Bouchard, Gary M. "The Curious Case of Robert Southwell, Gerard Hopkins, and a Princely Spanish Hawk." *Renascence* 51, no. 3 (spring 1999): 181-89.

[*In the following essay, Bouchard explores the influence of the imagery of a Southwell meditation on a poem by Gerard Manley Hopkins.*]

In 1962 Mother Mary Eleanor, S.H.C.J. published a short article entitled "Hopkins' 'Windhover' and Southwell's Hawk" in which she called "attention to a curiously parallel image in a little known book of meditations by Robert Southwell (1561-1595) on the Love of God" (21). Mother Eleanor's modest claim was that the image of Christ as a hawk in flight from "Meditation 56" of Southwell's *A Hundred Meditations on the Love of God* "may or may not provide a clue to the source of Hopkins' image; but it at least reinforces one's sense of the appropriateness of such an image, since it has occurred to another poet, formed in the same school of spirituality and arrested by the same fact of Christ's redeeming action" (21). This provocative discovery of Mother Eleanor's, a peculiar Renaissance needle in the vast haystack of literary influence, has been little heeded, scholarly readings of "The Windhover" having proceeded for the past thirty-five years as though her suggestion had never been made. This may be in part due to the considerable modesty with which she presented her case, but is attributable as well, no doubt, to the fact that she offered no external evidence to suggest how or why Hopkins, as a young nineteenth-century Jesuit, might have come to read, let alone borrow from, these little known meditations of his beheaded sixteenth-century Jesuit predecessor. How, in other words, did Hopkins stumble upon this same "needle" and who exactly put it in the haystack? I intend here to address these questions by considering an as yet unnoticed coincidence which connects the nineteenth century publication of *A Hundred Meditations on the Love of God* with Gerard Hopkins, and demonstrates the likelihood that Hopkins not only read at least some of the *Meditations,* but may have been guided in his reading by its editor, Father John Morris, S.J. who, as it turns out, would soon be one of Hopkins' professors, as

well as one of the few Jesuits to encourage Hopkins in his own efforts as a poet. Having presented this connection between Hopkins and the *Meditations*' editor, I then wish to return to the parallel imagery of "The Windhover" and Southwell's "Meditation 56," to argue Mother Eleanor's case afresh.

Let us begin with the peculiar history of *A Hundred Meditations Upon the Love of God.* Immediately after Robert Southwell's trial and gruesome public death in 1595 there followed, ironically, a prolific publication of his poetic works:

> The first editions of the poems in 1595 followed immediately upon the execution of Southwell in February. The popular demand for the poetry reflects the extraordinary response of the London crowd to Southwell himself. The first edition of **Saint Peters Complaint, with Other Poems,** appearing probably in March, was followed by a second edition before some of the type for the first edition had been distributed. When Gabriel Cawood secured the copyright in April and started his series of editions, he may have been confident that he had obtained the rights to a commercial success.
>
> (*Poems* lv)

By 1636 **Saint Peter's Complaint with Other Poems,** accompanied by a now famous dedicatory epistle, had been printed in London no fewer than eleven times. Nonetheless, *A Hundred Meditations Upon the Love of God,* which in its published form comprises some 538 pages of prose, survived unpublished and presumably unread in one transcribed copy at Stonyhurst College until 1873.

The person responsible for rescuing *A Hundred Meditations* from oblivion was Father John Morris, S.J., Lecturer of Ecclesiastical History at St. Bueno's Seminary in Wales, who, trusting in the "Transcriber's Dedication,"[1] believed incorrectly that he was bringing to light an extraordinary work of original recusant prose. In fact, however, the *Hundred Meditations* are not Southwell's original work, but an English translation which he made from an Italian version of a Spanish work, *Meditaciónes devotíssimas amor Dios* written by a Franciscan Friar, Fray Diego de Estella and published in Salamanca in 1576.[2] It is likely that Southwell translated an Italian version of Diego's work in order to help regain his competence in English after a decade on the continent. Whether Southwell knew that his Italian version of these meditations was a translation of Diego's Spanish work, or what his particular attraction to these meditations was, we can never know.

What is important to our present argument is not that Southwell's work was original, but that Father Morris believed that it was, and described it to his readers with a zeal appropriate to that belief. He wrote in his Preface:

> The interest of these Meditations is greatly enhanced by the recollection that it is a Martyr, at whose intercourse with God we are present. It is a revelation

to us of the interior union with God of a brave heart that aspired to and attained martyrdom. . . . In these Meditations, then, we see into a Martyr's heart, or rather . . . see the thoughts by which the heart was made heroic and apt for the great sacrifice of martyrdom. It was filled with the love of God. Everything spoke to it of the Love of God. It drew the love of God to itself from all around, and in its meditation all creatures, instead of weakening, helped to strengthen its love of God.

(*A Hundred Meditations* vii-viii)

One of Morris' motivations for publishing *A Hundred Meditations,* in fact, was to help "hasten the day when the Martyrs to whom we owe our inheritance shall receive their honors from the Church to which they were loyal unto death" (x). Southwell, along with the other English martyrs of the sixteenth-century recusant movement to whom Fr. Morris refers, would eventually be canonized, but not for another hundred years.

As for Morris' edition of *A Hundred Meditations,* it remains the only one to have ever been published, and while regarded until fairly recently as Southwell's original work, its audience has been comprised of, shall we say, a devout few. Extant copies of the text remain only in private collections, selected religious houses and in fewer than two dozen libraries world-wide. In fact, the greatest impact of Morris' unenviable labor may have been the unintentional spawning of Hopkins' extraordinary sonnet, "The Windhover" which the poet himself regarded as one of his finest poems. Just what do we know then about Fr. Morris and his eccentric pupil, Gerard Hopkins.

At the time at which Morris' edition of *A Hundred Meditations on the Love of God* was published, and during the previous three years while he was presumably working with the original manuscript at Stonyhurst, Gerard Hopkins was studying in the Jesuit Philosophate at St. Mary's Hall, Stonyhurst (1870-1873). That the two men would have met and conversed in some manner during this time seems quite possible as there were only thirty-five residents at St. Mary's Hall, including the three priests. That Morris may have brought to the young poet's attention his work upon what he believed were Robert Southwell's *A Hundred Meditations* is likewise possible since Morris admired Southwell's poetry, and, with Hopkins' composition of "Ad Mariam" at Stonyhurst, his own talent as a poet, or at the very least his interest in poetry, was known among his fellow Jesuits there. In any case, even if Morris and Hopkins completely escaped one another's notice at this time, they would meet three years later in Wales when Morris was now Hopkins' professor for both Canon Law as well as Ecclesiastical History at St. Beuno's.[3]

By this time, biographer Norman White suggests, "Hopkins must have been known to his colleagues as a poet. This reputation probably [having] followed him from Stonyhurst where he had written the Marian poems, and 'The Wreck of the Deutschland' would of course be known to the Rector" (262). What White does not mention is just what a very peculiar reputation "poet" would have been for Hopkins to have acquired among his fellow Jesuits, the order not being exactly overcrowded with would-be laureates. In a letter to R. W. Dixon in 1881, Hopkins himself would describe the scant Jesuit literary presence which preceded him:

We have had for three centuries often the flower of the youth of a country in numbers enter our body: among these how many poets, how many artists of all sorts, there must have been! But there have been very few Jesuit poets and, where they have been, I believe it would be found on examination that there was something exceptional in their circumstances or, so to say, counterbalancing in their career.

(*Correspondence* 92)

Hopkins then mentions three Jesuit poets:

Fr. Beschi who in Southern Hindustan composed an epic which has become one of the Tamul classics and is spoken of with unbounded admiration by those who can read it. . . . In England we had Fr. Southwell a poet, a minor poet but still a poet; but he wrote amidst terrible persecution and died a martyr, with circumstances of horrible barbarity: this is the counterpoise of his career. Then what a genius was Campion himself! Was not he a poet? Perhaps a great one, if he had chosen.

(*Correspondence* 94)

Since Campion did not choose to write poetry, and Beschi was Indian, Hopkins, by his own reckoning, is left with but one English Jesuit literary predecessor, Robert Southwell.

One other person who would be keenly aware that the English Jesuits had but one poet to speak of would, of course, have been Fr. Morris who refers in his Preface to "Mr. Grosart's admirable edition of Father Southwell's Poetical Works" (*A Hundred Meditations* v)[4] which was published in 1872, the year before his own edition of the *Hundred Meditations.* What Morris thought about Hopkins' poetry is suggested by an incident in 1876. For fittingly, this champion of Southwell's works was also responsible for the first and only printing of a Hopkins poem during Hopkins' own lifetime, "The Silver Jubilee."[5] In 1876 Fr. Morris had preached a special sermon on the occasion of Bishop James Brown's Jubilee visit to St. Beuno's that year. The sermon, the Bishop's address and the poem Hopkins composed for the occasion were subsequently published together in a pamphlet at the Bishop's request. When "Hopkins had protested against his poem being included . . . Fr. Morris had gracefully persuaded him that he needed its publication in order to entitle the sermon 'The Silver Jubilee'" (White 262). This incident may have been as simple and pragmatic as it sounds, although it suggests a tactful and sympathetic mentoring of the young poet away from excessive modesty and towards publication. It is, in any case, the small sum of what we know for certain about the relationship between Fr. Morris and Gerard Hopkins.

A year after writing "The Silver Jubilee" Hopkins would write "The Windhover." Before turning to the resemblances of this poem to "Meditation 56," we should note that from the 538 pages which comprise *A Hundred Meditations,* Fr. Morris offers a sampling of only five brief passages in his Preface, and the longest of these by far, and the one to which he gives the most attention, is the passage of the regal hawk in flight compared to Christ from "Meditation 56." Hence, Hopkins would not have had to read beyond Morris' Preface to discover this unusual metaphor. Although circumstantial, this evidence indicates that Hopkins may well have had his attention drawn to these meditations by Fr. Morris.

As to Hopkins' famous poem, it is easy to see why "The Windhover" was his favorite composition in what was a very creative year for the poet (White 282), and why many regard it as his single best poem, if for no other reason because of its extraordinary structural and formal characteristics. Never before or since, I think, has so much movement, rhythm, sound and emotion been so masterfully orchestrated within the confines of an Italian sonnet. Even so, a paraphrase of the poem's action is quite ordinary: an exuberant narrator admires the graceful flight and sudden descent of a kestrel. The poem's provocative dedication, "To Christ Our Lord," however, invites, perhaps requires, the reader to see the flight of the small bird with the same symbolic significance and accompanying excitement as the narrator:

> I caught this morning morning's minion, kingdom of
>   daylight's dauphin, dapple-dawn-drawn Falcon, in
>   his riding
>   Of the rolling level underneath him steady air, and
>   striding
> High there, how he rung upon the rein of a wimpling
>   wing
> In his Ecstasy! then off, off forth on swing,
>   As skate's heel sweeps smooth on a bow-bend: the
>   hurl and gliding
>   Rebuffed the wind. My heart in hiding
> Stirred for a bird,—the achieve of, the mastery of
>   thing!

If one insists upon reading this poem only as an extraordinary nature meditation, echoes of "Meditation 56" might be heard, though not significantly, as in "When the eagle-falcon, or ger-falcon, or any other kind of long-winged hawk, hath flown a high pitch, and skimming through the air hath mounted up to the clouds . . ." From this description may have been derived the more striking "rung upon the reign of a wimpling wing"

or the sweep of a skate's heel. But Hopkins, a keen observer of nature would need no primer on how to describe a hawk's flight.

If, on the other hand, one follows the prompting of the poet's dedication "To Christ Our Lord" and understands the flight as representative of Christ's own mastery of his destiny and ours, the potential significance of Fray Diego de Estella's "Meditation 56" as translated by Robert Southwell and published by Morris may be seen and heard in earnest. The passage from the meditation which Morris quotes in his Preface is as eloquent a summary of the religious meaning of "The Windhover" as any ever rendered:

> O Princely Hawk! which comest down from Heaven into the bowels of the Blessed Virgin, and from her womb unto the earth, and from the earth unto the desert, and from the desert unto the Cross, and from the Cross unto hell, and from hell unto Heaven, and madest those turnings to pursue our souls which Thou wert losing, and which without Thy helping hand had perished, is it much that Thou requirest our heart for reward of the travail and pains that Thou hast done to work our redemption? What hawk ever made such a brave flight, or lost so much blood in the pursuit of her game, as the salvation of our souls hath cost Thee, our God and our Lord?

> *(A Hundred Meditations* ix-x)

"O" we wait for Diego, via Southwell, to declare "my Chevalier!" For the parallel imagery between the two passages includes, not just the comparable flights of the hawks, but the awe at the hawk's regality and the consequent recognition of Christ's own kingship in the masterful flight. The essential spiritual movement of the two passages, in fact, is identical: the brave and redemptive life of the princely Christ witnessed in the flight and fall of a hawk, prompting the consequent stirring of the observer's heart.

The climactic spiritual awakening in Hopkins' poem, the inexplicably lovely fire which breaks from the kestrel at the moment of buckling, also has a precedent in Fray Diego's "Meditation 56." Consider first the opening three lines of Hopkins' sestet by which he arrives, in the last three words, at his famous version of "O Princely hawk!"

> Brute beauty and valour and act, oh, air, pride, plume,
>   here
> Buckle! AND the fire that breaks from thee then, a
>   billion
> Times told lovelier, more dangerous, O my chevalier!

Now consider what might pass for a prose paraphrase of these very lines rendered into English by Southwell some two hundred eighty years earlier:

> And is it much, O Lord, that I should offer unto Thy Divine Majesty my heart inflamed in Thy holy love, seeing that Thou, my God, didst so burn upon the Cross

with the fire of infinite love, whereon Thou didst put Thyself for my sake and for love of me, insomuch that there sprinkled out so many flames of fire from the sacred breast as there were wounds in Thy most sacred body?

(*A Hundred Meditations* 282)

The inflamed heart and the fire are themselves conventional religious images, but the "sprinkled out . . . flames of fire" within the context of the hawk's flight bear a persuasive resemblance, I think, to Hopkins' "fire that breaks from thee then" (line 10) which becomes in the poem's memorable final image: "blue-bleak embers" which "Fall, gall themselves, and gash gold-vermillion" (13-14).

Since the above passage from "Meditation 56" does not appear in Morris' Preface, Hopkins would have had to turn to the meditation himself, prompted, if he did so, by the passage in Morris' Preface, and believing that the words which he read there were those of Fr. Robert Southwell, the only English Jesuit poet to precede him.

It may be that the comparison of the redemptive life of Christ to the flight of a hawk, though novel to us, was in Hopkins' day a somewhat more conventional part of religious imagery which has since been lost, leaving behind a poem which seems more eccentric and original than it is. It is likewise possible that the imagery and imbedded spiritual argument of "The Windhover" are entirely the product of Gerard Manley Hopkins' experience of observing a kestrel in Wales and his own poetic fancy. Yet all works of art, and especially great ones, are, in some fashion, an imaginative compilation of certain things which have come before them. In the exclamation "ah my dear," of the poem's second to last line, for example, Norman White hears Hopkins borrowing from his favorite poet, George Herbert (White 283). My own suggestion is that the poem contains a much more substantial borrowing than these three words, that, unbeknownst to Gerard Hopkins or Mother Eleanor, "The Windhover" owes its origins to a sixteenth-century Spanish writer via two of Hopkins' brother Jesuits, Fr. Southwell who accomplished this, his most significant work of translation,[6] in virtual house arrest, and Fr. Morris who worked in immediate proximity to his future pupil, Gerard Hopkins, to bring to publication what he believed to be the original work of an important English poet and Jesuit predecessor.

The implications of the above case of influence should be of some interest to readers of Hopkins. In the first place, if Hopkins did read "Meditation 56," he may also have read some, though likely not all, of the other *Hundred Meditations On the Love of God* in Morris' edition. Certainly the first two meditations, stirring canticles to creation and the creator, would have engaged Hopkins' sensibilities and drawn him in, and

Diego's Franciscan-inspired love of nature, which is apparent in the imagery of nearly all the meditations, may well have had particular appeal to Hopkins. Since Hopkins never mentions *A Hundred Meditations* specifically in either his journals or correspondence, any other cases of influence must rest upon the external evidence I have presented here and any notable similarities between the two authors' texts. One other implication of the above argument is that Gerard Hopkins, as Jesuit poet, may have found in the example of Southwell and the encouragement of Morris something of a respite from the artistic isolation in which we have grown accustomed to imagine him. Whether or not this was the case, I hope, at the very least, to have demonstrated in this essay that the stirring imagery of "The Windhover" has a more richly textured presence and history than has heretofore been recognized by Hopkins' scholars. The needle which Mother Eleanor discovered in the literary haystack back in 1962 is, I believe, a significant (and significantly complex) one, far richer in its Spanish origins and its Italian and Elizabethan reconfigurations than she, or Fr. Morris, or Gerard Manley Hopkins himself had imagined.

*Notes*

1. Morris cannot be blamed for trusting himself to the claims of transcriber who was him/herself but making an honest mistake. The Dedication reads as follows: "TO THE RIGHT HONOURABLE AND VIRTUOUS LADY, THE LADY BEAUCHAMP. Noble Lady,—Having long had in my custody the original of these ensuing discourses, written with Mr. Robert Southwell's own hand (a gentleman for his holy life and happy death of eternal memory), and knowing certainly that he especially wrote and meant to have printed them for your holy mother's devotion, singularly by him honoured and affected, I have, in an eminent esteem which I profess myself to have of your virtuous and noble worth, moved also thereunto by one of your noblest and nearest kinswomen, presumed to make your honour partaker of such a treasury of devout discourses . . ." (*A Hundred Meditations Upon the Love of God* xix).

2. Fray Diego de Estella, whose worldly name was Diego Ballesteros y Cruzas, lived from 1524-1578. He is known, though not admired, for his authorship of *Meditaciones devotissimas amor Dios*. The work is regarded as an example of the sort of popular mystical works which were common at this time, primarily doctrinal rather than apologetic. His *Meditaciones* are filled with the abundant nature revelry typical of Franciscan spirituality.

3. See *Catalogus Provinciae Angliae Societatis Jesu* (Roehampton: Typographia Sancti Joseph, 1875), p. 10: "P. Joannes Morris, *Lect. hist. eccl.* . . ."

and *Catalogus Provinciae Angliae Societatis Jesu* (Roehampton: Typographia Sancti Joseph, 1876), p. 10: "P. Joannes Morris, *Lect. jur. can. et hist. eccl.* . . . ." I am grateful to Father Joseph Feeney, S.J. for securing this data on my behalf. Though we have no description of Fr. Morris as a lecturer, we are told of his reading of his Italian colleague, Fr Perini's lectures in English in the evenings (Alfred Thomas, S.J., *Hopkins the Jesuit: The Years of Training,* 1969).

4. The edition to which Morris refers is Alexander Grosart's *The Complete Poems of Robert South-well* (1872) which was the first collected edition of Southwell's poetry.

5. Says Norman White: "It was the first work he had published since entering the Society of Jesus, and it was also the only serious complete English poem written after he became a Jesuit which he would ever see in print" (White 262).

6. This according to Nancy Pollard Brown, editor of *The Poems of Robert Southwell* and of a forthcoming collection of his complete prose works.

## Works Cited

Eleanor, Mother Mary, S.H.C.J. "Hopkins' 'Windhover' and Southwell's Hawk." *Renascence* 15.1 (Fall 1962): 21-22, 27.

Hopkins, Gerard Manley. *The Correspondence of Gerard Manley Hopkins and Richard Watson Dixon.* Ed. Claude Colleer Abbott. Oxford: Oxford UP, 1935.

Hopkins, Gerard Manley. *The Poetical Works of Gerard Manley Hopkins.* Ed. Norman Mackenzie. Oxford: Clarendon Press, 1992.

Southwell, Robert. *A Hundred Meditations on the Love of God.* Ed. John Morris, S.J. London: Burns and Oates, 1873.

Southwell, Robert. *The Poems of Robert Southwell.* Ed. James H. McDonald and Nancy Pollard Brown. Oxford: Clarendon Press, 1967.

White, Norman. *Hopkins: A Literary Biography.* Oxford: Clarendon Press, 1992.

## Gary Kuchar (essay date March 2001)

SOURCE: Kuchar, Gary. "Southwell's 'A Vale of Tears': A Psychoanalysis of Form." *Mosaic* 34, no. 1 (March 2001): 107-20.

*[In the following essay, Kuchar approaches Southwell's "A Vale of Tears" from a psychoanalytic perspective, examining the formal features of the work to determine how it functions as a therapeutic text.]*

Putting psychoanalytic conceptions of self-transformation through speech in dialogue with early modern devotional techniques of spiritualizing the physical, this essay asks how Robert Southwell's poem **'A Vale of Tears"** constitutes a work of mourning.

Contemporary psychoanalytic discussions of subject formation attribute immense importance to processes of mourning. This concern with mourning in the work of post-Lacanian theorists, most notably Judith Butler and Julia Kristeva, is not simply a reflection on how one negotiates loss throughout one's life but more primarily how the subject is itself constituted by mourning: formed, that is, by and through loss. From this perspective, mourning is not simply something the subject engages in when confronted with abandonment; but, rather, the subject is itself an effect of loss—the product of a series of renunciations and compromise formations. For Lacan and his recent reformulaters, a primordial loss of an egoless sense of unity and fullness—the loss, in other words, of a past that could never have been present as such—is the condition of possibility for the emergence of a subject who is able to take itself as an object of its own thought. In order for self-consciousness to emerge, according to Lacan, a division (or Spaltung) between the emergent ego and the idealized mirror image with which the ego identifies, but which it subsequently fails to adequately incorporate, must take place. The ego's failure to incorporate the imago of this ideal ego results from the disjunction between the infant's actual motor incapacity, its real lack of bodily integrity, and the totality of the wholly integral self that it desires to emulate. To this extent, consciousness is structured by a disjointure, or gap, between the ego and its specular, imaginary Other that is set up within the self as both the condition and the effect of language. Self alienation, then, is the very basis of subjectivity-the ground of identity itself: "The only homogenous function of consciousness is the imaginary capture of the ego by its mirror reflection and the function of misrecognition which remains attached to it" (*Ecrits* 32). This formulation of the self as conditioned by self-difference, by an enabling emptiness or gap, has profound implications for the meaning and motivations of art and religion.

Indeed, Lacan states unequivocally, "In spite of [the formulation's] generality," at its heart, "religion [. . .] consists of avoiding this emptiness" (*Ethics* 130). Aesthetic and spiritual practices are, at bottom, modes of renegotiating identity, strategies of mourning aimed at confronting dividedness while living out imaginatively the sense of self-unity that the subject is constitutionally deprived of. As Kristeva puts it, symbolic language possesses therapeutic efficacy insofar as it "imposes itself as a means of countervailing the loss of Other and of meaning: a means more powerful than any other because more autonomous, [. . .] it fills

the [. . .] psychic need to confront separation, empti-
ness, death" (*Black Sun* 129-30). Lacan provides a more
specific view of the therapeutic efficacy of symbolic
language when he claims that the process of psycho-
therapy operates by enabling the patient to "reorder the
past contingent events by conferring on them the sense
of necessities to come" (*Language* 18). In short, it is
symbolic acts of interpretation that enable a subject to
transform objectifying and traumatizing events into
subjectively meaningful experiences. Devotional and
religious writings often present explicit examples of
this desire to mitigate feelings of meaningless and loss,
centring as they often tend to do around the desire for
identity with God as the absolute Subject, the source
and the delta of all meaning.

This therapeutic dimension of devotional writing is
evident in the work of the early modern Jesuit poet
Robert Southwell, particularly his poem **"A Vale of
Tears,"** published in the year of his execution, 1595.
Southwell's poem presents an unusually dramatic il-
lustration of how the therapeutic efficacy of early
modern religious poetry often derives from its careful
organization, its movement from a rhetoric of division,
emptiness, and loss to a language of union, identity, and
wholeness. This movement occurs through the speaker's
shifting disposition toward the Alpine landscape that he
confronts in the poem. When the speaker begins, he
perceives the landscape as a horror vacui, a wholly
godless, objectifying, and alienating unreality. Through
a process of poetic meditation, however, it emerges as
an appropriate setting for a spiritually meaningful
transformation of self that is enabled by an increased
sense of God's presence. In this respect, Southwell
presents a variation on the technique of spiritualizing
the physical, a well-established convention that consists,
as Saint Augustine says, in the knowledge that "every
good of ours either is God or comes from God" (27). In
**"A Vale of Tears,"** the devotional practice of spiritual-
izing the physical consists in the act of relating ele-
ments of creation that appear void of meaning because
they seem unrelated to God's goodness, back to their
divine source. Through the poem's emphasis on
paradox, visual and aural oppositions, and its insistent
representation of an objectless but omnipresent mourn-
ing, it expresses the speaker's feelings of loss and self-
division and his ultimate hope for union with God. The
formal dimensions of the poem perform this movement
from loss and division to the emergence of a meaning-
ful sense of spiritual purpose.

Although it is not my intention to evacuate **"A Vale of
Tears"** of its religiopolitical contexts, many of which
would illustrate the dramatic kinds of separation that
Southwell experienced as a Jesuit and eventual martyr,
my primary concern is to trace the poem's rhetorical
functioning. I trace the formal dimensions of the
speaker's development toward a sense of spiritual

identity at the end of the poem, examining how these
formal elements engage the reader throughout the read-
ing experience. By taking this psychoanalytically based
formalist approach to Southwell's text, I demonstrate
how its imagistic patterning, diction, meditative
features, and religious themes possess a certain cathartic
and sublimatory efficacy. In particular, I emphasize how
the speaker's translation of an alien physical landscape
into a symbolically significant expression of spiritual
identity constitutes a therapeutic scene; how it stages,
that is, the speaker's emerging awareness of his relation
to God. I conclude by explaining how Southwell's
translation of the Petrachan "plaint" for religious
purposes constitutes a literary analog to Lacan's inver-
sion of Freud's view of sublimation. And that this
translation presents a significant moment in the literary
articulation of desire as it develops in the early modern
religious lyric.

A Lytton Sells implicitly reveals why Southwell's cross-
ing of the Alps in 1586 provided an appropriate occa-
sion for staging a struggle for meaningful spiritual
identity when he observes that Southwell "could not but
judge the mountains [in St. Gothard Pass] from the
standpoint of his age which required 'nature' to be
perfected by 'art.' [. . .] But he stands apart from his
age in seeing something in this spectacle that does not
displease him" (330). The first part of Sells's comment
implies that a sixteenth-century mind like Southwell's
would have encountered the "wild, majestic and weird
scenery in the neighborhood of the St. Gothard pass"
(Janelle 278) as not only something imperfect or fallen
but also something quite literally unthinkable, a
paradoxical emblem, if you like, of that which stands
outside the symbolizable. As Southwell puts it, it is a
place "where nothing seemed wrong, yet nothing right"
(line 32). To this extent, the landscape presents an
encounter with meaninglessness, a scene, that is, where
God's presence remains indiscernible. The process of
bringing this empty and meaningless site into a
meaningful relation with the self is consistent with
locating signs of God's presence in the world, a process
that in turn enables the speaker to locate his own place
in relation to God. It is this process that leads Sells to
observe that Southwell sees "something in this spectacle
that does not displease him." In effect, what Southwell
comes to see in the landscape is his proper relation to
God through a deepened consciousness of sin.

Although Louis Martz's thesis regarding the direct influ-
ence of Ignatian meditation on Southwell's poetry has
been seriously challenged on a number of fronts, by
Joseph D. Scallon in particular, there seems little doubt
that certain Ignatian themes and meditative patterns are
significant to the poem and to the description of the
landscape in particular. The poem presents the speaker's
developing awareness of his consciousness of sin and
ends with an emphasis on the spiritual importance of

transforming "former faults" into "plainful thoughts" (69, 57). This thematic focus clearly resembles the meditative sentiments found in the meditations one sees in Saint Ignatius Loyola, where the practitioner "is to consider who God is against whom I have sinned, reflecting on the divine attributes and comparing them with their contraries in me; God's wisdom with my ignorance, God's omnipotence with my weakness, God's justice with my iniquity" (27).

This meditative process of focussing on one's lack in the face of God's perfection is, as Kristeva puts it in her reading of the Eucharist, to admit: "I am divided and lapsing with respect to my ideal, Christ, whose introjection [. . .] [incorporation] sanctifies me while reminding me of my incompletion" (Powers 118-19). To understand the therapeutic design of Southwell's **"A Vale of Tears"** is to recognize that the same logic of division and desire for union that is operating in Ignatian meditation also informs the structure of the poem. This is not to repeat Martz's thesis of a direct parallel between the tripartite organization of Ignatian meditation and early modern devotional poetry but to recognize a more general structural and psychological logic common to both. Indeed, Southwell's **"A Vale of Tears"** dramatizes the same feelings of longing and separation evident in Ignatian modes of meditation in which the practitioner implicates himself in the sufferings of Christ. W. W. Meissner, a practising psychoanalyst and member of the Jesuit order, sees Ignatius's *Spiritual Exercises* as, in part, "a manifestation of [Ignatius's] own psychic experience [that] reflects in some degree his internal world of dynamic and unconscious fantasy" (88). Meissner suggests that such unconscious fantasy is particularly apparent in the maternal imagery and its associated expression for union evident in the central Ignatian prayer Anima Christi:

> Soul of Christ, sanctify me.
> Body of Christ, saw me.
> Blood of Christ, inebriate me.
> Water from the side of Christ, wash me.
> Passion of Christi strengthen me.
>
> (Loyola 1-5)

Meissner suggests that the "imagery of protection, being enfolded within the sacred wounds, recalls associations to a fantasy of reunion with the lost mother" (89). Whatever the biographical significance of the imagery here, however, be it fantasy for the lost mother or otherwise, what is important about the therapeutic dimension of Ignatius's imagery is the way it places impersonal images that have potentially tragic dimensions (Christ's body and blood) into (inter)personally significant symbols of union and meaning. It is not the referential function of the images to Ignatius's unconscious that is of therapeutic and poetic interest here, but the form and process through which Ignatius and the

tradition to which he belongs that translates a scene of loss and non-meaning into a vision of union with the divine. Indeed, it is exactly this formal and thematic process—the process, that is, of translating a potentially meaningless and threatening encounter with an unfamiliar landscape into a spiritual and symbolically significant experience—that unfolds in Southwell's poem.

This process begins with Southwell's representation of the landscape in the opening three stanzas through the meditative dynamics of Ignatius's fourth exercise in the *Spiritual Exercises* (see Martz 207-08). This exercise calls for a meditation on hell in which the practitioner imagines hell using all five senses in order to envision its "length, breadth, and depth" (Loyola 29). Drawing on Ignatius's emphasis on the senses in the meditative process, Southwell begins his description of the Alpine landscape by evoking a world characterized by separation and loss. Between stanzas 2 and 3, the speaker moves from an emphasis on sight to sound re-creating the "composition of place" as practised in the Ignatian method: it is first a place "where eie-roume is from rockes to cloudie sky" (5) and then a site "where ears of other sound can have no choice / But various blustring of the stubburne winde" (9-10). What is most important about the influence of Ignatius's meditation on hell for the opening stanzas is that it provides an appropriate method for describing what initially appears as an outward and alien landscape.

Indeed, the opening line of **"A Vale of Tears"** initiates the dominating movement from high to low, from bright to dark, from vast space to encroaching sky, all of which create a disturbing effect of the landscape as a place of ubiquitous and incomprehensible loss: "A Vale there is enwrapt with dreadful shades / Which thicke of mourning pines shrouds from the sunne / Where hanging clifts yeld short and dumpish glades / And snowie floud with broken streames Both runne" (1-4). Although mourning is clearly a human activity, the landscape appears, nonetheless, objective to the speaker; it appears, that is, as a pure description of a world inaccessible to human intelligibility. Its motions are described as meaninglessly "diverse" as "eares of other sound can have no choice / But various blustering of the stubburne winde" (9-10, emph. mine). The Ignatian focus on the senses operates at this point precisely to undermine the power of human perception to locate signs of meaning in the landscape. This sense of alienation is most disturbing for the speaker as he views the "hollow clouds full fraught with thundering groans / With hideous thumps discharge their pregnant wombe" (15-16). The most terrifying element of the landscape remains its ability to reproduce its indiscernible and, at this point, terrifying features.

Having established his sense of terror at the meaninglessness of the landscape through visual and aural imagery, the speaker in **"A Vale of Tears"** thematizes its lack of discernible shape through the art/nature distinction so common in the period: "Resort there is of none but pilgrim wights, / That passe with trembling foot and panting heart, / With terror cast in cold and shivering frights, / They judge the place to terror framde by art: Yet Natures worke it is of arte untoucht" (21-25). An ambiguity begins to emerge here through the term resort that is crucial to the speaker's translation of the landscape from a site of division and meaninglessness to union and discernible form. On the one hand, these lines thematize the incomprehensibility of "Natures work" by emphasizing the sense that it is "of arte untoucht"; on the other hand, the term resort insinuates not only a "concourse or assemblage of people" but also "an opportunity for repair, retreat, or access to a place" (*OED*). This is the first point in the poem, in other words, where the speaker begins to advance toward a recognition of the "place" as a scene of repair, of communion, of meaning, rather than a site of sheer terror. To this extent, the speaker has implicitly begun to transform what is "of art untoucht" into spiritually and metaphorically meaningful terms. The poem develops by making this process of transformation increasingly explicit throughout. Indeed, the latent insinuation, in stanza 6, that the place is spiritually purposive rather than symbolically vacuous, becomes central in the following three stanzas. In the lines and stanzas immediately following the art/nature distinction, moreover, the coincidence of interior spiritual states and exterior physical motions is inscribed in the formal movements from alterity to identity, from opposition to union; rather than as an explicitly thematized recognition.

In stanzas 7 and 8, for instance, the oppositional elements of the landscape are tightly condensed into individual words set against one another, creating an uncomfortable sense of physical/spiritual dislocation: "Natures worke it is of arte untoucht [. . .] / With such disordered order strangely coucht, / And so with pleasing horror low and hie" (27-28). This dense juxtapositioning reaches its most condensed expression in the first line of stanza 9 as the word mated inscribes the dual senses of confusion and peace, loneliness and communion, fear and mutuality. Directly at the centre of the poem, the speaker tells us that the landscape is "a place for mated minds, an onely bower / Where every thing doth sooth a dumpish mood" (33-34). The term mated signifies both the sense of being "distraught" as in "the bitter smart that strained by mated mind" and a sense of likeness as in a "sweet union held of mated will" (*OED*). This sense of likeness or similarity refers simultaneously to the "Pilgrim blights" of stanza 6 as well as implicitly the identity of the speaker and the landscape itself. Thus the various forms of opposition articulated up to this point are momentarily united in this term, which carries multiple but not opposing meanings. The horrifying, alien landscape is now a "bower," providing a

brief moment of comfort. The unification of subject and object, of the speaker's inner world and the external physical world, is not registered in terms of content as such but, rather, through the productive ambiguity of the word mated. Indeed, it is here, at the centre of the poem, that Southwell's reader, one spiritual pilgrim among many, is invited into the meditational process that the text presents. The place for "mated minds" is no longer a specific place: it is now a shared existential/spiritual condition, a state of being where one seeks to reconcile feelings of dislocation from God. The term mated, then, makes more explicit what remained implicit in the word resort.

It is at this central moment in the poem, what we might call the typological juncture, that the speaker offers the reader the opportunity to imaginatively realign the oppositions formulated so far. The formal and spatial motions of the poem, its movement from opposition to unity, from geographic particularity to spiritual generality, invite the reader to reinterpret a similarity as an identity, thus furthering the symbolic sense of self-unity that the speaker seeks to attain. Indeed, the chaos and "horror of this fearful quier," the constant jarring motion from sky to earth, heat to cold, reaches a still point in the poem's middle as the reader is invited to imaginatively unite speaker and listener, external and internal. This unification is then registered in the images as the "earth lies forlorne, the cloudie skie doth lower, / The wind here weepes, here sighes, here cries aloude" (35-36). The previous cacophony is briefly translated into a harmonious, if still deeply mournful, choir of sound and sight.

Even at the point of momentary resolution, however, a dear ambiguity remains that reflects the speaker's imperfect sense of spiritual purpose. This is evident to the extent that "soothe" signifies not only "comfort" but also "show" or "declare" (*OED*). On the one hand, then, the lines express a sense of momentary ease, a sense of spiritual solidarity amongst the various "Pilgrim Wights" sharing the "bower"; and yet, on the other, they further signify the way that the landscape cannot help but to "betray" a sense of loss that remains disconnected from the consciousness of the speaker. The sense of comfort attained here is momentary and imperfect, an imperfection inscribed within the ambiguity of the diction itself. Indeed, the speaker's language and the reality of the external landscape remain imperfectly matched at this point. The connection, in other words, between the interior state of the speaker and the outward world of the landscape has yet to be deliberately thematized, recognized, that is, as a meaningful identity.

After this still point, the imagistic and rhetorical oppositions are explicitly taken up again as the meditative process begins anew by referring back to the imagery of the poem's opening stanza: "The pines thicke set, hie growne, and ever greene, / Still cloath the place with sad and mourning vaile" (41-42). The resolution achieved through the "mated minds" figure proves to be momentary, but it is nonetheless crucial to the reader's deepening consciousness that the speaker is struggling toward a meaningful vision of the self in relation to the previously terrifying landscape. By identifying with the speaker and thus made part of the community of "mated minds," the meditative focus aims to deepen the reader's awareness of sin in conscious relation to the landscape. The landscape now becomes a fit place for self-analysis and the redeeming power of sorrowful repentance: "All pangs and heavie passions here may find / A thousand motives suitly to their griefes, / To feed the sorrowes of their troubled minde, / And chase away dame pleasures vaine reliefes" (53-56). We have now begun to emerge into a deliberately thematic recognition of the appropriateness of the landscape for religious meditation; the landscape is, effectively, no longer entirely "of arte untoucht."

Indeed, the landscape is now said to "conspire"—which carries the Latinate meaning of "to breathe together"—with the speaker and his fellow pilgrims: "To plaining thoughts this vaile a rest may bee, / To which from worldly joyes they may retire. / Where sorrow springs from water, stone and tree, / Where everie thing with mourners doth conspire" (57-60). These lines resolve the earlier ambiguity in line 33 ("sooth a dumpish mood") by making explicit the sense that the speaker now derives comfort, or "rest," rather than discomfort and terror, from the reflection of his sorrow in the "conspiring" world around him. The sense of "conspire," however, still implies that the landscape stands in an objective relation to the speaker, that its mirroring effect is more coincidental than providential. This changes in the following three stanzas as a series of auditory images is reconciled and the speaker places the landscape within a familiar biblical and eschatological context.

The passive constructions of stanza 15 shift into deliberate meditation constructed through a series of imperative forms in the following stanzas: "Set here my soule maine streames of teares afloate / Here all thy sinfull foiles alone recount, / Of solemne tunes make thou the dolefulst note, / that to thy ditties dolor may amount" (61-64). The "heavy notes," "fearfull quier," "marble grones," and "roaring beates" of earlier stanzas are now deliberately translated into signs of inward griefs, of "solemn tunes," that are not only discernible but also spiritually efficacious. The following stanza is alone in situating the landscape within a recognizably biblical context, thus marking the most explicit point in the transition from alterity to meaning, emptiness to identity: "When Eccho doth repeat thy plainful cries / Thinke that the erie stones thy sinnes bewray, / And now accuse thee with their sad replies, / As heaven and

earth shall in the latter day" (65-68, emph. mine). The allusion to Luke 19:40 establishes the speaker's sense of self within a meaningful symbolic frame that explicitly extends into a view of eschatological history with the reference to the "latter day." The spiritual development of the speaker, then, is consistent with the development of the formal dimensions of the poem and the increasing thematization of the self's relation to the landscape: the initial resolution (at lines 33-35) occurs primarily in terms of a rhetorical still point, inscribing within it, nonetheless, a sense of unease about the relation between self and world, whereas the latter resolution functions thematically, as an explicit moment of reconciliation between the inward self and its outward expression. The reader, then, to the extent that he or she identifies with the speaker, moves from a state of unease regarding the discontinuity and ambiguity between self and landscape to a position of identity between interior and exterior worlds.

This process of securing a sense of identity and spiritual purpose by a recognition of the external state as an inward and symbolic reality is secured in the following stanza through a visual image that complements the auditory patterns concluded in stanzas 15 and 16. The imagistic dimension of this resolution is completed through the figure of the "Limbeck," which purifies the heart while providing a formal resolution, a means of retranslating division and cacophony into unity and harmony: "Let former faults be fuell of the fire, / For griefe in Limbecke of thy heart to still / Thy pensive thoughts, and dumps of thy desire, / And vapoure tears up to thy eies at will" (69-72). The pun on the word still, indicating both "distillation of sins and sorrows" and a sense of "stillness or peace," resolves the wanderings of desire at both imagistic and rhetorical levels (*OED*). Likewise, the figure "dumps," signifying both a musical composition characterized by its sad minor key (Brownlow 123) and the cavernous quality of the Alpine landscape, suggests the resolution of the visual and aural registers of desire initiated in stanzas 2 and 3. By resolving the imagistic and rhetorical oppositions in the poem, the speaker enacts the purifying or distilling process formally as well as thematically, moving from a consciousness of sin to the awareness of contrition, from noise to stillness, from physical and psychological division to imaginative unity. The function of ambiguity is no longer to insinuate division or opposition but rather similarity and identity.

The final stanza of the poem reveals the degree to which Southwell is self-conscious about his poem as both an imperative to, and an example of, the transformation of sorrow into song, of loss into an expression of the desire for union: "Let teares to tunes, and paines to plaints be prest, / And let this be the burdon of thy song, / Come deepe remorse, possess my sinfull brest / Delights adue, I harbourd you too long" (73-76, emph. mine). Southwell here thematizes his application of Petrachan motifs for religious purposes, changing as he does the object of the "plaint" from the courtly lady to God. The Petrachan figure of the "plaint," exploited by English sonneteers like Sir Thomas Wyatt, expresses, as Kenneth Graham argues, the speaker's desire for the courtly lady while implying an awareness of the speaker's unworthiness and lack of deserving of her love and desire (40-41). As a figure of the lover's "moan" or "sigh," the plaint tends to sign the inexpressibility of the lover's affection, as in Wyatt's plaining "without tongue" (Graham 42). In this sense, the emotional sincerity and the accompanying inexpressiveness of the lover's "plaint" might be opposed, as Graham explains, to the more self-consciously rhetorical and confident expression of a speaker's "complaint" (40-47). The figure of the plaint, indicating a sense of humbled "uncertainty" and "inexpressibility," is clearly ideal for the religious poet seeking union, through a deepened consciousness of sin, with the most inexpressible of objects, God. Indeed, Southwell emphasizes the sense of uncertainty around the figure of the plaint as an expression of "pensive thoughts" derived from "former faults" (69, 71). To this extent, the emphasis on plaint expresses the way that Southwell's speaker seeks to deepen his consciousness of separation from God to inspire his own worthiness for union. In Southwell, the "plainfull" speaker is the self-less speaker, a subject prepared to fully acknowledge his unworthiness and distance from the object of desire while hoping, nonetheless, that such an expression will conclude in union with the praised object.

Through this deepening consciousness of sin expressed as "plaining thoughts," Southwell's speaker seeks to meditatively inhabit the impossibly painful point of separation from the Father dramatized in the crucifixion. Kristeva describes this moment of division when she argues that the break, brief as might have been, in the bond linking Christ to his Father and to life introduces into the mythical representation of the Subject a fundamental and psychically necessary discontinuity. Such a caesura, which some have called a "hiatus," provides an image, at the same time as a narrative, for many separations that build up the psychic life of individuals. [. . .] It brought to consciousness the essential dramas that are internal to the becoming of each and every subject. It thus endows itself with a tremendous cathartic power. (Black 132)

The structural patterning and productive ambiguity of Southwell's poem aims to recreate, at the level of both form and theme, the cathartic power derived from the sorts of separations and unions found in the narrative dimensions of the Passion. Southwell's text seeks to spiritually purify its reader, inspire him or her to meditation to transform the wanderings of desire into contrite and purifying tears of repentance. By transforming a potentially meaningless and thus terrifying encounter with "Natures work" into a spiritually and symbolically significant meditative experience, Southwell anticipates the psychoanalytic principle that a therapeutic effect is evoked by "reordering the past contingent events by conferring on them the sense of necessities to come" (Lacan, *Language* 18). Moreover, by transforming the contingencies and "diverse noise" of "Natures work" into an occasion for contrite tears and by subsequently transforming those tears into "plaints" and "solemn songs," Southwell not only narrates the speaker's emergence into a sense of spiritual purpose, but he also thematizes the importance of what we can retrospectively locate as a particular understanding of sublimation. This view of sublimation reflects significant developments in the articulation of desire in the early modern religious lyric as well as its subsequent theorization by psychoanalysis.

This shift in the articulation of desire is evident to the extent that Southwell's transformation of the Petrachan figure of the "plaint" into a religious context presents a literary analogue to the principles behind Lacan's reversal of the Freudian view of sublimation. For Freud, sublimation simply consists in the displacement of instinct from an object that satisfies some direct material need to an object that bears no immediate relation to that need (39). For Lacan, however, the relation is inverted to the point that sublimation consists in investing a particular object, the example he uses is the lady of the courtly love lyric, with the sublime power associated with the source of one's lack, the emptiness around which one's identity is formed (*Ethics* 87-155). In the courtly lyric, the manifest desire for spiritual and sexual consummation covers over the masochistic reality that the lady functions as a stand-in for this nameless lack, which is the inaccessible source of the subject's desire, what Lacan calls the object-a. The courtly lady marks out, in other words, the emptiness that Kristeva speaks of concerning the "hiatus," or "break," represented in the Passion. From this perspective, the economy of sublimation in the courtly lyric tradition consists in the way that "the Object of desire itself coincides with the force that prevents its attainment—in a way, the object 'is' its own withdrawal, its own retraction" (Mek 96). In the courtly love lyric, this impossible situation remains implicit within the structure of the genre, in the way the speaker seeks, but must fail, to receive the lady's desire. In **"A Vale of Tears,"** however, the impossibly divine nature of the object of desire is made explicit, made, that is, a deliberate thematic issue.

This self-consciousness is apparent in Southwell's emphasis on his "plaining thoughts," "plainfull cries," and "plaints," which make dramatically explicit the fact that his lyric voice simultaneously expresses both his desire for God and his unworthiness to be the subject of God's desire (57, 65, 73). To this extent, Southwell makes the impossible nature of courtly desire a thematic dimension of his religious lyric. By displacing an economy of sublimation orchestrated around a human object, however it may be constituted in pseudo-divine terms, to God himself, Southwell makes explicit what remained more or less implicit in the structure of courtly lyric. In this sense, he poeticizes a mode of sublimation that Lacan later theorizes.

By elevating the object of desire from a woman to God, Southwell's speaker seeks to fill out his own lack in relation to what remains, insofar as he is a body as well as a soul, an impossible Object. Within the sublimatory economy of **"A Vale of Tears,"** then, the speaker, like the subject of Lacanian theory, knows himself by articulating his lack in relation to God (for Lacan the object-a) as the absolute aim and source of desire. For Southwell's speaker, the process of articulating a deepened consciousness of sin and the act of transforming this recognition into "plaining thoughts" of lack before God establishes his proper identity in relation to the Father. For Southwell, just as for Lacan, it is only by losing the self as ego, losing, that is, one's inwardly directed narcissistic certainty, in favour of a more consciously intersubjective understanding of the self, that a genuine subject emerges. By dramatizing the speaker's disavowal of "former faults" in favour of outwardly directed "solemn songs," Southwell poeticizes the psychoanalytic principle that a "genuine consciousness of self cannot be attained within the frame of phenomenological introspection but demands a frame of reference outside consciousness" (Lee 73). The speaker's encounter with a landscape that appears uninterpretable constitutes an occasion for inscribing his identity within an economy of sublimation where the self is understood as the subject of a desire for, as well as of, the Other.

Southwell's self-conscious thematization of religious desire in Petrachan terms reflects a significant moment in the history of anthropopathia (the rhetorical term for an expression of God's attributes in language that is normally reserved for describing human characteristics), as it occurs in the early modern religious lyric. By advocating a religious application of Petrachan modes, **"A Vale of Tears"** participated in a literary history that soon led to such radically anthropomorphic expressions of divine love as Donne's "Show me deare Christ" and "Batter my Heart." In these poems, Donne encourages his readers "to participate in the alarming extension of a traditional metaphor," drawing them into an "uneasy complicity" with the speaker's amorous passion for the divine (Kerrigan 338). Southwell's importance to the early modern lyric, then, is not simply a matter of his use of Ignatian exercises, which have been evoked in order to explain away Donne's violations of taste (338) but rather in his articulation and self-conscious understanding of religious desire in Petrachan terms.

This articulation of a subject whose identity is dependent upon an "undeserving" desire for a divine, and in this sense, "impossible" Object, anticipates the theorization of a psychoanalytic conception of the self as the subject of its own lack. Indeed, the early modern tradition of religious lyric that Southwell's **"A Vale of Tears"** participates in not only presents a therapeutic poetics of sublimation, but it also thematizes a view of the subject as a subject of loss, which unexpectedly foresees psychoanalysis.[1]

### Note

1. I would like to thank Mary Silcox and Sylvia Bowerbank for their comments on early drafts of this essay.

### Works Cited

Augustine, Saint. *On Christian Doctrine*. Trans. D. W. Robertson, Jr. Indianapolis: Bobbs Merrill, 1958.

Brownlow, F. W. *Robert Southwell*. London: Twayne, 1996.

Donne, John. *The Complete English Poems*. 1971. Ed. A. J. Smith. London: Penguin, 1986.

Freud, Sigmund. "Civilization and Its Discontents." *Civilization, Society, and Religion*. Vol. 12 of The Penguin Freud Library. Trans. James Strachey. London: Penguin, 1930, 1991. 243-340.

Graham, Kenneth J. E. *The Performance of Conviction: Plainness and Rhetoric in the Early English Renaissance*. Ithaca: Cornell UP, 1994.

Janelle, Pierre. *Robert Southwell: The Writer*. New York: Paul Appel, 1935.

Kerrigan, William. "The Fearful Accommodations of John Donne." *English Literary Renaissance* 4 (1974): 337-63.

Kristeva, Julia. *Black Sun*. New York: Columbia UP, 1989.

———. *Powers of Horror. An Essay in Abjection*. Trans. Leon S. Roudiez. New York: Columbia UP, 1982.

Lacan, Jacques. *Ecrits: A Selection*. New York: Norton, 1977.

———. *The Ethics of Psychoanalysis*. Trans. D. Porter. New York: Norton, 1992.

———. *The Language of the Self. The Function of Language in Psychoanalysis*. Trans. Anthony Wilden. Baltimore: Johns Hopkins UP, 1968.

Lee, Jonathan Scott. *Jacques Lacan*. Amherst: U of Massachusetts P, 1990.

Loyola, Saint Ignatius. *The Spiritual Exercises*. Trans. E. Tetlow. Boston: UP of America, 1987.

Martz, Louis. *The Poetry of Meditation*. New Haven: Yale UP, 1962.

Meissner, W. W. *Ignatius of Loyola: The Psychology of a Saint*, New Haven: Yale UP, 1992.

*Oxford English Dictionary*. 2nd ed (Compact). New York: Oxford UP, 1989.

Scallon, Joseph D. *The Poetry of Robert Southwell. S.J.* Salzburg: Institut fur Englische Sprache and Literatur, 1975.

Sells, A. Lytton. *The Italian Influence in English Poetry: From Chaucer to Southwell*. London: George Allen and Unwin, 1955.

Southwell, Robert. *The Poems of Robert Southwell*. Ed. J. Mcdonald and N. Brown. Oxford: Clarendon Press, 1967.

Mek, Slavoj. *The Metastases of Enjoyment: Six Essays on Woman and Causality*. New York: Verso, 1994.

### Kari Boyd McBride (essay date 2001)

SOURCE: McBride, Kari Boyd. "Gender and Judaism in Meditations on the Passion: Middleton, Southwell, Lanyer, and Fletcher." In *Discovering and (Re)Covering the Seventeenth Century Religious Lyric*, edited by Eugene R. Cunnar and Jeffrey Johnson, pp. 17-40. Pittsburgh: Duquesne University Press, 2001.

[*In the following essay, McBride compares the passion narratives of Southwell, Aemilia Lanyer, Elizabeth Middleton, and Giles Fletcher, examining their respective attitudes toward religion, gender, and nationality.*]

The four authors whose Passion narratives define this study all attempted to write themselves into some kind of literary identity through poetic meditations on the Passion.[1] Both the way we assess their self-fashioning and the status we accord their works depend significantly on our assumptions about literature, canonicity, and religious and literary subjectivity. The poetry of Robert Southwell has a continuous, if marginal, history, perhaps guaranteed by Ben Jonson's comment that he would have destroyed many of his own poems to have written **"The Burning Babe."** That poem is dutifully and widely anthologized, but scholarly interest in Southwell's poetry peaked with Louis Martz's 1954 book *The Poetry of Meditation* and more recent studies tend to concentrate on Southwell's recusancy and his prose works and letters.[2] Aemilia Lanyer's poems have lately been brought into the canon, if one counts anthologization as a sign of canonicity. There has been a small flood of works on Lanyer, which shows no sign of abating, but her relatively recent (re)discovery and the lack of contemporary comment on either her (as poet) or her

poetry, as well as the small size of her poetic corpus, circumscribe her influence on the development of genres and on the history of literature. Elizabeth Middleton's unique extant composition, which draws on Southwell's Passion poem, remains unpublished, and her identity unclear. That she is known at all is a testament to the feminist recuperative literary project rather than to either her generic influence or her poetic capacities. Giles Fletcher, whose poems had enthusiastic admirers in earlier centuries, has become a footnote to Milton scholarship because of the latter's admiration for Fletcher's work. His poems seem neither to be read nor studied today.

For all of these authors, Marshall Grossman's comment about Lanyer seems appropriate at some level: "[I]f, as appears to be the case, Lanyer's publication had, in fact, no historical consequence, failed to *cause* anything at all, in what sense (if any) was it a literary historical event? What does it mean—now—for Lanyer so belatedly to enter literary history?" Grossman answers these questions by showing how Lanyer's book and her treatment of the country house genre "present a specific resistance to the recollection of the past as *his*tory."[3] I wish to answer Grossman's question about authority and canonicity from another perspective, attending to genre, certainly, but looking at gender and other markers of identity as effects of poetry rather than simply precursors. I want to ask not how women as opposed to men deploy particular genres (a question that produces one set of illuminating answers), but rather how a particular genre, a poetic meditation on the Passion, can serve to construct a range of subjectivities.

The Passion narrative provides a particularly fruitful context for asking such questions, as its history is one of community and individual definition through the assignation of guilt and the definition of self by contrast to "other"—of apostle by apostate, of true believer by false, of Christian by Jew—in a generic context that has served to authorize the antisemitism and pogroms that mark the history of the West. As Michelle Cliff has noted, the distance between self-definition and self-justification for acts of persecution and violence is frighteningly small, for the process of identity construction can turn the enemy into an object whose distorted image replaces anything resembling the actual being in the oppressor's mind: "The actual being is then denied speech, denied self-definition, self-realization, . . . denied selfhood." It is this dehumanizing process, Cliff says, "that gives the impression of sanity to the process of oppression" and allows persecution to "be defended as logical."[4] I wish to suggest here that, by virtue of the authority and familiarity of the Passion narrative, the dynamics of that process of objectification could serve to construct various identities. The Christian subjectivity interpellated by the Passion narratives and the concomitant othering of the dehumanized Jews became merely subject and object positions available to be filled by alternative categories—"men" as distinguished from (and superior to) "women" or, vice versa, virtuous women in contrast to evil men. The Passion narrative thus functioned as a kind of universal subject/object machine productive of both community and individual identities.

The Passion narrative—the story of Jesus's betrayal, trial, execution, and burial—forms the climax of the four canonical gospels. Though the gospels differ in many details, in their rhetorical purposes, and in their christologies and theologies, they all agree that the Jewish people were primarily responsible for the death of Jesus, a contention that is not historically tenable. Although crucifixion was common throughout the ancient world,[5] and while the Jewish tradition of "crucifying" the already-dead bodies of criminals as public spectacle and deterrent gave way in Jerusalem to live crucifixion in the last centuries B.C.E., often under the authority of the Roman-delegated Jewish leadership, it is ultimately implausible that the Jewish crowds could demand and share in the act of crucifying Jesus over the objections—or even the apathy—of both Pilate and Caiaphas as they are reported to have done in the gospel accounts. That both Roman and Jewish authorities agreed in the judgment is likely;[6] that the Jewish *people* either were consulted or shared in the execution of the judgment is incredible.

Rather than representing historical fact, the gospel condemnation of the Jews represents the response of the early Christian communities to their political circumstances in the second half of the first century. The communities that produced the canonized gospels had particular reasons for blaming the Jews. Mark's point, for instance, is that those closest to Jesus, including his own family and his own people, are the very ones who fail to recognize his true nature, while outsiders, like the Roman centurion, saw that Jesus was "the son of God." Matthew, on the other hand, is written for relatively Jewish (as opposed to relatively Hellenized) Christians; it is concerned with intra-religious politics and blames the Pharisees in particular for their failure to recognize the divinity of Jesus. But the one fact that underlies every gospel portrayal of Jewish guilt is the power and presence of Rome; blaming the Romans for crucifying one's god might very well have been dangerous for gospel writers. So long as Christianity had less political standing than Judaism, the self-defensive fiction of Jewish culpability remained relatively innocuous; as Rome itself became Christian, the fiction of Jewish guilt became unnecessary at the very moment that it became—in the words of John Dominic Crossan—"lethal."[7]

It is at that moment that the gospel accounts of the Passion came to serve predominantly as another type of fiction, one of self-construction through othering.[8] Just

when the Passion narrative began to function to construct a corporate identity is hard to say, though I would suppose that identity based on distinction from the Jews would be dependent on the absolute break of Christianity from Judaism. This break from Judaism was precipitated both by the changes within Judaism that followed the destruction of Jerusalem in the year 70 and by the missionary impulse of Christianity, for by the final decades of the first century, the majority of Christians were non-Jews. For post-Constantinian Christians, the identity produced by the othering of the Jews would have taken on the kind of mythic quality that most effectively builds autonomous selfhood, especially as Christianity was increasingly coopted by the state and encouraged to articulate a theology of dominance rather than servanthood, a tendency that was developing long before the Edict of Milan gave Christianity official status.[9] Once Christianity is neither Jewish nor marginalized, Jews can become for Christians fundamentally and profoundly "not like us"— inhuman and demonized absolute others. This othering of the Jews also finesses the Jewishness of Jesus and his followers, who are oddly gentile in the Passion narratives of the gospels and in the developing Christian tradition, even in narratives with a relatively low christology.[10]

Thus, in a sense, the Passion narrative served as a kind of creation story, generative of identity in ways that even the Eden narrative could not match, though the Christian tradition read that story almost from the beginning as defining male identity by contrast to female.[11] And the centrality of the Passion narrative to the construction of a dominant Christian subjectivity was underscored by its repetition in both the weekly (or, later, daily) celebration of "The Lord's Supper," which contextualizes the eucharist in a recital of the Passion ("in the same night that he was betrayed, [Jesus] took bread . . .")[12] and in the yearly cycle of the church year whose climax is the dramatic (and dramatized) Holy Week reenactment of the Passion—from the Palm Sunday entrance into Jerusalem, through the Maundy Thursday Last Supper and the Good Friday remembrance of the crucifixion, to the Easter Sunday celebration of the resurrection—a pattern that developed early in the Middle Ages and that was elaborated (for instance, by the addition of the Good Friday Reproaches) over the centuries. The English Protestant reformers, who rejected some elements of the Palm Sunday celebration (like the blessing of the palms), retained the reading of the Passion narratives throughout Holy Week.[13] At the same time, the figure of the crucified Christ, which functioned as synecdochic icon for the entire Passion narrative, was a popular subject in stained glass, paint, and a variety of other media throughout the centuries. (Even Cromwellian iconoclasm in the seventeenth century failed to obliterate entirely that central devotional image from English practice.) Thus an early modern English Christian, Protestant or Catholic, would have been reminded, repeatedly and dramatically, publicly and privately, of the absolute otherness—the inhumanity—of the Jews, whose guilt functioned to construct dominance and identity.

In addition to the presence of these aural and visual representations of the Passion that were defined by liturgical and ecclesiastical forms, one must count the influence of meditative praxis, particularly that of the *Spiritual Exercises* (1548) of Ignatius Loyola, popularized not only by the dissemination of that text but by the many similar treatises spawned by the religious impulses that engendered Loyola's work, including Fray Luis de Granada's *Book of Prayer and Meditation* (1554), "the most popular of all these meditative writers in England at the beginning of the seventeenth century," according to Martz.[14] What all of these devotional exercises had in common was the goal of defining and refining the Christian self through meditation on vividly imagined scenes and events from the life of Christ. Paramount among these was the Passion; contemplation on the details of that narrative, the sense of being there and sharing the pain of Christ's suffering and the sorrow of his followers, produced humility and gratitude, the *sine qua non* of true devotion. Individual Christians, then, would have seen, heard, and rehearsed, publicly and privately, year in and year out, the heinous guilt of the Jews.

This absolute othering was reinforced in early modern England by the seeming absence of the Jews (since their expulsion in the thirteenth century[15]). In Spain, where Jews had lived in thriving communities alongside Christians—and Moslems—for many centuries, identity through othering must have taken a different form, even before Ferdinand and Isabella's Edict of Expulsion of 1492 that drove perhaps 200,000 Jews out of Spain and into the Levant but left behind probably hundreds of thousands of *Marranos,* or *Conversos,* who "chose" to convert rather than leave their homeland. In England, however, there were few Jews *until* the sixteenth century, and their renewed presence there was dramatically preceded, in a sense, (and certainly contextualized) by their demonic characterization in the familiar Passion narratives. James Shapiro has argued that, in England as elsewhere in Europe, the presence of converted Jews resulted in a "destabilization of cultural identity," an identity that was dependent on the essential yet unrecognizable difference between Christians and Jews that *Conversos* undermined.[16] The categories "Jew" and "Christian," thus, never entirely succeed in detaching one from the other; they are always and inevitably relational and only apparently dichotomous. Shapiro argues that the resulting national identity crisis produced various new narratives about difference that transformed the opposition "Christian versus Jew" into

"Englishman versus Jew" in a way that was productive of national identity. I would suggest here that the destabilized and destabilizing cultural context portrayed by Shapiro provided opportunities for the production of other individual and corporate identities; that is, the Passion narrative, understood to function as a kind of identity machine along the axes of race and religion, could produce identity along other axes, including nationality (as delineated by Shapiro) as well as gender and sexuality. I wish to suggest here that a variety of social markers in various combinations could be exploited in differing ways to produce authority and identity within the context of this founding narrative of Christianity.

Although Middleton's poem may have been the last of these poems to be written, I begin with it because it represents a kind of base line, the process of oppressive subject formation at its most virulent and explicit. Nothing is known of Middleton outside her one extant work; scholars have been unable to link her with the handful of contemporary women by that name (and nothing is known about any of those women that would provide clues to possible authorship). Middleton's poem, "The Death and Passion of our Lord Jesus Christ; As it was Acted by the Bloodye Jewes, And Registred by The Blessed Evangelists," exists in a unique (unpublished) Bodleian manuscript dated 1637.[17] (Of course, the poem may have been written years or decades earlier, though her quotation from Robert Southwell's *St. Peter's Complaint,* provides a *terminus a quo* of 1592.) Her meditation on the Passion is of that masochistic species of religious poetry that aims to prolong the reader's experience of spiritual ecstasy by making the gruesome relation of the Passion narrative last as long as possible, larding scriptural tags with superfluous words. Thus we get gems like this one: "The Spirritt fayne would doe it / But the weake fleshe Is hardly brought unto it" (115).[18] She spends 57 stanzas (of 173) on the agony in the garden, and the poem ends abruptly, with a two-line tag, the moment Jesus dies and there is no more bathos to be wrung from the telling. Middleton's poem, rather than illustrating the way an inventive poet could use the dynamics of the Passion narrative, shows the genre at its most hackneyed.

While the purpose of the poem is apparently meditative, it also functions to assess and assign guilt (and to construct identity through opposition, as the title suggests):

> Accompany Thy Saviour O my Soule
> In outward Signes of inward grieving woe
> Breake forth in sighes and with true teares condole
> The Dreadfull Horror that torments him soe
> Sith, for thy sake, sorrowe did pierce his Hart
> Good Reason, in his Griefe, thowe beare A Part.

(95)

Though the poet initially argues here that Jesus died to redeem the Christian soul, responsibility is quickly transferred to the Jews. Indeed, the poem is a textbook case illustrating the way in which dominant identity is produced through the othering of the Jews; if the poetry is unoriginal, it is nonetheless deadly. Here the inhuman, objectified portrait is produced by caricaturing the Jews' early modern role as bankers and merchants. And, as is often the case with such bigotry, there is in Middleton's poem an inverse relationship between vitriol and reason: the more heinous the portrait of the Jews, the less logical the argument. Only Judas has "sold" Christ for profit, but blind bigotry implicates the Jews, as well, who, by Middleton's logic, should be commended for "buying" Christ:

> Oh yee blood-thyrsty Jewes, that Chapmen weare
> Of this choyce Jewell;
>
> * * *
>
> Buy Truth and sell it not (sayes Holy writt)
> Christ is the Truthe, yet here both bought and sould
> Judas the Merchant, Jewes the Chapmen fitt
> For suche A merchandize, to be Enrould
> In Hells blacke booke. . . .
>
> * * *
>
> Unhappy Merchandize, that noe good brought
> To him that vented it, Nor any gayne
> Unto the chapmen, who this traffique bought.
> Only thay Gott theyre labour for theyre payne.
> Ill wynde (The Proverbe sayes) blowes no man good
> Suche are the fruites of sheading harmles blood.
>
> (36, 37, 39)

The mercantile metaphor has, of course, a long history in Christian theology. Christ's precious blood is a commodity exchanged for the souls of sinners; his death purchases human lives. But here the metaphor has been deformed to argue that Christians are saved precisely because Jews are damned.[19]

> Judas Hereby lost his owne Salvation,
> A Heavy losse; never to be Redeem'd.
> The Preistes and Jewes purchast theyre Damnation
> A woefull purchase, not to be esteem'd.
> Only wee Christians Reape the chiefest good
> For wee are Saved by his Precious blood.
>
> (40)

Only the deformed portrait of the Jews can make the persecution of them seem logical in this morass of bad poetry and worse argument. But this justified oppression is instantly productive of Christian identity, the "wee" of the poem.

In Middleton's account, furthermore, the "bloodthirsty Jewes" (153) are the agents of the entire drama. They

"brought . . . [Christ] before the Judgement Seat" (156), "put on him A purple Roabe," "smote him on the Head / And with theyre fillthy Spittle spauld his face" (157);

> Then to the place of Excecution
> They dragge this spotles Innocent to his End
> Where with A Hellishe Resolution
> Unanimous, They purpose, and intend
> Alive to nayle him to the Cursed Tree
> That not at once, but lingring he should Dye.
>
> (159)

Middleton, in a sense, completes the transfer of guilt from Romans to Jews that the gospel accounts began. Further, the account mitigates the Christian guilt that is the *raison d'être* of an atonement theology and of meditative practice. Thus the subjectivity produced by Middleton's poem escapes that spiritual abjection that a meditation on the Passion might otherwise produce. Christian responsibility or guilt is evoked only to be canceled out by the greater guilt of the Jews; the notion that "Christ died for our sins" is superseded by "Christ died at the hands of sinful Jews." Reading Middleton's poem, then, produces not compunction but rather a voyeuristic pleasure in which the subject is not implicated.

While little can be known about Middleton, there is significant and revealing biographical data available about Southwell, Lanyer, and, to a lesser extent, Fletcher. We can thus speculate about the historical and cultural positionings that inflect their elaborations on the Passion narrative. For these poets, the Passion narrative functioned to construct alternative, more complex identities than the simple opposition of Christian and Jew. Robert Southwell, recusant, Jesuit, finally martyr to the Roman cause in England in 1595, brought those histories with him to the project of writing *Saint Peters Complaint,* a work that he was probably composing just before his arrest in 1592.[20] The poem is a variation on the Passion narrative tradition, focusing on one scene, the denial of Peter. It is written in the persona of Peter, and borrows heavily from Luigi Tanzillo's *Le Lacrime di San Pietro.*[21] Southwell's poem is constructive of identity in a number of ways, but not most significantly of the identities one would most expect to find in a poem by the Jesuit head of the English Mission, such as Christian versus Jew, or Catholic versus Protestant. The Jews are mentioned only once, when their "Jewish tyrannies" are evoked as crimes *less* heinous than Peter's denial (127).[22] And while the distinction between orthodox Catholic and heretic Protestant is made early on in the poem, it provides merely a springboard to identities based on gender and sexuality that are more important to Southwell and that dominate the poem.

And the poem is manifestly about the construction of identity. The opening stanza of the preface from "The Author to the Reader" invites the reader to "learne by

[Peter's] faultes, what in thine owne to mend," that is, to construct a righteous self by contrast to a sinful one. But the concern of the poem quickly shifts from the scriptural contrast between sin and righteousness to a contemporary contrast between the "pagans" who write love lyrics and those who write in the service of Christianity:

> Still finest wits are stilling *Venus* rose.
> In Paynim toyes the sweetest vaines are spent:
> To Christian workes, few have their tallents lent.
>
> (16-18)

Succeeding stanzas again condemn those who "fill volumes with your forged Goddesse praise" and "Devote your fabling wits to lovers layes" (32, 34). This literary self-fashioning, however, soon becomes more complex than the simple dichotomies implied by subject and object, divine and secular, faithful and apostate. For the subjectivity that is being constructed is ultimately a male, homosocial identity constructed "between men," in the words of Eve Kosofsky Sedgwick,[23] across the bodies of women, initially the body of poetry about the bodies of beloved women, but finally a homoerotic subjectivity constructed upon the desirable body of Christ across the corrupt and corrupting bodies of all women. For in Southwell's portrait of Peter's denial, it is the humiliating fact that women prompted his denial of Christ—the servant-girls who assert, "You also were with Jesus the Galilean"—that makes his sin so heinous. (In fact, the number and gender of Peter's accusers vary according by gospel,[24] but the femaleness of the accusers is central to Southwell's argument, and he departs from the biblical text here.) Southwell's Peter reviles himself with the charge that "A puffe of womans wind bred all my fear," "a maidens easie breath / Did blow me down, and blast my soule to death" (150, 168).[25] These are not the ordinary, featureless women of the gospel accounts, but "homely droyles" (drudges or base servants), "ill grac'd" and "despisde" (314, 317), who with fearsome farts and dragon breath can "blast" a man's soul. Here women have assumed the object-position of the cloven-footed, demonic Jews in early modern iconography. Peter's denial becomes a type of Adam's seduction by Eve (who was also portrayed with demonic body parts in contemporary depictions)—the basest of sins by virtue of the baseness of women. So when Southwell summarizes women's nature, it is in the Augustinian tradition of original sin:

> O women, woe to men: traps for their falls,
> Still actors in all tragicall mischances:
> Earthes necessarie evils, captiving thralles,
> Now murdring with your tongs, now with your
>   glances,
> Parents of life, and love: spoylers of both,
> The theefes of Harts: fals do you love or loth.
>
> (319-24)

In contrast to this portrait of women, Southwell paints a picture of Jesus as the true object of desire, elaborating for 20 stanzas on the beauty of Christ (before calling himself back to the "real" purpose of his poem with the remark, "But O, how long demurre I on his eies" [445]), using the language of carnal love that provided the poet with an initial contrast productive of subjectivity. Jesus's eyes are the particular focus of this adoration:

> You flames devine that sparkle out your heats,
> And kindle pleasing fires in mortall hearts:
> You nectared Aumbryes of soule feeding meats,
> You graceful quivers of loves dearest darts:
> You did vouchsafe to warme, to wound, to feast:
> My cold, my stony, my now famishde breast.
>
> * * *
>
> These blasing comets, lightning flames of love,
> Made me their warming influence to know:
> My frozen hart their sacred force did prove,
> Which at their lookes did yeeld like melting snow.
>
> (349-54, 361-64)

Twice Jesus' eyes are praised in language that bears an uncanny resemblance to Shakespeare's homoerotic sonnet 20, "A woman's face with Nature's own hand painted." Shakespeare's beloved has

> An eye more bright than [women's], less false in roll-
>   ing,
> Gilding the object whereupon it gazeth;

and is

> A man in hue all hues in his controlling.
>
> (5-7)[26]

For Southwell's Peter, Jesus' eyes "make thinges nobler then in native hew, . . . all but your selves in light excelling" (369, 397).[27] The homoeroticism is underscored by images of fecundity that are portrayed not merely scatologically, but anally. Peter reproaches himself:

> Is this the harvest of his sowing toile?
> Did *Christ* manure thy hart to breed him bryars?
>
> * * *
>
> No: no: the Marle that perjuries do yeeld,
> May spoyle a good, not fat a barraine field.

Peter's sin also seems to have been one of role reversal in the amorous exchange. In the context of the relationship between holy and erotic poetry he has established, Southwell's mention of the "court" of Caiaphas recalls his court(ship) of Jesus the divine lover and an eroticized, penetrative relationship. Peter laments,

O, had I in that court much stronger bene:
Or not so strong as first to enter in.

(245-46)

Peter's sin is finally one of unfaithfulness or adultery to this true lover. His "hart," which should have been kept spotless and virginal for the holy lover Jesus, has been "deflowrde" (586) by heeding the servant girls' words.[28] Southwell uses the Passion narrative, then, as a context for the construction of a male, homosocial subjectivity, contrasting himself to false poets and linking Peter, Everyman and Catholic founder, with the true lover, Christ, across the bodies of debased women (servant girls, Eve, the inamorata of the sonnets). Identity is formed "between men" by fundamentally, as it were, distinguishing maleness from femaleness in the context of the Passion narrative.

The particular historical positioning Aemilia Lanyer brought to her *Salve Deus Rex Judaeorum* is more complex than Southwell's. Much has been made recently of Lanyer's Jewish origins through her father's family, the Bassanos (from Bassano del Grappa, near Venice).[29] This heritage is no doubt significant, but it is mediated by other religious and national positionings that inflected Lanyer's outlook. More formative in many ways than her father's origins would have been her mother's influence, not only because of the primacy of the mother in a young girl's life, but because her father died when Lanyer was seven. Her mother, Margaret Johnson (who was almost certainly Christian), lived until Lanyer was 18. Added to this is the likelihood that Lanyer spent at least some of her youth in the household of Susan Bertie, Countess of Kent, whose family was notable for the arch-Protestant politics that made them exiles during Mary's reign.[30] Further complicating the picture are the Roman Catholic roots of her husband's family, the Lanyers, who were also musicians like the Bassanos, who came to England, probably from Rouen, under Elizabeth, and whose given names—Innocent, Clement—read like a history of the popes.[31] Thus Lanyer was the product of multiple religious standpoints, none of which alone can define her particular religious positioning in the "Salve Deus." It is tempting to see her as pro-Jewish, but, while her Passion narrative is less antisemitic than Middleton's, it mentions the Jews more often than Southwell's, and more harshly.[32] I think it more accurate to call her pro-woman, but even that category is complicated by religious and, particularly, class issues: while she praises notably-Protestant women, she makes the Virgin Mary a principal player in the drama and identifies herself more adamantly and frequently with Christ than with her poetic assemblage of virtuous women. Instead of an overdetermined speaking subject, I would like, instead, to postulate Lanyer as a situated author, transforming and being transformed by the vortex of religious ideas that energized England in the sixteenth and seventeenth centuries and writing a self into existence through her poems.

Lanyer's "Salve Deus" is of interest not only because she constructs female subjectivity in contrast to male sinfulness, but for the way in which she subverts much of the oppressive potential of the narrative. That is, while Lanyer significantly substitutes the category "men" for "Jews" in her poem, men do not emerge from the poem so much as demonized but as sinners who, on account of their sin, do not have the right to lord it over women. While women are the focus of Lanyer's book, and the most holy person presented in the book is a woman—Margaret, Countess of Cumberland—neither Jews nor men as a group are damned. (Only Judas seems inescapably confined to hell because of his actions.) Indeed, Lanyer argues against the kind of divinely justified vengeance productive of persecution. Such behavior, she argues, is particularly abhorrent to Jesus. So the disciples' show of violence against the officials who come with Judas to arrest Jesus is contextualized by an analysis of the way decent people become persecutors. Jesus' enemies (Judas and the accusing Jews) are guilty, first, of rationalization: in them, "Falshood beares the shew of formall Right" (569). And violence born of objectifying, self-righteous hate is, for Lanyer, unchristian. So when Peter slashes off the ear of one of the soldiers, it "Offends [the] Lord, and is against the Lawes":

So much [Jesus] hates Revenge, so farre from Hate,
That he vouchsafes to heale, whom thou [Peter] dost wound;

\* \* \*

Nay, to his foes, his mercies so abound,
That he in pitty doth thy will restraine,
And heales the hurt, and takes away the paine.

(600-02, 606-08)

Rather than using the false accusation of Jesus as an impetus for revenge against the Jews, the scene becomes instead an occasion for condemning revenge and violence.

This is not to say that the poem ceases to construct identity, but that her self-fashioning is more complex than the simple contrasts "Christian versus Jew" or "woman versus man." Lanyer's poem initially shifts the blame for Christ's death from a bigoted category— "Jews"—to the actions of individual men. Judas (not the Jews, as in Middleton's poem) enacts a kind of *felix culpa*: human beings lost their standing "by *Adams* fall" but are "rais'd by a *Judas* kisse" (259-60). All the disciples are wrong in claiming they will not desert Jesus, but "poore *Peter,* he was most too blame, / That thought above them all, by Faith to clime" (355-56). Only after the mitigated condemnation of the two disciples ("rais'd by a *Judas* kisse," "poore *Peter*") are the Jews introduced. They are called "Fooles" (495) and "Monsters" (497), but their sins are human:

> How blinde were they could not discerne the Light!
> How dull! If not to understand the truth,
> How weake! If meekenesse overcame their might;
> How stony hearted, if not mov'd to ruth:
> How void of Pitie, and how full of Spight,
> Gainst him that was the Lord of Light and Truth:
> Here insolent Boldnesse checkt by Love and Grace,
> Retires, and falls before our Makers face.
>
> (505-12)

For Lanyer, the Jews are particularly misguided in their learning:

> Yet could their learned Ignorance apprehend
> No light of grace, to free themselves from blame:
> Zeale, Lawes, Religion, now they doe pretend
> Against the truth, untruths they seeke to frame:
> Now al their powres, their wits, their strengths, they
>   bend
> Against one siely, weake, unarmed man,
> Who no resistance makes, though much he can.
>
> (545-52)

They are contrasted to Jesus, whom Lanyer characterizes as the incarnation of Wisdom (e.g., 694, 701). When Jesus/Wisdom finally speaks, he shows his divinity by eschewing revenge and violence, by refusing to condemn the Jews:

> Then with so mild a Majestie he spake,
> As they might easily know from whence he came,
> His harmelesse tongue doth no exceptions take,
> Nor Priests, nor People, meanes he now to blame;
> But answers Folly, for true Wisdomes sake. . . .
>
> (697-701)

In addition, Lanyer returns, in the agony in the garden scene, to a condemnation of all the disciples who fail to stay awake and pray with Jesus and who all desert him after his arrest. At that moment, they form a culpable category: "Though they protest they never will forsake him, / They do like men, when dangers overtake them" (631-32). Rather than postulating Jewish guilt to minimize Christian responsibility and, thus, construct Christian identity in the manner of Middleton, Lanyer has multiplied the guilt and demonized violence. There is no divinely ordained retribution or persecution in Lanyer's theology—against the Jews, or men, or any individual.

Further, Lanyer, unlike Middleton, does not portray the Jews as responsible for the condemnation and execution of Jesus. Instead, in contradiction to the gospel traditions, she places the blame on Pilate (where it no doubt significantly belonged). Pilate is blamed not, however, as a representative of Rome (as opposed to Jerusalem), but as a representative of men, and his guilt arises significantly because he fails to listen to his wife, who pleads for Jesus' life. And rather than constructing Jesus' defense on his divinity or innocence, Pilate's wife contextualizes the error of Pilate's condemnation of Jesus in the Eden narrative. This abrupt shift is poetically surprising, but (theo)logically sound. The Christian tradition had seen Adam's fault as one of uxoriousness: had he not listened to Eve, he would not have sinned. This reading justified the silencing of women in the Pastoral epistles and in the misogynist tradition that followed them. (Included in this tradition is, of course, Southwell's *Saint Peters Complaint,* where the condemnation of Peter's heeding of the servant girls' words alludes to Adam's fault.) But Lanyer shows that Pilate will err precisely *because* he does not listen to his wife. The scene is a mirror of the exchange between Adam and Eve and, thus, reverses for Lanyer the relative guilt that had been assigned to Eve. Eve's sin, imputed to all women, had allowed men "to over-rule us all," says Pilate's wife, but Pilate's "indiscretion," imputed to all men, "sets us free" (760-61). So while Pilate's ultimate condemnation of Jesus does allow Lanyer to blame men rather than the Jews for the death of Jesus, and allows for the construction of autonomous female identity, her theology does not allow for the absolute othering of men. Rather, Pilate's action restores an equilibrium that was disturbed in Eden: as Mary's obedience was seen to correct Eve's disobedience, as Jesus' saving actions repaired Adam's loss, so men's implication in Pilate's sin rescinds men's authority over women and restores a gender balance. This is the context for Lanyer's demand for equality:

> Then let us have our Libertie againe,
> And challendge to your selves no Sov'raigntie;
>
> *  *  *
>
> Your fault beeing greater, why should you disdaine
> Our beeing your equals, free from tyranny?
> If one weake woman simply did offend,
> This sinne of yours, hath no excuse, nor end.
>
> (825-26, 829-32)

Like Southwell, Lanyer alters the subject/object dynamic in the Passion narrative to construct a gendered religious and poetic identity. She repeats accusations against the Jews but also accuses Peter, the disciples, and Pilate, significantly shifting the blame to men, who displace Jews as perpetrators of the crucifixion—and they are othered as coequals, not as subordinates. What effect her Jewish heritage might have had on these choices is difficult to say, though such self-knowledge may have made it impossible for her to portray the Jews as utterly inhuman. Nonetheless, a kind of thoughtless antisemitism is central to her portrayal; indeed, it is only in the context of a work like Middleton's that one can portray Lanyer's poem as moderate in this sense. One would have to credit her with a kind of Matthean prophetic voice—chastizing most harshly his own people for mistaking the identity of Jesus—to fit her negative portrayal of the Jews to her purported Jewish sense of identity, and nothing else in the text supports that reading. The ambient conversation about the "woman question" seems a more salient influence on her construction of subjectivity. Perhaps she shows herself, finally, to be more Protestant in her inclinations than Jewish, inclined to take seriously the contemporary injunctions of individual responsibility for individual salvation, working out a female subjectivity as she worked out a fit theology.

Lanyer's Passion narrative has recently been read in the context of Giles Fletcher's *Christ's Victorie and Triumph in Heaven, and Earth, over and after Death* (1610).[33] Janel Mueller has suggested that the two works share an analogous structure (*ottava rima* stanzas)[34] and patronage context, Fletcher making his suit to male patrons, and Lanyer, to female patrons of similar standing. For Mueller, these distinctions demonstrate, in part, Lanyer's "feminist poetics."[35] In this context, Mueller notes Fletcher's tendency to allegorize virtues (such as Mercy and Justice) as female, while Lanyer memorializes the virtues of real women like Margaret, Countess of Cumberland. The hagiography that developed around Fletcher's life resembles that tradition in the early memorials to George Herbert. Both were university scholars famous for their piety; after attending Cambridge and remaining there for several years as a "catechist," Fletcher was ordained and took a living in Suffolk "which is supposed to have hastened the period of his death":

> [H]e did not live long to reap the advantage of his preferment; the unhealthiness of the situation combined with the ignorance of his parishioners, to depress his spirits and exhaust his constitution; a lonely village in the maritime part of Suffolk, more than two hundred years ago, had few consolations to offer to one accustomed to the refined occupations of an University.[36]

The "refined occupations" of a university education are evident everywhere in Fletcher's poem, particularly in the characters from classical mythology that populate this biblical epic; indeed, the juxtaposition of Greek with Christian deities was disturbing to readers of earlier centuries.[37] The style, too, is explicitly imitative of Greek and Roman epics,[38] and Fletcher clearly means to establish poetic identity and authority in his appropriation of classical models. The shift from biblical to classical contexts nearly writes the Jews out of Fletcher's account. The crowds that clamor for Jesus' crucifixion are not identified as Jewish, but are rather called the "Fraile multitude" (31). And, when the sky darkens at

the moment of Jesus' death, a Jew's response is portrayed sympathetically alongside those of a philosopher and the Roman centurion:

> The wise philosopher cried, all agast,
> "The God of Nature surely languishèd!"
> The sad Centurion cried out as fast,
> The Sonne of God, the Sonne of God was dead;
> The headlong Iew hung downe his pensiue head,
> And homewards far'd; and euer, as he went,
> He smote his brest, half desperately bent:
> The verie woods and beasts did seeme His death lament.
>
> (39)

In Fletcher's poem, guilt is instead assigned to Satan and to Judas (40-51).

More significant in the context of this discussion is the way that Fletcher fashions a self through the Passion narrative, again as in Southwell's, between men, across the identities, or, at least, the characters, of Mary Magdalene and Mary, the mother of Jesus. For Fletcher, this initiatory poetic moment occurs after the death of Jesus when Joseph of Arimathea provides the tomb for Jesus' body. Though the story of Joseph of Arimathea is, of course, biblical in origin (appearing in all four canonical gospels),[39] in the biblical accounts, Joseph's presence at the tomb is quickly superseded by that of Mary Magdalene and other women (sometimes named as Joanna, or Mary, the mother of James, or Salome), who are the most significant players in the denouement of the Passion narrative. But in Fletcher's poem, Joseph displaces the "shole / Of Maries" (54), initially indistinguishable from each other, as he laments the death of Jesus. At that moment, he becomes a model for poetic and religious subjectivity and is urged by the narrator (in an apostrophe reminiscent of pastoral poetry) to "Sing, then, O sing aloude, thou Arimathean swaine!" (53). Displacing Mary, the mother of Jesus, Joseph holds Jesus' limp body, evoking an image of the Pietà, and then kisses the corpse:

> . . . long he stood, in his faint arms vpholding
> The fairest spoile heau'n euer forfeited,
> With such a silent passion griefe vnfoulding
> That, had the sheete but on himselfe beene spread,
> He for the corse might haue been buried:
>
> \* \* \*
>
> At length (kissing His lipps before he spake,
> As if from thence he fetcht againe His ghost)
> To Mary thus, with teares, his silence brake:
> "Ah, woefull soule! What ioy in all our cost,
> When Him we hould, we haue alreadie lost?"
>
> (54, 55)

After blazoning the healing powers of Christ's body (his eyes, his face, his feet, his hand, his lips), Joseph wishes for exile and death. In this, he displaces Mary

Magdalene, who, in the extra-biblical tradition, had become a hermit after Christ's death and was noted for her tears of sorrow and remorse.[40]

> Let mee, O let me neere some fountaine lie,
> That through the rocke heaues vp his sandie head;
> Or let me dwell vpon some mountaine high,
> Whose hollowe root and baser parts ar spread
> On fleeting waters, in his bowells bread,
> That I their streames, and they my teares may feed:
> Or, cloathèd in some hermit's ragged weed,
> Spend all my daies, in weeping for this cursèd deed.
>
> (62)

Fletcher's poetic identity and authority in this Passion narrative depends, then, on his figuration of Joseph as his antitype; Joseph, most faithful follower and poet, "sings" a poem about Jesus' death in Fletcher's poem about Jesus' death. The homoerotic connection between Joseph and Jesus relies on the co-option of extrabiblical traditions about both Mary Magdalene as holy lover and hermit and "the blessed Virgin" as Pietà. But, uniquely among the four poems I have discussed here, Fletcher's self-fashioning does not depend so much on othering as on displacement and effacement. It is not finally the contrast between Joseph and Mary Magdalene that constructs poetic vocation, but their likeness. Satan and his creature Judas bear the guilt (as, in "Christ's Victorie in Heaven," Satan bears responsibility for Adam's sin), but neither Jews, as in Middleton's account, nor women, as in Southwell's, nor men, as in Lanyer's, are othered to construct identity. Yet the context proves, again, to be productive of a poetic and religious self.

How, then, can we assess the significance of these authors' generically related yet very dissimilar poetic meditations? If we look for an answer in literary history and its byproduct, the canon, these four poems will not prove particularly revealing or illuminating and will remain footnotes to the biographies of major and minor poets—Middleton to Southwell, Southwell to Shakespeare, Fletcher to Milton—or exempla for revisionist literary scholarship reminiscent of Dr. Johnson's faint praise for the bipedal dog, as has partly been the case in Lanyer studies. But we mistake the context of these poems if we confine ourselves to a narrow vision of poetry and ignore the larger cultural and religious context within which they were written, including both public liturgy and private devotion. If seen as versions of a Passion narrative that was "performed" continuously in churches and homes throughout early modern England, the poems look different than if we see them as the oddities of a poetic corpus. In that larger cultural context, they reveal a spectrum of attitudes about nationality, religion, gender, and sexuality that the Passion narrative enabled because of its centrality to the Christian mythos and its long history as a producer of individual and corporate identities. The canon can il-

luminate. Like urban light pollution, it erases billions of dimmer stars and leaves us with a manageable set of constellations and bright suns. But it is sometimes interesting to travel to the desert, where darkness reveals the innumerable lights of the night sky and masks the relationships we thought we understood.

*Notes*

1. Thanks to John C. Ulreich and Herbert N. Schneidau for reading early versions of this study and making thoughtful suggestions. This paper (in a much abbreviated form) was originally delivered at the Southwest Regional Renaissance Conference at the Huntington Library, San Marino, 10 May 1996, supported by a travel grant from the Renaissance Conference of Southern California. A later version was given at the Conference on Medieval Studies in Kalamazoo in May 1999.

2. Louis Martz, *The Poetry of Meditation: A Study in English Religious Literature of the Seventeenth Century* (New Haven: New Haven Univ. Press, 1954). On Southwell, see, for instance, Ronald J. Corthell's "'The secrecy of man': Recusant Discourse and the Elizabethan Subject," *English Literary Renaissance* 19 (1989): 272-90, and F. W. Brownlow's *Robert Southwell* (New York: Twayne, 1996).

3. Marshall Grossman, "The Gendering of Genre: Literary History and the Canon." *Aemilia Lanyer: Gender, Genre, and the Canon,* ed. Marshall Grossman (Lexington: Univ. Press of Kentucky, 1998), 128, 140.

4. Michelle Cliff, "Object Into Subject: Some Thoughts On the Work of Black Women Artists," *Making Face, Making Soul/Haciendo Caras: Creative and Critical Perspectives by Feminists of Color,* ed. Gloria Anzaldúa (San Francisco: Aunt Lute Books, 1990), 271, 272, 274.

5. See Martin Hengel, *Crucifixion in the Ancient World and the Folly of the Message of the Cross* (Philadelphia: Fortress Press, 1977).

6. The Jewish historian Josephus recounts that "Pilate . . . hearing him accused by men of the highest standing amongst us . . . condemned him to be crucified" (qtd. in Crossan, 147). I am indebted to John Dominic Crossan's *Who Killed Jesus?: Exposing the Roots of Antisemitism in the Gospel Story of the Death of Jesus* (San Francisco: Harper, 1991) for much of my understanding of these ancient materials.

7. Crossan, *Who Killed Jesus?*, 152.

8. One could argue that the creation of identity by a kind of Saussurean negative relationship (knowing oneself by what one is not) has precedent in Juda-

ism: Jews are Jews because they are not Canaan-ites, they do not eat pork, they do not practice sacred prostitution or infanticide, they do not worship idols.

9. Note, for instance, the obsession of the early second century Pastoral Letters (1 and 2 Timothy and Titus) with obedience (by women, youth, and slaves to men, elders, and master) and with hierarchy in contrast to the earlier Pauline statement that in Christ "there is no longer Jew or Greek, . . . slave or free, . . . male and female" (Gal. 3.28).

10. Many Christians today and throughout the centuries have thought of Jesus, his followers, and his family as non-Jews. For instance, Elisabeth Schüssler Fiorenza relates a story of a woman who taught a parish adult education class on "Jesus, the Jew." At the end of the class, a participant said, "If you are so insistent that Jesus was Jewish, then you are probably right. But the Blessed Mother for sure is not." *In Memory of Her: A Feminist Theological Reconstruction of Christian Origins* (New York: Crossroad, 1985), 105-06.

11. Perhaps present in the singling out Eve as the one "deceived" in 2 Cor. 11.3; certainly a given in 1 Tim. 2.13 where Eve, and not Adam, is the one who was "deceived" and who "transgressed."

12. See *The Book of Common Prayer, 1559: The Elizabethan Prayer Book,* ed. John E. Booty (Charlottesville: Univ. Press of Virginia for the Folger Shakespeare Library, 1976). The text comes from 1 Cor. 11.23. Two factors might mitigate the impact of these eucharistic reminders of the Passion: the utter or relative incomprehensibility of the Latin Mass for most Christians and their rare and/or limited participation in the eucharistic liturgy. These factors must be weighed, however, against the portrayals of the Passion in graphic and plastic arts "readable" by all people, the popularity of Bible stories that had their own oral tradition throughout the premodern Christian world, and the existence of vernacular missals. Even so, literate laity and clergy would have an influence beyond their numbers on the creation of antisemitic rhetoric and policies.

13. The dramatic reenactment of Palm Sunday originated in fourth century Jerusalem and was practiced by the Roman church as early as the sixth century. The custom of reading the Passion narrative during Holy Week (from the four gospels, in canonical order) "goes back to very ancient times," and, by the Middle Ages, the Passion was being performed as a dramatic oratorio with cantors taking the various individual parts and the choir playing the Jews (a custom that was instrumental, of course, in reviving drama in the medieval world as the biblical enactments moved onto the church porch and then into the streets as Mystery plays). See Massey Hamilton Shepherd, Jr., *The Oxford American Prayer Book Commentary* (New York: Oxford Univ. Press, 1950), 134-37.

14. Louis Martz cites the studies of Helen C. White and Maria Hagedorn in *The Poetry of Meditation,* 5-6. See Helen C. White, *English Devotional Literature,* Wisconsin Studies in Language and Literature, no. 29 (Madison: [Univ. of Wisconsin], 1931), and Maria Hagedorn, *Reformation und spanische Andachtsliteratur: Luis de Granada in England* (Bonn: J. Duckwitz, 1934).

15. The 1290 expulsion of the Jews from England is traditionally attributed to Edward I. However, the 1290 date is largely symbolic, a final expulsion that followed on decades of persecution. For a discussion of the history of fixation on Edward I's 1290 expulsion, see James Shapiro, *Shakespeare and the Jews* (New York: Columbia Univ. Press, 1996), 46-55.

16. Shapiro, *Shakespeare and the Jews,* 15.

17. The manuscript context of the poem provides little help in identifying the author—in addition to her poem, it includes a Calvinist prose tract, "A Soveraign Antidote agayst [sic] Despayre fitt to be taken of all those who are afflicted eyther outwardlye in Boddy or Inwardly in Mynde, or both," and an incomplete version of William Austin's "Ecce Homo" in addition to Middleton's poem, which quotes extensively from Robert Southwell's "Saint Peter's Complaint." In *Kissing the Rod: An Anthology of Seventeenth-Century Women's Verse* (London: Virago, 1988), Germaine Greer et al. speculate that the presence of both Calvinist and Roman Catholic writings in the manuscript suggests that Middleton was related to a family of devout Anglicans with Puritan allies and English Catholic contacts. Unfortunately, Elizabeth was a popular given name in the three generations of Middletons who lived during the time when the poem could have been written (94-96).

18. Reference to Middleton's poem is by stanza number from Bod. Don. E.17. Actually, to be fair, Lanyer's rendering is pretty pedestrian:

> Although the Spirit was willing to obay,
> Yet what great weakeness in the Flesh was found!

But the lines that follow redeem it:

> They slept in Ease, whilst thou in Paine didst pray;
> Loe, they in Sleepe, and thou in Sorow drown'd."

(425-28)

All quotations from Lanyer are by line number from *The Poems of Aemilia Lanyer: Salve Deus Rex Judaeorum,* ed. Susanne Woods (New York: Oxford Univ. Press, 1993).

19. Thanks to John Ulreich for his reading of this passage.

20. See *The Poems of Robert Southwell, S. J.,* ed. James H. McDonald and Nancy Pollard Brown (Oxford: Clarendon Press, 1967), lxxxvi-xcii, for a discussion of the internal and historical arguments for dating the poem to the early 1590s.

21. See Mario Praz, "Robert Southwell's 'Saint Peter's Complaint' and its Italian Source," *Modern Language Review* 19 (1924): 273-90, and Louis Martz's discussion in *The Poetry of Meditation,* 194-95.

22. All quotations are from the McDonald and Brown edition of the *Poems,* cited by line number.

23. *Between Men: English Literature and Male Homosocial Desire* (New York: Columbia Univ. Press, 1985).

24. In Mark, a single servant girl accuses him twice, after which he is accused by "bystanders" (14.66-72). In Matthew, Peter is accused of being one of Jesus's followers by two different servant girls, and then by "bystanders" (26.69-75). In Luke, he is accused by a servant girl, then by "someone else," and then by "another" (22.54-62). In John, he is accused by "the woman who guarded the gate," by unidentified "they," and by "one of the slaves of the high priest" (18.15-27).

25. Significantly for my argument, Southwell borrows heavily from Tanzillo's the misogynistic tenor of Peter's "complaint," though the homoerotic elements I delineate in Southwell's poem seem to be original with him. I would argue, however, that, whatever the immediate source of particular images or descriptions, the self-fashioning achieved through the poem is no less Southwell's, just as Middleton's antisemitism must be attributed to her, whatever its larger context. Poets make choices from a variety of poetic and religious possibilities, and we can learn as much from their borrowings as from their seemingly original compositions.

26. Some biographers, including Alexander B. Grosart, who edited Southwell's works in the nineteenth century, have argued that Southwell had a wide and significant influence on Shakespeare. See Grosart's "Memorial-Introduction," in *The Complete Poems of Robert Southwell* (1872; reprint, Westport, CN: Greenwood Press, 1970) and Christopher Devlin's *Life of Robert Southwell, Poet and Martyr* (New York: Farrar, Straus and Cudahy, [1956]).

27. Lorna Hutson provides a contrast between the kind of male authority constructed in Shakespeare's sonnet—and, by implication, Southwell's poem—and the alternative authority Lanyer is attempting in the "Salve Deus":

> "All *Hews* in his controwling" thus indicates the reader's specifically masculine relation to the text. . . . The relation between masculine author and masculine patron/reader emerges as inherently "virtuous" (in the Renaissance sense of conducive to good action, rather than to theoretical speculation on the nature of good) by implicit comparison with the relation between masculine author and feminine pretext/reader, since the usual pretext of Petrarchan discourse—love for a woman—can only generate a "face" or textual surface of rhetorical colours to be exploited by men. . . . So, since only a man can effectively reproduce from a discourse which celebrates beauty, this power of discursive reproduction becomes his intrinsic beauty, and only a man can therefore be "truly" beautiful.

"Why the Lady's Eyes Are Nothing Like the Sun," in *Women, Texts and Histories 1575-1760,* ed. Clare Brant and Diane Purkiss (London: Routledge, 1992), 18.

28. Of course, this image of adulterous human and faithful God has precedents in the Hebrew prophets, who picture the syncretist Israelites as whoring after false gods.

29. Lanyer's Jewish background has been well established. See Leeds Barroll, "Looking for Patrons," in *Gender, Genre, and the Canon,* ed. Marshall Grossman (Lexington: Univ. Press of Kentucky), 29-48, and the sources he cites, especially David Lasocki with Roger Prior, *The Bassanos: Venetian Musicians and Instrument Makers in England, 1531-1665* (Aldershot: Scolar Press, 1995). However, see Susanne Woods, *Lanyer: A Renaissance Woman Poet* (Oxford Univ. Press, 1999), 5-7, where Woods argues that "[m]ore likely than Jewish origins is the possibility that Baptista [Bassano] and Margaret [Johnson, Lanyer's parents] were radical Protestant partisans" (7).

30. Leeds Barroll questions the likelihood of Lanyer's having known Bertie (32-34). However, Barroll is "looking for patrons" in Lanyer's life; her relationship with Bertie might not have been one of patronage in the literary sense at all (not even in some kind of nascent form). She might merely have been, as Barroll suggests, taken by her mother as a young child to Bertie's household where Lanyer's mother may have been serving Bertie. It would not be at all surprising for Lanyer to make more of this relationship than the circumstances warranted.

31. A. L. Rowse, *The Poems of Shakespeare's Dark Lady: Salve Deus Rex Judaeorum by Emilia Lanier* (London: Jonathan Cape, 1976), 14, 35-36.

32. See Catherine Keohane's discussion of Lanyer's Jewishness and its relationship to her portrayal of Jews in "'That Blindest Weakenesse Be Not Over-Bold': Aemilia Lanyer's Radical Unfolding of the Passion," in *English Literary History* 64 (1997), 359-89. Keohane quotes Janel Mueller's argument that "Lanyer's Jewish background may have enabled her to conceive the agency at issue in the Crucifixion in gendered terms rather than the ethnic ones that were commonplace throughout Christian Europe," but notes that "Lanyer does not fully exonerate the Jews," adding that "Lanyer's rewriting of the Passion story is not one that specifically seeks to absolve the Jews (only Jewish women perhaps)" (365).

33. *Christ's Victorie and Triumph in Heaven, and Earth, over and after Death* consists of four poems. The section "Christ's Triumph Over Death" is the Passion narrative. "Christ's Victorie in Heaven" portrays personified Mercy pleading with God for Adam's pardon; "Christ's Victorie on Earth" recounts the temptation in the desert; and "Christ's Triumph after Death" describes the resurrection, ascension, and the "beatificall vision of God . . . And of Christ" (The Argument), where Christ is figured as a type of Orpheus.

34. Though (as Mueller notes) Fletcher's stanzas conclude with an alexandrine, a form that produces a very different—Spenserian—effect. "The Feminist Poetics of 'Salve Deus Rex Judaeorum," *Aemilia Lanyer: Gender, Genre, and the Canon,* ed. Marshall Grossman (Lexington: Univ. Press of Kentucky).

35. Mueller, "Feminist Poetics," 107-08.

36. Quoted in Grosart, "Memorial-Introduction," *The Complete Poems of Giles Fletcher, B. D.* (London: Chatto and Windus, 1876), 15, from *The Poems of Phineas Fletcher. . . . ,* ed. Alexander Grosart, Fuller Worthies' Library (Blackburn: C. Tiplady, 1869).

37. Grosart, "Memorial-Introduction," 46-47.

38. For instance, note the epic echoes of the opening stanzas:

> The birth of Him that no beginning knewe,
> Yet giues beginning to all that are borne;

> \* \* \*

> How God and Man did both embrace each other,
> Met in one person, Heau'n and Earth did kiss;
> And how a Virgin did become a Mother,
> And bare that Sonne, Who the world's Father is,

> \* \* \*

> Is the first flame, wherewith my whiter Muse
> Doth burne in heauenly loue, such loue to tell.

> \* \* \*

> Ye Sacred Writings, in whose antique leaues
> The memories of Heau'n entreasur'd lie,
> Say, what might be the cause that Mercie heaues
> The dust and sinne aboue th'industrious skie,
> And lets it not to dust and ashes flie?

> (1,2,3,4)

Reference to Fletcher's poems is from Alexander B. Grosart's edition of *The Complete Poems of Giles Fletcher,* by stanza number.

39. In Matt. 27.57-60, Mark 15.43-46, Luke 23.50-53, and John 19.38. He is variously portrayed as "a disciple of Jesus" (Matt.); "a respected member of the council, who was also himself waiting expectantly for the kingdom of God" (Mark); "a good and righteous man . . . who, though a member of the council, had not agreed to their plan and action" (Luke); and "a disciple of Jesus, though a secret one because of his fear of the Jews" (John).

40. See Susan Haskins's *Mary Magdalene: Myth and Metaphor* (New York: Harcourt Brace, 1993) on Mary Magdalene's life as a hermit (105-13) and the importance of weeping in her iconography (187-90).

## Scott R. Pilarz (essay date 2001)

SOURCE: Pilarz, Scott R. "'To Help Souls': Recovering the Purpose of Southwell's Poetry and Prose." In *Discovering and (Re)Covering the Seventeenth Century Religious Lyric,* edited by Eugene R. Cunnar and Jeffrey Johnson, pp. 41-61. Pittsburgh: Duquesne University Press, 2001.

*[In the following essay, Pilarz examines recent scholarship on the Society of Jesus in an attempt to determine the main motivation behind Southwell's writing.]*

Robert Southwell belongs to the first generation of Jesuits. He entered the Society of Jesus fewer than 20 years after the death of Ignatius Loyola, the Order's founder, and religious historians maintain that those present at or near the birth of a religious movement best understand its particular charism.[1] This makes Southwell a Jesuit's Jesuit and, therefore, problematizes scholarship on his life and work. This essay argues that these complications should be embraced in order to recover his English poetry and prose.

Southwell had been a Jesuit for eight years before he returned to England to write again in the language of his boyhood.[2] His long and carefully prescribed course of religious formation largely determined his approach to literature. Furthermore, Jesuit foundational documents, including but not limited to Ignatius Loyola's *Spiritual Exercises,* supply "the primary language for [his] model of Christian selfhood" (Shuger 9).[3] This model of selfhood subsumed his approach to authorship and needs to be contextualized for the sake of rediscovering the most fundamental aspects of his work. As a Jesuit, Southwell wrote to "help souls" through reconciliation, confirmation, and consolation.

Everard Mercurian, the superior general of the Jesuits from 1572 to 1580, gave his subjects specific orders when he missioned them to England, and none of these instructions touched on what Louis Martz describes as "the poor estate of English religious poetry" (180). Contrary to the arguments of Martz and critics writing after him, Southwell did not return home with the intention of "reform[ing] English poetry by bringing to it certain arts he had found flourishing on the Continent: the practice of religious meditation [i.e., the *Spiritual Exercises*], and the conversion of the methods of profane poetry to the service of God" (183). This literary reformation would happen later and only as a result of Southwell's prior understanding of what the first Jesuits called their "way of proceeding."[4] After considerable resistance based upon fears of what would happen to his men, Mercurian sent Jesuits to England "to confirm Catholics in their faith, to absolve the lapsed, [and] not to battle with the heretics" (Basset 40).[5] My reading of Southwell's poetry and prose will show that he adhered so closely to these instructions that his writing should be understood as an exercise in pious utilitarianism. He used literature to achieve the three ends prescribed by his religious superiors, and these specific goals fulfill the original purpose of the Society of Jesus.

Bernard Basset describes how Mercurian, "groping in the dark and not too certain of conditions in England," sent his men with "a list of simple and prudent rules . . . in their pockets":

> Their commission, as Mercurian set it out, must be wholly spiritual. . . . The missionaries were urged to avoid all controversy and politics. They were not to mention politics in their letters and must never, save in private and on urgent occasions, join in conversations about the English Queen . . . "They must so behave that all men must see that the only gain they covet is that of souls."
>
> (40-41)[6]

As the primary purpose of the Society of Jesus, this "coveting" of souls explains Southwell's motive for returning home, as well as the various ministries he performed while in England.[7] Everything else, including the ministry of the *Spiritual Exercises* and producing literature, stands as secondary for Southwell. After eight

years of what he describes as "the restrained and severe Course" of Jesuit formation aimed at "victory over ourselves," Southwell understood this fundamental presupposition (*Supplication* 13).[8] Unfortunately, but understandably, most of his biographers and critics have not.

To date, many scholars have stressed Southwell's "Jesuitness," but in ways that do some injustice both to the poet and his religious order. Southwell's motivation for writing has everything to do with his understanding of the mission of the Society of Jesus, and while the formative value of the *Spiritual Exercises* and the pressures brought to bear by the Reformation should not be underestimated in this regard, they hardly account for all the energies that animate Southwell's work. Issues unexplained by Loyola's *Exercises* or the Protestant Reformation feature prominently in Southwell's poetry and prose, but most readers have been unable to appreciate this because they have worked without the benefit of recent historical scholarship on the Jesuits.[9]

Louis Martz's *The Poetry of Meditation,* published in 1954, marks the starting point in modern criticism of Southwell's work. In response to his argument for the predominant influence on Southwell's verse of the meditative structure of Loyola's *Exercises,* subsequent studies by Rosemond Tuve (1961), Richard Strier (1978), Barbara Lewalski (1979), and F. W. Brownlow (1996) have moved in other, but equally reductive, directions. Tuve, for example, reads Southwell in the tradition of sacred parody as practiced by polemicists of every early modern religious sort. Lewalski gives Southwell short shrift. To do otherwise would undermine her efforts to show that seventeenth century devotional poetry in England has more to do with native Protestant influences than with vestiges of continental Catholicism. Strier, too, discounts Southwell's importance, understanding him as a creature of the Counter-Reformation who paved the way for Crashaw and others to write poetry for the sake of "cultivating ecstasy" (37). Brownlow foregrounds Southwell's martyrdom, and in doing so stresses his "eccentricity and isolation." According to Brownlow, "Southwell made the decision, in some ways an extremely arrogant one, to be one of the absolutely excluded. He challenged his society to kill him . . . The effect, indeed the intention, of Southwell's work and life, was by violence to turn the world upside down in the spirit of the strongest gospel paradoxes and reversals" (xii-xiii). I do not dispute that Southwell wanted to conform his life to the pattern of the gospel, but I will argue that in his mind and art that pattern was refracted through a Jesuit lens, the dimensions of which need to be fully appreciated. Southwell may have been "isolated" and "excluded" from the perspective of Protestant Englishmen, but his poetry and prose place him at the center of the Society of Jesus. When asked who they were, Loyola and his first followers identified themselves as the *Compagnia di Gesu,* the Company of Jesus. Robert Southwell's writing reveals a company man.

According to its motto, *ad majorem Dei gloriam,* the Company of Jesus was founded to promote the greater glory of God. The number of times that this phrase appears in Jesuit foundational documents, however, pales in comparison to the more frequently used quotidian expression "to help souls" (O'Malley 18). This is news. Until recently, even Jesuits themselves labored under misconceptions about their original "way of proceeding." From the Order's inception, admirers and detractors alike have perennially confused its purpose because the Society represents, from the start, a revolutionary way of exercising ministry in the church. As John O'Malley reports, early Jesuits constantly had to insist, "we are not monks." They needed to explain to themselves and others that, while members of monastic orders flee the company of other human beings, "the essence of the Jesuits was to *seek* their company in order to help them." Nothing was to stand in their way, and especially not the familiar trappings of medieval religious life. Jesuits did not chant the Office in choir, nor did they wear monastic garb or live in monasteries or convents.[10] According to Loyola, Jesuits must understand that "the world is our house." Jeronimo Nadal, the man to whom Loyola entrusted the instruction of Jesuits in their "way of proceeding," interpreted this to mean that there was a virtue in mobility. According to Nadal, "the principal and most characteristic dwelling for Jesuits is not the professed houses, but in journeyings." He declares that "the most perfect houses of the Society are the journeys of the professed, by which they diligently seek to gain for Christ the sheep that are perishing."[11] Southwell, while journeying between recusant houses, writes poetry and prose for his English flock precisely as a means of inhabiting his worldly, Jesuit "home." He seeks the company of readers for the sake of "confirm[ing] Catholics in their faith, absolv[ing] the lapsed, and not to battle with heretics" (Basset 33).

Documenting misinterpretations of the Jesuits can be entertaining, especially their demonization by early modern Englishmen, but it is more profitable for reading Southwell to follow O'Malley's efforts "to understand the early Jesuits as they understood themselves" (3). In doing so, it is especially necessary because of the Jesuits' controversial English mission to dispel the single most common misperception about the founding of the Society. As O'Malley puts it, "although the Society of Jesus would have had a much different history, it would have come into being even if the Reformation had not happened, and it cannot be defined primarily in relation to it." Moreover, "in many parts of the world, the direct impact of the Reformation on the Jesuits ranged from minimal to practically nonexistent"

(17). Even in England, where the impact was considerable, Southwell and his fellow Jesuits "tended to understand the Reformation as primarily a pastoral problem": "They saw its fundamental causes and cures as related not so much to doctrinal issues as to the spiritual condition of the persons concerned, and they helped to perpetuate this interpretation, which correlated with their own understanding of what was most important in life" (O'Malley 16).[12] This insight illuminates Southwell's work. He writes as a pastor, not as a polemicist, and he is confident that his literary efforts will help souls by promoting reconciliation.

In several of his poems, Southwell reveals his preference for reconciliation to "battle" with reformers. Surprisingly, this preference even informs works on the Eucharist. Many of his contemporaries, Catholic and Protestant, came at Eucharistic issues with the intention of instigating arguments. But in **"Mary Magdalene's Complaint at Christ's Death,"** for example, Southwell sees the conciliatory advantage of adapting the form of a lover's lament. In the first stanza of the poem, Mary wants to die since the source of her life has parted. Without Christ in her life, she "lives by meere extortion" (4). Southwell characteristically moves from this emotional opening to a more rational and meditative second stanza in which he makes analogies between "seely starres" that "must needes leave shining, / When the sunne is shadowed" and "borrowed streames" that must "refraine their running, / When head springs are hindered" (7-10). In the absence of Christ, Mary desires death, unless there exists some means by which Christ can be really present to her again: "Let me die or live thou in mee" (18). Lines 19-24 of the poem allude to controversies surrounding Christ's presence, or lack thereof, in the Eucharist, but the tone is far from antagonistic:

> Where truth once was, and is not,
> Shadowes are but vanitie:
> Shewing want, that helpe they cannot:
> Signes, not salves of miserie.
> Paynted meate no hunger feedes,
> Dying life each death exceedes.

Southwell could have Protestant churches in mind when he contemplates sites which were once home to truth. Like Mary Magdalene, he mourns the substitution of "shadowes" and "signes" for that which once gave life. But lamentation differs inherently in tone from most Reformation-era literature concerning Communion. This speaker's voice is amorous; it does not anathematize. The poem ends with a loving apostrophe to the spear that pierced the side of Christ. Catholic iconography connects this piercing with the sacraments of Baptism and Eucharist since Scripture reports that water and blood flowed from Christ's side (John 19.34). Southwell sees a paradox in this piercing. It deprives Christ of life, but the release of Christ's blood also allows for the possibility that Christ can remain with Mary: "Though my life though drav'st away, / Maugre thee my love shall stay" (41-42). Southwell insists on the real presence of Christ to his followers through his blood, but he tempers this controversial assertion by the poem's pathos.

Given the contestatory attitudes of people on both sides of the Reformation divide, the reasonableness of Southwell's approach to the Eucharist should surprise us. Other Catholics were much less measured in their reactions to doctrinal challenges. As Peter Marshall reports,

> Confronted with growing evidence of disbelief in the real presence, some priests might be drawn to desperate measures to restore their credibility. In 1544 the London *Grey Friars' Chronicle* reported how a Kentish priest had been punished 'for cutting of his finger and making it bleed on the host at his mass for a false sacrifice,' a faked eucharistic miracle corresponding to the pattern familiar to the sermon literature and popular iconography of the middle ages.
>
> (75)

In responding to doubts about the Eucharist, Southwell, too, turns to the Middle Ages for his inspiration; but his solution relies more on good pastoral sense than on sham theatricality. In **"A Holy Hymne,"** entitled in the manuscripts, "St. Thomas of Aquinas Hymne. Read on Corpus Christi Day. Lauda Sion Salvatorem," Southwell translates and adapts traditional material in order to give it wider circulation. He points out how the feast was established for the purpose of celebrating the institution of the Eucharist at the Last Supper:

> A speciall theame of praise is read,
> A living and life giving bread
> Is on this day exhibited
> Which in the supper of our Lord,
> To twelve disciples at his bord,
> None doubted but was delivered.
>
> (7-12)

In arguing for the universal acceptance of what was "delivered" on Holy Thursday, Southwell avoids contemporary debates about Communion. Later in this long poem, he shows similar care when a priest performs the fraction rite during which the host is broken before reception:

> When the priest the hoast divideth,
> Know that in each part abideth
> All that the whole hoast covered,
> Form of bread not Christ is broken,
> Not of Christ but of his token
> Is state or stature altered.
>
> (55-60)

Southwell makes a typically conciliatory choice in describing this priestly action. The fraction rite was not controversial. Had Southwell wanted to provoke

Protestants, he would have shown his priest elevating the host rather than simply dividing it. Debates raged over the post-consecration elevation of the bread and wine. According to Marshall, "the elevation of the host, once the epitome of concord, now came to symbolize the divergence of religious attitudes" (974).[13] Southwell, following his superior's orders, does not want to foreground that divergence.

**"Content and Rich,"** a parody of Richard Dyer's "My Mind to Me a Kingdom Is," perhaps best exemplifies Southwell's conciliatory approach. Southwell writes,

> I wrastle not with rage,
> While furies flame doth burn:
> It is in vaine to stop the streame,
> Until the tide doth turn.
>
> But when the flame is out
> And ebbing wrath doth end:
> I turn a late enraged foe
> Into a quiet frend.
>
> (37-44)

While most of this poem responds line by line to Dyer's original, these two stanzas concern matters all Southwell's own. The speaker in Dyer's poem remains entirely self-absorbed. Others are mentioned simply as points of comparison to make the speaker's "bliss" all the more enviable. He "laugh[s] not at another's loss," nor does he "grudge . . . at an other's gaine" (31-32). Dyer has no interest in reconciliation, which Southwell makes a major focus of **"Content and Rich."**[14] Unlike Dyer, Southwell cannot be content until he befriends his "late enraged foe."

This intention of befriending "a late enraged foe" also informs one of Southwell's most carefully crafted prose works, *A Humble Supplication to Her Majestie*. His appeal, ostensibly written for Queen Elizabeth herself, responds to a 1591 "declaration of great troubles pretended against the Realme by a number of Seminarie Priests and Jesuits." The precarious political situation in the Netherlands, rumors of Spanish troops assembling in Normandy, and the threat of a second Armada occasioned the declaration. Elizabeth's Council introduced new measures to repress the recusant population lest they be tempted to join forces with potential invaders. Southwell's *Supplication* shows him at his conciliatory best. Instead of battling with heretics, he attempts to ingratiate himself with their recently excommunicated Queen.

The *Supplication* begins and ends with conventional courtly flattery, but the traditional language from the pen of a Catholic priest likely surprised sixteenth century readers. Without yielding any theological ground, Southwell petitions Elizabeth for clemency. She remains his "most mighty and most merciful, most feared and best beloved Princess" (1). In light of her "perfection in all Princely virtues," Southwell insists that she could never have countenanced "soe strange a Proclamation" filled with "Fictions" and "Counterfeit illusions" about her loyal Catholic subjects. It is equally impossible that she knows of the treatment of those subjects: "We presume that your maiestie seldome or never heareth the truth of our persecutions, your lenity and tendernesse being knowne to be soe professed and enemy to these Cruelties, that you would never permitt their Continuance, if they were expressed to your Highness as they are practiced upon us" (944).

After establishing this conciliatory tone, Southwell explains his mission to England in characteristically Jesuit terms. A natural love for his countrymen compels him "to winne soules" (4). For this end, and this end only, he and other Jesuits have been educated. The declaration that sparked Southwell's *Supplication* describes Jesuit colleges as "certaine receptacles made to live in, and there to be instructed in Schoole pointes of sedition" (Bald 60). Southwell corrects this by claiming that "nothing in those seminaryes is either intended or practiced, but the reliefe and good education of foresaken men, as from the stormes of our English shoare flie thither for a calmer Roade, till perfected in the Course of learning and vertue, they may returne to offer their blood for the recovery of souls" (5). The *Supplication* clarifies the issue of offering blood when Southwell explains how Jesuits will behave in the face of a foreign invasion. Instead of aiding and abetting the Spanish, "we doe assure your Maiestie, that what Army soever should come against you, we will rather yeald our brests to by broached by our Cuntrie swords then use our swords to th'effusion of our Cuntries bloud" (35). In response to the charge that he and his confreres are "Fugitives, Rebells, and Traytors," Southwell sums up his strategy and goal: "protesting upon our soules and salvations, and calling Allmighty god and his Angells for witnesses, . . . the whole and only intent of our coming into this Realme, is no other, but to labour for the salvation of soules, and in peaceable and quiet sort to confirme them in the auntient Catholique Faith in which their Forefathers lived and died these 1400 yeares" (11). When Southwell subsequently addresses Elizabeth as "gods annoynted" (33) and "your sacred self" (45), he dramatically confirms his own "peaceable" approach (33). He and other Jesuits, including the much maligned Robert Parsons, hope to "encline fury to Clemency, and rage to Compassion" (38).[15]

In describing recusants as "a bundle of broken reeds" who have "long enough been cut off from all Comfort" (45), Southwell informs readers of the *Supplication* why he needs to "confirm Catholics in their faith" and how he plans to do it. He will console them. When he arrives in England he realizes that his Catholic compatriots are "stinted to an endles taske of sorrows,

growing in griefs as we grow in yeares, one misery overtaking another, as if every one were but an earnest for harder payment" (45). They need consolation, and he writes to meet their need. Martz correctly observes that Southwell felt discouraged by what he discovered upon his return to England, but his reaction had less to do with literature than with the conditions of the Catholic community. His pastoral response to their situation draws upon what he learned during the course of his Jesuit formation. He will confirm them in the faith by means of "consolation." Promoting consolation ranks preeminently among the hallmarks of Jesuit ministry, and Southwell shapes his poetry and prose according to this purpose. Loyola defines consolation in the *Exercises*:

> By consolation I mean what occurs when some interior motion is caused within the soul through which it comes to be inflamed with love of its Creator and Lord. As a result it can love no created thing on the face of the earth itself, but only in the creator of all of them. Similarly, this consolation is experienced when the soul sheds tears that move it to love for its lord—whether they are tears of grief for its own sins or about the Passion of our Lord, or about other matters directly ordered to his service and praise. Finally, I include under the word consolation every increase in faith, hope and charity, and every interior joy that calls and attracts one to heavenly things and to the salvation of one's soul, by bringing it tranquility and peace in its creator and Lord
>
> (#316)

Southwell was surely familiar with this definition and with the importance of consolation in other foundational Jesuit documents. The *Formula of the Institute,* for example, lists "the spiritual consolation of all God's faithful" among the chief purposes for which the Society has been established (#1).

This clearly stated purpose inspires Southwell's earliest prose work, *The Epistle of Comfort.* In her introduction to *The Epistle,* Margaret Waugh compares Southwell's letter to Thomas More's *Dialogue of Comfort Against Tribulation.* While similar in title, the two works differ in "plan and execution": "St. Thomas More writes as a philosopher, musing and meditating in a heavenly manner of his fate; Southwell as a passionate pastor of souls" (xii).[16] He reveals his passion from the start when he writes about showing his "reverent affection" for recusants through these "Catholic, though broken, speeches" (4). With characteristic humility, Southwell likens himself to a "diseased physician" who "may prescribe some healthful physic" by enlarging "a few points which seem unto [him] the principal causes of consolation to those who suffer in God's quarrel" (4). Southwell suggests that Catholics can find consolation on account of their intimate relationship with Christ. He makes his pastoral appeal on the personal level. Rather than scoring doctrinal points, Southwell draws an analogy to the dynamics of friendship:

The love of a mortal friend not only moves us but enforces us to love him again, and his perils for us make us eager for his perils for him, because thereby both our love to him is best witnessed and his love to us most confirmed. And shall not this love on an immortal well-wisher, who tendereth us more than we ourselves, and in all respects better deserveth to have his love countervailed: shall it not, I say, be able to inflame us with desire to suffer for him and testify our affection in the midst of our torments if need so require.

(45)

In his reading of the *Epistle,* F. W. Brownlow describes Southwell as writing "without sorrow, regret, or sympathy" (34). He imagines the letter's primary recipient, the imprisoned Philip Arundel, as "the embodiment of the Southwellian man, his comfort a sheet of paper consigning him to the absolute as rigorously in its own way as his judges sentence" (34). Brownlow misses Southwell's appreciation of the potential of literature in relation to "the absolute." The "absolute," namely God, is, in Southwell's mind, the source of consolation; literature a possible means to it. As Southwell understands it, the sheet of paper upon which he writes can be transformed into a religious instrument.[17] Southwell admits the limitations of literature, recognizing that "neither the style nor the concept [of his *Epistle*] answereth to the weight and importance of the subject" (1). Nevertheless, he has confidence that his words on paper can cause "motions in the soul through which it can be inflamed with love." The only thing "rigorous" about Southwell's approach is the pressure he puts on himself to "labor" in "altering [his] style" so that his readers might experience "the full effect" of what he hopes will constitute an occasion of consolation (1).

Southwell's confidence that prose can mediate consolation is more than matched by his surety that poetry proves even more effective in moving souls. He turns to poetry, according to Josephine Evetts-Secker, precisely because he finds in verse a much needed "spiritual alchemy" (129). Poetic diction provides him with the means to recast the desolatory experiences of his audience. In his poetry Southwell not only presents "the mysterious paradox of finding life through death," but he also wants to "alter [his readers'] perception of reality, to mollify affliction by transforming it," so that they can "behold another truth and a more sublime reality" (129). Southwell distinguishes between poetry and prose in **"To the Reader,"** arguing that "tis a sweete repose, / With poets pleasing vaine to temper prose" (11-12). He describes recusants as "tyred spirits" who for "mirth must have a time" (6). The purpose of his "muses style," therefore, is to "delight" and "give sobrest countenance leave sometime to smyle" (2-3). Such delight is not superficial, nor should it be confused with enjoyment of the "profane conceits and fayning fits" so popular among his literary contemporaries. Southwell's poetry of consolation gives souls an opportunity to "take a

breathing flight," but it stays grounded in "vertue" and finds expression in "measured wordes" (15-16). Southwell considers "the true use of this measured and footed stile" to have been best exemplified by "men of greatest Pietie, in matters of most devotion" (The Author to his loving cosin 1-16). Old and New Testament authors, including Christ himself, provide Southwell with "a method to imitate," whereby he can promote worthy "affections" among his readers.

The specific affection that many of Southwell's poems cultivate, remorse, may strike modern readers as contrary to our concept of consolation. He wants his readers to feel remorse in preparation for sacramental confession. Along with confirming Catholics in their faith and avoiding controversies with reformers, Southwell had also been explicitly missioned to England to "absolve the lapsed." Some of his best known poems need to be recovered in terms of this characteristically Jesuit task. In all of their efforts to help souls, the founding members of the Society insisted that the sacrament of confession was "the centerpiece of Jesuit ministry" (O'Malley 20). It is not surprising, then, that it enjoys pride of place among the sacraments in Southwell's poems. As O'Malley observes, "for the Jesuits, Penance enjoyed . . . preeminence among the seven sacraments," and their confidence in the consoling power of penance was likely grounded in the experience of the *Spiritual Exercises.* The initial phase of this month-long retreat, made at least twice in the life of every Jesuit, climaxes with a confession of all the sins of one's life up to that point.[18] Given their own experience of the sacrament, "Jesuits consistently recommended it to others from all walks of life as the keystone and expression of their conversion," and they were quite specific about their priestly role in the consoling "drama of confession" (O'Malley 139). Jesuit confessors were instructed to "always incline in the more humane direction," and to fashion themselves as "vicars of the mild Christ" (142).

This image of a gentle God, deeply ingrained in Jesuit spirituality, manifests itself in Southwell's *Spiritual Exercises and Devotions.* In one entry he describes the consoling nature of his own relationship with God:

> If you love a friend so much, if he or she is so attractive that everything he asked of you, you would agree to; and if it is so sweet to sit and talk with him, describe your mishaps to him—then how much more should you betake yourself to God, the God of goodness, converse with him, show him your weakness and distress, for he has greater care of you than you have of yourself, indeed he is more intimately you than you are.

(66)

Several of Southwell's poems, including the shorter of his two efforts entitled *Saint Peter's Complaynte,* encourage readers to betake themselves to God in sacramental confession. Peter asks rhetorical questions which underscore his self-induced misery:

> How can I live, that have my life deny'de?
> What can I hope, that lost my hope in feare?
> What trust to one that trewth it selfe defyde?
> What good in him that did his God forsweare
>
>         (1-4)

Peter has forsworn his Lord out of fear; as a result, the church's "Chosen rocke" becomes "a pastor not to feed, but to betray" (24). Southwell reminds his readers that Peter is no ordinary penitent. He recounts the Apostle's great deeds and numbers the privileges granted to him by Christ, including the power to forgive sins: "I once designed Judge to lose and bynde / Now pleade at mercyes bar as guilty thrall" (43-44). The model disciple must now become the model convert in need of consolation. Peter, who once had faith enough to confess that Jesus was Lord, must now find remorse enough to confess his sins:

> O tongue, the first that did his godhedd sounde,
> How couldst thou utter such detesting wordes,
> That every word was to his hart a wounde,
> And lawnc'd him deeper than a thowsand swords?
>
>         (61-64)

After examining his conscience and recognizing the gravity of his offenses, Peter is moved to deep "remorse" signaled by "tears." In hope of future comfort, Peter asks Jesus to "lett myldness temper . . . deserved hate" (70). Jesus proves a perfectly mild confessor, and Southwell's readers should take consolation in this example and seek to imitate it by cultivating remorse for their own sins.

A companion piece, **"S. Peter's Remorse,"** reenforces the roles prescribed for penitent and priest. Again, the examination of a "selfe blaiming conscience" results in "streames of weeping eies" (2-4). These tears recall Loyola's definition of consolation. Peter models for Southwell's readers how motions can stir in a sinner's soul. He admits that fear has led him to "highest treasons," but he trusts that "mercy may relent and temper justice rod" (24-25). The sinner reminds himself and the reader that God is a "milde Lord" who can provide "comfort":

> O milde and mighty Lord,
> Amend what is amisse:
> My sinne my soare, thy love my salve,
> Thy cure my comfort is.
>
>         (53-56)

Southwell's most frequently anthologized piece, **"The Burning Babe,"** also stresses the mildness of Jesus in the act of forgiveness. The speaker employs a traditional Ignatian "composition of place" to summon up images of a "newly borne" Christ Child. Once the speaker sets the scene in vivid detail, the "pretty babe" cries because "none approach to warm their harts" (15). Were they to do so, the "fire" of his love would reduce their "shame and scornes" to ashes. Jesus invites those with "defiled souls" to approach him. He wants nothing else but "to work them to their good" (26). The Christ Child models behavior prescribed for confessors, and the speaker learns that his initial anxieties are groundless. He need not lift "a fearful eye" at this consoling vision. Even the purifying fire proves more comforting than harmful: "Mercie blowes on the coales" (22). While perhaps constituting an instance of alterity for us, writing a penitential poem to celebrate Christmas makes sense for Southwell. He connects the comforting feast of Christ's birth with a sacrament that also affords consolation, and he establishes a similar relationship between confession and Christ's death in **"Sinnes Heavie Load."** Here, the speaker's gaze fixes on the way of the cross, and his report foregrounds the dying Christ's kindness to sinners. The central images of the poem all concern "falling." The sinner has obviously fallen from grace, but Christ's fallings are more literal. Southwell imagines the scene in relation to sacramental confession. Again, Christ models behavior for future confessors. They should follow Christ in refusing to be "severe," even when circumstances warrant such a reaction. If Christ could be kind while enduring excruciating pain, all the more must confessors avoid severity in a sacramental context. The speaker admits that the weight of his sins causes Christ to stumble, but he learns to be glad of it: "But had they not to earth thus pressed thee, / Much more in hell would they have pestred me" (5-6).

After employing a stanza to apostrophize sin itself (13-18), the speaker speculates about sin's effects on him in the life to come: "Alas, if God himselfe sinke under sinne, / What will become of man that dies therein?" (17-18). He draws a parallel between Christ's three literal falls on the *via dolorosa* and his three "falls" in the course of salvation history. The latter include Christ's descent into Mary's womb at the Incarnation (20), his harrowing "sathans cave" (32), and his second coming. All these "falls" are acts of love, the contemplation of which should increase the sinner's hope for consolation. The speaker points out how Christ treats those who are "the cause of [his] unrest." In contrast to God the Father, who was "often . . . severe" (27), Christ reveals himself as exceedingly kind to those who sin against him: "O loving Lord that so doost love the foe, as thus to kiss the ground where he doth goe" (23-24). In forgiving sins, Christ "seal'st a peace with a bleeding kiss" (28). Confessors, therefore, should imitate their "Milde Lord" in granting pardon to sinners even when it involves personal cost. Sinners can see that they have nothing to fear.

At least two of Southwell's poems which touch on the consoling quality of sacramental confession strike a note of urgency. Readers should not delay in seeking forgiveness. In **"A Phansie Turned to a Sinners Complaint,"** Southwell's parody of Dyer's "A Fancy," the Jesuit turns the complaint of a spurned lover into a plea to sinners to confess while they can. The sinful speaker understands that his transgressions have not entirely blotted out the enduring power of grace. This grace, in fact, causes him a troubled conscience:

> Yet God's mist I remaine,
> By death, by wrong, by shame;
> I cannot blot out of my heart,
> The grace wrought in his name.
>
> (105-08)

He expresses remorse for his sins, admittedly adapting "the faining Poets stile" to "figure forth" his "greefe not fain'd" (146-49), and he worries that the time to repent is passing all too quickly. He fears that he will be found "Unworthy of reliefe / That craved it too late" (69-70). The same worry surfaces in **"Loss in Delaies."** Here, Southwell twists the *carpe diem* trope to make a case for confession. He employs imagery to describe the passing of time that rivals Marvell's in its oddity. While in "To His Coy Mistress" Marvell fixes on Time's masticating "slow-chapt power" (39-40), Southwell highlights his hairstyle:

> Time wears all his lockes before,
> Take thy hold upon his fore head,
> When he flies he turns no more,
> And behinde his scalpe is naked,
> Workes ajournd have many stayes,
> Long demurres breede new delaies.
>
> (13-18)

Southwell urges the sinner to seize the day, or the forelocks, as it were, and make a confession: "Happie man that soone doth knocke" (41). He ends by likening the consoling effects of confession to a "salve" (19).

This same urgency appears in Southwell's advice to his father, who had fallen away from the Roman Catholic church. One of Southwell's biographers, Christopher Devlin, notes that for Southwell, as well as for other English Jesuits, "the longing to bring spiritual help to his family played a great part in his vocation to an active [as opposed to monastic] order" (201).[19] In 1589, when the poet's father seemed close to death, Southwell wrote to him, urging him to return to the church by means of sacramental confession. He acknowledges his paradoxical position by writing that "He may be father to the soul that is a son to the body, and requite the benefit of his temporal life by reviving his parent from spiritual death" (*Triumphs* 42). After describing in no uncertain terms the proximity of his father's demise, he asks, "Why then do you not devote at least the small

remnant and surplusage of these your latter days, procuring to make atonement with God, and to free your conscience from such corruption as by your schism and fall hath crept into it?" (50). Southwell acknowledges his father's dire straits, but does so in terms designed to underscore the consolation which confession will bring:

> Howsoever therefore the soft gales of your morning pleasures lulled you in slumbery fits; howsoever the violent heats of noon might awake affections; yet now, in the cool and calm of the evening, retire to a Christian rest and close up the day of your life with a clear sunset: that leaving all darkness behind you and carrying in your conscience the light of grace, you may escape the horror of eternal night, and pass from a mortal day to an everlasting morrow.
>
> (64)

Southwell mentions the threat of hell, but does not dwell on it. Instead, here, as in so many of his poems, the syntax and substance of his prose mean to console.

Unlike most twentieth century readers, Southwell's closest contemporaries appreciated the points set forth here. Even those outside the Society understood the context of his literary work and read that work in relation to his mission. One of his literary executors, John Trussell, introduced a 1596 printed edition of Southwell's *Triumphs Over Death* with some verses of his own, and his poems put Southwell's work in its proper Jesuit perspective. Trussell prefaces the book by greeting the nieces and nephews of Philip Howard, the original recipient of the meditation that follows:

> To you succeeding hopes of mother's fame,
> I dedicate this fruit of Southwell's quill.
> He for your uncle's comfort first it writ:
> I for your consolation print and send you it.
>
> (*Triumphs* xi)[20]

Trussell understands his efforts as a continuation of Southwell's ministry of consolation. Only after clarifying the purpose of Southwell's work does his publisher praise him for his literary achievement. He describes the author as "Our Second-Ciceronian Southwell" famous for "persuasive pithy argument" (xii).

Given Southwell's priorities as a Jesuit missionary, he would have appreciated his publisher putting first things first. When writing for mission, function takes precedence over form, and substance outweighs style. Southwell estimates that his literary work amounts to "a few course threads" meant to show "how well verse and vertue sute together" (The Author to his loving Cosen, 2. 25-27). In Southwell's mind, virtue remains preeminent. Verse, and prose as well, constitute means for virtue's advancement. His primary purpose remains the fulfillment of his mission: "confirm[ing] Catholics in their faith, absolv[ing] the lapsed, and not to battle with heretics." Recovering Southwell's work requires us to understand that he wrote for the sake of "helping souls."

### Notes

1. This presumption is reflected in the Second Vatican Council's Decree on the Renewal of Religious Life which states, "the up-to-date renewal of religious life comprises . . . a constant return to the primitive inspiration of the institutes. . . . Therefore, the spirit and aims of each founder should be faithfully accepted and retained, as indeed should each institute's sound traditions, for all of these constitute the patrimony of an institute" (*Perfectae Caritatis #2*).

2. Southwell entered the Society on October 17, 1578. In the second year of his noviceship he was transferred to the Roman College, soon to become the Pontifical Gregorian University, to begin the study of philosophy. He pronounced his first vows on October 18, 1580, and completed his "Public Defense" in philosophy a year later. From the Roman College he moved to the English College where he would serve as a prefect and tutor to his fellow countrymen while completing his own training in theology. The exact date of his ordination is difficult to determine, but Parsons refers to him as "Father Southwell" in a letter of 1585 (Devlin 66).

3. Included among these documents are the *Formula of the Institute,* which is to the Jesuits what the Rule is to other religious orders; the *Constitutions,* which, according to John O'Malley, "articulated the broad principles according to which the Society was to achieve its goals and reduced the vague generalities of the *Formula* to concrete structures and procedures" (7); Ignatius's *Autobiography,* a narrated story of his life up to 1538, which best models the Jesuits' "way of proceeding"; and, lastly, Loyola's voluminous correspondence which "contains theory and ideals . . . interpreted against the background of everyday reality" (9).

4. According to O'Malley, this expression, *noster modus procedendi; nuestro modo de proceder,* was the Jesuits' "most inclusive and pregnant expression for their style of life and ministry," and "while it of course indicated official documentation, it transcended it by suggesting more spontaneous and actualized ideals and attitudes that distinguished Jesuit life and ministry from that of others" (8).

5. Mercurian's reluctance was at least twofold. As Basset reports, "part of the General's hesitancy about the proposed mission to England was due to

his knowledge that Jesuits were over committed in other parts of the world . . . [since] in 1579 Jesuits had been dispatched to India, Japan, the West Indies, Poland, and Syria" (30). The General was also concerned about committing his men to so dangerous an operation. He was so wary of things English that the Pope had to command him to have Jesuits assume control of the English College in Rome, which had been founded for the express purpose of training missionary priests who would return and reconvert their homeland. Once control of the College was forced upon Mercurian, the inevitability of missioning Jesuits to accompany their students became clear. "It was pointed out to the General," Basset explains, "that the Fathers could hardly train the English seminarians for so dangerous a mission if they were unwilling to share the risks" (33).

6. Claudio Aquaviva, Mercurian's successor, continued the policy of avoiding conflict. To this end he ordered Southwell and Garnet to steer clear of politics. As Philip Caraman reports, "They were not to meddle in the affairs of state; in their reports to Rome, they were to avoid political news and gossip; in company they were to shun talk about the Queen and were not to countenance it in others" (2).

7. Contrary to what earlier biographers surmised about Southwell's career, McDonald and Brown use the poet's letters to his superiors in Rome to show how he enjoyed "a most active pastoral and administrative career" (xvii). Southwell did not spend all his time hiding in the homes of Catholic aristocrats. He frequently visited prisons, provided shelter for priests who were newly arrived in London, and set up his secret printing press. Finally, in the year before his arrest his local superior, Henry Garnet, sent him on a tour of England during which he met with large numbers of recusants. He wrote his English prose and poetry while carrying on these activities, and "his achievement as a writer was already making his influence widespread among Catholic families of great distinction" (xxix).

8. Referring to his formation in *A Humble Supplication,* Southwell notes how "we must limit our myndes to the restrained and severe course of the Society of Jesus, . . . where the place is exile, the Rules strict, the government austere, our wills broken, our least faults chastised, and a most absolute vertue exacted" (7). The "end of all our warlike preparations," Southwell argues, are "the wrastling with our wills, the mortifying of our bodies, and a continual warfare with nature, to get victory over ourselves" (13).

9. John O'Malley's *The First Jesuits* is especially important in this regard. His work is a result of efforts launched in response to the Second Vatican Council's *Perfectae Caritatis,* a Decree on the Renewal of Religious Life. This document mandated that religious orders return to "the primitive inspiration" of their institutes by means of careful study and contemplation [2].

10. The dress of Jesuits in England was a source of criticism. For example, John Gee writes, "If, about Bloomesbury or Holborne, thou meet a smug young fellow in a gold-laced suit, a cloak lined thorow with velvet, one that hath gold rings on his fingers, a watch in his pocket, which he will value above 20 pounds, a very broad-laced band, a stiletto by his side, a man at his heeles, . . . then take heed of a Jesuit" (*Foote out of the Snare* 127). Southwell responds to such criticism in *A Humble Supplication,* insisting that "much more weighty is the salvation of our souls, than the external decency of our apparel; which though it be necessary in time and place; yet is it not so essential a point, as for the Care thereof to neglect the Charge of gods flock and the safety of our lives" (9).

11. Nadal's argument is treated at length by O'Malley in "To Travel to Any Part of the World: Jeronimo Nadal and the Jesuit Vocation," *Studies in the Spirituality of Jesuits* 16/2 (1984):7. This translation is taken from O'Malley's article.

12. Because so many have understood the Jesuits in terms of the Reformation for so long, there is warrant for belaboring this point. Ignatius himself reiterated it, often instructing his men to avoid "controversies" and "doubtful matters" in their preaching. He urged Jesuits in Prague, for example, "not to enter into polemics with the Protestants in the pulpit" (O'Malley 96). Promoting sound spirituality was, he insisted, "the bulwark against the errors of the times" (221). The attitudes of the first Jesuits to enter Germany is instructive in this regard. After careful observation they came to the conclusion that among the first and principal causes of "the calamity that afflicted Germany . . . were the depraved morals and vices of ecclesiastics." The solution was obvious enough: "If the bad lives of Christians were the cause of the Reformation, good lives must be the cure" (277).

13. For an insight into anxieties generated by the elevation of the host, see Richard McCoy's "The Wonderful Spectacle: The Civic Progress of Elizabeth I and the Troublesome Coronation." McCoy notes that "to confirmed Protestants, the elevation of the host was the essence of popish idolatry." Rather than witness the elevation at her Coronation Mass, and thereby alienate her Protestant subjects, the new queen is reported to have "retorned to her closet hearing the Consecration of the Mass" (220).

14. Dyer's "My Mind to Me a Kingdom is" can be found in McDonald and Brown, 150-51.

15. Southwell's remarks on Parsons may be wishful thinking. Not all Jesuits were as peaceable as Southwell, and Parsons is reputed to be among the most truculent. When Parsons seemed on the verge of advocating the assassination of Queen Elizabeth, the Jesuit general intervened. He warned Parsons, "it will behoove the Society to keep out of it, since it little becomes our Institute." Nevertheless, after James and Elizabeth ratified the Anglo-Scottish League on 5 July 1586, Parsons began instigating a Spanish invasion of England (Hicks 108-9).

16. In a survey of recusant consolatory writing, Josephine Evetts-Secker concurs that More's emphasis differs from Southwell's. More's *Dialogue,* written in the Tower in 1534, urges "euery man & euery woman both, [to] appoynt with goddes helpe in their owne mynd beforehand what thyng they intend to do yf the very worst fall." Southwell, writing his *Epistle* "in a medieval mode," dramatizes Christ as the "faithfull paramour of our soule," who languishes for our love (124; 128).

17. Evetts-Secker points out how Southwell admits that his appreciation of epistolary discourse is based on early Christian as well as Jesuit precedent (125). In his opening he writes, "It hath bene alwayes a laudable custome in Gods Church, for such were afflicted in time of persecution not onlye by continuall prayer, and good works, but also by letters and bookes to comforte one another" (*Epistle* 3).

18. Jesuits traditionally make the full 30-day version of the *Spiritual Exercises* shortly after entering the order and then again several years after they have been ordained to the priesthood. An abbreviated 8-day version of the retreat is made annually.

19. Southwell contemplated joining a Carthusian monastery before entering the Society. He discusses the process of discernment in a letter written in 1580: "I was in two minds about my vocation—tossed on a tide of suggestions, now making for the good ship 'Bruno,' now for the ship 'Ignatius,' and reaching neither; in fact I was drowning in a torrent of temptations, until at last I steered a sensible course and went to my Confessor. But he would say nothing except the same thing over and over again in different words: 'Stick to the Society, stick to your first vocation'" (Devlin 30-31).

20. Trussell writes to members of the Sackville family, who were the sons and daughters of Philip Howard's half sister, Lady Margaret Howard. Philip was the child of Lady Mary Fitzalan, the first wife of Thomas Howard, third Duke of Norfolk. Margaret was the daughter of his second wife, Margaret Audley. Margaret Howard married Robert Sackville. She died in 1521 at the age of 29, and it was to assuage her brother's grief that Southwell wrote *Triumphs Over Death*.

## Sadia Abbas (essay date fall 2003)

SOURCE: Abbas, Sadia. "Polemic and Paradox in Robert Southwell's Lyric Poems." *Criticism* 45, no. 4 (fall 2003): 453-82.

[*In the following essay, Abbas contends that the same argumentative and rhetorical styles that characterize Southwell's prose supplication also inform his poetry.*]

1

In 1591 Elizabeth I issued a proclamation that targeted Jesuits and seminary priests. It was "A declaration of great troubles pretended against the Realme by a number of Seminarie Priests and Jesuits sent, and very secretly dispersed to the same, to worke great Treasons under a false pretence of Religion, with a provision very necessary for remedy thereof."[1] Although the title paid lip service to a separation between the religious practice of the Catholics and the activity of seminary priests and Jesuits, portions of the text made explicit the longtime Elizabethan equation of Catholicism with treason.

The proclamation linked the presence of the Jesuits and seminary priests in England with Spain's expansionist aims. The men were called "Dissolute," "unnatural subjects," "Fugitives, Rebelles, and Traitors." They were accused of trying to "mooue, stirre up, and perswade as many of [Elizabeth's] subjects, as they dare deale withall, to renounce their naturall allegeance due to [the Queen and her] Crowne, and upon hope by a Spanish Invasion to be enriched and endowed." The priests were said to use the sacraments to make the Queen's subjects switch their allegiance to the King of Spain. Papal bulls and indulgences were also identified as tools of this treacherous persuasion.[2]

The proclamation went on to insist that no Catholic had to fear death for practicing his or her religion. Catholics only had to pay fines for not attending the British church. But by equating attendance at church with fealty to the state, the government had already made loyalty to any church other than its own treason. The rest of the proclamation made this clearer. Ecclesiastical members of the Church of England were asked to be diligent in teaching people to stay steadfast in their "profession of the Gospells, and in their duties to almightie God and us."[3]

The state was declared to be prepared for a sea battle with greater strength at sea than it had ever had. To aid in a confrontation on land, the realm had been divided into several "lieutenancies," so that the requisite steps could be taken to defend the country from within. Subjects were asked to defend their families, land, and "posterities" "against ravening strangers, willful destroyers of their native countrey and monstrous traytors."[4] Those who harbored Catholics were also to be "charged by law to their great danger."[5] Subjects of every estate and kind were to be asked if they knew of any such people. If such invaders were found, inquiries were to be made about where they had been for the previous year and whether they had attended church in accordance with the English laws. The Crown had appointed commissioners in every shire, city, and port to look for people who were attempting to make subjects relinquish their allegiance to the Queen, or "to acknowledge any kind of obedience to the Pope, or to the King of Spaine."[6] Subjects who had information and did not come forward within twenty days of the proclamation were to be punished as "abettors and mainteiners of traytors."[7] The choice between Queen and Pope, between country and Catholicism, could not have been more stark. To be Catholic was, in effect, to be a traitor.

In *An Humble Supplication to her Maiestie in Answere to the late Proclamation* (1591), Robert Southwell responded systematically to the government's charges. He dismissed the idea that Catholics were not persecuted for their religion and posed a series of impassioned questions:

> Was it not punishment for Religion, when a Company of honorable and worshipfull Ladies, and gentlewomen were most uncivilly lead through Cheapside, with their Priest before them, only for hearing Masse; and that before Priesthood was enacted to be Treason? Is not that very statute a most heavy oppression, now, when the most of the few *Queene Mary* Fathers that are left, are become soe old and impotent, that they cannot possibly supply Catholiques spiritual necessities, to make it by Law felony to receaue yonge Priests?
>
> (Southwell's italics)[8]

Southwell's argument exposed the fact that by targeting seminary priests, the government was, in effect, committed to the eradication of the old religion in England. If priests could not practice or be trained, in England, the pragmatics of the situation would result in quiet extinction. On the charge that Catholic priests and Jesuits were "unnaturall" subjects, he wrote:

> If we seeke with our deepest perills to plant [Catholicism] in our Realme, and to winne soules from misbelief unto it, we thinke that we owe a most sincere

and naturall love unto our Cuntrie (for even by *Christ's* own testimony, noe man's charity reacheth to any higher point than to yeald his life for the benefitt of his Friends).

(Southwell's italics)[9]

*An Humble Supplication* exhibits Southwell's speculative and rhetorical power, his habits of careful and systematic argument, and his sensitivity to contradictions. He identifies the conceptual crux of the assumptions in the proclamation and responds to it accordingly. Since Catholicism is equated insistently with treason, Southwell responds to the equation latent in this identification: treason requires a betrayal of one's compatriots, implicitly of one's friends, family, neighbors; but it would be a greater betrayal to let the souls of one's compatriots, friends, family, and neighbors be lost. For it is, after all, the height of charity to "yield one's life for the benefit of [one's] Friends." The opposition between body and soul occurs more explicitly twice in *An Humble Supplication.* No matter how priestly activity and Catholic belief are given the wrongful title of treason, "it will ever be Religion, and nothing but religion, for which we expose our blood to the hazard of these Lawes and for the benefit of our soules and yeald our bodies to all extremities."[10] In response to the law that even those who comfort priests will be punished, Southwell writes bitterly: "we are compelled to accuse those whom our conscience assureth us to be innocent . . . to whose Soules we be Pastors, and they the Fosterers of our bodies."[11]

In a letter to his father urging him to embrace Catholicism, Southwell writes: "he may be a father to the soul that is a son to the body, and requite the benefit of his temporal life by reviving his parent from a spiritual death."[12] Southwell allegorizes these variations on the theme of bodies and souls in **"Man's Civille Warre,"** which belongs to the subgenre of the body-and-soul poem but whose meaning is activated and layered by these implicit political and religious associations. I shall return to a discussion of **"Man's Civille Warre"** later in the essay.

Southwell's argumentative skills are very much in evidence in the first passage quoted from *An Humble Supplication,* as they are indeed throughout the piece. Without denying that he considers the saving of souls crucial, Southwell keeps his argument both precise and moving. He does not attack the Queen but rather acknowledges, a few lines later, that Elizabeth would be the highest "gayne of [their] deare purchase." If Catholic priests and Jesuits (the specific target of the proclamation) are to be martyred—as they expected to be even prior to it—the blood spilled as a result of Elizabeth's laws would be well worth it, if she too were to become a Catholic. Catholic blood would be the cur-

rency of this purchase of Elizabeth's redemption. The sacramental status granted to martyred Catholic blood here is of a piece with Southwell's frequent equation of Catholic suffering and sacrifice with Christ's redemptive blood.

In *An Epistle of Comfort*—which is meant, as its title suggests, to provide solace to English Catholics—Southwell insists that his readers should draw comfort from the fact "that we are moved to suffer Tribulation willingly, both by the precedent of Christ and the title of a Christian."[13] It is a felicity of language that "Christian" contains "Christ," one, moreover, that is bound to appeal to the poet for whom *imitatio Christi* has a literal and terrible resonance. As F. W. Brownlow remarks in his compelling and powerful study of Southwell: "the world in which the Incarnation is the central event is a world of figures, correspondences, symmetries, antitheses, and paradoxes, all wrought by God as artificer in the medium of life through the agency of time, grace, and nature."[14] In this world of correspondences and analogies, the suffering of Christ demands a similar, consciously analogic, sacrifice.

Secularizing the charge against the priests was intended to deny English Catholics the grounds of their Christian faith. Southwell is rhetorically sophisticated and insistent—though not unique—in asserting the religious component of Jesuit activity, almost as insistent, in fact, as the proclamation is on the *political* treachery of the Jesuits. He goes on to say, with a trace of bitterness, "but though they that hunt this fault in us, might best be their own prey (our Faith being the strongest ground of true and *naturall* fidelity) yet must we only be accounted *unnaturall*." Again, Southwell puts philosophical pressure on the government's argument: it is indeed the grounds of loyalty they are debating, but how should they decide where their loyalties ought to lie? This, Brownlow eloquently suggests, is the question posed by Southwell's career: "To whom, or what, and on what terms, and with what possible mitigations, is loyalty owed?"[15] The charge of betrayal that sits at the center of the accusation of treason allows Southwell to introduce the question of natural fidelity. Southwell drily reminds his Protestant opponents that, given their emphasis on justification by faith alone, they should be sympathetic to the attempt of English Catholics to keep theirs.

As the proclamation and *An Humble Supplication* show, in the 1580s and 1590s to be a practicing Catholic was simultaneously a political and a religious statement. The Catholic mass was illegal in England as early as 1559. After the Papal Bull of Excommunication of 1570, things started getting worse. By 1585 it was a capital offense to even aid or shelter Catholic priests. The situation was volatile and confusing, and it was made worse by the arrival of the first Jesuits in 1580.[16] Parliament presented three versions of the bill that would become

"The Act to retain the Queen's Majesty's subjects in their due obedience" when it met in 1581. The first two bills made the saying of Mass a felony, which would be punishable by the death penalty. Attending the mass was punishable by a fine of 200 marks and, in the second bill, imprisonment for six months. The second offense would result in the pains of praemunire (imprisonment and forfeiture of lands).[17] The statute based on the third bill reduced the penalty for saying Mass to a fine of 200 marks and the punishment for hearing it to 100 marks. The penalties for non-attendance for Catholic recusants were fines of £20 for the first month, £40 for the second, £100 for the third, and the pains of praemunire for the fourth.[18] It was the mutability of the situation that required, and elicited, the complex responses we see in Southwell's prose and in his poetry.

What interests me primarily in this discussion is the way in which the argumentative precision and detail and the rhetorical style we see in *An Humble Supplication* are refracted in Southwell's poetry. The inversions and paradoxes present throughout his poetry are seen in *An Humble Supplication* in their fully motivated context. In his poetry, Southwell returns repeatedly to the plight of English Catholics in seemingly nonpolemical, or at least not overtly political, contexts. He does so in order to provide solace to his brethren, but also to argue for the importance of fidelity to the Church.

Critics have tended to apologize for Southwell's style. He was too busy to polish his lyrics, too unfamiliar with the English language after his youth abroad. For Southwell—who left England secretly and, as Christopher Devlin's biography casts it, adventurously, in order to be trained at Douai in the old religion; who, on his return, is said to have told Henry Garnet that one day his head would be up on the spikes of the Tower of London; whose return to England was spent in hiding, illegally administering the sacraments to Catholics; and who was tortured by Topcliffe and eventually executed—biography can obscure, even as it grips.[19]

This state of affairs has begun to change in recent years. Brian Oxley and Brownlow have made the case for the complexity and intelligence of Southwell's style.[20] And as early modern Catholicism has begun to receive more attention, it has become possible to understand, in greater depth, the historical and political impetus of English Catholic literature.[21] I hope to build in this essay on Oxley's and Brownlow's case for Southwell's style, and to show how powerfully Southwell's political and social experience infuses his poetry. Understanding these motives allows us to retrieve what the poems might have meant to Southwell and to his Elizabethan readers, and enriches our valuation of his poetic ability and, consequently, of his poems. My assertion rests on an assumption that granting technical control and awareness to Southwell makes his poetry more interesting, because, as a result, we can see more clearly its discursive content, and its generation of meaning and argument through formal play.

The apology for Southwell's poetic style on grounds of his unfamiliarity with the tongue is perhaps least convincing. Southwell's tendency to use heavy alliteration, fourteeners, and versions of poulter's measure could, and I believe should, be as easily interpreted as evidence of his cultivation of a native, English, medieval style. The similarities between the style of Southwell's poems and the poems in *Tottel's Miscellany* (1557) and *The Paradyse of Dainty Devices* (1576) have been remarked and are clearly attributable to the tradition of sacred pardoy.[22] Brownlow seems right in suggesting that "the new Renaissance English style was too closely associated with either a protestant or a paganizing humanism for a recusant writer to adopt it, especially a Jesuit poet."[23] Southwell appears to have chosen a vernacular, alliterative style not only as a repudiation of contemporary poetic practice but also because such a style makes a statement about continuity and patriotism.

If critics have been tempted to apologize for Southwell it is because, after Herbert, we are accustomed to the minimizing of accent and of overt rhymes; we have been wary of anything that smacks of ballad, that lacks Herbert's stylistic reserve or Jonson's classical restraint. We are suspicious of poetry so overtly rhetorical and didactic. Nor do we have much by way of a critical discourse that would allow for talk about the formal aspects of what can, on occasion, look like the drab style. Southwell's poems reveal how much the understanding of poems that fall under the "drab" rubric depend upon context and biography. It is the very spareness and the familiarity of some of the metaphors of a poem such as **"Man's Civille Warre"** that makes our explications particularly dependent upon contextual information.

An additional reason for a resistance to Southwell's style is that he can be remarkably abstract, sometimes so much so that his more intricate figures "can seem to come untethered from the reality they should stand for."[24] Such abstraction can be alienating and, given a residual bias in favor of concrete imagery, can make the poetry seem far less dense and rich than it is. Furthermore, Southwell is an argumentative and partisan poet. When combined with all the other factors that work against him, the argumentative aspects of his style can be even more alienating to readers. Southwell can be tactful, but his is a poetry of abundant, accented argument. As a result, his poems demand to be read as structures wherein the argumentative shifts are charted through each line. The structures of the poems themselves invite attention to their arguments.

It is also my intention, in this essay, to revive and expand an older critical interest in the concept and function of paradox. Critical work that seeks to bring together political and formal concerns engages the specificity of the poet's oeuvre and context *and* the history and theory of form. It is my hope that examining the dialectic between the specifics of Southwell's case and the necessary conceptual generality of the idea of paradox will fruitfully enlarge our understanding of both.

Although I do not want to minimize the influence of his education on the Continent, from which Southwell clearly brought back some Baroque techniques, I do want to argue that Southwell's fondness for paradox, which has also incurred the charge of *preciosité,* derives in part from the paradoxes, uncertainties, and confusions rife in English national and religious history at the time.[25] The content motivates and earns the form.

The temptations of a heavily paradoxical style for Southwell lie both in the rich storehouse of paradoxical material the Bible provides and in the conceptual pressures arising from the identification of Catholicism with treason. For the religious group that went in a few years from dominance to recusancy, to being a persecuted minority in its own country, life must have seemed full of sudden reversals and paradoxes. In other words, a paradoxical style is appropriate if one's aim is to give an accurate rendition of the contrary layers of English Catholic experience. Moreover, if one's aim is to move people to stay true to a course of action that could lead to martyrdom, in which the paradox of the passion—a moment of great suffering and greater glory, great humiliation and even greater veneration—is a central hortatory figure, a paradoxical style is able to give an intricate and moving account of the world and its limits.

In her wonderful—and monumental—*Paradoxia Epidemica: The Renaissance Tradition of Paradox* (1966), Rosalie Colie suggests that "operating at the limits of discourse, redirecting thoughtful attention to the faulty or limited structures of thought, paradoxes play back and forth across terminal and categorical boundaries—that is, they play with human understanding, that most serious of all human activities."[26] Colie identifies three kinds of paradox: rhetorical, logical, and epistemological. Each generates and engages particular conceptual problems. "The rhetorical paradox criticizes the limitations and rigidity of argumentation," the logical "criticizes the limitations and rigidity of logic," and the epistemological "calls into question the process of human thought, as well as the categories thought out (by human thought) to express human thought."[27] The poet who could, in "Looke Home," write the phrase "what thought can think" would have appreciated Colie's explication.[28]

Paradox lends itself to the expression of religious ideas, especially Christian notions concerned with the doctrine of the incarnation, with its mix of divine inconceivability and worldly embodiment. As we shall see, paradox is also able to reflect upon and call into question the Elizabethan identification of Catholicism with treason. The Elizabethan nationalist enterprise required a historical narrative, and England's Christian history up to Henry VIII was Catholic. Southwell insists: "the whole and only intent of our coming into this Realme, is no other, but to labour for the salvation of souls, and in peaceable and quiet sort to confirm them *in the ancient Catholic Faith in which their forefathers lived and died these fourteen hundred years,* and out of which we believe it is impossible that any soul should be saved" (my italics).[29]

The practice of isolating English Catholics as part of the project of nation building put epistemological pressure on precisely the historical narrative that nationalism required, by obfuscating the "terminal," "categorical," and historical boundaries of Englishness, Christianity, Catholicism, treason. And it is this contrary epistemological tug that was identified with grim and poignant precision by Edmund Campion at his trial. If to be Catholic is to be a traitor, then English history is a history of traitors:

> The only thing we have to say is, that if our religion do make us traitors, we are worthy to be condemned. . . . In condemning us you condemn all that was once the glory of England, the island of saints, and the most devoted child of the see of Peter. For what have we taught, however you may qualify it with the odious name of treason, that they did not uniformly teach?[30]

As his execution, another Catholic martyr turned this historical paradox into a defiant joke aimed at his executioner:

> Lacey, now having the rope about his neck, was willed by Topcliffe to confess his treason. "For," saith he, "here are none but traitors who are of thy religion."
>
> "Then," said Lacey, "answer me. You yourself in Queen Mary's days was a Papist, at least in show. Tell, were you also a traitor?" At which, the people laughed aloud.[31]

The attempt to conceive of England as a national community required that an older, Catholic community be imagined out of existence. The Catholics posed a threat to the historical veracity and the conceptual foundations of the new national narrative.[32]

An important caveat is in order here: although recent revisionary writing on Catholicism has been very valuable, it can make the work of the Jesuit underground seem far more benign than it was by reading back the subsequent English persecution of Catholics into the history of Elizabethan Catholicism. It is worth remembering that, although Southwell's, Campion's, and Lacey's insistence on the religious component of their activities was understandable, the government's attitude was unsurprising. The punishments would have been at least as severe in other parts of sixteenth-century Europe; and other governments would have been no more inclined to view Catholic missionary activity as purely religious. William Allen and Robert Parsons, leaders of the English Catholic mission, openly advocated an invasion of England. The Catholic missionaries were trained with the financial help of the Pope and Spain, and under the patronage of the Pope.[33]

The political argument was also, of course, theologically layered and fit into continent-wide debates about the Eucharist and justification by faith. Thus, as we shall see, Southwell makes his poems do double, or even triple, work. **"Man's Civille Warre,"** a body-and-soul poem that could well have taken its theological content from Augustine, also becomes a polemic about the paradoxes and responsibilities of, and perils surrounding, the bodies and souls of English Catholics, engaged in their own silent civil war. In the **"Nativitie of Christ"** the mysteries of the Incarnation lead into a polemical defense of the doctrine of transubstantiation, which in turn transforms into a martyrological call to accept the host—and to imitate Christ. Paradox frequently turns into polemic in Southwell's poems.

## 2.

### "Man's Civille Warre"

My hovering thoughts would flie to heaven
And quiet nestle in the skie,
Faine would my ship in vertues shore
Without remove at anchor lie:

But mounting thoughts are hailed downe
With heavie poise of mortall load,
And blustring stormes denie my ship
In vertues haven secure aboade.

When inward eie to heavenly sights
Doth draw my longing harts desire,
The world with jesses of delights
Would to her pearch my thoughts retire.

Fond fancie traines to pleasures lure,
Though reason stiffly do repine.
Though wisdome wooe me to the saint,
Yet sense would win me to the shrine.

Where reason loathes, there fancie loves,
And overrules the captive will,
Foes senses are to vertues lore,
They draw the wit their wish to fill.

Neede craves consent of soule to sence,
Yet divers bents breed civil fray,
Hard hap where halves must disagree,
Or truce of halves the whole betray.

O cruell fight where fighting frend
With love doth kill a favoring foe,
Where peace with sense is warre with God,
And self delighte the seed of woe.

Dame pleasures drugges are steept in sinne,
Their sugred taste dothe breede annoye,
O fickle sense beware her ginne,
Sell not thy soule for brittle joy.

**"Man's Civille Warre"** is at once tense admonition against letting the body's desires merge with the soul's, lament for the necessity of war within the self, and exhortation to engage in this war. The poem begins with a vision of the soul's desire and ends in a homily meant to ensure that the body remains subordinate, in order to attain the soul's aim of "nestling quietly in the sky."

The beginning of the poem images the self's divisions as the body pulls the speaker's ascending thoughts down from a scene of repose, tranquillity and safety. The first stanza is the quietest in the poem. Its rhythms are slower. The comfort of thoughts nestling quietly in the sky is matched by the calm of the ship at shore. But the thoughts on their way upward are brought down by the weight of the body in the second stanza ("but mounting thoughts are hailed downe"). "Downe" weights the line with a thud. The vision of the ship at shore is disturbed by the actuality of "blustring stormes"; and "blustring" prepares the reader for the discomfort of the sixth stanza. The quiet and relatively musical rhythms of the first stanza are at war with the harder consonants and jerkier rhythms introduced by the second.

Janelle notes the presence of the nautical allegory in *Tottel's Miscellany* and *The Phoenix Nest* (1593).[34] Southwell also uses the image of the ship in the first chapter of *An Epistle of Comfort* ("The first cause of Comfort in Tribulation is that it is a great presumption that we are out of the devil's power"), which shows his ear for the rhythms of prose and the ways in which he can put alliteration to affective use.[35]

In our storm is their [the wicked's] time of singing, as is usual with the sirens, and they are the most sad in our calm and sorry in our comfort. And as the ship, while it is upon the main sea, is in a manner a castle or commonwealth by itself, and having all the souls hoisted up and swollen with the wind, and the banners displayed, danceth with a very lofty shew upon the waves and allureth every eye to behold its pride; but when it is come into the haven, it is straightway ransacked by the searcher, forced to pay custom; and the sails being gathered, the banners taken in, the anchors cast, it lieth quietly at ride and is little regarded. So they, who while they sailed upon the surge of wordly vanities and followed the tide of conscienceless course might range uncontrolled, and having the favorable gale of authority to waft them forward, and honours and pomps to set them forth, were admired of the people; but if they chance, by God's calling, to retire themselves into the port of true faith and virtuous life to work their salvation, they are straightway searched and sacked, their sails gathered, the accustomed wind set, their glory disgraced, and they little or nothing esteemed.[36]

Southwell turns the suffering of English Catholics into a cause of celebration—however ironic and inverted—and into a cautionary reminder that Catholics are not, as the title of the chapter suggests, out of the devil's power. As a result of their suffering they ought to be less likely to become spiritually complacent. This somewhat gloomy reassurance is part of the tradition of the literature of consolation.[37] The double figuration of the soul as a ship and of the ship as a commonwealth—which thus has some sovereign claim against the claims of the actual state—repoliticizes the Christian valuation of tribulation. For Southwell, the nautical metaphor comes with ideological and sociopolitical freight.

The Platonism of the poem turns it inward in the third stanza ("When inward eie to heavenly sights / Doth draw my longing harts desire"). The inward concentration combines with an upward pull; and one visualizes the kind of rapture one sees on the faces of figures in Mannerist painting.

The opposition the fourth stanza sets up between saint and shrine appears, for a moment, to concede the tension that is part of the iconoclastic challenge, which is also taken on by the Council of Trent's Decree on the "Invocation of Saints":

> the honour which is shown [saints] is referred to the prototypes which they represent, so that by means of the image which we kiss and before which we uncover the head and prostrate ourselves, we adore Christ and venerate the saints whose likeness they bear,

not because

> any divinity or virtue is believed to be in them by reason of which they are to be venerated, or that something is to be asked of them, or that trust is to be placed in image, as was done . . . by the Gentiles who place their trust in images.[38]

It goes on to say:

> great profit is derived from holy images . . . because through the saints the miracles of God and salutary examples are set before the eyes of the faithful, so that they may give God thanks for those things, may fashion their own life and conduct in imitation of the saints and be moved to adore and love God and cultivate piety.[39]

Southwell's Platonism in this poem is partly justified by the decree itself with its talk of "prototypes." He distills the essential parts of the decree into the last two lines of the stanza ("Though wisdome wooe me to the saint /

Yet sense would win me to the shrine") while giving the confused believer the benefit of the confusion: the attraction of the shrine is what makes us human, but wisdom will, or more properly ought to, mediate, by helping us distinguish intercession from idolatry, thing from image, by urging us to emulate the saint rather than venerate the image, indeed, by making it possible for the inward eye to apprehend the essence of divinity and of saintliness.

Two triangular relations are set up with argumentative clarity in the fifth stanza: one among reason, fancy, and will, the other among the senses, virtue, and wit. Each set of two lines can almost be diagrammed into a triangle. "Where reason loathes, there fancie loves, / And overrules the captive will" yields the opposing pulls of reason and fancy upon the will. "Foes senses are to vertues lore, / They draw the wit their wish to fill" sets up the tugs of the senses and virtue upon the wit. The phonetic closeness of "loathes" and "loves" reinforces the closeness of the forces at war and the difficulty of establishing the sovereignty of reason and virtue.

The sixth stanza draws together the problems set up in the previous ones; and the tensions are presented with exquisite deftness. If in the fifth stanza we see Southwell's ability to make compact clauses do hard, argumentative work, in the sixth we see him using paradox to great, poignant, and characteristically compact effect. The first surprise in the stanza is that discord is to be sought. It takes a moment to realize that it is a *good* thing that "diverse bents breed civil fray." Lament strains against the embedded exhortation. Not just a denial of the senses as vehicles for the body's appetites, the stanza is also a repudiation of the common sense that civil war is to be avoided at all costs. Alliteration intensifies the tension, as the double hardness of *c*'s ("crave's consent") modulates into the sibilance of "soule to sence." The second syllable of "consent" foreshadows "sence," continuing the play with (near) internal rhymes. One has to read the first two lines of the stanza slowly, as the rhyme and stanzaic structure, which hurry us along, work in tension with the phonetic elements, which demand to be pronounced with care. "Yet diverse bents breed civil fray" is hard to read, and its formal drama matches the contrary tugs of which it speaks. Again the alliteration is not just ornamental. The juxtaposition of "bents" and "breeds" is hard on the tongue. "Bents" is so heavily accented that it tenses the caesura.

"Or truce of halves the whole betray" concentrates the poem into its motivating and frightening irony: terrible though it is that the self must turn on itself, peace in this case would only destroy all the elements at war. The line has a hauntingly lingering tone, which comes from the length of the vowels in "truce," "halves," and "whole." "Betray" rhymes very closely with "fray," formally reinforcing the theme of closeness at odds with itself, suggesting also that betrayal is an inevitable consequence of civil fray.

In the first stanza of his parody of Edward Dyer's "A Fancy," Southwell makes four very careful changes:

> Hee that his mirth hath loste,
> Whose comfort is dismaid,
> Whose hope is vaine, whose faith is scornd,
> Whose trust is all betraid
>
> (Dyer, "A Fancy," 1-4)

> Hee that his mirth hath lost,
> Whose comfort is to rue,
> Whose hope is fallen, whose faith is cras'de,
> Whose trust is found untrue.
>
> (Southwell, **"A Phansie turned to a Sinner's Complaint,"** 1-4)

In the third line Southwell substitutes "fallen" for "vaine" and "cras'de" for "scorn'd." Even more interesting is the pointed substitution of the rhyme "rue" / "untrue" for "dismaid" / "betraid." The presence of "rue" in "untrue" would have appealed to a poet of Southwell's microcosmic bent, and his choice suggests that he was a careful and aware rhymer.

Where the end of the sixth stanza of **"Man's Civille Warre"** concentrates the poem into its central dilemma, the seventh draws outward and again expands on the strife the poem is about. "O cruell fight" governs both "where fighting frend / With love doth kill a favoring foe" and "where peace with sense is warre with God, / And self-delight the seed of woe." The cruel paradox is precisely that friends must fight each other. In this topsy-turvy world, friends fight and "kill with love"—in an ironically literal repositioning of a conceit from love poetry—foes favor, peace is war, delight is woe. Everything is inverted. Southwell's paradoxes are appropriate to this war which isn't. "Favoring foe" and "fighting friend" are in keeping with the paradoxes the poem has set up, but the exchange is explained in the third line of the stanza: "where peace with sense is war with God." An amity between the various aspects of the self can only sever the self from God, and this is the betrayal that bans the "truce of halves." We have already been prepared for this overriding connection by the third stanza: "inward eie" looks upward to "heavenly sights."

The final stanza's summary moral cannot quite match the tense paradoxes, or careful antitheses, of the earlier stanzas, but "ginne" continues the poem's doubleness. An obscure form of "ging" (troop or company), it can also mean skill, craft, artifice, cunning, or to catch in a trap or snare (*OED*). Pleasure may trap with its cunning or deceive with its artifice; it may defeat with the allurements and illusion of peace, or vanquish with its soldiery, which offers safety in exchange for quiescence.

All of **"Man's Civille Warre"** becomes an elaboration of the kind of figure (reflexive image, self-infolded simile—perhaps already formalized in the genre of the body and soul poem) Christopher Ricks has discussed in relation to Marvell in "Its Own Resemblance" and which William Keach has explained with regard to Percy Shelley.[40] Martz notes the foreshadowing in **"Looke Home"** of certain lines from Marvell's "The Garden."[41] Where Keach's discussion is primarily concerned with Shelley's interest in figuring "the operations of the human mind," Ricks makes the connection between self-infolded figures and civil wars. It is fortunate, then, that Southwell's most sustained elaboration of the self brings all these figures together.

Southwell is frequently concerned "with imaging the operations of the human mind," but in this poem he alludes elliptically to the silent civil war in which the Catholics in late Elizabethan England were engaged. It is perhaps no accident that Southwell shares a Platonism with Shelley. Southwell's art, heavily didactic, unabashedly partisan, allows itself a recourse that Marvell's does not. For Marvell's is a lighter—not more frivolous, but certainly more well lit—wryer art. The potentially infinite regress of the operations of the human mind can be settled by Southwell with a stabilizing recourse to God, and it is perhaps to an analogous quality Ricks refers when he complains of Crashaw that "there is no haunting interminability" in him.[42] Southwell, too, is too rapt and in many ways too insistent. The compression of paradox in his verse functions in a manner similar to *terza rima* in Dante: it confers a settling shape on ineffability, allows language to gather up and tighten inconceivability. We shall see a version of this in our discussion of **"The Nativitie of Christ"** as well.

Ricks tells us: "The shortcircuited comparison is itself apt to civil war. It is not only a language for civil war (desolatingly two and one), but also, in its strange self, a civil war of language and of the imaginable."[43] He goes on to quote Keach: "Reflexive images call unusual attention to the act of mind they presuppose, an act of mind which combines a moment of analysis and division, in which an aspect is separated from the idea to which it belongs, and a moment of synthesis and reunion. . . . A reflexive image makes the reader aware of the mind's ability not only to perceive relationships but to create them in a context of unity and identity."[44]

And it is precisely this act of mind calling attention to and elaborating upon its own divisions that Southwell explicates in **"Man's Civille Warre"** in order to make the divisions of the self figure the divisions of the country conceived as a larger self and to mourn the peculiar closeness and desolating separation of civil war. The line that perhaps best encapsulates the reflexive aspect of **"Man's Civille Warre"** occurs in **"At Home in Heaven"**: "O soule out of thy selfe seeke God alone." In **"Man's Civille Warre"** the figures of the division are stabilized to make them seem separate and independent entities, able to war, within the same structure, a formalization that has perhaps already taken place, as I suggested earlier, in the very conception of the body and soul poem.

An admonition to the soul within an explicitly Platonic context occurs again in **"At Home in Heaven,"** where God's love for humanity is to induce the soul to avoid corruption.[45]

> O soule do not thy noble thoughtes abase
> To lose thy loves in any mortall wight:
> Content thy eye at home with native grace,
> Sith God him selfe is ravisht with thy sight.
> If on thy beautie God enamored bee:
> Base is thy love of any less than hee.
>
> ("At Home in Heaven," ll. 25-30)

Alison Shell has suggested that Southwell's "audaciousness is . . . largely a question of doing away with neoplatonic machinery and other transitional figures between human and divine; his poetry seeks an apprehension of God with which even a heavenly muse would interfere."[46] Although it is true that Southwell does not use muses as a device very often (Shell counts two occasions), she construes Neoplatonism too narrowly. There is more to Neoplatonism then a reliance on muses. In **"Looke Home,"** Southwell writes: "The mind a creature is that can create, / To nature's pattern adding higher skills." Sells seems right in suggesting that these lines appear to be an expression of Plotinus's notion that the soul could create "the world of phenomena."[47] It is also the case that the abstraction and concentrated intensity of his poetry relies on the Platonic component within Christianity itself, as we shall see in the next section.

### 3.

### "The Nativitie of Christ"

> Behold the father, is his daughters sonne:
> The bird that built the nest, is hatched therein:
> The olde of yeares, an houre hath not out runne:
> Eternall life, to live doth now beginne.
> The word is dumme: the mirth of heaven doth weepe:
> Might feeble is: and force doth faintly creepe.
>
> O dying soules, beholde your living spring:
> O dasled eyes; behold your sonne of grace:
> Dull eares attend what word this word doth bring:
> Up heavie heartes: with joye your joye embrace.
> From death, from darke, from deafeness, from despaires:
> This life, this light, this word, this joy repaires.

> Gift better than himself, God doth not know:
> Gift better than his God, no man can see:
> This gift doth here the gever geven bestow:
> Gift to this gift let each receiver bee.
> God is my gift, himselfe he freely gave me:
> Gods gift am I, and none but God shall have me.
>
> Man altered was by sinne from man to beast:
> Beastes food is haye, haye is all mortall flesh:
> Now God is flesh, and lies in Manger prest:
> As haye, the brutest sinner to refresh:
> O happie fielde wherein the fodder grew,
> Whose taste, doth us from beasts to men renew.

Southwell's stylistic deliberateness is again apparent in **"The Nativitie of Christ"**—a series of paradoxes and inversions—from the Mary and Christ sequence, which Oxley has praised for its epigrammatic brilliance.[48] Unlike Southwell's four other nativity poems, this one is written in decasyllabic sixains, which we find frequently in his poetry. The *ababcc* rhyme scheme allows Southwell to set up a problem, or a set of paradoxes, in the quatrain and to appear to resolve it, or gather them together, in the couplet.

The first line launches the powerful paradoxes of the twenty-four-line poem. "Behold" announces that we are to witness something, that a scene is about to unfold, but what follows the imperative is not an event but an idea ("the father, is his daughters sonne"), and one of precisely the sort that cannot be "beheld." The second line fleshes out the concept "The bird that built the nest, is hatched therein." The metaphor makes the idea slightly more visual, but again we are to feel the strangeness of the idea, which is, as the circular metaphor tells us, outside our ken.

It is a commonplace of Southwell criticism, although one that has come under increasing and sophisticated pressure from Brownlow and Oxley, that the meditative method prescribed by Ignatius of Loyola in the *Spiritual Exercises* shapes Southwell's poetry. The method is usually taken to rely heavily upon a visual imagining of a scene from Christ's life. This may be true, but the mental image meant to trigger the meditation seems difficult to perceive when we are asked to "Behold" the father who is his daughter's son. What exactly would one imagine or visualize? Perhaps it could be suggested that the failed attempt to visualize the paradox enables a state of mental clarity, which in turn would enable meditation, that the *struggle* is necessary to achieving a meditative trance. In this case we need to reconsider our understanding of the apparatus required to induce meditation.

Southwell's imagery and practice in this poem betray more of a tendency the philosopher Gary Hatfield attributes to the influence of Augustinian rather than Ignatian meditation in his discussion of Descartes. What Hatfield says of Augustine appears to apply to Southwell as well: "By turning away from the senses and discovering his own intellect as an invisible, immaterial and yet mutable power, he was led to see with the fleshless eye of the mind the invisible, immaterial, immutable deity."[49]

If we were to compare Southwell's imagery to (say) Crashavian symbols, we might get a better sense of just how nonvisual Southwell's poems can be. To say this is not ultimately to vitiate the force of the point that, for Jesuits, Ignatius's exercises would have provided a model for habits of meditative thought that might, in turn, have influenced other habits and manifestations of intellection; it is rather to insist that such an influence could have, and in Southwell's case certainly seems to have, combined with other understandings of cognition. The "eye of the imagination" in this poem is turned strenuously toward thought. Southwell appears quite capable of combining traditions in order to achieve particular and various effects.

The two most explicit attempts I know of rendering the idea of God as the father of his mother are a figurine, part of the "vierges ouvrante" tradition, from around 1300 and a Flemish painting attributed to the school of Campin. The object is rather like a Russian doll: the figure of the Virgin Mary opens up to reveal the carved figure of God the Father (fig. 1). According to Barbara G. Lane, the body originally opened to show a "carved image of the Trinity" and is meant to "convey the idea that the Virgin contained the body of Christ in her womb as the tabernacle houses the altar."[50] The painting seems to make the problems of an attempted literal, visual representation even more evident (fig. 2). Mary holds the infant Christ as he caresses her chin while holding his penis, figuring his relation with Mary as begetter of himself.[51] The painting is distracting, because the worldliness of the sexual implication seems to compromise the sheerness of the paradox. The figurine merely banalizes the idea, making it seem paradoxically both ordinary and grotesque. It is the very bodiliness of the figurine that takes away from the teasing and elusive mysteriousness of God as the father of himself. Both the painting and the figurine seem as likely to orient attention away from the idea as to enable a mystical, or even meditative, apprehension of it.

Perhaps there is something to be said here about paradox and the relation between words and pictures. It is not so much that in this case paradox cannot be presented in pictorial form but rather that the pictures in a paradoxical context of the kind described in the poem require a narrative, a convention, or a set of symbols which themselves have a discursive content, which is supplied by the seer—understanding the paradox would require thinking about the story. By contrast, for example, Escher's etching of the waterfall where the water seems to be flowing upward calls attention to the act of seeing but does not require words—the medium supplies its own information and its own commentary upon itself.[52]

"The olde of yeares, an houre hath not out runne" introduces another paradox: the simultaneous agelessness and infancy of God in the form of the Christ child works with "Eternal life, to live doth now beginne" to develop further the theme of time introduced through the idea of God's age. The paradox of the agelessness of God and of the mystery of the birth of that which has no beginning in time works in tandem with the idea that by being born God gives "eternall life" to mankind, freeing mankind from death.

And since Christ gives life by surrendering his own, we are told the mourning has already begun in heaven. God is silent with grief, and the infant Christ cannot speak because he is a baby. The "mirth of heaven" weeps as it anticipates the crucifixion, and "Might feeble is: and force doth faintly creepe." The final line again holds world and heaven in suspension. "Might" highlights one of the central paradoxes of the nativity: that God would appear as helpless child. The word refers to God's "might," enfeebled by the knowledge of the suffering that is to befall Christ, and reminds us that Christ enfeebles the "might" of the tyrant. "And force doth faintly creepe" reiterates the first clause of the line; "force" is robbed of its power, which evokes, again, a sense of a dragging, grief-stricken God, of God as creeping child, on his way to Calvary or descended from the Cross, and of tyranny without power, "enfeebled might." The line manages to say all things simultaneously, twice. The final couplet glosses and sums up the stanza: God is born to his creation; the eternal "word" is a silent infant; and heaven is already grieving for the imminent pain of Christ—the happy child of heaven. By the end of the first stanza we have been reminded of the purpose of Christ's birth. Fittingly, the Incarnation is made to prefigure the Passion and announce the redemption.

Southwell restates this purpose in the first line of the second stanza by way of an injunction to "dying soules" to "behold" their "living spring." Again what we are told to observe is the *idea* of redemption embodied in the birth of Christ. "Dying soules," "dasled eyes," "dull eares," and "heavie heartes" are the salient features of mankind and act as counterpoint to this birth, which is "living spring," "sonne [sun] of grace," "word," and "joy." The first two lines of the stanza still adhere to the idea of "beholding" the qualities of Christ. The third and fourth lines, however, mobilize senses other than that of sight by way of "attend" and "embrace." The "word" this "word" brings needs to be "attended" to (both heard and sympathetically understood), and the "joy" this "joy" brings has to be embraced (both felt/ touched and accepted). Both lines evoke God's ability to both embody and create a feeling ("joy") or a thing/ idea ("word"). Aspects of the idea of joy are separated to show that God is all things and all feeling. Word as speech and action in the form of Christ's message is separated from the Word as God, embodying all things and ideas, both as the source and the thing itself. *The Gospel of John,* of course, offers rich and ample material for such linguistic and epistemological play. The idea of God as simultaneously source, pattern, and thing enables the exhortation to the imitation of Christ implicit in much of Southwell's writing.

The concluding couplet of this stanza tells us what the nativity will do by systematically listing the state of things before the birth and the conditions brought into the world by it. The birth will banish "death," "darke," "deafeness," and "despaire" with "life," "light," "word," and "joy"—all attributes here of God. The order of the list follows exactly the order in which its components appear in the first four lines of the stanza. Moreover, this "life," "light," "word," "joy" both fixes and withdraws from ("repaires") "death," "darke," "deafeness," "despaire."

The first two stanzas evoke, at least apparently, the reader's ability to "observe" the potent mix of attribute and promise the nativity presents. While building upon these, the third stanza presents the mystery of the nativity as a masterpiece of argumentative subtlety and of the divine ability to realize all the potential in the word "gift," mimicked by the poet's ability to do so. The act of generosity that is the nativity is celebrated through a play on "gift," that treats it as a form of the Word. Southwell takes the lines from *The Gospel of John,* "For God so loved the world that he gave his only Son, that whoever believes in him may have the eternal life" (John 3:16), imagines them back into a closer proximity to the beginning of the gospel, "In the beginning was the Word, and the Word was with God and the Word was God" (John 1:1), and transforms the entire stanza into a consideration of what it would mean for the Word to be "gift."

The first two lines of the stanza lay out two propositions. The first: God could not conceive of a better gift than himself. The second: man cannot "see" a better gift than God. The knowledge that man cannot see anything better than God mirrors God's inability to find a gift better than himself, and refers to a theological paradox: can God conceive of anything greater than himself? If not, there are limits to his conceiving. If so . . .

Particularly interesting is the play on "see," for it suggests either that man can "see" God or that God is to be appreciated by virtue of the knowledge that he is better than all else that one can see. The problem of seeing properly, beyond the deception of the senses and the snares of the world, is, of course, present throughout the Bible. Southwell's little joke here focuses another conceptual problem: whether we can visually compare two things if one has not been seen. How does one visually compare the inconceivable with the sensible, seeable, quotidian world? The poem relies on the idea of Christ in the manger but has not, so far, given us the image of the infant. It has given various versions of the idea(s) of the nativity but nowhere an image. Sight becomes a transcendent thing when anything is actually *seen* in the poem—when the "dasled eyes" invoked "behold" "the sonne of grace" they cannot actually see anything precisely because they are "dasled," blinded by the light of the "sonne [sun] of grace." Our eyes see by not seeing; and Southwell exploits the difference between linguistic and visual representation to make the Bible's point anew.

The stanza is an invitation to surrender oneself to the mystery, to accept God's gift by giving oneself to him. The construction of the final couplet is sophisticated: "himselfe he freely gave me" is perfectly poised between "God is my gift" and "Gods gift am I." If one privileges "God is my gift" as modifier, the medial clause comes to mean "he gave himself freely to me as a gift." If one takes "Gods gift am I" as the point to which the centered phrase leads, it comes to mean "he himself gave me freely to myself," in which freely can acquire the additional implication of the gift of free will. The narrative voice in this couplet is deliberately naive, particularly in the final clause, as the speaker simply accepts the gift and pledges himself to God. The effect of the feminine ending is to make the final clause trail and the sound to consequently linger on the speaker's gifting of himself. The rhyme "me/me" suggests a perfect reflexivity—to return oneself to oneself is to return oneself to God, bringing the *logos* full circle.

The third stanza concludes with the image of the conditions of man's redemption: "Gods gift am I, and none but God shall have me." Man has been persuaded by God's giving of himself to reciprocate and in the process has potentially, but also polemically ("and none but God shall have me"), redeemed himself, giving the gift of surrender to God through Christ—and Catholic Christianity.

In the chapter of an *An Epistle of Comfort,* where he explicitly invokes the "precedent of Christ," Southwell quotes St. Bernard:

> If I owe myself wholly for my first making, what can I
> add for my redeeming, especially seeing I was not so
> easily redeemed as I was made? In the first work he
> gave me myself, in the second himself, and when he
> gave me himself, he restored unto me myself. Therefore

thus given and restored, I owe myself for myself, and I owe myself twice. But now what I am able to repay my Lord for himself? For though I could repay myself a thousand time, what am I in comparison of my Lord?[53]

This chapter concludes with a call to martyrdom—perhaps the ultimate gift of oneself to God; and the right way of exchanging gifts is also at stake in the final stanza of **"The Nativitie,"** which further elaborates the relations this pledge entails. We shift to the manger; finally, we suppose, we will get an image of the infant Christ. Instead we get strange transfigurations between the literal, the metaphorical, and the conceptual, which move polemically into a defense of the Catholic position on the Eucharist.

The final stanza is a list of transformations: man to beast, flesh to hay, God to flesh to hay. The transformation of beasts back into men when they taste the hay is attainable in the earthly realm, the present tense suggests, and ensures mankind's eventual salvation, as by accepting the Catholic doctrine of the Eucharist one accepts the right path. The stanza turns the poem into an explication by allegory of Catholic doctrine. The multiple alterations reinforce the defense of transubstantiation and link the argument on the one (heavenly) end with the divinity of Christ (God is flesh) and on the other (bodily-earthly) end with the suggestion of the passion in "prest." The Passion leads into the Communion, where "the taste" of the fodder is to transform mankind from beasts to men, alluding to a function of the Communion—"remitting sin," although, as the Council of Trent insists, not the only, and not even the principal, "fruit" of the Communion.[54] Original sin remains distinguished from other sins in the poem: the beasts become men but do remain mortal.

Since the Catholic mass was forbidden in late Elizabethan England, accepting the doctrine of transubstantiation necessitated risking considerable penalties. However, Elizabeth's attitude toward the doctrine was characteristically hedged. When the 1552 prayer book was reinstituted in 1559, she inserted words from the 1549 version before the words celebrating the Communion: "The body of our Jesus Christ, which was given for thee, preserve thy body and soul unto everlasting life" (1549). "Take and eat this in remembrance that Christ died for thee, and feed on him in thy heart with thanksgiving" (1552). Patrick McGrath's suggestion that the Queen's insertion could be read as much more Catholic-friendly than was appreciated by the radical Protestants, who had become used to Calvinist liturgical practice while in exile, seems right.[55] Although the idea of commemoration is still present, this is not incompatible with the conciliar attitude at Trent, which acknowledges the necessity of commemoration but insists nevertheless that transubstantiation has taken place.[56]

One Southwellian argument for multiple alterations, assisted by the closeness of "may" and "made," "alter" and "altar," that allows Southwell to assert the relation

between conceivability and creation so important to religious belief, occurs in **"Of the Blessed Sacrament of the Alter":**[57]

> What god as auctour made he alter may,
> No change so harde as making all of nought:
> If Adame framed was of slymy claye,
> Bredd may to Cristes most sacred flesh be wrought.
> He may do this that made with mighty hande
> Of water wyne, a snake of Moyses wande.

**("Of the Blessed Sacrament of the Alter,"** 85-90)

Characteristically, Southwell's argument is conceptually subtle and simultaneously vigorous and insistent in the presentation: it is not beyond the bounds of conceivability that the inconceivable can make happen a particular of which we cannot conceive—and certainly not if the Christian doctrine of creation *ex nihilo* is to be given any weight. That he could compress the thought into a six-line stanza might be Southwell's real achievement.

Even in the final stanza of **"The Nativitie of Christ"** we are not given an image of the infant Christ. We are given instead an image of him transformed into hay, which is lying pressed in the manger. The metaphor of hay is an elaboration of the following verses from the Bible: "All flesh is grass . . . the grass withers, the flower fades; but the word of our God will stand for ever" (Isaiah 40:6-8). St. Peter, a figure of signal importance to Southwell, who made him the protagonist of several of his poems, rewrites this passage in his First Epistle: "All flesh is like grass and all its glory like the flower of grass. The grass withers, and the flower falls, but the word of the Lord abides forever" (1 Peter 1:24-25). God surrenders himself to the limitations of the created world by being incarnated as man, as grass. Peter goes on to write: "Since Christ suffered in the flesh, arm yourselves with the same thought, for whoever has suffered in the flesh has ceased from sin" (1 Peter 4:1). Peter's linking of the redemptive aspects of Christ's suffering gives additional warrant to the correspondences asserted in the poem. Man's relation with God through the sacrament of the Eucharist is suggested in the metaphor hay as well, but that explication works reticently through substitution:

> Man is beast.
> Beasts eat hay.
> Hay is flesh.
> Christ is flesh.
> Christ is hay.
> Beasts ("mortall flesh" = hay) become men ("mortall flesh" = hay) by being "refreshed" by hay.

By being refreshed—and even re-fleshed in the form of Christ—man regains his innocence. There are medieval accounts that suggest men are turned into beasts by sin.[58] And the poet of the *Ovide Moralisé* frequently compares Christ's assumption of human flesh to the pagan gods' transformation into animals.[59] Southwell draws these medieval and patristic metamorphic traditions together to make his case for the added metamorphosis of bread to Christ.

"Prest" is to be on loan, or a gift (*OED*); it is a variant of "pressed," and also of priest. So: God lies in the manger on loan, or, picking up on the third stanza, as a gift; swaddled (pressed) as an infant, or pressed from grass (the eternally living God) into hay (Christ = God as man = mortal flesh = hay), suggesting also the idea of man in the winepress of communion wine, or, in the sense of impresment: conscripted into fighting for mankind.[60] The word also alludes to the possibility of torture faced by those who might seek to imitate Christ in every respect, since one of the means of torture was contraction, using the instrument known as "the Scavenger's Daughter."[61] "Priest" was also used of Christ in his sacrificial and mediatorial character, and its etymology suggests an offerer of sacrifices, who also performs a mediating function between God and man. Christ, of course, *is* sacrifice, mediator, and both figures between whom he mediates. His existence *is* his mediation. "Prest" reinforces the richly metamorphic nature of the host and of the verbal and conceptual possibilities afforded by the first chapters of *The Gospel of St. John.* We can add this (metamorphic) Ovidianism to the (Heroidean) kind elaborated in Deborah Shuger's discussion of Southwell's *Mary Magdalens Funerall Teares* (1591).[62] The stanza prefigures Christ's suffering through the suggestion of him pressed in the manger, but unlike **"The Burning Babe"** and **"New Heaven, New Warre,"** the image is inconspicuously fleshless. This may also have something to do with the Council of Trent's insistence that the Eucharist "is a symbol of a sacred and a visible form of an invisible grace."[63] Although "prest" seems to alleviate the brutality of the image, the ironic tension between the idea of a protected infant and the image of grass pressed into hay, waiting to be eaten, actually intensifies it—as does the reminder of God's sacrifice in "prest" as loan. The metaphor, and image, of hay allows Southwell to retain a partially literal account of the host, while rerouting the idea of cannibalism which the Protestants had literalized in their polemics.

In his attack on the Jesuits, Phineas Fletcher powerfully satirized the implicit cannibalism of the Eucharist in *The Apollyonists* (1627) by literalizing the relations completely: "Of Men, nay Beasts: worse Monsters: worst of all, / Incarnate fiends, English Italianat, / Of Preists, O no, Masse-Priests, Priests-Cannibal, / Who make their Maker, chewe, grinde, feede, growe fat / With flesh divine."[64] Fletcher's pun on "make" in "make their Maker" suggests both that the mass is idolatrous, because motivated by the view that the maker can be created, and insufficiently reverent, for it implies the maker is then to be excreted, as another sense of the word (as in making water, urinating) is employed.

Southwell's complex juggling of the literal and the metaphorical is intended precisely to negate the basis of Fletcher's kind of polemic, not to mention earlier Reformation polemics. But Fletcher's poem does show how much the continued keeping of a balance between the literal and the metaphorical relies upon the cooperation of the audience.

In Southwell's **"Nativitie"** beasts eat hay and become men, and so the *eating* is literal, but *both* the eater and the eaten are other than themselves—man because his sin has already transformed him from his potential good self into a beast, and God because he is incarnated as man and, in the poem, further transformed into hay. It is this complicated dance between the literal and the metaphorical which makes the poem so powerful. Hay is ephemeral and transient and flesh is weak. Hay both eats and is eaten, is simultaneously agent and object. The poem is imagistically reticent about God the infant, as it is evasively suggestive about the eating of God. The act of beasts eating hay is presented as merely natural. The stanza toys with the brutal potency of Christ's suffering in the two lines: "Now God is flesh, and lies in Manger prest: / As haye, the brutest sinner to refresh." The colon after "prest" and the comma after "hay" generate an effect close to that of an enjambment, and simultaneously emphasize and bracket the horror of the image. We know already from line twenty that the circular reminder ("As hay") is not argumentatively necessary. It does, however, intensify *and* contain the rawness of the image. Southwell flirts with the bloody potential of the image and then moves on, with a punctuated stumble, to the *point* of Christ's nativity.

The stanza continues the poem's play with the withholding of images. We are given an illusion of visualness by the recurrence of "behold" earlier in the poem and by the evocation of the manger in this stanza. However, even when we think we get a picture ("Now God is flesh") we are actually getting the *idea* of Christ (God made flesh).

If, as Colie suggests, "The *logos* is the idea of all ideas, implying all other ideas, an idea in its essence paradoxical, reflexive, at once active and passive, sufficient to itself and creative of other modes," it is not outrageous that a poem structured around the Incarnation should be able to transform itself: first, to figure a polemic about the Eucharist, and then again to encode an injunction to Catholics to honor the sacrament of the Mass.[65]

The world in which the *logos* is the one and the many, and where God is seen as supreme artificer, is a world where it is the poet's duty to employ every linguistic turn, exploit every semantic possibility in order to render visible correspondences between the suffering of Catholics, the suffering of Christ, the art of the poet, and the artifice of God—to reveal, in essence, the Word in the world, and, of course, the world in the Word. Southwell's habits of complex abstraction are sanctioned by the idea of the *logos* as the "idea of all ideas."

It is the very abstractness of religious ideas and the generality of the patterns of paradox that make them so habitable by English Catholic experience. The content of a Christianity that is structured around the sacrifice of man (albeit also God) resonated with the Jesuit mission. A religion that could present its Messiah as saying the words quoted in the passage below not only allowed, but rather *demanded,* a political struggle where the country had to be saved from itself by the intervention of the Jesuit apostolate:

> I have not come to bring peace, but a sword. For I have come to set a man against his father, and a daughter against her mother, and a daughter-in-law against her mother-in-law; and a man's foes will be those of his own household. He who loves father or mother more than me is not worthy of me; and he who loves son or daughter more than me is not worthy of me; and who does not take his cross and follow me is not worthy of me. He who finds his life will lose it, and he who loses his life for my sake will find it.
>
> (Matt. 10:34-39)

The volatility and the potential for political change of the situation in England contributed to the uncertainties of Catholic existence. England's national identity was in the process of being shaped in the contest between Protestants and Catholics, and even within the Protestant and Catholic communities. The shifts in the religious position of the state made the question of the definition of treason a live and explosive one. The theological closeness—they were after all reliant on the same texts and tradition, no matter how differently they interpreted these—of all the sides involved meant that a language at once sinuous and compressed was required to access all the facets of the situation at the same time.

That the pressures of the historical situation made paradoxical the experience of English Catholics is evident. The multiple, punning, sophisticated linguistic techniques of a Baroque style were able to accommodate more easily the pressures of this paradoxical situation. Such a style was able to articulate the twists by which Catholics could become foreigners in their own land, English history could appear to be alienated from itself, God could become man, friend be foe, bread become Christ, suffering glory. Southwell's combination of these paradoxes, his use of habits of typological connection, and his amalgamation of these with a vernacular, indigenous style present an art, and a poet, formally, politically, theologically conscious, deliberate, and able.[66]

### Notes

1. See appendix I in Robert Southwell, *An Humble Supplication to her Maiestie in Answere to the Late Proclamation,* ed. R. C. Bald (Cambridge: Cambridge University Press, 1953), 59.

2. Ibid., 60.

3. Ibid., 62.

4. Ibid., 63.

5. Ibid., 64.

6. Ibid.

7. Ibid., 65.

8. Ibid., 40.

9. Ibid., 4.

10. Ibid., 31.

11. Ibid., 33.

12. "Epistle unto His Father," in Robert Southwell, S.J., *Two Letters and Short Rules of a Good Life,* ed. Nancy Pollard-Brown (Charlottesville: University of Virginia Press, 1973), 6-7.

13. Robert Southwell, *An Epistle of Comfort to the Reverend Priests and to the Honourable, Worshipful, and other of the Lay Sort, Restrained in Durance for the Catholic Faith,* ed. Margaret Waugh (Chicago: Loyola University Press, 1966), 29.

14. F. W. Brownlow, *Robert Southwell* (New York: Twayne, 1996), 106.

15. Ibid., 134.

16. John J. Larocca, S.J., "Popery and Pounds: The Effect of the Jesuit Mission on Penal Legislation," in *The Reckoned Expense: Edmund Campion and the Early English Jesuits; Essays in Celebration of the First Centenary of Campion Hall, Oxford (1896-1996),* ed. Thomas McCoog, S.J. (Suffolk: Boydell Press, 1996), 263.

17. J. E. Neale, *Elizabeth I and the Parliaments, 1559-1581* (New York: Norton, 1958), 389.

18. Ibid., 389.

19. Christopher Devlin, *The Life of Robert Southwell: Poet and Martyr* (London: Longmans, Green, 1956). Apologies for Southwell's style can be found in Louis Martz, *A Study in English Religious Literature of the Seventeenth Century* (New Haven: Yale University Press, 1962). They can also be found throughout Pierre Janelle's *Robert Southwell the Writer: A Study in Religious Inspiration* (New York: Sheed and Ward, 1935).

20. For treatments of Southwell's poetry that advance the case for Southwell's style, see the fourth and fifth chapters of Brownlow's *Robert Southwell.* See also Brian Oxley, "The Relation between Southwell's Neo-Latin and English Poetry," *Recusant History* 17, no. 3 (1985): 201-7, and "'Simples are by Compounds Farre Exceld': Southwell's Longer Latin Poems and St. Peter's Complaint," 17, no. 4 (1985): 330-40.

21. See, for instance, Christopher Haigh, *English Reformations: Religion, Politics, and Society under the Tudors* (Oxford: Clarendon Press, 1993); Eamon Duffy, *The Stripping of the Altars: Traditional Religion in England, 1400-1580* (New Haven: Yale University Press, 1992); Alison Shell, *Catholicism, Controversy, and the English Literary Imagination, 1558-1660* (Cambridge: Cambridge University Press, 1999); Arthur Marotti, ed., *Catholicism and Anti-Catholicism in Early Modern English Texts* (London: Macmillan, 1999).

22. Martz, *Study,* 198; Janelle, *Southwell the Writer,* 252.

23. Brownlow, *Southwell,* 80.

24. Ibid., 112.

25. The charge recurs throughout Janelle's book.

26. Rosalie Colie, *Paradoxia Epidemica: The Renaissance Tradition of Paradox* (Princeton: Princeton University Press, 1966), 7.

27. Ibid., 7.

28. James H. McDonald and Nancy Pollard Brown, *The Poems of Robert Southwell, S.J.* (Oxford: Clarendon Press, 1967), 57. All the Southwell poems quoted are from this edition.

29. Southwell, *Humble Supplications,* 11.

30. As quoted in Patrick McGrath, *Papists and Puritans under Elizabeth I* (London: Blandford Press, 1967), 73.

31. As quoted in Arthur Marotti's detailed and thorough "Manuscript Transmission and the Catholic Martyrdom Account in Early Modern England," in *Print, Manuscript, Performance: The Changing Relation of the Media in Early Modern England,* ed. Michael D. Bristol and Arthur F. Marotti (Columbus: Ohio State University Press, 2000), 184.

32. My terminology is, of course, borrowed from Benedict Anderson. See the first two chapters of *Imagined Communities: Reflections on the Origin and Spread of Nationalism* (London: Verso, 1983), 1-46.

33. Arnold Pritchard, *Catholic Loyalism in Elizabethan England* (Chapel Hill: University of North Carolina Press, 1979), 8. See also Peter Lake and Michael Questier, "Agency, Appropriation, and Rhetoric under the Gallows: Puritans, Romanists, and the State in Early Modern England," *Past and Present* 153 (November 1996): 65-66.

34. Janelle, *Study,* 218. A. Lytton Sells points out that the image of the poet's soul as a boat occurs in Petrarch's sonnet 189 in the *Rime sparse,* and

Southwell is known to have translated sonnet 134 into "What joy to live." *The Italian Influence in English Poetry: From Chaucer to Southwell* (London: Allen and Unwin, 1955), 320; Janelle, *Study,* 215. The image is also present in Dante in *Purgatorio,* canto i, and *Paradiso,* canto xxiii.

35. Southwell, *Epistle of Comfort,* 5.

36. Ibid., 8-10.

37. See Karen Batley, "Martyrdom in Sixteenth-Century English Jesuit Verse," *Unisa: English Studies* 26, no. 2 (1988): 3.

38. *Canons and Decrees of the Council of Trent,* trans. Rev. H. J. Schroeder, O.P. (Rockford: Tan Books and Publishers, 1978), 216.

39. Ibid.

40. Christopher Ricks, *The Force of Poetry* (New York: Oxford University Press, 1984); William Keach, *Shelley's Style* (New York: Methuen, 1984), esp. the chapter "Reflexive Imagery," 79-118.

41. Martz, *Study,* 206.

42. Ricks, *Force of Poetry,* 38.

43. Ibid., 55.

44. Ibid. See also Keach, *Shelley's Style,* 80.

45. For a discussion of the Platonism of "At Home in Heaven," see Sells, *Italian Influence,* 328.

46. Shell, *Catholicism,* 67.

47. Sells, *Italian Influences,* 328. For a more thorough discussion of Southwell's Neoplatonism and Platonism, see 328-29.

48. Oxley, "Southwell's Longer Latin Poems," 333.

49. Gary Hatfield, "The Senses and the Fleshless Eye: The Meditations as Cognitive Exercises," in *Essays on Descartes' Meditations,* ed. A. Rorty (Berkeley: University of California Press, 1986), 52.

50. Barbara G. Lane, *The Altar and the Altarpiece: Sacramental Themes in Early Netherlandish Painting* (New York: Harper and Row, 1984), 27.

51. On the chin-chuck and the sexuality of Christ see Leo Steinberg, *The Sexuality of Christ in Renaissance Art and Modern Oblivion* (Chicago: University of Chicago Press, 1983), 3-5.

52. My thanks to Kendall Walton for bringing this picture to my attention, and for discussion of these ideas.

53. Southwell, *Epistle of Comfort,* 52.

54. *Canons and Decrees,* 79.

55. McGrath, *Papists and Puritans,* 11.

56. *Canons and Decrees,* 74.

57. For a discussion of multiple alterations in South-well's "Christs Bloody Sweat" see Brian Oxley's illuminating "The Relation between Southwell's Neo-Latin and English Poetry."

58. Leonard Barkan, *The Gods Made Flesh: Metamorphosis and the Pursuit of Paganism* (New Haven: Yale University Press, 1986), 127.

59. Ibid., 115.

60. I am grateful to Claire Busse for suggesting this possibility.

61. Michael Schoenfeldt, *Prayer and Power: George Herbert and Renaissance Courtship* (Chicago: University of Chicago Press, 1991), 126-27.

62. Debora Kuller Shuger, "Saints and Lovers: Mary Magdalene and the Ovidian Evangel," in *The Renaissance Bible: Scholarship, Sacrifice, and Subjectivity* (Berkeley: University of California Press, 1994).

63. *Canons and Decrees,* 74.

64. Phineas Fletcher, *The Locust or Apollyonists,* Giles and Phineas Fletcher, *Poetical Works,* vol. 1, ed. Frederick S. Boas (Cambridge: Cambridge University Press, 1908), 128, canto I, ll. 1-5.

65. Colie, *Paradoxia Epidemica,* 28.

66. I would like to thank Claire Busse, Edwin Curley, William Keach, Steven Mullaney, Ian Proops, Michael Schoenfeldt, Kendall Walton and the scholars at the Renaissance Conference of Southern California, May 2000, for their invaluable comments on various drafts and fragments of this essay. Thanks also to an anonymous referee at this journal for very helpful criticisms.

## A. D. Cousins and R. J. Webb (essay date fall 2005)

SOURCE: Cousins, A. D., and R. J. Webb. "Southwell's 'The Presentation.'" *Explicator* 64, no. 1 (fall 2005): 2-3.

[*In the following essay, Cousins and Webb discuss "The Presentation," contending that the poem paradoxically obscures the role of Joseph and privileges the role of Simeon (and, by association, the role of the implied reader) in the presentation of the Christ child in the temple.*]

To be redeemed the world's Redeemer brought,
Two silly turtle doves for ransom pays,
O ware with empires worthy to be bought,
This easy rate doth sound not drown thy praise,

For sith no price can to thy worth amount,
A dove, yea love, due price thou dost account.

Old *Simeon,* cheap penny worth and sweet
Obtained when thee in arms he did embrace,
His weeping eyes thy smiling looks did meet,
Thy love his heart, thy kisses blest his face,
O eyes, O heart, mean sights and loves avoid,
Base not your selves, your best you have enjoyed.

O virgin pure thou dost these doves present
As due to law, not as an equal price,
To buy such ware thou wouldst thy life have spent,
The world to reach his worth could not suffice,
If God were to be bought, not worldly pelf,
But thou wert fittest price next God himself.[1]

Southwell's **"The Presentation"** is the ninth poem in his ***The Sequence on the Virgin Mary and Christ,*** a series of fourteen lyrics. ***The Sequence*** begins with celebration of the Virgin's conception and concludes with glorification of her assumption; the account of Christ's life goes no further than his childhood and is, of course, rendered within the framework of the Virgin's existence. In my view, **"The Presentation,"** as a meditative lyric based on Luke 2.22-38, covertly plays Simeon and the implied reader against the figure of Joseph, thus calculatedly disrupting the scriptural narrative of Christ's presentation in the temple.

The use of sacred paradox in the lyric is at once pedagogic and playful. In other words, the priestly and impersonal speaker's pastoral role is fulfilled through intermingled instruction and entertainment—a Horatian imperative familiarly iterated throughout early modern and, not least, Jesuit poetics.[2] Yet paradox seems to be more sophisticatedly and strategically used as a mode of communication in the poem than the obvious intermingling of the pedagogic with the playful might be thought to indicate.

The poem's central stanza is occupied by representation of Simeon holding the Christchild. Simeon, as an outsider to the Holy Family affectively witnessed—so to speak—in intimate contact with the infant Jesus (lines 8-10), becomes, in effect, a surrogate for the implied reader; that is, the reader seems meant to associate himself/herself with Simeon and thus to gain vicarious intimacy with the marvelous child: a tactic of meditative procedure concordant with Ignatius's theory of *compositio loci* and, hence, one not surprising in a meditative lyric by a Jesuit writer. Nevertheless, there is something noteworthy about the centerpiece to the lyric. That can broadly be described as the concealment of Joseph. Underplaying the role of Joseph in a portrayal of the Holy Family need not, in itself, be thought remarkable, because the custom in early modern painting (as in early modern verse) often was to marginalize Joseph lest the viewer or reader be tempted to see him, by reason simply of his closeness to Mary, as the father of Jesus. The obtrusive presence of Simeon—and the reader's placement with him in the poem's midst—very strongly emphasizes, however, Southwell's decision to hide Joseph, to occlude him. After all, **"The Presentation"** is a three-stanza poem elaborating on the brief, Lucan narrative concerning Mary and Joseph's presenting the infant Jesus in the temple. Reflection on the Christchild occupies the first stanza; praise of the Virgin, the last. One might expect that the third member of the Holy Family would occupy stanza 2—but, paradoxically, he does not. That omission may express a then-contemporary artistic convention; nevertheless, it also forms a deliberate disruption of scriptural narrative; the poem's Lucan source states that "they"—Mary and Joseph together—"brought him [the Christchild] up to Jerusalem to present him to the Lord" (verse 22).[3] Southwell's speaker offers no "they": instead, he conceals Joseph, focuses on Simeon, and thereby places, at the heart of the lyric, the implied reader in virtual contact with—or, at least, proximity to—the infant Jesus.[4]

The poem's impersonal speaker thus obscures Joseph and makes himself a present absence in order to involve the reader dramatically and centrally in the sacred tableau of **The Presentation.** Having become involved in that tableau and having (by way of the imagination) been made to acknowledge contact with Christ as the high point of human existence—for so the description of Simeon distinctly implies—the reader is therefore given what is de facto both motivation to concentrate his or her life on Christ and a foretaste of the beatific vision.

*Notes*

1. Robert Southwell, *The Poems,* ed. James H. McDonald and Nancy Pollard Brown (Oxford: Clarendon, 1967) 9. We have modernized the poem's spelling.

2. See Pierre Janelle, *Robert Southwell the Writer* (London: Sheed and Ward, 1935) 119; and A. D. Cousins, *The Catholic Religious Poets from Southwell to Crashaw: A Critical History* (London: Sheed and Ward, 1991) 16-17.

3. *Revised Standard Version* (1952; rpt. New York: Collins, 1972). The text in the Vulgate runs, at verse 22: "[T]ulerunt illum in Ierusalem, ut sisterent eum Domino [. . .]" See *Biblia Sacra,* ed. Alberto Colunga and Laurentio Turrado, 4th ed. (Madrid: Library of Christian Writers, 1965).

4. On early modern thinking about centrality and representations of it, see Alastair Fowler, *Triumphal Forms: Structural Patterns in Elizabethan Poetry* (Cambridge: Cambridge UP, 1970) 23-33.

---

# FURTHER READING

## Criticism

Grosart, Alexander B. "Memorial-Introduction." In *The Complete Poems of Robert Southwell,* edited by Alexander B. Grosart, pp. xxxv-c. New York: AMS Press, 1971.

> Originally written in 1872, offers an overview of Southwell's life and literary output.

Maurer, Warren R. "Spee, Southwell, and the Poetry of Meditation." *Comparative Literature* 15, no. 1 (winter 1963): 15-22.

> Examines similarities between the lives and writings of Southwell and Friedrich von Spee, contending that they were "the product of a very similar religious and literary environment."

McDonald, James H., and Nancy Pollard Brown. "Textual Introduction." In *The Poems of Robert Southwell, S.J.,* edited by James H. McDonald and Nancy Pollard Brown, pp. xxxv-civ. London: Oxford at the Clarendon Press, 1967.

> Study of the composition and publication history of Southwell's poetry.

White, Helen C. "Southwell: Metaphysical and Baroque." *Modern Philology* 61, no. 3 (February 1964): 159-68.

> Discusses Southwell as a pioneer in England of the Baroque style, which is typically considered a continental literary movement.

---

**Additional coverage of Southwell's life and career is contained in the following sources published by Gale:** *Dictionary of Literary Biography,* **Vol. 167;** *Literature Criticism 1400-1800,* **Vol. 108;** *Literature Resource Center;* *Reference Guide to English Literature,* **Ed. 2; and** *Twayne's English Authors.*

# How to Use This Index

## The main references

> **Calvino, Italo**
>     1923-1985 ....... CLC 5, 8, 11, 22, 33, 39,
>                                  73; SSC 3, 48

**list all author entries in the following Gale Literary Criticism series:**

*AAL* = *Asian American Literature*
*BG* = *The Beat Generation: A Gale Critical Companion*
*BLC* = *Black Literature Criticism*
*BLCS* = *Black Literature Criticism Supplement*
*CLC* = *Contemporary Literary Criticism*
*CLR* = *Children's Literature Review*
*CMLC* = *Classical and Medieval Literature Criticism*
*DC* = *Drama Criticism*
*FL* = *Feminism in Literature: A Gale Critical Companion*
*GL* = *Gothic Literature: A Gale Critical Companion*
*HLC* = *Hispanic Literature Criticism*
*HLCS* = *Hispanic Literature Criticism Supplement*
*HR* = *Harlem Renaissance: A Gale Critical Companion*
*LC* = *Literature Criticism from 1400 to 1800*
*NCLC* = *Nineteenth-Century Literature Criticism*
*NNAL* = *Native North American Literature*
*PC* = *Poetry Criticism*
*SSC* = *Short Story Criticism*
*TCLC* = *Twentieth-Century Literary Criticism*
*WLC* = *World Literature Criticism, 1500 to the Present*
*WLCS* = *World Literature Criticism Supplement*

## The cross-references

> See also CA 85-88, 116; CANR 23, 61;
> DAM NOV; DLB 196; EW 13; MTCW 1, 2;
> RGSF 2; RGWL 2; SFW 4; SSFS 12

**list all author entries in the following Gale biographical and literary sources:**

*AAYA* = *Authors & Artists for Young Adults*
*AFAW* = *African American Writers*
*AFW* = *African Writers*
*AITN* = *Authors in the News*
*AMW* = *American Writers*
*AMWR* = *American Writers Retrospective Supplement*
*AMWS* = *American Writers Supplement*
*ANW* = *American Nature Writers*
*AW* = *Ancient Writers*
*BEST* = *Bestsellers*
*BPFB* = *Beacham's Encyclopedia of Popular Fiction: Biography and Resources*
*BRW* = *British Writers*
*BRWS* = *British Writers Supplement*
*BW* = *Black Writers*
*BYA* = *Beacham's Guide to Literature for Young Adults*
*CA* = *Contemporary Authors*
*CAAS* = *Contemporary Authors Autobiography Series*
*CABS* = *Contemporary Authors Bibliographical Series*
*CAD* = *Contemporary American Dramatists*
*CANR* = *Contemporary Authors New Revision Series*
*CAP* = *Contemporary Authors Permanent Series*
*CBD* = *Contemporary British Dramatists*
*CCA* = *Contemporary Canadian Authors*
*CD* = *Contemporary Dramatists*
*CDALB* = *Concise Dictionary of American Literary Biography*

**CDALBS** = *Concise Dictionary of American Literary Biography Supplement*
**CDBLB** = *Concise Dictionary of British Literary Biography*
**CMW** = *St. James Guide to Crime & Mystery Writers*
**CN** = *Contemporary Novelists*
**CP** = *Contemporary Poets*
**CPW** = *Contemporary Popular Writers*
**CSW** = *Contemporary Southern Writers*
**CWD** = *Contemporary Women Dramatists*
**CWP** = *Contemporary Women Poets*
**CWRI** = *St. James Guide to Children's Writers*
**CWW** = *Contemporary World Writers*
**DA** = *DISCovering Authors*
**DA3** = *DISCovering Authors 3.0*
**DAB** = *DISCovering Authors: British Edition*
**DAC** = *DISCovering Authors: Canadian Edition*
**DAM** = *DISCovering Authors: Modules*
   **DRAM:** *Dramatists Module;* **MST:** *Most-studied Authors Module;*
   **MULT:** *Multicultural Authors Module;* **NOV:** *Novelists Module;*
   **POET:** *Poets Module;* **POP:** *Popular Fiction and Genre Authors Module*
**DFS** = *Drama for Students*
**DLB** = *Dictionary of Literary Biography*
**DLBD** = *Dictionary of Literary Biography Documentary Series*
**DLBY** = *Dictionary of Literary Biography Yearbook*
**DNFS** = *Literature of Developing Nations for Students*
**EFS** = *Epics for Students*
**EXPN** = *Exploring Novels*
**EXPP** = *Exploring Poetry*
**EXPS** = *Exploring Short Stories*
**EW** = *European Writers*
**FANT** = *St. James Guide to Fantasy Writers*
**FW** = *Feminist Writers*
**GFL** = *Guide to French Literature,* Beginnings to 1789, 1798 to the Present
**GLL** = *Gay and Lesbian Literature*
**HGG** = *St. James Guide to Horror, Ghost & Gothic Writers*
**HW** = *Hispanic Writers*
**IDFW** = *International Dictionary of Films and Filmmakers: Writers and Production Artists*
**IDTP** = *International Dictionary of Theatre: Playwrights*
**LAIT** = *Literature and Its Times*
**LAW** = *Latin American Writers*
**JRDA** = *Junior DISCovering Authors*
**MAICYA** = *Major Authors and Illustrators for Children and Young Adults*
**MAICYAS** = *Major Authors and Illustrators for Children and Young Adults Supplement*
**MAWW** = *Modern American Women Writers*
**MJW** = *Modern Japanese Writers*
**MTCW** = *Major 20th-Century Writers*
**NCFS** = *Nonfiction Classics for Students*
**NFS** = *Novels for Students*
**PAB** = *Poets: American and British*
**PFS** = *Poetry for Students*
**RGAL** = *Reference Guide to American Literature*
**RGEL** = *Reference Guide to English Literature*
**RGSF** = *Reference Guide to Short Fiction*
**RGWL** = *Reference Guide to World Literature*
**RHW** = *Twentieth-Century Romance and Historical Writers*
**SAAS** = *Something about the Author Autobiography Series*
**SATA** = *Something about the Author*
**SFW** = *St. James Guide to Science Fiction Writers*
**SSFS** = *Short Stories for Students*
**TCWW** = *Twentieth-Century Western Writers*
**WLIT** = *World Literature and Its Times*
**WP** = *World Poets*
**YABC** = *Yesterday's Authors of Books for Children*
**YAW** = *St. James Guide to Young Adult Writers*

# Literary Criticism Series
# Cumulative Author Index

**Appleman, Philip (Dean)** 1926- ........ **CLC 51**
See also CA 13-16R; 18; CANR 6, 29, 56

**Appleton, Lawrence**
See Lovecraft, H. P.

**Apteryx**
See Eliot, T(homas) S(tearns)

**Apuleius, (Lucius Madaurensis)** c. 125-c.
164 ........................................ **CMLC 1, 84**
See also AW 2; CDWLB 1; DLB 211;
RGWL 2, 3; SUFW; WLIT 8

**Aquin, Hubert** 1929-1977 ................... **CLC 15**
See also CA 105; DLB 53; EWL 3

**Aquinas, Thomas** 1224(?)-1274 ...... **CMLC 33**
See also DLB 115; EW 1; TWA

**Aragon, Louis** 1897-1982 ............ **CLC 3, 22;
TCLC 123**
See also CA 69-72; CAAS 108; CANR 28,
71; DAM NOV, POET; DLB 72, 258; EW
11; EWL 3; GFL 1789 to the Present;
GLL 2; LMFS 2; MTCW 1, 2; RGWL 2,
3

**Arany, Janos** 1817-1882 .................. **NCLC 34**

**Aranyos, Kakay** 1847-1910
See Mikszath, Kalman

**Aratus of Soli** c. 315B.C.-c.
240B.C. .................................... **CMLC 64**
See also DLB 176

**Arbuthnot, John** 1667-1735 .................... **LC 1**
See also DLB 101

**Archer, Herbert Winslow**
See Mencken, H(enry) L(ouis)

**Archer, Jeffrey** 1940- ........................ **CLC 28**
See also AAYA 16; BEST 89:3; BPFB 1;
CA 77-80; CANR 22, 52, 95, 136; CPW;
DA3; DAM POP; INT CANR-22; MTFW
2005

**Archer, Jeffrey Howard**
See Archer, Jeffrey

**Archer, Jules** 1915- ........................... **CLC 12**
See also CA 9-12R; CANR 6, 69; SAAS 5;
SATA 4, 85

**Archer, Lee**
See Ellison, Harlan

**Archilochus** c. 7th cent. B.C.- ........ **CMLC 44**
See also DLB 176

**Arden, John** 1930- .................. **CLC 6, 13, 15**
See also BRWS 2; CA 13-16R; 4; CANR
31, 65, 67, 124; CBD; CD 5, 6; DAM
DRAM; DFS 9; DLB 13, 245; EWL 3;
MTCW 1

**Arenas, Reinaldo** 1943-1990 .. **CLC 41; HLC
1; TCLC 191**
See also CA 128; CAAE 124; CAAS 133;
CANR 73, 106; DAM MULT; DLB 145;
EWL 3; GLL 2; HW 1; LAW; LAWS 1;
MTCW 2; MTFW 2005; RGSF 2; RGWL
3; WLIT 1

**Arendt, Hannah** 1906-1975 ....... **CLC 66, 98;
TCLC 193**
See also CA 17-20R; CAAS 61-64; CANR
26, 60; DLB 242; MTCW 1, 2

**Aretino, Pietro** 1492-1556 ................... **LC 12**
See also RGWL 2, 3

**Arghezi, Tudor** ................................ **CLC 80**
See Theodorescu, Ion N.
See also CA 167; CDWLB 4; DLB 220;
EWL 3

**Arguedas, Jose Maria** 1911-1969 .... **CLC 10,
18; HLCS 1; TCLC 147**
See also CA 89-92; CANR 73; DLB 113;
EWL 3; HW 1; LAW; RGWL 2, 3; WLIT
1

**Argueta, Manlio** 1936- ...................... **CLC 31**
See also CA 131; CANR 73; CWW 2; DLB
145; EWL 3; HW 1; RGWL 3

**Arias, Ron** 1941- ................................... **HLC 1**
See also CA 131; CANR 81, 136; DAM
MULT; DLB 82; HW 1, 2; MTCW 2;
MTFW 2005

**Ariosto, Lodovico**
See Ariosto, Ludovico
See also WLIT 7

**Ariosto, Ludovico** 1474-1533 ... **LC 6, 87; PC
42**
See Ariosto, Lodovico
See also EW 2; RGWL 2, 3

**Aristides**
See Epstein, Joseph

**Aristophanes** 450B.C.-385B.C. ....... **CMLC 4,
51; DC 2; WLCS**
See also AW 1; CDWLB 1; DA; DA3;
DAB; DAC; DAM DRAM, MST; DFS
10; DLB 176; LMFS 1; RGWL 2, 3;
TWA; WLIT 8

**Aristotle** 384B.C.-322B.C. ............ **CMLC 31;
WLCS**
See also AW 1; CDWLB 1; DA; DA3;
DAB; DAC; DAM MST; DLB 176;
RGWL 2, 3; TWA; WLIT 8

**Arlt, Roberto (Godofredo Christophersen)**
1900-1942 .................. **HLC 1; TCLC 29**
See also CA 131; CAAE 123; CANR 67;
DAM MULT; DLB 305; EWL 3; HW 1,
2; IDTP; LAW

**Armah, Ayi Kwei** 1939- . **BLC 1; CLC 5, 33,
136**
See also AFW; BRWS 10; BW 1; CA 61-
64; CANR 21, 64; CDWLB 3; CN 1, 2,
3, 4, 5, 6, 7; DAM MULT, POET; DLB
117; EWL 3; MTCW 1; WLIT 2

**Armatrading, Joan** 1950- .................. **CLC 17**
See also CA 186; CAAE 114

**Armin, Robert** 1568(?)-1615(?) ......... **LC 120**

**Armitage, Frank**
See Carpenter, John (Howard)

**Armstrong, Jeannette (C.)** 1948- ....... **NNAL**
See also CA 149; CCA 1; CN 6, 7; DAC;
DLB 334; SATA 102

**Arnette, Robert**
See Silverberg, Robert

**Arnim, Achim von (Ludwig Joachim von
Arnim)** 1781-1831 .. **NCLC 5, 159; SSC
29**
See also DLB 90

**Arnim, Bettina von** 1785-1859 ...... **NCLC 38,
123**
See also DLB 90; RGWL 2, 3

**Arnold, Matthew** 1822-1888 ..... **NCLC 6, 29,
89, 126; PC 5; WLC 1**
See also BRW 5; CDBLB 1832-1890; DA;
DAB; DAC; DAM MST, POET; DLB 32,
57; EXPP; PAB; PFS 2; TEA; WP

**Arnold, Thomas** 1795-1842 ............ **NCLC 18**
See also DLB 55

**Arnow, Harriette (Louisa) Simpson**
1908-1986 ...... **CLC 2, 7, 18; TCLC 196**
See also BPFB 1; CA 9-12R; CAAS 118;
CANR 14; CN 2, 3, 4; DLB 6; FW;
MTCW 1, 2; RHW; SATA 42; SATA-Obit
47

**Arouet, Francois-Marie**
See Voltaire

**Arp, Hans**
See Arp, Jean

**Arp, Jean** 1887-1966 ....... **CLC 5; TCLC 115**
See also CA 81-84; CAAS 25-28R; CANR
42, 77; EW 10

**Arrabal**
See Arrabal, Fernando

**Arrabal (Teran), Fernando**
See Arrabal, Fernando
See also CWW 2

**Arrabal, Fernando** 1932- ... **CLC 2, 9, 18, 58**
See Arrabal (Teran), Fernando
See also CA 9-12R; CANR 15; DLB 321;
EWL 3; LMFS 2

**Arreola, Juan Jose** 1918-2001 ....... **CLC 147;
HLC 1; SSC 38**
See also CA 131; CAAE 113; CAAS 200;
CANR 81; CWW 2; DAM MULT; DLB
113; DNFS 2; EWL 3; HW 1, 2; LAW;
RGSF 2

**Arrian** c. 89(?)-c. 155(?) ............... **CMLC 43**
See also DLB 176

**Arrick, Fran** .................................... **CLC 30**
See Gaberman, Judie Angell
See also BYA 6

**Arrley, Richmond**
See Delany, Samuel R., Jr.

**Artaud, Antonin (Marie Joseph)**
1896-1948 .............. **DC 14; TCLC 3, 36**
See also CA 149; CAAE 104; DA3; DAM
DRAM; DFS 22; DLB 258, 321; EW 11;
EWL 3; GFL 1789 to the Present; MTCW
2; MTFW 2005; RGWL 2, 3

**Arthur, Ruth M(abel)** 1905-1979 ..... **CLC 12**
See also CA 9-12R; CAAS 85-88; CANR
4; CWRI 5; SATA 7, 26

**Artsybashev, Mikhail (Petrovich)**
1878-1927 ........................... **TCLC 31**
See also CA 170; DLB 295

**Arundel, Honor (Morfydd)**
1919-1973 .................................. **CLC 17**
See also CA 21-22; CAAS 41-44R; CAP 2;
CLR 35; CWRI 5; SATA 4; SATA-Obit
24

**Arzner, Dorothy** 1900-1979 ............. **CLC 98**

**Asch, Sholem** 1880-1957 .................. **TCLC 3**
See also CAAE 105; DLB 333; EWL 3;
GLL 2; RGHL

**Ascham, Roger** 1516(?)-1568 ............ **LC 101**
See also DLB 236

**Ash, Shalom**
See Asch, Sholem

**Ashbery, John** 1927- ... **CLC 2, 3, 4, 6, 9, 13,
15, 25, 41, 77, 125, 221; PC 26**
See Berry, Jonas
See also AMWS 3; CA 5-8R; CANR 9, 37,
66, 102, 132; CP 1, 2, 3, 4, 5, 6, 7; DA3;
DAM POET; DLB 5, 165; DLBY 1981;
EWL 3; INT CANR-9; MAL 5; MTCW
1, 2; MTFW 2005; PAB; PFS 11; RGAL
4; TCLE 1:1; WP

**Ashbery, John Lawrence**
See Ashbery, John

**Ashdown, Clifford**
See Freeman, R(ichard) Austin

**Ashe, Gordon**
See Creasey, John

**Ashton-Warner, Sylvia (Constance)**
1908-1984 .................................. **CLC 19**
See also CA 69-72; CAAS 112; CANR 29;
CN 1, 2, 3; MTCW 1, 2

**Asimov, Isaac** 1920-1992 ..... **CLC 1, 3, 9, 19,
26, 76, 92**
See also AAYA 13; BEST 90:2; BPFB 1;
BYA 4, 6, 7, 9; CA 1-4R; CAAS 137;
CANR 2, 19, 36, 60, 125; CLR 12, 79;
CMW 4; CN 1, 2, 3, 4, 5; CPW; DA3;
DAM POP; DLB 8; DLBY 1992; INT
CANR-19; JRDA; LAIT 5; LMFS 2;
MAICYA 1, 2; MAL 5; MTCW 1, 2;
MTFW 2005; RGAL 4; SATA 1, 26, 74;
SCFW 1, 2; SFW 4; SSFS 17; TUS; YAW

**Askew, Anne** 1521(?)-1546 .................. **LC 81**
See also DLB 136

**Assis, Joaquim Maria Machado de**
See Machado de Assis, Joaquim Maria

**Astell, Mary** 1666-1731 ...................... **LC 68**
See also DLB 252, 336; FW

**Astley, Thea (Beatrice May)**
1925-2004 .................................. **CLC 41**
See also CA 65-68; CAAS 229; CANR 11,
43, 78; CN 1, 2, 3, 4, 5, 6, 7; DLB 289;
EWL 3

**Barker, Patricia**
    See Barker, Pat
**Barlach, Ernst (Heinrich)**
    1870-1938 ................................ **TCLC 84**
    See also CA 178; DLB 56, 118; EWL 3
**Barlow, Joel** 1754-1812 ................... **NCLC 23**
    See also AMWS 2; DLB 37; RGAL 4
**Barnard, Mary (Ethel)** 1909- .......... **CLC 48**
    See also CA 21-22; CAP 2; CP 1
**Barnes, Djuna** 1892-1982 .... **CLC 3, 4, 8, 11, 29, 127; SSC 3**
    See Steptoe, Lydia
    See also AMWS 3; CA 9-12R; CAAS 107; CAD; CANR 16, 55; CN 1, 2, 3; CWD; DLB 4, 9, 45; EWL 3; GLL 1; MAL 5; MTCW 1, 2; MTFW 2005; RGAL 4; TCLE 1:1; TUS
**Barnes, Jim** 1933- ............................ **NNAL**
    See also CA 175; 108, 175; 28; DLB 175
**Barnes, Julian** 1946- .................. **CLC 42, 141**
    See also BRWS 4; CA 102; CANR 19, 54, 115, 137; CN 4, 5, 6, 7; DAB; DLB 194; DLBY 1993; EWL 3; MTCW 2; MTFW 2005; SSFS 24
**Barnes, Julian Patrick**
    See Barnes, Julian
**Barnes, Peter** 1931-2004 .............. **CLC 5, 56**
    See also CA 65-68; 12; CAAS 230; CANR 33, 34, 64, 113; CBD; CD 5, 6; DFS 6; DLB 13, 233; MTCW 1
**Barnes, William** 1801-1886 ............ **NCLC 75**
    See also DLB 32
**Baroja, Pío** 1872-1956 ........ **HLC 1; TCLC 8**
    See also CA 247; CAAE 104; EW 9
**Baroja y Nessi, Pío**
    See Baroja, Pío
**Baron, David**
    See Pinter, Harold
**Baron Corvo**
    See Rolfe, Frederick (William Serafino Austin Lewis Mary)
**Barondess, Sue K(aufman)**
    1926-1977 ................................ **CLC 8**
    See Kaufman, Sue
    See also CA 1-4R; CAAS 69-72; CANR 1
**Baron de Teive**
    See Pessoa, Fernando (Antonio Nogueira)
**Baroness Von S.**
    See Zangwill, Israel
**Barres, (Auguste-)Maurice**
    1862-1923 ................................ **TCLC 47**
    See also CA 164; DLB 123; GFL 1789 to the Present
**Barreto, Afonso Henrique de Lima**
    See Lima Barreto, Afonso Henrique de
**Barrett, Andrea** 1954- ...................... **CLC 150**
    See also CA 156; CANR 92; CN 7; DLB 335; SSFS 24
**Barrett, Michele** .............................. **CLC 65**
**Barrett, (Roger) Syd** 1946-2006 ....... **CLC 35**
**Barrett, William (Christopher)**
    1913-1992 ................................ **CLC 27**
    See also CA 13-16R; CAAS 139; CANR 11, 67; INT CANR-11
**Barrett Browning, Elizabeth**
    1806-1861 ...... **NCLC 1, 16, 61, 66, 170; PC 6, 62; WLC 1**
    See also AAYA 63; BRW 4; CDBLB 1832-1890; DA; DA3; DAB; DAC; DAM MST, POET; DLB 32, 199; EXPP; FL 1:2; PAB; PFS 2, 16, 23; TEA; WLIT 4; WP
**Barrie, J(ames) M(atthew)**
    1860-1937 ................................ **TCLC 2, 164**
    See also BRWS 3; BYA 4, 5; CA 136; CAAE 104; CANR 77; CDBLB 1890-1914; CLR 16; CWRI 5; DA3; DAB;

DAM DRAM; DFS 7; DLB 10, 141, 156; EWL 3; FANT; MAICYA 1, 2; MTCW 2; MTFW 2005; SATA 100; SUFW; WCH; WLIT 4; YABC 1
**Barrington, Michael**
    See Moorcock, Michael
**Barrol, Grady**
    See Bograd, Larry
**Barry, Mike**
    See Malzberg, Barry N(athaniel)
**Barry, Philip** 1896-1949 .................. **TCLC 11**
    See also CA 199; CAAE 109; DFS 9; DLB 7, 228; MAL 5; RGAL 4
**Bart, Andre Schwarz**
    See Schwarz-Bart, Andre
**Barth, John (Simmons)** 1930- ... **CLC 1, 2, 3, 5, 7, 9, 10, 14, 27, 51, 89, 214; SSC 10, 89**
    See also AITN 1, 2; AMW; BPFB 1; CA 1-4R; CABS 1; CANR 5, 23, 49, 64, 113; CN 1, 2, 3, 4, 5, 6, 7; DAM NOV; DLB 2, 227; EWL 3; FANT; MAL 5; MTCW 1; RGAL 4; RGSF 2; RHW; SSFS 6; TUS
**Barthelme, Donald** 1931-1989 ... **CLC 1, 2, 3, 5, 6, 8, 13, 23, 46, 59, 115; SSC 2, 55**
    See also AMWS 4; BPFB 1; CA 21-24R; CAAS 129; CANR 20, 58; CN 1, 2, 3, 4; DA3; DAM NOV; DLB 2, 234; DLBY 1980, 1989; EWL 3; FANT; LMFS 2; MAL 5; MTCW 1, 2; MTFW 2005; RGAL 4; RGSF 2; SATA 7; SATA-Obit 62; SSFS 17
**Barthelme, Frederick** 1943- ...... **CLC 36, 117**
    See also AMWS 11; CA 122; CAAE 114; CANR 77; CN 4, 5, 6, 7; CSW; DLB 244; DLBY 1985; EWL 3; INT CA-122
**Barthes, Roland (Gerard)**
    1915-1980 ........ **CLC 24, 83; TCLC 135**
    See also CA 130; CAAS 97-100; CANR 66; DLB 296; EW 13; EWL 3; GFL 1789 to the Present; MTCW 1, 2; TWA
**Bartram, William** 1739-1823 ....... **NCLC 145**
    See also ANW; DLB 37
**Barzun, Jacques (Martin)** 1907- ..... **CLC 51, 145**
    See also CA 61-64; CANR 22, 95
**Bashevis, Isaac**
    See Singer, Isaac Bashevis
**Bashevis, Yitskhok**
    See Singer, Isaac Bashevis
**Bashkirtseff, Marie** 1859-1884 ....... **NCLC 27**
**Basho, Matsuo**
    See Matsuo Basho
    See also RGWL 2, 3; WP
**Basil of Caesaria** c. 330-379 ......... **CMLC 35**
**Basket, Raney**
    See Edgerton, Clyde (Carlyle)
**Bass, Kingsley B., Jr.**
    See Bullins, Ed
**Bass, Rick** 1958- ........ **CLC 79, 143; SSC 60**
    See also AMWS 16; ANW; CA 126; CANR 53, 93, 145; CSW; DLB 212, 275
**Bassani, Giorgio** 1916-2000 ............... **CLC 9**
    See also CA 65-68; CAAS 190; CANR 33; CWW 2; DLB 128, 177, 299; EWL 3; MTCW 1; RGHL; RGWL 2, 3
**Bastian, Ann** ..................................... **CLC 70**
**Bastos, Augusto Roa**
    See Roa Bastos, Augusto
**Bataille, Georges** 1897-1962 ............ **CLC 29; TCLC 155**
    See also CA 101; CAAS 89-92; EWL 3
**Bates, H(erbert) E(rnest)**
    1905-1974 ................... **CLC 46; SSC 10**
    See also CA 93-96; CAAS 45-48; CANR 34; CN 1; DA3; DAB; DAM POP; DLB 162, 191; EWL 3; EXPS; MTCW 1, 2; RGSF 2; SSFS 7

**Bauchart**
    See Camus, Albert
**Baudelaire, Charles** 1821-1867 . **NCLC 6, 29, 55, 155; PC 1; SSC 18; WLC 1**
    See also DA; DA3; DAB; DAC; DAM MST, POET; DLB 217; EW 7; GFL 1789 to the Present; LMFS 2; PFS 21; RGWL 2, 3; TWA
**Baudouin, Marcel**
    See Peguy, Charles (Pierre)
**Baudouin, Pierre**
    See Peguy, Charles (Pierre)
**Baudrillard, Jean** 1929-2007 ............. **CLC 60**
    See also CA 252; CAAS 258; DLB 296
**Baum, L(yman) Frank** 1856-1919 .. **TCLC 7, 132**
    See also AAYA 46; BYA 16; CA 133; CAAE 108; CLR 15, 107; CWRI 5; DLB 22; FANT; JRDA; MAICYA 1, 2; MTCW 1, 2; NFS 13; RGAL 4; SATA 18, 100; WCH
**Baum, Louis F.**
    See Baum, L(yman) Frank
**Baumbach, Jonathan** 1933- .......... **CLC 6, 23**
    See also CA 13-16R; 5; CANR 12, 66, 140; CN 3, 4, 5, 6, 7; DLBY 1980; INT CANR-12; MTCW 1
**Bausch, Richard** 1945- ...................... **CLC 51**
    See also AMWS 7; CA 101; 14; CANR 43, 61, 87, 164; CN 7; CSW; DLB 130; MAL 5
**Bausch, Richard Carl**
    See Bausch, Richard
**Baxter, Charles** 1947- .................. **CLC 45, 78**
    See also AMWS 17; CA 57-60; CANR 40, 64, 104, 133; CPW; DAM POP; DLB 130; MAL 5; MTCW 2; MTFW 2005; TCLE 1:1
**Baxter, George Owen**
    See Faust, Frederick (Schiller)
**Baxter, James K(eir)** 1926-1972 ....... **CLC 14**
    See also CA 77-80; CP 1; EWL 3
**Baxter, John**
    See Hunt, E. Howard
**Bayer, Sylvia**
    See Glassco, John
**Bayle, Pierre** 1647-1706 .................... **LC 126**
    See also DLB 268, 313; GFL Beginnings to 1789
**Baynton, Barbara** 1857-1929 ......... **TCLC 57**
    See also DLB 230; RGSF 2
**Beagle, Peter S.** 1939- ................. **CLC 7, 104**
    See also AAYA 47; BPFB 1; BYA 9, 10, 16; CA 9-12R; CANR 4, 51, 73, 110; DA3; DLBY 1980; FANT; INT CANR-4; MTCW 2; MTFW 2005; SATA 60, 130; SUFW 1, 2; YAW
**Beagle, Peter Soyer**
    See Beagle, Peter S.
**Bean, Normal**
    See Burroughs, Edgar Rice
**Beard, Charles A(ustin)**
    1874-1948 ................................ **TCLC 15**
    See also CA 189; CAAE 115; DLB 17; SATA 18
**Beardsley, Aubrey** 1872-1898 .......... **NCLC 6**
**Beattie, Ann** 1947- ..... **CLC 8, 13, 18, 40, 63, 146; SSC 11**
    See also AMWS 5; BEST 90:2; BPFB 1; CA 81-84; CANR 53, 73, 128; CN 4, 5, 6, 7; CPW; DA3; DAM NOV, POP; DLB 218, 278; DLBY 1982; EWL 3; MAL 5; MTCW 1, 2; MTFW 2005; RGAL 4; RGSF 2; SSFS 9; TUS
**Beattie, James** 1735-1803 ............... **NCLC 25**
    See also DLB 109

**Beauchamp, Kathleen Mansfield** 1888-1923
See Mansfield, Katherine
See also CA 134; CAAE 104; DA; DA3;
DAC; DAM MST; MTCW 2; TEA

**Beaumarchais, Pierre-Augustin Caron de**
1732-1799 .......................... DC 4; LC 61
See also DAM DRAM; DFS 14, 16; DLB
313; EW 4; GFL Beginnings to 1789;
RGWL 2, 3

**Beaumont, Francis** 1584(?)-1616 .. DC 6; LC
33
See also BRW 2; CDBLB Before 1660;
DLB 58; TEA

**Beauvoir, Simone de** 1908-1986 .... CLC 1, 2,
4, 8, 14, 31, 44, 50, 71, 124; SSC 35;
WLC 1
See also BPFB 1; CA 9-12R; CAAS 118;
CANR 28, 61; DA; DA3; DAB; DAC;
DAM MST, NOV; DLB 72; DLBY 1986;
EW 12; EWL 3; FL 1:5; FW; GFL 1789
to the Present; LMFS 2; MTCW 1, 2;
MTFW 2005; RGSF 2; RGWL 2, 3; TWA

**Beauvoir, Simone Lucie Ernestine Marie**
**Bertrand de**
See Beauvoir, Simone de

**Becker, Carl (Lotus)** 1873-1945 ..... TCLC 63
See also CA 157; DLB 17

**Becker, Jurek** 1937-1997 ............... CLC 7, 19
See also CA 85-88; CAAS 157; CANR 60,
117; CWW 2; DLB 75, 299; EWL 3;
RGHL

**Becker, Walter** 1950- ......................... CLC 26

**Becket, Thomas a** 1118(?)-1170 ...... CMLC 83

**Beckett, Samuel** 1906-1989 ... CLC 1, 2, 3, 4,
6, 9, 10, 11, 14, 18, 29, 57, 59, 83; DC
22; SSC 16, 74; TCLC 145; WLC 1
See also BRWC 2; BRWR 1; BRWS 1; CA
5-8R; CAAS 130; CANR 33, 61; CBD;
CDBLB 1945-1960; CN 1, 2, 3, 4; CP 1,
2, 3, 4; DA; DA3; DAB; DAC; DAM
DRAM, MST, NOV; DFS 2, 7, 18; DLB
13, 15, 233, 319, 321, 329; DLBY 1990;
EWL 3; GFL 1789 to the Present; LATS
1:2; LMFS 2; MTCW 1, 2; MTFW 2005;
RGSF 2; RGWL 2, 3; SSFS 15; TEA;
WLIT 4

**Beckford, William** 1760-1844 ........ NCLC 16
See also BRW 3; DLB 39, 213; GL 2; HGG;
LMFS 1; SUFW

**Beckham, Barry (Earl)** 1944- ............. BLC 1
See also BW 1; CA 29-32R; CANR 26, 62;
CN 1, 2, 3, 4, 5, 6; DAM MULT; DLB 33

**Beckman, Gunnel** 1910- .................... CLC 26
See also CA 33-36R; CANR 15, 114; CLR
25; MAICYA 1, 2; SAAS 9; SATA 6

**Becque, Henri** 1837-1899 .... DC 21; NCLC 3
See also DLB 192; GFL 1789 to the Present

**Becquer, Gustavo Adolfo**
1836-1870 ............. HLCS 1; NCLC 106
See also DAM MULT

**Beddoes, Thomas Lovell** 1803-1849 .. DC 15;
NCLC 3, 154
See also BRWS 11; DLB 96

**Bede** c. 673-735 .............................. CMLC 20
See also DLB 146; TEA

**Bedford, Denton R.** 1907-(?) ............. NNAL

**Bedford, Donald F.**
See Fearing, Kenneth (Flexner)

**Beecher, Catharine Esther**
1800-1878 ........................... NCLC 30
See also DLB 1, 243

**Beecher, John** 1904-1980 .................... CLC 6
See also AITN 1; CA 5-8R; CAAS 105;
CANR 8; CP 1, 2, 3

**Beer, Johann** 1655-1700 ...................... LC 5
See also DLB 168

**Beer, Patricia** 1924- ......................... CLC 58
See also CA 61-64; CAAS 183; CANR 13,
46; CP 1, 2, 3, 4, 5, 6; CWP; DLB 40;
FW

**Beerbohm, Max**
See Beerbohm, (Henry) Max(imilian)

**Beerbohm, (Henry) Max(imilian)**
1872-1956 ......................... TCLC 1, 24
See also BRWS 2; CA 154; CAAE 104;
CANR 79; DLB 34, 100; FANT; MTCW
2

**Beer-Hofmann, Richard**
1866-1945 ............................... TCLC 60
See also CA 160; DLB 81

**Beg, Shemus**
See Stephens, James

**Begiebing, Robert J(ohn)** 1946- ....... CLC 70
See also CA 122; CANR 40, 88

**Begley, Louis** 1933- ......................... CLC 197
See also CA 140; CANR 98; DLB 299;
RGHL; TCLE 1:1

**Behan, Brendan (Francis)**
1923-1964 ............. CLC 1, 8, 11, 15, 79
See also BRWS 2; CA 73-76; CANR 33,
121; CBD; CDBLB 1945-1960; DAM
DRAM; DFS 7; DLB 13, 233; EWL 3;
MTCW 1, 2

**Behn, Aphra** 1640(?)-1689 .. DC 4; LC 1, 30,
42, 135; PC 13; WLC 1
See also BRWS 3; DA; DA3; DAB; DAC;
DAM DRAM, MST, NOV, POET; DFS
16, 24; DLB 39, 80, 131; FW; TEA;
WLIT 3

**Behrman, S(amuel) N(athaniel)**
1893-1973 ............................... CLC 40
See also CA 13-16; CAAS 45-48; CAD;
CAP 1; DLB 7, 44; IDFW 3; MAL 5;
RGAL 4

**Bekederemo, J. P. Clark**
See Clark Bekederemo, J.P.
See also CD 6

**Belasco, David** 1853-1931 ................ TCLC 3
See also CA 168; CAAE 104; DLB 7; MAL
5; RGAL 4

**Belcheva, Elisaveta Lyubomirova**
1893-1991 .................................. CLC 10
See also Bagryana, Elisaveta

**Beldone, Phil "Cheech"**
See Ellison, Harlan

**Beleno**
See Azuela, Mariano

**Belinski, Vissarion Grigoryevich**
1811-1848 ................................ NCLC 5
See also DLB 198

**Belitt, Ben** 1911- ............................. CLC 22
See also CA 13-16R; 4; CANR 7, 77; CP 1,
2, 3, 4, 5, 6; DLB 5

**Belknap, Jeremy** 1744-1798 .............. LC 115
See also DLB 30, 37

**Bell, Gertrude (Margaret Lowthian)**
1868-1926 ............................... TCLC 67
See also CA 167; CANR 110; DLB 174

**Bell, J. Freeman**
See Zangwill, Israel

**Bell, James Madison** 1826-1902 ........ BLC 1;
TCLC 43
See also BW 1; CA 124; CAAE 122; DAM
MULT; DLB 50

**Bell, Madison Smartt** 1957- ..... CLC 41, 102,
223
See also AMWS 10; BPFB 1; CA 183; 111,
183; CANR 28, 54, 73, 134; CN 5, 6, 7;
CSW; DLB 218, 278; MTCW 2; MTFW
2005

**Bell, Marvin (Hartley)** 1937- ...... CLC 8, 31;
PC 79
See also CA 21-24R; 14; CANR 59, 102;
CP 1, 2, 3, 4, 5, 6, 7; DAM POET; DLB
5; MAL 5; MTCW 1; PFS 25

**Bell, W. L. D.**
See Mencken, H(enry) L(ouis)

**Bellamy, Atwood C.**
See Mencken, H(enry) L(ouis)

**Bellamy, Edward** 1850-1898 ..... NCLC 4, 86,
147
See also DLB 12; NFS 15; RGAL 4; SFW
4

**Belli, Gioconda** 1948- ....................... HLCS 1
See also CA 152; CANR 143; CWW 2;
DLB 290; EWL 3; RGWL 3

**Bellin, Edward J.**
See Kuttner, Henry

**Bello, Andres** 1781-1865 ............... NCLC 131
See also LAW

**Belloc, (Joseph) Hilaire (Pierre Sebastien**
**Rene Swanton)** 1870-1953 ......... PC 24;
TCLC 7, 18
See also CA 152; CAAE 106; CLR 102;
CWRI 5; DAM POET; DLB 19, 100, 141,
174; EWL 3; MTCW 2; MTFW 2005;
SATA 112; WCH; YABC 1

**Belloc, Joseph Peter Rene Hilaire**
See Belloc, (Joseph) Hilaire (Pierre Sebas-
tien Rene Swanton)

**Belloc, Joseph Pierre Hilaire**
See Belloc, (Joseph) Hilaire (Pierre Sebas-
tien Rene Swanton)

**Belloc, M. A.**
See Lowndes, Marie Adelaide (Belloc)

**Belloc-Lowndes, Mrs.**
See Lowndes, Marie Adelaide (Belloc)

**Bellow, Saul** 1915-2005 ...... CLC 1, 2, 3, 6, 8,
10, 13, 15, 25, 33, 34, 63, 79, 190, 200;
SSC 14, 101; WLC 1
See also AITN 2; AMW; AMWC 2; AMWR
2; BEST 89:3; BPFB 1; CA 5-8R; CAAS
238; CABS 1; CANR 29, 53, 95, 132;
CDALB 1941-1968; CN 1, 2, 3, 4, 5, 6,
7; DA; DA3; DAB; DAC; DAM MST,
NOV, POP; DLB 2, 28, 299, 329; DLBD
3; DLBY 1982; EWL 3; MAL 5; MTCW
1, 2; MTFW 2005; NFS 4, 14, 26; RGAL
4; RGHL; RGSF 2; SSFS 12, 22; TUS

**Belser, Reimond Karel Maria de** 1929-
See Ruyslinck, Ward
See also CA 152

**Bely, Andrey** ........................ PC 11; TCLC 7
See Bugayev, Boris Nikolayevich
See also DLB 295; EW 9; EWL 3

**Belyi, Andrei**
See Bugayev, Boris Nikolayevich
See also RGWL 2, 3

**Bembo, Pietro** 1470-1547 .................... LC 79
See also RGWL 2, 3

**Benary, Margot**
See Benary-Isbert, Margot

**Benary-Isbert, Margot** 1889-1979 .... CLC 12
See also CA 5-8R; CAAS 89-92; CANR 4,
72; CLR 12; MAICYA 1, 2; SATA 2;
SATA-Obit 21

**Benavente (y Martinez), Jacinto**
1866-1954 .... DC 26; HLCS 1; TCLC 3
See also CA 131; CAAE 106; CANR 81;
DAM DRAM, MULT; DLB 329; EWL 3;
GLL 2; HW 1, 2; MTCW 1, 2

**Benchley, Peter** 1940-2006 ............. CLC 4, 8
See also AAYA 14; AITN 2; BPFB 1; CA
17-20R; CAAS 248; CANR 12, 35, 66,
115; CPW; DAM NOV, POP; HGG;
MTCW 1, 2; MTFW 2005; SATA 3, 89,
164

**Benchley, Peter Bradford**
See Benchley, Peter

**Benchley, Robert (Charles)**
1889-1945 ......................... TCLC 1, 55
See also CA 153; CAAE 105; DLB 11;
MAL 5; RGAL 4

**Benda, Julien** 1867-1956 ................. **TCLC 60**
See also CA 154; CAAE 120; GFL 1789 to
the Present

**Benedict, Ruth** 1887-1948 ............. **TCLC 60**
See also CA 158; CANR 146; DLB 246

**Benedict, Ruth Fulton**
See Benedict, Ruth

**Benedikt, Michael** 1935- ............ **CLC 4, 14**
See also CA 13-16R; CANR 7; CP 1, 2, 3,
4, 5, 6, 7; DLB 5

**Benet, Juan** 1927-1993 ..................... **CLC 28**
See also CA 143; EWL 3

**Benet, Stephen Vincent** 1898-1943 ..... **PC 64;
SSC 10, 86; TCLC 7**
See also AMWS 11; CA 152; CAAE 104;
DA3; DAM POET; DLB 4, 48, 102, 249,
284; DLBY 1997; EWL 3; HGG; MAL 5;
MTCW 2; MTFW 2005; RGAL 4; RGSF
2; SSFS 22; SUFW; WP; YABC 1

**Benet, William Rose** 1886-1950 ..... **TCLC 28**
See also CA 152; CAAE 118; DAM POET;
DLB 45; RGAL 4

**Benford, Gregory** 1941- ..................... **CLC 52**
See also BPFB 1; CA 175; 69-72, 175; 27;
CANR 12, 24, 49, 95, 134; CN 7; CSW;
DLBY 1982; MTFW 2005; SCFW 2;
SFW 4

**Benford, Gregory Albert**
See Benford, Gregory

**Bengtsson, Frans (Gunnar)**
1894-1954 ............................... **TCLC 48**
See also CA 170; EWL 3

**Benjamin, David**
See Slavitt, David R.

**Benjamin, Lois**
See Gould, Lois

**Benjamin, Walter** 1892-1940 .......... **TCLC 39**
See also CA 164; DLB 242; EW 11; EWL
3

**Ben Jelloun, Tahar** 1944- ............... **CLC 180**
See also CA 135, 162; CANR 100, 166;
CWW 2; EWL 3; RGWL 3; WLIT 2

**Benn, Gottfried** 1886-1956 .. **PC 35; TCLC 3**
See also CA 153; CAAE 106; DLB 56;
EWL 3; RGWL 2, 3

**Bennett, Alan** 1934- ..................... **CLC 45, 77**
See also BRWS 8; CA 103; CANR 35, 55,
106, 157; CBD; CD 5, 6; DAB; DAM
MST; DLB 310; MTCW 1, 2; MTFW
2005

**Bennett, (Enoch) Arnold**
1867-1931 ........................... **TCLC 5, 20**
See also BRW 6; CA 155; CAAE 106; CD-
BLB 1890-1914; DLB 10, 34, 98, 135;
EWL 3; MTCW 2

**Bennett, Elizabeth**
See Mitchell, Margaret (Munnerlyn)

**Bennett, George Harold** 1930-
See Bennett, Hal
See also BW 1; CA 97-100; CANR 87

**Bennett, Gwendolyn B.** 1902-1981 .... **HR 1:2**
See also BW 1; CA 125; DLB 51; WP

**Bennett, Hal** ........................................ **CLC 5**
See Bennett, George Harold
See also CA 13; DLB 33

**Bennett, Jay** 1912- ............................ **CLC 35**
See also AAYA 10, 73; CA 69-72; CANR
11, 42, 79; JRDA; SAAS 4; SATA 41, 87;
SATA-Brief 27; WYA; YAW

**Bennett, Louise** 1919-2006 .. **BLC 1; CLC 28**
See also BW 2, 3; CA 151; CAAS 252; CD-
WLB 3; CP 1, 2, 3, 4, 5, 6, 7; DAM
MULT; DLB 117; EWL 3

**Bennett, Louise Simone**
See Bennett, Louise

**Bennett-Coverley, Louise**
See Bennett, Louise

**Benoit de Sainte-Maure** fl. 12th cent.
- ............................................... **CMLC 90**

**Benson, A. C.** 1862-1925 ............... **TCLC 123**
See also DLB 98

**Benson, E(dward) F(rederic)**
1867-1940 ............................... **TCLC 27**
See also CA 157; CAAE 114; DLB 135,
153; HGG; SUFW 1

**Benson, Jackson J.** 1930- ................. **CLC 34**
See also CA 25-28R; DLB 111

**Benson, Sally** 1900-1972 ................... **CLC 17**
See also CA 19-20; CAAS 37-40R; CAP 1;
SATA 1, 35; SATA-Obit 27

**Benson, Stella** 1892-1933 ............... **TCLC 17**
See also CA 154, 155; CAAE 117; DLB
36, 162; FANT; TEA

**Bentham, Jeremy** 1748-1832 ......... **NCLC 38**
See also DLB 107, 158, 252

**Bentley, E(dmund) C(lerihew)**
1875-1956 ............................... **TCLC 12**
See also CA 232; CAAE 108; DLB 70;
MSW

**Bentley, Eric** 1916- ............................ **CLC 24**
See also CA 5-8R; CAD; CANR 6, 67;
CBD; CD 5, 6; INT CANR-6

**Bentley, Eric Russell**
See Bentley, Eric

**ben Uzair, Salem**
See Horne, Richard Henry Hengist

**Beolco, Angelo** 1496-1542 ................... **LC 139**

**Beranger, Pierre Jean de**
1780-1857 ............................... **NCLC 34**

**Berdyaev, Nicolas**
See Berdyaev, Nikolai (Aleksandrovich)

**Berdyaev, Nikolai (Aleksandrovich)**
1874-1948 ............................... **TCLC 67**
See also CA 157; CAAE 120

**Berdyayev, Nikolai (Aleksandrovich)**
See Berdyaev, Nikolai (Aleksandrovich)

**Berendt, John** 1939- .......................... **CLC 86**
See also CA 146; CANR 75, 83, 151

**Berendt, John Lawrence**
See Berendt, John

**Beresford, J(ohn) D(avys)**
1873-1947 ............................... **TCLC 81**
See also CA 155; CAAE 112; DLB 162,
178, 197; SFW 4; SUFW 1

**Bergelson, David (Rafailovich)**
1884-1952 ............................... **TCLC 81**
See Bergelson, Dovid
See also CA 220; DLB 333

**Bergelson, Dovid**
See Bergelson, David (Rafailovich)
See also EWL 3

**Berger, Colonel**
See Malraux, (Georges-)Andre

**Berger, John** 1926- ........................ **CLC 2, 19**
See also BRWS 4; CA 81-84; CANR 51,
78, 117, 163; CN 1, 2, 3, 4, 5, 6, 7; DLB
14, 207, 319, 326

**Berger, John Peter**
See Berger, John

**Berger, Melvin H.** 1927- ................... **CLC 12**
See also CA 5-8R; CANR 4, 142; CLR 32;
SAAS 2; SATA 5, 88, 158; SATA-Essay
124

**Berger, Thomas** 1924- .... **CLC 3, 5, 8, 11, 18,
38**
See also BPFB 1; CA 1-4R; CANR 5, 28,
51, 128; CN 1, 2, 3, 4, 5, 6, 7; DAM
NOV; DLB 2; DLBY 1980; EWL 3;
FANT; INT CANR-28; MAL 5; MTCW
1, 2; MTFW 2005; RHW; TCLE 1:1;
TCWW 1, 2

**Bergman, Ingmar** 1918-2007 ..... **CLC 16, 72,
210**
See also AAYA 61; CA 81-84; CAAS 262;
CANR 33, 70; CWW 2; DLB 257;
MTCW 2; MTFW 2005

**Bergson, Henri(-Louis)** 1859-1941 . **TCLC 32**
See also CA 164; DLB 329; EW 8; EWL 3;
GFL 1789 to the Present

**Bergstein, Eleanor** 1938- ..................... **CLC 4**
See also CA 53-56; CANR 5

**Berkeley, George** 1685-1753 ................. **LC 65**
See also DLB 31, 101, 252

**Berkoff, Steven** 1937- ......................... **CLC 56**
See also CA 104; CANR 72; CBD; CD 5, 6

**Berlin, Isaiah** 1909-1997 ................ **TCLC 105**
See also CA 85-88; CAAS 162

**Bermant, Chaim (Icyk)** 1929-1998 ... **CLC 40**
See also CA 57-60; CANR 6, 31, 57, 105;
CN 2, 3, 4, 5, 6

**Bern, Victoria**
See Fisher, M(ary) F(rances) K(ennedy)

**Bernanos, (Paul Louis) Georges**
1888-1948 ................................. **TCLC 3**
See also CA 130; CAAE 104; CANR 94;
DLB 72; EWL 3; GFL 1789 to the
Present; RGWL 2, 3

**Bernard, April** 1956- ........................... **CLC 59**
See also CA 131; CANR 144

**Bernard, Mary Ann**
See Soderbergh, Steven

**Bernard of Clairvaux** 1090-1153 .. **CMLC 71**
See also DLB 208

**Bernard Silvestris** fl. c. 1130-fl. c.
1160 ......................................... **CMLC 87**
See also DLB 208

**Berne, Victoria**
See Fisher, M(ary) F(rances) K(ennedy)

**Bernhard, Thomas** 1931-1989 ..... **CLC 3, 32,
61; DC 14; TCLC 165**
See also CA 85-88; CAAS 127; CANR 32,
57; CDWLB 2; DLB 85, 124; EWL 3;
MTCW 1; RGHL; RGWL 2, 3

**Bernhardt, Sarah (Henriette Rosine)**
1844-1923 ............................... **TCLC 75**
See also CA 157

**Bernstein, Charles** 1950- ............... **CLC 142,**
See also CA 129; 24; CANR 90; CP 4, 5, 6,
7; DLB 169

**Bernstein, Ingrid**
See Kirsch, Sarah

**Beroul** fl. c. 12th cent. - ................. **CMLC 75**

**Berriault, Gina** 1926-1999 ....... **CLC 54, 109;
SSC 30**
See also CA 129; CAAE 116; CAAS 185;
CANR 66; DLB 130; SSFS 7,11

**Berrigan, Daniel** 1921- ......................... **CLC 4**
See also CA 187; 33-36R, 187; 1; CANR
11, 43, 78; CP 1, 2, 3, 4, 5, 6, 7; DLB 5

**Berrigan, Edmund Joseph Michael, Jr.**
1934-1983
See Berrigan, Ted
See also CA 61-64; CAAS 110; CANR 14,
102

**Berrigan, Ted** ...................................... **CLC 37**
See Berrigan, Edmund Joseph Michael, Jr.
See also CP 1, 2, 3; DLB 5, 169; WP

**Berry, Charles Edward Anderson** 1931-
See Berry, Chuck
See also CA 115

**Berry, Chuck** ...................................... **CLC 17**
See Berry, Charles Edward Anderson

**Berry, Jonas**
See Ashbery, John
See also GLL 1

**Berry, Wendell** 1934- .... **CLC 4, 6, 8, 27, 46;
PC 28**
See also AITN 1; AMWS 10; ANW; CA
73-76; CANR 50, 73, 101, 132; CP 1, 2,
3, 4, 5, 6, 7; CSW; DAM POET; DLB 5,
6, 234, 275; MTCW 2; MTFW 2005;
TCLE 1:1

**Borowski, Tadeusz** 1922-1951 ........... **SSC 48; TCLC 9**
See also CA 154; CAAE 106; CDWLB 4; DLB 215; EWL 3; RGHL; RGSF 2; RGWL 3; SSFS 13

**Borrow, George (Henry)**
1803-1881 ............................... **NCLC 9**
See also BRWS 12; DLB 21, 55, 166

**Bosch (Gaviño), Juan** 1909-2001 ..... **HLCS 1**
See also CA 151; CAAS 204; DAM MST, MULT; DLB 145; HW 1, 2

**Bosman, Herman Charles**
1905-1951 ............................... **TCLC 49**
See Malan, Herman
See also CA 160; DLB 225; RGSF 2

**Bosschere, Jean de** 1878(?)-1953 ... **TCLC 19**
See also CA 186; CAAE 115

**Boswell, James** 1740-1795 ... **LC 4, 50; WLC 1**
See also BRW 3; CDBLB 1660-1789; DA; DAB; DAC; DAM MST; DLB 104, 142; TEA; WLIT 3

**Bottomley, Gordon** 1874-1948 ..... **TCLC 107**
See also CA 192; CAAE 120; DLB 10

**Bottoms, David** 1949- ...................... **CLC 53**
See also CA 105; CANR 22; CSW; DLB 120; DLBY 1983

**Boucicault, Dion** 1820-1890 ........... **NCLC 41**

**Boucolon, Maryse**
See Conde, Maryse

**Bourdieu, Pierre** 1930-2002 ............ **CLC 198**
See also CA 130; CAAS 204

**Bourget, Paul (Charles Joseph)**
1852-1935 ............................... **TCLC 12**
See also CA 196; CAAE 107; DLB 123; GFL 1789 to the Present

**Bourjaily, Vance (Nye)** 1922- ........ **CLC 8, 62**
See also CA 1-4R; 1; CANR 2, 72; CN 1, 2, 3, 4, 5, 6, 7; DLB 2, 143; MAL 5

**Bourne, Randolph S(illiman)**
1886-1918 ............................... **TCLC 16**
See also AMW; CA 155; CAAE 117; DLB 63; MAL 5

**Bova, Ben** 1932- .............................. **CLC 45**
See also AAYA 16; CA 5-8R; 18; CANR 11, 56, 94, 111, 157; CLR 3, 96; DLBY 1981; INT CANR-11; MAICYA 1, 2; MTCW 1; SATA 6, 68, 133; SFW 4

**Bova, Benjamin William**
See Bova, Ben

**Bowen, Elizabeth (Dorothea Cole)**
1899-1973 . **CLC 1, 3, 6, 11, 15, 22, 118; SSC 3, 28, 66; TCLC 148**
See also BRWS 2; CA 17-18; CAAS 41-44R; CANR 35, 105; CAP 2; CDBLB 1945-1960; CN 1; DA3; DAM NOV; DLB 15, 162; EWL 3; FW; HGG; MTCW 1, 2; MTFW 2005; NFS 13; RGSF 2; SSFS 5, 22; SUFW 1; TEA; WLIT 4

**Bowering, George** 1935- .............. **CLC 15, 47**
See also CA 21-24R; 16; CANR 10; CN 7; CP 1, 2, 3, 4, 5, 6, 7; DLB 53

**Bowering, Marilyn R(uthe)** 1949- .... **CLC 32**
See also CA 101; CANR 49; CP 4, 5, 6, 7; CWP; DLB 334

**Bowers, Edgar** 1924-2000 .................. **CLC 9**
See also CA 5-8R; CAAS 188; CANR 24; CP 1, 2, 3, 4, 5, 6, 7; CSW; DLB 5

**Bowers, Mrs. J. Milton** 1842-1914
See Bierce, Ambrose (Gwinett)

**Bowie, David** ................................... **CLC 17**
See Jones, David Robert

**Bowles, Jane (Sydney)** 1917-1973 ..... **CLC 3, 68**
See Bowles, Jane Auer
See also CA 19-20; CAAS 41-44R; CAP 2; CN 1; MAL 5

**Bowles, Jane Auer**
See Bowles, Jane (Sydney)
See also EWL 3

**Bowles, Paul** 1910-1999 ..... **CLC 1, 2, 19, 53; SSC 3, 98**
See also AMWS 4; CA 1-4R; 1; CAAS 186; CANR 1, 19, 50, 75; CN 1, 2, 3, 4, 5, 6; DA3; DLB 5, 6, 218; EWL 3; MAL 5; MTCW 1, 2; MTFW 2005; RGAL 4; SSFS 17

**Bowles, William Lisle** 1762-1850 . **NCLC 103**
See also DLB 93

**Box, Edgar**
See Vidal, Gore

**Boyd, James** 1888-1944 ................. **TCLC 115**
See also CA 186; DLB 9; DLBD 16; RGAL 4; RHW

**Boyd, Nancy**
See Millay, Edna St. Vincent
See also GLL 1

**Boyd, Thomas (Alexander)**
1898-1935 ............................... **TCLC 111**
See also CA 183; CAAE 111; DLB 9; DLBD 16, 316

**Boyd, William (Andrew Murray)**
1952- ............................ **CLC 28, 53, 70**
See also CA 120; CAAE 114; CANR 51, 71, 131; CN 4, 5, 6, 7; DLB 231

**Boyesen, Hjalmar Hjorth**
1848-1895 ............................... **NCLC 135**
See also DLB 12, 71; DLBD 13; RGAL 4

**Boyle, Kay** 1902-1992 ........ **CLC 1, 5, 19, 58, 121; SSC 5, 102**
See also CA 13-16R; 1; CAAS 140; CANR 29, 61, 110; CN 1, 2, 3, 4, 5; CP 1, 2, 3, 4, 5; DLB 4, 9, 48, 86; DLBY 1993; EWL 3; MAL 5; MTCW 1, 2; MTFW 2005; RGAL 4; RGSF 2; SSFS 10, 13, 14

**Boyle, Mark**
See Kienzle, William X.

**Boyle, Patrick** 1905-1982 ................... **CLC 19**
See also CA 127

**Boyle, T. C.**
See Boyle, T. Coraghessan
See also AMWS 8

**Boyle, T. Coraghessan** 1948- ..... **CLC 36, 55, 90; SSC 16**
See Boyle, T. C.
See also AAYA 47; BEST 90:4; BPFB 1; CA 120; CANR 44, 76, 89, 132; CN 6, 7; CPW; DA3; DAM POP; DLB 218, 278; DLBY 1986; EWL 3; MAL 5; MTCW 2; MTFW 2005; SSFS 13, 19

**Boz**
See Dickens, Charles (John Huffam)

**Brackenridge, Hugh Henry**
1748-1816 ............................... **NCLC 7**
See also DLB 11, 37; RGAL 4

**Bradbury, Edward P.**
See Moorcock, Michael
See also MTCW 2

**Bradbury, Malcolm (Stanley)**
1932-2000 ............................ **CLC 32, 61**
See also CA 1-4R; CANR 1, 33, 91, 98, 137; CN 1, 2, 3, 4, 5, 6, 7; CP 1; DA3; DAM NOV; DLB 14, 207; EWL 3; MTCW 1, 2; MTFW 2005

**Bradbury, Ray** 1920- ... **CLC 1, 3, 10, 15, 42, 98, 235; SSC 29, 53; WLC 1**
See also AAYA 15; AITN 1, 2; AMWS 4; BPFB 1; BYA 4, 5, 11; CA 1-4R; CANR 2, 30, 75, 125; CDALB 1968-1988; CN 1, 2, 3, 4, 5, 6, 7; CPW; DA; DA3; DAB; DAC; DAM MST, NOV, POP; DLB 2, 8; EXPN; EXPS; HGG; LAIT 3, 5; LATS 1:2; LMFS 2; MAL 5; MTCW 1, 2; MTFW 2005; NFS 1, 22; RGAL 4; RGSF 2; SATA 11, 64, 123; SCFW 1, 2; SFW 4; SSFS 1, 20; SUFW 1, 2; TUS; YAW

**Braddon, Mary Elizabeth**
1837-1915 ............................... **TCLC 111**
See also BRWS 8; CA 179; CAAE 108; CMW 4; DLB 18, 70, 156; HGG

**Bradfield, Scott** 1955- ..................... **SSC 65**
See also CA 147; CANR 90; HGG; SUFW 2

**Bradfield, Scott Michael**
See Bradfield, Scott

**Bradford, Gamaliel** 1863-1932 ....... **TCLC 36**
See also CA 160; DLB 17

**Bradford, William** 1590-1657 ............. **LC 64**
See also DLB 24, 30; RGAL 4

**Bradley, David, Jr.** 1950- ... **BLC 1; CLC 23, 118**
See also BW 1, 3; CA 104; CANR 26, 81; CN 4, 5, 6, 7; DAM MULT; DLB 33

**Bradley, David Henry, Jr.**
See Bradley, David, Jr.

**Bradley, John Ed** 1958- ..................... **CLC 55**
See also CA 139; CANR 99; CN 6, 7; CSW

**Bradley, John Edmund, Jr.**
See Bradley, John Ed

**Bradley, Marion Zimmer**
1930-1999 ............................... **CLC 30**
See Chapman, Lee; Dexter, John; Gardner, Miriam; Ives, Morgan; Rivers, Elfrida
See also AAYA 40; BPFB 1; CA 57-60; 10; CAAS 185; CANR 7, 31, 51, 75, 107; CPW; DA3; DAM POP; FANT; FW; MTCW 1, 2; MTFW 2005; SATA 90, 139; SATA-Obit 116; SFW 4; SUFW 2; YAW

**Bradshaw, John** 1933- ...................... **CLC 70**
See also CA 138; CANR 61

**Bradstreet, Anne** 1612(?)-1672 ....... **LC 4, 30, 130; PC 10**
See also AMWS 1; CDALB 1640-1865; DA; DA3; DAC; DAM MST, POET; DLB 24; EXPP; FW; PFS 6; RGAL 4; TUS; WP

**Brady, Joan** 1939- ............................ **CLC 86**
See also CA 141

**Bragg, Melvyn** 1939- ....................... **CLC 10**
See also BEST 89:3; CA 57-60; CANR 10, 48, 89, 158; CN 1, 2, 3, 4, 5, 6, 7; DLB 14, 271; RHW

**Brahe, Tycho** 1546-1601 ...................... **LC 45**
See also DLB 300

**Braine, John (Gerard)** 1922-1986 . **CLC 1, 3, 41**
See also CA 1-4R; CAAS 120; CANR 1, 33; CDBLB 1945-1960; CN 1, 2, 3, 4; DLB 15; DLBY 1986; EWL 3; MTCW 1

**Braithwaite, William Stanley (Beaumont)**
1878-1962 ......... **BLC 1; HR 1:2; PC 52**
See also BW 1; CA 125; DAM MULT; DLB 50, 54; MAL 5

**Bramah, Ernest** 1868-1942 ............. **TCLC 72**
See also CA 156; CMW 4; DLB 70; FANT

**Brammer, Billy Lee**
See Brammer, William

**Brammer, William** 1929-1978 .......... **CLC 31**
See also CA 235; CAAS 77-80

**Brancati, Vitaliano** 1907-1954 ........ **TCLC 12**
See also CAAE 109; DLB 264; EWL 3

**Brancato, Robin F(idler)** 1936- ........ **CLC 35**
See also AAYA 9, 68; BYA 6; CA 69-72; CANR 11, 45; CLR 32; JRDA; MAICYA 2; MAICYAS 1; SAAS 9; SATA 97; WYA; YAW

**Brand, Dionne** 1953- ....................... **CLC 192**
See also BW 2; CA 143; CANR 143; CWP; DLB 334

**Brand, Max**
See Faust, Frederick (Schiller)
See also BPFB 1; TCWW 1, 2

**Brooks, Gwendolyn** 1917-2000 .......... **BLC 1; CLC 1, 2, 4, 5, 15, 49, 125; PC 7; WLC 1**
See also AAYA 20; AFAW 1, 2; AITN 1; AMWS 3; BW 2, 3; CA 1-4R; CAAS 190; CANR 1, 27, 52, 75, 132; CDALB 1941-1968; CLR 27; CP 1, 2, 3, 4, 5, 6, 7; CWP; DA; DA3; DAC; DAM MST, MULT, POET; DLB 5, 76, 165; EWL 3; EXPP; FL 1:5; MAL 5; MBL; MTCW 1, 2; MTFW 2005; PFS 1, 2, 4, 6; RGAL 4; SATA 6; SATA-Obit 123; TUS; WP

**Brooks, Mel** 1926-
See Kaminsky, Melvin
See also CA 65-68; CANR 16; DFS 21

**Brooks, Peter (Preston)** 1938- .......... **CLC 34**
See also CA 45-48; CANR 1, 107

**Brooks, Van Wyck** 1886-1963 .......... **CLC 29**
See also AMW; CA 1-4R; CANR 6; DLB 45, 63, 103; MAL 5; TUS

**Brophy, Brigid (Antonia)**
1929-1995 ................. **CLC 6, 11, 29, 105**
See also CA 5-8R; 4; CAAS 149; CANR 25, 53; CBD; CN 1, 2, 3, 4, 5, 6; CWD; DA3; DLB 14, 271; EWL 3; MTCW 1, 2

**Brosman, Catharine Savage** 1934- ..... **CLC 9**
See also CA 61-64; CANR 21, 46, 149

**Brossard, Nicole** 1943- .... **CLC 115, 169; PC 80**
See also CA 122; 16; CANR 140; CCA 1; CWP; CWW 2; DLB 53; EWL 3; FW; GLL 2; RGWL 3

**Brother Antoninus**
See Everson, William (Oliver)

**Brothers Grimm**
See Grimm, Jacob Ludwig Karl; Grimm, Wilhelm Karl

**The Brothers Quay**
See Quay, Stephen; Quay, Timothy

**Broughton, T(homas) Alan** 1936- ..... **CLC 19**
See also CA 45-48; CANR 2, 23, 48, 111

**Broumas, Olga** 1949- ................... **CLC 10, 73**
See also CA 85-88; CANR 20, 69, 110; CP 5, 6, 7; CWP; GLL 2

**Broun, Heywood** 1888-1939 ......... **TCLC 104**
See also DLB 29, 171

**Brown, Alan** 1950- ........................... **CLC 99**
See also CA 156

**Brown, Charles Brockden**
1771-1810 ................. **NCLC 22, 74, 122**
See also AMWS 1; CDALB 1640-1865; DLB 37, 59, 73; FW; GL 2; HGG; LMFS 1; RGAL 4; TUS

**Brown, Christy** 1932-1981 ................ **CLC 63**
See also BYA 13; CA 105; CAAS 104; CANR 72; DLB 14

**Brown, Claude** 1937-2002 ... **BLC 1; CLC 30**
See also AAYA 7; BW 1, 3; CA 73-76; CAAS 205; CANR 81; DAM MULT

**Brown, Dan** 1964- .......................... **CLC 209**
See also AAYA 55; CA 217; MTFW 2005

**Brown, Dee** 1908-2002 ................ **CLC 18, 47**
See also AAYA 30; CA 13-16R; 6; CAAS 212; CANR 11, 45, 60, 150; CPW; CSW; DA3; DAM POP; DLBY 1980; LAIT 2; MTCW 1, 2; MTFW 2005; NCFS 5; SATA 5, 110; SATA-Obit 141; TCWW 1, 2

**Brown, Dee Alexander**
See Brown, Dee

**Brown, George**
See Wertmueller, Lina

**Brown, George Douglas**
1869-1902 .............................. **TCLC 28**
See Douglas, George
See also CA 162

**Brown, George Mackay** 1921-1996 ... **CLC 5, 48, 100**
See also BRWS 6; CA 21-24R; 6; CAAS 151; CANR 12, 37, 67; CN 1, 2, 3, 4, 5, 6; CP 1, 2, 3, 4, 5, 6; DLB 14, 27, 139, 271; MTCW 1; RGSF 2; SATA 35

**Brown, James Wllie**
See Komunyakaa, Yusef

**Brown, James Wllie, Jr.**
See Komunyakaa, Yusef

**Brown, Larry** 1951-2004 ................... **CLC 73**
See also CA 134; CAAE 130; CAAS 233; CANR 117, 145; CSW; DLB 234; INT CA-134

**Brown, Moses**
See Barrett, William (Christopher)

**Brown, Rita Mae** 1944- ........ **CLC 18, 43, 79**
See also BPFB 1; CA 45-48; CANR 2, 11, 35, 62, 95, 138; CN 5, 6, 7; CPW; CSW; DA3; DAM NOV, POP; FW; INT CANR-11; MAL 5; MTCW 1, 2; MTFW 2005; NFS 9; RGAL 4; TUS

**Brown, Roderick (Langmere) Haig-**
See Haig-Brown, Roderick (Langmere)

**Brown, Rosellen** 1939- ............. **CLC 32, 170**
See also CA 77-80; 10; CANR 14, 44, 98; CN 6, 7

**Brown, Sterling Allen** 1901-1989 ...... **BLC 1; CLC 1, 23, 59; HR 1:2; PC 55**
See also AFAW 1, 2; BW 1, 3; CA 85-88; CAAS 127; CANR 26; CP 3, 4; DA3; DAM MULT, POET; DLB 48, 51, 63; MAL 5; MTCW 1, 2; MTFW 2005; RGAL 4; WP

**Brown, Will**
See Ainsworth, William Harrison

**Brown, William Hill** 1765-1793 .......... **LC 93**
See also DLB 37

**Brown, William Larry**
See Brown, Larry

**Brown, William Wells** 1815-1884 ...... **BLC 1; DC 1; NCLC 2, 89**
See also DAM MULT; DLB 3, 50, 183, 248; RGAL 4

**Browne, Clyde Jackson**
See Browne, Jackson

**Browne, Jackson** 1948(?)- ................ **CLC 21**
See also CA 120

**Browne, Sir Thomas** 1605-1682 ......... **LC 111**
See also BRW 2; DLB 151

**Browning, Robert** 1812-1889 . **NCLC 19, 79; PC 2, 61; WLCS**
See also BRW 4; BRWC 2; BRWR 2; CD-BLB 1832-1890; CLR 97; DA; DA3; DAB; DAC; DAM MST, POET; DLB 32, 163; EXPP; LATS 1:1; PAB; PFS 1, 15; RGEL 2; TEA; WLIT 4; WP; YABC 1

**Browning, Tod** 1882-1962 ................ **CLC 16**
See also CA 141; CAAS 117

**Brownmiller, Susan** 1935- ............. **CLC 159**
See also CA 103; CANR 35, 75, 137; DAM NOV; FW; MTCW 1, 2; MTFW 2005

**Brownson, Orestes Augustus**
1803-1876 ............................... **NCLC 50**
See also DLB 1, 59, 73, 243

**Bruccoli, Matthew J(oseph)** 1931- ... **CLC 34**
See also CA 9-12R; CANR 7, 87; DLB 103

**Bruce, Lenny** ...................................... **CLC 21**
See Schneider, Leonard Alfred

**Bruchac, Joseph** 1942- ...................... **NNAL**
See also AAYA 19; CA 256; 33-36R, 256; CANR 13, 47, 75, 94, 137, 161; CLR 46; CWRI 5; DAM MULT; JRDA; MAICYA 2; MAICYAS 1; MTCW 2; MTFW 2005; SATA 42, 89, 131, 176; SATA-Essay 176

**Bruin, John**
See Brutus, Dennis

**Brulard, Henri**
See Stendhal

**Brulls, Christian**
See Simenon, Georges (Jacques Christian)

**Brunetto Latini** c. 1220-1294 ........ **CMLC 73**

**Brunner, John (Kilian Houston)**
1934-1995 ............................ **CLC 8, 10**
See also CA 1-4R; 8; CAAS 149; CANR 2, 37; CPW; DAM POP; DLB 261; MTCW 1, 2; SCFW 1, 2; SFW 4

**Bruno, Giordano** 1548-1600 ............... **LC 27**
See also RGWL 2, 3

**Brutus, Dennis** 1924- ... **BLC 1; CLC 43; PC 24**
See also AFW; BW 2, 3; CA 49-52; 14; CANR 2, 27, 42, 81; CDWLB 3; CP 1, 2, 3, 4, 5, 6, 7; DAM MULT, POET; DLB 117, 225; EWL 3

**Bryan, C(ourtlandt) D(ixon) B(arnes)**
1936- ...................................... **CLC 29**
See also CA 73-76; CANR 13, 68; DLB 185; INT CANR-13

**Bryan, Michael**
See Moore, Brian
See also CCA 1

**Bryan, William Jennings**
1860-1925 ............................... **TCLC 99**
See also DLB 303

**Bryant, William Cullen** 1794-1878 . **NCLC 6, 46; PC 20**
See also AMWS 1; CDALB 1640-1865; DA; DAB; DAC; DAM MST, POET; DLB 3, 43, 59, 189, 250; EXPP; PAB; RGAL 4; TUS

**Bryusov, Valery Yakovlevich**
1873-1924 ............................... **TCLC 10**
See also CA 155; CAAE 107; EWL 3; SFW 4

**Buchan, John** 1875-1940 ................. **TCLC 41**
See also CA 145; CAAE 108; CMW 4; DAB; DAM POP; DLB 34, 70, 156; HGG; MSW; MTCW 2; RGEL 2; RHW; YABC 2

**Buchanan, George** 1506-1582 ............... **LC 4**
See also DLB 132

**Buchanan, Robert** 1841-1901 ....... **TCLC 107**
See also CA 179; DLB 18, 35

**Buchheim, Lothar-Guenther**
1918-2007 ................................... **CLC 6**
See also CA 85-88; CAAS 257

**Buchner, (Karl) Georg**
1813-1837 ........................... **NCLC 26, 146**
See also CDWLB 2; DLB 133; EW 6; RGSF 2; RGWL 2, 3; TWA

**Buchwald, Art** 1925-2007 ................. **CLC 33**
See also AITN 1; CA 5-8R; CAAS 256; CANR 21, 67, 107; MTCW 1, 2; SATA 10

**Buchwald, Arthur**
See Buchwald, Art

**Buck, Pearl S(ydenstricker)**
1892-1973 ................. **CLC 7, 11, 18, 127**
See also AAYA 42; AITN 1; AMWS 2; BPFB 1; CA 1-4R; CAAS 41-44R; CANR 1, 34; CDALBS; CN 1; DA; DA3; DAB; DAC; DAM MST, NOV; DLB 9, 102, 329; EWL 3; LAIT 3; MAL 5; MTCW 1, 2; MTFW 2005; NFS 25; RGAL 4; RHW; SATA 1, 25; TUS

**Buckler, Ernest** 1908-1984 ............... **CLC 13**
See also CA 11-12; CAAS 114; CAP 1; CCA 1; CN 1, 2, 3; DAC; DAM MST; DLB 68; SATA 47

**Buckley, Christopher** 1952- ........... **CLC 165**
See also CA 139; CANR 119

**Buckley, Christopher Taylor**
See Buckley, Christopher

**Buckley, Vincent (Thomas)**
1925-1988 ................................. **CLC 57**
See also CA 101; CP 1, 2, 3, 4; DLB 289

**Buckley, William F., Jr.** 1925- ..... **CLC 7, 18, 37**
See also AITN 1; BPFB 1; CA 1-4R; CANR 1, 24, 53, 93, 133; CMW 4; CPW; DA3; DAM POP; DLB 137; DLBY 1980; INT CANR-24; MTCW 1, 2; MTFW 2005; TUS

**Buechner, Frederick** 1926- ..... **CLC 2, 4, 6, 9**
See also AMWS 12; BPFB 1; CA 13-16R; CANR 11, 39, 64, 114, 138; CN 1, 2, 3, 4, 5, 6, 7; DAM NOV; DLBY 1980; INT CANR-11; MAL 5; MTCW 1, 2; MTFW 2005; TCLE 1:1

**Buell, John (Edward)** 1927- ............. **CLC 10**
See also CA 1-4R; CANR 71; DLB 53

**Buero Vallejo, Antonio** 1916-2000 ... **CLC 15, 46, 139, 226; DC 18**
See also CA 106; CAAS 189; CANR 24, 49, 75; CWW 2; DFS 11; EWL 3; HW 1; MTCW 1, 2

**Bufalino, Gesualdo** 1920-1996 ......... **CLC 74**
See also CA 209; CWW 2; DLB 196

**Bugayev, Boris Nikolayevich** 1880-1934 ..................... **PC 11; TCLC 7**
See Bely, Andrey; Belyi, Andrei
See also CA 165; CAAE 104; MTCW 2; MTFW 2005

**Bukowski, Charles** 1920-1994 ... **CLC 2, 5, 9, 41, 82, 108; PC 18; SSC 45**
See also CA 17-20R; CAAS 144; CANR 40, 62, 105; CN 4, 5; CP 1, 2, 3, 4, 5; CPW; DA3; DAM NOV, POET; DLB 5, 130, 169; EWL 3; MAL 5; MTCW 1, 2; MTFW 2005

**Bulgakov, Mikhail** 1891-1940 .......... **SSC 18; TCLC 2, 16, 159**
See also AAYA 74; BPFB 1; CA 152; CAAE 105; DAM DRAM, NOV; DLB 272; EWL 3; MTCW 2; MTFW 2005; NFS 8; RGSF 2; RGWL 2, 3; SFW 4; TWA

**Bulgakov, Mikhail Afanasevich**
See Bulgakov, Mikhail

**Bulgya, Alexander Alexandrovich** 1901-1956 ..................... **TCLC 53**
See Fadeev, Aleksandr Aleksandrovich; Fadeev, Alexandr Alexandrovich; Fadeyev, Alexander
See also CA 181; CAAE 117

**Bullins, Ed** 1935- ... **BLC 1; CLC 1, 5, 7; DC 6**
See also BW 2, 3; CA 49-52; 16; CAD; CANR 24, 46, 73, 134; CD 5, 6; DAM DRAM, MULT; DLB 7, 38, 249; EWL 3; MAL 5; MTCW 1, 2; MTFW 2005; RGAL 4

**Bulosan, Carlos** 1911-1956 ................... **AAL**
See also CA 216; DLB 312; RGAL 4

**Bulwer-Lytton, Edward (George Earle Lytton)** 1803-1873 ............. **NCLC 1, 45**
See also DLB 21; RGEL 2; SFW 4; SUFW 1; TEA

**Bunin, Ivan**
See Bunin, Ivan Alexeyevich

**Bunin, Ivan Alekseevich**
See Bunin, Ivan Alexeyevich

**Bunin, Ivan Alexeyevich** 1870-1953 ... **SSC 5; TCLC 6**
See also CAAE 104; DLB 317, 329; EWL 3; RGSF 2; RGWL 2, 3; TWA

**Bunting, Basil** 1900-1985 ....... **CLC 10, 39, 47**
See also BRWS 7; CA 53-56; CAAS 115; CANR 7; CP 1, 2, 3, 4; DAM POET; DLB 20; EWL 3; RGEL 2

**Bunuel, Luis** 1900-1983 ... **CLC 16, 80; HLC 1**
See also CA 101; CAAS 110; CANR 32, 77; DAM MULT; HW 1

**Bunyan, John** 1628-1688 .. **LC 4, 69; WLC 1**
See also BRW 2; BYA 5; CDBLB 1660-1789; DA; DAB; DAC; DAM MST; DLB 39; RGEL 2; TEA; WCH; WLIT 3

**Buravsky, Alexandr** ......................... **CLC 59**

**Burchill, Julie** 1959- ......................... **CLC 238**
See also CA 135; CANR 115, 116

**Burckhardt, Jacob (Christoph)** 1818-1897 ............................... **NCLC 49**
See also EW 6

**Burford, Eleanor**
See Hibbert, Eleanor Alice Burford

**Burgess, Anthony** . **CLC 1, 2, 4, 5, 8, 10, 13, 15, 22, 40, 62, 81, 94**
See Wilson, John (Anthony) Burgess
See also AAYA 25; AITN 1; BRWS 1; CD-BLB 1960 to Present; CN 1, 2, 3, 4, 5; DAB; DLB 14, 194, 261; DLBY 1998; EWL 3; RGEL 2; RHW; SFW 4; YAW

**Burke, Edmund** 1729(?)-1797 ........ **LC 7, 36; WLC 1**
See also BRW 3; DA; DA3; DAB; DAC; DAM MST; DLB 104, 252, 336; RGEL 2; TEA

**Burke, Kenneth (Duva)** 1897-1993 ... **CLC 2, 24**
See also AMW; CA 5-8R; CAAS 143; CANR 39, 74, 136; CN 1, 2; CP 1, 2, 3, 4, 5; DLB 45, 63; EWL 3; MAL 5; MTCW 1, 2; MTFW 2005; RGAL 4

**Burke, Leda**
See Garnett, David

**Burke, Ralph**
See Silverberg, Robert

**Burke, Thomas** 1886-1945 .............. **TCLC 63**
See also CA 155; CAAE 113; CMW 4; DLB 197

**Burney, Fanny** 1752-1840 ....... **NCLC 12, 54, 107**
See also BRWS 3; DLB 39; FL 1:2; NFS 16; RGEL 2; TEA

**Burney, Frances**
See Burney, Fanny

**Burns, Robert** 1759-1796 ... **LC 3, 29, 40; PC 6; WLC 1**
See also AAYA 51; BRW 3; CDBLB 1789-1832; DA; DA3; DAB; DAC; DAM MST, POET; DLB 109; EXPP; PAB; RGEL 2; TEA; WP

**Burns, Tex**
See L'Amour, Louis

**Burnshaw, Stanley** 1906-2005 ..... **CLC 3, 13, 44**
See also CA 9-12R; CAAS 243; CP 1, 2, 3, 4, 5, 6, 7; DLB 48; DLBY 1997

**Burr, Anne** 1937- ................................. **CLC 6**
See also CA 25-28R

**Burroughs, Edgar Rice** 1875-1950 . **TCLC 2, 32**
See also AAYA 11; BPFB 1; BYA 4, 9; CA 132; CAAE 104; CANR 131; DA3; DAM NOV; DLB 8; FANT; MTCW 1, 2; MTFW 2005; RGAL 4; SATA 41; SCFW 1, 2; SFW 4; TCWW 1, 2; TUS; YAW

**Burroughs, William S.** 1914-1997 . **CLC 1, 2, 5, 15, 22, 42, 75, 109; TCLC 121; WLC 1**
See Lee, William; Lee, Willy
See also AAYA 60; AITN 2; AMWS 3; BG 1:2; BPFB 1; CA 9-12R; CAAS 160; CANR 20, 52, 104; CN 1, 2, 3, 4, 5, 6; CPW; DA; DA3; DAB; DAC; DAM MST, NOV, POP; DLB 2, 8, 16, 152, 237; DLBY 1981, 1997; EWL 3; HGG; LMFS 2; MAL 5; MTCW 1, 2; MTFW 2005; RGAL 4; SFW 4

**Burroughs, William Seward**
See Burroughs, William S.

**Burton, Sir Richard F(rancis)** 1821-1890 ................................ **NCLC 42**
See also DLB 55, 166, 184; SSFS 21

**Burton, Robert** 1577-1640 ................... **LC 74**
See also DLB 151; RGEL 2

**Buruma, Ian** 1951- ............................... **CLC 163**
See also CA 128; CANR 65, 141

**Busch, Frederick** 1941-2006 .. **CLC 7, 10, 18, 47, 166**
See also CA 33-36R; 1; CAAS 248; CANR 45, 73, 92, 157; CN 1, 2, 3, 4, 5, 6, 7; DLB 6, 218

**Busch, Frederick Matthew**
See Busch, Frederick

**Bush, Barney (Furman)** 1946- .......... **NNAL**
See also CA 145

**Bush, Ronald** 1946- ............................ **CLC 34**
See also CA 136

**Bustos, F(rancisco)**
See Borges, Jorge Luis

**Bustos Domecq, H(onorio)**
See Bioy Casares, Adolfo; Borges, Jorge Luis

**Butler, Octavia E.** 1947-2006 .... **BLCS; CLC 38, 121, 240**
See also AAYA 18, 48; AFAW 2; AMWS 13; BPFB 1; BW 2, 3; CA 73-76; CAAS 248; CANR 12, 24, 38, 73, 145, 240; CLR 65; CN 7; CPW; DA3; DAM MULT, POP; DLB 33; LATS 1:2; MTCW 1, 2; MTFW 2005; NFS 8, 21; SATA 84; SCFW 2; SFW 4; SSFS 6; TCLE 1:1; YAW

**Butler, Octavia Estelle**
See Butler, Octavia E.

**Butler, Robert Olen, (Jr.)** 1945- ...... **CLC 81, 162**
See also AMWS 12; BPFB 1; CA 112; CANR 66, 138; CN 7; CSW; DAM POP; DLB 173, 335; INT CA-112; MAL 5; MTCW 2; MTFW 2005; SSFS 11, 22

**Butler, Samuel** 1612-1680 ............. **LC 16, 43**
See also DLB 101, 126; RGEL 2

**Butler, Samuel** 1835-1902 ......... **TCLC 1, 33; WLC 1**
See also BRWS 2; CA 143; CDBLB 1890-1914; DA; DA3; DAB; DAC; DAM MST, NOV; DLB 18, 57, 174; RGEL 2; SFW 4; TEA

**Butler, Walter C.**
See Faust, Frederick (Schiller)

**Butor, Michel (Marie Francois)** 1926- ................ **CLC 1, 3, 8, 11, 15, 161**
See also CA 9-12R; CANR 33, 66; CWW 2; DLB 83; EW 13; EWL 3; GFL 1789 to the Present; MTCW 1, 2; MTFW 2005

**Butts, Mary** 1890(?)-1937 ............... **TCLC 77**
See also CA 148; DLB 240

**Buxton, Ralph**
See Silverstein, Alvin; Silverstein, Virginia B(arbara Opshelor)

**Buzo, Alex**
See Buzo, Alexander (John)
See also DLB 289

**Buzo, Alexander (John)** 1944- .......... **CLC 61**
See also CA 97-100; CANR 17, 39, 69; CD 5, 6

**Buzzati, Dino** 1906-1972 ................... **CLC 36**
See also CA 160; CAAS 33-36R; DLB 177; RGWL 2, 3; SFW 4

**Byars, Betsy** 1928- ............................ **CLC 35**
See also AAYA 19; BYA 3; CA 183; 33-36R, 183; CANR 18, 36, 57, 102, 148; CLR 1, 16, 72; DLB 52; INT CANR-18; JRDA; MAICYA 1, 2; MAICYAS 1; MTCW 1; SAAS 1; SATA 4, 46, 80, 163; SATA-Essay 108; WYA; YAW

**Byars, Betsy Cromer**
See Byars, Betsy

**Byatt, Antonia Susan Drabble**
See Byatt, A.S.
**Byatt, A.S.** 1936- ........ **CLC 19, 65, 136, 223; SSC 91**
See also BPFB 1; BRWC 2; BRWS 4; CA 13-16R; CANR 13, 33, 50, 75, 96, 133; CN 1, 2, 3, 4, 5, 6; DA3; DAM NOV, POP; DLB 14, 194, 319, 326; EWL 3; MTCW 1, 2; MTFW 2005; RGSF 2; RHW; TEA
**Byrd, William II** 1674-1744 ............... **LC 112**
See also DLB 24, 140; RGAL 4
**Byrne, David** 1952- ............................ **CLC 26**
See also CA 127
**Byrne, John Keyes** 1926-
See Leonard, Hugh
See also CA 102; CANR 78, 140; INT CA-102
**Byron, George Gordon (Noel)**
1788-1824 ..... **DC 24; NCLC 2, 12, 109, 149; PC 16; WLC 1**
See also AAYA 64; BRW 4; BRWC 2; CD-BLB 1789-1832; DA; DA3; DAB; DAC; DAM MST, POET; DLB 96, 110; EXPP; LMFS 1; PAB; PFS 1, 14; RGEL 2; TEA; WLIT 3; WP
**Byron, Robert** 1905-1941 ............... **TCLC 67**
See also CA 160; DLB 195
**C. 3. 3.**
See Wilde, Oscar
**Caballero, Fernan** 1796-1877 ......... **NCLC 10**
**Cabell, Branch**
See Cabell, James Branch
**Cabell, James Branch** 1879-1958 .... **TCLC 6**
See also CA 152; CAAE 105; DLB 9, 78; FANT; MAL 5; MTCW 2; RGAL 4; SUFW 1
**Cabeza de Vaca, Alvar Nunez**
1490-1557(?) ................................ **LC 61**
**Cable, George Washington**
1844-1925 .................... **SSC 4; TCLC 4**
See also CA 155; CAAE 104; DLB 12, 74; DLBD 13; RGAL 4; TUS
**Cabral de Melo Neto, Joao**
1920-1999 ................................ **CLC 76**
See Melo Neto, Joao Cabral de
See also CA 151; DAM MULT; DLB 307; LAW; LAWS 1
**Cabrera Infante, G.** 1929-2005 ... **CLC 5, 25, 45, 120; HLC 1; SSC 39**
See also CA 85-88; CAAS 236; CANR 29, 65, 110; CDWLB 3; CWW 2; DA3; DAM MULT; DLB 113; EWL 3; HW 1, 2; LAW; LAWS 1; MTCW 1, 2; MTFW 2005; RGSF 2; WLIT 1
**Cabrera Infante, Guillermo**
See Cabrera Infante, G.
**Cade, Toni**
See Bambara, Toni Cade
**Cadmus and Harmonia**
See Buchan, John
**Caedmon** fl. 658-680 ...................... **CMLC 7**
See also DLB 146
**Caeiro, Alberto**
See Pessoa, Fernando (Antonio Nogueira)
**Caesar, Julius** .............................. **CMLC 47**
See Julius Caesar
See also AW 1; RGWL 2, 3; WLIT 8
**Cage, John (Milton), (Jr.)**
1912-1992 ..................... **CLC 41; PC 58**
See also CA 13-16R; CAAS 169; CANR 9, 78; DLB 193; INT CANR-9; TCLE 1:1
**Cahan, Abraham** 1860-1951 .......... **TCLC 71**
See also CA 154; CAAE 108; DLB 9, 25, 28; MAL 5; RGAL 4
**Cain, G.**
See Cabrera Infante, G.
**Cain, Guillermo**
See Cabrera Infante, G.

**Cain, James M(allahan)** 1892-1977 .. **CLC 3, 11, 28**
See also AITN 1; BPFB 1; CA 17-20R; CAAS 73-76; CANR 8, 34, 61; CMW 4; CN 1, 2; DLB 226; EWL 3; MAL 5; MSW; MTCW 1; RGAL 4
**Caine, Hall** 1853-1931 .................... **TCLC 97**
See also RHW
**Caine, Mark**
See Raphael, Frederic (Michael)
**Calasso, Roberto** 1941- ..................... **CLC 81**
See also CA 143; CANR 89
**Calderon de la Barca, Pedro**
1600-1681 . **DC 3; HLCS 1; LC 23, 136**
See also DFS 23; EW 2; RGWL 2, 3; TWA
**Caldwell, Erskine** 1903-1987 ... **CLC 1, 8, 14, 50, 60; SSC 19; TCLC 117**
See also AITN 1; AMW; BPFB 1; CA 1-4R; 1; CAAS 121; CANR 2, 33; CN 1, 2, 3, 4; DA3; DAM NOV; DLB 9, 86; EWL 3; MAL 5; MTCW 1, 2; MTFW 2005; RGAL 4; RGSF 2; TUS
**Caldwell, (Janet Miriam) Taylor (Holland)**
1900-1985 ........................ **CLC 2, 28, 39**
See also BPFB 1; CA 5-8R; CAAS 116; CANR 5; DA3; DAM NOV, POP; DLBD 17; MTCW 2; RHW
**Calhoun, John Caldwell**
1782-1850 ................................ **NCLC 15**
See also DLB 3, 248
**Calisher, Hortense** 1911- ..... **CLC 2, 4, 8, 38, 134; SSC 15**
See also CA 1-4R; CANR 1, 22, 117; CN 1, 2, 3, 4, 5, 6, 7; DA3; DAM NOV; DLB 2, 218; INT CANR-22; MAL 5; MTCW 1, 2; MTFW 2005; RGAL 4; RGSF 2
**Callaghan, Morley Edward**
1903-1990 ..... **CLC 3, 14, 41, 65; TCLC 145**
See also CA 9-12R; CAAS 132; CANR 33, 73; CN 1, 2, 3, 4; DAC; DAM MST; DLB 68; EWL 3; MTCW 1, 2; MTFW 2005; RGEL 2; RGSF 2; SSFS 19
**Callimachus** c. 305B.C.-c.
240B.C. ................................ **CMLC 18**
See also AW 1; DLB 176; RGWL 2, 3
**Calvin, Jean**
See Calvin, John
See also DLB 327; GFL Beginnings to 1789
**Calvin, John** 1509-1564 ...................... **LC 37**
See Calvin, Jean
**Calvino, Italo** 1923-1985 .... **CLC 5, 8, 11, 22, 33, 39, 73; SSC 3, 48; TCLC 183**
See also AAYA 58; CA 85-88; CAAS 116; CANR 23, 61, 132; DAM NOV; DLB 196; EW 13; EWL 3; MTCW 1, 2; MTFW 2005; RGHL; RGSF 2; RGWL 2, 3; SFW 4; SSFS 12; WLIT 7
**Camara Laye**
See Laye, Camara
See also EWL 3
**Camden, William** 1551-1623 ............... **LC 77**
See also DLB 172
**Cameron, Carey** 1952- ..................... **CLC 59**
See also CA 135
**Cameron, Peter** 1959- ....................... **CLC 44**
See also AMWS 12; CA 125; CANR 50, 117; DLB 234; GLL 2
**Camoens, Luis Vaz de** 1524(?)-1580
See Camoes, Luis de
See also EW 2
**Camoes, Luis de** 1524(?)-1580 . **HLCS 1; LC 62; PC 31**
See Camoens, Luis Vaz de
See also DLB 287; RGWL 2, 3
**Campana, Dino** 1885-1932 .............. **TCLC 20**
See also CA 246; CAAE 117; DLB 114; EWL 3

**Campanella, Tommaso** 1568-1639 ....... **LC 32**
See also RGWL 2, 3
**Campbell, Bebe Moore** 1950-2006 . **CLC 246**
See also AAYA 26; BW 2, 3; CA 139; CAAS 254; CANR 81, 134; DLB 227; MTCW 2; MTFW 2005
**Campbell, John W(ood, Jr.)**
1910-1971 .................................... **CLC 32**
See also CA 21-22; CAAS 29-32R; CANR 34; CAP 2; DLB 8; MTCW 1; SCFW 1, 2; SFW 4
**Campbell, Joseph** 1904-1987 .......... **CLC 69; TCLC 140**
See also AAYA 3, 66; BEST 89:2; CA 1-4R; CAAS 124; CANR 3, 28, 61, 107; DA3; MTCW 1, 2
**Campbell, Maria** 1940- ....... **CLC 85; NNAL**
See also CA 102; CANR 54; CCA 1; DAC
**Campbell, (John) Ramsey** 1946- ..... **CLC 42; SSC 19**
See also AAYA 51; CA 228; 57-60, 228; CANR 7, 102; DLB 261; HGG; INT CANR-7; SUFW 1, 2
**Campbell, (Ignatius) Roy (Dunnachie)**
1901-1957 ................................... **TCLC 5**
See also AFW; CA 155; CAAE 104; DLB 20, 225; EWL 3; MTCW 2; RGEL 2
**Campbell, Thomas** 1777-1844 ....... **NCLC 19**
See also DLB 93, 144; RGEL 2
**Campbell, Wilfred** ......................... **TCLC 9**
See Campbell, William
**Campbell, William** 1858(?)-1918
See Campbell, Wilfred
See also CAAE 106; DLB 92
**Campbell, William Edward March**
1893-1954
See March, William
See also CAAE 108
**Campion, Jane** 1954- ................. **CLC 95, 229**
See also AAYA 33; CA 138; CANR 87
**Campion, Thomas** 1567-1620 ............. **LC 78**
See also CDBLB Before 1660; DAM POET; DLB 58, 172; RGEL 2
**Camus, Albert** 1913-1960 ...... **CLC 1, 2, 4, 9, 11, 14, 32, 63, 69, 124; DC 2; SSC 9, 76; WLC 1**
See also AAYA 36; AFW; BPFB 1; CA 89-92; CANR 131; DA; DA3; DAB; DAC; DAM DRAM, MST, NOV; DLB 72, 321, 329; EW 13; EWL 3; EXPN; EXPS; GFL 1789 to the Present; LATS 1:2; LMFS 2; MTCW 1, 2; MTFW 2005; NFS 6, 16; RGHL; RGSF 4; RGWL 2, 3; SSFS 4; TWA
**Canby, Vincent** 1924-2000 ................. **CLC 13**
See also CA 81-84; CAAS 191
**Cancale**
See Desnos, Robert
**Canetti, Elias** 1905-1994 .. **CLC 3, 14, 25, 75, 86; TCLC 157**
See also CA 21-24R; CAAS 146; CANR 23, 61, 79; CDWLB 2; CWW 2; DA3; DLB 85, 124, 329; EW 12; EWL 3; MTCW 1, 2; MTFW 2005; RGWL 2, 3; TWA
**Canfield, Dorothea F.**
See Fisher, Dorothy (Frances) Canfield
**Canfield, Dorothea Frances**
See Fisher, Dorothy (Frances) Canfield
**Canfield, Dorothy**
See Fisher, Dorothy (Frances) Canfield
**Canin, Ethan** 1960- ............. **CLC 55; SSC 70**
See also CA 135; CAAE 131; DLB 335; MAL 5
**Cankar, Ivan** 1876-1918 ............... **TCLC 105**
See also CDWLB 4; DLB 147; EWL 3
**Cannon, Curt**
See Hunter, Evan

Cao, Lan 1961- ............................ **CLC 109**
See also CA 165
**Cape, Judith**
See Page, P(atricia) K(athleen)
See also CCA 1
**Capek, Karel** 1890-1938 ........ **DC 1; SSC 36;**
**TCLC 6, 37, 192; WLC 1**
See also CA 140; CAAE 104; CDWLB 4;
DA; DA3; DAB; DAC; DAM DRAM,
MST, NOV; DFS 7, 11; DLB 215; EW
10; EWL 3; MTCW 2; MTFW 2005;
RGSF 2; RGWL 2, 3; SCFW 1, 2; SFW 4
**Capella, Martianus** fl. 4th cent. - .. **CMLC 84**
**Capote, Truman** 1924-1984 . **CLC 1, 3, 8, 13,**
**19, 34, 38, 58; SSC 2, 47, 93; TCLC**
**164; WLC 1**
See also AAYA 61; AMWS 3; BPFB 1; CA
5-8R; CAAS 113; CANR 18, 62; CDALB
1941-1968; CN 1, 2, 3; CPW; DA; DA3;
DAB; DAC; DAM MST, NOV, POP;
DLB 2, 185, 227; DLBY 1980, 1984;
EWL 3; EXPS; GLL 1; LAIT 3; MAL 5;
MTCW 1, 2; MTFW 2005; NCFS 2;
RGAL 4; RGSF 2; SATA 91; SSFS 2;
TUS
**Capra, Frank** 1897-1991 ................... **CLC 16**
See also AAYA 52; CA 61-64; CAAS 135
**Caputo, Philip** 1941- .......................... **CLC 32**
See also AAYA 60; CA 73-76; CANR 40,
135; YAW
**Caragiale, Ion Luca** 1852-1912 ...... **TCLC 76**
See also CA 157
**Card, Orson Scott** 1951- ....... **CLC 44, 47, 50**
See also AAYA 11, 42; BPFB 1; BYA 5, 8;
CA 102; CANR 27, 47, 73, 102, 106, 133;
CLR 116; CPW; DA3; DAM POP; FANT;
INT CANR-27; MTCW 1, 2; MTFW
2005; NFS 5; SATA 83, 127; SCFW 2;
SFW 4; SUFW 2; YAW
**Cardenal, Ernesto** 1925- .......... **CLC 31, 161;**
**HLC 1; PC 22**
See also CA 49-52; CANR 2, 32, 66, 138;
CWW 2; DAM MULT, POET; DLB 290;
EWL 3; HW 1, 2; LAWS 1; MTCW 1, 2;
MTFW 2005; RGWL 2, 3
**Cardinal, Marie** 1929-2001 ............. **CLC 189**
See also CA 177; CWW 2; DLB 83; FW
**Cardozo, Benjamin N(athan)**
1870-1938 ............................... **TCLC 65**
See also CA 164; CAAE 117
**Carducci, Giosue (Alessandro Giuseppe)**
1835-1907 ................... **PC 46; TCLC 32**
See also CA 163; DLB 329; EW 7; RGWL
2, 3
**Carew, Thomas** 1595(?)-1640 . **LC 13; PC 29**
See also BRW 2; DLB 126; PAB; RGEL 2
**Carey, Ernestine Gilbreth**
1908-2006 ............................... **CLC 17**
See also CA 5-8R; CAAS 254; CANR 71;
SATA 2; SATA-Obit 177
**Carey, Peter** 1943- ......... **CLC 40, 55, 96, 183**
See also BRWS 12; CA 127; CAAE 123;
CANR 53, 76, 117, 157; CN 4, 5, 6, 7;
DLB 289, 326; EWL 3; INT CA-127;
MTCW 1, 2; MTFW 2005; RGSF 2;
SATA 94
**Carleton, William** 1794-1869 .......... **NCLC 3**
See also DLB 159; RGEL 2; RGSF 2
**Carlisle, Henry (Coffin)** 1926- .......... **CLC 33**
See also CA 13-16R; CANR 15, 85
**Carlsen, Chris**
See Holdstock, Robert
**Carlson, Ron** 1947- ........................... **CLC 54**
See also CA 189; 105, 189; CANR 27, 155;
DLB 244
**Carlson, Ronald F.**
See Carlson, Ron
**Carlyle, Jane Welsh** 1801-1866 ... **NCLC 181**
See also DLB 55

**Carlyle, Thomas** 1795-1881 ..... **NCLC 22, 70**
See also BRW 4; CDBLB 1789-1832; DA;
DAB; DAC; DAM MST; DLB 55, 144,
254, 338; RGEL 2; TEA
**Carman, (William) Bliss** 1861-1929 ... **PC 34;**
**TCLC 7**
See also CA 152; CAAE 104; DAC; DLB
92; RGEL 2
**Carnegie, Dale** 1888-1955 .............. **TCLC 53**
See also CA 218
**Carossa, Hans** 1878-1956 .............. **TCLC 48**
See also CA 170; DLB 66; EWL 3
**Carpenter, Don(ald Richard)**
1931-1995 ............................... **CLC 41**
See also CA 45-48; CAAS 149; CANR 1,
71
**Carpenter, Edward** 1844-1929 ....... **TCLC 88**
See also BRWS 13; CA 163; GLL 1
**Carpenter, John (Howard)** 1948- ... **CLC 161**
See also AAYA 2, 73; CA 134; SATA 58
**Carpenter, Johnny**
See Carpenter, John (Howard)
**Carpentier (y Valmont), Alejo**
1904-1980 . **CLC 8, 11, 38, 110; HLC 1;**
**SSC 35**
See also CA 65-68; CAAS 97-100; CANR
11, 70; CDWLB 3; DAM MULT; DLB
113; EWL 3; HW 1, 2; LAW; LMFS 2;
RGSF 2; RGWL 2, 3; WLIT 1
**Carr, Caleb** 1955- .............................. **CLC 86**
See also CA 147; CANR 73, 134; DA3
**Carr, Emily** 1871-1945 ..................... **TCLC 32**
See also CA 159; DLB 68; FW; GLL 2
**Carr, John Dickson** 1906-1977 .......... **CLC 3**
See Fairbairn, Roger
See also CA 49-52; CAAS 69-72; CANR 3,
33, 60; CMW 4; DLB 306; MSW; MTCW
1, 2
**Carr, Philippa**
See Hibbert, Eleanor Alice Burford
**Carr, Virginia Spencer** 1929- ........... **CLC 34**
See also CA 61-64; DLB 111
**Carrere, Emmanuel** 1957- ................ **CLC 89**
See also CA 200
**Carrier, Roch** 1937- ...................... **CLC 13, 78**
See also CA 130; CANR 61, 152; CCA 1;
DAC; DAM MST; DLB 53; SATA 105,
166
**Carroll, James Dennis**
See Carroll, Jim
**Carroll, James P.** 1943(?)- ................. **CLC 38**
See also CA 81-84; CANR 73, 139; MTCW
2; MTFW 2005
**Carroll, Jim** 1951- ...................... **CLC 35, 143**
See also AAYA 17; CA 45-48; CANR 42,
115; NCFS 5
**Carroll, Lewis** ...... **NCLC 2, 53, 139; PC 18,**
**74; WLC 1**
See Dodgson, Charles L(utwidge)
See also AAYA 39; BRW 5; BYA 5, 13; CD-
BLB 1832-1890; CLR 2, 18, 108; DLB
18, 163, 178; DLBY 1998; EXPN; EXPP;
FANT; JRDA; LAIT 1; NFS 7; PFS 11;
RGEL 2; SUFW 1; TEA; WCH
**Carroll, Paul Vincent** 1900-1968 ...... **CLC 10**
See also CA 9-12R; CAAS 25-28R; DLB
10; EWL 3; RGEL 2
**Carruth, Hayden** 1921- ..... **CLC 4, 7, 10, 18,**
**84; PC 10**
See also AMWS 16; CA 9-12R; CANR 4,
38, 59, 110; CP 1, 2, 3, 4, 5, 6, 7; DLB 5,
165; INT CANR-4; MTCW 1, 2; MTFW
2005; PFS 26; SATA 47
**Carson, Anne** 1950- ........... **CLC 185; PC 64**
See also AMWS 12; CA 203; CP 7; DLB
193; PFS 18; TCLE 1:1
**Carson, Ciaran** 1948- ...................... **CLC 201**
See also BRWS 13; CA 153; CAAE 112;
CANR 113; CP 6, 7; PFS 26

**Carson, Rachel**
See Carson, Rachel Louise
See also AAYA 49; DLB 275
**Carson, Rachel Louise** 1907-1964 .... **CLC 71**
See Carson, Rachel
See also AMWS 9; ANW; CA 77-80; CANR
35; DA3; DAM POP; FW; LAIT 4; MAL
5; MTCW 1, 2; MTFW 2005; NCFS 1;
SATA 23
**Carter, Angela** 1940-1992 ...... **CLC 5, 41, 76;**
**SSC 13, 85; TCLC 139**
See also BRWS 3; CA 53-56; CAAS 136;
CANR 12, 36, 61, 106; CN 3, 4, 5; DA3;
DLB 14, 207, 261, 319; EXPS; FANT;
FW; GL 2; MTCW 1, 2; MTFW 2005;
RGSF 2; SATA 66; SATA-Obit 70; SFW
4; SSFS 4, 12; SUFW 2; WLIT 4
**Carter, Angela Olive**
See Carter, Angela
**Carter, Nick**
See Smith, Martin Cruz
**Carver, Raymond** 1938-1988 ..... **CLC 22, 36,**
**53, 55, 126; PC 54; SSC 8, 51, 104**
See also AAYA 44; AMWS 3; BPFB 1; CA
33-36R; CAAS 126; CANR 17, 34, 61,
103; CN 4; CPW; DA3; DAM NOV; DLB
130; DLBY 1984, 1988; EWL 3; MAL 5;
MTCW 1, 2; MTFW 2005; PFS 17;
RGAL 4; RGSF 2; SSFS 3, 6, 12, 13, 23;
TCLE 1:1; TCWW 2; TUS
**Cary, Elizabeth, Lady Falkland**
1585-1639 ............................... **LC 30, 141**
**Cary, (Arthur) Joyce (Lunel)**
1888-1957 ....................... **TCLC 1, 29, 196**
See also BRW 7; CA 164; CAAE 104; CD-
BLB 1914-1945; DLB 15, 100; EWL 3;
MTCW 2; RGEL 2; TEA
**Casal, Julian del** 1863-1893 ......... **NCLC 131**
See also DLB 283; LAW
**Casanova, Giacomo**
See Casanova de Seingalt, Giovanni Jacopo
See also WLIT 7
**Casanova de Seingalt, Giovanni Jacopo**
1725-1798 ............................... **LC 13**
See Casanova, Giacomo
**Casares, Adolfo Bioy**
See Bioy Casares, Adolfo
See also RGSF 2
**Casas, Bartolome de las** 1474-1566
See Las Casas, Bartolome de
See also WLIT 1
**Case, John**
See Hougan, Carolyn
**Casely-Hayford, J(oseph) E(phraim)**
1866-1903 ................... **BLC 1; TCLC 24**
See also BW 2; CA 152; CAAE 123; DAM
MULT
**Casey, John (Dudley)** 1939- ............. **CLC 59**
See also BEST 90:2; CA 69-72; CANR 23,
100
**Casey, Michael** 1947- ......................... **CLC 2**
See also CA 65-68; CANR 109; CP 2, 3;
DLB 5
**Casey, Patrick**
See Thurman, Wallace (Henry)
**Casey, Warren (Peter)** 1935-1988 .... **CLC 12**
See also CA 101; CAAS 127; INT CA-101
**Casona, Alejandro** .......................... **CLC 49**
See Alvarez, Alejandro Rodriguez
See also EWL 3
**Cassavetes, John** 1929-1989 ............. **CLC 20**
See also CA 85-88; CAAS 127; CANR 82
**Cassian, Nina** 1924- ......................... **PC 17**
See also CWP; CWW 2
**Cassill, R(onald) V(erlin)**
1919-2002 ............................... **CLC 4, 23**
See also CA 9-12R; 1; CAAS 208; CANR
7, 45; CN 1, 2, 3, 4, 5, 6, 7; DLB 6, 218;
DLBY 2002

**Chapman, George** 1559(?)-1634 . **DC 19; LC 22, 116**
See also BRW 1; DAM DRAM; DLB 62, 121; LMFS 1; RGEL 2

**Chapman, Graham** 1941-1989 ......... **CLC 21**
See Monty Python
See also CA 116; CAAS 129; CANR 35, 95

**Chapman, John Jay** 1862-1933 ....... **TCLC 7**
See also AMWS 14; CA 191; CAAE 104

**Chapman, Lee**
See Bradley, Marion Zimmer
See also GLL 1

**Chapman, Walker**
See Silverberg, Robert

**Chappell, Fred (Davis)** 1936- .... **CLC 40, 78, 162**
See also CA 198; 5-8R, 198; 4; CANR 8, 33, 67, 110; CN 6; CP 6, 7; CSW; DLB 6, 105; HGG

**Char, Rene(-Emile)** 1907-1988 .... **CLC 9, 11, 14, 55; PC 56**
See also CA 13-16R; CAAS 124; CANR 32; DAM POET; DLB 258; EWL 3; GFL 1789 to the Present; MTCW 1, 2; RGWL 2, 3

**Charby, Jay**
See Ellison, Harlan

**Chardin, Pierre Teilhard de**
See Teilhard de Chardin, (Marie Joseph) Pierre

**Chariton** fl. 1st cent. (?)- ................ **CMLC 49**

**Charlemagne** 742-814 .................... **CMLC 37**

**Charles I** 1600-1649 ............................. **LC 13**

**Charriere, Isabelle de** 1740-1805 .. **NCLC 66**
See also DLB 313

**Chartier, Alain** c. 1392-1430 ............... **LC 94**
See also DLB 208

**Chartier, Emile-Auguste**
See Alain

**Charyn, Jerome** 1937- ............. **CLC 5, 8, 18**
See also CA 5-8R; 1; CANR 7, 61, 101, 158; CMW 4; CN 1, 2, 3, 4, 5, 6, 7; DLBY 1983; MTCW 1

**Chase, Adam**
See Marlowe, Stephen

**Chase, Mary (Coyle)** 1907-1981 ........... **DC 1**
See also CA 77-80; CAAS 105; CAD; CWD; DFS 11; DLB 228; SATA 17; SATA-Obit 29

**Chase, Mary Ellen** 1887-1973 .......... **CLC 2; TCLC 124**
See also CA 13-16; CAAS 41-44R; CAP 1; SATA 10

**Chase, Nicholas**
See Hyde, Anthony
See also CCA 1

**Chateaubriand, Francois Rene de** 1768-1848 ......................... **NCLC 3, 134**
See also DLB 119; EW 5; GFL 1789 to the Present; RGWL 2, 3; TWA

**Chatelet, Gabrielle-Emilie Du**
See du Chatelet, Emilie
See also DLB 313

**Chatterje, Sarat Chandra** 1876-1936(?)
See Chatterji, Saratchandra
See also CAAE 109

**Chatterji, Bankim Chandra** 1838-1894 ................................ **NCLC 19**

**Chatterji, Saratchandra** ................ **TCLC 13**
See Chatterje, Sarat Chandra
See also CA 186; EWL 3

**Chatterton, Thomas** 1752-1770 ....... **LC 3, 54**
See also DAM POET; DLB 109; RGEL 2

**Chatwin, (Charles) Bruce** 1940-1989 ..................... **CLC 28, 57, 59**
See also AAYA 4; BEST 90:1; BRWS 4; CA 85-88; CAAS 127; CPW; DAM POP; DLB 194, 204; EWL 3; MTFW 2005

**Chaucer, Daniel**
See Ford, Ford Madox
See also RHW

**Chaucer, Geoffrey** 1340(?)-1400 .. **LC 17, 56; PC 19, 58; WLCS**
See also BRW 1; BRWC 1; BRWR 2; CD-BLB Before 1660; DA; DA3; DAB; DAC; DAM MST, POET; DLB 146; LAIT 1; PAB; PFS 14; RGEL 2; TEA; WLIT 3; WP

**Chavez, Denise** 1948- .......................... **HLC 1**
See also CA 131; CANR 56, 81, 137; DAM MULT; DLB 122; FW; HW 1; LLW; MAL 5; MTCW 2; MTFW 2005

**Chaviaras, Strates** 1935-
See Haviaras, Stratis
See also CA 105

**Chayefsky, Paddy** ............................. **CLC 23**
See Chayefsky, Sidney
See also CAD; DLB 7, 44; DLBY 1981; RGAL 4

**Chayefsky, Sidney** 1923-1981
See Chayefsky, Paddy
See also CA 9-12R; CAAS 104; CANR 18; DAM DRAM

**Chedid, Andree** 1920- ....................... **CLC 47**
See also CA 145; CANR 95; EWL 3

**Cheever, John** 1912-1982 ..... **CLC 3, 7, 8, 11, 15, 25, 64; SSC 1, 38, 57; WLC 2**
See also AAYA 65; AMWS 1; BPFB 1; CA 5-8R; CAAS 106; CABS 1; CANR 5, 27, 76; CDALB 1941-1968; CN 1, 2, 3; CPW; DA; DA3; DAB; DAC; DAM MST, NOV, POP; DLB 2, 102, 227; DLBY 1980, 1982; EWL 3; EXPS; INT CANR-5; MAL 5; MTCW 1, 2; MTFW 2005; RGAL 4; RGSF 2; SSFS 2, 14; TUS

**Cheever, Susan** 1943- ................. **CLC 18, 48**
See also CA 103; CANR 27, 51, 92, 157; DLBY 1982; INT CANR-27

**Chekhonte, Antosha**
See Chekhov, Anton (Pavlovich)

**Chekhov, Anton (Pavlovich)** 1860-1904 ....... **DC 9; SSC 2, 28, 41, 51, 85, 102; TCLC 3, 10, 31, 55, 96, 163; WLC 2**
See also AAYA 68; BYA 14; CA 124; CAAE 104; DA; DA3; DAB; DAC; DAM DRAM, MST; DFS 1, 5, 10, 12; DLB 277; EW 7; EWL 3; EXPS; LAIT 3; LATS 1:1; RGSF 2; RGWL 2, 3; SATA 90; SSFS 5, 13, 14; TWA

**Cheney, Lynne V.** 1941- .................... **CLC 70**
See also CA 89-92; CANR 58, 117; SATA 152

**Chernyshevsky, Nikolai Gavrilovich**
See Chernyshevsky, Nikolay Gavrilovich
See also DLB 238

**Chernyshevsky, Nikolay Gavrilovich** 1828-1889 ................................ **NCLC 1**
See Chernyshevsky, Nikolai Gavrilovich

**Cherry, Carolyn Janice** .................... **CLC 35**
See Cherryh, C.J.
See also AAYA 24; BPFB 1; DLBY 1980; FANT; SATA 93; SCFW 2; SFW 4; YAW

**Cherryh, C.J.** 1942-
See Cherry, Carolyn Janice
See also CA 65-68; CANR 10, 147; SATA 172

**Chesnutt, Charles W(addell)** 1858-1932 .... **BLC 1; SSC 7, 54; TCLC 5, 39**
See also AFAW 1, 2; AMWS 14; BW 1, 3; CA 125; CAAE 106; CANR 76; DAM MULT; DLB 12, 50, 78; EWL 3; MAL 5; MTCW 1, 2; MTFW 2005; RGAL 4; RGSF 2; SSFS 11

**Chester, Alfred** 1929(?)-1971 ............ **CLC 49**
See also CA 196; CAAS 33-36R; DLB 130; MAL 5

**Chesterton, G(ilbert) K(eith)** 1874-1936 . **PC 28; SSC 1, 46; TCLC 1, 6, 64**
See also AAYA 57; BRW 6; CA 132; CAAE 104; CANR 73, 131; CDBLB 1914-1945; CMW 4; DAM NOV, POET; DLB 10, 19, 34, 70, 98, 149, 178; EWL 3; FANT; MSW; MTCW 1, 2; MTFW 2005; RGEL 2; RGSF 2; SATA 27; SUFW 1

**Chettle, Henry** 1560-1607(?) ............. **LC 112**
See also DLB 136; RGEL 2

**Chiang, Pin-chin** 1904-1986
See Ding Ling
See also CAAS 118

**Chief Joseph** 1840-1904 .................... **NNAL**
See also CA 152; DA3; DAM MULT

**Chief Seattle** 1786(?)-1866 ................. **NNAL**
See also DA3; DAM MULT

**Ch'ien, Chung-shu** 1910-1998 ......... **CLC 22**
See Qian Zhongshu
See also CA 130; CANR 73; MTCW 1, 2

**Chikamatsu Monzaemon** 1653-1724 ... **LC 66**
See also RGWL 2, 3

**Child, Francis James** 1825-1896 . **NCLC 173**
See also DLB 1, 64, 235

**Child, L. Maria**
See Child, Lydia Maria

**Child, Lydia Maria** 1802-1880 .. **NCLC 6, 73**
See also DLB 1, 74, 243; RGAL 4; SATA 67

**Child, Mrs.**
See Child, Lydia Maria

**Child, Philip** 1898-1978 .............. **CLC 19, 68**
See also CA 13-14; CAP 1; CP 1; DLB 68; RHW; SATA 47

**Childers, (Robert) Erskine** 1870-1922 ................................ **TCLC 65**
See also CA 153; CAAE 113; DLB 70

**Childress, Alice** 1920-1994 . **BLC 1; CLC 12, 15, 86, 96; DC 4; TCLC 116**
See also AAYA 8; BW 2, 3; BYA 2; CA 45-48; CAAS 146; CAD; CANR 3, 27, 50, 74; CLR 14; CWD; DA3; DAM DRAM, MULT, NOV; DFS 2, 8, 14; DLB 7, 38, 249; JRDA; LAIT 5; MAICYA 1, 2; MAI-CYAS 1; MAL 5; MTCW 1, 2; MTFW 2005; RGAL 4; SATA 7, 48, 81; TUS; WYA; YAW

**Chin, Frank (Chew, Jr.)** 1940- .... **AAL; CLC 135; DC 7**
See also CA 33-36R; CAD; CANR 71; CD 5, 6; DAM MULT; DLB 206, 312; LAIT 5; RGAL 4

**Chin, Marilyn (Mei Ling)** 1955- ......... **PC 40**
See also CA 129; CANR 70, 113; CWP; DLB 312

**Chislett, (Margaret) Anne** 1943- ...... **CLC 34**
See also CA 151

**Chitty, Thomas Willes** 1926- ............ **CLC 11**
See Hinde, Thomas
See also CA 5-8R; CN 7

**Chivers, Thomas Holley** 1809-1858 ................................ **NCLC 49**
See also DLB 3, 248; RGAL 4

**Choi, Susan** 1969- ........................... **CLC 119**
See also CA 223

**Chomette, Rene Lucien** 1898-1981
See Clair, Rene
See also CAAS 103

**Chomsky, Avram Noam**
See Chomsky, Noam

**Chomsky, Noam** 1928- .................... **CLC 132**
See also CA 17-20R; CANR 28, 62, 110, 132; DA3; DLB 246; MTCW 1, 2; MTFW 2005

**Chona, Maria** 1845(?)-1936 ............... **NNAL**
See also CA 144

**Chopin, Kate** ............ SSC 8, 68; TCLC 127; WLCS
See Chopin, Katherine
See also AAYA 33; AMWR 2; AMWS 1; BYA 11, 15; CDALB 1865-1917; DA; DAB; DLB 12, 78; EXPN; EXPS; FL 1:3; FW; LAIT 3; MAL 5; MBL; NFS 1; RGAL 4; RGSF; SSFS 2, 13, 17; TUS

**Chopin, Katherine** 1851-1904
See Chopin, Kate
See also CA 122; CAAE 104; DA3; DAC; DAM MST, NOV

**Chretien de Troyes** c. 12th cent. - . CMLC 10
See also DLB 208; EW 1; RGWL 2, 3; TWA

**Christie**
See Ichikawa, Kon

**Christie, Agatha (Mary Clarissa)**
1890-1976 .. CLC 1, 6, 8, 12, 39, 48, 110
See also AAYA 9; AITN 1, 2; BPFB 1; BRWS 2; CA 17-20R; CAAS 61-64; CANR 10, 37, 108; CBD; CDBLB 1914-1945; CMW 4; CN 1, 2; CPW; CWD; DA3; DAB; DAC; DAM NOV; DFS 2; DLB 13, 77, 245; MSW; MTCW 1, 2; MTFW 2005; NFS 8; RGEL 2; RHW; SATA 36; TEA; YAW

**Christie, Philippa** ............................ CLC 21
See Pearce, Philippa
See also BYA 5; CANR 109; CLR 9; DLB 161; MAICYA 1; SATA 1, 67, 129

**Christine de Pisan**
See Christine de Pizan
See also FW

**Christine de Pizan** 1365(?)-1431(?) ...... LC 9, 130; PC 68
See Christine de Pisan; de Pizan, Christine
See also DLB 208; FL 1:1; RGWL 2, 3

**Chuang-Tzu** c. 369B.C.-c. 286B.C. .................................... CMLC 57

**Chubb, Elmer**
See Masters, Edgar Lee

**Chulkov, Mikhail Dmitrievich**
1743-1792 .................................... LC 2
See also DLB 150

**Churchill, Caryl** 1938- ....... CLC 31, 55, 157; DC 5
See Churchill, Chick
See also BRWS 4; CA 102; CANR 22, 46, 108; CBD; CD 6; CWD; DFS 12, 16; DLB 13, 310; EWL 3; FW; MTCW 1; RGEL 2

**Churchill, Charles** 1731-1764 ................ LC 3
See also DLB 109; RGEL 2

**Churchill, Chick**
See Churchill, Caryl
See also CD 5

**Churchill, Sir Winston (Leonard Spencer)**
1874-1965 ............................. TCLC 113
See also BRW 6; CA 97-100; CDBLB 1890-1914; DA3; DLB 100, 329; DLBD 16; LAIT 4; MTCW 1, 2

**Chute, Carolyn** 1947- ........................ CLC 39
See also CA 123; CANR 135; CN 7

**Ciardi, John (Anthony)** 1916-1986 . CLC 10, 40, 44, 129; PC 69
See also CA 5-8R; 2; CAAS 118; CANR 5, 33; CLR 19; CP 1, 2, 3, 4; CWRI 5; DAM POET; DLB 5; DLBY 1986; INT CANR-5; MAICYA 1, 2; MAL 5; MTCW 1, 2; MTFW 2005; RGAL 4; SAAS 26; SATA 1, 65; SATA-Obit 46

**Cibber, Colley** 1671-1757 .................... LC 66
See also DLB 84; RGEL 2

**Cicero, Marcus Tullius**
106B.C.-43B.C. ................. CMLC 3, 81
See also AW 1; CDWLB 1; DLB 211; RGWL 2, 3; WLIT 8

**Cimino, Michael** 1943- ..................... CLC 16
See also CA 105

**Cioran, E(mil) M.** 1911-1995 ............ CLC 64
See also CA 25-28R; CAAS 149; CANR 91; DLB 220; EWL 3

**Cisneros, Sandra** 1954- .... CLC 69, 118, 193; HLC 1; PC 52; SSC 32, 72
See also AAYA 9, 53; AMWS 7; CA 131; CANR 64, 118; CLR 123; CN 7; CWP; DA3; DAM MULT; DLB 122, 152; EWL 3; EXPN; FL 1:5; FW; HW 1, 2; LAIT 5; LATS 1:2; LLW; MAICYA 2; MAL 5; MTCW 2; MTFW 2005; NFS 2; PFS 19; RGAL 4; RGSF 2; SSFS 3, 13; WLIT 1; YAW

**Cixous, Helene** 1937- ....................... CLC 92
See also CA 126; CANR 55, 123; CWW 2; DLB 83, 242; EWL 3; FL 1:5; FW; GLL 2; MTCW 1, 2; MTFW 2005; TWA

**Clair, Rene** ...................................... CLC 20
See Chomette, Rene Lucien

**Clampitt, Amy** 1920-1994 .... CLC 32; PC 19
See also AMWS 9; CA 110; CAAS 146; CANR 29, 79; CP 4, 5; DLB 105; MAL 5; PFS 27

**Clancy, Thomas L., Jr.** 1947-
See Clancy, Tom
See also CA 131; CAAE 125; CANR 62, 105; DA3; INT CA-131; MTCW 1, 2; MTFW 2005

**Clancy, Tom** ............................. CLC 45, 112
See Clancy, Thomas L., Jr.
See also AAYA 9, 51; BEST 89:1, 90:1; BPFB 1; BYA 10, 11; CANR 132; CMW 4; CPW; DAM NOV, POP; DLB 227

**Clare, John** 1793-1864 .. NCLC 9, 86; PC 23
See also BRWS 11; DAB; DAM POET; DLB 55, 96; RGEL 2

**Clarin**
See Alas (y Urena), Leopoldo (Enrique Garcia)

**Clark, Al C.**
See Goines, Donald

**Clark, Brian (Robert)**
See Clark, (Robert) Brian
See also CD 6

**Clark, (Robert) Brian** 1932- ............. CLC 29
See Clark, Brian (Robert)
See also CA 41-44R; CANR 67; CBD; CD 5

**Clark, Curt**
See Westlake, Donald E.

**Clark, Eleanor** 1913-1996 ............ CLC 5, 19
See also CA 9-12R; CAAS 151; CANR 41; CN 1, 2, 3, 4, 5, 6; DLB 6

**Clark, J. P.**
See Clark Bekederemo, J.P.
See also CDWLB 3; DLB 117

**Clark, John Pepper**
See Clark Bekederemo, J.P.
See also AFW; CD 5; CP 1, 2, 3, 4, 5, 6, 7; RGEL 2

**Clark, Kenneth (Mackenzie)**
1903-1983 ............................. TCLC 147
See also CA 93-96; CAAS 109; CANR 36; MTCW 1, 2; MTFW 2005

**Clark, M. R.**
See Clark, Mavis Thorpe

**Clark, Mavis Thorpe** 1909-1999 ...... CLC 12
See also CA 57-60; CANR 8, 37, 107; CLR 30; CWRI 5; MAICYA 1, 2; SAAS 5; SATA 8, 74

**Clark, Walter Van Tilburg**
1909-1971 ................................ CLC 28
See also CA 9-12R; CAAS 33-36R; CANR 63, 113; CN 1; DLB 9, 206; LAIT 2; MAL 5; RGAL 4; SATA 8; TCWW 1, 2

**Clark Bekederemo, J.P.** 1935- . BLC 1; CLC 38; DC 5
See Bekederemo, J. P. Clark; Clark, J. P.; Clark, John Pepper
See also BW 1; CA 65-68; CANR 16, 72; DAM DRAM, MULT; DFS 13; EWL 3; MTCW 2; MTFW 2005

**Clarke, Arthur C.** 1917- .... CLC 1, 4, 13, 18, 35, 136; SSC 3
See also AAYA 4, 33; BPFB 1; BYA 13; CA 1-4R; CANR 2, 28, 55, 74, 130; CLR 119; CN 1, 2, 3, 4, 5, 6, 7; CPW; DAM POP; DLB 261; JRDA; LAIT 5; MAICYA 1, 2; MTCW 1, 2; MTFW 2005; SATA 13, 70, 115; SCFW 1, 2; SFW 4; SSFS 4, 18; TCLE 1:1; YAW

**Clarke, Austin** 1896-1974 ................ CLC 6, 9
See also CA 29-32; CAAS 49-52; CAP 2; CP 1, 2; DAM POET; DLB 10, 20; EWL 3; RGEL 2

**Clarke, Austin C.** 1934- . BLC 1; CLC 8, 53; SSC 45
See also BW 1; CA 25-28R; 16; CANR 14, 32, 68, 140; CN 1, 2, 3, 4, 5, 6, 7; DAC; DAM MULT; DLB 53, 125; DNFS 2; MTCW 1; MTFW 2005; RGSF 2

**Clarke, Gillian** 1937- ........................ CLC 61
See also CA 106; CP 3, 4, 5, 6, 7; CWP; DLB 40

**Clarke, Marcus (Andrew Hislop)**
1846-1881 ................ NCLC 19; SSC 94
See also DLB 230; RGEL 2; RGSF 2

**Clarke, Shirley** 1925-1997 ................. CLC 16
See also CA 189

**Clash, The**
See Headon, (Nicky) Topper; Jones, Mick; Simonon, Paul; Strummer, Joe

**Claudel, Paul (Louis Charles Marie)**
1868-1955 ........................... TCLC 2, 10
See also CA 165; CAAE 104; DLB 192, 258, 321; EW 8; EWL 3; GFL 1789 to the Present; RGWL 2, 3; TWA

**Claudian** 370(?)-404(?) .................... CMLC 46
See also RGWL 2, 3

**Claudius, Matthias** 1740-1815 ....... NCLC 75
See also DLB 97

**Clavell, James** 1925-1994 ....... CLC 6, 25, 87
See also BPFB 1; CA 25-28R; CAAS 146; CANR 26, 48; CN 5; CPW; DA3; DAM NOV, POP; MTCW 1, 2; MTFW 2005; NFS 10; RHW

**Clayman, Gregory** ........................... CLC 65

**Cleaver, (Leroy) Eldridge**
1935-1998 ............. BLC 1; CLC 30, 119
See also BW 1, 3; CA 21-24R; CAAS 167; CANR 16, 75; DA3; DAM MULT; MTCW 2; YAW

**Cleese, John (Marwood)** 1939- ......... CLC 21
See Monty Python
See also CA 116; CAAE 112; CANR 35; MTCW 1

**Cleishbotham, Jebediah**
See Scott, Sir Walter

**Cleland, John** 1710-1789 ................ LC 2, 48
See also DLB 39; RGEL 2

**Clemens, Samuel Langhorne** 1835-1910
See Twain, Mark
See also CA 135; CAAE 104; CDALB 1865-1917; DA; DA3; DAB; DAC; DAM MST, NOV; DLB 12, 23, 64, 74, 186, 189; JRDA; LMFS 1; MAICYA 1, 2; NCFS 4; NFS 20; SATA 100; YABC 2

**Clement of Alexandria**
150(?)-215(?) ........................... CMLC 41

**Cleophil**
See Congreve, William

**Clerihew, E.**
See Bentley, E(dmund) C(lerihew)

Clerk, N. W.
See Lewis, C.S.

Cleveland, John 1613-1658 ................ **LC 106**
See also DLB 126; RGEL 2

Cliff, Jimmy ................................ **CLC 21**
See Chambers, James
See also CA 193

Cliff, Michelle 1946- ........... **BLCS; CLC 120**
See also BW 2; CA 116; CANR 39, 72; CD-WLB 3; DLB 157; FW; GLL 2

Clifford, Lady Anne 1590-1676 .......... **LC 76**
See also DLB 151

Clifton, Lucille 1936- ... **BLC 1; CLC 19, 66, 162; PC 17**
See also AFAW 2; BW 2, 3; CA 49-52; CANR 2, 24, 42, 76, 97, 138; CLR 5; CP 2, 3, 4, 5, 6, 7; CSW; CWP; CWRI 5; DA3; DAM MULT, POET; DLB 5, 41; EXPP; MAICYA 1, 2; MTCW 1, 2; MTFW 2005; PFS 1, 14; SATA 20, 69, 128; WP

Clinton, Dirk
See Silverberg, Robert

Clough, Arthur Hugh 1819-1861 .. **NCLC 27, 163**
See also BRW 5; DLB 32; RGEL 2

Clutha, Janet Paterson Frame 1924-2004
See Frame, Janet
See also CA 1-4R; CAAS 224; CANR 2, 36, 76, 135; MTCW 1, 2; SATA 119

Clyne, Terence
See Blatty, William Peter

Cobalt, Martin
See Mayne, William (James Carter)

Cobb, Irvin S(hrewsbury)
1876-1944 ................................ **TCLC 77**
See also CA 175; DLB 11, 25, 86

Cobbett, William 1763-1835 .......... **NCLC 49**
See also DLB 43, 107, 158; RGEL 2

Coburn, D(onald) L(ee) 1938- .......... **CLC 10**
See also CA 89-92; DFS 23

Cocteau, Jean 1889-1963 ... **CLC 1, 8, 15, 16, 43; DC 17; TCLC 119; WLC 2**
See also AAYA 74; CA 25-28; CANR 40; CAP 2; DA; DA3; DAB; DAC; DAM DRAM, MST, NOV; DFS 24; DLB 65, 258, 321; EW 10; EWL 3; GFL 1789 to the Present; MTCW 1, 2; RGWL 2, 3; TWA

Cocteau, Jean Maurice Eugene Clement
See Cocteau, Jean

Codrescu, Andrei 1946- ............. **CLC 46, 121**
See also CA 33-36R; 19; CANR 13, 34, 53, 76, 125; CN 7; DA3; DAM POET; MAL 5; MTCW 2; MTFW 2005

Coe, Max
See Bourne, Randolph S(illiman)

Coe, Tucker
See Westlake, Donald E.

Coen, Ethan 1958- .......................... **CLC 108**
See also AAYA 54; CA 126; CANR 85

Coen, Joel 1955- ............................ **CLC 108**
See also AAYA 54; CA 126; CANR 119

The Coen Brothers
See Coen, Ethan; Coen, Joel

Coetzee, J.M. 1940- ...... **CLC 23, 33, 66, 117, 161, 162**
See also AAYA 37; AFW; BRWS 6; CA 77-80; CANR 41, 54, 74, 114, 133; CN 4, 5, 6, 7; DA3; DAM NOV; DLB 225, 326, 329; EWL 3; LMFS 2; MTCW 1, 2; MTFW 2005; NFS 21; WLIT 2; WWE 1

Coetzee, John Maxwell
See Coetzee, J.M.

Coffey, Brian
See Koontz, Dean R.

Coffin, Robert P(eter) Tristram
1892-1955 ................................ **TCLC 95**
See also CA 169; CAAE 123; DLB 45

Cohan, George M. 1878-1942 ........ **TCLC 60**
See also CA 157; DLB 249; RGAL 4

Cohan, George Michael
See Cohan, George M.

Cohen, Arthur A(llen) 1928-1986 ...... **CLC 7, 31**
See also CA 1-4R; CAAS 120; CANR 1, 17, 42; DLB 28; RGHL

Cohen, Leonard 1934- ............... **CLC 3, 38**
See also CA 21-24R; CANR 14, 69; CN 1, 2, 3, 4, 5, 6; CP 1, 2, 3, 4, 5, 6, 7; DAC; DAM MST; DLB 53; EWL 3; MTCW 1

Cohen, Leonard Norman
See Cohen, Leonard

Cohen, Matt(hew) 1942-1999 ............ **CLC 19**
See also CA 61-64; 18; CAAS 187; CANR 40; CN 1, 2, 3, 4, 5, 6; DAC; DLB 53

Cohen-Solal, Annie 1948- ................. **CLC 50**
See also CA 239

Colegate, Isabel 1931- ...................... **CLC 36**
See also CA 17-20R; CANR 8, 22, 74; CN 4, 5, 6, 7; DLB 14, 231; INT CANR-22; MTCW 1

Coleman, Emmett
See Reed, Ishmael

Coleridge, Hartley 1796-1849 ........ **NCLC 90**
See also DLB 96

Coleridge, M. E.
See Coleridge, Mary E(lizabeth)

Coleridge, Mary E(lizabeth)
1861-1907 ................................. **TCLC 73**
See also CA 166; CAAE 116; DLB 19, 98

Coleridge, Samuel Taylor
1772-1834 .... **NCLC 9, 54, 99, 111, 177; PC 11, 39, 67; WLC 2**
See also AAYA 66; BRW 4; BRWR 2; BYA 4; CDBLB 1789-1832; DA; DA3; DAB; DAC; DAM MST, POET; DLB 93, 107; EXPP; LATS 1:1; LMFS 1; PAB; PFS 4, 5; RGEL 2; TEA; WLIT 3; WP

Coleridge, Sara 1802-1852 ............. **NCLC 31**
See also DLB 199

Coles, Don 1928- ............................. **CLC 46**
See also CA 115; CANR 38; CP 5, 6, 7

Coles, Robert (Martin) 1929- ......... **CLC 108**
See also CA 45-48; CANR 3, 32, 66, 70, 135; INT CANR-32; SATA 23

Colette, (Sidonie-Gabrielle)
1873-1954 .. **SSC 10, 93; TCLC 1, 5, 16**
See Willy, Colette
See also CA 131; CAAE 104; DA3; DAM NOV; DLB 65; EW 9; EWL 3; GFL 1789 to the Present; MTCW 1, 2; MTFW 2005; RGWL 2, 3; TWA

Collett, (Jacobine) Camilla (Wergeland)
1813-1895 ................................ **NCLC 22**

Collier, Christopher 1930- ................ **CLC 30**
See also AAYA 13; BYA 2; CA 33-36R; CANR 13, 33, 102; JRDA; MAICYA 1, 2; SATA 16, 70; WYA; YAW 1

Collier, James Lincoln 1928- .............. **CLC 30**
See also AAYA 13; BYA 2; CA 9-12R; CANR 4, 33, 60, 102; CLR 3; DAM POP; JRDA; MAICYA 1, 2; SAAS 21; SATA 8, 70, 166; WYA; YAW 1

Collier, Jeremy 1650-1726 .................... **LC 6**
See also DLB 336

Collier, John 1901-1980 . **SSC 19; TCLC 127**
See also CA 65-68; CAAS 97-100; CANR 10; CN 1, 2; DLB 77, 255; FANT; SUFW 1

Collier, Mary 1690-1762 ...................... **LC 86**
See also DLB 95

Collingwood, R(obin) G(eorge)
1889(?)-1943 ........................... **TCLC 67**
See also CA 155; CAAE 117; DLB 262

Collins, Billy 1941- .............................. **PC 68**
See also AAYA 64; CA 151; CANR 92; CP 7; MTFW 2005; PFS 18

Collins, Hunt
See Hunter, Evan

Collins, Linda 1931- .......................... **CLC 44**
See also CA 125

Collins, Tom
See Furphy, Joseph
See also RGEL 2

Collins, (William) Wilkie
1824-1889 ....... **NCLC 1, 18, 93; SSC 93**
See also BRWS 6; CDBLB 1832-1890; CMW 4; DLB 18, 70, 159; GL 2; MSW; RGEL 2; RGSF 2; SUFW 1; WLIT 4

Collins, William 1721-1759 ...... **LC 4, 40; PC 72**
See also BRW 3; DAM POET; DLB 109; RGEL 2

Collodi, Carlo ............................... **NCLC 54**
See Lorenzini, Carlo
See also CLR 5, 120; WCH; WLIT 7

Colman, George
See Glassco, John

Colman, George, the Elder
1732-1794 ................................. **LC 98**
See also RGEL 2

Colonna, Vittoria 1492-1547 ................ **LC 71**
See also RGWL 2, 3

Colt, Winchester Remington
See Hubbard, L. Ron

Colter, Cyrus J. 1910-2002 ............... **CLC 58**
See also BW 1; CA 65-68; CAAS 205; CANR 10, 66; CN 2, 3, 4, 5, 6; DLB 33

Colton, James
See Hansen, Joseph
See also GLL 1

Colum, Padraic 1881-1972 ............... **CLC 28**
See also BYA 4; CA 73-76; CAAS 33-36R; CANR 35; CLR 36; CP 1; CWRI 5; DLB 19; MAICYA 1, 2; MTCW 1; RGEL 2; SATA 15; WCH

Colvin, James
See Moorcock, Michael

Colwin, Laurie (E.) 1944-1992 .... **CLC 5, 13, 23, 84**
See also CA 89-92; CAAS 139; CANR 20, 46; DLB 218; DLBY 1980; MTCW 1

Comfort, Alex(ander) 1920-2000 ........ **CLC 7**
See also CA 1-4R; CAAS 190; CANR 1, 45; CN 1, 2, 3, 4; CP 1, 2, 3, 4, 5, 6, 7; DAM POP; MTCW 2

Comfort, Montgomery
See Campbell, (John) Ramsey

Compton-Burnett, I(vy)
1892(?)-1969 ........ **CLC 1, 3, 10, 15, 34; TCLC 180**
See also BRW 7; CA 1-4R; CAAS 25-28R; CANR 4; DAM NOV; DLB 36; EWL 3; MTCW 1, 2; RGEL 2

Comstock, Anthony 1844-1915 ...... **TCLC 13**
See also CA 169; CAAE 110

Comte, Auguste 1798-1857 ............. **NCLC 54**

Conan Doyle, Arthur
See Doyle, Sir Arthur Conan
See also BPFB 1; BYA 4, 5, 11

Conde (Abellan), Carmen
1901-1996 ................................ **HLCS 1**
See also CA 177; CWW 2; DLB 108; EWL 3; HW 2

Conde, Maryse 1937- ..... **BLCS; CLC 52, 92**
See also BW 2, 3; CA 190; 110, 190; CANR 30, 53, 76; CWW 2; DAM MULT; EWL 3; MTCW 2; MTFW 2005

Condillac, Etienne Bonnot de
1714-1780 ................................. **LC 26**
See also DLB 313

**Condon, Richard** 1915-1996 ...... **CLC 4, 6, 8, 10, 45, 100**
See also BEST 90:3; BPFB 1; CA 1-4R; 1; CAAS 151; CANR 2, 23, 164; CMW 4; CN 1, 2, 3, 4, 5, 6; DAM NOV; INT CANR-23; MAL 5; MTCW 1, 2

**Condon, Richard Thomas**
See Condon, Richard

**Condorcet** .......................................... **LC 104**
See Condorcet, marquis de Marie-Jean-Antoine-Nicolas Caritat
See also GFL Beginnings to 1789

**Condorcet, marquis de Marie-Jean-Antoine-Nicolas Caritat** 1743-1794
See Condorcet
See also DLB 313

**Confucius** 551B.C.-479B.C. .... **CMLC 19, 65; WLCS**
See also DA; DA3; DAB; DAC; DAM MST

**Congreve, William** 1670-1729 ... **DC 2; LC 5, 21; WLC 2**
See also BRW 2; CDBLB 1660-1789; DA; DAB; DAC; DAM DRAM, MST, POET; DFS 15; DLB 39, 84; RGEL 2; WLIT 3

**Conley, Robert J(ackson)** 1940- ........ **NNAL**
See also CA 41-44R; CANR 15, 34, 45, 96; DAM MULT; TCWW 2

**Connell, Evan S., Jr.** 1924- ....... **CLC 4, 6, 45**
See also AAYA 7; AMWS 14; CA 1-4R; 2; CANR 2, 39, 76, 97, 140; CN 1, 2, 3, 4, 5, 6; DAM NOV; DLB 2, 335; DLBY 1981; MAL 5; MTCW 1, 2; MTFW 2005

**Connelly, Marc(us Cook)** 1890-1980 . **CLC 7**
See also CA 85-88; CAAS 102; CAD; CANR 30; DFS 12; DLB 7; DLBY 1980; MAL 5; RGAL 4; SATA-Obit 25

**Connor, Ralph** ............................... **TCLC 31**
See Gordon, Charles William
See also DLB 92; TCWW 1, 2

**Conrad, Joseph** 1857-1924 ..... **SSC 9, 67, 69, 71; TCLC 1, 6, 13, 25, 43, 57; WLC 2**
See also AAYA 26; BPFB 1; BRW 6; BRWC 1; BRWR 2; BYA 2; CA 131; CAAE 104; CANR 60; CDBLB 1890-1914; DA; DA3; DAB; DAC; DAM MST, NOV; DLB 10, 34, 98, 156; EWL 3; EXPN; EXPS; LAIT 2; LATS 1:1; LMFS 1; MTCW 1, 2; MTFW 2005; NFS 2, 16; RGEL 2; RGSF 2; SATA 27; SSFS 1, 12; TEA; WLIT 4

**Conrad, Robert Arnold**
See Hart, Moss

**Conroy, Pat** 1945- ....................... **CLC 30, 74**
See also AAYA 8, 52; AITN 1; BPFB 1; CA 85-88; CANR 24, 53, 129; CN 7; CPW; CSW; DA3; DAM NOV, POP; DLB 6; LAIT 5; MAL 5; MTCW 1, 2; MTFW 2005

**Constant (de Rebecque), (Henri) Benjamin** 1767-1830 ........................ **NCLC 6, 182**
See also DLB 119; EW 4; GFL 1789 to the Present

**Conway, Jill K(er)** 1934- ................. **CLC 152**
See also CA 130; CANR 94

**Conybeare, Charles Augustus**
See Eliot, T(homas) S(tearns)

**Cook, Michael** 1933-1994 ................. **CLC 58**
See also CA 93-96; CANR 68; DLB 53

**Cook, Robin** 1940- .......................... **CLC 14**
See also AAYA 32; BEST 90:2; BPFB 1; CA 111; CAAE 108; CANR 41, 90, 109; CPW; DA3; DAM POP; HGG; INT CA-111

**Cook, Roy**
See Silverberg, Robert

**Cooke, Elizabeth** 1948- ..................... **CLC 55**
See also CA 129

**Cooke, John Esten** 1830-1886 .......... **NCLC 5**
See also DLB 3, 248; RGAL 4

**Cooke, John Estes**
See Baum, L(yman) Frank

**Cooke, M. E.**
See Creasey, John

**Cooke, Margaret**
See Creasey, John

**Cooke, Rose Terry** 1827-1892 ...... **NCLC 110**
See also DLB 12, 74

**Cook-Lynn, Elizabeth** 1930- ........... **CLC 93; NNAL**
See also CA 133; DAM MULT; DLB 175

**Cooney, Ray** ................................... **CLC 62**
See also CBD

**Cooper, Anthony Ashley** 1671-1713 .. **LC 107**
See also DLB 101, 336

**Cooper, Dennis** 1953- ...................... **CLC 203**
See also CA 133; CANR 72, 86; GLL 1; HGG

**Cooper, Douglas** 1960- ...................... **CLC 86**

**Cooper, Henry St. John**
See Creasey, John

**Cooper, J. California** (?)- ................. **CLC 56**
See also AAYA 12; BW 1; CA 125; CANR 55; DAM MULT; DLB 212

**Cooper, James Fenimore** 1789-1851 ..................... **NCLC 1, 27, 54**
See also AAYA 22; AMW; BPFB 1; CDALB 1640-1865; CLR 105; DA3; DLB 3, 183, 250, 254; LAIT 1; NFS 25; RGAL 4; SATA 19; TUS; WCH

**Cooper, Susan Fenimore** 1813-1894 ............................... **NCLC 129**
See also ANW; DLB 239, 254

**Coover, Robert** 1932- .. **CLC 3, 7, 15, 32, 46, 87, 161; SSC 15, 101**
See also AMWS 5; BPFB 1; CA 45-48; CANR 3, 37, 58, 115; CN 1, 2, 3, 4, 5, 6, 7; DAM NOV; DLB 2, 227; DLBY 1981; EWL 3; MAL 5; MTCW 1, 2; MTFW 2005; RGAL 4; RGSF 2

**Copeland, Stewart (Armstrong)** 1952- .......................................... **CLC 26**

**Copernicus, Nicolaus** 1473-1543 ......... **LC 45**

**Coppard, A(lfred) E(dgar)** 1878-1957 .................. **SSC 21; TCLC 5**
See also BRWS 8; CA 167; CAAE 114; DLB 162; EWL 3; HGG; RGEL 2; RGSF 2; SUFW 1; YABC 1

**Coppee, Francois** 1842-1908 .......... **TCLC 25**
See also CA 170; DLB 217

**Coppola, Francis Ford** 1939- ... **CLC 16, 126**
See also AAYA 39; CA 77-80; CANR 40, 78; DLB 44

**Copway, George** 1818-1869 ............... **NNAL**
See also DAM MULT; DLB 175, 183

**Corbiere, Tristan** 1845-1875 .......... **NCLC 43**
See also DLB 217; GFL 1789 to the Present

**Corcoran, Barbara (Asenath)** 1911- ..................................... **CLC 17**
See also AAYA 14; CA 191; 21-24R, 191; 2; CANR 11, 28, 48; CLR 50; DLB 52; JRDA; MAICYA 2; MAICYAS 1; RHW; SAAS 20; SATA 3, 77; SATA-Essay 125

**Cordelier, Maurice**
See Giraudoux, Jean(-Hippolyte)

**Corelli, Marie** ............................... **TCLC 51**
See Mackay, Mary
See also DLB 34, 156; RGEL 2; SUFW 1

**Corinna** c. 225B.C.-c. 305B.C. ...... **CMLC 72**

**Corman, Cid** .................................... **CLC 9**
See Corman, Sidney
See also CA 2; CP 1, 2, 3, 4, 5, 6, 7; DLB 5, 193

**Corman, Sidney** 1924-2004
See Corman, Cid
See also CA 85-88; CAAS 225; CANR 44; DAM POET

**Cormier, Robert** 1925-2000 ........ **CLC 12, 30**
See also AAYA 3, 19; BYA 1, 2, 6, 8, 9; CA 1-4R; CANR 5, 23, 76, 93; CDALB 1968-1988; CLR 12, 55; DA; DAB; DAC; DAM MST, NOV; DLB 52; EXPN; INT CANR-23; JRDA; LAIT 5; MAICYA 1, 2; MTCW 1, 2; MTFW 2005; NFS 2, 18; SATA 10, 45, 83; SATA-Obit 122; WYA; YAW

**Corn, Alfred (DeWitt III)** 1943- ....... **CLC 33**
See also CA 179; 179; 25; CANR 44; CP 3, 4, 5, 6, 7; CSW; DLB 120, 282; DLBY 1980

**Corneille, Pierre** 1606-1684 .. **DC 21; LC 28, 135**
See also DAB; DAM MST; DFS 21; DLB 268; EW 3; GFL Beginnings to 1789; RGWL 2, 3; TWA

**Cornwell, David**
See le Carre, John

**Cornwell, Patricia** 1956- ................ **CLC 155**
See also AAYA 16, 56; BPFB 1; CA 134; CANR 53, 131; CMW 4; CPW; CSW; DAM POP; DLB 306; MSW; MTCW 2; MTFW 2005

**Cornwell, Patricia Daniels**
See Cornwell, Patricia

**Corso, Gregory** 1930-2001 .... **CLC 1, 11; PC 33**
See also AMWS 12; BG 1:2; CA 5-8R; CAAS 193; CANR 41, 76, 132; CP 1, 2, 3, 4, 5, 6, 7; DA3; DLB 5, 16, 237; LMFS 2; MAL 5; MTCW 1, 2; MTFW 2005; WP

**Cortazar, Julio** 1914-1984 ... **CLC 2, 3, 5, 10, 13, 15, 33, 34, 92; HLC 1; SSC 7, 76**
See also BPFB 1; CA 21-24R; CANR 12, 32, 81; CDWLB 3; DA3; DAM MULT, NOV; DLB 113; EWL 3; EXPS; HW 1, 2; LAW; MTCW 1, 2; MTFW 2005; RGSF 2; RGWL 2, 3; SSFS 3, 20; TWA; WLIT 1

**Cortes, Hernan** 1485-1547 ................... **LC 31**

**Corvinus, Jakob**
See Raabe, Wilhelm (Karl)

**Corwin, Cecil**
See Kornbluth, C(yril) M.

**Cosic, Dobrica** 1921- ......................... **CLC 14**
See also CA 138; CAAE 122; CDWLB 4; CWW 2; DLB 181; EWL 3

**Costain, Thomas B(ertram)** 1885-1965 .................................. **CLC 30**
See also BYA 3; CA 5-8R; CAAS 25-28R; DLB 9; RHW

**Costantini, Humberto** 1924(?)-1987 . **CLC 49**
See also CA 131; CAAS 122; EWL 3; HW 1

**Costello, Elvis** 1954- .......................... **CLC 21**
See also CA 204

**Costenoble, Philostene**
See Ghelderode, Michel de

**Cotes, Cecil V.**
See Duncan, Sara Jeannette

**Cotter, Joseph Seamon Sr.** 1861-1949 .................. **BLC 1; TCLC 28**
See also BW 1; CA 124; DAM MULT; DLB 50

**Couch, Arthur Thomas Quiller**
See Quiller-Couch, Sir Arthur (Thomas)

**Coulton, James**
See Hansen, Joseph

**Couperus, Louis (Marie Anne)** 1863-1923 ................................. **TCLC 15**
See also CAAE 115; EWL 3; RGWL 2, 3

**Coupland, Douglas** 1961- ......... **CLC 85, 133**
See also AAYA 34; CA 142; CANR 57, 90, 130; CCA 1; CN 7; CPW; DAC; DAM POP; DLB 334

**Court, Wesli**
See Turco, Lewis (Putnam)

**Crustt**
See Crumb, R.
**Crutchfield, Les**
See Trumbo, Dalton
**Cruz, Victor Hernandez** 1949- ... **HLC 1; PC 37**
See also BW 2; CA 65-68; 17; CANR 14, 32, 74, 132; CP 1, 2, 3, 4, 5, 6, 7; DAM MULT, POET; DLB 41; DNFS 1; EXPP; HW 1, 2; LLW; MTCW 2; MTFW 2005; PFS 16; WP
**Cryer, Gretchen (Kiger)** 1935- ........ **CLC 21**
See also CA 123; CAAE 114
**Csath, Geza** ...................................... **TCLC 13**
See Brenner, Jozef
See also CAAE 111
**Cudlip, David R(ockwell)** 1933- ....... **CLC 34**
See also CA 177
**Cullen, Countee** 1903-1946 . **BLC 1; HR 1:2; PC 20; TCLC 4, 37; WLCS**
See also AFAW 2; AMWS 4; BW 1; CA 124; CAAE 108; CDALB 1917-1929; DA; DA3; DAC; DAM MST, MULT, POET; DLB 4, 48, 51; EWL 3; EXPP; LMFS 2; MAL 5; MTCW 1, 2; MTFW 2005; PFS 3; RGAL 4; SATA 18; WP
**Culleton, Beatrice** 1949- ..................... **NNAL**
See also CA 120; CANR 83; DAC
**Cum, R.**
See Crumb, R.
**Cumberland, Richard**
1732-1811 ............................... **NCLC 167**
See also DLB 89; RGEL 2
**Cummings, Bruce F(rederick)** 1889-1919
See Barbellion, W. N. P.
See also CAAE 123
**Cummings, E(dward) E(stlin)**
1894-1962 .. **CLC 1, 3, 8, 12, 15, 68; PC 5; TCLC 137; WLC 2**
See also AAYA 41; AMW; CA 73-76; CANR 31; CDALB 1929-1941; DA; DA3; DAB; DAC; DAM MST, POET; DLB 4, 48; EWL 3; EXPP; MAL 5; MTCW 1, 2; MTFW 2005; PAB; PFS 1, 3, 12, 13, 19; RGAL 4; TUS; WP
**Cummins, Maria Susanna**
1827-1866 ............................... **NCLC 139**
See also DLB 42; YABC 1
**Cunha, Euclides (Rodrigues Pimenta) da**
1866-1909 ................................ **TCLC 24**
See also CA 219; CAAE 123; DLB 307; LAW; WLIT 1
**Cunningham, E. V.**
See Fast, Howard
**Cunningham, J(ames) V(incent)**
1911-1985 .............................. **CLC 3, 31**
See also CA 1-4R; CAAS 115; CANR 1, 72; CP 1, 2, 3, 4; DLB 5
**Cunningham, Julia (Woolfolk)**
1916- ..................................... **CLC 12**
See also CA 9-12R; CANR 4, 19, 36; CWRI 5; JRDA; MAICYA 1, 2; SAAS 2; SATA 1, 26, 132
**Cunningham, Michael** 1952- .... **CLC 34, 243**
See also AMWS 15; CA 136; CANR 96, 160; CN 7; DLB 292; GLL 2; MTFW 2005; NFS 23
**Cunninghame Graham, R. B.**
See Cunninghame Graham, Robert (Gallnigad) Bontine
**Cunninghame Graham, Robert (Gallnigad) Bontine** 1852-1936 ................. **TCLC 19**
See Graham, R(obert) B(ontine) Cunninghame
See also CA 184; CAAE 119
**Curnow, (Thomas) Allen (Monro)**
1911-2001 ................................... **PC 48**
See also CA 69-72; CAAS 202; CANR 48, 99; CP 1, 2, 3, 4, 5, 6, 7; EWL 3; RGEL 2

**Currie, Ellen** 19(?)- ............................. **CLC 44**
**Curtin, Philip**
See Lowndes, Marie Adelaide (Belloc)
**Curtin, Phillip**
See Lowndes, Marie Adelaide (Belloc)
**Curtis, Price**
See Ellison, Harlan
**Cusanus, Nicolaus** 1401-1464 .............. **LC 80**
See Nicholas of Cusa
**Cutrate, Joe**
See Spiegelman, Art
**Cynewulf** c. 770- ............................. **CMLC 23**
See also DLB 146; RGEL 2
**Cyrano de Bergerac, Savinien de**
1619-1655 ................................ **LC 65**
See also DLB 268; GFL Beginnings to 1789; RGWL 2, 3
**Cyril of Alexandria** c. 375-c. 430 . **CMLC 59**
**Czaczkes, Shmuel Yosef Halevi**
See Agnon, S(hmuel) Y(osef Halevi)
**Dabrowska, Maria (Szumska)**
1889-1965 ................................ **CLC 15**
See also CA 106; CDWLB 4; DLB 215; EWL 3
**Dabydeen, David** 1955- .................... **CLC 34**
See also BW 1; CA 125; CANR 56, 92; CN 6, 7; CP 5, 6, 7
**Dacey, Philip** 1939- ........................... **CLC 51**
See also CA 231; 37-40R, 231; 17; CANR 14, 32, 64; CP 4, 5, 6, 7; DLB 105
**Dacre, Charlotte** c. 1772-1825(?) . **NCLC 151**
**Dafydd ap Gwilym** c. 1320-c. 1380 ..... **PC 56**
**Dagerman, Stig (Halvard)**
1923-1954 ................................ **TCLC 17**
See also CA 155; CAAE 117; DLB 259; EWL 3
**D'Aguiar, Fred** 1960- ...................... **CLC 145**
See also CA 148; CANR 83, 101; CN 7; CP 5, 6, 7; DLB 157; EWL 3
**Dahl, Roald** 1916-1990 ...... **CLC 1, 6, 18, 79; TCLC 173**
See also AAYA 15; BPFB 1; BRWS 4; BYA 5; CA 1-4R; CAAS 133; CANR 6, 32, 37, 62; CLR 1, 7, 41, 111; CN 1, 2, 3, 4; CPW; DA3; DAB; DAC; DAM MST, NOV, POP; DLB 139, 255; HGG; JRDA; MAICYA 1, 2; MTCW 1, 2; MTFW 2005; RGSF 2; SATA 1, 26, 73; SATA-Obit 65; SSFS 4; TEA; YAW
**Dahlberg, Edward** 1900-1977 .. **CLC 1, 7, 14**
See also CA 9-12R; CAAS 69-72; CANR 31, 62; CN 1, 2; DLB 48; MAL 5; MTCW 1; RGAL 4
**Daitch, Susan** 1954- ........................ **CLC 103**
See also CA 161
**Dale, Colin** ...................................... **TCLC 18**
See Lawrence, T(homas) E(dward)
**Dale, George E.**
See Asimov, Isaac
**d'Alembert, Jean Le Rond**
1717-1783 ................................ **LC 126**
**Dalton, Roque** 1935-1975(?) ..... **HLCS 1; PC 36**
See also CA 176; DLB 283; HW 2
**Daly, Elizabeth** 1878-1967 ................ **CLC 52**
See also CA 23-24; CAAS 25-28R; CANR 60; CAP 2; CMW 4
**Daly, Mary** 1928- ........................... **CLC 173**
See also CA 25-28R; CANR 30, 62, 166; FW; GLL 1; MTCW 1
**Daly, Maureen** 1921-2006 ................ **CLC 17**
See also AAYA 5, 58; BYA 6; CAAS 253; CANR 37, 83, 108; CLR 96; JRDA; MAICYA 1, 2; SAAS 1; SATA 2, 129; SATA-Obit 176; WYA; YAW
**Damas, Leon-Gontran** 1912-1978 .... **CLC 84**
See also BW 1; CA 125; CAAS 73-76; EWL 3

**Dana, Richard Henry Sr.**
1787-1879 ............................... **NCLC 53**
**Daniel, Samuel** 1562(?)-1619 .............. **LC 24**
See also DLB 62; RGEL 2
**Daniels, Brett**
See Adler, Renata
**Dannay, Frederic** 1905-1982 ............. **CLC 11**
See Queen, Ellery
See also CA 1-4R; CAAS 107; CANR 1, 39; CMW 4; DAM POP; DLB 137; MTCW 1
**D'Annunzio, Gabriele** 1863-1938 ... **TCLC 6, 40**
See also CA 155; CAAE 104; EW 8; EWL 3; RGWL 2, 3; TWA; WLIT 7
**Danois, N. le**
See Gourmont, Remy(-Marie-Charles) de
**Dante** 1265-1321 .... **CMLC 3, 18, 39, 70; PC 21; WLCS**
See Alighieri, Dante
See also DA; DA3; DAB; DAC; DAM MST, POET; EFS 1; EW 1; LAIT 1; RGWL 2, 3; TWA; WP
**d'Antibes, Germain**
See Simenon, Georges (Jacques Christian)
**Danticat, Edwidge** 1969- . **CLC 94, 139, 228; SSC 100**
See also AAYA 29; CA 192; 152, 192; CANR 73, 129; CN 7; DNFS 1; EXPS; LATS 1:2; MTCW 2; MTFW 2005; SSFS 1, 25; YAW
**Danvers, Dennis** 1947- ..................... **CLC 70**
**Danziger, Paula** 1944-2004 ............... **CLC 21**
See also AAYA 4, 36; BYA 6, 7, 14; CA 115; CAAE 112; CAAS 229; CANR 37, 132; CLR 20; JRDA; MAICYA 1, 2; MTFW 2005; SATA 36, 63, 102, 149; SATA-Brief 30; SATA-Obit 155; WYA; YAW
**Da Ponte, Lorenzo** 1749-1838 ........ **NCLC 50**
**d'Aragona, Tullia** 1510(?)-1556 ......... **LC 121**
**Dario, Ruben** 1867-1916 ....... **HLC 1; PC 15; TCLC 4**
See also CA 131; CANR 81; DAM MULT; DLB 290; EWL 3; HW 1, 2; LAW; MTCW 1, 2; MTFW 2005; RGWL 2, 3
**Darley, George** 1795-1846 ............... **NCLC 2**
See also DLB 96; RGEL 2
**Darrow, Clarence (Seward)**
1857-1938 ............................... **TCLC 81**
See also CA 164; DLB 303
**Darwin, Charles** 1809-1882 ............. **NCLC 57**
See also BRWS 7; DLB 57, 166; LATS 1:1; RGEL 2; TEA; WLIT 4
**Darwin, Erasmus** 1731-1802 ........ **NCLC 106**
See also DLB 93; RGEL 2
**Daryush, Elizabeth** 1887-1977 ...... **CLC 6, 19**
See also CA 49-52; CANR 3, 81; DLB 20
**Das, Kamala** 1934- ............. **CLC 191; PC 43**
See also CA 101; CANR 27, 59; CP 1, 2, 3, 4, 5, 6, 7; CWP; DLB 323; FW
**Dasgupta, Surendranath**
1887-1952 ............................... **TCLC 81**
See also CA 157
**Dashwood, Edmee Elizabeth Monica de la Pasture** 1890-1943
See Delafield, E. M.
See also CA 154; CAAE 119
**da Silva, Antonio Jose**
1705-1739 ............................... **NCLC 114**
**Daudet, (Louis Marie) Alphonse**
1840-1897 ............................... **NCLC 1**
See also DLB 123; GFL 1789 to the Present; RGSF 2
**Daudet, Alphonse Marie Leon**
1867-1942 ............................... **SSC 94**
See also CA 217

Cumulative Author Index

**de la Parra, (Ana) Teresa (Sonojo)**
1890(?)-1936 .......................... **TCLC 185**
See Parra Sanojo, Ana Teresa de la
See also CA 178; HW 2

**De La Ramee, Marie Louise** 1839-1908
See Ouida
See also CA 204; SATA 20

**de la Roche, Mazo** 1879-1961 .......... **CLC 14**
See also CA 85-88; CANR 30; DLB 68;
RGEL 2; RHW; SATA 64

**De La Salle, Innocent**
See Hartmann, Sadakichi

**de Laureamont, Comte**
See Lautreamont

**Delbanco, Nicholas** 1942- ..... **CLC 6, 13, 167**
See also CA 189; 17-20R, 189; 2; CANR
29, 55, 116, 150; CN 7; DLB 6, 234

**Delbanco, Nicholas Franklin**
See Delbanco, Nicholas

**del Castillo, Michel** 1933- ................ **CLC 38**
See also CA 109; CANR 77

**Deledda, Grazia (Cosima)**
1875(?)-1936 ......................... **TCLC 23**
See also CA 205; CAAE 123; DLB 264,
329; EWL 3; RGWL 2, 3; WLIT 7

**Deleuze, Gilles** 1925-1995 ............. **TCLC 116**
See also DLB 296

**Delgado, Abelardo (Lalo) B(arrientos)**
1930-2004 ...................................... **HLC 1**
See also CA 131; 15; CAAS 230; CANR
90; DAM MST, MULT; DLB 82; HW 1,
2

**Delibes, Miguel** .......................... **CLC 8, 18**
See Delibes Setien, Miguel
See also DLB 322; EWL 3

**Delibes Setien, Miguel** 1920-
See Delibes, Miguel
See also CA 45-48; CANR 1, 32; CWW 2;
HW 1; MTCW 1

**DeLillo, Don** 1936- ..... **CLC 8, 10, 13, 27, 39,**
**54, 76, 143, 210, 213**
See also AMWC 2; AMWS 6; BEST 89:1;
BPFB 1; CA 81-84; CANR 21, 76, 92,
133; CN 3, 4, 5, 6, 7; CPW; DA3; DAM
NOV, POP; DLB 6, 173; EWL 3; MAL 5;
MTCW 1, 2; MTFW 2005; RGAL 4; TUS

**de Lisser, H. G.**
See De Lisser, H(erbert) G(eorge)
See also DLB 117

**De Lisser, H(erbert) G(eorge)**
1878-1944 ............................... **TCLC 12**
See de Lisser, H. G.
See also BW 2; CA 152; CAAE 109

**Deloire, Pierre**
See Peguy, Charles (Pierre)

**Deloney, Thomas** 1543(?)-1600 .... **LC 41; PC**
**79**
See also DLB 167; RGEL 2

**Deloria, Ella (Cara)** 1889-1971(?) ..... **NNAL**
See also CA 152; DAM MULT; DLB 175

**Deloria, Vine, Jr.** 1933-2005 .... **CLC 21, 122;**
**NNAL**
See also CA 53-56; CAAS 245; CANR 5,
20, 48, 98; DAM MULT; DLB 175;
MTCW 1; SATA 21; SATA-Obit 171

**Deloria, Vine Victor, Jr.**
See Deloria, Vine, Jr.

**del Valle-Inclan, Ramon (Maria)**
See Valle-Inclan, Ramon (Maria) del
See also DLB 322

**Del Vecchio, John M(ichael)** 1947- .. **CLC 29**
See also CA 110; DLBD 9

**de Man, Paul (Adolph Michel)**
1919-1983 ................................. **CLC 55**
See also CA 128; CAAS 111; CANR 61;
DLB 67; MTCW 1, 2

**DeMarinis, Rick** 1934- ..................... **CLC 54**
See also CA 184; 57-60, 184; 24; CANR 9,
25, 50, 160; DLB 218; TCWW 2

**de Maupassant, (Henri Rene Albert) Guy**
See Maupassant, (Henri Rene Albert) Guy
de

**Dembry, R. Emmet**
See Murfree, Mary Noailles

**Demby, William** 1922- ......... **BLC 1; CLC 53**
See also BW 1, 3; CA 81-84; CANR 81;
DAM MULT; DLB 33

**de Menton, Francisco**
See Chin, Frank (Chew, Jr.)

**Demetrius of Phalerum** c.
307B.C.- .................................. **CMLC 34**

**Demijohn, Thom**
See Disch, Thomas M.

**De Mille, James** 1833-1880 .......... **NCLC 123**
See also DLB 99, 251

**Deming, Richard** 1915-1983
See Queen, Ellery
See also CA 9-12R; CANR 3, 94; SATA 24

**Democritus** c. 460B.C.-c. 370B.C. . **CMLC 47**

**de Montaigne, Michel (Eyquem)**
See Montaigne, Michel (Eyquem) de

**de Montherlant, Henry (Milon)**
See Montherlant, Henry (Milon) de

**Demosthenes** 384B.C.-322B.C. ...... **CMLC 13**
See also AW 1; DLB 176; RGWL 2, 3;
WLIT 8

**de Musset, (Louis Charles) Alfred**
See Musset, Alfred de

**de Natale, Francine**
See Malzberg, Barry N(athaniel)

**de Navarre, Marguerite** 1492-1549 ... **LC 61;**
**SSC 85**
See Marguerite d'Angouleme; Marguerite
de Navarre
See also DLB 327

**Denby, Edwin (Orr)** 1903-1983 ........ **CLC 48**
See also CA 138; CAAS 110; CP 1

**de Nerval, Gerard**
See Nerval, Gerard de

**Denham, John** 1615-1669 .................... **LC 73**
See also DLB 58, 126; RGEL 2

**Denis, Julio**
See Cortazar, Julio

**Denmark, Harrison**
See Zelazny, Roger

**Dennis, John** 1658-1734 ...................... **LC 11**
See also DLB 101; RGEL 2

**Dennis, Nigel (Forbes)** 1912-1989 ...... **CLC 8**
See also CA 25-28R; CAAS 129; CN 1, 2,
3, 4; DLB 13, 15, 233; EWL 3; MTCW 1

**Dent, Lester** 1904-1959 ................... **TCLC 72**
See also CA 161; CAAE 112; CMW 4;
DLB 306; SFW 4

**De Palma, Brian** 1940- ..................... **CLC 20**
See also CA 109

**De Palma, Brian Russell**
See De Palma, Brian

**de Pizan, Christine**
See Christine de Pizan
See also FL 1:1

**De Quincey, Thomas** 1785-1859 ..... **NCLC 4,**
**87**
See also BRW 4; CDBLB 1789-1832; DLB
110, 144; RGEL 2

**Deren, Eleanora** 1908(?)-1961
See Deren, Maya
See also CA 192; CAAS 111

**Deren, Maya** ............................. **CLC 16, 102**
See Deren, Eleanora

**Derleth, August (William)**
1909-1971 ................................. **CLC 31**
See also BPFB 1; BYA 9, 10; CA 1-4R;
CAAS 29-32R; CANR 4; CMW 4; CN 1;
DLB 9; DLBD 17; HGG; SATA 5; SUFW
1

**Der Nister** 1884-1950 ..................... **TCLC 56**
See Nister, Der

**de Routisie, Albert**
See Aragon, Louis

**Derrida, Jacques** 1930-2004 ...... **CLC 24, 87,**
**225**
See also CA 127; CAAE 124; CAAS 232;
CANR 76, 98, 133; DLB 242; EWL 3;
LMFS 2; MTCW 2; TWA

**Derry Down Derry**
See Lear, Edward

**Dersonnes, Jacques**
See Simenon, Georges (Jacques Christian)

**Der Stricker** c. 1190-c. 1250 .......... **CMLC 75**
See also DLB 138

**Desai, Anita** 1937- ......... **CLC 19, 37, 97, 175**
See also BRWS 5; CA 81-84; CANR 33,
53, 95, 133; CN 1, 2, 3, 4, 5, 6, 7; CWRI
5; DA3; DAB; DAM NOV; DLB 271,
323; DNFS 2; EWL 3; FW; MTCW 1, 2;
MTFW 2005; SATA 63, 126

**Desai, Kiran** 1971- .......................... **CLC 119**
See also BYA 16; CA 171; CANR 127

**de Saint-Luc, Jean**
See Glassco, John

**de Saint Roman, Arnaud**
See Aragon, Louis

**Desbordes-Valmore, Marceline**
1786-1859 ............................... **NCLC 97**
See also DLB 217

**Descartes, Rene** 1596-1650 ............ **LC 20, 35**
See also DLB 268; EW 3; GFL Beginnings
to 1789

**Deschamps, Eustache** 1340(?)-1404 .. **LC 103**
See also DLB 208

**De Sica, Vittorio** 1901(?)-1974 .......... **CLC 20**
See also CAAS 117

**Desnos, Robert** 1900-1945 ............... **TCLC 22**
See also CA 151; CAAE 121; CANR 107;
DLB 258; EWL 3; LMFS 2

**Destouches, Louis-Ferdinand**
1894-1961 ............................... **CLC 9, 15**
See Celine, Louis-Ferdinand
See also CA 85-88; CANR 28; MTCW 1

**de Tolignac, Gaston**
See Griffith, D(avid Lewelyn) W(ark)

**Deutsch, Babette** 1895-1982 ............. **CLC 18**
See also BYA 3; CA 1-4R; CAAS 108;
CANR 4, 79; CP 1, 2, 3; DLB 45; SATA
1; SATA-Obit 33

**Devenant, William** 1606-1649 ............. **LC 13**

**Devkota, Laxmiprasad** 1909-1959 . **TCLC 23**
See also CAAE 123

**De Voto, Bernard (Augustine)**
1897-1955 ............................... **TCLC 29**
See also CA 160; CAAE 113; DLB 9, 256;
MAL 5; TCWW 1, 2

**De Vries, Peter** 1910-1993 ..... **CLC 1, 2, 3, 7,**
**10, 28, 46**
See also CA 17-20R; CAAS 142; CANR
41; CN 1, 2, 3, 4, 5; DAM NOV; DLB 6;
DLBY 1982; MAL 5; MTCW 1, 2;
MTFW 2005

**Dewey, John** 1859-1952 ................... **TCLC 95**
See also CA 170; CAAE 114; CANR 144;
DLB 246, 270; RGAL 4

**Dexter, John**
See Bradley, Marion Zimmer
See also GLL 1

**Dexter, Martin**
See Faust, Frederick (Schiller)

**Dexter, Pete** 1943- ...................... **CLC 34, 55**
See also BEST 89:2; CA 131; CAAE 127;
CANR 129; CPW; DAM POP; INT CA-
131; MAL 5; MTCW 1; MTFW 2005

**Diamano, Silmang**
See Senghor, Leopold Sedar

**Diamant, Anita** 1951- ...................... **CLC 239**
See also CA 145; CANR 126

**Diamond, Neil** 1941- ........................ **CLC 30**
See also CA 108**

**Donoso (Yanez), Jose** 1924-1996 ... **CLC 4, 8, 11, 32, 99; HLC 1; SSC 34; TCLC 133**
See also CA 81-84; CAAS 155; CANR 32, 73; CDWLB 3; CWW 2; DAM MULT; DLB 113; EWL 3; HW 1, 2; LAW; LAWS 1; MTCW 1, 2; MTFW 2005; RGSF 2; WLIT 1

**Donovan, John** 1928-1992 ................ **CLC 35**
See also AAYA 20; CA 97-100; CAAS 137; CLR 3; MAICYA 1, 2; SATA 72; SATA-Brief 29; YAW

**Don Roberto**
See Cunninghame Graham, Robert (Gallnigad) Bontine

**Doolittle, Hilda** 1886-1961 . **CLC 3, 8, 14, 31, 34, 73; PC 5; WLC 3**
See H. D.
See also AAYA 66; AMWS 1; CA 97-100; CANR 35, 131; DA; DAC; DAM MST, POET; DLB 4, 45; EWL 3; FW; GLL 1; LMFS 2; MAL 5; MBL; MTCW 1, 2; MTFW 2005; PFS 6; RGAL 4

**Doppo, Kunikida** ........................... **TCLC 99**
See Kunikida Doppo

**Dorfman, Ariel** 1942- ......... **CLC 48, 77, 189; HLC 1**
See also CA 130; CAAE 124; CANR 67, 70, 135; CWW 2; DAM MULT; DFS 4; EWL 3; HW 1, 2; INT CA-130; WLIT 1

**Dorn, Edward (Merton)**
1929-1999 ........................... **CLC 10, 18**
See also CA 93-96; CAAS 187; CANR 42, 79; CP 1, 2, 3, 4, 5, 6, 7; DLB 5; INT CA-93-96; WP

**Dor-Ner, Zvi** ................................. **CLC 70**

**Dorris, Michael** 1945-1997 ............ **CLC 109; NNAL**
See also AAYA 20; BEST 90:1; BYA 12; CA 102; CAAS 157; CANR 19, 46, 75; CLR 58; DA3; DAM MULT, NOV; DLB 175; LAIT 5; MTCW 2; MTFW 2005; NFS 3; RGAL 4; SATA 75; SATA-Obit 94; TCWW 2; YAW

**Dorris, Michael A.**
See Dorris, Michael

**Dorsan, Luc**
See Simenon, Georges (Jacques Christian)

**Dorsange, Jean**
See Simenon, Georges (Jacques Christian)

**Dorset**
See Sackville, Thomas

**Dos Passos, John (Roderigo)**
1896-1970 ... **CLC 1, 4, 8, 11, 15, 25, 34, 82; WLC 2**
See also AMW; BPFB 1; CA 1-4R; CAAS 29-32R; CANR 3; CDALB 1929-1941; DA; DA3; DAB; DAC; DAM MST, NOV; DLB 4, 9, 274, 316; DLBD 1, 15; DLBY 1996; EWL 3; MAL 5; MTCW 1, 2; MTFW 2005; NFS 14; RGAL 4; TUS

**Dossage, Jean**
See Simenon, Georges (Jacques Christian)

**Dostoevsky, Fedor Mikhailovich**
1821-1881 .. **NCLC 2, 7, 21, 33, 43, 119, 167; SSC 2, 33, 44; WLC 2**
See Dostoevsky, Fyodor
See also AAYA 40; DA; DA3; DAB; DAC; DAM MST, NOV; EW 7; EXPN; NFS 3, 8; RGSF 2; RGWL 2, 3; SSFS 8; TWA

**Dostoevsky, Fyodor**
See Dostoevsky, Fedor Mikhailovich
See also DLB 238; LATS 1:1; LMFS 1, 2

**Doty, M. R.**
See Doty, Mark

**Doty, Mark** 1953(?)- .......... **CLC 176; PC 53**
See also AMWS 11; CA 183; 161, 183; CANR 110; CP 7

**Doty, Mark A.**
See Doty, Mark

**Doty, Mark Alan**
See Doty, Mark

**Doughty, Charles M(ontagu)**
1843-1926 ............................. **TCLC 27**
See also CA 178; CAAE 115; DLB 19, 57, 174

**Douglas, Ellen** ................................. **CLC 73**
See Haxton, Josephine Ayres; Williamson, Ellen Douglas
See also CN 5, 6, 7; CSW; DLB 292

**Douglas, Gavin** 1475(?)-1522 ............... **LC 20**
See also DLB 132; RGEL 2

**Douglas, George**
See Brown, George Douglas
See also RGEL 2

**Douglas, Keith (Castellain)**
1920-1944 ............................. **TCLC 40**
See also BRW 7; CA 160; DLB 27; EWL 3; PAB; RGEL 2

**Douglas, Leonard**
See Bradbury, Ray

**Douglas, Michael**
See Crichton, Michael

**Douglas, (George) Norman**
1868-1952 ............................. **TCLC 68**
See also BRW 6; CA 157; CAAE 119; DLB 34, 195; RGEL 2

**Douglas, William**
See Brown, George Douglas

**Douglass, Frederick** 1817(?)-1895 ..... **BLC 1; NCLC 7, 55, 141; WLC 2**
See also AAYA 48; AFAW 1, 2; AMWC 1; AMWS 3; CDALB 1640-1865; DA; DA3; DAC; DAM MST, MULT; DLB 1, 43, 50, 79, 243; FW; LAIT 2; NCFS 2; RGAL 4; SATA 29

**Dourado, (Waldomiro Freitas) Autran**
1926- ...................................... **CLC 23, 60**
See also CA 25-28R, 179; CANR 34, 81; DLB 145, 307; HW 2

**Dourado, Waldomiro Freitas Autran**
See Dourado, (Waldomiro Freitas) Autran

**Dove, Rita** 1952- .. **BLCS; CLC 50, 81; PC 6**
See also AAYA 46; AMWS 4; BW 2; CA 109; 19; CANR 27, 42, 68, 76, 97, 132; CDALBS; CP 5, 6, 7; CSW; CWP; DA3; DAM MULT, POET; DLB 120; EWL 3; EXPP; MAL 5; MTCW 2; MTFW 2005; PFS 1, 15; RGAL 4

**Dove, Rita Frances**
See Dove, Rita

**Doveglion**
See Villa, Jose Garcia

**Dowell, Coleman** 1925-1985 ............. **CLC 60**
See also CA 25-28R; CAAS 117; CANR 10; DLB 130; GLL 2

**Downing, Major Jack**
See Smith, Seba

**Dowson, Ernest (Christopher)**
1867-1900 ............................. **TCLC 4**
See also CA 150; CAAE 105; DLB 19, 135; RGEL 2

**Doyle, A. Conan**
See Doyle, Sir Arthur Conan

**Doyle, Sir Arthur Conan**
1859-1930 ..... **SSC 12, 83, 95; TCLC 7; WLC 2**
See Conan Doyle, Arthur
See also AAYA 14; BRWS 2; CA 122; CAAE 104; CANR 131; CDBLB 1890-1914; CLR 106; CMW 4; DA; DA3; DAB; DAC; DAM MST, NOV; DLB 18, 70, 156, 178; EXPS; HGG; LAIT 2; MSW; MTCW 1, 2; MTFW 2005; RGEL 2; RGSF 2; RHW; SATA 24; SCFW 1, 2; SFW 4; SSFS 2; TEA; WCH; WLIT 4; WYA; YAW

**Doyle, Conan**
See Doyle, Sir Arthur Conan

**Doyle, John**
See Graves, Robert

**Doyle, Roddy** 1958- ................... **CLC 81, 178**
See also AAYA 14; BRWS 5; CA 143; CANR 73, 128, 168; CN 6, 7; DA3; DLB 194, 326; MTCW 2; MTFW 2005

**Doyle, Sir A. Conan**
See Doyle, Sir Arthur Conan

**Dr. A**
See Asimov, Isaac; Silverstein, Alvin; Silverstein, Virginia B(arbara Opshelor)

**Drabble, Margaret** 1939- ...... **CLC 2, 3, 5, 8, 10, 22, 53, 129**
See also BRWS 4; CA 13-16R; CANR 18, 35, 63, 112, 131; CDBLB 1960 to Present; CN 1, 2, 3, 4, 5, 6, 7; CPW; DA3; DAB; DAC; DAM MST, NOV, POP; DLB 14, 155, 231; EWL 3; FW; MTCW 1, 2; MTFW 2005; RGEL 2; SATA 48; TEA

**Drakulic, Slavenka** 1949- ............... **CLC 173**
See also CA 144; CANR 92

**Drakulic-Ilic, Slavenka**
See Drakulic, Slavenka

**Drapier, M. B.**
See Swift, Jonathan

**Drayham, James**
See Mencken, H(enry) L(ouis)

**Drayton, Michael** 1563-1631 ................. **LC 8**
See also DAM POET; DLB 121; RGEL 2

**Dreadstone, Carl**
See Campbell, (John) Ramsey

**Dreiser, Theodore** 1871-1945 ........... **SSC 30; TCLC 10, 18, 35, 83; WLC 2**
See also AMW; AMWC 2; AMWR 2; BYA 15, 16; CA 132; CAAE 106; CDALB 1865-1917; DA; DA3; DAC; DAM MST, NOV; DLB 9, 12, 102, 137; DLBD 1; EWL 3; LAIT 2; LMFS 2; MAL 5; MTCW 1, 2; MTFW 2005; NFS 8, 17; RGAL 4; TUS

**Dreiser, Theodore Herman Albert**
See Dreiser, Theodore

**Drexler, Rosalyn** 1926- ................... **CLC 2, 6**
See also CA 81-84; CAD; CANR 68, 124; CD 5, 6; CWD; MAL 5

**Dreyer, Carl Theodor** 1889-1968 ...... **CLC 16**
See also CAAS 116

**Drieu la Rochelle, Pierre**
1893-1945 ............................. **TCLC 21**
See also CA 250; CAAE 117; DLB 72; EWL 3; GFL 1789 to the Present

**Drieu la Rochelle, Pierre-Eugene** 1893-1945
See Drieu la Rochelle, Pierre

**Drinkwater, John** 1882-1937 ......... **TCLC 57**
See also CA 149; CAAE 109; DLB 10, 19, 149; RGEL 2

**Drop Shot**
See Cable, George Washington

**Droste-Hulshoff, Annette Freiin von**
1797-1848 .......................... **NCLC 3, 133**
See also CDWLB 2; DLB 133; RGSF 2; RGWL 2, 3

**Drummond, Walter**
See Silverberg, Robert

**Drummond, William Henry**
1854-1907 ............................. **TCLC 25**
See also CA 160; DLB 92

**Drummond de Andrade, Carlos**
1902-1987 ............. **CLC 18; TCLC 139**
See Andrade, Carlos Drummond de
See also CA 132; CAAS 123; DLB 307; LAW

**Drummond of Hawthornden, William**
1585-1649 ............................. **LC 83**
See also DLB 121, 213; RGEL 2

**Drury, Allen (Stuart)** 1918-1998 ....... **CLC 37**
See also CA 57-60; CAAS 170; CANR 18, 52; CN 1, 2, 3, 4, 5, 6; INT CANR-18

FL 1:5; LAIT 5; LATS 1:2; MAL 5; MTCW 1, 2; MTFW 2005; NFS 5; PFS 14; RGAL 4; SATA 94, 141; SSFS 14, 22; TCWW 2

**Erenburg, Ilya (Grigoryevich)**
    See Ehrenburg, Ilya (Grigoryevich)

**Erickson, Stephen Michael**
    See Erickson, Steve

**Erickson, Steve** 1950- ........................ **CLC 64**
    See also CA 129; CANR 60, 68, 136; MTFW 2005; SFW 4; SUFW 2

**Erickson, Walter**
    See Fast, Howard

**Ericson, Walter**
    See Fast, Howard

**Eriksson, Buntel**
    See Bergman, Ingmar

**Eriugena, John Scottus** c. 810-877 ................................... **CMLC 65**
    See also DLB 115

**Ernaux, Annie** 1940- .................. **CLC 88, 184**
    See also CA 147; CANR 93; MTFW 2005; NCFS 3, 5

**Erskine, John** 1879-1951 ............... **TCLC 84**
    See also CA 159; CAAE 112; DLB 9, 102; FANT

**Erwin, Will**
    See Eisner, Will

**Eschenbach, Wolfram von**
    See von Eschenbach, Wolfram
    See also RGWL 3

**Eseki, Bruno**
    See Mphahlele, Ezekiel

**Esenin, S.A.**
    See Esenin, Sergei
    See also EWL 3

**Esenin, Sergei** 1895-1925 .................. **TCLC 4**
    See Esenin, S.A.
    See also CAAE 104; RGWL 2, 3

**Esenin, Sergei Aleksandrovich**
    See Esenin, Sergei

**Eshleman, Clayton** 1935- .................... **CLC 7**
    See also CA 212; 33-36R, 212; 6; CANR 93; CP 1, 2, 3, 4, 5, 6, 7; DLB 5

**Espada, Martin** 1957- ........................ **PC 74**
    See also CA 159; CANR 80; CP 7; EXPP; LLW; MAL 5; PFS 13, 16

**Espriella, Don Manuel Alvarez**
    See Southey, Robert

**Espriu, Salvador** 1913-1985 ............... **CLC 9**
    See also CA 154; CAAS 115; DLB 134; EWL 3

**Espronceda, Jose de** 1808-1842 ..... **NCLC 39**

**Esquivel, Laura** 1950(?)- ... **CLC 141; HLCS 1**
    See also AAYA 29; CA 143; CANR 68, 113, 161; DA3; DNFS 2; LAIT 3; LMFS 2; MTCW 2; MTFW 2005; NFS 5; WLIT 1

**Esse, James**
    See Stephens, James

**Esterbrook, Tom**
    See Hubbard, L. Ron

**Estleman, Loren D.** 1952- ................. **CLC 48**
    See also AAYA 27; CA 85-88; CANR 27, 74, 139; CMW 4; CPW; DA3; DAM NOV, POP; DLB 226; INT CANR-27; MTCW 1, 2; MTFW 2005; TCWW 1, 2

**Etherege, Sir George** 1636-1692 . **DC 23; LC 78**
    See also BRW 2; DAM DRAM; DLB 80; PAB; RGEL 2

**Euclid** 306B.C.-283B.C. .................. **CMLC 25**

**Eugenides, Jeffrey** 1960(?)- ....... **CLC 81, 212**
    See also AAYA 51; CA 144; CANR 120; MTFW 2005; NFS 24

**Euripides** c. 484B.C.-406B.C. ....... **CMLC 23, 51; DC 4; WLCS**
    See also AW 1; CDWLB 1; DA; DA3; DAB; DAC; DAM DRAM, MST; DFS 1, 4, 6; DLB 176; LAIT 1; LMFS 1; RGWL 2, 3; WLIT 8

**Evan, Evin**
    See Faust, Frederick (Schiller)

**Evans, Caradoc** 1878-1945 ... **SSC 43; TCLC 85**
    See also DLB 162

**Evans, Evan**
    See Faust, Frederick (Schiller)

**Evans, Marian**
    See Eliot, George

**Evans, Mary Ann**
    See Eliot, George
    See also NFS 20

**Evarts, Esther**
    See Benson, Sally

**Evelyn, John** 1620-1706 .................... **LC 144**
    See also BRW 2; RGEL 2

**Everett, Percival**
    See Everett, Percival L.
    See also CSW

**Everett, Percival L.** 1956- ................. **CLC 57**
    See Everett, Percival
    See also BW 2; CA 129; CANR 94, 134; CN 7; MTFW 2005

**Everson, R(onald) G(ilmour)** 1903-1992 ........................... **CLC 27**
    See also CA 17-20R; CP 1, 2, 3, 4; DLB 88

**Everson, William (Oliver)** 1912-1994 ........................... **CLC 1, 5, 14**
    See Antoninus, Brother
    See also BG 1:2; CA 9-12R; CAAS 145; CANR 20; CP 2, 3, 4, 5; DLB 5, 16, 212; MTCW 1

**Evtushenko, Evgenii Aleksandrovich**
    See Yevtushenko, Yevgeny (Alexandrovich)
    See also CWW 2; RGWL 2, 3

**Ewart, Gavin (Buchanan)** 1916-1995 ........................... **CLC 13, 46**
    See also BRWS 7; CA 89-92; CAAS 150; CANR 17, 46; CP 1, 2, 3, 4, 5, 6; DLB 40; MTCW 1

**Ewers, Hanns Heinz** 1871-1943 ..... **TCLC 12**
    See also CA 149; CAAE 109

**Ewing, Frederick R.**
    See Sturgeon, Theodore (Hamilton)

**Exley, Frederick (Earl)** 1929-1992 .... **CLC 6, 11**
    See also AITN 2; BPFB 1; CA 81-84; CAAS 138; CANR 117; DLB 143; DLBY 1981

**Eynhardt, Guillermo**
    See Quiroga, Horacio (Sylvestre)

**Ezekiel, Nissim (Moses)** 1924-2004 .. **CLC 61**
    See also CA 61-64; CAAS 223; CP 1, 2, 3, 4, 5, 6, 7; DLB 323; EWL 3

**Ezekiel, Tish O'Dowd** 1943- ............. **CLC 34**
    See also CA 129

**Fadeev, Aleksandr Aleksandrovich**
    See Bulgya, Alexander Alexandrovich
    See also DLB 272

**Fadeev, Alexandr Alexandrovich**
    See Bulgya, Alexander Alexandrovich
    See also EWL 3

**Fadeyev, A.**
    See Bulgya, Alexander Alexandrovich

**Fadeyev, Alexander** ........................ **TCLC 53**
    See Bulgya, Alexander Alexandrovich

**Fagen, Donald** 1948- ........................ **CLC 26**

**Fainzil'berg, Il'ia Arnol'dovich**
    See Fainzilberg, Ilya Arnoldovich

**Fainzilberg, Ilya Arnoldovich** 1897-1937 ............................... **TCLC 21**
    See Il'f, Il'ia
    See also CA 165; CAAE 120; EWL 3

**Fair, Ronald L.** 1932- ........................ **CLC 18**
    See also BW 1; CA 69-72; CANR 25; DLB 33

**Fairbairn, Roger**
    See Carr, John Dickson

**Fairbairns, Zoe (Ann)** 1948- ............. **CLC 32**
    See also CA 103; CANR 21, 85; CN 4, 5, 6, 7

**Fairfield, Flora**
    See Alcott, Louisa May

**Fairman, Paul W.** 1916-1977
    See Queen, Ellery
    See also CAAS 114; SFW 4

**Falco, Gian**
    See Papini, Giovanni

**Falconer, James**
    See Kirkup, James

**Falconer, Kenneth**
    See Kornbluth, C(yril) M.

**Falkland, Samuel**
    See Heijermans, Herman

**Fallaci, Oriana** 1930-2006 ......... **CLC 11, 110**
    See also CA 77-80; CAAS 253; CANR 15, 58, 134; FW; MTCW 1

**Faludi, Susan** 1959- ........................ **CLC 140**
    See also CA 138; CANR 126; FW; MTCW 2; MTFW 2005; NCFS 3

**Faludy, George** 1913- ........................ **CLC 42**
    See also CA 21-24R

**Faludy, Gyoergy**
    See Faludy, George

**Fanon, Frantz** 1925-1961 ... **BLC 2; CLC 74; TCLC 188**
    See also BW 1; CA 116; CAAS 89-92; DAM MULT; DLB 296; LMFS 2; WLIT 2

**Fanshawe, Ann** 1625-1680 .................... **LC 11**

**Fante, John (Thomas)** 1911-1983 .... **CLC 60; SSC 65**
    See also AMWS 11; CA 69-72; CAAS 109; CANR 23, 104; DLB 130; DLBY 1983

**Far, Sui Sin** ........................................... **SSC 62**
    See Eaton, Edith Maude
    See also SSFS 4

**Farah, Nuruddin** 1945- ...... **BLC 2; CLC 53, 137**
    See also AFW; BW 2, 3; CA 106; CANR 81, 148; CDWLB 3; CN 4, 5, 6, 7; DAM MULT; DLB 125; EWL 3; WLIT 2

**Fargue, Leon-Paul** 1876(?)-1947 .... **TCLC 11**
    See also CAAE 109; CANR 107; DLB 258; EWL 3

**Farigoule, Louis**
    See Romains, Jules

**Farina, Richard** 1936(?)-1966 ............. **CLC 9**
    See also CA 81-84; CAAS 25-28R

**Farley, Walter (Lorimer)** 1915-1989 ................................ **CLC 17**
    See also CA 17-20R; BYA 14; CA 17-20R; CANR 8, 29, 84; DLB 22; JRDA; MAICYA 1, 2; SATA 2, 43, 132; YAW

**Farmer, Philip Jose** 1918- ............. **CLC 1, 19**
    See also AAYA 28; BPFB 1; CA 1-4R; CANR 4, 35, 111; DLB 8; MTCW 1; SATA 93; SCFW 1, 2; SFW 4

**Farquhar, George** 1677-1707 ............... **LC 21**
    See also BRW 2; DAM DRAM; DLB 84; RGEL 2

**Farrell, J(ames) G(ordon)** 1935-1979 ................................ **CLC 6**
    See also CA 73-76; CAAS 89-92; CANR 36; CN 1, 2; DLB 14, 271, 326; MTCW 1; RGEL 2; RHW; WLIT 4

**Farrell, James T(homas)** 1904-1979 . **CLC 1, 4, 8, 11, 66; SSC 28**
    See also AMW; BPFB 1; CA 5-8R; CAAS 89-92; CANR 9, 61; CN 1, 2; DLB 4, 9, 86; DLBD 2; EWL 3; MAL 5; MTCW 1, 2; MTFW 2005; RGAL 4

**Findley, Timothy (Irving Frederick)**
　　1930-2002 ...................... **CLC 27, 102**
　　See also CA 25-28R; CAAS 206; CANR
　　12, 42, 69, 109; CCA 1; CN 4, 5, 6, 7;
　　DAC; DAM MST; DLB 53; FANT; RHW

**Fink, William**
　　See Mencken, H(enry) L(ouis)

**Firbank, Louis** 1942-
　　See Reed, Lou
　　See also CAAE 117

**Firbank, (Arthur Annesley) Ronald**
　　1886-1926 ............................ **TCLC 1**
　　See also BRWS 2; CA 177; CAAE 104;
　　DLB 36; EWL 3; RGEL 2

**Firdawsi, Abu al-Qasim**
　　See Ferdowsi, Abu'l Qasem
　　See also WLIT 6

**Fish, Stanley**
　　See Fish, Stanley Eugene

**Fish, Stanley E.**
　　See Fish, Stanley Eugene

**Fish, Stanley Eugene** 1938- ............ **CLC 142**
　　See also CA 132; CAAE 112; CANR 90;
　　DLB 67

**Fisher, Dorothy (Frances) Canfield**
　　1879-1958 ............................ **TCLC 87**
　　See also CA 136; CAAE 114; CANR 80;
　　CLR 71; CWRI 5; DLB 9, 102, 284;
　　MAICYA 1, 2; MAL 5; YABC 1

**Fisher, M(ary) F(rances) K(ennedy)**
　　1908-1992 ...................... **CLC 76, 87**
　　See also AMWS 17; CA 77-80; CAAS 138;
　　CANR 44; MTCW 2

**Fisher, Roy** 1930- .............................. **CLC 25**
　　See also CA 81-84; 10; CANR 16; CP 1, 2,
　　3, 4, 5, 6, 7; DLB 40

**Fisher, Rudolph** 1897-1934 . **BLC 2; HR 1:2;
　　SSC 25; TCLC 11**
　　See also BW 1, 3; CA 124; CAAE 107;
　　CANR 80; DAM MULT; DLB 51, 102

**Fisher, Vardis (Alvero)** 1895-1968 .... **CLC 7;
　　TCLC 140**
　　See also CA 5-8R; CAAS 25-28R; CANR
　　68; DLB 9, 206; MAL 5; RGAL 4;
　　TCWW 1, 2

**Fiske, Tarleton**
　　See Bloch, Robert (Albert)

**Fitch, Clarke**
　　See Sinclair, Upton

**Fitch, John IV**
　　See Cormier, Robert

**Fitzgerald, Captain Hugh**
　　See Baum, L(yman) Frank

**FitzGerald, Edward** 1809-1883 ...... **NCLC 9,
　　153; PC 79**
　　See also BRW 4; DLB 32; RGEL 2

**Fitzgerald, F(rancis) Scott (Key)**
　　1896-1940 ... **SSC 6, 31, 75; TCLC 1, 6,
　　14, 28, 55, 157; WLC 2**
　　See also AAYA 24; AITN 1; AMW; AMWC
　　2; AMWR 1; BPFB 1; CA 123; CAAE
　　110; CDALB 1917-1929; DA; DA3;
　　DAB; DAC; DAM MST, NOV; DLB 4,
　　9, 86, 219, 273; DLBD 1, 15, 16; DLBY
　　1981, 1996; EWL 3; EXPN; EXPS; LAIT
　　3; MAL 5; MTCW 1, 2; MTFW 2005;
　　NFS 2, 19, 20; RGAL 4; RGSF 2; SSFS
　　4, 15, 21, 25; TUS

**Fitzgerald, Penelope** 1916-2000 . **CLC 19, 51,
　　61, 143**
　　See also BRWS 5; CA 85-88; 10; CAAS
　　190; CANR 56, 86, 131; CN 3, 4, 5, 6, 7;
　　DLB 14, 194, 326; EWL 3; MTCW 2;
　　MTFW 2005

**Fitzgerald, Robert (Stuart)**
　　1910-1985 ................................ **CLC 39**
　　See also CA 1-4R; CAAS 114; CANR 1;
　　CP 1, 2, 3, 4; DLBY 1980; MAL 5

**FitzGerald, Robert D(avid)**
　　1902-1987 ................................ **CLC 19**
　　See also CA 17-20R; CP 1, 2, 3, 4; DLB
　　260; RGEL 2

**Fitzgerald, Zelda (Sayre)**
　　1900-1948 ............................ **TCLC 52**
　　See also AMWS 9; CA 126; CAAE 117;
　　DLBY 1984

**Flanagan, Thomas (James Bonner)**
　　1923-2002 ...................... **CLC 25, 52**
　　See also CA 108; CAAS 206; CANR 55;
　　CN 3, 4, 5, 6, 7; DLBY 1980; INT CA-
　　108; MTCW 1; RHW; TCLE 1:1

**Flaubert, Gustave** 1821-1880 .... **NCLC 2, 10,
　　19, 62, 66, 135, 179, 185; SSC 11, 60;
　　WLC 2**
　　See also DA; DA3; DAB; DAC; DAM
　　MST, NOV; DLB 119, 301; EW 7; EXPS;
　　GFL 1789 to the Present; LAIT 2; LMFS
　　1; NFS 14; RGSF 2; RGWL 2, 3; SSFS
　　6; TWA

**Flavius Josephus**
　　See Josephus, Flavius

**Flecker, Herman Elroy**
　　See Flecker, (Herman) James Elroy

**Flecker, (Herman) James Elroy**
　　1884-1915 ................................ **TCLC 43**
　　See also CA 150; CAAE 109; DLB 10, 19;
　　RGEL 2

**Fleming, Ian** 1908-1964 ... **CLC 3, 30; TCLC
　　193**
　　See also AAYA 26; BPFB 1; CA 5-8R;
　　CANR 59; CDBLB 1945-1960; CMW 4;
　　CPW; DA3; DAM POP; DLB 87, 201;
　　MSW; MTCW 1, 2; MTFW 2005; RGEL
　　2; SATA 9; TEA; YAW

**Fleming, Ian Lancaster**
　　See Fleming, Ian

**Fleming, Thomas** 1927- ...................... **CLC 37**
　　See also CA 5-8R; CANR 10, 102, 155;
　　INT CANR-10; SATA 8

**Fleming, Thomas James**
　　See Fleming, Thomas

**Fletcher, John** 1579-1625 .......... **DC 6; LC 33**
　　See also BRW 2; CDBLB Before 1660;
　　DLB 58; RGEL 2; TEA

**Fletcher, John Gould** 1886-1950 .... **TCLC 35**
　　See also CA 167; CAAE 107; DLB 4, 45;
　　LMFS 2; MAL 5; RGAL 4

**Fleur, Paul**
　　See Pohl, Frederik

**Flieg, Helmut**
　　See Heym, Stefan

**Flooglebuckle, Al**
　　See Spiegelman, Art

**Flora, Fletcher** 1914-1969
　　See Queen, Ellery
　　See also CA 1-4R; CANR 3, 85

**Flying Officer X**
　　See Bates, H(erbert) E(rnest)

**Fo, Dario** 1926- .... **CLC 32, 109, 227; DC 10**
　　See also CA 128; CAAE 116; CANR 68,
　　114, 134, 164; CWW 2; DA3; DAM
　　DRAM; DFS 23; DLB 330; DLBY 1997;
　　EWL 3; MTCW 1, 2; MTFW 2005; WLIT
　　7

**Foden, Giles** 1967- .......................... **CLC 231**
　　See also CA 240; DLB 267; NFS 15

**Fogarty, Jonathan Titulescu Esq.**
　　See Farrell, James T(homas)

**Follett, Ken** 1949- .............................. **CLC 18**
　　See also AAYA 6, 50; BEST 89:4; BPFB 1;
　　CA 81-84; CANR 13, 33, 54, 102, 156;
　　CMW 4; CPW; DA3; DAM NOV, POP;
　　DLB 87; DLBY 1981; INT CANR-33;
　　MTCW 1

**Follett, Kenneth Martin**
　　See Follett, Ken

**Fondane, Benjamin** 1898-1944 ..... **TCLC 159**

**Fontane, Theodor** 1819-1898 . **NCLC 26, 163**
　　See also CDWLB 2; DLB 129; EW 6;
　　RGWL 2, 3; TWA

**Fonte, Moderata** 1555-1592 ............... **LC 118**

**Fontenelle, Bernard Le Bovier de**
　　1657-1757 ............................ **LC 140**
　　See also DLB 268, 313; GFL Beginnings to
　　1789

**Fontenot, Chester** .......................... **CLC 65**

**Fonvizin, Denis Ivanovich**
　　1744(?)-1792 ............................ **LC 81**
　　See also DLB 150; RGWL 2, 3

**Foote, Horton** 1916- ...................... **CLC 51, 91**
　　See also CA 73-76; CAD; CANR 34, 51,
　　110; CD 5, 6; CSW; DA3; DAM DRAM;
　　DFS 20; DLB 26, 266; EWL 3; INT
　　CANR-34; MTFW 2005

**Foote, Mary Hallock** 1847-1938 .. **TCLC 108**
　　See also DLB 186, 188, 202, 221; TCWW
　　2

**Foote, Samuel** 1721-1777 ................... **LC 106**
　　See also DLB 89; RGEL 2

**Foote, Shelby** 1916-2005 ........... **CLC 75, 224**
　　See also AAYA 40; CA 5-8R; CAAS 240;
　　CANR 3, 45, 74, 131; CN 1, 2, 3, 4, 5, 6,
　　7; CPW; CSW; DA3; DAM NOV, POP;
　　DLB 2, 17; MAL 5; MTCW 2; MTFW
　　2005; RHW

**Forbes, Cosmo**
　　See Lewton, Val

**Forbes, Esther** 1891-1967 ................. **CLC 12**
　　See also AAYA 17; BYA 2; CA 13-14;
　　CAAS 25-28R; CAP 1; CLR 27; DLB 22;
　　JRDA; MAICYA 1, 2; RHW; SATA 2,
　　100; YAW

**Forche, Carolyn** 1950- .. **CLC 25, 83, 86; PC
　　10**
　　See also CA 117; CAAE 109; CANR 50,
　　74, 138; CP 4, 5, 6, 7; CWP; DA3; DAM
　　POET; DLB 5, 193; INT CA-117; MAL
　　5; MTCW 2; MTFW 2005; PFS 18;
　　RGAL 4

**Forche, Carolyn Louise**
　　See Forche, Carolyn

**Ford, Elbur**
　　See Hibbert, Eleanor Alice Burford

**Ford, Ford Madox** 1873-1939 ... **TCLC 1, 15,
　　39, 57, 172**
　　See Chaucer, Daniel
　　See also BRW 6; CA 132; CAAE 104;
　　CANR 74; CDBLB 1914-1945; DA3;
　　DAM NOV; DLB 34, 98, 162; EWL 3;
　　MTCW 1, 2; RGEL 2; TEA

**Ford, Henry** 1863-1947 ................... **TCLC 73**
　　See also CA 148; CAAE 115

**Ford, Jack**
　　See Ford, John

**Ford, John** 1586-1639 .............. **DC 8; LC 68**
　　See also BRW 2; CDBLB Before 1660;
　　DA3; DAM DRAM; DFS 7; DLB 58;
　　IDTP; RGEL 2

**Ford, John** 1895-1973 ...................... **CLC 16**
　　See also AAYA 75; CA 187; CAAS 45-48

**Ford, Richard** 1944- ........... **CLC 46, 99, 205**
　　See also AMWS 5; CA 69-72; CANR 11,
　　47, 86, 128, 164; CN 5, 6, 7; CSW; DLB
　　227; EWL 3; MAL 5; MTCW 2; MTFW
　　2005; NFS 25; RGAL 4; RGSF 2

**Ford, Webster**
　　See Masters, Edgar Lee

**Foreman, Richard** 1937- ................... **CLC 50**
　　See also CA 65-68; CAD; CANR 32, 63,
　　143; CD 5, 6

**Forester, C(ecil) S(cott)** 1899-1966 . **CLC 35;
　　TCLC 152**
　　See also CA 73-76; CAAS 25-28R; CANR
　　83; DLB 191; RGEL 2; RHW; SATA 13

**Freneau, Philip Morin** 1752-1832 .. **NCLC 1, 111**
See also AMWS 2; DLB 37, 43; RGAL 4

**Freud, Sigmund** 1856-1939 ............ **TCLC 52**
See also CA 133; CAAE 115; CANR 69; DLB 296; EW 8; EWL 3; LATS 1:1; MTCW 1, 2; MTFW 2005; NCFS 3; TWA

**Freytag, Gustav** 1816-1895 .......... **NCLC 109**
See also DLB 129

**Friedan, Betty** 1921-2006 ................. **CLC 74**
See also CA 65-68; CAAS 248; CANR 18, 45, 74; DLB 246; FW; MTCW 1, 2; MTFW 2005; NCFS 5

**Friedan, Betty Naomi**
See Friedan, Betty

**Friedlander, Saul** 1932- .................... **CLC 90**
See also CA 130; CAAE 117; CANR 72; RGHL

**Friedman, B(ernard) H(arper)**
1926- ................................. **CLC 7**
See also CA 1-4R; CANR 3, 48

**Friedman, Bruce Jay** 1930- ...... **CLC 3, 5, 56**
See also CA 9-12R; CAD; CANR 25, 52, 101; CD 5, 6; CN 1, 2, 3, 4, 5, 6, 7; DLB 2, 28, 244; INT CANR-25; MAL 5; SSFS 18

**Friel, Brian** 1929- .... **CLC 5, 42, 59, 115; DC 8; SSC 76**
See also BRWS 5; CA 21-24R; CANR 33, 69, 131; CBD; CD 5, 6; DFS 11; DLB 13, 319; EWL 3; MTCW 1; RGEL 2; TEA

**Friis-Baastad, Babbis Ellinor**
1921-1970 ............................ **CLC 12**
See also CA 17-20R; CAAS 134; SATA 7

**Frisch, Max** 1911-1991 ...... **CLC 3, 9, 14, 18, 32, 44; TCLC 121**
See also CA 85-88; CAAS 134; CANR 32, 74; CDWLB 2; DAM DRAM, NOV; DLB 69, 124; EW 13; EWL 3; MTCW 1, 2; MTFW 2005; RGHL; RGWL 2, 3

**Fromentin, Eugene (Samuel Auguste)**
1820-1876 ...................... **NCLC 10, 125**
See also DLB 123; GFL 1789 to the Present

**Frost, Frederick**
See Faust, Frederick (Schiller)

**Frost, Robert** 1874-1963 . **CLC 1, 3, 4, 9, 10, 13, 15, 26, 34, 44; PC 1, 39, 71; WLC 2**
See also AAYA 21; AMW; AMWR 1; CA 89-92; CANR 33; CDALB 1917-1929; CLR 67; DA; DA3; DAB; DAC; DAM MST, POET; DLB 54, 284; DLBD 7; EWL 3; EXPP; MAL 5; MTCW 1, 2; MTFW 2005; PAB; PFS 1, 2, 3, 4, 5, 6, 7, 10, 13; RGAL 4; SATA 14; TUS; WP; WYA

**Frost, Robert Lee**
See Frost, Robert

**Froude, James Anthony**
1818-1894 ............................... **NCLC 43**
See also DLB 18, 57, 144

**Froy, Herald**
See Waterhouse, Keith (Spencer)

**Fry, Christopher** 1907-2005 ... **CLC 2, 10, 14**
See also BRWS 3; CA 17-20R; 23; CAAS 240; CANR 9, 30, 74, 132; CBD; CD 5, 6; CP 1, 2, 3, 4, 5, 6, 7; DAM DRAM; DLB 13; EWL 3; MTCW 1, 2; MTFW 2005; RGEL 2; SATA 66; TEA

**Frye, (Herman) Northrop**
1912-1991 ........ **CLC 24, 70; TCLC 165**
See also CA 5-8R; CAAS 133; CANR 8, 37; DLB 67, 68, 246; EWL 3; MTCW 1, 2; MTFW 2005; RGAL 4; TWA

**Fuchs, Daniel** 1909-1993 .............. **CLC 8, 22**
See also CA 81-84; 5; CAAS 142; CANR 40; CN 1, 2, 3, 4, 5; DLB 9, 26, 28; DLBY 1993; MAL 5

**Fuchs, Daniel** 1934- ......................... **CLC 34**
See also CA 37-40R; CANR 14, 48

**Fuentes, Carlos** 1928- .. **CLC 3, 8, 10, 13, 22, 41, 60, 113; HLC 1; SSC 24; WLC 2**
See also AAYA 4, 45; AITN 2; BPFB 1; CA 69-72; CANR 10, 32, 68, 104, 138; CDWLB 3; CWW 2; DA; DA3; DAB; DAC; DAM MST, MULT, NOV; DLB 113; DNFS 2; EWL 3; HW 1, 2; LAIT 3; LATS 1:2; LAW; LAWS 1; LMFS 2; MTCW 1, 2; MTFW 2005; NFS 8; RGSF 2; RGWL 2, 3; TWA; WLIT 1

**Fuentes, Gregorio Lopez y**
See Lopez y Fuentes, Gregorio

**Fuertes, Gloria** 1918-1998 .................... **PC 27**
See also CA 178, 180; DLB 108; HW 2; SATA 115

**Fugard, (Harold) Athol** 1932- . **CLC 5, 9, 14, 25, 40, 80, 211; DC 3**
See also AAYA 17; AFW; CA 85-88; CANR 32, 54, 118; CD 5, 6; DAM DRAM; DFS 3, 6, 10, 24; DLB 225; DNFS 1, 2; EWL 3; LATS 1:2; MTCW 1; MTFW 2005; RGEL 2; WLIT 2

**Fugard, Sheila** 1932- ......................... **CLC 48**
See also CA 125

**Fujiwara no Teika** 1162-1241 ....... **CMLC 73**
See also DLB 203

**Fukuyama, Francis** 1952- .............. **CLC 131**
See also CA 140; CANR 72, 125

**Fuller, Charles (H.), (Jr.)** 1939- ......... **BLC 2; CLC 25; DC 1**
See also BW 2; CA 112; CAAE 108; CAD; CANR 87; CD 5, 6; DAM DRAM, MULT; DFS 8; DLB 38, 266; EWL 3; INT CA-112; MAL 5; MTCW 1

**Fuller, Henry Blake** 1857-1929 .... **TCLC 103**
See also CA 177; CAAE 108; DLB 12; RGAL 4

**Fuller, John (Leopold)** 1937- ............ **CLC 62**
See also CA 21-24R; CANR 9, 44; CP 1, 2, 3, 4, 5, 6, 7; DLB 40

**Fuller, Margaret**
See Ossoli, Sarah Margaret (Fuller)
See also AMWS 2; DLB 183, 223, 239; FL 1:3

**Fuller, Roy (Broadbent)** 1912-1991 ... **CLC 4, 28**
See also BRWS 7; CA 5-8R; 10; CAAS 135; CANR 53, 83; CN 1, 2, 3, 4, 5; CP 1, 2, 3, 4, 5; CWRI 5; DLB 15, 20; EWL 3; RGEL 2; SATA 87

**Fuller, Sarah Margaret**
See Ossoli, Sarah Margaret (Fuller)

**Fuller, Sarah Margaret**
See Ossoli, Sarah Margaret (Fuller)
See also DLB 1, 59, 73

**Fuller, Thomas** 1608-1661 .................. **LC 111**
See also DLB 151

**Fulton, Alice** 1952- ............................. **CLC 52**
See also CA 116; CANR 57, 88; CP 5, 6, 7; CWP; DLB 193; PFS 25

**Furphy, Joseph** 1843-1912 .............. **TCLC 25**
See Collins, Tom
See also CA 163; DLB 230; EWL 3; RGEL 2

**Fuson, Robert H(enderson)** 1927- .... **CLC 70**
See also CA 89-92; CANR 103

**Fussell, Paul** 1924- ............................. **CLC 74**
See also BEST 90:1; CA 17-20R; CANR 8, 21, 35, 69, 135; INT CANR-21; MTCW 1, 2; MTFW 2005

**Futabatei, Shimei** 1864-1909 ......... **TCLC 44**
See Futabatei Shimei
See also CA 162; MJW

**Futabatei Shimei**
See Futabatei, Shimei
See also DLB 180; EWL 3

**Futrelle, Jacques** 1875-1912 .......... **TCLC 19**
See also CA 155; CAAE 113; CMW 4

**Gaboriau, Emile** 1835-1873 ........... **NCLC 14**
See also CMW 4; MSW

**Gadda, Carlo Emilio** 1893-1973 ...... **CLC 11; TCLC 144**
See also CA 89-92; DLB 177; EWL 3; WLIT 7

**Gaddis, William** 1922-1998 ... **CLC 1, 3, 6, 8, 10, 19, 43, 86**
See also AMWS 4; BPFB 1; CA 17-20R; CAAS 172; CANR 21, 48, 148; CN 1, 2, 3, 4, 5, 6; DLB 2, 278; EWL 3; MAL 5; MTCW 1, 2; MTFW 2005; RGAL 4

**Gage, Walter**
See Inge, William (Motter)

**Gaiman, Neil** 1960- ........................... **CLC 195**
See also AAYA 19, 42; CA 133; CANR 81, 129; CLR 109; DLB 261; HGG; MTFW 2005; SATA 85, 146; SFW 4; SUFW 2

**Gaiman, Neil Richard**
See Gaiman, Neil

**Gaines, Ernest J.** 1933- .. **BLC 2; CLC 3, 11, 18, 86, 181; SSC 68**
See also AAYA 18; AFAW 1, 2; AITN 1; BPFB 2; BW 2, 3; BYA 6; CA 9-12R; CANR 6, 24, 42, 75, 126; CDALB 1968-1988; CLR 62; CN 1, 2, 3, 4, 5, 6, 7; CSW; DA3; DAM MULT; DLB 2, 33, 152; DLBY 1980; EWL 3; EXPN; LAIT 5; LATS 1:2; MAL 5; MTCW 1, 2; MTFW 2005; NFS 5, 7, 16; RGAL 4; RGSF 2; RHW; SATA 86; SSFS 5; YAW

**Gaitskill, Mary** 1954- ......................... **CLC 69**
See also CA 128; CANR 61, 152; DLB 244; TCLE 1:1

**Gaitskill, Mary Lawrence**
See Gaitskill, Mary

**Gaius Suetonius Tranquillus**
See Suetonius

**Galdos, Benito Perez**
See Perez Galdos, Benito
See also EW 7

**Gale, Zona** 1874-1938 ...................... **TCLC 7**
See also CA 153; CAAE 105; CANR 84; DAM DRAM; DFS 17; DLB 9, 78, 228; RGAL 4

**Galeano, Eduardo** 1940- ... **CLC 72; HLCS 1**
See also CA 29-32R; CANR 13, 32, 100, 163; HW 1

**Galeano, Eduardo Hughes**
See Galeano, Eduardo

**Galiano, Juan Valera y Alcala**
See Valera y Alcala-Galiano, Juan

**Galilei, Galileo** 1564-1642 ................... **LC 45**

**Gallagher, Tess** 1943- ....... **CLC 18, 63; PC 9**
See also CA 106; CP 3, 4, 5, 6, 7; CWP; DAM POET; DLB 120, 212, 244; PFS 16

**Gallant, Mavis** 1922- ..... **CLC 7, 18, 38, 172; SSC 5, 78**
See also CA 69-72; CANR 29, 69, 117; CCA 1; CN 1, 2, 3, 4, 5, 6, 7; DAC; DAM MST; DLB 53; EWL 3; MTCW 1, 2; MTFW 2005; RGEL 2; RGSF 2

**Gallant, Roy A(rthur)** 1924- .............. **CLC 17**
See also CA 5-8R; CANR 4, 29, 54, 117; CLR 30; MAICYA 1, 2; SATA 4, 68, 110

**Gallico, Paul (William)** 1897-1976 ..... **CLC 2**
See also AITN 1; CA 5-8R; CAAS 69-72; CANR 23; CN 1, 2; DLB 9, 171; FANT; MAICYA 1, 2; SATA 13

**Gallo, Max Louis** 1932- .................... **CLC 95**
See also CA 85-88

**Gallois, Lucien**
See Desnos, Robert

**Gallup, Ralph**
See Whitemore, Hugh (John)

**Galsworthy, John** 1867-1933 ............ **SSC 22; TCLC 1, 45; WLC 2**
See also BRW 6; CA 141; CAAE 104; CANR 75; CDBLB 1890-1914; DA; DA3; DAB; DAC; DAM DRAM, MST, NOV; DLB 10, 34, 98, 162, 330; DLBD 16; EWL 3; MTCW 2; RGEL 2; SSFS 3; TEA

**Galt, John** 1779-1839 ............... **NCLC 1, 110**
See also DLB 99, 116, 159; RGEL 2; RGSF 2

**Galvin, James** 1951- .......................... **CLC 38**
See also CA 108; CANR 26

**Gamboa, Federico** 1864-1939 ........ **TCLC 36**
See also CA 167; HW 2; LAW

**Gandhi, M. K.**
See Gandhi, Mohandas Karamchand

**Gandhi, Mahatma**
See Gandhi, Mohandas Karamchand

**Gandhi, Mohandas Karamchand**
1869-1948 ................................ **TCLC 59**
See also CA 132; CAAE 121; DA3; DAM MULT; DLB 323; MTCW 1, 2

**Gann, Ernest Kellogg** 1910-1991 ..... **CLC 23**
See also AITN 1; BPFB 2; CA 1-4R; CAAS 136; CANR 1, 83; RHW

**Gao Xingjian** 1940- .......................... **CLC 167**
See Xingjian, Gao
See also MTFW 2005

**Garber, Eric** 1943(?)-
See Holleran, Andrew
See also CANR 89, 162

**Garcia, Cristina** 1958- ...................... **CLC 76**
See also AMWS 11; CA 141; CANR 73, 130; CN 7; DLB 292; DNFS 1; EWL 3; HW 2; LLW; MTFW 2005

**Garcia Lorca, Federico** 1898-1936 ...... **DC 2; HLC 2; PC 3; TCLC 1, 7, 49, 181; WLC 2**
See Lorca, Federico Garcia
See also AAYA 46; CA 131; CAAE 104; CANR 81; DA; DA3; DAC; DAM DRAM, MST, MULT, POET; DFS 4, 10; DLB 108; EWL 3; HW 1, 2; LATS 1:2; MTCW 1, 2; MTFW 2005; TWA

**Garcia Marquez, Gabriel** 1928- .... **CLC 2, 3, 8, 10, 15, 27, 47, 55, 68, 170; HLC 1; SSC 8, 83; WLC 3**
See also AAYA 3, 33; BEST 89:1, 90:4; BPFB 2; BYA 12, 16; CA 33-36R; CANR 10, 28, 50, 75, 82, 128; CDWLB 3; CPW; CWW 2; DA; DA3; DAB; DAC; DAM MST, MULT, NOV, POP; DLB 113, 330; DNFS 1, 2; EWL 3; EXPN; EXPS; HW 1, 2; LAIT 2; LATS 1:2; LAW; LAWS 1; LMFS 2; MTCW 1, 2; MTFW 2005; NCFS 3; NFS 1, 5, 10; RGSF 2; RGWL 2, 3; SSFS 1, 6, 16, 21; TWA; WLIT 1

**Garcia Marquez, Gabriel Jose**
See Garcia Marquez, Gabriel

**Garcilaso de la Vega, El Inca**
1539-1616 ................... **HLCS 1; LC 127**
See also DLB 318; LAW

**Gard, Janice**
See Latham, Jean Lee

**Gard, Roger Martin du**
See Martin du Gard, Roger

**Gardam, Jane** 1928- ........................ **CLC 43**
See also CA 49-52; CANR 2, 18, 33, 54, 106, 167; CLR 12; DLB 14, 161, 231; MAICYA 1, 2; MTCW 1; SAAS 9; SATA 39, 76, 130; SATA-Brief 28; YAW

**Gardam, Jane Mary**
See Gardam, Jane

**Gardner, Herb(ert George)**
1934-2003 ................................ **CLC 44**
See also CA 149; CAAS 220; CAD; CANR 119; CD 5, 6; DFS 18, 20

**Gardner, John, Jr.** 1933-1982 ... **CLC 2, 3, 5, 7, 8, 10, 18, 28, 34; SSC 7; TCLC 195**
See also AAYA 45; AITN 1; AMWS 6; BPFB 2; CA 65-68; CAAS 107; CANR 33, 73; CDALBS; CN 2, 3; CPW; DA3; DAM NOV, POP; DLB 2; DLBY 1982; EWL 3; FANT; LATS 1:2; MAL 5; MTCW 1, 2; MTFW 2005; NFS 3; RGAL 4; RGSF 2; SATA 40; SATA-Obit 31; SSFS 8

**Gardner, John** 1926-2007 ................. **CLC 30**
See also CA 103; CANR 15, 69, 127; CMW 4; CPW; DAM POP; MTCW 1

**Gardner, John Edmund**
See Gardner, John

**Gardner, Miriam**
See Bradley, Marion Zimmer
See also GLL 1

**Gardner, Noel**
See Kuttner, Henry

**Gardons, S. S.**
See Snodgrass, W.D.

**Garfield, Leon** 1921-1996 ................. **CLC 12**
See also AAYA 8, 69; BYA 1, 3; CA 17-20R; CAAS 152; CANR 38, 41, 78; CLR 21; DLB 161; JRDA; MAICYA 1, 2; MAICYAS 1; SATA 1, 32, 76; SATA-Obit 90; TEA; WYA; YAW

**Garland, (Hannibal) Hamlin**
1860-1940 ................. **SSC 18; TCLC 3**
See also CAAE 104; DLB 12, 71, 78, 186; MAL 5; RGAL 4; RGSF 2; TCWW 1, 2

**Garneau, (Hector de) Saint-Denys**
1912-1943 ................................ **TCLC 13**
See also CAAE 111; DLB 88

**Garner, Alan** 1934- ........................... **CLC 17**
See also AAYA 18; BYA 3, 5; CA 178; 73-76, 178; CANR 15, 64, 134; CLR 20; CPW; DAB; DAM POP; DLB 161, 261; FANT; MAICYA 1, 2; MTCW 1, 2; MTFW 2005; SATA 18, 69; SATA-Essay 108; SUFW 1, 2; YAW

**Garner, Hugh** 1913-1979 ................... **CLC 13**
See Warwick, Jarvis
See also CA 69-72; CANR 31; CCA 1; CN 1, 2; DLB 68

**Garnett, David** 1892-1981 .................. **CLC 3**
See also CA 5-8R; CAAS 103; CANR 17, 79; CN 1, 2; DLB 34; FANT; MTCW 2; RGEL 2; SFW 4; SUFW 1

**Garnier, Robert** c. 1545-1590 ........... **LC 119**
See also DLB 327; GFL Beginnings to 1789

**Garrett, George (Palmer, Jr.)** 1929- . **CLC 3, 11, 51; SSC 30**
See also AMWS 7; BPFB 2; CA 202; 1-4R, 202; 5; CANR 1, 42, 67, 109; CN 1, 2, 3, 4, 5, 6, 7; CP 1, 2, 3, 4, 5, 6, 7; CSW; DLB 2, 5, 130, 152; DLBY 1983

**Garrick, David** 1717-1779 .................. **LC 15**
See also DAM DRAM; DLB 84, 213; RGEL 2

**Garrigue, Jean** 1914-1972 .............. **CLC 2, 8**
See also CA 5-8R; CAAS 37-40R; CANR 20; CP 1; MAL 5

**Garrison, Frederick**
See Sinclair, Upton

**Garrison, William Lloyd**
1805-1879 .............................. **NCLC 149**
See also CDALB 1640-1865; DLB 1, 43, 235

**Garro, Elena** 1920(?)-1998 .. **HLCS 1; TCLC 153**
See also CA 131; CAAS 169; CWW 2; DLB 145; EWL 3; HW 1; LAWS 1; WLIT 1

**Garth, Will**
See Hamilton, Edmond; Kuttner, Henry

**Garvey, Marcus (Moziah, Jr.)**
1887-1940 ... **BLC 2; HR 1:2; TCLC 41**
See also BW 1; CA 124; CAAE 120; CANR 79; DAM MULT

**Gary, Romain** ................................ **CLC 25**
See Kacew, Romain
See also DLB 83, 299; RGHL

**Gascar, Pierre** ................................. **CLC 11**
See Fournier, Pierre
See also EWL 3; RGHL

**Gascoigne, George** 1539-1577 ........... **LC 108**
See also DLB 136; RGEL 2

**Gascoyne, David (Emery)**
1916-2001 ................................ **CLC 45**
See also CA 65-68; CAAS 200; CANR 10, 28, 54; CP 1, 2, 3, 4, 5, 6, 7; DLB 20; MTCW 1; RGEL 2

**Gaskell, Elizabeth Cleghorn**
1810-1865 .... **NCLC 5, 70, 97, 137; SSC 25, 97**
See also BRW 5; CDBLB 1832-1890; DAB; DAM MST; DLB 21, 144, 159; RGEL 2; RGSF 2; TEA

**Gass, William H.** 1924- . **CLC 1, 2, 8, 11, 15, 39, 132; SSC 12**
See also AMWS 6; CA 17-20R; CANR 30, 71, 100; CN 1, 2, 3, 4, 5, 6, 7; DLB 2, 227; EWL 3; MAL 5; MTCW 1, 2; MTFW 2005; RGAL 4

**Gassendi, Pierre** 1592-1655 ................. **LC 54**
See also GFL Beginnings to 1789

**Gasset, Jose Ortega y**
See Ortega y Gasset, Jose

**Gates, Henry Louis, Jr.** 1950- ... **BLCS; CLC 65**
See also BW 2, 3; CA 109; CANR 25, 53, 75, 125; CSW; DA3; DAM MULT; DLB 67; EWL 3; MAL 5; MTCW 2; MTFW 2005; RGAL 4

**Gatos, Stephanie**
See Katz, Steve

**Gautier, Theophile** 1811-1872 .. **NCLC 1, 59; PC 18; SSC 20**
See also DAM POET; DLB 119; EW 6; GFL 1789 to the Present; RGWL 2, 3; SUFW; TWA

**Gay, John** 1685-1732 ........................... **LC 49**
See also BRW 3; DAM DRAM; DLB 84, 95; RGEL 2; WLIT 3

**Gay, Oliver**
See Gogarty, Oliver St. John

**Gay, Peter** 1923- ............................. **CLC 158**
See also CA 13-16R; CANR 18, 41, 77, 147; INT CANR-18; RGHL

**Gay, Peter Jack**
See Gay, Peter

**Gaye, Marvin (Pentz, Jr.)**
1939-1984 ................................ **CLC 26**
See also CA 195; CAAS 112

**Gebler, Carlo** 1954- .......................... **CLC 39**
See also CA 133; CAAE 119; CANR 96; DLB 271

**Gee, Maggie** 1948- ........................... **CLC 57**
See also CA 130; CANR 125; CN 4, 5, 6, 7; DLB 207; MTFW 2005

**Gee, Maurice** 1931- .......................... **CLC 29**
See also AAYA 42; CA 97-100; CANR 67, 123; CLR 56; CN 2, 3, 4, 5, 6, 7; CWRI 5; EWL 3; MAICYA 2; RGSF 2; SATA 46, 101

**Gee, Maurice Gough**
See Gee, Maurice

**Geiogamah, Hanay** 1945- .................. **NNAL**
See also CA 153; DAM MULT; DLB 175

**Gelbart, Larry**
See Gelbart, Larry (Simon)
See also CAD; CD 5, 6

**Gelbart, Larry (Simon)** 1928- .... **CLC 21, 61**
See Gelbart, Larry
See also CA 73-76; CANR 45, 94

**Gelber, Jack** 1932-2003 ...... **CLC 1, 6, 14, 79**
See also CA 1-4R; CAAS 216; CAD;
CANR 2; DLB 7, 228; MAL 5

**Gellhorn, Martha (Ellis)**
1908-1998 ......................... **CLC 14, 60**
See also CA 77-80; CAAS 164; CANR 44;
CN 1, 2, 3, 4, 5, 6 7; DLBY 1982, 1998

**Genet, Jean** 1910-1986 .. **CLC 1, 2, 5, 10, 14,
44, 46; DC 25; TCLC 128**
See also CA 13-16R; CANR 18; DA3;
DAM DRAM; DFS 10; DLB 72, 321;
DLBY 1986; EW 13; EWL 3; GFL 1789
to the Present; GLL 1; LMFS 2; MTCW
1, 2; MTFW 2005; RGWL 2, 3; TWA

**Genlis, Stephanie-Felicite Ducrest**
1746-1830 .............................. **NCLC 166**
See also DLB 313

**Gent, Peter** 1942- ............................ **CLC 29**
See also AITN 1; CA 89-92; DLBY 1982

**Gentile, Giovanni** 1875-1944 .......... **TCLC 96**
See also CAAE 119

**Geoffrey of Monmouth** c.
1100-1155 ............................ **CMLC 44**
See also DLB 146; TEA

**George, Jean**
See George, Jean Craighead

**George, Jean Craighead** 1919- ......... **CLC 35**
See also AAYA 8, 69; BYA 2, 4; CA 5-8R;
CANR 25; CLR 1; 80; DLB 52; JRDA;
MAICYA 1, 2; SATA 2, 68, 124, 170;
WYA; YAW

**George, Stefan (Anton)** 1868-1933 . **TCLC 2,
14**
See also CA 193; CAAE 104; EW 8; EWL
3

**Georges, Georges Martin**
See Simenon, Georges (Jacques Christian)

**Gerald of Wales** c. 1146-c. 1223 ... **CMLC 60**

**Gerhardi, William Alexander**
See Gerhardie, William Alexander

**Gerhardie, William Alexander**
1895-1977 ............................... **CLC 5**
See also CA 25-28R; CAAS 73-76; CANR
18; CN 1, 2; DLB 36; RGEL 2

**Gerson, Jean** 1363-1429 ....................... **LC 77**
See also DLB 208

**Gersonides** 1288-1344 ................... **CMLC 49**
See also DLB 115

**Gerstler, Amy** 1956- .......................... **CLC 70**
See also CA 146; CANR 99

**Gertler, T.** ........................................ **CLC 34**
See also CA 121; CAAE 116

**Gertsen, Aleksandr Ivanovich**
See Herzen, Aleksandr Ivanovich

**Ghalib** ...................................... **NCLC 39, 78**
See Ghalib, Asadullah Khan

**Ghalib, Asadullah Khan** 1797-1869
See Ghalib
See also DAM POET; RGWL 2, 3

**Ghelderode, Michel de** 1898-1962 ..... **CLC 6,
11; DC 15; TCLC 187**
See also CA 85-88; CANR 40, 77; DAM
DRAM; DLB 321; EW 11; EWL 3; TWA

**Ghiselin, Brewster** 1903-2001 .......... **CLC 23**
See also CA 13-16R; 10; CANR 13; CP 1,
2, 3, 4, 5, 6, 7

**Ghose, Aurabinda** 1872-1950 ......... **TCLC 63**
See Ghose, Aurobindo
See also CA 163

**Ghose, Aurobindo**
See Ghose, Aurabinda
See also EWL 3

**Ghose, Zulfikar** 1935- ................ **CLC 42, 200**
See also CA 65-68; CANR 67; CN 1, 2, 3,
4, 5, 6, 7; CP 1, 2, 3, 4, 5, 6, 7; DLB 323;
EWL 3

**Ghosh, Amitav** 1956- ................. **CLC 44, 153**
See also CA 147; CANR 80, 158; CN 6, 7;
DLB 323; WWE 1

**Giacosa, Giuseppe** 1847-1906 .......... **TCLC 7**
See also CAAE 104

**Gibb, Lee**
See Waterhouse, Keith (Spencer)

**Gibbon, Edward** 1737-1794 ................. **LC 97**
See also BRW 3; DLB 104, 336; RGEL 2

**Gibbon, Lewis Grassic** ................... **TCLC 4**
See Mitchell, James Leslie
See also RGEL 2

**Gibbons, Kaye** 1960- .......... **CLC 50, 88, 145**
See also AAYA 34; AMWS 10; CA 151;
CANR 75, 127; CN 7; CSW; DA3; DAM
POP; DLB 292; MTCW 2; MTFW 2005;
NFS 3; RGAL 4; SATA 117

**Gibran, Kahlil** 1883-1931 . **PC 9; TCLC 1, 9**
See also CA 150; CAAE 104; DA3; DAM
POET, POP; EWL 3; MTCW 2; WLIT 6

**Gibran, Khalil**
See Gibran, Kahlil

**Gibson, Mel** 1956- ............................ **CLC 215**

**Gibson, William** 1914- ...................... **CLC 23**
See also CA 9-12R; CAD; CANR 9, 42, 75,
125; CD 5, 6; DA; DAB; DAC; DAM
DRAM, MST; DFS 2; DLB 7; LAIT 2;
MAL 5; MTCW 2; MTFW 2005; SATA
66; YAW

**Gibson, William** 1948- ....... **CLC 39, 63, 186,
192; SSC 52**
See also AAYA 12, 59; AMWS 16; BPFB
2; CA 133; CAAE 126; CANR 52, 90,
106; CN 6, 7; CPW; DA3; DAM POP;
DLB 251; MTCW 2; MTFW 2005; SCFW
2; SFW 4

**Gibson, William Ford**
See Gibson, William

**Gide, Andre (Paul Guillaume)**
1869-1951 ...... **SSC 13; TCLC 5, 12, 36,
177; WLC 3**
See also CA 124; CAAE 104; DA; DA3;
DAB; DAC; DAM MST, NOV; DLB 65,
321, 330; EW 8; EWL 3; GFL 1789 to
the Present; MTCW 1, 2; MTFW 2005;
NFS 21; RGSF 2; RGWL 2, 3; TWA

**Gifford, Barry (Colby)** 1946- ........... **CLC 34**
See also CA 65-68; CANR 9, 30, 40, 90

**Gilbert, Frank**
See De Voto, Bernard (Augustine)

**Gilbert, W(illiam) S(chwenck)**
1836-1911 ................................ **TCLC 3**
See also CA 173; CAAE 104; DAM DRAM,
POET; RGEL 2; SATA 36

**Gilbert of Poitiers** c. 1085-1154 .... **CMLC 85**

**Gilbreth, Frank B(unker), Jr.**
1911-2001 ................................. **CLC 17**
See also CA 9-12R; SATA 2

**Gilchrist, Ellen (Louise)** 1935- .. **CLC 34, 48,
143; SSC 14, 63**
See also BPFB 2; CA 116; CAAE 113;
CANR 41, 61, 104; CN 4, 5, 6, 7; CPW;
CSW; DAM POP; DLB 130; EWL 3;
EXPS; MTCW 1, 2; MTFW 2005; RGAL
4; RGSF 2; SSFS 9

**Giles, Molly** 1942- ............................ **CLC 39**
See also CA 126; CANR 98

**Gill, Eric** ........................................ **TCLC 85**
See Gill, (Arthur) Eric (Rowton Peter
Joseph)

**Gill, (Arthur) Eric (Rowton Peter Joseph)**
1882-1940
See Gill, Eric
See also CAAE 120; DLB 98

**Gill, Patrick**
See Creasey, John

**Gillette, Douglas** .............................. **CLC 70**

**Gilliam, Terry** 1940- ................. **CLC 21, 141**
See Monty Python
See also AAYA 19, 59; CA 113; CAAE 108;
CANR 35; INT CA-113

**Gilliam, Terry Vance**
See Gilliam, Terry

**Gillian, Jerry**
See Gilliam, Terry

**Gilliatt, Penelope (Ann Douglass)**
1932-1993 .................. **CLC 2, 10, 13, 53**
See also AITN 2; CA 13-16R; CAAS 141;
CANR 49; CN 1, 2, 3, 4, 5; DLB 14

**Gilligan, Carol** 1936- ...................... **CLC 208**
See also CA 142; CANR 121; FW

**Gilman, Charlotte (Anna) Perkins (Stetson)**
1860-1935 ...... **SSC 13, 62; TCLC 9, 37,
117**
See also AAYA 75; AMWS 11; BYA 11;
CA 150; CAAE 106; DLB 221; EXPS;
FL 1:5; FW; HGG; LAIT 2; MBL; MTCW
2; MTFW 2005; RGAL 4; RGSF 2; SFW
4; SSFS 1, 18

**Gilmour, David** 1946- ....................... **CLC 35**

**Gilpin, William** 1724-1804 ............. **NCLC 30**

**Gilray, J. D.**
See Mencken, H(enry) L(ouis)

**Gilroy, Frank D(aniel)** 1925- .............. **CLC 2**
See also CA 81-84; CAD; CANR 32, 64,
86; CD 5, 6; DFS 17; DLB 7

**Gilstrap, John** 1957(?)- ...................... **CLC 99**
See also AAYA 67; CA 160; CANR 101

**Ginsberg, Allen** 1926-1997 .... **CLC 1, 2, 3, 4,
6, 13, 36, 69, 109; PC 4, 47; TCLC
120; WLC 3**
See also AAYA 33; AITN 1; AMWC 1;
AMWS 2; BG 1:2; CA 1-4R; CAAS 157;
CANR 2, 41, 63, 95; CDALB 1941-1968;
CP 1, 2, 3, 4, 5, 6; DA; DA3; DAB; DAC;
DAM MST, POET; DLB 5, 16, 169, 237;
EWL 3; GLL 1; LMFS 2; MAL 5; MTCW
1, 2; MTFW 2005; PAB; PFS 5; RGAL 4;
TUS; WP

**Ginzburg, Eugenia** ............................ **CLC 59**
See Ginzburg, Evgeniia

**Ginzburg, Evgeniia** 1904-1977
See Ginzburg, Eugenia
See also DLB 302

**Ginzburg, Natalia** 1916-1991 ....... **CLC 5, 11,
54, 70; SSC 65; TCLC 156**
See also CA 85-88; CAAS 135; CANR 33;
DFS 14; DLB 177; EW 13; EWL 3;
MTCW 1, 2; MTFW 2005; RGHL;
RGWL 2, 3

**Giono, Jean** 1895-1970 .... **CLC 4, 11; TCLC
124**
See also CA 45-48; CAAS 29-32R; CANR
2, 35; DLB 72, 321; EWL 3; GFL 1789
to the Present; MTCW 1; RGWL 2, 3

**Giovanni, Nikki** 1943- ....... **BLC 2; CLC 2, 4,
19, 64, 117; PC 19; WLCS**
See also AAYA 22; AITN 1; BW 2, 3; CA
29-32R; 6; CANR 18, 41, 60, 91, 130;
CDALBS; CLR 6, 73; CP 2, 3, 4, 5, 6, 7;
CSW; CWP; CWRI 5; DA; DA3; DAB;
DAC; DAM MST, MULT, POET; DLB 5,
41; EWL 3; EXPP; INT CANR-18; MAI-
CYA 1, 2; MAL 5; MTCW 1, 2; MTFW
2005; PFS 17; RGAL 4; SATA 24, 107;
TUS; YAW

**Giovene, Andrea** 1904-1998 ................ **CLC 7**
See also CA 85-88

**Gippius, Zinaida (Nikolaevna)** 1869-1945
See Hippius, Zinaida (Nikolaevna)
See also CA 212; CAAE 106

**Giraudoux, Jean(-Hippolyte)**
1882-1944 ............................ **TCLC 2, 7**
See also CA 196; CAAE 104; DAM
DRAM; DLB 65, 321; EW 9; EWL 3;
GFL 1789 to the Present; RGWL 2, 3;
TWA

**GoodWeather, Harley**
See King, Thomas

**Googe, Barnabe** 1540-1594 ................. **LC 94**
See also DLB 132; RGEL 2

**Gordimer, Nadine** 1923- ...... **CLC 3, 5, 7, 10, 18, 33, 51, 70, 123, 160, 161; SSC 17, 80; WLCS**
See also AAYA 39; AFW; BRWS 2; CA 5-8R; CANR 3, 28, 56, 88, 131; CN 1, 2, 3, 4, 5, 6, 7; DA; DA3; DAB; DAC; DAM MST, NOV; DLB 225, 326, 330; EWL 3; EXPS; INT CANR-28; LATS 1:2; MTCW 1, 2; MTFW 2005; NFS 4; RGEL 2; RGSF 2; SSFS 2, 14, 19; TWA; WLIT 2; YAW

**Gordon, Adam Lindsay**
1833-1870 ................................. **NCLC 21**
See also DLB 230

**Gordon, Caroline** 1895-1981 . **CLC 6, 13, 29, 83; SSC 15**
See also AMW; CA 11-12; CAAS 103; CANR 36; CAP 1; CN 1, 2; DLB 4, 9, 102; DLBD 17; DLBY 1981; EWL 3; MAL 5; MTCW 1, 2; MTFW 2005; RGAL 4; RGSF 2

**Gordon, Charles William** 1860-1937
See Connor, Ralph
See also CAAE 109

**Gordon, Mary** 1949- .. **CLC 13, 22, 128, 216; SSC 59**
See also AMWS 4; BPFB 2; CA 102; CANR 44, 92, 154; CN 4, 5, 6, 7; DLB 6; DLBY 1981; FW; INT CA-102; MAL 5; MTCW 1

**Gordon, Mary Catherine**
See Gordon, Mary

**Gordon, N. J.**
See Bosman, Herman Charles

**Gordon, Sol** 1923- .............................. **CLC 26**
See also CA 53-56; CANR 4; SATA 11

**Gordone, Charles** 1925-1995 .. **CLC 1, 4; DC 8**
See also BW 1, 3; CA 180; 93-96, 180; CAAS 150; CAD; CANR 55; DAM DRAM; DLB 7; INT CA-93-96; MTCW 1

**Gore, Catherine** 1800-1861 ........... **NCLC 65**
See also DLB 116; RGEL 2

**Gorenko, Anna Andreevna**
See Akhmatova, Anna

**Gorky, Maxim** .... **SSC 28; TCLC 8; WLC 3**
See Peshkov, Alexei Maximovich
See also DAB; DFS 9; DLB 295; EW 8; EWL 3; TWA

**Goryan, Sirak**
See Saroyan, William

**Gosse, Edmund (William)**
1849-1928 ............................... **TCLC 28**
See also CAAE 117; DLB 57, 144, 184; RGEL 2

**Gotlieb, Phyllis (Fay Bloom)** 1926- .. **CLC 18**
See also CA 13-16R; CANR 7, 135; CN 7; CP 1, 2, 3, 4; DLB 88, 251; SFW 4

**Gottesman, S. D.**
See Kornbluth, C(yril) M.; Pohl, Frederik

**Gottfried von Strassburg** fl. c.
1170-1215 ............................... **CMLC 10**
See also CDWLB 2; DLB 138; EW 1; RGWL 2, 3

**Gotthelf, Jeremias** 1797-1854 ....... **NCLC 117**
See also DLB 133; RGWL 2, 3

**Gottschalk, Laura Riding**
See Jackson, Laura (Riding)

**Gould, Lois** 1932(?)-2002 ............. **CLC 4, 10**
See also CA 77-80; CAAS 208; CANR 29; MTCW 1

**Gould, Stephen Jay** 1941-2002 ....... **CLC 163**
See also AAYA 26; BEST 90:2; CA 77-80; CAAS 205; CANR 10, 27, 56, 75, 125; CPW; INT CANR-27; MTCW 1, 2; MTFW 2005

**Gourmont, Remy(-Marie-Charles) de**
1858-1915 ............................... **TCLC 17**
See also CA 150; CAAE 109; GFL 1789 to the Present; MTCW 2

**Gournay, Marie le Jars de**
See de Gournay, Marie le Jars

**Govier, Katherine** 1948- ................... **CLC 51**
See also CA 101; CANR 18, 40, 128; CCA 1

**Gower, John** c. 1330-1408 ....... **LC 76; PC 59**
See also BRW 1; DLB 146; RGEL 2

**Goyen, (Charles) William**
1915-1983 .................... **CLC 5, 8, 14, 40**
See also AITN 2; CA 5-8R; CAAS 110; CANR 6, 71; CN 1, 2, 3; DLB 2, 218; DLBY 1983; EWL 3; INT CANR-6; MAL 5

**Goytisolo, Juan** 1931- .... **CLC 5, 10, 23, 133; HLC 1**
See also CA 85-88; CANR 32, 61, 131; CWW 2; DAM MULT; DLB 322; EWL 3; GLL 2; HW 1, 2; MTCW 1, 2; MTFW 2005

**Gozzano, Guido** 1883-1916 ................. **PC 10**
See also CA 154; DLB 114; EWL 3

**Gozzi, (Conte) Carlo** 1720-1806 .... **NCLC 23**

**Grabbe, Christian Dietrich**
1801-1836 ................................. **NCLC 2**
See also DLB 133; RGWL 2, 3

**Grace, Patricia Frances** 1937- .......... **CLC 56**
See also CA 176; CANR 118; CN 4, 5, 6, 7; EWL 3; RGSF 2

**Gracian y Morales, Baltasar**
1601-1658 ................................. **LC 15**

**Gracq, Julien** 1910-2007 ............. **CLC 11, 48**
See Poirier, Louis
See also CA 126; CAAE 122; CANR 141; CWW 2; DLB 83; GFL 1789 to the present

**Grade, Chaim** 1910-1982 ................. **CLC 10**
See also CA 93-96; CAAS 107; DLB 333; EWL 3; RGHL

**Grade, Khayim**
See Grade, Chaim

**Graduate of Oxford, A**
See Ruskin, John

**Grafton, Garth**
See Duncan, Sara Jeannette

**Grafton, Sue** 1940- ......................... **CLC 163**
See also AAYA 11, 49; BEST 90:3; CA 108; CANR 31, 55, 111, 134; CMW 4; CPW; CSW; DA3; DAM POP; DLB 226; FW; MSW; MTFW 2005

**Graham, John**
See Phillips, David Graham

**Graham, Jorie** 1950- .... **CLC 48, 118; PC 59**
See also AAYA 67; CA 111; CANR 63, 118; CP 4, 5, 6, 7; CWP; DLB 120; EWL 3; MTFW 2005; PFS 10, 17; TCLE 1:1

**Graham, R(obert) B(ontine) Cunninghame**
See Cunninghame Graham, Robert (Gallnigad) Bontine
See also DLB 98, 135, 174; RGEL 2; RGSF 2

**Graham, Robert**
See Haldeman, Joe

**Graham, Tom**
See Lewis, (Harry) Sinclair

**Graham, W(illiam) S(ydney)**
1918-1986 ................................. **CLC 29**
See also BRWS 7; CA 73-76; CAAS 118; CP 1, 2, 3, 4; DLB 20; RGEL 2

**Graham, Winston (Mawdsley)**
1910-2003 ................................. **CLC 23**
See also CA 49-52; CAAS 218; CANR 2, 22, 45, 66; CMW 4; CN 1, 2, 3, 4, 5, 6, 7; DLB 77; RHW

**Grahame, Kenneth** 1859-1932 ...... **TCLC 64, 136**
See also BYA 5; CA 136; CAAE 108; CANR 80; CLR 5; CWRI 5; DA3; DAB; DLB 34, 141, 178; FANT; MAICYA 1, 2; MTCW 2; NFS 20; RGEL 2; SATA 100; TEA; WCH; YABC 1

**Granger, Darius John**
See Marlowe, Stephen

**Granin, Daniil** 1918- ......................... **CLC 59**
See also DLB 302

**Granovsky, Timofei Nikolaevich**
1813-1855 ................................. **NCLC 75**
See also DLB 198

**Grant, Skeeter**
See Spiegelman, Art

**Granville-Barker, Harley**
1877-1946 ................................. **TCLC 2**
See Barker, Harley Granville
See also CA 204; CAAE 104; DAM DRAM; RGEL 2

**Granzotto, Gianni**
See Granzotto, Giovanni Battista

**Granzotto, Giovanni Battista**
1914-1985 ................................. **CLC 70**
See also CA 166

**Grasemann, Ruth Barbara**
See Rendell, Ruth

**Grass, Guenter**
See Grass, Gunter
See also CWW 2; DLB 330; RGHL

**Grass, Gunter** 1927- .. **CLC 1, 2, 4, 6, 11, 15, 22, 32, 49, 88, 207; WLC 3**
See Grass, Guenter
See also BPFB 2; CA 13-16R; CANR 20, 75, 93, 133; CDWLB 2; DA; DA3; DAB; DAC; DAM MST, NOV; DLB 75, 124; EW 13; EWL 3; MTCW 1, 2; MTFW 2005; RGWL 2, 3; TWA

**Grass, Gunter Wilhelm**
See Grass, Gunter

**Gratton, Thomas**
See Hulme, T(homas) E(rnest)

**Grau, Shirley Ann** 1929- ....... **CLC 4, 9, 146; SSC 15**
See also CA 89-92; CANR 22, 69; CN 1, 2, 3, 4, 5, 6, 7; CSW; DLB 2, 218; INT CA-89-92; CANR-22; MTCW 1

**Gravel, Fern**
See Hall, James Norman

**Graver, Elizabeth** 1964- ................... **CLC 70**
See also CA 135; CANR 71, 129

**Graves, Richard Perceval**
1895-1985 ................................. **CLC 44**
See also CA 65-68; CANR 9, 26, 51

**Graves, Robert** 1895-1985 ... **CLC 1, 2, 6, 11, 39, 44, 45; PC 6**
See also BPFB 2; BRW 7; BYA 4; CA 5-8R; CAAS 117; CANR 5, 36; CDBLB 1914-1945; CN 1, 2, 3; CP 1, 2, 3, 4; DA3; DAB; DAC; DAM MST, POET; DLB 20, 100, 191; DLBD 18; DLBY 1985; EWL 3; LATS 1:1; MTCW 1, 2; MTFW 2005; NCFS 2; NFS 21; RGEL 2; RHW; SATA 45; TEA

**Graves, Valerie**
See Bradley, Marion Zimmer

**Gray, Alasdair** 1934- ......................... **CLC 41**
See also BRWS 9; CA 126; CANR 47, 69, 106, 140; CN 4, 5, 6, 7; DLB 194, 261, 319; HGG; INT CA-126; MTCW 1, 2; MTFW 2005; RGSF 2; SUFW 2

**Gray, Amlin** 1946- ............................. **CLC 29**
See also CA 138

**Gray, Francine du Plessix** 1930- ..... **CLC 22, 153**
    See also BEST 90:3; CA 61-64; 2; CANR 11, 33, 75, 81; DAM NOV; INT CANR-11; MTCW 1, 2; MTFW 2005
**Gray, John (Henry)** 1866-1934 ...... **TCLC 19**
    See also CA 162; CAAE 119; RGEL 2
**Gray, John Lee**
    See Jakes, John
**Gray, Simon** 1936- .................. **CLC 9, 14, 36**
    See also AITN 1; CA 21-24R; 3; CANR 32, 69; CBD; CD 5, 6; CN 1, 2, 3; DLB 13; EWL 3; MTCW 1; RGEL 2
**Gray, Simon James Holliday**
    See Gray, Simon
**Gray, Spalding** 1941-2004 ........ **CLC 49, 112; DC 7**
    See also AAYA 62; CA 128; CAAS 225; CAD; CANR 74, 138; CD 5, 6; CPW; DAM POP; MTCW 2; MTFW 2005
**Gray, Thomas** 1716-1771 ..... **LC 4, 40; PC 2, 80; WLC 3**
    See also BRW 3; CDBLB 1660-1789; DA; DA3; DAB; DAC; DAM MST; DLB 109; EXPP; PAB; PFS 9; RGEL 2; TEA; WP
**Grayson, David**
    See Baker, Ray Stannard
**Grayson, Richard (A.)** 1951- ........... **CLC 38**
    See also CA 210; 85-88, 210; CANR 14, 31, 57; DLB 234
**Greeley, Andrew M.** 1928- ............... **CLC 28**
    See also BPFB 2; CA 5-8R; 7; CANR 7, 43, 69, 104, 136; CMW 4; CPW; DA3; DAM POP; MTCW 1, 2; MTFW 2005
**Green, Anna Katharine** 1846-1935 ................................ **TCLC 63**
    See also CA 159; CAAE 112; CMW 4; DLB 202, 221; MSW
**Green, Brian**
    See Card, Orson Scott
**Green, Hannah**
    See Greenberg, Joanne (Goldenberg)
**Green, Hannah** 1927(?)-1996 ............. **CLC 3**
    See also CA 73-76; CANR 59, 93; NFS 10
**Green, Henry** ........................ **CLC 2, 13, 97**
    See Yorke, Henry Vincent
    See also BRWS 2; CA 175; DLB 15; EWL 3; RGEL 2
**Green, Julian** ........................ **CLC 3, 11, 77**
    See Green, Julien (Hartridge)
    See also EWL 3; GFL 1789 to the Present; MTCW 2
**Green, Julien (Hartridge)** 1900-1998
    See Green, Julian
    See also CA 21-24R; CAAS 169; CANR 33, 87; CWW 2; DLB 4, 72; MTCW 1, 2; MTFW 2005
**Green, Paul (Eliot)** 1894-1981 ......... **CLC 25**
    See also AITN 1; CA 5-8R; CAAS 103; CAD; CANR 3; DAM DRAM; DLB 7, 9, 249; DLBY 1981; MAL 5; RGAL 4
**Greenaway, Peter** 1942- .................. **CLC 159**
    See also CA 127
**Greenberg, Ivan** 1908-1973
    See Rahv, Philip
    See also CA 85-88
**Greenberg, Joanne (Goldenberg)** 1932- ...................................... **CLC 7, 30**
    See also AAYA 12, 67; CA 5-8R; CANR 14, 32, 69; CN 6, 7; DLB 335; NFS 23; SATA 25; YAW
**Greenberg, Richard** 1959(?)- ........... **CLC 57**
    See also CA 138; CAD; CD 5, 6; DFS 24
**Greenblatt, Stephen J(ay)** 1943- ...... **CLC 70**
    See also CA 49-52; CANR 115

**Greene, Bette** 1934- .......................... **CLC 30**
    See also AAYA 7, 69; BYA 3; CA 53-56; CANR 4, 146; CLR 2; CWRI 5; JRDA; LAIT 4; MAICYA 1, 2; NFS 10; SAAS 16; SATA 8, 102, 161; WYA; YAW
**Greene, Gael** ...................................... **CLC 8**
    See also CA 13-16R; CANR 10, 166
**Greene, Graham** 1904-1991 .. **CLC 1, 3, 6, 9, 14, 18, 27, 37, 70, 72, 125; SSC 29; WLC 3**
    See also AAYA 61; AITN 2; BPFB 2; BRWR 2; BRWS 1; BYA 3; CA 13-16R; CAAS 133; CANR 35, 61, 131; CBD; CDBLB 1945-1960; CMW 4; CN 1, 2, 3, 4; DA; DA3; DAB; DAC; DAM MST, NOV; DLB 13, 15, 77, 100, 162, 201, 204; DLBY 1991; EWL 3; MSW; MTCW 1, 2; MTFW 2005; NFS 16; RGEL 2; SATA 20; SSFS 14; TEA; WLIT 4
**Greene, Robert** 1558-1592 .................. **LC 41**
    See also BRWS 8; DLB 62, 167; IDTP; RGEL 2; TEA
**Greer, Germaine** 1939- .................... **CLC 131**
    See also AITN 1; CA 81-84; CANR 33, 70, 115, 133; FW; MTCW 1, 2; MTFW 2005
**Greer, Richard**
    See Silverberg, Robert
**Gregor, Arthur** 1923- .......................... **CLC 9**
    See also CA 25-28R; 10; CANR 11; CP 1, 2, 3, 4, 5, 6, 7; SATA 36
**Gregor, Lee**
    See Pohl, Frederik
**Gregory, Lady Isabella Augusta (Persse)** 1852-1932 ........................ **TCLC 1, 176**
    See also BRW 6; CA 184; CAAE 104; DLB 10; IDTP; RGEL 2
**Gregory, J. Dennis**
    See Williams, John A(lfred)
**Gregory of Nazianzus, St.** 329-389 .................................... **CMLC 82**
**Grekova, I.** ......................................... **CLC 59**
    See Ventsel, Elena Sergeevna
    See also CWW 2
**Grendon, Stephen**
    See Derleth, August (William)
**Grenville, Kate** 1950- .......................... **CLC 61**
    See also CA 118; CANR 53, 93, 156; CN 7; DLB 325
**Grenville, Pelham**
    See Wodehouse, P(elham) G(renville)
**Greve, Felix Paul (Berthold Friedrich)** 1879-1948
    See Grove, Frederick Philip
    See also CA 141, 175; CAAE 104; CANR 79; DAC; DAM MST
**Greville, Fulke** 1554-1628 .................... **LC 79**
    See also BRWS 11; DLB 62, 172; RGEL 2
**Grey, Lady Jane** 1537-1554 ................. **LC 93**
    See also DLB 132
**Grey, Zane** 1872-1939 ...................... **TCLC 6**
    See also BPFB 2; CA 132; CAAE 104; DA3; DAM POP; DLB 9, 212; MTCW 1, 2; MTFW 2005; RGAL 4; TCWW 1, 2; TUS
**Griboedov, Aleksandr Sergeevich** 1795(?)-1829 .......................... **NCLC 129**
    See also DLB 205; RGWL 2, 3
**Grieg, (Johan) Nordahl (Brun)** 1902-1943 ................................ **TCLC 10**
    See also CA 189; CAAE 107; EWL 3
**Grieve, C(hristopher) M(urray)** 1892-1978 ............................ **CLC 11, 19**
    See MacDiarmid, Hugh; Pteleon
    See also CA 5-8R; CAAS 85-88; CANR 33, 107; DAM POET; MTCW 1; RGEL 2
**Griffin, Gerald** 1803-1840 ............... **NCLC 7**
    See also DLB 159; RGEL 2

**Griffin, John Howard** 1920-1980 ..... **CLC 68**
    See also AITN 1; CA 1-4R; CAAS 101; CANR 2
**Griffin, Peter** 1942- ........................... **CLC 39**
    See also CA 136
**Griffith, D(avid Lewelyn) W(ark)** 1875(?)-1948 ............................ **TCLC 68**
    See also CA 150; CAAE 119; CANR 80
**Griffith, Lawrence**
    See Griffith, D(avid Lewelyn) W(ark)
**Griffiths, Trevor** 1935- ............... **CLC 13, 52**
    See also CA 97-100; CANR 45; CBD; CD 5, 6; DLB 13, 245
**Griggs, Sutton (Elbert)** 1872-1930 ........................ **TCLC 77**
    See also CA 186; CAAE 123; DLB 50
**Grigson, Geoffrey (Edward Harvey)** 1905-1985 ............................ **CLC 7, 39**
    See also CA 25-28R; CAAS 118; CANR 20, 33; CP 1, 2, 3, 4; DLB 27; MTCW 1, 2
**Grile, Dod**
    See Bierce, Ambrose (Gwinett)
**Grillparzer, Franz** 1791-1872 ............. **DC 14; NCLC 1, 102; SSC 37**
    See also CDWLB 2; DLB 133; EW 5; RGWL 2, 3; TWA
**Grimble, Reverend Charles James**
    See Eliot, T(homas) S(tearns)
**Grimke, Angelina (Emily) Weld** 1880-1958 ................................ **HR 1:2**
    See Weld, Angelina (Emily) Grimke
    See also BW 1; CA 124; DAM POET; DLB 50, 54
**Grimke, Charlotte L(ottie) Forten** 1837(?)-1914
    See Forten, Charlotte L.
    See also BW 1; CA 124; CAAE 117; DAM MULT, POET
**Grimm, Jacob Ludwig Karl** 1785-1863 ............. **NCLC 3, 77; SSC 36**
    See Grimm Brothers
    See also CLR 112; DLB 90; MAICYA 1, 2; RGSF 2; RGWL 2, 3; SATA 22; WCH
**Grimm, Wilhelm Karl** 1786-1859 .. **NCLC 3, 77; SSC 36**
    See Grimm Brothers
    See also CDWLB 2; CLR 112; DLB 90; MAICYA 1, 2; RGSF 2; RGWL 2, 3; SATA 22; WCH
**Grimm and Grim**
    See Grimm, Jacob Ludwig Karl; Grimm, Wilhelm Karl
**Grimm Brothers** ............................... **SSC 88**
    See Grimm, Jacob Ludwig Karl; Grimm, Wilhelm Karl
    See also CLR 112
**Grimmelshausen, Hans Jakob Christoffel von**
    See Grimmelshausen, Johann Jakob Christoffel von
    See also RGWL 2, 3
**Grimmelshausen, Johann Jakob Christoffel von** 1621-1676 ................................ **LC 6**
    See Grimmelshausen, Hans Jakob Christoffel von
    See also CDWLB 2; DLB 168
**Grindel, Eugene** 1895-1952
    See Eluard, Paul
    See also CA 193; CAAE 104; LMFS 2
**Grisham, John** 1955- ........................ **CLC 84**
    See also AAYA 14, 47; BPFB 2; CA 138; CANR 47, 69, 114, 133; CMW 4; CN 6, 7; CPW; CSW; DA3; DAM POP; MSW; MTCW 2; MTFW 2005
**Grosseteste, Robert** 1175(?)-1253 . **CMLC 62**
    See also DLB 115

**Grossman, David** 1954- ............. **CLC 67, 231**
See also CA 138; CANR 114; CWW 2;
DLB 299; EWL 3; RGHL; WLIT 6

**Grossman, Vasilii Semenovich**
See Grossman, Vasily (Semenovich)
See also DLB 272

**Grossman, Vasily (Semenovich)**
1905-1964 .................................. **CLC 41**
See also Grossman, Vasilii Semenovich
See also CA 130; CAAE 124; MTCW 1;
RGHL

**Grove, Frederick Philip** .................. **TCLC 4**
See Greve, Felix Paul (Berthold Friedrich)
See also DLB 92; RGEL 2; TCWW 1, 2

**Grubb**
See Crumb, R.

**Grumbach, Doris** 1918- ........ **CLC 13, 22, 64**
See also CA 5-8R; 2; CANR 9, 42, 70, 127;
CN 6, 7; INT CANR-9; MTCW 2; MTFW
2005

**Grundtvig, Nikolai Frederik Severin**
1783-1872 ......................... **NCLC 1, 158**
See also DLB 300

**Grunge**
See Crumb, R.

**Grunwald, Lisa** 1959- ........................ **CLC 44**
See also CA 120; CANR 148

**Gryphius, Andreas** 1616-1664 ............. **LC 89**
See also CDWLB 2; DLB 164; RGWL 2, 3

**Guare, John** 1938- .... **CLC 8, 14, 29, 67; DC 20**
See also CA 73-76; CAD; CANR 21, 69,
118; CD 5, 6; DAM DRAM; DFS 8, 13;
DLB 7, 249; EWL 3; MAL 5; MTCW 1,
2; RGAL 4

**Guarini, Battista** 1537-1612 ............... **LC 102**

**Gubar, Susan (David)** 1944- .......... **CLC 145**
See also CA 108; CANR 45, 70, 139; FW;
MTCW 1; RGAL 4

**Gudjonsson, Halldor Kiljan** 1902-1998
See Halldor Laxness
See also CA 103; CAAS 164

**Guenter, Erich**
See Eich, Gunter

**Guest, Barbara** 1920-2006 ... **CLC 34; PC 55**
See also BG 1:2; CA 25-28R; CAAS 248;
CANR 11, 44, 84; CP 1, 2, 3, 4, 5, 6, 7;
CWP; DLB 5, 193

**Guest, Edgar A(lbert)** 1881-1959 ... **TCLC 95**
See also CA 168; CAAE 112

**Guest, Judith** 1936- ...................... **CLC 8, 30**
See also AAYA 7, 66; CA 77-80; CANR
15, 75, 138; DA3; DAM NOV, POP;
EXPN; INT CANR-15; LAIT 5; MTCW
1, 2; MTFW 2005; NFS 1

**Guevara, Che** ................... **CLC 87; HLC 1**
See Guevara (Serna), Ernesto

**Guevara (Serna), Ernesto**
1928-1967 .................... **CLC 87; HLC 1**
See Guevara, Che
See also CA 127; CAAS 111; CANR 56;
DAM MULT; HW 1

**Guicciardini, Francesco** 1483-1540 ..... **LC 49**

**Guido delle Colonne** c. 1215-c.
1290 ........................................ **CMLC 90**

**Guild, Nicholas M.** 1944- ................. **CLC 33**
See also CA 93-96

**Guillemin, Jacques**
See Sartre, Jean-Paul

**Guillen, Jorge** 1893-1984 . **CLC 11; HLCS 1;
PC 35**
See also CA 89-92; CAAS 112; DAM
MULT, POET; DLB 108; EWL 3; HW 1;
RGWL 2, 3

**Guillen, Nicolas (Cristobal)**
1902-1989 .... **BLC 2; CLC 48, 79; HLC
1; PC 23**
See also BW 2; CA 125; CAAE 116; CAAS
129; CANR 84; DAM MST, MULT,
POET; DLB 283; EWL 3; HW 1; LAW;
RGWL 2, 3; WP

**Guillen y Alvarez, Jorge**
See Guillen, Jorge

**Guillevic, (Eugene)** 1907-1997 .......... **CLC 33**
See also CA 93-96; CWW 2

**Guillois**
See Desnos, Robert

**Guillois, Valentin**
See Desnos, Robert

**Guimaraes Rosa, Joao** 1908-1967 .... **HLCS 2**
See Rosa, Joao Guimaraes
See also CA 175; LAW; RGSF 2; RGWL 2,
3

**Guiney, Louise Imogen**
1861-1920 ............................... **TCLC 41**
See also CA 160; DLB 54; RGAL 4

**Guinizelli, Guido** c. 1230-1276 ...... **CMLC 49**
See Guinizzelli, Guido

**Guinizzelli, Guido**
See Guinizelli, Guido
See also WLIT 7

**Guiraldes, Ricardo (Guillermo)**
1886-1927 ............................... **TCLC 39**
See also CA 131; EWL 3; HW 1; LAW;
MTCW 1

**Gumilev, Nikolai (Stepanovich)**
1886-1921 ............................... **TCLC 60**
See Gumilyov, Nikolay Stepanovich
See also CA 165; DLB 295

**Gumilyov, Nikolay Stepanovich**
See Gumilev, Nikolai (Stepanovich)
See also EWL 3

**Gump, P. Q.**
See Card, Orson Scott

**Gunesekera, Romesh** 1954- ............... **CLC 91**
See also BRWS 10; CA 159; CANR 140;
CN 6, 7; DLB 267, 323

**Gunn, Bill** .................................... **CLC 5**
See Gunn, William Harrison
See also DLB 38

**Gunn, Thom(son William)**
1929-2004 . **CLC 3, 6, 18, 32, 81; PC 26**
See also BRWS 4; CA 17-20R; CAAS 227;
CANR 9, 33, 116; CDBLB 1960 to
Present; CP 1, 2, 3, 4, 5, 6, 7; DAM
POET; DLB 27; INT CANR-33; MTCW
1; PFS 9; RGEL 2

**Gunn, William Harrison** 1934(?)-1989
See Gunn, Bill
See also AITN 1; BW 1, 3; CA 13-16R;
CAAS 128; CANR 12, 25, 76

**Gunn Allen, Paula**
See Allen, Paula Gunn

**Gunnars, Kristjana** 1948- ................. **CLC 69**
See also CA 113; CCA 1; CP 6, 7; CWP;
DLB 60

**Gunter, Erich**
See Eich, Gunter

**Gurdjieff, G(eorgei) I(vanovich)**
1877(?)-1949 ........................... **TCLC 71**
See also CA 157

**Gurganus, Allan** 1947- ...................... **CLC 70**
See also BEST 90:1; CA 135; CANR 114;
CN 6, 7; CPW; CSW; DAM POP; GLL 1

**Gurney, A. R.**
See Gurney, A(lbert) R(amsdell), Jr.
See also DLB 266

**Gurney, A(lbert) R(amsdell), Jr.**
1930- ............................... **CLC 32, 50, 54**
See Gurney, A. R.
See also AMWS 5; CA 77-80; CAD; CANR
32, 64, 121; CD 5, 6; DAM DRAM; EWL
3

**Gurney, Ivor (Bertie)** 1890-1937 ... **TCLC 33**
See also BRW 6; CA 167; DLBY 2002;
PAB; RGEL 2

**Gurney, Peter**
See Gurney, A(lbert) R(amsdell), Jr.

**Guro, Elena (Genrikhovna)**
1877-1913 ............................... **TCLC 56**
See also DLB 295

**Gustafson, James M(oody)** 1925- ... **CLC 100**
See also CA 25-28R; CANR 37

**Gustafson, Ralph (Barker)**
1909-1995 ............................... **CLC 36**
See also CA 21-24R; CANR 8, 45, 84; CP
1, 2, 3, 4, 5, 6; DLB 88; RGEL 2

**Gut, Gom**
See Simenon, Georges (Jacques Christian)

**Guterson, David** 1956- ...................... **CLC 91**
See also CA 132; CANR 73, 126; CN 7;
DLB 292; MTCW 2; MTFW 2005; NFS
13

**Guthrie, A(lfred) B(ertram), Jr.**
1901-1991 ............................... **CLC 23**
See also CA 57-60; CAAS 134; CANR 24;
CN 1, 2, 3; DLB 6, 212; MAL 5; SATA
62; SATA-Obit 67; TCWW 1, 2

**Guthrie, Isobel**
See Grieve, C(hristopher) M(urray)

**Guthrie, Woodrow Wilson** 1912-1967
See Guthrie, Woody
See also CA 113; CAAS 93-96

**Guthrie, Woody** ............................ **CLC 35**
See Guthrie, Woodrow Wilson
See also DLB 303; LAIT 3

**Gutierrez Najera, Manuel**
1859-1895 ............. **HLCS 2; NCLC 133**
See also DLB 290; LAW

**Guy, Rosa (Cuthbert)** 1925- ............. **CLC 26**
See also AAYA 4, 37; BW 2; CA 17-20R;
CANR 14, 34, 83; CLR 13; DLB 33;
DNFS 1; JRDA; MAICYA 1, 2; SATA 14,
62, 122; YAW

**Gwendolyn**
See Bennett, (Enoch) Arnold

**H. D.** ........... **CLC 3, 8, 14, 31, 34, 73; PC 5**
See Doolittle, Hilda
See also FL 1:5

**H. de V.**
See Buchan, John

**Haavikko, Paavo Juhani** 1931- .. **CLC 18, 34**
See also CA 106; CWW 2; EWL 3

**Habbema, Koos**
See Heijermans, Herman

**Habermas, Juergen** 1929- ............... **CLC 104**
See also CA 109; CANR 85, 162; DLB 242

**Habermas, Jurgen**
See Habermas, Juergen

**Hacker, Marilyn** 1942- ...... **CLC 5, 9, 23, 72,
91; PC 47**
See also CA 77-80; CANR 68, 129; CP 3,
4, 5, 6, 7; CWP; DAM POET; DLB 120,
282; FW; GLL 2; MAL 5; PFS 19

**Hadewijch of Antwerp** fl. 1250- ... **CMLC 61**
See also RGWL 3

**Hadrian** 76-138 ............................. **CMLC 52**

**Haeckel, Ernst Heinrich (Philipp August)**
1834-1919 ............................... **TCLC 83**
See also CA 157

**Hafiz** c. 1326-1389(?) ..................... **CMLC 34**
See also RGWL 2, 3; WLIT 6

**Hagedorn, Jessica T(arahata)**
1949- ..................................... **CLC 185**
See also CA 139; CANR 69; CWP; DLB
312; RGAL 4

MST, NOV, POET; DLB 18, 19, 135, 284; EWL 3; EXPN; EXPP; LAIT 2; MTCW 1, 2; MTFW 2005; NFS 3, 11, 15, 19; PFS 3, 4, 18; RGEL 2; RGSF 2; TEA; WLIT 4

**Hare, David** 1947- . **CLC 29, 58, 136; DC 26**
See also BRWS 4; CA 97-100; CANR 39, 91; CBD; CD 5, 6; DFS 4, 7, 16; DLB 13, 310; MTCW 1; TEA

**Harewood, John**
See Van Druten, John (William)

**Harford, Henry**
See Hudson, W(illiam) H(enry)

**Hargrave, Leonie**
See Disch, Thomas M.

**Hariri, Al- al-Qasim ibn 'Ali Abu Muhammad al-Basri**
See al-Hariri, al-Qasim ibn 'Ali Abu Muhammad al-Basri

**Harjo, Joy** 1951- ..... **CLC 83; NNAL; PC 27**
See also AMWS 12; CA 114; CANR 35, 67, 91, 129; CP 6, 7; CWP; DAM MULT; DLB 120, 175; EWL 3; MTCW 2; MTFW 2005; PFS 15; RGAL 4

**Harlan, Louis R(udolph)** 1922- ........ **CLC 34**
See also CA 21-24R; CANR 25, 55, 80

**Harling, Robert** 1951(?)- ................... **CLC 53**
See also CA 147

**Harmon, William (Ruth)** 1938- ........ **CLC 38**
See also CA 33-36R; CANR 14, 32, 35; SATA 65

**Harper, F. E. W.**
See Harper, Frances Ellen Watkins

**Harper, Frances E. W.**
See Harper, Frances Ellen Watkins

**Harper, Frances E. Watkins**
See Harper, Frances Ellen Watkins

**Harper, Frances Ellen**
See Harper, Frances Ellen Watkins

**Harper, Frances Ellen Watkins**
1825-1911 ..... **BLC 2; PC 21; TCLC 14**
See also AFAW 1, 2; BW 1, 3; CA 125; CAAE 111; CANR 79; DAM MULT; POET; DLB 50, 221; MBL; RGAL 4

**Harper, Michael S(teven)** 1938- ... **CLC 7, 22**
See also AFAW 2; BW 1; CA 224; 33-36R, 224; CANR 24, 108; CP 2, 3, 4, 5, 6, 7; DLB 41; RGAL 4; TCLE 1:1

**Harper, Mrs. F. E. W.**
See Harper, Frances Ellen Watkins

**Harpur, Charles** 1813-1868 ......... **NCLC 114**
See also DLB 230; RGEL 2

**Harris, Christie**
See Harris, Christie (Lucy) Irwin

**Harris, Christie (Lucy) Irwin**
1907-2002 .................................. **CLC 12**
See also CA 5-8R; CANR 6, 83; CLR 47; DLB 88; JRDA; MAICYA 1, 2; SAAS 10; SATA 6, 74; SATA-Essay 116

**Harris, Frank** 1856-1931 ................. **TCLC 24**
See also CA 150; CAAE 109; CANR 80; DLB 156, 197; RGEL 2

**Harris, George Washington**
1814-1869 ....................... **NCLC 23, 165**
See also DLB 3, 11, 248; RGAL 4

**Harris, Joel Chandler** 1848-1908 ..... **SSC 19, 103; TCLC 2**
See also CA 137; CAAE 104; CANR 80; CLR 49; DLB 11, 23, 42, 78, 91; LAIT 2; MAICYA 1, 2; RGSF 2; SATA 100; WCH; YABC 1

**Harris, John (Wyndham Parkes Lucas) Beynon** 1903-1969
See Wyndham, John
See also CA 102; CAAS 89-92; CANR 84; SATA 118; SFW 4

**Harris, MacDonald** ....................... **CLC 9**
See Heiney, Donald (William)

**Harris, Mark** 1922-2007 .................. **CLC 19**
See also CA 5-8R; 3; CAAS 260; CANR 2, 55, 83; CN 1, 2, 3, 4, 5, 6, 7; DLB 2; DLBY 1980

**Harris, Norman** ................................. **CLC 65**

**Harris, (Theodore) Wilson** 1921- .... **CLC 25, 159**
See also BRWS 5; BW 2, 3; CA 65-68; 16; CANR 11, 27, 69, 114; CDWLB 3; CN 1, 2, 3, 4, 5, 6, 7; CP 1, 2, 3, 4, 5, 6, 7; DLB 117; EWL 3; MTCW 1; RGEL 2

**Harrison, Barbara Grizzuti**
1934-2002 .................................. **CLC 144**
See also CA 77-80; CAAS 205; CANR 15, 48; INT CANR-15

**Harrison, Elizabeth (Allen) Cavanna**
1909-2001
See Cavanna, Betty
See also CA 9-12R; CAAS 200; CANR 6, 27, 85, 104, 121; MAICYA 2; SATA 142; YAW

**Harrison, Harry (Max)** 1925- ........... **CLC 42**
See also CA 1-4R; CANR 5, 21, 84; DLB 8; SATA 4; SCFW 2; SFW 4

**Harrison, James**
See Harrison, Jim

**Harrison, James Thomas**
See Harrison, Jim

**Harrison, Jim** 1937- ........ **CLC 6, 14, 33, 66, 143; SSC 19**
See also AMWS 8; CA 13-16R; CANR 8, 51, 79, 142; CN 5, 6; CP 1, 2, 3, 4, 5, 6; DLBY 1982; INT CANR-8; RGAL 4; TCWW 2; TUS

**Harrison, Kathryn** 1961- .......... **CLC 70, 151**
See also CA 144; CANR 68, 122

**Harrison, Tony** 1937- ............... **CLC 43, 129**
See also BRWS 5; CA 65-68; CANR 44, 98; CBD; CD 5, 6; CP 2, 3, 4, 5, 6, 7; DLB 40, 245; MTCW 1; RGEL 2

**Harriss, Will(ard Irvin)** 1922- .......... **CLC 34**
See also CA 111

**Hart, Ellis**
See Ellison, Harlan

**Hart, Josephine** 1942(?)- ................... **CLC 70**
See also CA 138; CANR 70, 149; CPW; DAM POP

**Hart, Moss** 1904-1961 ...................... **CLC 66**
See also CA 109; CAAS 89-92; CANR 84; DAM DRAM; DFS 1; DLB 7, 266; RGAL 4

**Harte, (Francis) Bret(t)**
1836(?)-1902 ... **SSC 8, 59; TCLC 1, 25; WLC 3**
See also AMWS 2; CA 140; CAAE 104; CANR 80; CDALB 1865-1917; DA; DA3; DAC; DAM MST; DLB 12, 64, 74, 79, 186; EXPS; LAIT 2; RGAL 4; RGSF 2; SATA 26; SSFS 3; TUS

**Hartley, L(eslie) P(oles)** 1895-1972 ... **CLC 2, 22**
See also BRWS 7; CA 45-48; CAAS 37-40R; CANR 33; CN 1; DLB 15, 139; EWL 3; HGG; MTCW 1, 2; MTFW 2005; RGEL 2; RGSF 2; SUFW 1

**Hartman, Geoffrey H.** 1929- ............. **CLC 27**
See also CA 125; CAAE 117; CANR 79; DLB 67

**Hartmann, Sadakichi** 1869-1944 ... **TCLC 73**
See also CA 157; DLB 54

**Hartmann von Aue** c. 1170-c. 1210 ........................................ **CMLC 15**
See also CDWLB 2; DLB 138; RGWL 2, 3

**Hartog, Jan de**
See de Hartog, Jan

**Haruf, Kent** 1943- ............................. **CLC 34**
See also AAYA 44; CA 149; CANR 91, 131

**Harvey, Caroline**
See Trollope, Joanna

**Harvey, Gabriel** 1550(?)-1631 .............. **LC 88**
See also DLB 167, 213, 281

**Harwood, Ronald** 1934- .................... **CLC 32**
See also CA 1-4R; CANR 4, 55, 150; CBD; CD 5, 6; DAM DRAM, MST; DLB 13

**Hasegawa Tatsunosuke**
See Futabatei, Shimei

**Hasek, Jaroslav (Matej Frantisek)**
1883-1923 ................... **SSC 69; TCLC 4**
See also CA 129; CAAE 104; CDWLB 4; DLB 215; EW 9; EWL 3; MTCW 1, 2; RGSF 2; RGWL 2, 3

**Hass, Robert** 1941- ... **CLC 18, 39, 99; PC 16**
See also AMWS 6; CA 111; CANR 30, 50, 71; CP 3, 4, 5, 6, 7; DLB 105, 206; EWL 3; MAL 5; MTFW 2005; RGAL 4; SATA 94; TCLE 1:1

**Hastings, Hudson**
See Kuttner, Henry

**Hastings, Selina** ................................. **CLC 44**
See also CA 257

**Hastings, Selina Shirley**
See Hastings, Selina

**Hathorne, John** 1641-1717 .................. **LC 38**

**Hatteras, Amelia**
See Mencken, H(enry) L(ouis)

**Hatteras, Owen** ............................... **TCLC 18**
See Mencken, H(enry) L(ouis); Nathan, George Jean

**Hauff, Wilhelm** 1802-1827 ........... **NCLC 185**
See also DLB 90; SUFW 1

**Hauptmann, Gerhart (Johann Robert)**
1862-1946 ................... **SSC 37; TCLC 4**
See also CA 153; CAAE 104; CDWLB 2; DAM DRAM; DLB 66, 118, 330; EW 8; EWL 3; RGSF 2; RGWL 2, 3; TWA

**Havel, Vaclav** 1936- ..... **CLC 25, 58, 65, 123; DC 6**
See also CA 104; CANR 36, 63, 124; CDWLB 4; CWW 2; DA3; DAM DRAM; DFS 10; DLB 232; EWL 3; LMFS 2; MTCW 1, 2; MTFW 2005; RGWL 3

**Haviaras, Stratis** ............................. **CLC 33**
See Chaviaras, Strates

**Hawes, Stephen** 1475(?)-1529(?) .......... **LC 17**
See also DLB 132; RGEL 2

**Hawkes, John** 1925-1998 .. **CLC 1, 2, 3, 4, 7, 9, 14, 15, 27, 49**
See also BPFB 2; CA 1-4R; CAAS 167; CANR 2, 47, 64; CN 1, 2, 3, 4, 5, 6; DLB 2, 7, 227; DLBY 1980, 1998; EWL 3; MAL 5; MTCW 1, 2; MTFW 2005; RGAL 4

**Hawking, S. W.**
See Hawking, Stephen W.

**Hawking, Stephen W.** 1942- ..... **CLC 63, 105**
See also AAYA 13; BEST 89:1; CA 129; CAAE 126; CANR 48, 115; CPW; DA3; MTCW 2; MTFW 2005

**Hawkins, Anthony Hope**
See Hope, Anthony

**Hawthorne, Julian** 1846-1934 ........ **TCLC 25**
See also CA 165; HGG

**Hawthorne, Nathaniel** 1804-1864 ... **NCLC 2, 10, 17, 23, 39, 79, 95, 158, 171; SSC 3, 29, 39, 89; WLC 3**
See also AAYA 18; AMW; AMWC 1; AMWR 1; BPFB 2; BYA 3; CDALB 1640-1865; CLR 103; DA; DA3; DAB; DAC; DAM MST, NOV; DLB 1, 74, 183, 223, 269; EXPN; EXPS; GL 2; HGG; LAIT 1; NFS 1, 20; RGAL 4; RGSF 2; SSFS 1, 7, 11, 15; SUFW 1; TUS; WCH; YABC 2

**Hawthorne, Sophia Peabody**
1809-1871 ............................... **NCLC 150**
See also DLB 183, 239

**Haxton, Josephine Ayres** 1921-
See Douglas, Ellen
See also CA 115; CANR 41, 83

**Hayaseca y Eizaguirre, Jorge**
See Echegaray (y Eizaguirre), Jose (Maria Waldo)

**Hayashi, Fumiko** 1904-1951 .......... **TCLC 27**
See Hayashi Fumiko
See also CA 161

**Hayashi Fumiko**
See Hayashi, Fumiko
See also DLB 180; EWL 3

**Haycraft, Anna** 1932-2005
See Ellis, Alice Thomas
See also CA 122; CAAS 237; CANR 90, 141; MTCW 2; MTFW 2005

**Hayden, Robert E(arl)** 1913-1980 ..... **BLC 2; CLC 5, 9, 14, 37; PC 6**
See also AFAW 2; AMWS 2; BW 1, 3; CA 69-72; CAAS 97-100; CABS 2; CANR 24, 75, 82; CDALB 1941-1968; CP 1, 2, 3; DA; DAC; DAM MST, MULT, POET; DLB 5, 76; EWL 3; EXPP; MAL 5; MTCW 1, 2; PFS 1; RGAL 4; SATA 19; SATA-Obit 26; WP

**Haydon, Benjamin Robert**
1786-1846 ............................. **NCLC 146**
See also DLB 110

**Hayek, F(riedrich) A(ugust von)**
1899-1992 ............................ **TCLC 109**
See also CA 93-96; CAAS 137; CANR 20; MTCW 1, 2

**Hayford, J(oseph) E(phraim) Casely**
See Casely-Hayford, J(oseph) E(phraim)

**Hayman, Ronald** 1932- ..................... **CLC 44**
See also CA 25-28R; CANR 18, 50, 88; CD 5, 6; DLB 155

**Hayne, Paul Hamilton** 1830-1886 . **NCLC 94**
See also DLB 3, 64, 79, 248; RGAL 4

**Hays, Mary** 1760-1843 ................. **NCLC 114**
See also DLB 142, 158; RGEL 2

**Haywood, Eliza (Fowler)**
1693(?)-1756 ............................ **LC 1, 44**
See also BRWS 12; DLB 39; RGEL 2

**Hazlitt, William** 1778-1830 ...... **NCLC 29, 82**
See also BRW 4; DLB 110, 158; RGEL 2; TEA

**Hazzard, Shirley** 1931- ............. **CLC 18, 218**
See also CA 9-12R; CANR 4, 70, 127; CN 1, 2, 3, 4, 5, 6, 7; DLB 289; DLBY 1982; MTCW 1

**Head, Bessie** 1937-1986 ...... **BLC 2; CLC 25, 67; SSC 52**
See also AFW; BW 2, 3; CA 29-32R; CAAS 119; CANR 25, 82; CDWLB 3; CN 1, 2, 3, 4; DA3; DAM MULT; DLB 117, 225; EWL 3; EXPS; FL 1:6; FW; MTCW 1, 2; MTFW 2005; RGSF; SSFS 5, 13; WLIT 2; WWE 1

**Headon, (Nicky) Topper** 1956(?)- ..... **CLC 30**

**Heaney, Seamus** 1939- . **CLC 5, 7, 14, 25, 37, 74, 91, 171, 225; PC 18; WLCS**
See also AAYA 61; BRWR 1; BRWS 2; CA 85-88; CANR 25, 48, 75, 91, 128; CD-BLB 1960 to Present; CP 1, 2, 3, 4, 5, 6, 7; DA3; DAB; DAM POET; DLB 40, 330; DLBY 1995; EWL 3; EXPP; MTCW 1, 2; MTFW 2005; PAB; PFS 2, 5, 8, 17; RGEL 2; TEA; WLIT 4

**Hearn, (Patricio) Lafcadio (Tessima Carlos)**
1850-1904 ............................. **TCLC 9**
See also CA 166; CAAE 105; DLB 12, 78, 189; HGG; MAL 5; RGAL 4

**Hearne, Samuel** 1745-1792 ................. **LC 95**
See also DLB 99

**Hearne, Vicki** 1946-2001 ................. **CLC 56**
See also CA 139; CAAS 201

**Hearon, Shelby** 1931- ........................ **CLC 63**
See also AITN 2; AMWS 8; CA 25-28R; 11; CANR 18, 48, 103, 146; CSW

**Heat-Moon, William Least** ............. **CLC 29**
See Trogdon, William (Lewis)
See also AAYA 9

**Hebbel, Friedrich** 1813-1863 . **DC 21; NCLC 43**
See also CDWLB 2; DAM DRAM; DLB 129; EW 6; RGWL 2, 3

**Hebert, Anne** 1916-2000 . **CLC 4, 13, 29, 246**
See also CA 85-88; CAAS 187; CANR 69, 126; CCA 1; CWP; CWW 2; DA3; DAC; DAM MST, POET; DLB 68; EWL 3; GFL 1789 to the Present; MTCW 1, 2; MTFW 2005; PFS 20

**Hecht, Anthony (Evan)** 1923-2004 .... **CLC 8, 13, 19; PC 70**
See also AMWS 10; CA 9-12R; CAAS 232; CANR 6, 108; CP 1, 2, 3, 4, 5, 6, 7; DAM POET; DLB 5, 169; EWL 3; PFS 6; WP

**Hecht, Ben** 1894-1964 ..... **CLC 8; TCLC 101**
See also CA 85-88; DFS 9; DLB 7, 9, 25, 26, 28, 86; FANT; IDFW 3, 4; RGAL 4

**Hedayat, Sadeq** 1903-1951 ............. **TCLC 21**
See also CAAE 120; EWL 3; RGSF 2

**Hegel, Georg Wilhelm Friedrich**
1770-1831 ........................ **NCLC 46, 151**
See also DLB 90; TWA

**Heidegger, Martin** 1889-1976 ........... **CLC 24**
See also CA 81-84; CAAS 65-68; CANR 34; DLB 296; MTCW 1, 2; MTFW 2005

**Heidenstam, (Carl Gustaf) Verner von**
1859-1940 ................................ **TCLC 5**
See also CAAE 104; DLB 330

**Heidi Louise**
See Erdrich, Louise

**Heifner, Jack** 1946- ........................... **CLC 11**
See also CA 105; CANR 47

**Heijermans, Herman** 1864-1924 .... **TCLC 24**
See also CAAE 123; EWL 3

**Heilbrun, Carolyn G(old)**
1926-2003 ............................ **CLC 25, 173**
See Cross, Amanda
See also CA 45-48; CAAS 220; CANR 1, 28, 58, 94; FW

**Hein, Christoph** 1944- ..................... **CLC 154**
See also CA 158; CANR 108; CDWLB 2; CWW 2; DLB 124

**Heine, Heinrich** 1797-1856 ....... **NCLC 4, 54, 147; PC 25**
See also CDWLB 2; DLB 90; EW 5; RGWL 2, 3; TWA

**Heinemann, Larry** 1944- ................. **CLC 50**
See also CA 110; 21; CANR 31, 81, 156; DLBD 9; INT CANR-31

**Heinemann, Larry Curtiss**
See Heinemann, Larry

**Heiney, Donald (William)** 1921-1993
See Harris, MacDonald
See also CA 1-4R; CAAS 142; CANR 3, 58; FANT

**Heinlein, Robert A.** 1907-1988 .. **CLC 1, 3, 8, 14, 26, 55; SSC 55**
See also AAYA 17; BPFB 2; BYA 4, 13; CA 1-4R; CAAS 125; CANR 1, 20, 53; CLR 75; CN 1, 2, 3, 4; CPW; DA3; DAM POP; DLB 8; EXPS; JRDA; LAIT 5; LMFS 2; MAICYA 1, 2; MTCW 1, 2; MTFW 2005; RGAL 4; SATA 9, 69; SATA-Obit 56; SCFW 1, 2; SFW 4; SSFS 7; YAW

**Helforth, John**
See Doolittle, Hilda

**Heliodorus** fl. 3rd cent. - ................ **CMLC 52**
See also WLIT 8

**Hellenhofferu, Vojtech Kapristian z**
See Hasek, Jaroslav (Matej Frantisek)

**Heller, Joseph** 1923-1999 . **CLC 1, 3, 5, 8, 11, 36, 63; TCLC 131, 151; WLC 3**
See also AAYA 24; AITN 1; AMWS 4; BPFB 2; BYA 1; CA 5-8R; CAAS 187; CABS 1; CANR 8, 42, 66, 126; CN 1, 2, 3, 4, 5, 6; CPW; DA; DA3; DAB; DAC; DAM MST, NOV, POP; DLB 2, 28, 227; DLBY 1980, 2002; EWL 3; EXPN; INT CANR-8; LAIT 4; MAL 5; MTCW 1, 2; MTFW 2005; NFS 1; RGAL 4; TUS; YAW

**Hellman, Lillian** 1906-1984 . **CLC 2, 4, 8, 14, 18, 34, 44, 52; DC 1; TCLC 119**
See also AAYA 47; AITN 1, 2; AMWS 1; CA 13-16R; CAAS 112; CAD; CANR 33; CWD; DA3; DAM DRAM; DFS 1, 3, 14; DLB 7, 228; DLBY 1984; EWL 3; FL 1:6; FW; LAIT 3; MAL 5; MBL; MTCW 1, 2; MTFW 2005; RGAL 4; TUS

**Helprin, Mark** 1947- ......... **CLC 7, 10, 22, 32**
See also CA 81-84; CANR 47, 64, 124; CDALBS; CN 7; CPW; DA3; DAM NOV, POP; DLB 335; DLBY 1985; FANT; MAL 5; MTCW 1, 2; MTFW 2005; SSFS 25; SUFW 2

**Helvetius, Claude-Adrien** 1715-1771 .. **LC 26**
See also DLB 313

**Helyar, Jane Penelope Josephine** 1933-
See Poole, Josephine
See also CA 21-24R; CANR 10, 26; CWRI 5; SATA 82, 138; SATA-Essay 138

**Hemans, Felicia** 1793-1835 ...... **NCLC 29, 71**
See also DLB 96; RGEL 2

**Hemingway, Ernest (Miller)**
1899-1961 .... **CLC 1, 3, 6, 8, 10, 13, 19, 30, 34, 39, 41, 44, 50, 61, 80; SSC 1, 25, 36, 40, 63; TCLC 115; WLC 3**
See also AAYA 19; AMW; AMWC 1; AMWR 1; BPFB 2; BYA 2, 3, 13, 15; CA 77-80; CANR 34; CDALB 1917-1929; DA; DA3; DAB; DAC; DAM MST, NOV; DLB 4, 9, 102, 210, 308, 316, 330; DLBD 1, 15, 16; DLBY 1981, 1987, 1996, 1998; EWL 3; EXPN; EXPS; LAIT 3, 4; LATS 1:1; MAL 5; MTCW 1, 2; MTFW 2005; NFS 1, 5, 6, 14; RGAL 4; RGSF 2; SSFS 17; TUS; WYA

**Hempel, Amy** 1951- ......................... **CLC 39**
See also CA 137; CAAE 118; CANR 70, 166; DA3; DLB 218; EXPS; MTCW 2; MTFW 2005; SSFS 2

**Henderson, F. C.**
See Mencken, H(enry) L(ouis)

**Henderson, Sylvia**
See Ashton-Warner, Sylvia (Constance)

**Henderson, Zenna (Chlarson)**
1917-1983 ................................ **SSC 29**
See also CA 1-4R; CAAS 133; CANR 1, 84; DLB 8; SATA 5; SFW 4

**Henkin, Joshua** ................................ **CLC 119**
See also CA 161

**Henley, Beth** ................... **CLC 23; DC 6, 14**
See Henley, Elizabeth Becker
See also AAYA 70; CABS 3; CAD; CD 5, 6; CSW; CWD; DFS 2, 21; DLBY 1986; FW

**Henley, Elizabeth Becker** 1952-
See Henley, Beth
See also CA 107; CANR 32, 73, 140; DA3; DAM DRAM, MST; MTCW 1, 2; MTFW 2005

**Henley, William Ernest** 1849-1903 .. **TCLC 8**
See also CA 234; CAAE 105; DLB 19; RGEL 2

**Hennissart, Martha** 1929-
See Lathen, Emma
See also CA 85-88; CANR 64

**Henry VIII** 1491-1547 ........................ **LC 10**
See also DLB 132

Henry, O. . SSC 5, 49; TCLC 1, 19; WLC 3
See Porter, William Sydney
See also AAYA 41; AMWS 2; EXPS; MAL
5; RGAL 4; RGSF 2; SSFS 2, 18; TCWW
1, 2

Henry, Patrick 1736-1799 ............... LC 25
See also LAIT 1

Henryson, Robert 1430(?)-1506(?) ..... LC 20,
110; PC 65
See also BRWS 7; DLB 146; RGEL 2

Henschke, Alfred
See Klabund

Henson, Lance 1944- ......................... NNAL
See also CA 146; DLB 175

Hentoff, Nat(han Irving) 1925- ......... CLC 26
See also AAYA 4, 42; BYA 6; CA 1-4R; 6;
CANR 5, 25, 77, 114; CLR 1, 52; INT
CANR-25; JRDA; MAICYA 1, 2; SATA
42, 69, 133; SATA-Brief 27; WYA; YAW

Heppenstall, (John) Rayner
1911-1981 ................................. CLC 10
See also CA 1-4R; CAAS 103; CANR 29;
CN 1, 2; CP 1, 2, 3; EWL 3

Heraclitus c. 540B.C.-c. 450B.C. ... CMLC 22
See also DLB 176

Herbert, Frank 1920-1986 ... CLC 12, 23, 35,
44, 85
See also AAYA 21; BPFB 2; BYA 4, 14;
CA 53-56; CAAS 118; CANR 5, 43;
CDALBS; CPW; DAM POP; DLB 8; INT
CANR-5; LAIT 5; MTCW 1, 2; MTFW
2005; NFS 17; SATA 9, 37; SATA-Obit
47; SCFW 1, 2; SFW 4; YAW

Herbert, George 1593-1633 . LC 24, 121; PC
4
See also BRW 2; BRWR 2; CDBLB Before
1660; DAB; DAM POET; DLB 126;
EXPP; PFS 25; RGEL 2; TEA; WP

Herbert, Zbigniew 1924-1998 ..... CLC 9, 43;
PC 50; TCLC 168
See also CA 89-92; CAAS 169; CANR 36,
74; CDWLB 4; CWW 2; DAM POET;
DLB 232; EWL 3; MTCW 1; PFS 22

Herbst, Josephine (Frey)
1897-1969 ................................. CLC 34
See also CA 5-8R; CAAS 25-28R; DLB 9

Herder, Johann Gottfried von
1744-1803 ........................... NCLC 8, 186
See also DLB 97; EW 4; TWA

Heredia, Jose Maria 1803-1839 ....... HLCS 2
See also LAW

Hergesheimer, Joseph 1880-1954 ... TCLC 11
See also CA 194; CAAE 109; DLB 102, 9;
RGAL 4

Herlihy, James Leo 1927-1993 .......... CLC 6
See also CA 1-4R; CAAS 143; CAD;
CANR 2; CN 1, 2, 3, 4, 5

Herman, William
See Bierce, Ambrose (Gwinett)

Hermogenes fl. c. 175- ..................... CMLC 6

Hernandez, Jose 1834-1886 ............ NCLC 17
See also LAW; RGWL 2, 3; WLIT 1

Herodotus c. 484B.C.-c. 420B.C. .. CMLC 17
See also AW 1; CDWLB 1; DLB 176;
RGWL 2, 3; TWA; WLIT 8

Herr, Michael 1940(?)- ................... CLC 231
See also CA 89-92; CANR 68, 142; DLB
185; MTCW 1

Herrick, Robert 1591-1674 ....... LC 13; PC 9
See also BRW 2; BRWC 2; DA; DAB;
DAC; DAM MST, POP; DLB 126; EXPP;
PFS 13; RGAL 4; RGEL 2; TEA; WP

Herring, Guilles
See Somerville, Edith Oenone

Herriot, James 1916-1995 ................ CLC 12
See Wight, James Alfred
See also AAYA 1, 54; BPFB 2; CAAS 148;
CANR 40; CLR 80; CPW; DAM POP;
LAIT 3; MAICYA 2; MAICYAS 1;
MTCW 2; SATA 86, 135; TEA; YAW

Herris, Violet
See Hunt, Violet

Herrmann, Dorothy 1941- ................ CLC 44
See also CA 107

Herrmann, Taffy
See Herrmann, Dorothy

Hersey, John 1914-1993 .. CLC 1, 2, 7, 9, 40,
81, 97
See also AAYA 29; BPFB 2; CA 17-20R;
CAAS 140; CANR 33; CDALBS; CN 1,
2, 3, 4, 5; CPW; DAM POP; DLB 6, 185,
278, 299; MAL 5; MTCW 1, 2; MTFW
2005; RGHL; SATA 25; SATA-Obit 76;
TUS

Herzen, Aleksandr Ivanovich
1812-1870 ........................... NCLC 10, 61
See Herzen, Alexander

Herzen, Alexander
See Herzen, Aleksandr Ivanovich
See also DLB 277

Herzl, Theodor 1860-1904 ............. TCLC 36
See also CA 168

Herzog, Werner 1942- ............... CLC 16, 236
See also CA 89-92

Hesiod c. 8th cent. B.C.- .................. CMLC 5
See also AW 1; DLB 176; RGWL 2, 3;
WLIT 8

Hesse, Hermann 1877-1962 ... CLC 1, 2, 3, 6,
11, 17, 25, 69; SSC 9, 49; TCLC 148,
196; WLC 3
See also AAYA 43; BPFB 2; CA 17-18;
CAP 2; CDWLB 2; DA; DA3; DAB;
DAC; DAM MST, NOV; DLB 66, 330;
EW 9; EWL 3; EXPN; LAIT 1; MTCW
1, 2; MTFW 2005; NFS 6, 15, 24; RGWL
2, 3; SATA 50; TWA

Hewes, Cady
See De Voto, Bernard (Augustine)

Heyen, William 1940- ................. CLC 13, 18
See also CA 220; 33-36R, 220; 9; CANR
98; CP 3, 4, 5, 6, 7; DLB 5; RGHL

Heyerdahl, Thor 1914-2002 ............. CLC 26
See also CA 5-8R; CAAS 207; CANR 5,
22, 66, 73; LAIT 4; MTCW 1, 2; MTFW
2005; SATA 2, 52

Heym, Georg (Theodor Franz Arthur)
1887-1912 ................................... TCLC 9
See also CA 181; CAAE 106

Heym, Stefan 1913-2001 ................... CLC 41
See also CA 9-12R; CAAS 203; CANR 4;
CWW 2; DLB 69; EWL 3

Heyse, Paul (Johann Ludwig von)
1830-1914 ................................... TCLC 8
See also CA 209; CAAE 104; DLB 129,
330

Heyward, (Edwin) DuBose
1885-1940 ................... HR 1:2; TCLC 59
See also CA 157; CAAE 108; DLB 7, 9,
45, 249; MAL 5; SATA 21

Heywood, John 1497(?)-1580(?) ......... LC 65
See also DLB 136; RGEL 2

Heywood, Thomas 1573(?)-1641 ....... LC 111
See also DAM DRAM; DLB 62; LMFS 1;
RGEL 2; TEA

Hiaasen, Carl 1953- ....................... CLC 238
See also CA 105; CANR 22, 45, 65, 113,
133, 168; CMW 4; CPW; CSW; DA3;
DLB 292; MTCW 2; MTFW 2005

Hibbert, Eleanor Alice Burford
1906-1993 ................................... CLC 7
See Holt, Victoria
See also BEST 90:4; CA 17-20R; CAAS
140; CANR 9, 28, 59; CMW 4; CPW;
DAM POP; MTCW 2; MTFW 2005;
RHW; SATA 2; SATA-Obit 74

Hichens, Robert (Smythe)
1864-1950 ................................. TCLC 64
See also CA 162; DLB 153; HGG; RHW;
SUFW

Higgins, Aidan 1927- ......................... SSC 68
See also CA 9-12R; CANR 70, 115, 148;
CN 1, 2, 3, 4, 5, 6, 7; DLB 14

Higgins, George V(incent)
1939-1999 .................. CLC 4, 7, 10, 18
See also BPFB 2; CA 77-80; 5; CAAS 186;
CANR 17, 51, 89, 96; CMW 4; CN 2, 3,
4, 5, 6; DLB 2; DLBY 1981, 1998; INT
CANR-17; MSW; MTCW 1

Higginson, Thomas Wentworth
1823-1911 ............................... TCLC 36
See also CA 162; DLB 1, 64, 243

Higgonet, Margaret ......................... CLC 65

Highet, Helen
See MacInnes, Helen (Clark)

Highsmith, Patricia 1921-1995 ...... CLC 2, 4,
14, 42, 102
See Morgan, Claire
See also AAYA 48; BRWS 5; CA 1-4R;
CAAS 147; CANR 1, 20, 48, 62, 108;
CMW 4; CN 1, 2, 3, 4, 5; CPW; DA3;
DAM NOV, POP; DLB 306; MSW;
MTCW 1, 2; MTFW 2005; SSFS 25

Highwater, Jamake (Mamake)
1942(?)-2001 ............................. CLC 12
See also AAYA 7, 69; BPFB 2; CA
65-68; 7; CAAS 199; CANR 10, 34, 84;
CLR 17; CWRI 5; DLB 52; DLBY 1985;
JRDA; MAICYA 1, 2; SATA 32, 69;
SATA-Brief 30

Highway, Tomson 1951- ...... CLC 92; NNAL
See also CA 151; CANR 75; CCA 1; CD 5,
6; CN 7; DAC; DAM MULT; DFS 2;
DLB 334; MTCW 2

Hijuelos, Oscar 1951- .......... CLC 65; HLC 1
See also AAYA 25; AMWS 8; BEST 90:1;
CA 123; CANR 50, 75, 125; CPW; DA3;
DAM MULT, POP; DLB 145; HW 1, 2;
LLW; MAL 5; MTCW 2; MTFW 2005;
NFS 17; RGAL 4; WLIT 1

Hikmet, Nazim 1902-1963 ................. CLC 40
See Nizami of Ganja
See also CA 141; CAAS 93-96; EWL 3;
WLIT 6

Hildegard von Bingen 1098-1179 . CMLC 20
See also DLB 148

Hildesheimer, Wolfgang 1916-1991 .. CLC 49
See also CA 101; CAAS 135; DLB 69, 124;
EWL 3; RGHL

Hill, Geoffrey (William) 1932- ...... CLC 5, 8,
18, 45
See also BRWS 5; CA 81-84; CANR 21,
89; CDBLB 1960 to Present; CP 1, 2, 3,
4, 5, 6, 7; DAM POET; DLB 40; EWL 3;
MTCW 1; RGEL 2; RGHL

Hill, George Roy 1921-2002 ............. CLC 26
See also CA 122; CAAE 110; CAAS 213

Hill, John
See Koontz, Dean R.

Hill, Susan 1942- ....................... CLC 4, 113
See also CA 33-36R; CANR 29, 69, 129;
CN 2, 3, 4, 5, 6, 7; DAB; DAM MST,
NOV; DLB 14, 139; HGG; MTCW 1;
RHW; SATA 183

Hill, Susan Elizabeth
See Hill, Susan

Hillard, Asa G. III ......................... CLC 70

Hillerman, Tony 1925- ............. CLC 62, 170
See also AAYA 40; BEST 89:1; BPFB 2;
CA 29-32R; CANR 21, 42, 65, 97, 134;
CMW 4; CPW; DA3; DAM POP; DLB
206, 306; MAL 5; MSW; MTCW 2;
MTFW 2005; RGAL 4; SATA 6; TCWW
2; YAW

Hillesum, Etty 1914-1943 ............... TCLC 49
See also CA 137; RGHL

Hilliard, Noel (Harvey) 1929-1996 ... CLC 15
See also CA 9-12R; CANR 7, 69; CN 1, 2,
3, 4, 5, 6

**Hillis, Rick** 1956- ............................... **CLC 66**
See also CA 134

**Hilton, James** 1900-1954 ................. **TCLC 21**
See also AAYA 76; CA 169; CAAE 108;
DLB 34, 77; FANT; SATA 34

**Hilton, Walter** (?)-1396 ................... **CMLC 58**
See also DLB 146; RGEL 2

**Himes, Chester (Bomar)** 1909-1984 .. **BLC 2;**
**CLC 2, 4, 7, 18, 58, 108; TCLC 139**
See also AFAW 2; AMWS 16; BPFB 2; BW
2; CA 25-28R; CAAS 114; CANR 22, 89;
CMW 4; CN 1, 2, 3; DAM MULT; DLB
2, 76, 143, 226; EWL 3; MAL 5; MSW;
MTCW 1, 2; MTFW 2005; RGAL 4

**Himmelfarb, Gertrude** 1922- ........... **CLC 202**
See also CA 49-52; CANR 28, 66, 102, 166

**Hinde, Thomas** ............................ **CLC 6, 11**
See Chitty, Thomas Willes
See also CN 1, 2, 3, 4, 5, 6; EWL 3

**Hine, (William) Daryl** 1936- ............. **CLC 15**
See also CA 1-4R; 15; CANR 1, 20; CP 1,
2, 3, 4, 5, 6, 7; DLB 60

**Hinkson, Katharine Tynan**
See Tynan, Katharine

**Hinojosa, Rolando** 1929- ..................... **HLC 1**
See Hinojosa-Smith, Rolando
See also CA 131; 16; CANR 62; DAM
MULT; DLB 82; HW 1, 2; LLW; MTCW
2; MTFW 2005; RGAL 4

**Hinton, S.E.** 1950- ...................... **CLC 30, 111**
See also AAYA 2, 33; BPFB 2; BYA 2, 3;
CA 81-84; CANR 32, 62, 92, 133;
CDALBS; CLR 3, 23; CPW; DA; DA3;
DAB; DAC; DAM MST, NOV; JRDA;
LAIT 5; MAICYA 1, 2; MTCW 1, 2;
MTFW 2005; NFS 5, 9, 15, 16; SATA 19,
58, 115, 160; WYA; YAW

**Hippius, Zinaida (Nikolaevna)** ....... **TCLC 9**
See Gippius, Zinaida (Nikolaevna)
See also DLB 295; EWL 3

**Hiraoka, Kimitake** 1925-1970
See Mishima, Yukio
See also CA 97-100; CAAS 29-32R; DA3;
DAM DRAM; GLL 1; MTCW 1, 2

**Hirsch, E.D., Jr.** 1928- ...................... **CLC 79**
See also CA 25-28R; CANR 27, 51, 146;
DLB 67; INT CANR-27; MTCW 1

**Hirsch, Edward** 1950- .................. **CLC 31, 50**
See also CA 104; CANR 20, 42, 102, 167;
CP 6, 7; DLB 120; PFS 22

**Hirsch, Eric Donald, Jr.**
See Hirsch, E.D., Jr.

**Hitchcock, Alfred (Joseph)**
1899-1980 ................................... **CLC 16**
See also AAYA 22; CA 159; CAAS 97-100;
SATA 27; SATA-Obit 24

**Hitchens, Christopher** 1949- .......... **CLC 157**
See also CA 152; CANR 89, 155

**Hitchens, Christopher Eric**
See Hitchens, Christopher

**Hitler, Adolf** 1889-1945 ................... **TCLC 53**
See also CA 147; CAAE 117

**Hoagland, Edward (Morley)** 1932- .. **CLC 28**
See also ANW; CA 1-4R; CANR 2, 31, 57,
107; CN 1, 2, 3, 4, 5, 6, 7; DLB 6; SATA
51; TCWW 2

**Hoban, Russell** 1925- ..................... **CLC 7, 25**
See also BPFB 2; CA 5-8R; CANR 23, 37,
66, 114, 138; CLR 3, 69; CN 4, 5, 6, 7;
CWRI 5; DAM NOV; DLB 52; FANT;
MAICYA 1, 2; MTCW 1, 2; MTFW 2005;
SATA 1, 40, 78, 136; SFW 4; SUFW 2;
TCLE 1:1

**Hobbes, Thomas** 1588-1679 ......... **LC 36, 142**
See also DLB 151, 252, 281; RGEL 2

**Hobbs, Perry**
See Blackmur, R(ichard) P(almer)

**Hobson, Laura Z(ametkin)**
1900-1986 ............................ **CLC 7, 25**
See also BPFB 2; CA 17-20R; CAAS 118;
CANR 55; CN 1, 2, 3, 4; DLB 28; SATA
52

**Hoccleve, Thomas** c. 1368-c. 1437 ...... **LC 75**
See also DLB 146; RGEL 2

**Hoch, Edward D(entinger)** 1930-
See Queen, Ellery
See also CA 29-32R; CANR 11, 27, 51, 97;
CMW 4; DLB 306; SFW 4

**Hochhuth, Rolf** 1931- ............... **CLC 4, 11, 18**
See also CA 5-8R; CANR 33, 75, 136;
CWW 2; DAM DRAM; DLB 124; EWL
3; MTCW 1, 2; MTFW 2005; RGHL

**Hochman, Sandra** 1936- ................. **CLC 3, 8**
See also CA 5-8R; CP 1, 2, 3, 4, 5; DLB 5

**Hochwaelder, Fritz** 1911-1986 ......... **CLC 36**
See Hochwalder, Fritz
See also CA 29-32R; CAAS 120; CANR
42; DAM DRAM; MTCW 1; RGWL 3

**Hochwalder, Fritz**
See Hochwaelder, Fritz
See also EWL 3; RGWL 2

**Hocking, Mary (Eunice)** 1921- ......... **CLC 13**
See also CA 101; CANR 18, 40

**Hodgins, Jack** 1938- .......................... **CLC 23**
See also CA 93-96; CN 4, 5, 6, 7; DLB 60

**Hodgson, William Hope**
1877(?)-1918 ............................... **TCLC 13**
See also CA 164; CAAE 111; CMW 4; DLB
70, 153, 156, 178; HGG; MTCW 2; SFW
4; SUFW 1

**Hoeg, Peter** 1957- ...................... **CLC 95, 156**
See also CA 151; CANR 75; CMW 4; DA3;
DLB 214; EWL 3; MTCW 2; MTFW
2005; NFS 17; RGWL 3; SSFS 18

**Hoffman, Alice** 1952- ........................ **CLC 51**
See also AAYA 37; AMWS 10; CA 77-80;
CANR 34, 66, 100, 138; CN 4, 5, 6, 7;
CPW; DAM NOV; DLB 292; MAL 5;
MTCW 1, 2; MTFW 2005; TCLE 1:1

**Hoffman, Daniel (Gerard)** 1923- . **CLC 6, 13,**
**23**
See also CA 1-4R; CANR 4, 142; CP 1, 2,
3, 4, 5, 6, 7; DLB 5; TCLE 1:1

**Hoffman, Eva** 1945- ........................ **CLC 182**
See also AMWS 16; CA 132; CANR 146

**Hoffman, Stanley** 1944- ...................... **CLC 5**
See also CA 77-80

**Hoffman, William** 1925- ................. **CLC 141**
See also CA 21-24R; CANR 9, 103; CSW;
DLB 234; TCLE 1:1

**Hoffman, William M.**
See Hoffman, William M(oses)
See also CAD; CD 5, 6

**Hoffman, William M(oses)** 1939- ..... **CLC 40**
See Hoffman, William M.
See also CA 57-60; CANR 11, 71

**Hoffmann, E(rnst) T(heodor) A(madeus)**
1776-1822 ..... **NCLC 2, 183; SSC 13, 92**
See also CDWLB 2; DLB 90; EW 5; GL 2;
RGSF 2; RGWL 2, 3; SATA 27; SUFW
1; WCH

**Hofmann, Gert** 1931-1993 ................. **CLC 54**
See also CA 128; CANR 145; EWL 3;
RGHL

**Hofmannsthal, Hugo von** 1874-1929 ... **DC 4;**
**TCLC 11**
See also CA 153; CAAE 106; CDWLB 2;
DAM DRAM; DFS 17; DLB 81, 118; EW
9; EWL 3; RGWL 2, 3

**Hogan, Linda** 1947- ..... **CLC 73; NNAL; PC**
**35**
See also AMWS 4; ANW; BYA 12; CA 226;
120, 226; CANR 45, 73, 129; CWP; DAM
MULT; DLB 175; SATA 132; TCWW 2

**Hogarth, Charles**
See Creasey, John

**Hogarth, Emmett**
See Polonsky, Abraham (Lincoln)

**Hogarth, William** 1697-1764 ............. **LC 112**
See also AAYA 56

**Hogg, James** 1770-1835 ............ **NCLC 4, 109**
See also BRWS 10; DLB 93, 116, 159; GL
2; HGG; RGEL 2; SUFW 1

**Holbach, Paul-Henri Thiry**
1723-1789 ................................... **LC 14**
See also DLB 313

**Holberg, Ludvig** 1684-1754 ................... **LC 6**
See also DLB 300; RGWL 2, 3

**Holcroft, Thomas** 1745-1809 ......... **NCLC 85**
See also DLB 39, 89, 158; RGEL 2

**Holden, Ursula** 1921- ......................... **CLC 18**
See also CA 101; 8; CANR 22

**Holderlin, (Johann Christian) Friedrich**
1770-1843 ............. **NCLC 16, 187; PC 4**
See also CDWLB 2; DLB 90; EW 5; RGWL
2, 3

**Holdstock, Robert** 1948- .................... **CLC 39**
See also CA 131; CANR 81; DLB 261;
FANT; HGG; SFW 4; SUFW 2

**Holdstock, Robert P.**
See Holdstock, Robert

**Holinshed, Raphael** fl. 1580- ............... **LC 69**
See also DLB 167; RGEL 2

**Holland, Isabelle (Christian)**
1920-2002 ................................... **CLC 21**
See also AAYA 11, 64; CA 181; 21-24R;
CAAS 205; CANR 10, 25, 47; CLR 57;
CWRI 5; JRDA; LAIT 4; MAICYA 1, 2;
SATA 8, 70; SATA-Essay 103; SATA-Obit
132; WYA

**Holland, Marcus**
See Caldwell, (Janet Miriam) Taylor
(Holland)

**Hollander, John** 1929- .......... **CLC 2, 5, 8, 14**
See also CA 1-4R; CANR 1, 52, 136; CP 1,
2, 3, 4, 5, 6, 7; DLB 5; MAL 5; SATA 13

**Hollander, Paul**
See Silverberg, Robert

**Holleran, Andrew** ............................ **CLC 38**
See Garber, Eric
See also CA 144; GLL 1

**Holley, Marietta** 1836(?)-1926 ........ **TCLC 99**
See also CAAE 118; DLB 11; FL 1:3

**Hollinghurst, Alan** 1954- ............. **CLC 55, 91**
See also BRWS 10; CA 114; CN 5, 6, 7;
DLB 207, 326; GLL 1

**Hollis, Jim**
See Summers, Hollis (Spurgeon, Jr.)

**Holly, Buddy** 1936-1959 ................. **TCLC 65**
See also CA 213

**Holmes, Gordon**
See Shiel, M(atthew) P(hipps)

**Holmes, John**
See Souster, (Holmes) Raymond

**Holmes, John Clellon** 1926-1988 ...... **CLC 56**
See also BG 1:2; CA 9-12R; CAAS 125;
CANR 4; CN 1, 2, 3, 4; DLB 16, 237

**Holmes, Oliver Wendell, Jr.**
1841-1935 ............................... **TCLC 77**
See also CA 186; CAAE 114

**Holmes, Oliver Wendell**
1809-1894 ............. **NCLC 14, 81; PC 71**
See also AMWS 1; CDALB 1640-1865;
DLB 1, 189, 235; EXPP; PFS 24; RGAL
4; SATA 34

**Holmes, Raymond**
See Souster, (Holmes) Raymond

**Holt, Victoria**
See Hibbert, Eleanor Alice Burford
See also BPFB 2

**Holub, Miroslav** 1923-1998 ................. **CLC 4**
See also CA 21-24R; CAAS 169; CANR
10; CDWLB 4; CWW 2; DLB 232; EWL
3; RGWL 3

**Huch, Ricarda (Octavia)**
1864-1947 ................................. **TCLC 13**
See also CA 189; CAAE 111; DLB 66;
EWL 3

**Huddle, David** 1942- .......................... **CLC 49**
See also CA 57-60, 261; 20; CANR 89;
DLB 130

**Hudson, Jeffrey**
See Crichton, Michael

**Hudson, W(illiam) H(enry)**
1841-1922 ............................... **TCLC 29**
See also CA 190; CAAE 115; DLB 98, 153,
174; RGEL 2; SATA 35

**Hueffer, Ford Madox**
See Ford, Ford Madox

**Hughart, Barry** 1934- ......................... **CLC 39**
See also CA 137; FANT; SFW 4; SUFW 2

**Hughes, Colin**
See Creasey, John

**Hughes, David (John)** 1930-2005 ..... **CLC 48**
See also CA 129; CAAE 116; CAAS 238;
CN 4, 5, 6, 7; DLB 14

**Hughes, Edward James**
See Hughes, Ted
See also DA3; DAM MST, POET

**Hughes, (James Mercer) Langston**
1902-1967 ..... **BLC 2; CLC 1, 5, 10, 15,
35, 44, 108; DC 3; HR 1:2; PC 1, 53;
SSC 6, 90; WLC 3**
See also AAYA 12; AFAW 1, 2; AMWR 1;
AMWS 1; BW 1, 3; CA 1-4R; CAAS 25-
28R; CANR 1, 34, 82; CDALB 1929-
1941; CLR 17; DA; DA3; DAB; DAC;
DAM DRAM, MST, MULT, POET; DFS
6, 18; DLB 4, 7, 48, 51, 86, 228, 315;
EWL 3; EXPP; EXPS; JRDA; LAIT 3;
LMFS 2; MAICYA 1, 2; MAL 5; MTCW
1, 2; MTFW 2005; NFS 21; PAB; PFS 1,
3, 6, 10, 15; RGAL 4; RGSF 2; SATA 4,
33; SSFS 4, 7; TUS; WCH; WP; YAW

**Hughes, Richard (Arthur Warren)**
1900-1976 ............................. **CLC 1, 11**
See also CA 5-8R; CAAS 65-68; CANR 4;
CN 1, 2; DAM NOV; DLB 15, 161; EWL
3; MTCW 1; RGEL 2; SATA 8; SATA-
Obit 25

**Hughes, Ted** 1930-1998 . **CLC 2, 4, 9, 14, 37,
119; PC 7**
See Hughes, Edward James
See also BRWC 2; BRWR 2; BRWS 1; CA
1-4R; CAAS 171; CANR 1, 33, 66, 108;
CLR 3; CP 1, 2, 3, 4, 5, 6; DAB; DAC;
DLB 40, 161; EWL 3; EXPP; MAICYA
1, 2; MTCW 1, 2; MTFW 2005; PAB;
PFS 4, 19; RGEL 2; SATA 49; SATA-
Brief 27; SATA-Obit 107; TEA; YAW

**Hugo, Richard**
See Huch, Ricarda (Octavia)

**Hugo, Richard F(ranklin)**
1923-1982 .......... **CLC 6, 18, 32; PC 68**
See also AMWS 6; CA 49-52; CAAS 108;
CANR 3; CP 1, 2, 3; DAM POET; DLB
5, 206; EWL 3; MAL 5; PFS 17; RGAL 4

**Hugo, Victor (Marie)** 1802-1885 .... **NCLC 3,
10, 21, 161, 189; PC 17; WLC 3**
See also AAYA 28; DA; DA3; DAB; DAC;
DAM DRAM, MST, NOV, POET; DLB
119, 192, 217; EFS 2; EW 6; EXPN; GFL
1789 to the Present; LAIT 1, 2; NFS 5,
20; RGWL 2, 3; SATA 47; TWA

**Huidobro, Vicente**
See Huidobro Fernandez, Vicente Garcia
See also DLB 283; EWL 3; LAW

**Huidobro Fernandez, Vicente Garcia**
1893-1948 ............................... **TCLC 31**
See Huidobro, Vicente
See also CA 131; HW 1

**Hulme, Keri** 1947- ..................... **CLC 39, 130**
See also CA 125; CANR 69; CN 4, 5, 6, 7;
CP 6, 7; CWP; DLB 326; EWL 3; FW;
INT CA-125; NFS 24

**Hulme, T(homas) E(rnest)**
1883-1917 ............................... **TCLC 21**
See also BRWS 6; CA 203; CAAE 117;
DLB 19

**Humboldt, Alexander von**
1769-1859 ............................. **NCLC 170**
See also DLB 90

**Humboldt, Wilhelm von**
1767-1835 ............................. **NCLC 134**
See also DLB 90

**Hume, David** 1711-1776 ................. **LC 7, 56**
See also BRWS 3; DLB 104, 252, 336;
LMFS 1; TEA

**Humphrey, William** 1924-1997 ........ **CLC 45**
See also AMWS 9; CA 77-80; CAAS 160;
CANR 68; CN 1, 2, 3, 4, 5, 6; CSW; DLB
6, 212, 234, 278; TCWW 1, 2

**Humphreys, Emyr Owen** 1919- ........ **CLC 47**
See also CA 5-8R; CANR 3, 24; CN 1, 2,
3, 4, 5, 6, 7; DLB 15

**Humphreys, Josephine** 1945- ..... **CLC 34, 57**
See also CA 127; CAAE 121; CANR 97;
CSW; DLB 292; INT CA-127

**Huneker, James Gibbons**
1860-1921 ............................... **TCLC 65**
See also CA 193; DLB 71; RGAL 4

**Hungerford, Hesba Fay**
See Brinsmead, H(esba) F(ay)

**Hungerford, Pixie**
See Brinsmead, H(esba) F(ay)

**Hunt, E. Howard** 1918-2007 .............. **CLC 3**
See also AITN 1; CA 45-48; CAAS 256;
CANR 2, 47, 103, 160; CMW 4

**Hunt, Everette Howard, Jr.**
See Hunt, E. Howard

**Hunt, Francesca**
See Holland, Isabelle (Christian)

**Hunt, Howard**
See Hunt, E. Howard

**Hunt, Kyle**
See Creasey, John

**Hunt, (James Henry) Leigh**
1784-1859 ............... **NCLC 1, 70; PC 73**
See also DAM POET; DLB 96, 110, 144;
RGEL 2; TEA

**Hunt, Marsha** 1946- .......................... **CLC 70**
See also BW 2, 3; CA 143; CANR 79

**Hunt, Violet** 1866(?)-1942 .............. **TCLC 53**
See also CA 184; DLB 162, 197

**Hunter, E. Waldo**
See Sturgeon, Theodore (Hamilton)

**Hunter, Evan** 1926-2005 .............. **CLC 11, 31**
See McBain, Ed
See also AAYA 39; BPFB 2; CA 5-8R;
CAAS 241; CANR 5, 38, 62, 97, 149;
CMW 4; CN 1, 2, 3, 4, 5, 6, 7; CPW;
DAM POP; DLB 306; DLBY 1982; INT
CANR-5; MSW; MTCW 1; SATA 25;
SATA-Obit 167; SFW 4

**Hunter, Kristin**
See Lattany, Kristin (Elaine Eggleston)
Hunter
See also CN 1, 2, 3, 4, 5, 6

**Hunter, Mary**
See Austin, Mary (Hunter)

**Hunter, Mollie** 1922- .......................... **CLC 21**
See McIlwraith, Maureen Mollie Hunter
See also AAYA 13, 71; BYA 6; CANR 37,
78; CLR 25; DLB 161; JRDA; MAICYA
1, 2; SAAS 7; SATA 54, 106, 139; SATA-
Essay 139; WYA; YAW

**Hunter, Robert** (?)-1734 ........................ **LC 7**

**Hurston, Zora Neale** 1891-1960 ........ **BLC 2;
CLC 7, 30, 61; DC 12; HR 1:2; SSC 4,
80; TCLC 121, 131; WLCS**
See also AAYA 15, 71; AFAW 1, 2; AMWS
6; BW 1, 3; BYA 12; CA 85-88; CANR
61; CDALBS; DA; DA3; DAC; DAM
MST, MULT, NOV; DFS 6; DLB 51, 86;
EWL 3; EXPN; EXPS; FL 1:6; FW; LAIT
3; LATS 1:1; LMFS 2; MAL 5; MBL;
MTCW 1, 2; MTFW 2005; NFS 3; RGAL
4; RGSF 2; SSFS 1, 6, 11, 19, 21; TUS;
YAW

**Husserl, E. G.**
See Husserl, Edmund (Gustav Albrecht)

**Husserl, Edmund (Gustav Albrecht)**
1859-1938 ............................. **TCLC 100**
See also CA 133; CAAE 116; DLB 296

**Huston, John (Marcellus)**
1906-1987 ............................... **CLC 20**
See also CA 73-76; CAAS 123; CANR 34;
DLB 26

**Hustvedt, Siri** 1955- .......................... **CLC 76**
See also CA 137; CANR 149

**Hutten, Ulrich von** 1488-1523 ............. **LC 16**
See also DLB 179

**Huxley, Aldous (Leonard)**
1894-1963 ....... **CLC 1, 3, 4, 5, 8, 11, 18,
35, 79; SSC 39; WLC 3**
See also AAYA 11; BPFB 2; BRW 7; CA
85-88; CANR 44, 99; CDBLB 1914-1945;
DA; DA3; DAB; DAC; DAM MST, NOV;
DLB 36, 100, 162, 195, 255; EWL 3;
EXPN; LAIT 5; LMFS 2; MTCW 1, 2;
MTFW 2005; NFS 6; RGEL 2; SATA 63;
SCFW 1, 2; SFW 4; TEA; YAW

**Huxley, T(homas) H(enry)**
1825-1895 ............................... **NCLC 67**
See also DLB 57; TEA

**Huygens, Constantijn** 1596-1687 ....... **LC 114**
See also RGWL 2, 3

**Huysmans, Joris-Karl** 1848-1907 ... **TCLC 7,
69**
See also CA 165; CAAE 104; DLB 123;
EW 7; GFL 1789 to the Present; LMFS 2;
RGWL 2, 3

**Hwang, David Henry** 1957- .... **CLC 55, 196;
DC 4, 23**
See also CA 132; CAAE 127; CAD; CANR
76, 124; CD 5, 6; DA3; DAM DRAM;
DFS 11, 18; DLB 212, 228, 312; INT CA-
132; MAL 5; MTCW 2; MTFW 2005;
RGAL 4

**Hyde, Anthony** 1946- .......................... **CLC 42**
See Chase, Nicholas
See also CA 136; CCA 1

**Hyde, Margaret O(ldroyd)** 1917- ..... **CLC 21**
See also CA 1-4R; CANR 1, 36, 137; CLR
23; JRDA; MAICYA 1, 2; SAAS 8; SATA
1, 42, 76, 139

**Hynes, James** 1956(?)- ...................... **CLC 65**
See also CA 164; CANR 105

**Hypatia** c. 370-415 ........................ **CMLC 35**

**Ian, Janis** 1951- ................................. **CLC 21**
See also CA 187; CAAE 105

**Ibanez, Vicente Blasco**
See Blasco Ibanez, Vicente
See also DLB 322

**Ibarbourou, Juana de**
1895(?)-1979 ............................. **HLCS 2**
See also DLB 290; HW 1; LAW

**Ibarguengoitia, Jorge** 1928-1983 ..... **CLC 37;
TCLC 148**
See also CA 124; CAAS 113; EWL 3; HW
1

**Ibn Battuta, Abu Abdalla**
1304-1368(?) ........................... **CMLC 57**
See also WLIT 2

Cumulative Author Index

**Ibn Hazm** 994-1064 ........................ **CMLC 64**
**Ibn Zaydun** 1003-1070 ................... **CMLC 89**
**Ibsen, Henrik (Johan)** 1828-1906 ........ **DC 2;**
  **TCLC 2, 8, 16, 37, 52; WLC 3**
    See also AAYA 46; CA 141; CAAE 104;
    DA; DA3; DAB; DAC; DAM DRAM,
    MST; DFS 1, 6, 8, 10, 11, 15, 16; EW 7;
    LAIT 2; LATS 1:1; MTFW 2005; RGWL
    2, 3
**Ibuse, Masuji** 1898-1993 ................... **CLC 22**
    See Ibuse Masuji
    See also CA 127; CAAS 141; MJW; RGWL
    3
**Ibuse Masuji**
    See Ibuse, Masuji
    See also CWW 2; DLB 180; EWL 3
**Ichikawa, Kon** 1915- .......................... **CLC 20**
    See also CA 121
**Ichiyo, Higuchi** 1872-1896 .............. **NCLC 49**
    See also MJW
**Idle, Eric** 1943- ............................... **CLC 21**
    See Monty Python
    See also CA 116; CANR 35, 91, 148
**Idris, Yusuf** 1927-1991 ...................... **SSC 74**
    See also AFW; EWL 3; RGSF 2, 3; RGWL
    3; WLIT 2
**Ignatieff, Michael** 1947- ................... **CLC 236**
    See also CA 144; CANR 88, 156; CN 6, 7;
    DLB 267
**Ignatieff, Michael Grant**
    See Ignatieff, Michael
**Ignatow, David** 1914-1997 ....... **CLC 4, 7, 14,**
    **40; PC 34**
    See also CA 9-12R; 3; CAAS 162; CANR
    31, 57, 96; CP 1, 2, 3, 4, 5, 6; DLB 5;
    EWL 3; MAL 5
**Ignotus**
    See Strachey, (Giles) Lytton
**Ihimaera, Witi (Tame)** 1944- ............ **CLC 46**
    See also CA 77-80; CANR 130; CN 2, 3, 4,
    5, 6, 7; RGSF 2; SATA 148
**Il'f, Il'ia**
    See Fainzilberg, Ilya Arnoldovich
    See also DLB 272
**Ilf, Ilya**
    See Fainzilberg, Ilya Arnoldovich
**Illyes, Gyula** 1902-1983 ...................... **PC 16**
    See also CA 114; CAAS 109; CDWLB 4;
    DLB 215; EWL 3; RGWL 2, 3
**Imalayen, Fatima-Zohra**
    See Djebar, Assia
**Immermann, Karl (Lebrecht)**
    1796-1840 ............................ **NCLC 4, 49**
    See also DLB 133
**Ince, Thomas H.** 1882-1924 ............ **TCLC 89**
    See also IDFW 3, 4
**Inchbald, Elizabeth** 1753-1821 ...... **NCLC 62**
    See also DLB 39, 89; RGEL 2
**Inclan, Ramon (Maria) del Valle**
    See Valle-Inclan, Ramon (Maria) del
**Infante, G(uillermo) Cabrera**
    See Cabrera Infante, G.
**Ingalls, Rachel** 1940- .......................... **CLC 42**
    See also CA 127; CAAE 123; CANR 154
**Ingalls, Rachel Holmes**
    See Ingalls, Rachel
**Ingamells, Reginald Charles**
    See Ingamells, Rex
**Ingamells, Rex** 1913-1955 .............. **TCLC 35**
    See also CA 167; DLB 260
**Inge, William (Motter)** 1913-1973 ..... **CLC 1,**
    **8, 19**
    See also CA 9-12R; CAD; CDALB 1941-
    1968; DA3; DAM DRAM; DFS 1, 3, 5,
    8; DLB 7, 249; EWL 3; MAL 5; MTCW
    1, 2; MTFW 2005; RGAL 4; TUS
**Ingelow, Jean** 1820-1897 ........ **NCLC 39, 107**
    See also DLB 35, 163; FANT; SATA 33

**Ingram, Willis J.**
    See Harris, Mark
**Innaurato, Albert (F.)** 1948(?)- ... **CLC 21, 60**
    See also CA 122; CAAE 115; CAD; CANR
    78; CD 5, 6; INT CA-122
**Innes, Michael**
    See Stewart, J(ohn) I(nnes) M(ackintosh)
    See also DLB 276; MSW
**Innis, Harold Adams** 1894-1952 .... **TCLC 77**
    See also CA 181; DLB 88
**Insluis, Alanus de**
    See Alain de Lille
**Iola**
    See Wells-Barnett, Ida B(ell)
**Ionesco, Eugene** 1912-1994 ... **CLC 1, 4, 6, 9,**
    **11, 15, 41, 86; DC 12; WLC 3**
    See also CA 9-12R; CAAS 144; CANR 55,
    132; CWW 2; DA; DA3; DAB; DAC;
    DAM DRAM, MST; DFS 4, 9; DLB 321;
    EW 13; EWL 3; GFL 1789 to the Present;
    LMFS 2; MTCW 1, 2; MTFW 2005;
    RGWL 2, 3; SATA 7; SATA-Obit 79;
    TWA
**Iqbal, Muhammad** 1877-1938 ........ **TCLC 28**
    See also CA 215; EWL 3
**Ireland, Patrick**
    See O'Doherty, Brian
**Irenaeus St.** 130- ............................... **CMLC 42**
**Irigaray, Luce** 1930- ........................ **CLC 164**
    See also CA 154; CANR 121; FW
**Iron, Ralph**
    See Schreiner, Olive (Emilie Albertina)
**Irving, John** 1942- . **CLC 13, 23, 38, 112, 175**
    See also AAYA 8, 62; AMWS 6; BEST
    89:3; BPFB 2; CA 25-28R; CANR 28, 73,
    112, 133; CN 3, 4, 5, 6, 7; CPW; DA3;
    DAM NOV, POP; DLB 6, 278; DLBY
    1982; EWL 3; MAL 5; MTCW 1, 2;
    MTFW 2005; NFS 12, 14; RGAL 4; TUS
**Irving, John Winslow**
    See Irving, John
**Irving, Washington** 1783-1859 . **NCLC 2, 19,**
    **95; SSC 2, 37, 104; WLC 3**
    See also AAYA 56; AMW; CDALB 1640-
    1865; CLR 97; DA; DA3; DAB; DAC;
    DAM MST; DLB 3, 11, 30, 59, 73, 74,
    183, 186, 250, 254; EXPS; GL 2; LAIT
    1; RGAL 4; RGSF 2; SSFS 1, 8, 16;
    SUFW 1; TUS; WCH; YABC 2
**Irwin, P. K.**
    See Page, P(atricia) K(athleen)
**Isaacs, Jorge Ricardo** 1837-1895 ... **NCLC 70**
    See also LAW
**Isaacs, Susan** 1943- .......................... **CLC 32**
    See also BEST 89:1; BPFB 2; CA 89-92;
    CANR 20, 41, 65, 112, 134, 165; CPW;
    DA3; DAM POP; INT CANR-20; MTCW
    1, 2; MTFW 2005
**Isherwood, Christopher** 1904-1986 ... **CLC 1,**
    **9, 11, 14, 44; SSC 56**
    See also AMWS 14; BRW 7; CA 13-16R;
    CAAS 117; CANR 35, 97, 133; CN 1, 2,
    3; DA3; DAM DRAM, NOV; DLB 15,
    195; DLBY 1986; EWL 3; IDTP; MTCW
    1, 2; MTFW 2005; RGAL 4; RGEL 2;
    TUS; WLIT 4
**Ishiguro, Kazuo** 1954- . **CLC 27, 56, 59, 110,**
    **119**
    See also AAYA 58; BEST 90:2; BPFB 2;
    BRWS 4; CA 120; CANR 49, 95, 133;
    CN 5, 6, 7; DA3; DAM NOV; DLB 194,
    326; EWL 3; MTCW 1, 2; MTFW 2005;
    NFS 13; WLIT 4; WWE 1
**Ishikawa, Hakuhin**
    See Ishikawa, Takuboku
**Ishikawa, Takuboku** 1886(?)-1912 ..... **PC 10;**
    **TCLC 15**
    See Ishikawa Takuboku
    See also CA 153; CAAE 113; DAM POET

**Iskander, Fazil (Abdulovich)** 1929- .. **CLC 47**
    See Iskander, Fazil' Abdulevich
    See also CA 102; EWL 3
**Iskander, Fazil' Abdulevich**
    See Iskander, Fazil (Abdulovich)
    See also DLB 302
**Isler, Alan (David)** 1934- ................... **CLC 91**
    See also CA 156; CANR 105
**Ivan IV** 1530-1584 .............................. **LC 17**
**Ivanov, V.I.**
    See Ivanov, Vyacheslav
**Ivanov, Vyacheslav** 1866-1949 ........ **TCLC 33**
    See also CAAE 122; EWL 3
**Ivanov, Vyacheslav Ivanovich**
    See Ivanov, Vyacheslav
**Ivask, Ivar Vidrik** 1927-1992 ........... **CLC 14**
    See also CA 37-40R; CAAS 139; CANR 24
**Ives, Morgan**
    See Bradley, Marion Zimmer
    See also GLL 1
**Izumi Shikibu** c. 973-c. 1034 ........ **CMLC 33**
**J. R. S.**
    See Gogarty, Oliver St. John
**Jabran, Kahlil**
    See Gibran, Kahlil
**Jabran, Khalil**
    See Gibran, Kahlil
**Jackson, Daniel**
    See Wingrove, David
**Jackson, Helen Hunt** 1830-1885 .... **NCLC 90**
    See also DLB 42, 47, 186, 189; RGAL 4
**Jackson, Jesse** 1908-1983 .................. **CLC 12**
    See also BW 1; CA 25-28R; CAAS 109;
    CANR 27; CLR 28; CWRI 5; MAICYA
    1, 2; SATA 2, 29; SATA-Obit 48
**Jackson, Laura (Riding)** 1901-1991 .... **PC 44**
    See Riding, Laura
    See also CA 65-68; CAAS 135; CANR 28,
    89; DLB 48
**Jackson, Sam**
    See Trumbo, Dalton
**Jackson, Sara**
    See Wingrove, David
**Jackson, Shirley** 1919-1965 . **CLC 11, 60, 87;**
    **SSC 9, 39; TCLC 187; WLC 3**
    See also AAYA 9; AMWS 9; BPFB 2; CA
    1-4R; CAAS 25-28R; CANR 4, 52;
    CDALB 1941-1968; DA; DA3; DAC;
    DAM MST; DLB 6, 234; EXPS; HGG;
    LAIT 4; MAL 5; MTCW 2; MTFW 2005;
    RGAL 4; RGSF 2; SATA 2; SSFS 1;
    SUFW 1, 2
**Jacob, (Cyprien-)Max** 1876-1944 .... **TCLC 6**
    See also CA 193; CAAE 104; DLB 258;
    EWL 3; GFL 1789 to the Present; GLL 2;
    RGWL 2, 3
**Jacobs, Harriet A(nn)**
    1813(?)-1897 ................... **NCLC 67, 162**
    See also AFAW 1, 2; DLB 239; FL 1:3; FW;
    LAIT 2; RGAL 4
**Jacobs, Jim** 1942- .............................. **CLC 12**
    See also CA 97-100; INT CA-97-100
**Jacobs, W(illiam) W(ymark)**
    1863-1943 ............... **SSC 73; TCLC 22**
    See also CA 167; CAAE 121; DLB 135;
    EXPS; HGG; RGEL 2; RGSF 2; SSFS 2;
    SUFW 1
**Jacobsen, Jens Peter** 1847-1885 .... **NCLC 34**
**Jacobsen, Josephine (Winder)**
    1908-2003 ............... **CLC 48, 102; PC 62**
    See also CA 33-36R; 18; CAAS 218; CANR
    23, 48; CCA 1; CP 2, 3, 4, 5, 6, 7; DLB
    244; PFS 23; TCLE 1:1
**Jacobson, Dan** 1929- ...... **CLC 4, 14; SSC 91**
    See also AFW; CA 1-4R; CANR 2, 25, 66;
    CN 1, 2, 3, 4, 5, 6, 7; DLB 14, 207, 225,
    319; EWL 3; MTCW 1; RGSF 2

**Johnson, B(ryan) S(tanley William)**
1933-1973 .......................... **CLC 6, 9**
See also CA 9-12R; CAAS 53-56; CANR
9; CN 1; CP 1, 2; DLB 14, 40; EWL 3;
RGEL 2

**Johnson, Benjamin F., of Boone**
See Riley, James Whitcomb

**Johnson, Charles (Richard)** 1948- .... **BLC 2;**
**CLC 7, 51, 65, 163**
See also AFAW 2; AMWS 6; BW 2, 3; CA
116; 18; CANR 42, 66, 82, 129; CN 5, 6,
7; DAM MULT; DLB 33, 278; MAL 5;
MTCW 2; MTFW 2005; RGAL 4; SSFS
16

**Johnson, Charles S(purgeon)**
1893-1956 ................................ **HR 1:3**
See also BW 1, 3; CA 125; CANR 82; DLB
51, 91

**Johnson, Denis** 1949- . **CLC 52, 160; SSC 56**
See also CA 121; CAAE 117; CANR 71,
99; CN 4, 5, 6, 7; DLB 120

**Johnson, Diane** 1934- ...... **CLC 5, 13, 48, 244**
See also BPFB 2; CA 41-44R; CANR 17,
40, 62, 95, 155; CN 4, 5, 6, 7; DLBY
1980; INT CANR-17; MTCW 1

**Johnson, E(mily) Pauline** 1861-1913 . **NNAL**
See also CA 150; CCA 1; DAC; DAM
MULT; DLB 92, 175; TCWW 2

**Johnson, Eyvind (Olof Verner)**
1900-1976 ................................ **CLC 14**
See also CA 73-76; CAAS 69-72; CANR
34, 101; DLB 259, 330; EW 12; EWL 3

**Johnson, Fenton** 1888-1958 ................ **BLC 2**
See also BW 1; CA 124; CAAE 118; DAM
MULT; DLB 45, 50

**Johnson, Georgia Douglas (Camp)**
1880-1966 ................................ **HR 1:3**
See also BW 1; CA 125; DLB 51, 249; WP

**Johnson, Helene** 1907-1995 ............... **HR 1:3**
See also CA 181; DLB 51; WP

**Johnson, J. R.**
See James, C(yril) L(ionel) R(obert)

**Johnson, James Weldon** 1871-1938 .. **BLC 2;**
**HR 1:3; PC 24; TCLC 3, 19, 175**
See also AAYA 73; AFAW 1, 2; BW 1, 3;
CA 125; CAAE 104; CANR 82; CDALB
1917-1929; CLR 32; DA3; DAM MULT;
POET; DLB 51; EWL 3; EXPP; LMFS 2;
MAL 5; MTCW 1, 2; MTFW 2005; NFS
22; PFS 1; RGAL 4; SATA 31; TUS

**Johnson, Joyce** 1935- ....................... **CLC 58**
See also BG 1:3; CA 129; CAAE 125;
CANR 102

**Johnson, Judith (Emlyn)** 1936- .... **CLC 7, 15**
See Sherwin, Judith Johnson
See also CA 25-28R, 153; CANR 34; CP 6,
7

**Johnson, Lionel (Pigot)**
1867-1902 ................................ **TCLC 19**
See also CA 209; CAAE 117; DLB 19;
RGEL 2

**Johnson, Marguerite Annie**
See Angelou, Maya

**Johnson, Mel**
See Malzberg, Barry N(athaniel)

**Johnson, Pamela Hansford**
1912-1981 ......................... **CLC 1, 7, 27**
See also CA 1-4R; CAAS 104; CANR 2,
28; CN 1, 2, 3; DLB 15; MTCW 1, 2;
MTFW 2005; RGEL 2

**Johnson, Paul** 1928- ........................ **CLC 147**
See also BEST 89:4; CA 17-20R; CANR
34, 62, 100, 155

**Johnson, Paul Bede**
See Johnson, Paul

**Johnson, Robert** ............................... **CLC 70**

**Johnson, Robert** 1911(?)-1938 ........ **TCLC 69**
See also BW 3; CA 174

**Johnson, Samuel** 1709-1784 . **LC 15, 52, 128;**
**PC 81; WLC 3**
See also BRW 3; BRWR 1; CDBLB 1660-
1789; DA; DAB; DAC; DAM MST; DLB
39, 95, 104, 142, 213; LMFS 1; RGEL 2;
TEA

**Johnson, Uwe** 1934-1984 .. **CLC 5, 10, 15, 40**
See also CA 1-4R; CAAS 112; CANR 1,
39; CDWLB 2; DLB 75; EWL 3; MTCW
1; RGWL 2, 3

**Johnston, Basil H.** 1929- ..................... **NNAL**
See also CA 69-72; CANR 11, 28, 66;
DAC; DAM MULT; DLB 60

**Johnston, George (Benson)** 1913- .... **CLC 51**
See also CA 1-4R; CANR 5, 20; CP 1, 2, 3,
4, 5, 6, 7; DLB 88

**Johnston, Jennifer (Prudence)**
1930- ........................... **CLC 7, 150, 228**
See also CA 85-88; CANR 92; CN 4, 5, 6,
7; DLB 14

**Joinville, Jean de** 1224(?)-1317 ..... **CMLC 38**

**Jolley, Elizabeth** 1923-2007 ..... **CLC 46; SSC**
**19**
See also CA 127; 13; CAAS 257; CANR
59; CN 4, 5, 6, 7; DLB 325; EWL 3;
RGSF 2

**Jolley, Monica Elizabeth**
See Jolley, Elizabeth

**Jones, Arthur Llewellyn** 1863-1947
See Machen, Arthur
See also CA 179; CAAE 104; HGG

**Jones, D(ouglas) G(ordon)** 1929- ..... **CLC 10**
See also CA 29-32R; CANR 13, 90; CP 1,
2, 3, 4, 5, 6, 7; DLB 53

**Jones, David (Michael)** 1895-1974 .... **CLC 2,**
**4, 7, 13, 42**
See also BRW 6; BRWS 7; CA 9-12R;
CAAS 53-56; CANR 28; CDBLB 1945-
1960; CP 1, 2; DLB 20, 100; EWL 3;
MTCW 1; PAB; RGEL 2

**Jones, David Robert** 1947-
See Bowie, David
See also CA 103; CANR 104

**Jones, Diana Wynne** 1934- ................ **CLC 26**
See also AAYA 12; BYA 6, 7, 9, 11, 13, 16;
CA 49-52; CANR 4, 26, 56, 120, 167;
CLR 23, 120; DLB 161; FANT; JRDA;
MAICYA 1, 2; MTFW 2005; SAAS 7;
SATA 9, 70, 108, 160; SFW 4; SUFW 2;
YAW

**Jones, Edward P.** 1950- ............. **CLC 76, 223**
See also AAYA 71; BW 2, 3; CA 142;
CANR 79, 134; CSW; MTFW 2005; NFS
26

**Jones, Gayl** 1949- ...... **BLC 2; CLC 6, 9, 131**
See also AFAW 1, 2; BW 2, 3; CA 77-80;
CANR 27, 66, 122; CN 4, 5, 6, 7; CSW;
DA3; DAM MULT; DLB 33, 278; MAL
5; MTCW 1, 2; MTFW 2005; RGAL 4

**Jones, James** 1921-1977 ...... **CLC 1, 3, 10, 39**
See also AITN 1, 2; AMWS 11; BPFB 2;
CA 1-4R; CAAS 69-72; CANR 6; CN 1,
2; DLB 2, 143; DLBD 17; DLBY 1998;
EWL 3; MAL 5; MTCW 1; RGAL 4

**Jones, John J.**
See Lovecraft, H. P.

**Jones, LeRoi** .............. **CLC 1, 2, 3, 5, 10, 14**
See Baraka, Amiri
See also CN 1, 2; CP 1, 2, 3; MTCW 2

**Jones, Louis B.** 1953- ......................... **CLC 65**
See also CA 141; CANR 73

**Jones, Madison** 1925- ......................... **CLC 4**
See also CA 13-16R; 11; CANR 7, 54, 83,
158; CN 1, 2, 3, 4, 5, 6, 7; CSW; DLB
152

**Jones, Madison Percy, Jr.**
See Jones, Madison

**Jones, Mervyn** 1922- ................... **CLC 10, 52**
See also CA 45-48; 5; CANR 1, 91; CN 1,
2, 3, 4, 5, 6, 7; MTCW 1

**Jones, Mick** 1956(?)- .......................... **CLC 30**

**Jones, Nettie (Pearl)** 1941- ............... **CLC 34**
See also BW 2; CA 137; 20; CANR 88

**Jones, Peter** 1802-1856 ...................... **NNAL**

**Jones, Preston** 1936-1979 ................. **CLC 10**
See also CA 73-76; CAAS 89-92; DLB 7

**Jones, Robert F(rancis)** 1934-2003 .... **CLC 7**
See also CA 49-52; CANR 2, 61, 118

**Jones, Rod** 1953- .............................. **CLC 50**
See also CA 128

**Jones, Terence Graham Parry**
1942- ................................... **CLC 21**
See Jones, Terry; Monty Python
See also CA 116; CAAE 112; CANR 35,
93; INT CA-116; SATA 127

**Jones, Terry**
See Jones, Terence Graham Parry
See also SATA 67; SATA-Brief 51

**Jones, Thom (Douglas)** 1945(?)- ..... **CLC 81;**
**SSC 56**
See also CA 157; CANR 88; DLB 244;
SSFS 23

**Jong, Erica** 1942- ........... **CLC 4, 6, 8, 18, 83**
See also AITN 1; AMWS 5; BEST 90:2;
BPFB 2; CA 73-76; CANR 26, 52, 75,
132, 166; CN 3, 4, 5, 6, 7; CP 2, 3, 4, 5,
6, 7; CPW; DA3; DAM NOV, POP; DLB
2, 5, 28, 152; FW; INT CANR-26; MAL
5; MTCW 1, 2; MTFW 2005

**Jonson, Ben(jamin)** 1572(?)-1637 . **DC 4; LC**
**6, 33, 110; PC 17; WLC 3**
See also BRW 1; BRWC 1; BRWR 1; CD-
BLB Before 1660; DA; DAB; DAC;
DAM DRAM, MST, POET; DFS 4, 10;
DLB 62, 121; LMFS 1; PFS 23; RGEL 2;
TEA; WLIT 3

**Jordan, June** 1936-2002 .. **BLCS; CLC 5, 11,**
**23, 114, 230; PC 38**
See also AAYA 2, 66; AFAW 1, 2; BW 2,
3; CA 33-36R; CAAS 206; CANR 25, 70,
114, 154; CLR 10; CP 3, 4, 5, 6, 7; CWP;
DAM MULT, POET; DLB 38; GLL 2;
LAIT 5; MAICYA 1, 2; MTCW 1; SATA
4, 136; YAW

**Jordan, June Meyer**
See Jordan, June

**Jordan, Neil** 1950- ............................ **CLC 110**
See also CA 130; CAAE 124; CANR 54,
154; CN 4, 5, 6, 7; GLL 2; INT CA-130

**Jordan, Neil Patrick**
See Jordan, Neil

**Jordan, Pat(rick M.)** 1941- ............... **CLC 37**
See also CA 33-36R; CANR 121

**Jorgensen, Ivar**
See Ellison, Harlan

**Jorgenson, Ivar**
See Silverberg, Robert

**Joseph, George Ghevarughese** ........ **CLC 70**

**Josephson, Mary**
See O'Doherty, Brian

**Josephus, Flavius** c. 37-100 ..... **CMLC 13, 93**
See also AW 2; DLB 176; WLIT 8

**Josiah Allen's Wife**
See Holley, Marietta

**Josipovici, Gabriel** 1940- ...... **CLC 6, 43, 153**
See also CA 224; 37-40R, 224; 8; CANR
47, 84; CN 3, 4, 5, 6, 7; DLB 14, 319

**Josipovici, Gabriel David**
See Josipovici, Gabriel

**Joubert, Joseph** 1754-1824 ............... **NCLC 9**

**Jouve, Pierre Jean** 1887-1976 .......... **CLC 47**
See also CA 252; CAAS 65-68; DLB 258;
EWL 3

**Jovine, Francesco** 1902-1950 .......... **TCLC 79**
See also DLB 264; EWL 3

**Kazakov, Yuri Pavlovich** 1927-1982 . **SSC 43**
See Kazakov, Iurii Pavlovich; Kazakov, Yury
See also CA 5-8R; CANR 36; MTCW 1; RGSF 2

**Kazakov, Yury**
See Kazakov, Yuri Pavlovich
See also EWL 3

**Kazan, Elia** 1909-2003 ........... **CLC 6, 16, 63**
See also CA 21-24R; CAAS 220; CANR 32, 78

**Kazantzakis, Nikos** 1883(?)-1957 .... **TCLC 2, 5, 33, 181**
See also BPFB 2; CA 132; CAAE 105; DA3; EW 9; EWL 3; MTCW 1, 2; MTFW 2005; RGWL 2, 3

**Kazin, Alfred** 1915-1998 ..... **CLC 34, 38, 119**
See also AMWS 8; CA 1-4R; 7; CANR 1, 45, 79; DLB 67; EWL 3

**Keane, Mary Nesta (Skrine)** 1904-1996
See Keane, Molly
See also CA 114; CAAE 108; CAAS 151; RHW

**Keane, Molly** ...................................... **CLC 31**
See Keane, Mary Nesta (Skrine)
See also CN 5, 6; INT CA-114; TCLE 1:1

**Keates, Jonathan** 1946(?)- ................. **CLC 34**
See also CA 163; CANR 126

**Keaton, Buster** 1895-1966 ................. **CLC 20**
See also CA 194

**Keats, John** 1795-1821 ...... **NCLC 8, 73, 121; PC 1; WLC 3**
See also AAYA 58; BRW 4; BRWR 1; CD-BLB 1789-1832; DA; DA3; DAB; DAC; DAM MST, POET; DLB 96, 110; EXPP; LMFS 1; PAB; PFS 1, 2, 3, 9, 17; RGEL 2; TEA; WLIT 3; WP

**Keble, John** 1792-1866 ................... **NCLC 87**
See also DLB 32, 55; RGEL 2

**Keene, Donald** 1922- .......................... **CLC 34**
See also CA 1-4R; CANR 5, 119

**Keillor, Garrison** 1942- ..... **CLC 40, 115, 222**
See also AAYA 2, 62; AMWS 16; BEST 89:3; BPFB 2; CA 117; CAAE 111; CANR 36, 59, 124; CPW; DA3; DAM POP; DLBY 1987; EWL 3; MTCW 1, 2; MTFW 2005; SATA 58; TUS

**Keith, Carlos**
See Lewton, Val

**Keith, Michael**
See Hubbard, L. Ron

**Keller, Gottfried** 1819-1890 .... **NCLC 2; SSC 26**
See also CDWLB 2; DLB 129; EW; RGSF 2; RGWL 2, 3

**Keller, Nora Okja** 1965- ................. **CLC 109**
See also CA 187

**Kellerman, Jonathan** 1949- ............... **CLC 44**
See also AAYA 35; BEST 90:1; CA 106; CANR 29, 51, 150; CMW 4; CPW; DA3; DAM POP; INT CANR-29

**Kelley, William Melvin** 1937- ........... **CLC 22**
See also BW 1; CA 77-80; CANR 27, 83; CN 1, 2, 3, 4, 5, 6, 7; DLB 33; EWL 3

**Kellogg, Marjorie** 1922-2005 ............. **CLC 2**
See also CA 81-84; CAAS 246

**Kellow, Kathleen**
See Hibbert, Eleanor Alice Burford

**Kelly, Lauren**
See Oates, Joyce Carol

**Kelly, M(ilton) T(errence)** 1947- ...... **CLC 55**
See also CA 97-100; 22; CANR 19, 43, 84; CN 6

**Kelly, Robert** 1935- ........................... **SSC 50**
See also CA 17-20R; 19; CANR 47; CP 1, 2, 3, 4, 5, 6, 7; DLB 5, 130, 165

**Kelman, James** 1946- .................. **CLC 58, 86**
See also BRWS 5; CA 148; CANR 85, 130; CN 5, 6, 7; DLB 194, 319, 326; RGSF 2; WLIT 4

**Kemal, Yasar**
See Kemal, Yashar
See also CWW 2; EWL 3; WLIT 6

**Kemal, Yashar** 1923(?)- ............... **CLC 14, 29**
See also CA 89-92; CANR 44

**Kemble, Fanny** 1809-1893 ............. **NCLC 18**
See also DLB 32

**Kemelman, Harry** 1908-1996 ............. **CLC 2**
See also AITN 1; BPFB 2; CA 9-12R; CAAS 155; CANR 6, 71; CMW 4; DLB 28

**Kempe, Margery** 1373(?)-1440(?) ... **LC 6, 56**
See also BRWS 12; DLB 146; FL 1:1; RGEL 2

**Kempis, Thomas a** 1380-1471 ............. **LC 11**

**Kendall, Henry** 1839-1882 ............ **NCLC 12**
See also DLB 230

**Keneally, Thomas** 1935- .... **CLC 5, 8, 10, 14, 19, 27, 43, 117**
See also BRWS 4; CA 85-88; CANR 10, 50, 74, 130, 165; CN 1, 2, 3, 4, 5, 6, 7; CPW; DA3; DAM NOV; DLB 289, 299, 326; EWL 3; MTCW 1, 2; MTFW 2005; NFS 17; RGEL 2; RGHL; RHW

**Keneally, Thomas Michael**
See Keneally, Thomas

**Kennedy, A(lison) L(ouise)** 1965- ... **CLC 188**
See also CA 213; 168, 213; CANR 108; CD 5, 6; CN 6, 7; DLB 271; RGSF 2

**Kennedy, Adrienne (Lita)** 1931- ........ **BLC 2; CLC 66; DC 5**
See also AFAW 2; BW 2, 3; CA 103; 20; CABS 3; CAD; CANR 26, 53, 82; CD 5, 6; DAM MULT; DFS 9; DLB 38; FW; MAL 5

**Kennedy, John Pendleton**
1795-1870 ................................. **NCLC 2**
See also DLB 3, 248, 254; RGAL 4

**Kennedy, Joseph Charles** 1929-
See Kennedy, X. J.
See also CA 201; 1-4R, 201; CANR 4, 30, 40; CWRI 5; MAICYA 2; MAICYAS 1; SATA 14, 86, 130; SATA-Essay 130

**Kennedy, William** 1928- .. **CLC 6, 28, 34, 53, 239**
See also AAYA 1, 73; AMWS 7; BPFB 2; CA 85-88; CANR 14, 31, 76, 134; CN 4, 5, 6, 7; DA3; DAM NOV; DLB 143; DLBY 1985; EWL 3; INT CANR-31; MAL 5; MTCW 1, 2; MTFW 2005; SATA 57

**Kennedy, X. J.** ............................. **CLC 8, 42**
See Kennedy, Joseph Charles
See also AMWS 15; CA 9; CLR 27; CP 1, 2, 3, 4, 5, 6, 7; DLB 5; SAAS 22

**Kenny, Maurice (Francis)** 1929- ..... **CLC 87; NNAL**
See also CA 144; 22; CANR 143; DAM MULT; DLB 175

**Kent, Kelvin**
See Kuttner, Henry

**Kenton, Maxwell**
See Southern, Terry

**Kenyon, Jane** 1947-1995 ...................... **PC 57**
See also AAYA 63; AMWS 7; CA 118; CAAS 148; CANR 44, 69; CP 6, 7; CWP; DLB 120; PFS 9, 17; RGAL 4

**Kenyon, Robert O.**
See Kuttner, Henry

**Kepler, Johannes** 1571-1630 ............... **LC 45**

**Ker, Jill**
See Conway, Jill K(er)

**Kerkow, H. C.**
See Lewton, Val

**Kerouac, Jack** 1922-1969 ...... **CLC 1, 2, 3, 5, 14, 29, 61; TCLC 117; WLC**
See Kerouac, Jean-Louis Lebris de
See also AAYA 25; AMWC 1; AMWS 3; BG 3; BPFB 2; CDALB 1941-1968; CP 1; CPW; DLB 2, 16, 237; DLBD 3; DLBY 1995; EWL 3; GLL 1; LATS 1:2; LMFS 2; MAL 5; NFS 8; RGAL 4; TUS; WP

**Kerouac, Jean-Louis Lebris de** 1922-1969
See Kerouac, Jack
See also AITN 1; CA 5-8R; CAAS 25-28R; CANR 26, 54, 95; DA; DA3; DAB; DAC; DAM MST, NOV, POET, POP; MTCW 1, 2; MTFW 2005

**Kerr, (Bridget) Jean (Collins)**
1923(?)-2003 .............................. **CLC 22**
See also CA 5-8R; CAAS 212; CANR 7; INT CANR-7

**Kerr, M. E.** ................................. **CLC 12, 35**
See Meaker, Marijane
See also AAYA 2, 23; BYA 1, 7, 8; CLR 29; SAAS 1; WYA

**Kerr, Robert** ...................................... **CLC 55**

**Kerrigan, (Thomas) Anthony** 1918- .. **CLC 4, 6**
See also CA 49-52; 11; CANR 4

**Kerry, Lois**
See Duncan, Lois

**Kesey, Ken** 1935-2001 .... **CLC 1, 3, 6, 11, 46, 64, 184; WLC 3**
See also AAYA 25; BG 1:3; BPFB 2; CA 1-4R; CAAS 204; CANR 22, 38, 66, 124; CDALB 1968-1988; CN 1, 2, 3, 4, 5, 6, 7; CPW; DA; DA3; DAB; DAC; DAM MST, NOV, POP; DLB 2, 16, 206; EWL 3; EXPN; LAIT 4; MAL 5; MTCW 1, 2; MTFW 2005; NFS 2; RGAL 4; SATA 66; SATA-Obit 131; TUS; YAW

**Kesselring, Joseph (Otto)**
1902-1967 .................................. **CLC 45**
See also CA 150; DAM DRAM, MST; DFS 20

**Kessler, Jascha (Frederick)** 1929- ...... **CLC 4**
See also CA 17-20R; CANR 8, 48, 111; CP 1

**Kettelkamp, Larry (Dale)** 1933- ....... **CLC 12**
See also CA 29-32R; CANR 16; SAAS 3; SATA 2

**Key, Ellen (Karolina Sofia)**
1849-1926 ................................. **TCLC 65**
See also DLB 259

**Keyber, Conny**
See Fielding, Henry

**Keyes, Daniel** 1927- ........................... **CLC 80**
See also AAYA 23; BYA 11; CA 181; 17-20R, 181; CANR 10, 26, 54, 74; DA; DA3; DAC; DAM MST, NOV; EXPN; LAIT 4; MTCW 2; MTFW 2005; NFS 2; SATA 37; SFW 4

**Keynes, John Maynard**
1883-1946 ................................. **TCLC 64**
See also CA 162, 163; CAAE 114; DLBD 10; MTCW 2; MTFW 2005

**Khanshendel, Chiron**
See Rose, Wendy

**Khayyam, Omar** 1048-1131 ... **CMLC 11; PC 8**
See Omar Khayyam
See also DA3; DAM POET; WLIT 6

**Kherdian, David** 1931- ..................... **CLC 6, 9**
See also AAYA 42; CA 192; 21-24R, 192; 2; CANR 39, 78; CLR 24; JRDA; LAIT 3; MAICYA 1, 2; SATA 16, 74; SATA-Essay 125

**Khlebnikov, Velimir** ...................... **TCLC 20**
See Khlebnikov, Viktor Vladimirovich
See also DLB 295; EW 10; EWL 3; RGWL 2, 3

**Khlebnikov, Viktor Vladimirovich** 1885-1922
See Khlebnikov, Velimir
See also CA 217; CAAE 117

**Khodasevich, V.F.**
See Khodasevich, Vladislav

**Khodasevich, Vladislav**
1886-1939 ............................. **TCLC 15**
See also CAAE 115; DLB 317; EWL 3

**Khodasevich, Vladislav Felitsianovich**
See Khodasevich, Vladislav

**Kielland, Alexander Lange**
1849-1906 ................................. **TCLC 5**
See also CAAE 104

**Kiely, Benedict** 1919-2007 . **CLC 23, 43; SSC 58**
See also CA 1-4R; CAAS 257; CANR 2, 84; CN 1, 2, 3, 4, 5, 6, 7; DLB 15, 319; TCLE 1:1

**Kienzle, William X.** 1928-2001 ......... **CLC 25**
See also CA 93-96; 1; CAAS 203; CANR 9, 31, 59, 111; CMW 4; DA3; DAM POP; INT CANR-31; MSW; MTCW 1, 2; MTFW 2005

**Kierkegaard, Soren** 1813-1855 ..... **NCLC 34, 78, 125**
See also DLB 300; EW 6; LMFS 2; RGWL 3; TWA

**Kieslowski, Krzysztof** 1941-1996 .... **CLC 120**
See also CA 147; CAAS 151

**Killens, John Oliver** 1916-1987 ........ **CLC 10**
See also BW 2; CA 77-80; 2; CAAS 123; CANR 26; CN 1, 2, 3, 4; DLB 33; EWL 3

**Killigrew, Anne** 1660-1685 .............. **LC 4, 73**
See also DLB 131

**Killigrew, Thomas** 1612-1683 ............. **LC 57**
See also DLB 58; RGEL 2

**Kim**
See Simenon, Georges (Jacques Christian)

**Kincaid, Jamaica** 1949- ...... **BLC 2; CLC 43, 68, 137, 234; SSC 72**
See also AAYA 13, 56; AFAW 2; AMWS 7; BRWS 7; BW 2, 3; CA 125; CANR 47, 59, 95, 133; CDALBS; CDWLB 3; CLR 63; CN 4, 5, 6, 7; DA3; DAM MULT, NOV; DLB 157, 227; DNFS 1; EWL 3; EXPS; FW; LATS 1:2; LMFS 2; MAL 5; MTCW 2; MTFW 2005; NCFS 1; NFS 3; SSFS 5, 7; TUS; WWE 1; YAW

**King, Francis (Henry)** 1923- ....... **CLC 8, 53, 145**
See also CA 1-4R; CANR 1, 33, 86; CN 1, 2, 3, 4, 5, 6, 7; DAM NOV; DLB 15, 139; MTCW 1

**King, Kennedy**
See Brown, George Douglas

**King, Martin Luther, Jr.** 1929-1968 . **BLC 2; CLC 83; WLCS**
See also BW 2, 3; CA 25-28; CANR 27, 44; CAP 2; DA; DA3; DAB; DAC; DAM MST, MULT; LAIT 5; LATS 1:2; MTCW 1, 2; MTFW 2005; SATA 14

**King, Stephen** 1947- ....... **CLC 12, 26, 37, 61, 113, 228, 244; SSC 17, 55**
See also AAYA 1, 17; AMWS 5; BEST 90:1; BPFB 2; CA 61-64; CANR 1, 30, 52, 76, 119, 134, 168; CN 7; CPW; DA3; DAM NOV, POP; DLB 143; DLBY 1980; HGG; JRDA; LAIT 5; MTCW 1, 2; MTFW 2005; RGAL 4; SATA 9, 55, 161; SUFW 1, 2; WYAS 1; YAW

**King, Stephen Edwin**
See King, Stephen

**King, Steve**
See King, Stephen

**King, Thomas** 1943- .... **CLC 89, 171; NNAL**
See also CA 144; CANR 95; CCA 1; CN 6, 7; DAC; DAM MULT; DLB 175, 334; SATA 96

**Kingman, Lee** ................................... **CLC 17**
See Natti, (Mary) Lee
See also CWRI 5; SAAS 3; SATA 1, 67

**Kingsley, Charles** 1819-1875 .......... **NCLC 35**
See also CLR 77; DLB 21, 32, 163, 178, 190; FANT; MAICYA 2; MAICYAS 1; RGEL 2; WCH; YABC 2

**Kingsley, Henry** 1830-1876 .......... **NCLC 107**
See also DLB 21, 230; RGEL 2

**Kingsley, Sidney** 1906-1995 .............. **CLC 44**
See also CA 85-88; CAAS 147; CAD; DFS 14, 19; DLB 7; MAL 5; RGAL 4

**Kingsolver, Barbara** 1955- ......... **CLC 55, 81, 130, 216**
See also AAYA 15; AMWS 7; CA 134; CAAE 129; CANR 60, 96, 133; CDALBS; CN 7; CPW; CSW; DA3; DAM POP; DLB 206; INT CA-134; LAIT 5; MTCW 2; MTFW 2005; NFS 5, 10, 12, 24; RGAL 4; TCLE 1:1

**Kingston, Maxine Hong** 1940- .... **AAL; CLC 12, 19, 58, 121; WLCS**
See also AAYA 8, 55; AMWS 5; BPFB 2; CA 69-72; CANR 13, 38, 74, 87, 128; CDALBS; CN 6, 7; DA3; DAM MULT, NOV; DLB 173, 212, 312; DLBY 1980; EWL 3; FL 1:6; FW; INT CANR-13; LAIT 5; MAL 5; MBL; MTCW 1, 2; MTFW 2005; NFS 6; RGAL 4; SATA 53; SSFS 3; TCWW 2

**Kinnell, Galway** 1927- ..... **CLC 1, 2, 3, 5, 13, 29, 129; PC 26**
See also AMWS 3; CA 9-12R; CANR 10, 34, 66, 116, 138; CP 1, 2, 3, 4, 5, 6, 7; DLB 5; DLBY 1987; EWL 3; INT CANR-34; MAL 5; MTCW 1, 2; MTFW 2005; PAB; PFS 9, 26; RGAL 4; TCLE 1:1; WP

**Kinsella, Thomas** 1928- ....... **CLC 4, 19, 138; PC 69**
See also BRWS 5; CA 17-20R; CANR 15, 122; CP 1, 2, 3, 4, 5, 6, 7; DLB 27; EWL 3; MTCW 1, 2; MTFW 2005; RGEL 2; TEA

**Kinsella, W.P.** 1935- ............ **CLC 27, 43, 166**
See also AAYA 7, 60; BPFB 2; CA 222; 97-100, 222; 7; CANR 21, 35, 66, 75, 129; CN 4, 5, 6, 7; CPW; DAC; DAM NOV, POP; FANT; INT CANR-21; LAIT 5; MTCW 1, 2; MTFW 2005; NFS 15; RGSF 2

**Kinsey, Alfred C(harles)**
1894-1956 ................................. **TCLC 91**
See also CA 170; CAAE 115; MTCW 2

**Kipling, (Joseph) Rudyard** 1865-1936 . **PC 3; SSC 5, 54; TCLC 8, 17, 167; WLC 3**
See also AAYA 32; BRW 6; BRWC 1, 2; BYA 4; CA 120; CAAE 105; CANR 33; CDBLB 1890-1914; CLR 39, 65; CWRI 5; DA; DA3; DAB; DAC; DAM MST, POET; DLB 19, 34, 141, 156, 330; EWL 3; EXPS; FANT; LAIT 3; LMFS 1; MAICYA 1, 2; MTCW 1, 2; MTFW 2005; NFS 21; PFS 22; RGEL 2; RGSF 2; SATA 100; SFW 4; SSFS 8, 21, 22; SUFW 1; TEA; WCH; WLIT 4; YABC 2

**Kircher, Athanasius** 1602-1680 ......... **LC 121**
See also DLB 164

**Kirk, Russell (Amos)** 1918-1994 .. **TCLC 119**
See also AITN 1; CA 1-4R; 9; CAAS 145; CANR 1, 20, 60; HGG; INT CANR-20; MTCW 1, 2

**Kirkham, Dinah**
See Card, Orson Scott

**Kirkland, Caroline M.** 1801-1864 . **NCLC 85**
See also DLB 3, 73, 74, 250, 254; DLBD 13

**Kirkup, James** 1918- .......................... **CLC 1**
See also CA 1-4R; 4; CANR 2; CP 1, 2, 3, 4, 5, 6, 7; DLB 27; SATA 12

**Kirkwood, James** 1930(?)-1989 .......... **CLC 9**
See also AITN 2; CA 1-4R; CAAS 128; CANR 6, 40; GLL 2

**Kirsch, Sarah** 1935- ......................... **CLC 176**
See also CA 178; CWW 2; DLB 75; EWL 3

**Kirshner, Sidney**
See Kingsley, Sidney

**Kis, Danilo** 1935-1989 ..................... **CLC 57**
See also CA 118; CAAE 109; CAAS 129; CANR 61; CDWLB 4; DLB 181; EWL 3; MTCW 1; RGSF 2; RGWL 2, 3

**Kissinger, Henry A(lfred)** 1923- .... **CLC 137**
See also CA 1-4R; CANR 2, 33, 66, 109; MTCW 1

**Kittel, Frederick August**
See Wilson, August

**Kivi, Aleksis** 1834-1872 .................. **NCLC 30**

**Kizer, Carolyn** 1925- ..... **CLC 15, 39, 80; PC 66**
See also CA 65-68; 5; CANR 24, 70, 134; CP 1, 2, 3, 4, 5, 6, 7; CWP; DAM POET; DLB 5, 169; EWL 3; MAL 5; MTCW 2; MTFW 2005; PFS 18; TCLE 1:1

**Klabund** 1890-1928 ......................... **TCLC 44**
See also CA 162; DLB 66

**Klappert, Peter** 1942- ....................... **CLC 57**
See also CA 33-36R; CSW; DLB 5

**Klein, A(braham) M(oses)**
1909-1972 ................................. **CLC 19**
See also CA 101; CAAS 37-40R; CP 1; DAB; DAC; DAM MST; DLB 68; EWL 3; RGEL 2; RGHL

**Klein, Joe**
See Klein, Joseph

**Klein, Joseph** 1946- ........................ **CLC 154**
See also CA 85-88; CANR 55, 164

**Klein, Norma** 1938-1989 ................... **CLC 30**
See also AAYA 2, 35; BPFB 2; BYA 6, 7, 8; CA 41-44R; CAAS 128; CANR 15, 37; CLR 2, 19; INT CANR-15; JRDA; MAICYA 1, 2; SAAS 1; SATA 7, 57; WYA; YAW

**Klein, T.E.D.** 1947- .......................... **CLC 34**
See Klein, Theodore Eibon Donald
See also CA 119; CANR 44, 75, 167; HGG

**Klein, Theodore Eibon Donald**
See Klein, T.E.D.

**Kleist, Heinrich von** 1777-1811 ...... **NCLC 2, 37; SSC 22**
See also CDWLB 2; DAM DRAM; DLB 90; EW 5; RGSF 2; RGWL 2, 3

**Klima, Ivan** 1931- ..................... **CLC 56, 172**
See also CA 25-28R; CANR 17, 50, 91; CDWLB 4; CWW 2; DAM NOV; DLB 232; EWL 3; RGWL 3

**Klimentev, Andrei Platonovich**
See Klimentov, Andrei Platonovich

**Klimentov, Andrei Platonovich**
1899-1951 ................. **SSC 42; TCLC 14**
See Platonov, Andrei Platonovich; Platonov, Andrey Platonovich
See also CA 232; CAAE 108

**Klinger, Friedrich Maximilian von**
1752-1831 .............................. **NCLC 1**
See also DLB 94

**Klingsor the Magician**
See Hartmann, Sadakichi

**Klopstock, Friedrich Gottlieb**
1724-1803 ................................ **NCLC 11**
See also DLB 97; EW 4; RGWL 2, 3

**Kluge, Alexander** 1932- .................... **SSC 61**
See also CA 81-84; CANR 163; DLB 75

**Knapp, Caroline** 1959-2002 ............. **CLC 99**
See also CA 154; CAAS 207

**Knebel, Fletcher** 1911-1993 ............. **CLC 14**
See also AITN 1; CA 1-4R; 3; CAAS 140; CANR 1, 36; CN 1, 2, 3, 4, 5; SATA 36; SATA-Obit 75

**Knickerbocker, Diedrich**
See Irving, Washington

**Knight, Etheridge** 1931-1991 ... **BLC 2; CLC 40; PC 14**
See also BW 1, 3; CA 21-24R; CAAS 133; CANR 23, 82; CP 1, 2, 3, 4, 5; DAM POET; DLB 41; MTCW 2; MTFW 2005; RGAL 4; TCLE 1:1

**Knight, Sarah Kemble** 1666-1727 ......... **LC 7**
See also DLB 24, 200

**Knister, Raymond** 1899-1932 ......... **TCLC 56**
See also CA 186; DLB 68; RGEL 2

**Knowles, John** 1926-2001 ... **CLC 1, 4, 10, 26**
See also AAYA 10, 72; AMWS 12; BPFB 2; BYA 3; CA 17-20R; CAAS 203; CANR 40, 74, 76, 132; CDALB 1968-1988; CLR 98; CN 1, 2, 3, 4, 5, 6, 7; DA; DAC; DAM MST, NOV; DLB 6; EXPN; MTCW 1, 2; MTFW 2005; NFS 2; RGAL 4; SATA 8, 89; SATA-Obit 134; YAW

**Knox, Calvin M.**
See Silverberg, Robert

**Knox, John** c. 1505-1572 ...................... **LC 37**
See also DLB 132

**Knye, Cassandra**
See Disch, Thomas M.

**Koch, C(hristopher) J(ohn)** 1932- .... **CLC 42**
See also CA 127; CANR 84; CN 3, 4, 5, 6, 7; DLB 289

**Koch, Christopher**
See Koch, C(hristopher) J(ohn)

**Koch, Kenneth** 1925-2002 ....... **CLC 5, 8, 44; PC 80**
See also AMWS 15; CA 1-4R; CAAS 207; CAD; CANR 6, 36, 57, 97, 131; CD 5, 6; CP 1, 2, 3, 4, 5, 6, 7; DAM POET; DLB 5; INT CANR-36; MAL 5; MTCW 2; MTFW 2005; PFS 20; SATA 65; WP

**Kochanowski, Jan** 1530-1584 .............. **LC 10**
See also RGWL 2, 3

**Kock, Charles Paul de** 1794-1871 . **NCLC 16**

**Koda Rohan**
See Koda Shigeyuki

**Koda Rohan**
See Koda Shigeyuki
See also DLB 180

**Koda Shigeyuki** 1867-1947 ............. **TCLC 22**
See Koda Rohan
See also CA 183; CAAE 121

**Koestler, Arthur** 1905-1983 ... **CLC 1, 3, 6, 8, 15, 33**
See also BRWS 1; CA 1-4R; CAAS 109; CANR 1, 33; CDBLB 1945-1960; CN 1, 2, 3; DLBY 1983; EWL 3; MTCW 1, 2; MTFW 2005; NFS 19; RGEL 2

**Kogawa, Joy Nozomi** 1935- ...... **CLC 78, 129**
See also AAYA 47; CA 101; CANR 19, 62, 126; CN 6, 7; CP 1; CWP; DAC; DAM MST, MULT; DLB 334; FW; MTCW 2; MTFW 2005; NFS 3; SATA 99

**Kohout, Pavel** 1928- ........................... **CLC 13**
See also CA 45-48; CANR 3

**Koizumi, Yakumo**
See Hearn, (Patricio) Lafcadio (Tessima Carlos)

**Kolmar, Gertrud** 1894-1943 .......... **TCLC 40**
See also CA 167; EWL 3; RGHL

**Komunyakaa, Yusef** 1947- .. **BLCS; CLC 86, 94, 207; PC 51**
See also AFAW 2; AMWS 13; CA 147; CANR 83, 164; CP 6, 7; CSW; DLB 120; EWL 3; PFS 5, 20; RGAL 4

**Konrad, George**
See Konrad, Gyorgy

**Konrad, Gyorgy** 1933- ............ **CLC 4, 10, 73**
See also CA 85-88; CANR 97; CDWLB 4; CWW 2; DLB 232; EWL 3

**Konwicki, Tadeusz** 1926- ....... **CLC 8, 28, 54, 117**
See also CA 101; 9; CANR 39, 59; CWW 2; DLB 232; EWL 3; IDFW 3; MTCW 1

**Koontz, Dean R.** 1945- .............. **CLC 78, 206**
See also AAYA 9, 31; BEST 89:3, 90:2; CA 108; CANR 19, 36, 52, 95, 138; CMW 4; CPW; DA3; DAM NOV, POP; DLB 292; HGG; MTCW 1; MTFW 2005; SATA 92, 165; SFW 4; SUFW 2; YAW

**Koontz, Dean Ray**
See Koontz, Dean R.

**Kopernik, Mikolaj**
See Copernicus, Nicolaus

**Kopit, Arthur (Lee)** 1937- ...... **CLC 1, 18, 33**
See also AITN 1; CA 81-84; CABS 3; CAD; CD 5, 6; DAM DRAM; DFS 7, 14, 24; DLB 7; MAL 5; MTCW 1; RGAL 4

**Kopitar, Jernej (Bartholomaus)**
1780-1844 .............................. **NCLC 117**

**Kops, Bernard** 1926- .......................... **CLC 4**
See also CA 5-8R; CANR 84, 159; CBD; CN 1, 2, 3, 4, 5, 6, 7; CP 1, 2, 3, 4, 5, 6, 7; DLB 13; RGHL

**Kornbluth, C(yril) M.** 1923-1958 .... **TCLC 8**
See also CA 160; CAAE 105; DLB 8; SCFW 1, 2; SFW 4

**Korolenko, V.G.**
See Korolenko, Vladimir G.

**Korolenko, Vladimir**
See Korolenko, Vladimir G.

**Korolenko, Vladimir G.**
1853-1921 ................................ **TCLC 22**
See also CAAE 121; DLB 277

**Korolenko, Vladimir Galaktionovich**
See Korolenko, Vladimir G.

**Korzybski, Alfred (Habdank Skarbek)**
1879-1950 ................................ **TCLC 61**
See also CA 160; CAAE 123

**Kosinski, Jerzy** 1933-1991 ..... **CLC 1, 2, 3, 6, 10, 15, 53, 70**
See also AMWS 7; BPFB 2; CA 17-20R; CAAS 134; CANR 9, 46; CN 1, 2, 3, 4; DA3; DAM NOV; DLB 2, 299; DLBY 1982; EWL 3; HGG; MAL 5; MTCW 1, 2; MTFW 2005; NFS 12; RGAL 4; RGHL; TUS

**Kostelanetz, Richard (Cory)** 1940- .. **CLC 28**
See also CA 13-16R; 8; CANR 38, 77; CN 4, 5, 6; CP 2, 3, 4, 5, 6, 7

**Kostrowitzki, Wilhelm Apollinaris de**
1880-1918
See Apollinaire, Guillaume
See also CAAE 104

**Kotlowitz, Robert** 1924- ..................... **CLC 4**
See also CA 33-36R; CANR 36

**Kotzebue, August (Friedrich Ferdinand) von**
1761-1819 ................................ **NCLC 25**
See also DLB 94

**Kotzwinkle, William** 1938- ..... **CLC 5, 14, 35**
See also BPFB 2; CA 45-48; CANR 3, 44, 84, 129; CLR 6; CN 7; DLB 173; FANT; MAICYA 1, 2; SATA 24, 70, 146; SFW 4; SUFW 2; YAW

**Kowna, Stancy**
See Szymborska, Wislawa

**Kozol, Jonathan** 1936- ...................... **CLC 17**
See also AAYA 46; CA 61-64; CANR 16, 45, 96; MTFW 2005

**Kozoll, Michael** 1940(?)- .................. **CLC 35**

**Kramer, Kathryn** 19(?)- .................... **CLC 34**

**Kramer, Larry** 1935- ............. **CLC 42; DC 8**
See also CA 126; CAAE 124; CANR 60, 132; DAM POP; DLB 249; GLL 1

**Krasicki, Ignacy** 1735-1801 ............. **NCLC 8**

**Krasinski, Zygmunt** 1812-1859 ....... **NCLC 4**
See also RGWL 2, 3

**Kraus, Karl** 1874-1936 ................... **TCLC 5**
See also CA 216; CAAE 104; DLB 118; EWL 3

**Kreve (Mickevicius), Vincas**
1882-1954 ................................ **TCLC 27**
See also CA 170; DLB 220; EWL 3

**Kristeva, Julia** 1941- ................. **CLC 77, 140**
See also CA 154; CANR 99; DLB 242; EWL 3; FW; LMFS 2

**Kristofferson, Kris** 1936- .................. **CLC 26**
See also CA 104

**Krizanc, John** 1956- .......................... **CLC 57**
See also CA 187

**Krleza, Miroslav** 1893-1981 ........ **CLC 8, 114**
See also CA 97-100; CAAS 105; CANR 50; CDWLB 4; DLB 147; EW 11; RGWL 2, 3

**Kroetsch, Robert (Paul)** 1927- .... **CLC 5, 23, 57, 132**
See also CA 17-20R; CANR 8, 38; CCA 1; CN 2, 3, 4, 5, 6, 7; CP 6, 7; DAC; DAM POET; DLB 53; MTCW 1

**Kroetz, Franz**
See Kroetz, Franz Xaver

**Kroetz, Franz Xaver** 1946- .............. **CLC 41**
See also CA 130; CANR 142; CWW 2; EWL 3

**Kroker, Arthur (W.)** 1945- ............... **CLC 77**
See also CA 161

**Kroniuk, Lisa**
See Berton, Pierre (Francis de Marigny)

**Kropotkin, Peter (Aleksieevich)**
1842-1921 ................................ **TCLC 36**
See Kropotkin, Petr Alekseevich
See also CA 219; CAAE 119

**Kropotkin, Petr Alekseevich**
See Kropotkin, Peter (Aleksieevich)
See also DLB 277

**Krotkov, Yuri** 1917-1981 ................... **CLC 19**
See also CA 102

**Krumb**
See Crumb, R.

**Krumgold, Joseph (Quincy)**
1908-1980 ................................ **CLC 12**
See also BYA 1, 2; CA 9-12R; CAAS 101; CANR 7; MAICYA 1, 2; SATA 1, 48; SATA-Obit 23; YAW

**Krumwitz**
See Crumb, R.

**Krutch, Joseph Wood** 1893-1970 ..... **CLC 24**
See also ANW; CA 1-4R; CAAS 25-28R; CANR 4; DLB 63, 206, 275

**Krutzch, Gus**
See Eliot, T(homas) S(tearns)

**Krylov, Ivan Andreevich**
1768(?)-1844 ............................ **NCLC 1**
See also DLB 150

**Kubin, Alfred (Leopold Isidor)**
1877-1959 ................................ **TCLC 23**
See also CA 149; CAAE 112; CANR 104; DLB 81

**Kubrick, Stanley** 1928-1999 ........... **CLC 16; TCLC 112**
See also AAYA 30; CA 81-84; CAAS 177; CANR 33; DLB 26

**Kumin, Maxine** 1925- .... **CLC 5, 13, 28, 164; PC 15**
See also AITN 2; AMWS 4; ANW; CA 1-4R; 8; CANR 1, 21, 69, 115, 140; CP 2, 3, 4, 5, 6, 7; CWP; DA3; DAM POET; DLB 5; EWL 3; EXPP; MTCW 1, 2; MTFW 2005; PAB; PFS 18; SATA 12

**Kundera, Milan** 1929- . **CLC 4, 9, 19, 32, 68, 115, 135, 234; SSC 24**
See also AAYA 2, 62; BPFB 2; CA 85-88; CANR 19, 52, 74, 144; CDWLB 4; CWW 2; DA3; DAM NOV; DLB 232; EW 13; EWL 3; MTCW 1, 2; MTFW 2005; NFS 18; RGSF 2; RGWL 3; SSFS 10

**Lange, John**
See Crichton, Michael

**Langer, Elinor** 1939- .......................... **CLC 34**
See also CA 121

**Langland, William** 1332(?)-1400(?) .... **LC 19, 120**
See also BRW 1; DA; DAB; DAC; DAM MST, POET; DLB 146; RGEL 2; TEA; WLIT 3

**Langstaff, Launcelot**
See Irving, Washington

**Lanier, Sidney** 1842-1881 . **NCLC 6, 118; PC 50**
See also AMWS 1; DAM POET; DLB 64; DLBD 13; EXPP; MAICYA 1; PFS 14; RGAL 4; SATA 18

**Lanyer, Aemilia** 1569-1645 .... **LC 10, 30, 83; PC 60**
See also DLB 121

**Lao-Tzu**
See Lao Tzu

**Lao Tzu** c. 6th cent. B.C.-3rd cent.
B.C. ............................................. **CMLC 7**

**Lapine, James (Elliot)** 1949- ............. **CLC 39**
See also CA 130; CAAE 123; CANR 54, 128; INT CA-130

**Larbaud, Valery (Nicolas)**
1881-1957 .................................... **TCLC 9**
See also CA 152; CAAE 106; EWL 3; GFL 1789 to the Present

**Larcom, Lucy** 1824-1893 .............. **NCLC 179**
See also AMWS 13; DLB 221, 243

**Lardner, Ring**
See Lardner, Ring(gold) W(ilmer)
See also BPFB 2; CDALB 1917-1929; DLB 11, 25, 86, 171; DLBD 16; MAL 5; RGAL 4; RGSF 2

**Lardner, Ring W., Jr.**
See Lardner, Ring(gold) W(ilmer)

**Lardner, Ring(gold) W(ilmer)**
1885-1933 ............. **SSC 32; TCLC 2, 14**
See Lardner, Ring
See also AMW; CA 131; CAAE 104; MTCW 1, 2; MTFW 2005; TUS

**Laredo, Betty**
See Codrescu, Andrei

**Larkin, Maia**
See Wojciechowska, Maia (Teresa)

**Larkin, Philip (Arthur)** 1922-1985 ... **CLC 3, 5, 8, 9, 13, 18, 33, 39, 64; PC 21**
See also BRWS 1; CA 5-8R; CAAS 117; CANR 24, 62; CDBLB 1960 to Present; CP 1, 2, 3, 4; DA3; DAB; DAM MST, POET; DLB 27; EWL 3; MTCW 1, 2; MTFW 2005; PFS 3, 4, 12; RGEL 2

**La Roche, Sophie von**
1730-1807 .............................. **NCLC 121**
See also DLB 94

**La Rochefoucauld, Francois**
1613-1680 .................................. **LC 108**

**Larra (y Sanchez de Castro), Mariano Jose
de** 1809-1837 .................. **NCLC 17, 130**

**Larsen, Eric** 1941- ........................... **CLC 55**
See also CA 132

**Larsen, Nella** 1893(?)-1963 ....... **BLC 2; CLC 37; HR 1:3**
See also AFAW 1, 2; BW 1; CA 125; CANR 83; DAM MULT; DLB 51; FW; LATS 1:1; LMFS 2

**Larson, Charles R(aymond)** 1938- ... **CLC 31**
See also CA 53-56; CANR 4, 121

**Larson, Jonathan** 1960-1996 ........... **CLC 99**
See also AAYA 28; CA 156; DFS 23; MTFW 2005

**La Sale, Antoine de** c. 1386-1460(?) . **LC 104**
See also DLB 208

**Las Casas, Bartolome de**
1474-1566 ....................... **HLCS; LC 31**
See Casas, Bartolome de las
See also DLB 318; LAW

**Lasch, Christopher** 1932-1994 ........ **CLC 102**
See also CA 73-76; CAAS 144; CANR 25, 118; DLB 246; MTCW 1, 2; MTFW 2005

**Lasker-Schueler, Else** 1869-1945 ... **TCLC 57**
See Lasker-Schuler, Else
See also CA 183; DLB 66, 124

**Lasker-Schuler, Else**
See Lasker-Schueler, Else
See also EWL 3

**Laski, Harold J(oseph)** 1893-1950 . **TCLC 79**
See also CA 188

**Latham, Jean Lee** 1902-1995 ........... **CLC 12**
See also AITN 1; BYA 1; CA 5-8R; CANR 7, 84; CLR 50; MAICYA 1, 2; SATA 2, 68; YAW

**Latham, Mavis**
See Clark, Mavis Thorpe

**Lathen, Emma** ........................... **CLC 2**
See Hennissart, Martha; Latsis, Mary J(ane)
See also BPFB 2; CMW 4; DLB 306

**Lathrop, Francis**
See Leiber, Fritz (Reuter, Jr.)

**Latsis, Mary J(ane)** 1927-1997
See Lathen, Emma
See also CA 85-88; CAAS 162; CMW 4

**Lattany, Kristin**
See Lattany, Kristin (Elaine Eggleston) Hunter

**Lattany, Kristin (Elaine Eggleston) Hunter**
1931- ........................................ **CLC 35**
See Hunter, Kristin
See also AITN 1; BW 1; BYA 3; CA 13-16R; CANR 13, 108; CLR 3; CN 7; DLB 33; INT CANR-13; MAICYA 1, 2; SAAS 10; SATA 12, 132; YAW

**Lattimore, Richmond (Alexander)**
1906-1984 .................................. **CLC 3**
See also CA 1-4R; CAAS 112; CANR 1; CP 1, 2, 3; MAL 5

**Laughlin, James** 1914-1997 .............. **CLC 49**
See also CA 21-24R; 22; CAAS 162; CANR 9, 47; CP 1, 2, 3, 4, 5, 6; DLB 48; DLBY 1996, 1997

**Laurence, Margaret** 1926-1987 ..... **CLC 3, 6, 13, 50, 62; SSC 7**
See also BYA 13; CA 5-8R; CAAS 121; CANR 33; CN 1, 2, 3, 4; DAC; DAM MST; DLB 53; EWL 3; FW; MTCW 1, 2; MTFW 2005; NFS 11; RGEL 2; RGSF 2; SATA-Obit 50; TCWW 2

**Laurent, Antoine** 1952- ..................... **CLC 50**

**Lauscher, Hermann**
See Hesse, Hermann

**Lautreamont** 1846-1870 .. **NCLC 12; SSC 14**
See Lautreamont, Isidore Lucien Ducasse
See also GFL 1789 to the Present; RGWL 2, 3

**Lautreamont, Isidore Lucien Ducasse**
See Lautreamont
See also DLB 217

**Lavater, Johann Kaspar**
1741-1801 .............................. **NCLC 142**
See also DLB 97

**Laverty, Donald**
See Blish, James (Benjamin)

**Lavin, Mary** 1912-1996 . **CLC 4, 18, 99; SSC 4, 67**
See also CA 9-12R; CAAS 151; CANR 33; CN 1, 2, 3, 4, 5, 6; DLB 15, 319; FW; MTCW 1; RGEL 2; RGSF 2; SSFS 23

**Lavond, Paul Dennis**
See Kornbluth, C(yril) M.; Pohl, Frederik

**Lawes, Henry** 1596-1662 .................... **LC 113**
See also DLB 126

**Lawler, Ray**
See Lawler, Raymond Evenor
See also DLB 289

**Lawler, Raymond Evenor** 1922- ....... **CLC 58**
See Lawler, Ray
See also CA 103; CD 5, 6; RGEL 2

**Lawrence, D(avid) H(erbert Richards)**
1885-1930 .......... **PC 54; SSC 4, 19, 73; TCLC 2, 9, 16, 33, 48, 61, 93; WLC 3**
See Chambers, Jessie
See also BPFB 2; BRW 7; BRWR 2; CA 121; CAAE 104; CANR 131; CDBLB 1914-1945; DA; DA3; DAB; DAC; DAM MST, NOV, POET; DLB 10, 19, 36, 98, 162, 195; EWL 3; EXPP; EXPS; LAIT 2, 3; MTCW 1, 2; MTFW 2005; NFS 18, 26; PFS 6; RGEL 2; RGSF 2; SSFS 2, 6; TEA; WLIT 4; WP

**Lawrence, T(homas) E(dward)**
1888-1935 .............................. **TCLC 18**
See Dale, Colin
See also BRWS 2; CA 167; CAAE 115; DLB 195

**Lawrence of Arabia**
See Lawrence, T(homas) E(dward)

**Lawson, Henry (Archibald Hertzberg)**
1867-1922 ................. **SSC 18; TCLC 27**
See also CA 181; CAAE 120; DLB 230; RGEL 2; RGSF 2

**Lawton, Dennis**
See Faust, Frederick (Schiller)

**Layamon** fl. c. 1200- ...................... **CMLC 10**
See also DLB 146; RGEL 2

**Laye, Camara** 1928-1980 ..... **BLC 2; CLC 4, 38**
See Camara Laye
See also AFW; BW 1; CA 85-88; CAAS 97-100; CANR 25; DAM MULT; MTCW 1, 2; WLIT 2

**Layton, Irving** 1912-2006 ..... **CLC 2, 15, 164**
See also CA 1-4R; CAAS 247; CANR 2, 33, 43, 66, 129; CP 1, 2, 3, 4, 5, 6, 7; DAC; DAM MST, POET; DLB 88; EWL 3; MTCW 1, 2; PFS 12; RGEL 2

**Layton, Irving Peter**
See Layton, Irving

**Lazarus, Emma** 1849-1887 ...... **NCLC 8, 109**

**Lazarus, Felix**
See Cable, George Washington

**Lazarus, Henry**
See Slavitt, David R.

**Lea, Joan**
See Neufeld, John (Arthur)

**Leacock, Stephen (Butler)**
1869-1944 ................... **SSC 39; TCLC 2**
See also CA 141; CAAE 104; CANR 80; DAC; DAM MST; DLB 92; EWL 3; MTCW 2; MTFW 2005; RGEL 2; RGSF 2

**Lead, Jane Ward** 1623-1704 ............... **LC 72**
See also DLB 131

**Leapor, Mary** 1722-1746 ..................... **LC 80**
See also DLB 109

**Lear, Edward** 1812-1888 ..... **NCLC 3; PC 65**
See also AAYA 48; BRW 5; CLR 1, 75; DLB 32, 163, 166; MAICYA 1, 2; RGEL 2; SATA 18, 100; WCH; WP

**Lear, Norman (Milton)** 1922- .......... **CLC 12**
See also CA 73-76

**Leautaud, Paul** 1872-1956 ............. **TCLC 83**
See also CA 203; DLB 65; GFL 1789 to the Present

**Leavis, F(rank) R(aymond)**
1895-1978 .................................. **CLC 24**
See also BRW 7; CA 21-24R; CAAS 77-80; CANR 44; DLB 242; EWL 3; MTCW 1, 2; RGEL 2

**Marut, Ret**
See Traven, B.

**Marut, Robert**
See Traven, B.

**Marvell, Andrew** 1621-1678 .... **LC 4, 43; PC 10; WLC 4**
See also BRW 2; BRWR 2; CDBLB 1660-1789; DA; DAB; DAC; DAM MST, POET; DLB 131; EXPP; PFS 5; RGEL 2; TEA; WP

**Marx, Karl (Heinrich)** 1818-1883 ........................ **NCLC 17, 114**
See also DLB 129; LATS 1:1; TWA

**Masaoka, Shiki** -1902 ........................ **TCLC 18**
See Masaoka, Tsunenori
See also RGWL 3

**Masaoka, Tsunenori** 1867-1902
See Masaoka, Shiki
See also CA 191; CAAE 117; TWA

**Masefield, John (Edward)** 1878-1967 ................ **CLC 11, 47; PC 78**
See also CA 19-20; CAAS 25-28R; CANR 33; CAP 2; CDBLB 1890-1914; DAM POET; DLB 10, 19, 153, 160; EWL 3; EXPP; FANT; MTCW 1, 2; PFS 5; RGEL 2; SATA 19

**Maso, Carole** 1955(?)- ........................ **CLC 44**
See also CA 170; CANR 148; CN 7; GLL 2; RGAL 4

**Mason, Bobbie Ann** 1940- ... **CLC 28, 43, 82, 154; SSC 4, 101**
See also AAYA 5, 42; AMWS 8; BPFB 2; CA 53-56; CANR 11, 31, 58, 83, 125, 169; CDALBS; CN 5, 6, 7; CSW; DA3; DLB 173; DLBY 1987; EWL 3; EXPS; INT CANR-31; MAL 5; MTCW 1, 2; MTFW 2005; NFS 4; RGAL 4; RGSF 2; SSFS 3, 8, 20; TCLE 1:2; YAW

**Mason, Ernst**
See Pohl, Frederik

**Mason, Hunni B.**
See Sternheim, (William Adolf) Carl

**Mason, Lee W.**
See Malzberg, Barry N(athaniel)

**Mason, Nick** 1945- ........................ **CLC 35**

**Mason, Tally**
See Derleth, August (William)

**Mass, Anna** ........................ **CLC 59**

**Mass, William**
See Gibson, William

**Massinger, Philip** 1583-1640 ................ **LC 70**
See also BRWS 11; DLB 58; RGEL 2

**Master Lao**
See Lao Tzu

**Masters, Edgar Lee** 1868-1950 ...... **PC 1, 36; TCLC 2, 25; WLCS**
See also AMWS 1; CA 133; CAAE 104; CDALB 1865-1917; DA; DAC; DAM MST, POET; DLB 54; EWL 3; EXPP; MAL 5; MTCW 1, 2; MTFW 2005; RGAL 4; TUS; WP

**Masters, Hilary** 1928- ........................ **CLC 48**
See also CA 217; 25-28R, 217; CANR 13, 47, 97; CN 6, 7; DLB 244

**Mastrosimone, William** 1947- .......... **CLC 36**
See also CA 186; CAD; CD 5, 6

**Mathe, Albert**
See Camus, Albert

**Mather, Cotton** 1663-1728 ................ **LC 38**
See also AMWS 2; CDALB 1640-1865; DLB 24, 30, 140; RGAL 4; TUS

**Mather, Increase** 1639-1723 ................ **LC 38**
See also DLB 24

**Mathers, Marshall**
See Eminem

**Mathers, Marshall Bruce**
See Eminem

**Matheson, Richard (Burton)** 1926- .. **CLC 37**
See also AAYA 31; CA 97-100; CANR 88, 99; DLB 8, 44; HGG; INT CA-97-100; SCFW 1, 2; SFW 4; SUFW 2

**Mathews, Harry** 1930- ................ **CLC 6, 52**
See also CA 21-24R; 6; CANR 18, 40, 98, 160; CN 5, 6, 7

**Mathews, John Joseph** 1894-1979 .. **CLC 84; NNAL**
See also CA 19-20; CAAS 142; CANR 45; CAP 2; DAM MULT; DLB 175; TCWW 1, 2

**Mathias, Roland** 1915-2007 ............. **CLC 45**
See also CA 97-100; CANR 19, 41; CP 1, 2, 3, 4, 5, 6, 7; DLB 27

**Mathias, Roland Glyn**
See Mathias, Roland

**Matsuo Basho** 1644(?)-1694 ...... **LC 62; PC 3**
See Basho, Matsuo
See also DAM POET; PFS 2, 7, 18

**Mattheson, Rodney**
See Creasey, John

**Matthews, (James) Brander** 1852-1929 ................ **TCLC 95**
See also CA 181; DLB 71, 78; DLBD 13

**Matthews, Greg** 1949- ........................ **CLC 45**
See also CA 135

**Matthews, William (Procter III)** 1942-1997 ........................ **CLC 40**
See also AMWS 9; CA 29-32R; 18; CAAS 162; CANR 12, 57; CP 2, 3, 4, 5, 6; DLB 5

**Matthias, John (Edward)** 1941- ......... **CLC 9**
See also CA 33-36R; CANR 56; CP 4, 5, 6, 7

**Matthiessen, F(rancis) O(tto)** 1902-1950 ........................ **TCLC 100**
See also CA 185; DLB 63; MAL 5

**Matthiessen, Peter** 1927- ... **CLC 5, 7, 11, 32, 64, 245**
See also AAYA 6, 40; AMWS 5; ANW; BEST 90:4; BPFB 2; CA 9-12R; CANR 21, 50, 73, 100, 138; CN 1, 2, 3, 4, 5, 6, 7; DA3; DAM NOV; DLB 6, 173, 275; MAL 5; MTCW 1, 2; MTFW 2005; SATA 27

**Maturin, Charles Robert** 1780(?)-1824 ........................ **NCLC 6, 169**
See also BRWS 8; DLB 178; GL 3; HGG; LMFS 1; RGEL 2; SUFW

**Matute (Ausejo), Ana Maria** 1925- .. **CLC 11**
See also CA 89-92; CANR 129; CWW 2; DLB 322; EWL 3; MTCW 1; RGSF 2

**Maugham, W. S.**
See Maugham, W(illiam) Somerset

**Maugham, W(illiam) Somerset** 1874-1965 .. **CLC 1, 11, 15, 67, 93; SSC 8, 94; WLC 4**
See also AAYA 55; BPFB 2; BRW 6; CA 5-8R; CAAS 25-28R; CANR 40, 127; CDBLB 1914-1945; CMW 4; DA; DA3; DAB; DAC; DAM DRAM, MST, NOV; DFS 22; DLB 10, 36, 77, 100, 162, 195; EWL 3; LAIT 3; MTCW 1, 2; MTFW 2005; NFS 23; RGEL 2; RGSF 2; SATA 54; SSFS 17

**Maugham, William Somerset**
See Maugham, W(illiam) Somerset

**Maupassant, (Henri Rene Albert) Guy de** 1850-1893 . **NCLC 1, 42, 83; SSC 1, 64; WLC 4**
See also BYA 14; DA; DA3; DAB; DAC; DAM MST; DLB 123; EW 7; EXPS; GFL 1789 to the Present; LAIT 2; LMFS 1; RGSF 2; RGWL 2, 3; SSFS 4, 21; SUFW; TWA

**Maupin, Armistead** 1944- ................ **CLC 95**
See also CA 130; CAAE 125; CANR 58, 101; CPW; DA3; DAM POP; DLB 278; GLL 1; INT CA-130; MTCW 2; MTFW 2005

**Maupin, Armistead Jones, Jr.**
See Maupin, Armistead

**Maurhut, Richard**
See Traven, B.

**Mauriac, Claude** 1914-1996 ................ **CLC 9**
See also CA 89-92; CAAS 152; CWW 2; DLB 83; EWL 3; GFL 1789 to the Present

**Mauriac, Francois (Charles)** 1885-1970 ........... **CLC 4, 9, 56; SSC 24**
See also CA 25-28; CAP 2; DLB 65, 331; EW 10; EWL 3; GFL 1789 to the Present; MTCW 1, 2; MTFW 2005; RGWL 2, 3; TWA

**Mavor, Osborne Henry** 1888-1951
See Bridie, James
See also CAAE 104

**Maxwell, Glyn** 1962- ........................ **CLC 238**
See also CA 154; CANR 88; CP 6, 7; PFS 23

**Maxwell, William (Keepers, Jr.)** 1908-2000 ........................ **CLC 19**
See also AMWS 8; CA 93-96; CAAS 189; CANR 54, 95; CN 1, 2, 3, 4, 5, 6, 7; DLB 218, 278; DLBY 1980; INT CA-93-96; MAL 5; SATA-Obit 128

**May, Elaine** 1932- ........................ **CLC 16**
See also CA 142; CAAE 124; CAD; CWD; DLB 44

**Mayakovski, Vladimir (Vladimirovich)** 1893-1930 ........................ **TCLC 4, 18**
See Maiakovskii, Vladimir; Mayakovsky, Vladimir
See also CA 158; CAAE 104; EWL 3; MTCW 2; MTFW 2005; SFW 4; TWA

**Mayakovsky, Vladimir**
See Mayakovski, Vladimir (Vladimirovich)
See also EW 11; WP

**Mayhew, Henry** 1812-1887 ............. **NCLC 31**
See also DLB 18, 55, 190

**Mayle, Peter** 1939(?)- ........................ **CLC 89**
See also CA 139; CANR 64, 109, 168

**Maynard, Joyce** 1953- ........................ **CLC 23**
See also CA 129; CAAE 111; CANR 64, 169

**Mayne, William (James Carter)** 1928- ........................ **CLC 12**
See also AAYA 20; CA 9-12R; CANR 37, 80, 100; CLR 25, 123; FANT; JRDA; MAICYA 1, 2; MAICYAS 1; SAAS 11; SATA 6, 68, 122; SUFW 2; YAW

**Mayo, Jim**
See L'Amour, Louis

**Maysles, Albert** 1926- ........................ **CLC 16**
See also CA 29-32R

**Maysles, David** 1932-1987 ................ **CLC 16**
See also CA 191

**Mazer, Norma Fox** 1931- ................ **CLC 26**
See also AAYA 5, 36; BYA 1, 8; CA 69-72; CANR 12, 32, 66, 129; CLR 23; JRDA; MAICYA 1, 2; SAAS 1; SATA 24, 67, 105, 168; WYA; YAW

**Mazzini, Guiseppe** 1805-1872 ........ **NCLC 34**

**McAlmon, Robert (Menzies)** 1895-1956 ........................ **TCLC 97**
See also CA 168; CAAE 107; DLB 4, 45; DLBD 15; GLL 1

**McAuley, James Phillip** 1917-1976 .. **CLC 45**
See also CA 97-100; CP 1, 2; DLB 260; RGEL 2

**McBain, Ed**
See Hunter, Evan
See also MSW

**McNickle, (William) D'Arcy**
1904-1977 ............... **CLC 89; NNAL**
See also CA 9-12R; CAAS 85-88; CANR
5, 45; DAM MULT; DLB 175, 212;
RGAL 4; SATA-Obit 22; TCWW 1, 2

**McPhee, John** 1931- ............... **CLC 36**
See also AAYA 61; AMWS 3; ANW; BEST
90:1; CA 65-68; CANR 20, 46, 64, 69,
121, 165; CPW; DLB 185, 275; MTCW
1, 2; MTFW 2005; TUS

**McPhee, John Angus**
See McPhee, John

**McPherson, James Alan** 1943- . **BLCS; CLC
19, 77; SSC 95**
See also BW 1, 3; CA 25-28R; 17; CANR
24, 74, 140; CN 3, 4, 5, 6; CSW; DLB
38, 244; EWL 3; MTCW 1, 2; MTFW
2005; RGAL 4; RGSF 2; SSFS 23

**McPherson, William (Alexander)**
1933- ............................ **CLC 34**
See also CA 69-72; CANR 28; INT
CANR-28

**McTaggart, J. McT. Ellis**
See McTaggart, John McTaggart Ellis

**McTaggart, John McTaggart Ellis**
1866-1925 .................... **TCLC 105**
See also CAAE 120; DLB 262

**Mead, George Herbert** 1863-1931 . **TCLC 89**
See also CA 212; DLB 270

**Mead, Margaret** 1901-1978 .............. **CLC 37**
See also AITN 1; CA 1-4R; CAAS 81-84;
CANR 4; DA3; FW; MTCW 1, 2; SATA-
Obit 20

**Meaker, Marijane** 1927-
See Kerr, M. E.
See also CA 107; CANR 37, 63, 145; INT
CA-107; JRDA; MAICYA 1, 2; MAIC-
YAS 1; MTCW 1; SATA 20, 61, 99, 160;
SATA-Essay 111; YAW

**Mechthild von Magdeburg** c. 1207-c.
1282 ............................ **CMLC 91**
See also DLB 138

**Medoff, Mark (Howard)** 1940- .... **CLC 6, 23**
See also AITN 1; CA 53-56; CAD; CANR
5; CD 5, 6; DAM DRAM; DFS 4; DLB
7; INT CANR-5

**Medvedev, P. N.**
See Bakhtin, Mikhail Mikhailovich

**Meged, Aharon**
See Megged, Aharon

**Meged, Aron**
See Megged, Aharon

**Megged, Aharon** 1920- ................. **CLC 9**
See also CA 49-52; 13; CANR 1, 140; EWL
3; RGHL

**Mehta, Deepa** 1950- .................... **CLC 208**

**Mehta, Gita** 1943- ...................... **CLC 179**
See also CA 225; CN 7; DNFS 2

**Mehta, Ved** 1934- ........................ **CLC 37**
See also CA 212; 1-4R, 212; CANR 2, 23,
69; DLB 323; MTCW 1; MTFW 2005

**Melanchthon, Philipp** 1497-1560 ........ **LC 90**
See also DLB 179

**Melanter**
See Blackmore, R(ichard) D(oddridge)

**Meleager** c. 140B.C.-c. 70B.C. ...... **CMLC 53**

**Melies, Georges** 1861-1938 ............ **TCLC 81**

**Melikow, Loris**
See Hofmannsthal, Hugo von

**Melmoth, Sebastian**
See Wilde, Oscar

**Melo Neto, Joao Cabral de**
See Cabral de Melo Neto, Joao
See also CWW 2; EWL 3

**Meltzer, Milton** 1915- ..................... **CLC 26**
See also AAYA 8, 45; BYA 2, 6; CA 13-
16R; CANR 38, 92, 107; CLR 13; DLB
61; JRDA; MAICYA 1, 2; SAAS 1; SATA
1, 50, 80, 128; SATA-Essay 124; WYA;
YAW

**Melville, Herman** 1819-1891 ..... **NCLC 3, 12,
29, 45, 49, 91, 93, 123, 157, 181; PC 82;
SSC 1, 17, 46, 95; WLC 4**
See also AAYA 25; AMW; AMWR 1;
CDALB 1640-1865; DA; DA3; DAB;
DAC; DAM MST, NOV; DLB 3, 74, 250,
254; EXPN; EXPS; GL 3; LAIT 1, 2; NFS
7, 9; RGAL 4; RGSF 2; SATA 59; SSFS
3; TUS

**Members, Mark**
See Powell, Anthony

**Membreno, Alejandro** ..................... **CLC 59**

**Menand, Louis** 1952- ..................... **CLC 208**
See also CA 200

**Menander** c. 342B.C.-c. 293B.C. .... **CMLC 9,
51; DC 3**
See also AW 1; CDWLB 1; DAM DRAM;
DLB 176; LMFS 1; RGWL 2, 3

**Menchu, Rigoberta** 1959- .. **CLC 160; HLCS
2**
See also CA 175; CANR 135; DNFS 1;
WLIT 1

**Mencken, H(enry) L(ouis)**
1880-1956 ............................ **TCLC 13**
See also AMW; CA 125; CAAE 105;
CDALB 1917-1929; DLB 11, 29, 63, 137,
222; EWL 3; MAL 5; MTCW 1, 2;
MTFW 2005; NCFS 4; RGAL 4; TUS

**Mendelsohn, Jane** 1965- ................... **CLC 99**
See also CA 154; CANR 94

**Mendelssohn, Moses** 1729-1786 ........ **LC 142**
See also DLB 97

**Mendoza, Inigo Lopez de**
See Santillana, Inigo Lopez de Mendoza,
Marques de

**Menton, Francisco de**
See Chin, Frank (Chew, Jr.)

**Mercer, David** 1928-1980 ................... **CLC 5**
See also CA 9-12R; CAAS 102; CANR 23;
CBD; DAM DRAM; DLB 13, 310;
MTCW 1; RGEL 2

**Merchant, Paul**
See Ellison, Harlan

**Meredith, George** 1828-1909 .. **PC 60; TCLC
17, 43**
See also CA 153; CAAE 117; CANR 80;
CDBLB 1832-1890; DAM POET; DLB
18, 35, 57, 159; RGEL 2; TEA

**Meredith, William** 1919-2007 ...... **CLC 4, 13,
22, 55; PC 28**
See also CA 9-12R; 14; CAAS 260; CANR
6, 40, 129; CP 1, 2, 3, 4, 5, 6, 7; DAM
POET; DLB 5; MAL 5

**Meredith, William Morris**
See Meredith, William

**Merezhkovsky, Dmitrii Sergeevich**
See Merezhkovsky, Dmitry Sergeyevich
See also DLB 295

**Merezhkovsky, Dmitry Sergeevich**
See Merezhkovsky, Dmitry Sergeyevich
See also EWL 3

**Merezhkovsky, Dmitry Sergeyevich**
1865-1941 ............................ **TCLC 29**
See Merezhkovsky, Dmitrii Sergeevich;
Merezhkovsky, Dmitry Sergeevich
See also CA 169

**Merimee, Prosper** 1803-1870 ... **NCLC 6, 65;
SSC 7, 77**
See also DLB 119, 192; EW 6; EXPS; GFL
1789 to the Present; RGSF 2; RGWL 2,
3; SSFS 8; SUFW

**Merkin, Daphne** 1954- ..................... **CLC 44**
See also CA 123

**Merleau-Ponty, Maurice**
1908-1961 ............................ **TCLC 156**
See also CA 114; CAAS 89-92; DLB 296;
GFL 1789 to the Present

**Merlin, Arthur**
See Blish, James (Benjamin)

**Mernissi, Fatima** 1940- .................... **CLC 171**
See also CA 152; FW

**Merrill, James** 1926-1995 ...... **CLC 2, 3, 6, 8,
13, 18, 34, 91; PC 28; TCLC 173**
See also AMWS 3; CA 13-16R; CAAS 147;
CANR 10, 49, 63, 108; CP 1, 2, 3, 4;
DA3; DAM POET; DLB 5, 165; DLBY
1985; EWL 3; INT CANR-10; MAL 5;
MTCW 1, 2; MTFW 2005; PAB; PFS 23;
RGAL 4

**Merrill, James Ingram**
See Merrill, James

**Merriman, Alex**
See Silverberg, Robert

**Merriman, Brian** 1747-1805 .......... **NCLC 70**

**Merritt, E. B.**
See Waddington, Miriam

**Merton, Thomas (James)**
1915-1968 . **CLC 1, 3, 11, 34, 83; PC 10**
See also AAYA 61; AMWS 8; CA 5-8R;
CAAS 25-28R; CANR 22, 53, 111, 131;
DA3; DLB 48; DLBY 1981; MAL 5;
MTCW 1, 2; MTFW 2005

**Merwin, W.S.** 1927- ..... **CLC 1, 2, 3, 5, 8, 13,
18, 45, 88; PC 45**
See also AMWS 3; CA 13-16R; CANR 15,
51, 112, 140; CP 1, 2, 3, 4, 5, 6, 7; DA3;
DAM POET; DLB 5, 169; EWL 3; INT
CANR-15; MAL 5; MTCW 1, 2; MTFW
2005; PAB; PFS 5, 15; RGAL 4

**Metastasio, Pietro** 1698-1782 ............ **LC 115**
See also RGWL 2, 3

**Metcalf, John** 1938- ............ **CLC 37; SSC 43**
See also CA 113; CN 4, 5, 6, 7; DLB 60;
RGSF 2; TWA

**Metcalf, Suzanne**
See Baum, L(yman) Frank

**Mew, Charlotte (Mary)** 1870-1928 .. **TCLC 8**
See also CA 189; CAAE 105; DLB 19, 135;
RGEL 2

**Mewshaw, Michael** 1943- ................... **CLC 9**
See also CA 53-56; CANR 7, 47, 147;
DLBY 1980

**Meyer, Conrad Ferdinand**
1825-1898 ................. **NCLC 81; SSC 30**
See also DLB 129; EW; RGWL 2, 3

**Meyer, Gustav** 1868-1932
See Meyrink, Gustav
See also CA 190; CAAE 117

**Meyer, June**
See Jordan, June

**Meyer, Lynn**
See Slavitt, David R.

**Meyers, Jeffrey** 1939- ...................... **CLC 39**
See also CA 186; 73-76, 186; CANR 54,
102, 159; DLB 111

**Meynell, Alice (Christina Gertrude
Thompson)** 1847-1922 ............... **TCLC 6**
See also CA 177; CAAE 104; DLB 19, 98;
RGEL 2

**Meyrink, Gustav** ........................... **TCLC 21**
See Meyer, Gustav
See also DLB 81; EWL 3

**Michaels, Leonard** 1933-2003 ..... **CLC 6, 25;
SSC 16**
See also AMWS 16; CA 61-64; CAAS 216;
CANR 21, 62, 119; CN 3, 4, 5, 6, 7; DLB
130; MTCW 1; TCLE 1:2

**Michaux, Henri** 1899-1984 ......... **CLC 8, 19**
See also CA 85-88; CAAS 114; DLB 258;
EWL 3; GFL 1789 to the Present; RGWL
2, 3

**Mitchell, W(illiam) O(rmond)**
1914-1998 ................................. **CLC 25**
See also CA 77-80; CAAS 165; CANR 15,
43; CN 1, 2, 3, 4, 5, 6; DAC; DAM MST;
DLB 88; TCLE 1:2

**Mitchell, William (Lendrum)**
1879-1936 ................................. **TCLC 81**
See also CA 213

**Mitford, Mary Russell** 1787-1855 ... **NCLC 4**
See also DLB 110, 116; RGEL 2

**Mitford, Nancy** 1904-1973 ................ **CLC 44**
See also BRWS 10; CA 9-12R; CN 1; DLB
191; RGEL 2

**Miyamoto, (Chujo) Yuriko**
1899-1951 ................................. **TCLC 37**
See Miyamoto Yuriko
See also CA 170, 174

**Miyamoto Yuriko**
See Miyamoto, (Chujo) Yuriko
See also DLB 180

**Miyazawa, Kenji** 1896-1933 .......... **TCLC 76**
See Miyazawa Kenji
See also CA 157; RGWL 3

**Miyazawa Kenji**
See Miyazawa, Kenji
See also EWL 3

**Mizoguchi, Kenji** 1898-1956 .......... **TCLC 72**
See also CA 167

**Mo, Timothy (Peter)** 1950- ...... **CLC 46, 134**
See also CA 117; CANR 128; CN 5, 6, 7;
DLB 194; MTCW 1; WLIT 4; WWE 1

**Modarressi, Taghi (M.)** 1931-1997 ... **CLC 44**
See also CA 134; CAAE 121; INT CA-134

**Modiano, Patrick (Jean)** 1945- ........ **CLC 18,
218**
See also CA 85-88; CANR 17, 40, 115;
CWW 2; DLB 83, 299; EWL 3; RGHL

**Mofolo, Thomas (Mokopu)**
1875(?)-1948 .............. **BLC 3; TCLC 22**
See also AFW; CA 153; CAAE 121; CANR
83; DAM MULT; DLB 225; EWL 3;
MTCW 2; MTFW 2005; WLIT 2

**Mohr, Nicholasa** 1938- ........ **CLC 12; HLC 2**
See also AAYA 8, 46; CA 49-52; CANR 1,
32, 64; CLR 22; DAM MULT; DLB 145;
HW 1, 2; JRDA; LAIT 5; LLW; MAICYA
2; MAICYAS 1; RGAL 4; SAAS 8; SATA
8, 97; SATA-Essay 113; WYA; YAW

**Moi, Toril** 1953- ............................... **CLC 172**
See also CA 154; CANR 102; FW

**Mojtabai, A(nn) G(race)** 1938- ..... **CLC 5, 9,
15, 29**
See also CA 85-88; CANR 88

**Moliere** 1622-1673 ..... **DC 13; LC 10, 28, 64,
125, 127; WLC 4**
See also DA; DA3; DAB; DAC; DAM
DRAM, MST; DFS 13, 18, 20; DLB 268;
EW 3; GFL Beginnings to 1789; LATS
1:1; RGWL 2, 3; TWA

**Molin, Charles**
See Mayne, William (James Carter)

**Molnar, Ferenc** 1878-1952 .............. **TCLC 20**
See also CA 153; CAAE 109; CANR 83;
CDWLB 4; DAM DRAM; DLB 215;
EWL 3; RGWL 2, 3

**Momaday, N. Scott** 1934- ...... **CLC 2, 19, 85,
95, 160; NNAL; PC 25; WLCS**
See also AAYA 11, 64; AMWS 4; ANW;
BPFB 2; BYA 12; CA 25-28R; CANR 14,
34, 68, 134; CDALBS; CN 2, 3, 4, 5, 6,
7; CPW; DA; DA3; DAB; DAC; DAM
MST, MULT, NOV, POP; DLB 143, 175,
256; EWL 3; EXPP; INT CANR-14;
LAIT 4; LATS 1:2; MAL 5; MTCW 1, 2;
MTFW 2005; NFS 10; PFS 2, 11; RGAL
4; SATA 48; SATA-Brief 30; TCWW 1,
2; WP; YAW

**Monette, Paul** 1945-1995 .................. **CLC 82**
See also AMWS 10; CA 139; CAAS 147;
CN 6; GLL 1

**Monroe, Harriet** 1860-1936 ............ **TCLC 12**
See also CA 204; CAAE 109; DLB 54, 91

**Monroe, Lyle**
See Heinlein, Robert A.

**Montagu, Elizabeth** 1720-1800 ....... **NCLC 7,
117**
See also FW

**Montagu, Mary (Pierrepont) Wortley**
1689-1762 ................... **LC 9, 57; PC 16**
See also DLB 95, 101; FL 1:1; RGEL 2

**Montagu, W. H.**
See Coleridge, Samuel Taylor

**Montague, John (Patrick)** 1929- ..... **CLC 13,
46**
See also CA 9-12R; CANR 9, 69, 121; CP
1, 2, 3, 4, 5, 6, 7; DLB 40; EWL 3;
MTCW 1; PFS 12; RGEL 2; TCLE 1:2

**Montaigne, Michel (Eyquem) de**
1533-1592 ................ **LC 8, 105; WLC 4**
See also DA; DAB; DAC; DAM MST;
DLB 327; EW 2; GFL Beginnings to
1789; LMFS 1; RGWL 2, 3; TWA

**Montale, Eugenio** 1896-1981 ... **CLC 7, 9, 18;
PC 13**
See also CA 17-20R; CAAS 104; CANR
30; DLB 114, 331; EW 11; EWL 3;
MTCW 1; PFS 22; RGWL 2, 3; TWA;
WLIT 7

**Montesquieu, Charles-Louis de Secondat**
1689-1755 ............................... **LC 7, 69**
See also DLB 314; EW 3; GFL Beginnings
to 1789; TWA

**Montessori, Maria** 1870-1952 ...... **TCLC 103**
See also CA 147; CAAE 115

**Montgomery, (Robert) Bruce** 1921(?)-1978
See Crispin, Edmund
See also CA 179; CAAS 104; CMW 4

**Montgomery, L(ucy) M(aud)**
1874-1942 ........................ **TCLC 51, 140**
See also AAYA 12; BYA 1; CA 137; CAAE
108; CLR 8, 91; DA3; DAC; DAM MST;
DLB 92; DLBD 14; JRDA; MAICYA 1,
2; MTCW 2; MTFW 2005; RGEL 2;
SATA 100; TWA; WCH; WYA; YABC 1

**Montgomery, Marion, Jr.** 1925- ......... **CLC 7**
See also AITN 1; CA 1-4R; CANR 3, 48,
162; CSW; DLB 6

**Montgomery, Marion H.** 1925-
See Montgomery, Marion, Jr.

**Montgomery, Max**
See Davenport, Guy (Mattison, Jr.)

**Montherlant, Henry (Milon) de**
1896-1972 ............................ **CLC 8, 19**
See also CA 85-88; CAAS 37-40R; DAM
DRAM; DLB 72, 321; EW 11; EWL 3;
GFL 1789 to the Present; MTCW 1

**Monty Python**
See Chapman, Graham; Cleese, John
(Marwood); Gilliam, Terry; Idle, Eric;
Jones, Terence Graham Parry; Palin,
Michael (Edward)
See also AAYA 7

**Moodie, Susanna (Strickland)**
1803-1885 ........................ **NCLC 14, 113**
See also DLB 99

**Moody, Hiram** 1961-
See Moody, Rick
See also CA 138; CANR 64, 112; MTFW
2005

**Moody, Minerva**
See Alcott, Louisa May

**Moody, Rick** .................................... **CLC 147**
See Moody, Hiram

**Moody, William Vaughan**
1869-1910 ............................... **TCLC 105**
See also CA 178; CAAE 110; DLB 7, 54;
MAL 5; RGAL 4

**Mooney, Edward** 1951-
See Mooney, Ted
See also CA 130

**Mooney, Ted** .................................... **CLC 25**
See Mooney, Edward

**Moorcock, Michael** 1939- ...... **CLC 5, 27, 58,
236**
See Bradbury, Edward P.
See also AAYA 26; CA 45-48; 5; CANR 2,
17, 38, 64, 122; CN 5, 6, 7; DLB 14, 231,
261, 319; FANT; MTCW 1, 2; MTFW
2005; SATA 93, 166; SCFW 1, 2; SFW 4;
SUFW 1, 2

**Moorcock, Michael John**
See Moorcock, Michael

**Moore, Alan** 1953- .......................... **CLC 230**
See also AAYA 51; CA 204; CANR 138;
DLB 261; MTFW 2005; SFW 4

**Moore, Brian** 1921-1999 ... **CLC 1, 3, 5, 7, 8,
19, 32, 90**
See Bryan, Michael
See also BRWS 9; CA 1-4R; CAAS 174;
CANR 1, 25, 42, 63; CCA 1; CN 1, 2, 3,
4, 5, 6; DAB; DAC; DAM MST; DLB
251; EWL 3; FANT; MTCW 1, 2; MTFW
2005; RGEL 2

**Moore, Edward**
See Muir, Edwin
See also RGEL 2

**Moore, G. E.** 1873-1958 ................... **TCLC 89**
See also DLB 262

**Moore, George Augustus**
1852-1933 ................... **SSC 19; TCLC 7**
See also BRW 6; CA 177; CAAE 104; DLB
10, 18, 57, 135; EWL 3; RGEL 2; RGSF
2

**Moore, Lorrie** ....................... **CLC 39, 45, 68**
See Moore, Marie Lorena
See also AMWS 10; CN 5, 6, 7; DLB 234;
SSFS 19

**Moore, Marianne (Craig)**
1887-1972 .... **CLC 1, 2, 4, 8, 10, 13, 19,
47; PC 4, 49; WLCS**
See also AMW; CA 1-4R; CAAS 33-36R;
CANR 3, 61; CDALB 1929-1941; CP 1;
DA; DA3; DAB; DAC; DAM MST,
POET; DLB 45; DLBD 7; EWL 3; EXPP;
FL 1:6; MAL 5; MBL; MTCW 1, 2;
MTFW 2005; PAB; PFS 14, 17; RGAL 4;
SATA 20; TUS; WP

**Moore, Marie Lorena** 1957- .......... **CLC 165**
See Moore, Lorrie
See also CA 116; CANR 39, 83, 139; DLB
234; MTFW 2005

**Moore, Michael** 1954- ..................... **CLC 218**
See also AAYA 53; CA 166; CANR 150

**Moore, Thomas** 1779-1852 ....... **NCLC 6, 110**
See also DLB 96, 144; RGEL 2

**Moorhouse, Frank** 1938- ................... **SSC 40**
See also CA 118; CANR 92; CN 3, 4, 5, 6,
7; DLB 289; RGSF 2

**Mora, Pat** 1942- ................................. **HLC 2**
See also AMWS 13; CA 129; CANR 57,
81, 112; CLR 58; DAM MULT; DLB 209;
HW 1, 2; LLW; MAICYA 2; MTFW
2005; SATA 92, 134

**Moraga, Cherrie** 1952- ...... **CLC 126; DC 22**
See also CA 131; CANR 66, 154; DAM
MULT; DLB 82, 249; FW; GLL 1; HW 1,
2; LLW

**Morand, Paul** 1888-1976 .... **CLC 41; SSC 22**
See also CA 184; CAAS 69-72; DLB 65;
EWL 3

**Morante, Elsa** 1918-1985 ............. **CLC 8, 47**
See also CA 85-88; CAAS 117; CANR 35;
DLB 177; EWL 3; MTCW 1, 2; MTFW
2005; RGHL; RGWL 2, 3; WLIT 7

**Muir, John** 1838-1914 ...................... **TCLC 28**
    See also AMWS 9; ANW; CA 165; DLB
    186, 275

**Mujica Lainez, Manuel** 1910-1984 ... **CLC 31**
    See Lainez, Manuel Mujica
    See also CA 81-84; CAAS 112; CANR 32;
    EWL 3; HW 1

**Mukherjee, Bharati** 1940- ..... **AAL; CLC 53,**
    **115, 235; SSC 38**
    See also AAYA 46; BEST 89:2; CA 232;
    107, 232; CANR 45, 72, 128; CN 5, 6, 7;
    DAM NOV; DLB 60, 218, 323; DNFS 1,
    2; EWL 3; FW; MAL 5; MTCW 1, 2;
    MTFW 2005; RGAL 4; RGSF 2; SSFS 7,
    24; TUS; WWE 1

**Muldoon, Paul** 1951- .......... **CLC 32, 72, 166**
    See also BRWS 4; CA 113; CAAE 113;
    CANR 52, 91; CP 2, 3, 4, 5, 6, 7; DAM
    POET; DLB 40; INT CA-129; PFS 7, 22;
    TCLE 1:2

**Mulisch, Harry (Kurt Victor)**
    1927- ................................. **CLC 42**
    See also CA 9-12R; CANR 6, 26, 56, 110;
    CWW 2; DLB 299; EWL 3

**Mull, Martin** 1943- ........................... **CLC 17**
    See also CA 105

**Muller, Wilhelm** ............................. **NCLC 73**

**Mulock, Dinah Maria**
    See Craik, Dinah Maria (Mulock)
    See also RGEL 2

**Multatuli** 1820-1881 ..................... **NCLC 165**
    See also RGWL 2, 3

**Munday, Anthony** 1560-1633 ............... **LC 87**
    See also DLB 62, 172; RGEL 2

**Munford, Robert** 1737(?)-1783 ............. **LC 5**
    See also DLB 31

**Mungo, Raymond** 1946- ................... **CLC 72**
    See also CA 49-52; CANR 2

**Munro, Alice** 1931- .... **CLC 6, 10, 19, 50, 95,**
    **222; SSC 3, 95; WLCS**
    See also AITN 2; BPFB 2; CA 33-36R;
    CANR 33, 53, 75, 114; CCA 1; CN 1, 2,
    3, 4, 5, 6, 7; DA3; DAC; DAM MST,
    NOV; DLB 53; EWL 3; MTCW 1, 2;
    MTFW 2005; RGEL 2; RGSF 2; SATA
    29; SSFS 5, 13, 19; TCLE 1:2; WWE 1

**Munro, H(ector) H(ugh)** 1870-1916
    See Saki
    See also AAYA 56; CA 130; CAAE 104;
    CANR 104; CDBLB 1890-1914; DA;
    DA3; DAB; DAC; DAM MST, NOV;
    DLB 34, 162; EXPS; MTCW 1, 2; MTFW
    2005; RGEL 2; SSFS 15

**Murakami, Haruki** 1949- ............... **CLC 150**
    See Murakami Haruki
    See also CA 165; CANR 102, 146; MJW;
    RGWL 3; SFW 4; SSFS 23

**Murakami Haruki**
    See Murakami, Haruki
    See also CWW 2; DLB 182; EWL 3

**Murasaki, Lady**
    See Murasaki Shikibu

**Murasaki Shikibu** 978(?)-1026(?) .. **CMLC 1,**
    **79**
    See also EFS 2; LATS 1:1; RGWL 2, 3

**Murdoch, Iris** 1919-1999 .. **CLC 1, 2, 3, 4, 6,**
    **8, 11, 15, 22, 31, 51; TCLC 171**
    See also BRWS 1; CA 13-16R; CAAS 179;
    CANR 8, 43, 68, 103, 142; CBD; CD-
    BLB 1960 to Present; CN 1, 2, 3, 4, 5, 6;
    CWD; DA3; DAB; DAC; DAM MST,
    NOV; DLB 14, 194, 233, 326; EWL 3;
    INT CANR-8; MTCW 1, 2; MTFW 2005;
    NFS 18; RGEL 2; TCLE 1:2; TEA; WLIT
    4

**Murfree, Mary Noailles** 1850-1922 .. **SSC 22;**
    **TCLC 135**
    See also CA 176; CAAE 122; DLB 12, 74;
    RGAL 4

**Murglie**
    See Murnau, F.W.

**Murnau, Friedrich Wilhelm**
    See Murnau, F.W.

**Murnau, F.W.** 1888-1931 ................ **TCLC 53**
    See also CAAE 112

**Murphy, Richard** 1927- ..................... **CLC 41**
    See also BRWS 5; CA 29-32R; CP 1, 2, 3,
    4, 5, 6, 7; DLB 40; EWL 3

**Murphy, Sylvia** 1937- ........................ **CLC 34**
    See also CA 121

**Murphy, Thomas (Bernard)** 1935- ... **CLC 51**
    See Murphy, Tom
    See also CA 101

**Murphy, Tom**
    See Murphy, Thomas (Bernard)
    See also DLB 310

**Murray, Albert** 1916- ........................ **CLC 73**
    See also BW 2; CA 49-52; CANR 26, 52,
    78, 160; CN 7; CSW; DLB 38; MTFW
    2005

**Murray, Albert L.**
    See Murray, Albert

**Murray, James Augustus Henry**
    1837-1915 ............................. **TCLC 117**

**Murray, Judith Sargent**
    1751-1820 ............................... **NCLC 63**
    See also DLB 37, 200

**Murray, Les(lie Allan)** 1938- ............ **CLC 40**
    See also BRWS 7; CA 21-24R; CANR 11,
    27, 56, 103; CP 1, 2, 3, 4, 5, 6, 7; DAM
    POET; DLB 289; DLBY 2001; EWL 3;
    RGEL 2

**Murry, J. Middleton**
    See Murry, John Middleton

**Murry, John Middleton**
    1889-1957 ............................... **TCLC 16**
    See also CA 217; CAAE 118; DLB 149

**Musgrave, Susan** 1951- ............... **CLC 13, 54**
    See also CA 69-72; CANR 45, 84; CCA 1;
    CP 2, 3, 4, 5, 6, 7; CWP

**Musil, Robert (Edler von)**
    1880-1942 ............... **SSC 18; TCLC 12, 68**
    See also CAAE 109; CANR 55, 84; CD-
    WLB 2; DLB 81, 124; EW 9; EWL 3;
    MTCW 2; RGSF 2; RGWL 2, 3

**Muske, Carol** ..................................... **CLC 90**
    See Muske-Dukes, Carol (Anne)

**Muske-Dukes, Carol (Anne)** 1945-
    See Muske, Carol
    See also CA 203; 65-68, 203; CANR 32,
    70; CWP; PFS 24

**Musset, Alfred de** 1810-1857 . **DC 27; NCLC**
    **7, 150**
    See also DLB 192, 217; EW 6; GFL 1789
    to the Present; RGWL 2, 3; TWA

**Musset, Louis Charles Alfred de**
    See Musset, Alfred de

**Mussolini, Benito (Amilcare Andrea)**
    1883-1945 ............................... **TCLC 96**
    See also CAAE 116

**Mutanabbi, Al-**
    See al-Mutanabbi, Ahmad ibn al-Husayn
    Abu al-Tayyib al-Jufi al-Kindi
    See also WLIT 6

**My Brother's Brother**
    See Chekhov, Anton (Pavlovich)

**Myers, L(eopold) H(amilton)**
    1881-1944 ............................... **TCLC 59**
    See also CA 157; DLB 15; EWL 3; RGEL
    2

**Myers, Walter Dean** 1937- .. **BLC 3; CLC 35**
    See Myers, Walter M.
    See also AAYA 4, 23; BW 2; BYA 6, 8, 11;
    CA 33-36R; CANR 20, 42, 67, 108; CLR
    4, 16, 35, 110; DAM MULT, NOV; DLB
    33; INT CANR-20; JRDA; LAIT 5; MAI-

CYA 1, 2; MAICYAS 1; MTCW 2;
    MTFW 2005; SAAS 2; SATA 41, 71, 109,
    157; SATA-Brief 27; WYA; YAW

**Myers, Walter M.**
    See Myers, Walter Dean

**Myles, Symon**
    See Follett, Ken

**Nabokov, Vladimir (Vladimirovich)**
    1899-1977 ....... **CLC 1, 2, 3, 6, 8, 11, 15,**
    **23, 44, 46, 64; SSC 11, 86; TCLC 108,**
    **189; WLC 4**
    See also AAYA 45; AMW; AMWC 1;
    AMWR 1; BPFB 2; CA 5-8R; CAAS 69-
    72; CANR 20, 102; CDALB 1941-1968;
    CN 1, 2; CP 2; DA; DA3; DAB; DAC;
    DAM MST, NOV; DLB 2, 244, 278, 317;
    DLBD 3; DLBY 1980, 1991; EWL 3;
    EXPS; LATS 1:2; MAL 5; MTCW 1, 2;
    MTFW 2005; NCFS 4; NFS 9; RGAL 4;
    RGSF 2; SSFS 6, 15; TUS

**Naevius** c. 265B.C.-201B.C. ........... **CMLC 37**
    See also DLB 211

**Nagai, Kafu** ..................................... **TCLC 51**
    See Nagai, Sokichi
    See also DLB 180

**Nagai, Sokichi** 1879-1959
    See Nagai, Kafu
    See also CAAE 117

**Nagy, Laszlo** 1925-1978 ..................... **CLC 7**
    See also CA 129; CAAS 112

**Naidu, Sarojini** 1879-1949 ............. **TCLC 80**
    See also EWL 3; RGEL 2

**Naipaul, Shiva** 1945-1985 .......... **CLC 32, 39;**
    **TCLC 153**
    See also CA 112; CAAE 110; CAAS 116;
    CANR 33; CN 2, 3; DA3; DAM NOV;
    DLB 157; DLBY 1985; EWL 3; MTCW
    1, 2; MTFW 2005

**Naipaul, V.S.** 1932- .. **CLC 4, 7, 9, 13, 18, 37,**
    **105, 199; SSC 38**
    See also BPFB 2; BRWS 1; CA 1-4R;
    CANR 1, 33, 51, 91, 126; CDBLB 1960
    to Present; CDWLB 3; CN 1, 2, 3, 4, 5,
    6, 7; DA3; DAB; DAC; DAM MST,
    NOV; DLB 125, 204, 207, 326, 331;
    DLBY 1985, 2001; EWL 3; LATS 1:2;
    MTCW 1, 2; MTFW 2005; RGEL 2;
    RGSF 2; TWA; WLIT 4; WWE 1

**Nakos, Lilika** 1903(?)-1989 ............... **CLC 29**

**Napoleon**
    See Yamamoto, Hisaye

**Narayan, R.K.** 1906-2001 ...... **CLC 7, 28, 47,**
    **121, 211; SSC 25**
    See also BPFB 2; CA 81-84; CAAS 196;
    CANR 33, 61, 112; CN 1, 2, 3, 4, 5, 6, 7;
    DA3; DAM NOV; DLB 323; DNFS 1;
    EWL 3; MTCW 1, 2; MTFW 2005; RGEL
    2; RGSF 2; SATA 62; SSFS 5; WWE 1

**Nash, (Frediric) Ogden** 1902-1971 . **CLC 23;**
    **PC 21; TCLC 109**
    See also CA 13-14; CAAS 29-32R; CANR
    34, 61; CAP 1; CP 1; DAM POET; DLB
    11; MAICYA 1, 2; MAL 5; MTCW 1, 2;
    RGAL 4; SATA 2, 46; WP

**Nashe, Thomas** 1567-1601(?) . **LC 41, 89; PC**
    **82**
    See also DLB 167; RGEL 2

**Nathan, Daniel**
    See Dannay, Frederic

**Nathan, George Jean** 1882-1958 .... **TCLC 18**
    See Hatteras, Owen
    See also CA 169; CAAE 114; DLB 137;
    MAL 5

**Natsume, Kinnosuke**
    See Natsume, Soseki

**Natsume, Soseki** 1867-1916 ........ **TCLC 2, 10**
    See Natsume Soseki; Soseki
    See also CA 195; CAAE 104; RGWL 2, 3;
    TWA

**Natsume Soseki**
See Natsume, Soseki
See also DLB 180; EWL 3

**Natti, (Mary) Lee** 1919-
See Kingman, Lee
See also CA 5-8R; CANR 2

**Navarre, Marguerite de**
See de Navarre, Marguerite

**Naylor, Gloria** 1950- ..... **BLC 3; CLC 28, 52, 156; WLCS**
See also AAYA 6, 39; AFAW 1, 2; AMWS 8; BW 2, 3; CA 107; CANR 27, 51, 74, 130; CN 4, 5, 6, 7; CPW; DA; DA3; DAC; DAM MST, MULT, NOV, POP; DLB 173; EWL 3; FW; MAL 5; MTCW 1, 2; MTFW 2005; NFS 4, 7; RGAL 4; TCLE 1:2; TUS

**Neal, John** 1793-1876 .................... **NCLC 161**
See also DLB 1, 59, 243; FW; RGAL 4

**Neff, Debra** ........................ **CLC 59**

**Neihardt, John Gneisenau** 1881-1973 ........................ **CLC 32**
See also CA 13-14; CANR 65; CAP 1; DLB 9, 54, 256; LAIT 2; TCWW 1, 2

**Nekrasov, Nikolai Alekseevich** 1821-1878 .............................. **NCLC 11**
See also DLB 277

**Nelligan, Emile** 1879-1941 ............. **TCLC 14**
See also CA 204; CAAE 114; DLB 92; EWL 3

**Nelson, Willie** 1933- ........................... **CLC 17**
See also CA 107; CANR 114

**Nemerov, Howard** 1920-1991 .... **CLC 2, 6, 9, 36; PC 24; TCLC 124**
See also AMW; CA 1-4R; CAAS 134; CABS 2; CANR 1, 27, 53; CN 1, 2, 3; CP 1, 2, 3, 4, 5; DAM POET; DLB 5, 6; DLBY 1983; EWL 3; INT CANR-27; MAL 5; MTCW 1, 2; MTFW 2005; PFS 10, 14; RGAL 4

**Nepos, Cornelius** c. 99B.C.-c. 24B.C. ...................................... **CMLC 89**
See also DLB 211

**Neruda, Pablo** 1904-1973 .. **CLC 1, 2, 5, 7, 9, 28, 62; HLC 2; PC 4, 64; WLC 4**
See also CA 19-20; CAAS 45-48; CANR 131; CAP 2; DA; DA3; DAB; DAC; DAM MST, MULT, POET; DLB 283, 331; DNFS 2; EWL 3; HW 1; LAW; MTCW 1, 2; MTFW 2005; PFS 11; RGWL 2, 3; TWA; WLIT 1; WP

**Nerval, Gerard de** 1808-1855 ... **NCLC 1, 67; PC 13; SSC 18**
See also DLB 217; EW 6; GFL 1789 to the Present; RGSF 2; RGWL 2, 3

**Nervo, (Jose) Amado (Ruiz de)** 1870-1919 ................ **HLCS 2; TCLC 11**
See also CA 131; CAAE 109; DLB 290; EWL 3; HW 1; LAW

**Nesbit, Malcolm**
See Chester, Alfred

**Nessi, Pio Baroja y**
See Baroja, Pio

**Nestroy, Johann** 1801-1862 ........... **NCLC 42**
See also DLB 133; RGWL 2, 3

**Netterville, Luke**
See O'Grady, Standish (James)

**Neufeld, John (Arthur)** 1938- .......... **CLC 17**
See also AAYA 11; CA 25-28R; CANR 11, 37, 56; CLR 52; MAICYA 1, 2; SAAS 3; SATA 6, 81, 131; SATA-Essay 131; YAW

**Neumann, Alfred** 1895-1952 ......... **TCLC 100**
See also CA 183; DLB 56

**Neumann, Ferenc**
See Molnar, Ferenc

**Neville, Emily Cheney** 1919- ............. **CLC 12**
See also BYA 2; CA 5-8R; CANR 3, 37, 85; JRDA; MAICYA 1, 2; SAAS 2; SATA 1; YAW

**Newbound, Bernard Slade** 1930-
See Slade, Bernard
See also CA 81-84; CANR 49; CD 5; DAM DRAM

**Newby, P(ercy) H(oward)** 1918-1997 ............................. **CLC 2, 13**
See also CA 5-8R; CAAS 161; CANR 32, 67; CN 1, 2, 3, 4, 5, 6; DAM NOV; DLB 15, 326; MTCW 1; RGEL 2

**Newcastle**
See Cavendish, Margaret Lucas

**Newlove, Donald** 1928- ....................... **CLC 6**
See also CA 29-32R; CANR 25

**Newlove, John (Herbert)** 1938- ........ **CLC 14**
See also CA 21-24R; CANR 9, 25; CP 1, 2, 3, 4, 5, 6, 7

**Newman, Charles** 1938-2006 ......... **CLC 2, 8**
See also CA 21-24R; CAAS 249; CANR 84; CN 3, 4, 5, 6

**Newman, Charles Hamilton**
See Newman, Charles

**Newman, Edwin (Harold)** 1919- ...... **CLC 14**
See also AITN 1; CA 69-72; CANR 5

**Newman, John Henry** 1801-1890 . **NCLC 38, 99**
See also BRWS 7; DLB 18, 32, 55; RGEL 2

**Newton, (Sir) Isaac** 1642-1727 ...... **LC 35, 53**
See also DLB 252

**Newton, Suzanne** 1936- ..................... **CLC 35**
See also BYA 7; CA 41-44R; CANR 14; JRDA; SATA 5, 77

**New York Dept. of Ed.** ..................... **CLC 70**

**Nexo, Martin Andersen** 1869-1954 ................................. **TCLC 43**
See also CA 202; DLB 214; EWL 3

**Nezval, Vitezslav** 1900-1958 ........... **TCLC 44**
See also CAAE 123; CDWLB 4; DLB 215; EWL 3

**Ng, Fae Myenne** 1957(?)- ................. **CLC 81**
See also BYA 11; CA 146

**Ngema, Mbongeni** 1955- ................... **CLC 57**
See also BW 2; CA 143; CANR 84; CD 5, 6

**Ngugi, James T.** ............... **CLC 3, 7, 13, 182**
See Ngugi wa Thiong'o
See also CN 1, 2

**Ngugi, James Thiong'o**
See Ngugi wa Thiong'o

**Ngugi wa Thiong'o** 1938- ... **BLC 3; CLC 36, 182**
See Ngugi, James T.
See also AFW; BRWS 8; BW 2; CA 81-84; CANR 27, 58, 164; CD 3, 4, 5, 6, 7; CD-WLB 3; DAM MULT, NOV; DLB 125; DNFS 2; EWL 3; MTCW 1, 2; MTFW 2005; RGEL 2; WWE 1

**Niatum, Duane** 1938- .......................... **NNAL**
See also CA 41-44R; CANR 21, 45, 83; DLB 175

**Nichol, B(arrie) P(hillip)** 1944-1988 . **CLC 18**
See also CA 53-56; CP 1, 2, 3, 4; DLB 53; SATA 66

**Nicholas of Cusa** 1401-1464 ................. **LC 80**
See also DLB 115

**Nichols, John** 1940- ........................... **CLC 38**
See also AMWS 13; CA 190; 9-12R, 190; 2; CANR 6, 70, 121; DLBY 1982; LATS 1:2; MTFW 2005; TCWW 1, 2

**Nichols, Leigh**
See Koontz, Dean R.

**Nichols, Peter (Richard)** 1927- .... **CLC 5, 36, 65**
See also CA 104; CANR 33, 86; CBD; CD 5, 6; DLB 13, 245; MTCW 1

**Nicholson, Linda** ............................ **CLC 65**

**Ni Chuilleanain, Eilean** 1942- ............. **PC 34**
See also CA 126; CANR 53, 83; CP 5, 6, 7; CWP; DLB 40

**Nicolas, F. R. E.**
See Freeling, Nicolas

**Niedecker, Lorine** 1903-1970 ..... **CLC 10, 42; PC 42**
See also CA 25-28; CAP 2; DAM POET; DLB 48

**Nietzsche, Friedrich (Wilhelm)** 1844-1900 ................... **TCLC 10, 18, 55**
See also CA 121; CAAE 107; CDWLB 2; DLB 129; EW 7; RGWL 2, 3; TWA

**Nievo, Ippolito** 1831-1861 ............... **NCLC 22**

**Nightingale, Anne Redmon** 1943-
See Redmon, Anne
See also CA 103

**Nightingale, Florence** 1820-1910 ... **TCLC 85**
See also CA 188; DLB 166

**Nijo Yoshimoto** 1320-1388 ............. **CMLC 49**
See also DLB 203

**Nik. T. O.**
See Annensky, Innokenty (Fyodorovich)

**Nin, Anais** 1903-1977 ..... **CLC 1, 4, 8, 11, 14, 60, 127; SSC 10**
See also AITN 2; AMWS 10; BPFB 2; CA 13-16R; CAAS 69-72; CANR 22, 53; CN 1, 2; DAM NOV, POP; DLB 2, 4, 152; EWL 3; GLL 2; MAL 5; MBL; MTCW 1, 2; MTFW 2005; RGAL 4; RGSF 2

**Nisbet, Robert A(lexander)** 1913-1996 ............................... **TCLC 117**
See also CA 25-28R; CAAS 153; CANR 17; INT CANR-17

**Nishida, Kitaro** 1870-1945 ............... **TCLC 83**

**Nishiwaki, Junzaburo** 1894-1982 ........ **PC 15**
See Junzaburo, Nishiwaki
See also CA 194; CAAS 107; MJW; RGWL 3

**Nissenson, Hugh** 1933- ................... **CLC 4, 9**
See also CA 17-20R; CANR 27, 108, 151; CN 5, 6; DLB 28, 335

**Nister, Der**
See Der Nister
See also DLB 333; EWL 3

**Niven, Larry** 1938-
See Niven, Laurence VanCott
See also CA 207; 21-24R, 207; 12; CANR 14, 44, 66, 113, 155; CPW; DAM POP; MTCW 1, 2; SATA 95, 171; SFW 4

**Niven, Laurence VanCott** .................. **CLC 8**
See Niven, Larry
See also AAYA 27; BPFB 2; BYA 10; DLB 8; SCFW 1, 2

**Nixon, Agnes Eckhardt** 1927- ........... **CLC 21**
See also CA 110

**Nizan, Paul** 1905-1940 .................... **TCLC 40**
See also CA 161; DLB 72; EWL 3; GFL 1789 to the Present

**Nkosi, Lewis** 1936- .............. **BLC 3; CLC 45**
See also BW 1, 3; CA 65-68; CANR 27, 81; CBD; CD 5, 6; DAM MULT; DLB 157, 225; WWE 1

**Nodier, (Jean) Charles (Emmanuel)** 1780-1844 ............................... **NCLC 19**
See also DLB 119; GFL 1789 to the Present

**Noguchi, Yone** 1875-1947 ............... **TCLC 80**

**Nolan, Christopher** 1965- .............. **CLC 58**
See also CA 111; CANR 88

**Noon, Jeff** 1957- ................................. **CLC 91**
See also CA 148; CANR 83; DLB 267; SFW 4

**Norden, Charles**
See Durrell, Lawrence (George)

**Nordhoff, Charles Bernard** 1887-1947 ............................... **TCLC 23**
See also CA 211; CAAE 108; DLB 9; LAIT 1; RHW 1; SATA 23

**Norfolk, Lawrence** 1963- ................... **CLC 76**
See also CA 144; CANR 85; CN 6, 7; DLB 267

**Norman, Marsha (Williams)** 1947- . **CLC 28, 186; DC 8**
See also CA 105; CABS 3; CAD; CANR 41, 131; CD 5, 6; CSW; CWD; DAM DRAM; DFS 2; DLB 266; DLBY 1984; FW; MAL 5

**Normyx**
See Douglas, (George) Norman

**Norris, (Benjamin) Frank(lin, Jr.)** 1870-1902 ........ **SSC 28; TCLC 24, 155**
See also AAYA 57; AMW; AMWC 2; BPFB 2; CA 160; CAAE 110; CDALB 1865-1917; DLB 12, 71, 186; LMFS 2; MAL 5; NFS 12; RGAL 4; TCWW 1, 2; TUS

**Norris, Leslie** 1921-2006 .................... **CLC 14**
See also CA 11-12; CAAS 251; CANR 14, 117; CAP 1; CP 1, 2, 3, 4, 5, 6, 7; DLB 27, 256

**North, Andrew**
See Norton, Andre

**North, Anthony**
See Koontz, Dean R.

**North, Captain George**
See Stevenson, Robert Louis (Balfour)

**North, Captain George**
See Stevenson, Robert Louis (Balfour)

**North, Milou**
See Erdrich, Louise

**Northrup, B. A.**
See Hubbard, L. Ron

**North Staffs**
See Hulme, T(homas) E(rnest)

**Northup, Solomon** 1808-1863 ...... **NCLC 105**

**Norton, Alice Mary**
See Norton, Andre
See also MAICYA 1; SATA 1, 43

**Norton, Andre** 1912-2005 .................. **CLC 12**
See Norton, Alice Mary
See also AAYA 14; BPFB 2; BYA 4, 10, 12; CA 1-4R; CAAS 237; CANR 2, 31, 68, 108, 149; CLR 50; DLB 8, 52; JRDA; MAICYA 2; MTCW 1; SATA 91; SUFW 1, 2; YAW

**Norton, Caroline** 1808-1877 .......... **NCLC 47**
See also DLB 21, 159, 199

**Norway, Nevil Shute** 1899-1960
See Shute, Nevil
See also CA 102; CAAS 93-96; CANR 85; MTCW 2

**Norwid, Cyprian Kamil** 1821-1883 .............................. **NCLC 17**
See also RGWL 3

**Nosille, Nabrah**
See Ellison, Harlan

**Nossack, Hans Erich** 1901-1977 ......... **CLC 6**
See also CA 93-96; CAAS 85-88; CANR 156; DLB 69; EWL 3

**Nostradamus** 1503-1566 ........................ **LC 27**

**Nosu, Chuji**
See Ozu, Yasujiro

**Notenburg, Eleanora (Genrikhovna) von**
See Guro, Elena (Genrikhovna)

**Nova, Craig** 1945- .......................... **CLC 7, 31**
See also CA 45-48; CANR 2, 53, 127

**Novak, Joseph**
See Kosinski, Jerzy

**Novalis** 1772-1801 .................. **NCLC 13, 178**
See also CDWLB 2; DLB 90; EW 5; RGWL 2, 3

**Novick, Peter** 1934- .......................... **CLC 164**
See also CA 188

**Novis, Emile**
See Weil, Simone (Adolphine)

**Nowlan, Alden (Albert)** 1933-1983 ... **CLC 15**
See also CA 9-12R; CANR 5; CP 1, 2, 3; DAC; DAM MST; DLB 53; PFS 12

**Noyes, Alfred** 1880-1958 ...... **PC 27; TCLC 7**
See also CA 188; CAAE 104; DLB 20; EXPP; FANT; PFS 4; RGEL 2

**Nugent, Richard Bruce**
1906(?)-1987 .............................. **HR 1:3**
See also BW 1; CA 125; DLB 51; GLL 2

**Nunn, Kem** ........................................ **CLC 34**
See also CA 159

**Nussbaum, Martha Craven** 1947- .. **CLC 203**
See also CA 134; CANR 102

**Nwapa, Flora (Nwanzuruaha)**
1931-1993 ...................... **BLCS; CLC 133**
See also BW 2; CA 143; CANR 83; CD-WLB 3; CWRI 5; DLB 125; EWL 3; WLIT 2

**Nye, Robert** 1939- ........................ **CLC 13, 42**
See also BRWS 10; CA 33-36R; CANR 29, 67, 107; CN 1, 2, 3, 4, 5, 6, 7; CP 1, 2, 3, 4, 5, 6, 7; CWRI 5; DAM NOV; DLB 14, 271; FANT; HGG; MTCW 1; RHW; SATA 6

**Nyro, Laura** 1947-1997 .................... **CLC 17**
See also CA 194

**Oates, Joyce Carol** 1938- .. **CLC 1, 2, 3, 6, 9, 11, 15, 19, 33, 52, 108, 134, 228; SSC 6, 70; WLC 4**
See also AAYA 15, 52; AITN 1; AMWS 2; BEST 89:2; BPFB 2; BYA 11; CA 5-8R; CANR 25, 45, 74, 113, 129, 165; CDALB 1968-1988; CN 1, 2, 3, 4, 5, 6, 7; CP 5, 6, 7; CPW; CWP; DA; DA3; DAB; DAC; DAM MST, NOV, POP; DLB 2, 5, 130; DLBY 1981; EWL 3; EXPS; FL 1:6; FW; GL 3; HGG; INT CANR-25; LAIT 4; MAL 5; MBL; MTCW 1, 2; MTFW 2005; NFS 8, 24; RGAL 4; RGSF 2; SATA 159; SSFS 1, 8, 17; SUFW 2; TUS

**O'Brian, E. G.**
See Clarke, Arthur C.

**O'Brian, Patrick** 1914-2000 ............ **CLC 152**
See also AAYA 55; BRWS 12; CA 144; CAAS 187; CANR 74; CPW; MTCW 2; MTFW 2005; RHW

**O'Brien, Darcy** 1939-1998 ................ **CLC 11**
See also CA 21-24R; CAAS 167; CANR 8, 59

**O'Brien, Edna** 1932- ..... **CLC 3, 5, 8, 13, 36, 65, 116, 237; SSC 10, 77**
See also BRWS 5; CA 1-4R; CANR 6, 41, 65, 102, 169; CDBLB 1960 to Present; CN 1, 2, 3, 4, 5, 6, 7; DA3; DAM NOV; DLB 14, 231, 319; EWL 3; FW; MTCW 1, 2; MTFW 2005; RGSF 2; WLIT 4

**O'Brien, Fitz-James** 1828-1862 ..... **NCLC 21**
See also DLB 74; RGAL 4; SUFW

**O'Brien, Flann** .......... **CLC 1, 4, 5, 7, 10, 47**
See O Nuallain, Brian
See also BRWS 2; DLB 231; EWL 3; RGEL 2

**O'Brien, Richard** 1942- .................... **CLC 17**
See also CA 124

**O'Brien, Tim** 1946- ........ **CLC 7, 19, 40, 103, 211; SSC 74**
See also AAYA 16; AMWS 5; CA 85-88; CANR 40, 58, 133; CDALBS; CN 5, 6, 7; CPW; DA3; DAM POP; DLB 152; DLBD 9; DLBY 1980; LATS 1:2; MAL 5; MTCW 2; MTFW 2005; RGAL 4; SSFS 5, 15; TCLE 1:2

**Obstfelder, Sigbjoern** 1866-1900 .... **TCLC 23**
See also CAAE 123

**O'Casey, Sean** 1880-1964 .... **CLC 1, 5, 9, 11, 15, 88; DC 12; WLCS**
See also BRW 7; CA 89-92; CANR 62; CBD; CDBLB 1914-1945; DA3; DAB; DAC; DAM DRAM, MST; DFS 19; DLB 10; EWL 3; MTCW 1, 2; MTFW 2005; RGEL 2; TEA; WLIT 4

**O'Cathasaigh, Sean**
See O'Casey, Sean

**Occom, Samson** 1723-1792 .... **LC 60; NNAL**
See also DLB 175

**Occomy, Marita (Odette) Bonner**
1899(?)-1971
See Bonner, Marita
See also BW 2; CA 142; DFS 13; DLB 51, 228

**Ochs, Phil(ip David)** 1940-1976 ........ **CLC 17**
See also CA 185; CAAS 65-68

**O'Connor, Edwin (Greene)**
1918-1968 .................................. **CLC 14**
See also CA 93-96; CAAS 25-28R; MAL 5

**O'Connor, (Mary) Flannery**
1925-1964 .... **CLC 1, 2, 3, 6, 10, 13, 15, 21, 66, 104; SSC 1, 23, 61, 82; TCLC 132; WLC 4**
See also AAYA 7; AMW; AMWR 2; BPFB 3; BYA 16; CA 1-4R; CANR 3, 41; CDALB 1941-1968; DA; DA3; DAB; DAC; DAM MST, NOV; DLB 2, 152; DLBD 12; DLBY 1980; EWL 3; EXPS; LAIT 5; MAL 5; MBL; MTCW 1, 2; MTFW 2005; NFS 3, 21; RGAL 4; RGSF 2; SSFS 2, 7, 10, 19; TUS

**O'Connor, Frank** ................ **CLC 23; SSC 5**
See O'Donovan, Michael Francis
See also DLB 162; EWL 3; RGSF 2; SSFS 5

**O'Dell, Scott** 1898-1989 .................... **CLC 30**
See also AAYA 3, 44; BPFB 3; BYA 1, 2, 3, 5; CA 61-64; CAAS 129; CANR 12, 30, 112; CLR 1, 16; DLB 52; JRDA; MAICYA 1, 2; SATA 12, 60, 134; WYA; YAW

**Odets, Clifford** 1906-1963 ..... **CLC 2, 28, 98; DC 6**
See also AMWS 2; CA 85-88; CAD; CANR 62; DAM DRAM; DFS 3, 17, 20; DLB 7, 26; EWL 3; MAL 5; MTCW 1, 2; MTFW 2005; RGAL 4; TUS

**O'Doherty, Brian** 1928- .................... **CLC 76**
See also CA 105; CANR 108

**O'Donnell, K. M.**
See Malzberg, Barry N(athaniel)

**O'Donnell, Lawrence**
See Kuttner, Henry

**O'Donovan, Michael Francis**
1903-1966 .................................. **CLC 14**
See O'Connor, Frank
See also CA 93-96; CANR 84

**Oe, Kenzaburo** 1935- .. **CLC 10, 36, 86, 187; SSC 20**
See Oe Kenzaburo
See also CA 97-100; CANR 36, 50, 74, 126; DA3; DAM NOV; DLB 182, 331; DLBY 1994; LATS 1:2; MJW; MTCW 1, 2; MTFW 2005; RGSF 2; RGWL 2, 3

**Oe Kenzaburo**
See Oe, Kenzaburo
See also CWW 2; EWL 3

**O'Faolain, Julia** 1932- .... **CLC 6, 19, 47, 108**
See also CA 81-84; 2; CANR 12, 61; CN 2, 3, 4, 5, 6, 7; DLB 14, 231, 319; FW; MTCW 1; RHW

**O'Faolain, Sean** 1900-1991 ...... **CLC 1, 7, 14, 32, 70; SSC 13; TCLC 143**
See also CA 61-64; CAAS 134; CANR 12, 66; CN 1, 2, 3, 4; DLB 15, 162; MTCW 1, 2; MTFW 2005; RGEL 2; RGSF 2

**O'Flaherty, Liam** 1896-1984 ....... **CLC 5, 34; SSC 6**
See also CA 101; CAAS 113; CANR 35; CN 1, 2, 3; DLB 36, 162; DLBY 1984; MTCW 1, 2; MTFW 2005; RGEL 2; RGSF 2; SSFS 5, 20

**Ogai**
See Mori Ogai
See also MJW

**Ogilvy, Gavin**
See Barrie, J(ames) M(atthew)

**Parkin, Frank** 1940- .......................... **CLC 43**
   See also CA 147

**Parkman, Francis, Jr.** 1823-1893 .. **NCLC 12**
   See also AMWS 2; DLB 1, 30, 183, 186,
   235; RGAL 4

**Parks, Gordon** 1912-2006 .... **BLC 3; CLC 1,**
   **16**
   See also AAYA 36; AITN 2; BW 2, 3; CA
   41-44R; CAAS 249; CANR 26, 66, 145;
   DA3; DAM MULT; DLB 33; MTCW 2;
   MTFW 2005; SATA 8, 108; SATA-Obit
   175

**Parks, Suzan-Lori** 1964(?)- ................. **DC 23**
   See also AAYA 55; CA 201; CAD; CD 5,
   6; CWD; DFS 22; RGAL 4

**Parks, Tim(othy Harold)** 1954- ...... **CLC 147**
   See also CA 131; CAAE 126; CANR 77,
   144; CN 7; DLB 231; INT CA-131

**Parmenides** c. 515B.C.-c.
   450B.C. .................................... **CMLC 22**
   See also DLB 176

**Parnell, Thomas** 1679-1718 ................. **LC 3**
   See also DLB 95; RGEL 2

**Parr, Catherine** c. 1513(?)-1548 ......... **LC 86**
   See also DLB 136

**Parra, Nicanor** 1914- ... **CLC 2, 102; HLC 2;**
   **PC 39**
   See also CA 85-88; CANR 32; CWW 2;
   DAM MULT; DLB 283; EWL 3; HW 1;
   LAW; MTCW 1

**Parra Sanojo, Ana Teresa de la**
   1890-1936 ................................... **HLCS 2**
   See de la Parra, (Ana) Teresa (Sonojo)
   See also LAW

**Parrish, Mary Frances**
   See Fisher, M(ary) F(rances) K(ennedy)

**Parshchikov, Aleksei** 1954- ............... **CLC 59**
   See Parshchikov, Aleksei Maksimovich

**Parshchikov, Aleksei Maksimovich**
   See Parshchikov, Aleksei
   See also DLB 285

**Parson, Professor**
   See Coleridge, Samuel Taylor

**Parson Lot**
   See Kingsley, Charles

**Parton, Sara Payson Willis**
   1811-1872 ................................. **NCLC 86**
   See also DLB 43, 74, 239

**Partridge, Anthony**
   See Oppenheim, E(dward) Phillips

**Pascal, Blaise** 1623-1662 ...................... **LC 35**
   See also DLB 268; EW 3; GFL Beginnings
   to 1789; RGWL 2, 3; TWA

**Pascoli, Giovanni** 1855-1912 ......... **TCLC 45**
   See also CA 170; EW 7; EWL 3

**Pasolini, Pier Paolo** 1922-1975 .. **CLC 20, 37,**
   **106; PC 17**
   See also CA 93-96; CAAS 61-64; CANR
   63; DLB 128, 177; EWL 3; MTCW 1;
   RGWL 2, 3

**Pasquini**
   See Silone, Ignazio

**Pastan, Linda (Olenik)** 1932- ........... **CLC 27**
   See also CA 61-64; CANR 18, 40, 61, 113;
   CP 3, 4, 5, 6, 7; CSW; CWP; DAM
   POET; DLB 5; PFS 8, 25

**Pasternak, Boris** 1890-1960 ... **CLC 7, 10, 18,**
   **63; PC 6; SSC 31; TCLC 188; WLC 4**
   See also BPFB 3; CA 127; CAAS 116; DA;
   DA3; DAB; DAC; DAM MST, NOV,
   POET; DLB 302, 331; EW 10; MTCW 1,
   2; MTFW 2005; NFS 26; RGSF 2; RGWL
   2, 3; TWA; WP

**Patchen, Kenneth** 1911-1972 .... **CLC 1, 2, 18**
   See also BG 1:3; CA 1-4R; CAAS 33-36R;
   CANR 3, 35; CN 1; CP 1; DAM POET;
   DLB 16, 48; EWL 3; MAL 5; MTCW 1;
   RGAL 4

**Patchett, Ann** 1963- .......................... **CLC 244**
   See also AAYA 69; AMWS 12; CA 139;
   CANR 64, 110, 167; MTFW 2005

**Pater, Walter (Horatio)** 1839-1894 . **NCLC 7,**
   **90, 159**
   See also BRW 5; CDBLB 1832-1890; DLB
   57, 156; RGEL 2; TEA

**Paterson, A(ndrew) B(arton)**
   1864-1941 ................................. **TCLC 32**
   See also CA 155; DLB 230; RGEL 2; SATA
   97

**Paterson, Banjo**
   See Paterson, A(ndrew) B(arton)

**Paterson, Katherine** 1932- .......... **CLC 12, 30**
   See also AAYA 1, 31; BYA 1, 2, 7; CA 21-
   24R; CANR 28, 59, 111; CLR 7, 50;
   CWRI 5; DLB 52; JRDA; LAIT 4; MAI-
   CYA 1, 2; MAICYAS 1; MTCW 1; SATA
   13, 53, 92, 133; WYA; YAW

**Paterson, Katherine Womeldorf**
   See Paterson, Katherine

**Patmore, Coventry Kersey Dighton**
   1823-1896 ..................... **NCLC 9; PC 59**
   See also DLB 35, 98; RGEL 2; TEA

**Paton, Alan** 1903-1988 ..... **CLC 4, 10, 25, 55,**
   **106; TCLC 165; WLC 4**
   See also AAYA 26; AFW; BPFB 3; BRWS
   2; BYA 1; CA 13-16; CAAS 125; CANR
   22; CAP 1; CN 1, 2, 3, 4; DA; DA3;
   DAB; DAC; DAM MST, NOV; DLB 225;
   DLBD 17; EWL 3; EXPN; LAIT 4;
   MTCW 1, 2; MTFW 2005; NFS 3, 12;
   RGEL 2; SATA 11; SATA-Obit 56; TWA;
   WLIT 2; WWE 1

**Paton Walsh, Gillian**
   See Paton Walsh, Jill
   See also AAYA 47; BYA 1, 8

**Paton Walsh, Jill** 1937- ..................... **CLC 35**
   See Paton Walsh, Gillian; Walsh, Jill Paton
   See also AAYA 11; CA 262; 262; CANR
   38, 83, 158; CLR 2, 65; DLB 161; JRDA;
   MAICYA 1, 2; SAAS 3; SATA 4, 72, 109;
   YAW

**Patsauq, Markoosie** 1942- ................. **NNAL**
   See also CA 101; CLR 23; CWRI 5; DAM
   MULT

**Patterson, (Horace) Orlando (Lloyd)**
   1940- ......................................... **BLCS**
   See also BW 1; CA 65-68; CANR 27, 84;
   CN 1, 2, 3, 4, 5, 6

**Patton, George S(mith), Jr.**
   1885-1945 ................................. **TCLC 79**
   See also CA 189

**Paulding, James Kirke** 1778-1860 ... **NCLC 2**
   See also DLB 3, 59, 74, 250; RGAL 4

**Paulin, Thomas Neilson**
   See Paulin, Tom

**Paulin, Tom** 1949- ...................... **CLC 37, 177**
   See also CA 128; CAAE 123; CANR 98;
   CP 3, 4, 5, 6, 7; DLB 40

**Pausanias** c. 1st cent. - ................. **CMLC 36**

**Paustovsky, Konstantin (Georgievich)**
   1892-1968 ................................... **CLC 40**
   See also CA 93-96; CAAS 25-28R; DLB
   272; EWL 3

**Pavese, Cesare** 1908-1950 .... **PC 13; SSC 19;**
   **TCLC 3**
   See also CA 169; CAAE 104; DLB 128,
   177; EW 12; EWL 3; PFS 20; RGSF 2;
   RGWL 2, 3; TWA; WLIT 7

**Pavic, Milorad** 1929- .......................... **CLC 60**
   See also CA 136; CDWLB 4; CWW 2; DLB
   181; EWL 3; RGWL 3

**Pavlov, Ivan Petrovich** 1849-1936 . **TCLC 91**
   See also CA 180; CAAE 118

**Pavlova, Karolina Karlovna**
   1807-1893 ............................... **NCLC 138**
   See also DLB 205

**Payne, Alan**
   See Jakes, John

**Payne, Rachel Ann**
   See Jakes, John

**Paz, Gil**
   See Lugones, Leopoldo

**Paz, Octavio** 1914-1998 . **CLC 3, 4, 6, 10, 19,**
   **51, 65, 119; HLC 2; PC 1, 48; WLC 4**
   See also AAYA 50; CA 73-76; CAAS 165;
   CANR 32, 65, 104; CWW 2; DA; DA3;
   DAB; DAC; DAM MST, MULT, POET;
   DLB 290, 331; DLBY 1990, 1998; DNFS
   1; EWL 3; HW 1, 2; LAW; LAWS 1;
   MTCW 1, 2; MTFW 2005; PFS 18;
   RGWL 2, 3; SSFS 13; TWA; WLIT 1

**p'Bitek, Okot** 1931-1982 .... **BLC 3; CLC 96;**
   **TCLC 149**
   See also AFW; BW 2, 3; CA 124; CAAS
   107; CANR 82; CP 1, 2, 3; DAM MULT;
   DLB 125; EWL 3; MTCW 1, 2; MTFW
   2005; RGEL 2; WLIT 2

**Peabody, Elizabeth Palmer**
   1804-1894 ............................... **NCLC 169**
   See also DLB 1, 223

**Peacham, Henry** 1578-1644(?) ........... **LC 119**
   See also DLB 151

**Peacock, Molly** 1947- ....................... **CLC 60**
   See also CA 262; 103, 262; 21; CANR 52,
   84; CP 5, 6, 7; CWP; DLB 120, 282

**Peacock, Thomas Love**
   1785-1866 ............................... **NCLC 22**
   See also BRW 4; DLB 96, 116; RGEL 2;
   RGSF 2

**Peake, Mervyn** 1911-1968 ............. **CLC 7, 54**
   See also CA 5-8R; CAAS 25-28R; CANR
   3; DLB 15, 160, 255; FANT; MTCW 1;
   RGEL 2; SATA 23; SFW 4

**Pearce, Philippa** 1920-2006
   See Christie, Philippa
   See also CA 5-8R; CAAS 255; CANR 4,
   109; CWRI 5; FANT; MAICYA 2; SATA-
   Obit 179

**Pearl, Eric**
   See Elman, Richard (Martin)

**Pearson, Jean Mary**
   See Gardam, Jane

**Pearson, T. R.** 1956- .......................... **CLC 39**
   See also CA 130; CAAE 120; CANR 97,
   147; CSW; INT CA-130

**Pearson, Thomas Reid**
   See Pearson, T. R.

**Peck, Dale** 1967- ................................ **CLC 81**
   See also CA 146; CANR 72, 127; GLL 2

**Peck, John (Frederick)** 1941- ............. **CLC 3**
   See also CA 49-52; CANR 3, 100; CP 4, 5,
   6, 7

**Peck, Richard** 1934- .......................... **CLC 21**
   See also AAYA 1, 24; BYA 1, 6, 8, 11; CA
   85-88; CANR 19, 38, 129; CLR 15; INT
   CANR-19; JRDA; MAICYA 1, 2; SAAS
   2; SATA 18, 55, 97, 110, 158; SATA-
   Essay 110; WYA; YAW

**Peck, Richard Wayne**
   See Peck, Richard

**Peck, Robert Newton** 1928- ............. **CLC 17**
   See also AAYA 3, 43; BYA 1, 6; CA 182;
   81-84, 182; CANR 31, 63, 127; CLR 45;
   DA; DAC; DAM MST; JRDA; LAIT 3;
   MAICYA 1, 2; SAAS 1; SATA 21, 62,
   111, 156; SATA-Essay 108; WYA; YAW

**Peckinpah, David Samuel**
   See Peckinpah, Sam

**Peckinpah, Sam** 1925-1984 ............. **CLC 20**
   See also CA 109; CAAS 114; CANR 82

**Pedersen, Knut** 1859-1952
   See Hamsun, Knut
   See also CA 119; CAAE 104; CANR 63;
   MTCW 1, 2

**Peele, George** 1556-1596 ....... **DC 27; LC 115**
　　See also BRW 1; DLB 62, 167; RGEL 2
**Peeslake, Gaffer**
　　See Durrell, Lawrence (George)
**Peguy, Charles (Pierre)**
　　1873-1914 ............................. **TCLC 10**
　　See also CA 193; CAAE 107; DLB 258;
　　EWL 3; GFL 1789 to the Present
**Peirce, Charles Sanders**
　　1839-1914 .............................. **TCLC 81**
　　See also CA 194; DLB 270
**Pelecanos, George P.** 1957- ............. **CLC 236**
　　See also CA 138; CANR 122, 165; DLB
　　306
**Pelevin, Victor** 1962- ........................ **CLC 238**
　　See Pelevin, Viktor Olegovich
　　See also CA 154; CANR 88, 159
**Pelevin, Viktor Olegovich**
　　See Pelevin, Victor
　　See also DLB 285
**Pellicer, Carlos** 1897(?)-1977 ............ **HLCS 2**
　　See also CA 153; CAAS 69-72; DLB 290;
　　EWL 3; HW 1
**Pena, Ramon del Valle y**
　　See Valle-Inclan, Ramon (Maria) del
**Pendennis, Arthur Esquir**
　　See Thackeray, William Makepeace
**Penn, Arthur**
　　See Matthews, (James) Brander
**Penn, William** 1644-1718 .................... **LC 25**
　　See also DLB 24
**PEPECE**
　　See Prado (Calvo), Pedro
**Pepys, Samuel** 1633-1703 ... **LC 11, 58; WLC
　　4**
　　See also BRW 2; CDBLB 1660-1789; DA;
　　DA3; DAB; DAC; DAM MST; DLB 101,
　　213; NCFS 4; RGEL 2; TEA; WLIT 3
**Percy, Thomas** 1729-1811 ............... **NCLC 95**
　　See also DLB 104
**Percy, Walker** 1916-1990 ....... **CLC 2, 3, 6, 8,
　　14, 18, 47, 65**
　　See also AMWS 3; BPFB 3; CA 1-4R;
　　CAAS 131; CANR 1, 23, 64; CN 1, 2, 3,
　　4; CPW; CSW; DA3; DAM NOV, POP;
　　DLB 2; DLBY 1980, 1990; EWL 3; MAL
　　5; MTCW 1, 2; MTFW 2005; RGAL 4;
　　TUS
**Percy, William Alexander**
　　1885-1942 ............................... **TCLC 84**
　　See also CA 163; MTCW 2
**Perec, Georges** 1936-1982 ......... **CLC 56, 116**
　　See also CA 141; DLB 83, 299; EWL 3;
　　GFL 1789 to the Present; RGHL; RGWL
　　3
**Pereda (y Sanchez de Porrua), Jose Maria
　　de** 1833-1906 .......................... **TCLC 16**
　　See also CAAE 117
**Pereda y Porrua, Jose Maria de**
　　See Pereda (y Sanchez de Porrua), Jose
　　Maria de
**Peregoy, George Weems**
　　See Mencken, H(enry) L(ouis)
**Perelman, S(idney) J(oseph)**
　　1904-1979 .. **CLC 3, 5, 9, 15, 23, 44, 49;
　　SSC 32**
　　See also AITN 1, 2; BPFB 3; CA 73-76;
　　CAAS 89-92; CANR 18; DAM DRAM;
　　DLB 11, 44; MTCW 1, 2; MTFW 2005;
　　RGAL 4
**Peret, Benjamin** 1899-1959 .... **PC 33; TCLC
　　20**
　　See also CA 186; CAAE 117; GFL 1789 to
　　the Present
**Peretz, Isaac Leib**
　　See Peretz, Isaac Loeb
　　See also CA 201; DLB 333

**Peretz, Isaac Loeb** 1851(?)-1915 ...... **SSC 26;
　　TCLC 16**
　　See Peretz, Isaac Leib
　　See also CAAE 109
**Peretz, Yitzkhok Leibush**
　　See Peretz, Isaac Loeb
**Perez Galdos, Benito** 1843-1920 ..... **HLCS 2;
　　TCLC 27**
　　See Galdos, Benito Perez
　　See also CA 153; CAAE 125; EWL 3; HW
　　1; RGWL 2, 3
**Peri Rossi, Cristina** 1941- .. **CLC 156; HLCS
　　2**
　　See also CA 131; CANR 59, 81; CWW 2;
　　DLB 145, 290; EWL 3; HW 1, 2
**Perlata**
　　See Peret, Benjamin
**Perloff, Marjorie G(abrielle)**
　　1931- ...................................... **CLC 137**
　　See also CA 57-60; CANR 7, 22, 49, 104
**Perrault, Charles** 1628-1703 ........... **LC 2, 56**
　　See also BYA 4; CLR 79; DLB 268; GFL
　　Beginnings to 1789; MAICYA 1, 2;
　　RGWL 2, 3; SATA 25; WCH
**Perry, Anne** 1938- .......................... **CLC 126**
　　See also CA 101; CANR 22, 50, 84, 150;
　　CMW 4; CN 6, 7; CPW; DLB 276
**Perry, Brighton**
　　See Sherwood, Robert E(mmet)
**Perse, St.-John**
　　See Leger, (Marie-Rene Auguste) Alexis
　　Saint-Leger
**Perse, Saint-John**
　　See Leger, (Marie-Rene Auguste) Alexis
　　Saint-Leger
　　See also DLB 258, 331; RGWL 3
**Persius** 34-62 ................................. **CMLC 74**
　　See also AW 2; DLB 211; RGWL 2, 3
**Perutz, Leo(pold)** 1882-1957 ......... **TCLC 60**
　　See also CA 147; DLB 81
**Peseenz, Tulio F.**
　　See Lopez y Fuentes, Gregorio
**Pesetsky, Bette** 1932- ....................... **CLC 28**
　　See also CA 133; DLB 130
**Peshkov, Alexei Maximovich** 1868-1936
　　See Gorky, Maxim
　　See also CA 141; CAAE 105; CANR 83;
　　DA; DAC; DAM DRAM, MST, NOV;
　　MTCW 2; MTFW 2005
**Pessoa, Fernando (Antonio Nogueira)**
　　1888-1935 ..... **HLC 2; PC 20; TCLC 27**
　　See also CA 183; CAAE 125; DAM MULT;
　　DLB 287; EW 10; EWL 3; RGWL 2, 3;
　　WP
**Peterkin, Julia Mood** 1880-1961 ...... **CLC 31**
　　See also CA 102; DLB 9
**Peters, Joan K(aren)** 1945- .............. **CLC 39**
　　See also CA 158; CANR 109
**Peters, Robert L(ouis)** 1924- .............. **CLC 7**
　　See also CA 13-16R; 8; CP 1, 5, 6, 7; DLB
　　105
**Petofi, Sandor** 1823-1849 ............... **NCLC 21**
　　See also RGWL 2, 3
**Petrakis, Harry Mark** 1923- .............. **CLC 3**
　　See also CA 9-12R; CANR 4, 30, 85, 155;
　　CN 1, 2, 3, 4, 5, 6, 7
**Petrarch** 1304-1374 ............... **CMLC 20; PC 8**
　　See also DA3; DAM POET; EW 2; LMFS
　　1; RGWL 2, 3; WLIT 7
**Petronius** c. 20-66 .......................... **CMLC 34**
　　See also AW 2; CDWLB 1; DLB 211;
　　RGWL 2, 3; WLIT 8
**Petrov, Evgeny** .............................. **TCLC 21**
　　See Kataev, Evgeny Petrovich
**Petry, Ann (Lane)** 1908-1997 .. **CLC 1, 7, 18;
　　TCLC 112**
　　See also AFAW 1, 2; BPFB 3; BW 1, 3;
　　BYA 2; CA 5-8R; 6; CAAS 157; CANR
　　4, 46; CLR 12; CN 1, 2, 3, 4, 5, 6; DLB

76; EWL 3; JRDA; LAIT 1; MAICYA 1,
　　2; MAICYAS 1; MTCW 1; RGAL 4;
　　SATA 5; SATA-Obit 94; TUS
**Petursson, Halligrimur** 1614-1674 ........ **LC 8**
**Peychinovich**
　　See Vazov, Ivan (Minchov)
**Phaedrus** c. 15B.C.-c. 50 ................. **CMLC 25**
　　See also DLB 211
**Phelps (Ward), Elizabeth Stuart**
　　See Phelps, Elizabeth Stuart
　　See also FW
**Phelps, Elizabeth Stuart**
　　1844-1911 ............................. **TCLC 113**
　　See Phelps (Ward), Elizabeth Stuart
　　See also CA 242; DLB 74
**Philips, Katherine** 1632-1664 . **LC 30; PC 40**
　　See also DLB 131; RGEL 2
**Philipson, Ilene J.** 1950- ................... **CLC 65**
　　See also CA 219
**Philipson, Morris H.** 1926- .............. **CLC 53**
　　See also CA 1-4R; CANR 4
**Phillips, Caryl** 1958- ..... **BLCS; CLC 96, 224**
　　See also BRWS 5; BW 2; CA 141; CANR
　　63, 104, 140; CBD; CD 5, 6; CN 5, 6, 7;
　　DA3; DAM MULT; DLB 157; EWL 3;
　　MTCW 2; MTFW 2005; WLIT 4; WWE
　　1
**Phillips, David Graham**
　　1867-1911 ............................... **TCLC 44**
　　See also CA 176; CAAE 108; DLB 9, 12,
　　303; RGAL 4
**Phillips, Jack**
　　See Sandburg, Carl (August)
**Phillips, Jayne Anne** 1952- ........ **CLC 15, 33,
　　139; SSC 16**
　　See also AAYA 57; BPFB 3; CA 101;
　　CANR 24, 50, 96; CN 4, 5, 6, 7; CSW;
　　DLBY 1980; INT CANR-24; MTCW 1,
　　2; MTFW 2005; RGAL 4; RGSF 2; SSFS
　　4
**Phillips, Richard**
　　See Dick, Philip K.
**Phillips, Robert (Schaeffer)** 1938- .... **CLC 28**
　　See also CA 17-20R; 13; CANR 8; DLB
　　105
**Phillips, Ward**
　　See Lovecraft, H. P.
**Philostratus, Flavius** c. 179-c.
　　244 ....................................... **CMLC 62**
**Piccolo, Lucio** 1901-1969 ................... **CLC 13**
　　See also CA 97-100; DLB 114; EWL 3
**Pickthall, Marjorie L(owry) C(hristie)**
　　1883-1922 ............................... **TCLC 21**
　　See also CAAE 107; DLB 92
**Pico della Mirandola, Giovanni**
　　1463-1494 .................................. **LC 15**
　　See also LMFS 1
**Piercy, Marge** 1936- .... **CLC 3, 6, 14, 18, 27,
　　62, 128; PC 29**
　　See also BPFB 3; CA 187; 21-24R, 187; 1;
　　CANR 13, 43, 66, 111; CN 3, 4, 5, 6, 7;
　　CP 1, 2, 3, 4, 5, 6, 7; CWP; DLB 120,
　　227; EXPP; FW; MAL 5; MTCW 1, 2;
　　MTFW 2005; PFS 9, 22; SFW 4
**Piers, Robert**
　　See Anthony, Piers
**Pieyre de Mandiargues, Andre** 1909-1991
　　See Mandiargues, Andre Pieyre de
　　See also CA 103; CAAS 136; CANR 22,
　　82; EWL 3; GFL 1789 to the Present
**Pilnyak, Boris** 1894-1938 . **SSC 48; TCLC 23**
　　See Vogau, Boris Andreyevich
　　See also EWL 3
**Pinchback, Eugene**
　　See Toomer, Jean

**Prishvin, Mikhail Mikhailovich**
See Prishvin, Mikhail
See also DLB 272; EWL 3

**Pritchard, William H(arrison)**
1932- ........................................ **CLC 34**
See also CA 65-68; CANR 23, 95; DLB
111

**Pritchett, V(ictor) S(awdon)**
1900-1997 ... **CLC 5, 13, 15, 41; SSC 14**
See also BPFB 3; BRWS 3; CA 61-64;
CAAS 157; CANR 31, 63; CN 1, 2, 3, 4,
5, 6; DA3; DAM NOV; DLB 15, 139;
EWL 3; MTCW 1, 2; MTFW 2005; RGEL
2; RGSF 2; TEA

**Private 19022**
See Manning, Frederic

**Probst, Mark** 1925- ........................... **CLC 59**
See also CA 130

**Procaccino, Michael**
See Cristofer, Michael

**Proclus** c. 412-c. 485 ...................... **CMLC 81**

**Prokosch, Frederic** 1908-1989 ...... **CLC 4, 48**
See also CA 73-76; CAAS 128; CANR 82;
CN 1, 2, 3, 4; CP 1, 2, 3, 4; DLB 48;
MTCW 2

**Propertius, Sextus** c. 50B.C.-c.
16B.C. .......................................... **CMLC 32**
See also AW 2; CDWLB 1; DLB 211;
RGWL 2, 3; WLIT 8

**Prophet, The**
See Dreiser, Theodore

**Prose, Francine** 1947- .............. **CLC 45, 231**
See also AMWS 16; CA 112; CAAE 109;
CANR 46, 95, 132; DLB 234; MTFW
2005; SATA 101, 149

**Protagoras** c. 490B.C.-420B.C. ...... **CMLC 85**
See also DLB 176

**Proudhon**
See Cunha, Euclides (Rodrigues Pimenta)
da

**Proulx, Annie**
See Proulx, E. Annie

**Proulx, E. Annie** 1935- .............. **CLC 81, 158**
See also AMWS 7; BPFB 3; CA 145;
CANR 65, 110; CN 6, 7; CPW 1; DA3;
DAM POP; DLB 335; MAL 5; MTCW 2;
MTFW 2005; SSFS 18, 23

**Proulx, Edna Annie**
See Proulx, E. Annie

**Proust, (Valentin-Louis-George-Eugene)
Marcel** 1871-1922 ..... **SSC 75; TCLC 7,
13, 33; WLC 5**
See also AAYA 58; BPFB 3; CA 120;
CAAE 104; CANR 110; DA; DA3; DAB;
DAC; DAM MST, NOV; DLB 65; EW 8;
EWL 3; GFL 1789 to the Present; MTCW
1, 2; MTFW 2005; RGWL 2, 3; TWA

**Prowler, Harley**
See Masters, Edgar Lee

**Prudentius, Aurelius Clemens** 348-c.
405 ........................................... **CMLC 78**
See also EW 1; RGWL 2, 3

**Prudhomme, Rene Francois Armand**
1839-1907
See Sully Prudhomme, Rene-Francois-
Armand
See also CA 170

**Prus, Boleslaw** 1845-1912 .............. **TCLC 48**
See also RGWL 2, 3

**Pryor, Aaron Richard**
See Pryor, Richard

**Pryor, Richard** 1940-2005 ................. **CLC 26**
See also CA 152; CAAE 122; CAAS 246

**Pryor, Richard Franklin Lenox Thomas**
See Pryor, Richard

**Przybyszewski, Stanislaw**
1868-1927 ................................. **TCLC 36**
See also CA 160; DLB 66; EWL 3

**Pseudo-Dionysius the Areopagite** fl. c. 5th
cent. - ...................................... **CMLC 89**
See also DLB 115

**Pteleon**
See Grieve, C(hristopher) M(urray)
See also DAM POET

**Puckett, Lute**
See Masters, Edgar Lee

**Puig, Manuel** 1932-1990 .... **CLC 3, 5, 10, 28,
65, 133; HLC 2**
See also BPFB 3; CA 45-48; CANR 2, 32,
63; CDWLB 3; DA3; DAM MULT; DLB
113; DNFS 1; EWL 3; GLL 1; HW 1, 2;
LAW; MTCW 1, 2; MTFW 2005; RGWL
2, 3; TWA; WLIT 1

**Pulitzer, Joseph** 1847-1911 ............. **TCLC 76**
See also CAAE 114; DLB 23

**Pullman, Philip** 1946- ..................... **CLC 245**
See also AAYA 15, 41; BRWS 13; BYA 8,
13; CA 127; CANR 50, 77, 105, 134;
CLR 20, 62, 84; JRDA; MAICYA 1, 2;
MAICYAS 1; MTFW 2005; SAAS 17;
SATA 65, 103, 150; SUFW 2; WYAS 1;
YAW

**Purchas, Samuel** 1577(?)-1626 ............. **LC 70**
See also DLB 151

**Purdy, A(lfred) W(ellington)**
1918-2000 ................... **CLC 3, 6, 14, 50**
See also CA 81-84; 17; CAAS 189; CANR
42, 66; CP 1, 2, 3, 4, 5, 6, 7; DAC; DAM
MST, POET; DLB 88; PFS 5; RGEL 2

**Purdy, James (Amos)** 1923- .... **CLC 2, 4, 10,
28, 52**
See also AMWS 7; CA 33-36R; 1; CANR
19, 51, 132; CN 1, 2, 3, 4, 5, 6, 7; DLB
2, 218; EWL 3; INT CANR-19; MAL 5;
MTCW 1; RGAL 4

**Pure, Simon**
See Swinnerton, Frank Arthur

**Pushkin, Aleksandr Sergeevich**
See Pushkin, Alexander (Sergeyevich)
See also DLB 205

**Pushkin, Alexander (Sergeyevich)**
1799-1837 ....... **NCLC 3, 27, 83; PC 10;
SSC 27, 55, 99; WLC 5**
See Pushkin, Aleksandr Sergeevich
See also DA; DA3; DAB; DAC; DAM
DRAM, MST, POET; EW 5; EXPS; RGSF
2; RGWL 2, 3; SATA 61; SSFS 9; TWA

**P'u Sung-ling** 1640-1715 ....... **LC 49; SSC 31**

**Putnam, Arthur Lee**
See Alger, Horatio, Jr.

**Puttenham, George** 1529(?)-1590 ...... **LC 116**
See also DLB 281

**Puzo, Mario** 1920-1999 ........ **CLC 1, 2, 6, 36,
107**
See also BPFB 3; CA 65-68; CAAS 185;
CANR 4, 42, 65, 99, 131; CN 1, 2, 3, 4,
5, 6; CPW; DA3; DAM NOV, POP; DLB
6; MTCW 1, 2; MTFW 2005; NFS 16;
RGAL 4

**Pygge, Edward**
See Barnes, Julian

**Pyle, Ernest Taylor** 1900-1945
See Pyle, Ernie
See also CA 160; CAAE 115

**Pyle, Ernie** ....................................... **TCLC 75**
See Pyle, Ernest Taylor
See also DLB 29; MTCW 2

**Pyle, Howard** 1853-1911 ................. **TCLC 81**
See also AAYA 57; BYA 2, 4; CA 137;
CAAE 109; CLR 22, 117; DLB 42, 188;
DLBD 13; LAIT 1; MAICYA 1, 2; SATA
16, 100; WCH; YAW

**Pym, Barbara (Mary Crampton)**
1913-1980 .............. **CLC 13, 19, 37, 111**
See also BPFB 3; BRWS 2; CA 13-14;
CAAS 97-100; CANR 13, 34; CAP 1;
DLB 14, 207; DLBY 1987; EWL 3;
MTCW 1, 2; MTFW 2005; RGEL 2; TEA

**Pynchon, Thomas** 1937- .. **CLC 2, 3, 6, 9, 11,
18, 33, 62, 72, 123, 192, 213; SSC 14,
84; WLC 5**
See also AMWS 2; BEST 90:2; BPFB 3;
CA 17-20R; CANR 22, 46, 73, 142; CN
1, 2, 3, 4, 5, 6, 7; CPW 1; DA; DA3;
DAB; DAC; DAM MST, NOV, POP;
DLB 2, 173; EWL 3; MAL 5; MTCW 1,
2; MTFW 2005; NFS 23; RGAL 4; SFW
4; TCLE 1:2; TUS

**Pythagoras** c. 582B.C.-c. 507B.C. . **CMLC 22**
See also DLB 176

**Q**
See Quiller-Couch, Sir Arthur (Thomas)

**Qian, Chongzhu**
See Ch'ien, Chung-shu

**Qian, Sima** 145B.C.-c. 89B.C. ....... **CMLC 72**

**Qian Zhongshu**
See Ch'ien, Chung-shu
See also CWW 2; DLB 328

**Qroll**
See Dagerman, Stig (Halvard)

**Quarles, Francis** 1592-1644 .............. **LC 117**
See also DLB 126; RGEL 2

**Quarrington, Paul (Lewis)** 1953- ..... **CLC 65**
See also CA 129; CANR 62, 95

**Quasimodo, Salvatore** 1901-1968 .... **CLC 10;
PC 47**
See also CA 13-16; CAAS 25-28R; CAP 1;
DLB 114, 332; EW 12; EWL 3; MTCW
1; RGWL 2, 3

**Quatermass, Martin**
See Carpenter, John (Howard)

**Quay, Stephen** 1947- ......................... **CLC 95**
See also CA 189

**Quay, Timothy** 1947- ......................... **CLC 95**
See also CA 189

**Queen, Ellery** ............................... **CLC 3, 11**
See Dannay, Frederic; Davidson, Avram
(James); Deming, Richard; Fairman, Paul
W.; Flora, Fletcher; Hoch, Edward
D(entinger); Kane, Henry; Lee, Manfred
B.; Marlowe, Stephen; Powell, (Oval) Tal-
mage; Sheldon, Walter J(ames); Sturgeon,
Theodore (Hamilton); Tracy, Don(ald
Fiske); Vance, Jack
See also BPFB 3; CMW 4; MSW; RGAL 4

**Queen, Ellery, Jr.**
See Dannay, Frederic; Lee, Manfred B.

**Queneau, Raymond** 1903-1976 ..... **CLC 2, 5,
10, 42**
See also CA 77-80; CAAS 69-72; CANR
32; DLB 72, 258; EW 12; EWL 3; GFL
1789 to the Present; MTCW 1, 2; RGWL
2, 3

**Quevedo, Francisco de** 1580-1645 ....... **LC 23**

**Quiller-Couch, Sir Arthur (Thomas)**
1863-1944 ................................. **TCLC 53**
See also CA 166; CAAE 118; DLB 135,
153, 190; HGG; RGEL 2; SUFW 1

**Quin, Ann** 1936-1973 ......................... **CLC 6**
See also CA 9-12R; CAAS 45-48; CANR
148; CN 1; DLB 14, 231

**Quin, Ann Marie**
See Quin, Ann

**Quincey, Thomas de**
See De Quincey, Thomas

**Quindlen, Anna** 1953- ..................... **CLC 191**
See also AAYA 35; AMWS 17; CA 138;
CANR 73, 126; DA3; DLB 292; MTCW
2; MTFW 2005

**Quinn, Martin**
See Smith, Martin Cruz

**Quinn, Peter** 1947- ......................... **CLC 91**
See also CA 197; CANR 147

**Quinn, Peter A.**
See Quinn, Peter

**Quinn, Simon**
See Smith, Martin Cruz

**Richter, Conrad (Michael)**
    1890-1968 ................... **CLC 30**
    See also AAYA 21; BYA 2; CA 5-8R;
    CAAS 25-28R; CANR 23; DLB 9, 212;
    LAIT 1; MAL 5; MTCW 1, 2; MTFW
    2005; RGAL 4; SATA 3; TCWW 1, 2;
    TUS; YAW
**Ricostranza, Tom**
    See Ellis, Trey
**Riddell, Charlotte** 1832-1906 ......... **TCLC 40**
    See Riddell, Mrs. J. H.
    See also CA 165; DLB 156
**Riddell, Mrs. J. H.**
    See Riddell, Charlotte
    See also HGG; SUFW
**Ridge, John Rollin** 1827-1867 ...... **NCLC 82;**
    **NNAL**
    See also CA 144; DAM MULT; DLB 175
**Ridgeway, Jason**
    See Marlowe, Stephen
**Ridgway, Keith** 1965- ...................... **CLC 119**
    See also CA 172; CANR 144
**Riding, Laura** ............................... **CLC 3, 7**
    See Jackson, Laura (Riding)
    See also CP 1, 2, 3, 4, 5; RGAL 4
**Riefenstahl, Berta Helene Amalia** 1902-2003
    See Riefenstahl, Leni
    See also CA 108; CAAS 220
**Riefenstahl, Leni** ..................... **CLC 16, 190**
    See Riefenstahl, Berta Helene Amalia
**Riffe, Ernest**
    See Bergman, Ingmar
**Riffe, Ernest Ingmar**
    See Bergman, Ingmar
**Riggs, (Rolla) Lynn**
    1899-1954 ................... **NNAL; TCLC 56**
    See also CA 144; DAM MULT; DLB 175
**Riis, Jacob A(ugust)** 1849-1914 ..... **TCLC 80**
    See also CA 168; CAAE 113; DLB 23
**Riley, James Whitcomb** 1849-1916 .... **PC 48;**
    **TCLC 51**
    See also CA 137; CAAE 118; DAM POET;
    MAICYA 1, 2; RGAL 4; SATA 17
**Riley, Tex**
    See Creasey, John
**Rilke, Rainer Maria** 1875-1926 ........... **PC 2;**
    **TCLC 1, 6, 19, 195**
    See also CA 132; CAAE 104; CANR 62,
    99; CDWLB 2; DA3; DAM POET; DLB
    81; EW 9; EWL 3; MTCW 1, 2; MTFW
    2005; PFS 19, 27; RGWL 2, 3; TWA; WP
**Rimbaud, (Jean Nicolas) Arthur**
    1854-1891 ... **NCLC 4, 35, 82; PC 3, 57;**
    **WLC 5**
    See also DA; DA3; DAB; DAC; DAM
    MST, POET; DLB 217; EW 7; GFL 1789
    to the Present; LMFS 2; RGWL 2, 3;
    TWA; WP
**Rinehart, Mary Roberts**
    1876-1958 ............................... **TCLC 52**
    See also BPFB 3; CA 166; CAAE 108;
    RGAL 4; RHW
**Ringmaster, The**
    See Mencken, H(enry) L(ouis)
**Ringwood, Gwen(dolyn Margaret) Pharis**
    1910-1984 ............................... **CLC 48**
    See also CA 148; CAAS 112; DLB 88
**Rio, Michel** 1945(?)- .......................... **CLC 43**
    See also CA 201
**Rios, Alberto** 1952- ............................ **PC 57**
    See also AAYA 66; AMWS 4; CA 113;
    CANR 34, 79, 137; CP 6, 7; DLB 122;
    HW 2; MTFW 2005; PFS 11
**Ritsos, Giannes**
    See Ritsos, Yannis
**Ritsos, Yannis** 1909-1990 ........ **CLC 6, 13, 31**
    See also CA 77-80; CAAS 133; CANR 39,
    61; EW 12; EWL 3; MTCW 1; RGWL 2,
    3

**Ritter, Erika** 1948(?)- ..................... **CLC 52**
    See also CD 5, 6; CWD
**Rivera, Jose Eustasio** 1889-1928 ... **TCLC 35**
    See also CA 162; EWL 3; HW 1, 2; LAW
**Rivera, Tomas** 1935-1984 ................. **HLCS 2**
    See also CA 49-52; CANR 32; DLB 82;
    HW 1; LLW; RGAL 4; SSFS 15; TCWW
    2; WLIT 1
**Rivers, Conrad Kent** 1933-1968 ........ **CLC 1**
    See also BW 1; CA 85-88; DLB 41
**Rivers, Elfrida**
    See Bradley, Marion Zimmer
    See also GLL 1
**Riverside, John**
    See Heinlein, Robert A.
**Rizal, Jose** 1861-1896 ..................... **NCLC 27**
**Roa Bastos, Augusto** 1917-2005 ...... **CLC 45;**
    **HLC 2**
    See also CA 131; CAAS 238; CWW 2;
    DAM MULT; DLB 113; EWL 3; HW 1;
    LAW; RGSF 2; WLIT 1
**Roa Bastos, Augusto Jose Antonio**
    See Roa Bastos, Augusto
**Robbe-Grillet, Alain** 1922- .... **CLC 1, 2, 4, 6,**
    **8, 10, 14, 43, 128**
    See also BPFB 3; CA 9-12R; CANR 33,
    65, 115; CWW 2; DLB 83; EW 13; EWL
    3; GFL 1789 to the Present; IDFW 3, 4;
    MTCW 1, 2; MTFW 2005; RGWL 2, 3;
    SSFS 15
**Robbins, Harold** 1916-1997 ................ **CLC 5**
    See also BPFB 3; CA 73-76; CAAS 162;
    CANR 26, 54, 112, 156; DA3; DAM
    NOV; MTCW 1, 2
**Robbins, Thomas Eugene** 1936-
    See Robbins, Tom
    See also CA 81-84; CANR 29, 59, 95, 139;
    CN 7; CPW; CSW; DA3; DAM NOV,
    POP; MTCW 1, 2; MTFW 2005
**Robbins, Tom** ......................... **CLC 9, 32, 64**
    See Robbins, Thomas Eugene
    See also AAYA 32; AMWS 10; BEST 90:3;
    BPFB 3; CN 3, 4, 5, 6, 7; DLBY 1980
**Robbins, Trina** 1938- ....................... **CLC 21**
    See also AAYA 61; CA 128; CANR 152
**Robert de Boron** fl. 12th cent. - .... **CMLC 94**
**Roberts, Charles G(eorge) D(ouglas)**
    1860-1943 ................... **SSC 91; TCLC 8**
    See also CA 188; CAAE 105; CLR 33;
    CWRI 5; DLB 92; RGEL 2; RGSF 2;
    SATA 88; SATA-Brief 29
**Roberts, Elizabeth Madox**
    1886-1941 ............................... **TCLC 68**
    See also CA 166; CAAE 111; CLR 100;
    CWRI 5; DLB 9, 54, 102; RGAL 4;
    RHW; SATA 33; SATA-Brief 27; TCWW
    2; WCH
**Roberts, Kate** 1891-1985 ................. **CLC 15**
    See also CA 107; CAAS 116; DLB 319
**Roberts, Keith (John Kingston)**
    1935-2000 ............................... **CLC 14**
    See also BRWS 10; CA 25-28R; CANR 46;
    DLB 261; SFW 4
**Roberts, Kenneth (Lewis)**
    1885-1957 ............................... **TCLC 23**
    See also CA 199; CAAE 109; DLB 9; MAL
    5; RGAL 4; RHW
**Roberts, Michele** 1949- ............. **CLC 48, 178**
    See also CA 115; CANR 58, 120, 164; CN
    6, 7; DLB 231; FW
**Roberts, Michele Brigitte**
    See Roberts, Michele
**Robertson, Ellis**
    See Ellison, Harlan; Silverberg, Robert
**Robertson, Thomas William**
    1829-1871 ............................... **NCLC 35**
    See Robertson, Tom
    See also DAM DRAM

**Robertson, Tom**
    See Robertson, Thomas William
    See also RGEL 2
**Robeson, Kenneth**
    See Dent, Lester
**Robinson, Edwin Arlington**
    1869-1935 ......... **PC 1, 35; TCLC 5, 101**
    See also AAYA 72; AMW; CA 133; CAAE
    104; CDALB 1865-1917; DA; DAC;
    DAM MST, POET; DLB 54; EWL 3;
    EXPP; MAL 5; MTCW 1, 2; MTFW
    2005; PAB; PFS 4; RGAL 4; WP
**Robinson, Henry Crabb**
    1775-1867 ............................... **NCLC 15**
    See also DLB 107
**Robinson, Jill** 1936- ......................... **CLC 10**
    See also CA 102; CANR 120; INT CA-102
**Robinson, Kim Stanley** 1952- ........... **CLC 34**
    See also AAYA 26; CA 126; CANR 113,
    139; CN 6, 7; MTFW 2005; SATA 109;
    SCFW 2; SFW 4
**Robinson, Lloyd**
    See Silverberg, Robert
**Robinson, Marilynne** 1944- ...... **CLC 25, 180**
    See also AAYA 69; CA 116; CANR 80, 140;
    CN 4, 5, 6, 7; DLB 206; MTFW 2005;
    NFS 24
**Robinson, Mary** 1758-1800 .......... **NCLC 142**
    See also BRWS 13; DLB 158; FW
**Robinson, Smokey** ........................... **CLC 21**
    See Robinson, William, Jr.
**Robinson, William, Jr.** 1940-
    See Robinson, Smokey
    See also CAAE 116
**Robison, Mary** 1949- .................. **CLC 42, 98**
    See also CA 116; CAAE 113; CANR 87;
    CN 4, 5, 6, 7; DLB 130; INT CA-116;
    RGSF 2
**Roches, Catherine des** 1542-1587 ...... **LC 117**
    See also DLB 327
**Rochester**
    See Wilmot, John
    See also RGEL 2
**Rod, Edouard** 1857-1910 ................ **TCLC 52**
**Roddenberry, Eugene Wesley** 1921-1991
    See Roddenberry, Gene
    See also CA 110; CAAS 135; CANR 37;
    SATA 45; SATA-Obit 69
**Roddenberry, Gene** ........................... **CLC 17**
    See Roddenberry, Eugene Wesley
    See also AAYA 5; SATA-Obit 69
**Rodgers, Mary** 1931- ....................... **CLC 12**
    See also BYA 5; CA 49-52; CANR 8, 55,
    90; CLR 20; CWRI 5; INT CANR-8;
    JRDA; MAICYA 1, 2; SATA 8, 130
**Rodgers, W(illiam) R(obert)**
    1909-1969 ............................... **CLC 7**
    See also CA 85-88; DLB 20; RGEL 2
**Rodman, Eric**
    See Silverberg, Robert
**Rodman, Howard** 1920(?)-1985 ........ **CLC 65**
    See also CAAS 118
**Rodman, Maia**
    See Wojciechowska, Maia (Teresa)
**Rodo, Jose Enrique** 1871(?)-1917 .... **HLCS 2**
    See also CA 178; EWL 3; HW 2; LAW
**Rodolph, Utto**
    See Ouologuem, Yambo
**Rodriguez, Claudio** 1934-1999 ......... **CLC 10**
    See also CA 188; DLB 134
**Rodriguez, Richard** 1944- .... **CLC 155; HLC**
    **2**
    See also AMWS 14; CA 110; CANR 66,
    116; DAM MULT; DLB 82, 256; HW 1,
    2; LAIT 5; LLW; MTFW 2005; NCFS 3;
    WLIT 1
**Roelvaag, O(le) E(dvart)** 1876-1931
    See Rolvaag, O(le) E(dvart)
    See also AAYA 75; CA 171; CAAE 117

**Roethke, Theodore (Huebner)**
1908-1963 ......... **CLC 1, 3, 8, 11, 19, 46, 101; PC 15**
See also AMW; CA 81-84; CABS 2; CDALB 1941-1968; DA3; DAM POET; DLB 5, 206; EWL 3; EXPP; MAL 5; MTCW 1, 2; PAB; PFS 3; RGAL 4; WP

**Rogers, Carl R(ansom)**
1902-1987 ............................. **TCLC 125**
See also CA 1-4R; CAAS 121; CANR 1, 18; MTCW 1

**Rogers, Samuel** 1763-1855 ............. **NCLC 69**
See also DLB 93; RGEL 2

**Rogers, Thomas** 1927-2007 .............. **CLC 57**
See also CA 89-92; CAAS 259; CANR 163; INT CA-89-92

**Rogers, Thomas Hunton**
See Rogers, Thomas

**Rogers, Will(iam Penn Adair)**
1879-1935 .............. **NNAL; TCLC 8, 71**
See also CA 144; CAAE 105; DA3; DAM MULT; DLB 11; MTCW 2

**Rogin, Gilbert** 1929- ......................... **CLC 18**
See also CA 65-68; CANR 15

**Rohan, Koda**
See Koda Shigeyuki

**Rohlfs, Anna Katharine Green**
See Green, Anna Katharine

**Rohmer, Eric** ................................... **CLC 16**
See Scherer, Jean-Marie Maurice

**Rohmer, Sax** ................................. **TCLC 28**
See Ward, Arthur Henry Sarsfield
See also DLB 70; MSW; SUFW

**Roiphe, Anne** 1935- ......................... **CLC 3, 9**
See also CA 89-92; CANR 45, 73, 138; DLBY 1980; INT CA-89-92

**Roiphe, Anne Richardson**
See Roiphe, Anne

**Rojas, Fernando de** 1475-1541 ... **HLCS 1, 2; LC 23**
See also DLB 286; RGWL 2, 3

**Rojas, Gonzalo** 1917- ......................... **HLCS 2**
See also CA 178; HW 2; LAWS 1

**Roland (de la Platiere), Marie-Jeanne**
1754-1793 ..................................... **LC 98**
See also DLB 314

**Rolfe, Frederick (William Serafino Austin Lewis Mary)** 1860-1913 ......... **TCLC 12**
See Al Siddik
See also CA 210; CAAE 107; DLB 34, 156; RGEL 2

**Rolland, Romain** 1866-1944 .......... **TCLC 23**
See also CA 197; CAAE 118; DLB 65, 284, 332; EWL 3; GFL 1789 to the Present; RGWL 2, 3

**Rolle, Richard** c. 1300-c. 1349 ...... **CMLC 21**
See also DLB 146; LMFS 1; RGEL 2

**Rolvaag, O(le) E(dvart)** ................. **TCLC 17**
See Roelvaag, O(le) E(dvart)
See also DLB 9, 212; MAL 5; NFS 5; RGAL 4

**Romain Arnaud, Saint**
See Aragon, Louis

**Romains, Jules** 1885-1972 ................. **CLC 7**
See also CA 85-88; CANR 34; DLB 65, 321; EWL 3; GFL 1789 to the Present; MTCW 1

**Romero, Jose Ruben** 1890-1952 .... **TCLC 14**
See also CA 131; CAAE 114; EWL 3; HW 1; LAW

**Ronsard, Pierre de** 1524-1585 . **LC 6, 54; PC 11**
See also DLB 327; EW 2; GFL Beginnings to 1789; RGWL 2, 3; TWA

**Rooke, Leon** 1934- ..................... **CLC 25, 34**
See also CA 25-28R; CANR 23, 53; CCA 1; CPW; DAM POP

**Roosevelt, Franklin Delano**
1882-1945 ................................. **TCLC 93**
See also CA 173; CAAE 116; LAIT 3

**Roosevelt, Theodore** 1858-1919 ..... **TCLC 69**
See also CA 170; CAAE 115; DLB 47, 186, 275

**Roper, William** 1498-1578 ................... **LC 10**

**Roquelaure, A. N.**
See Rice, Anne

**Rosa, Joao Guimaraes** 1908-1967 ... **CLC 23; HLCS 1**
See Guimaraes Rosa, Joao
See also CAAS 89-92; DLB 113, 307; EWL 3; WLIT 1

**Rose, Wendy** 1948- . **CLC 85; NNAL; PC 13**
See also CA 53-56; CANR 5, 51; CWP; DAM MULT; DLB 175; PFS 13; RGAL 4; SATA 12

**Rosen, R. D.**
See Rosen, Richard (Dean)

**Rosen, Richard (Dean)** 1949- .......... **CLC 39**
See also CA 77-80; CANR 62, 120; CMW 4; INT CANR-30

**Rosenberg, Isaac** 1890-1918 .......... **TCLC 12**
See also BRW 6; CA 188; CAAE 107; DLB 20, 216; EWL 3; PAB; RGEL 2

**Rosenblatt, Joe** ........................... **CLC 15**
See Rosenblatt, Joseph
See also CP 3, 4, 5, 6, 7

**Rosenblatt, Joseph** 1933-
See Rosenblatt, Joe
See also CA 89-92; CP 1, 2; INT CA-89-92

**Rosenfeld, Samuel**
See Tzara, Tristan

**Rosenstock, Sami**
See Tzara, Tristan

**Rosenstock, Samuel**
See Tzara, Tristan

**Rosenthal, M(acha) L(ouis)**
1917-1996 ................................. **CLC 28**
See also CA 1-4R; 6; CAAS 152; CANR 4, 51; CP 1, 2, 3, 4, 5, 6; DLB 5; SATA 59

**Ross, Barnaby**
See Dannay, Frederic; Lee, Manfred B.

**Ross, Bernard L.**
See Follett, Ken

**Ross, J. H.**
See Lawrence, T(homas) E(dward)

**Ross, John Hume**
See Lawrence, T(homas) E(dward)

**Ross, Martin** 1862-1915
See Martin, Violet Florence
See also DLB 135; GLL 2; RGEL 2; RGSF 2

**Ross, (James) Sinclair** 1908-1996 ... **CLC 13; SSC 24**
See also CA 73-76; CANR 81; CN 1, 2, 3, 4, 5, 6; DAC; DAM MST; DLB 88; RGEL 2; RGSF 2; TCWW 1, 2

**Rossetti, Christina** 1830-1894 ... **NCLC 2, 50, 66, 186; PC 7; WLC 5**
See also AAYA 51; BRW 5; BYA 4; CLR 115; DA; DA3; DAB; DAC; DAM MST, POET; DLB 35, 163, 240; EXPP; FL 1:3; LATS 1:1; MAICYA 1, 2; PFS 10, 14, 27; RGEL 2; SATA 20; TEA; WCH

**Rossetti, Christina Georgina**
See Rossetti, Christina

**Rossetti, Dante Gabriel** 1828-1882 . **NCLC 4, 77; PC 44; WLC 5**
See also AAYA 51; BRW 5; CDBLB 1832-1890; DA; DAB; DAC; DAM MST, POET; DLB 35; EXPP; RGEL 2; TEA

**Rossi, Cristina Peri**
See Peri Rossi, Cristina

**Rossi, Jean-Baptiste** 1931-2003
See Japrisot, Sebastien
See also CA 201; CAAS 215

**Rossner, Judith** 1935-2005 ........ **CLC 6, 9, 29**
See also AITN 2; BEST 90:3; BPFB 3; CA 17-20R; CAAS 242; CANR 18, 51, 73; CN 4, 5, 6, 7; DLB 6; INT CANR-18; MAL 5; MTCW 1, 2; MTFW 2005

**Rossner, Judith Perelman**
See Rossner, Judith

**Rostand, Edmond (Eugene Alexis)**
1868-1918 ............... **DC 10; TCLC 6, 37**
See also CA 126; CAAE 104; DA; DA3; DAB; DAC; DAM DRAM; DFS 1; DLB 192; LAIT 1; MTCW 1; RGWL 2, 3; TWA

**Roth, Henry** 1906-1995 ..... **CLC 2, 6, 11, 104**
See also AMWS 9; CA 11-12; CAAS 149; CANR 38, 63; CAP 1; CN 1, 2, 3, 4, 5, 6; DA3; DLB 28; EWL 3; MAL 5; MTCW 1, 2; MTFW 2005; RGAL 4

**Roth, (Moses) Joseph** 1894-1939 ... **TCLC 33**
See also CA 160; DLB 85; EWL 3; RGWL 2, 3

**Roth, Philip** 1933- ... **CLC 1, 2, 3, 4, 6, 9, 15, 22, 31, 47, 66, 86, 119, 201; SSC 26, 102; WLC 5**
See also AAYA 67; AMWR 2; AMWS 3; BEST 90:3; BPFB 3; CA 1-4R; CANR 1, 22, 36, 55, 89, 132; CDALB 1968-1988; CN 3, 4, 5, 6, 7; CPW 1; DA; DA3; DAB; DAC; DAM MST, NOV, POP; DLB 2, 28, 173; DLBY 1982; EWL 3; MAL 5; MTCW 1, 2; MTFW 2005; NFS 25; RGAL 4; RGHL; RGSF 2; SSFS 12, 18; TUS

**Roth, Philip Milton**
See Roth, Philip

**Rothenberg, Jerome** 1931- ........... **CLC 6, 57**
See also CA 45-48; CANR 1, 106; CP 1, 2, 3, 4, 5, 6, 7; DLB 5, 193

**Rotter, Pat** ........................................ **CLC 65**

**Roumain, Jacques (Jean Baptiste)**
1907-1944 ................... **BLC 3; TCLC 19**
See also BW 1; CA 125; CAAE 117; DAM MULT; EWL 3

**Rourke, Constance Mayfield**
1885-1941 ................................. **TCLC 12**
See also CA 200; CAAE 107; MAL 5; YABC 1

**Rousseau, Jean-Baptiste** 1671-1741 ...... **LC 9**

**Rousseau, Jean-Jacques** 1712-1778 .... **LC 14, 36, 122; WLC 5**
See also DA; DA3; DAB; DAC; DAM MST; DLB 314; EW 4; GFL Beginnings to 1789; LMFS 1; RGWL 2, 3; TWA

**Roussel, Raymond** 1877-1933 ........ **TCLC 20**
See also CA 201; CAAE 117; EWL 3; GFL 1789 to the Present

**Rovit, Earl (Herbert)** 1927- ............... **CLC 7**
See also CA 5-8R; CANR 12

**Rowe, Elizabeth Singer** 1674-1737 ..... **LC 44**
See also DLB 39, 95

**Rowe, Nicholas** 1674-1718 .................... **LC 8**
See also DLB 84; RGEL 2

**Rowlandson, Mary** 1637(?)-1678 ......... **LC 66**
See also DLB 24, 200; RGAL 4

**Rowley, Ames Dorrance**
See Lovecraft, H. P.

**Rowley, William** 1585(?)-1626 ... **LC 100, 123**
See also DFS 22; DLB 58; RGEL 2

**Rowling, J.K.** 1965- ................. **CLC 137, 217**
See also AAYA 34; BYA 11, 13, 14; CA 173; CANR 128, 157; CLR 66, 80, 112; MAICYA 2; MTFW 2005; SATA 109, 174; SUFW 2

**Rowling, Joanne Kathleen**
See Rowling, J.K.

**Rowson, Susanna Haswell**
1762(?)-1824 ............... **NCLC 5, 69, 182**
See also AMWS 15; DLB 37, 200; RGAL 4

**Sarraute, Nathalie** 1900-1999 .... **CLC 1, 2, 4, 8, 10, 31, 80; TCLC 145**
See also BPFB 3; CA 9-12R; CAAS 187; CANR 23, 66, 134; CWW 2; DLB 83, 321; EW 12; EWL 3; GFL 1789 to the Present; MTCW 1, 2; MTFW 2005; RGWL 2, 3

**Sarton, May** 1912-1995 ... **CLC 4, 14, 49, 91; PC 39; TCLC 120**
See also AMWS 8; CA 1-4R; CAAS 149; CANR 1, 34, 55, 116; CN 1, 2, 3, 4, 5, 6; CP 1, 2, 3, 4, 5, 6; DAM POET; DLB 48; DLBY 1981; EWL 3; FW; INT CANR-34; MAL 5; MTCW 1, 2; MTFW 2005; RGAL 4; SATA 36; SATA-Obit 86; TUS

**Sartre, Jean-Paul** 1905-1980 . **CLC 1, 4, 7, 9, 13, 18, 24, 44, 50, 52; DC 3; SSC 32; WLC 5**
See also AAYA 62; CA 9-12R; CAAS 97-100; CANR 21; DA; DA3; DAB; DAC; DAM DRAM, MST, NOV; DFS 5; DLB 72, 296, 321, 332; EW 12; EWL 3; GFL 1789 to the Present; LMFS 2; MTCW 1, 2; MTFW 2005; NFS 21; RGHL; RGSF 2; RGWL 2, 3; SSFS 9; TWA

**Sassoon, Siegfried (Lorraine)** 1886-1967 ............. **CLC 36, 130; PC 12**
See also BRW 6; CA 104; CAAS 25-28R; CANR 36; DAB; DAM MST, NOV, POET; DLB 20, 191; DLBD 18; EWL 3; MTCW 1, 2; MTFW 2005; PAB; RGEL 2; TEA

**Satterfield, Charles**
See Pohl, Frederik

**Satyremont**
See Peret, Benjamin

**Saul, John (W. III)** 1942- .................. **CLC 46**
See also AAYA 10, 62; BEST 90:4; CA 81-84; CANR 16, 40, 81; CPW; DAM NOV, POP; HGG; SATA 98

**Saunders, Caleb**
See Heinlein, Robert A.

**Saura (Atares), Carlos** 1932-1998 .... **CLC 20**
See also CA 131; CAAE 114; CANR 79; HW 1

**Sauser, Frederic Louis**
See Sauser-Hall, Frederic

**Sauser-Hall, Frederic** 1887-1961 ...... **CLC 18**
See Cendrars, Blaise
See also CA 102; CAAS 93-96; CANR 36, 62; MTCW 1

**Saussure, Ferdinand de** 1857-1913 ............................... **TCLC 49**
See also DLB 242

**Savage, Catharine**
See Brosman, Catharine Savage

**Savage, Richard** 1697(?)-1743 ............. **LC 96**
See also DLB 95; RGEL 2

**Savage, Thomas** 1915-2003 ............... **CLC 40**
See also CA 132; 15; CAAE 126; CAAS 218; CN 6, 7; INT CA-132; SATA-Obit 147; TCWW 2

**Savan, Glenn** 1953-2003 .................... **CLC 50**
See also CA 225

**Sax, Robert**
See Johnson, Robert

**Saxo Grammaticus** c. 1150-c. 1222 ........................................ **CMLC 58**

**Saxton, Robert**
See Johnson, Robert

**Sayers, Dorothy L(eigh)** 1893-1957 . **SSC 71; TCLC 2, 15**
See also BPFB 3; BRWS 3; CA 119; CAAE 104; CANR 60; CDBLB 1914-1945; CMW 4; DAM POP; DLB 10, 36, 77, 100; MSW; MTCW 1, 2; MTFW 2005; RGEL 2; SSFS 12; TEA

**Sayers, Valerie** 1952- .................. **CLC 50, 122**
See also CA 134; CANR 61; CSW

**Sayles, John (Thomas)** 1950- ....... **CLC 7, 10, 14, 198**
See also CA 57-60; CANR 41, 84; DLB 44

**Scamander, Newt**
See Rowling, J.K.

**Scammell, Michael** 1935- .................. **CLC 34**
See also CA 156

**Scannell, Vernon** 1922-2007 ............. **CLC 49**
See also CA 5-8R; CANR 8, 24, 57, 143; CN 1, 2; CP 1, 2, 3, 4, 5, 6, 7; CWRI 5; DLB 27; SATA 59

**Scarlett, Susan**
See Streatfeild, (Mary) Noel

**Scarron** 1847-1910
See Mikszath, Kalman

**Scarron, Paul** 1610-1660 .................... **LC 116**
See also GFL Beginnings to 1789; RGWL 2, 3

**Schaeffer, Susan Fromberg** 1941- ..... **CLC 6, 11, 22**
See also CA 49-52; CANR 18, 65, 160; CN 4, 5, 6, 7; DLB 28, 299; MTCW 1, 2; MTFW 2005; SATA 22

**Schama, Simon** 1945- ..................... **CLC 150**
See also BEST 89:4; CA 105; CANR 39, 91, 168

**Schama, Simon Michael**
See Schama, Simon

**Schary, Jill**
See Robinson, Jill

**Schell, Jonathan** 1943- ..................... **CLC 35**
See also CA 73-76; CANR 12, 117

**Schelling, Friedrich Wilhelm Joseph von** 1775-1854 .......................... **NCLC 30**
See also DLB 90

**Scherer, Jean-Marie Maurice** 1920-
See Rohmer, Eric
See also CA 110

**Schevill, James (Erwin)** 1920- ............ **CLC 7**
See also CA 5-8R; 12; CAD; CD 5, 6; CP 1, 2, 3, 4, 5

**Schiller, Friedrich von** 1759-1805 ...... **DC 12; NCLC 39, 69, 166**
See also CDWLB 2; DAM DRAM; DLB 94; EW 5; RGWL 2, 3; TWA

**Schisgal, Murray (Joseph)** 1926- ....... **CLC 6**
See also CA 21-24R; CAD; CANR 48, 86; CD 5, 6; MAL 5

**Schlee, Ann** 1934- ............................. **CLC 35**
See also CA 101; CANR 29, 88; SATA 44; SATA-Brief 36

**Schlegel, August Wilhelm von** 1767-1845 ......................... **NCLC 15, 142**
See also DLB 94; RGWL 2, 3

**Schlegel, Friedrich** 1772-1829 ........ **NCLC 45**
See also DLB 90; EW 5; RGWL 2, 3; TWA

**Schlegel, Johann Elias (von)** 1719(?)-1749 ............................ **LC 5**

**Schleiermacher, Friedrich** 1768-1834 ............................... **NCLC 107**
See also DLB 90

**Schlesinger, Arthur M., Jr.** 1917-2007 ................................... **CLC 84**
See Schlesinger, Arthur Meier
See also AITN 1; CA 1-4R; CAAS 257; CANR 1, 28, 58, 105; DLB 17; INT CANR-28; MTCW 1, 2; SATA 61; SATA-Obit 181

**Schlink, Bernhard** 1944- ................. **CLC 174**
See also CA 163; CANR 116; RGHL

**Schmidt, Arno (Otto)** 1914-1979 ...... **CLC 56**
See also CA 128; CAAS 109; DLB 69; EWL 3

**Schmitz, Aron Hector** 1861-1928
See Svevo, Italo
See also CA 122; CAAE 104; MTCW 1

**Schnackenberg, Gjertrud** 1953- ...... **CLC 40; PC 45**
See also AMWS 15; CAAE 116; CANR 100; CP 5, 6, 7; CWP; DLB 120, 282; PFS 13, 25

**Schnackenberg, Gjertrud Cecelia**
See Schnackenberg, Gjertrud

**Schneider, Leonard Alfred** 1925-1966
See Bruce, Lenny
See also CA 89-92

**Schnitzler, Arthur** 1862-1931 ..... **DC 17; SSC 15, 61; TCLC 4**
See also CAAE 104; CDWLB 2; DLB 81, 118; EW 8; EWL 3; RGSF 2; RGWL 2, 3

**Schoenberg, Arnold Franz Walter** 1874-1951 ............................... **TCLC 75**
See also CA 188; CAAE 109

**Schonberg, Arnold**
See Schoenberg, Arnold Franz Walter

**Schopenhauer, Arthur** 1788-1860 . **NCLC 51, 157**
See also DLB 90; EW 5

**Schor, Sandra (M.)** 1932(?)-1990 ..... **CLC 65**
See also CAAS 132

**Schorer, Mark** 1908-1977 .................. **CLC 9**
See also CA 5-8R; CAAS 73-76; CANR 7; CN 1, 2; DLB 103

**Schrader, Paul (Joseph)** 1946- . **CLC 26, 212**
See also CA 37-40R; CANR 41; DLB 44

**Schreber, Daniel** 1842-1911 ......... **TCLC 123**

**Schreiner, Olive (Emilie Albertina)** 1855-1920 ........................... **TCLC 9**
See also AFW; BRWS 2; CA 154; CAAE 105; DLB 18, 156, 190, 225; EWL 3; FW; RGEL 2; TWA; WLIT 2; WWE 1

**Schulberg, Budd (Wilson)** 1914- .. **CLC 7, 48**
See also BPFB 3; CA 25-28R; CANR 19, 87; CN 1, 2, 3, 4, 5, 6, 7; DLB 6, 26, 28; DLBY 1981, 2001; MAL 5

**Schulman, Arnold**
See Trumbo, Dalton

**Schulz, Bruno** 1892-1942 .. **SSC 13; TCLC 5, 51**
See also CA 123; CAAE 115; CANR 86; CDWLB 4; DLB 215; EWL 3; MTCW 2; MTFW 2005; RGSF 2; RGWL 2, 3

**Schulz, Charles M.** 1922-2000 .......... **CLC 12**
See also AAYA 39; CA 9-12R; CAAS 187; CANR 6, 132; INT CANR-6; MTFW 2005; SATA 10; SATA-Obit 118

**Schulz, Charles Monroe**
See Schulz, Charles M.

**Schumacher, E(rnst) F(riedrich)** 1911-1977 .................................. **CLC 80**
See also CA 81-84; CAAS 73-76; CANR 34, 85

**Schumann, Robert** 1810-1856 ...... **NCLC 143**

**Schuyler, George Samuel** 1895-1977 . **HR 1:3**
See also BW 2; CA 81-84; CAAS 73-76; CANR 42; DLB 29, 51

**Schuyler, James Marcus** 1923-1991 .. **CLC 5, 23**
See also CA 101; CAAS 134; CP 1, 2, 3, 4, 5; DAM POET; DLB 5, 169; EWL 3; INT CA-101; MAL 5; WP

**Schwartz, Delmore (David)** 1913-1966 . **CLC 2, 4, 10, 45, 87; PC 8; SSC 105**
See also AMWS 2; CA 17-18; CAAS 25-28R; CANR 35; CAP 2; DLB 28, 48; EWL 3; MAL 5; MTCW 1, 2; MTFW 2005; PAB; RGAL 4; TUS

**Schwartz, Ernst**
See Ozu, Yasujiro

**Schwartz, John Burnham** 1965- ....... **CLC 59**
See also CA 132; CANR 116

**Schwartz, Lynne Sharon** 1939- ........ **CLC 31**
See also CA 103; CANR 44, 89, 160; DLB 218; MTCW 2; MTFW 2005

**Sewall, Samuel** 1652-1730 .................... **LC 38**
  See also DLB 24; RGAL 4
**Sexton, Anne (Harvey)** 1928-1974 ..... **CLC 2, 4, 6, 8, 10, 15, 53, 123; PC 2, 79; WLC 5**
  See also AMWS 2; CA 1-4R; CAAS 53-56; CABS 2; CANR 3, 36; CDALB 1941-1968; CP 1, 2; DA; DA3; DAB; DAC; DAM MST, POET; DLB 5, 169; EWL 3; EXPP; FL 1:6; FW; MAL 5; MBL; MTCW 1, 2; MTFW 2005; PAB; PFS 4, 14; RGAL 4; RGHL; SATA 10; TUS
**Shaara, Jeff** 1952- ............................ **CLC 119**
  See also AAYA 70; CA 163; CANR 109; CN 7; MTFW 2005
**Shaara, Michael** 1929-1988 .............. **CLC 15**
  See also AAYA 71; AITN 1; BPFB 3; CA 102; CAAS 125; CANR 52, 85; DAM POP; DLBY 1983; MTFW 2005; NFS 26
**Shackleton, C.C.**
  See Aldiss, Brian W.
**Shacochis, Bob** ............................... **CLC 39**
  See Shacochis, Robert G.
**Shacochis, Robert G.** 1951-
  See Shacochis, Bob
  See also CA 124; CAAE 119; CANR 100; INT CA-124
**Shadwell, Thomas** 1641(?)-1692 ........ **LC 114**
  See also DLB 80; IDTP; RGEL 2
**Shaffer, Anthony** 1926-2001 ............ **CLC 19**
  See also CA 116; CAAE 110; CAAS 200; CBD; CD 5, 6; DAM DRAM; DFS 13; DLB 13
**Shaffer, Anthony Joshua**
  See Shaffer, Anthony
**Shaffer, Peter** 1926- ... **CLC 5, 14, 18, 37, 60; DC 7**
  See also BRWS 1; CA 25-28R; CANR 25, 47, 74, 118; CBD; CD 5, 6; CDBLB 1960 to Present; DA3; DAB; DAM DRAM, MST; DFS 5, 13; DLB 13, 233; EWL 3; MTCW 1, 2; MTFW 2005; RGEL 2; TEA
**Shakespeare, William** 1564-1616 ....... **WLC 5**
  See also AAYA 35; BRW 1; CDBLB Before 1660; DA; DA3; DAB; DAC; DAM DRAM, MST, POET; DFS 20, 21; DLB 62, 172, 263; EXPP; LAIT 1; LATS 1:1; LMFS 1; PAB; PFS 1, 2, 3, 4, 5, 8, 9; RGEL 2; TEA; WLIT 3; WP; WS; WYA
**Shakey, Bernard**
  See Young, Neil
**Shalamov, Varlam (Tikhonovich)** 1907-1982 ................................. **CLC 18**
  See also CA 129; CAAS 105; DLB 302; RGSF 2
**Shamloo, Ahmad**
  See Shamlu, Ahmad
**Shamlou, Ahmad**
  See Shamlu, Ahmad
**Shamlu, Ahmad** 1925-2000 .............. **CLC 10**
  See also CA 216; CWW 2
**Shammas, Anton** 1951- ..................... **CLC 55**
  See also CA 199
**Shandling, Arline**
  See Berriault, Gina
**Shange, Ntozake** 1948- ... **BLC 3; CLC 8, 25, 38, 74, 126; DC 3**
  See also AAYA 9, 66; AFAW 1, 2; BW 2; CA 85-88; CABS 3; CAD; CANR 27, 48, 74, 131; CD 5, 6; CP 5, 6, 7; CWD; CWP; DA3; DAM DRAM, MULT; DFS 2, 11; DLB 38, 249; FW; LAIT 4, 5; MAL 5; MTCW 1, 2; MTFW 2005; NFS 11; RGAL 4; SATA 157; YAW
**Shanley, John Patrick** 1950- ............. **CLC 75**
  See also AAYA 74; AMWS 14; CA 133; CAAE 128; CAD; CANR 83, 154; CD 5, 6; DFS 23

**Shapcott, Thomas W(illiam)** 1935- .. **CLC 38**
  See also CA 69-72; CANR 49, 83, 103; CP 1, 2, 3, 4, 5, 6, 7; DLB 289
**Shapiro, Jane** 1942- ......................... **CLC 76**
  See also CA 196
**Shapiro, Karl** 1913-2000 ... **CLC 4, 8, 15, 53; PC 25**
  See also AMWS 2; CA 1-4R; 6; CAAS 188; CANR 1, 36, 66; CP 1, 2, 3, 4, 5, 6; DLB 48; EWL 3; EXPP; MAL 5; MTCW 1, 2; MTFW 2005; PFS 3; RGAL 4
**Sharp, William** 1855-1905 .............. **TCLC 39**
  See Macleod, Fiona
  See also CA 160; DLB 156; RGEL 2
**Sharpe, Thomas Ridley** 1928-
  See Sharpe, Tom
  See also CA 122; CAAE 114; CANR 85; INT CA-122
**Sharpe, Tom** ................................... **CLC 36**
  See Sharpe, Thomas Ridley
  See also CN 4, 5, 6, 7; DLB 14, 231
**Shatrov, Mikhail** ........................... **CLC 59**
**Shaw, Bernard**
  See Shaw, George Bernard
  See also DLB 10, 57, 190
**Shaw, G. Bernard**
  See Shaw, George Bernard
**Shaw, George Bernard** 1856-1950 ..... **DC 23; TCLC 3, 9, 21, 45; WLC 5**
  See Shaw, Bernard
  See also AAYA 61; BRW 6; BRWC 1; BRWR 2; CA 128; CAAE 104; CDBLB 1914-1945; DA; DA3; DAB; DAC; DAM DRAM, MST; DFS 1, 3, 6, 11, 19, 22; DLB 332; EWL 3; LAIT 3; LATS 1:1; MTCW 1, 2; MTFW 2005; RGEL 2; TEA; WLIT 4
**Shaw, Henry Wheeler** 1818-1885 .. **NCLC 15**
  See also DLB 11; RGAL 4
**Shaw, Irwin** 1913-1984 ........... **CLC 7, 23, 34**
  See also AITN 1; BPFB 3; CA 13-16R; CAAS 112; CANR 21; CDALB 1941-1968; CN 1, 2, 3; CPW; DAM DRAM, POP; DLB 6, 102; DLBY 1984; MAL 5; MTCW 1, 21; MTFW 2005
**Shaw, Robert (Archibald)** 1927-1978 ................................. **CLC 5**
  See also AITN 1; CA 1-4R; CAAS 81-84; CANR 4; CN 1, 2; DLB 13, 14
**Shaw, T. E.**
  See Lawrence, T(homas) E(dward)
**Shawn, Wallace** 1943- ..................... **CLC 41**
  See also CA 112; CAD; CD 5, 6; DLB 266
**Shaykh, al- Hanan**
  See al-Shaykh, Hanan
  See also CWW 2; EWL 3
**Shchedrin, N.**
  See Saltykov, Mikhail Evgrafovich
**Shea, Lisa** 1953- ............................. **CLC 86**
  See also CA 147
**Sheed, Wilfrid (John Joseph)** 1930- . **CLC 2, 4, 10, 53**
  See also CA 65-68; CANR 30, 66; CN 1, 2, 3, 4, 5, 6, 7; DLB 6; MAL 5; MTCW 1, 2; MTFW 2005
**Sheehy, Gail** 1937- .......................... **CLC 171**
  See also CA 49-52; CANR 1, 33, 55, 92; CPW; MTCW 1
**Sheldon, Alice Hastings Bradley** 1915(?)-1987
  See Tiptree, James, Jr.
  See also CA 108; CAAS 122; CANR 34; INT CA-108; MTCW 1
**Sheldon, John**
  See Bloch, Robert (Albert)
**Sheldon, Walter J(ames)** 1917-1996
  See Queen, Ellery
  See also AITN 1; CA 25-28R; CANR 10

**Shelley, Mary Wollstonecraft (Godwin)** 1797-1851 ........ **NCLC 14, 59, 103, 170; SSC 92; WLC 5**
  See also AAYA 20; BPFB 3; BRW 3; BRWC 2; BRWS 3; BYA 5; CDBLB 1789-1832; DA; DA3; DAB; DAC; DAM MST, NOV; DLB 110, 116, 159, 178; EXPN; FL 1:3; GL 3; HGG; LAIT 1; LMFS 1, 2; NFS 1; RGEL 2; SATA 29; SCFW 1, 2; SFW 4; TEA; WLIT 3
**Shelley, Percy Bysshe** 1792-1822 .. **NCLC 18, 93, 143, 175; PC 14, 67; WLC 5**
  See also AAYA 61; BRW 4; BRWR 1; CD-BLB 1789-1832; DA; DA3; DAB; DAC; DAM MST, POET; DLB 96, 110, 158; EXPP; LMFS 1; PAB; PFS 2, 27; RGEL 2; TEA; WLIT 3; WP
**Shepard, James R.**
  See Shepard, Jim
**Shepard, Jim** 1956- .......................... **CLC 36**
  See also AAYA 73; CA 137; CANR 59, 104, 160; SATA 90, 164
**Shepard, Lucius** 1947- ...................... **CLC 34**
  See also CA 141; CAAE 128; CANR 81, 124; HGG; SCFW 2; SFW 4; SUFW 2
**Shepard, Sam** 1943- .... **CLC 4, 6, 17, 34, 41, 44, 169; DC 5**
  See also AAYA 1, 58; AMWS 3; CA 69-72; CABS 3; CAD; CANR 22, 120, 140; CD 5, 6; DA3; DAM DRAM; DFS 3, 6, 7, 14; DLB 7, 212; EWL 3; IDFW 3, 4; MAL 5; MTCW 1, 2; MTFW 2005; RGAL 4
**Shepherd, Jean (Parker)** 1921-1999 ................. **TCLC 177**
  See also AAYA 69; AITN 2; CA 77-80; CAAS 187
**Shepherd, Michael**
  See Ludlum, Robert
**Sherburne, Zoa (Lillian Morin)** 1912-1995 ................................. **CLC 30**
  See also AAYA 13; CA 1-4R; CAAS 176; CANR 3, 37; MAICYA 1, 2; SAAS 18; SATA 3; YAW
**Sheridan, Frances** 1724-1766 ................. **LC 7**
  See also DLB 39, 84
**Sheridan, Richard Brinsley** 1751-1816 . **DC 1; NCLC 5, 91; WLC 5**
  See also BRW 3; CDBLB 1660-1789; DA; DAB; DAC; DAM DRAM, MST; DFS 15; DLB 89; WLIT 3
**Sherman, Jonathan Marc** 1968- ....... **CLC 55**
  See also CA 230
**Sherman, Martin** 1941(?)- ................ **CLC 19**
  See also CA 123; CAAE 116; CAD; CANR 86; CD 5, 6; DFS 20; DLB 228; GLL 1; IDTP; RGHL
**Sherwin, Judith Johnson**
  See Johnson, Judith (Emlyn)
  See also CANR 85; CP 2, 3, 4, 5; CWP
**Sherwood, Frances** 1940- ................. **CLC 81**
  See also CA 220; 146, 220; CANR 158
**Sherwood, Robert E(mmet)** 1896-1955 ................................. **TCLC 3**
  See also CA 153; CAAE 104; CANR 86; DAM DRAM; DFS 11, 15, 17; DLB 7, 26, 249; IDFW 3, 4; MAL 5; RGAL 4
**Shestov, Lev** 1866-1938 ................. **TCLC 56**
**Shevchenko, Taras** 1814-1861 ........ **NCLC 54**
**Shiel, M(atthew) P(hipps)** 1865-1947 ................................. **TCLC 8**
  See Holmes, Gordon
  See also CA 160; CAAE 106; DLB 153; HGG; MTCW 2; MTFW 2005; SCFW 1, 2; SFW 4; SUFW
**Shields, Carol** 1935-2003 .. **CLC 91, 113, 193**
  See also AMWS 7; CA 81-84; CAAS 218; CANR 51, 74, 98, 133; CCA 1; CN 6, 7; CPW; DA3; DAC; DLB 334; MTCW 2; MTFW 2005; NFS 23

**Spacks, Barry (Bernard)** 1931- ........ **CLC 14**
See also CA 154; CANR 33, 109; CP 3, 4, 5, 6, 7; DLB 105

**Spanidou, Irini** 1946- .......................... **CLC 44**
See also CA 185

**Spark, Muriel** 1918-2006 ....... **CLC 2, 3, 5, 8, 13, 18, 40, 94, 242; PC 72; SSC 10**
See also BRWS 1; CA 5-8R; CAAS 251; CANR 12, 36, 76, 89, 131; CDBLB 1945-1960; CN 1, 2, 3, 4, 5, 6, 7; CP 1, 2, 3, 4, 5, 6, 7; DA3; DAB; DAC; DAM MST, NOV; DLB 15, 139; EWL 3; FW; INT CANR-12; LAIT 4; MTCW 1, 2; MTFW 2005; NFS 22; RGEL 2; TEA; WLIT 4; YAW

**Spark, Muriel Sarah**
See Spark, Muriel

**Spaulding, Douglas**
See Bradbury, Ray

**Spaulding, Leonard**
See Bradbury, Ray

**Speght, Rachel** 1597-c. 1630 ................ **LC 97**
See also DLB 126

**Spence, J. A. D.**
See Eliot, T(homas) S(tearns)

**Spencer, Anne** 1882-1975 ...... **HR 1:3; PC 77**
See also BW 2; CA 161; DLB 51, 54

**Spencer, Elizabeth** 1921- .... **CLC 22; SSC 57**
See also CA 13-16R; CANR 32, 65, 87; CN 1, 2, 3, 4, 5, 6, 7; CSW; DLB 6, 218; EWL 3; MTCW 1; RGAL 4; SATA 14

**Spencer, Leonard G.**
See Silverberg, Robert

**Spencer, Scott** 1945- .......................... **CLC 30**
See also CA 113; CANR 51, 148; DLBY 1986

**Spender, Stephen** 1909-1995 ..... **CLC 1, 2, 5, 10, 41, 91; PC 71**
See also BRWS 2; CA 9-12R; CAAS 149; CANR 31, 54; CDBLB 1945-1960; CP 1, 2, 3, 4, 5, 6; DA3; DAM POET; DLB 20; EWL 3; MTCW 1, 2; MTFW 2005; PAB; PFS 23; RGEL 2; TEA

**Spengler, Oswald (Arnold Gottfried)** 1880-1936 .............................. **TCLC 25**
See also CA 189; CAAE 118

**Spenser, Edmund** 1552(?)-1599 ...... **LC 5, 39, 117; PC 8, 42; WLC 5**
See also AAYA 60; BRW 1; CDBLB Before 1660; DA; DA3; DAB; DAC; DAM MST, POET; DLB 167; EFS 2; EXPP; PAB; RGEL 2; TEA; WLIT 3; WP

**Spicer, Jack** 1925-1965 .......... **CLC 8, 18, 72**
See also BG 1:3; CA 85-88; DAM POET; DLB 5, 16, 193; GLL 1; WP

**Spiegelman, Art** 1948- .............. **CLC 76, 178**
See also AAYA 10, 46; CA 125; CANR 41, 55, 74, 124; DLB 299; MTCW 2; MTFW 2005; RGHL; SATA 109, 158; YAW

**Spielberg, Peter** 1929- ........................ **CLC 6**
See also CA 5-8R; CANR 4, 48; DLBY 1981

**Spielberg, Steven** 1947- ............ **CLC 20, 188**
See also AAYA 8, 24; CA 77-80; CANR 32; SATA 32

**Spillane, Frank Morrison**
See Spillane, Mickey
See also BPFB 3; CMW 4; DLB 226; MSW

**Spillane, Mickey** 1918-2006 .. **CLC 3, 13, 241**
See Spillane, Frank Morrison
See also CA 25-28R; CAAS 252; CANR 28, 63, 125; DA3; MTCW 1, 2; MTFW 2005; SATA 66; SATA-Obit 176

**Spinoza, Benedictus de** 1632-1677 .. **LC 9, 58**

**Spinrad, Norman (Richard)** 1940- ... **CLC 46**
See also BPFB 3; CA 233; 37-40R, 233; 19; CANR 20, 91; DLB 8; INT CANR-20; SFW 4

**Spitteler, Carl** 1845-1924 ................ **TCLC 12**
See also CAAE 109; DLB 129, 332; EWL 3

**Spitteler, Karl Friedrich Georg**
See Spitteler, Carl

**Spivack, Kathleen (Romola Drucker)** 1938- ............................................... **CLC 6**
See also CA 49-52

**Spivak, Gayatri Chakravorty** 1942- ....................................... **CLC 233**
See also CA 154; CAAE 110; CANR 91; FW; LMFS 2

**Spofford, Harriet (Elizabeth) Prescott** 1835-1921 ................................... **SSC 87**
See also CA 201; DLB 74, 221

**Spoto, Donald** 1941- ........................ **CLC 39**
See also CA 65-68; CANR 11, 57, 93

**Springsteen, Bruce** 1949- .................. **CLC 17**
See also CA 111

**Springsteen, Bruce F.**
See Springsteen, Bruce

**Spurling, Hilary** 1940- ...................... **CLC 34**
See also CA 104; CANR 25, 52, 94, 157

**Spurling, Susan Hilary**
See Spurling, Hilary

**Spyker, John Howland**
See Elman, Richard (Martin)

**Squared, A.**
See Abbott, Edwin A.

**Squires, (James) Radcliffe** 1917-1993 .................................. **CLC 51**
See also CA 1-4R; CAAS 140; CANR 6, 21; CP 1, 2, 3, 4, 5

**Srivastava, Dhanpat Rai** 1880(?)-1936
See Premchand
See also CA 197; CAAE 118

**Stacy, Donald**
See Pohl, Frederik

**Stael**
See Stael-Holstein, Anne Louise Germaine Necker
See also EW 5; RGWL 2, 3

**Stael, Germaine de**
See Stael-Holstein, Anne Louise Germaine Necker
See also DLB 119, 192; FL 1:3; FW; GFL 1789 to the Present; TWA

**Stael-Holstein, Anne Louise Germaine Necker** 1766-1817 .............. **NCLC 3, 91**
See Stael; Stael, Germaine de

**Stafford, Jean** 1915-1979 .. **CLC 4, 7, 19, 68; SSC 26, 86**
See also CA 1-4R; CAAS 85-88; CANR 3, 65; CN 1, 2; DLB 2, 173; MAL 5; MTCW 1, 2; MTFW 2005; RGAL 4; RGSF 2; SATA-Obit 22; SSFS 21; TCWW 1, 2; TUS

**Stafford, William (Edgar)** 1914-1993 ............. **CLC 4, 7, 29; PC 71**
See also AMWS 11; CA 5-8R; CAAS 142; CANR 5, 22; CP 1, 2, 3, 4, 5; DAM POET; DLB 5, 206; EXPP; INT CANR-22; MAL 5; PFS 2, 8, 16; RGAL 4; WP

**Stagnelius, Eric Johan** 1793-1823 . **NCLC 61**

**Staines, Trevor**
See Brunner, John (Kilian Houston)

**Stairs, Gordon**
See Austin, Mary (Hunter)

**Stalin, Joseph** 1879-1953 ................ **TCLC 92**

**Stampa, Gaspara** c. 1524-1554 .. **LC 114; PC 43**
See also RGWL 2, 3; WLIT 7

**Stampflinger, K. A.**
See Benjamin, Walter

**Stancykowna**
See Szymborska, Wislawa

**Standing Bear, Luther** 1868(?)-1939(?) ............................ **NNAL**
See also CA 144; CAAE 113; DAM MULT

**Stanislavsky, Constantin** 1863(?)-1938 .......................... **TCLC 167**
See also CAAE 118

**Stanislavsky, Konstantin**
See Stanislavsky, Constantin

**Stanislavsky, Konstantin Sergeievich**
See Stanislavsky, Constantin

**Stanislavsky, Konstantin Sergeivich**
See Stanislavsky, Constantin

**Stanislavsky, Konstantin Sergeyevich**
See Stanislavsky, Constantin

**Stannard, Martin** 1947- ..................... **CLC 44**
See also CA 142; DLB 155

**Stanton, Elizabeth Cady** 1815-1902 .............................. **TCLC 73**
See also CA 171; DLB 79; FL 1:3; FW

**Stanton, Maura** 1946- ......................... **CLC 9**
See also CA 89-92; CANR 15, 123; DLB 120

**Stanton, Schuyler**
See Baum, L(yman) Frank

**Stapledon, (William) Olaf** 1886-1950 .............................. **TCLC 22**
See also CA 162; CAAE 111; DLB 15, 255; SCFW 1, 2; SFW 4

**Starbuck, George (Edwin)** 1931-1996 .............................. **CLC 53**
See also CA 21-24R; CAAS 153; CANR 23; CP 1, 2, 3, 4, 5, 6; DAM POET

**Stark, Richard**
See Westlake, Donald E.

**Statius** c. 45-c. 96 ......................... **CMLC 91**
See also AW 2; DLB 211

**Staunton, Schuyler**
See Baum, L(yman) Frank

**Stead, Christina (Ellen)** 1902-1983 ... **CLC 2, 5, 8, 32, 80**
See also BRWS 4; CA 13-16R; CAAS 109; CANR 33, 40; CN 1, 2, 3; DLB 260; EWL 3; FW; MTCW 1, 2; MTFW 2005; RGEL 2; RGSF 2; WWE 1

**Stead, William Thomas** 1849-1912 .............................. **TCLC 48**
See also BRWS 13; CA 167

**Stebnitsky, M.**
See Leskov, Nikolai (Semyonovich)

**Steele, Richard** 1672-1729 ................... **LC 18**
See also BRW 3; CDBLB 1660-1789; DLB 84, 101; RGEL 2; WLIT 3

**Steele, Timothy (Reid)** 1948- ........... **CLC 45**
See also CA 93-96; CANR 16, 50, 92; CP 5, 6, 7; DLB 120, 282

**Steffens, (Joseph) Lincoln** 1866-1936 .............................. **TCLC 20**
See also CA 198; CAAE 117; DLB 303; MAL 5

**Stegner, Wallace (Earle)** 1909-1993 .. **CLC 9, 49, 81; SSC 27**
See also AITN 1; AMWS 4; ANW; BEST 90:3; BPFB 3; CA 1-4R; 9; CAAS 141; CANR 1, 21, 46; CN 1, 2, 3, 4, 5; DAM NOV; DLB 9, 206, 275; DLBY 1993; EWL 3; MAL 5; MTCW 1, 2; MTFW 2005; RGAL 4; TCWW 1, 2; TUS

**Stein, Gertrude** 1874-1946 .... **DC 19; PC 18; SSC 42, 105; TCLC 1, 6, 28, 48; WLC 5**
See also AAYA 64; AMW; AMWC 2; CA 132; CAAE 104; CANR 108; CDALB 1917-1929; DA; DA3; DAB; DAC; DAM MST, NOV, POET; DLB 4, 54, 86, 228; DLBD 15; EWL 3; EXPS; FL 1:6; GLL 1; MAL 5; MBL; MTCW 1, 2; MTFW 2005; NCFS 4; RGAL 4; RGSF 2; SSFS 5; TUS; WP

**Thucydides** c. 455B.C.-c. 395B.C. . **CMLC 17**
  See also AW 1; DLB 176; RGWL 2, 3;
  WLIT 8

**Thumboo, Edwin Nadason** 1933- ........ **PC 30**
  See also CA 194; CP 1

**Thurber, James (Grover)**
  1894-1961 .. **CLC 5, 11, 25, 125; SSC 1,
  47**
  See also AAYA 56; AMWS 1; BPFB 3;
  BYA 5; CA 73-76; CANR 17, 39; CDALB
  1929-1941; CWRI 5; DA; DA3; DAB;
  DAC; DAM DRAM, MST, NOV; DLB 4,
  11, 22, 102; EWL 3; EXPS; FANT; LAIT
  3; MAICYA 1, 2; MAL 5; MTCW 1, 2;
  MTFW 2005; RGAL 4; RGSF 2; SATA
  13; SSFS 1, 10, 19; SUFW; TUS

**Thurman, Wallace (Henry)**
  1902-1934 ..... **BLC 3; HR 1:3; TCLC 6**
  See also BW 1, 3; CA 124; CAAE 104;
  CANR 81; DAM MULT; DLB 51

**Tibullus** c. 54B.C.-c. 18B.C. .......... **CMLC 36**
  See also AW 2; DLB 211; RGWL 2, 3;
  WLIT 8

**Ticheburn, Cheviot**
  See Ainsworth, William Harrison

**Tieck, (Johann) Ludwig**
  1773-1853 ..... **NCLC 5, 46; SSC 31, 100**
  See also CDWLB 2; DLB 90; EW 5; IDTP;
  RGSF 2; RGWL 2, 3; SUFW

**Tiger, Derry**
  See Ellison, Harlan

**Tilghman, Christopher** 1946- .......... **CLC 65**
  See also CA 159; CANR 135, 151; CSW;
  DLB 244

**Tillich, Paul (Johannes)**
  1886-1965 ................................. **CLC 131**
  See also CA 5-8R; CAAS 25-28R; CANR
  33; MTCW 1, 2

**Tillinghast, Richard (Williford)**
  1940- ..................................... **CLC 29**
  See also CA 29-32R; 23; CANR 26, 51, 96;
  CP 2, 3, 4, 5, 6, 7; CSW

**Tillman, Lynne** (?)- ......................... **CLC 231**
  See also CA 173; CANR 144

**Timrod, Henry** 1828-1867 ............. **NCLC 25**
  See also DLB 3, 248; RGAL 4

**Tindall, Gillian (Elizabeth)** 1938- ...... **CLC 7**
  See also CA 21-24R; CANR 11, 65, 107;
  CN 1, 2, 3, 4, 5, 6, 7

**Tiptree, James, Jr.** ...................... **CLC 48, 50**
  See Sheldon, Alice Hastings Bradley
  See also DLB 8; SCFW 1, 2; SFW 4

**Tirone Smith, Mary-Ann** 1944- ........ **CLC 39**
  See also CA 136; CAAE 118; CANR 113;
  SATA 143

**Tirso de Molina** 1580(?)-1648 ........... **DC 13;
  HLCS 2; LC 73**
  See also RGWL 2, 3

**Titmarsh, Michael Angelo**
  See Thackeray, William Makepeace

**Tocqueville, Alexis (Charles Henri Maurice
  Clerel Comte) de** 1805-1859 .. **NCLC 7,
  63**
  See also EW 6; GFL 1789 to the Present;
  TWA

**Toer, Pramoedya Ananta**
  1925-2006 ............................. **CLC 186**
  See also CA 197; CAAS 251; RGWL 3

**Toffler, Alvin** 1928- ......................... **CLC 168**
  See also CA 13-16R; CANR 15, 46, 67;
  CPW; DAM POP; MTCW 1, 2

**Toibin, Colm** 1955- ......................... **CLC 162**
  See also CA 142; CANR 81, 149; CN 7;
  DLB 271

**Tolkien, John Ronald Reuel**
  See Tolkien, J.R.R

**Tolkien, J.R.R** 1892-1973 ...... **CLC 1, 2, 3, 8,
  12, 38; TCLC 137; WLC 6**
  See also AAYA 10; AITN 1; BPFB 3;
  BRWC 2; BRWS 2; CA 17-18; CAAS 45-
  48; CANR 36, 134; CAP 2; CDBLB
  1914-1945; CLR 56; CN 1; CPW 1;
  CWRI 5; DA; DA3; DAB; DAC; DAM
  MST, NOV, POP; DLB 15, 160, 255; EFS
  2; EWL 3; FANT; JRDA; LAIT 1; LATS
  1:2; LMFS 2; MAICYA 1, 2; MTCW 1,
  2; MTFW 2005; NFS 8, 26; RGEL 2;
  SATA 2, 32, 100; SATA-Obit 24; SFW 4;
  SUFW; TEA; WCH; WYA; YAW

**Toller, Ernst** 1893-1939 .................. **TCLC 10**
  See also CA 186; CAAE 107; DLB 124;
  EWL 3; RGWL 2, 3

**Tolson, M. B.**
  See Tolson, Melvin B(eaunorus)

**Tolson, Melvin B(eaunorus)**
  1898(?)-1966 ........ **BLC 3; CLC 36, 105**
  See also AFAW 1, 2; BW 1, 3; CA 124;
  CAAS 89-92; CANR 80; DAM MULT,
  POET; DLB 48, 76; MAL 5; RGAL 4

**Tolstoi, Aleksei Nikolaevich**
  See Tolstoi, Alexey Nikolaevich

**Tolstoi, Lev**
  See Tolstoy, Leo (Nikolaevich)
  See also RGSF 2; RGWL 2, 3

**Tolstoy, Aleksei Nikolaevich**
  See Tolstoi, Alexey Nikolaevich
  See also DLB 272

**Tolstoy, Alexey Nikolaevich**
  1882-1945 ................................. **TCLC 18**
  See also Tolstoi, Aleksei Nikolaevich
  See also CA 158; CAAE 107; EWL 3; SFW
  4

**Tolstoy, Leo (Nikolaevich)**
  1828-1910 . **SSC 9, 30, 45, 54; TCLC 4,
  11, 17, 28, 44, 79, 173; WLC 6**
  See Tolstoi, Lev
  See also AAYA 56; CA 123; CAAE 104;
  DA; DA3; DAB; DAC; DAM MST, NOV;
  DLB 238; EFS 2; EW 7; EXPS; IDTP;
  LAIT 2; LATS 1:1; LMFS 1; NFS 10;
  SATA 26; SSFS 5; TWA

**Tolstoy, Count Leo**
  See Tolstoy, Leo (Nikolaevich)

**Tomalin, Claire** 1933- ..................... **CLC 166**
  See also CA 89-92; CANR 52, 88, 165;
  DLB 155

**Tomasi di Lampedusa, Giuseppe** 1896-1957
  See Lampedusa, Giuseppe (Tomasi) di
  See also CAAE 111; DLB 177; EWL 3;
  WLIT 7

**Tomlin, Lily** 1939(?)-
  See Tomlin, Mary Jean
  See also CAAE 117

**Tomlin, Mary Jean** ......................... **CLC 17**
  See Tomlin, Lily

**Tomline, F. Latour**
  See Gilbert, W(illiam) S(chwenck)

**Tomlinson, (Alfred) Charles** 1927- .... **CLC 2,
  4, 6, 13, 45; PC 17**
  See also CA 5-8R; CANR 33; CP 1, 2, 3, 4,
  5, 6, 7; DAM POET; DLB 40; TCLE 1:2

**Tomlinson, H(enry) M(ajor)**
  1873-1958 ................................. **TCLC 71**
  See also CA 161; CAAE 118; DLB 36, 100,
  195

**Tonna, Charlotte Elizabeth**
  1790-1846 ............................. **NCLC 135**
  See also DLB 163

**Tonson, Jacob** fl. 1655(?)-1736 ........... **LC 86**
  See also DLB 170

**Toole, John Kennedy** 1937-1969 ..... **CLC 19,
  64**
  See also BPFB 3; CA 104; DLBY 1981;
  MTCW 2; MTFW 2005

**Toomer, Eugene**
  See Toomer, Jean

**Toomer, Eugene Pinchback**
  See Toomer, Jean

**Toomer, Jean** 1894-1967 .. **BLC 3; CLC 1, 4,
  13, 22; HR 1:3; PC 7; SSC 1, 45;
  TCLC 172; WLCS**
  See also AFAW 1, 2; AMWS 3, 9; BW 1;
  CA 85-88; CDALB 1917-1929; DA3;
  DAM MULT; DLB 45, 51; EWL 3; EXPP;
  EXPS; LMFS 2; MAL 5; MTCW 1, 2;
  MTFW 2005; NFS 11; RGAL 4; RGSF 2;
  SSFS 5

**Toomer, Nathan Jean**
  See Toomer, Jean

**Toomer, Nathan Pinchback**
  See Toomer, Jean

**Torley, Luke**
  See Blish, James (Benjamin)

**Tornimparte, Alessandra**
  See Ginzburg, Natalia

**Torre, Raoul della**
  See Mencken, H(enry) L(ouis)

**Torrence, Ridgely** 1874-1950 .......... **TCLC 97**
  See also DLB 54, 249; MAL 5

**Torrey, E. Fuller** 1937- ................... **CLC 34**
  See also CA 119; CANR 71, 158

**Torrey, Edwin Fuller**
  See Torrey, E. Fuller

**Torsvan, Ben Traven**
  See Traven, B.

**Torsvan, Benno Traven**
  See Traven, B.

**Torsvan, Berick Traven**
  See Traven, B.

**Torsvan, Berwick Traven**
  See Traven, B.

**Torsvan, Bruno Traven**
  See Traven, B.

**Torsvan, Traven**
  See Traven, B.

**Tourneur, Cyril** 1575(?)-1626 .............. **LC 66**
  See also BRW 2; DAM DRAM; DLB 58;
  RGEL 2

**Tournier, Michel** 1924- .... **CLC 6, 23, 36, 95;
  SSC 88**
  See also CA 49-52; CANR 3, 36, 74, 149;
  CWW 2; DLB 83; EWL 3; GFL 1789 to
  the Present; MTCW 1, 2; SATA 23

**Tournier, Michel Edouard**
  See Tournier, Michel

**Tournimparte, Alessandra**
  See Ginzburg, Natalia

**Towers, Ivar**
  See Kornbluth, C(yril) M.

**Towne, Robert (Burton)** 1936(?)- ..... **CLC 87**
  See also CA 108; DLB 44; IDFW 3, 4

**Townsend, Sue** ................................. **CLC 61**
  See Townsend, Susan Lilian
  See also AAYA 28; CA 127; CAAE 119;
  CANR 65, 107; CBD; CD 5, 6; CPW;
  CWD; DAB; DAC; DAM MST; DLB
  271; INT CA-127; SATA 55, 93; SATA-
  Brief 48; YAW

**Townsend, Susan Lilian** 1946-
  See Townsend, Sue

**Townshend, Pete**
  See Townshend, Peter (Dennis Blandford)

**Townshend, Peter (Dennis Blandford)**
  1945- ................................... **CLC 17, 42**
  See also CA 107

**Tozzi, Federigo** 1883-1920 ............. **TCLC 31**
  See also CA 160; CANR 110; DLB 264;
  EWL 3; WLIT 7

**Tracy, Don(ald Fiske)** 1905-1970(?)
  See Queen, Ellery
  See also CA 1-4R; CAAS 176; CANR 2

**Trafford, F. G.**
  See Riddell, Charlotte

**Walser, Martin** 1927- ................ **CLC 27, 183**
See also CA 57-60; CANR 8, 46, 145;
CWW 2; DLB 75, 124; EWL 3

**Walser, Robert** 1878-1956 ..... **SSC 20; TCLC 18**
See also CA 165; CAAE 118; CANR 100;
DLB 66; EWL 3

**Walsh, Gillian Paton**
See Paton Walsh, Jill

**Walsh, Jill Paton** ............................ **CLC 35**
See Paton Walsh, Jill
See also CLR 2, 65; WYA

**Walter, Villiam Christian**
See Andersen, Hans Christian

**Walters, Anna L(ee)** 1946- ................ **NNAL**
See also CA 73-76

**Walther von der Vogelweide** c.
1170-1228 .............................. **CMLC 56**

**Walton, Izaak** 1593-1683 .............. **LC 72**
See also BRW 2; CDBLB Before 1660;
DLB 151, 213; RGEL 2

**Walzer, Michael (Laban)** 1935- ...... **CLC 238**
See also CA 37-40R; CANR 15, 48, 127

**Wambaugh, Joseph, Jr.** 1937- ...... **CLC 3, 18**
See also AITN 1; BEST 89:3; BPFB 3; CA
33-36R; CANR 42, 65, 115, 167; CMW
4; CPW 1; DA3; DAM NOV, POP; DLB
6; DLBY 1983; MSW; MTCW 1, 2

**Wambaugh, Joseph Aloysius**
See Wambaugh, Joseph, Jr.

**Wang Wei** 699(?)-761(?) ...................... **PC 18**
See also TWA

**Warburton, William** 1698-1779 .......... **LC 97**
See also DLB 104

**Ward, Arthur Henry Sarsfield** 1883-1959
See Rohmer, Sax
See also CA 173; CAAE 108; CMW 4;
HGG

**Ward, Douglas Turner** 1930- ........... **CLC 19**
See also BW 1; CA 81-84; CAD; CANR
27; CD 5, 6; DLB 7, 38

**Ward, E. D.**
See Lucas, E(dward) V(errall)

**Ward, Mrs. Humphry** 1851-1920
See Ward, Mary Augusta
See also RGEL 2

**Ward, Mary Augusta** 1851-1920 ... **TCLC 55**
See Ward, Mrs. Humphry
See also DLB 18

**Ward, Nathaniel** 1578(?)-1652 .......... **LC 114**
See also DLB 24

**Ward, Peter**
See Faust, Frederick (Schiller)

**Warhol, Andy** 1928(?)-1987 ............. **CLC 20**
See also AAYA 12; BEST 89:4; CA 89-92;
CAAS 121; CANR 34

**Warner, Francis (Robert Le Plastrier)**
1937- ........................................ **CLC 14**
See also CA 53-56; CANR 11; CP 1, 2, 3, 4

**Warner, Marina** 1946- .............. **CLC 59, 231**
See also CA 65-68; CANR 21, 55, 118; CN
5, 6, 7; DLB 194; MTFW 2005

**Warner, Rex (Ernest)** 1905-1986 ...... **CLC 45**
See also CA 89-92; CAAS 119; CN 1, 2, 3,
4; CP 1, 2, 3, 4; DLB 15; RGEL 2; RHW

**Warner, Susan (Bogert)**
1819-1885 ...................... **NCLC 31, 146**
See also DLB 3, 42, 239, 250, 254

**Warner, Sylvia (Constance) Ashton**
See Ashton-Warner, Sylvia (Constance)

**Warner, Sylvia Townsend**
1893-1978 .. **CLC 7, 19; SSC 23; TCLC 131**
See also BRWS 7; CA 61-64; CAAS 77-80;
CANR 16, 60, 104; CN 1, 2; DLB 34,
139; EWL 3; FANT; FW; MTCW 1, 2;
RGEL 2; RGSF 2; RHW

**Warren, Mercy Otis** 1728-1814 ..... **NCLC 13**
See also DLB 31, 200; RGAL 4; TUS

**Warren, Robert Penn** 1905-1989 .. **CLC 1, 4, 6, 8, 10, 13, 18, 39, 53, 59; PC 37; SSC 4, 58; WLC 6**
See also AITN 1; AMW; AMWC 2; BPFB
3; BYA 1; CA 13-16R; CAAS 129; CANR
10, 47; CDALB 1968-1988; CN 1, 2, 3,
4; CP 1, 2, 3, 4; DA; DA3; DAB; DAC;
DAM MST, NOV, POET; DLB 2, 48, 152,
320; DLBY 1980, 1989; EWL 3; INT
CANR-10; MAL 5; MTCW 1, 2; MTFW
2005; NFS 13; RGAL 4; RGSF 2; RHW;
SATA 46; SATA-Obit 63; SSFS 8; TUS

**Warrigal, Jack**
See Furphy, Joseph

**Warshofsky, Isaac**
See Singer, Isaac Bashevis

**Warton, Joseph** 1722-1800 ... **LC 128; NCLC 118**
See also DLB 104, 109; RGEL 2

**Warton, Thomas** 1728-1790 .......... **LC 15, 82**
See also DAM POET; DLB 104, 109, 336;
RGEL 2

**Waruk, Kona**
See Harris, (Theodore) Wilson

**Warung, Price** ............................. **TCLC 45**
See Astley, William
See also DLB 230; RGEL 2

**Warwick, Jarvis**
See Garner, Hugh
See also CCA 1

**Washington, Alex**
See Harris, Mark

**Washington, Booker T(aliaferro)**
1856-1915 .................... **BLC 3; TCLC 10**
See also BW 1; CA 125; CAAE 114; DA3;
DAM MULT; LAIT 2; RGAL 4; SATA
28

**Washington, George** 1732-1799 .......... **LC 25**
See also DLB 31

**Wassermann, (Karl) Jakob**
1873-1934 ................................. **TCLC 6**
See also CA 163; CAAE 104; DLB 66;
EWL 3

**Wasserstein, Wendy** 1950-2006 . **CLC 32, 59, 90, 183; DC 4**
See also AAYA 73; AMWS 15; CA 129;
CAAE 121; CAAS 247; CABS 3; CAD;
CANR 53, 75, 128; CD 5, 6; CWD; DA3;
DAM DRAM; DFS 5, 17; DLB 228;
EWL 3; FW; INT CA-129; MAL 5;
MTCW 2; MTFW 2005; SATA 94; SATA-
Obit 174

**Waterhouse, Keith (Spencer)** 1929- . **CLC 47**
See also BRWS 13; CA 5-8R; CANR 38,
67, 109; CBD; CD 6; CN 1, 2, 3, 4, 5, 6,
7; DLB 13, 15; MTCW 1, 2; MTFW 2005

**Waters, Frank (Joseph)** 1902-1995 .. **CLC 88**
See also CA 5-8R; 13; CAAS 149; CANR
3, 18, 63, 121; DLB 212; DLBY 1986;
RGAL 4; TCWW 1, 2

**Waters, Mary C.** ............................ **CLC 70**

**Waters, Roger** 1944- ......................... **CLC 35**

**Watkins, Frances Ellen**
See Harper, Frances Ellen Watkins

**Watkins, Gerrold**
See Malzberg, Barry N(athaniel)

**Watkins, Gloria Jean**
See hooks, bell

**Watkins, Paul** 1964- .......................... **CLC 55**
See also CA 132; CANR 62, 98

**Watkins, Vernon Phillips**
1906-1967 ................................. **CLC 43**
See also CA 9-10; CAAS 25-28R; CAP 1;
DLB 20; EWL 3; RGEL 2

**Watson, Irving S.**
See Mencken, H(enry) L(ouis)

**Watson, John H.**
See Farmer, Philip Jose

**Watson, Richard F.**
See Silverberg, Robert

**Watts, Ephraim**
See Horne, Richard Henry Hengist

**Watts, Isaac** 1674-1748 ........................ **LC 98**
See also DLB 95; RGEL 2; SATA 52

**Waugh, Auberon (Alexander)**
1939-2001 ................................... **CLC 7**
See also CA 45-48; CAAS 192; CANR 6,
22, 92; CN 1, 2, 3; DLB 14, 194

**Waugh, Evelyn (Arthur St. John)**
1903-1966 .. **CLC 1, 3, 8, 13, 19, 27, 44, 107; SSC 41; WLC 6**
See also BPFB 3; BRW 7; CA 85-88; CAAS
25-28R; CANR 22; CDBLB 1914-1945;
DA; DA3; DAB; DAC; DAM MST, NOV,
POP; DLB 15, 162, 195; EWL 3; MTCW
1, 2; MTFW 2005; NFS 13, 17; RGEL 2;
RGSF 2; TEA; WLIT 4

**Waugh, Harriet** 1944- ......................... **CLC 6**
See also CA 85-88; CANR 22

**Ways, C. R.**
See Blount, Roy (Alton), Jr.

**Waystaff, Simon**
See Swift, Jonathan

**Webb, Beatrice (Martha Potter)**
1858-1943 ................................. **TCLC 22**
See also CA 162; CAAE 117; DLB 190;
FW

**Webb, Charles (Richard)** 1939- ......... **CLC 7**
See also CA 25-28R; CANR 114

**Webb, Frank J.** .............................. **NCLC 143**
See also DLB 50

**Webb, James, Jr.**
See Webb, James

**Webb, James** 1946- .......................... **CLC 22**
See also CA 81-84; CANR 156

**Webb, James H.**
See Webb, James

**Webb, James Henry**
See Webb, James

**Webb, Mary Gladys (Meredith)**
1881-1927 ................................. **TCLC 24**
See also CA 182; CAAS 123; DLB 34; FW;
RGEL 2

**Webb, Mrs. Sidney**
See Webb, Beatrice (Martha Potter)

**Webb, Phyllis** 1927- .......................... **CLC 18**
See also CA 104; CANR 23; CCA 1; CP 1,
2, 3, 4, 5, 6, 7; CWP; DLB 53

**Webb, Sidney (James)** 1859-1947 .. **TCLC 22**
See also CA 163; CAAE 117; DLB 190

**Webber, Andrew Lloyd** .................... **CLC 21**
See Lloyd Webber, Andrew
See also DFS 7

**Weber, Lenora Mattingly**
1895-1971 ................................. **CLC 12**
See also CA 19-20; CAAS 29-32R; CAP 1;
SATA 2; SATA-Obit 26

**Weber, Max** 1864-1920 .................. **TCLC 69**
See also CA 189; CAAE 109; DLB 296

**Webster, John** 1580(?)-1634(?) ...... **DC 2; LC 33, 84, 124; WLC 6**
See also BRW 2; CDBLB Before 1660; DA;
DAB; DAC; DAM DRAM, MST; DFS
17, 19; DLB 58; IDTP; RGEL 2; WLIT 3

**Webster, Noah** 1758-1843 .............. **NCLC 30**
See also DLB 1, 37, 42, 43, 73, 243

**Wedekind, Benjamin Franklin**
See Wedekind, Frank

**Wedekind, Frank** 1864-1918 ........... **TCLC 7**
See also CA 153; CAAE 104; CANR 121,
122; CDWLB 2; DAM DRAM; DLB 118;
EW 8; EWL 3; LMFS 2; RGWL 2, 3

**Wehr, Demaris** ............................... **CLC 65**

**Weidman, Jerome** 1913-1998 ............. **CLC 7**
See also AITN 2; CA 1-4R; CAAS 171;
CAD; CANR 1; CD 1, 2, 3, 4, 5; DLB 28

MAL 5; MBL; MTCW 1, 2; MTFW 2005; NFS 5, 11, 15, 20; RGAL 4; RGSF 2; RHW; SSFS 6, 7; SUFW; TUS

**Wharton, James**
See Mencken, H(enry) L(ouis)

**Wharton, William (a pseudonym)**
1925- ..................................... **CLC 18, 37**
See also CA 93-96; CN 4, 5, 6, 7; DLBY 1980; INT CA-93-96

**Wheatley (Peters), Phillis**
1753(?)-1784 ... **BLC 3; LC 3, 50; PC 3; WLC 6**
See also AFAW 1, 2; CDALB 1640-1865; DA; DA3; DAC; DAM MST, MULT, POET; DLB 31, 50; EXPP; FL 1:1; PFS 13; RGAL 4

**Wheelock, John Hall** 1886-1978 ....... **CLC 14**
See also CA 13-16R; CAAS 77-80; CANR 14; CP 1, 2; DLB 45; MAL 5

**Whim-Wham**
See Curnow, (Thomas) Allen (Monro)

**Whisp, Kennilworthy**
See Rowling, J.K.

**Whitaker, Rod** 1931-2005
See Trevanian
See also CA 29-32R; CAAS 246; CANR 45, 153; CMW 4

**White, Babington**
See Braddon, Mary Elizabeth

**White, E. B.** 1899-1985 ......... **CLC 10, 34, 39**
See also AAYA 62; AITN 2; AMWS 1; CA 13-16R; CAAS 116; CANR 16, 37; CDALBS; CLR 1, 21, 107; CPW; DA3; DAM POP; DLB 11, 22; EWL 3; FANT; MAICYA 1, 2; MAL 5; MTCW 1, 2; MTFW 2005; NCFS 5; RGAL 4; SATA 2, 29, 100; SATA-Obit 44; TUS

**White, Edmund** 1940- ............... **CLC 27, 110**
See also AAYA 7; CA 45-48; CANR 3, 19, 36, 62, 107, 133; CN 5, 6, 7; DA3; DAM POP; DLB 227; MTCW 1, 2; MTFW 2005

**White, Elwyn Brooks**
See White, E. B.

**White, Hayden V.** 1928- .................. **CLC 148**
See also CA 128; CANR 135; DLB 246

**White, Patrick (Victor Martindale)**
1912-1990 ...... **CLC 3, 4, 5, 7, 9, 18, 65, 69; SSC 39; TCLC 176**
See also BRWS 1; CA 81-84; CAAS 132; CANR 43; CN 1, 2, 3, 4; DLB 260, 332; EWL 3; MTCW 1; RGEL 2; RGSF 2; RHW; TWA; WWE 1

**White, Phyllis Dorothy James** 1920-
See James, P. D.
See also CA 21-24R; CANR 17, 43, 65, 112; CMW 4; CN 7; CPW; DA3; DAM POP; MTCW 1, 2; MTFW 2005; TEA

**White, T(erence) H(anbury)**
1906-1964 ................................. **CLC 30**
See also AAYA 22; BPFB 3; BYA 4, 5; CA 73-76; CANR 37; DLB 160; FANT; JRDA; LAIT 1; MAICYA 1, 2; RGEL 2; SATA 12; SUFW 1; YAW

**White, Terence de Vere** 1912-1994 ... **CLC 49**
See also CA 49-52; CAAS 145; CANR 3

**White, Walter**
See White, Walter F(rancis)

**White, Walter F(rancis)** 1893-1955 ... **BLC 3; HR 1:3; TCLC 15**
See also BW 1; CA 124; CAAE 115; DAM MULT; DLB 51

**White, William Hale** 1831-1913
See Rutherford, Mark
See also CA 189; CAAE 121

**Whitehead, Alfred North**
1861-1947 ................................. **TCLC 97**
See also CA 165; CAAE 117; DLB 100, 262

**Whitehead, Colson** 1970- ............... **CLC 232**
See also CA 202; CANR 162

**Whitehead, E(dward) A(nthony)**
1933- ......................................... **CLC 5**
See Whitehead, Ted
See also CA 65-68; CANR 58, 118; CBD; CD 5; DLB 310

**Whitehead, Ted**
See Whitehead, E(dward) A(nthony)
See also CD 6

**Whiteman, Roberta J. Hill** 1947- ...... **NNAL**
See also CA 146

**Whitemore, Hugh (John)** 1936- ....... **CLC 37**
See also CA 132; CANR 77; CBD; CD 5, 6; INT CA-132

**Whitman, Sarah Helen (Power)**
1803-1878 ................................. **NCLC 19**
See also DLB 1, 243

**Whitman, Walt(er)** 1819-1892 .. **NCLC 4, 31, 81; PC 3; WLC 6**
See also AAYA 42; AMW; AMWR 1; CDALB 1640-1865; DA; DA3; DAB; DAC; DAM MST, POET; DLB 3, 64, 224, 250; EXPP; LAIT 2; LMFS 1; PAB; PFS 2, 3, 13, 22; RGAL 4; SATA 20; TUS; WP; WYAS 1

**Whitney, Isabella** fl. 1565-fl. 1575 ..... **LC 130**
See also DLB 136

**Whitney, Phyllis A(yame)** 1903- ....... **CLC 42**
See also AAYA 36; AITN 2; BEST 90:3; CA 1-4R; CANR 3, 25, 38, 60; CLR 59; CMW 4; CPW; DA3; DAM POP; JRDA; MAICYA 1, 2; MTCW 2; RHW; SATA 1, 30; YAW

**Whittemore, (Edward) Reed, Jr.**
1919- ......................................... **CLC 4**
See also CA 219; 9-12R, 219; 8; CANR 4, 119; CP 1, 2, 3, 4, 5, 6, 7; DLB 5; MAL 5

**Whittier, John Greenleaf**
1807-1892 ................................. **NCLC 8, 59**
See also AMWS 1; DLB 1, 243; RGAL 4

**Whittlebot, Hernia**
See Coward, Noel (Peirce)

**Wicker, Thomas Grey** 1926-
See Wicker, Tom
See also CA 65-68; CANR 21, 46, 141

**Wicker, Tom** ......................................... **CLC 7**
See Wicker, Thomas Grey

**Wideman, John Edgar** 1941- ... **BLC 3; CLC 5, 34, 36, 67, 122; SSC 62**
See also AFAW 1, 2; AMWS 10; BPFB 4; BW 2, 3; CA 85-88; CANR 14, 42, 67, 109, 140; CN 4, 5, 6, 7; DAM MULT; DLB 33, 143; MAL 5; MTCW 2; MTFW 2005; RGAL 4; RGSF 2; SSFS 6, 12, 24; TCLE 1:2

**Wiebe, Rudy** 1934- ......... **CLC 6, 11, 14, 138**
See also CA 37-40R; CANR 42, 67, 123; CN 1, 2, 3, 4, 5, 6, 7; DAC; DAM MST; DLB 60; RHW; SATA 156

**Wiebe, Rudy Henry**
See Wiebe, Rudy

**Wieland, Christoph Martin**
1733-1813 ....................... **NCLC 17, 177**
See also DLB 97; EW 4; LMFS 1; RGWL 2, 3

**Wiene, Robert** 1881-1938 ............... **TCLC 56**

**Wieners, John** 1934- ............................. **CLC 7**
See also BG 1:3; CA 13-16R; CP 1, 2, 3, 4, 5, 6, 7; DLB 16; WP

**Wiesel, Elie** 1928- ...... **CLC 3, 5, 11, 37, 165; WLCS**
See also AAYA 7, 54; AITN 1; CA 5-8R; 4; CANR 8, 40, 65, 125; CDALBS; CWW 2; DA; DA3; DAB; DAC; DAM MST, NOV; DLB 83, 299; DLBY 1987; EWL 3; INT CANR-8; LAIT 4; MTCW 1, 2; MTFW 2005; NCFS 4; NFS 4; RGHL; RGWL 3; SATA 56; YAW

**Wiesel, Eliezer**
See Wiesel, Elie

**Wiggins, Marianne** 1947- .................. **CLC 57**
See also AAYA 70; BEST 89:3; CA 130; CANR 60, 139; CN 7; DLB 335

**Wigglesworth, Michael** 1631-1705 .... **LC 106**
See also DLB 24; RGAL 4

**Wiggs, Susan** ................................... **CLC 70**
See also CA 201

**Wight, James Alfred** 1916-1995
See Herriot, James
See also CA 77-80; SATA 55; SATA-Brief 44

**Wilbur, Richard** 1921- .. **CLC 3, 6, 9, 14, 53, 110; PC 51**
See also AAYA 72; AMWS 3; CA 1-4R; CABS 2; CANR 2, 29, 76, 93, 139; CDALBS; CP 1, 2, 3, 4, 5, 6, 7; DA; DAB; DAC; DAM MST, POET; DLB 5, 169; EWL 3; EXPP; INT CANR-29; MAL 5; MTCW 1, 2; MTFW 2005; PAB; PFS 11, 12, 16; RGAL 4; SATA 9, 108; WP

**Wilbur, Richard Purdy**
See Wilbur, Richard

**Wild, Peter** 1940- ............................ **CLC 14**
See also CA 37-40R; CP 1, 2, 3, 4, 5, 6, 7; DLB 5

**Wilde, Oscar** 1854(?)-1900 ... **DC 17; SSC 11, 77; TCLC 1, 8, 23, 41, 175; WLC 6**
See also AAYA 49; BRW 5; BRWC 1, 2; BRWR 2; BYA 15; CA 119; CAAE 104; CANR 112; CDBLB 1890-1914; CLR 114; DA; DA3; DAB; DAC; DAM DRAM, MST, NOV; DFS 4, 8, 9, 21; DLB 10, 19, 34, 57, 141, 156, 190; EXPS; FANT; GL 3; LATS 1:1; NFS 20; RGEL 2; RGSF 2; SATA 24; SSFS 7; SUFW; TEA; WCH; WLIT 4

**Wilde, Oscar Fingal O'Flahertie Willis**
See Wilde, Oscar

**Wilder, Billy** ...................................... **CLC 20**
See Wilder, Samuel
See also AAYA 66; DLB 26

**Wilder, Samuel** 1906-2002
See Wilder, Billy
See also CA 89-92; CAAS 205

**Wilder, Stephen**
See Marlowe, Stephen

**Wilder, Thornton (Niven)**
1897-1975 .. **CLC 1, 5, 6, 10, 15, 35, 82; DC 1, 24; WLC 6**
See also AAYA 29; AITN 2; AMW; CA 13-16R; CAAS 61-64; CAD; CANR 40, 132; CDALBS; CN 1, 2; DA; DA3; DAB; DAC; DAM DRAM, MST, NOV; DFS 1, 4, 16; DLB 4, 7, 9, 228; DLBY 1997; EWL 3; LAIT 3; MAL 5; MTCW 1, 2; MTFW 2005; NFS 24; RGAL 4; RHW; WYAS 1

**Wilding, Michael** 1942- ...... **CLC 73; SSC 50**
See also CA 104; CANR 24, 49, 106; CN 4, 5, 6, 7; DLB 325; RGSF 2

**Wiley, Richard** 1944- ........................ **CLC 44**
See also CA 129; CAAE 121; CANR 71

**Wilhelm, Kate** ....................................... **CLC 7**
See Wilhelm, Katie
See also AAYA 20; BYA 16; CA 5; DLB 8; INT CANR-17; SCFW 2

**Wilhelm, Katie** 1928-
See Wilhelm, Kate
See also CA 37-40R; CANR 17, 36, 60, 94; MTCW 1; SFW 4

**Wilkins, Mary**
See Freeman, Mary E(leanor) Wilkins

**Willard, Nancy** 1936- .................... **CLC 7, 37**
See also BYA 5; CA 89-92; CANR 10, 39, 68, 107, 152; CLR 5; CP 2, 3, 4, 5; CWP; CWRI 5; DLB 5, 52; FANT; MAICYA 1, 2; MTCW 1; SATA 37, 71, 127; SATA-Brief 30; SUFW 2; TCLE 1:2

**William of Malmesbury** c. 1090B.C.-c.
1140B.C. .................................. **CMLC 57**

**William of Moerbeke** c. 1215-c.
1286 ........................................ **CMLC 91**

**William of Ockham** 1290-1349 ..... **CMLC 32**

**Williams, Ben Ames** 1889-1953 ..... **TCLC 89**
See also CA 183; DLB 102

**Williams, Charles**
See Collier, James Lincoln

**Williams, Charles (Walter Stansby)**
1886-1945 ............................ **TCLC 1, 11**
See also BRWS 9; CA 163; CAAE 104;
DLB 100, 153, 255; FANT; RGEL 2;
SUFW 1

**Williams, C.K.** 1936- .......... **CLC 33, 56, 148**
See also CA 37-40R; 26; CANR 57, 106;
CP 1, 2, 3, 4, 5, 6, 7; DAM POET; DLB
5; MAL 5

**Williams, Ella Gwendolen Rees**
See Rhys, Jean

**Williams, (George) Emlyn**
1905-1987 .............................. **CLC 15**
See also CA 104; CAAS 123; CANR 36;
DAM DRAM; DLB 10, 77; IDTP; MTCW
1

**Williams, Hank** 1923-1953 ............. **TCLC 81**
See Williams, Hiram King

**Williams, Helen Maria**
1761-1827 ............................ **NCLC 135**
See also DLB 158

**Williams, Hiram Hank**
See Williams, Hank

**Williams, Hiram King**
See Williams, Hank
See also CA 188

**Williams, Hugo (Mordaunt)** 1942- ... **CLC 42**
See also CA 17-20R; CANR 45, 119; CP 1,
2, 3, 4, 5, 6, 7; DLB 40

**Williams, J. Walker**
See Wodehouse, P(elham) G(renville)

**Williams, John A(lfred)** 1925- . **BLC 3; CLC
5, 13**
See also AFAW 2; BW 2, 3; CA 195; 53-
56, 195; 3; CANR 6, 26, 51, 118; CN 1,
2, 3, 4, 5, 6, 7; CSW; DAM MULT; DLB
2, 33; EWL 3; INT CANR-6; MAL 5;
RGAL 4; SFW 4

**Williams, Jonathan (Chamberlain)**
1929- .................................. **CLC 13**
See also CA 9-12R; 12; CANR 8, 108; CP
1, 2, 3, 4, 5, 6, 7; DLB 5

**Williams, Joy** 1944- .......................... **CLC 31**
See also CA 41-44R; CANR 22, 48, 97,
168; DLB 335; SSFS 25

**Williams, Norman** 1952- ................... **CLC 39**
See also CA 118

**Williams, Roger** 1603(?)-1683 ........... **LC 129**
See also DLB 24

**Williams, Sherley Anne** 1944-1999 ... **BLC 3;
CLC 89**
See also AFAW 2; BW 2, 3; CA 73-76;
CAAS 185; CANR 25, 82; DAM MULT,
POET; DLB 41; INT CANR-25; SATA
78; SATA-Obit 116

**Williams, Shirley**
See Williams, Sherley Anne

**Williams, Tennessee** 1911-1983 . **CLC 1, 2, 5,
7, 8, 11, 15, 19, 30, 39, 45, 71, 111; DC
4; SSC 81; WLC 6**
See also AAYA 31; AITN 1, 2; AMW;
AMWC 1; CA 5-8R; CAAS 108; CABS
3; CAD; CANR 31, 132; CDALB 1941-
1968; CN 1, 2, 3; DA; DA3; DAB; DAC;
DAM DRAM, MST; DFS 17; DLB 7;
DLBD 4; DLBY 1983; EWL 3; GLL 1;
LAIT 4; LATS 1:2; MAL 5; MTCW 1, 2;
MTFW 2005; RGAL 4; TUS

**Williams, Thomas (Alonzo)**
1926-1990 ............................... **CLC 14**
See also CA 1-4R; CAAS 132; CANR 2

**Williams, William C.**
See Williams, William Carlos

**Williams, William Carlos**
1883-1963 .... **CLC 1, 2, 5, 9, 13, 22, 42,
67; PC 7; SSC 31; WLC 6**
See also AAYA 46; AMW; AMWR 1; CA
89-92; CANR 34; CDALB 1917-1929;
DA; DA3; DAB; DAC; DAM MST,
POET; DLB 4, 16, 54, 86; EWL 3; EXPP;
MAL 5; MTCW 1, 2; MTFW 2005; NCFS
4; PAB; PFS 1, 6, 11; RGAL 4; RGSF 2;
TUS; WP

**Williamson, David (Keith)** 1942- ..... **CLC 56**
See also CA 103; CANR 41; CD 5, 6; DLB
289

**Williamson, Ellen Douglas** 1905-1984
See Douglas, Ellen
See also CA 17-20R; CAAS 114; CANR 39

**Williamson, Jack** ............................... **CLC 29**
See Williamson, John Stewart
See also CA 8; DLB 8; SCFW 1, 2

**Williamson, John Stewart** 1908-2006
See Williamson, Jack
See also AAYA 76; CA 17-20R; CAAS 255;
CANR 23, 70, 153; SFW 4

**Willie, Frederick**
See Lovecraft, H. P.

**Willingham, Calder (Baynard, Jr.)**
1922-1995 ......................... **CLC 5, 51**
See also CA 5-8R; CAAS 147; CANR 3;
CN 1, 2, 3, 4, 5; CSW; DLB 2, 44; IDFW
3, 4; MTCW 1

**Willis, Charles**
See Clarke, Arthur C.

**Willy**
See Colette, (Sidonie-Gabrielle)

**Willy, Colette**
See Colette, (Sidonie-Gabrielle)
See also GLL 1

**Wilmot, John** 1647-1680 ........ **LC 75; PC 66**
See Rochester
See also BRW 2; DLB 131; PAB

**Wilson, A.N.** 1950- ........................... **CLC 33**
See also BRWS 6; CA 122; CAAE 112;
CANR 156; CN 4, 5, 6, 7; DLB 14, 155,
194; MTCW 2

**Wilson, Andrew Norman**
See Wilson, A.N.

**Wilson, Angus (Frank Johnstone)**
1913-1991 . **CLC 2, 3, 5, 25, 34; SSC 21**
See also BRWS 1; CA 5-8R; CAAS 134;
CANR 21; CN 1, 2, 3, 4; DLB 15, 139,
155; EWL 3; MTCW 1, 2; MTFW 2005;
RGEL 2; RGSF 2

**Wilson, August** 1945-2005 .. **BLC 3; CLC 39,
50, 63, 118, 222; DC 2; WLCS**
See also AAYA 16; AFAW 2; AMWS 8; BW
2, 3; CA 122; CAAE 115; CAAS 244;
CAD; CANR 42, 54, 76, 128; CD 5, 6;
DA; DA3; DAB; DAC; DAM DRAM,
MST, MULT; DFS 3, 7, 15, 17, 24; DLB
228; EWL 3; LAIT 4; LATS 1:2; MAL 5;
MTCW 1, 2; MTFW 2005; RGAL 4

**Wilson, Brian** 1942- ........................... **CLC 12**

**Wilson, Colin (Henry)** 1931- ........ **CLC 3, 14**
See also CA 1-4R; 5; CANR 1, 22, 33, 77;
CMW 4; CN 1, 2, 3, 4, 5, 6; DLB 14, 194;
HGG; MTCW 1; SFW 4

**Wilson, Dirk**
See Pohl, Frederik

**Wilson, Edmund** 1895-1972 .. **CLC 1, 2, 3, 8,
24**
See also AMW; CA 1-4R; CAAS 37-40R;
CANR 1, 46, 110; CN 1; DLB 63; EWL
3; MAL 5; MTCW 1, 2; MTFW 2005;
RGAL 4; TUS

**Wilson, Ethel Davis (Bryant)**
1888(?)-1980 ............................ **CLC 13**
See also CA 102; CN 1, 2; DAC; DAM
POET; DLB 68; MTCW 1; RGEL 2

**Wilson, Harriet**
See Wilson, Harriet E. Adams
See also DLB 239

**Wilson, Harriet E.**
See Wilson, Harriet E. Adams
See also DLB 243

**Wilson, Harriet E. Adams**
1827(?)-1863(?) ......... **BLC 3; NCLC 78**
See Wilson, Harriet; Wilson, Harriet E.
See also DAM MULT; DLB 50

**Wilson, John** 1785-1854 ................... **NCLC 5**

**Wilson, John (Anthony) Burgess** 1917-1993
See Burgess, Anthony
See also CA 1-4R; CAAS 143; CANR 2,
46; DA3; DAC; DAM NOV; MTCW 1,
2; MTFW 2005; NFS 15; TEA

**Wilson, Katharina** .......................... **CLC 65**

**Wilson, Lanford** 1937- .. **CLC 7, 14, 36, 197;
DC 19**
See also CA 17-20R; CABS 3; CAD; CANR
45, 96; CD 5, 6; DAM DRAM; DFS 4, 9,
12, 16, 20; DLB 7; EWL 3; MAL 5; TUS

**Wilson, Robert M.** 1941- ................. **CLC 7, 9**
See also CA 49-52; CAD; CANR 2, 41; CD
5, 6; MTCW 1

**Wilson, Robert McLiam** 1964- ......... **CLC 59**
See also CA 132; DLB 267

**Wilson, Sloan** 1920-2003 ................... **CLC 32**
See also CA 1-4R; CAAS 216; CANR 1,
44; CN 1, 2, 3, 4, 5, 6

**Wilson, Snoo** 1948- .......................... **CLC 33**
See also CA 69-72; CBD; CD 5, 6

**Wilson, William S(mith)** 1932- ......... **CLC 49**
See also CA 81-84

**Wilson, (Thomas) Woodrow**
1856-1924 .............................. **TCLC 79**
See also CA 166; DLB 47

**Winchilsea, Anne (Kingsmill) Finch**
1661-1720
See Finch, Anne
See also RGEL 2

**Winckelmann, Johann Joachim**
1717-1768 ............................... **LC 129**
See also DLB 97

**Windham, Basil**
See Wodehouse, P(elham) G(renville)

**Wingrove, David** 1954- ..................... **CLC 68**
See also CA 133; SFW 4

**Winnemucca, Sarah** 1844-1891 .... **NCLC 79;
NNAL**
See also DAM MULT; DLB 175; RGAL 4

**Winstanley, Gerrard** 1609-1676 .......... **LC 52**

**Wintergreen, Jane**
See Duncan, Sara Jeannette

**Winters, Arthur Yvor**
See Winters, Yvor

**Winters, Janet Lewis** ....................... **CLC 41**
See Lewis, Janet
See also DLBY 1987

**Winters, Yvor** 1900-1968 .. **CLC 4, 8, 32; PC
82**
See also AMWS 2; CA 11-12; CAAS 25-
28R; CAP 1; DLB 48; EWL 3; MAL 5;
MTCW 1; RGAL 4

**Winterson, Jeanette** 1959- ........ **CLC 64, 158**
See also BRWS 4; CA 136; CANR 58, 116;
CN 5, 6, 7; CPW; DA3; DAM POP; DLB
207, 261; FANT; FW; GLL 1; MTCW 2;
MTFW 2005; RHW

**Winthrop, John** 1588-1649 .......... **LC 31, 107**
See also DLB 24, 30

**Wirth, Louis** 1897-1952 ................. **TCLC 92**
See also CA 210

**Wiseman, Frederick** 1930- ............... **CLC 20**
See also CA 159

**Wister, Owen** 1860-1938 ..... **SSC 100; TCLC 21**
See also BPFB 3; CA 162; CAAE 108; DLB 9, 78, 186; RGAL 4; SATA 62; TCWW 1, 2

**Wither, George** 1588-1667 .................. **LC 96**
See also DLB 121; RGEL 2

**Witkacy**
See Witkiewicz, Stanislaw Ignacy

**Witkiewicz, Stanislaw Ignacy** 1885-1939 .................................. **TCLC 8**
See also CA 162; CAAE 105; CDWLB 4; DLB 215; EW 10; EWL 3; RGWL 2, 3; SFW 4

**Wittgenstein, Ludwig (Josef Johann)** 1889-1951 ................................ **TCLC 59**
See also CA 164; CAAE 113; DLB 262; MTCW 2

**Wittig, Monique** 1935-2003 .............. **CLC 22**
See also CA 135; CAAE 116; CAAS 212; CANR 143; CWW 2; DLB 83; EWL 3; FW; GLL 1

**Wittlin, Jozef** 1896-1976 .................. **CLC 25**
See also CA 49-52; CAAS 65-68; CANR 3; EWL 3

**Wodehouse, P(elham) G(renville)** 1881-1975 . **CLC 1, 2, 5, 10, 22; SSC 2; TCLC 108**
See also AAYA 65; AITN 2; BRWS 3; CA 45-48; CAAS 57-60; CANR 3, 33; CD-BLB 1914-1945; CN 1, 2; CPW 1; DA3; DAB; DAC; DAM NOV; DLB 34, 162; EWL 3; MTCW 1, 2; MTFW 2005; RGAL 2; RGSF 2; SATA 22; SSFS 10

**Woiwode, L.**
See Woiwode, Larry (Alfred)

**Woiwode, Larry (Alfred)** 1941- ... **CLC 6, 10**
See also CA 73-76; CANR 16, 94; CN 3, 4, 5, 6, 7; DLB 6; INT CANR-16

**Wojciechowska, Maia (Teresa)** 1927-2002 .................................. **CLC 26**
See also AAYA 8, 46; BYA 3; CA 183; 9-12R, 183; CAAS 209; CANR 4, 41; CLR 1; JRDA; MAICYA 1, 2; SAAS 1; SATA 1, 28, 83; SATA-Essay 104; SATA-Obit 134; YAW

**Wojtyla, Karol (Josef)**
See John Paul II, Pope

**Wojtyla, Karol (Jozef)**
See John Paul II, Pope

**Wolf, Christa** 1929- ....... **CLC 14, 29, 58, 150**
See also CA 85-88; CANR 45, 123; CD-WLB 2; CWW 2; DLB 75; EWL 3; FW; MTCW 1; RGWL 2, 3; SSFS 14

**Wolf, Naomi** 1962- .......................... **CLC 157**
See also CA 141; CANR 110; FW; MTFW 2005

**Wolfe, Gene** 1931- ........................... **CLC 25**
See also AAYA 35; CA 57-60; 9; CANR 6, 32, 60, 152; CPW; DAM POP; DLB 8; FANT; MTCW 2; MTFW 2005; SATA 118, 165; SCFW 2; SFW 4; SUFW 2

**Wolfe, Gene Rodman**
See Wolfe, Gene

**Wolfe, George C.** 1954- ........ **BLCS; CLC 49**
See also CA 149; CAD; CD 5, 6

**Wolfe, Thomas (Clayton)** 1900-1938 ...... **SSC 33; TCLC 4, 13, 29, 61; WLC 6**
See also AMW; BPFB 3; CA 132; CAAE 104; CANR 102; CDALB 1929-1941; DA; DA3; DAB; DAC; DAM MST, NOV; DLB 9, 102, 229; DLBD 2, 16; DLBY 1985, 1997; EWL 3; MAL 5; MTCW 1, 2; NFS 18; RGAL 4; SSFS 18; TUS

**Wolfe, Thomas Kennerly, Jr.** 1931- ............................................ **CLC 147**
See Wolfe, Tom
See also CA 13-16R; CANR 9, 33, 70, 104; DA3; DAM POP; DLB 185; EWL 3; INT CANR-9; MTCW 1, 2; MTFW 2005; TUS

**Wolfe, Tom** ................ **CLC 1, 2, 9, 15, 35, 51**
See Wolfe, Thomas Kennerly, Jr.
See also AAYA 8, 67; AITN 2; AMWS 3; BEST 89:1; BPFB 3; CN 5, 6, 7; CPW; CSW; DLB 152; LAIT 5; RGAL 4

**Wolff, Geoffrey** 1937- ........................ **CLC 41**
See also CA 29-32R; CANR 29, 43, 78, 154

**Wolff, Geoffrey Ansell**
See Wolff, Geoffrey

**Wolff, Sonia**
See Levitin, Sonia (Wolff)

**Wolff, Tobias** 1945- .... **CLC 39, 64, 172; SSC 63**
See also AAYA 16; AMWS 7; BEST 90:2; BYA 12; CA 117; 22; CAAE 114; CANR 54, 76, 96; CN 5, 6, 7; CSW; DA3; DLB 130; EWL 3; INT CA-117; MTCW 2; MTFW 2005; RGAL 4; RGSF 2; SSFS 4, 11

**Wolitzer, Hilma** 1930- ........................ **CLC 17**
See also CA 65-68; CANR 18, 40; INT CANR-18; SATA 31; YAW

**Wollstonecraft, Mary** 1759-1797 .... **LC 5, 50, 90**
See also BRWS 3; CDBLB 1789-1832; DLB 39, 104, 158, 252; FL 1:1; FW; LAIT 1; RGEL 2; TEA; WLIT 3

**Wonder, Stevie** 1950- ......................... **CLC 12**
See also CAAE 111

**Wong, Jade Snow** 1922-2006 ............ **CLC 17**
See also CA 109; CAAS 249; CANR 91; SATA 112; SATA-Obit 175

**Wood, Ellen Price**
See Wood, Mrs. Henry

**Wood, Mrs. Henry** 1814-1887 ...... **NCLC 178**
See also CMW 4; DLB 18; SUFW

**Wood, James** 1965- .......................... **CLC 238**
See also CA 235

**Woodberry, George Edward** 1855-1930 ................................ **TCLC 73**
See also CA 165; DLB 71, 103

**Woodcott, Keith**
See Brunner, John (Kilian Houston)

**Woodruff, Robert W.**
See Mencken, H(enry) L(ouis)

**Woodward, Bob**
See Woodward, Robert Upshur

**Woodward, Robert Upshur** 1943- .. **CLC 240**
See also CA 69-72; CANR 31, 67, 107; MTCW 1

**Woolf, (Adeline) Virginia** 1882-1941 .. **SSC 7, 79; TCLC 1, 5, 20, 43, 56, 101, 123, 128; WLC 6**
See also AAYA 44; BPFB 3; BRW 7; BRWC 2; BRWR 1; CA 130; CAAE 104; CANR 64, 132; CDBLB 1914-1945; DA; DA3; DAB; DAC; DAM MST, NOV; DLB 36, 100, 162; DLBD 10; EWL 3; EXPS; FL 1:6; FW; LAIT 3; LATS 1:1; LMFS 2; MTCW 1, 2; MTFW 2005; NCFS 2; NFS 8, 12; RGEL 2; RGSF 2; SSFS 4, 12; TEA; WLIT 3

**Woollcott, Alexander (Humphreys)** 1887-1943 ................................. **TCLC 5**
See also CA 161; CAAE 105; DLB 29

**Woolrich, Cornell** ............................ **CLC 77**
See Hopley-Woolrich, Cornell George
See also MSW

**Woolson, Constance Fenimore** 1840-1894 ................. **NCLC 82; SSC 90**
See also DLB 12, 74, 189, 221; RGAL 4

**Wordsworth, Dorothy** 1771-1855 . **NCLC 25, 138**
See also DLB 107

**Wordsworth, William** 1770-1850 .. **NCLC 12, 38, 111, 166; PC 4, 67; WLC 6**
See also AAYA 70; BRW 4; BRWC 1; CD-BLB 1789-1832; DA; DA3; DAB; DAC; DAM MST, POET; DLB 93, 107; EXPP; LATS 1:1; LMFS 1; PAB; PFS 2; RGEL 2; TEA; WLIT 3; WP

**Wotton, Sir Henry** 1568-1639 .............. **LC 68**
See also DLB 121; RGEL 2

**Wouk, Herman** 1915- ................. **CLC 1, 9, 38**
See also BPFB 3; CA 5-8R; CANR 6, 33, 67, 146; CDALBS; CN 1, 2, 3, 4, 5, 6; CPW; DA3; DAM NOV, POP; DLBY 1982; INT CANR-6; LAIT 4; MAL 5; MTCW 1, 2; MTFW 2005; NFS 7; TUS

**Wright, Charles** 1935- ... **CLC 6, 13, 28, 119, 146**
See also AMWS 5; CA 29-32R; 7; CANR 23, 36, 62, 88, 135; CP 3, 4, 5, 6, 7; DLB 165; DLBY 1982; EWL 3; MTCW 1, 2; MTFW 2005; PFS 10

**Wright, Charles Stevenson** 1932- ..... **BLC 3; CLC 49**
See also BW 1; CA 9-12R; CANR 26; CN 1, 2, 3, 4, 5, 6, 7; DAM MULT, POET; DLB 33

**Wright, Frances** 1795-1852 ............ **NCLC 74**
See also DLB 73

**Wright, Frank Lloyd** 1867-1959 .... **TCLC 95**
See also AAYA 33; CA 174

**Wright, Harold Bell** 1872-1944 .... **TCLC 183**
See also BPFB 3; CAAE 110; DLB 9; TCWW 2

**Wright, Jack R.**
See Harris, Mark

**Wright, James (Arlington)** 1927-1980 ....... **CLC 3, 5, 10, 28; PC 36**
See also AITN 2; AMWS 3; CA 49-52; CAAS 97-100; CANR 4, 34, 64; CDALBS; CP 1, 2; DAM POET; DLB 5, 169; EWL 3; EXPP; MAL 5; MTCW 1, 2; MTFW 2005; PFS 7, 8; RGAL 4; TUS; WP

**Wright, Judith** 1915-2000 ... **CLC 11, 53; PC 14**
See also CA 13-16R; CAAS 188; CANR 31, 76, 93; CP 1, 2, 3, 4, 5, 6, 7; CWP; DLB 260; EWL 3; MTCW 1, 2; MTFW 2005; PFS 8; RGEL 2; SATA 14; SATA-Obit 121

**Wright, L(aurali) R.** 1939- ................ **CLC 44**
See also CA 138; CMW 4

**Wright, Richard (Nathaniel)** 1908-1960 ... **BLC 3; CLC 1, 3, 4, 9, 14, 21, 48, 74; SSC 2; TCLC 136, 180; WLC 6**
See also AAYA 5, 42; AFAW 1, 2; AMW; BPFB 3; BW 1; BYA 2; CA 108; CANR 64; CDALB 1929-1941; DA; DA3; DAB; DAC; DAM MST, MULT, NOV; DLB 76, 102; DLBD 2; EWL 3; EXPN; LAIT 3, 4; MAL 5; MTCW 1, 2; MTFW 2005; NCFS 1; NFS 1, 7; RGAL 4; RGSF 2; SSFS 3, 9, 15, 20; TUS; YAW

**Wright, Richard B(ruce)** 1937- ......... **CLC 6**
See also CA 85-88; CANR 120; DLB 53

**Wright, Rick** 1945- ........................... **CLC 35**

**Wright, Rowland**
See Wells, Carolyn

**Wright, Stephen** 1946- ...................... **CLC 33**
See also CA 237

**Wright, Willard Huntington** 1888-1939
See Van Dine, S. S.
See also CA 189; CAAE 115; CMW 4; DLBD 16

**Wright, William** 1930- ...................... **CLC 44**
See also CA 53-56; CANR 7, 23, 154

**Wroth, Lady Mary** 1587-1653(?) ....... **LC 30, 139; PC 38**
See also DLB 121

**Wu Ch'eng-en** 1500(?)-1582(?) ............. **LC 7**

**Wu Ching-tzu** 1701-1754 ..................... **LC 2**

**Wulfstan** c. 10th cent. -1023 .......... **CMLC 59**

**Wurlitzer, Rudolph** 1938(?)- .... **CLC 2, 4, 15**
See also CA 85-88; CN 4, 5, 6, 7; DLB 173

**Zimmerman, Robert**
 See Dylan, Bob
**Zindel, Paul** 1936-2003 ...... **CLC 6, 26; DC 5**
 See also AAYA 2, 37; BYA 2, 3, 8, 11, 14;
  CA 73-76; CAAS 213; CAD; CANR 31,
  65, 108; CD 5, 6; CDALBS; CLR 3, 45,
  85; DA; DA3; DAB; DAC; DAM DRAM,
  MST, NOV; DFS 12; DLB 7, 52; JRDA;
  LAIT 5; MAICYA 1, 2; MTCW 1, 2;
  MTFW 2005; NFS 14; SATA 16, 58, 102;
  SATA-Obit 142; WYA; YAW
**Zinger, Yisroel-Yehoyshue**
 See Singer, Israel Joshua
**Zinger, Yitskhok**
 See Singer, Isaac Bashevis
**Zinn, Howard** 1922- ........................ **CLC 199**
 See also CA 1-4R; CANR 2, 33, 90, 159
**Zinov'Ev, A.A.**
 See Zinoviev, Alexander
**Zinov'ev, Aleksandr**
 See Zinoviev, Alexander
 See also DLB 302

**Zinoviev, Alexander** 1922-2006 ......... **CLC 19**
 See Zinov'ev, Aleksandr
 See also CA 133; 10; CAAE 116; CAAS
  250
**Zinoviev, Alexander Aleksandrovich**
 See Zinoviev, Alexander
**Zizek, Slavoj** 1949- .......................... **CLC 188**
 See also CA 201; MTFW 2005
**Zoilus**
 See Lovecraft, H. P.
**Zola, Emile (Edouard Charles Antoine)**
  1840-1902 .. **TCLC 1, 6, 21, 41; WLC 6**
 See also CA 138; CAAE 104; DA; DA3;
  DAB; DAC; DAM MST, NOV; DLB 123;
  EW 7; GFL 1789 to the Present; IDTP;
  LMFS 1, 2; RGWL 2; TWA
**Zoline, Pamela** 1941- ........................ **CLC 62**
 See also CA 161; SFW 4
**Zoroaster** 628(?)B.C.-551(?)B.C. ... **CMLC 40**
**Zorrilla y Moral, Jose** 1817-1893 .... **NCLC 6**
**Zoshchenko, Mikhail** 1895-1958 ...... **SSC 15;**
  **TCLC 15**
 See also CA 160; CAAE 115; EWL 3;
  RGSF 2; RGWL 3

**Zoshchenko, Mikhail Mikhailovich**
 See Zoshchenko, Mikhail
**Zuckmayer, Carl** 1896-1977 ........... **CLC 18;**
  **TCLC 191**
 See also CA 69-72; DLB 56, 124; EWL 3;
  RGWL 2, 3
**Zuk, Georges**
 See Skelton, Robin
 See also CCA 1
**Zukofsky, Louis** 1904-1978 ... **CLC 1, 2, 4, 7,**
  **11, 18; PC 11**
 See also AMWS 3; CA 9-12R; CAAS 77-
  80; CANR 39; CP 1, 2; DAM POET; DLB
  5, 165; EWL 3; MAL 5; MTCW 1; RGAL
  4
**Zweig, Paul** 1935-1984 ................ **CLC 34, 42**
 See also CA 85-88; CAAS 113
**Zweig, Stefan** 1881-1942 ................. **TCLC 17**
 See also CA 170; CAAE 112; DLB 81, 118;
  EWL 3; RGHL
**Zwingli, Huldreich** 1484-1531 ............. **LC 37**
 See also DLB 179

# *PC* Cumulative Nationality Index

## AMERICAN

Ai **72**
Aiken, Conrad (Potter) **26**
Alexie, Sherman **53**
Ammons, A(rchie) R(andolph) **16**
Angelou, Maya **32**
Ashbery, John (Lawrence) **26**
Auden, W(ystan) H(ugh) **1**
Baca, Jimmy Santiago **41**
Baraka, Amiri **4**
Bell, Marvin **79**
Benét, Stephen Vincent **64**
Berry, Wendell (Erdman) **28**
Berryman, John **64**
Bishop, Elizabeth **3, 34**
Bly, Robert (Elwood) **39**
Bogan, Louise **12**
Bradstreet, Anne **10**
Braithwaite, William **52**
Brodsky, Joseph **9**
Brooks, Gwendolyn (Elizabeth) **7**
Brown, Sterling Allen **55**
Bryant, William Cullen **20**
Bukowski, Charles **18**
Cage, John **58**
Carruth, Hayden **10**
Carver, Raymond **54**
Cervantes, Lorna Dee **35**
Chin, Marilyn (Mei Ling) **40**
Ciardi, John **69**
Cisneros, Sandra **52**
Clampitt, Amy **19**
Clifton, (Thelma) Lucille **17**
Collins, Billy **68**
Corso, (Nunzio) Gregory **33**
Crane, (Harold) Hart **3**
Crane, Stephen **80**
Creeley, Robert **73**
Cullen, Countée **20**
Cummings, E(dward) E(stlin) **5**
Dickey, James (Lafayette) **40**
Dickinson, Emily (Elizabeth) **1**
Doolittle, Hilda **5**
Doty, Mark **53**
Dove, Rita (Frances) **6**
Dunbar, Paul Laurence **5**
Duncan, Robert (Edward) **2, 75**
Dylan, Bob **37**
Eberhart, Richard **76**
Eliot, T(homas) S(tearns) **5, 31**
Emerson, Ralph Waldo **18**
Erdrich, Louise **52**
Espada, Martín **74**
Ferlinghetti, Lawrence (Monsanto) **1**
Forché, Carolyn (Louise) **10**
Francis, Robert (Churchill) **34**

Frost, Robert (Lee) **1, 39, 71**
Gallagher, Tess **9**
Ginsberg, Allen **4, 47**
Giovanni, Nikki **19**
Glück, Louise (Elisabeth) **16**
Graham, Jorie **59**
Guest, Barbara **55**
Hacker, Marilyn **47**
Hall, Donald **70**
Hammon, Jupiter **16**
Harjo, Joy **27**
Harper, Frances Ellen Watkins **21**
Hass, Robert **16**
Hayden, Robert E(arl) **6**
H. D. **5**
Hecht, Anthony **70**
Hogan, Linda **35**
Holmes, Oliver Wendell **71**
Hongo, Garrett Kaoru **23**
Howe, Julia Ward **81**
Howe, Susan **54**
Hughes, (James) Langston **1, 53**
Hugo, Richard **68**
Ignatow, David **34**
Jackson, Laura (Riding) **44**
Jacobsen, Josephine **62**
Jarrell, Randall **41**
Jeffers, (John) Robinson **17**
Johnson, James Weldon **24**
Jordan, June **38**
Justice, Donald **64**
Kaufman, Bob **74**
Kenyon, Jane **57**
Kinnell, Galway **26**
Kizer, Carolyn **66**
Knight, Etheridge **14**
Koch, Kenneth **80**
Komunyakaa, Yusef **51**
Kumin, Maxine (Winokur) **15**
Kunitz, Stanley (Jasspon) **19**
Lanier, Sidney **50**
Levertov, Denise **11**
Levine, Philip **22**
Lindsay, (Nicholas) Vachel **23**
Longfellow, Henry Wadsworth **30**
Lorde, Audre (Geraldine) **12**
Lowell, Amy **13**
Lowell, Robert (Traill Spence Jr.) **3**
Loy, Mina **16**
MacLeish, Archibald **47**
Mackey, Nathaniel **49**
Madhubuti, Haki R. **5**
Masters, Edgar Lee **1, 36**
McHugh, Heather **61**
Melville, Herman **82**
Meredith, William (Morris) **28**

Merrill, James (Ingram) **28**
Merton, Thomas **10**
Merwin, W. S. **45**
Millay, Edna St. Vincent **6, 61**
Momaday, N(avarre) Scott **25**
Moore, Marianne (Craig) **4, 49**
Mueller, Lisel **33**
Nash, (Fredric) Ogden **21**
Nemerov, Howard (Stanley) **24**
Niedecker, Lorine **42**
O'Hara, Frank **45**
Olds, Sharon **22**
Oliver, Mary **75**
Olson, Charles (John) **19**
Oppen, George **35**
Ortiz, Simon J(oseph) **17**
Paredes, Américo **83**
Parker, Dorothy (Rothschild) **28**
Piercy, Marge **29**
Pinsky, Robert **27**
Plath, Sylvia **1, 37**
Poe, Edgar Allan **1, 54**
Pound, Ezra (Weston Loomis) **4**
Quintana, Leroy V. **36**
Ransom, John Crowe **61**
Reed, Ishmael **68**
Reese, Lizette Woodworth **29**
Rexroth, Kenneth **20**
Rich, Adrienne (Cecile) **5**
Riley, James Whitcomb **48**
Ríos, Alberto **57**
Robinson, Edwin Arlington **1, 35**
Roethke, Theodore (Huebner) **15**
Rose, Wendy **13**
Rukeyser, Muriel **12**
Sanchez, Sonia **9**
Sandburg, Carl (August) **2, 41**
Sarton, (Eleanor) May **39**
Schwartz, Delmore (David) **8**
Schnackenberg, Gjertrud **45**
Schwerner, Armand **42**
Sexton, Anne (Harvey) **2, 79**
Shapiro, Karl (Jay) **25**
Silverstein, Shel **49**
Simic, Charles **69**
Snodgrass, W. D. **74**
Snyder, Gary (Sherman) **21**
Song, Cathy **21**
Soto, Gary **28**
Spencer, Anne **77**
Spicer, Jack **78**
Stafford, William **71**
Stein, Gertrude **18**
Stevens, Wallace **6**
Stone, Ruth **53**
Strand, Mark **63**

459

Nationality Index

# *PC*-83 Title Index